# A HISTORY OF
# FRENCH PASSIONS

## 1848–1945

BY

THEODORE ZELDIN

*Volume Two*
INTELLECT, TASTE AND
ANXIETY

CLARENDON PRESS · OXFORD

*Oxford University Press, Walton Street, Oxford* OX2 6DP
*Oxford New York Toronto*
*Delhi Bombay Calcutta Madras Karachi*
*Kuala Lumpur Singapore Hong Kong Tokyo*
*Nairobi Dar es Salaam Cape Town*
*Melbourne Auckland Madrid*
*and associated companies in*
*Berlin Ibadan*

*Oxford is a trade mark of Oxford University Press*

*Published in the United States*
*by Oxford University Press Inc., New York*

© *Theodore Zeldin 1977*

*First published 1973*
*First issued as a paperback 1993*

*British Library Cataloguing in Publication Data*
*Data available*

*Library of Congress Cataloging in Publication Data*
*Data available*
*ISBN 0–19–822178–9*

*Printed in Great Britain*
*on acid-free paper by*
*J. W. Arrowsmith Ltd, Bristol*

OXFORD HISTORY OF

*General Editors*

LORD BULLOCK *and* SIR WILLIAM DEAKIN

*Oxford History of Modern Europe*

# CONTENTS

# LIST OF MAPS AND GRAPHS

# Part I

# 1. The National Identity

I N 1864, an inspector of education, touring in the mountains of the Lozère, asked the children at a village school: 'In what country is the Lozère situated?' Not a single pupil knew the answer. 'Are you English or Russian?' he demanded. They could not say. This was in one of the remoter parts of France, but the incident illustrates how Frenchmen only gradually became aware of what it was that distinguished them from other men. The French nation had to be created. The slogan *Vive la France!* was not just a formal salute but a positive assertion of faith in the virtues of patriotism.

Because the spread of this faith was largely the work of the middle classes, it has been said that modern France, as it emerged in this period, was essentially bourgeois. But the bourgeoisie was so varied, and bourgeois ideals were so complex, that no satisfactory explanation of French behaviour can be provided simply in these terms.[1] One should not indeed unquestioningly assume that the French were a single people, clearly defined by their political boundaries. The process by which their unification was attempted continued throughout this period: the resistance that patriotism met, the varieties of allegiance that resulted from the clash of innovation and tradition, exactly what was involved in being French and how the sense of belonging to the nation was spread among different groups, all this is usually glossed over, because the division of Europe into nation-states has been regarded as natural and inevitable. But even the ideals that Frenchmen set themselves, the image of themselves that they formed, were not clear or distinct.

The politicians were the principal architects of national unity: the fact that Frenchmen willingly died for their country in several wars (though not with equal enthusiasm) seems to imply that the politicians were largely successful. However, France's political history also shows that the acceptance of

[1] See Volume 1, part 1.

common ideals was vigorously denied and that profound differences about what communal life involved continued unabated. I have argued[1] that the French were not only confused about what held them together, but that they consistently exaggerated their differences and that emphasis on diversity was an essential part of their society. One needs to go beyond political history to see the extent and the limits of these divergencies. National unity was fashioned not only by politics but also by the schools. The educational experience of Frenchmen needs to be investigated with care, to uncover the pressures to which they were subject, and to assess just how much they resisted those pressures. Having probed *la France bourgeoise*, it is necessary to analyse *la France*.[2]

In political terms, France was one of the first 'nation-states' in Europe, but for long its unity was felt consciously more by its rulers than by its people. In the seventeenth century, La Bruyère justly pointed out that men served the state from 'interest or desire for glory' and that they considered themselves to be servants of their prince, rather than of the community. The idea of France having a common personality and interest —as distinct from its all being the possession of one king—did not emerge till the eighteenth century, when the word nation first came to be used in a combative sense, to mean the sovereign people, as opposed to its despotic rulers. A despotic country could not be considered a *patrie*—a word adopted almost as a political slogan by the revolutionaries in 1789—a patriot being the opposite of an aristocrat.

Montesquieu had said that love of the *patrie* was the distinguishing mark of republicans, because it meant love of equality. Voltaire, in his *Philosophical Dictionary*, had added that the poor could have no *patrie*, and neither could the philosopher, who

[1] Volume 1, part 3.
[2] Carlton J. H. Hayes, *France. A Nation of Patriots* (New York, 1930); W. C. Brownell, *French Traits* (New York, 1888); Vicomte d'Avenel, *Les Français de mon temps* (n.d., about 1900); Barrett Wendel, *La France d'aujourd'hui* (1909); Gustave Rodrigues, *La France éternelle* (1919); E. R. Curtius, *Essai sur la France* (1931); Fortunat Strowski, *Nationalisme ou patriotisme* (1933); Wladimir d'Ormesson, *Qu'est-ce qu'un Français* (1934); Paul Distelbarth, *La Personne France* (1935); Lucien Maury, *Définitions de la France* (1941); Alexandre Eckhardt, *Le Génie français* (1942); Marcel Raymond, *Génies de France* (Cahiers du Rhône, Neuchâtel, May 1942); M. M. Martin, *Histoire de l'unité française* (1949); A. Siegfried, *L'Âme des peuples* (1950); Raoul Girardet, *Le Nationalisme français* (1966); Z. Sternhell, *Maurice Barrès et le nationalisme français* (1972).

loved all humanity—in the same way as Montaigne had said that all men everywhere were his compatriots. The *ancien régime* had failed to instil any real sense of belonging into the country at large. Turgot told Louis XVI that ordinary villagers knew little about their links with the state. 'They are rather badly informed of their family duties and not at all of those which they owe to the state. Families barely know what holds them to this state of which they are part, they do not know in what way. They regard the exercise of authority in the collection of taxes, which serve to maintain order, as the law of the strongest, seeing no reason to yield to it other than their powerlessness to resist, and they believe in avoiding them whenever they can. There is no public spirit, because there is no common, known, visible interest.' When in 1787 the Academy of Châlons-sur-Marne held an essay-competition on 'the best means of giving birth to and encouraging patriotism in a monarchy', it awarded its prize to the entry which said that patriotism was only possible if the monarch pursued the happiness of his people, so that all citizens were satisfied. When the Revolution broke out, different ways of securing this happiness were seen and not all involved national unity. Only 35 per cent of the *cahiers de doléances* demanded a national programme of reform as the solution for France's discontents; 30 per cent looked to the church against the monarchy, to the parishes as defences against the central government, and to class privilege against the idea of the nation; and 34 per cent, though willing to increase the central power to a certain extent, favoured federalism, and the preservation of local privileges.[1] On the whole, it was only the old provinces, around Paris, which identified themselves with France; the frontier ones demanded the confirmation of their ancient prerogatives and Navarre even refused to attend the Estates General on the ground that it was independent. It was only in 1789 that the unity of the country was proclaimed, after the different estates and regions renounced their privileges in 'a heroic suicide of particularism', and that the equality of all was accepted. There were, however, some who rejected this new order: first the Girondin federalists and then the royalist émigrés, who

[1] Beatrice F. Hyslop, *French Nationalism in 1789 according to the General Cahiers* (New York, 1934), 198–228.

even co-operated with the rest of Europe to fight the French revolutionary armies. It was in these armies that patriotism received its baptism, and for long after it remained warlike, 'liberal', implying the liberation of subject peoples from tyrannical rule, and therefore inevitably as much partisan as national.[1] Paradoxically therefore, patriotism and nationalism were things that could divide Frenchmen, as much as expressing what they felt in common.

Nationalism was an ideal as much as a fact, and it is important to distinguish between the two, between the way the nation was idealised and held up as an object of veneration, and the way the people viewed it and responded to it in real life, even though their reactions might be very different in the course of ordinary routine and in times of war or crisis. The idealisers put forward theories as to what France ought to represent, and by force of repetition these theories have sometimes been accepted as descriptions of what France in fact was. Here, too, it is necessary to be clear as to what one is talking about.

The first and most influential theory about France was that it stood for 'civilisation'. To be a Frenchman, in the fullest sense, meant to be civilised, which required that one accepted the models of thought, behaviour and expression held in esteem in Paris. At one level, to accept civilisation meant to accept cultural uniformity and centralisation. By this definition, to be a Frenchman meant more than to be born in France, or to be a mere peasant; it involved adherence to a set of values, but in return one could hope to benefit from all the rewards that the state showered on those who adopted those values. *Civilisation* (like *nation*) was a new word, first used in 1766, and admitted into the dictionary of the French Academy only in 1798 (the year in which the word *nationalism* was first used in France). The idea of course was much older, though it is significant that the word formerly used was *civility*: this implied politeness, urbanity, a rejection of savagery and rurality, aspiration towards justice, order, education.[2] But at the beginning of the nineteenth century civilisation was still a contro-

[1] A. Aulard, *Le Patriotisme français de la renaissance à la révolution* (1921), 39, 102–5.

[2] George Huppert, 'The Idea of Civilisation in the Sixteenth Century', in A. Molho and J. A. Tedeschi, *Renaissance Studies in honour of Hans Baron* (Florence, 1971), 759–69.

versial idea.[1] On the one hand conservatives rejected it, because it seemed to imply change: Montlosier equated it with the Rights of Man, and the public prosecutor in a treason trial in 1822 declared that just as humans perished from excessive plumpness, so societies perished from an excess of civilisation. On the other hand Fourier denied that civilisation could be the ultimate destiny of man and invented a utopia to replace it. A Société de Civilisation was founded in 1832; Lamartine called the journal he founded in 1852 *Le Civilisateur*. The arguments were all complicated by the fact that the romantics—in the tradition of Rousseau who had praised the noble savage—imagined that the 'barbarians', the poor masses, being uncorrupted, were destined to give new life to a civilisation already considered decadent. But the basic idea behind 'civilisation' was that it was a state of movement and development. Guizot was the man who propagated this idea, and who worked out the theory that France was the country which led this movement. 'One can say, without flattery', he declared in his Sorbonne lectures on 'The General History of Civilisation in Europe' (1828), 'that France has been the centre, the home of civilisation in Europe.' 'It would be going too far,' he admitted, 'to pretend that it has always, and in every instance, marched at the head of the nations.' He acknowledged that Italy had at times led the world in art, and England in political institutions, but France possessed certain unique qualities, which meant that 'civilising ideas and institutions born in other lands have been in some way forced to undergo a further development in France whenever they wanted to transplant themselves, to become fruitful and general, to act for the common benefit of European civilisation; and it is from France, as from a second, more fecund and richer fatherland, that they have launched themselves to conquer Europe. There has been hardly any great idea, any great principle of civilisation, which, seeking to spread everywhere, has not first passed through France.' Guizot defined civilisation as the broadening and improvement of life, both by the amelioration of relations between men and by the elevation of the intellectual and moral condition of individuals. Civilisation meant progress in the way society organised itself and

[1] L. Febvre, *Pour une histoire à part entière* (1962), 'Civilisation, le mot, l'idée', 481–528.

behaved, it required an increasingly equitable distribution of goods and enlightenment between men, but it existed only when all the ingredients which made it up were found together. No one factor should be favoured at the expense of the others. Civilisation meant at once the perfecting of the individual and of society. It was therefore something very new, for the ancient world had never succeeded in achieving all of this and had reached a high level only in one particular sphere. Guizot saw an essential link between civilisation and national, representative government: the development of centralised states made possible the introduction of the benefits of civilisation to all classes; the adoption of liberal institutions meant that all classes could participate in deciding the direction civilisation took. Civilisation was a moral idea, and a humane idea, but also an artistic one, because it involved proselytisation. That is why France was at the head of European civilisation, because its instinct for sociability, its sympathy for generous ideas, the clarity of its language, made it best capable of understanding its goals and explaining them to others.[1] One thus became a better man by being civilised—more educated, polite, understanding—and one's country became a better place to live in —with more justice, liberty and prosperity—but acquiring civilisation involved not just receiving advantages but also preaching the gospel and helping others in the same path. Civilisation implied a whole social, economic and political programme, to be carried out in co-operation with like-minded citizens and, inevitably, against those whom one would label as obscurantist and reactionary. It was egalitarian but also elitist. It was universal, but also nationalist. These ambivalences were to remain as a constant feature in the French patriotic ideal.

At different times in this period, different facets of it were stressed more or less. Thus in the Second Empire Napoleon III presented every instance of technical progress, agricultural modernisation or improvement in communications as a triumph for civilisation and France's every political act as proof that it was 'the advanced sentinel and first soldier of civilisation'. Catholics like Veuillot complained that this was too materialist an interpretation of France's mission; the Pope

[1] F. Guizot, *Cours d'histoire moderne. Histoire générale de la civilisation en Europe* (1828), lecture i.

condemned 'modern civilisation' altogether in 1864; but Catholics were happy to support French colonial expansion, and the conversion and westernisation of their new subjects in the name of civilisation. For a long time this certainty that French values were so superior that they had to be communicated to others possessed even the most liberal thinkers. The republican Edgar Quinet wrote that some other countries had indeed succeeded in acquiring supremacy in one field—Italy in art, Germany in science and religion, Britain in industry, the United States in liberty—but their achievements were always partial. France alone had 'the instinct of civilisation, the need to take the initiative in a general way to bring about progress in modern society. . . . It is this disinterested though imperious need . . . which makes French unity, which gives sense to its history and a soul to the country. This civilising force, this desire for external influence is the best part of France, its art, its genius, its happiness.'[1] The vagueness and variety of these grandiloquent statements meant that people defined civilisation in ways totally unacceptable to many Frenchmen. Adolphe Thiers, who was often regarded as the mouthpiece of the common-sensical, realist bourgeoisie, saw civilisation as the movement 'from the desert to the city, from cruelty to gentleness, from ignorance to knowledge'. But he concluded that its very foundation was private property 'without which there can be no civilisation'. He had no use for generosity and sacrifice in this matter and still less in the preservation of the national interest, which he insisted should be defended by military force, in exactly the same way as the Bourbon kings of the *ancien régime* had done. Important elements of the old monarchical ideals of grandeur and even conquest survived the Revolution, even if they put on new clothes. It was never really clear what aspect of civilisation France represented, or what aspect of France was being vaunted at any particular time. Civilisation was, to some extent, a war cry, preaching peace.[2]

An alternative tradition was that what made a man French

[1] E. Quinet, *De l'Allemagne et de la Révolution* (1832).

[2] R. A. Lochore, *History of the Idea of Civilisation in France 1830–1870* (Bonn, 1935), written by a student of Curtius; P. C. Roux-Lavergne, *De la philosophie de l'histoire* (1850), chapter one on 'Civilisation'; Antoine Arago, *Étude sur le rôle politique de la France* (1859).

was his race. This had a wider and longer vogue than is now generally admitted. It used to be thought that the French were descended from the Franks, who themselves came from Troy, and, until the eighteenth century, genealogies going back to Priam were dutifully memorised by schoolboys. Politics then complicated this theory. The bourgeoisie began to trace their descent back to the Gallo-Roman cities, and to claim the legacy of their liberties and privileges. Boulainvilliers (1658–1722) worked this into a theory whereby the nobles of France were Franks, while the third estate were Gauls.[1] The popularity of this view is seen in the way many people, Siéyès for example, saw the Revolution as a racial victory for the Gauls against the Frankish conquerors.[2] In the eighteenth century the noble Franks claimed to represent the freedom of the German forests against the despotic monarchy, but then in the nineteenth it was the Gauls who stood for democratic freedom. Napoleon, considering himself the heir of both the Roman Caesar and the German Charlemagne, dissociated the Gauls from the Romans and attributed the faults in the French character to the Gallic elements in it; but Augustin Thierry devoted his life to championing the Gallic third estate and his brother Amédée wrote a *History of the Gauls* (1828) which went through ten editions by 1881. The issue was complicated by the discovery of the Celts or Kymris (Bretons), a race less influenced by Rome, more indigenously French, who were praised as endowed with many qualities.

The scientists rallied to the support of the historians and declared that these racial varieties could still be discerned, in the shape of the skulls of living Frenchmen; and phrenology allowed them, moreover, to attribute moral characteristics to each race.[3] Physical anthropology grew into a fashionable and active science from the 1860s, stimulated by the dedication of Paul Broca (1824–80), the Protestant doctor who founded the Anthropological Society in 1859, which at first consisted entirely of doctors of medicine. Broca, who was appointed

---

[1] Boulainvilliers, *Essai sur la noblesse de France* (1732).

[2] Jacques Barzun, *The French Race: Theories of its Origins and their Social and Political Implications prior to the Revolution*, Ph.D. Columbia (New York, 1932).

[3] W. Edwards (founder of the Ethnological Society of Paris in 1838), *Des Caractéristiques physiologiques des races humaines considérées dans leur rapport avec l'histoire* (1829).

professor at the Paris faculty of medicine in 1867 and ended as a senator of the republic, had originally been watched by the police, for fear that his materialist doctrines might be dangerous, but in the 1870s his work was subsidised both by the Paris municipal council and by the state. He invented a large number of instruments for measuring men, particularly their skulls, from which he and his disciples drew varying conclusions.[1] The disputes about just how many races France contained grew complicated. Broca studied the height of conscripts and showed how the inhabitants of Brittany, the Massif Central and the Alps were between 8 and 17 per cent shorter than elsewhere. Comparing the heads of doctors and male nurses at his hospital, he discovered that the former were considerably larger. This led to more and more skulls being measured. One craniologist took this to the point of being able to make 5,000 measurements on a single skull. Bigger heads were sometimes declared to be better, but then that required the Auvergnats to be placed at the head of civilisation, while the Corsicans had to be relegated to the supposedly inferior level of the Chinese and the Eskimos. But then the theory that protruding foreheads were signs of civilisation made the Corsicans world leaders by this criterion. Collignon, a military doctor, interpreted the class struggle in France as a racial war between narrow-headed 'dolichocephalics'—who had arrived in France more recently, and represented innovation and adventure—and the round-headed 'brachycephalics' who were conservative peasants. He prophesied the victory of the latter. He measured the cephalic indexes of 16,000 people, and produced a map of their regional distribution. Professor Tropinard, in the 1880s, examined the colouring of 200,000 Frenchmen, assisted by a whole phalanx of interested doctors, and showed that twenty-two departments of France had a predominance of blonds and twenty-two of dark complexions, the rest being mixed. Basing himself on these and other studies, Deniker divided France into six different races; and Montandon in 1935 summarised all previous work in a new map, which divided France into three races and seven subraces. The simple generalisations about the Gauls were thus

[1] Dr. Samuel Pozzi, *Paul Broca, biographie, bibliographie* (1880); Paul Broca, *Instructions générales pour les recherches et observations anthropologiques* (1865), id., *Instructions craniologiques et craniométriques* (1868). Broca's bibliography lists 450 articles.

broken down into patterns too complicated to have more than a negative significance.[1] Science in the end confirmed the view which many people had held in any case, that France was not a unity from a racial point of view.

But this did not end the debate. Theorists argued how these disparate elements ought to be combined. Darwin was used freely to support conflicting arguments. Old Dr. Cabanis had laid it down that the mixing of races produced an improvement. But then the comte de Gobineau (1816–82) started the idea that it was precisely mixture that was ruining French civilisation, for though mixture at first led to the creation of higher qualities, continuation of it produced increasing amounts of the characteristics of the inferior race and the superior race inevitably disappeared. This was his explanation of the rise and fall of civilisations.[2]

The extremes to which these racial theories were taken may be seen in criminal anthropology, which at the turn of the century favoured the view that criminals were a distinct race, recognisable by their long jaws, flattened noses, scanty beard and other peculiarities supposedly denoting a reversion to savagery. The discovery that the shape of the famous murderer Vacher's skull was identical with Gambetta's was not enough to discredit this. In 1915 Dr. Edgar Berillon conveniently 'discovered' that Germans had intestines nine feet longer than all other humans, as well as being prone to polychesia (excessive defecation) and bromidrosis (body odour), by which criteria Berillon was able to uncover German spies and Germans masquerading as Alsatians.[3] However absurd this pushing of racial ideas to their utmost extremes may now appear, it was nevertheless long possible to appear both erudite and scientific

[1] P. Broca, 'Sur l'ethnologie de la France', *Mémoires de la Société d'Anthropologie de Paris* (1860), vol. 1 and (1868) vol. 3; Jacques de Boisjolin, *Les Peuples en France* (1878); Gustave Lagneau, *Anthropologie de la France* (1879); René Collignon, 'Étude anthropométrique élémentaire des principales races de France', *Bulletin de la Société d'Anthropologie de Paris* (1883), 3rd series, vol. 6; J. Tropinard, *L'Homme dans la nature* (1891); J. Deniker, *Les Races de l'Europe* (1899–1908); Dr. G. Montandon, *L'Ethnie française* (1935), 168–9.

[2] J. A. de Gobineau, *Essai sur l'inégalité des races humaines* (1853–5); Janine Buenzod, *La Formation de la pensée de Gobineau* (1967); M. D. Biddiss, *Gobineau* (1970); cf. G. Vacher de Lapouge, *L'Aryen, son rôle social* (1899).

[3] Jacques Barzun, *Race. A Study in modern Superstition* (1938), 240. Cf. Jean Finot, *Le Préjugé des races* (1905); Christine Bolt, *Victorian Attitudes to Race* (1971).

with almost any variation on this theme. Taine himself had espoused race as one of the three determining factors behind human behaviour: he had attributed characteristics to different nations on this basis; and his works were standard textbooks in every school. It was on the basis of such respectable authorities, and of all this scientific research, that the nationalist movements of the twentieth century built their theories about the need to exclude foreigners from France and to 'keep the French race pure'.

But the research also fitted an equally powerful tradition, that race played no part in creating French nationality. France would have had to surrender considerable areas on its borders, and perhaps have granted independence to whole regions, if it had been simply racialist. The loss of Alsace and Lorraine, like the annexation of Savoy, made this obvious, and stressed the need to have an alternative theory. It was Ernest Renan who supplied it. In a lecture at the Sorbonne given in 1882, which was much publicised and reprinted, he asked the question, 'What is a nation?'. Race, he declared, was no longer an adequate basis: the French were 'Celtic, Iberic and German', the Germans were 'German, Celtic and Slav'. Race was an interesting subject for historians to investigate but it could have no place in politics. It meant different things in any case, depending on whether one studied it anthropologically or philologically. Neither blood, nor appearance, could describe a man, because men were essentially reasonable and moral entities. The language men spoke did not say what their nationality was, because both English and Americans spoke the same language, and besides Switzerland showed that a common language was not indispensable. It is clear that Renan was arguing not from first premisses, but from the nineteenth-century situation: his theory, like the theories of so many historians, was designed to justify the *status quo*. Religion, he went on, was nowadays a personal matter, so it could not make a nation; nor could community of interests: the Zollverein was a commercial, not a national arrangement. He concluded, in a peroration that was to become famous: 'A nation is a soul, a spiritual principle . . . [it is based on] the common possession of a rich legacy of memories from the past and consent in the present, the desire to live together and the will to continue to develop one's heritage.' Nations cannot be improvised: they are 'the result of a long history of effort, sacrifice and devotion'. Nations existed therefore because of the will of their members, reiterated in a silent daily plebiscite: they implied that the members had done great things together, and wanted to do more in the same company. They represented 'a great solidarity, constituted by the feelings created by sacrifices borne together and the wish to bear further ones'. If there were any doubts about their frontiers, they could easily be resolved by asking the people.[1]

Renan's principle, however, was seldom fully accepted, even by himself. He rather contradictorily objected to the annexation of Nice and Savoy, even though these two provinces had voted in a plebiscite to join France: he declared it would have more inconveniences than advantages, and was probably worried that they were clerical and conservative areas. Michelet was likewise uncertain as to what he thought, despite his democratic instincts. He declared that 'France was not a race, as Germany was, but a nation. Its origin is mixture. Individuals in it derive their glory from their voluntary participation in it.' He maintained, however, both that 'the immense majority of Frenchmen are Celts' and that 'language is the principal sign of nationality'.[2] In the same way, Émile Ollivier, who wrote one of the most interesting works on the 'Principle of Nationalities' (1895), argued that any group of people, of whatever number or race, had the right to form independent states if they wished; he did not think nations necessarily had to be large, though he expected that the unification of Germany and Italy would in due course lead to a Confederation of Europe. The racial idea, he said, was 'barbarous and retrograde'. Civilisation consisted in destroying primitive groups so as to form by free will contractual groups which would be far more solidly cemented than those born from chance. But in 1870 he declared war on Germany, on the ground that the whole nation wanted war, implying that free self-determination could be stopped by a foreign neighbour where 'dignity and honour' were insulted by it.[3] Not everyone who believed in nations

---

[1] E. Renan, Qu'est-ce qu'une nation (1882).

[2] J. Michelet, Tableau de la France (1875), 1, 14; id., La France devant l'Europe (1870).

[3] É. Ollivier, Du principe des nationalités (1895), vol. 1 of L'Empire libéral, and further references in T. Zeldin, Emile Ollivier (1963), 168–72.

based on the popular will accepted that it required only a plebiscite to set up a new country. Proudhon disliked large countries and wanted to divide the great powers of Europe into sixty different states.

Since nationalists were usually imperialists, they were faced with the problem of reconciling their belief in the superiority of the French race with a willingness to admit conquered peoples into the fold of the nation. Some controversy arose about the extent to which the French were free from racial prejudice. There were those who claimed French colonisation was marked by an exceptional readiness to assimilate people of other colours. It will be shown, in due course, that this was only superficially true.[1] And when, in 1963, the first scientific inquiry into racial prejudice in France was carried out, on a sample drawn mainly from the liberal professions, it was shown that racism remained very strong, with much use of insult, rejection of contact, and even violence towards people of other races. Interestingly enough, it was found that the peasants were the least racist, particularly in areas which had little contact with foreigners. In the departments of Lot and Corrèze there was no patois word for Jew until the Occupation and the peasants there discovered the Jew only then.[2] After the war of 1914–18, quite a few Frenchmen rejected the right of the Germans to be one nation, and twisted their theories so as to justify the setting-up of a buffer Rhine state.[3] The French law on nationality certainly never accepted the view that anyone could elect to be a Frenchman, though, as the number of Frenchmen declined relatively to the population of other powers, naturalisation was facilitated, and foreigners allowed to enter freely. This new admixture of alien races, however, stimulated protests against the 'métèques', who were adulterating 'purer blood'.

Whatever may have been France's racial composition in the days of Caesar and Charlemagne, in modern times it was distinguished by the large number of foreigners living in it. Though it obviously could not be compared with the U.S.A., France had some of America's problems regarding the

[1] See chapter 18.
[2] P. H. Maucorps, *Les Français et le racisme* (1965), 155.
[3] René Johannet, *Le Principe des nationalités* (1918); Louis Le Fur, *Races, nationalités, états* (1922); Judith M. Hughes, *To The Maginot Line* (Cambridge, Mass., 1971).

absorption of newly arrived citizens. The statistics of foreign residents were:

| | | | |
|---|---|---|---|
| 1851 | 380,000 | 1901 | 1,034,000 |
| 1861 | 497,000 | 1911 | 1,116,000 |
| 1872 | 741,000 | 1921 | 1,496,000 |
| 1881 | 1,001,000 | 1931 | 2,613,000 |
| 1891 | 1,130,000 | | |

This, however, does not accurately reveal the total number of foreigners, for naturalised immigrants were deducted. The figures for these latter rose rapidly:

*Naturalisations*

| | | | |
|---|---|---|---|
| 1851 | 13,500 | 1891 | 170,700 |
| 1861 | 15,300 | 1901 | 221,800 |
| 1872 | 15,300 | 1911 | 252,000 |
| 1881 | 77,000 | | |

Between 1889 and 1927 1,330,000 foreigners were naturalised, and between 1927 and 1940 another 967,000. So in 1940 it was estimated that 1,750,000 naturalised Frenchmen needed to be added to the 2,600,000 unnaturalised foreigners. But in addition many Frenchmen were the children of mixed marriages. In 1888 (when the first figures on this subject were compiled) there were about 8,000 mixed marriages; in the 1920s there were about 17,000 per annum. Originally, the foreigners who came into France were mainly from border regions, notably Belgians,[1] Italians,[2] Germans,[3] Portuguese and Spaniards. But after the war there was an immense influx of Poles into France —412,000 according to the French statistics and half as many again according to the Polish ones.[4] Half a million Russian, half a million Spanish, and 30,000 Jewish political refugees escaped into France. How many settled is not clear. Perhaps one-third of the Jews stayed on. The Spaniards mainly went back to Spain: in 1951 only 165,000 of them were still in France.[5]

[1] 33 per cent in 1851, 47 per cent in 1872, 24 per cent in 1911.

[2] 16 per cent in 1851 rising gradually to 36 per cent in 1911.

[3] 15 per cent in 1851, 17 per cent in 1861, declining gradually to between 8 and 10 per cent.

[4] S. Wlocewski, *L'Établissement des Polonais en France* (1936); Pierre Depoid, *Les Naturalisations en France 1870–1940* (Études Démographiques, no. 3) (1942); Henri Bunle, *Mouvements immigratoires entre la France et l'étranger* (1943), 70–2.

[5] Guy Hermet, *Les Espagnols en France* (1967).

How quickly those who stayed came to consider themselves and came to be considered as Frenchmen has not been investigated. The Russians certainly formed a separate community for a long time, with their own cathedral and at one stage as many as forty different churches and chapels in the Paris region alone. They had sixty-two newspapers and reviews. The princes (and others) who became taxi drivers were numerous enough to have a Russian newspaper for themselves, *Le Chauffeur russe*, a review (*Au volant*), libraries, garages, canteens of their own. Passy became almost a Russian town. The pretender, Grand Duke Vladimir, lived in Brittany (Saint-Brieuc-sur-Mer) from 1921 to 1944. But many Russians were in varying degrees assimilated, particularly if they entered the service of the French state: Gorky's adopted son, Zinovy Pechkoff, became a brigadier-general; Michel Garder, professor at the School of War, became a leading French strategist; Serge Lifar transformed the art of ballet; two authors, Kessel and Troyat, were even elected to the French Academy. Prince Youssoupoff, one of the murderers of Rasputin, set up as a couturier.[1]

France was considered capable of absorbing such varied populations—not only foreign ones, but also the different types at its extremities—because the possession of French culture was another definition of what constituted a Frenchman. This meant that a peasant, as much as an immigrant, had to be made French, and that it was the inculcation of the traditional values, particularly through the schools and the army, that was primarily responsible for creating the nation. The institution of compulsory, free and lay education was a major step, therefore, in the diffusion of patriotism—which underlines how much effort had to be put to stimulate that sentiment. It will be seen, in the chapters on education, how the teaching of civic and moral duties was an important part of the school curriculum, how love for the nation was preached as something expected of the child, in the same way as love for his mother. It was explained to him how much he owed to France, and how therefore no sacrifice was too great to repay his debt. Now, to acquire French culture meant first of all to obtain mastery of its language, and language, it was believed, contained the key to the art both of

[1] Banine, *La France étrangère* (1968).

behaving and of thinking. No one has given a better statement of how much was expected of the French language than Joseph de Maistre, himself of course a Savoyard, for whom therefore France was a freely chosen ideal. France, he said, may not have succeeded in dominating the world by force of arms, but it enjoyed 'another kind of domination, much more honourable, that of opinion . . . and to exercise this, it has a dominating language . . . which, even before it made itself illustrious by masterpieces of all kinds, was recognised as supreme by Europe. People loved it and considered it an honour to speak it. What is called the art of speaking is eminently the talent of the French, and it is by the art of speaking that one rules over men. Someone has said that an idea is never adopted by the world until a writer of genius takes hold of it and expresses it well . . . That is presumably the source of the influence of France: the good writers of this nation express things better than those of all other nations, and make their ideas spread throughout Europe in less time than a writer of another country would need to get his ideas known in his province. It is this talent, this distinctive quality, this extraordinary gift that has made the French the distributors of fame . . . Self-love—more insidious and stronger than national pride—revealed this truth to all the famous men of the whole world who had the more or less open ambition to win the approbation of the French, because they could not conceal from themselves that they were condemned to a local reputation until Paris consented to make them famous . . . English literature owes all its celebrity to the French: it was completely unknown to the rest of Europe until France took a liking to the literary productions of its rival . . . Perhaps nothing is properly understood in Europe until the French have explained it.'[1]

It should not be thought, however, that the interest in language was confined to writers seeking fame. The peculiarity of the French situation was that, from a very early period, to speak and write well, according to the manner laid down in turn by the Court, the Academy, the University, and Paris became a mark of distinction in all classes. The French language acquired its prestige first of all because it liberated men

[1] J. de Maistre, *Trois Fragments sur la France*, printed in *Œuvres inédites du comte J. de Maistre* (1870), 7–9.

from isolation, enabled them to get beyond the patois of their families and villages, to mix on equal terms with anybody, to participate in the most sociable and most cultivated of the arts, conversation. It has been seen how to this very day, uneducated workers regret above all that they lack mastery of the language, because they see it as the passport to social intercourse and to full equality.[1] This attitude could probably be found in other countries, but nowhere was language so highly esteemed as embodying the national genius. When Paul Valéry, in 1941, was asked to say what France represented, he replied that 'the first thing to examine if one wants to appreciate the mental life of this people and its evolution . . . is its language, the first intellectual fruit of a nation'.[2] Its literature and philosophy were 'nothing but the exploitation of certain properties' of this language. Even though Saussure pointed out that 'the generally accepted view that language reflects the psychological character of a nation' was not supported by even the most elementary investigation of linguistics,[3] it nevertheless was an ineradicable superstition that by speaking French a man gave expression to the values the country admired. 'Whatever is not clear is not French', Rivarol had said in 1783 in the essay with which he won the competition set by the Academy of Berlin, asking why French was a universal language, why it deserved this status and whether it was likely to keep it.[4] French was then the language of diplomacy and remained so until 1919 when English was admitted as its equal at the Peace Conference of Versailles. That the claims of French were less and less accepted was seen in 1945 when the peace treaties were drawn up in English and Russian, with French being added only after protests from France. When the United Nations planned to have English, Spanish and Russian as its three working languages, French had again to be forced in as a fourth.[5] In the age of the enlightenment, most educated people could speak French, but the advent of democracy ironically revealed

[1] Vol. 1, 273.
[2] Paul Valéry et al., La France et la civilisation contemporaine (1941), 8–9.
[3] F. de Saussure, Cours de linguistique général (1916), 310–11; cf. Georges A. Heuse, La Psychologie ethnique (1953), 39.
[4] A. de Rivarol, Discours sur l'universalité de la langue française (1784).
[5] Firmin Roz and Maurice Honoré, Le Rayonnement de la langue française dans le monde (1957).

French to be very much a minority tongue. It is wrong to think that French retained its supremacy as an international language until the end of this period. In diplomacy it may have done so, but in other fields, notably in commerce, industry and outside Europe, English was very often an easily successful rival. Already in 1859 a French critic was remarking 'in our generation, dominance is passing more and more to the English language'.[1]

Nevertheless it was argued that French was unbeatable if one wanted clarity. The French language was supposed to give expression to the great French quality of logic. 'Logic governs our speech,' wrote Jules Simon, 'affecting even the very form of our periods . . . It is impossible to be unreasonable or equivocal when one speaks French, without it being immediately obvious that it is not French that one is speaking.' The language was supposed to reflect the good sense and clarity of mind that all Frenchmen inherited from Descartes.[2] This myth, as will be seen,[3] represented some very confused thinking. French, as the Danish linguist Otto Jespersen pointed out, was not a particularly logical language by any professional test—Chinese and English were both more logical.[4] But what Frenchmen stressed was that the order of words in French was governed by strict rules, in contrast with German where the weight of words counted for more than meaning in determining order. Subordinate clauses had to be introduced by definite conjunctions, unlike English which allowed greater freedom, so that the links between phrases were less clearly defined. It was claimed that in French it was impossible to lapse into Germanic 'verbal diarrhoea'. What this meant was that French had rules which were more clear-cut, defended on the ground that they represented the triumph of reason, taste and art over chaos. These rules encouraged people to order their ideas in a certain way, to classify them according to a set pattern, and to present them with a due degree of abstraction. The conclusion was rather hastily drawn that other nations lacked the

---

[1] J. Lemoine, *Nouvelles études critiques et biographiques* (1863), article on 'Grandeur et décadence de la langue française' written in 1859, 362–71.

[2] *Alliance Française*, pamphlet in British Museum, 1601/193 (1889), 29.

[3] See chapter 5.

[4] Otto Jespersen, *The Growth and Structure of the English Language* (1938, New York reprint), 1–16. Cf. N. Chomsky, *Cartesian Linguistics* (1966), 28–31, 93–5.

French power of abstraction. To many people, form was all important; the way a man expressed himself mattered almost as much as what he said. Politicians were admired for their oratory quite as much as for their principles, and some quite second-rate people with beautiful voices could, largely on the ground that they could roll out harmonious periods loaded with the right allusions and rhythm, reach the highest positions in the state. Viviani, who became prime minister in 1914, took lessons at the Comédie-Française in the art of declamation and used to spend long hours practising his parliamentary speeches, as though they were songs. To be able to classify material in an orderly, traditional manner often appeared as the sign of intellectual superiority, even when it only involved the application of old rules. Pedantry, as opposed to efficiency, could thus often become the ideal of junior employees in the civil service and the rising mass of clerks who mistook the form for the essence.

To those who had acquired mastery of the French language only by personal effort, in family surroundings where patois was supreme, French did indeed represent more than a means of expression. Jean-Paul Sartre recalled how his grandfather Charles Schweitzer, an Alsatian, was 'still amazed by the French language at the age of seventy, because he had learnt it with difficulty and had not quite made it his own; he used to play with it, he enjoyed the words and liked saying them, and his merciless diction did not spare me a syllable.' He and his grandson wrote to each other in verse: 'bound by a new link, they talked, like Indians or the pimps of Montmartre, in a language forbidden to women'. Sartre has shown the effects of this on behaviour. He had discovered the world through language and so 'for a long time I mistook language for the world. To exist was to have a registered trade-name somewhere in the infinite Tables of the Word.' Observing the world meant not investigating it, but 'catching living things in the trap of phrases', imposing names on them, and taking pleasure above all in words.[1] In politics, the tendency to confuse words with action, to think one had dealt with a situation by making a fine speech about it, by defining it precisely in a beautiful piece of prose, was an inevitable consequence of this attitude.

But not all Frenchmen spoke good French or fulfilled the

[1] J.-P. Sartre, *Les Mots* (1964); Penguin translation *Words* (1967), 89, 115.

ideals of the grammarians. Linguists showed that almost every village had its own peculiarities of style, vocabulary and pronunciation.[1] Pronunciation certainly long remained very diverse. In the 1930s to say cinq francs was considered vulgar and men of distinction still did not do it. At the end of the nineteenth century people used to pronounce sept francs sè francs, differentiating it from c'est franc only by spelling. Popular pressure fought against such ambiguities imposed by formal rules, but also created ambiguities of its own which the rules forbade. Uniformity in speech had not even been established among the most highly educated élite of the country at the turn of the century, so that they could hardly set a model to others. A German linguist had the idea of recording phonetically the speech of a number of eminent writers in Paris, and he was amazed by the wide discrepancies in their pronunciations.[2] The way most Frenchmen pronounce r, which appears as one of their most characteristic idiosyncrasies, is quite a recent phenomenon. The r used to be pronounced in a full, rolled way (with the point of the tongue in the same position as for l, but with a vibration of both tongue and vocal chords). The Parisian r (with the back of the tongue against the palate) appeared only in the eighteenth century, as an urban phenomenon. It came to be used independently at the same time in the city of Marseille, so that in a vaudeville played in Toulouse in 1850, an actor who had the part of a Marseillais used the guttural r to show his origin. This pronunciation spread to other towns and to the northern part of France in the course of the next century under the joint influence of women and education, but without being totally victorious; and the regionalist movement may well halt it in its tracks. All the while professors of singing continued to teach their pupils to pronounce r in a rolled way, so that, for example, Edith Piaf, born and bred in Paris, sang as though she came from Carcassonne. But until the 1890s, the majority of Frenchmen still used the rolled r. In the same way the pronouncing of both consonants where two are found side by side,

[1] J. Gilliéron and E. Edmond, Atlas linguistique de la France (1902–20); on patois, see below, chapter 2, and M. de Certeau, D. Julia and J. Revel, Une Politique de la langue: La Révolution française et la langue. L'Enquête de Grégoire (1975).
[2] Eduard Koschwitz, Les Parlers parisiens (1893). Cf. Marguerite Durand, Le Genre grammatical en français parlé à Paris et dans la région parisienne (1936) for changes in popular speech in the previous fifty years.

as in *grammaire*, was a development of this period, stimulated partly by teachers, who liked to enunciate clearly in order to help their pupils in dictation, partly by the snobs of the Second Empire, copying the Italian singers, fashionable then, and finally by the radio announcers, who, as one chansonnier said, even put three *ts* in *attendre*. This again was a form which was developed mainly in the north.[1]

If French was a logical language in the fullest sense, it could have adapted its spelling to changes in pronunciation. Because it is a language which has experienced rapid evolution, the discrepancy between the two is considerable. But the Academy has been reluctant to modernise spelling: it once agreed, for example, under the influence of Émile Faguet, to replace the plural ending *x* by *s* and to return to the medieval simplicity of *chous*; but it never implemented its decision. Spelling survives therefore which is antiquated and complicated by the pedantry of Renaissance rhetoricians who introduced parasitic letters to satisfy the demands of false etymologies and by legal bureaucrats who added double letters and multiplied *h* and *y* in order to make words look more beautiful in their fine script. Illogicalities like *honneur* and *honorer* remain. How difficult the Academy itself finds it to be logical was shown when it debated the question of whether *automobile* should be masculine or feminine—genders in French are of course unreasonable, the neuter has illogically been allowed to die. The Conseil d'État, which needed to issue a decree using the word, was inclined to make *automobile* masculine, which is what it was in popular parlance at first, but the Academy decided it was a *voiture* and should therefore be feminine, which people gradually accepted.

The slowness with which the Academy has revised its dictionary and the way it has resisted change should not be taken at their face value. In eighteenth-century France, inventing new words was considered acceptable. It was only in the nineteenth century that the French Academy became timid about neologisms, so that when it produced a new edition of its dictionary in 1835, critics complained that it had left out about one-third of the spoken language. Littré, whose dictionary (1863–72) remained the standard authority for nearly a hundred years, gave himself the objective of producing a record of

[1] A. Dauzat, *Le Génie de la langue française* (1943), 37–9.

'contemporary' language and he added vastly to the Academy's vocabulary, not only technical terms but also words from daily speech, including dialects (and particularly the dialect of Normandy). But he interpreted contemporary to mean France since the beginning of the seventeenth century and he also inserted older words left out of the Academy's dictionary; his examples were drawn very largely from authors before 1830. Under Louis XVI, d'Alembert protested against dictionaries laying down the law; but now the major ones were generally accepted as authoritative.[1] However, the language continued to change all the same. Argot as well as patois survived and both developed actively in this period. The rules of style and even of grammar have been broken, on the one hand, by successive literary movements, so that the ideal of classical abstraction has long been challenged, even though it still retains certain well-entrenched positions, and on the other hand by journalists, scientists and travellers, who have introduced modes of speech which have never won literary admiration, but have been used none the less. English has made deep inroads into French. Philosophers have borrowed heavily from German, and a certain kind of obscurity has become fully accepted, despite all the traditions against it. In 1937 the leading linguist in the country, Ferdinand Brunot, assisted by many dignitaries like Paul Valéry, established the Office of the French Language to 'prevent the nomenclature of new things being left to the arbitrary decision of individuals, especially at a time when pedantry and pretentiousness are supreme'. The French language, the Office declared, 'because of the fantasies of certain industrialists, engineers, merchants and journalists, is in the process of becoming a ridiculous carnival'. This body of course had no effect. Archaism was not a characteristic of the French language in this period; the language was in constant movement; and that is why the notion that it gave expression to French nationalism was either naïve or too complicated to be useful.[2]

The principles of civilisation, the bonds of race and the

---

[1] Georges Matoré, *Histoire des dictionnaires français* (1968); Eugène Ritter, *Les Quatres Dictionnaires français* (Geneva, 1905), 24–5.

[2] Michel Bréal, 'Le langage et les nationalités', *Revue des Deux Mondes* (1 Dec. 1891), 615–39; Henri Bauche, *Le Langage populaire* (1920); F. Brunot, *La Pensée et la*

French language as an expression of these, were put forward as the main factors which made the inhabitants of France into Frenchmen, conscious of their nationality. French 'nationalism', as a creed, went far beyond this. Paradoxically, nationalism was a source of division among Frenchmen, because it became the instrument through which quite different political ideas were propagated. Thus on the one hand, nationalism was at first equated with liberalism or revolution: it was the Jacobin doctrine of the emancipation of oppressed peoples; the leaders of the Third Republic, from Gambetta to Clemenceau, proclaimed themselves heirs of this tradition, and the conservatives attacked them. On the other hand, nationalism, at the turn of the century, emerged also as a reactionary doctrine, protesting against the way French life was developing: Barrès found in anti-Semitism a passion around which Frenchmen could reunite, against what he called decadence; Maurras was anxious that his generation should not be 'the last of the French'. All the different varieties of nationalism therefore aroused bitter hostility among Frenchmen, for they always emphasised only one aspect of the nation's values. The League of Patriots was strongly opposed by the League of the Rights of Man. Neither of these, however, involved more than small minorities.[1] The most important kind of nationalism was that which gave no reasons. Michelet had defined it as a new religion. That was in effect what the schools preached, when they urged children to love France 'with an exclusive and jealous affection'.[2] General de Gaulle explained what this meant when he defined his own nationalism as being essentially sentimental, based on the 'instinct' that Providence meant France to enjoy an eminent and exceptional destiny. France was not itself except when it was in the first rank: it could not exist without 'grandeur'; and if it ever fell into mediocrity that was an 'absurd anomaly'

langue (1922); Charles Bally, Le Langage et la vie (1952); Georges Matoré, Le Vocabulaire et la société sous Louis-Philippe (1951).

[1] The League of Patriots (founded in 1882) had at most 100,000 members in 1888–9. Peter M. Rutkoff, 'The Ligue des Patriotes', French Historical Studies (Fall, 1974), 585–603. See also Eugen Weber, The Nationalist Revival in France 1905–14 (U. of California Press, 1959), 9–10, 58, 89. For the development of nationalism, see below, ch. 23.

[2] Pierre Nora, 'Ernest Lavisse: son rôle dans la formation du sentiment national', Revue historique (July 1962), 99.

B

due to the faults of individuals, and not to the 'genius of the fatherland'.[1]

One needs to explain how this state of mind could develop; and one needs to balance the loyalty people felt to the nation against their other loyalties. The nation, of course, meant not only grand principles, great literature and art but also taxation, compulsory schooling, military service. It was no easy matter judging the benefits that membership of the nation bestowed against the price that had to be paid. What ordinary citizens thought about this is very difficult to discover, because nationalism, like religion, was something which they seldom analysed. The history of nationalism is still in the state that the history of religion was before the sociology of religion was invented, to ask not what doctrines churches proclaimed, or how governments and bishops quarrelled, but how religion affected the masses and was felt by them. However, two eminent sociologists did direct their attention to the problem of the ties that held the people together. The relations of the individual and the community had of course been a principal object of interest to most political thinkers, but they had hitherto examined it from the point of view of rights and obligations, law and morals. Durkheim, while not indifferent to these considerations, concentrated on what the bonds between the individual and other groups actually were, regarding them simply as a sociological phenomenon. Durkheim's conclusions should have worried the nationalists, if they had not written him off as a Jewish socialist. He maintained that the old loyalties of the village, the family and the province were withering away and had ceased to awaken any 'profound sentiments'. 'The provincial spirit has vanished without hope of return; local patriotism has become an archaism which cannot be restored at will.' Local government interested people only in so far as it affected their personal concerns. Society had become 'an infinite powder of unorganised individuals which a hypertrophied state tries to contain and to hold in check'. But the state was too far away from the individual and had contacts with him which were too intermittent to be able to 'penetrate much into their consciences and to socialise them internally'. Moreover, as society developed, individuals increasingly freed themselves from the collective

[1] C. de Gaulle, *Mémoires de guerre*, vol. 1 (1954), 1–3.

personality and their diversities increased. Durkheim noted that the fraternity and solidarity which the Revolution and the republic had stood for had not been achieved in practice. He diagnosed, at the turn of the century, what men like Comte and Tocqueville had argued, with less elaboration, some time before, a widespread state of *anomie*. Comte's solution had been a strong government to produce the missing unity, particularly by means of moral education and the inculcation of altruism. The Third Republic to a certain extent tried to implement these ideas. Durkheim on the one hand believed in them too, and wrote a book on moral education to develop them; but he also noted the failure of fifty years of effort to produce a harmonious nation by this means. He advocated the additional use of social institutions, notably professional corporations, to diminish the individual's isolation. But alienation became an increasingly frequent theme among commentators in France as in the industrialising nations.[1]

At about the same time, Gustave Le Bon, in his *Psychology of Crowds* (1895), argued that it was necessary to distinguish between what people believed as individuals and the views they expressed when they formed groups. The nation was therefore far more than the sum of its parts. Crowds gave the individual a sense of invincible power, which allowed him to yield to instincts he forcibly repressed when he was alone; they allowed him to lose his sense of responsibility; they diminished his critical powers, aroused the intolerant, authoritarian and conservative elements in him, increased his suggestibility and made him an easy prey for leaders with skill at repeating slogans and formulas. The key to understanding national behaviour was therefore to be found in the unconscious 'collective soul': it was only when an idea penetrated into the unconscious that it could lead to effective action.[2] Nations thus became considerably more mysterious, but also much more influential. This was a conclusion very different from Durkheim's. Le Bon, however, did not provide much detailed evidence to support his theory: he was one of the pioneers of social psychology, but he was also an old-fashioned polymath doctor, who was interested

---

[1] É. Durkheim, *De la division du travail social* (1902, 2nd edition with a new preface), XXXII, 341.
[2] G. Le Bon, *La Psychologie des foules* (1895).

in almost everything, from atomic energy, photography and sound recording to the dangers of smoking and the training of horses, and it was on the basis of his observation of horses that he developed his views on crowds. Durkheim, for his part, supported his theory with a study of suicide, which, though it was of seminal importance in the development of sociology, left a great many questions unanswered.[1] Both of them in fact offered methodological guidelines more than conclusions based on a thorough investigation of anything like all the loyalties that were influential in the society of their day.

It is not enough to quote the opinion poll, held in April 1945, asking Frenchmen what nationality they would choose, if they were free to: 74 per cent said they would still like to be French.[2] How nationalism was seen in practice, how a national way of thinking was propagated, and indeed, how far it ever existed, need further examination. And to begin with, one can look at the contrast between Parisians and provincials, and between the provincials of different parts of the country.

[1] Steven Lukes, *Émile Durkheim* (1973), 191–226.
[2] H. Cantril, *Public Opinion 1935–46* (Princeton, 1951), 508. Three per cent said they would like to be American, 2 per cent English, 2 per cent Russian, 9 per cent Swiss, 1 per cent Swedish.

# 2. Provincials

THE inferiority complex of provincials in this period is one of the most important and deceptive factors in the image that France had as a nation. It is as a result of this complex that historians have been able to present France as a single unified entity, assuming that what happened in Paris was decisive in the country as a whole. The self-flattery of governments has been accorded the status of accepted truth. Governments liked to believe that their laws would be obeyed throughout the land, and that they represented the whole nation. This was, of course, to a considerable extent, wishful thinking. Historians, by concentrating on the doings of these governments, have strengthened the myth. Though the history of governments tells one a great deal about the country, and even more about the mentalities of politicians, it is important to supplement one's investigation of them by asking how far and in what variety of ways their laws were implemented, and how much national uniformity there really was.

This chapter will attempt to delve beneath the nationalist platitudes to assess the survival of regional individuality. The contempt Parisians have shown for the whole idea of 'provincialism', and the oblivion to which they have attempted to condemn this, cannot be dissociated from the fact that most Parisians in this period had been provincials only a generation or two before. Throughout this period, as will be shown in due course, less than half of Parisians had been born in Paris. Provincialism is therefore an idea full of ambivalence.

Balzac can be used to illustrate the condemnation of the provinces which has done so much to sap their self-confidence. Balzac described provincials as dominated by routine and monotony; their small towns 'apart from a few usages, are all the same'. Provincials were like moles burrowing about in their little plots, or frogs at the bottom of their puddles, engaged in sordid, trivial rivalries, moved by petty jealousies, avarice and material interests. Since they do not think about anything serious, 'the passions shrink while getting excited about tiny things. That is the reason for the greed and gossip which plague provincial life.' There was gossip in Paris too, but provincial life was so narrow that gossip assumed far greater importance there. Provincials had to 'live in public'; they could have no secrets. 'In the provinces, you are not allowed to be original, because this means to have ideas others cannot understand, and people want similarity of minds as well as similarity of manners.' So the main activity must be to live as your father did, to eat four meals a day and watch over your property. Morals are stuffy, dictated by interest and fear of what others will say rather than by virtue. So the monotony can be relieved only by faction and malice.[1]

Over a century later, in 1951, a public opinion poll revealed that, to a considerable extent, this view was still accepted. Forty-six per cent of the Parisians questioned reproached provincials for these same faults: narrowness, meanness, hypocrisy, prejudice, avarice, backwardness, too much interest in others' private lives, and lack of elegance. Forty-five per cent of Parisians, it is true, did not support these accusations. But then only 24 per cent of provincials criticised Parisians (for pretentiousness, superficiality, egoism, noisiness, cynicism, loose morals and wasting money), while 64 per cent spoke well of them. The majority of provincials accepted their inferiority: 64 per cent said they would like to live in Paris, and 50 per cent thought they would improve personally and in terms of education, and broader outlook, if they did. It is true provincials had a limited knowledge of what Paris represented: thus only 42 per cent of them (as opposed to 79 per cent of Parisians) knew who J.-P. Sartre was—others described him variously as a street, a deputy, a painter and a dress designer.[2] But a constant feature of modern French history is that provincials have tried to turn themselves into Parisians.

The peculiarity of France is that people migrated from the countryside to Paris far more than to local regional capitals. This at once destroys part of the image of the provincial as one who stays put where he was born. The population of the pro-

---

[1] Jared Wanger, 'The Province and the Provinces in the Work of Honoré de Balzac' (Princeton Ph.D. thesis, 1937).

[2] *Sondages* (1951), no. 2, 3–42.

vinces was far from being static. If one takes, for example, the villages of the canton of Confolens (Charente), one finds that between 1900 and 1967, 3,233 people born there died. Of these only 797 died in the commune where they were born. 585 died in the same canton, but outside their commune; 360 died in communes bordering on their canton; and 530 in rural areas of neighbouring departments. 359 died in towns in neighbouring departments, 227 in Paris and 372 in the rest of France. Thus about 30 per cent of the children in these villages abandoned their province altogether; but the town which attracted the largest number among them was Paris. Only 98 went to Limoges, only 84 to Angoulême, 57 to Bordeaux, 47 to Poitiers, even though Paris was 375 kilometres away. People born in small towns migrated to Paris in even larger numbers. Thus of the 3,078 deaths of natives of Châtellerault (Vienne) between 1901 and 1967, only 31 per cent occurred in that town; 12 per cent were in the department of Vienne, 12 per cent in neighbouring departments, 25 per cent in Paris, and 18 per cent in the rest of France. Thus only 128 died in Poitiers, even though it was ten times nearer than Paris, where 788 people ended their days. In the canton of Castries (Hérault) twice as many left for Paris as for Marseille, even though the latter was five times nearer.[1]

Because of this polarity, it has always been common to make blanket generalisations about the provinces as a whole. François Mauriac, in a book written between the two world wars, and which he reprinted in 1964, considering it still to be true, showed that the contrast of Paris and the provinces continued to be seen very much to the disadvantage of the latter, even when analysed with profound psychological insight. Mauriac saw provincial life, first of all, as incompatible with intelligence. 'The horror of the provinces', he wrote, 'consists in the certainty that we can find no one who speaks our own language, and at the same time in the fact that we cannot spend a single second unobserved.' An intelligent provincial was plagued by loneliness, 'neither intelligence, nor wit, nor talent counting for anything . . . Conversation is a pleasure the provinces do not know. People get together to eat, or to play cards, but not to talk.' Provincial hostesses do not know how to bring together

[1] Jean Pitié, *Exode rural et migrations intérieures en France. L'exemple de la Vienne et du Poitou-Charentes* (Poitiers, 1971).

men who otherwise would not meet. The reason was the 'terrible law that one can only accept a politeness which one can return', with the result that social life and conversation were killed. Men were devoured by their professions and very seldom avoided being forced to play the roles which these imposed on them. They moved therefore in definite and limited circles. They hardly ever invited people from outside their own *milieu* or *monde*. In Paris, the artist or writer was welcomed everywhere; he could enjoy as much isolation as he wanted, but could emerge from it when he felt like it; he was not constantly watched, nor forced into hypocritical conformity. He was not sat upon by his family as he would be in the provinces, where the family was all-powerful. There, individuals were worth only what their family was worth. Families intermarried and so were able to suffice unto themselves, killing true social life, and setting up stifling controls on their members. 'What is known as family life often comes down to every member of the family being watched by the others, and shows itself in the passionate attention with which they spite each other.' Their furious internal rivalries—as to who could marry his daughters quickest, who could find the richest spouse, who could keep his servants longest—were what preoccupied them. Their meals were the main events of the day. The kitchen was the most important room in the house, to the extent that the rich had two kitchens, one for the cook and one for the mistress of the house, where she could make her *terrines* and *confits* and receive her sharecroppers. Secondly, therefore, Mauriac saw provincial life as an almighty barrage of obstacles set up against the passions. It was based on envy, repression and hypocrisy. Religion and social hierarchy restrained the expression of greed, hate, love and pride, which accumulated bitterly. The provinces knew how to hate as no one else, and they passed their hates on to their children. 'The French provinces are peopled by young beings consumed by unsatisfied appetites. All these repressed ambitions, decupled in intensity by their repression, ensure that later these provincials win the first places in politics, literature and business. . . . The provinces are a nursery of ambitious people, so starved that they can never be satisfied in later life.' Emma Bovary lived in many a soul. The result of this was that the provinces could create deep animosity against

virtue and religion, because they produced such awful caricatures of them. Paris got its population from the provinces, but
gave it back its worst features—like its fashions—and kept for
itself everything worth keeping, like painting and music.[1]

In 1934 *L'Avenir de l'Yonne*, a regional newspaper, carried
out an inquiry into intellectual life in the provinces, seeking
out the opinion of writers, teachers and notables all over France.
Though many of them voluntarily preferred to live in the
country, they were nevertheless often scathing about its satisfactions. They were very much influenced by the fact that the
state system of promotion sent the junior members of the civil
service to the most distant posts, with least population, and
then gradually promoted them to larger towns, before giving
them the crowning glory of a Parisian appointment. This
implied that anyone who stayed in the provinces all his life was
incompetent. Even writers who devoted themselves to singing
the praises of their region admitted the 'obsessive tyranny of
the capital which thinks it is the unique brain of the country'.
There were intelligent men who devoted themselves to local
causes and local studies, which gave them much satisfaction;
and many said they could keep up with new developments,
in Paris and elsewhere, perfectly well by reading books and
reviews. Some nationally famous authors were able to ply their
trade without difficulty from obscure provincial retreats. But
very few lesser intellectuals were able to view the world independently of Paris. Many, while enjoying the countryside,
condemned regionalism as absurd or anachronistic. Maurice
Grammont, for example, professor of phonetics at Montpellier
(and therefore very much the sort of man who might be expected
to become a self-conscious advocate of his regional dialect) said
he took his job because he liked the climate and he had never
responded to the advances of the regionalist movement. A
provincial town like Montpellier, he said, had the disadvantage
that an expert like himself had no one to talk to about his
subject. Those bourgeois who wanted to occupy their leisure in
an intellectual way usually studied history, 'one of the domains
in which one can most easily give oneself the illusion of writing
remarkable books', but they were amateurs without training and 'what they produce is usually without value'. Most

[1] François Mauriac, *La Province* (1964 edition).

provincial literature was 'worthless'. Jean Azais, a judge of the
peace in the Haute-Garonne, said regional pride was good in
theory but in practice it expressed itself in boring and ridiculous
little societies, inadequate libraries, symphonic associations
producing bad music, and periodical reviews with less than a
hundred readers. Jean Dayma, though he devoted himself to
salvaging Gascon dialect and tradition, lamented the indifference he encountered. Daniel Bourchenin, the president of the
Academy of Mountauban, one of the founders of the Society of
Popular Traditions (1882), a member of the Feminist Federation of the south-west, of the Society of French Folklore, of the
Society of Writers, of the Historical Society of Niort (where he
was born), placed limits on what the provinces should claim:
he said he was against their developing an 'excessively proud
consciousness of their originality and respective merits'; he
was against regional *fanfaronnade* or autonomy. Paul Cazin,
who lived in Autun, translating Polish literature, reiterated the
old criticism that the provinces 'lacked altruism'. 'The clan and
the tribe still survive in small towns and in the countryside . . .
People entrenched themselves in their little properties, with
their petty interests, and petty grievances . . . mistrustful of
young talent . . . oblivious of the great problems of the world.'
It was no wonder the young fled to Paris.[1]

Such opinions were banal, but they were not the whole truth.
The attacks on provincial life came from a certain kind of
person, who was involved in the political or cultural climb to
Paris, or regretting in some way that he was not. The tentacles
of the capital did not reach everywhere, however, and one finds
an extremely rich variety of thought and feeling, which deserves
independent study. One reason why the capital ignored this was
that knowledge of France—in the simplest geographical sense—
was still astonishingly primitive, even at the end of the nineteenth century. It should not be taken for granted that most
people had any clear idea of what the rest of the country, outside their own part of it, was like. The first complete and
accurate map of France was made only in 1750–89 by Cassini,
and some of it remained unpublished till 1815 because Napoleon

[1] Ch. J. Millon, *La Vie intellectuelle en province* (Sens, 1934), 10–16, 42, 94,
71–2, 101.

considered it a military secret. It suffered from a rather elementary depiction of relief, in that little dells were indicated with the same marks as the deepest valleys and abysses; and its scale was only 1:86,400. A new map, attempting greater legibility and capable of being used by all the public services, was produced between 1818 and 1866, but it was still on the scale 1:80,000. (A one-inch Ordnance Survey map is on the scale 1:2,500.) Despite the consciousness of the need for more detailed maps, even a 1:20,000 map was considered too expensive to contemplate, and by 1914 only a few sheets of a new map, coloured and contoured, at 1:50,000, had appeared.[1]

During the Second Empire, the study of geography was still largely historical, concentrating on the frontiers and administrative divisions of ancient Persia, Rome or Byzantium. Geography at school meant essentially the memorising of place-names; and the best introduction to it was still Jules Verne, which is partly why he was so popular. Only in 1872, when Émile Levasseur was appointed to the Collège de France as professor of geography, history and economic statistics (the breadth of his scope shows how limited was that of geography), did the study of modern France acquire the status of an academic subject. At first the emphasis was statistical, digesting the results of the government's demographic statistics, and industrial, agricultural and social inquiries.[2] It was still possible for Élysée Reclus (1830–1905), when not active as an anarchist agitator, to write almost single-handed a *Universal Geography* in nineteen volumes (1876–94). Reclus had been virtually forced to travel abroad, because he was expelled for political reasons from France, first by Louis Napoleon in 1851 and then in 1871 for his part in the Commune. His monumental work is important because it attempted to go beyond description, and to produce general explanations. This approach was taken further by Paul Vidal de la Blache (1845–1918), who, after starting as an ancient historian, began teaching geography at the École Normale in 1875 and was professor at the

[1] See the history of French map-making in the appendix to Jean Brunhes, *Géographie humaine de la France* (1920), 2. 617 ff.

[2] B. Gille, *Les Sources statistiques de l'histoire de France: Des enquêtes du 17ᵉ siècle à 1870* (1964); É. Levasseur, *L'Étude et l'enseignement de la géographie* (1872); id., *Précis de la géographie physique, politique et économique de la France et de ses colonies* (1886); P. Joanne, *Dictionnaire géographique et administratif de la France* (1888–1905).

Sorbonne from 1899 to 1909. His *Historical and Geographical Atlas* (1894) was the first which did not concentrate on place-names. He founded the tradition of walking as a means of learning about geography. His method was to collect facts, group them, show how various factors combined to produce the total result, making geography a science which sought to generalise and explain. He was attacked by students of other subjects who claimed there was no room for geography; Durkheim, for example, battled with him, claiming that 'social morphology' should replace geography. Vidal de La Blache was highly influential in developing first 'general geography' (based on the view that all lands belong to a 'type') and in urging his pupils to embark on 'regional geography'. How much still needed to be accomplished, however, may be seen from the way he purposely excluded the study of social and economic factors from geography, on the grounds that they were controversial and therefore difficult to be impartial about. He gave greatest weight to politics as the factor which determined the extent of a region.

In his *Portrait of the Geography of France* (1903) which was published as an introduction to Lavisse's multi-volume history of France, he devoted 180 pages to the Paris region, because that was where 'national history essentially took place', but only 27 pages to the Massif Central, and 15 to the Mediterranean South. Regional geography had still to be created. Adolphe Joanne's famous series of department geographies (1868–9) were mainly lists of railway stations and rivers. Geographical theses had till then usually been historical. This marriage of history and geography has remained one of the strongest features of the French approach to geography, but it was only at the turn of the century that the decisive alliance with economics and social studies was effected. The outstanding theses of Jules Sion on Normandy[1] and Albert Demangeon on Picardy,[2] which gave a total picture of society, linking human activity with physical features, for the first time brought out the profound originality of different regions of France. Instead of simply trying to categorise each region, as an example of a

---

[1] J. Sion, *Les Paysans de la Normandie orientale: étude géographique* (1909).
[2] A. Demangeon, *La Picardie et les régions voisines* (1905); cf. id., *Les Sources de la géographie de la France aux Archives nationales* (1905).

type within a framework provided by general geography, they studied each for its own sake; investigating whatever special problems each presented. Some of the most original thinking about France has been embodied in these regional geographical theses, which revealed the country in a new light, making correlations and distinctions where none had been suspected. André Siegfried analysed the links of politics and geography, Albert Demangeon showed the contribution geography could make to economics and to planning.[1] Geographers thus looked beyond the artificial administrative divisions of the country, and sought to delimit real entities, with a uniform mode of life. A vast number of theories followed as to how France could most satisfactorily be divided, and as to what elements created it. In 1912 a chair in human geography was founded at the Collège de France for Jean Brunhes (1869–1930), one of its most active popularisers. In 1928 the *Annales* review was started by a group of geographers and historians, which did a great deal to broaden the sort of question that was asked by both.

There were certainly gaps in this discovery of France. How much remained to be done was shown by the outpouring of theses on regions still unstudied after 1945. Thus urban geography was slow to develop. Demangeon's thesis on Picardy gave Amiens only one page, and in 1929 Pierre Denis in his geography of South America gave no more to Buenos Aires or Rio de Janeiro. Raoul Blanchard's pioneering work on Grenoble (1912) was followed by only a few between the two World Wars. Rural problems tended to preoccupy the geographers, perhaps because they knew more medieval than modern history. Morphology, because it seemed more scientific, turned many geographers away from human problems altogether. Emmanuel de Martonne (1873–1955), La Blache's son-in-law, led this reaction with his *Treatise of Physical Geography* (1908–9). As a result the important review *Annales de géographie* (founded 1891), which in 1902–11 had only 44 per cent of its articles devoted to morphology, printed 57 per cent on it in 1912–21 and 80 per cent in 1922–31. In 1928 the International Congress of Geographers, attended by 547 specialists, included 42 French representatives; ten years later, 147 out of the 1,217 participants were French. The way French geographers altered their

[1] On Siegfried, see vol. 1, 367–74; A. Demangeon, *Le Déclin de l'Europe* (1920).

countrymen's self-consciousness and awareness of their complicated heritage deserves further study. They included an exceptionally large number of outstandingly able men. But the
'French school' of geography, which has won international
admiration for its breadth and liveliness, itself contained
diverse elements, and it should no more be regarded as mono-
lithically uniform than should the France whose diversity they
revealed.[1]

It was easy for Parisians, and for reluctant provincials, to
decry the intellectual life of the provinces, and to suggest that
nothing original or interesting happened there, but this was not
true. The provincial academies and learned societies, whose
importance in the *ancien régime* is generally conceded, were
indeed temporarily abolished at the Revolution, but they
quickly revived, and by the end of the century there were
roughly three times as many societies in the provinces as in
Paris: about 1,100 as opposed to 375 in Paris. Almost every
town which could claim that title had some kind of intellectual
activity. Mâcon, for example, (population 18,000) had in
1903 an Academy, known also as the Society of Arts, Sciences,
Belles-Lettres and Agriculture of Saône-et-Loire, with 347
members and an uninterrupted history dating back to 1805. It
also had an Agricultural Society (founded 1880) with 450
members, a Natural History Society (founded 1893) with 140
members, a Horticultural Society (1841) with 450 members;
and all of these produced publications and journals. In Agen
(population also 18,000) the Society of Agriculture, Sciences
and Arts of Agen (founded in the Year VI) issued three different
periodicals. A city like Lyon had about 30 different more or less
intellectual societies in 1903 which are worth listing to show
the kind of activities that were popular.

| Society | Founded | Members |
|---|---|---|
| Academy of Sciences, Belles-Lettres and Arts | 1700 | 232 |
| Society of Agriculture, Sciences and Industry | 1761 | 173 |
| Literary, Historical and Archaeological Society | 1778 | 94 |
| Medical Society | 1789 | 76 |
| Pharmaceutical Society | 1806 | 67 |
| Linnean Society | 1822 | 95 |
| Architectural Society | 1830 | 182 |

[1] André Meynier, *Histoire de la pensée géographique en France* (1969) is an invaluable
starting-point.

| Society | Founded | Members |
|---|---|---|
| Educational Society | 1830 | 80 |
| Society of Practical Horticulture | 1843 | 609 |
| Pomological Society (publishing *La Pomologie française*, monthly) | 1856 | 450 |
| Society of Medical Sciences (*Lyon-Médicale*, weekly) | 1861 | 211 |
| Book-readers Society | 1862 | 406 |
| Rhône Society for Professional Education | 1864 | 800 |
| Society of Political and Social Economy | 1864 | 385 |
| Viticultural Society (*La Vigne américaine*, fortnightly) | 1870 | 372 |
| Horticultural Association | 1872 | 1,050 |
| Botanic Society | 1872 | 154 |
| Lyon section, French Alpine Club | 1875 | 605 |
| Geographical Society | 1875 | 626 |
| Association of Steam Engine Owners | 1876 | 850 |
| Architectural Union | 1879 | 86 |
| Anthropological Society | 1881 | 218 |
| Bibliophiles Society (limited membership) | 1885 | 20 |
| Provincial Association of French Architects | 1886 | 597 |
| Society of Fine Arts | 1887 | 1,000 |
| Photo Club | 1888 | 100 |
| Cercle Pierre Dupont (artistic and literary) | 1894 | 403 |
| Rhône Pedagogical Union | 1896 | 450 |
| Society of Veterinary Sciences | 1898 | 510 |

It is true that gardening emerges as the most popular society, and that some societies had less than a hundred members, but they all busily published proceedings, bulletins and reviews, at annual, monthly or even fortnightly intervals.[1]

No one has gone through all these publications systematically to assess their worth, partly perhaps because the encyclopedic knowledge required is beyond the modern specialist. In the eighteenth century, one of the sources of the importance of the provincial academies had been that they were privileged to print without permission from the Censor. In the nineteenth century their publications became even more numerous, more bulky and more regular than in the eighteenth. They still offered prizes which were sought out by the young: Léon Faucher, Thiers, Guizot, Mignet and Louis Blanc were among the prizewinners who were thus launched on the path to fame. Though the academies had lost a great deal of their property at the Revolution, they had accumulated more from new donations and from local subsidies, and they were therefore patrons of learning on a substantial scale. The Academies of Lyon, Bordeaux, Rouen, Caen and Marseille were able to

[1] H. Delaunay, *Annuaire international des sociétés savantes* (1903).

offer a large number of prizes. The subjects they set for competition not only reveal what they were interested in, but also directed research into these fields. Thus the Academy of Lyon managed a prize of 1,500 francs established by Arlès-Dufour for an essay on the amelioration of the lot of women. It also had an income of 1,800 francs, bequeathed by the scientist Ampère, to enable a young man of talent to complete his education. Besançon had a similar one, founded by Suard, from which Proudhon benefited. The Academy of Caen awarded a prize of as much as 4,000 francs for an essay on botany. There were some who thought that all this provincial activity ought to be organised, to form a counterweight to Paris. In 1833 Arcisse de Caumont, a wealthy nobleman who devoted his fortune and forty years of activity to this cause, attending more learned society meetings probably than anyone ever has, held the first Congress of Provincial Societies and in 1839 founded the Institut des Provinces. This, however, appeared to be a challenge to the national and official Institut de France, particularly since Caumont was constantly attacking the latter for supporting the centralisation of the country and for refusing to put itself at the head of the provincial intellectuals. In the eighteenth century there had been close ties between the Paris and provincial academies: individual members of the Académie française or (in the case of Montpellier and Bordeaux, which specialised in medicine and physics respectively) the Académie des Sciences constituted themselves protectors of the provincial academies, which for their part were given the right to send deputies to Paris, to report on their work and to receive comments and compliments on it. The sense of isolation which the provinces felt in the nineteenth century was partly the result of the ending of this tradition. The Congress of Learned Societies, which Caumont also started in 1850 (with 120 participants, rising to 200 in 1875), was designed to remedy this, but the large academies boycotted it, because it was open to all, and did not seek to be exclusive as they were. They claimed that only second-rate scholars attended, and that since papers on any subject under the sun could be presented, there was no possibility of useful discussion.

The government too was jealous of this independent body, and so founded a similar one of its own, with an identical title, but crowned by official prizes awarded by the ministry of education in an annual ceremony at the Sorbonne. This second and official Congress of Learned Societies was an outgrowth of the Historical Committee Guizot had established in 1833 when he was minister of education, to publish historical records. It had doled out subsidies to local scholars who spent lifetimes editing medieval manuscripts for publication, at a snail's pace, for forty years later only 258 volumes had been published at a cost of 130,000 francs a year. During the Second Empire this subsidy system was reorganised, so that it could be spread out more thinly to more people: other subjects apart from history were encouraged. The competition for these grants kept quite a lot of provincials busy; it also stimulated bitter antagonisms, because the grants and prizes tended to be given out on a geographical basis, with special favour shown to new and as yet undistinguished societies. Eminent scholars and the more ancient academies resented that they were not justly recognised. This effort to bring provincial intellectuals closer to the government, through the bait of honours and decorations, was hardly successful. The really active provincial scholars were stimulated to stress their independence. An academician of Lyon, when told off by the minister of education in 1857 for criticising the government's policy towards the provinces, replied that he had no need of ministerial permission, he could speak as he pleased, for the academies were 'little republics which administered themselves . . . living off their own income, and once instituted by decree of the head of state, they were no longer subject to anybody'.[1]

There were plenty of bookshops, journals and newspapers in the provinces to allow them an independent life. In 1860 there were 622 bookshops in Paris (publishers and booksellers being combined in this figure), and about 1,180 printing firms of all kinds. Marseille, which had a population of 233,000 compared to Paris's 1,500,000, had at least 33 bookshops, and 65 printers. Proportionately, Paris had about three times as many bookshops and publishers, but Marseille had enough, in however modest a way, to have a personality of its own. Moreover, every town in the surrounding department of

[1] F. Bouillier, *L'Institut et les académies de province* (1879); E. de Robillard de Beaurepaire, *M. de Caumont* (1874).

Bouches-du-Rhône had its own bookshops too. Aix, with only 26,000 inhabitants, had five bookshops, Arles (population 24,000) four, Tarascon (13,000) three, Salon (7,000) two, Gardane (2,700) one, etc., and there were in addition fifteen printing firms in these towns. Lyon (292,000) had at least eighty bookshops and publishers and eighty printers. The sub-prefecture of Baume-les-Dames (2,615) had three bookshops and one printer. The distribution was unequal. The department of Morbihan for example was underprovided: Vannes (14,000) had four bookshops and three printers, while Beauvais, with the same population had twice as many of each.[1] Some authors claimed that unless their books were published in Paris, they could not regard themselves as successful, but that was because they demanded a certain kind of success. In 1934 there were a very substantial number of provincial publishers to produce their works. Paris now had around 800 publishers, but the provinces had almost 400. Paris had about 3,700 printers, but the provinces had about 3,800. Paris had 820 bookshops, and the provinces 3,250.[2] An *Annuaire des poètes* produced in 1935 listed 800 people claiming to be poets, most of them living and writing in the provinces. Massive local bibliographies testify to the productivity of authors whom neither Paris nor posterity noticed. The single arrondissement of Le Havre, for example, counted 2,038 writers publishing between 1850 and 1900. They were men of all professions: the director of the Havre branch of the Bank of France, the chaplain of the hospital, the conductor of the orchestra, many doctors, teachers, solicitors, a 'poète géologue', a clerk in the navy, etc.[3] Between 1918 and 1936 the publications of Alsace were voluminous enough to require a bibliography of six bulky tomes just to list them.[4] A list of Breton authors published in 1886 included 915 names under the letter A, and seems to have petered out, because of the immensity of the task of producing a full catalogue, halfway

[1] Jules Delalain, *Annuaire de la librairie, de l'imprimerie, de la papeterie* (1860); *Recherches statistiques sur la ville de Paris, d'après les ordres de M. le baron Haussmann*, vol. 6 (1860).

[2] *Annuaire-agenda des auteurs, éditeurs, imprimeurs, etc.* (1934). These are very rough statistics, and include many publishers who only issued reviews.

[3] A. Lechevalier (instituteur), *Bio-bibliographie des écrivains de l'arrondissement du Havre* (Le Havre, 1902–3).

[4] *Bibliographie alsacienne*, published by the Faculty of Strasbourg (1918–36).

through the letter B.[1] The town of Mulhouse produced over 3,000 works about itself between 1870 and 1960.[2] In addition to all this, there was the immensely active local newspaper press, which will be discussed separately.

As an example of what a provincial intellectual could do, one can look at the career of Raoul de la Grasserie (1839–1914). Born in Rennes, he spent the whole of his life in Brittany, as a judge, mainly in Rennes and in Nantes. He published over 360 books and articles. The range of his interests and his competence is astounding. He wrote about psychology (social, ethnic and religious), sociology (theoretical, political and criminal), linguistics (comparative, semantic and North American), law, literature, politics, 'anti-feminist prejudices', 'sexuality in language'. There was almost no contemporary social or theoretical issue on which he did not have something—and often something interesting—to say. He belonged to many learned societies and corresponded with some foreign ones. He showed a knowledge of the latest trends in European scholarship far superior to many a Paris professor. He was making use of Frazer's *Golden Bough*, for example, within a few years of its publication, to analyse the religion of the Bretons.[3]

## Provence

The most obvious division of France was between north and south. When Mérimée came down the Rhône to visit Provence for the first time, and got off his boat at Avignon, he declared that he felt as though he was landing in a foreign country.[4] The language of the people, indeed the landscape, the climate, the way of life were all in marked contrast to the north, whereas the links with Italy and Spain were striking. The economic unity of France was only in the process of being achieved in

---

[1] R. Kerviler, *Répertoire de bio-bibliographie bretonne* (1886).

[2] Denise May and Noë Richter, *Bibliographie mulhousienne 1870–1960*, published by the municipal library of Mulhouse (1966); cf. Ed. Vimont, *Catalogue des livres imprimés de la ville de Clermont-Ferrand . . . relatifs à l'Auvergne* (Clermont, 1878), with 3,419 items; Académie Nationale de Metz, *Bibliographie lorraine*, vol. 1 (Metz, 1970), lists 654 authors whose names begin with the letter A.

[3] The municipal library of Rennes has the fullest collection and bibliography of his works.

[4] P. Mérimée, *Notes d'un voyage dans le Midi de la France* (1835), 131; Stendhal, *Mémoires d'un touriste* (1838).

the second half of the nineteenth century. While the north of the country exported wheat and sugar, the south imported it. Protection was bitterly opposed by Marseille, which regarded it as a sign of its oppression by the northerners. The Mediterranean trade gave the south an outlook towards Africa, the Levant and the Far East. This was even accentuated after 1870, when Marseille lost its position as the busiest port of the continent to Rotterdam, Hamburg and Antwerp, for it then became an industrial city specialising in producing for markets in underdeveloped countries. Politically, the south had a distinctively revolutionary character, supporting radicals, socialists and communists in turn.[1] Psychologically, it constantly complained of being underprivileged, even though it paid less taxes than the north and had a disproportionate share of representatives in parliament.[2] The political leaders it produced in great numbers were, rather vaguely, seen as orators and operators who typically embodied its faults—though there was not all that much in common between Guizot of Nîmes, Thiers and Émile Ollivier of Marseille, Gambetta of Cahors, Paul Reynaud of Barcelonette and Daladier of Carpentras.

The belief that the people of the south were a different kind of people, with a distinct mentality, was widely held and actively propagated by the southerners themselves. The man who perhaps more than anybody made the southerner a distinct type was Alphonse Daudet, with his novels *Tartarin*, *Numa Roumestan* and *L'Arlésienne*. Daudet popularised the notion that the southerners were above all people of unbridled imagination, as though the sun, which dominated their civilisation, created mirages for them. According to him, they were not so much liars as exhibitionists, who deceived themselves, who were carried away by their own inventions and ingenuity and who found in their exaggerations a necessary *bouquet* to season reality. They loved the theatrical stance; they liked giving themselves up to passion, eloquence 'with short and terrible rages, ostentatious and grimacing, always a little simulated even when they were sincere, making tragedy or comedy of everything', then relapsing into indolence and torpor. They

---

[1] See maps in vol. 1, pp. 367–9.
[2] *Questions du Jour* (July 1935), special number on regionalism, gives figures 167–75. Cf. also, vol. 1, p. 710.

were men of words and gestures, who had a great need to communicate their feelings and who never fully experienced an emotion unless they told others about it. 'When I do not speak, I do not think,' said Numa Roumestan. Their words, however, always said more than they meant. They regarded the idea of a home as a northern one, for they lived out of doors, but they were also devoted to family and tradition, 'resembling Orientals in their fidelity to the clan and the tribe, in their taste for sweet foods and in that incurable contempt for women, which did not stop them being passionate and voluptuous to the point of delirium'. They were superstitious and idolatrous while also vigorously anticlerical; they forgot their gods in daily life but ran back to them in sickness or misfortune. They loved gaiety and laughing though they were also malicious; they were optimistic even though they had an exaggerated fear of death and illness. Alphonse Daudet came from a ruined family of silk weavers in Nîmes; he made his fortune in Paris and stayed there. His portrait of the south was that of an émigré who had escaped. He declared that he mocked the south because that was his way of loving it. Southerners complained that he had caricatured them, so that no one could take them seriously any more.[1]

However, writers about Provence developed this idea that the people of the south had a distinct psychology. One, J. Aurouze, obtained a doctorate of letters in 1907 from the Faculty of Aix (which had established a chair of Provençal history in 1894) by putting these claims into scientific jargon and proving them with Taine's theory of race, milieu and moment. Even if the Provençals were not biologically a race, he said, 'centuries of peculiar habits had been building up in their brains and souls' to produce a 'psychological alluvium', which made them unique and distinct. It was the beauty of the landscape which had developed their 'noble and harmonious gestures'; the fact that their agriculture consisted principally of fruit and vine, and so did not require hard work from them, made them gay and happy; the warmth of the climate explained their great powers of perception

---

[1] Alexander Krugicoff, *Alphonse Daudet et la Provence* (1936); Louis Michel, *Le Langage méridional dans l'œuvre d'Alphonse Daudet* (1961); Jean Camp, 'Le Midi dans l'œuvre d'Alphonse Daudet', *Nouvelle Revue du Midi* (1924), 65–84; A. Daudet, *Numa Roumestan* (1881), postscript.

and sensation and their curiosity.[1] He, and many others, protested against the feelings of inferiority which had been instilled into provincials, because they could not speak properly, because they were not Parisians. In a reaction against this, the peculiarities of southerners were dissected, explained and turned into positive advantages. Self-denigration was replaced by pride in those very traits which had formerly been held against them. It used to be said that patois was incapable of expressing ideas, or thought, and was only useful for the farmyard and practical daily life. Now Provençal was exalted as being the only medium by which the 'true emotions and obscure sentiments' of the Provençals could develop and express themselves.[2] Such ideas were paradoxically strengthened by the realisation that the Provençals were racially one of the most mixed regions of France. The birth-rate was comparatively low, emigration was frequent, and there was a great deal of immigration.[3] The Provençal mentality thus emerged as similar in kind to the American one, imposed, as a rather clever book by a doctor argued in 1883, by neighbours more than inherited from ancestors. This book suggested that most Provençals did not have the mentality in any full sense because they had not had time to acquire it. However, immigrants were quick to call themselves Provençals. So there were many varieties of the mentality, and Provençals could be divided into three generations. The first had immigrated from the French Alps (65 per cent) or the Italian Alps (Piedmont and Genoa, 20 per cent), the Cévennes and Pyrenees (5 per cent), the centre or north of France (5 per cent), Corsica (2 per cent) and other countries (3 per cent). A quarter of them were foreigners, and 90 per cent of them men from mountainous regions, poor, seldom very successful, but hard-working, respectful towards authority, thrifty and prolific of children. Only in the second generation did they develop their ambition and imagination and begin to talk more. It was the third generation, consisting

[1] J. Aurouze, *Histoire critique de la renaissance méridionale au XIX^e siècle* (Avignon, 1907), 1. 53.

[2] Cf., e.g. Émilien Cazes (inspecteur d'Académie à Marseille), *La Provence et les Provençaux* (n.d., about 1895), 192; Abbé J. Mascle, *La Provence et l'âme provençale* (Aix, 1911), discours prononcé à la distribution des prix du Collège Catholique d'Aix.

[3] Cf. Pierre Merlin, *La Dépopulation des plateaux de Haute-Provence* (1969).

of only 25 per cent of the population, which exhibited the psychology popularly attributed to the typical Provençal. It was these men, who had made good, who were loquacious and conceited and who constantly felt the need to tell and show everybody how clever and beautiful they were. They now sought to solve their difficulties not by hard work but by wit, imagination and family relations: they gambled, drank, confided in anyone willing to take them seriously, in order to conceal their troubles and maintain a superficial decorum. They sought to stupefy their neighbours by acts of incredible bravura like giving fantastic banquets, with food brought from Paris by express railway. They mocked and criticised their compatriots a lot, so it was difficult for them to become prophets in their own part of the country, but they had a great enthusiasm for causes, and because they loved attracting attention, politics played a great part in their lives. After politics, they gave their energy to societies of all sorts, and for preference musical ones, which, like politics, they valued because these gave splendid opportunities for exhibitionism, the wearing of decorations and the waving of flags. They seized on every occasion—marriage, burial, promotion—to parade, to play music, to hold enormous processions with ribbons and fanfares.[1]

Though the majority of Provençals continued to take the well-known path of careerism towards Paris, and assimilated themselves as Frenchmen, a small but increasingly vocal minority stressed their affinities with other Mediterranean peoples, rather than with the French. They expressed pride in traditions they claimed to have inherited from the Arabs, and the Spaniards, and sang the praises of Raymond Lull, the prolific thirteenth-century Catalonian author, whom they portrayed as a Mediterranean man, uniting the races, religions and philosophies of its two coasts.[2] They claimed that their love of poetry, for example, had more in common with that of Arabs, such as Ibn Dawoud or Ibn Hazm, than with Ovid, and criticised Renan for saying that there was an unbridgeable abyss between Roman and Arab literature. They saw themselves

[1] L. J. B. Bérenger-Féraud, Les Provençaux à travers les âges (1900); id., La Race provençale (1883); cf. Lucien Duc, En Provence, études de mœurs (1895).

[2] See the thesis by J. H. Probst, Caractère et origine des idées du bienheureux Raymond Lull (Toulouse, 1912).

as heretics in Christendom, heirs of the Cathar creed of the twelfth and thirteenth centuries which France had brutally repressed but which still survived among them. They argued that the Manichaean heresy accurately embodied the deepest and continuing inclinations of the Provençals. Provençals, they claimed, did not see good and evil as contradictory; they had no hierarchy of values, no moral imperatives; they saw life as an art, to be played with coquetry and dilettantism; they did not judge other people on the basis of the qualities they had, but accepted their right to be what they were, and appreciated an individual in proportion to the extent that he lived up to his own ideal. They did not judge the ideal. Unlike the northerner who believed in absolute truth, they valued men for the way each one lived with himself and coped with his characteristics. Thus they identified themselves with Ulysses, whom they saw as the eternal prototype of the Mediterranean man, and whose essential quality was ambivalence. Ulysses might be considered a liar, but lying was not disapproved of in the Mediterranean. Lying indeed was neither a game nor a psychosis, but a rite and a ceremonial. Ulysses coloured reality, because he liked to see himself as its creator. He did not fear death, because Mediterraneans did not think about death, but only about funerals, as Mediterranean cemeteries showed. They did not live in order to obtain rewards in the next world, but sought to enjoy the present, to please themselves, to create an image of themselves as agreeable, noble, beautiful. Love in the south was different from what it was in the north. Provençals did not condemn passion; they did not hold up faithfulness to one woman as the supreme virtue; they stressed man's superiority over woman, respecting her above all as Mother. All this, they claimed, made the 'Occitane genius' and the Mediterranean mind totally different from that of Paris, with its rules of taste and of reason. They had a different philosophy, poetry, religion. They had a different way of feeling. Their culture was based on oral tradition, not on literature.[1]

In the nineteenth century, the richness of the Provençal inheritance was rediscovered, partly by foreign scholars who

[1] 'Le Génie d'Oc et l'homme méditerranéen', *Cahiers du Sud*, special number 249, Aug.–Oct. 1942. For legal peculiarities, see Charles Tavernier, *Usages et règlements locaux ayant force de loi dans le département des Bouches-du-Rhône* (Aix, 1859).

took an interest in it before the Parisians, and partly by southern erudites, many of them amateurs but with the leisure to devote a whole lifetime to local study.[1] The discovery of the poetry of the Troubadours revealed Provence as the seat of one of the most magnificent literatures of medieval Europe, expressed in a language which could now be seen to be no mere dialect, or corruption of French, but its equal, developing simultaneously with and independently of French. This medieval lyricism appealed strongly to the romantics. Augustin Thierry presented French history as a clash of north and south, with the south as the home of liberty, envied for its rich fields and large towns, crushed by the military despots of the north, whose language the Provençals had once likened to the barking of dogs. In Guizot's histories, too, Provence emerged as a conquered land. In 1831, when Fauriel was appointed professor of foreign literature at the Sorbonne, he lectured on the history of Provençal poetry and published a book about Southern Gaul dominated by the conquering Germans.[2] In 1851, when Hippolyte Fortoul of Digne, professor at Aix, became minister of education, he sent emissaries into the provinces to collect popular songs and ballads, which 'literature' had so far disdained.[3] François Raynouard, a barrister of Aix and Brignoles (1761–1836), published a dictionary, a compendium of laws and an anthology of the poetry of Provence.[4] Louis Méry protested against 'the Parisianisms which are infecting the Provençals'.[5] Dr. S. J. Honnorat of Digne, who had been brought up to speak Provençal, and who had then taught himself French, produced a dictionary of Provençal five times larger than any previously available.[6] All this was on a small scale: Honnorat's dictionary was remaindered, even though the ministry of education bought a hundred copies. It was only

[1] For example, A. Bruce Whyte, *Histoire des langues romanes et de leur littérature depuis leur origine jusqu'au 14e siècle* (3 vols., 1841).
[2] C. C. Fauriel, *Histoire de la Gaule méridionale sous la domination des conquérants Germains* (4 vols., 1836); id., *Histoire de la poésie provençale* (3 vols., 1846).
[3] F. Mistral, *Un Poète bilingue, Adolphe Dumas* (1927).
[4] F. J. M. Raynouard, *Choix des poésies originales des troubadours* (6 vols., 1816–21); id., *Lexique roman ou dictionnaire de la langue des troubadours, comparée avec les autres langues de l'Europe latine* (6 vols., 1838–44).
[5] Louis Méry, *Histoire de Provence* (1830–7).
[6] S. J. Honnorat, *Dictionnaire provençal-français ou dictionnaire de la langue d'oc, ancienne et moderne* (4 vols., Digne, 1846–9).

a modest counter-attack against the far more numerous works which sought to make the Provençals abandon their dialect and to teach them how to pronounce and speak French 'correctly'.[1] It was essentially erudition, and only when this erudition was popularised did it produce really significant results.

This popularisation was above all the work of Frédéric Mistral (1830–1914) whose lyrical genius gave Provençal poetry an international status. In 1905 Mistral was awarded the Nobel Prize. One is immediately led to ask why the Provençal regional movement, of which he was the head, never got much success beyond its poetry, by contrast with that of Catalonia, with which for a while Mistral maintained close relations, and whose literary festival he attended in 1868. The answer is that the Catalan movement had a backing of economic forces which the Provençal one never did. Catalonia was in the forefront in the industrialisation of Iberia; but its businessmen and commercial leaders also took an active part in its literary renaissance. The secretary of the Metallurgical Employers Union was a poet; philologists were also engineers. It was the adoption of Catalan by the upper classes, and their total rejection of Spain, which made Catalan particularism so powerful—a condition never attained in Provence. Catalan was thus installed as the first language of all classes, but Provençal never had the same status against French.[2] The Provençals continued to seek their fortune in Paris or in the civil service. When industrialisation finally did come to the south, it was largely with capital from outside and with managers drawn from other regions. The railway network of the PLM made it easy to go north, but difficult to move across the south. The leaders of the Provençal regionalist movement were survivors of the old economy, looking backward to a glorious past. Mistral was the son of a *ménager*, that is a small landowner halfway between a peasant and a bourgeois, and he inherited just enough to enable him to live modestly. After obtaining his degree in law at Aix, he devoted himself to poetry. He made friends with young

[1] For example J. F. Rolland, *Dictionnaire des expressions vicieuses et des fautes de prononciation les plus communes dans les Hautes et les Basses-Alpes, accompagnées de leur correction* (Gap, 1810).

[2] Pierre Vilar, *La Catalogne dans l'Espagne moderne. Recherches sur les fondements économiques des structures nationales* (1962), 1. 30 ff.

men of similar status, who met to read their poems to each other, and in 1854 seven of them, meeting at Font-Ségugne, founded the Félibrige, a society for the propagation of Provençal. Their creed was populist and linguistic. They believed that the people's patois had wrongly been considered fit only to express 'low or droll subjects'. There had been numerous popular poets in the south, before the Félibres—men like Pierre Bellot, the stocking manufacturer of Marseille, whose Provençal tales, in four volumes, had sold 2,000 copies in 1840. He had made his characters speak each in his own tongue, Provençal, Gascon, Italian and various degrees of French. Victor Gelu (1806–85), son of a baker of Marseille, had sung realistically about the troubles of his fellow citizens, a southern version of Bérenger. Mistral continued and expanded this popular literature, but with a skill unequalled before, and with a youthful zest which makes him a precursor of the modern popular American singers and musicians who have likewise expressed a whole way of life. He announced his programme in the first issue of the *Provençal Almanach* (1855), which contained new poems by him and his friends:

> Nous sommes des amis, des frères,
> Étant les chanteurs du pays!
> Tout jeune enfant aime sa mère,
> Tout oisillon aime son nid;
> Notre ciel bleu, notre terroir,
> Sont pour nous autres, un paradis.

*Refrain:*

> Tous des amis, joyeux et libres,
> De la Provence tous épris,
> C'est nous qui sont les Félibres,
> Les gais Félibres provençaux.

The Almanach's first edition consisted of only 500 copies, but it later sold about 10,000 copies a year, which Mistral claimed meant that it had about 50,000 readers.[1] However, the aim of the Félibres was not simply to give expression to popular feelings in the language of the people, but also to reform, improve and standardise Provençal. This was a major purpose of

[1] Frédéric Mistral, *Mémoires et récits; correspondance*, ed. Pierre Rollet (1969), 463.

their congresses, and also a major stumbling-block to harmony. Provence had some twenty different variants of its dialect, and this was itself different from that of other southern provinces—Toulouse, Béarn, Languedoc, Auvergne, Limousin, etc. In view of this, it was amazing that the Félibres won so much support over so wide an area. In old age, Mistral became a kind of patriarch, almost a king, surrounded by a court, treated with veneration by disciples who came long distances to pay him homage. In 1876 a Félibre constitution divided up the south into regions or 'maintenances', each with its own dignitaries, reviews, periodical meetings and squabbles. A history of literature names over 500 writers in the Oc dialect, as being particularly noteworthy, and there were many more.[1]

However, the Félibres remained a small minority and failed to acquire mass influence, because they were torn by fundamental disagreements which paralysed them. Mistral himself was not content to be simply the poet of Provence. He always had an eye on Paris. It was indeed Adolphe Dumas, Fortoul's emissary in the search for popular songs, who discovered him, invited him to Paris and introduced him to Lamartine. Mistral published his first masterpiece, *Mireille*, with a French translation which was as carefully worked at as the Provençal. Lamartine hailed it as a new *Iliad* and Mistral as a new Homer. Mistral was never able to resist these blandishments. He lacked the resolution or vigour to be a party leader. He was at first a republican and appreciated Proudhon as a federalist; but after the defeat of 1870 and the Commune, he was frightened into dropping his support of Provençal autonomy, and became the poet of tradition, and the old provincial life, even going so far as to favour Catholicism (though never practising). With time, the delirious enthusiasm people felt for him waned. He was accused of singing only about Provence in the sunshine, about its rural beauties, about his own feelings, ignoring the problems of industrialisation and never speaking of Marseille. It was said that he made Provence into a folkloric curiosity—and indeed he used his Nobel prize money to start a museum at Arles in which he collected and catalogued the dress and tools

---

[1] Robert Lafont and Christian Anatole, *Nouvelle Histoire de la littérature occitane* (2 vols., 1970), is an excellent guide.

of the peasantry, as though he was an ethnographer. He did not in fact know much about the south beyond the district immediately around where he lived: for his poem on the Rhone, he read tourist books and then took a steamboat excursion to collect further detail. His retrospective idealisations prevented him from becoming more than a poet. In the end his message appeared negative: his search for the ideal, for perfection, which is the constant theme running through his poetry, was a search which he declared wellnigh impossible to complete. He created illusions in order to take refuge in them. As he said, he had 'a violent distate for the artificial world in which I was shut up' and he was drawn to 'a vague ideal I saw distantly blue on the horizon'.

Mistral's friends were considerably more reactionary than he was. Joseph Roumanille (1818–91), the son of a poor gardener, was a teacher and then a printer's proof-reader. He had been destined for the priesthood and remained religious; his inclinations were conservative, pious, virtuous, moralising; the Catholic polemicist Veuillot acknowledged him as an ally. Théodore Aubanel (1829–86) was also pious, son of the Pope's well-to-do official printer at Avignon, although his autobiographic love poem, about his hopeless love for a poor girl who ended up as a nun, was condemned as obscene by the clergy. Aubanel was very much an urban poet, describing the sordid side of life, rejecting the Félibres' idealisation of Provence; he was a sort of provincial counterpart to Baudelaire. He was the most professional of the Félibres, making friends with the leading Parisian writers of his day. When Mistral and Roumanille united in a conservative front in 1876, Aubanel emerged as the leader of a liberal, anti-provincial movement centred round the young Félibres of Paris, for there was also a school of provincials who rejected provincialism or who wanted to combine it with what was best in French culture. These few tergiversations give only a small idea of the constant disagreements which divided individuals, towns and regions, in an infinite variety of ideological positions. Marseille and Montpellier, for example, had strongly anticlerical branches of the Félibre movement which contradicted many of the master's teachings. The Montpellier Reds were led by L. X. de Ricard (1843–1911) who was the son of a marquis and general of Napoleon III's reign, and who had rebelled to republicanism at the age of twenty. Victor Gelu, the popular poet of Marseille, despised the Félibres as pretentious and preferred to show provincialism as dying, doomed in the age of industrialisation. Another tendency was to promote the 'Latin idea', in which Italians, Catalans and Romanians were united; this was launched with a Festival at Montpellier in 1878.[1] But the unity of the south was never established. Roumanille's langue d'Oc, which Mistral adopted, was only one dialect; they claimed it should be the national language of the south, but it was not. Mistral, who in 1892 had combined with Maurras and Amouretti to launch a federalist manifesto for France, typically retracted during the Dreyfus Affair and formed the Ligue de la Patrie française. When the vinegrowers of the south revolted in 1907,[2] he refused to put himself at their head. He disliked the dynamism of the young men who came forward to head the movement at the turn of the century, like the Protestant Paul Devoluy. The traditional divisions of the south, expressed with their usual vigour, were all reflected in the Félibre movement. It could not decide what precisely it represented.[3]

## The Bretons

The national self-consciousness of the Bretons has been considerably more forceful. It has carried separatism to the point where some Bretons in 1939 refused to fight for France against the Germans and it has produced the only autonomist movement using violence. This independence has a long history. Under the *ancien régime* Brittany succeeded in resisting centralisation and modernisation more effectively than most provinces; and it was hit all the more noticeably by the reinvigorated centralisation of the nineteenth century. It stood out in France as the most steadfastly religious province, and it was regarded with particular fear by modernisers, who attributed this piety to its economic backwardness. Breton religion was something few outsiders understood. It was quite different, for example, from that of Spain. Its strength came from the reinforcement of

[1] See *La Revue du Monde latin*, 1883–6 and *Le Félibrige latin*, 1890.
[2] See vol. 1, pp. 706–7.
[3] Émile Ripert, *La Renaissance provençale 1800–60* (n.d., about 1917); Beatrice Elliott, *Émile Ripert* (Avignon, 1938).

Catholicism by much older pagan beliefs and practices. The basis of Breton religion was superstition and magic, against which the Catholic clergy had at first fought hard, but which it had usually been forced to incorporate into its own system. Thus the ancient magic fountains were turned into objects of Catholic pilgrimage. Magic became an inferior demoniac religion. Fairies survived: 'the Bretons speak of them with complaisance as though they were a delicious forbidden fruit.' The Church tried to condemn them as evil spirits but the peasants refused to believe this and continued to use them. The worship of saints (after whom most Breton villages are named), though given an external Catholic respectability, continued in forms which were barely Christian. Most of the saints were local ones, unknown to Rome. Every parish had at least a couple of chapels in their honour, often as many as six: Plouaret (population 3,300) had twenty-four chapels. Each saint had a particular and definite purpose. Religion was powerful here because it was useful and practised from self-interest. Each saint could grant specific favours and each required different rewards. St. Onenne cured dropsy, St. Trémeur cured neuralgia, St. Brandon cured ulcers. Every species of animal also had its own saint. St. Avoye required white hens before he would do anything, St. Majan (who cured headaches) accepted hair as his offering. And when saints refused to grant their favours, they were forced to. Renan tells how his father went to a saint to cure a fever: he took the village blacksmith with him, complete with his tools; the blacksmith heated up an iron till it was red hot, held it up to the saint's face and said, 'If you do not cure this child of this fever I shall shoe you like a horse'. The saint obeyed. The Bretons did not communicate with God except through saints, and indeed had no dealings with God, but only with the saints, with whom they were involved in a ceaseless commerce, exchanging services. The Christian God was turned into a kind of constitutional monarch, above the details of daily life. The saints, unrecognised elsewhere, gave the Bretons a provincial allegiance; because there were so many of them, the individualism of the Bretons was respected; because they provided opportunities for so many social activities, they were valued for the fun as well as for the consolation they provided. The Breton 'pardons' and pilgrimages were outings on a mass scale carried out long before the holiday excursion. But this religion turned the Bretons always towards their past; every ceremony was linked with the worship of their ancestors, to the extent even of holding funeral memorial services as part of wedding celebrations. Breton piety was not exempt from doubt. The three great writers of nineteenth-century Brittany—Chateaubriand, Lamennais and Renan—were all involved in doubt or unorthodoxy. This doubt was all the more disconcerting because it was countered with sentiment rather than reason. There was thus a mysterious element at the bottom of Breton religion, and the Bretons were religious in an original way.[1]

The Breton language distinguishes this people still further, since it is a Celtic tongue totally incomprehensible to Frenchmen and having much more in common with Welsh and Gaelic. It has been estimated that in 1806 one million people normally spoke Breton, in 1886 1,300,000, and in 1970 about 600,000 to 700,000 used it daily. In the course of the nineteenth century in this province as in others, it became a mark of education and progress to forget Breton, which disappeared most rapidly in the towns. More recently, since 1920, Breton has been taken up again with pride by intellectuals, so that it is no longer simply a language for peasants. Its importance can be seen from an inquiry conducted in 1927 which revealed that out of 635 communes questioned, 474 had sermons entirely in Breton and 397 taught the catechism in Breton. Seventy had sermons mainly in Breton, 21 in both languages, 21 mainly in French and 49 entirely in French.[2] Religion and language combined to produce another distinctly individual tradition—that of an extremely vigorous popular theatre. In 1929 there were still over a hundred theatrical troupes in Brittany, performing plays which were at once traditional and demanding of imagination. These were not the hobby of middle-class people with leisure, but the recreation of men of all classes and all ages. (Women were allowed to act only in the towns.)[3]

[1] Cf. Émile Jobbé-Duval, *Les Idées primitives dans la Bretagne contemporaine* (1920).
[2] The figures for catechisms mainly in Breton are 72, in both languages 30, mainly in French 33, entirely in French 103. P. Sérant, *La Bretagne et la France* (1970), 205.
[3] A. Le Braz, *Essai sur l'histoire du théâtre celtique* (1904), doctoral thesis by a lecturer at the University of Rennes who became a leading advocate of the language.

Celtic literature had been as brilliant and as individual as that
of Provence in the Middle Ages, and in the nineteenth century
its traditions were revived by a large number of writers who,
for obvious reasons, have not reached the French textbooks.
In 1879 the Society of Breton Bibliophiles published a list of
nineteenth-century Breton poets which contained over 200
names. By 1914 there were about fifty associations in Brittany
devoted to Breton art and literature, and some thirty more in
Paris.[1] All this activity allowed Arthur Le Moyne de La Borderie to say in his inaugural lecture, when taking up the chair
of Breton history in 1891, that Brittany had all the bases of
national originality—a language, a national character, a
history and a poetry of its own.[2]

This view could be challenged. Brittany had four, if not
five, different dialects. Part of the province, Basse Bretagne,
was largely Francised, or at least spoke French—though it was
significantly here that the Breton separatist movement made
most headway. The juxtaposition of these two cultures was
comparable to that prevailing in Belgium. But the province
was exceptionally divided geographically and economically.
There were very different conditions on the sea coast and in the
interior—the former having a density of population twice that
of the latter. The Bretons' political and religious behaviour was
by no means as uniform as appeared at first glance, so that
there were exceptions to almost every generalisation about
them. The intense mistrust and rivalry between the villages,
which often broke out into bloody battles, made united action
difficult. Though the Bretons had a very high birth-rate, they
appeared to be a vanishing race, because they emigrated in
such enormous numbers, providing Paris with its prostitutes
and the army with its private soldiers: no province lost as many
men in 1914–18 as Brittany did. Émile Souvestre wrote a book
about them in 1836 entitled *The Last Bretons*, as though they
were disappearing like the Amerindians. But very little was
really known about Brittany then. Souvestre claimed that
travel books about it simply copied from each other, all of
them written in a style reminiscent of Christopher Columbus's

---

[1] Camille Le Mercier d'Erm, *La Bretagne vue par les écrivains et les artistes*
(1929).
[2] Cf. A. Le Moyne de La Borderie, *Histoire de Bretagne* (6 vols., 1896–1914).

C

discovery of an unknown race of savages.[1] The self-consciousness of the Bretons had to be created by intellectuals and this is what happened, even while—and perhaps because—the province was exporting its children to the rest of France to the extent that no city in Brittany contained anywhere near as many Bretons as did Paris. And the Bretons outside Brittany, despite the nostalgia which they exhibited in the early years of exile, quickly assimilated themselves to their new surroundings: they were not nearly as active as, for example, the Auvergnats, in keeping together and preserving the memory of their homeland.[2] The Breton revival of this period has been likened to Zionism in its early years. Both movements were an answer to maltreatment in various degrees, for Brittany resented its poverty and its neglect by the government. Both were the creation of determined and able individuals.

In 1870 the Army of Brittany, under the command of Kératry (a great-grandson of a president of the Estates of Brittany), formed to repulse the Prussians, had so frightened the republican leaders, as potentially a dangerous and alienated force, that it was left virtually without arms. 'I beg you', telegraphed Freycinet to Kératry, 'to forget that you are a Breton and remember only that you are French.'[3] There were a number of people who refused to forget their origins and rejected assimilation.

The man who put Brittany on the map as a nation with a distinguished past, at a time when it was considered a backward and bigoted bogland, was Théodore Hersart de La Villemarqué (1815–95). In 1839 he published *Barzaz-Breiz* which purported to be a collection of the popular songs of Brittany collected by himself. He seems in fact to have contributed a lot to their composition, so that it was more creative poetry than folklorism (the word folklore, it might be added, was first used in 1846, by an Englishman). His book was written for Parisians, and he himself was a Breton émigré to Paris, who had become interested in Brittany only after he had settled in the capital.

---

[1] Émile Souvestre, *Les Derniers Bretons* (1836, new larger edition 1854).

[2] The *Annuaire des Bretons de Paris* (1911) said that only 2 per cent of Bretons in Paris were members of Breton associations: its list of Breton addresses in Paris contained only 3,600 names out of an estimated 200,000.

[3] C. Le Mercier d'Erm, *L'Étrange Aventure de l'armée de Bretagne* (first published, privately, 1935, reprinted 1970), 110.

A year before, the minister of education had given him a grant of 600 francs to attend the Eistedfodd at Abergavenny and to search the library of Jesus College, Oxford, for historical records. Such places, and the École des Chartes in Paris, which he attended, were paradoxically the most convenient sources from which one could obtain the information needed to re-create the idea of Breton nationality. La Villemarqué's book came out looking very much like the *Popular Songs of Modern Greece* which Fauriel had published in 1824. Only 500 copies were printed, and, over the century, no more than an average of 25 copies were sold each year. But George Sand declared after reading it that no one could henceforth pass a Breton in the street without taking his hat off to him. It made a very considerable impression on a few influential people. La Ville-marqué was elected to the Institut and he became the centre of a Bretons-in-exile fraternity, devoted to reviving the use of the ancient language. Already in 1841 the *Dictionnaire encyclopédique* talked of the 'Breton nationality'.[1] Le Gonidec's Breton–French dictionary, published posthumously in 1847, was the work of an exile too, who managed to compile its 835 double-columned quarto pages without setting foot in Brittany between 1804 and his death in 1838. Joseph Loth, another of the pioneers of the study of ancient Breton literature, went to learn Gaelic in Wales, married a Welsh girl, and only then, in 1884, started lecturing on Celtic literature at the Faculty of Rennes. There a whole line of distinguished pupils were to continue his work.

The Breton movement had three different strands in it. The first was Celtic, erudite, essentially interested in the study of the past, and principally linguistic. An *Association bretonne*, founded in 1834, was suppressed by Napoleon III who, how-ever, did not obstruct the Académie bardique (1855), which was purely cultural. The College of Druids, founded at the end of the century, modelled its statutes on those of its Welsh counterparts, and held annual competitions in the same way. Later it organised examinations in Breton for children and even offered prizes for Breton advertising slogans. By the 1930s, however, its activities were scorned by the younger genera-tion, who criticised the Druids for dressing up for the benefit

[1] Francis Gourvil, *T. C. H. Hersart de La Villemarqué (1815–95) et le 'Barzaz-Breiz'* (Rennes, 1960), 21, 28, 77, 147.

of tourists, for closing their minds to changing economic conditions and even for being hypocritical, when the Grand Druid
Taldir, who wrote a celebrated anti-alcoholic tract, was revealed to be a cider merchant. The scholarly side of the Celtic
movement, however, had some very formidable men in it, who
in 1898 founded the Breton Regionalist Union. This included
the leading Breton authors of the day—Anatole Le Braz, Charles
Le Goffic, Camille Vallée, with the marquis de L'Estourbeillon
as president. Its main interest was the teaching of the Breton
language in schools, and up to *baccalauréat* standard, arguing
that Breton had as much right to be officially recognised as
Arabic, Annamite and Malagache, which were optional
parts of the syllabus. Its slogan was 'Children: speak Breton to
your parents'. It also pressed for the economic development of
Brittany, but it abstained from any serious political activity and
so had comparatively little influence.

The really important development in the revival of Breton
was the foundation of Gwalarm (meaning north-west), which
lasted from 1915 to 1940. This was a publishing house, directed
by Roparz Hemon, a teacher of English at Brest. Its achievement was to turn Breton into a modern language, in the way
that Hebrew was later revived in Israel. It published a large
number of books, novels, poems, plays and, not least, works on
every subject including science—all in Breton. It arranged for
numerous translations of European classics into Breton, from
Aeschylus to Alexander Blok. It commissioned a new history of
the world in Breton, as well as physics and geometry textbooks.
It was particularly successful with Breton children's books,
with stories generally derived from Irish or Danish sagas, or
definitely non-French sources like Finnish. It supplemented its
publishing by language classes, correspondence courses and a
summer university. It paid no royalties, and all the work, which
made Breton into an authentic and modern vehicle of self-
expression, rather than a folkloric survival, was done by
amateurs.[1] At the level of the primary schools, Yann Sohier, the
communist *instituteur* of the village of Plourivo, in 1928 began

[1] Roparz Hemon, *Les Mots du breton usuel classés d'après le sens* (Brest, 1936); id.,
*Petit Dictionnaire pratique breton–français* (Brest, 1928); id., *L'Orthographie bretonne*
(Brest, 1929); id., *Dictionnaire breton–français* (second revised edition, La Baule,
1948).

speaking to his pupils in Breton and corrected their mistakes in Breton as severely as those they made in French. He discussed current events with them in Breton and sought to end their feelings of guilt about using a language normally associated with the uneducated and the poor. The School Inspector could do nothing about it because the pupils were the best in the canton in French, and Sohier won the approval of their parents. In 1933, together with some other primary teachers, he founded *Ar Falz* (*The Sickle*), a review and a movement which spread this new method widely in the schools of the province.

The second strand in the Breton revival was that of the conservative aristocrats. Little is written about this, though the influence normally attributed to the aristocrats would make their activities worth investigating. The paradox of their situation was that though they favoured greater autonomy for the Bretons, they also wanted to change the Bretons, to reform them, so that they would accept their dominance. The comte de Lantivy-Trédion, who was a disciple of La Tour du Pin, and who wrote a book on 'The Breton Question' in 1909, was severe in his criticisms of the Breton peasants. He castigated them for being egoistic, anarchistic, irrational, only superficially religious, attending *pardons* simply in order to get drunk. He feared the Druids because they were pagan and because they had links with Protestant England. He denounced that wayward Breton imagination which had led men like Lamennais on the dangerous paths of heresy. La Tour du Pin's efforts to establish the Free Estates of Dauphiné had failed because they had lacked popular support. The lesson was to form the masses into professional corporations who, it was hoped, would accept an aristocratic constitution. Something of this kind was mooted again under the Vichy régime. But it was never a powerful trend.[1]

What attracted more public attention was the third, more violent and demanding aspect of the Breton movement. In 1911 Camille Le Mercier d'Erm founded the Breton Nationalist Party, which asked for national independence. It declared that Brittany was an enslaved nation, like Ireland and Poland, and only independence could free it. His was a party of young men, ready to go to prison for their beliefs. At the unveiling

[1] Comte de Lantivy-Trédion, *La Question bretonne* (1909).

of a new statue in Rennes in 1912 commemorating the union
of Brittany and France, Le Mercier d'Erm organised the first
public demonstration of separatist protest against France, and
was himself the first Breton to be arrested for his nationalism.
His party and his paper *Breiz Dishual* (*Free Brittany*) disappeared
with the war of 1914. But immediately after this, *Breiz Atao*
(*Brittany Always*) was founded, a review which grew into a
movement. Its programme was to fight tuberculosis, alcoholism and French domination, the three scourges of Brittany.
In 1927 it started the Breton Autonomist Party; in 1929 the
review became a weekly; in 1930 it put up a candidate for
parliament, unsuccessfully. The review normally sold about
5,000 copies, though occasional issues were five times as large.
It tried to be neutral in social and religious questions. Its
slogan was: 'Neither red nor blue'. It adopted the Celtic cross
as its symbol, signifying peace and union (until Hitler's demonstrations caused it to abandon this, in favour of the flag of nine
black-and-white stripes—standing for the nine *pays* of Brittany). It expressed itself in very strong language, which worried some of its supporters, on the evils resulting from French
imperialism in Brittany. Its stickers, bearing slogans about how
Bretons were discriminated against, how taxes they paid were
used to develop other regions, etc., spread its message beyond
the faithful who read the review. It had some difficulty, however, in deciding what tactics to follow. For a while it steered
clear of separatism, merely talking about autonomy. It was
rather vague for a few years about what kind of federation it
wanted, suggesting occasionally that Brittany should be part
of a reorganised Europe as much as of a decentralised France.

Though its emphases were modified from time to time, its
1929 Manifesto gives the best idea of its general line of attack.
This began by insisting that it was not retrograde. Old Brittany had gone for ever, and it did not want to resurrect it,
though it respected it. It denied being anti-French, but it
declared that French rule was illegitimate, contrary to the
wishes of the Bretons and in violation of the Treaty of 1532,
which had united them to France on condition that their
customs were respected. It opposed French centralism and
French imperialism 'which exposes us to new wars for interests
which are not ours. We are rising against France's indifference

towards our economic needs, its inability to understand our cultural and moral aspirations, its militant animosity against our language. We note France's inability to accord with the rhythm of the world's general evolution. We think that what it is usual to call France is not a Nation, but a State, containing a certain number of nationalities, and we cannot accept that our demands should be opposed by the mystical dogma of a Nation "one and indivisible", which is today left way behind by all the enlightened people of the globe.' Breiz Atao was the first movement to denounce French 'imperialism' within metropolitan France itself, and to coin the slogan which has, since the 1960s, been widely adopted by other people. 'Brittany', it declared, 'has been an exploited colony.' Brittany was a nation born of events entirely foreign to the history of France, as a result of emigration from Great Britain. It was a nation 'and every nation which does not administer itself rapidly falls into decadence'. This had happened to Brittany, and that is why it now demanded its own parliament, controlling its own executive, with particular concern for the organisation of education and the revival of the arts 'in conformity with our Western and Nordic genius, to expel the Latin obscenities with which the novels, songs, theatres and newspapers of Paris poison us'. It wanted a religious settlement 'in accord with the wishes of our people', social legislation adapted to their needs, the abolition of France's prefectoral and departmental system which was out-dated in an age of improved communications, to be replaced by communes free from administrative interference. France would lose nothing if it granted all this, because its centralisation had paralysed it: it was outdistanced in social legislation, economic equipment, education, dramatic and architectural production, hygiene and urbanisation by many other countries, notably Germany, England, Switzerland, Holland, Czechoslovakia and Scandinavia. The interesting feature of this programme was the way it looked to Europe, beyond France (rather than the U.S.A.). As a model for federalism it sometimes quoted Switzerland; for its cultural inspiration it looked to a wide variety of Nordic countries. 'We believe', it declared, 'that Europe is destined to form, sooner or later, an economic unity', which was the only way to stop it fighting. 'But this unity will not be constituted by a federation of the present states, which are arbitrary aggregations, the products of chance, violence and guile, and which are not as eternal as the politicians so emphatically claim.'[1]

How to deal with this problem of federalism produced divisions and resignations. Some—'the federalists'—wanted to make Brittany a general international question, while 'the nationalists' wanted to concentrate on the internal problems of Brittany itself. In 1936 the latter set up a *Front Breton* to support candidates for parliament who would accept the Breton demands: forty-one did accept and of these fifteen were elected, constituting a 'committee for the defence of Breton interests'. But the government got worried by this agitation, and in 1938 the Breiz Atao leaders, Michel Debauvais and Olier Mordrel, were arrested and put on trial at Rennes, and in 1939 their party (now called the Breton National Party) was banned. The demands of the Breton movement were thus completely rejected by the French. When a young Breton heckled Daladier, at a public meeting about this, Daladier scornfully replied: 'Do you want us to go back to the Gauls?' The Breton programme was too savage an attack on France's pride in its achievements and on the progress it claimed to incarnate. So as soon as war broke out in 1939, Debauvais and Mordrel went to Berlin and issued a manifesto inviting the Bretons to remain neutral in a war that did not concern them. They believed that by this bold gesture they could turn Brittany into a second Ireland, and that it required only a few hundred determined men to bring this about. It was a complete miscalculation. This was because, first of all, the Breton movement had been too divided and ambivalent about its attitude to France to allow any enthusiastic and widespread support for such a drastic course. Secondly, Pétain presented an apparently viable alternative—he was a regionalist peasant, in his own way. The Bretons at first got no response from him to their requests for autonomy, but in 1942 a Lorrainer, Jean Quenette, became regional prefect of Brittany, and created a Breton Consultative Committee—the first recognition they had ever had. This appears to have given some satisfaction; it made Breton a subject in the primary school-leaving certificate and increased

[1] René Barbin, *L'Autonomisme breton 1815–1930* (1934, no place of publication), 136.

the teaching of the language. Thirdly, the Germans, though they allowed Mordrel and Debauvais to try and form (without much success) a Breton Corps from Breton prisoners of war, who were segregated into a special camp, had their own plans for dealing with France. The 'reconciliation' of France and Germany was a greater prize, so they could not offend France by dismembering it. Otto Abetz, who was married to a Frenchwoman, effectively killed the hopes of Mordrel: he thought the best that should be done for him was to offer him a professorship in Celtic at the University of Tübingen.

Olier Mordrel, twice condemned to death for treason, in 1940 and 1946, published his memoirs in 1973, after twenty-two years of exile in Argentina. He was just eighteen when he helped to found Breiz Atao and he shows how it needed only a few young men to produce and maintain the agitation. In 1927 the movement had only about 100 active members; in the 1930s, they never even dreamed of having more than 20,000 'potential supporters'; and in 1938 their congress at Guincamp was attended by only 1,500 people. They were not pro-German and still less Nazis: their contacts with Germans had been with outsiders and eccentrics like themselves, who proved powerless to obtain official aid for them. If they had a foreign model, it was rather the Irish Republican Army, from which they got some arms. They had a small dissident faction, which formed a tiny 'army', determined to use violence, and this was particularly active during the war. Mordrel took the risk of going to Berlin, conscious that he would be called a traitor if he failed, but convinced that the Bretons' only hope of success was to seize the opportunity presented by France's involvement in war. His memoirs are written with a remarkable serenity and modesty, which contrasts strangely with his inextinguishable optimism.[1]

The Bretons were torn by the war in a particularly acute way, because while many joined the Resistance, a small group of antagonists waged war against these, and a series of bitter reprisals followed. In 1944–5 many Breton autonomists were arrested, which hardened their hostility to the French, turning moderates into separatists. After a lull of some years, the Breton movement revived with considerably greater popularity, and

[1] Olier Mordrel, *Breiz Atao: Histoire et actualité du nationalisme breton* (1973).

more will no doubt be heard of it.[1] But a good many years will elapse before enough historians will have had the time to work through the vast amount of material that needs to be looked at. A bibliography of Breton periodical publications, published in 1898, shows that in Nantes alone there were 60 journals produced before 1848 and about 130 between 1848 and 1896. The list for the single department of Loire-Inférieure was 583 items long.[2] It is not surprising that the French never became aware of all this literary activity, which was essentially local, particularly because the more independent reviews were not sold openly at railway stations, but went straight to subscribers, and the really Breton bookshops were obscurely tucked away in back streets. It will be interesting to see in due course how the 'Breton character' is redefined, whether melancholy and taciturnity—even in love—obstinacy, indolence, asceticism, violent alternations between gravity and drunken festivity, religiosity and anarchism, continue to be regarded as basic traits, or simply the product of a poor and isolated civilisation. In 1905 Raoul de La Grasserie claimed that the Breton character was inseparable from its surroundings and collapsed in emigration. It is curious that when a national public opinion poll asked people what made them feel attached to their native province, the Bretons stressed the 'temperament' of their people less than others, but laid twice as much emphasis as others did on 'folkloric traditions'. But the factor stressed more than any other was the same with them as with all the Frenchmen: having been born in Brittany or having many relations there. The increasing mobility of labour no longer takes the form of onion sellers coming to England seasonally (the Bodleian Library has a drawing of one of these dated 1753), nor adventure beyond the seas (there is a colony of 90,000 Bretons in New York). Bretons have sought work all over France for many generations now and have become assimilated there. There are about 600,000 today, born in Brittany, who live elsewhere in France, and there are 200,000 natives of other regions of France living in Brittany.[3]

[1] The best accounts of it are in P. Sérant, op. cit., Barbin, op. cit. A vigorous contemporary document is Morvan Lebesque, *Comment peut-on être Breton?* (1970).

[2] René Kerviler, *Essai d'une bibliographie des publications périodiques de la Bretagne* (Rennes, 1884–98).

[3] Poll in Sérant, 166. For Bretons abroad, see Olivier Vincent Lossouarn, *Les Bretons dans le monde* (1969) and Jean Choleau, *Les Bretons à l'aventure* (1950). For

That is why the new generation of autonomists is redefining what it stands for, in a wider European context which must have more general relevance.

## The Auvergnats

It would take too long to list all the regional parties and groups, seldom mentioned in French national histories, which flourished with more or (usually) less success in these years. However, they raise some important general questions about the degree to which French culture was assimilated. The regions were of two kinds. Some were frontier regions, whose inhabitants shared a non-French language with people living under other governments—like the Basques, the Flemish, the Alsatians, the Catalans, the Corsicans. The central regions of France were not subject to this tension, but they showed strong signs of independence and individuality all the same, though in different ways. Thus the Auvergnats had a distinctive consciousness both of the outside world and of their own poor province. They had fewer illusions about themselves. They admitted the accusation, which seems to have been almost universally made, that they were above all interested in making money. They prided themselves on being honest, hard-working, thrifty, persevering and practical. Their ideal was the man who showed good judgement, who gave sensible opinions, who always kept practical aims in view, and who concentrated on amassing money and land. Even one of their most venerated writers, Ajalbert, talked of their 'absolute contempt for anything which was not money'. At most, they enjoyed music and dancing, but had little use for art and less for utopianism. Jules Romains, another of their sons who had made good in Paris, lamented that they 'did not contribute enough to the expression of the national genius' or 'make their weight felt in the common consciousness of the country'.[1]

'Breton psychology', see Raoul de La Grasserie, *Essai d'une psychologie du peuple breton* (Nantes, 1905); Anatole Le Braz, *La Bretagne* (1925) and Stéphane Strowski, *Les Bretons, essai de psychologie et de caractérologie provinciales* (Rennes, 1952); Marquis de L'Estourbeillon, *L'Immuabilité de l'âme bretonne* (1914); Charles Le Goffic, *L'Âme bretonne* (1902–8); Y. Le Febvre, *La Pensée bretonne* (1914); M. Duhamel, *La Question bretonne* (1929).

[1] Max Giraudet, *Les Auvergnats découverts et jugés par un Parisien* (1912); Joseph Desaymard, *L'Auvergne dans les lettres contemporaines* (1943); Vercin-Rhétorix,

They had a long tradition of emigrating, usually for about twenty years of their adult life, to make their fortunes. Already in the seventeenth century, the French ambassador in Madrid reported that there were at least 200,000 of them in Spain. They worked as merchants, usurers, pedlars in Andalusia and Castile. They were bakers in Madrid. In 1936 their factories in Valencia and Candette were still responsible for importing half the jute used in Spain to make the soles of espadrilles.

The Auvergne's most respected modern poet, Arsène Vermenouze (1850–1910), came from a family which had long had a small business in Illescas. Each member of the family usually went there for two years at a time, known as a 'campaign', and then came home for ten months. Young men would spend their first six or eight years of work as itinerant pedlars until they were admitted as full members of the company at around the age of thirty; they then spent most of their time in the shop. (The smuggling of goods into Spain was a specialised trade.) Most Auvergnat papers usually had a regular column of news about Spain. Vermenouze himself spent his youth reading not just Hugo, but Calderón, Cervantes, Moratín and Lope de Vega, and when he finally brought his profits home to settle in Auvergne, he still treasured his memories of Spain as 'his second fatherland'. But this migration to Spain diminished considerably in the nineteenth century and had largely dried up by 1875.[1] Instead the Auvergnats made their way to Paris, whither they had long travelled, first as chapmen and water-carriers, but increasingly as building workers, coal dealers, café and hotel keepers. They provided a lot of the labour which rebuilt Paris, and many of the hotels which its rapid growth necessitated. They specialised in buying up crumbling houses, refitting them and turning them gradually into respectable and highly profitable businesses. Paris became the city in France with most Auvergnats, who were all the more noticeable because they became famous for the way they stuck together

L'Auvergne aux Auvergnats (Clermont-Ferrand, 1969); Dr. A. Béal, Passe-temps d'un practicien d'Auvergne. Causeries sur l'hygiène et autres sujets joyeux (1900), interesting on Cantal cheese, among other things.

[1] M. Trillat, 'L'Émigration de la Haute-Auvergne en Espagne du 17e au 20e siècle', Revue de la Haute-Auvergne (1954–5), vol. 34, 257–94; Société française de littérature comparée, Actes du quatrième congrès national: Espagne et la littérature française (Toulouse, 1960).

and helped each other out. By the Second World War, there were 147 friendly societies for Auvergnats in Paris, some general ones, but most of them for individual villages, cantons or departments. In 1927, for example, the Friendly Society of Parisians from Cayrol (Aveyron) held a banquet attended by 227 people, followed by a ball to which 350 others came. Cayrol itself then had a total population still living there of only 646. The banquet was presided over by the mayor of Cayrol, aged 80, who came to Paris for the purpose and recalled how he had lived in the capital from 1887 to 1915, before retiring with his profits from the wine trade. The Auvergnats had their own newspaper in Paris (*L'Auvergnat de Paris*) founded in 1882 by Louis Bonnet, who also started the *Trains-Bonnet*, cheap special transport to allow his countrymen to spend the summer at home. Every new arrival in Paris, if he did not have relatives or friends, could go to what called itself the Auvergnat Embassy—a wine merchants' shop in fact—which issued references or 'passports', and gave help. All this organisation was designed, as one of its leaders said, 'to stop the Auvergnats being treated as pariahs in the capital', to ensure that the government recognised their importance, and to arrange that when a man set up a business or entered the liberal professions, he should be provided with Auvergnat clients to start him off. Any one of them who succeeded in national terms was invited to preside over their banquets (which sometimes had over 1,000 diners) and to use his influence on their behalf. The community life of the Auvergnats was essentially practical, though it also manifested itself in sport and dancing.[1]

However, there was also a literary side to their particularism, which had some curious characteristics. The first writers in Auvergnat patois were priests, like the abbé Courchinoux (1859–1902), professor of history at the seminary of St. Flour (whence he visited Jerusalem), subsequently promoted director of studies at the École Gerson in Paris, and abbé Pierre Gérand, professor of sciences and English at the seminary of Pléaux,

---

[1] Antoine Bonnefoy, *Les Auvergnats de Paris* (1925); Roger Béteille, 'Les Rouergats à Paris, aux 19ᵉ et 20ᵉ siècles. Le rôle du clergé dans l'émigration', *Études de la région parisienne* (Jan. 1972), 9–18; cf. Marcel Berthou, *Les Associations professionnelles et ouvrières en Auvergne au 18ᵉ siècle* (Clermont-Ferrand, 1935, Poitiers law thesis).

tutor successively to the princes of Bavaria, the French ambassador in Madrid and the prince of Romania. Auvergnats travelled far. Other notable pioneers were J. B. Veyre (1798–1876), an *instituteur*, who was the first major poet in Auvergnat, until he died of drink, and Auguste Bancharel (†1889), who founded a newspaper, *L'Avenir du Cantal*, to publish the works of these men. In 1894 a correspondent of *La Dépêche de Toulouse* at Aurillac got the Auvergnat writers to affiliate themselves to the Southern Félibrige, and a new paper, *Lo Cobreto*, was founded to spread the word. It is significant that this was set on its feet by a banquet held in Paris (attended by 1,200), as a result of which the director of the *Auvergnat de Paris* promised to take 6,000 copies, out of the 7,000 it printed for his subscribers. Considerable contact with the Félibres of other regions followed, and pious pilgrimages to Mistral.[1] The outstanding lyrical poetry of Vermenouze gave national recognition to the individuality of Auvergnat literature. It is not surprising that this poetry, though all in praise of the beauty of the Auvergne forests and mountains, was not the product of a solitary or withdrawn backwoodsman. Vermenouze, as has been mentioned, had spent his youth in Spain. He then set up as a liqueur and lemonade manufacturer in Aurillac. He did his commercial travelling in the surrounding regions, taking with him his dog and his rifle, for hunting was another of his passions; he brought back business orders, game and poems at the same time. He travelled also to Italy, to Algiers to see his brother, to Normandy to see a cousin, to other provinces to partake in Félibre banquets, to Paris to advance his literary fame, and after his retirement at the age of 50 (by which time he had converted his 10,000 francs investment into 60,000 francs) to numerous spas where he met other ageing dignitaries. Another side of his life was his political activity. Though a republican in the early 1870s, he was alienated by the regime's anticlericalism, and wrote a great deal of polemic against freemasons, against Jews, against England, and in praise of General Boulanger and Joan of Arc, urging revenge on Germany. He was one of the principal writers for *La Croix du Cantal*, the weekly local supplement of the virulent Catholic

---

[1] Duc de La Salle de Rochemaure, *Régionalisme auvergnat* (Aurillac, 1909) and *Régionalisme et Félibrige* (Aurillac, 1911). Rochemaure was a Papal Duke.

newspaper. His anti-Semitism was of long standing, and was noteworthy because the Auvergnats engaged in precisely the same commercial and social activities for which the Jews were criticised. He worked hard to become famous, and a whole network of compatriots was got busy in Paris to propagate his name among the literary establishment. He put in several times for the prizes of the French Academy and eventually won one. Coppée deigned to express a wish to see 'this peasant, this savage'. Vermenouze's friends obtained long reviews for him in the Paris press. In time, he graduated to becoming a literary glory, and was invited to make speeches at school prize-givings. Auvergnat regionalism was thus no challenge to French unity in any way. Vermenouze's career was a literary counterpart of the Paris business success-stories of his region. But it shows how the Auvergnats stuck together and worked for their success. They were a powerful element in French life.[1]

## The Normans

As one examines in turn the image which each province had of itself, it becomes clear that 'French culture', or the French ideal, as presented by the most celebrated national writers, is not the sum total obtained by adding up all the regional variations, and that it is not even a reconciliation of them. This can be seen once again if one looks at the Normans. They too had a region-alist movement, though it was not influential. A speaker at a banquet held by the Old Boys' Association of a school at Flers in 1911 (and this kind of occasion is one of the best sources of banal opinions, on which everybody agreed) lamented that even in the single department of the Orne, there was no 'fusion of ideas or of manners, no conformity of religious habits or social relationships'. The idea that the provinces were each more of a moral unity than the country as a whole was also a myth, the creation of men who sought something greater than their own village to attach themselves to. To the local inhabi-tants, the Pays d'Auge, the Pays Bas and the Perche appeared quite distinct in their attitudes. Nevertheless, it was claimed

---

[1] Jean Marzières, *Arsène Vermenouze (1850–1910) et la Haute-Auvergne de son temps* (1965); A. Vermenouze's *Œuvres complètes* (published in 1950–1 in four volumes); H. Pourrat, *Ceux d'Auvergne, types et coutumes* (1928).

that over and above these differences, the Norman could be distinguished by the energy and skill with which he pursued his own interest. Prudence was his favourite virtue. He had cold common sense, practicality and repugnance for risky theories; he avoided all extremes in politics; he respected the past; he was cautious towards the future, and 'without committing himself, he drew the best he could out of the present'. He had a reputation for being quibbling and litigious, but that was because he had a 'refined sense of law and of mine and thine'. He liked the rules to be followed always.[1]

More gifted regionalist writers elevated these mundane attributes into much more exciting qualities. La Varende made much of the Normans as descendants of the Vikings, and if Scandinavian beauty could not always be recognised in them, this was because they had an admixture of Andalusian and Castilian blood. It was the Vikings, searching for a better life, who explain why the Normans were keen on money and good living; if the Normans were often miserly, this was because their ancestors were poor. What gaiety they had owed nothing to the Gauls; and conversely the melancholy everybody saw as one of their characteristics was German in origin. This melancholy nevertheless had its individuality. It was not avowed; it was not the result of disillusionment, but of the acceptance of the world as it was. Thus Norman funerals were seldom emotional and death was accepted readily. Religion, when it existed, was combined with materialism, with a barter system carried on through local saints, with superstition and devil worship. Melancholy therefore remained reasonable, and it did not lead to sterile romanticism. If there was an internal conflict among the Normans, it was between their passion for the land and their love of adventure: the heirs of the Corsairs were the Norman businessmen. But it could be argued that compromise, which is what the Normans had settled for, was the result of the clash between their Viking desire for action, and French centralisation, which frustrated it. That was a good regionalist explanation, which kept hope and idealism alive. But then that was one of the functions of regionalism. La Varende even

---

[1] S. Guesdon, *Toast à l'occasion du millénaire de la Normandie, prononcé au banquet de l'association amicale des anciens élèves de l'Immaculée-Conception à Flers* (15 June 1911, pamphlet), 8–10.

managed to sing the praises of the rain of Normandy, so preferable, he declared, to the 'stupid and stupefying sun' of the south. He even defended the high illegitimate birth-rate in Normandy, by saying that, though he had a profound respect for Christianity and the family, bastardy was a most valuable element in Norman society and a condition of its success, because it was the product of vigorous blood, rather than marriages of convenience fixed by old notaries. This kind of regionalism was a protest against the oecumenical character of the French culture, which sought to appeal throughout and beyond the frontiers of the country, which imported and exported values. France, as Montherlant was to say, represented a 'great conspiracy against the naïve and the natural'. The regionalists claimed that they wished to preserve the 'real' personality of the people, as against the model and the ideal invented by Paris.[1]

## The Savoyards

In 1860 Savoy, which was then part of the kingdom of Piedmont and Sardinia, became French, as part of the deal by which Italy was unified with Napoleon III's help. This event gives one an opportunity to study how France absorbed a hitherto foreign province, how French culture penetrated, how the natives reacted, and what vestiges of particularism survived. But France had already spread its influence over Savoy long before annexation. The language universally spoken was French; the leisured classes were imbued with French culture; Joseph de Maistre, the political philosopher of Chambéry, though he was not a French citizen, though he was educated at Turin and though he did not visit Paris till he was 73, was very much absorbed by French problems and thought that the dismemberment of France would be a great calamity.[2] Bishop Dupanloup, a major French Catholic leader, and Buloz (1803–77), a key figure in the French literary world as editor of the *Revue des Deux Mondes*, were both Savoyard by birth. At a humbler level, Paris, Lyon and Marseille each had some

[1] Jean Datain, *La Varende et les valeurs normandes. Essai régionaliste* (Saint-Lô, 1953); J. de La Varende, *Pays d'Ouche 1740–1933* (1934); R. Lelièvre, *La Varende* (1963).
[2] J. de Maistre, *Considérations sur la France* (1797).

10,000 Savoyards for at least part of the year (as did Geneva also), for in many mountainous regions, up to 50 per cent of the young men migrated seasonally in search of supplementary income. The sense of belonging to a separate 'nation' existed—for that word was used of Savoy—but subject to two qualifications. First, it was the well-to-do rather than the masses who ever thought about Savoy in this general sense. They were involved, as electors and as civil servants, in dealings with Piedmont, and their main aim was to preserve their independence and their privileges. It was partly because Piedmont adopted an anticlerical and Italian policy that these men were alienated from it and supported annexation by France. The change in their attitude came with the revolutions of 1848, which threatened their aristocratic rule. In a united Italy, Savoy would be an appendage, speaking a different language, whereas in the original kingdom of Piedmont, presided over by the House of Savoy, it could be certain of a large influence. Secondly, the idea of the Savoyard nation was modified by very strong local particularisms within it. Savoy became two departments when it was annexed by France because Chambéry contained a wealthy aristocracy, which made its contempt for the petty bourgeoisie of Annecy too evident. Annexation by France gave equality at last to the latter, and made their town into a departmental capital. And again beyond this rivalry in the bourgeoisie, each village had a very strong sense of its own independence and, apparently, even a particularity of dialect which enabled it to be distinguished from all others. The result of this was seen in Paris, where the Savoyard colony was divided into no less than forty different societies, one, more or less, for each village or groups of villages. These societies maintained a strong sense of loyalty between the émigrés in Paris and those who had remained at home, and they regularly sent donations and gifts to help the villages whenever they suffered from fire, flood or other misfortune. This particularism should not be exaggerated, however, for the Savoyards still met as such; 6,000 of them celebrated the anniversary of the union of Savoy and France in 1910 at the Trocadéro. Those who had emigrated to the U.S.A. had a single society, Les Allobroges de New York, founded in 1901, and maintained in some prosperity through the generosity of J. B. Martin, owner of one of the city's largest French cafés, which was said to employ some 400 Savoyards.[1] The paradox of Savoy was that it contained a mass of isolated and inaccessible valleys but that it also had a tradition of migration, so that Savoyards often had more contact with distant cities than with their own immediate neighbours.

The Savoyards voted to join France overwhelmingly in the plebiscite held in 1860. They believed that they would benefit from the union by the abolition of the customs barriers of France; imports would be cheaper and they would have good markets for their own produce; the jobs of the massive French civil service would be opened to them; they would have a shorter military service (seven years, as opposed to eleven years in Piedmont). But before the plebiscite the local leaders visited Paris and extracted assurances that their own positions and their special usages would be respected. Savoy thus entered France rather like the old provinces, with guarantees, though the world noticed only the plebiscite. France did start by trying to honour its undertakings. Missions were sent to study local usages. But after a few months in which every care was taken to tread carefully and tactfully, the French centralising machine began to knock everything down, as it had always done, because it could not easily behave in any other way. There was no question of giving Savoy any autonomy. It soon became clear that France would not give all the best jobs to Savoyards (who, by the unofficial agreement, had a right to the same jobs as they had held in Piedmont, or their equivalent). Disillusion rapidly set in; there was much haggling over claims and endless delays while 'notables' sought compensation. Most of the Savoyard 'syndics' were kept on as mayors, but when they proved unsatisfactory instruments of the French bureaucracy, French *instituteurs* were sent in, with special additional training in administration, to serve as secretaries to the mayors. Schooling cost more, the French forest administration was more severe, and the new roads, which were perhaps the most striking visible sign of French rule, failed to bring prosperity. Napoleon III, who seems to have appealed to the Savoyards and whose personal prestige seems to have played some part in attracting them into France, was soon replaced by anticlerical

[1] Alphonse Buinoud, *Les Savoyards à Paris* (1910), 267.

republicans who seemed as bad as Cavour and Garibaldi—
exactly what the Savoyards had tried to escape. Emigration
increasingly emptied the region, until Savoy was saved by an
unforeseen boon—the tourist trade—which gave it a new role
to play in France and indeed in Europe. Just when Savoy became French, the first Englishmen were arriving to climb the
mountains. Savoy then had at most 20,000 tourists a year. The
largest single group went to Aix-les-Bains, which had only
ten hotels and eight pensions, accommodating about 5,000
bathers, 3,000 of them French. These numbers increased
rapidly, and when watering-places lost their attractions,
skiing became fashionable, so that by 1960 at least one and a
quarter million tourists visited Savoy annually. Even with the
change of tastes, Aix in 1934 still had 45,000 bathers, and
Évian 30,000. Savoy thus became one of France's playgrounds
and in this cosmopolitan and changing function, there was no
longer cause to ruminate about whether it was a separate
nation. By 1925, 26 per cent of the permanent residents had
been born outside the region. Formerly, Savoyards had intermarried so closely that, stricken by thyroid hypertrophy,
cretinism and goitre, they showed in their physical appearance
pronounced signs of backwardness. In 1800 35 per cent of
Savoyards were under 5 feet tall (150 cm) and 20 per cent
were even under 4 feet 10 inches (145 cm). In the years 1800–
1850 they gained on average 2 inches in height, and between
1850 and 1950 another 2 inches. St-Jean-de-Maurienne, in
1925, still had some of the smallest men in France, and still
had the highest amount of consanguinity, but such villages
were now the exception. Savoy as a whole was absorbed into
France, and found a function to fulfil, in its leisure activities, as
respectable as Paris or any other region had in its own speciality. This is an instance of economic and social change making
regionalism irrelevant.[1]

[1] Ginette Billy, *La Savoie, anthropologie physique et raciale* (1962, Paris thesis for
the doctorate in natural sciences); Jacques Lovie, *La Savoie dans la vie française de
1860 à 1875* (1963); Charles Montmayeur (an *instituteur*), *Choses de Savoie vers 1860*
(1911), 28, 30; *Mémorial de Savoie: le livre du centenaire 1860–1960* (Chambéry and
Annecy, 1960, with a preface by Henry Bordeaux), 125, 313, 366; Henry Bordeaux,
*Portrait de la Savoie par ses écrivains* (1960). For regionalist feeling see the *Revue
Savoisienne*. For other regionalisms see Roland Moreau, *Histoire de l'âme basque*
(Bordeaux, 1970); Émile Coonaert, *La Flandre française de langue flamande* (1970).
For an instructive comparison, H. J. Hanham, *Scottish Nationalism* (1969).

## Alsace

In the case of Alsace-Lorraine, however, regionalism became an important political issue, because when the provinces, which the Germans annexed in 1871, were recovered in 1918, it was too easily assumed that they would welcome the restoration of French sovereignty without reservations. In fact forty-eight years of German government had brought about profound changes in a territory which in any case had only just started to become French when it was lost. Alsace-Lorraine was ceded to France in 1648, with reservations, and finally only in 1697. In the eighteenth century it enjoyed much autonomy and no attempt was made to incorporate it systematically into France —its legal and customs arrangements remained peculiar to it. Voltaire visiting Colmar in 1753 described it as 'half German, half French and totally Iroquois'; eighty years later Michelet still could not decide whether it was French or German. Its patriotic attachment to France was greatly stimulated during the Napoleonic wars, to which it contributed a large number of soldiers and a quite exceptional proportion of generals and marshals; and in the nineteenth century nowhere did the Napoleonic cult flourish more vigorously. However, French culture had made but slight inroads.[1] In 1870 only the bourgeoisie habitually spoke French; most of the peasants spoke Alsatian, which is a German dialect; and German was the language in which both Catholics and Protestants (a minority of about 20 per cent) were taught their religion. There were small areas, particularly around Metz, which spoke French, but it was only at the close of the Second Empire that an attempt was made to make French the principal language taught in schools. In 1871, 12·5 per cent of the population opted to keep their French nationality and to migrate to France: these were mainly members of the middle classes, and so the provinces lost precisely those elements who were most French. After 1871 the Germans systematically pursued a policy of 'deforeignisation'. German became the sole official language; and the spread of French was halted and indeed reversed. By 1918 it could be said that five-sixths of the population normally

[1] Paul Leuillot, *L'Alsace au début du XIXᵉ siècle* (1959); F. L'Huillier, *L'Alsace en 1870-71* (Strasbourg, 1971).

spoke German; and three-quarters had done their military service in the German army.

However, the Germans made the mistake of pursuing their national aims too vigorously, without tact or consideration for the traditions and interests of the natives. Alsace-Lorraine was made a Reichsland—subject directly to the emperor, and not an equal of the other members of the federation, like for example Bavaria. It was in effect Germany's first colony, and it was treated as a colony. It was administered by a civil service composed very largely of Prussians. Power was concentrated in the hands of a nominee of the emperor; the local assembly was without influence and when in 1911 a new constitution established a Landtag this turned out to be an empty sham, for the ministers continued to be responsible to the emperor.[1] The Germans certainly brought efficient administration (even if it involved little popular participation), the most advanced social security system in Europe and reasonable economic prosperity.[2] But this was not enough to win the Alsatians' loyalty. It is true that in 1914 there was little enthusiasm amongst them for reunion with France;[3] and the Ligue Patriotique had only a few hundred members. During the first fifteen years of German rule, the Alsatians merely sent opposition deputies to the Reichstag, but after that a movement for local autonomy won increasing influence, until it obtained almost universal support. It demanded more jobs for natives, the use of the local dialect by the civil service, the expenditure of locally levied taxes for Alsatian purposes, the reintroduction of French teaching in schools and the elimination from textbooks of deprecating reflections on the ancestors of the new generation of Alsatians. 'Français ne peux, Prussien ne veux, Alsacien suis.' The Germans made the Alsatians a self-conscious nation, aware of their unique position, and anxious to remain in cultural contact with both their neighbours. This movement was not so much directed at Germany as against the arrogance and

[1] Jean-Marie Mayeur, *Autonomie et politique en Alsace: la constitution de 1911* (1970).

[2] Joseph Weydmann, ancien député, 'L'Évolution de la législation sociale en Alsace-Lorraine de 1870 à 1918', *L'Alsace contemporaine: études politiques, économiques et sociales*, published by the Société savante d'Alsace et des régions de l'est (Strasbourg, 1950).

[3] Coleman Phillipson, *Alsace-Lorraine. Past, Present and Future* (1918), 198, a valuable impartial study of the German period.

persecuting spirit of the conquerors (for there were sons of German immigrants among the autonomists); a change of regime might well have satisfied them.

The idea that Alsace-Lorraine wished to be fully absorbed into French life was largely the creation of the Alsatians who emigrated to France after 1871. These formed an important pressure group in French politics—emerging into the limelight in the Dreyfus Affair.[1] Their departure had created a vacuum of power in Alsatian politics, and the leadership of the people was assumed in their stead by the clergy. Under Germany the Catholics were a minority in a Protestant country; after 1918 they were an anomaly in a France that had adopted anti-clerical principles. In 1918 Alsace was still subject to the Concordat, the clergy were paid by the state, the Loi Falloux was still in force and members of religious orders taught in schools, where religious education was compulsory. The French realised that serious problems would be created by reannexation, so they promised full respect for Alsatian traditions. The French armies were therefore received with great enthusiasm, as liberators.

This enthusiasm soon disappeared, for the French made the same mistakes as the Germans and possibly even more. They wrongly assumed that the autonomists were pro-German and gave them no sympathy. They did not keep their promises for long. Millerand, appointed Commissaire général de la république for Alsace-Lorraine, introduced a bill to give the two provinces a regional council: this might both have satisfied the Alsatians and prepared the way for a general decentralisation of French administration, in fulfilment of the ideas of the regionalists who were pressing for a drastic revision of the Napoleonic system. But parliament rejected this, as it rejected anything which appeared too radical.[2] Millerand's successor Alapetite (1920–4) instead achieved the full reintegration of the provinces into France and in 1924 his post and the Consultative Council (which was a kind of regional parliament) were abolished. Alsace was ruled once more from Paris—

[1] On the Alsatian clique, see e.g. Paul Appell, *Souvenirs d'un Alsacien* (1923); his brother Charles, leader of the Alsatian pro-French party, spent ten years in prison.

[2] A. Millerand, *Le Retour de l'Alsace-Lorraine à la France* (1923), particularly the introduction.

though until 1940 the three prefects remained responsible to the prime minister instead of the minister of the interior, and a special department was established in his office to supervise Alsatian affairs. This was largely because the incorporation of Alsace presented very difficult problems. French law could not be reintroduced at once and in 1940 there were still numerous legal differences—for example, in local government, public health, civil law, in addition of course to the special pre-1870 religious laws. The province's laws—a mixture of German, French and Alsatian—were a veritable labyrinth of confusion.[1] Disillusionment with the French regime was rapid. The provinces were invaded by French civil servants, as they had previously been flooded by Prussian ones. The misfortune of the Alsatians was that very few of them had obtained senior administrative experience under German rule, and they seemed unfitted to take over the running of their country. They found they were paying far higher taxes than the rest of France because their municipal system involved local taxes four or five times greater than French ones; the French state elsewhere paid for services which in Alsace were the responsibility of the communes.[2] German property was confiscated and sold at fantastically low prices, with a great deal of corruption and profiteering, which seems to make previous financial scandals pale into insignificance.[3] The Alsatian railways, which had till then been making a profit, were taken over by the French state, with an agreement by which most of those profits went to help the French railways. The potash mines were also bought by the state at a very low price, and only a fraction of the profits were ploughed back into Alsace. The autonomists claimed that twenty-five milliard francs disappeared through corruption. All but one of the local Alsatian banks were taken over by the large French ones in the economic crisis of 1928–32, and it was claimed that Alsatian money deposited in them was used elsewhere: the banks were said to have refused to help out

[1] Jacques Fonlupt-Esperaber, ancien secrétaire général du Haut Commissariat de la république à Strasbourg, *Alsace et Lorraine: Hier, aujourd'hui, demain* (1945), 39–125.

[2] Georges Lasch, 'Politiques municipales', *L'Alsace depuis son retour à la France*, published by the Comité Alsacien d'études et d'information (Strasbourg, 1932–3), 1. 277–88.

[3] See Cluzel's report, *Journal officiel*, 1928.

the local textile firms when they got into difficulties, so that they collapsed or were absorbed by French concerns. Alsace, it was said, became a colony of France, exploited for French ends, in the same way as it had been of Germany. Certainly the prosperity of the provinces declined. They had been in the van of progress before 1870, but the readaptation to the German market had slowed down growth, and again in 1918 the attempt to find a place in the French market proved very difficult. Political uncertainty had greatly reduced investment. Between the wars this once flourishing province was economically almost stagnant.

Even more important, the French aroused the hostility of the clergy, who had consolidated their hold on the masses by closely linking religious and social activities in the village. They insisted on making French the primary language everywhere and on teaching it by the direct method, so that there should be no interposition of German. German was maintained but only as a secondary language, which was not taught to the very young. This was to attack the language of prayer, as well as the mother tongue of the majority. The clergy protested under their leader abbé Haegy, the editor of the *Elsässer Kurier* of Colmar and inspirer of many other Catholic journals (whose vigour and number were a further element in the clergy's power). Abbé Haegy, it has been written, 'succeeded in exercising over the militant clergy of the Union Populaire Républicaine (the Catholic party) a veritable dictatorship. Already under German rule he had the reputation of an obstinate member of the opposition. He always placed the interests of the Church, as he understood them, above the national interest, which he had never tried to understand. Ignorant of all things French, with which he deliberately avoided making contact, abbé Haegy was haunted by the idea of a Jacobin France having no aim but to laicise Alsace.'[1] In 1924 Herriot, ignoring the strength of the Alsatian Catholics, announced his intention of introducing the republic's lay legislation into Alsace. This led to violent agitation and to the foundation, in

---

[1] Albert Wolff, *La Loi Falloux et son application en Alsace et Lorraine* (1939), 128–9 n. A thorough piece of work. On the clergy's power see also Odette d'Allerit, 'Une enquête de sociologie religieuse en milieu rural', *Paysans d'Alsace*, published by the Société Savante d'Alsace et des régions de l'est (Strasbourg, 1959), 523–57.

1927, of an Autonomist Party. The government replied by twenty-five arrests and a dramatic trial for plotting against the safety of the state. It was said that the autonomists had clandestine depots of German arms and a plan for armed insurrection. Certainly the Germans were active and generous in their support of the autonomists, flooding the provinces with cheap literature and subsidising the autonomist press.[1] But the autonomist movement was no puppet of the Germans; and the trial was unable to prove anything much; most of the accused were acquitted; and two of the four imprisoned were immediately elected to parliament. The election results in the interwar period confirmed the strength of the autonomists. They obtained few concrete gains from their agitation beyond thwarting an attempt by Blum to keep Alsatians at primary school for an additional year so as to improve their knowledge of French. Successive governments in Paris showed a complete inability to understand autonomism: they did not realise that there were several different attitudes concealed behind this general label. The separatists, who wanted a return to Germany, were a small minority, confined to some Protestant rural districts, led by Lutheran pastors trained in Germany, but including also some workers who refused to learn French. There were others who wanted to erect the provinces into a buffer Rhineland state, and demanded equality between the *Muttersprache* and French. The vast majority were however simply regionalists, wishing to maintain local traditions against French centralisation, as they had opposed German centralisation. The radicals and socialists, who were firm believers in centralisation, had no sympathy for this view, and they therefore lost most of their influence and votes. The communists profited a little from this, and by taking up the autonomist programme, they were able, with the assistance of the Catholics, to elect a communist mayor of Strasbourg. But the main result of the republic's hostility was that Alsace-Lorraine became largely 'Christian democrat' and 'Centre'.[2] Ultimately, this was to be the way that it came to be integrated

[1] Édouard Helsey, *Notre Alsace. L'Enquête du* Journal *et le procès de Colmar* (1927).

[2] F. Eccard, Sénateur du Bas-Rhin, in *L'Alsace depuis son retour à la France* (Strasbourg, 1932–3), 164; Jean Dumser, *Confessions d'un autonomiste alsacien lorrain* (1929), on the press; François G. Dreyfus, *La Vie politique en Alsace 1919–1936* (1969).

into France. The M.R.P. and Gaullist movements were the natural heirs of this political nuance, which came into its own after 1945. They ended the identification of France with anti-clericalism and the provinces could therefore at last find a satisfactory place, and no longer a marginal one, in French politics. The rise of Nazism was decisive too, for it dealt a mortal blow to autonomism: Hitler did more for the French cause than two centuries of French rule had done; he was much more savage in his repression of Alsatian particularism. In 1945, therefore, the government was able to have only French taught in the primary schools, to the exclusion of German, even though it supported its legislation by an advertising campaign with the slogan 'It is *chic* to speak French'. However, the linguistic problem remained: knowledge of German declined among the young generation, but in 1952 German was restored as an optional subject: about 85 per cent of parents declared their wish that their children should study it. A new *modus vivendi* has developed. It was fitting that Strasbourg should have been chosen as the seat of the Council of Europe.[1]

The movement to decentralise France and to give these regions a greater share and independence in its administration has a long history, which is worth mentioning even though it had no significant results till the 1960s. At first decentralisation was principally a royalist doctrine, by which the nobles expected to regain their waning influence. This was one reason why it was so vigorously resisted not only by those in power, but also by many republicans who were willing to sacrifice their liberal principles to keep the royalists out. But during the Second Empire an important breakthrough occurred when some liberals agreed to join people of all but the Bonapartist party in a manifesto, known as the Programme of Nancy (1865), which demanded that at least a beginning should be made in reducing centralisation. In 1870 a certain Charles de Gaulle (a schoolmaster, uncle of the general), together with the comte de Charencey and H. Gaidoz, petitioned parliament

---

[1] Paul Sérant, *La France des minorités* (1965), 312; Pierre Pflimlin and René Ulrich, *L'Alsace, destin et volonté* (1963); Pierre Maugué, *Le Particularisme alsacien 1918–67* (1970). For a German view, see Dr. Christian Hallier, *La Lutte de l'élément ethnique allemand d'Alsace et de Lorraine pour son existence 1918–40* (Brussels, n.d.).

asking that chairs of regional languages and literatures should
be established in the provincial universities, that teachers in
schools should have the right to teach in the local dialect, and
that in future all new teachers should have to prove, in an
examination, their knowledge of the local language. Governments, however, still feared these languages as instruments
of reaction and resistance to progress, maintaining the belief
expressed by Barrère during the first Revolution that they
represented 'superstition and error'. The commissions which
were set up by Émile Ollivier's liberal empire in 1870 and by
Ribot in 1895 came to nothing, any more than did the twenty-
five different bills introduced into parliament between 1887
and 1910. Briand, when he became prime minister in the latter
year, promised that he would take up the cause—but without
result. The cause was certainly winning increasing support from
many moderate republicans, including a considerable number
who had no special reason to be personally dissatisfied with
things as they were, like Paul Deschanel and Paul-Boncour. By
1903 the *Figaro* could say that regionalism was 'a sort of new
faith', or, as another journal put it in 1906, 'today the question
is no longer whether one is a regionalist, but how'. That was
the problem. Each proposal offered a different solution. No
agreement could be reached as to what should constitute a
region. The National Regionalist League founded in 1895,
the Regionalist Federation founded in 1900 and its review
*L'Action régionaliste*, started in 1907, aired the issues without
making much progress. There was division even on whether
local languages should be encouraged, for those who spoke
nothing but French opposed the revival of obstacles to mutual
comprehension. J. Charles-Brun (1870–1946), who was the
most active organiser of the federalist movement, liked to link
his views with those of Proudhon. He lectured on the Serbo-
Croats to show, as he thought, how people of different languages could live together. Jean Hennessy of the Cognac
family, ambassador at Berne (1924), minister of agriculture
(1928–30), a deputy, who was also active in support of the
League of Nations, and who in 1940 advocated Franco-
British union, was another leading advocate of regionalism: he
saw Switzerland as a model. He, Étienne Clémentel (minister
of commerce 1915–20) and the historian Henri Hauser were

among the few who were conscious of the importance of having economic bases for regional decentralisation, but this was an aspect which was widely and more fully studied only after the Second World War. It will be seen how the Vichy regime tried to do something about regionalism, because by then it was generally accepted as a necessary reform, but of course wartime was hardly propitious for such experiments.[1] Only in 1951 did the Loi Deixonne allow the teaching of local languages—optionally—in schools and provide for their examination in the *baccalauréat*, but it did not make any arrangements for the teaching, so the law was largely a dead letter. It was in the 1960s that regionalism finally became a live issue, but in new conditions, and it is too early to assess its consequences.[2]

[1] F. Jean-Desthieux, *L'Évolution régionaliste, du Félibrige au fédéralisme* (1918); J. Charles-Brun, *Le Régionalisme* (1911); Jean Hennessy and J. Charles-Brun, *Le Principe fédératif* (1940); François Prevet, *Le Régionalisme économique* (with a preface by E. Clémentel), 1929; H. Hauser, *Le Problème du régionalisme* (1924).

[2] R. Lafont, *La Révolution régionaliste* (1967); J. F. Gravier, *La Question régionale* (1970); T. Flory, *Le Mouvement régionaliste français* (1966); M. Philipponneau, *La Gaule et les régions* (1967); K. Allen and M. C. MacLennan, *Regional problems and policies in Italy and France* (1970).

# 3. Attitudes to Foreigners

FRANCE was defined as a nation not only by the policies of its rulers—or, alternatively, by the peculiarities of the provinces from which it was formed—but also by the way it distinguished itself from the nations that surrounded it. To understand France, one must appreciate the complexity of its attitudes towards foreigners.

## Travel

The first question is, what did Frenchmen know of foreigners? They could claim that they had no need to go abroad, because their country was the centre of the world, which everybody who mattered was obliged to visit. A very large number of people did indeed visit France in this period. As soon as statistics of tourism began to be kept, France was revealed as the country which was almost the major tourist attraction in Europe.[1] Already in 1910 it was estimated that France was earning 350 million francs from its tourists compared to the 200 million francs earned by Switzerland and the 318 million francs by Italy. International travel appears to have roughly doubled in the 1920s: 1929 was the peak year, after which travel collapsed back to its 1920 level. In 1929 the credit and debit account in tourism showed France as a country which imported far more tourists than it exported. France earned £80 million from tourists, while its nationals spent only £12 million as tourists abroad. The U.S.A. received £37 million from visitors, but spent £178 million. Britain earned £22 million and spent £32. Germany earned £8·8 million and spent £14·6 million. Visitors to France, moreover, spent more money there than they did elsewhere—on average £40 a head, compared to only £21 spent in Italy; and the American visitor spent £120 a head in France. The British were probably always the most numerous visitors to France, as these figures for 1929 show:

[1] The Italians started keeping statistics in 1899, but comparative figures for Europe are available only after 1919.

*Visitors to France (1929)*

| From | | |
|------|------|------|
| | Britain | 881,000 |
| | Spain | 350,000 |
| | U.S.A. | 296,000 |
| | South America | 150,000 |
| | Netherlands | 55,000 |
| | Switzerland | 45,000 |
| | Belgium | 38,000 |
| | Germany | 35,000 |
| | Austria | 30,000 |
| | Other countries | 30,000 |
| | TOTAL | 1,910,000 |

France in 1929 had more visitors than any country except Switzerland, which had 2,154,000; it had more than Austria's 1,849,000 and was far ahead of Italy, which had 1,290,000. But the balance of curiosity between France and its visitors was far from being reciprocal. Thus in return for the 881,000 British visitors to France, France sent only 55,000 visitors to Britain: though it is fair to add that, even so, the French were the second most numerous tourists in Britain (representing 13·6 per cent of the total who visited Britain), coming after the U.S.A. (33·7 per cent, or 137,000 people), but ahead of the Germans (49,000, 12·1 per cent) and the Dutch who came fourth (8·2 per cent, 33,000). When the great depression reduced American visitors to Britain to 66,000 in 1933, the French still continued to come at the same rate: 55,000 in 1933. France was the favourite country for British travellers, but when the French travelled abroad, they preferred first of all Switzerland and then Italy.

*Comparison of travel abroad by the British and the French (1929)*

| | | British Travellers | French Travellers |
|------|------|------|------|
| To | Switzerland | 204,000 | 104,000 |
| | Italy | 132,000 | 97,000 |
| | France | 881,000 | .. |
| | England | .. | 55,000 |
| | Norway | 28,000 | 3,136 |
| | Japan | 6,391 | 883 |

One striking feature in these unequal exchanges is that the French barely visited Germany, and few Germans came to

France. In 1929, 297,000 Italians visited France, but only 35,215 Germans. Seventeen per cent of visitors to Germany were Americans, 11 per cent were British, only 2·6 per cent were French. The Germans preferred to go to Italy, 313,000 of them in 1930, accounting for 24·3 per cent of all tourists in Italy, whereas the French comprised only 7·6 per cent.

*Visitors to Italy (1930)*

| Germans | 313,000 |
|---------|---------|
| Swiss | 148,000 |
| Austrians | 143,000 |
| Americans | 133,000 |
| Britons | 132,000 |
| French | 97,000 |

The Germans also dominated tourism in Switzerland, where in 1929 38·8 per cent of tourists were German, 13·7 per cent British, 13·2 per cent American and only 9·4 per cent French. The statistics are too imperfect to make a map of European travel possible, but they reveal enough to show that the political alignments did not necessarily reflect popular knowledge or taste.[1]

They show also that the French did travel to a considerable extent, even if not on the same scale as the British. There certainly were far fewer Frenchmen abroad than there were Britons; but their numbers were not insignificant. French emigration has a long history. Without going back to the 60,000 Normans who are said to have invaded England in 1066, and the even larger number who settled in Spain between the sixteenth and eighteenth centuries, one has around half a million Huguenots leaving France in 1660–1710. Many Frenchmen went to fight in foreign armies: the Prussian army is said to have contained 25,000 Frenchmen in 1773. Between three and four hundred thousand may have emigrated at the Revolution (1789–95) though many of them later returned. Only some 25,000 had left for Canada by the time it became British, but at the end of the *ancien régime* it was estimated that there were about 230,000 Frenchmen abroad: 90,000 of them were in Europe, and 74,000 in French colonies. The total increased

[1] A. J. Norval, *The Tourist Industry* (1936); F. W. Ogilvie, *The Tourist Industry. An Economic Study* (1933).

rapidly during the century covered by this book (as shown in the accompanying table).

*Frenchmen Abroad*

| In | 1861 | 1881–6 | 1901 | 1911 | 1931 |
|---|---|---|---|---|---|
| Britain | 13,000 | 26,600 | 22,450 | 32,000 | 15,000 |
| Jersey | 2,780 | ? | 8,100 | 8,500 | 7,000 |
| Belgium | 35,000 | 52,000 | 56,580 | 80,000 | 80,000 |
| Russia | 2,479 | 5,760 | 8,000 | 12,000 | 1,500 |
| Germany | 6,429 | 1,756 | 20,480 | 19,000 | 15,000 |
| Switzerland | 45,000 | 54,260 | 58,520 | 64,000 | 40,000 |
| Italy | 4,718 | 10,900 | 6,950 | 8,000 | 9,000 |
| Spain | 10,642 | 17,600 | 20,560 | 20,000 | 20,000 |
| TOTAL EUROPE | 128,000 | 185,000 | 220,000 | 269,000 | 220,000 |
| Egypt | 14,207 | 15,700 | 10,200 | 11,500 | 18,000 |
| Asia (mainly China) | 4,000 | 5,000 | 7,000 | 10,000 | 11,000 |
| U.S.A. | 108,870 | 106,900 | 104,000 | 125,000 | 127,000 |
| Canada | 3,173 | 4,400 | 7,900 | 25,000 | 21,000 |
| Mexico | — | 8,800 | 4,000 | 4,000 | 6,000 |
| Argentina | 29,196 | 60,000(?) | 94,100 | 100,000 | 80,000 |
| Brazil | 592 | 68,000 | 10,000 | 14,000 | 14,000 |
| Chile | 1,650 | 4,198 | 7,800 | 10,000 | 6,000 |
| Uruguay | 23,000 | 14,300 | 12,900 | 9,500 | 8,000 |
| TOTAL FOR SOUTH AMERICA | 56,000 | 92,000 | 130,000 | 138,000 | 113,000 |
| TOTAL FOR WORLD | 318,000 | 426,000 | 495,000 | 600,000 | 535,000 |

Source: État Français, Service National des Statistiques, *Études démographiques* no. 4, *Mouvements migratoires entre la France et l'étranger* (1943) [by Henri Bunle], 33–4.

The figures give only a very rough and general idea of the extent to which the French moved around the world, for the statistics are, as usual, unreliable. Many people left France without any government department knowing: emigration was most active in the frontier regions which had strong traditions in smuggling and in the evasion of military service, and where Frenchmen participated to some extent in the large-scale movements which drove so many Italians, Germans and Spaniards to the new world. Thus Alsatians went to America with the assistance of the German businessmen who specialised in transporting their own countrymen; the Savoyards emigrated as part of the Italian exodus, and the Basques travelled to South

America through Spain. In 1857 the department which had the highest rate of emigration was the Basses-Pyrénées (the second was Paris). By 1860 emigration had become so active that France had no less than thirty-one authorised emigration agencies. The major shipping lines which linked France with the U.S.A. (there were ten of them by the end of the Second Empire) co-operated with these, since they wanted passengers to fill up their boats, sent out to fetch American cotton. The government, however, tried hard to restrict and obstruct emigration, because it was keen that if any Frenchmen did leave, they should go to Algeria. But France's emigration was difficult to control, because it was somewhat different in character to that of the rest of Europe. The people who went out from France were in general not driven out by poverty or unemployment; many of them were enterprising individuals, making their own choice, rather than participating in a mass movement; they were often artisans or even professional men anxious to make a fortune and to use their skills in a new environment. In 1858–60 only 21·2 per cent of passports issued for emigration were granted to peasants. The people who went to Algeria were of a special kind, and (apart from 1848, when some 13,500 Parisians went out—and quickly returned—and from 1871, when some Alsatians tried it) generally from southern France. The Bretons, by contrast, went to Paris for the most part. No accurate figures are available for emigration from France: in 1860–70 four times more Frenchmen arrived in the U.S.A. than were supposed to have left France. About 7,000 appear to have left for the U.S.A. in, for example, 1840, but 20,000 in 1846; more or less this level may have been maintained till 1860, despite the supposed prosperity of the Second Empire. In 1871–6 about 8,000 or 9,000 went each year to the U.S.A. (and 4–5,000 to Argentina); in 1888 the figure was 17,000, in 1889 27,000, in 1890 17,000. But the departures for the new world were probably considerably less frequent than emigration, permanent or temporary, to Europe, where the French presence was always more consciously felt, instead of being absorbed.[1] It has been estimated that between a third and a half of French emigration was to Europe. That to the colonies accounted for between one- and

---

[1] L. Chevalier, 'L'Émigration française au dix-neuvième siècle', *Études d'histoire moderne et contemporaine* (1947), 127–71.

two-fifths.[1] After the exodus to South America (highest in 1875–87), the colonies and Europe thus attracted the largest share of French emigrants.

The French often liked to make a virtue of the supposed fact that they seldom travelled abroad, but the stay-at-home Frenchman was something of a myth. The French were quite active travellers even in the nineteenth century. Already in 1864 a doctor writing a medical guide for travellers (and many such were published) declared that one of the most noticeable characteristics of the century and indeed one of its 'most intense and active passions' was the desire to travel.[2] It is true there were also moralists, and particularly clergymen, who considered this a dangerous development. The timid abbé Hulot—who was worried by every new or old amusement, from dancing to novel-reading—published little books to urge people to stay at home, rather than face the hazards of corruption in public carriages full of strangers: and if you absolutely had to travel, he advised, pretend to be asleep, so as to avoid conversation.[3] As late as 1878 a travel guide urged men who ventured on trains alone to arm themselves with a revolver or cane.[4] Some young women long continued to express terror at the idea of travelling by train as they later feared aeroplanes; some doctors claimed to share these fears, for they reassured their patients that travel was not dangerous provided it was endured under medical supervision. Commercial travellers had special diets composed for them because of the troubles their constant movement produced. But, though dangerous, travel was also highly valued as a cure for many diseases. A doctor writing in 1864 described it as 'a fashionable remedy', and there was indeed a whole science behind the different prescriptions of it which could be issued. Climate, it was agreed, had direct influence on temperament and a change of climate could therefore modify temperament. Italy was thus recommended for the cure of 'moral diseases, profound sorrows, hallucinations and monomania', though it

---

[1] 27% (1851–60), 19% (1861–90), 30% (1891–1900), 13% (1901–20), 35·6% (1921–30), 43% (1931–5).

[2] Dr. Émile Decaisne, *Guide médical et hygiénique du voyageur* (1864), iii, vii.

[3] Abbé Hulot, *Instructions sur la danse* (1821), *Instructions sur les spectacles* (1823), *Instructions sur les mauvaises chansons* (1824), *Instructions sur les romans* (1825), *Instructions sur l'abstinence* (1830).

[4] Eugène Chapus, *Voyageur, prenez garde à vous* [1878], 51.

would not help nervousness. Obesity could be cured by travel, in the case of lymphatics, though those of sanguine temperament were made worse by it. 'Thin women with disordered imaginations, unbridled passions, jealous characters and worried dispositions', and indeed the vast number of people of both sexes who plagued doctors with complaints about nervousness and headaches—'nothing is more common than the complaint *J'ai mal aux nerfs*'—were recommended to travel, because medicine could find no other cure.[1]

Travel for one's health did not necessarily mean travel abroad. Very often it meant going to a watering-place. The fashion for this was one of the major reasons that kept the French in their own country, and brought foreigners to France. Interest in mineral waters for medical purposes was of course very old, and a French author who produced a work on them in 1785 was able to list no less than 1,140 titles in his bibliography. At that date, Parisians could take the waters at Passy and a whole host of little resorts in what are now the suburbs; Plombières was then beginning to rival Baden, offering, it was said, much better food at half the price. Voltaire and Saint-Simon went to Forges, the rising rival to Bagnères-de-Bigorre which was the most fashionable French resort of the eighteenth century, with thirty-two different springs and over 10,000 visitors a year. But it was during the Second Empire that taking the waters became a widespread middle-class recreation and also the subject of a new and vigorous medical science. In 1853 Dr. Isadore Guitard founded the Société de Médecine du Midi appliquée à l'Hydrologie, and in the same year the Société d'Hydrologie médicale de Paris was established, producing learned annual publications. In 1858 the bi-monthly *Gazette des eaux*, which in the next century was renamed the *Presse thermale et climatique*, started a flood of periodicals devoted exclusively to this subject. By 1871 it was such a busy industry that a Mineral Waters Agency was set up in Paris, publishing the *Conseiller des villes d'eaux*. In 1886 the first international congress of hydrology was held at Biarritz, to be followed by about a dozen more. In 1887 'hydrological caravans' were started by Dr. Carron de la Carrière (and long continued by such eminent doctors as

[1] J. F. Dancel, *De l'influence des voyages sur l'homme et sur ses maladies. Ouvrage spécialement destiné aux gens du monde* (1846), viii, 186–7, 482.

Landouzy and Laignel-Lavastine), by which interested doctors travelled around the resorts examining their merits. In 1891 the first chair of medical hydrology was founded at Toulouse for Félix Garrigou (born 1835), one of the pioneers of 'hydrochemistry'; by 1928 all faculties of medicine had similar chairs; in 1933 the *agrégation* in hydrology was established. The speed at which taking the waters became popular may be seen from a few statistics. In 1822 about 30,000 people visited spas; in 1852 the figure was 93,000; in 1855 140,000. This sudden increase in a few years was related partly to the building of the railways and partly to the development of the spas on an ambitious commercial scale. Vichy, which had belonged to the state since Francis I, was now suddenly made one of the great attractions in the country by lavish building and by the opening-up of new springs. In the 1850s, second- and third-class bathing establishments were built there to draw a far wider clientele. Napoleon III transformed the town with splendid boulevards; he built himself a private chalet, to use during his repeated visits. Magnificent and huge hotels appeared, and innumerable doctors set up private clinics offering as many varieties of treatment. The municipality then acquired an energetic mayor in a pharmacist who specialised in embalming the corpses of foreigners who died in the town, for dispatch to their native countries; between them, the doctors, pharmacists and hoteliers formed a powerful lobby, which knew both how to advertise their services and how to obtain subsidies from the state. In 1903 the crowning glory of Vichy, a new first-class bathing house, replaced the old one which had itself been greatly admired. The number of visitors, which had been a mere 575 in 1833 and 2,543 in 1840, rose to around 20,000 in 1860 and perhaps 100,000 by 1890. The attraction of Vichy of course was not simply medical, or perhaps even predominantly so, for the great watering-places were beautiful towns, offering amusements and a social life which even Paris could barely rival. The basis of their prosperity was the decree of 24 June 1806 which forbade gambling houses in France but exempted those in watering-places, and gambling drew hordes of idle rich, and so hordes of mothers and daughters in search of husbands. The best resorts organised a wide variety of entertainments, excursions and concerts: one of the most successful *coups* carried out by Vichy was to entice Isaac Strauss from Aix in 1853 to conduct its symphony orchestra.

But the craze for taking the waters would not have been particularly important if it had affected only fashionable people, even though the number of those who aspired to be so was constantly rising. There were several hundred spas, each of which came to attract a different kind of clientele. It was not just that each claimed different medicinal virtues: an enormous literature poured forth analysing these, making elaborate recommendations about where to go, and what to do, for every kind of complaint. Sets of people got into the habit of meeting in a particular resort in the summer; fashions were established and then waned. Thus Cauterets, though an old established resort, had only a small clientele until in the latter years of the century it was 'discovered' as a place where people who were 'really ill' could go and be very well looked after. Then many actors and actresses, including Sarah Bernhardt, took to going there, since it claimed to cure throat troubles, and it attracted as many as 25,000 visitors a year. Eaux-Bonnes and Mont-Doré were frequented by actors and singers, and also many priests, for the cure of sore throats too. Saint-Sauveur specialised in aristocratic ladies with neuralgia, hysteria and hypochondria, and Plombières acquired a reputation for treating other female diseases. Luchon by contrast was a gay gambling place, which had the advantage, as had Aix-les-Bains also, that its public baccarat rooms were open to both sexes. Royat, owned by the chocolate manufacturer of that town, had not only two casinos but also an English church. And depending on one's taste, one could choose between the grape cure, the milk and whey cure, the earth cure (for gout, particularly good at Arcachon and Dax), or one could be massaged under a shower at Aix and then carried home in a basket, wrapped in a warmed blanket.

In 1882 France had no less than 1,102 mineral sources. Prices suited all pockets, and they remained relatively stable till 1914. Thus at Flourens, near Toulouse, board and lodging could be had at the hotels for 4 francs a day, eating at the 'best table', 3 francs at the 'second table' and 2 francs at the servants' table. One could spend a month at Cauterets for 65–70 francs, but many people, for whom even this was too much, brought their own food with them. Foreign guides suggested 10 francs a day as the minimum and foreigners were no doubt often charged much more. A lot depended on which doctor one chose. Increasingly, fashionable doctors set up practices in the fashionable resorts, and even famous Parisian ones opened clinics there for the season, because there were such enormous profits to be made.

The trade in bottled mineral waters rose constantly. It had already been big business in the eighteenth century, but in the nineteenth shops selling them issued catalogues listing as many as 300 different types, each with its own elaborate medical analysis. But in the 1890s, four-fifths of all the bottled water consumed in France came from Saint-Galmier: it cost only 30 centimes a bottle, whereas Vichy cost 70 centimes. The label on a bottle however meant little in itself: in 1908 an industrialist was found guilty of having taken three million litres of Paris tap water and selling it fraudulently as Vichy water.

Bottled mineral water continued to increase in popularity, and to become an important industry, but by the turn of the nineteenth century the visiting of watering-places had reached its peak and after 1914 they went into rapid decline. If they had been popularised by the railways—and they had been very good at getting special cheap excursion tickets from the railway companies—the bicycle and the motor car offered people a wider choice of recreation. The seaside and sports of all kinds provided alternative attractions. But the decisive factor in their downfall was that they failed to win a place in the social security system of the new welfare state. The law of 1893 did not include water cures among the free medical assistance it offered. Instead, a law of 1907 levied a 15 per cent tax on gambling in casinos, which yielded 6·8 million francs. The railway companies took to offering very cheap excursions to the seaside, but offered only minimal reductions for trips to watering-places, and in the case of the Est and PLM railways, no reductions at all. The rise of the Côte d'Azur has something to do with this. The final blow came after 1958 when the social security system, which had hitherto subsidised 75 per cent of patients at the watering-places, greatly reduced its grants. So, when figures were compared in 1965, France was shown to have only half a million people taking the waters in that year, representing only 1 per cent of its population. By contrast the Federal Republic of Germany had 2·2 per cent, Czechoslovakia 5 per cent and Hungary 6 per cent. It was not simply that the seaside and warm sun were now preferred: Italy had one million visitors to its watering-places. Foreigners almost ceased to come: their numbers fell from 500,000 in 1952 to 17,000 in 1970. In the latter year, 'thermalism' was an industry with a turnover of 750 to 1,000 million francs a year, which was still a little more than the cinema industry, but a little less than the jewellery industry. But the production and distribution of bottled water had reached a figure of 1,400 million francs a year.[1]

The French tourist industry developed along lines which were slightly different from those of its neighbours. There were few large hotels in France at the beginning of the period, and though an increasing number were built after 1860, they were long confined to a few tourist towns and were designed as much for foreigners as for Frenchmen. To stay in a hotel was still something of a luxury in 1900 and to a certain extent it remained so till the 1960s. In 1961 only 22 per cent of French holiday-makers in France stayed in hotels or boarding-houses; 12·5 per cent rented houses or rooms, but 45 per cent lodged with their families or friends; 10 per cent stayed in second homes owned by themselves, 10 per cent went camping. By contrast 45 per cent of British holiday-makers stayed at hotels and boarding-houses, 8 per cent in rented accommodation, 26 per cent were with family or friends, and 17 per cent camped. In 1967 France still had only 13,000 approved hotels (giving only 350,000 rooms) and 50,000 unofficial hotels. But 950,000 people had second homes in the country or at the seaside. In Lille, 30 per cent of employers and members of the liberal professions had a second home and 3 per cent of the workers, but the poor were not always as underprivileged as this might suggest, for many had family homes (even if they did not own them) in their village

[1] E. H. Guitard, *Le Prestigieux Passé des eaux minérales. Histoire du thermalisme et de l'hydrologie des origines à 1950* (1951); Dr. Grellety, *De l'importance sociale des villes d'eaux* (Mâcon, 1895); Marcel Craponne, *Les Neurasthéniques aux villes d'eaux* (1914); *Troisième Congrès des villes d'eaux, bains de mer et stations climatiques tenu à Paris du 11 au 14 décembre 1911, rapports et comptes rendus* (1912); François Delooz, *Le Thermalisme à Néris-les-Bains* (unpublished mémoire, Institut d'Études politiques, Paris, 1971); E. Decaisne and X. Gorecki, *Dictionnaire élémentaire de médecine* (1877); F. Engerand, *Les Amusements des villes d'eaux à travers les âges* (1936); M. L. Pailleron, *Les Buveurs d'eaux* (Grenoble, 1935); Thomas Linn, M.D., *The Health Resorts of Europe* (7th edition, 1899); A. Mallat and J. Cornillon, *Histoire des eaux minérales de Vichy* (Vichy, 1906); A. Mallat, *Histoire contemporaine de Vichy de 1789 à 1889* (Vichy, 1921).

of origin. Many of these second homes were let to holiday-makers. Money thus went into homes rather than into hotels. At La Baule, for example, in 1900 there were 2,300 hotel rooms but 7,000 villas. The point made by these figures is that there was a strong tendency to confine one's movement between the place where one lived and the province from which one came; and to save up to buy a house to which one could retire. This basic travel was supplemented by relatively short trips to the seaside or other resorts, and by the occasional pilgrimage. In 1867 the railway network reached Lourdes; by 1872 100,000 pilgrims were visiting it and in the jubilee year of 1908 no less than 300,000 pilgrims were counted. The Touring Club de France, founded in 1890, had 20,000 members in 1895 and 100,000 members by 1905, so that there was quite a large minority keen on travelling from the beginning of the twentieth century. It is true the club's publications warned members that prices were high in England, that 'the food does not always suit stomachs accustomed to French cuisine' and that hotel accommodation in many countries was primitive; and there were also organisations set up in the 1900s to urge Frenchmen to spend their honeymoons in France rather than be charged fancy prices in Switzerland.[1] It is true also that it was easier to travel in France than abroad because the foreign holiday with all accommodation arranged in advance was almost unknown, while on the contrary there were innumerable reduced-price tickets offered by the French railway companies. There was nothing to compare with the low-cost tours organised for Englishmen by Thomas Cook, who in 1867 was able to offer four days in Paris for only £1·80, and who in that year transported over 12,000 Englishmen to the Paris exhibition, lodging half of them in special accommodation he had built in Passy.[2] The French

---

[1] Touring Club de France, *Annuaire des pays étrangers* (1912), I. 25; *Le Compagnon de voyage*, published by the Société Anonyme pour la propagation des voyages en France (1909). *L'Indicateur du tourisme*, published by the Office central des voyages et excursions (first issue 1910), encouraged travel in France by producing very good maps, with suggested routes and excursions. For an early example of a practical travel magazine, see *Revue des voyages* (started April 1852), for which Jacques Offenbach wrote the gossip column.

[2] Thirty-six shillings is the price quoted by W. Fraser Rae, *The Business of Travel* (1891), but Thomas Cook and Son, *Cook's Tours* (1875), *Cook's Guide to Paris* (1878), 101, give the normal 4-day tour to Paris as costing between £4·55 and £5·35.

preferred, or had, to make their own arrangements. Whereas Thomas Cook advised his customers to save money by sharing one meal between two—for good meals, he said, could be got only at the top restaurants, the others being 'varied and showy rather than wholesome'—the French seemed to have tried to economise by renting very cheap accommodation in the country, often of a primitive kind, and they usually did not go very far.

There was, moreover, no dramatic change in travelling habits produced by longer holidays. The rich had long spent part of the year on their country estates and part in town. The poor went away when they were out of work. The idea of the 'holiday' was slow to penetrate. In 1900 in the Paris department stores, employees had a right to seven days of unpaid leave every seven years, if they preferred to accumulate it this way, rather than have one day off a year. The working class won the right to paid holidays in 1936, but they were too poor to take advantage of this and the number of long-distance tickets sold in the years following increased by only 10 per cent (it was the number of weekend tickets which doubled). The idea of the holiday spread slowly from the schools. Education had for long been seasonal and irregular, particularly at the primary level. However, the secondary schools, which were more serious, had tried to limit holidays to the very minimum, because they believed in control-ling the whole life of their pupils; they provided recreation in the form of military exercises. But in the course of the nineteenth century, a reaction set in against 'overwork' in schools (*sur-menage*). In 1834 school holidays were fixed at only six weeks a year. In 1894 they were increased to eight weeks. They were put up to two and a half months in secondary schools in 1912 and in other schools in 1935. The notion of the 'holiday' can perhaps be dated to around 1900. In 1912 an article on this subject said that fifty years ago, to take a holiday was very odd, but now not to take one was odd. (This of course referred to the bourgeoisie.) But it took another half century for new habits to develop in regard to what one did on holiday. In 1961 still 14 per cent of holidays were taken abroad; in 1966 18 per cent. These years mark the beginning of the democratisation of foreign travel.[1]

[1] Françoise Cribier, *La Grande Migration d'été des citadins en France* (1969); Henri Boiraud, *Contribution à l'étude historique des congés et des vacances scolaires en France du*

However, the statistics of railway travel show France lagging far behind England.[1]

*Railway Passengers (in millions)*

|      | France | England |
|------|--------|---------|
| 1870 |        | 336     |
| 1880 |        | 603     |
| 1884 | 211    |         |
| 1890 |        | 817     |
| 1894 | 336    |         |
| 1900 | 443    | 1,142   |
| 1913 | 547    | 1,549   |
| 1924 | 796    | 1,746   |
| 1933 |        | 1,575   |
| 1935 | 585    |         |
| 1937 |        | 1,819   |

The number of people able or anxious to travel in the first and second class in France fell very significantly after 1900; the increase in third-class passengers, though continuous, was not large enough to raise France, in the 1930s, even to the level of England in 1890.

*Travel by classes (million passengers)*

|      | First Class | Second Class | Third Class |
|------|-------------|--------------|-------------|
| 1884 | 16          | 71           | 124         |
| 1894 | 20          | 106          | 210         |
| 1900 | 22          | 148          | 271         |
| 1910 | 22          | 109          | 378         |
| 1935 | 11          | 83           | 490         |

Nor did France compensate by writing more letters. In the 1880s, Englishmen were posting almost exactly twice as many letters as Frenchmen and four times as many postcards. English

*Moyen Âge à 1914* (1971); Victor Parant, *Le Problème du tourisme populaire* (1939); Albert Dauzat, *Pour qu'on voyage. Essai sur l'état de bien voyager* (1911).

[1] Based on *Statistiques des chemins de fer français* (to be found, incomplete, in the offices of the Ministry of Transport, Paris). English figures from H. J. Dyos and D. H. Alcroft, *British Transport* (Leicester, 1969), 148, and P. S. Bagwell, *The Transport Revolution* (1974), 253: English figures to 1912 exclude season ticket holders. A comparison made in 1905, of 'kilometre-travellers per inhabitant' showed 250 as the average for Europe, 539 as the figure for England, 477 for Switzerland, 427 for Germany and 370 for France. É. Levasseur, *Histoire du commerce en France* (1912), 2. 689 n.

figures are not statistically comparable in the 1920s, but
German ones are and they show the Germans exchanging twice
as many letters as the French and fifteen times more postcards
(1927). But for letters sent abroad, France was, interestingly, less
far behind:[1]

*Number of letters sent per inhabitant*

|             | 1882 | 1892 |
| ----------- | ---- | ---- |
| France      | 16   | 16   |
| England     | 40   | 51   |
| Germany     | 17   | 24   |
| Switzerland | 25   | 29   |
| Italy       | 7    | 6    |
| Spain       | 5    | 5    |

*Letters sent abroad (1927) in millions*

|                | France | Germany | England | Italy | Japan | Russia |
| -------------- | ------ | ------- | ------- | ----- | ----- | ------ |
| Letters        | 122    | 152     | 174     | 51    | 69    | 12     |
| Postcards      | 14     | 55      | 6       | 10    | 48    | 2      |
| Printed papers | 81     | 109     | 131     | 14    | 36    | 1      |

### France and England

The odd thing about the relations of France and England in this
period is that at no stage was there a war between them. It was
the first time they had spent a whole century at peace. The
explanation is to be found partly in the growth of new circumstances in international relations, but partly simply in accident.
For the animosity, rivalry and incomprehension between them
was not extinguished, as will be seen. On several occasions they
were on the very brink of war. The phrase Entente Cordiale was
first coined in the early 1840s, in a reaction to the crisis of 1840,
when Thiers had wanted to fight England over Egypt, but new
sources of conflict quickly arose. The Entente Cordiale of 1904,
again, was not the solemnisation of a friendship but the settlement of a few colonial disputes, at a time when the two countries
were almost ready to fight each other, but felt they would rather

[1] *Statistique générale du service postal dans les pays de l'Union postale universelle*, publiée
par le bureau international des postes (1882, 1890, 1927).

settle with other enemies first. They quarrelled vigorously even as joint victors at the end of the 1914–18 war, and in 1940, when France signed the armistice with Germany, the entente cordiale reached its lowest ebb. Though General de Gaulle revived it, there was no love lost between the governments of the two countries, even when they were supposedly allies. However, there were two main reasons why animosity never went further than words in this century. First, the rise of Germany altered the balance of power so drastically that both England and France were equally menaced by it and had to co-operate to keep it in check. Secondly, there grew up, from around 1815, a notion that England and France represented liberalism in a world threatened by the despotic governments of Russia, Austria and Prussia, and that there was therefore an ideological cause in which they were, more or less, brothers. This was a rather woolly notion, because Napoleon III could hardly qualify as a liberal monarch in English eyes, and yet England was willing to have his help in the Crimean War. The liberal–autocratic divide in Europe was a little like the Catholic–Protestant, or Christian–Muslim one of former times, which people used when it suited them.

Nevertheless, this sense of possessing a common ideology did have a basis in fact. In the eighteenth century France had discovered the English constitution and a fashion of Anglomania was firmly established, to last, among a certain class, ever since. In the fight against the absolute monarchy of the *ancien régime*, England's parliamentary government was held up by people like Voltaire, Montesquieu and Mounier as the ideal; and then after the restoration in 1815, liberal royalists like Guizot and even extreme ones like Polignac argued that France needed to learn from England if it wished to enjoy the political stability and freedom, which, they believed, flourished as nowhere else on the other side of the Channel. Their political heirs continued this tradition well into the 1870s. Charles de Rémusat declared in 1865: 'I confess willingly that the dream of my life has been the English system of government in French society.'[1] The 'republic of dukes' of 1871–9 was deeply impregnated by Anglophilism, as were also liberal Catholics of the school of Montalembert, Orleanists like Passy and Odilon Barrot, and liberal

[1] C. de Rémusat, *L'Angleterre au 18ᵉ siècle* (1865), I. 11.

economists like Leroy-Beaulieu and Michel Chevalier.[1] The snag about a lot of the Anglophilism, however, was that it involved admiration for aristocracy, in one form or another, and that was difficult to reconcile with democracy. Most of the admirers of England were not democrats. Guizot, who considered that fourteenth-century England provided a model for representative government, was careful to point out that he did not wish to copy nineteenth-century England, because by then the king had lost too much of his power to parliament, and Guizot was hostile to parliamentary rule, as he was to popular sovereignty. All these people agreed that what gave England its stability was its gentry, controlling local government with disinterested 'public spirit'. Many of them therefore suggested that France should try and replace its decayed nobility by a new class of local notables, who should be given considerable power in a reorganised, decentralised constitution. The appeal of this programme was inevitably limited to men who considered themselves to be notables. Even Guizot found it too much, for he said that England had achieved liberty, but not equality, and he laid much stress on that also, as he did on the rule of merit. So, though Anglophilism was bolstered by a whole philosophical apparatus, and by the raising of moralists like Reid and Dugald Stewart to the rank of major thinkers (with Cousin, who could recite whole works of theirs by heart, recommending them for study in schools), in the end England remained a model for only a small class of snobs.[2]

The English dandy became a model in France in the early nineteenth century. It became fashionable to wear English

[1] G. Bonno, *La Constitution anglaise devant l'opinion française de Montesquieu à Bonaparte* (1931); L. de Carné, *Du gouvernement représentatif en France et en Angleterre* (1841); D. Nisard, *Les Classes moyennes en Angleterre et la bourgeoisie en France* (1850); Paul Leroy-Beaulieu, *L'Administration locale en France et en Angleterre* (1872); C. de Franqueville, *Les Institutions politiques, judiciaires et administratives de l'Angleterre* (1863); Victor de Broglie, *Vues sur le gouvernement de la France* (2nd edition, 1872); O. Barrot, *De la centralisation* (1861); C. de Montalembert, *De l'avenir politique de l'Angleterre* (3rd edition, 1856); Michel Chevalier, 'La Constitution de l'Angleterre', *Revue des Deux Mondes* (1 Dec. 1867), 529–55.

[2] F. Guizot, *Histoire des origines du gouvernement représentatif en Europe* (1820–2, revised edition 1851), 2. 264; id., *Mélanges politiques et historiques* (1869), 47, 74–5; id., *Mémoires pour servir à l'histoire de mon temps* (1858–64), 1. 110–11, 171, 318–22; 5. 8; 8. 3–5; M. de Barante, *La Vie politique de M. Royer-Collard* (1863), 1. 215–19; 2. 232–3; Theodore Zeldin, 'English Ideals in French Politics', *Cambridge Historical Journal* (1959), 1. 40–58.

clothes, and a whole host of French garments began to be called spencers, jerseys, waterproofs, machintoshes, and macfarlanes. 'High life' now involved tying one's tie in a special way, holding one's cane and mounting a horse as, supposedly, the English did. French courtesy was disdained in favour of the frigid haughtiness of the English gentleman. Anglo-American taverns sprang up all over Paris. A new race of sportsmen appeared, copying first the aristocratic English pastimes of horse-racing and then pretty well every other English game (on which more below). The Jockey Club was founded in Paris in 1833. The jargon of the English turf was taken over, clubs and whist drives were organised. French children began to be dressed up in 'Queen Anne' clothes, based on the highly popular fashions set by Kate Greenaway.[1] The romantics introduced Shakespeare, Milton, Ossian, Byron and Walter Scott. The last had numerous imitators in French as well as being a best seller. Seven translations of Scott were published in the years 1830–5 alone. In 1832 there was already a Paris bookshop and lending library which claimed in its advertisements that it received 140 English newspapers and had 40,000 volumes, mainly in English. After 1848, Dickens succeeded Scott in popularity, but obscure women novelists like Miss M. S. Cummins and Mrs. Elizabeth Wetherell went through edition after edition during the Second Empire.[2] 'Humour' was added to wit in social intercourse. Strong spirits and beer became fashionable drinks.[3] The dates at which *franglais* words were first used in French provide an archaeology of the new mixed culture that was growing up: bifteck (1786), fashionable (1803), lunch, dandy (1820), corned beef (1826), pyjama (1837), high life (1845), baby (1850), shirting (1855), cocktail (1860), breakfast (1877), flirt (1879), five o'clock tea (1885), smoking (jacket) (1889), grill room (1893), lavatory (1902), shorts (1933).[4] By the end of the nineteenth century, there were Frenchmen who argued that, despite the pre-eminence of French culture, the English system of education,

[1] Ruth Hill Viguers, *The Kate Greenaway Treasury* (1968). Between 1878 and 1905 932,100 copies of her books were produced.

[2] M. G. Devonshire, *The English Novel in France 1830–70* (1929), 67, 327, 395.

[3] Georges Renard, 'L'Influence de l'Angleterre sur la France depuis 1830', *Nouvelle Revue* (1885), vol. 35. 673–715, vol. 36. 35–76.

[4] R. Leslie-Melville, 'English Words in French', *Notes and Queries* (28 Sept. 1940), 225–8, (5 Oct. 1940), 246–8.

which trained character, had much to be said for it and deserved to be imitated.[1]

Though it was regretfully concluded that England could not be copied politically, given the inalterably different conditions of France, nevertheless admiration for England continued in modified form, following a new approach to the question inaugurated by Hippolyte Taine. He more than any man created the image of England held by Frenchmen between 1870 and 1939. His *History of English Literature* (1863-9) claimed to be based on a scientific analysis which distilled the essential character of the English 'race', though in fact, and significantly, it was based almost entirely on book reading. Though he did visit England for six weeks, he did so only after he had worked out his theories, and he was happy to note that observation confirmed them. His theories were influential not only because they were 'scientific' but also because they were systematic and clear. It was a part of them that books were an excellent instrument for understanding a civilisation and 'almost always capable of replacing the actual physical sight of it'. (His pronunciation of English was so bad that when he ordered potatoes, he got buttered toast.) Politically, Taine admired English self-government, the justices of the peace, private philanthropy and the educational system—he claimed an Eton schoolboy knew more about politics than most French deputies. But though he admired the aristocracy, he contradictorily could not stomach the 'humiliating inequality' which went with it—to the extent even of disliking the distinction between nobles, commoners and scholars at Oxford, each wearing a different gown. Though an unbeliever, he loved the broad church of England and thought —without much hope—that France would be transformed by Protestantism of this kind. These institutional observations were however impractical and irrelevant, because his view was that there were distinct English and French characters, which naturally developed the institutions that suited them. He therefore tended to stress the differences between the two countries. He distilled their peculiarities into two distinct 'types'. The English type was incarnated in the gentleman. He had pride, but also tenacity, practical business sense and the ability to concentrate on his ambitions and achieve them. That is why

[1] É. Desmolins, *A quoi tient la supériorité des Anglo-Saxons?* (c. 1897).

England had become a great industrial and colonial power. It represented will power, but it lacked the capacity to form abstract ideas, to converse pleasantly and wittily, which was where Frenchmen excelled. This is not to say that he saw England as simply a nation of shopkeepers and squires. Far from it. England, he said, had the best poetry in Europe and its prose equalled that of France—though it was weak in criticism and in art. To admire English literature—as opposed to English ideals—thus became fashionable.[1]

Taine's theories were elaborated by Émile Boutmy, the first director of the Paris School of Political Sciences, which Taine helped to found, to remedy France's inferiority to Eton schoolboys, and which became one of the mainstays of this new kind of Anglophilism. Using the same positivist methods of analysis, Boutmy argued that the grey and misty climate of England encouraged vigorous action, morose thoughts and an ardent imagination feeding itself on internal reverie rather than observation. But the most interesting statements by Boutmy are the ones he makes, by way of contrast, about France, which show how the French sense of national identity was developing, or rather was consolidating itself in its traditional mould. In France, he said, the air is limpid, the light is brilliant and varied, so sensations are extremely distinct and infinitely diversified. The French therefore have clear ideas: 'these classify themselves automatically in the brain, which enjoys reviewing them, and expressing them in polysyllabic, joyous and sonorous words, pronounced slowly in a warm air which carries them back whole to the ear. Thought and speech are in France naturally analytical; both are at once a representation of reality and a source of enchantment; they absorb, like a theatre stage, the successive march, the ordered deployment of ideas and images; they become in some way part of the external world.' Words thus become objects. 'Enjoying himself amid so many varied and delicate impressions, the Frenchman only regretfully tears himself away to act, and he hastens to return to the animated spectacle that nature and his own intelligence provide him with at all times.' From this contemplation come the abstract ideas at which the French were said to be so good and the English so hopeless.

[1] F. C. Roe, *Taine et l'Angleterre* (1923); H. Taine, *Notes sur l'Angleterre* (1872).

The English have therefore failed to satisfy what is most basic in man, to dissipate the sadness with which their heavy clouded sky oppresses them. They have gross humour, but not delicate wit. They are more poetic than the Latins, more creative, but less artistic, because they have too much arbitrary freedom in the way they express themselves; they disdain clarity, harmony, plausibility, without which (to a Frenchman believing in classical rules, as Boutmy does) art is impossible. Thus he criticises the English novel for trying 'to portray life in all its infinite variety, in contrast to French novels which restricted themselves to studying two or three characters, around whom they arranged the other characters hierarchically, in a gradually diminishing order of importance'. Art for the Frenchman meant rules, ordered development, crisis and solution, because art was inspired by the desire for clarity, order, unity. Boutmy saw the French as trying to order the world in their ideas, loving to contemplate beauty, while the English were filled with a desire for action and efficiency, because they felt the need to master themselves: Protestantism was the religion of internal self-government. Thus, he said, English puritanism concealed a deep and violent sexuality. 'Anyone who has lived long in England knows the bestiality of the majority of the race. Sport, gambling and drunkenness are among the pleasures the English appreciate most. In sexual relations, they are interested in the direct satisfaction of the senses . . . The Englishman goes straight to the object of his desires, instead of combining love-making with light entertainment and with the pleasures of conversation. The sensuality of the upper classes is concealed by a heavy hypocrisy . . . the lower classes can amuse themselves only grossly and violently.'

The result of this was, on the one hand, that English literature provided marvellous insights into the emotions, but, on the other hand, the English were able to show 'unequalled inhumanity' in dealing with colonial peoples. The English had not learnt how to enjoy themselves, because they did not know how to 'enjoy the superfluous, which gives charm to life, and which the French cultivated'. The English succeeded in business and industry because they were always direct, practical and concentrated on definite aims. By contrast, in France, action was the result of abstract ideas, which were complicated and involved many problems which needed discussion. So the French were likely to stop half-way and to move constantly from one novelty to another. 'That is why the French are revolutionaries, while the English do not go beyond eccentricity.' That, too, is why the English were the 'provincials of Europe', self-sufficient, suspicious of continental ideas, unaffected by what they saw abroad, and incapable of intermarrying with any other race. They were the most solitary and unsociable of people, the very opposite of the French, and, as Montesquieu said, 'The French cannot make friends in England'. The English were not naturally polite, as the French were: 'it is because the Englishman is not naturally a gentleman that England has a class of gentlemen'. Gentility represented the result of hard effort over many generations to overcome a natural boorishness: the masses realised how difficult it was to achieve and most did not aspire to so exalted a state. The French by contrast were 'poets and orators by birth', who were naturally graceful and who, with only a few months of acclimatisation, could modify their manners to make them equal to those of any class. That is why they were egalitarian.

The English got a lot of satisfaction from their work, even the most lowly of them, because of their passion for action, and that was another reason why the poor did not revolt, even though English employers were unequalled for their 'brutal insensitiveness'. The English had a 'slow intelligence' which 'rarely gave itself the time for profound deliberation'. Politics therefore was not about issues, but trials of strength, and since the English believed that will-power triumphed (rather than ideas) the aristocracy readily yielded. The masses willingly accepted the constant changes of their position, however contradictory, provided such changes did not appear to show weakness of will in the leaders. Rapid change was possible in England, because the rich were very rich and therefore able to take risks, and the poor, having nothing to lose, took risks too. The spirit of initiative was partly the result of the 'scandalously disproportionate distribution of property'. Boutmy concluded that though England was changing, it remained and would always remain individualist, incapable of feeling sympathy for others and not caring about whether it had the sympathy of others, very proud, contemptuous of other races and incapable of mixing with them, unable

to unite ideas into syntheses, preferring to follow a great statesman rather than principles, having no revolutionary spirit but
many individual eccentrics. Boutmy's ingenious arguments thus
end up with admiration for England whittled down to virtues
which France is shown as being better without. Even this Anglophile concludes that the two countries are incompatible, and
that ultimately he prefers to be French.[1]

This conclusion is important, because it meant that the pro-
English party in France, aside from its superficial snobbery,
ultimately came to adopt many of the criticisms of the anti-
English, who were more numerous and had a longer tradition.
Even among conservatives, England was far from being universally accepted as a model. Joseph de Maistre had said in 1814:
'In philosophy, wisdom begins with contempt for English
ideas.'[2] Most conservatives abominated England's Protestantism, its Civil War, its empiricism: they insisted that a French
constitution should be based on French, not foreign, traditions,
and that truth came from God, not from Bacon or Locke. The
abbé de Genoude, one of the legitimists' leaders, was not even
impressed by England's prosperity, for, he said, it was based on
commerce, whereas that of France was founded on glory: 'In
England power and intelligence are very developed, but the
heart is arid . . . Cupidity is the universal motive. The question
everybody asks about a man is, How much is he worth? Even
the aristocracy has prostrated itself at the feet of the golden calf
. . . The arts are a nullity.'[3] This materialism was frequently
stressed, until it was transferred as an accusation against the
Americans: it is striking that the two countries were disapproved
of for the same reasons. The desire to make money, said the
journalist Alphonse Esquiros, whose descriptions of England
were widely read during the Second Empire, was not simply
universal in England, but particularly characteristic, because
men obtained not only comfort from it but also consideration.[4]
England's industrialisation aroused more repulsion than wonder: the quality of life had been ruined, and the destruction of
agriculture meant that England was far more vulnerable than

---

[1] Émile Boutmy, *Essai d'une psychologie politique du peuple anglais au 19ᵉ siècle*(1901);
cf. É. Levasseur, 'Boutmy et l'école', *Annales des sciences politiques* (1906), 141–79.

[2] F. Holdsworth, *Joseph de Maistre et l'Angleterre* (1935), 26.

[3] M. de Genoude, *Lettres sur l'Angleterre* (1842), 26.

[4] Alphonse Esquiros, *L'Angleterre et la vie anglaise* (5 vols., 1869), 4. 174.

a balanced country like France.[1] Léon Faucher, who wrote one of the most detailed descriptions of English society in the mid-nineteenth century, painted a horrific picture of poverty and crime in cities like Liverpool and Birmingham, and vigorously attacked the upper and middle classes for inhumanity and selfishness. Though he wrote generously in praise of English liberty, he argued that the French were generally misinformed about this and did not see the vices which accompanied it. Political liberty was balanced by severe moral intolerance, equality of rights by the most extreme economic inequalities. Love of money was supreme, and went hand in hand with a deep religiosity, but there was no real stability or unity as a result, as outsiders imagined. The inequalities of wealth were driving the poor to emigration, but agitation among them was increasing. So, though the aristocracy was omnipotent, it was unable to sleep in peace. Faucher's remarkable criticism was reproduced in many other attacks on the dangers of following England's course. An early decadence was predicted for England.[2] Edgar Quinet declared that though he breathed more freely in England, he would not advise emigration to it. To crown all its political and economic faults, England was boring: it was the home of spleen. Even the poorest Corsican was happier than the worker of Birmingham. The slave-like conditions in the factories, the endless hard labour, represented France's revenge for Waterloo. If Merry England ever existed, it must have been a very long time ago.[3]

All these old views and prejudices survived into the twentieth century and indeed to 1939. Complaints that Taine's views were out of date had little effect.[4] The translation of Bernard Shaw, who was not only popular but even adopted as a set book in the official school syllabuses, showed that wit, paradox, play with ideas and advanced socialist doctrine could all come from this supposedly decadent country, but the result was only to raise

---

[1] Boucher de Perthes, *De la suprématie de l'Angleterre et de sa durée* (1862), 19, predicted that Australia would replace England as leader of the empire; id., *Voyage en Angleterre, Écosse et Irlande en 1860* (1868), 66.

[2] Léon Faucher, *Études sur l'Angleterre* (1843–4, 2nd edition, expanded, 1856); A. A. Ledru-Rollin, *De la décadence de l'Angleterre* (1850).

[3] Pierre Reboul, *Le Mythe anglais dans la littérature française sous la restauration* (Lille, 1962) is an excellent guide, unfortunately for only a limited period.

[4] P. Mantoux, *A Travers l'Angleterre contemporaine* (1909).

still further the prestige of English literature rather than the image of the English people. By 1914, indeed, knowledge of English literature was regarded as essential to anyone claiming to be cultured. Gide, Proust and Claudel were among the leading writers who published translations from English. But the idea the French had of England's way of life remained almost static. It is true that there were a few historians—notably Élie Halévy and Paul Mantoux—who made important contributions to understanding English society and a few minor authors who observed England with accuracy. Pierre Hamp, for example, who worked as a cook at the Savoy Hotel under Escoffier, and Louis Hémon, who sold electric lamps in England (1903–11), produced vivid descriptions of working-class life. However, the authors who were regarded as the main experts on England were interested much more in the aristocracy, Oxford and that old-world England which was blown up into an ideal all the more as it ceased to have any basis in the new democratic age. France thus had pumped into it a fairy-land dream of England which could have little relevance in the inter-war years. Paul Bourget wrote some of his novels in the Randolph Hotel, Oxford, but his first visit to England was in 1880, his last in 1897, and yet his novels long continued to be accepted as though they were about real life. Abel Hermant was another popular novelist, who again loved Oxford, though he also penetrated as far as Newcastle where one of his stories takes place. The most successful Anglophile novelist of all was André Maurois, who fell in love with England during the war when he was a liaison officer with the British troops in France, and who then visited England regularly; but his most famous books were about the old Victorian England, about elegant and proper officers with their good-humoured batmen, and though he knew about it, he seldom referred to unemployment or slums. There were many minor novelists who wrote about England as though it was an island of poetry, aesthetes and athletes, beautiful young men and no women: in Paris, Oscar Wilde was its representative, and when English females did appear in French novels, they were usually simply governesses, the 'miss'. This kind of England enabled Frenchmen steeped in the classics to reconstruct a sort of mirage of ancient Greece. Behind the pastoral calm, many authors also found a fascinating but un-French eroticism:

even Maurois's Dr. O'Grady confesses: 'Englishmen are more bashful because their desires are more violent. One finds even in the most austere of them, crises of sadism which astound one, considering how carefully their souls are cleaned.' *Mœurs oxfordiennes* became synonymous with homosexuality. *Lady Chatterley's Lover*, for the translation of which André Maurois wrote a preface, served to bring out from under Victorian England the bestiality Frenchmen had always claimed existed beneath the surface; and it was more mysterious than attractive, because, as Gide said, 'the more their ideas become emancipated, the more they stick to their morals, to the point that no one is more puritan than some English free-thinkers'. François Mauriac wrote: 'I do not understand and I do not like the English, except when they are dead and a thousand commentators, a thousand published letters, intimate diaries, information supplied by Maurois and good translations finally convince me that they are not Martians but brothers.'[1]

The inter-war writers on England were largely second rank. The most admired French authors drew no inspiration from English life, even if, like Gide, they read a lot of English literature; they were more interested in Russia and the East. The impressions of those who did visit England were superficial: Maurras went only to look at the Parthenon (Elgin) marbles: Jules Romains noticed only the 'chic' of London. The cult of the English gentleman was losing its appeal in a world preoccupied with Marxism, conscious of the decay of imperialism and the strains of capitalism. French books hostile to England were far more numerous than the favourable ones. The treatment of the Irish and the Indians was denounced as proof of English inhumanity and hypocrisy: Pierre Benoit and Henri Béraud wrote best-selling attacks on England, the latter declaring, 'I hate this people, as much from instinct as by tradition'.[2] What is most striking is that, despite the fact that so much was written by Frenchmen about England, they remained profoundly ignorant of how life was changing in it and of how complex its problems and aspirations were. The few carefully documented studies of contemporary conditions—and there were some very perspicacious ones—were little read and made far less impression than

[1] F. Mauriac, *Journal* (1937), 2. 16.
[2] Henri Béraud, *Faut-il réduire l'Angleterre en esclavage?* (1935), 19.

the old stereotypes, reproduced from Bourget to Maurois. One of the most popular of English novelists in France was Charles Morgan, because he wrote of the only England the French wanted to hear about, with its country-houses, its humour and its vicarage tea-parties. The English for their part translated Maurois's *Silences of Colonel Bramble*, but they paid no attention to Pierre Benoit's *Châtelaine du Liban* (1924), a violent attack on them which had far larger sales.

There was thus a rather curious situation in 1939. English literature was better known in France than it had ever been before, and greatly admired, but the French as a whole thought of England as Victorian, out of date, with nothing new to say about the urgent problems of the world. All the ancient animosities, far from dying, were sharpened by the numerous conflicts between the two governments. One can understand therefore why, during the 1939–45 war, Vichy's hostile attitude to England was possible and popular to such an extent that de Gaulle, even while benefiting from English aid, kept up a very reserved attitude towards his ally. In July 1940, it has been said, 90 per cent of Frenchmen hated the English. The navy, which had considerable influence under Vichy, was anti-English by tradition and had more recent scores to settle. Many thus felt that England had abandoned and betrayed France, in the old perfidious style. The Resistance was far from being entirely pro-English: careful archival study has revealed how much variation there was on a regional basis, the west and north-east being most favourable to England, while parts of the south-west remained hostile. The Resistance movement itself, carrying out an inquiry in November 1943 in the Saint-Étienne region, found that only 40 per cent were pro-English, 30–35 per cent opportunistic and 25–30 per cent anti-English. Young people in general everywhere and in all classes seem to have been more favourable to England. Perhaps half of the petty bourgeoisie were indifferent as to whether England or Germany should win the war; but they were most hostile of all to Russia. Feelings towards the different powers changed a lot in the course of the war, so no simple generalisation is possible, except that, for the majority, to be pro-English meant above all to be anti-German. The memories of old colonial rivalries were still powerful. The quip in the manifesto of 8 March 1942 signed by well-known writers

rang true to many: 'Great Britain . . . the country of millionaires
and the dole . . . always shows the most profound contempt for
the colonial peoples it conquered, remains faithful to its view
that the niggers begin at Calais.' Ideologically, the U.S.A.
seemed the more dynamic ideal of democracy, and those who
thought otherwise turned to Russia rather than to England. But
at one time or another probably most people hoped for an
English victory and to that extent there was a collective feeling
in favour of England. The ambivalence of this conclusion summarises the attraction, the animosity and the mystery inspired
by France's ally and oldest enemy.[1]

### France and Germany

France's involvement with Germany was much more intense,
more important to France, more complicated. It manifested
itself in a love–hate relationship which continually tormented
and frustrated Frenchmen. If France was married to any country, it was to Germany. The three wars they fought in this
period did not end their fascination with each other. The French
interest in England was, by comparison, not much more than
a flirtation or an affair. When France became really interested
in Anglo-Saxon civilisation, it was the U.S.A. that attracted its
attention, in a way much more profound than England did. But
Franco-German relations reveal best of all the complexity of
France's position in Europe. This is a particularly striking case,
in which the study of these relations in purely diplomatic terms
gives a positively misleading picture of what went on in the
minds of people outside the political arena. Germany was the
land of Kant, Goethe, Wagner, Marx and Nietzsche to more
people than that it was that of Bismarck and Hitler.

France's interest in Germany was from the beginning passionate. It was kept alive by a constant sense of discovery, and a

[1] Marius-François Guyard, *La Grande Bretagne dans le roman français 1914–40*
(1954), one of the best works in comparative literature; Manuela Semidei, 'La
Grande Bretagne dans l'opinion française pendant les années de guerre 1940–4'
(typescript doctoral thesis in the Paris School of Political Sciences library, 1960),
based on much original material; Pierre Bourdon, *Perplexités et grandeur de l'Angleterre* (1945); Pierre de Coulevain, *L'Île inconnue* (1906); F. Delattre, *Dickens et la
France* (1927); G. Tabouis, *Albion perfide ou loyale* (1938); A. Siegfried, *L'Angleterre
d'aujourd'hui* (1924); id., *La Crise britannique au 20ᵉ siècle* (1931); P. Morand, *Londres*
(1933); F. Crouzet, *Revue historique* (July–Sept. 1975), 105–34.

sense that these discoveries were immediately relevant and important. Little was known of Germany, and little interest shown, until Madame de Staël suddenly found in Germany the land of liberty, in contrast with France oppressed by the despotism of Napoleon, who promptly banned her book, *De l'Allemagne* (1810). What was particularly attractive to her, and others after her, was that Germany accorded an unusually large role to writers and philosophers, since politically the country was still dismembered and of the second rank. Madame de Staël—who in fact saw very little of Germany and could not speak the language—proclaimed that here at last was a country where men's minds were free, where 'there was no fixed taste on anything, where everything is independence and individuality'. Almost every peasant was musical; the humbler villages had people who loved literature and philosophy: 'they argue in the domain of intellectual speculation, and they leave the realities of life to the great of this earth'. They were primitive, spontaneous, emotional, sociable. Whereas the proud Englishman considered his dignity and the vain Frenchman wondered what others would think, the German gave himself up to reverie and to science. Germany was seized on as the country which would liberate France, from classicism in literature, from materialism in philosophy, and in general revivify it with the qualities that it lacked. The irony of it was that the Germany the French discovered had largely ceased to exist just when they began praising it, so that to a considerable extent the Germany they admired was their own creation. On the theoretical plane, that did not matter, because the influx of ideas proved immensely stimulating, but in practical terms it repeatedly presented French intellectuals with terrifying situations, in which the object of their interest behaved in a way totally different from what they expected. These sudden revelations of unsuspected reality created moral crises as profound as the discoveries they repudiated.

In 1826 Victor Cousin wrote to Hegel: 'Hegel, tell me the truth. I shall pass on to my country as much as it can understand.' Hegel said derisively: 'M. Cousin has taken a few fish from me, but he has well and truly drowned them in his sauce.' Despite all rebuffs, French fascination with German philosophy continued throughout this period. Kant, whom Cousin proclaimed to be one of the origins of the French Revolution, became one of the tutelary dignitaries of French thinking, not merely because he was a set book in the schools, but because he was a decisive influence on most philosophers, from Renouvier onwards, so that he held second place only to Descartes. Marx, Hegel and Nietzsche were a major source of inspiration, particularly between the two world wars; Freud, though long resisted—as is shown in another chapter—finally invaded France after 1945. It is barely possible to disentangle the German contribution to French philosophy—in the widest sense of that word—because it is so universally pervasive. It was much more important than that of England—whose presence was felt more in literature—because it penetrated to the very roots of French attitudes. The philosophical marriage was so close indeed that some French writers, from the 1930s, even lost their taste for clarity, and tortuous obscurity became fashionable—and remains so—in some circles. When the French tired of one German influence, they replaced it by another German one, even though they sometimes disguised the fact. Thus around 1900 Nietzsche became the symbol of liberation from Kant, and people claimed that though he might be German by nationality, his education and his ideas were French.[1] Jaurès wrote his thesis on German socialism and while the republican politicians declared Germany to be the enemy, the socialists proclaimed them allies.

Just how deep this involvement with Germany went can be seen by the way even defeat at Germany's hands was unable to end it. It was to a considerable extent the French intellectuals who stopped France from obstructing the unification of Germany. Germany was seen as one of the pillars of the cosmopolitanism so fashionable in 1848. Traditionally French policy towards Germany had been to keep it disunited. Under the Second Empire, Thiers was one of the few politicians who still believed that this was the right attitude. He looked on Prussian ambitions simply in terms of power and military advantage. Edgar Quinet, once Cousin's pupil, translator of Herder (though significantly he translated it from the English translation), had once said that to study philosophy meant to study Germany, but he had with time become disillusioned and complained of the

[1] G. Bianquis, *Nietzsche en France* (1928).

'unanimous servility with which Frenchmen bow before German doctrines, without discussion or precision, to the point of completely exaggerating and distorting them'. He had spent longer in Germany than most of his colleagues, and had seen the identification of German philosophers with a narrow nationalism, which other Frenchmen did not want to notice, because it contradicted their view that the Germans were, as Flaubert said in his *Dictionary of Received Ideas*, a 'people of dreamers'. But Quinet's protests against 'Teutomania' and Heine's satire of it in his book *On Germany* (1835) completely failed to change the image Madame de Staël had created. Lamartine proclaimed: 'My policy is eminently German: it is the only one that suits this age dominated by the eastern question.' Russia was the great barbarian enemy, and, as Émile Ollivier said, 'the land of Mozart and Beethoven . . . democratic, liberal, cultivated', was France's natural ally against Russia, 'our rampart, our veritable avant-garde'. Michelet talked passionately of 'my Germany, the scientific power that alone has made me study questions deeply, and given me Kant, Beethoven and a new faith'. Victor Hugo wrote of it 'No nation is greater'. Renan declared, 'I studied Germany and I felt as though I was entering a temple; everything I have found there is pure, elevated, moral, beautiful and touching. Ah! How sweet and strong they are! . . . I considered that this advent of a new spirit is a fact analogous to the birth of Christianity.' German idealism had saved French philosophy from English empiricism, which reduced 'all to the miserable level of pleasure and utility'. The romantics saw Germany as rejuvenating the world. A *Revue germanique* was founded in 1857 to 'build a bridge across the Rhine', and many eminent writers contributed to it. The co-operation of the countries which had produced the two greatest movements in modern history, the Reformation and the Revolution, the union of their different talents, was seen as the herald of immense progress. The days of narrow nationalism were declared to be over.[1] Taine wrote in 1867: 'The Germans are the initiators and perhaps the masters of the modern spirit', and he wanted the French, who specialised in making ideas clear, to co-operate to spread it so that it became 'the universal spirit'. He had some doubts about how far this supremacy extended beyond science and

---

[1] Charles Dollfuss, *De l'esprit français et de l'esprit allemand* (1864).

philosophy: during a visit to Germany in the spring of 1870 he was dismayed by the regimentation, and declared that Germany was 'ready for slavery'. But it was considered illiberal to oppose German unification, which many in any case considered to be a necessary preliminary to the confederation of Europe. So it was only when France's 'honour' was slighted that Napoleon III declared war on Prussia.[1]

The defeat—on one level—shook the whole country profoundly. Revenge and the recovery of Alsace-Lorraine became a principal object of French policy for the next forty years. That Germany was France's enemy became the basic fact of international relations. The cosmopolitan, fraternal aspect of France received a crushing blow—though the socialists revived it—and a new strident, inward-looking nationalism developed, demanding rearmament if not war. The liberal illusion appeared to have been unmasked and a return to the chauvinist, power-conscious, egocentric traditions of the old monarchy was demanded. And in due course France fought Germany again and having defeated it, tried to dismember it, or at least to exact savage reparations from it—with a bitterness unequalled by any other belligerent. There is a vast amount of evidence on the animosity that estranged the two countries.

But—at another level—France recovered from its humiliation with astonishing speed, perhaps because it saw it as a justified humiliation at the hands of a country whose superiority in certain fields was manifest and inescapable. So, though French tourists kept away from Germany, co-operation between the two countries was not only resumed in practical terms, but vastly increased. Their economic and financial relations became closer and more extensive, at the same time as the two governments hurled insults at each other. The Paris Universal Exhibition of 1900 publicly revealed this. More Germans attended it than all other foreigners put together, far outnumbering the English and the Russians; and they were awarded nearly 2,000 prizes for their exhibits, their leadership in the electrical, chemical and optical industries being internationally acclaimed. The

[1] Michael Howard, *The Franco-Prussian War* (1961) for the war. For opinion before it, E. Quinet, *La France et l'Allemagne* (1867); L. A. Prévost-Paradol, *La France nouvelle* (1868); E. About, *La Prusse en 1860* (1860); A. Dumas, *La Terreur prussienne* (1867).

nationalist politicians issued cries of alarm about the penetration of German capital into France, but when one looks at this impartially, as an economic historian has recently done in an important thesis, one sees it as part of a co-operation which businessmen and investors found mutually advantageous. The French in fact invested about three times as much in Germany as the Germans did in France, because the investment opportunities were so attractive. In 1914, 445 million francs' worth of shares owned by Germans were sequestrated in France, while Frenchmen owned about 800 million francs' worth of German shares, plus 480 million francs' worth of Alsatian shares. French property in Germany—of all kinds—was worth 3,000 million. What raised the alarm was that the French policy of protection meant that subterfuges had to be found by the Germans to make trade easier. Between 1893 and 1913 French imports from Germany increased threefold and exports to Germany doubled. In the 1890s, a quarter of the beer consumed in France was produced in Germany; the bulk of textile dyes used in France came from Germany; the Lorraine metallurgical industry imported 39 per cent of its fuel from Germany (in 1891); Germany was France's main supplier of coke (whereas England supplied coal). In return, French exports to Germany were raw materials (one-third of the total) and agricultural produce (another third). Though in the statistics of around 1900, England appears still to buy more from France than from any other country, many German goods travelled to England through the Low Countries, so that in fact the figures were about equal. The economic rivalry between France and Germany was blown up out of proportion by the politicians, even though it was true that France lost ground to Germany in world trade. But the two countries were to a considerable extent active in different parts of the world. Thus French investments were predominantly European (see table). This uses official figures: investments in Germany were obviously higher; those in Spain are also estimated to be nearer 5,000 million; those in Egypt nearer 2,700 million. Germany had something like 2,500 million francs more invested in the U.S.A. than France had, and more also in Central America, especially Mexico. In South America, the two countries were roughly equal, notably in Argentina, but Germany had more in Chile and Venezuela, and France more in

Brazil and Colombia. In Africa, Germany concentrated on southern Africa, France on Egypt. The French interest in Turkey was older and therefore larger than Germany's. Germany tended to invest in industry, and outside Europe, while France bought up the state bonds particularly in Europe.

*French investments abroad (1902)*

| French investments in | Million francs | French investments in | Million francs |
|---|---|---|---|
| Russia | 6966 | China | 651 |
| Spain | 2974 | Turkey in Asia | 354 |
| Austria–Hungary | 2850 | Russia in Asia | 60 |
| Turkey in Europe | 1818 | British Africa | 1592 |
| Italy | 1430 | Egypt | 1436 |
| England | 1000 | Tunis | 512 |
| Portugal | 900 | Argentina | 923 |
| Belgium | 600 | Brazil | 696 |
| Switzerland | 455 | U.S.A. | 600 |
| Romania | 438 | Mexico | 300 |
| Norway | 290 | Colombia | 246 |
| Greece | 283 | Chile | 226 |
| Serbia | 201 | Uruguay | 219 |
| Netherlands | 200 | Canada | 138 |
| Monaco | 158 | Venezuela | 130 |
| Denmark | 131 | Cuba | 126 |
| Sweden | 123 | Peru | 107 |
| Germany | 85 | Haiti | 78 |
| Luxembourg | 62 | Bolivia | 70 |
| Bulgaria | 48 | Central America | 42 |

There was certainly industrial rivalry, as for example in Bulgaria, where Krupp and Schneider fought for military contracts, and in Morocco, where imports from Germany quadrupled between 1894 and 1898; but there was also a lot of financial co-operation between the banks. They collaborated, for example, in the Crédit Foncier Égyptien, apparently an eminently French bank, but in 1908 this had three German directors on its board. The Crédit Lyonnais was represented in Brazil by the German–Brazilian Bank; and here even Cail and Schneider got themselves represented by German firms. Though the Baghdad Railway was an instrument of German expansion, which produced bitter political rivalry, the Germans had French help in financing it: the hostility came from the French government, not the French banks. The German government forbade the establishment of a German Chamber of Commerce in Paris for political reasons, and in 1911 financial co-operation was virtually halted. But in the preceding decade, the Germans had been buying themselves into French industry, particularly with a view to ensuring their supplies of iron ore from Normandy and Lorraine, while the French steelmakers were buying a stake in the German coalfields. The concessions bought by the Germans frightened public opinion, but not the industrialists, who had plenty of iron and wanted coal in return. Germany was an increasingly serious competitor in world trade, but that was partly because the French were so notoriously inefficient as salesmen. In many regions, French banks had helped Germany expand, though after 1910 the Germans got the feeling that the French were putting obstacles in their way. Till then, there were strong pressures for an economic rapprochement between them.[1]

In the same way, at the intellectual level, Germany continued to be a source of inspiration, even though there was also widespread bewilderment and uncertainty as to how to deal with it. There were always academics and writers who denounced the Germans as brutal barbarians—men as distinguished as Fustel de Coulanges and Émile Durkheim, both of whom owed a lot to German thought, wrote violent polemics against the German in war-time.[2] Instead of admitting that they had failed to study Germany carefully enough, they castigated the Germans as hypocrites. In some circles it became fashionable to condemn Germans as barbarians. The generation which had preached Franco-German friendship up to 1870 was terribly shaken. Some took up the attitude that the defeat marked the end of France as a leader in Europe. Taine had already written in 1867: 'Our role is finished, at least for the time being. The future rests with Prussia, America and England.' French hegemony in Europe, as a result of which the principle of equality had been introduced, was over, just as Italian hegemony had ended in the sixteenth century. Taine now gave his life to

---

[1] Raymond Poidevin, *Les Relations économiques et financières entre la France et l'Allemagne de 1898 à 1914* (1969), a masterly study. For a description of German activity in France, see Louis Bruneau, *L'Allemagne en France: enquêtes économiques* (1914).

[2] Fustel de Coulanges, *L'Alsace est-elle allemande ou française. Réponse à M. Mommsen* (1870); É. Durkheim, 'L'Allemagne au dessus de tout', *La Mentalité allemande et la guerre* (1915).

studying French history so as to discover the reasons for this defeat, and he found it in what he considered to be the poisoning influence of French classicism and Jacobinism. France was at fault and his belief in German relativism, traditionalism, Protestantism and science thus remained undamaged. The effect of his *Origins of Contemporary France* was thus not to turn Frenchmen against Germany, but to urge them to move on the same conservative, indeed reactionary, path that Germany was following. The new French nationalism did not simply reflect hostility to Germany; in many cases it was also imitative of Germany, which was seen as leading a new, inexorably successful march in the direction of traditionalism. Renan likewise turned conservative, even monarchist, though he also became more critical of Germany, criticising even the values he had once praised, saying that Germany was 'heavy and obstinate'. Younger people did not even need to make Germany their scapegoat: they put the blame for the defeat on Napoleon III and condemned not Germany, but war itself. Many of them, after an initial revulsion against the victor, declared that it was the Second Empire, not France, that had been defeated, or alternatively that it was 'science' that had triumphed, and the answer lay in more education. Socialism, with its international ideals, was an alternative to nationalism, and many people thus revived the old cosmopolitanism of the romantics, in which German ideas kept pride of place alongside French ones. The notion that there were two Germanies was popular: the left admired liberal, intellectual anticlerical Germany, and regretted only that this was unfortunately balanced by the Hohenzollern, despotic Germany. The right admired its monarchist power, and regretted that it was materialist and Protestant. The school manuals did not become anti-German: most denounced war, they preached patriotism but within the context of humanitarianism, in the tradition of Kant.

Germany perhaps was no longer admired so blindly: the historian Seignobos in 1881 suggested that praise of German universities was exaggerated; Durkheim in 1887 was also, to a certain extent, critical of German philosophy; Lucien Herr declared that Germany was living on its past; but nevertheless the intellectuals continued to visit Germany, to write reports on it, and the prestige of its science, its education, its music and

E

its socialism survived. Even Barrès, who attacked French schoolmasters for spreading the doctrines of Kant, got some of his own ideas from Hartmann's *Philosophy of the Unconscious*, which was translated into French in 1877, and he praised Wagner in whom he thought he could find his own doctrine of the Cult of the Ego. It is true that in course of time Barrès became increasingly anti-German, but he never completely abandoned the French tradition of universality. It was Maurras who finally carried egoism to its ultimate conclusion and urged the purging of all foreign influence from France. When in 1895 the *Mercure de France* held an inquiry on Franco-German intellectual relations, practically all the Frenchmen it questioned said they were in favour of more contact and exchange of ideas. Another inquiry in 1902–3 was considerably less enthusiastic: many people were following the same path as Barrès. As the threat of war grew, books and novels appeared in increasing numbers saying that to be pacifist was to play into the hands of a Germany which hated France; and even people like Péguy joined those who demanded a victory over Germany, to put right the insult to French supremacy.[1] But not all people reacted in this way, for not all were worried in the same way by the notion of France in fact (as opposed to ideally) being inferior. As Germany's population, which had been equal to that of France in 1870, reached 68 million in 1913, and as its industrialisation was accentuated, some people saw Germany as the herald of a new kind of civilisation, with urbanisation, efficiency and a new kind of wealth, in direct contrast to the old romantic, pastoral myth. And Romain Rolland spent twelve years writing a long novel, *Jean-Christophe* (1904–12), studying the question of Franco-German relations, with the conclusion that both countries had faults and virtues. He wanted them to combine to create something better than either; his hesitations about the war, which he ultimately accepted as inevitable, show how divided the French intellectuals were about patriotism. In 1869, when Sarcey was lecturing on Horace at the Collège de France, he illustrated his argument about families being separated by war, by asking his audience to imagine what would happen if war should break out between France and

---

[1] e.g. Marcel Prévost, *Monsieur et Madame Moloch* (1906); André Lichtenberger, *Juste Lobel, Alsacien* (1911); Agathon, *Les Jeunes Gens d'aujourd'hui* (1913).

Germany. The audience protested, and a man shouted, 'The supposition is impious . . . it is unpatriotic'. That attitude never quite died.[1]

During the 1914–18 war, and as a result of it, there was a widespread, deeply felt desire to solve the German problem by destroying Germany. War propaganda portrayed the 'Boches' as violent, inhuman barbarians. Clemenceau incarnated this total opposition to them. But it should not be forgotten that he had to lock up Caillaux, one of the country's leading politicians who enjoyed much support and who wanted an amicable settlement of differences between the two countries. It is striking that while France was trying to force the rest of Europe to take extreme measures against the Germans in the 1920s, the intellectuals once more took up their role as advocates of conciliation and spiritual union. There was a great increase of interest in German literature between the wars, with numerous translations in particular of the German romantics. In 1927 *La Revue d'Allemagne* was founded, supported by Jean Giraudoux, Lévy-Bruhl, Paul Langevin, Jules Romains, as well as Robert Curtius and Thomas Mann, to stimulate friendly discussion about the arts and literature. The years 1926–9 were notable for many congresses and meetings arranged between writers of the two countries. In 1929 the École Normale Supérieure petitioned for a united, disarmed Europe. The surrealists took their hate of French bourgeois culture to the point of shouting 'Down with France, Up with Germany'. Such attitudes were stimulated by the belief that sentimental, cultured Germany, discovered by Madame de Staël, and brutal Prussia, revealed by Bismarck, were neither of them the 'real' Germany. Rather it was argued that Germany had no unalterable character, but was malleable, educable, and that precisely was its charm and the source of its youth; whereas by contrast classical France was inescapably satisfied with itself and immobile. Giraudoux, who had studied German literature at the École Normale Supérieure, and who soon recovered his optimism about Germany after the war, particularly urged this view; in 1928 he staged a play, *Siegfried*, which advocated reconciliation and which was well received. He said the Germans

[1] Claude Digeon, *La Crise allemande de la pensée française 1870–1914* (1959) is the essential guide to this question, with a full bibliography.

were not warlike: 'it was the desire to travel that excited them all into war'. This showed just how full of energy they were; their own Kultur was a failure; but they had irreplaceable characteristics which Europe should value. Jacques Rivière likewise published his memoirs of his prisoner-of-war days without bitterness, arguing that Germans were neither poets nor barbarians but characterless people, unable to distinguish between truth and falsehood, between right and wrong; they were capable of making of themselves anything they pleased, by an act of will. They had no innate taste for war. So they should be used to create a new Europe, since co-operation with them was preferable to fighting them. It is not clear how far Rivière distinguished between romanticism, which he hated, and the Germans, whom he criticised as so confused that their Kultur simply represented an inability to think clearly: they thought of ideals as things to be realised, and therefore had only practical goals. Their domination would destroy the individual and the arts. He saw them not as barbarians but as a flabby, over-emotional people, who needed to be taken in hand. Rivière said in 1923: 'Germany continues to attract and repel me in equal measure.' He refused to reject all things German, or to make French interests the sole guide of policy. Peace could only be obtained by co-operation; Germany should therefore not be frustrated, but made into the industrial region of Europe. Even Barrès, who in 1919 was one of those who warned against forgiving the Germans, came to distinguish between good and bad Germans: he very conveniently produced the theory that the good ones lived mainly in the Rhineland, where they had the benefit of Latin influence, and which should now become France's buffer against bad Germany. His solution was therefore to take over part of Germany.

The 1930s showed how the French tended to look at Germany in ways which suited their ideology. Thus Alain, the philosopher of the individual against authority, wrote on 25 June 1933: 'I have not reacted much in face of the Hitler crisis. Distant events do not move me much. From my very youth, Germany has always been painted as . . . guilty of threats, ruses, lies and torture, given to singing and gorging itself with beer. I believed none of this, and I hope our rulers will free themselves of these phantoms. On the contrary, in every German I have seen, I have promptly recognised the man.' A lot of confusion followed, as people tried to decide whether Nazism should alter their attitude—a confusion which will be studied in another chapter. Left and right, it will be seen, reversed their positions: many pacifists now wanted war, many nationalists now talked of peace with Germany. The net result was that once again France was divided about its attitude to the Germans. But once again there were enough influential people, sufficiently certain of their attitude, to risk co-operating with them.[1]

The belief in France's intellectual superiority did not die. In the interwar period there was a lot of discussion of this matter. French and Germans wrote books about each other's civilisation, translated them and debated them. Both sides ended up with a feeling that their own was, ultimately, best. The Germans accused the French of being static, basically hostile to real innovation, deriving their ideas from Rome— whereas the Germans represented revolt and dynamism. To a considerable extent the French accepted this. The attacks on them made them rise in defence of what were considered their traditional attributes. They replied that their function had been to impose rules of taste, based on reason, upon the chaos of life; that they saw the need to reinvigorate their civilisation, but they were unwilling to make any drastic changes in it. Change, wrote even the future collaborationist Louis Reynaud, should always be carried out 'within the iron framework of certain forms which represent conquests of proved value, which are above argument, and outside which there is only chaos, individual arbitrariness, bad taste and barbarism'. He said Germany also had important qualities: 'a powerful and obscure understanding of the deeper needs of life', of instinct and emotion, and an ability, because their thought was so chaotic, occasionally to produce unexpected truths by putting things together which no one had joined before. They were capable of dealing with the indistinct, the uncertain, and the idea of development was one of their great discoveries; but they also had an unrivalled ability to collect facts, which they combined

---

[1] J. M. Carré, *Les Écrivains français et le mirage allemand 1800–1940* (1947); B. D. Kingstone, 'The View of the German Character in French Literature 1918–39' (unpublished D.Phil. Oxford thesis, 1965); Jacques Body, *Giraudoux et l'Allemagne* (1975).

to produce great speculative edifices. In this way they had renewed European scholarship, and also triumphed as business-men and industrialists. France and Germany thus had different priorities but their views were not necessarily antagonistic. It could be claimed that they should complement each other, and that though they would always have difficulty in agree-ing, it was not impossible for them, meanwhile, to reconcile their immediate practical interests. But it was only when the grandiose ideas of absolute supremacy which both countries held, finally became too unreal after 1945 that they were able to do this.[1]

Paris still has no German restaurants (they call themselves Alsatian). In a poll held in 1966 the French still thought of the Germans as disciplined, proud, romantic, heavy and bellicose and of themselves as elegant, individualistic, logical, frivolous and vain. The Germans agreed about French elegance but not about French logic; German girls, however, while condemning wars, said they liked officers and uniforms. Twenty years of a new kind of propaganda had failed to alter the stereotypes.[2] But perhaps now these mattered much less, because the decisive criteria were no longer spiritual, but economic.

### France and the U.S.A.

France was very conscious of America throughout these years. Diplomatic history perhaps inevitably sees France as a Euro-pean power and its relations with America as of secondary importance. But reflexion on the American experience, which was so different to that of France, caused many Frenchmen to redefine their own culture, to stress its originality and to defend it more self-consciously in the face of the power which by 1940 was clearly surpassing it in an increasing number of fields. The new attitudes which appeared in France in the 1950s, and made possible its rapid economic expansion and the unprecedented growth in its population, were, to a considerable extent, prepared by this reflexion.

[1] Louis Reynaud, *L'Âme allemande* (1933)—who was then a professor at the faculty of Lyon; Alexandre Arnoux, de l'Académie Goncourt, *Contacts allemands. Journal d'un demi siècle* (1950), an enlightening and honest personal history.

[2] Yvon Bourdet, *Préjugés français et préjugés allemands* (n.d., about 1967), 29, 38, 61.

Talk of the Americanisation of Europe began very early. Philarète Chasles in 1851 was already saying that 'American ideas are invading us'. The constitution of 1848 had brought the American political model to the highest degree of popularity it was ever to enjoy. But in 1855 Baudelaire, in a much wider context, referred to 'this century americanised by its zoocratic and industrial philosophers'. The fears were certainly premature. In 1850 France and England were still both ahead of the U.S.A. as commercial powers, though the latter's merchant fleet was already second only to England's. In the 1851 Universal Exhibition, England exhibited as much as all the other nations put together, and it won seventy-seven of the medals for outstanding originality, compared to fifty-six given to France and only five to the U.S.A. America was noted then, from the technical point of view, largely for its agricultural machines.[1] Though Singer invented the sewing machine in 1851, Bell the telephone in 1876 and Edison the electric lamp in 1891, the great industrial power was still England. It was only in 1887 that the U.S.A. produced more steel than England, 1890 that it produced more iron and 1899 more coal. By 1890 it had more steam horsepower than England. In 1901 for the first time England received an American loan. In 1891 the U.S.A. produced as much wheat as France and Russia combined. While England was the leading industrial nation, France maintained a very active intellectual resistance to industrialisation, though this did have many French admirers. But it was much more the U.S.A. that finally convinced France that it should abandon its protest and at least some of the values, which, paradoxically, the Americans had admired more than any other nation.

At the beginning of the nineteenth century the French still had rather elementary ideas about America. They relied on such books as those of the abbé Raynal (1770), Volney (1802) and Chateaubriand (1827), and argued about such questions as whether the American climate was conducive to civilisation or was bound to create degeneration. They read unflattering works by English writers such as Mrs. Trollope (1831) which the

---

[1] H. Koht, *The American Spirit in Europe. A Study of Transatlantic Influences* (Philadelphia, 1949); cf. Crane Brinton, *The Americans and the French* (Cambridge, Mass., 1968).

eminent philosopher Jouffroy took seriously enough to devote
three long articles to them in the *Revue des Deux Mondes*. French
emigrants had very little notion of America's size and some
imagined it to be no bigger than a French department. The
President of the Chamber of Deputies himself in 1834 described
Pennsylvania as a desert. Ostensibly respectable French guide-
books thought Boston was the capital of Virginia. But all this
was rapidly changed in the course of the July Monarchy and
the years following it. Between 1815 and 1852 between eight
and ten books on the U.S.A. appeared in France each year—
three to four hundred in all. Benjamin Franklin's *Way to
Wealth* was translated into French, went through fifty editions
by 1852 to become perhaps the most popular foreign book in
France, probably as widely read as La Fontaine and certainly
one of the most widely accepted guides to conduct, because it
was acceptable to all parties. Fenimore Cooper came to live in
Paris 1826–8 and 1830–3 and his highly successful novels gave
Frenchmen a concrete, even if misleading, picture of the new
world, to be complemented in due course by *Uncle Tom's Cabin*,
of which eleven different French translations were published in
ten months. Michel Chevalier spent two years in the U.S.A.
before writing his book on it (1834) which also appeared in the
*Journal des Débats*, so reaching a wide audience. Tocqueville's
*Democracy in America* (1825) made the U.S.A. immediately
relevant to anyone interested in France's post-revolutionary
development. Democrats made Washington one of France's
heroes, to counter the autocratic Napoleon. The American
constitution, which the republic of 1848 partly copied, might
well have exerted great influence if that republic had not
collapsed so catastrophically. Frenchmen quickly became
aware of America in economic relations because trade increased
rapidly, American cotton being exchanged for silk and wine
and also—for the French did not always disdain to adapt their
products—such things as wallpaper with special 'American'
scenes. The export of French paintings to America was already
active under Louis-Philippe and soon became important to
both 'academic' and 'modern' artists. In the course of these
years, therefore, the image of America in France changed
from being the land of the eighteenth-century noble savage
into one of a commercial power. But as it was studied more,

criticism increased and people began to see the two countries as representing opposing kinds of civilisation. There were some who praised Americans for their inventiveness, their enterprise and common sense, for incarnating the ideal of the self-made man who would also be a philanthropist. But it became rather more fashionable to caricature Americans as coarse, materialist bores, interested only in making money, narrowly puritan, incapable of conversing in a polished way. That is why the French identified rather with the southern states, which seemed to value aristocracy, leisure and pleasure more, though they disliked the way the southerners treated the Indians and Blacks and deplored the extravagance of their religious sects.[1]

The characteristic feature of America which struck the French most powerfully was perhaps its women. Tocqueville's book on Democracy was complemented by a novel, *Marie* (1835), by his friend Beaumont, and this was only one of a whole host of others discussing the strikingly different relations between the sexes across the Atlantic. The professor of comparative legislation at the Collège de France, Édouard Laboulaye, who had never visited the United States but who was regarded as France's greatest expert on it, likewise complemented his lectures on the American constitution by a novel, *Paris in America* (1862), which went through eight editions in its first year and had been reprinted thirty-five times by 1887.[2] Many other novels appeared in the 1860s which showed American girls in casual clothes and shorter skirts, never troubled by modesty and never lowering their eyes, not voluptuous but simply straightforward. Maurice Sand, in *Miss Mary* (1867), thought this placed an almost unbridgeable gulf between them and Frenchmen. Alfred Assollant, in *Un Quaker à Paris* (1866), depicted American women dominating over the males. Mario Uchard, in *Inès Parker* (1880), which was serialised in the *Revue des Deux Mondes*, claimed that the American principle was that every woman was sovereign, while the French held that every woman was prey. His conservative conclusion was that women needed to be protected by barriers because they were creatures of instinct, not of reason. But there

---

[1] There is an excellent survey of this early period by René Rémond, *Les États-Unis devant l'opinion français 1815–52* (2 vols., 1962).
[2] Laboulaye was also the translator of Channing.

were also others who spoke in favour of American girls, like the French consul in San Francisco, Paulin Neboyet, in *L'Américaine* (1875), who held them up as an ideal, because they were free of preciousness, prudery, superstition, feebleness or puritanism. Just how quickly the debate became active even outside the circles which read books may be seen from the 1852 vaudeville, *The Bloomerists or The Reform of the Skirts*, and from Sardou's highly successful play *Strong Women* (1860) which satirised 'Americomaniac' women with masculine ambitions. In his *The Benoiton Family* (1865), which had 300 consecutive performances, Sardou makes a French father forbid his two girls to go on a walk alone: they reply: 'Oh! What a French papa! Why not alone, like in America?' Sardou kept up his attack on this, saying 'This America I attack has invaded us so successfully that I am very fearful I shall be defeated in the struggle I am undertaking'.[1] The arguments about this continued for a whole century, so the battle was by no means decisive. But when Simone de Beauvoir said she had identified herself with Jo, the intellectual in *Little Women*, she probably was speaking for many other girls whom the American example urged on the path of greater independence.

The American male was for a long time denigrated as being coarse and clumsy, above all inadequate as a lover, in which role the French imagined themselves to be supreme. Novels often portrayed him as a self-made millionaire, rapacious, exclusively practical, with a commercial attitude even towards religion. One novel, entitled *Miss Million* (1880), by Alphonse Brot, described the sordid squabbling of American oil magnates to produce as the hero a French engineer who eventually succeeds in building the pipe-line. Detective stories about New York started appearing as early as 1877 and the cowboys of the Far West became famous after 1889, following their personal appearance, complete with Indians, at the International Exhibition. Jules Verne was the first novelist to introduce Americans regularly into his works: in about twenty of his novels, Americans have important roles. Verne liked their ready enthusiasm for even the maddest and most dangerous schemes. He portrayed them as having a passion for action, and believing that anything was possible to achieve; but they also

[1] S. Jeune, *Les Types américains dans le roman et le théâtre français 1861–1917* (1963).

had sound common sense, and they relied not simply on human energy but also on technical progress. Verne, who appeared to be one of the great advocates of the indefinite improvement of the world by machines, was perhaps the novelist who was most sympathetic to the Americans, and his enormous sales throughout this period made his sympathy worth a lot. It is true he also admired the English, whom he considered to be equally determined, pursuing their aims with obstinacy and cold passion, but after the increase in Anglo-French colonial rivalry, the English sometimes began to appear a little as villains, too proud, and too certain of their superiority. But this did not mean Verne denigrated his own countrymen: he still praised their wit, intelligence, good humour, elegance, love of glory, and their contempt for material gain.

The opposition between French and American attitudes to life was skilfully analysed by the philosopher Émile Boutroux in 1912, during a series of lectures organised by the France–America Committee in Paris. France and America, he said, both started with the view that all men were equal; that, as Descartes said, common sense was the best shared thing in the world. But the French believed that man needed to be perfected by culture, and as Pascal had pointed out, though man had natural instincts for good, these were often repressed by blind impulses and disordered passions. Art was needed to impose rules and discipline on man, but art by itself was not enough, because it could too easily take itself as its own end and so become artificial. Perfect culture came from the union of art and nature, of mind and heart. But this again was not an aim in itself. The French had an ideal of man with certain qualities which could be developed only in social intercourse, 'that habitual meeting of a certain number of chosen people, where each one tries hard to think and speak in a manner that will win the approbation of all . . . to surpass himself in order to be heard, and where distinction, delicacy, ingeniousness, fine judgement and wit are imposed'. It is in surroundings of this kind, in effect the *salon*, that the French had created the ideal man. They expected from him first of all reason, which could apply all the faculties to understand anything, and this meant taste and sensibility as well as intelligence; secondly, the cult of 'simple and natural sentiments', notably love of the family and of humanity, so that he naturally sided with the weak; thirdly, generosity, devotion to disinterested ends, glory, the honour of France and the good of humanity. The French language had been developed in *salons* of this kind to give expression to the ideals that were valued in them: clarity, precision, elegance. Boutroux argued that the Americans shared the French concern for democracy, humanity, simplicity, cordiality; they had remarkable public spirit and generous philanthropists, who used their millions for cultural purposes. But he felt that they had not quite understood what the perfect man should be like. They sought each of his characteristics independently, they saw the ideal as a synthesis, whereas the French viewed it as a creation.[1]

This was a condescending conclusion, but it showed how far the Americans had risen in the esteem of the French by the First World War. The image of the brutal millionaire was rapidly displaced as the French became increasingly aware of America's cultural achievements, and got to know more of its distinguished people. Bourget, after visiting the U.S.A. for eight months, published a highly successful book on it, *Overseas* (1895), which praised it for reconciling Christianity, democracy and science. He declared that the American businessman was an 'intellectual force' as remarkable as any traditional hero, and that the prejudice of the *lettré* against him was unjustified. Jules Cambon, French ambassador in Washington 1897–1902, could not speak English, but his successor J. J. Jusserand (1902–20) knew it so well that he wrote his memoirs in English, to record the important work he had done to bring the two countries closer together.[2] In 1896, Gabriel Hanotaux, the minister for foreign affairs, had talked about the American menace to Europe, as had also quite a few others, urging European union as the answer;[3] but by 1913 he had changed his attitude completely. In 1895 a meeting was held in Paris, at the house of T. E. Evans, the famous American dentist, of American and French scholars, including the poet Mallarmé,

[1] E. Boutroux, *Les États-Unis et la France* (1914), 10–21.

[2] J. J. Jusserand, *What Me Befell* (1933).

[3] G. Hanotaux, 'Le Péril prochain: l'Europe et ses rivaux', *Revue des Deux Mondes* (1 Apr. 1896); Octave Noël, 'Le Péril américain', *Le Correspondant* (25 Mar. and 10 Apr. 1899); Augustin Leger, 'L'Américanisation du monde', ibid. (25 Apr. 1902); D'Estournelles de Constant, *Les États-Unis d'Amérique* (1913), with a preface by Hanotaux.

to discuss how cultural contacts could be improved. In 1897 the French established the *doctorat d'université*, to provide an equivalent to the Ph.D. In 1898 Harvard established a visiting lectureship to enable it to invite distinguished Frenchmen, using a benefaction from James H. Hyde (once owner of the Equitable Insurance Company), who had settled in France. Exchanges of scholars were arranged, and people as eminent as Émile Boutroux and Gustave Lanson went to lecture in the U.S.A. The interest in America at this time is revealed by the success of E.-M. de Vogüé's novel *The Master of the Sea* (1903) about the struggle between a Frenchman and an American, which went through twenty editions in three months, and was placed by the critic Faguet on the same level as *War and Peace* and *The Red and the Black*. The characters were apparently based on Colonel Marchand and Pierpont Morgan, and the thesis behind it taken from W. T. Stead's *The Americanisation of the World* (1901). Vogüé showed his millionaire as a Homeric hero, whose wealth in no way made him despicable; he seemed to be arguing that the American achievement was compatible with intelligence and generosity, and that economic progress benefited not just the rich but all men.[1] André Tardieu's *Notes on the U.S.A.* (1908) said that America was interesting for its industry but no less for its intellectual and moral life: America was not just a piano factory.[2]

France indeed began receiving numerous benefactions from American millionaires to preserve its cultural heritage: Edward Tuck made possible the restoration of Malmaison in 1911–12, Rockefeller bought Pasteur's house in Dôle and donated it to the town. French noblemen had for some time already been marrying American heiresses: a book published in 1898 listed no less than thirty-two such marriages as having taken place since 1875; and it should be added that there were also three prime ministers who married Americans: Clemenceau, Waddington and Ribot.[3] What was seen as even more significant was

[1] E.-M. de Vogüé, *Le Maître de la Mer* (1903); cf. Paul Adam, *Vues d'Amérique* (1906) and *Le Trust* (1910); Georges Ohnet, *Mariage américain* (1907); Henry Gréville, *Roi des milliards* (1907), all favourable.

[2] For a favourable view of American industry see E. Levasseur, *The American Workman* (Baltimore, 1900, based on a visit in 1893).

[3] F. E. Johanet, *Autour du monde millionnaire américain* (1898); L. de Norvins, *Les Milliardaires américains* (1900).

that Frenchwomen began marrying Americans. The Americans in Paris became numerous enough for the American Express to open its Paris office in 1895; the colony in France was large enough in 1905 to produce a directory.[1] Direct observation of America by French travellers was not inconsiderable, for between 1765 and 1932 no less than 1,583 books were published by such visitors.[2] The French could hardly take no notice of a country in which cultural appreciation has reached such a point that New York itself had become an important centre for the French theatre: in each of the years 1900, 1904 and 1907, thirteen new French plays were staged there, and in 1909 and 1910 no less than eighteen.[3] But Henry Van Dyke was right to say in 1910 that, despite all this, Americans still tended to look on France as the 'home of the Yellow Novel and the Everlasting Dance', while Frenchmen as a whole still thought of the United States as a country of 'skyscrapers and the almighty dollar'.

The study of America in French universities had got off to an early start. There was little room in the school syllabus for American history or literature, but already in 1840 the 'independence of the U.S.A.' was introduced as a subject in the *baccalauréat*; in 1843 the 'history of the United States from the beginning of colonisation to the death of Washington' was set as the examination subject in the history *agrégation*. In 1864 Washington Irving's *Sketch Book* became a set text for the *agrégation*; between 1884 and 1914 American subjects were set in the geographical examination for this degree eleven times, and ten times in history; in English there was one American book set almost every other year. Forty-three doctorates about America were awarded 1887–1918. This compares with nineteen theses on American literature—and eighty-two on Shakespeare—passed in Germany, 1898–1918. The number of people who had a thorough knowledge of American life was still insignificant, but already many courses had been set up on different aspects of it, and many English departments in universities had American sections: only Germany and Switzerland had anything to compare with

---

[1] Alden Hatch, *American Express* (New York, 1950).

[2] Frank Monaghan, *French Travellers in the U.S. 1765–1932* (New York, 1961).

[3] Hamilton Mason, *French Theatre in New York, a List of Plays, 1899–1939* (New York, 1940), 9. For American views of France see Elizabeth Brett White, *American Opinion of France, from Lafayette to Poincaré* (New York, 1927).

France's achievement, and in France American studies were probably better established as a normal part of the university curriculum. In 1917 France was the first European country to establish a specialised university post in American literature and civilisation; in 1922 Anglo-Saxon was dropped as a compulsory subject for a degree in English and a more detailed examination in American literature introduced. Between 1920 and 1934, 118 doctoral theses on American subjects were written. But in 1952, when the Sorbonne had 16,000 students, 1,400 of them were doing English and of these 650 tried for the American certificate. In 1954 only 10 per cent of teachers of English had been to the U.S.A. Despite the introduction of some American studies, the French educational system was still very traditional. The opportunities for reading about America, and indeed about foreign countries in general, remained distinctly limited. Thus the English department of Bordeaux University in 1954 had only 400 English books in its library and very few on America. Lille had about 900 American books, half of them donated by the U.S. Information Library. Perhaps the most influential discovery of America took place outside the classroom, with the advent of the American film and novelists like Faulkner, Dos Passos, Hemingway, Caldwell and Steinbeck.[1]

Though America enabled France to emerge victorious from the First World War, the political relations between them were not always friendly. Napoleon III had won a bad name for himself by interfering in Mexico and by supporting the South. In 1870 President Grant congratulated Prussia on its victory. After 1918 disillusionment set in rapidly, particularly because the French failed to pay their war debts. In 1940, the United States maintained relations with the Vichy government and was slow to accept de Gaulle.[2] So in the first half of the twentieth century, the French still had many causes for suspicion. There were Americanists who pointed out the virtues which were the counterpart of the faults the French complained about: thus when American children were said to have little respect for their parents, it was answered that they were also remarkable for their initiative; it was agreed they lacked

[1] Sigmund Skard, *American Studies in Europe. Their History and Organisation* (Philadelphia, 1958), 131–208.
[2] D. C. McKay, *The United States and France* (Cambridge, Mass., 1951).

intellectual discipline of the French kind, but then they were better informed about politics, economics and sociology than their French counterparts. American universities had weaknesses, but they did much more for society than the French ones, educating not just future teachers; Harvard was said to have a larger annual budget than the whole higher education system in France. Mass production did not necessarily produce shoddy goods. For all their supposed coarseness, the Americans published more books on religion than novels.[1] Paul Morand wrote in praise of the U.S.A. in 1930 in a way which showed that some Frenchmen at least were very conscious that Paris was no longer the centre of civilisation. 'I love New York', he said, 'because it is the largest city in the universe and because it is inhabited by the strongest people in the world, the only one which, since the war, has succeeded in organising itself, the only one which does not live off credit from its past, the only one, apart from Italy, which is not demolishing but on the contrary has been able to construct . . . Everyone adores victory.' It was a double-sided compliment, but he added that New York was now to young artists what Rome had been to Corot and Poussin. 'Only New York offers the superfluous, and the superfluous is father of the arts.' One could no longer understand the world unless one visited New York. He praised even the New York lunch.[2]

Others took up opposite positions. Robert Aron and André Dandieu attacked *The American Cancer* (1931); anarchists and socialists attacked American capitalism.[3] Above all, Georges Duhamel in 1930 produced one of the most all-embracing attacks on American civilisation ever made, in beautiful prose, which showed that the old conservative French bourgeois was still very much alive. He complained angrily of the insufferable bureaucracy of the U.S. immigration authorities; the obsession with calories; the canned music; the illiterate cinema—'I would not exchange one play by Molière, one picture by Rembrandt, or one fugue by Bach for the whole of this celluloid

---

[1] Charles Cestre, *Production industrielle et justice sociale en Amérique* (1921); id. *Les Américains* (1945); E. Servan-Schreiber, *L'Exemple américain* (1917).

[2] Paul Morand, *New York* (1930), 51, 257–81.

[3] R. Aron and A. Dandieu, *Le Cancer américain* (1931); L. F. Céline, *Le Voyage au bout de la nuit* (1932); V. Pozner, *États désunis* (1938). Cyrille Arnavon, *L'Américanisme et nous* (1958) is a useful history, by a professor of English studies at Lyon and Lille, who had also been a visiting professor at Harvard and Columbia.

production' which, because it required no effort from the audience, could not claim to be an art. He objected to controls on the drinking of alcohol—would they propose to control his love-making next? He found that their liberty was superficial, for they were slaves to hygiene, to puritanism, and to experts. The women had identically beautiful legs but laughed identically like Hollywood stars. The motor car was used as the 'revenge of the vain and the incapable'. Everybody was in a hurry; the countryside was being ruined. What artists there were fled the country. Omnipresent advertising was an insult to the public. Their idea of sport was a joke, since it culminated 'in twenty-five boys playing, watched by 40,000 immobile louts smoking and catching colds'. The U.S.A., he concluded, had not made a contribution to European civilisation, but represented deviance and a break from it. That was to him condemnation in itself.[1]

In 1953 a public opinion poll was held asking Frenchmen what they thought of America. To the question 'What foreign country do you like most?' 19 per cent answered Switzerland, 16 per cent answered the United States, 13 per cent the Benelux countries, 11 per cent Britain, 9 per cent the U.S.S.R., 9 per cent Italy and Spain. Thirty-nine per cent thought that the Americans were uncultured, but 43 per cent said they were not; 66 per cent thought they were interested only in money, but 22 per cent disagreed; 46 per cent thought they had bad taste, but 31 per cent did not. 38 per cent said they would use American methods if they were running a business or factory, 21 per cent said they would not, 41 per cent did not know. Only 2 per cent of those questioned had been to the United States—which must be an exaggeration; 56 per cent said they would like to visit it, but 22 per cent said they definitely did not want to. When asked what they liked about the United States, these rather striking replies were made:

| Do you like | Very much | Quite | Not at all | No answer |
| --- | --- | --- | --- | --- |
| Jazz | 12 | 29 | 54 | 5 |
| American films | 6 | 38 | 43 | 13 |
| Coca-cola | 5 | 12 | 61 | 22 |
| American cigarettes | 23 | 33 | 36 | 8 |
| American household appliances | 52 | 21 | 9 | 18 |

[1] G. Duhamel, *Scènes de la vie future* (1930).

It is perhaps this last answer which is significant.[1] In the 1950s the other-wordly values of the intellectuals, heirs of the clergy, had ceased to hold unchallenged sway. The Americans knew how to make life more comfortable, and comfort was not necessarily incompatible with culture. Perhaps the new direction of French behaviour after 1950 came from the feeling that culture by itself had not produced the promised utopia and that the priorities should now be altered.

The contrast of Frenchman and foreigner was thus by no means one of direct opposition. The national identity was not an exclusive one. It may seem, however, that if one considers the matter at a humbler level, in the schools, for example, one will find a simplified and standardised version of it, which could win acceptance from the masses. This is an illusion. Education only looks as though it conveys a simple message if it is viewed superficially, or from the vantage point of the politicians who direct it. It is necessary to examine what the schools did in fact achieve in some detail, for their history reveals that the national message was understood and transmitted in different ways by the different levels in the educational system. The schools were indeed almost as much a divisive as a unifying force. They show that the French way of thinking—if that is what the schools ultimately sought to instil—had many varieties to it.

[1] *Réalités* (September 1953), no. 34 'America as the French see it'. Cf. the Harvard thesis of Charles W. Brooks and the Oxford thesis of Thomas A. Sancton.

# 4. Education and Hope

AMONG the labels by which one can, summarily but not too inaccurately, characterise this century, one undoubtedly is the Age of Education. It was in this period that Frenchmen were made universally literate; it was in this period that the solution to practically every problem was widely believed to lie in the spread of education. Schools came to be considered indispensable amenities, which every state must provide for all its citizens. Five, then ten and ultimately as much as twenty years of people's lives were, partly by developing usage and partly by governmental sanctions, devoted to supervised study. Education assumed a place second only to that of earning one's bread. Education seemed to hold the key to social prestige, wealth, wisdom, and, some even claimed, happiness.[1]

But it is not satisfactory to examine the history of education simply as one manifestation of Progress. This is perhaps one sphere of life where the historian finds it particularly difficult to detach himself from his subject, for he is usually both a product and a servant of that educational system, which—for all the changes it has undergone—remains omnipresent today, accepted almost as part of the natural order of things. Since the results of education are so difficult to assess, and since the precise details of its work are susceptible of infinite variation, controversy about syllabuses and organisation, about what schools should and should not attempt, have absorbed the attention of most writers on it. So though there are a vast number of books about education, they are virtually all by participants: pretty well every author has been to school. It is impossible to find independent, outside observers or critics, as one can in, for example, activities like coalmining (where the trouble is the opposite one, that there are not enough accounts from inside). The history of education is usually presented in an institutional way, beginning with the chronicle of a particular school by an old boy and ending with the narrative, in

[1] The best bibliography is in Antoine Prost, *Histoire de l'enseignement en France 1800–1967* (1968), which is itself an excellent survey.

much the same way, of the growth of national systems which gradually obtain universal acceptance and practise more and more advanced methods. These may be criticisms or apologias but the focus of attention tends to be the school and the materials put into it—buildings, textbooks, teachers—rather than the mentality of the child who is the victim of these attentions or the adolescent who emerges scathed or unscathed from them. How different did people become as a result of going to school?

This is a key question in the history of France, because there education became almost a substitute for religion; belief in its virtues reached exceptionally high levels. The Third Republic prided itself on its educational achievement as much as or more than on anything else, and the appellation *la république des professeurs* was neither scorned nor unjustified. It becomes all the more important, therefore, to establish precisely what the role of teachers in this society was, what cause exactly they thought they were serving, and how far this image corresponded with the reality. Placing education at the very centre of national preoccupations highlights an essential trait of the period, but it also distorts history. Just as in politics, the proclamation of grand principles and the formation of parties were usually purely superficial, at best a sublimation of other concerns, external to most men's lives and to the vast bulk of intrigues and relationships, so at least to an equal extent in education there was an enormous gap between the legislation, pedagogic theories and changes in official programmes, on the one hand, and what, on the other hand, actually happened. By itself, the history of the instructions issued is profoundly misleading. The instructions tell one about a certain class of men. The history of the masses must be written, for the most part, from other sources.

Mass education had results which were of three different kinds. First, it altered the character of politics. It made it possible for democracy and universal suffrage to function with greater reality; it vastly increased the possibilities of communication between the government and the people; it enabled the masses to watch over those whom they appointed to administer the country. But it also made them even more subject to propaganda and to brainwashing, and to persuasion that they should sacrifice their immediate interests and desires

to supposedly more important national causes—such as glory
or war—which their teachers had the task of enlightening them
about. It increased their articulacy, but it also increased
the power of the press, which simultaneously told them what to
think and spoke in their name. It was in principle egalitarian,
but in practice the very opposite, because there were so many
different gradations in education that the possession simply of
'primary' education came to be held as a mark of inadequacy.
The kind of education that was dispensed was in any case not
necessarily democratic, for though the paternalist reformers
who universalised it claimed they were doing so in order to
educate the electorate—their new masters—the values preached
by the teachers were not on the whole values inspired by the
masses. Rather, mass education could be seen as an attempt by
the élite to avoid a mass civilisation, and to impose aristocratic
values on the people. The political significance of the Age of
Education is thus ambiguous in the extreme and needs careful
analysis.

Secondly, the spread of education had a profound influence
on social relationships. It was one of the greatest stimulants of
national uniformity, while at the same time, to a certain
extent, it also heightened contrasts between Frenchmen and
other people. It represented an organised onslaught on regional
and local eccentricity, in the name of good taste and higher
culture. Just as monetary inflation could suddenly undermine
the economic power of a whole class, so education created a
sudden appreciation of the value of certain literary and verbal
skills. Birth or wealth, by themselves, no longer sufficed to
ensure consideration or influence. New dividing lines cut across
old social barriers. A new mandarinate emerged with a complicated hierarchical organisation, and a largely self-recruiting
membership. Public examinations and school certificates
became a new way of judging people, clashing with the
traditional and still powerful systems of nepotism and clientele.
The irony of it all was that the teachers were not the beneficiaries of this cultural revolution they carried out. One needs
to discover who was.

Thirdly, important psychological consequences followed
from the transformation of a largely illiterate nation into one
in which the written word became the key to many activities.

The usual assumption is that education stamped out superstition, that what the schools stood for—science, progress, rationalism—replaced traditionalism and routine as the ideals of society. In some vague way, these changes are linked up with industrialisation, which makes the change from the old to the new appear complete. But one needs to look more carefully at the changes in mentality that the schools brought about. One needs to investigate the contrast between rural and urban mentalities. Education was, to some extent, a conquest of the countryside by the towns; but the victory was not as total as is usually thought. The schools attempted to discredit certain ways of thinking and of behaving but they were by no means successful in abolishing them. This is a problem which needs to be linked with the debate about the distinction between oral and literate cultures, which unfortunately has generally been confined to 'primitive' tribes. In France, the fact that literature enjoyed such prestige did not mean that another world with different rules did not coexist beside it. When judging the results of literacy campaigns, it is not enough to consider simply the direct benefits in reading skills, nor to establish that literate factory workers have higher productivity levels than illiterate ones (which is by no means always the case).

The demand for education did not originally come from the masses. There was no pressure for it, as there was among the landless for land, or among the workers for economic independence. In 1833, when inspectors were sent round the country to investigate the state of the schools and popular attitudes towards them, they were almost unanimous in being struck by the indifference of parents. They were often greeted, as one of them reported, in the same way as tax-collectors come to inspect the wine-sellers' stocks of bottles. They were told: 'You would do better to turn your attention to the state of the roads. We are not much interested in schools. Our children will be what our fathers were. Look at so-and-so who can read: he is no richer than us who cannot.' The inspectors attributed this inability of the illiterate to appreciate the benefits of education to the combined influence of ignorance, poverty and self-interest. Children were economic assets from the age of five or six; they could earn sums which, though small, were indispensable to the balancing of the family budget. 'Weighed down under the yoke of poverty, they have no worry but that of their subsistence.' The rise of factories could, at first, be a direct hindrance to the spread of education. The better-off classes were in general doubtful or suspicious: they feared that once the children of the peasantry could read, they would desert the countryside; it would be impossible to find labourers or share-croppers. The political consequences were also frightening. Several mayors of the Gironde said that education for all would produce peasants who would be 'indocile, fainéant et raison-neur'. The notaries of the Corrèze, reported another inspector, were preventing grants of public money being given to schools because 'when everybody could sign, they would have fewer powers of attorney and fewer documents'. Mass education was an obvious challenge to many vested interests; but those at the bottom of the social scale generally did not see in it an obvious remedy for their troubles.[1] But there were two exceptions to this attitude.

In 1789 the north and east of France had far more schools, far higher attendance and far greater literacy than the rest of the country. The accompanying map illustrates this clear division, which reflected both a different history and a different pattern of settlement. The basic fact about education is that schools existed originally in towns, and it was still the towns which were best provided with them. This meant not simply the main cities but also small conglomerations, which were more than simply agricultural. In purely rural areas, the school was situated in the *bourg*, and, as Roger Thabaut recounted in the case of his village of Mazières-en-Gâtine, it was the trades-men and artisans, living right next to the school, who sent their children to it, while the peasants in their isolated farms re-mained suspicious and indifferent. The north-east of France began with the advantage that its inhabitants lived in com-pact villages, as distinct from scattered hamlets, and this made the spread of literacy much more rapid. But the arrival of a teacher in a village at all has still to be explained. A decisive factor was religion: the Protestants laid great stress on education

[1] The essential works on primary education are M. Gontard, *L'Enseignement primaire en France de la Révolution à la loi Guizot 1789–1833* (1959) and *Les Écoles primaires de la France bourgeoise 1833–75* (duplicated, Toulouse, 1964). See also A. Léaud and E. Glay, *L'École primaire en France* (1934).

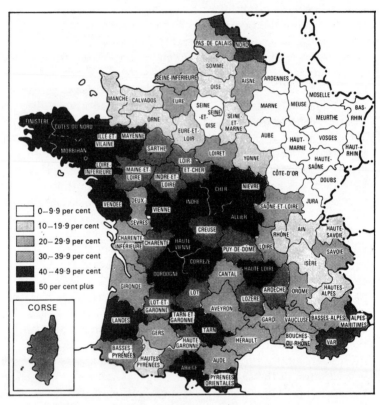

Map 1. Illiteracy (1862). Men aged twenty unable to read or write. Based on
J. Simon, *L'École* (1865), 219.

and on teaching the truth as they saw it to their adherents. The Catholics, in areas where they were thus challenged, replied by founding rival schools of their own. Literacy was the fruit of these quarrels. In the late nineteenth century a new attack on the Catholic Church, this time by the republicans (many of them Protestants), repeated the process in areas where the Church had hitherto been supreme. Till then, popular education had been basically religious, the concern of the Church, and it was very much in keeping with this tradition that the republicans made their primary schools concentrate on morals. But the Church cannot be held to have generally failed in its mission of rescuing the poor from their benighted ignorance. People on the verge of starvation had no leisure for useless learning. But in certain regions it was precisely learning which was discovered to be a possible escape from poverty. On some arid, overpopulated soils, where tillage and cattle could not keep the inhabitants alive all the year, the peasants sometimes turned to artisan activities like weaving, or to seasonal migration. On the isolated slopes of the Alps and the Pyrenees, the people chose learning as the source of their supplementary income, and in winter migrated to supply the plains of southern France with its teachers. Each of these different reasons for going to school implied a different attitude to education. Much more still needs to be discovered about the origins of popular attitudes in this matter; but these instances are enough to confirm that the poor viewed it in their own—and varied—way.

The second major exception to the general indifference towards education was the peculiar and complex attitude of the leaders of the working class. In the mid-nineteenth century the skilled Paris artisans often demanded education as a right, in the same way as they demanded the right to strike, to form unions and to earn a decent wage. Universal education meant, for them, the establishment of true equality, the necessary complement to universal suffrage, the ending of invidious distinctions, the 'fusion of classes'. But their attitude towards learning was ambiguous and often even hostile; and there was considerable uncertainty among them as to what kind of education they wanted. Thus even the supposedly democratic idea that all children should be given the opportunity to develop their individual talents did not receive anything like universal assent. Fourier was the great advocate of individuals being allowed to express themselves freely, but Proudhon did not like the idea of vocation. He dismissed this as a petty bourgeois dream. 'The masses do not believe in the reality of what you call *vocation*', he wrote. 'They think that every man who is sound in mind and body and who is duly taught, can and ought to be capable, with a few natural exceptions, of doing everything ... Genius ... was a halting of natural growth rather than an indication of talent. Children must accustom themselves to eat everything: that is the first parental lesson a poor child receives.' The artisan-politician Corbon, who had himself worked in about five different trades, was likewise a believer in general rather than specialised professional training. (He made a distinction between artists and scientists—whom he called *fantaisistes* and *précisionnistes*—which he saw running right through every form of labour, depending on how much 'geometrical skill' was needed. The making of fashionable objects, decoration and jewellery, for example, was in the first category, carpentry and mechanical trades in the second.) The workers were not necessarily interested in an education which would enable them to escape from their artisan condition, for, as even Corbon said, 'I like my trade; I like my tools as much as my books and even if I could live by my pen, I should not want to stop being a locksmith'.[1] Their discussions of education were very largely concerned with professional, technical training. For them, public schools teaching practical skills meant above all the ending of the secrecy surrounding artisan activity, with a master confiding his special knowledge to a chosen apprentice. They had to establish democracy within their own class before bothering about the bourgeoisie. They were keen on physical education, because they were conscious that the poor were often physically inferior. They had no wish to be turned into 'artists' by the schools; and they often had a certain contempt for the schoolmaster. The idea of a teacher appointed by the state was anathema to Proudhon, who wanted education to be as much as possible a family affair: bachelors— still less nuns—were unfit to teach. The demand was for straight-forward scientific information, but there was also deep suspicion of the technical schools. The remedy for 'secrecy' was

[1] A. Corbon, *De l'enseignement professionnel* (1859), 69.

often just as bad as the disease. The Arts and Crafts Schools were criticised for being too theoretical; conservatives and revolutionaries agreed about this. Blanqui said the technical schools were 'seminaries to produce Chinamen', with the 'fixed idea of incarcerating the workers in a trade and so returning to the system of castes'; Thiers said they 'were good only for producing little Americans'. It was the factory workers, as opposed to the artisans, who were interested in this kind of specialised training. The artisans, moreover, were by no means hostile to Latin or the traditional upper-class syllabus. The autodidacts among them loved the classics: Perdiguier wanted every journeyman to read Homer and Virgil and produced a list of some fifty works from every century as an ideal workers' library, which barely differed from what a good *lycée* pupil would choose. They deplored only the brutality and rigour of the state's schools, and saw the wage earner and the secondary schoolboy united by the link that they were both oppressed. But these were views held at a distance, for the workers had little to say in general about the education of the bourgeoisie, which was too remote from their preoccupations. It was not with the university that they had dealings, neither with its professors nor its textbooks. They got their ideas above all from the newspapers, the journals popularising knowledge and cheap novelettes—that side of bourgeois activity which was officially despised and to which the university turned a blind eye. The workers would not be the first recruits of the educational reformers: they were in many ways—in their attitude towards school discipline for example—deeply conservative.[1]

Education was offered to the people from above, and then enforced upon them. This was done in the name of a variety of ideals, often contradictory, so that though more or less the same subjects were taught at school, the purpose of all the effort varied very considerably. The increasing provision of schools should not be seen as constant evolution in the same direction. It is important to be clear at the outset, therefore, about the deeper motives of the advocates and legislators of education.

The Catholic Church knew exactly what it was doing, though it aroused so much animosity against itself that many otherwise

[1] G. Duveau, *La Pensée ouvrière sur l'éducation pendant la seconde république et le second empire* (1947).

intelligent men got strangely muddled about what this was. As Pius IX put it in his Syllabus of 1864: 'The schools for the masses are established principally with a view to giving the people religious instruction, to bringing them to piety and to a truly Christian moral discipline.' The function of Catholic schools, which before the nineteenth century, meant virtually all French elementary schools, was essentially religious and moral, to produce Christians and to teach whatever was needed to effect this. It laid great stress on the catechism, to the extent of insisting that children should memorise it even if they did not understand it. It sought to cultivate a pious and receptive attitude, to prepare children above all for their first communion, which if received in the right spirit, could, it was thought, be the decisive event in their lives. It treated education as a battle of good against evil, designed to instil horror of ill-doing, consciousness that duty and happiness were inseparable, that the origin of sin was human and that service of God was the prime purpose of life. For long the church schools dispensed education as though it was a mystic initiation into sacred truths. As one textbook said, 'In order to teach letters properly, children must first be taught to make the sign of the cross.' Though children were allowed to keep their hats on during writing and arithmetic classes, they were forbidden to read unless they were bare-headed, as they had to be at prayers also. It was this reverence for books—which the Church treated almost as holy—that explains the acceptance of the Index, the horror of 'evil books', the constant denunciation of sacrilege by modern authors who did not respect Christian dogma. Traditional Catholic teaching was designed not to awaken the child but to teach him that desire could never be satisfied, except in the next world. It sought to fill him with humility, to warn him of God's severity as well as of his justice and mercy. But because Catholic schools tended to use very old textbooks, which were often difficult to understand, their pupils probably absorbed only parts of what they were taught, and invented their own meaning, and often a different meaning each time, for the edifying exhortations they had to spell out. These methods aroused the scorn of lay reformers, who accused the Catholics of standing in the way of enlightenment and progress. Such attacks were only partly justified. There is no doubt that the Church, under attack, tended to entrench itself in the repetition of its dogmas, to divert its efforts to the organisation of spectacular pilgrimages and charitable works, so that the majority of its clergymen were unable to participate on equal terms in intellectual debate with their enemies. But the Church also had some quite outstanding teachers, whose ideas were influential on the whole field of education, lay as well as religious. These included men who were remarkable defenders of the 'rights of the child', as one of them, Bishop Dupanloup, put it. Catholic education was not necessarily more oppressive than that with which the republic tried to replace it. A Catholic manual of 1868 listed nine different reasons why the teacher should *respect* the child, who should not be regarded as an object to be brainwashed.[1] Bishop Dupanloup was one of the first writers on education to protest against the repression of children by over-affectionate mothers and over-ambitious fathers.[2]

The Church held the monopoly of education for so long and kept its teaching at such an elementary level, because the notables on the whole considered that it was providing exactly the service demanded of it. Richelieu had warned against the dangers of having too many learned men in the country, who would be too proud and presumptuous to be obedient. The Parlement of Aix, just before the Revolution, instructed the church schools to limit their admissions and under no circumstances to teach the sons of peasants, for fear that agriculture would lack an adequate labour force. Voltaire ended up by agreeing, saying that the populace 'had neither the time nor the capacity to acquire learning': they should be satisfied with modelling themselves on the example of their superiors. It was only the bourgeoisie, he thought, who ought to be educated. La Chalotais, when drawing up his *Essay on National Education* (1763), agreed with him. Destutt de Tracy insisted that every civilised society necessarily had two classes, living respectively from manual and intellectual labour. The working class needed little knowledge, and could afford little time to obtain it, for parents required the assistance of their children and the children had to be accustomed early to the habits necessary in the

[1] J. B. Furet, *Sentences, leçons, avis* (1868), 464–8.
[2] See vol. 1, p. 323; and Pierre Zind, *L'Enseignement religieux dans l'instruction primaire publique en France de 1850 à 1873* (Lyon, 1971).

'painful work to which they were destined'. This was a situation 'which no human will could change, following necessarily from the very nature of men and societies'. So it was right that there should be two entirely separate systems of education— one very brief and elementary for the masses, and a fuller one confined to the élite which had the leisure and the need for it.[1] Such views continued to be held well into the nineteenth century, and by men who were politically known as liberals. It should not be forgotten that many of these were religious men, and that the university was firmly Catholic at least until the 1880s. Thus Eugène Rendu, a leading inspector and administrator of primary education during the Second Empire, while urging universal education, insisted that its purpose should not be intellectual but moral. It did not matter very much whether the masses could read or not, for civilisation with large-scale illiteracy had proved possible in the past. What worried him was that the Church was losing its grip on the people, materialism was advancing, and something had to be done to provide the moral and religious education which children were no longer getting from the church or from their parents. The main purpose of primary schools should be not just to teach arithmetic but to 'purify the sentiments' of the poor, 'to give them some dignity'.[2] The liberals often simply wanted to do what the church used to do or was failing to do.

Those who advocated education frequently did so with very conservative or reactionary ends in view. Guizot considered that 'ignorance renders the masses turbulent and ferocious; it makes them an instrument to be used by the factions'. When passing his law requiring every village to have a primary school (1833) he told his prefects: 'We have tried to create in every commune a moral force which the government can use at need.' He wanted the teacher to preach submission, respect for the law, love of order in exactly the same way as the church had done, though perhaps even more explicitly, and indeed he wanted the education dispensed by these schools to be essentially religious.[3] His purpose was not diabolically political. He

---

[1] Destutt de Tracy, *Observations sur le système actuel d'instruction publique* (1800).
[2] E. Rendu, *Mémoire sur l'enseignement obligatoire* (1853).
[3] F. Guizot, *Essai sur l'histoire et sur l'état actuel de l'instruction publique en France* (1816), 5.

genuinely wanted to increase the happiness of the masses, and
he believed that this could best be attained by teaching them
to accept their lot in life, and to see in the regular fulfilment of
their painful daily tasks the source of their contentment.

Against such people, it is natural to contrast those who believed that education would solve most human problems and
lead to a better world, though these optimists, like the pessimists, completely misjudged the effect of their proposals, and
neither the one nor the other in the end obtained what they
wanted. Education was not only one of the causes which raised
the highest hopes, but one which has disappointed the reformers
most constantly. The real leader of all those who expected
education to achieve utopia was Condorcet. His doctrines were
the inspiration of many generations of republicans. He believed
that mass education would ensure the indefinite progress and
happiness of humanity. Liberty and democracy would follow
from it, because enlightened citizens would know how to order
public affairs; equality would be advanced, because the hidden
talents of the poor would be revealed; morality would be perfected, because intelligent men would no longer feel the boredom
which led the ignorant to distract themselves 'through sensations
as opposed to ideas'; family life would be strengthened, because
women would be able to share in their husbands' interests.
These facile expectations were raised into dogmas and endlessly
repeated throughout the century. Napoleon III, who had a
talent for turning into original-sounding slogans the commonest platitudes of his time, laid it down that the nation with
the most schools would be the first nation in the world, in its
enjoyment of material prosperity, order and liberty; and that
by spreading education he was winning 'to religion, morals and
comfort' that enormous part of the population 'that barely
knew the precepts of Christ'. The victory of the Germans over
France in 1870 was held to be due above all to the work of the
Prussian schools. Zola repeated, 'France will be what the
primary teacher makes it'. This became one of those fundamental truths which, like proverbs, were on everybody's lips, though
no one completely believed them in practical life.

It inspired the Education League (Ligue de l'Enseignement),
founded in the 1860s by Jean Macé, joined by people of all
classes, and ultimately one of the most active pressure groups

in the country. Macé became an official hero of the Third Republic, symbolising the struggle of the humble to acquire knowledge. His life, and that of his society, deserve to be better known, because the hagiography surrounding them has obscured the disagreements behind their demands and the complexity of the whole movement for popular education. Macé was the son of a carrier or cart-driver and called himself a *camionneur d'idées*. He was taught to read by his *curé*, and won a scholarship to the Catholic College Stanislas, while his sister went off to be a nun. Because his League came to support lay education, the fact that he was a religious man has been overlooked. He always insisted that the great plague of the century was the lack of religious beliefs and of awareness of God: the soul had its needs as well as the body and Sunday rest was essential to enable one to think of higher things. What he objected to was the incompetence of the clergy, who were not implementing the true spirit of their Church. Macé was always very much a man of 1848, in whom religiosity, emotion and politics combined in the belief that the great need of the time— and of himself—was to love and be loved. His frustration expressed itself in a marriage with an illiterate worker, thirteen years older than himself, who became both a mother and a wife to him, and in a vocation, to which he devoted his life, for teaching girls. He had won top prizes at Stanislas, but rejected a career in the university; 'his independent temperament and his need of an open-air life', as he himself wrote, 'led him to spend the first years of his youth obscurely in adventures'. He was a poor boy who had made good (disproving yet again the view that the poor were cut off from secondary education), but he felt ill at ease in the establishment, and too emotionally hungry to be respectable. He became a Saint-Simonian and then a Fourierist. As a schoolteacher at Mademoiselle Verenet's boarding establishment for girls at Beblenheim, where he continued to teach even when he had acquired national fame, he dispensed a very unorthodox form of education, of Fourierist flavour, totally different from that of the regimented primary public system he worked so hard to spread. The traditional schools, he said, gave their pupils very little knowledge, and a disgust for studying which they would retain all their lives. Macé, in his own teaching, avoided memorising, dryness, overwork; he introduced intellectual work only 'as a second string, in hours of rest' after physical and manual education. He abolished compulsory homework; he used feasts, the theatre and country walks as ways of arousing the individual interests and talents of his pupils, who organised their own discipline and who were not forced to live in drab uniforms. 'Coquetry' was accepted, in keeping with Fourier's opposition to repressing natural instincts. Girls should have the same education as boys, so that they could be true companions to men, who were incomplete without them. He became a best-selling author with chatty little books he wrote for the girls, explaining the facts of life and of science, which Hetzel published side by side with the novels of Jules Verne. The purpose of all this was to give dignity and self-respect. Macé did not wish to end economic inequalities: 'What the poor man has the greatest difficulty in forgiving the rich man for is not his wealth, but his contempt.' For Macé, the republic's main function was to end this contempt. That was what his educational campaigns were for and he stressed that his league was essentially political. He had been terrified by the proclamation of universal suffrage, which he had considered dangerous. He wanted to stop the masses from being surly people who provided fodder for barricades. His aim was 'the embourgeoisement of the masses'.[1] He admitted this in precisely these words; but it is important to realise all the ambiguity contained in the idea of embourgeoisement, as revealed in Mace's own career, which in many ways defied the bourgeois order.

Moreover, the Education League became very different from what Macé had intended it to be. His skill had shown itself in deliberately linking the league to the Freemasons, as a result of which he soon had a nationwide organisation. He had a friend in the Havas news agency, which he was able to use as an advertising medium. The Eastern Railway gave him a free pass to travel on its lines. Napoleon III's prefects gave him their blessing. A Fourierist philanthropist, Faustin Moigneau, provided him with funds. There was a very strange combination of forces behind the league. That did not worry Macé, who was all in favour of each locality enjoying complete autonomy in the running of its educational programme. But the Paris

<hr>

[1] Letter to Buls, 11 January 1868.

branch of the league, to his consternation, then began assuming leadership of it. Its secretary was a commercial traveller, Emmanuel Vauchez (1836–1926), who gave up his lucrative occupation to devote himself completely to the cause. This man had a passion for organisation, administration and centralisation. He personally wrote 7,000 letters and sent out 80,000 circulars in a campaign lasting fifteen months, as a result of which he collected 1,267,000 signatures for a petition in favour of more education. However, even he could not escape the fact that the league's supporters were divided about exactly what they wanted. Only 348,000 were signatures in favour of free, compulsory and lay education; 383,000 wanted it to be compulsory and free but not lay, and 116,000 wanted it to be simply compulsory.[1] It was Vauchez who made the league adopt laicisation as its demand, then add military training as a supplement to education. Macé was opposed to both of these. Vauchez turned the league into a far more militant, anticlerical, centralised, patriotic organisation than its founder had intended. Having succeeded in getting lay education established, he concentrated its efforts on encouraging those things that the government was not doing, particularly distributing suitably republican books to local libraries, stimulating nationalism through shooting clubs, giving scholarships to primary teachers and turning its attention to adolescents over the compulsory school age. In 1907 the league bought up a dissolved abbey off the rue de Sèvres and built itself a magnificent headquarters.[2] By then it had become part of the establishment, with men like Leon Bourgeois at its head. Increasingly the professors of the university took it over and turned it into a 'cultural centre', where they met to discuss the benefits of keeping the church out of education. Benevolent merchants bequeathed sizeable gifts to it. But it is curious that this temple of reason was in its early years supported by the Kardec sect of spiritualists, and Vauchez, in his retirement, devoted himself to the study of the esoteric. It is important not to take its rationalist proclamations too literally.[3]

The administrators and ministers who set up and ran the

---

[1] The details of the remaining signatures are not known.
[2] Later to become the Récamier Cinema and Theatre.
[3] Édouard Petit, *Jean Macé, sa vie, son œuvre* (n.d.) [*c.* 1922], is the best, but

primary education system in this period represented two additional approaches, which were different once again. One was Protestant, the other was positivist. There was a surprisingly large Protestant group, who naturally recruited like-minded assistants, at the head of the republic's primary schools. Their leader was Ferdinand Buisson (1841–1932), director of primary education from 1879 to 1896, editor of the *Dictionnaire de pédagogie* (1882–93), which was the *instituteurs'* principal guide for several generations, president of the Radical Party's executive committee, president of the League of the Rights of Man, president of the Education League, and winner of the Nobel Peace Prize in 1926: his accumulated honours show how high a place mass education held in the priorities of his day. Buisson was a Protestant who attempted to reform and update the religion of his fathers, in a way which combined revolt against the domination of the past and of traditional institutions with acceptance of their moral doctrines and of their approach to life. Taking refuge in Switzerland during the Second Empire, he wrote in favour of a *Liberal Christianity* (1865); he presented a doctoral thesis on Sébastien Castellion, the sixteenth-century Protestant divine whom he hailed as a pioneer of toleration and true religion combined. He distinguished between the body and soul of religion, arguing that the institutions, hierarchy and dogmas of the church were oppressive, but that its ethics were an indispensable basis of society. Religion—which he thus equated with morality—needed to be preserved and the battle for laicisation which he led was therefore a purely political one. The church should be deprived of control of the schools so that its doctrines, duly purified and reformed, could be taught to children as they should always have been. He deliberately called what he hoped to instil into them *la foi laïque*—a new kind of religion. Though, as a passionate believer in the principles of the revolution of 1789, he had infinite faith in the progress of humanity, he was, as a Protestant, also deeply conscious of man's imperfections and

of the presence of evil. He combined the two ideas by a definition of religion as that which leads man towards perfection,
towards the true, the good and the beautiful, but through
rational not mystical processes, not by grace but always by
protracted personal effort. Religion was the sentiment that
gave man, though conscious of his weakness, the strength to
undergo the sufferings necessary to improve himself and to
advance progress. He added patriotism as its necessary corollary, for this was a respectable and natural manifestation of
human solidarity, but in no way incompatible with belief in
peace and international arbitration. In this neo-Protestant
doctrine, Buisson also incorporated Kantism. The philosopher
Renouvier (1815–1903) had shown how the mixture could be
carried out. Renouvier was another Christian heretic who spent
his life attacking the Church and writing textbooks of republican morals for teachers, but he was constantly obsessed by the
problems of religion: in 1873 he declared his conversion to
Protestantism and set up a journal, *La Critique philosophique*
(1872–89), to argue that the conversion of France to Protestantism would solve its problems. With the help of the doctrines
of Kant, who henceforth became one of the main sources of
republican inspiration,[1] he developed a *Science of Morals* (1869)
independent of religion. The educational implication of this
was the training of will-power and self-control above all else.
But paradoxically, Renouvier felt dissatisfied with his intellectual creation and in 1894 disowned it: 'Everybody seems to
believe in progress, despite everything,' he wrote. 'I no longer
do. In our time, it is preferable to try to believe in another world
better than this one.'[2] One constantly finds this kind of hesitation among the more thoughtful educational theorists; but the
simplification of their doctrines should not be regarded as the
inevitable result of popularisation. Many teachers, though with
less complicated arguments, seem to have been conscious of
these philosophical difficulties. The educational system gave
the impression, in its slogans, that it had a coherent doctrine
but the reality was more uncertain.

Positivism provided another inspiration of the reformers.
Jules Ferry declared his allegiance to it; and it was the schools

[1] J. Benda, *Kant* (1950).
[2] Marcel Méry, *La Critique du Christianisme chez Renouvier* (1952), 2. 15.

which did as much as anything to preserve Comte's popularity, by giving him a prominent place in the syllabus.[1] The education theory of Comte was never succinctly formulated, and, as is known, Comte's ideas developed considerably during his lifetime, so here again theoretical guidance could be very diversely interpreted. What was indubitable was that education held a very high place in his system, and the teacher too, though Comte wanted the teacher to be the mother in early childhood; after that, an independent, autonomous corporation of intellectuals should take over. (That was the theoretical justification of Ferry's making the University a self-governing body, instead of a government department as Napoleon had it.) Comte stressed the importance of emotional and aesthetic education, the need to teach the observation of concrete phenomena, using active methods: he called Froebel 'the only pedagogue who understood the need for harmony between individual education and activity in social life'. Comte wanted great attention to be paid to the development of sentiments of sociability. He greatly admired the Jesuits' educational skills; he wanted his teachers to instil 'active and voluntary submission' as opposed to 'sterile or disorganised discussion'; but he criticised the Jesuits for cutting off their schools from the real world. Comte was not interested in vocational or technical education (as the Saint-Simonians were) and insisted on the primacy of moral education, to be achieved through general studies, as opposed to the acquisition of particular scientific skills.[2] Durkheim repeated Comte's views that education 'must be essentially a matter of authority', but he concentrated his attention on discipline, self-control, effort, duty, in an intellectualist way which was narrower than that of Comte, who was very conscious of the importance of emotionality. For Durkheim, the family was a failure, and the school must replace it.[3] It was against such doctrines that the *École Nouvelle* movement, to be discussed later, rebelled, proposing an approach to education from the very opposite angle, that is, from the needs of the child rather than of society. The disagreements about

[1] On Ferry, see vol. 1, 621–32; on positivism in general see vol. 2, ch. 12.

[2] Paul Arbousse-Bastide, *La Doctrine de l'éducation universelle dans la philosophie d'Auguste Comte* (1957) is the fullest account; L. Legrand, *L'Influence du positivisme dans l'œuvre scolaire de Jules Ferry* (1961).

[3] É. Durkheim, *L'Éducation morale* (1925).

what schools should do were thus very considerable indeed. And since it was difficult to study just what effects they did in fact have, the theoretical basis for education was always controversial, uncertain and vague.

## The Instituteurs

This review of some of the main ideas which inspired the advocates of popular education points to one obvious reason why the movement bred so much frustration and disappointment, even though it succeeded in bringing all children into schools. The ideas themselves were too varied, if not contradictory, for it to be possible even to find a common criterion by which to judge its consequences, beyond the mere enumeration of examination results. At the same time, the basis of these ideas was a holistic view of man, an expectation that there was one fundamental need in everybody, which schools could satisfy, and that they alone could provide a unique and necessary preparation for life. Just how divorced these notions were from reality may be seen by examining the growth and development of the profession of primary-school teachers. Even they implemented the ideas of the philosophers only very partially and with infinite modifications. The way they fulfilled their function of intermediaries of this new culture illuminates its complex character, and also brings one nearer the actual, practical manifestations of culture in daily life.

The history of the *instituteurs* is one of dedication and struggle. The *instituteurs* came to be seen as symbols of all that was noble and idealistic in the work of the republic; they were praised as the missionaries of its anticlerical doctrines (and vilified by Catholics for the same reason). They came to form an enormous, apparently uniform army: 150,000 in the first decade of the twentieth century, 120,000 after 1918. It is only recently that the full significance of their experience has begun to emerge from the polemic surrounding them. One can see now that too much was expected of them. The elementary schoolmaster at the beginning of the nineteenth century was still, as he had been under the *ancien régime*, a very humble man indeed. Far from having any professional status, he was very often an unemployed peasant or artisan, a 'pedlar of participles' who might hawk pots and pans one year and offer to teach another. He wore one, two or three quills in his hat, to indicate that he could teach reading, writing and arithmetic; and there were few who could manage all of these. His wife might be a washerwoman or keep a grocer's shop, for he could seldom live on the pittance he earned. As soon as spring arrived, his pupils would desert him to help their parents in the fields and he would have to seek another occupation till the winter. Only in the towns could he hope to get a regular clientele. Often families carried on the trade of teaching from father to son. A lecturer at the University of Paris–Nanterre recently unearthed the papers of his ancestors who had been teachers in this way. The first had taken up teaching after failing in trade in 1833. His son opened up a school of his own in 1845, in a stable. He left a pathetic account of his troubles, of poverty so extreme that his children died of starvation or grew up deformed.[1] Other memoirs confirm that this was in no way exceptional—hunger, atrocious living conditions, bullying by the village notables and the *curé*, who used them as jacks-of-all-trades—which they had to be, to get enough to survive on—this was their regular lot. The teacher was poorer than a labourer: Michelet said a baker might be six times richer. In 1840, the minimum salary of a village teacher was 200 francs a year (£8) and 23,000 communes paid precisely that amount. In addition the teacher could expect a small sum (of between 30 centimes and 2 francs a month) for each child who came to school, but he had much trouble in collecting this, and the poor were in any case exempted from paying at all. This poverty was something the teachers never escaped from. Even when they were made civil servants and the state took to paying them salaries, they were the lowest paid of all civil servants. In 1914, teachers in Alsace–Lorraine (under German sovereignty) received twice as much pay as their French counterparts and in an international survey French primary teachers were classified as the worst paid in Europe, coming twenty-fifth, equal with those of Montenegro. The result was that people generally became teachers to escape from something worse or as a stepping-stone to other things. They were sometimes weakling or deformed peasant children, who had to

[1] Yves Sandré, *Marchands de participes* (1962).

use their wits to make up for their physical defects, or they saw in education a means of avoiding the grinding labour of the fields. Few saw it as lifetime's career. One of the ways the government attracted recruits was to offer exemption from military service, provided ten years were spent in teaching. The teacher was very often therefore a young man, waiting to enter the lower ranks of the civil service, through examinations for which his education fitted him. There were of course also teachers who had retired from other occupations—such as the army; and others still whom family tradition kept in the profession. But increasingly, the sons of *instituteurs* attempted to become secondary-school masters; and their sons might aspire to become professors. But this was for long an over-ambitious dream. A survey of kindergarten teachers in the department of the Seine in 1959 showed that 45 per cent of them had grandfathers who had been *instituteurs*, and 25 per cent of these had sons who became *instituteurs*. More often it was the *instituteurs*' daughters who followed them in the same job, while sons moved on to higher things.[1] The teacher training colleges were always definitely proletarian: in Saint-Lô, in 1880–4, 53 per cent of the students were sons of peasants, 28 per cent sons of artisans and shopkeepers, 3·4 per cent sons of workers and clerks. Forty years later peasants no longer found it worth while—9 per cent were sons of peasants, 12·5 per cent sons of artisans and shopkeepers, and 49·5 per cent sons of workers. Between the wars, girls who took up teaching were of slightly higher social origin, but generally they had not gone through the training colleges: they were drop-outs from higher education who had failed to obtain degrees (22 per cent in Ida Berger's survey). When questioned, almost a half of the primary teachers in Paris said they would prefer to teach in more senior schools, even if there was no difference in pay or conditions. Elementary teaching was thus not made attractive as a profession in itself, and it was only a minority who entered it with a sense of vocation.

At the same time as they were given the mission of bringing civilisation to the masses, the *instituteurs* were savagely humiliated to prevent them from demanding anything like

---

[1] Ida Berger, *Les Maternelles. Étude sociologique sur les institutrices des écoles maternelles de la Seine* (1959), 57.

proportionate rewards for their pains: the faith in education · was surrounded by an elaborate hypocrisy. Guizot, the minister of public instruction, and a former university professor, who first organised training colleges on a uniform basis in 1832–4, gave firm orders that these colleges should avoid 'fomenting in the pupil-teachers that distate for their very modest situation, that excessive thirst for material well-being that today torments the destiny of so many men, and corrupts their character'. An enormous amount was demanded of them, but in the spirit of self-sacrifice. The discipline in the colleges should be 'severe' so that they would know how to instil the same obedience into children, because it was school discipline which determined whether 'people in later life had a proper respect for legitimate authority'. The pupil-teachers must not be taught anything beyond what was strictly necessary for the carrying-out of their duties: 'more general, vague and superficial subjects, unsuited to the modest functions of a village teacher' should be avoided. 'I expect a lot of you,' wrote Guizot. 'There will be, so to speak, no private life for you: the state asks not only for the tribute of your intelligence and know-ledge, but for the whole man.' But in return teachers 'must expect neither fame nor fortune, and must be content with the austere pleasure of having served their fellow men, obtaining nothing beyond their obscure and laborious condition'. The philosopher Jouffroy, in discussing the role of teachers at the Academy of Moral and Political Sciences in 1840, insisted that 'a critical spirit' was suitable only for the élite, who received secondary and higher education, and not for mere primary teachers. Victor Cousin said their job was noble but essentially humble, and the 'spirit of poverty' was essential to it. The *instituteurs* thus closely resembled the curés, who came from the same poor background, were also exempted from military service, and earned the same miserable pittance. The government was terrified, in the case of both of them, that they might win too much influence.

The republicans did a certain amount to raise their morale, by making them their chosen agents for the distribution of political propaganda. The historian Martin and the philosopher Renouvier wrote republican textbooks in the form of catechisms, which were sent out to the teachers. A journal,

*L'Écho des instituteurs* (1845–50), started up to defend their interests; and some of them played an active role in left-wing electioneering in 1848. This was enough for Thiers to accuse all 37,000 of them of being 'socialists and communists, veritable anti-*curés* . . . of consuming ambition', and to warn against the dangers of too much education for the masses. In 1851 some 3,000 *instituteurs* were dismissed as dangerous. The Second Empire at first shared these fears: it showered circulars upon them, forbidding them to play at politics, to visit cabarets or cafés, to frequent 'any society which was not in keeping with the gravity and dignity of their functions'. But it then saw them as valuable allies in its war against the Church; it invited them in 1860 to send in their views on education—an unprecedented piece of consultation: 5,940 of them sent in essays which showed a great sense of responsibility as well as of misery. A newspaper in 1863 commented: 'Constantly at the mercy of an inspector's report, or a denunciation, transferred frequently and on the least pretext, the *instituteurs* in the countryside had reached such a degree of moral wretchedness that every one among them who felt he had any good in him was emigrating to the civil service, the railways or private industry.' The government now began treating them with a little more respect: in 1867 it invited 700 of them to Paris to see the International Exhibition and Napoleon III himself entertained them. The Third Republic finally hailed them as the vanguard of progress, and the chosen instrument of the new enlightenment, and its school-building programme frequently gave the *instituteur* the most splendid house in the village from which to operate. A Pedagogical Museum was founded in 1879, and professorships of pedagogy established, to raise teaching to the status of a science. Leading politicians and philosophers took to writing textbooks to guide the *instituteurs*, so that they became participants in what was supposed to be a great national movement. But the republic was slow to raise their wages; in 1889, in the name of equality, their military exemption was ended; and it was by no means clear that they were the republic's favourites except in the rhetoric of politicians.

The *instituteurs* in due course became disabused and began to organise themselves against the government—but this was a slow process, because they were far from all being revolutionaries. At first they formed friendly societies (*amicales*) which by 1914 claimed 97,000 members; but these were largely controlled by the inspectors and headmasters, whose authoritarian methods some of the rank and file were beginning to resent. When, following the law on associations of 1884, some tried to form a trade union, the minister forbade it, for they were civil servants and 'to allow the regimentation of functionaries without the participation of their superiors, and even against their superiors, would be to consent in advance to the collapse of the whole civil service'. But revolutionary syndicalist ideas gained ground among some *instituteurs* after 1900, and in 1905 this small minority of extremists decided to form themselves into a union, affiliated to the Bourses du Travail and the C.G.T. They wanted better wages but, even more, self-government for the teachers, and liberation from the favouritism and arbitrariness of their superiors. Headmasters were still treating *instituteurs* like eighteenth-century ushers, forbidding them to visit cafés, insisting on their taking their meals as the headmaster's paying guests, at high rates: one example of a complaint was that the headmaster ate trout while the *instituteurs* were given herrings. In the 1904–5 elections for the consultative departmental councils, all the inspectors and headmasters were eliminated and replaced by ordinary *instituteurs*. In 1919 the *amicales*, following the lead of the syndicalists, turned themselves into a trade union (Syndicat National des Instituteurs), and at last in 1924–5 the government agreed to treat with it. Henceforth promotions and transfers had to be carried out in consultation with the union; but *instituteurs* were not able to gain any large wage increases, and the fact that an exceptionally large proportion of them became union members (about 80 per cent) meant that the older, more conservative elements directed their policy. They continued to repeat pre-war slogans, they continued to preach the pacifism of 1914 during the Spanish Civil War and even in the face of Hitler's violence. By 1939 they were strangely isolated within the nation, forming an idiosyncratic type, but not a model.[1]

One explanation is the training they received. The training colleges (*écoles normales*) were at first almost indistinguishable

---

[1] Max Ferré, *Histoire du mouvement syndicaliste révolutionnaire chez les instituteurs* (1955) unfortunately stops in 1922.

from ecclesiastical seminaries. The trainees were all boarders, sleeping in dormitories, with their lives regulated to the smallest detail from the moment they rose at 5 a.m. to their bedtime at 9. They were forbidden to go out without the director's special permission. Their drink allowance was fixed by ministerial decree at one-third of a litre of wine a day (mixed with twice as much water). The subjects taught were the very same things primary schoolboys learnt, and no more. Only in the Second Empire was the syllabus gradually increased to include music 'so that the *instituteurs* could contribute to the pomp of religious ceremonies and conduct tastefully and intelligently musical societies which are such a desirable form of competition to the cabarets'. The standard for admission was very low: the École Normale of the Rhône had fourteen new entrants in 1864, but eight of them could barely write. Many of these colleges were tiny, with just a couple of people on their staff. They were usually housed in old buildings, former nunneries or even wings of prisons. What held them together was a passionate dedication to hard work, a firm belief in slogging memorisation, a peasant determination to make good. They were dry, rigid, very institutional. It is true that in 1865 and again in the 1880s discipline was relaxed, the offence of 'insubordination' was abolished, seven weeks' holidays were allowed. Then the lecturers at the colleges got their emancipation, were no longer required to live in, or to attend to domestic arrangements. Two *écoles normales supérieures*, one for men and one for women, were established at St. Cloud and Fontenay-aux-Roses, which produced more sophisticated and dedicated lecturers, whose teaching methods were much more theoretical, and indeed often high-flown, 'marked by Parisian approval'. The syllabuses at the colleges were broadened, entry standards raised; in the 1880s they began teaching much the same syllabus as the lower forms of secondary schools; after 1905 the third year at training colleges was almost like the top forms or like the first year of the faculties, with a long essay which the trainees pompously called their 'thesis'; after 1920 the stimulation of 'intellectual curiosity' became an official purpose of the colleges. The colleges were thus gradually raised from primary to secondary status in fact, if not in name: in 1937 the minister Jean Zay proposed to send all the trainees to secondary schools and make the *écoles normales* provide simply short professional courses; and in 1940 the Vichy government did just this. The result, not unexpectedly, was catastrophic for teacher recruitment, because once the trainees were inserted into the secondary system, 80 per cent of them abandoned the idea of becoming *instituteurs* and moved on to better jobs. The expansion of the educational system meant that there were far more opportunities for promotion, and the best graduates of the training colleges preferred to become administrators or training-college lecturers, or to work for higher qualifications. But while they lasted, the *écoles normales* gave the *instituteurs* a sense of corporate identity; their old pupil associations were very vigorous; and an *instituteur*'s best friends were very often other *instituteurs*. From around the turn of the century, it became quite frequent for *instituteurs* to marry *institutrices*. Formerly, it had been considered scandalous for a woman teacher to marry and continue to work; but now the government decided that since it could not give them a living wage, the best solution was for the male and female teachers to combine in couples and earn two wages. The effect of this, however, was to accentuate the separation of the teachers from other professions.[1]

The *instituteurs* always had to contend with a great deal of hostility, both political and social, and it was almost inevitable that they should turn to their own unions and associations for strength. The peasants looked on them as wily children who had succeeded in avoiding the hard work that ordinary people had to accept; they resented their long holidays, short hours and the fixed wage they received regularly whatever the weather. The *instituteurs* were not quite bourgeois but neither were they peasants and they had difficulty in finding friends among either. The *instituteurs*, besides, sometimes had their pride: as one of them wrote, 'We had such a high view of our function that we considered ourselves bound to be extremely reserved and at least to have the appearance of distinction.' But as prosperity spread among the peasantry, they could less

---

[1] M. Gontard, *La Question des écoles normales primaires de la Révolution de 1789 à nos jours* (Toulouse, 2nd edition, 1964); M. Vallée, *L'École normale des instituteurs de Vesoul* (Vesoul, 1901); J. Ozouf, 'Les Instituteurs de la Manche et leur associations au début du xxᵉ siècle', *Revue d'histoire moderne et contemporaine* (Jan.–Mar. 1966), 95–114; J. P. David, *L'Établissement de l'enseignement primaire au 19ᵉ siècle dans le département de Maine-et-Loire 1816–79* (Angers, 1967).

and less be looked on as children who had made good. One cannot generalise too much about attitudes towards them, because these varied enormously according to local conditions, individual personalities and the roles they assumed. Thus in the department of the Manche, they were treated with deference on the coast but shunned by many peasants in the interior. In certain religious areas, the state's *instituteurs* might have classes of only half a dozen or even two children, because the majority attended the church school: here they were totally isolated. But when the balance of opinion was more even, the *instituteurs* could and often did enjoy enormous influence. They could become leaders of the left-wing party and be responsible for organising most of its social activities, which assumed a much greater importance because they were in constant competition with those of the church. One *instituteur* of the Deux-Sèvres (born in 1884) described how he worked in a village with 'two schools, two musical societies, two public libraries, two sporting clubs (gymnastics on the right, shooting on the left), two friendly societies, two public meeting halls, two electoral committees (the republican, and the Catholics of Poitou); two different annual festivals for the boys called up to the army, with only the republican one displaying the tricolour. Only the firemen formed a single subdivision, responsible to the Prefecture, or there would have been left wing and right wing fires.' All businesses likewise had their political label, except that when a trader wanted to keep the custom of both sides he sent his daughter to the church school and his son to the state one. Since the *instituteurs* were the main cause or symbol of this division, they became village notables. They won influence, however, not so much from their political opinions but from what they contributed to village life. More than half of them, at the end of the nineteenth century, were secretary to the mayor, in which capacity they were indispensable intermediaries for most dealings with the authorities. The *instituteurs* who also knew how to measure land, how to carry out calculations, and write letters for the peasants, on those subjects which concerned their daily lives, and who themselves cultivated a plot of land in their spare time, would be esteemed in a special way. It was often to their advantage if they were indistinguishable from peasants in physical appearance.

Nevertheless the peasants saw them as something apart, and in personal, as opposed to administrative, difficulties, shy peasants might well prefer to consult the *curé*. However, the stereotype of the *instituteur* at war with the *curé* was by no means universally true. For long the *instituteur* was his subordinate, and in some localities they lived in harmony. The stereotype indeed is proved inaccurate the more one studies the details of the lives of these men, who have left autobiographies and documents revealing an impressive independence of thought and much individual strength of will.

A Savoyard *instituteur*, born in 1844, has left some interesting memoirs which show the problems and the satisfactions of this first generation of popular *instituteurs*. He was the son of a peasant; by great sacrifices, he got into a training college; when his father died, it gave him a quarter scholarship—the rest of his fees to be a loan. 'Accustomed to the authority of my father, I accepted the discipline of the college willingly enough.' It was run by a priest and he was taught that his mission was to assist the priest of his village, to reinforce religion. At nineteen, he became an assistant *instituteur* with a hundred pupils, but on a wage of 400 francs which left him so hungry that he used to walk home, 33 kilometres each way, whenever he could, in order to get a square meal. But even his brothers and sisters thought he was not working properly, and profiting from the labours of others. The peasants envied the *instituteur* his ready cash, assuming that he must therefore be rich. On one occasion, a peasant asked him to lend him his salary of 400 francs, not realising that he had no other resources, no land, and that he had to live off his pay. His religious duties were almost as heavy as his teaching. He had to teach the choir to sing, to ring the church bells at five o'clock, to serve mass and to sing on Sunday both at mass and vespers, and generally to be at the beck and call of the *curé*. He had no holidays at Christmas or Easter because these were religious feasts. In addition he was secretary to the mayor. He also played the violin, so he was in demand at parties; and he could measure lands, so could be useful to the peasants. But when he offended the *curé* by marrying the *institutrice*, he was sacked; and he had to take another job on lower pay, and his wife could not get a teaching post there. He walked a hundred kilometres to the capital to see the inspector about this and get a transfer. Two of their children died of hunger; his wife got 'neurasthenia' from the worry, an illness that bore down on the rest of their lives. But he received a present of a dictionary of medicine from some grateful pupils, and his wife therefore took up advising women on their illnesses. Teaching was always only part of his life. He also took boarders; he learnt carpentry, and spent the vacations making rustic furniture. He quarrelled with one *curé*; but then the next *curé* treated him well, telling him to walk on his left while the mayor walked on his right; so he kept the cross in the school-room despite official orders. In his retirement, he was able to continue with his hobbies. Though his life had been very hard, there was an impressive stoicism about it. In 1870 he had voted *No* against Napoleon III, exclaiming, 'O magic power of universal suffrage, which gives the humblest man the right to affirm, for once, his personality, and to count as much as the most powerful.'[1]

This history may be compared with that of an *institutrice* two generations later. She entered the profession after 1945; but her memoirs reveal that abysmally primitive physical conditions could still survive, particularly in backward regions of France where time moved slowly. She started in the Lozère, in a school with fourteen pupils, aged five to fourteen. The school was so damp, she had two centimetres of water on the floor and lessons were taken wearing rubber boots. She had to live in a room upstairs, without running water or sanitation. André Maurois by chance learnt of this, protested to the authorities and within a few weeks the water arrived. It needed the intervention of a Parisian demigod to change things. The inspector answered complaints by saying nothing could be done; that he too had started in one of these depressed regions, in similarly bad conditions; promotion was the only way out.[2] These are just two stories: they are not typical, because there was always too much variety for that to be possible; but they show what could and did happen.

There were *instituteurs* who behaved like peasants, spoke rarely and slowly, did not hesitate to use the local dialect, and played boules with the villagers in the evening or cards in winter.

[1] C. Brun, *Trois plumes au chapeau, ou l'Instituteur d'autrefois* (Grenoble, 1950).
[2] Huguette Bastide, *Institutrice de Village* (1971).

But there were an extraordinarily large number who either could not or would not visit the café, and when they did, perhaps once a week, sat alone. The older ones, who had abandoned ideas of leaving their profession, who became trade union leaders, or who had lost their interest in sport, cultivated virtues of solidity. Some never read a book if they could help it—they were by no means all intellectuals—while others became experts in local history or geology. Many devoted the whole of their lives to teaching and were totally absorbed in their work. In general, they were serious people, having little in common with the dilettante iconoclasm of Paris: they accepted the need for order, they believed in what they were doing, they had faith in the power of knowledge. What distinguished them from the rest of the population more than anything else was perhaps their rejection of monetary and material ideals—a characteristic they shared only with the clergy, who were paradoxically seen as their enemies.

In the course of the twentieth century two new features altered the image and ambitions of the *instituteurs*. First, the men began leaving the profession. In 1891 for the first time more women than men were recuited; women could teach boys, but men could not teach in single-sex girls' schools. The *institutrices* had less political dedication and less desire to be active outside the world of education. Secondly, the men took on educational work which was not just 'primary'—a word which no longer meant elementary, for the *écoles primaires supérieures* and the *écoles normales* could reach *baccalauréat* standard. The hierarchy in the primary sector became elaborate. In 1914 when an *instituteur*'s maximum salary was 2,450 francs, teachers at the *écoles primaires supérieures* earned between 2,100 and 4,100 francs, lecturers in training colleges 2,900 to 4,900, and directors of training colleges got an additional 1,000 to 1,600 francs. Primary inspectors earned 3,700 to 5,500; *inspecteurs d'académie* 7,166 to 8,666; inspectors-general 10,000 to 12,000 and rectors 13,000 to 18,000.[1] Innumerable grades and pay scales within these different jobs produced constant worries and grievances. The inspectors had a lot of power, so that their tours were dreaded: every *instituteur* got a mark when he was inspected, as though to impress upon him that by becoming a teacher he

[1] A. Lantenois, *Ce que l'instituteur doit savoir* (4th edition, 1928), 562-3.

had opted to remain at school. But the inspectors also had too many schools to inspect, so that they could not do their work properly and were often seen simply as arbitrary, bureaucratic obstacles. So the *instituteurs* had more and more internal battles to fight, which concerned only themselves.

An inquiry by two sociologists among the primary teachers of the Seine, published in 1964, showed just how far they had evolved. They were on the whole still left wing, but whereas 59 per cent of the men thought that 'present-day society is antagonistic to what I want from life', only 43 per cent of the women did, and there were even 7 per cent of men and 23 per cent of women who thought present-day society was good. 64 per cent of the men and 46 of the women were unbelievers, but 30 and 42 per cent were believers. This still implied that teachers were less religious than the population as a whole, but only 23 per cent of the men and 9 of the women were opposed to religion as such. All agreed that their prestige had sunk even though their paper qualifications had risen, but 65 per cent of the women (as opposed to 46 per cent of the men) declared themselves satisfied with their jobs. The repressed, aggressive male *instituteur* was thus being replaced by more contented women, who saw teaching as an emancipation in itself. These women were not blue-stockings—only 28 per cent of them were unmarried (as opposed to 15 per cent bachelors) and only 10 per cent thought it all right for a woman to have a better job than her husband (whereas 26 per cent of the men had no objection to this). Nearly three-quarters, of both men and women, said they belonged to the middle class, or the petite bourgeoisie. Their identification with the workers was gone (only 22 per cent of men and 9 per cent of women said they belonged to the working class). The primary school thus failed to identify itself with the proletariat, though it was designed for it; it remained the intermediary by which the proletariat—led by the *instituteurs* themselves—tried to escape.[1] This should not be seen as a failure or a betrayal. If the majority of the proletariat wanted to escape from that condition, then the *instituteurs* were in one sense clearing the path for them; but in the process they set up and were absorbed by a system which was too distant from the ordinary working world. The

[1] Ida Berger and Roger Benjamin, *L'Univers des instituteurs* (1964).

*instituteurs* were never really all that much more politically committed than the people at large. It was only a minority that took part in elections; only a tiny minority were freemasons; in most cases what they valued most was professional and intellectual independence—in exactly the same way as the peasant or the worker. But their weakness was that there were too many pressures on them, from the state, from politicians, from the church, from parents, from the children, from their superiors and their colleagues, not to mention the full share of family and personal worries that tormented them.[1] No other profession had to serve so many masters and it is not surprising that they fully satisfied nobody. They needed faith to survive in such conditions and they evolved one, which gave most of them a sense of satisfaction in having tried to advance the cause of progress. But they were judged in terms of the society that employed them.[2]

## Teaching Methods and their Consequences

These different forces in French education led to the use of techniques which made the relation between school and the world outside it distinctly formal and uncompromising. The reactions of pupils to what they were taught, and the permanent results of their schooling, may be seen, first of all, in the way they were introduced to reading and writing. It is usual to isolate several methods, each claiming to be more modern than the previous one, and to say that, after vigorous battles between them, they gradually supplanted each other; but in fact the legacy of the past was seldom entirely lost, and one had rather an accumulation of methods superimposed. The continuity behind the revolutionary battles is as remarkable in education as in politics and government—even though there were many important changes in detail. Thus, to begin with, the method of teaching reading changed drastically around the middle of the century, with the adoption of the phonetic system. Formerly,

[1] Cf. Roger Crinier, *Caractérologie des instituteurs* (1963).

[2] J. Ozouf, *Nous, les maîtres d'école* (1967), the best study pending the completion of his thesis on the *instituteurs*; G. Duveau, *Les Instituteurs* (1957); André Ferré, *L'Instituteur* (1954); Serge Jeanneret, *La Vérité sur les instituteurs* (1941); Émile Glay and Henry Champeau, *L'Instituteur* (1928), by their trade union leaders; Henri Bibert, *Les Bourriques* (1911); C. Brun, op. cit.

reading lessons used to begin with memorising letters, then words, then sentences, as opposed to learning how each letter was pronounced and composing syllables from that. Though the second method, propagated by Hachette and especially Peigné after 1831, aroused much enthusiasm among its partisans, and though the Brothers of the Christian Schools adopted it in 1847, teachers were divided into two camps on the subject until at least 1870, and even in 1889 when the phonetic method had the support of the immense majority, there were still departments in the west, and some religious schools, which preferred the traditional one.[1] It used to be the practice to learn to read in Latin, partly because there were no unpronounced letters, and partly also because many parents and teachers considered they had done enough if they taught children to read their prayers and Sunday offices. Boys in larger schools were divided into 'latinists', the lowest grade, 'Frenchmen' when they moved on to read their own language, and they became 'writers' only after that, since it was a principle that the three Rs should be tackled in turn and not simultaneously. *Instituteurs*, besides, could not always teach all three, and a boy might thus learn to read but not to count or calculate. In 1880 the Inspector-General of Rennes reported that many *instituteurs* still believed this was a good thing, and children were not even given a pen or pencil till their second year at school. The fact that many schools at that time still did not have desks for their pupils to write on made any desire for change irrelevant. It was J. B. La Salle, the founder of the Brothers of the Christian Schools, who first broke with the Latin tradition, by producing his French spelling book, but he did not alter the religious character of the exercise: boys were taught to read out of his *Christian Duties* and *Christian Behaviour*, which consisted of lists of religious and moral principles.[2] Exactly the same kind of reading books were used in other schools in the mid-nineteenth century—for example, *Reading and Moral Exercises* by Émile Delapalme, a magistrate and brother-in-law

[1] I. Carré, *L'Enseignement de la lecture, de l'écriture et de la langue française dans les écoles primaires* (1889) (Mémoires et documents scolaires publiés par le Musée pédagogique, deuxième série, fasc. 27).

[2] H. C. Rudon and Ph. Friot, *Un Siècle de pédagogie dans les écoles primaires (1820–1940). Histoire des méthodes et des manuels utilisés dans l'Institut des Frères de l'instruction chrétienne de Ploërmel* (1962) is one of the few histories of teaching methods.

of Napoleon III's minister Baroche.[1] This book was reprinted thirty-eight times between 1843 and 1908, showing how long traditions survive. A great change occurred at the beginning of the Third Republic, with the wildfire success of *Francinet* and *Le Tour de France par deux enfants*, which were reading books with an interesting story and with a lot of factual information, but the content was still very moralising. After the decline of religion, great stress was laid on choosing only the very best prose, by the most admired writers. Reading, indeed education as a whole, continued to be seen as the conquest of values. Though the child was no longer regarded as sinful, he was now considered to be nothing in himself, infinitely malleable, and the aim was to raise him quickly to adult life and to participation in the achievements of humanity. This was the way the religious traditionalists and the new positivists met on common ground. 'To read', wrote the republican philosopher Alain, 'that is the true cult. That is why I am far from believing that the child must understand all that he reads and recites.' Alain's pupil, Jean Chateau (b. 1908) likewise insisted that no object was properly perceived until it was named: 'The word is the portmanteau to which the idea attaches itself. So vocabulary must at first be learnt by heart.'[2] Memorising, no longer of religious doctrines but now of admired prose and poetry, continued to occupy a major part of the children's efforts. There was an attack on this at the end of the nineteenth century, but it was only temporary and a reaction then set in once again. As a result, small children were made familiar with 'literature' in a very thorough way at an early age: even if they could not understand it, they could recite it, as they had once been able to recite their prayers.

Grammar likewise continued to be studied in great detail, if not in quite the same way as had been the practice when Latin was the language taught, at least in a similar spirit.

---

[1] E. Delapalme [1793–1868], *Exercices de lecture et de leçons de morale* (1843); id., *Premier Livre de l'enfance*, 43 editions 1849–1908; id., *Bibliothèque d'enseignement élémentaire à l'usage des instituteurs primaires* (1829–30), 25 vols. Compare the survival of the *Méthode de lecture* (1958) by Frères Théodorit and Job of the Christian Schools, the 57th edition of which appeared in 1923.

[2] Louis Legrand, *L'Enseignement du français à l'école élémentaire: problèmes et perspectives* (Neuchâtel, 1966), by a former *instituteur* and *inspecteur primaire* who obtained a doctorate and became chef du service de la recherche pédagogique—one of the most interesting analysts in this field.

The positivists loved grammar, because they saw in it a method of getting the child to pass from the 'intuitive' stage to a clear understanding of the rules and structure of language; they retained a belief in the value of abstract grammatical definitions, on the assumption that these would be spontaneously transferred to ordinary speech. So here again, after the temporary discrediting of grammar under the Second Empire, there was a revival of it. At the beginning of the nineteenth century, the standard grammar book was Lhomond's (1727–94), based on Latin models and containing simply a summary of the rules, without any exercises.[1] Then Noël and Chapsal produced their *New French Grammar* in 1823, which became extremely popular, reaching its eightieth edition in 1889, not counting pirated versions. Chapsal (1788–1858) was a teacher at Louis le Grand and Noël (1755–1841) was a renegade priest who sided with the Revolution, became a diplomat, prefect and Inspector-General of Education. They must be counted among the best-selling authors of the century: the titles of Noël's numerous textbooks and dictionaries occupy twenty-one pages in the Bibliothèque Nationale catalogue. They were not innovators, but they succeeded in giving the rules of grammar in a clear and orderly way, with simple formulae to explain them. They set a new fashion for the grammatical analysis of French, even if the result was not all that different from the old. Their greatest contribution was that they added exercises at the bottom of each page, in the form of a catechism. The book begins: 'French grammar is the art of speaking and writing correctly in French. To speak and write, one uses words. Words are composed of letters. There are two kinds of letters.' And the questions for the pupil at the bottom of the page were: 'What is grammar, what are words composed of?' Definitions of every part of speech were set out, complete with an enormous number of infinitely subtle distinctions, all to be memorised.[2] Napoleon III's ministers waged a war against this method, as encouraging parrot learning. Instead the principle was proclaimed that grammar should go from the concrete to the abstract, from example to rule; and in 1877 two other teachers, Fleury and

---

[1] C. F. Lhomond, *Éléments de grammaire française* (1780).

[2] F. J. M. Noël and C. P. Chapsal, *Nouvelle Grammaire française sur un plan très méthodique* (56th edition, 1875).

Larive, produced a new textbook which, claiming to carry this out, achieved even greater success, reaching its 229th edition in 1953.[1] In fact, it was not all that different in content to its predecessor, but had the advantage that it reorganised its facts between three different books, elementary, middle and senior, to suit the threefold division of primary schools just introduced.[2] With time, *instituteurs* varied the methods and made them increasingly flexible and inductive, but the stress on grammar survived. French children in the 1950s were learning analyses of verb and subject at the age of seven, when Swiss children did not attempt it till ten.

Accurate spelling continued to be valued very highly, and tests by Binet and others have shown that standards have risen since 1904, even in working-class districts of Paris (though Genevan children still spell better, as they did earlier).[3] The stress on accuracy in written French was associated with the continued use of dictation. This traditional practice was maintained with a whole new barrage of arguments about its virtues: it gave pupils practice in handling sentences; it directed their attention to grammatical constructions; it gave them models to follow in spelling, punctuation and capitalisation; it enlarged the vocabulary, and, not least, it prevented them from separating the spoken language from the written. An American professor who visited a French school in 1912 found, by tests, that French children of twelve could spell considerably better than American college freshmen. Good spelling, as the French Academy pointed out in 1694, was 'what distinguishes men of letters from the ignorant and from simple women'; the fondness for strict rules in this matter has increased very considerably with time, good spelling becoming a kind of social passport.[4] In 1889 an official commentator asserted that for long the study of French was above all the study of spelling, by reading, copying and taking down dictation, and that it was only in 1880

[1] J. F. B. Fleury and Larive, *La Première Année de grammaire* (1871, 201st edition 1917).
[2] Fleury was the father of Madame Durand, alias 'Henri Greville', author of the best-selling textbook on morals for primary schools. Fleury and Larive's textbook is said to have sold twelve million copies.
[3] Legrand, op. cit., 77, 109.
[4] Rollo W. Brown, *How the French Boy Learns to Write* (Cambridge, Mass., 1924), 60–1; Legrand, op. cit., 119.

that composition, which had hitherto been considered the preserve of the secondary system, was introduced. But in 1966 an equally authoritative expert complained that primary education had continued to be dominated by spelling and dictation: certainly a dictation every day remained normal; but it is true that dictation gradually came to be treated with less respect and a child would lose only a quarter or half a mark, instead of a whole one, for a spelling mistake. It was the same with handwriting. This used to be taught as an art in several varieties and one of the *instituteurs'* time-consuming functions had been to sharpen quills (until around 1870), but beautiful handwriting then came to be considered a sign of immaturity, and the smart *instituteurs* from the *écoles normales* liked to despise it as old fashioned. One of the causes of its downfall was that there was disagreement as to which style should be taught, while the civil service, which used to be one of the major patrons of calligraphy, increasingly cultivated illegibility, so that a new form of esoterism succeeded the old.

What struck American observers of the French system was the large place writing held in the schools and in their routine. 'The ideal of writing well has been held up before the schoolboy so long, and with such seriousness, that he attaches more importance to ability of this kind than the average American boy could at present be led to comprehend' (1915).[1] Composition was introduced into the system by Jules Ferry in association with *la leçon de choses*—one of the most popular slogans of the reformers—which was supposed to sharpen the child's powers of observation, in a properly scientific spirit. But though this produced far more interesting lessons, on subjects which would not ordinarily have been treated at school, it also involved spending a great deal of time in the study of words, in a far more thorough way than would be found in either England or America. Thus the pupil would be required to define a word, give examples of its various uses, learn its original meaning, compare it with synonyms and above all contrast it with its opposites. 'It is scarcely too much to say that the basis of all word-teaching is contrast rather than likeness.' The consequences of this should not be exaggerated, for they indicate only the mental attitudes the educators admired. But children

[1] R. W. Brown, op. cit., 47.

were trained to use words which did not come naturally to them. 'The feeling for words which the pupil develops', wrote the same American professor, 'becomes a permanent part of his life. The boy who has had training of this kind may still use slangy or worn speech, but he is at least aware of what he does. And he will often avoid the colorless word not because he simply knows that it should be avoided, but because his quickened nature instinctively revolts aganst it.'[1] It will be seen in due course how these tendencies were developed and pushed further in the secondary schools. But even the primary schoolchild, despite the warnings of ministers and inspectors who liked to insist that this level should remain essentially practical and working class, was given a training that had more than a hint of the literary in it. Each pupil was required to keep a notebook in which most of his written work was collected. The ideal was that nothing should be finally consigned to that notebook until it was absolutely correct. And the compositions collected for the International Exhibition of 1878 showed that the system could work very efficiently: even those sent in by children are incredibly mature, while those sent in by their teachers were very impressive, thoughtful and interesting.[2] However, just how responsibility for the fluency of these exercises should be shared between parents and teachers is not clear. Recent investigations have suggested that home background still plays a more decisive role in school success than any other factor (except perhaps in mathematics). This was always an important limitation upon the primary schools.

## Moral Education

However, the heart of the new primary education developed by the Third Republic was moral and civic training. This was what the reformers considered to be their most original contribution;[3] this is what aroused most controversy among their opponents; and paradoxically, this was perhaps the part of the syllabus which had least practical effect. It represented, more than anything else, the intervention of theorists and professors

[1] Ibid. 57.

[2] *Devoirs d'écoliers français recueillis à l'exposition universelle de Paris, 1878*, edited by Bagnaux, Berger, Buisson *et al.* (1879).

[3] H. Marion, *Le Mouvement des idées pédagogiques en France depuis 1870* (1889), 31.

into primary education, of which they had little personal knowledge, imposing methods strangely out of touch with reality. They wanted to create a society whose members would be more than oppressed subjects, held to the observance of the laws simply by fear of punishment. Universal suffrage was a terrifying prospect when large sections of the population were considered 'savages' and 'barbarians' and the working classes were labelled 'the dangerous classes'.[1] For many, a common French language was the essential preliminary for national unity, but just as pressing was the need to gain acceptance for the moral values for which the new France stood. The first and second republics had both made a start; Hippolyte Carnot, as minister of education in 1848, had distributed little books (of roughly the same size as the *Thoughts of Chairman Mao*) which combined republican propaganda with exhortations to virtue and philosophical explanations of why one should be both virtuous and republican.[2] But it was Jules Ferry and Paul Bert who made this an integral part of the school syllabus. After 1881-2, the day's work had to be preceded by a little lesson on morals, in place of prayers. The ministerial instructions were drawn up by Henri Marion and the syllabus by Paul Janet, both professors at the Sorbonne. They declared that the lay teacher of morals should aim to complete what the priest and the father began, or failed to accomplish: he had to ensure that every child 'served an effectual moral apprenticeship'. Whereas the Church, by defining its dogmas, stressed what separated Catholics from others, the lay school, while avoiding religious controversy, would show children what they should have in common, above any disagreements—'those essential notions of human morality common to all doctrines and necessary to all civilised mankind'. These philosophers were of course no revolutionaries, and Ferry rightly summarised their ambition when he said that all they hoped to teach was 'the good old morality we learnt from our fathers and mothers'.

Because this seemed to infringe the rights of the clergy, because the approach of moral education was deist and rationalist as opposed to Catholic, and because it brought out into the open, before the children, political and religious disputes, moral

---

[1] L. Chevalier, *Classes laborieuses et classes dangereuses* (1958).
[2] Cf. Augustin Sicard, *L'Éducation morale et civique 1700-1808* (1884).

education became the object of a vast hostile campaign by the Church. A great attack was launched on the textbooks. It is necessary to see what this protest was about, but it will be shown that, from the educational point of view, the fuss was largely one about theory, not practice. The practical interest of moral education, it will be suggested, lies elsewhere. The textbooks which the republicans now produced, and which the Church immediately placed on the Index, were less important for what they achieved than interesting for what they revealed about their authors. Republican morality was distinctly conservative. Its great innovation was that it sought the rational assent of children to the generally agreed rules of society. It therefore reduced these to a level which was at once banal and immensely striking, because it dared say, in a few words, things which critical minds would want qualified and elaborated. Living together seemed a grim business when the rules were spelt out: the sight of the very skeleton on which all else rested was disconcerting. The exercise revealed just how unoriginal and old-fashioned the advocates of progress and science were—but they were terrifying none the less.

The trouble with the moral textbooks was that they were written for children, but almost none were produced to give guidance on how the subject should be taught. The teachers were left with the relatively brief instructions issued by the ministry; but these vacillated confusingly. In 1882 Ferry laid it down that the morals lesson should appeal above all to the emotions. A great deal depended on the way the teacher succeeded in arousing the feelings of his pupils. 'The teacher is not required to fill the child's memory, but to teach his heart, to make him feel, by an immediate experience, the majesty of the moral law.' But then in 1888 Octave Gréard (for several decades a powerful civil servant in the ministry of education) said the method should not be emotional, but intellectual. 'Coldness is preferable to declamation, lack of emotion to the pretence of emotion.' The nature of duty should be clarified and proved necessary by reason. Then again in 1923 the minister said that the approach should be to 'sensibility' and that the effectiveness of the teaching depended on its intensity and warmth of conviction. At this point, though the old regulations continued to be officially reissued, the ministry seems to have lost courage somewhat, and instead of demanding uniformity, declared that each teacher had better follow his own inclinations, and certainly prefer them to the textbooks.[1]

Moral education therefore reached the children in many different guises. Though from reading about the debates on the textbooks, one might imagine a revolution was being fomented in the classrooms in the 1880s, the programme took at least twenty years to get going. Many *instituteurs*, particularly in the west, just did nothing about it. They were not so much worried by exactly how God was discussed in the textbooks, as unaccustomed to, and uninterested in, dealing in these abstractions. An inspector reporting on the department of Morbihan in 1895–1900 said that the state schools were continuing to teach the Catholic catechism, just as though there had been no Ferry laws at all. Only a few *instituteurs* here had acquired the new moral textbooks; some at first simply refused to teach the new subject. But by 1900 the large majority had got into the habit of giving about three lessons a week on morals. They usually began by writing a moral maxim on the blackboard, reading it out and explaining it. Then the pupils copied it down and learnt it by heart. The 'practical' side consisted in putting up notices in the village saying: 'Alcohol is the Enemy', cutting out reports from the local papers of accidents and misfortunes caused by alcohol, and making 'respectful remonstrances' to parents when they were seen drinking. This naturally was not the kind of teaching parents wanted to encourage. So it might all end with just a Table of Honour listing virtuous deeds by moral pupils, for example X found a purse containing two francs: 'putting into practice the lesson he had learnt at school, he immediately brought it to his teacher'.[2] The inspector of Lons-le-Saulnier wrote (in 1889): 'The lessons are generally pale imitations of the country priest's sermons: they are either grotesque, declamatory and hollow, or banal, vague and embarrassed.' Another wrote: 'Morals are taught as formerly the catechism was, by question and answer, by yes and no.' The

[1] Brouard and Ch. Defodon, *Les Nouveaux Programmes des écoles primaires* (1914), 43–5; H. Gossot and F. Brunot, *L'Enseignement du premier degré: de la théorie à la pratique (c. 1939)*.

[2] A. Aignan, Inspecteur d'Académie, *Notes et documents sur l'enseignement de la morale. Écoles laïques du Morbihan 1895–1900* (Vannes, 1900, copy in the Musée pédagogique).

inspector of Limoges found an *institutrice* 'disserting on the distinction between the body and the soul to little mites of seven or eight years', but that otherwise 'the teaching of morals does not exist in the schools of my district'. Some gave the lesson perfunctorily in five minutes; some turned it into 'a sort of public confession', getting their pupils to tell the class what good deeds they had done or seen. The subject was thus not popular with either parents, teachers or pupils. The textbooks which were preferred were not the philosophically disputatious ones, but those, like Lavisse's, which dealt with one virtue per lesson, with each precept numbered, so that teaching could be systematic.[1] Patriotism was probably the idea which was most widely propagated as a result, though one inspector, from Ribérac, claimed that his teachers were unanimously agreed their lessons had made lying less frequent.[2]

The hope that moral education would give young children a sort of elementary version of the *culture générale* that the secondary schools dispensed, or a condensed summary of accumulated human wisdom, was never fulfilled, despite numerous debates and constantly revised textbooks. Perhaps the nearest it got to success was at the École Normale at Fontenay-aux-Roses, the chief training college for *institutrices*, at the head of which Ferry placed Félix Pécaut, who exerted a profound influence on its graduates. He was a Protestant pastor who had in 1859 published a book, *Christ and Conscience*, which anticipated and even surpassed the audacity of Renan's *Life of Jesus*: in it he argued that Christ was not divine, his teaching was not perfect, but was capable of being improved with time. It was this attitude, of the extreme left of Protestantism, that Pécaut tried to give his pupils, in early-morning lectures, which were on the borderline of morals and religion, and which became so famous that they were printed in the *Revue pédagogique*. His pupils are said to have venerated him; spiritual life at the college was 'intense', with the accent on introspection, self-knowledge and moral rectitude.[3] But this was something that affected only an élite of *institutrices;* and it did not solve the problem of how to teach young children.

[1] E. Lavisse's moral books were published under the pseudonym of Pierre Laloi: *Les Récits de Pierre Laloi* (1888).

[2] F. Lichtenberger, *L'Éducation morale dans les écoles primaires* (1889) (Mémoires et documents scolaires publiés par le Musée pédagogique, deuxième série, fasc. 28).

[3] F. Pécaut, *Éducation publique et vie nationale* (1897).

In 1914 an inspector-general admitted that the methods for moral education 'in large part not only needed to be set out, but needed to be discovered'. The extent of his bewilderment may be judged from his suggestion that perhaps the lay theorists should look more closely at the methods of the Catholic Church, which used ceremonies, symbolism and group feelings, though he would not concede that it was necessarily more successful.[1] In 1953 a director of a teacher training college with long experience of this subject admitted that all those involved in it had been sadly disappointed with its results; he doubted whether it was worth teaching at all; with many people so sceptical, any advocate of it was likely to be laughed at.[2]

The experiment was essentially a product of a rationalist approach to education, and this is perhaps its main interest. It revealed how the approach survived despite the discoveries of psychology, which remained, as it were, locked up in a separate compartment. A sample lesson in moral education may perhaps show how this worked. It is taken from a pedagogic treatise by the inspector who specialised in the subject. The lesson was on gratitude. The teacher was told to begin with a definition of gratitude. He should explain gratitude to parents, teachers and benefactors, and he should contrast it with ingratitude. He would then show how gratitude was a duty, and how detestable ingratitude was. 'Speak of the satisfaction experienced in repaying a kindness received and of the loving and powerful bond formed between men by gratitude: give examples from school life.' The lesson should conclude with a summary: 'All benefits received lay upon us the duty of gratitude. Ingratitude is detestable; the fulfilment of the duty of gratitude gives the soul real joy.' The 'maxim' to be remembered was 'The heart also has its memory, its name is gratitude; ingratitude is a sort of treason'. The children should then memorise and recite two relevant fables from La Fontaine and a story from a reading book by Guyau, author of *Morals Without Religion*.[3]

The explanation of this kind of lesson is belief in the importance of the training of the will. Until around the 1880s, the

[1] R. Allier, G. Belot *et al.*, *Morale religieuse et morale laïque* (1914), 51.
[2] Robert Mériaux, *La Formation morale à l'école primaire. Du sentiment à la raison* (1953).
[3] I. Carré, *Traité de pédagogie scolaire* (1897), 397.

view upheld by most philosophers, under the influence of Cousin, was that of Kant, that the will should train itself, by self-imposed effort; and that the categorical imperative would lead men to be good. A contradictory view, stemming from Rousseau, that the child was basically good, and should simply be allowed to develop naturally, away from corrupting influences, won, as will be seen, some support among infant teachers, but never got far beyond this. Moral education in primary education stood uncertainly between these two theories: the theories of the different levels of education were never coherent.[1] The authors of the first syllabuses for the primary schools were products of the Cousin–Kant school. Buisson, however, stood halfway between them and the new psychologists. He favoured making school life more enjoyable but he warned against turning it simply into an entertainment. Effort and hard work were necessary at school, for otherwise they would disappear from adult life too. Borrowing from Dr. F. Lagrange's pedagogy of physical education and Ribot's theories on the psychology of the will, he argued that the education of the will should be a prime purpose of the schools, but that the child should be assisted towards a rational mastery of himself by training, in the same way as muscles needed to be exercised. Obedience of the will to its own law—moral autonomy—should still be the ultimate goal. Reason and conscience must be the basis of education.[2] Gréard had insisted: 'Education is the work of reason, addressing itself to reason and using reason.' Jules Payot, Rector of Aix University, though critical of these doctrines, produced a treatise on 'The Education of the Will' which gave a preponderant role to 'meditation'.[3] By the time Piaget showed, in his *Moral Judgements of Children* (1932), how up to the age of about 8 children equated good with obedience, how they gradually acquired notions of solidarity and co-operation between the ages of 8 and 12, and how logic

---

[1] Cf. Debs, *Tableau de l'activité volontaire pour servir à la science de l'éducation* (Amiens, 1844).

[2] F. Buisson, *Education of the Will* (Washington, 1903), a summary of his unpublished lectures on pedagogy given at the Sorbonne in 1899; id., *Conférences et causeries pédagogiques* (1888), especially on 'ensignement intuitif'; id., *La Religion, la morale et la science: leur conflit dans l'éducation contemporaine* (1900), 178–80, and *passim*, shows some of the contradictions. Cf. above, 1. 717, 730 and 2. 155.

[3] Jules Payot, *L'Éducation de la volonté* (1907, 27th edition 1920).

and morals cannot be used to explain each other, the French system of moral education was already discredited in practice, but it survived in the syllabus. It was really only after 1945 that it was seen that this system, which claimed to develop the will, in fact did not require enough effort from the child, because it neglected his individual personality. As Hubert, another Rector wrote in 1948, 'Morals are not a lesson that one learns after having had them put into a formula; they are a discovery made at the price of personal efforts, an experience that one conquers.'[1]

Moral education was distinct from, but closely linked with, civic education. On this subject, again, there was disagreement. Jules Ferry wanted civic education to be purely factual and informative, instruction on the organisation of society and government. But more optimistic people hoped it would be something more, that it would 'bend children to the obedience that the laws required' and 'inspire in them respect for these'. The lessons were brief, adding up to only one hour a week. It was soon obvious that 'the results were almost nil'. The teachers' arguments that the laws should be obeyed because they represented justice and reason came up against the 'suspicious and defiant instinct of unenlightened children', as one expert put it in 1889, and the subject remained at 'a purely verbal level'.[2] The loss of faith in it can be seen by looking at Paul Bert's textbook of 1882 (a fascinating defence of patriotism and the French Revolution—with bitter denigration of the *ancien régime*—a paean in favour at once of progress and the *status quo*, arguing that inequality of wealth, which was 'natural', did not make France any the less a fraternal society, because equality of opportunity existed); this was 176 pages long; but by the 1920s the most widely used book, by Primaire, was a

[1] R. Hubert, *L'Éducation morale* (1948), 73–4. For a vigorous critique of French methods, see Gustav Spiller, *Moral Education in Eighteen Countries* (1899), published by the International Union of Ethical Societies, 206–31. For modern psychological views, Arlette Bourcier, *La Nouvelle Éducation morale* (1966). Cf. Arnould Clausse, *Pédagogie rationaliste* (1968); F. Alengry, *Psychologie et morale appliquées en éducation* (n.d., about 1907); Albin Liangminas, *L'Enseignement de la morale, essai sur sa nature et ses méthodes* (1938); Groupe des étudiants socialistes révolutionnaires internationalistes, *Comment l'État enseigne la morale* (1897).

[2] Léopold Mabilleau, *L'Instruction civique* (1889) (Mémoires . . . musée pédagogique, deuxième série, fasc. 29.) Cf. id., *Cours d'instruction civique* (1884, 6th edition 1909).

mere sixteen pages.[1] Some textbooks had been pretty controversial, urging the case for votes for women, regionalism, pacifism and even listing the faults of Frenchmen side by side with their supposed qualities. In 1920, instead of either civic or moral education, teacher training colleges, in their second year, taught 'sociology'. This caused something of a sensation, but the minister responsible assured parliament that sociology should frighten no one, because 'it produces not a sceptical indifference, but the justification of our moral practices'.[2] Another manifestation of civic education was the introduction of military training and gymnastics into schools. This contributed to reinforcing the military atmosphere that flourished in France till 1914, sustaining values which some claimed were redolent of the *ancien régime*. In 1906, a vistor from Teachers College, Columbia, reported that gymnastic apparatus was almost unknown; practically all the swimming exercises referred to in the official syllabus were performed on dry land; the boxing was a series of formal movements against imaginary opponents.[3] The teachers were much worried by their legal liability for accidents that might occur.

There can be no doubt that some teachers, with powerful personalities, did manage to make something of this moral education. In particular, it was possible to have a practical effect on children's behaviour by encouraging such things as kindness towards animals. But there was always a basic contradiction between the theories of equality and fraternity the teacher preached, and the autocratic authoritarianism he exercised in his class. It was rightly pointed out that though he attacked the despotism of the *ancien régime*, he was often a perfect example of despotism. The whole disciplinary system of the schools, moreover, was inconsistent with its theories: effort was demanded in return for prizes and marks. 'I have yet to find a single class where the teacher ever rose to any ethical basis above the idea of reward and punishment,' wrote an American professor.[4]

[1] Paul Bert, *L'Instruction civique à l'école* (1882).

[2] Jean Beigbeder, *La Formation du futur citoyen à l'école primaire publique* (Paris thesis, Alençon, 1923, reprinted Paris, 1924), 260.

[3] F. E. Farrington, *The Public Primary School System of France* (New York, 1906), 114.

[4] Ibid. 107.

## Infant Schools

It was in infant education that most innovation was achieved, because this was a new branch with fewer traditions and vested interests to raise obstacles. *Salles d'asile* (rather than schools) had been started in some large towns to keep toddlers off the streets. They were the creation of private philanthropists; by 1837 there were only 800 of them, providing for 23,000 children. Though the intentions of these men were admirable, the results were grim. Many of the asylums were huge barrack-like structures, often with 200 or even 400 children in one room, with bitumen floors, and rows of benches on which they were tightly packed. A supervisor watched to make sure they sat still; a bell rang to get them to rise simultaneously, or blow their noses all at once. In 1840 an enterprising contractor offered to build *salles* capable of holding 6,000 children, so arranged that a single teacher on a high platform could see them all. In 1847 the minister of education himself believed that these establishments 'need no class equipment': the children indeed had no tables to write on, and they ate their meals from plates on their knees. Only in 1881 were tables prescribed, though most municipalities refused to buy them. It was in that year that Ferry abolished the *salles d'asiles* and renamed them *écoles maternelles*, with the mission, no longer of drilling infants in the parrot-like repetition of words they could not understand, but of giving them 'the *care* that their physical, moral and intellectual development required'. The emphasis was now to be on their general well-being, with an attempt to provide 'affectionate and indulgent gentleness', to bring enjoyment into their lives, habits of cleanliness, politeness, attention and obedience, which they were to acquire in organised games. The theorists behind this were a series of remarkable women: Madame Millet, who after visiting England introduced Buchanan's methods; Madame Pape-Carpentier, director of a training college for infant teachers in the rue des Ursulines, 1847–74, who was influenced by Fourierism, and attacked the punishment of children;[1] and above all Madame Pauline Kergomard (1838–1925). She was the daughter of a primary school inspector, the

---

[1] See her *Conseils sur la direction des salles d'asile* (1845).

niece of a Protestant pastor, and the cousin of the famous anarchist Reclus brothers. In 1879 Ferry appointed her inspector-general in charge of infant education. She tried to reduce classes to a maximum of 50—though in 1910 she herself reported that there were still classes of over 100: her intentions were never matched by the funds at her disposal. She attacked cramming, punishment, repression, the segregation of the sexes; she was an ardent feminist and wanted the equality of the sexes to start from childhood, but she also condemned single-sex schools because they 'killed children's sense of modesty (*pudeur*)' She was for great freedom, for a 'family atmosphere', but she wanted children to be given a 'social sense', rather than be left undisciplined. One of her first acts had been to get rid of any Froebel equipment she came across, saying it was too complicated; she opposed to 'the German method' 'the method of reason, common sense, personal independence, vivified by that fund of good humour, vivacity and natural wit which is peculiar to our national temperament'.[1] Later, there was no enthusiasm for the methods of Montessori either; these, it was claimed, did no more than what the French had already done in the *écoles maternelles*, and besides, Montessori owed her ideas partly to two French doctors, Itard and Séguin. But in 1900, the *maternelles* were attended by only one-quarter of children between 2 and 6; after that, they declined, following the closure of church schools, and between the wars only one-seventh of eligible children attended them. They appear to have been somewhat uneven in quality; but teachers had more independence, they broke the official rules, both in a liberal sense, to make them more practical, and also restrictively, when resources were inadequate for the grandiose projects the rules ordered. Some of the graduates of the new training college organised by Madame Kergomard were outward looking, and paid visits, for example, to the Decroly school in Belgium and the J.-J. Rousseau Institute in Geneva, but there were many more untrained teachers, barely aware of advances in the psychological or physiological sciences.[2]

[1] But a Froebel Society was established in 1880.

[2] Madame Pauline Kergomard, *Les Écoles maternelles de 1837 jusqu'en 1910* (1910); Ch. Charrier, *La Pédagogie vécue à l'école des petits* (1965 edition); Madame S. Herbinière-Lebert, 'Pédagogie de l'école maternelle' in R. Cousinet, *Leçons de pédagogie* (1950), 180–226.

## Expansion

The *maternelles* had to wage a constant battle against many parents, who wanted their children to be taught the three Rs as early as possible, insisting on visible and rapid results. This pressure to extend the syllabus manifested itself throughout the primary system, so that the schools tried to do more and more. This led to a rather interesting result, in that primary education became almost autonomous, doing many of the things previously associated with secondary schools, but giving them a peculiar stamp, which was sometimes but by no means always 'practical'. The distinctive 'concentric' method introduced by Octave Gréard into the primary schools was that they should be divided into three classes, junior, middle and senior, all of which would have the same syllabus, but with different degrees of intensity. This applied the view that there was a basic body of knowledge which these schools should instil; a pupil who left early would thus have at least some smattering of it all. 'Since primary education is an education of principles,' wrote Gréard, 'and since principles cannot be too often represented if they are to penetrate, it is necessary that the child should pass constantly over the same ground.' The aim was also to end the old anarchy which left *instituteurs* alone to make as much progress as they could: henceforth the programme of the school was fixed in detail month by month, week by week. A child who moved from one town to another would thus miss nothing. Gréard, described by an admirer as a 'melancholy optimist', was descended from a long line of administrators, and he was a great believer in order, which he did his best to imprint on the schools. He was keen that they should not attempt to do too much: they must 'open access for everybody to careers where study is not necessary, they must give satisfaction to legitimate ambitions, but without over-exciting blind pretensions, which are as disappointing to individuals as they are fatal to society'. They must therefore be, first, practical and, secondly, moral. He wrote his thesis on 'Plutarch as a Moralist', whom he admired for preaching common virtues, in moderation and with no heroic element. Though serving the lay state, he was a Catholic, who regretted the decline in religious beliefs. He had been an efficient teacher of philosophy and 'he would have been a perfect man if he had ever consented to amuse himself'. This cultured, intelligent, methodical model of a civil servant told the *instituteurs* that they must make the schools enjoyable, but he had no fear that the systematic repetition he advocated might also breed boredom.[1] Of course, the 'concentric method' could barely be applied in small rural schools; and despite all ministerial injunctions, in 1906 it was estimated that at least 11 per cent of primary pupils were still being taught by some form of the Bell and Lancaster system, in which the older ones taught the younger ones. This had been forbidden over fifty years before, but died hard. Similarly, one should not imagine Gréard's instructions were accurately implemented.

Geography and history were seen as part of moral and civic education. The syllabus concentrated heavily on France; the fostering of pride in the national heritage, both human and physical, was the main purpose. There is no doubt that patriotism was advanced by these lessons. Good pupils memorised a large number of dates, names and statistics about their country; they could draw freehand a complete map of France, divided into departments, and insert the names of all the subprefectures. It was only in the junior form that world geography was studied; in the upper two forms, three-quarters of the lessons were on France. Reformers protested that the syllabus tried to make children memorise the directories of the post office, magistrature and army and the railway time-table; reforms were decreed, but in general the primary schools did not benefit from the brilliant development of French geography. A different plan prevailed in history teaching. The first two years were devoted to France, and the third to revision, plus the addition of ancient history from Egypt to Rome. The 'concentric method' required that the whole of French history be covered each year: in practice this meant that the French middle ages were taught and retaught most thoroughly—a strange result for the republic to achieve. The Merovingians who started the course got a month, as much as the Revolution, Consulate and Empire, which came last and was not always

---

[1] M. P. Bourgain, *Gréard, un moraliste éducateur* (1907) 64-5, 96, 113-14, 364; O. Gréard, *Éducation et instruction*, vol. 1; *Enseignement primaire* (1887); Farrington, op. cit., 101.

completed. There were demands from an early date that *Kulturgeschichte* should replace anecdotal history, but it is unlikely that any whisper of the *Annales* school ever reached the primary classes.[1] Instructions were repeatedly issued by the ministry, in history and in geography as also in the study of the French language, that the teachers must relate their lessons to the experience of their pupils, that Ferry's formula, *la leçon de choses,* should replace the theoretical memorising. But, as the ministry's instructions of 1945 themselves stated, these orders were seldom carried out: 'Too often, *la leçon de choses* came down to the study of a textbook or a summary: the pupils remember only words which have no meaning for them. So exercises which could make an important contribution to their intellectual development are valueless and even harmful.'[2]

Another way by which the schools and the outside world were supposed to be linked was manual education. This was inspired partly by the thesis of Rousseau, Pestalozzi, Froebel and Fourier, but even more it was seen as a practical answer to France's industrial problems, to the decline of apprenticeship, and to the fear that the best pupils of the primary schools would increasingly try to become officials or clerks. The republican worker-author Corbon, in his book *Professional Education* (1859), criticised the traditional apprentice who simply knew his little speciality and had no aspirations after improving his mind; he demanded that the schools should combine education with professional training, to produce a sort of workers' *culture générale*.[3] These ideas were taken up by G. Salicis, a junior teacher at the Polytechnic, who in 1873 got an official grant to start manual education experimentally in one Paris school. In 1882 Ferry made it a compulsory part of every primary syllabus and appointed Salicis inspector-general in charge. The teachers used were artisans, paid by the hour; the numbers of hours devoted to the subject was gradually increased as the children grew older. A model school of a new kind, with even more emphasis on manual work (so that boys in their final year spent nearly the whole of their time on it) was founded at

---

[1] H. Lemonnier, *L'Enseignement de l'histoire dans les écoles primaires* (1889); P. Dupuy, *La Géographie dans l'enseignement primaire* (1889).

[2] Instructions of 1945, quoted by Prost, 279.

[3] A. Corbon, *De l'enseignement professionnelle* (1859).

Vierzon. Altogether, 12,000 schools tried it out (which shows once again how 'compulsory' subjects could be ignored by the majority). Only half of them had properly equipped workshops; the amateur teachers proved unsatisfactory; so an attempt was made to train ordinary *instituteurs* in manual work, which they resented, because it meant going on compulsory vacation courses. A special training college was founded but closed down two years later for lack of funds. Salicis argued that it was contradictory that the infant schools should develop manual dexterity and that the primary schools should then largely forget about it; but the tendency towards theory was too powerful for him. After his death in 1889, manual work became less and less manual. René Leblanc, editor of a journal, *L'Enseignement manuel*, began preaching that it should be regarded as part of science, as an intellectual training, and that once it became so, the *instituteurs* would drop their opposition to it. His ideas were adopted by the city of Paris, which abandoned the preparation for professional training and replaced it by simpler activities, like making objects out of paper; freed from any industrial purpose, it was made almost a part of geometry. But this does not seem to have had much effect outside Paris, where the whole idea languished. In rural areas, manual work became almost entirely agriculture, but this was kept theoretical: 'The child has in his head the names of grasses he has never seen, of fertilisers of whose composition and properties he is alike ignorant.' The most interesting work in manual education was probably done in a few private establishments, like that founded at Creil by the industrialist Somasco.[1]

Instead, the academic status of the primary system was strengthened by its extension beyond the education of young children by means of *écoles primaires supérieures*, which could keep pupils until the age of 17. These schools had two sections, general and professional, but the vast majority of pupils enrolled in the general courses, so that it was essentially an academic education that they received. The only difference between these schools and the *lycées* was that they claimed to adapt their syllabus to industry and commerce, and in fact they trained

[1] A. Panthier, *Enquête historique sur l'enseignement manuel dans les écoles non techniques* (1906); G. Salicis, *Enseignement du travail manuel* (1889); René Leblanc, *L'Enseignement professionnel en France au début du 20ᵉ siècle* (1905).

the growing body of clerks and junior supervisory ranks. They
were accordingly very successful; they got the most ambitious
pupils of the primary schools. In 1890 there were 296 of them;
in 1937, 579. Some reached a very high standard and prepared,
with excellent results, for the *baccalauréat*. The model was the
Collège Chaptal, which attempted to copy the German
*Realschulen*: founded in 1844, it expanded until by 1877 it had
1,300 pupils. In the early Third Republic several imitations of it
were established in Paris and gradually the provinces followed
suit. Some primary schools simply offered a 'cours complé-
mentaire', which had the advantage that no fixed syllabus was
officially laid down for it and this was one of the few areas in
which local initiative had more or less free rein. But the teachers
were the ordinary *instituteurs*. The *écoles primaires supérieures*, by
contrast, developed into a self-contained system, with their own
teachers trained to a higher level and earning more. Increasingly
they performed much the same function as the 'modern'
sections of the *lycées*. The aim of the inventors of these schools
was thus foiled: these were schools for the people, but they did
not provide technical training. Technical education had to be
started as an independent system. Thus the number of parallel
systems multiplied, each living its own life, not quite as though
inhabiting different countries, but proud of its own approach
and values. This was all the odder, because in fact they were
moving closer in what they taught.[1]

## New Methods

Not surprisingly, therefore, there were protests against these
traditions and some interesting experiments were undertaken
in order to correct their shortcomings; but if one is studying
schoolchildren as a whole, one must at once admit that the
experiments affected only a small minority of them, and a very
small minority of teachers. For in these years France lost its
leadership in educational ideas. It produced only a few of the
major educational figures of the century, and much of its
innovation consisted in borrowing from the more adventurous

---

[1] This is a sphere of education of which no history has been written. For the
origins, see O. Gréard, op. cit. 139–72; statistics in A. de Mouzie and L. Febvre,
*Encyclopédie française*, vol. 15 (1939), chapter 1.

experiments in the U.S.A., Switzerland, Germany and England. But there was considerable resistance to such borrowing, and when borrowings were made, for example, from Froebel, or from Baden-Powell, a lot of effort was spent pointing out that the French adaptation was specifically French, purged of nasty foreign elements. The xenophobia was by no means general: one is struck by the very considerable knowledge of foreign work which the leading educationists showed. Buisson was as well informed as anyone in the world about what was going on abroad, and he had visited many foreign countries. Education might well have been the subject in which knowledge of foreign developments was greatest: the reports on foreign educational systems, by official investigators, came out at regular intervals.[1] What is significant is that comparatively little resulted from all this interest.

The first move was to look at education more from the point of view of the child, to see what he wanted from it and to measure how far he was getting it. Progress in child psychology did not necessarily and immediately lead to changes in school methods, first because the new ideas were controversial, and secondly because they were studied for themselves, with little emphasis on practical application.[2] This is what Alfred Binet (1857–1911) tried to put right. He had studied in turn law, medicine, histology (his thesis was on the Nervous Intestinal System of Insects (1894)) and finally psychology. He was struck by the way discussion of educational questions was so often based on purely subjective polemic, without any effort to collect facts scientifically. He vigorously criticised in particular a debate held at the Academy of Medicine on overwork in schools, complaining that the statistical and medical observations were largely lacking. He wrote a book on *Intellectual Exhaustion* (1898) which concluded that no conclusion was possible until a great deal more research was done. He called for a *new pedagogy*, which would break away from the *old*, which he condemned as 'too generalising, too vague, too literary, too moralising, too verbalistic, too preaching . . . It solves the

---

[1] For example, see the work of C. Hippeau, *L'Instruction publique aux États-Unis* (1869), *L'Instruction publique en Angleterre* (1872), . . . *en Allemagne* (1873), . . . *en Italie* (1874), . . . *en Suède, Norvège et Danemark* (1876), etc.

[2] For the psychology of children, see vol. 1, ch. 12, and vol. 2, chs. 15–17.

gravest problems by literary quotations from Quintilian and Bossuet; it replaces facts by exhortations and sermons; the word which characterises it best is *verbiage*'—an approach hardly conducive to winning him friends among the more or less conservative teachers. In 1899 Buisson and he founded the Société libre pour l'étude psychologique de l'enfant, renamed the Société Alfred Binet after his death, to inaugurate a new method, founded on observation and experiment. Here he first tried using questionnaires (borrowed from the American Stanley Hall) but since these often produced unconvincing results—they were rather inefficiently administered—he took to organising research by teams, each to solve a particular problem. These teams studied an enormous variety of subjects, such as methods of teaching writing, reading, spelling, and of preventing laziness etc. As a basis for all this, Binet, with his disciples Simon and Vanney, developed the intelligence test, which was to be his most celebrated achievement, as well as other scales for measuring educational attainment. People recognised that Binet's intentions were admirably scientific, but there was no denying that the immediate results of his investigations were not as helpful as his fine-sounding manifesto had led them to hope. Binet often had to admit that he had made mistakes which invalidated his work: it was one of his merits that he never hesitated to make these admissions publicly. Some complained that he used a great deal of effort to prove what was obvious: Binet held complicated experiments to prove that his intelligence tests were less arbitrary than the marks of teachers in examinations, but he aroused vigorous opposition. He had a long controversy in 1907 with Jules Payot, who was then editor of *Le Volume*, a weekly journal for *instituteurs*. Payot had launched an attack on dictation and spelling, arguing that children remembered whole words, rather than built them up from individual letters. Binet refused to accept as evidence simply the general impressions Payot adduced on the basis of his long experience as an inspector. He insisted on devising tests, and these proved that the teaching of spelling was useful. Vitriolic attacks were exchanged in the process. He also tried to prove that children who started to read at the age of six—as the kindergarten movement was urging—did no worse than those who began at five, as the primary school officials demanded.

He invaded a multitude of subjects sanctified by tradition and taught by highly experienced teachers, casting doubts on almost sacred principles like the examination system and even the religious neutrality of lay schools. He asked searching questions: he demanded an inquiry into whether neutrality was in fact achieved and, if so, what exact consequences it had on the mentality of children. Binet's importance came from an extra-ordinary capacity to detach himself from the accepted plati-tudes of his time, but he had never actually taught in a school, or indeed anywhere, so that he could be accused of being out of touch with reality. Nevertheless, his work encouraged a new way of approaching the problem of the abilities and aptitudes of children. It was to yield fruits also in more effective vocational guidance, and in the establishment of schools for sub-normal children—a subject which particularly interested him. But the linking of the psychological investigations his disciples pursued, and actual educational reform, was a slow business.[1]

More immediately effective was the work of Roger Cousinet, who was able, as an inspector of primary schools, and therefore in close touch with the *instituteurs*, to start experiments in group methods, first in Sedan (1920) and then in thirty-seven schools in Paris. The schools were not completely reorganised, according to the principles advocated by the *École Nouvelle* movement, of which he was a leading light, and the pupils were given only a certain degree of participation in the running of their work. The idea behind this was that children should be encouraged to work in small teams, guided by their own interests and apti-tudes, rather than sit passively in large classes. The initial experiment appears to have been a failure, both because the children found it difficult to adapt to this new demand on their initiative, and because the *instituteurs* complained that the new method increased instead of diminishing their hours of work. Cousinet had more success in applying group methods to play, as opposed to work.[2] At about the same time Profit, inspector of primary schools at Saint-Jean-d'Angély, introduced

[1] François Zuza, *Alfred Binet et la pédagogie expérimentale* (Louvain, 1948), contains a good bibliography. See especially A. Binet, *Les Idées modernes sur les enfants* (1909); F. L. Bertrand, *Alfred Binet et son œuvre* (1930).

[2] Roger Cousinet, 'Petite chronologie de l'éducation nouvelle', *L'École nouvelle française* (Mar. 1954); R. Cousinet and F. Chatelain, 'L'État présent de l'éduca-tion nouvelle', ibid. (Oct. 1953); P. Foulquié, *Les Écoles nouvelles* (1948).

the co-operative idea into the schools of his district (1918), making the children themselves create school museums and organise scientific experiments on their own. This was designed to turn the school into the children's own institution. In 1939 some 9,000 such co-operatives were in existence, of varying effectiveness.[1]

The history of these efforts has still to be written, but just how much trouble an advocate of anti-authoritarian ideas could have was shown by the career of Freinet. Cousinet was an inspector who eventually won considerable administrative power, but even that was not enough to get his ideas adopted on more than a trial basis. Freinet was a humble *instituteur*, who worked on his own. Freinet never had any official pedagogical training, having followed a shortened course at an *école normale* after the 1914–18 war. He was the son of a peasant and a washerwoman; he suffered from tuberculosis; his weak health made traditional methods, with the teacher as orator, impractical for him. In 1920 he was appointed assistant *instituteur* at the little village of Bar-sur-Couz (Alpes-Maritimes). The headmaster was one of the old type of peasant-teachers, who knew, with no worries about technique, how to get his pupils through examinations and who spent half his time in the fields. Freinet read Pestalozzi, and Ferrière; he met Cousinet at the International Congress of the New Education; he was interested by Marx, Lenin, anarchism and the Geneva psychologists. But the theories he learnt about seemed too grandiose for his hovel of a school and he was not at home in the 'laboratory' atmosphere of the intellectual discussions of pedagogy. He wanted simply to do the best he could for the children in his school, to liberate them from the repressions forced on them by the traditional methods, with the ultimate goal of thereby renovating society as a whole. His first act was to abandon textbooks, which he denounced as contributing to 'the idolatry of the printed word, as a world apart, as something almost divine, whose assertions one always hesitates to dispute'; they killed the critical faculties, and enslaved the teachers, who used them to further the cult of examinations. With his meagre savings, he bought a printing press and made printing the centre of the

[1] Georges Prévot, *Pédagogie de la coopération scolaire* (1960); B. Profit, *La Coopération à l'école primaire* (1922); F. and L. Cattier, *Les Coopératives scolaires* (1937).

children's school activity: he used it to teach the child to distinguish between letters, to understand punctuation, and in discussion of the proofs, grammar and style could be studied with direct interest, because the children printed their own reading material, in the form of a school newspaper. In this way he hoped to salvage 'the treasures of good sense and originality' of humble people, to enable the child to educate himself, with the help of a teacher in the background.

He was an anarchist-communist, so he was not satisfied with the people like Ferrière who thought the ideal school could be established: Freinet insisted that a reorganisation of society was necessary first. He was keen to produce a unity between the school and life outside, to make the children accept that they would be workers, rather than try to become something else. Thus he complained that the teaching of mathematics was concerned with the problems of merchants, speculators and civil servants—with problems of profits and sales and interest—and that it needed fundamental reform. He began exchanging his school newspaper with other schools who took up the same idea: by 1939 there were several hundred of them. Freinet had to move from his village to a larger one, so as to get a double job with his wife, who was also a teacher and who assisted him with the increasing administrative labours involved in running what had become a sizeable movement. When he began, he had been unable to afford the paper for the printing, and only the friendship of the mayor's secretary enabled him to start on the back of voting ballots left over from an election. Now the production of printing presses, of newspapers, of a filing-card system which he started, to replace textbooks, showed how much unofficial action could achieve. But his political involvement aroused opposition in his new post. His inspector complained that his pupils knew none of the dates of ancient history, that they sat where they pleased, that the disorder in the classroom was anarchic. Quarrels with parents and local officials ended in riots, which led to his suspension. The administration had tolerated, even encouraged, him in his first post, but the limits of its tolerance were now revealed: it could not absorb an extreme left-wing movement. In 1940 Freinet was arrested. His was probably the most exciting achievement of an individual teacher in the interwar period. But it affected only a few.

Purged of its politics, so far as was possible, it was partially absorbed by the *Éducation Nouvelle* movement. After 1945 this became quasi-official, with headquarters in the Musée pédagogique: Freinet had become increasingly hostile to it, seeing in it a hideout of products of the bourgeois secondary system. The reformers were almost as bitterly divided amongst themselves as they were opposed to the traditional system.[1]

The history of France's education produces the same conclusion as the history of its politics, that the theories propagated do not provide an accurate guide to what actually happened. The educational world was full of bright ideas, of constant demand for reform, of innumerable projects; rival factions, speaking in the name of religion, morals, freedom, modernity and other causes, fought against each other in a whole array of specialist periodicals. But one needs to look beyond the legislators and inspectors in order to judge the effects of the schools. It certainly cannot be said that France lacked able men at the head of its educational system, but it may be questioned whether these were not, to a considerable degree, prisoners of the system they served. Because teachers and those interested in education vented their grievances in public, the paralysing effects of administrative hierarchy, centralisation and routine can be seen here with exceptional clarity. Thus for example, the inspectorate which controlled large parts of the system often succeeded in obstructing experiment and adaptation to local conditions, because its function was to ensure that the rules were obeyed; but its knowledge of what was going on was often superficial, and one is also amazed at the extent to which the rules were disobeyed. The inspectors appointed before 1880 seldom had direct experience of primary teaching; they were usually men who had escaped from secondary teaching into the quieter havens of administration; they were invariably ageing, if not old. The inspectors-general throughout this period had hardly ever worked in primary schools: they of course were never young and were so busy writing letters and reports that they had time only for rapid tours in the provinces. Their

[1] Élise Freinet, *Naissance d'une pédagogie populaire. Histoire de l'école moderne (Méthodes Freinet)* (1968), is a lively biography by his widow. Cf. Freinet, *L'École moderne française* (1945).

custom seems to have been to come in the fine weather of spring, summon all the local inspectors, get them to fill in long question-naires: every chief had to write a personal appreciation of his subordinate: every official had to report, in triplicate, that he still had the same name and birthday as at the last inspection; and when all this paper had been collected, the inspector-general selected one school in the whole academy to look at, which was regarded as typical and which was decisive for his assessment of the situation. That was how uniformity and blindness to the lack of it were simultaneously preserved; and the existence of this rigid hierarchy of course meant that everyone was able to disclaim responsibility for what happened.

It was not easy to make suggestions for really fundamental changes, because universal education and the republic became inextricably identified with each other, and few people there-fore dared say that the system was a source of confusion as well as of new opportunities.[1] But the administrators should not be blamed for its defects without it being added that they could not respond favourably to all the contradictory pressures upon them. If they were accused by the left of enforcing an excessively traditional or bourgeois syllabus, they could answer that the workers were very uncertain as to what they would put in its place. This was forcibly revealed when the Institut Supérieur Ouvrier was founded in the 1930s, to revive the old *universités populaires* (which had appeared and quickly died at the turn of the century) but this time with the aim of doing without bourgeois co-operation, going beyond the system of unconnected lectures, and establishing team-work, in the image of the society of the future. It turned out that even this militant minority of workers were not quite clear whether they did want a separate 'workers' culture' or not. In 1935 only about 2,000 people were induced to participate in their grand-sounding experiment, Zoretti, who was a leading theorist of mass education, spoke rather vaguely of group methods, but could think of nothing more original than football (as a means of 'concretising ideas of collective discipline and mastering the excess of indivi-dualism'), or scouting, rebaptised the Red Falcons, with its

[1] Cf. Ch. Drouard, *Les Écoles urbaines* (2nd edition, 1902), 72; T. Nandy, *L'Enseignement primaire et ce qu'il devrait être* (7ᵉ Cahiers de la quinzaine, 14ᵉ série, 1913).

leaders obligatorily members of the Confédération Générale du Travail or the socialist party.[1]

Similarly, parents did not know what they wanted. Liberal complaints about the schools' disciplinary methods were certainly justified. There was a flagrant contradiction between the schools' desire to develop fraternity and morality and their encouragement of competitiveness, which they took over uncritically from the past. Success in academic work was what had got the teachers where they were, and they praised it as the highest of goals. The award of marks in every exercise, the constant classification of pupils by order of merit, the obsession with examinations, introduced a new factor into popular culture. (The certificate of primary studies was introduced, unsuccessfully, in 1834, reactivated in 1866 and finally made a national, as opposed to a local, award in 1880; later, a variety of more senior certificates were added.) This was perhaps the key instrument that subordinated primary school children to values of those who were more privileged than themselves. Almost automatically it was designed to breed frustration or disappointment in children who did not come first: it pitilessly subjected whole generations of less-endowed children to repeated public humiliations. The theory of meritocracy did not concern itself overmuch with those who were unsuccessful, though they formed a high proportion of the pupils. The elaborate system of rewards and punishments reduced morals to a form of accountancy: good points or tickets were granted in every lesson, and others for general behaviour, punctuality and various virtues: each week these points could be exchanged for *billets de satisfactions;* they were used almost as current coin, to pay for points lost by inattentiveness or other faults, though serious offences were not redeemable in this way. All this compensated for an important achievement of Napoleon's, which more or less effectively abolished corporal punishment. But it does not appear that there was any serious opposition from parents to these methods. On the contrary, many parents, in their effort to keep recalcitrant children under control, pressed for even firmer and more authoritarian punishments by the schools. The educators felt therefore that they had to

[1] L. Zoretti, *Pour l'éducation des masses* (1935); Maurice Poussin, *L'Éducation populaire et le socialisme* (1933); Lucien Gachon, *Les Écoles du peuple* (1942).

educate parents. The École des Parents, founded in 1928 by Madame Vérine, sought to reconcile the old principles of paternal authority with new ideas about the autonomy and personality of the child: it held annual congresses and organised lectures, and in 1942–3 it obtained a state subsidy. But when in 1956 it carried out an inquiry among its 'correspondents', 60 per cent of these still said that they used 'authoritarian' methods with their children, including corporal punishment; 20 per cent said they had tried all methods, including liberal ones. Only 14 per cent said they had lost faith in authoritarian methods and only 21 per cent said they believed in liberal methods. The three great worries of parents regarding children were given as their *nervosité*, their poor academic results and indiscipline, though it is true that worry about school results was eight times more frequent with boys than with girls.[1] The teachers could thus be said to have contributed to the general atmosphere of anxiety. It should be added that most parents who expressed opinions were middle class, and the anxiety probably only gradually spread down the social scale.

Employers, for their part, clamoured for more practical teaching from the schools and less theory. They seemed to have little regard for the knowledge the primary schools provided. Michelin in 1911, advertising jobs in his factory, said that all he demanded from recruits was a good character, honesty and ambition: he would undertake to teach them what they needed to know to do their work. Private employers, often without formal educational qualifications themselves, were most ready to ignore school results; but increasingly the possession of paper qualifications was required, even though they were despised.[2]

The quarrel about church participation in education was part of this general ambivalence towards the schools. The republicans, like the Catholics, wanted everyone to have the same kind of education: both sides tried to force all children into the same mould; neither appears to have had public opinion behind it. In 1850 the situation was that boys went predominantly to state schools, but 50 per cent of girls went to

[1] André Isambert, *L'Éducation des parents* (1959, 2nd edition 1968), 62; C. Hippeau, *L'Éducation et l'instruction considérées dans leurs rapports avec le bien-être social et le perfectionnement de l'esprit humain* (1885), 181.

[2] Pierre Dufrenne, *La Réforme de l'école primaire* (1919), 71.

schools run by religious orders. In 1848 there were only 2,136 male church teachers (*frères*) but 10,371 female ones (*sœurs*) By 1863 these numbers trebled to 7,161 *frères* and 36,397 *sœurs*; and by 1875 roughly one-quarter of boys were being taught by the *frères* and two-thirds of the girls by *sœurs*. In the eight years 1852–60 alone, the nuns involved in girls' education received no less than 10 million francs in donations, and they were able to buy property worth 23 million francs. This was at a time when the state was spending only about 6 million francs a year, while parents contributed 18 million in fees (1862). One cannot conclude that these facts necessarily mean that the majority of parents wanted their children educated by nuns, because they were not always given a free choice, but despite the admitted incompetence and ignorance of many of the nuns, who were usually totally untrained, they enjoyed considerable popularity. The effect of the republic was to give most boys and girls the same education. By 1914 boys were almost entirely taught by laymen and only a quarter of girls remained in church schools. This was achieved very gradually, because the government, having proclaimed the principle, had to accept that local opinion often would not accept its policy. The laicisation of schools between 1879 and 1890 was carried out at a rate of only 600 schools a year, and at half that rate after then: not until 1897 did the last boys' school run by a religious order disappear. But there were then still over 5,000 girls' schools run by nuns, and in addition some 7,000 nuns were teaching in state schools, principally in Catholic regions. The second wave of anti-clericalism succeeded in closing down the remaining church schools, but about 60 per cent of them immediately reappeared with their teachers 'secularised', that is, nominally lay.[1] So the Church managed to retain about 20 per cent of primary school children. This meant, not that there was a small minority of dissidents dotted thinly around the country but rather that certain regions refused to accept the laicisation. In 1914 in the department of Morbihan, 48·9 per cent of pupils were in Catholic

[1] Maurice Gontard, *Les Écoles primaires de la France bourgeoise 1833–75* (Toulouse, 1964), 133; id., *L'Œuvre scolaire de la troisième république: l'enseignement primaire en France de 1876 à 1914* (Toulouse, 1967), 118. These works, as well as M. Gontard's *La Question des écoles normales primaires* (Toulouse, 1964) and his thesis, *L'Enseignement primaire en France 1789–1833* (1959), provide the fullest history of the subject, and are indispensable.

schools, while only 2 per cent in the Basses-Alpes were. In 1965 the eight westernmost departments of France had between 35 and 49 per cent of their children in Catholic schools, and certain regions of the north and centre had between 15 and 34 per cent.[1] The ideal of uniformity was thus only partially attained. Many people were still willing to pay for a religious education, even when a free public one was available, and this shows the failure of the republic to create a new morality which would effectively reconcile and sum up the basic belief of the nation. There was no such thing. The war against church education was also a war against patois, which was another reason why it was resented. 'The clergy', wrote Duruz in 1866, 'make it a matter of conscience to fight French as the language of impiety. [The Alsatian dialect], one of them has said, is a preservative against dangerous books and a safeguard against religious indifference.' A Breton priest declared: 'It is in French that evil books are published.' The victory of the republic was supposed to be a victory for a uniform Parisian culture.[2]

That is what it superficially seemed to be, and partly was, but one must not accept this without further investigation. It is usual to sum up the results of the spread of primary education by graphs showing the decline of illiteracy. Illiteracy, which was already diminishing very rapidly under the Second Empire, fell from 14·6 per cent in 1882 to 4·3 per cent in 1900 for men, and from 22·6 per cent to 6·3 per cent for women. But the tests of illiteracy were so simple that they meant little. Full attendance at school up to the age of 13 was not really achieved in this period: it needed the establishment of family allowances to prevent parents being forced to send their children out to work. In 1902 only one half of France's communes had carried out the provisions of the law of 1882 requiring them to establish *caisses d'écoles* to help poor children with the expenses of schooling.[3] So, though in 1914 the official method of classifying illiterates led the army to call only 1·92 of its conscripts illiterate, further

---

[1] See map in Prost, 479, and for a study of the obstacles to laicisation, Bernard Ménager, *La Laïcisation des écoles communales dans le département du Nord 1879–99* (Lille, 1971).

[2] Pierre Zind, *L'Enseignement religieux dans l'instruction primaire publique en France de 1850 à 1873* (Lyon, 1971), 249. But contrast M. Bréal, *Les Langues vivantes dans l'enseignement primaire* (1889), 2–3, which urges acceptance of patois by the schools.

[3] Farrington, op. cit. 48.

interrogation caused it to say that 35 per cent had an 'education which is nil or inadequate', in that they could barely do more than read and write in the most elementary fashion.[1] In 1920, the figure went up to 41 per cent. Marc Sangnier carried out some tests on conscripts in 1920 which showed how little of what the schools taught was remembered. History and geography in particular seem to have been totally forgotten: the most widely known fact was that Gambetta escaped by balloon from Paris, but many also believed that Napoleon had been burnt alive at St. Helena. This does not mean that the conscripts had no political or other opinions, and were not capable of expressing them forcefully and clearly, particularly in conversation.[2] It is important to discover just what these opinions were, what the school did not teach. Another chapter will suggest that the oral traditional culture of the nation survived more powerfully than is realised, and that what the schools attempted to inculcate was frequently shrugged off, or continued to live side by side, only half assimilated, with a totally different set of beliefs.[3]

One must weigh all this against the obvious fact that, in the course of this period, primary education came to be accepted, and demanded, as the essential basis of human dignity and equality, that it became the indispensable stepping-stone to advancement and social mobility, and that by joining forces with ambition, it emerged as one of the forces which affected society most powerfully.

---

[1] This compares with the 25 per cent of the men enlisted into the U.S. Army classified as being unable to read a newspaper or write a letter home. E. Ginsburg and D. W. Bray, *The Uneducated* (1953).

[2] See Beigbeder, op. cit. 166, 289.                    [3] See chapter 9.

# 5. Logic and Verbalism

IT may be that the mark by which one could recognise a Frenchman was often not so much his appearance—for that varied enormously—not necessarily even the fact that he spoke French—since not all did, and besides French had, to a certain extent, succeeded Latin as the universal language—but something much deeper and much subtler: the way he used language, the way he thought, the way he argued. This was by no means true of all Frenchmen and the traditional generalisation about their being logical or 'Cartesian' cannot be accepted at its face value, but it points to a genuine idiosyncrasy, which requires explanation. This was something of which the French were both very proud and mercilessly, if slightly ingenuously, critical. In 1871 Amiel wrote in his diary: 'The French always place a school of thought, a formula, convention, *a priori* arguments, abstraction, and artificiality above reality; they prefer clarity to truth, words to things, rhetoric to science . . . They understand nothing though they chop logic about everything. They are clever at distinguishing, classifying, perorating, but they stop at the threshold of philosophy . . . They emerge from description only to hurl themselves into precipitate generalisations. They imagine they understand man in his entirety, whereas they cannot break the hard shell of their personalities, and they do not understand a single nation apart from themselves.'[1]

The institution which specialised in developing, instilling and defending these qualities was the secondary school system. But one should not simplistically imagine that one can explain a national characteristic, or what passed for one, by showing that teachers professed it and pupils memorised it. The behaviour of certain groups was wrongly held up as being typical of the nation. The schools may have been maintained by the taxes, or the fees, of the rich, but they did not obediently serve their

[1] F. Amiel, Journal intime, 30 September 1871, quoted by A. Canivez, *J. Lagneau* (1965), 289.

interests. The theory that the rise of capitalist industrialisation caused education to serve capitalist ends, and no longer aristocratic or religious ones, does not fit the facts, if only because, as has been shown, capitalist power had not attained anything like supremacy in this period. The sociological platitude that every society's education reflects its values is equally impossible to use as a guiding explanation, because of the infinitely fragmented nature of French society, which allowed the teachers to develop their own independent values, peculiar to themselves. It has become common practice to write the history of French education in social terms, with the question of class bias as the dominating theme, the moral being that the principal function of the schools—rigidly divided into bourgeois and plebeian ones—was to maintain class divisions. There is much to be learnt from such a perspective, but it is also a misleading one, as misleading as the older perspective it has largely displaced, which saw education as a battle of enlightenment against obscurantism, with the fight about religious schools as central and decisive.

The history of education, perhaps more than any other form of history, has been captured by other disciplines and made subservient to politics, or sociology, or, not least, the hagiographical self-esteem of the teachers themselves. This book will argue, by contrast, that while industrialisation increased, parallel with it and largely independent of it, 'educationism' developed. This period was the age of education, and of educational illusions, as much as of industry and the transformations it produced. In France, in particular, the teachers, and politicians who followed them, made claims on behalf of education to challenge those of industry. At certain times, when the educational budget grew to unprecedented levels, when key positions in the state were held by schoolmasters, whose knowledge of philosophy or literature had somehow appeared to open all doors, it did indeed seem as though a new mandarinate had seized power. But the idea that they came to dominate the country was an illusion, a figment of their own imaginations, to which the loudness of their mutual praise and their near-monopoly of the written word gave a superficial plausibility. The extent of their influence reached only as far as they could see, and that was not far, for they lived in a closed world.

Their idealism, in any case, was rudely shattered by their head-on crash with reality in the two world wars of the twentieth century. After these, the self-proclaimed age of the mandarin vanished like a dream. The doctrine of the post-war era was productivity, and the new hero was the industrialist, the businessman, the materialist. These had been firmly entrenched in their own way of life all the while.

To understand the complex preoccupations which the secondary schools expressed, one must pull apart their different, and by no means mutually sustaining, activities, and look very closely at what they taught, and how they did it. A great deal is revealed, first of all, by philosophy, their crowning glory. French schools distinguished themselves from those of most of Europe by teaching philosophy to children; the senior forms in the secondary schools were the *classes de philosophie*. This was highly significant. To finish off their education, the élite of the nation were neither given responsibility as prefects, nor encouraged into athletic distractions, as were British children, but instead were offered a very peculiar intellectual training. It is easy to argue from this that the philosophy class was the means by which the influence of Descartes was perpetuated, and with official blessing, for the class was a state institution. It was there that Frenchmen learned their characteristic abstract and pompous vocabulary, their skill in classification and synthesis, in solving problems by rearranging them verbally, their rationalism and scepticism—paradoxically conformist—and their ability to argue elegantly and apparently endlessly. But this requires much more careful scrutiny.

The philosophy class was born by accident. Philosophy was a subject which originally was taught in the faculties of arts. In the fifteenth century, schools, attempting to make good the deficiencies of the decadent universities, began teaching it, so that it was no longer limited to clerics studying theology. But only the very best, most prosperous schools had the resources for this luxury: it was impossible for them to develop any really independent doctrines or methods of their own, so they remained in the medieval tradition. Philosophy, supposedly the instrument of rational liberation of the schoolboy, thus in fact kept him firmly tied to the past. Medieval philosophy was not a method of making discoveries or of advancing knowledge. All

that could be known was known and the philosopher confined
himself to exposing the truth, to inventing or tabulating
objections to it, and then to refuting these. It did not involve
research, but only disputation. It sought not to unshackle the
mind but to inculcate uncontested dogmas; it provided intellectual security and a ready way of handling all that threatened
this. It was for most people essentially a game, a sporting
activity for those who did not engage in real-life battles. It
certainly called for, and its practice developed, skills which were
valued in scholastic circles: philosophers had to have not only
knowledge, but also quickness of wit, vigour and aggressiveness
in disputation, self-possession, a certain showmanship, a love
of competition but also of communal life. Inevitably, superficial cleverness, the appearance of thoughtfulness combined
with a tireless verbosity, the ability to dispute about anything,
publicly and at all times, were the criteria of success. Arguments were therefore cultivated for their own sake, not from
an interest in truth; a complete lack of intellectual curiosity
was easily compatible with this verbal fencing; books existed
mainly as arsenals of arguments. This scholastic philosophy was
not dead in the nineteenth century. Both Cousin and Cournot
praised it, because, as will be seen, their view of philosophy was
not all that different. There can be no doubt, besides, that
scholasticism did teach people to express their thoughts, to
spread the conviction that conduct must be based on principles,
that principles could be discovered in all conduct, and that
the discussion of these was more important, or more interesting,
than action itself. The form in which arguments were presented
was given much attention. Some cultivated obscurity, jargon
and subtleties incomprehensible to outsiders. Others laid all
stress on beautiful presentation, turning philosophy into
rhetoric. This was a conflict which remained throughout the
centuries, for the scholastic tradition was by no means uniform.
The rhetorical strand in it was absorbed into the cult of the
humanities, which, after the Renaissance, became more
fashionable than philosophy. But in the eighteenth century,
though the mere professor of philosophy had sunk to the status
of a contemptible pedant, the *philosophe* emerged in a new guise,
as a man of the world who could discuss all subjects—a genera-
list rather than a specialist—who appealed to common sense

and to all classes, and who was at home equally in literature, science and art. It might appear that the greatest change of all was that the *philosophe* now revolted systematically against accepted ideas but though this was true, to a certain extent, as far as the leading lights were concerned, humbler imitators, following in their footsteps, adopted their poses in studiously conformist ways: they had discovered a new way of arguing. One is still dealing, however, with a very small number of people: philosophers were rare birds; in 1812 the subject was taught only in about sixty schools, and only eleven of these had enough pupils to warrant distributing prizes in the subject. It was only in the course of the nineteenth century that the French state took to creating a special class of civil servants who were professional philosophers in public pay, charged with multiplying their kind or at least giving schoolboys an outward philosophical veneer before they went out into the world. France was the only country in Europe to make philosophising a career, paying a good salary, and to have enough of these official philosophers, distributed over the whole country, for them to form a significant social and intellectual force.

This profession owed its growth first to the fact that it claimed the mission of defending the *status quo*, of reconciling the traditions of the past with the needs of the present, and of showing civilisation the dangers that menaced it. The man who set it up in this role was Victor Cousin, probably the most influential French philosopher of the nineteenth century, influential far beyond the boundaries of his specialisation, and the first of the species to become a minister.[1] He controlled the training and appointment of philosophy teachers during the July Monarchy and the Second Empire, long enough to imprint a lasting pattern on them, and he gave them a powerful protection which allowed their high pretensions to take root. Cousin developed a philosophical syllabus for schools which survived in its essentials for a hundred and thirty years. His own works remained as set books till 1880, and when they were dethroned, they were replaced by those of his faithful disciple Jouffroy, which survived till 1927—a typical piece of bogus modernisation. Cousin entrenched philosophy so firmly in the schools because he deliberately adapted it to the tastes of the

[1] For a fuller discussion of Victor Cousin, see below, 409–11.

middle classes, whom he recognised as being firmly conservative in moral attitudes; by making it the most important subject in the final examination of the *baccalauréat*, he gave it official status as the necessary hallmark of an educated man. But though the schools were told to teach little more than common sense, the distilled wisdom of the past and the slick skills of classification, there was the constant worry that they were undermining religion, for reason was regarded as a dangerous instrument. Philosophy was under heavy attack from the right wing up to the 1880s, and particularly during the Restoration and the Second Empire. Its teachers were spied on and denounced; their opinions were minutely studied by the authorities and the slightest suggestion of nonconformity could lead to their disgrace. Cousin warned his regiment that even a hint of irreligion would lead to instant dismissal. He has been much maligned for this, but if he had not protected the profession in this way, it would never have been given the chance to establish its roots. Moreover, Cousin's rule was never as complete as it appeared to be: the emissaries of reason were really quite few in number: he once claimed he had 200 of them, but a truer figure was 75. It was the distinction of many of them, the amount they talked about each other and got themselves talked about that gave the impression of a national force. The capacity to blow up their own importance was something they never lost.

Under Napoleon III, a terrified government for a time abolished philosophy altogether in schools, as too dangerous in a time of crisis. Cousin was attacked by some of his former pupils with a savagery that academic life was already developing. Amédée Jacques was sacked for atheism, which he admitted; Vacherot preached the very opposite of Cousin's eclecticism, that reason, faith and observation yielded different kinds of knowledge which could never be reconciled, and he was sacked too; Taine, and a number of lesser men, were penalised for challenging orthodoxy. But despite the flowering of all these dangerous doctrines, the philosophers persuaded the government that their subject was indispensable. In 1863, when philosophy was restored to the *baccalauréat*, it was Cousin's syllabus that was revived: his tradition was too firm to dislodge. As the profession grew, control over its uniformity became less and less possible. Lachelier (1832–1918) was perhaps the last man to attempt to hold the teachers within a mental framework that perpetuated the ideals of Cousin. Lachelier, the inspector-general in charge of the subject, ran the *agrégation* examinations on the principle that all that could be said in philosophy had been said, there was no more to discover or invent, and what teachers needed to do was simply to present the known facts in a lively way. He was determined to keep them from flirting with new subjects like anthropology or social science. Thus he twice failed Charles Andler, who took the *agrégation* in 1887 and 1888, largely because he disliked his excessive bias in favour of German philosophy. Andler therefore sat for the German literature *agrégation* in the following year, came first, and only under the auspices of modern languages was he able to write his important book on Nietzsche. However, the philosophers were with time left increasingly free; power in the subject became less concentrated; but that led to the rise of the *patron*, with his little clique of devotees, and the rebel counter-clique which challenged and replaced it, only to fall in turn.

It was under the Third Republic that the philosophy teachers' pretensions to social superiority reached their highest level. Under the July Monarchy they derived their standing from their role as emissaries of Parisian culture. Francisque Bouillier, who came first in the philosophy *agrégation* in 1837 and two years later was appointed professor at the faculty of Lyon, at the age of twenty-four, began his inaugural lecture with these words: 'I shall teach in the name of a school which has already caused some stir in the world, which has even, if I dare say it, already had a salutary influence in it and which I hope will lend some authority to my words.'[1] Jules Simon arrived in Caen at the age of twenty-one, the proud representative of the already proud École Normale Supérieure, and preached the pure doctrine of his master Cousin, with fluent charm and fashionable elegance. Bright men like him quickly left the provinces for Paris, while the humbler drudges who served out their time in obscure outposts benefited from their reflected glory.[2] Under the Second Empire, orthodoxy and

---

[1] C. Latreille, *Francisque Bouillier, le dernier des Cartésiens* (1907), 49.

[2] M. Chauvet, 'L'Enseignement philosophique à Caen depuis 1830. Souvenirs d'un vieux professeur', *Mémoires de l'Académie nationale des sciences, arts et belles-lettres de Caen* (Caen, 1891), 105–63.

adherence to the official truncated syllabus was more easily enforced in the *lycées* of country towns; there were still plenty of clergymen teaching philosophy who were happy to plod on with the methods of the *ancien régime*, dictating old notes about lifeless texts.[1] But even graduates of the École Normale, as an eminent inspector-general, Cournot, said in 1860, often merely 'translated into catechistic formulae the brilliant utterances of their teachers', and finding the teaching of philosophy of the mind too difficult, they retreated to the construction of syllogisms, to what was virtually the old scholasticism, rehashing the old textbooks 'which they covered with a completely transparent veneer of modernity'. At this stage, the teacher of literature was more highly esteemed, as Renan rightly observed, than the teacher of philosophy, because the latter was regarded, and regarded himself, as simply one who put into more or less fine phrases a doctrine which was supposed to be fixed once and for all.

Two factors changed this. First, the philosophy teachers began making friends with their pupils, building them up into clienteles of admirers, who when they made their way in the world raised up their former mentors to the status of important thinkers, intellectual and moral guides. In the provinces, the philosophy class was often quite small—half a dozen boys—and the teacher was sometimes not much older than the pupils: together they could make the last year at school into an intoxicating experience, permanently memorable as the moment at which intellectual adulthood and independence was achieved. The teachers began dabbling in politics or the world of letters; they published articles in journals they declared to be fashionable; they acquired a standing in the world outside the school. The most famous of them obtained the teaching jobs in Paris, where they might have as many as a hundred pupils in their class: they were admired from afar, but they also won the affection of the dozen or so favourites they would select for special attention, inviting them to their own homes and helping to launch them into literary circles. Secondly, the teachers formed pressure groups which spread their influence beyond the intellectual élite. In particular, they joined the socialist party

---

[1] Ch. Bénard, *L'Enseignement actuel de la philosophie dans les lycées et les collèges* (1862), 25.

and played a leading role in it. Jaurès, a professor of philosophy, and seventeen *agrégés* founded *L'Humanité*: this was a great change from *La République française* founded by Gambetta and his group of barristers (though there was already one philosophy teacher in his set). In 1945 likewise Jean-Paul Sartre and three other *agrégés de philosophie* founded *Les Temps modernes*. The success of Marxist and other left-wing ideologies added greatly to the power of these teachers who knew how to manipulate dialectics and play with German metaphysics. It was no accident that they were attracted to this particular brand of political debate. Their skill was to give the impression that they were 'advanced', and leading a radically new crusade; they lost the mask of pedantry and even became fashionable, or at least there were sets which thought them so. But to appreciate more exactly the balance of innovation and tradition in their outlook one needs to look at them more carefully and individually.

The most celebrated philosophy teacher of the Third Republic was Émile Chartier (1868–1951), who, under the pseudonym of Alain, wrote, in his spare time, articles for the *Dépêche de Rouen* and *Les Libres Propos*. He produced several thousand of these; reprinted in book form they became best-sellers and they have been given the accolade of inclusion in the Bibliothèque de la Pléiade. By the time of his death, 785 books and articles had been published about him. Exhibitions have been held in Alain's honour, and there is a society to perpetuate his memory. His pupils included many authors who paid generous tribute to what they owed him, and helped him on to his pedestal of fame. Very little is in fact known about Alain as a personality, because he took care that he should appear to the world as a thinker, as a collection of ideas rather than of emotions. He refused to write an autobiography, and produced only a *History of my Thoughts*, in which he dismissed his childhood in a few pages as a period, like all childhoods, of foolishness. The purpose of wise living was to overcome and eliminate this foolishness. Significantly, however, he recalled that as a boy he used to spend long hours telling himself stories in which he was always the imperturbable and invincible hero: they were always military adventures; and all his life his reveries were of the same kind, in which he exterminated enemies. He interpreted this as revealing the basic pugnacity of humans, with their desire for honour and power; he admitted that these instincts of childhood remained throughout life; but he considered that 'virile resolution' and will-power could repress them and dispatch them into impotence. His whole life was indeed devoted to creating a personality, for himself and his pupils, which was the product of self-conscious and rational effort: that was what education meant. To achieve this, he made use of a carefully nurtured self-confidence, which led him to refuse all criticism of his writing, to the point that he made it a rule to refuse to allow a publisher to see his manuscript before agreeing to publish it. The literary world he entered was one where he could act more freely than in any other—writing exactly what he pleased, as much as he pleased—and where he could, without moving anything but his pen, 'pulverise' those who contradicted him. Literature and ideas were supreme in his eyes; and the school was therefore all-important as the vehicle of their transmission. He said he had nothing worth saying about his family, because he never thought much about it. This was one reason why 'family virtues' were seen as conflicting with the subversive criticism of the schools. This attitude, also, provides an explanation of why Alain could reject Freud, Einstein and other novelties with such firm assurance. The only man Alain fully admired, 'the only god he recognised', was his own philosophy teacher, Jules Lagneau, and he added that it was not insignificant that this man should also have had the best handwriting he had ever seen.[1]

Alain's idea of philosophy was based on the rejection of originality as either desirable or even possible. 'All has been said,' he wrote, 'but nothing has been finally understood. Plato thought for himself, not for me.' The philosopher therefore must rethink the thoughts of Plato. Invention was outside his scope: he could aim only at the discovery of what already existed. The great philosophers who deserved study advocated different systems, but they had in common an attitude towards human problems, and it was this attitude that was the essence

[1] Suzanne Dewit, *Alain, Essai de bibliographie* (Brussels, 1961); Alain, *Histoire de mes pensées* (1936), 19, 71, 90, 99; Henri Mondor, *Alain* (1953); Paul Foulquié, *Alain* (1965); 'Hommage à Alain', *Mercure de France* (1 Dec. 1951), 583–653; 'Hommage à Alain', *Nouvelle Revue française* (1952, special issue); Olivier Reboul, *L'Homme et ses passions d'après Alain* (1968).

of philosophy. 'Philosophy is not a system, it is a style.' Alain
was not really interested in ideas, but longed for commitment,
action, personal involvement. The fruit of philosophical study
must be the power of judgement, of making decisions. He denied
that objective certainty was possible: 'man is prejudice' he said.
He followed Plato (in Cousin's translation, of course) in thinking
that man was governed by reason, emotion and appetite, which
were in constant conflict, so that all he could aim for was
serenity and a sense of freedom of action, based on developed
powers of reflection. This was not all that different from
Christian salvation, except that for Alain salvation was something each individual settled with himself. Alain's masters were
Plato, Descartes, Kant and Comte: he was certain that meditation on the great works of the past was the way to wisdom.
The assertion of individuality concealed, therefore, a profound
traditionalism. Alain harboured a whole mass of prejudices
which his much-vaunted rationalism never questioned. He
accepted Comte's view that the black race was 'affective', the
yellow race 'active' and the white race 'intellectual'; he
remained a believer, like Comte, in phrenology and the
theory of four temperaments; he completely and vigorously
rejected Freud.[1] His teaching methods were therefore based on
a primitive psychology, which totally denied that children had
any special problems: the one thing he never wrote about was
childhood. Like so many other leading French educators, he
was himself childless; he was a bachelor until his retirement,
when he married his secretary. His influence on youth came
perhaps because he treated his pupils as adults. He argued that
children have no need for play: they do play only because they
are fed by adults and so have nothing more urgent to do. Things
should not be made easy for them, because what they enjoyed
above all in their games, and in all else too, was solving
problems, winning victories. 'The child is a little man: one must
respect his seriousness'; he lived in a magic world only because
he was unable to link his experiences, and because he could
not grasp the real world. The teacher should not therefore
try to understand the child and develop elaborate pedagogic
methods for him: he will get to know him by teaching him,
because the child's true nature is created in education: 'it is by

[1] Georges Pascal, *L'Idée de philosophie chez Alain* (1970).

teaching him to sing that I shall discover whether he is a musician'. So the teacher had no need to be a psychologist. But he could benefit from studying the sociology of the school. The school, thought Alain, was not like a family, and the teacher ought not to try and love his pupils like a father. On the contrary, a father was incapable of teaching his child precisely because he loved him; he could get obedience through emotional pressures, which a teacher could not. The school must have an impersonal, mechanical discipline, without anger and without pardon; it must be different from the outside world and indeed aim to keep the child protected from the outside world and from the realities of life. This was precisely the opposite of what the reformers of the primary school argued: it was in the tradition of the priest's seminary; and it was an ideal far more influential than the supposed bolstering of 'bourgeois' values.

Alain thought the child had to be prepared for the world on the model of Plato's myth of the cave: he had to be given ideas with which to master and understand the world, before he was let out into it. It is for this reason that he stressed intellectual education as vital: experience and apprenticeship were quite inadequate, because they failed to teach the art of reflection. Human society was based on the 'cult of the dead', and that is why education required a historical approach: the study of contemporary man was unsatisfactory because distance was needed to free the judgement from passion; and besides it was best to seek accord not just with a few of one's fellows in the present; one should aim at agreement with the greatest minds of all times. One needed the mediation of the finest examples of humanity of all ages in order to be fully human oneself, and to discover what was universally true. It did not matter if children did not understand all they were taught—it was best to start with the form and move to the content; obscurity had to precede clarity. Alain's syllabus placed the greatest emphasis on the education of the will: the school must teach children to work hard and to control themselves, for evil and bad judgement were the result of lack of will-power. He hated modern theories of education which tried to make things easy for the pupil. Not that he did not see the value of encouragement: he always folded up corrected exercises he returned, so that the mark he gave should remain secret. But he was hostile to the new primary school ideas about the value of teaching practical facts, and placing the child in concrete situations. His aim was to teach not facts, but how to think. This did not mean uniformity, for he had a modest view of the educator's powers: no one could make a crocodile anything but a crocodile, he said. But a teacher could help the child to develop his faculties in certain ways.[1]

Alain cannot be considered a typical philosophy teacher, but his ideas—expressed more fully than any other teacher attempted—reveal the complexities of the *classe de philosophie*, elitist, but attempting to make a doctrine out of common sense, rationalist but still bearing the imprint of scholasticism, at once other-worldly and partisan, individualist but also inspired by the past, historical, but picking out from history only what fitted in with its prejudices, encouraging cleverness and originality until they became routine. Philosophy could survive all revolutions, because it said that all doctrines were equally worthy of study and of criticism: what really mattered was the style with which this was done.

What was supposed to distinguish French philosophy from that of other countries was that it tried to be not a technical speciality, but a general survey of the whole of life, bringing together all the disparate information the child had accumulated into a meaningful and coherent synthesis. It sought not to inculcate knowledge but to stimulate reflection. More particularly, it tried to encourage reflection about general and universal problems. The teacher set an example because the method especially favoured was the 'personal lecture', in which he expressed his own opinions, while giving due consideration to those of others. The pupils were taught to think for themselves by regularly having to write *dissertations* (short essays) in which rigorous reasoning and accurate use of language were demanded. Though there was a syllabus, the teacher was not bound to follow it, and the most famous of them followed it least. But the basis of all their teaching was the interpretation and criticism of texts. Personal experience and converse with great minds were thus used to enable the young to meditate on the difficulties of the human condition, to be aware of a wide range of problems and to learn how to discuss them. The

[1] G. Pascal, *Alain éducateur* (1969).

H

purpose of the philosophy class was frequently debated, because it was so uncertain what it achieved, but there was a remarkable coincidence of views as to what it ought to be. A circular by the minister of education, Monzie, in 1925 summarised the generally accepted doctrine when it said that the function of the class was to 'allow young people to understand better, by this new kind of intellectual effort, the significance and value of those very studies, scientific or literary, that they had pursued till then, and to produce some sort of synthesis out of them'. Before going on to specialise for their individual careers, they were armed by it 'with a method of reflection and some general principles of intellectual and moral life to sustain them in their new lives, so that they should be men with a trade, but capable of seeing beyond their trade, citizens capable of exercising that enlightened and independent judgement that our democratic society needs'. But it was significant that the circular then warned against a host of abuses to which the class was liable, and it was clear that these abuses existed: abstraction, memorising, scholasticism, dictation, cramming. The *baccalauréat* made philosophy into a subject of widespread study but it also very nearly killed it by imposing on it all the restraints and compromises that examinations inevitably involve.[1]

As rival disciplines developed in the secondary syllabus, so the protests against this claim to supremacy were increasingly challenged. Gustave Monod, founder of the *Revue historique* (1876), demanded that philosophy should be altogether abolished in schools: it was justified only when the faculties were not functioning properly: but now that higher education was being revived, it should return where it belonged. As it was, boys were being accustomed 'to talk and write about things they did not understand'. Either they did not take philosophy seriously, or else it led them to 'contract a dangerous over-excitation of the brain'. The army of philosophers the system created had not made France any better at philosophy, for its prestige abroad in the subject was not high: French philosophy was 'distinguished by its obscurity and its subtlety'. It did not

---

[1] *Pour et contre l'enseignement philosophique* (1894), articles reprinted from *La Revue bleue* (1894) by F. Vandérem, T. Ribot, E. Boutroux *et al.*; U.N.E.S.C.O., *The Teaching of Philosophy: An International Enquiry* (1953), contribution by Georges Canguilhem, inspector-general in charge of philosophy teaching in France.

dare tell boys of sixteen all its doubts, so it got out of it by
enveloping itself in clouds. 'Philosophic loquacity and gibberish
are, in my view, among the most certain causes of the intellectual decadence from which we suffer.' The psychologist
Ribot, though a philosopher by training, agreed that philosophy
was above most pupils' heads: it bored the majority of them,
and intoxicated the rest with generalisations and formulae they
could not really use, because it needed years to be able to
make sense of them. A journalist claimed that perhaps only 15
per cent of pupils understood what it was about.[1] This was in
the 1890s. In 1968 the philosophy class was attacked in exactly
the same way, and not least because it had been incapable of
moving with the times. Seminars were held at the University of
Vincennes and elsewhere to uncover its reactionary implications. It was pointed out that though it claimed to avoid
dogmatism, it took as its starting-point individual consciousness;
its basic doctrine was subjectivity; it was inescapably the
vehicle of an ideology. It was consistently hostile to materialism,
from the time when, under Napoleon III, Fortoul ordered it to
'show the invisible and immutable plan of the Divine Wisdom'
at work in the world, and Duruy justified it as 'the best remedy
against materialism', to Monzie in 1925 warning against
'extreme ideas' and 'doctrines which attract by their novelty or
trenchant character'. It continued to equate truth with beauty,
from Cousin to Simone Weil; Marx entered the syllabus only
in 1960. It was sustained by a deep conceit, from the traditional
first lesson devoted to self-praise at the expense of science, art,
religion and 'vulgar ideas'. It taught self-knowledge 'as a
thinking being': it played down emotion and the unconscious.
(There was a curious reason why 'the passions' were excluded
from its syllabus: they used to be studied in rhetoric: they
belonged to another syllabus, and when rhetoric was abolished,
so were the passions.) It perpetuated not only Cousin's spiritualism, but also his eclecticism, for the method was always
synthetic, aiming to reconcile as many authors as possible, to give
at least partial satisfaction to different traditions. It perpetuated
his historical approach also, for it always went back to past
texts. Originality did not go beyond quoting a philosopher

[1] F. Vandérem, 'L'Enseignement de la philosophie', *Revue politique et littéraire*
(*Revue bleue*), Jan. 1894, 1. 125.

whom everyone else had forgotten. Its criticism was superficial, because as soon as a new author like Hegel, Marx or Freud, was forced upon the philosophers, they did their best to integrate him into the system. They would cut down a little on Malebranche or Lucretius to find room for Lévi-Strauss or Sartre. Philosophy half-heartedly tried to find room for more and more as the natural and social sciences grew, so that it became increasingly superficial.[1]

There can be no denying the stultification of the examination questions. Thus though some teachers were doubtless brilliant and independent, the manufacture of textbooks and, even worse, model answers was a flourishing industry. One such book, for example, was published in 1897 by an Academy Inspector, *professeur agrégé de philosophie*: it listed 770 questions asked during the period 1867–1891, rearranged them under a smaller number of headings and provided fully written-out essays as model answers. The thirteenth edition of this book was published in 1939, without any modifications: the questions of 1867 were still considered relevant.[2] The reports of examiners in the *baccalauréat* show that candidates had difficulty in absorbing even these potted formulae. One report analysed in detail sixty-seven answers to a question about the will. Twenty-five candidates seemed to know nothing of any philosophical theory on this subject; and nearly all the others were aware of only one.[3] A question on Aristotle's dictum, 'Man is a political animal' could get an answer that 'There are nevertheless men who are not interested in politics'. In 1948 a question on the contrast between the thinker and the man of action produced the notary and the clerk as examples of the former and the cook and the merchant as examples of the latter. In 1957 a question on behaviourism revealed that there were those who attributed this theory to Monsieur Behavior.[4] The cramming books—of which there were extraordinarily large numbers—divided

[1] François Châtelet, *La Philosophie des professeurs* (1970); Lucien Sève, *La Philosophie française contemporaine* (1962); Roboald Marcas, *Précis de philosophie moderne* (1968)—a parody of a philosophy textbook.

[2] E. Rayot, *La Composition de philosophie* (13th edition, 1939).

[3] G. Texier, 'Que savent les candidats?', *Revue de l'enseignement philosophique* (Oct.–Nov. 1953), 33–5.

[4] René Manblanc, 'La Classe de philosophie: son présent et son avenir' *Cahiers rationalistes*, no. 179 (Apr.–May 1959), 102–31.

philosophy into a number of -isms and showed how standard
questions could be answered by standard replies. What they
said was often quite sensible, but capable of being misused to
result in parrot-like sophistry.[1]

One witty teacher sarcastically produced a 'perpetual answer'
or 'master key' which could be applied to any question, on the
basis, as he said, of long experience of marking *baccalauréat*
scripts, where he had found the same introductions, arguments
and conclusions being endlessly repeated. The typical essay
would read as follows: 'The problem of (copy the question) is
one of the most important in philosophy and since earliest
antiquity, men have not ceased to produce solutions as numerous as they have been varied. Some have tried to solve it in one
way (do not say how), others in other ways. It is at once
obvious, however, that both positions (no details) are much
exaggerated and that a solution can only be found in a harmonious synthesis of the two points of view, for as the Sage (do
not say who) said, *in medio stat virtus*.' This is the introduction.
The 'development' must concentrate on not revealing ignorance:
'Man has an innate curiosity, a need to know the cause of
things (no details). Already the young child (girls should say
"the little baby") demands to know . . .' There are endless
variations of these platitudes, like 'Science advances with giant
footsteps' or 'Man cannot live alone'. Quotations should be
added, but they need to be attributed only to a 'great French
writer' or a 'celebrated thinker'. (Many teachers used to
dictate quotations of all sorts for their pupils to memorise.)
These platitudes should then be submitted, for a paragraph, to
'criticism': 'A totally new light is cast on the problem by this
definition . . . However, this affirmation seems to us to be open
to criticism'; and when the pupil is quite lost, he should end
the paragraph, 'Consequently, what we have argued follows
clearly from this'. The conclusion should either copy the
introduction, beginning: 'That is why we can say . . .', or,
more elegantly: 'What ought one to think of such a problem?
Philosophers are still debating it.' The 'national ending' should
round it off: 'And so we can say that X is truly French.' This
was not too wild a caricature of what many pupils churned out.[2]

[1] e.g. Robert Lenoble, *Conseils pratiques aux jeunes philosophes* (1939).
[2] Jean Brun, 'Modeste projet en faveur d'un corrigé perpétuel de dissertation

With time, the distance separating the best from the worst may well have increased. Some able teachers encouraged their clever pupils to read widely, and the subjects covered by them ranged over increasingly varied topics, though politics, psychology and ethics were the most popular. Many writers have recorded the exhilaration they experienced as new intellectual horizons were opened to them in this class. The teachers encouraged the taste for obscure and original studies because they aimed above all at winning successes for their pupils in the *concours général* and the entrance examination for the École Normale Supérieure. The bright pupils benefited from the freedom and the guidance they received. But as science became more popular, philosophy was taken increasingly as a soft option by those least suited to academic work of any kind. Between the wars the proportion taking philosophy diminished, though the total numbers rose because of the large influx of girls into the subject. Whereas in the 1920s only about 10 per cent of candidates were girls, in 1950 77 per cent (in the Paris Academy) were girls. Though philosophy was supposed to be a general subject, surveying all the others in the syllabus, and above them, it had by then lost its supremacy, and become a speciality like any other, locked in its obscure jargon, contemptuous of the sciences and in rivalry with them.[1]

The generalisations about France's philosophical spirit, and the philosophy class as the instrument propagating it, must be interpreted with due allowance for the vagueness of the notions and the imprecision of the instrument. There can be no doubt that France did develop, in this period, an official philosophical army, led by the *agrégés*, and with soldiers in every *lycée*. Cousin declared in 1850 that 'a philosophy teacher is a functionary in the service of moral order, appointed by the state to cultivate minds and souls', but Renan laughed at the idea of a government having an official philosophy, saying it was as absurd as having a governmental doctrine on chemistry or geology. Though paid by the state, the philosophy teachers

philosophique', *Revue de l'enseignement philosophique* (July–Aug. 1951), 35–8. This review also reproduces the winning essays of the *concours général*.

[1] D. Dreyfus, 'La Philosophie peut-elle s'enseigner?', *Revue de l'enseignement philosophique* (July–Sept. 1952), 3–6, and debate on the function of the philosophy class, ibid. 55–68. On girls, see Françoise Mayeur's forthcoming thesis.

were not tame propagandists preaching an authorised doctrine: they valued their security as civil servants but they reacted against the implication of subservience by increasingly assuming independent attitudes. During the Second Empire, they had to be obedient, because they were brutally sacked if they were not, but under the Third Republic teaching was orthodox because of an absolutely self-imposed tyranny: they had been the victors of the examinations in their youth, and they then taught their pupils to play the same game. But this was a game played at school; only a small proportion of the school population stayed on long enough to participate; even fewer learnt to do so with any skill; so the number of those actually permanently marked by the philosophy class was very small. It is true that they included many highly intelligent and articulate people who made a stir in the world. Certain branches of literature, some serious newspapers and periodicals echoed their language, in so far as they were run by them, or by writers who admired them; and this no doubt widened the circle of those who cultivated the philosophical style in speech and writing—in all its variations from clarity to verbosity. Because they were at the top of the educational hierarchy, those who wished to appear educated might ape them; and in this period, when education was new to most people, their influence had the attraction of novelty. The examination system sustained it. But the philosophical style was very far from being universal in France. It did however help to produce a certain kind of Frenchman, with high pretensions. These pretensions should not be taken at their face value, but in certain groups they were.

The statement that the French nation was 'Cartesian' is untenable, and it is doubly so, because Cartesianism in fact had a very chequered history. The identification with Descartes was certainly made frequently: thus even a respectable philosopher, in a study of Descartes written between the wars, concluded that Marshal Foch was the last contemporary incarnation of the Cartesian spirit and it was this that had won the war. A German critic writing at the same time explained extraordinary claims of this kind by saying that Descartes's ideas had been so simplified that they had come to represent simply the common sense that every French peasant was supposed to possess; that the French were not really interested in philosophy for its own sake, as the Germans were or the ancient Greeks had been; their culture was literary; philosophy had accepted this tutelage and Descartes was the greatest of French philosophers because he had identified himself at once with clarity and good French prose.

Descartes has had many different incarnations over the last three hundred years. He has by no means always been praised by the French; he has had violent opponents; his significance can (like Rousseau's) be interpreted in many ways and Paul Valéry rightly talked of 'a plurality of plausible Descartes'. If he does epitomise something permanent in French attitudes, then people were a long time in recognising it. He was paradoxically first raised into a symbol and a hero by various religious groups, the Oratorians and Jansenists, who used him against the Jesuits. The Jesuits put him on the Index and set the Sorbonne to condemn him; but then they found him a useful instrument in other battles and produced an anodyne version of him. Cartesianism is loosely supposed to mean the triumph of individual reason, the proclamation of reason's ability to understand and solve all problems, the rejection of authority, the questioning of all dogmas, the universal doubt, the assertion that man is above all a thinking being, who is not dependent on sensations and experience for his ideas or for the discovery of truth. All this has not found equal acceptance. Thus the French Academy in 1765 crowned A. L. Thomas's oration in praise of Descartes as the greatest of all thinkers since Aristotle, but Voltaire at around the same time declared that Descartes's influence had vanished after 1730. Some contributors to the eighteenth-century Encyclopedia identified themselves with Descartes, developing what they considered to be his materialist and mechanistic message, but in the nineteenth century Cousin used him precisely to destroy the influence of the Encyclopedists, declaring him to be the father of spiritualism. In the 1860s, it was said that 'the teaching of the state is founded entirely on Cartesian ideas'.[1] The philosopher Fouillée in 1893 praised Descartes as 'perhaps the greatest of all Frenchmen', who was responsible for a revolution as important as that of 1789.[2] But in 1896, the rising star of the world of literary

---

[1] *Larousse du dix-neuvième siècle* (1864–76), 'Descartes'.
[2] A. Fouillée, *Descartes* (1893), 6.

criticism, Gustave Lanson, denied that Cartesianism had exerted any such profound influence, and asserted that the method of arguing from simple principles was 'a profound and permanent disposition of the French mind'. Cartesianism was mathematical and incapable of generating an aesthetic; it had even destroyed respect for classical antiquity and so for poetry and art; though it was true that it had set a fashion for writing on specialised topics in language which all could understand.[1]

Opposing schools have continued to interpret Descartes in opposing ways. There are of course many types of rationalism; and it is possible to argue that Descartes's was not a sceptical variety, not essentially critical at all, that it used doubt only to build a new dogmatism more soundly, in which reason could know the world adequately because it was reason which participated in the reason of God. There were certainly profound variations in the nature of rationalism in each of the centuries since Descartes's time. The Cartesian rationalism of the Cousin school was thus definitely not individualistic; and the rationalism of Comte was not Cartesian, since it tried to separate science and metaphysics.[2] Descartes has obviously been a flag flown to indicate support for a number of different causes. But the uncertainty about his precise significance is the key to understanding his influence, or, more precisely, the place of Cartesianism in French life. If that means rationalism, then rationalism had several faces to it, worn at one extreme by the Jesuits and at the other by the sceptics and the materialists. The French could identify with this doctrine because it could be interpreted so variously. Cartesianism, like *la France bourgeoise*,

---

[1] G. Lanson, 'L'influence de la philosophie cartésienne sur la littérature française', *Revue de métaphysique* (1896), reprinted in his *Études d'histoire littéraire* (1929), 58–96.

[2] A. L. Thomas, *Éloge de Descartes* (1765); Francisque Bouillier, *Histoire et critique de la révolution cartésienne* (Lyon, 1842); Robert Aron, *Les Frontaliers du Néant* (1949); Roger Lefèvre, *Le Criticisme de Descartes* (1958), id., *La Pensée existentielle de Descartes* (1965); Roger Verneaux, *Les Sources cartésiennes et kantiennes de l'idéalisme français* (1936); Jean Laporte, *Le Rationalisme de Descartes* (1945); C. Latreille, *Francisque Bouillier, le dernier des cartésiens* (1907); Henri Mongin, 'L'esprit encyclopédique et la tradition philosophique française', *La Pensée* (1945) 5. 8–18 and (1946) 6. 25–38; C. J. Beyer, 'Du cartésianisme à la philosophie des lumières', *Romanic Review* (New York, Feb. 1943), 18–39; G. Sortais, 'Le cartésianisme chez les Jésuites français', *Archives de philosophie* (1929), vol. 6, cahier 3.

is a very woolly notion and that is its strength. Most people could in some degree accept something in it. In that sense, it was a characteristic Frenchmen shared.

The philosophy class has been both praised and attacked by various writers. It could make a powerful impression on clever children. It could alter the whole course of a life as it did for Maurice Barrès, who in *Les Déracinés* made the philosophy teacher a dangerous maniac specialising in cutting boys away from all traditional values, so as to get them to worship abstract gods. André Maurois, looking back on his own adolescence more benignly, thought the philosophy class filled him with self-confidence. He could henceforth spout quotations to prove he was always right. 'I gave the impression of being a pedant, a prig, a scoffer. With women I affected a high-handed manner; I behaved as though I were in a play by Marivaux or Musset, by Dumas fils or Becque.' In his courtships, instead of making pretty speeches, he talked about Spinoza. This kind of pretentiousness was superficial. With some it may have lasted all their lives. With others, it was a veneer which could conceal timidity and even compassion. But there were some who reacted vigorously against philosophy. Lévi-Strauss claimed he became an ethnologist because he realised, in his first year as a philosophy teacher, that there was no more to be learnt once he had mastered the tricks of this game: he would repeat his lessons for the rest of his career. It was a game by which every problem, serious or futile, could be given the appearance of being solved simply by applying a method, which was always identical: show that the common-sense view of it was liable to criticism, but then how this critical theory was in turn false, and conclude, by an analysis of vocabulary or a play on words, that the truth had two sides to it and all these arguments could be accommodated within it. 'These exercises', said Lévi-Strauss, 'quickly become verbal, based on skill at making puns, which becomes a substitute for reflection, on assonances between terms, on homophony and ambiguity, which combine to provide the raw material for these speculative *coups de théâtre*: ingenuity in them is the mark of good philosophical work.' Not only did this reduce the subject to a boring uniformity, with a unique method which provided a passkey to everything in it, but it removed any possibility of scientific exploration, and deflated it with the aesthetic contemplation of consciousness by itself.[1]

But it may well be asked whether Lévi-Strauss ever escaped completely from this tradition. He condemns philosophy's games with illusion and being, the continuous and the discontinuous, essence and existence, but his own work was centred around similar oppositions, like the raw and the cooked. He is an author whose reputation was won also because he wrote so beautifully. The distinction between philosophical writing and beautiful writing needs to be explained further. The relationship between the two will provide the key to one of the most important sources of unity among the educated classes.

### Rhetoric

French philosophy, in this period, was with few exceptions not original and it aroused little interest in other countries. This may partly have been due to the fact that it was, at least in the way it was taught, to a great extent a literary exercise, in which the studied expression of obvious ideas in impressive language took precedence over the solution of problems. Originality that might have been philosophical was channelled into political and social theory, which was outside the scope of the schools and not subject to its rules. Philosophy was not an autonomous study. Even though it was taught at the conclusion of the school course, it was much influenced by the literary preoccupations which predominated over the syllabus as a whole; and to understand therefore why philosophers expressed themselves in the way they did, one must examine not only the traditionalism of their subject-matter, but also their style, which they picked up partly from the teachers of rhetoric and belles-lettres, who had pretensions as high as theirs.

All languages have some differences between their spoken and their written forms, and the differences have important social and psychological connotations. Democracy and widespread literacy reduce the differences to a minimum, as in America, while societies where learning is confided to a small élite can have a written language almost unintelligible to the uneducated, as in Arabic. In France, the schools remained the

---

[1] C. Lévi-Strauss, *Tristes tropiques* (1955), 54–5.

heirs of classical traditions, admirers and guardians of what they considered polite language, as enshrined in the great works of literature of the past. They were, however, revolutionary as well as conservative, for they saw their mission as the spread of this polite language, conquering dialect, accent and vulgarity, so that ideally people would talk as they wrote. The implication was that they would also learn to think as they were supposed to write, in an orderly and logical way. The mechanisms they employed were not always the same ones. Until the mid-nineteenth century, the way an educated Frenchman learnt to write good French was first to learn to write Latin, and secondly to read French authors whose style had been approved by universal consensus, usually after the lapse of a century or more. Imitation of ancient models was therefore what schoolmasters sought to inculcate. This was the basis of the *classe de rhétorique*, the final class but one, but the point at which many pupils left school; philosophy was often considered superfluous, while rhetoric was at times so popular that some pupils, with no academic ambitions, stayed on in the class for two years.

The rhetoric class taught the *discours*, the art of making speeches, writing letters and expressing oneself in a way that would show one's taste, education and dignity. The models the pupils had to follow were those of ancient Greece and Rome, partly because this raised them above vulgar dialects, partly because it presented them with noble and moral heroes and partly because it removed them from contact with the con-taminating controversies of contemporary life. Artificiality was the essence of this ideal: since man was not only sinful but disgusting, the way to make him pleasing was to dress him up in clothes which, it was hoped, would make him have elevated thoughts, and gravity and nobility in expressing them. The writing of speeches as though one were a Roman Emperor was designed to encourage not sincerity but conformity. It helped powerfully to produce what Michel Bréal called that 'intellec-tual illness which consists in paying each other with words, shutting oneself up in a role and drawing out of one's head passions one does not feel'. To call this an illness, to label it all as typical and institutionalised bourgeois hypocrisy, is, how-ever, to do it an injustice. All education, almost by definition, involves the encouragement of artificiality and the holding-up of values of one sort or another. The passion for words as fascinating in themselves was not surprising in people whom words introduced to new experiences. Jean-Paul Sartre recalled that as a boy the sight of a plane-tree in the Luxembourg gardens encouraged him not to observe it carefully but rather to find adjectives or phrases to describe it: in this way, he said, 'I enriched the universe with a mass of shimmering leaves'. He could 'raise up cathedrals of words' from simple sights.[1] In such a situation, literature could almost be confused with prayer. Pushing the claims of literature still further, the professional handlers of words could think that the preservation of these constructions was their principal duty. This has remained a powerful element in the attitude of the schools towards the teaching of language; and it is in keeping with it that the new science of linguistics has been welcomed as the key to universal understanding. It is not surprising that many teachers of literature took a long time to accept the opening-up of the secondary schools to all and sundry. Sincerely republican and democratic though they were, they considered that mastery of the language required such delicacy of taste, that it could not be picked up by anybody. In the early twentieth century, Lanson, a leading professor of literature, insisted that the increasing hordes of schoolchildren were too 'practical and scientific' in their attitude to be able to appreciate literature; the majority came from uncultured homes, where respect for books had either never been acquired, or had vanished before the invasion of the newspaper. He saw the 'primary school spirit' as a danger that threatened the secondary schools; elitism was a literary creed for him.[2]

The teaching of French came late to the secondary schools. In 1803 a selection of French classics were recommended for study, mainly in the *classe de belles lettres*, which was then the name for the second year of the rhetoric class, but French was regarded as subsidiary to the main subject of study, which was the Greek and Latin classics. Bossuet was designed to act as a counterpart to Livy, for example, but far less attention was paid to him, or indeed to any French author. In 1840 Cousin instituted an oral examination on a French text in the

[1] J.-P. Sartre, *Words* (Penguin translation, 1967), 89, 113–15.
[2] G. Lanson, *L'Enseignement du Français. Conférences du musée pédagogique* (1909), 9.

*baccalauréat* and enjoined that it should be studied with as much care as ancient texts, but in 1850 French was still generally being given only ten minutes a day, usually at the end of the classics lesson. It was only in 1880 that a larger selection of French set books was prescribed—Bossuet, Pascal, Voltaire. Only in 1885 was the study of nineteenth-century authors permitted, but 'with prudence'; only in 1890 was the injunction to prudence dropped. Thus the ancient classics surrendered their dominance of the syllabus to French literature only in the second decade of the Third Republic. But there was much disagreement as to what this new subject should involve.

When the study of French was still part of the study of rhetoric, it was on form and presentation that the teachers concentrated. They followed the methods perfected by a whole host of distinguished predecessors, over many centuries, among whom Aristotle, Cicero and Quintilian, however, still held pride of place. Though rhetoric, in the early twentieth century, came to have a pejorative meaning, it survived so long because it provided an exceptionally comprehensive and orderly analysis of human speech. It studied what to say, how to order it and how to express it (*inventio, dispositio, elocutio*); it distinguished between the different aims a speaker could set himself, and showed how he could best attain what he was setting out to do; it showed the different methods to be used in judiciary, deliberative and demonstrative rhetoric, how to persuade, how to move and how to please; and it went into great detail to place this advice on such a systematic basis, that eloquence was almost reduced to a mechanical operation: almost, but not quite, for it did not claim that simply following its rules would make one automatically eloquent. Intellectual, social and physical gifts were needed to excel, but the rhetorician could put these to their best use, and could warn of the dangers to be avoided—in logic, in gesture, in tactics. Just how interesting this kind of study could be may be seen from the *Course in Literature, Rhetoric, Poetics and Literary History* by E. Geruzez, professor at the Sorbonne, published in 1841 and reprinted over fifty times in the next fifty years. This was the standard textbook used in schools during this period. It presented rhetoric as 'a science of observation based on the study of the human mind and on the masterpieces of eloquence'. It defended rhetoric as being to eloquence what poetics is to poetry, what logic is to reasoning, because it facilitated the operations of the mind and analysed what would now be called the psychology of inter-personal relations. It argued that by teaching people to express themselves well it was forging 'the best possible instrument man could have for the advancement of letters and of science, and for the commerce of life.' The weakness of schoolboys following this course, however, had traditionally been their almost total ignorance of literary history, so that they studied the 'extracts' presented to them divorced from the context in which they were written. Geruzez attempted to remedy this, saying that 'the history of literature has become in our time a veritable science', which showed the links between ideas and events, and 'revealed in a new light the revolution of empires'. At the same time, rhetoric was, as it had always aimed to be, a course in morals, seeking to inspire good conduct by the contemplation of literary beauty. 'The domain of literature embraces the whole expanse of human thought'; even if it avoided going into the details of science or erudition, it surveyed their general results.[1]

These were large claims, and Geruzez was himself aware that the aims of rhetoric would be attained only by gifted people. It was a dangerous subject, because it could so easily degen-erate into trivial classification and tiresome pedantry. One of the principal activities of the schools was indeed to reduce it, for the majority of their pupils, to the level of banality, imita-tion and interminable repetitiveness. That is why under the Second Empire there was a revolt against rhetoric. Dionysus Ordinaire, one of Gambetta's lieutenants, led the protest with what seemed a radical challenge: rhetoric, he declared, could not be taught, and fashions, besides, were changing: the epic was dead, antique tragedy had been replaced by popular drama, the novel had arrived, the very idea of eloquence with its measured gestures had become bourgeois, usable only in the boring circles of respectable worthies. Eloquence was a natural gift, and the best way to develop it was to avoid getting embog-ged in the rules of the rhetoricians. Instead of studying them, it would be more sensible to see what the great masters of literature

[1] E. Geruzez, *Cours de littérature, rhétorique, poétique, histoire littéraire* (26th edition 1887), v–vi, 137.

had done, and to concentrate on modern and contemporary masters. The motto he held up was: 'Be yourself, imitate no one'. Demosthenes was popular not because he followed the rules but because he loved his country. Conviction was the most irresistible of charms. One can see the links here between political developments, the new democracy and the educational syllabus. But one should not exaggerate the practical significance of this challenge. Having made his protest, Ordinaire nevertheless went on to describe all the old rules; he insisted that the proof of their value was that they had continued to be repeated without change since Aristotle; and he ended with a long commentary on Cicero's *Rhetorical Art*.[1]

In the 1880s, there were still questions being set in the *baccalauréat* about the rules of rhetoric.[2] In the French composition practised at school at this time, the great virtue encouraged in pupils was docility, respect for accepted ideals. Teachers tended to do most of the thinking for their pupils, to give them headings for each paragraph, to confine contributions to strict limits, four paragraphs being generally demanded, as though an essay was an architectural edifice, to be constructed in the same way irrespective of the ideas it contained. A certain kind of harmony was thus required between the paragraphs, which had to be of predetermined length. The subject-matter had preferably to be turned to a moral purpose, so that a 'speech by Henri IV on the Edict of Nantes' would turn into a eulogy of liberty of conscience. This was encouraged as a means of teaching pupils to see general ideas behind details, but it inevitably produced a lot of empty phraseology, and all the more so since the most esteemed approach was to argue by allusion, to suggest one knew more than one said. The detailed attention to style certainly taught people to express themselves methodically and in an orderly fashion, even if it did impose a pattern of formalism and pretentiousness. It taught them to know the works of a few authors very thoroughly, in that it was customary to limit the study of French literature to a few books. But French composition was more than just style, because the

[1] D. Ordinaire, *Rhétorique nouvelle* (1867); cf. E. Laboulaye, *Rhétorique populaire* (1869).

[2] James Condamin, *La Composition française: conseils et plans synoptiques pour traiter 850 sujets proposés aux candidats au baccalauréat* (Lyon, 9th edition 1886), 1–8.

subject-matter on which pupils wrote gradually expanded: though the content was mainly classical, French literature, history, morals and aesthetics were also written about. In the 1890s developments in these subjects, and the rise of new social sciences, led to French composition becoming increasingly abstract. The details of literary texts were skimmed over, and instead pupils were asked to draw out of them the 'immutable general laws' which ruled them. Poems and plays were used as a basis for comparison and generalisation designed to produce complex classifications and universal formulae. The bright teachers of these years would ask their pupils what they were really interested in: they often got the answer that it was geography or literary history (it was the age of Vidal de La Blache and Brunetière) and they would accordingly ask their pupils to write their compositions about these. This 'philosophic method' appeared to be exciting and broadening, but it was based on superficiality if not total ignorance, and it gave rise to even more angry accusations that these so-called literary studies taught people simply hollow verbiage of a high-sounding kind. Examination questions were now so general that there was no chance that the candidates could possibly have the information necessary to answer them. No concession was made to their youth and the questions at the *baccalauréat* were not significantly different from those at the *agrégation*.[1] The result was that the spirit of the old rhetoric lived on: pupils simply could not avoid padding their essays with empty declamation.

The enemies of rhetoric triumphed in 1902, when the subject was removed from the syllabus. The principle behind the republic's education since Ferry's time was that it should be factual, based on observation and not memory. This had been difficult to apply. But gradually the literature specialists developed it into the *explication des textes*, which now became the basis of the teaching of French. At its best, when properly executed, this could be a quite extraordinarily thorough analysis of language and ideas, drawn from a short piece of prose or verse. Imitation was now replaced by analysis; the aim was the cultivation not of style but of understanding. The pupil was asked not to express his personal feelings on reading the

[1] F. Lhomme and E. Petit, *La Composition française aux examens et aux concours* (6th edition, 1917), covering the years 1882–1916, preface.

text, but to produce a methodical and careful explanation of it, trying as far as possible to put himself into the author's skin, to understand him as fully as possible. He had to show what the general sense of the text was, how the dominant idea was developed; what the text's aesthetic or moral character was, what kind of intention or spirit it conveyed, how it came to be written, how it fitted in the rest of the author's work, how valid were its arguments, how it was received and how influential it had been. He had to dissect the language used, examine the words and sentences, their origins, their musical and picturesque qualities, and compare the style to that of contemporaries. Finally he had to show what general questions the text posed, say whether it solved some general problems of composition or style, whether it threw light on the working of the literary imagination, or on the forms of expression. An example of *explication de textes* by a teacher, published as a model, ran to twenty-six pages in a commentary on as many lines of verse by Victor Hugo. In its thoroughness and comprehensiveness, it set new standards.[1] This method has remained the basis of French literary studies ever since; it has provided the framework for a great deal of penetrating and ingenious research, and it has been the model influencing many other forms of writing.

However, the teachers undermined the value of what was one of their most important contributions to society by two developments of it, in opposing directions: they were too ambitious in the range of subjects they tried to apply it to, and they bastardised it by producing all sorts of ruinous short cuts to help their pupils pass their examinations. Pretentiousness was often their answer to the contempt they saw around them, while the *baccalauréat* brought out what was worst in them. The study of grammar was increasingly considered too pedestrian. It used to be a major preoccupation in the study of Latin, and French grammar used to be modelled on that; but as Latin was replaced by modern languages, the interest in the rules diminished. The result was that examiners regularly complained that candidates could not write grammatical French, could not spell, and even could not understand it—though it is fair to add they had been complaining about the

[1] G. Rudler, *L'Explication française. Principes et applications* (1902).

inability to understand throughout the nineteenth century. There was considerable evidence to support those who claimed that schoolboys played with words they could not comprehend. At the same time, however, as a reaction against grammatical study set in, teachers tried to make their subject more intellectualist, more concerned with ideas, making even greater demands of their pupils. The tradition lived on that study of great authors should be a moral experience, teaching artistic and literary ideals. This had been easier to do in the eighteenth century, when there was a precise code of taste and fixed rules, so that pupils could recognise the application and violation of these; they knew what to look for; but now individual sensibility and appreciation entered the scene and vastly complicated the activity. Some teachers thought it was enough to get the pupils to understand the spirit of an author and the meaning of his text, so that being able to read him out aloud with full expressiveness should be the ultimate aim. This was the tradition of *elocutio*, which also survived, and skill in reading aloud continues to be cultivated with impressive success. Some teachers were willing to leave it to the pupils to take the initiative in asking questions about the texts. But the most ambitious teachers of French aspired to making their subject the vehicle for the moulding of their pupils' minds. They said that whereas previously somebody like Bossuet might be studied as a work of art, now he ought to be read also for the theology, the history and the ideas he contained. From this they moved on to using the authors as commentators on 'the principal human questions', which became the central object of the lesson. 'What is Science?' might be one such question; 'How did reason progress in the eighteenth century?' or 'What were the political ideas of Montesquieu?'. As one distinguished teacher said, literature was the 'popularisation of philosophy'. Pupils were thus introduced to the deepest problems at a remarkably early age, and expected to write about them with maturity.

But, of course, since they also had to pass examinations, they were helped along by a whole variety of cribs and textbooks. The informal, often highly personal lecture by the teacher, which could make these French lessons so inspiring, was supplemented by the dictation of model answers, potted definitions and summaries, which were laboriously copied into different exercise books and mercilessly memorised. While on the one hand the pupil was encouraged to use his own judgement, he was on the other hand told what the right answers were, even if they were well above his head. So in examinations, his intelligence had to be displayed by the ingenuity with which he presented the facts and attitudes expected of him. The writing of essays became above all a matter of *dispositio*. The plan of the essay was all-important. Much effort was devoted to practising its construction. Those who sought simply to pass their examination would be content with a symmetrical construction, divided into parts, as the old rhetoricians had taught. It was more ambitious to add movement and progression to these different parts and to lead up to a climax in the argument. But then the ideal became to have a dialectical progression. An ordinary progression would simply, for example, describe a man first physically, then intellectually, then morally. If one wanted to 'dialecticise', one would make these into thesis, antithesis and synthesis, which was increasingly recommended. A leading guide on how to write essays, published in 1955, said 'The essay is like a universe where nothing is free, an enslaved universe, a world from which everthing which does not serve the discussion of a fundamental problem must be excluded, and where autonomous development is the gravest fault one can imagine'. The key to success was to spot the most general problem into which the subject fitted; and no one trained properly should ever be 'really surprised by any general subject'.[1] But it was naïve to imagine that the essay should be simply about the general problem. Rather it had to be about what people thought of the problem. Ultimately, therefore, at this level, a beautiful style was no longer as useful as brilliance in producing formulae; the proliferation of memorised quotations was now replaced by skill in producing analyses and paraphrases. The passionate interest in how ideas should be expressed was cultivated from an early age; and it spread beyond the school. The civil service, which in the eighteenth century had prided itself on writing beautiful prose, indistinguishable from that of men of letters, always gave great weight to the way reports were written; in the nineteenth it paraded pomposity and verbiage, no doubt from misplaced notions of

[1] A. Chassang and Ch. Senninger, *La Dissertation littéraire générale* (1955), 6, 8.

traditionalism; more recently, it too has stressed the importance of the plan, of precision and analysis.[1]

At the same time, however, another trend was increasing the scientific character of the study of French, stressing erudition and objectivity. This involved transforming it, to a great extent, into literary history. The key figure in this movement was Gustave Lanson (1857–1934), author of the history of French literature which reigned supreme in the first half of the twentieth century. One must beware of making him into too much of a symbol, or of attributing too much success to his methods. His textbook is regarded as having ousted that of René Doumic (1860–1937), but the two men were exact contemporaries. Doumic was both perpetual secretary of the French Academy and editor of the *Revue des Deux Mondes*, where he maintained the cult of classical taste and animosity against any new ideas. The Academy and the schools were not necessarily on the same side.[2] But Lanson wanted the study of French literature to have all the vigour, exactitude and gravity of a science. He thought that commentaries on authors were not justified unless they were based on 'exhaustive' study, that nothing should be left out of their bibliographies, that all available texts should be scrutinised and compared, that influences and sources should be chased to the farthest limits. He aimed to turn the study of French literature into a rigorous discipline: he gave lectures which could sometimes be nothing but an enormous bibliography, catalogued inexorably, which, however, his audience would copy down with religious respect, for this, at last, seemed true scholarship. There were complaints that all this was too Germanic, and that his critical editions, with their mysterious symbols, looked like works of geometry. This was indeed how some people interpreted and applied what they thought was his method: the study of texts could thus be reduced to a laborious palaeography, from which capricious taste could be banished and hard work assured of its reward.

Lanson, however, was in real life a many-sided man and a remarkably gifted teacher. It is true he appeared cold, radiating

[1] Jean Datain, *L'Art d'écrire et le style des administrations* (1953, 15e mille 1970), 12; G. Genette, 'Enseignement et rhétorique au 20e siècle', *Annales*, vol. 21 (Jan.–June 1966), 292–305.

[2] R. Doumic, *Histoire de la littérature française* (1900) reached its 25th printing in 1908, and a new edition was published in 1947.

intelligence rather than warmth, but this was a superficial impression. He was the son of a glove manufacturer, his mother was the daughter of a mirror merchant; he came from an unfrivolous and determined background, where people were bent on improving themselves. He was contemptuous of those who thought they could acquire good taste without effort. He graduated, top of his year, from the École Normale in 1879, defended his thesis in 1887, where he first revealed his extraordinary powers of argumentation, vigour, obstinacy, imperturbable calm and self-control, which were to make him the dominant figure in every conference and meeting he attended. He was appointed to a post at the Sorbonne at an exceptionally young age, and rose to be Director of the École Normale.[1] But he was most at ease, perhaps, lecturing to girl teacher trainees at Sèvres, where there was less wildness and independence than in the rue d'Ulm; and *The Principles of Composition and of Style*, which he published in 1887 when he was still a schoolmaster at the Lycée Charlemagne, give a fairer picture of what his methods were at the level of secondary education. They show that he was not the advocate of an exclusive or narrow doctrine: all attempts to analyse teaching methods inevitably oversimplify, and neglect the large middle ground on which contending parties were agreed. Lanson was aware of all the faults conscientious teaching could lead to. He declared himself, at the beginning of this book of precepts, to be against precepts and against formulae which would simply be memorised: he castigated vagueness and verbosity. He said that in teaching literary style he was aiming to teach how to think well, and how to judge books. Sterile criticism was the result of failing to see how much effort was needed to do it properly. He advocated intellectual effort, not at the expense of sincerity of sentiment, but because only an exercised mind could express exactly what a person felt. He urged his pupils to read a lot, but also to argue with the authors they read, so as to benefit their intelligence as well as their memory. Conversation used to be the main source of instruction: it was now a dead art, but it could be fruitful if it was an instrument to clarify ideas and if it was treated as more than a distraction. Introspection was necessary too, to educate one's sensibility by asking oneself

[1] For his work there, see chapter 7.

what one was feeling—dissipating the confusion of one's emotions into clear ideas, distinguishing, for example, between one's love for one's mother, one's dog, one's clothes and one's favourite poet. He had an ideal, which he thought existed in the eighteenth-century *salons*, of a general education, produced by the assiduous cultivation of clarity; and it was this that produced a good style of writing. He repeated the injunctions to seek out the general idea, to study the *lieux communs* which were at the basis of all thought, to free principles from all personal and local circumstances so that they could be clearly understood, and indeed he divided his book in the traditional way of rhetoric, into Invention, Disposition and Elocution. It is true he added a chapter on the relationship of words and things, warning against mistaking abstract names for concrete realities, which he claimed was a vice women were particularly liable to. (He complained that foreigners had too stereotyped an idea of Frenchmen, but he had a similar, contemptuous view of women.)[1]

With time, he became pessimistic about the possibility of spreading taste and refinement to the mass of pupils. He looked back nostalgically to the days when the teacher was allowed to concentrate on a handful of bright pupils while the others 'were content to have sat on the same benches as this élite'. The fathers of those who were ignored did not complain, but were proud of the few successes the *lycée* won in the national examinations. The pressure of examinations had indeed turned French into a mere speciality, and morals and history had won their independence. So pupils were now simply being exercised in mental games, taught to write paradoxical and over-clever answers, which 'they deformed into gross and pretentious affirmations from which the fine grain of justice had disappeared'. There was little point in getting them to regurgitate 'strange pot-pourris' of the leading critics and textbooks. The danger now was that French literature might be regarded as 'the realm of vagueness, arbitrariness and whim'. Its sights, in the new schools for the masses, should therefore be lowered. It should cease to appeal to the imagination which was only 'an apprenticeship in pretentiousness and false elegance'. It could

<hr/>

[1] G. Lanson, *Principes de composition et de style* (1887, 5th edition 1912); cf. his *Conseils sur l'art d'écrire* (1890, 10th edition 1918).

not hope to make the majority of its pupils into artists. It should
be content to teach them 'to produce a good report, a straightforward statement, in a precise, clear and orderly style, without
literary qualities but with method and exactness'. The primary
schools were supposed to teach this; the secondary schools could
not be doing badly if they succeeded in achieving it.[1] This does
not mean that Lanson wished to abolish the role of sensibility
in the study of French. It is true that he insisted that 'reason was
the most perfect and noble of human faculties' and that it was
the intellectual element in prose that, above all else, gave value
to it; but he valued the pleasures to be obtained from artistic
form. He argued, however, that spontaneous taste was inadequate: only when it was based on reflection, and on historical
study, could it yield worthwhile fruits. One should value one's
personal impressions, but one should also try to understand why
one felt as one did. He tried to be even more scientific than
Taine, which is why he was suspicious of theories of literary
evolution: ultimately it was the creative genius of the individual
writer that interested him.[2]

These controversies among the teachers of French are
significant in several ways. First, they show that beneath the
various arguments there was a considerable amount of consensus. Learning the language was to Frenchmen more than the
acquisition of a practical tool. It involved the training of the
mind also, and the development of certain ways of thinking
which they valued. This meant, secondly, that they tried to
encourage an intellectualist approach to all the problems that
language could express; they tried to get their pupils to see
general principles behind details, and to place their arguments
under the protection of universal laws. So, thirdly, they insisted
on a great deal of attention being paid to the presentation of
arguments, to ordering them in a way that appeared logical,
clear, well planned and divided, as far as possible, into three
parts. But, finally, they were not innovating as much as they
imagined; their new pedagogical methods were not all as new
as they thought. They were in many ways still imprisoned in the

[1] G. Lanson, *L'Enseignement du Français* (1909), 1–24.
[2] *Gustave Lanson 1857–1934*, published by the Société des Amis de l'École Normale Supérieure (1958).

old laws of rhetoric, though they might have varied their emphasis. The teachers did not therefore transform the character of social relationships by imposing a new usage of language. But it is certain that they popularised among a far larger audience ways of expression which had once been confined to an élite or to pedants, and to this extent their efforts were rewarded by many Frenchmen sounding different, arguing differently. The question, however, which they did not ask themselves, was whether this form of discourse was suited to the non-literary world, where what one said, and how one said it, could have practical and serious consequences. The prestige of their academic certificates, guaranteed by the state, led many people to adopt their way of talking, and so to imagine that a problem was solved once it had been clarified. A veneer of principle became almost necessary to anyone who wished to appear educated. But it is not certain that they therefore made the articulate section of the country into a class that was genuinely united in its mental mechanisms. A professor who has studied the oratory of politicians has shown how each party has its own particular style—the left makes longer speeches than the right, uses more metaphors, more adjectives and adverbs, while General de Gaulle employed twice as many subordinate clauses as his rivals.[1]

No doubt one could take this kind of analysis further to show the differences in the style of different professions and different social groups. Until more research is done, therefore, it is not possible to conclude firmly about the results of the schools' cult of rhetoric, but any exposition of its influence must be qualified in two ways. What the schools taught was assimilated with varying degrees of comprehension, and much speech and writing attempting to conform to their noble ideals was only a parody of it: they could never fully approve of the mediocrity they engendered. Their claim, that they contributed to increasing clarity, must be judged by studying how Frenchmen behaved in practice. If the resolution of daily problems into abstract terms was one consequence, then it may be that this not infrequently also complicated people's lives and created more disagreements than might otherwise have been noticed. But that was perhaps the way they came to like it.

[1] Jean Roche, *Le Style des candidats à la présidence de la république 1965–9. Étude quantitative de stylistique* (Toulouse, 1971).

Whatever their direct results, the prestige of rhetoric and philosophy also led to some paradoxical and unexpected consequences. Precisely because their methods could be dogmatic, they stimulated fecund rebellion: they produced not just conformity but also innovation, and sociology, for example, was one of the children of the rebellion against philosophy. Philosophy's ambition to be universal in its interests could mean superficiality, but it was also one of the most important stimuli for the introduction of foreign ideas into France, and in particular it was constantly building new bridges to Germany. By itself, philosophy often seemed to be sterile, but it was like a celibate having constant affairs, and in combination it could be highly fruitful. Rhetoric, for its part, might be hollow, but it could also create enthusiasm. French ideas were often presented in a way that gave the impression that new continents were being discovered, or rather were about to be discovered. The excitement generated made intellectual life probably more exhilarating than anywhere else in the world, even if the excitement had to be paid for with the subsequent gloom of disappointment.

# 6. Privilege and Culture

## Practical v. Useless Learning

'IT is not with fine words that one manufactures beet sugar; it is not with Alexandrine verses that one extracts sodium from sea salt.' So said the scientist Arago in parliament in 1837, in a debate in which the preoccupation of the schools with the classics and with useless knowledge was challenged. But the poet Lamartine, soon to be made head of the Republic, replied that, 'If the human race were condemned to lose entirely one of these two sets of truths—either all mathematical truths or all moral truths—I say that it ought not to hesitate to sacrifice mathematics. For if all mathematical truths are lost, the industrial world and the material world would no doubt suffer great harm and immense detriment, but if man were to lose a single one of those moral truths, of which literary studies are the vehicle, it would be man himself, it would be the whole of humanity which would perish.' The attitudes of France towards material and literary values were mirrored in the controversies about the school syllabus, in the struggle of the arts against the sciences.

A superficial view of the educational system might lead one to suppose that this was a country in which literature was held in quite exceptional esteem; and it seems consistent with this that it should also be a country which long resisted industrialisation. There is truth in this view, but it is not the whole truth. It was indeed the case that the schools had their attention turned above all to the study of the past, and in particular of past literature—a preoccupation justified in the interests of perpetuating 'the humanities'. It was also the case that the schools fought endless battles to preserve Latin as the basis of their syllabus and opposed the introduction of scientific subjects into it. But, as so often happened in France, the dust generated by these controversies obscured the fact that quite a significant number of pupils did specialise as scientists and that a lot of modernisation of the syllabus did take place. The *lycée*, concentrating on rhetoric and philosophy, was the most esteemed of educational institutions, particularly among those who had been to it, but it coexisted with other types of schools which many people preferred. Moreover, even within the *lycée*, there were mathematicians who avoided the rule of the classics almost completely. A picture of the educational system which suggested that it was all of one type, or that it was exclusively retrograde would be inaccurate. The way it undertook its modernisation, and the place it accorded to science are, indeed, highly revealing about the organisation of society as a whole.

The *lycées* represented the preservation of the secondary schools of the *ancien régime*. In the 1790s, an attempt had been made to break away from this tradition, by setting up a radically different system, known as the *écoles centrales*. These did not have classes of boys of the same age, placed under one master and subject to strict discipline, but instead offered courses given by specialised teachers, which the pupils could take according to their inclinations. Their syllabus had as its basis not Latin, but drawing, designed to teach decoration and to serve as the basis both for scientific and artistic training—and over ten times more pupils enrolled for this than for the course in belles-lettres. It included modern as well as ancient languages (each province choosing the language of its nearest foreign neighbour); it transformed the old grammar into general, philosophical grammar, seeking to penetrate the ideas and logic of language; it abandoned ancient for contemporary history and added a course in contemporary politics and legislation; it made belles-lettres into a study of the psychology behind literature; it introduced courses in experimental physics and chemistry, as well as mathematics, requiring each school to have a laboratory, a library and a garden. The teachers were given security of tenure, independence and self-government. The pupils were liberated from disciplinary controls; boarding was abolished; hours of work were gradually reduced as pupils got older, so that they could read on their own. This was supposed to be an education directed at instilling not worship of the past but a spirit of inquiry into the present and into the facts of real life. The school was no longer to be a retreat from the world. But these *écoles centrales* were the pipe dream of the Ideologues, who themselves had an inadequate appreciation of what the world was like. The schools were too peculiar to appeal to the middle classes; few pupils were sent to them; and there were not enough teachers qualified to offer the courses, most of which were never in fact given. The whole idea was soon condemned as dangerously revolutionary and it vanished as all but a utopia, which, moreover, never had more than a tiny group of believers in it.[1] Henceforth, those who were keen on practical education diverted their endeavours towards the primary schools, and those interested in more science put their hopes in the faculties. The secondary schools remained the bastion of literary studies.

The heritage of the Jesuits was that only one side of the Renaissance tradition was preserved—the study of antiquity, but not that of science; their aim to produce polished and fluent conversationalists overrode the interest, which some people, like Cardinal Richelieu and Abbé Fleury, had expressed in the seventeenth century, that the schools should train different types of pupils, and not simply for the world of fashion, of letters and of the liberal professions.[2] So the compromise between mathematics and the classics, briefly attempted by the Consulate, was abandoned under the Empire. Science was postponed till after the child had acquired a literary training. The *classe de mathématiques* was relegated to the final year, as an alternative to the *classe de philosophie*, and virtually limited to those seeking admission to the Polytechnic and other advanced scientific schools. Mathematics was taught in an abstract way, with no applications. In 1846 no natural science was taught in *lycées* in the first three years, and it was offered only as an optional subject, for one hour a week, to be taken on the Thursday holiday. An inquiry held in that year brought to the fore the demands of the scientists, led by the chemist J. B. Dumas, for a change in this state of affairs, but the Revolution prevented any actual reform being brought about, and, as will be seen, change was diverted from the general programme of the *lycées*, to the idea of creating special schools for scientists. The literary vested interests remained impregnable. Too many other battles were being fought

[1] But one of these was Francisque Vial, Director of Secondary Education: see his *Trois Siècles d'histoire de l'enseignement secondaire* (1936), 71–153, for an adulatory account of the *écoles centrales*.

[2] C. Falcucci, *L'Humanisme dans l'enseignement secondaire en France au dix-neuvième siècle* (Toulouse, 1939) is an erudite thesis recounting the history of the controversy.

at the same time for scientific education to be capable of becoming a major issue. It is quite wrong to suppose that republicans were in favour of it. They were absorbed by the struggle with the Church; they placed their faith in moral education, and there were many of them who were firm believers in the classics. They put their efforts into upholding the educational value of pagan antiquity, against those clergymen who, while defending the study of Latin, wanted to make it the study of Christian Latinity.[1]

The Second Empire changed the situation in two ways. First, it introduced *bifurcation*, which meant that pupils were able to opt between science and letters after their third year. It did not separate the two specialisations completely, for the scientists had to do some literary studies and the classicists got a smattering of science. The idea behind this was to make it possible for preparation for the scientific *grandes écoles* to start earlier, rather than be concentrated into intensive cramming after the *baccalauréat*; and it was also an attempt to make the *lycée* more competitive against the church schools, offering a distinctive syllabus, directed once again towards state service. Enormous howls of protest greeted this reform and most historians have continued to malign Fortoul, the minister responsible for it. The trouble with it was that it was bound up with other, clearly repressive moves, based on fear of the small minority of revolutionary teachers. The classicists were indignant that their age-old supremacy was being challenged; the philosophers cried loudest because their subject was abolished altogether, and turned into logic (alias scientific methodology). *Bifurcation*, however, was not all that much of an innovation; it simply reorganised the methods by which pupils could specialise in science from about the age of 14, which a few already used to do in any case, but it tried to turn this specialisation into a coherent education. The study of letters remained the basis of the new scientific syllabus: 'The Emperor', declared Fortoul, 'does not wish there to be two nations in the *lycées*'; his aim is to divert some of the growing mass of unemployable arts graduates into training that would fit them for industry. The classicists replied that this watering-down of their syllabus destroyed all its moral value,

[1] Abbé J. Gaume, *Le Ver rongeur des sociétés modernes, ou le paganisme dans l'éducation* (1851).

and that scientific education could have none. Many scientists, paradoxically, shared their prejudice. This was an important reason why science never sought pride of place at school: the science teachers often accepted the claims of the classicists, and they liked *bifurcation* because, by keeping some literature in the scientific syllabus, it gave it a more respectable status. Other scientists, however, regretted *bifurcation*, because they were intent on developing their own purely scientific schools, and knew that this would damage their separatist cause. Nevertheless, despite the enormous amount of disagreement in political and teaching circles, the new system was popular among parents. Within a year of the new system being started, the pupils opting for science outnumbered those who stayed on with the classics in forty-five out of sixty *lycées*. Some Paris *lycées* were divided equally, and some in small towns, which catered for a traditionalist clientele, but the large provincial *lycées* on the whole favoured the new system and some went on to establish strong and lasting scientific traditions. Those in the ports and on the eastern frontier, which prepared for the naval and military schools, found it suited them well. But it was never given a proper chance. As Pasteur said, there were just not enough science teachers to allow a sudden expansion. In practice, some continued to teach what they had always taught. The industrialists, moreover, were at this very time abandoning their support for science in the schools. This can be seen in a particularly striking way at Mulhouse, where, early in the nineteenth century, they had established a school for their children, to give them a scientific education. But during the Second Empire they gradually increased the literary content and henceforth they preferred to obtain the literary *baccalauréat*, as a surer mark of respectability.[1] Some declared that it was important to cultivate 'French taste' because that was what made French products distinctive and saleable. The doctors dealt *bifurcation* its final blow: it had allowed admission to medical schools simply with a *baccalauréat ès sciences*: they protested that this would introduce uncultured ignoramuses into the profession and in 1858 got the *baccalauréat ès lettres* restored as a compulsory qualification for medical studies. In the early 1860s between a third and a quarter of headmasters were still in favour of *bifurcation*, but it

[1] R. Oberlé, *L'Enseignement à Mulhouse de 1789 à 1870* (1961).

was, for practical reasons, doomed. The isolation of the scientists in *math préparatoire* was restored: this was limited *bifurcation* for a few but without the common literary education which was the real essence of *bifurcation*.[1]

The historian Victor Duruy, Napoleon III's most famous minister of public instruction, had been horrified, when he had had to tour the country as an inspector-general, by the obvious uselessness of the classical syllabus for so many people. He had watched the sons of well-to-do farmers stuttering with pain and incomprehension through their Latin translation, simply because that was the only respectable education which someone who was making his way up in the world could buy. Duruy protested that 'we are stealing these people's money'. The boys would become farmers in their turn; their smattering of Latin was wasted and soon forgotten. So when he became minister, he started up a new branch of 'special secondary education' designed for the agricultural, commercial and industrial classes. This, again, was not a totally new thing, for the *lycées* had long had 'special courses', which were supplementary, practical classes given in *lycées*, usually by less qualified teachers, for the benefit of pupils who left school early and had no ambition to enter the liberal professions. Duruy developed these into an autonomous system, making them less technical, including in their syllabus history and literary history, modern languages (but not Latin) and morals (but not philosophy). Special education was not industrial training, and indeed only partly secondary. It was aimed at a lower social class than the classical *lycée*: Duruy said it would provide the non-commissioned officers of the industrial army. His often-praised liberalism had its limits: he believed in education corresponding to people's social status, even though he also talked about the rule of merit, and the people who sent their children to these new forms were indeed of the lower middle classes. Duruy tried, however, to modify the traditional approach by making them less theoretical and involving more 'applications': 'no metaphysics, no abstraction:

[1] R. D. Anderson, 'Some Developments in French Secondary Education during the Second Empire' (unpublished Oxford D.Phil. thesis 1967), particularly chapters 4, 5 and 8, using the Fortoul papers. Maurice Gontard has since written a biography of Fortoul. For an excellent general survey of all levels of education under the Second Empire see R. D. Anderson, *Education in France 1848–70* (Oxford, 1975).

let the word concrete be held in honour', he said. He established an *agrégation spéciale* to give the teachers a respectability equal to that of the classical teachers, which they sorely needed, for most were former primary teachers. A special teacher training college was established at Cluny, in three sections—applied science, modern languages, and literature and economics. This survived till 1891, when special education was fully absorbed into the secondary system and became 'modern education'.[1]

Neither special nor modern education gave a scientific training. These were not revivals of the *écoles centrales*. The dominance of literature was seen in the study of the ancient world being replaced largely by that of modern languages. Special education was an education for clerks and shopkeepers, more than for factory managers, useful though it might be. There was not all that much to distinguish it from the *écoles primaires supérieures*, apart from the quite significant fact that it was more expensive, in that it charged the same fees as the *lycées*. Between 1866 and 1880 only 5 per cent of its pupils completed the whole course; and 45 per cent left in the first two years of their schooling. But in 1886 the course was lengthened from four to six years. It ceased therefore to be limited mainly to those who had not the time to do a full *lycée* course and it graduated into a comparable alternative to classical education. It still lacked prestige, in the eyes of those who had received a classical education, but it was popular all the same. Side by side with the traditional classical course, which tended to absorb the attention of historians and indeed most writers, there was that of 'modern humanities', as it was called, which had rather different pretensions. By the turn of the century, half the secondary school population was opting for it. Between 1865 and 1880, 68 per cent of secondary pupils were 'classical' and 32 per cent were modern. In 1894, however, after the incorporation of special education into the secondary system, the classics fell to 53 per cent and the moderns rose to 47 per cent. In 1899 the classics and the moderns were exactly equal. In 1900 the moderns were in the majority, with 52 per cent. But this was not the triumph of science. For a time during the Second Empire, almost the same number of *baccalauréats* were awarded in science as in letters: in 1854 and 1855, indeed, there were even a few more scientists than classicists:

---

[1] The best account is in Anderson, op. cit.

I

but in the years 1870–90, there were roughly four classical *bacheliers* to every three scientific ones. The establishment of a modern *baccalauréat* (in 1881) made little difference to this: it was not taken by many people at first: pupils who opted for modern education were not interested in certificates, and it was not science that they studied in any case. The ministry of commerce, indeed, even granted holders of the modern *baccalauréat* various privileges, in its competition, over holders of the science *baccalauréat*. But modern education increasingly became a caricature of classical education, more and more literary, with only the ancient languages left out: the teachers lost the opportunity to make something really positive out of it and it fell into the status of a poor relation. In the period between the two world wars, by which time the modern *baccalauréat* had been abolished and incorporated into a general examination, there were regularly twice as many pupils obtaining the *baccalauréat* in letters as obtained that in science—and sometimes more than that. So whereas in 1891 nearly 3,000 obtained the science *baccalauréat*, in 1935 there were still only 3,365. At the same time the *bacheliers* in letters rose from 4,142 to 8,574.[1] This is explained not only by the failure of 'modern' pupils to finish their courses, but also by the amount of time given to science in schools, as shown in the accompanying table.

*Percentage of time spent by pupils in the course*
*of their seven years at secondary school*

I: If they chose the most classical options:

|      | Philosophy | Letters | Modern Languages | History & Geography | Science |
|------|------------|---------|------------------|---------------------|---------|
| 1852 | 2          | 67      | 5                | 13                  | 13      |
| 1864 | 5·5        | 60      | 6·5              | 12·5                | 15·5    |
| 1880 | 5          | 52      | 11·5             | 15                  | 16      |
| 1890 | 5          | 58·3    | 7·3              | 13·8                | 15·4    |
| 1902 | 6          | 49      | 14               | 17                  | 16      |
| 1925 | 5          | 48      | 13               | 15                  | 25      |
| 1938 | 5·4        | 43·5    | 11·7             | 14·5                | 25·2    |
| 1952 | 5·8        | 44      | 14·2             | 15·9                | 20      |
| 1962 | 6          | 42      | 14·3             | 15·1                | 22·7    |

[1] Statistics in J. B. Piobetta, *Le Baccalauréat* (1937), 304–8.

II: If they chose the most modern options:

| | Philosophy | Letters | Modern Languages | History & Geography | Science |
|---|---|---|---|---|---|
| 1852 | 2 | 47 | 5 | 13 | 32 |
| 1865 | 0 | 15·5 | 17·5 | 13 | 54 |
| 1882 | 8 | 20 | 16 | 12 | 43 |
| 1891 | 6 | 20 | 27 | 13 | 31 |
| 1904 | 2 | 16 | 23 | 13 | 36 |
| 1925 | 2 | 24 | 27 | 16 | 31 |
| 1938 | 1·9 | 24 | 27·8 | 14·4 | 31·7 |
| 1952 | 2 | 21·4 | 27·8 | 15·1 | 35 |
| 1962 | 2 | 21·2 | 26·7 | 14·9 | 36·1 |

Based on V. Isambert-Jamati, *Crises de la société* (1970), appendix II.

Except for a brief period during and a little after the Second Empire, science, even in the most 'modern' option, was never given more than one-third of the pupils' time; and mathematics was always given at least half of this time, so that the bulk of scientific teaching was theoretical. Until 1902 (and in some schools long after that) the standard textbook in geometry, for example, was that of Legendre, first published in 1794, the main effect of which was to require pupils simply to memorise definitions and proofs.[1]

It was not for lack of trying that the state failed to provide the types of education people wanted, or needed. The secondary syllabus was altered no less than fifteen times in the course of the nineteenth century and between 1802 and 1887 no less than seventy-five decrees of various kinds modified the organisation of the schools. In 1899–1902, a major effort was made to consult all sections of opinion, in a parliamentary inquiry whose findings filled seven large volumes. As a result of this, a law of 1902 attempted to diversify the options open to pupils, by setting up four different combinations of study—from the old Greek and Latin specialisation at one extreme to sciences and modern languages at the other, with Latin, science and one modern language as a third option, and Latin and two modern languages

[1] A.-M. Legendre [1752–1834], *Éléments de géométrie* (1794, 14th edition 1839, 11th revised edition 1868; translated into Spanish 1826, into Turkish 1841, Argentinian edition 1886). For the reform of teaching in geometry, see Charles Meray, *L'Enseignement des mathématiques* (1901) and *Nouveaux Éléments de géométrie* (1874, new edition 1903).

as a fourth. The partisans of the classics got better terms than they had a right to expect, for over the previous fifteen years the number of pupils specialising in the classics had fallen by over a third. Latin and, even more, Greek were already, and noticeably, losing their popularity after 1885, but the generation educated on the classics were in power and loath to condemn knowledge which they thought had made them what they were. So much so, indeed, that in 1923 a conservative government even tried to reintroduce compulsory classics for everybody during the first three years of secondary schooling. But at the same time this government also saw the need for more science, and invented the formula of 'scientific equality', proposing that all options should also have a common scientific basis. This is what the radicals established in 1925, but only by increasing the length of the school day. In 1941 the Vichy regime yielded to the protests about overwork and returned to the four options, with science as a specialisation. It was clearly impossible to conciliate all interests and it is unjust to condemn these different systems, since no one had a generally acceptable alternative. The triumph of science would have destroyed too many traditions. Paul Appell, dean of the Faculty of Sciences of Paris and rector of the Academy of the capital, considered that the *lycées* had made certain characteristics—'imported by the Jesuits from China' as he liked to say—so specifically their own, that they left no room for a genuine acceptance of the scientific approach. The *baccalauréat*, towards which everything in the *lycée* was directed, meant that the memorising of correct answers, rather than the spirit of inquiry and research, was supreme: 'everywhere it is the book that rules'. Theory was preferred to experiment; and even the pupils best endowed for science were forced to go through the same syllabus two or three times in order to gain admission to the Polytechnic: stamina in repetition, not independent thought, was the quality encouraged. He placed his hopes therefore on the universities, lamenting that the products of the *lycées*, devoted to literary studies, could not be got to change their ways.[1]

These educational controversies revealed the existence of several different types of ambition, which sought gratification through the schools in different ways; and that is why, in prac-

[1] Paul Appell, *Éducation et enseignement* (1922), 90–7, 113–24.

tice, so many varieties of schools developed, despite the passion for uniformity and monopoly that tormented the politicians. At the inquiry of 1899 it was pointed out by several witnesses that the syllabus was only one out of many factors that mattered to parents. Those who were involved in state service and the liberal professions were interested in the *baccalauréat*, which raised their children into membership of what people did not hesitate to call the ruling caste. There were parents who believed that the classics were a necessary foundation for a truly educated man, but, apart from some whose literary attainments qualified them to make such a judgement, the majority saw in Latin simply a way of entering certain jobs, or of distinguishing themselves from the lower orders, because they could afford to cultivate the superfluous. But Édouard Aynard, a banker from Lyon, noted that the idle rich were now under attack and the ideal of being a man of leisure and pleasure was becoming discredited. Previously, dandy young men used to refuse to enter the family business and so allowed the graduates of the *lycées* and the universities, often of humble origin, to make their way into important positions in industry and commerce. But now the rich were agreeing to follow in their fathers' footsteps and the best jobs were thus being kept within the family. The only way for one without fortune to make his way (unless he was exceptionally brilliant) was to start at the bottom. The holders of *baccalauréats* had to resign themselves to this. But employers saw that they were resigned, discontented, feeling that society owed them something better; and so they might often prefer to take on a boy of fifteen without any certificate or pretensions, who would do as he was told. The constant confusion in secondary education was due to its overproduction of boys with diplomas which were useful only in certain limited professions, and to its directing its efforts above all to preparing its pupils for admission to the universities, which most, in this period, did not want to enter. The teachers inevitably thought that the best pupils should become teachers. But the lower middle classes, which were faithful clients of the *lycées*, had other horizons than the civil service. A teacher of a 'modern' course told the inquiry that the parents of his pupils did not care much what their boys learnt: 'the essential thing was to have their children brought up in a bourgeois institution . . . The *petit bourgeois* puts his son into a *lycée*, not to make a learned man out of him, but so as not to put him in the same school as that to which the sons of his servant and his concierge go.'[1] An investigation carried out in the 1880s in Paris showed clearly that 'modern' education appealed to a distinct class—the foremen, clerks, small business men.[2] The aspirations of these people did not press the state to increase scientific education. 'Modern' education was therefore also largely useless, for the literary methods of the classics were simply transferred to modern languages.

If they wanted more practical advantages from their schooling, it was to the Church more than the state that these people turned. The Church was not restricted by the all-important distinction between primary and secondary, and it was infinitely more flexible. Despite the increase in population, the state had established only one new *lycée* in Paris between Napoleon's day and Ferry's. In 1880, indeed, Berlin had five times as many gymnasia as Paris had *lycées*. The number of pupils at the ten *collèges* of Paris in 1789 was 5,000; in 1880 the *lycées* that succeeded them had only 6,792. The state thus provided for a small circle of people that had dealings with it. Other people looked elsewhere and the Church created schools of all kinds to meet their diverse needs. Its flexibility was even more notable in the provinces, where uniform *lycées* were distributed without regard for the demand. Thus one of the first results of the invention of special secondary education was that the Church transformed about fifty of its *écoles primaires supérieures* into 'special' colleges, giving them a new social status, but also keeping the practical primary bent. At the same time, it continued to establish and develop its aristocratic schools, which emphasised character training rather than examinations. It provided a whole range of schools—contrasting with the more fixed pattern of the *lycées* —catering for every degree of snobbishness, and at every price. But, of course, science was not the Church's strong point. The modernisation of the syllabus thus, to a certain extent, used up its impetus in the creation of numerous new gradations of social differentiation, rather than in introducing new teaching methods.

---

[1] *Enquête sur l'enseignement secondaire* (1899), 2.108, and Annexe (rapport général), 34.

[2] O. Gréard, *Éducation et instruction* (1887), 2. 55.

Keeping up with the times was no easy matter when so many forces were pushing the schools in different directions. Thus on the one hand the *lycées* had to perform what they considered their traditional function, of training the élite of the literary and civil service worlds, but their traditional methods were breaking down before the increase in pupil numbers: these doubled between 1850 and 1920, and doubled again between 1930 and 1938. The attractions of the civil service were, moreover, diminishing; new opportunities were being offered in commerce—previously despised; new ambitions were developing and new ideals were being invented. The school-teachers were faced not only with the problem of how to react to these changes and how to reassess their work in relation to them, but also with the need to defend and improve their own status when traditional values were everywhere being undermined. They had the alternative of trying to forecast which trends would be victorious, or of making the schools guardians of the truths they had grown up with and on the whole continued to cherish. That is why one cannot see the schools as simply 'reflecting society' and propagating its ideals, quite apart from the fact that the schools had a long history of providing a retreat from the world. A sociologist, Madame Isambert-Jamati, has attempted to study the attitudes of the schools towards society on a quantitative basis, taking as her source 2,000 speeches made at school prize-givings between 1860 and 1965. The exhortations and platitudes uttered at these ceremonies are taken as evidence of what head-masters, senior teachers and local dignitaries thought they were doing. The results of this computerised study are highly instructive in that they do show marked and interesting adaptations. The dating of the changing attitudes cannot be too precise, because the people who make speeches on these occasions are nearly always old men; they could easily be expressing ideas picked up thirty or even fifty years earlier. The processing of this mass of banality through computers is designed to produce averages, which are inevitably simplifications.

Nevertheless, it is the case that under the Second Empire, many of these speakers praised the *lycées* as a training ground for the country's élite 'whom the favour of Providence', as one speaker put it, 'has placed on the best rung of the social scale: you are destined to rule'. But different types of speakers looked for different results from this training: the arts masters stressed the development of taste, the science masters and administrators, following the current governmental policy, thought the schools were providing intellectual exercises to equip people to cope better with problems; while the 'notables' were not very interested by the syllabus but saw in the schools institutions which were preparing boys to enter their own class and become like themselves. Much was made of the need to obey authority, to maintain discipline. But averaging out all the points made, this was the period when most stress was placed on the school as a retreat from the dangers of the world, as protecting children; and also on its helping to inculcate the values society cherished —the true, the good and the beautiful, as defined by Victor Cousin.

In the founding years of the Third Republic, 1876–85, numerous changes were made to the syllabus, introducing more French, history and geography; more stress was laid on developing the individual judgement of pupils; and much was made of the republic as the regime of the rule of merit. But only 20 per cent of prize-givings mentioned this ideal of education being open to all. Thirty-two per cent still talked of the *lycée* as training an élite (a proportion even higher than under Napoleon III); and the liberal professions were still regarded as the natural outlet for pupils (87 per cent of speeches, as against 57 per cent mentioning technical jobs). Those who favoured 'discipline' were now balanced almost exactly by those who spoke in favour of individual initiative, just as those who continued to believe in the school as a retreat from the world were now balanced equally by those who were discarding this idea. The most popular theme was now patriotism (75 per cent), followed by the need to improve the world, the need for action, rather than just preserving old values. This new attitude was common ground between the notables and the history teachers, but the literature masters were still interested in styles of life and the importance of knowing languages. These divergences give one a hint of the sort of things teachers said to their pupils, as asides, as they glossed the same old set books: they obviously did not all say the same thing, and apart from a general agreement on flag-waving, a good half of them probably rejected the ideals of Ferry, with which the period is usually associated.

With time, as more and more reforms rained on them, many teachers retreated into attitudes of self-defence. By the turn of the century, the notables were being threatened also in their privileges. So in the years 1906–1930 the most frequent topic at prize-givings became the importance of disinterested knowledge and the preservation of taste. The teachers had once included many advocates of modernity, but when modernity actually arrived, and they saw their pupils abandoning the classics, and actually preferring action to education, they were horrified. Now they stressed instead the value of education for its own sake; there were references to science in only 9 per cent of the speeches. In the 1930s this attitude was altered slightly, in that education was now praised as developing the critical faculties and mental qualities such as clarity and precision, which could serve society better. There was no more preaching of adherence to social values, but this implied that the schools were now confident in values of their own. Children were seen less as adults in the making, than as having problems of their own, which the schools catered for, and this to a certain extent was a modification of the old idea of the school as a refuge. The study of the past was no longer mentioned as the main concern of schools, but it was not contemporary politics or economics that attracted comment: instead it was 'human nature' in the abstract that was now held up as what pupils should be taught to understand, and it is significant that, for this, it was to the literature of the seventeenth and eighteenth centuries that speakers turned most for their illustrations. The schools were thus redeveloping as small societies, seeking out roles for themselves which were not modelled on what the politicians were preaching in this highly agitated period: agitation outside could produce a search for the opposite inside the schools.

One explanation of this independence is that the relations of teachers and pupils were changing. The old authoritarianism was discredited. One teacher told his pupils: 'Be our friends, be our teachers.' This was the period when adolescence won a new respect, so that the whole idea of teaching was in danger of being challenged. By the 1950s, teachers could no longer easily think of themselves as superior to their pupils, and their function in society became very difficult to define. While the world outside absorbed itself in economic reconstruction and profiteering,

the literature teachers condemned efficiency as vulgar, and proclaimed the grandeur of disinterested effort, of taste. References
to science were now made in only 10 per cent of prize-givings—
no more than references to philosophy, which was mentioned
ten times more than in the 1930s, because it was now emerging
as a provider of a common cultural language for those who were
above the fray and claimed to judge it. Philosophy had the advantage that it was more esoteric than literature—still the most
widely respected subject for developing taste—and it went
beyond taste. The philosophers were the new élite who spoke
Latin when few people did, or better still Greek or Hebrew.
Only in the 1960s did the study of contemporary man and
society become the goal most frequently urged. Even after due
allowance is made for the limited value of these prize-giving
speeches as indications of general trends, they do at least suggest
that the schools were often as concerned to defend themselves
as to serve society and play up to its latest obsession.[1] That is
an important reason why one cannot look to the schools for
simple explanations of changing attitudes in the country as a
whole, or talk of the influence of teachers in general terms.
Some teachers were articulate out of all proportion to their
numbers, and created the illusion that society as a whole was
worried by their problems; while, on the other hand, the
teachers in the 'modern' schools were not given to proclaiming
grand principles or to rationalising their activities, and their
work—which affected half the pupils in the secondary schools—
has gone largely unrecorded.

### Rebellion, Discipline and Competitiveness

If the question of the influence of schools is to be understood,
the relations between teachers and pupils must first be examined
more closely.

'Merchants of Greek! Merchants of Latin! Hacks! Bulldogs!
Philistines! Magisters! I hate you, pedagogues!
Because, with your grave self-assurance, infallibility, stupidity,
You deny ideals, grace and beauty!

[1] V. Isambert-Jamati, *Crises de la société, crises de l'enseignement. Sociologie de
l'enseignement secondaire français* (1970).

Because your texts, your laws, your rules are fossils!
Because, with your profound airs, you are imbeciles!
Because you teach everything and know nothing! . . .'[1]

This translation of a verse by Victor Hugo presents the other
side of the school, the resistance it generated to so much that
was taught, simply because it was taught. There were an
extraordinarily large number of Frenchmen who recalled their
schooldays in these years with horror and pain: even if life later
brought them more serious misfortunes, schooling was probably
a disagreeable experience for the majority who went through it.
With time, more and more children had to undergo it: the
proportion of those whose temperaments and interests it did not
suit may well have increased. Until scholars dig up and scrutin-
ise a vast mass of end-of-term reports, it will be impossible to
say how the reactions of children varied at different periods and
whether, when schooling was made compulsory for everybody,
it was accepted more or less willingly. But schoolchildren certainly had grievances of a very positive nature. Following the
new situation created by the events of 1968, their opinions and
protests have been collected and analysed in great detail by
sociologists. It is striking that these do not differ very much from
those of the previous century—though knowledge of their discontents in the past is of course far more fragmentary. Just as
the teachers' refusal to allow their pupils to wear long hair or
mini-skirts was a source of bitter resentment in 1968, so in the
1840s there is a record of a *lycée* going on strike because its headmaster forbade the senior pupils to wear beards and expelled
one who protested insolently to him.[2] During the Second Empire, the irate pupils of the *lycée* at Poitiers barricaded themselves in their dormitories and were expelled only when the
troops forced their way in, under the command of the garrison
general himself. In 1870 no less than twenty-one pupil revolts
were recorded. But the real crisis of pupil–teacher relations
occurred in 1882–3. It began with a mutiny at Toulouse, in
protest against excessively strict discipline and as a result also
of grievances against individual teachers. The headmaster,
backed by the Inspector and the Rector, dealt with it firmly by

[1] V. Hugo, *Les Contemplations* (1856).
[2] *Lycée Henri Poincaré: le livre des centenaires* (Nancy, 1954), 56.

mass expulsions, sending telegrams to the parents to remove their boys at once and escorting these to the station without delay. The pupils were defeated by their lack of unity. Soon afterwards the *lycéens* of Montpellier therefore called a congress, which was attended by representatives of a dozen *lycées*, mainly from the south, but from as far as Lyon, Nantes and Nevers too —though the congress had to change its venue secretly to Albi, to avoid repression. It produced a petition demanding the establishment of committees of pupils to act as intermediaries between the boys and the administration, a five-day week, the taxation of concierges who exploited boarders, an amnesty for boys involved in the mutinies and—on the academic plane— that Greek and Latin should be made optional, but that two modern languages should be compulsory. A newspaper entitled *The Rights of Youth* appeared. The boys of the Lycée Condorcet demanded that headmasters should be elected. It was, however, at Louis-le-Grand, the largest of the Paris *lycées*, that the most serious agitation occurred, to be reported extensively by the national press. Following a protest against the punishment of a boy, considered too severe, the headmaster had expelled five leaders of the protest. Violent demonstrations followed: the pupils smashed the furniture and resisted with iron rods the police who were summoned to quell them. The headmaster got permission from the Under-Secretary of State to expel the whole of the top form if necessary. He sent telegrams to their parents to remove them. Ninety-three pupils were expelled from Louis-le-Grand and twelve others were forbidden to attend any other state school.[1] These disturbances led to the whole question of discipline and authority being re-examined and new regulations were introduced in 1890, which considerably diminished the rigour of school life. To some extent, therefore, there were two periods in the history of school discipline, before and after these events. But many underlying features survived into the Fifth Republic, even if punishments could no longer be doled out as they once had been. However, the repetitive way in which, at intervals, leading authorities in the educational world proclaimed that there was a 'crisis of authority and of discipline'

---

[1] R. H. Guerrand, *Lycéens révoltés: étudiants révolutionnaires au 19ᵉ siècle* (1969), 66. O. Gréard, 'L'Esprit de discipline dans l'éducation', in his *Éducation et instruction: Enseignement secondaire* (1887), 2. 163, gives the figure 89, not 93.

shows that there were constant and fundamental problems, to which solutions were not found.

The French were proud that they had been the first people to abolish corporal punishment. Already in 1769 when new regulations were drawn up for Louis-le-Grand, there was no mention of beating, but instead 240 articles spelling out an elaborate variety of non-violent methods of control. In 1809 Napoleon simply generalised these. In 1854 Napoleon III made them somewhat less severe, by abolishing three of the sanctions still in use: imprisonment, relegation to a 'table of penitence' and 'deprivation of uniform'. The pupils were thus controlled by black marks, detentions of varying types, and expulsion. The law did not interfere with the *lycées*' brutal initiation rites and 'sending to Coventry' but there was nothing like the English fagging system, which was judged highly offensive to the doctrine of social equality. The physical conditions to which the boys were subjected were, however, often grim in the extreme. Most *lycées* were started in old church buildings confiscated at the Revolution, old hospitals, barracks and convents. In 1887 only one-fifth of them were purpose-built. An inspector visiting the college of Pertuis in 1877 wrote: 'Is this a school, a farm, or an inn, this vast ramshackle hut with rotting shutters and a bare courtyard?' At Grasse the college was a former perfume-distillery in ruins 'sordidly poor and completely neglected. Nothing has been mended, nothing cleaned: there is no desire to live.' At the *lycée* of Nancy, academically one of the best in the provinces, pupils complained, during the July Monarchy, that the mattresses they slept on—stuffed with straw or maize leaves—were so infested with lice as to make sleep difficult: the modernisation which followed involved the introduction of iron beds, and the provision of a bedside table for each one, instead of the single shelf which was all they had had to keep their property on. But in 1842 visiting inspectors were 'suffocated' by the smell of the latrines. In the 1860s a new bathroom was installed for the washing of feet, which was made obligatory once a fortnight. But in 1969 schoolchildren were still complaining about dormitories with seventy beds in long rows, saying that their buildings were like prisons—complete with grilles—but also dirty, ramshackle, uncomfortable, and noisy; they were still protesting, as they put it, against 'Napoleonic discipline' and furious punishments—like 700 lines.[1] Food—though a major preoccupation and provided with varying skill by bursars intent on economy—does not appear to have aroused anything like the dissatisfaction common in English schools. Boys, however, had a constant war directed at them to repress their sexuality—hard beds and coarse sheets were provided as anti-aphrodisiacs—and in 1969 they were still saying that homosexuality was one of the greatest problems of the schoolboy's life. Futile rules were made to control their leisure reading: in 1920 a pupil was expelled from the Lycée Buffon after a pornographic work, which the headmaster euphemistically called 'a particularly ignoble paper' was found in his possession: it was in vain that the boy protested he had picked it up at a religious club. In 1928 a ministerial order was issued forbidding pupils 'to form associations which elect a president and officials, sport insignia and claim to impose rules of any kind on members. In establishments of public education there is only one authority, that of the staff charged with administration, teaching and surveillance. Pupils, of whatever seniority, may not have relations with their teachers except individual ones, and collective representations may be allowed only in exceptional circumstances, and when they directly and exclusively concern academic work.' The government of the Liberation repealed this regulation in 1945.[2]

In the academic subjects they taught, the schools were confident that they were giving their pupils not only knowledge, but also the intellectual qualities needed to cope with life, to see its meaning and to judge the value of competing claims made upon them. But these mental powers—even if they were developed—were undermined by several contradictions in the emotional education which was offered. In the first place, though the schools preached respect for parents, they also saw themselves as rivals of the family. Boarding, the *internat*, was the expression of this ambivalence. In 1809, 63 per cent of all pupils in the *lycées* were boarders. This was seen as an indispensable part of the idea of the school as a closed world of its own, reinforced by the use of the *lycée* as a training ground for state servants, and by the desire to open it to merit, irrespective of where the parents resided. These various aims did not mix too

---

[1] Gérard Vincent, *Les Lycéens* (1971), based on 5,000 essays by schoolchildren, 66, 75.       [2] Guerrand, op. cit. 36.

well, for dissatisfaction with the way the *internat* worked in the *lycées* increased steadily. Part of the trouble was that the state delegated the duties of looking after the material side of the boys' lives to a separate class of despised and underpaid *surveillants*, known colloquially as *pions*. These were of two kinds. Some were youths who aspired to become teachers but, having no qualifications, took on the task of waking the boys up in the morning, keeping them in order during their meals, recreations and homework periods and supervising their discipline in general. They were supposed to study in their spare time, but they were on duty from when the boys rose to when they went to bed; they were paid a derisory pittance; they were lodged in attics and boxrooms without any comforts: it was the lowest possible job a youth could get: 'not even the most junior clerk, not even the convict was less happy than he'.[1] Most of them tried to move to something better as soon as they could; but some despaired of escaping and lived on, resigned, despised. The boys had no reason to respect them, so that a war waged between them, with vicious discipline being counteracted by merciless teasing and practical joking on the part of the pupils.[2] These ushers were employed by the headmaster on the same terms as servants, dismissible without notice. In the 1880s they formed themselves into an association and gradually won better conditions; but in 1900 only 3 per cent of them managed to get teaching jobs.[3] In 1923 they won guarantees against arbitrary dismissal; in 1937 they had a law requiring them to hold a *baccalauréat* and to have six hours a day free for study; they were dignified with the title of *maître d'internat*. Though their status improved in time, they continued to bear resentments. They opposed the relaxation of discipline, which they said would make them victims of the pupils' whims instead of those of the headmaster: liberty should not be given to the children until it was given to them.[4] The system by which the teacher just gave his

[1] Édouard Ourliac, *Physiologie de l'écolier* (1850), 107.

[2] For a description of the *pion's* life, see Alphonse Daudet, *Le Petit Chose* (1868).

[3] Paul Verdun, *Un Lycée sous la troisième république* (1888); Louis Durien, *Le Pion* (1880); Roger Rabaté, *De la situation économique et morale du personnel inférieur des lycées* (Paris law thesis, 1909); *L'Enquête sur l'enseignement secondaire* (1899), rapport, chapter 3.

[4] Maurice Loi, *Guide du surveillant* (1949) by the secretary-general of *L'Union du personnel de surveillance*.

classes and then went away, like a university professor, meant that sending one's boy to a *lycée* involved having him brought up by men who were regarded as little better than failures. This was very different from church schools, where at least the ushers were priests. The result was that the number of boarders in the *lycées* fell drastically under the Third Republic, to only 29 per cent in 1908. Parents who were compelled to send their children away from home increasingly preferred the church schools, which had over half of their pupils as boarders.[1] It was not irrelevant that boarding cost substantially more in state, as opposed to church schools, because the state tried to make a profit out of it, to subsidise the salaries of its teachers. During the July Monarchy and the Second Empire, a frequent compromise was to live in a private *pensionnat* and attend the *lycée* as a day boy; even pupils of church schools used to attend lectures at the *lycée*; and teachers used to move between the public and private sector. But this virtually disappeared during the Third Republic as the *lycée* hardened in its hostility to its rivals.[2]

As Alain defined it, the role of the *lycée* was to be a forcing house, to lead its pupils to the highest intellectual attainments, but in doing so, to compel them to become adults as soon as possible. In the name of Kant's categorical imperative, it saw its mission as liberating the child from his animality by imposing self-discipline on him, for the child who was indulged would remain savage all his life. The *lycée*'s disciplinary system had once been military. Under the republic it was reconstituted on a liberal basis, with much pedagogical and philosophical justification, but in practice it turned out to be highly authoritarian still. Thus Jules Payot, one of the new theorists, hoped that there would be voluntary submission to the teacher who showed calm, firmness and tact, but he still saw the teacher as a figure in authority.[3] Bergson opposed to the old system of breaking children in like horses, the authority based on charisma and the influence of the teacher seen as a model and hero. The experts were fully aware that severity produced 'rebellion, maladjustment, bitter or mistrustful pride', and that the teacher's

---

[1] 55% boarders in *petits séminaires*, 50% in diocesan schools, 47% in schools run by secular priests, 43% in independent lay schools, 30% in state *collèges* and 26% in *lycées*. Figures given in *L'Enquête*, rapport général (1899), 55.

[2] Jacques Rocafort, *L'Éducation morale au lycée* (1899).

[3] Albert Autin, *Autorité et discipline en matière d'éducation* (1920).

power could be an instrument of 'institutionalised sadism'. But routine was one of the strongest elements in the schools, and not least because many teachers self-confessedly became teachers in order to get their own back for the humiliations they had suffered as pupils. In 1968, a survey showed that 89 per cent of *lycée* pupils thought their teachers humiliated them, at least sometimes: they did not mean by that that teachers exercised authority over them, for they agreed overwhelmingly with the teachers that 'authority' was the most important quality a teacher had to have. But, next to that, the pupils valued love of children in teachers, while the teachers thought knowledge was more important; the majority of pupils complained against favouritism, which almost invariably went to those who were academically most successful; they wanted affection independently of their performance and that is what they did not get. The teachers replied that their classes were too large for them to take an interest in everybody.[1]

The result was that the pupils devised methods of protecting themselves, which considerably reduced the influence of their teachers. In memories of their schooldays, what they remembered most frequently was the ragging of teachers, which incidentally enabled them to forget the sufferings they underwent at their teachers' hands. Ragging was the reverse side of discipline, and between them they reveal how great the resistance of the pupils could be. During the July Monarchy Edmond Saisset thought he was performing his duties as a *lycée* teacher adequately simply by having a conversation with the best boys in the class, who sat in the front rows; he left the rest to their own devices; when the noise in the room became too great, he came down from his rostrum to hear what his 'dear disciples' were saying. This was quite common; to ignore a 'half-silence' was considered an achievement; which shows how, paradoxically, the teachers succeeded gradually in imposing their dominance over their pupils, despite their protestations of liberalism. The pupils replied to the favouritism shown to the successful by giving their admiration to the brave, who defied the teacher and could go furthest in flouting the rules of discipline. This attitude was organised into a formidable institution by the formation of cliques and gangs. Marcel Pagnol recounts that when he entered

[1] Vincent, op. cit. 61.

the Lycée Thiers at Marseille, he at once became part of a self-sufficient group of friends: as a *demi-pensionnaire* he spent eleven hours a day at school, so he knew nothing of the family of even his best friends. In these cliques, the pupils developed rules of their own, which neither parents nor teachers could influence much. One of these was exclusiveness: the claim to superiority, hostility to the *externes*, the day-boys (who however were used as emissaries, agents and pimps, to bring forbidden food and books into the school, and who could introduce fashions from the outside world).[1] Often these groups would choose leaders who would have precisely the opposite characteristics of the teachers—brutal ones if the teacher was weak, or cordial ones if he was severe; and with effective leaders, they could wage veritable wars of attrition against selected victims. The friendships formed here might last throughout their schooldays and sometimes throughout their lives: that was their positive side; but lying, cheating against teachers, bullying against the weak, group loyalty before all else were also developed. The school was partly responsible for allowing this, because it based its teaching methods on the encouragement of emulation and rivalry between the pupils. The sociability the politicians talked about was demanded only on a certain level. One of the major weaknesses of the school was that it did not appreciate how its pupils developed two different personalities, indeed two languages—an official one used in relations with teachers, and a slangy one, used among themselves. The influence of the teachers could not penetrate into this second world of the cliques. It has been suggested, in the chapter on primary education, that the *instituteur* failed to dislodge the primitive or superstitious mentality that his pupils inherited from their traditional backgrounds. Primary pupils seldom formed cliques, or threw up leaders, to resist their teachers. Unity was developed only in the secondary schools, and it was there that an additional way of life was developed, with moral attitudes different in many ways from that advocated by the schools. At the secondary level, there were thus three superimposed but independent cultures to which the pupils belonged: the academic, the adolescent and the family. The teachers, and the successful, academically

---

[1] J. Fontanel, *Psychologie de l'adolescence — Nos lycéens* (1913); Roger Ikor, *Les Cas de conscience du professeur* (1966), 212–19.

inclined children, were perhaps the only ones who reconciled these—by subordinating them to a single ambition. But for the majority, the tensions between them were both a source of conflict and a method by which the pressures of any one of them could be limited.[1]

Another of the contradictions between the intellectual and emotional work of the schools emanated from their attitude towards competitiveness. The problem had quickly been spotted during the first Revolution: in 1801 the Institut offered a prize for an essay on the question 'Is emulation a good means of education?'. The Jesuits (as will be seen) had made it the very basis of their school system, urging on their pupils to excel by stimulating rivalry between them and by an elaborate variety of honours and rewards. The winner of the prize concluded that some change was needed, that emulation under the *ancien régime* had been 'monarchical' but a democratic republic ought to find some alternative. There had been philosophers in the eighteenth century such as Bernardin de Saint-Pierre, who had thought that emulation ought to be eradicated; Rousseau had wanted to limit it to emulation against oneself; and some opponents of the Jesuits had protested that it was contrary to Christian humility. But the revolutionary doctrine of both fraternity and equality was in practice somehow reconciled with the maintenance of competitiveness. The nineteenth century, indeed, not only generalised it but sharpened and institutionalised it, and most notably of all, in the secondary schools, through the examination system. There was ample theoretical justification produced for it. Prévost-Paradol, the liberal moralist, declared that the desire for glory was one of the purest of emotions, that ambition was commendable provided it was directed at winning a reputation and men. Those who wanted money or pleasure were not ambitious but simply greedy or voluptuous. The ambition 'to make others adopt one's will and so . . . to will through them and act through them . . . gave one something like the Divine power': it extended one's strength, it elevated and indeed transformed human nature. Henri Marion, the republican philosopher of education, despite some reservations, thought emulation ought to be maintained, because it was the best way

[1] R. M. Mossé-Bastide, *L'Autorité du maître* (Neuchâtel, 1966); and chapter 12, of the first volume of this book.

of getting pupils to stretch themselves to the limit. An inspector-general, who gave a lecture in 1913 'On the utility of rewards and particularly of school prizes', defended the honours, medals, honourable mentions and constant classification by merit, which were studiously maintained by the teachers (who had of course themselves been the victors of this system) : he insisted that these were not the product of French vanity. Prizes were necessary because children were not perfect and would not work well simply to obey the categorical imperative. The struggle they involved was a useful preparation for the struggles of life. Some-how, the jealousies and disappointments they engendered must be mitigated; but no better method was proposed than the award of yet more prizes, for 'good conduct', which everybody, however stupid, had a chance of winning.[1]

Constant comparison of pupils against each other was a basic element in the schools. Marks were awarded for every exercise. One zealous teacher is even reported to have given three marks for every exercise: one which judged the work itself, a second which graded it by comparison with previous work and a third by comparison with the standard reached by other pupils. The state greatly increased the competitiveness by making pupils of the whole country compete against each other in national *concours généraux*. These were previously limited to the Paris *lycées*: in 1865 Duruy, in a spirit of democracy, drew the provincial schools in. Complaints about the ill-effects led to the abolition of the *concours* in 1903, but, by public demand, they were restored in 1922—the habit was too ingrained for it to be exorcised, any more than alcoholism could be. An inspector-general wrote in 1879 of his youth that these *concours généraux*, by which every child in the country could hope to be marked out as the best of his generation, were 'the sole preoccupation of everybody—headmasters, teachers and pupils. We were ceaselessly reminded of the great day, when we would have to bear the school's flag: it was to this goal that all our exercises, all our efforts were directed.' Parents were willing to play the game, even if their children were bound, except in very rare cases, to lose. The newspapers reported the details—as they still

[1] E. Jacoulet, 'Émulation', in F. Buisson, *Nouveau Dictionnaire pédagogique* (1911), 1. 544–8; Frédéric Queyrat, *L'Émulation et son rôle dans l'éducation. Étude de psychologie appliquée* (1919); Henri Marion, *L'Éducation dans l'université* (1890), 280–9.

do—even publishing the winning essays. It was acceptable, perhaps, because it was an alternative to the national lottery.

The *baccalauréat* was established by Napoleon as a method by which the state could test the abilities of those whom it recruited to serve it. At first, it involved only an oral examination, lasting half or three-quarters of an hour, during which the candidate was given a passage from a book he had previously studied and questioned on it. Eight candidates could be examined simultaneously by the 'jury', who would often correct and comment on the answers: 'I have never had a better Latin lesson', said Gréard, 'than the day I presented myself for the *baccalauréat*.'[1] Pupils of seminaries could get the certificate without any examination at all, simply on the presentation of a certificate from their teacher and their bishop; and the pupils of the *lycées* generally found that their examiners were their own teachers, acting as members of the faculty. Under Napoleon, it concerned very few people: in 1810–14, the Paris faculty of letters awarded between 67 and 164 *baccalauréats* annually, plus about 10 *baccalauréats* in science. No one worried about it then. Only those who needed the certificate, to enter the faculties of theology, law and medicine, bothered to obtain it. But under the Restoration, it became necessary for admission to the civil service and the liberal professions; in 1830 the written examination was introduced; in 1841 Cousin tried to increase uniformity of standards, for some faculties were notoriously lenient; in 1847 schoolteachers were no longer allowed to examine, and the faculties were developed as examination bodies. In this period, there were definite questions the candidates could prepare for—2,500 of them in all—and one was chosen out of a box. This resulted in textbooks being published to provide the right answers and crammers known as *boîtes à bachot* or *fours à bachot* sprouting, often on the basis of no fees being demanded unless the candidate passed, and some guaranteeing a pass within two months —a reasonable enough proposal, since it was simply a matter of memorising certain facts. The satirical magazine *Le Charivari* in 1849 carried seventy-eight advertisements of this sort, placed between a cure for venereal diseases and the announcement of a public ball. The historian Lavisse complained that the result of this was that the *baccalauréat* ceased to be proof of ten years of

[1] J. B. Piobetta, *Examens et concours* (1943), 11.

classical education and became something one could cram for
in a few weeks: he was of course looking back to a golden age
that never existed. Protests against it multiplied: the anticlerical
prime minister Combes inveighed against it as an obstacle to
true learning, which ought to be replaced by a straightforward
school-leaving certificate. But when the parliamentary inquiry
of 1899 collected public opinion on the subject, it discovered that
the spokesmen of local government—the *conseils généraux*—were
generally in favour of it: that of the department of the Rhône
said firmly: 'Secondary education is very well organised.' The
president of the inquiry castigated the *baccalauréat* as a social
institution which divided France into two castes, one of which
claimed the right to monopolise all public offices. But it had by
now also become a vested interest and a goal for ambition
among too many people. It easily survived all attacks.[1]

A new science arose to study examinations—'docimology'. In
the 1920s, there were protests that it was time to clarify exactly
what the *baccalauréat* was testing, whether intelligence, culture,
memory, writing skills, rapid reflexes or efficient teaching.
Psychologists carried out experiments which showed that different examiners could mark the same answers in wildly different
ways: in French composition the maximum divergence between
them could be as much as 13 out of 20 (i.e. when answers were
marked on a scale from 0 to 20, the same script could get a mark
of say 3 from one examiner and 16 from another); in philosophy
it could be as much as 12, and even 8 in physics. The average
variation in philosophy was 3·36 out of 20; and 23 per cent of
philosophy scripts, when marked by more than one examiner,
received marks which diverged by five or more points. These
differences were due partly to some examiners giving most of
their marks around the middle range, while others, reacting
with more emotion, frequently touched the extremes; some
examiners marked down heavily when they encountered one
important mistake, while others ignored it; but apart from these
different techniques, there were also straightforward disagreements about quality which could not be reconciled. Relevance
was very important to some in French composition, and its lack
taken as a sign of an inability to concentrate; a logical presentation, with a preamble, paragraphs and a conclusion, seemed

[1] J. B. Piobetta, *Le Baccalauréat* (1937).

indispensable to others; while originality appealed to still others.[1] Officialdom replied that these were faults it was aware of and was trying to remedy; more skilful and experienced examiners could avoid these pitfalls; and besides, since 1890, it was permissible for pupils to produce the record of their school performance at the *baccalauréat*, so that it could be taken into consideration in deciding the result. The examination system was defended not simply as an unfortunate necessity but as having positive virtues. Piobetta, the university official in charge of the *baccalauréat* between the world wars, declared that 'examinations and competitions are part of our way of life. Some of them are an integral part of our oldest institutions. All of them have become the pivot of our social hierarchy. Careers, public or private, that do not require the possession of a diploma are becoming increasingly rare. Titles and grades, with the official stamp on them, constitute veritable letters of nobility to which rights and prerogatives are attached.' This was as it should be, for merit had thus triumphed over favouritism and intrigue. Examinations were not just a test of knowledge, but also of will, temperament and personality. They showed people that one had to work and fight in order to succeed, and so they prepared children for the struggles of life. Examinations, he concluded, were 'beautiful and good'. He agreed they had their limitations: if in 1942 for example, all candidates who mis-spelt the word session in their application forms had been failed, then 10 per cent, i.e. 3,000 pupils, would have been eliminated. It was true that 'standards were falling', that cramming was dangerous, and the mandarinate of China was a terrible warning. But that was reason only to improve the system, not to abolish it.[2]

Strangely, Piobetta had public opinion behind him. Children may have hated the *baccalauréat*, but parents valued the status it accorded, and the prizes in this loaded lottery were enough to make people forget the disappointments it caused. Even in 1968, when traditional educational institutions were attacked as they never had been before, the *baccalauréat* still had its defenders. Significantly, the most prominent of these was the president of

[1] International Institute Examinations Inquiry. Commission française pour l'enquête Carnegie sur les examens et concours en France, *La Correction des épreuves écrites dans les examens. Enquête expérimentale sur le baccalauréat* (1936), 129, 198.
[2] J. B. Piobetta, *Examens et concours* (1943), 86–101.

the Federation of Parents' Associations, who, while conscious of
its faults, complained only that not enough children were able
to obtain it: he did not want to abolish it, but to alter it so that
as many children as possible could obtain it; and he wanted it
to give automatic right of admission into universities. By then,
many university teachers, overwhelmed by the enormous increase in the numbers of students, were demanding the right to
select only the ones they judged suitable, arguing that a *baccalauréat* was no proof of the qualities higher education valued.
Those who breached the *baccalauréat* barrier found that new ones
were being raised beyond it.[1]

If the *baccalauréat* was indeed the crowning glory of the secondary education system, then that system must inevitably be
judged to have been a failure, because only a small minority of
those who entered it succeeded in obtaining the certificate. Its
failure rate, as its critics put it, was such that it would have gone
out of business long ago, were it not bolstered by these social
prejudices. The year 1846 was the first in which more than 4,000
pupils obtained the *baccalauréat*, 1869 the first year the figure
reached 6,000, 1891 7,000, 1904 8,000, 1919 10,000. Between
1885 and 1918 altogether only 200,000 people obtained the
ambiguous honour of belonging to the 'prolétariat des bacheliers'. This was at a time when the secondary school population
was growing as follows:

| | | Pupils in secondary *lycées* and *collèges* | |
|---|---|---|---|
| 1850 | 30,000 | 1930 | 66,870 |
| 1860 | 35,000 | 1935 | 99,250 |
| 1871 | 39,000 | 1938 | 119,870 |
| 1881 | 53,000 | 1942 | 147,560 |
| 1890 | 56,000 | 1946 | 166,740 |
| 1900 | 58,800 | 1955 | 217,750 |
| 1910 | 62,000 | 1960 | 342,840 |
| 1920 | 62,000 | 1964 | 564,210 |

The pass rate of those who took the examination was on average

[1] Jean Cornec, *Pour le baccalauréat* (1968). For the qualities required in the
*baccalauréat*, see the advice of André Piot, *L'Art de concourir enseigné aux étudiants*
(Avignon, 1944), and J. B. Piobetta, *Le Succès aux examens* (1954).

only about 50 per cent. (In 1932, to take a year at random, it was 42·45 per cent; in the 1960s it was about 60 per cent.) But most secondary pupils did not even try to obtain it: they left school early. In 1900, 40 per cent of pupils had left by the end of their third year, and naturally it was the poorer children who dropped out most. In 1967, it was still the case that 76 per cent of pupils admitted into the *lycées* did not obtain the *baccalauréat*, and of those who did sit for it, one-third failed to obtain it, even after three successive tries. The success record of the *lycées* thus did not rise above 24 per cent. One failure, as the president of the parents' association said, was a 'family drama', but 100,000 failures a year was a 'national disaster'.

It is not surprising that there were complaints that the examination system was creating a whole mass of people whose 'energy was often irreparably destroyed, and who became melancholic, enervated, agitated and *abouliques*'.[1] Already in 1848 a commission was appointed to 'examine the effects produced on the health of pupils by the relationship between hours devoted to study and those given to sleep, recreation, gymnastics and promenade'. The overburdening of the syllabus became a constant theme of debate, but with little practical result since the virtues of hard work, approval of the desire to succeed, and the ambition to provide a complete general education all contributed to maintaining the maximum pressure on children. The advance of knowledge inevitably increased the amount that had to be learnt, at an accelerating rate: and in the 1960s candidates for the *baccalauréat* were expected to read twice as much as those of 1930. In 1963 an inquiry revealed that the minimum preparation required to pass that examination was sixty-one hours a week for the mathematicians, fifty hours for the experimental scientists and forty-nine and a half for the philosophers, though if optional subjects were added the totals were raised to sixty-six, fifty-seven and fifty-two hours.[2] The *baccalauréat* produced a distinctive physical type. In 1906, 33 per cent of the boarders of a *lycée* in Lyon were found to be short-sighted and 18 per cent of the day boys, and as they progressed into the senior classes, the percentage increased. In the Collège Rollin, 10 per cent of pupils in the bottom class were short-sighted and 55 per cent

---

[1] Jules Payot, *La Faillite de l'enseignement* (1937), 79.
[2] Jean Capelle, *Contre le baccalauréat* (1968), 62.

of those in the *classe de philosophie*.[1] But little research was attempted on how children reacted to the failure which the majority were bound to encounter. The problem of how far this failure was due to difficulties in adapting themselves to school life, to temperament and background, quite apart from the question of intelligence, was seen to be important by some, but it was only in the 1930s that vocational guidance began to be practised even on a small scale.[2] No one has yet calculated how much the schools, with their competitiveness and their dedication to examinations, contributed to the creation of all that depression, nervousness, neurasthenia and melancholy, which is studied in another chapter.

## State and Private Education

The schools might once have been expected to study the same Latin passage at the same time, in every classroom throughout the country, but in practice there was infinite variation created by the eccentricities of the teachers and the pressures of local conditions. Centralisation gave them status, but human weakness made them what they were. No ministerial order could be enforced until it had travelled through the hierarchy; but officials, headmasters and teachers often hated, despised or feared each other, and these animosities stirred up resistance which could completely transform the spirit in which the orders were applied. Francisque Sarcey, a successful journalist, began his life as a secondary teacher under Napoleon III. His experiences show how the struggles of the political world were reproduced in microcosm: just as the elector resented the power of the government and was constantly ridiculing it and getting round its laws, while trying to derive all possible benefits from it, so the teachers hated the headmasters and inspectors, whom they condemned as failed teachers. They ganged up against the administrators in almost childish ways. Sarcey's headmaster passed on to him a ministerial order that every teacher should keep a notebook with a full record of the lessons he gave and the

[1] Union des Associations d'anciens élèves des lycées et collèges français, *Bulletin trimestriel* (Oct. 1906), 22.

[2] André Le Gall, *Les Insuccès scolaires* (1954); Dr. Jean Philippe et Dr. G. Paul-Boncour, *Les Anomalies mentales chez les écoliers. Étude médico-pédagogique* (1905); Dr. Jean Philippe, *La Psychologie des écoliers* (1906).

marks he awarded, and the progress made by each pupil daily. Sarcey protested that it was impossible to assess progress daily, but was forced to obey orders. So he invented a different adjective for each day: incessant, extraordinary, unheard-of, incredible, stupefying progress. He was summoned by the furious headmaster, but he replied that he had been appointed by the minister to assess the pupils' progress and only he could do it: if he was stupefied by it, then it was his duty to say that the progress was stupefying. This kind of sniping was a permanent feature. But on the other hand most teachers had a profound faith in the values of what they were doing, and despite the limitations of their own knowledge, they taught with a conviction which sustained the system much more than the regulations. Sarcey recalled how in the *lycée* at Chaumont in 1851—a third-rate school at which he, who had failed the *agrégation*, was among the most distinguished members of the staff—it was precisely those teachers who were academically weakest who exercised most influence on the boys. The professor of philosophy had dictated the same lessons for twenty years, rearranging the same materials only very slightly to accommodate them within the different syllabuses which were introduced from time to time, and continuing to teach the lectures of Larouviguière, from whom in his youth he had picked up all he knew of philosophy. But he was more respected than the fashionable youngsters with the latest theories; and his influence must be measured not in terms of what he taught but of the way he did it, and of the relationship he established with each pupil. The generalisations about the schools need to make allowance for the infinite variations of individual personality. The teacher of literature in this school taught the classics mainly by reading them out to the accompaniment of dithyrambic praise after each phrase— a method which was once fashionable and had by then ceased to be so, but some pupils were deeply moved and roused to a similar admiration; others looked back on it as proof of the puerility of teachers.[1]

The atmosphere of each institution, moreover, was special to it and schools built up traditions which became more tenacious than the vagaries of governments or staff. Thus the *lycée* of Nancy, founded in 1803 to replace a Jesuit school, was highly

[1] Francisque Sarcey, *Souvenirs de jeunesse* (1885), 183–94.

responsive to local demand. Though it resembled a barracks under Napoleon and a monastery under the Restoration, the headmaster, conscious of parental anxieties, promised his pupils 'the love of a father, the benevolence of a protector and the zeal of a friend': in 1840 an inspector complained that the boarders were left very much to their own devices: 'the discipline was completely negative and there was total lack of moral direction'. In 1831 the school started 'industrial classes' to prepare for professions which did not need Latin; in 1836 it had a 'modern laboratory', in 1838 an 'electromagnetic apparatus', in 1851 a commercial course and in 1854 a gymnastics teacher. Under the Second Empire the school developed its scientific specialisation, thanks to a headmaster, V. A. Davau, who was an *agrégé des mathématiques* from the École Normale Supérieure. It had four mathematics teachers, and all was organised with a view to winning admission to the *grandes écoles*. In 1860, 200 out of the 261 boys in the top forms were scientists. Between 1856 and 1870 no less than seventy-four pupils went on to the Polytechnic; in the early years of the Third Republic as many as fifteen used to get into it each year, though the numbers fell to between five and ten after 1900 and only one or two by 1939, as it became the fashion to go to the Paris *lycées* for a final year, from which the chances of success were considered (not altogether justifiably) better. The pupils were taught intensively, not only by their very able teachers, who received extra pay to give extra discussion and revision classes and mock examinations, but also by successful former pupils, who had been through the *écoles speciales* and came back to give occasional lessons. Weekly tests were a regular feature. Literature was not neglected in the school as a whole; the philosophy and mathematics classes were indeed roughly equal in numbers; but Latin was dropped by more than half the boys, and there was not the same competitiveness among the classicists. The number of classicists from the whole of France who could hope to get into the École Normale Supérieure was small (about thirty a year), compared to the 200 scientists admitted annually to the Polytechnic. This was the main reason why preparation for the former was quickly concentrated at a few Paris *lycées*, mainly Henri IV and Louis-le-Grand, and why the victors in this struggle were such a clearly defined clique. Nancy thus did not have an autonomous *Khagne* (classical top class, preparing for the École Normale Supérieure) and Lucien Febvre, one of its pupils, went to Paris to finish his schooling. By contrast, Nancy had a very strong *Corniche* (scientific top class, preparing for the military school of Saint-Cyr), which in the years 1880–1914 had on average fifty-one pupils, with a success rate of between 27 and 48 per cent, so that no less than 1,310 pupils of Nancy went on to Saint-Cyr between 1806 and 1953. Saint-Cyr was easier to get into than the Polytechnic; it did not require ceaseless hard work; and the *Corniche* had a slightly less intellectual and more social atmosphere than the other top forms, with a solemn annual dinner to celebrate the battle of Austerlitz, ghastly initiation rites, fines on freshmen for breaking the rules, and a special badge to differentiate them. A *classe d'Agro* catered for the sons of the local landowners; others prepared for the Haute École Commerciale, the École Centrale, the École Vétérinaire, etc.; in 1945 Nancy and Bordeaux were the two provincial *lycées* which also established a *Colo* (preparing for admission to the École Coloniale). The *lycée* of Nancy was the school that produced Maurice Barrès—who was desperately lonely, crying every night in his dormitory—Marshal Lyautey, President Albert Lebrun, the mathematician Poincaré, and above all the civil servants, lawyers and engineers of the region. It owed its unusual success to the fact that it performed a service better than any rival. It was conscious of the competition of the local church schools, and it could not meet it on the social level. By 1938 its boarding pupils were down to 236 out of 1,140, partly because the boarding fees were twice as high as those of the cheapest *internat* in the region. It introduced sports, excursions, hobbies like beekeeping and aeromodelling, but its function was above all intellectual, oriented towards examinations. This meant that it appealed only to certain types of families, and different specialisations, such as *Khagne* and *Corniche*, attracted boys from noticeably different backgrounds. In 1950 an analysis of its 1,600 pupils showed that only 8 per cent had well-to-do parents and 36 per cent poor ones; nearly 10 per cent were orphans. Attempts had been made before the war to take in more pupils from primary schools, but without much success, because these preferred to go to the *école primaire supérieure*, which had a shorter course. The *lycée* had a character of its own, though when one places it—and schools like it—under a microscope, one sees still more minute societies within it.[1]

However, the measure of the failure of the state *lycées* to provide, even in all their varied forms, the kind of education parents wanted is the rapid revival of church schools. Once freedom was given to the Church, it recruited very nearly one-half of all secondary pupils, even though the state replied by making its own *lycées* partly free. In the first half of the nineteenth century, there was a lot of private enterprise in providing secondary education, and up to one-third of pupils were taught in lay private schools, but these, mainly second-rate crammers, virtually vanished in the second half of the century, to be replaced by church schools.[2] These statistics are not entirely comparable, since not all schools provided teaching right up to the *baccalauréat*. In 1842 the private schools entered only 6 per cent of the 5,000 candidates for the *baccalauréat*, but by 1932 they entered 55 per cent of the 14,640 candidates.

*Proportion of Pupils in Public and Private Secondary Schools* (%)

|  | State *lycées* and *collèges* | Lay Private Schools | Church Private Schools |
|---|---|---|---|
| 1855 | 42 | 36 | 22 |
| 1867 | 47 | 28 | 25 |
| 1887 | 56 | 13 | 31 |
| 1899 | 51 | 6 | 43 |
| 1920 | 59 | 41 | |
| 1930 | 56 | 44 | |
| 1937 | 51 | 49 | |
| 1951 | 57 | 43 | |
| 1965–6 | 79 | 21 | |

'If I had a son, I would rather send him out as a cabin boy on a fishing boat than have him exposed to the dangers which I myself ran in the schools of the university.'[3] So wrote Montalembert, one of the most active opponents of the state's monopoly of education, and a lot of people agreed with him, for the rise of the church schools was the result not of the efforts of a

[1] Lycée Henri Poincaré, *Le Livre des centenaires* (Nancy, 1954).

[2] For a history of a lay private school, see G. Ruhlmann, *Cinq siècles au collège Sainte-Barbe* (1960). This school, whose pupils included Eiffel, Péguy, Herriot, Louis Blériot and Léon Gaumont, went bankrupt in 1900 but was saved by the state's generosity.

[3] A. Trannoy, *Le Romantisme politique de Montalembert avant 1843* (1942), 64.

centralised government, but of the totally uncoordinated initiative of many individuals and small societies. Their competition was exacerbated by political disputes, but they also represented quite widespread feelings about how children ought to be brought up. It was the Jesuits who had set the pattern which these schools were more or less to follow. By the middle of the eighteenth century, the Society of Jesus had no less than 699 schools all over the world, ninety-one of them in France. These last had been closed following the expulsion of the order, but in 1849 the first Jesuit school of the nineteenth century was founded in Avignon and by 1880, when they were again expelled, they had established twenty-seven, with over 10,000 pupils. Their popularity was such that at Vannes, for example, their school, opened in 1850, had 400 pupils within four years; in Paris, their Collège de l'Immaculée-Conception, started in 1852, had 600 pupils in 1867 and 800 in 1875, and the Collège Vaugirard rejected as many applicants as it admitted. Originally the Jesuit schools had been entirely free, and they had only day-boys, but the pressure from parents was now such that in the nineteenth century they were predominantly for boarders. Church schools had the advantage that, because they employed mainly priests, they had far lower expenses on salaries, and their fees were usually lower; but it was not just cheapness that made them popular. In 1865, the average annual fees in the different types of school were as follows (in francs):

|  | Boarders | Day-boys |
|---|---|---|
| Lycées | 739 | 110 |
| Municipal collèges | 649 | 72 |
| Catholic schools | 630 | 97 |
| Jesuit schools | 764 | 70 |

Some of the most expensive schools were Catholic as well as some of the cheapest; the Catholics awarded scholarships, in the same way as the state did. They were thus able to cater for an even wider range of social groups than the state's secondary schools. The Jesuits attracted the sons of the aristocracy and of the high bourgeoisie; by the late 1870s their fees for boarders in Paris were 1,400 francs. At the other end of the scale were the *petits séminaires*, designed for the poor and frequented mainly by peasants. They always included poor boys, picked out by the *curé* as the brightest in the village and destined for the priest-hood, but the majority of pupils in the *petits séminaires* never became priests. In Savoy, these schools collected their fees in kind—corn or wine—to put themselves within reach of even the humblest. It was customary for the church schools, in any case, to charge fees according to the ability of the parents to pay. Between these two extremes there grew up a multitude of schools, started by individuals or by different orders, and responding to local conditions and the demands of different classes in a far more flexible way than the more uniform state system. In particularly religious regions, the state schools were often largely staffed by priests, at least during the Second Empire and the early years of the Third Republic, so the con-trast between public and private education was not always ob-vious.[1]

The church schools sought to distinguish themselves in the way they looked after the moral and physical welfare of the boys. Taine, touring the provinces as a state inspector of educa-tion and therefore not predisposed in favour of its rivals, reported in the 1860s that the Jesuits were popular because they were fashionable, 'because the food and the personal care are reputed to be better, because good contacts are made there . . . The Fathers make themselves comrades of the students, while [in the *lycée*] the teacher is cold and the usher (*surveillant*) is an enemy . . . Very great attention to the food, the dress, the manners of the students.'[2] The Jesuits conceived of the schools as partly religious communities, organised as families, and partly a re-action against the Napoleonic idea of the school as a barracks. They addressed their pupils not as *élèves*, nor *messieurs* (as in the *lycée*), but as *mes enfants*. They gave each class a single principal teacher who, as far as possible, progressed with the pupils from year to year, and who was expected to get to know each pupil individually and intimately. These were priests and so too were the *surveillants*, who were not considered inferior, but just as essential a part of the school. Their task was 'to help their

[1] Robert Anderson, 'Catholic Secondary Schools (1850–70): A Reappraisal', in Theodore Zeldin, *Conflicts in French Society* (1971), 51–93; J. W. Padberg, S.J., *Colleges in Controversy: The Jesuit Schools in France from Revival to Suppression 1815–80* (Cambridge, Mass., 1969).

[2] H. Taine, *Carnets de voyage: notes sur la province 1863–5* (1897), 225–8.

pupils' work, to put the finishing touches to their education, to form their character and to enlighten and develop their religious feelings, in order to make them faithful to God and useful to their country'. The *surveillant* was also in charge of games, which were much encouraged, and in extraordinary variety.[1] Since many of the schools were rural, often splendid country mansions, long walks were a frequent relaxation, as well as gymnastics.[2] Lay teachers were brought in on a part-time basis for drawing, fencing, music and foreign languages: César Franck, for example, taught at the Jesuits' Vaugirard school for a number of years. The boys were given 'offices of trust' to develop their sense of responsibility, as bell-ringers, librarians, sacristans, 'quaestors' (to deal with lost property), 'aediles' (to report necessary repairs) and treasurers of the poor (to collect alms). The ushers were instructed to 'command with extreme gentleness', as a much quoted book of advice on discipline put it.[3] 'How can you expect the yoke of authority to be bearable without gentleness?' The boys should be treated with respect, 'because they are deserving of respect', 'because they are stronger than we think' and 'because it is the only way to persuade them'. They must be got to behave well but freely, since force will only make them hypocrites. They must be persuaded that happiness was not to be found in the enjoyment of sensual pleasures and external advantages, but in moral satisfactions. Their evil inclinations must be opposed by showing them the evil consequences they bring about. But all children were different and the character of each one should be carefully studied, his fears, his sorrows and his faults. Children cannot be made to work hard 'as are battalions of soldiers': great care must be taken not to anger them. Punishment should be used only 'with extreme discretion', and teachers should 'wait patiently for the results of the child's efforts'.[4] The state's experts on pedagogy were well aware of much of this, and men like Henri Marion, for example, had his

[1] C. de Nadaillac, S.J., *Les Jeux de collège* (1875).

[2] For photographs of church schools, see the *Annuaire de l'enseignement libre français* (e.g. 1927).

[3] Amédée de Damas, S.J., *Le Surveillant dans un collège catholique* (1857), 156.

[4] On Amédée de Damas (1821–1903), author of about 44 educational and religious pamphlets, see the biography by J. Burnichon (1908). Cf. Abbé Simon, *De la direction des enfants dans un internat des garçons* (1904); and Emmanuel Barbier, S.J., *La Discipline dans les écoles secondaires libres. Manuel pratique du surveillant* (1888, 3rd edition, 1897).

book *Education in the University* recommended to priests training as teachers. The deeply humane attitudes of some religious teachers were, however, counterbalanced by a terror of homosexuality and indeed of all sexuality. Friendships between just two boys, or between a teacher and any one boy, were to be avoided at all costs, as every manual repeated. One, for example, insisted that 'in bathing, pupils must be forbidden to touch each other under any pretext, even under the pretext of helping others to swim'.[1] The rapid expansion of the church schools meant that standards were, in some orders, lower even than those to be found in the obscure municipal colleges; animosities could flourish despite the religious atmosphere, with teachers and pupils denouncing each other in the name of virtue.[2] But there does seem to have been a greater confidence in these schools on the part of parents, who probably went to see the teachers more frequently than in the *lycées*; and the teachers felt they owed more to the parents, who paid them.[3] The headmasters of church schools—unlike the *proviseurs* of *lycées*—were not simply administrators, but played an important educational and moral role; and they were able to attract parents by the personal stamp they could imprint on their schools.

It was the Jesuits who had originally developed emulation into a fundamental educational method. Contests of all kinds were constantly being organised, with prizes, rank listings, fanciful Roman titles, and an 'Academy' to which the best pupils were elected. The lengths to which this could go are illustrated by the (rather unusual) habit of one teacher at Saint-Acheul School, Amiens, to offer a pinch of snuff at the end of each day to the best pupil of the day; and the best pupil of the week was given the privilege not only of satisfying his own appetite but also of offering a pinch from the teacher's snuffbox to his classmates who had received high marks. The pupils were also divided into two camps, Romans and Carthaginians, with an *imperator* or consul at the head of each, assisted by tribunes, praetors and senators, and subdivided into decuries, all arranged hierarchically, and every individual pupil was allocated a definite

[1] Abbé Charles Guillemant, supérieur du petit séminaire d'Arras, *Précis de pédagogie à l'usage des jeunes professeurs de l'enseignement secondaire* (Arras, 1905), 62.
[2] Firmin Counort, *A travers les pensionnats des Frères* (1902).
[3] Gérard Avelane, *Carnet d'un professeur de troisième* (1969).

rival in another decury.[1] How far these methods gave better academic results than were obtained at state schools is difficult to say: by the nineteenth century there was probably not much to choose between the two systems from the point of view of the amount of emulation they encouraged. Both systems recruited from so wide a spectrum of society that one cannot say that the pupils of either came from more ambitious backgrounds. The quality of the teaching varied considerably. The Church's teachers probably always had inferior academic qualifications but that sometimes meant only that they had not been through the official university channels. The Jesuits in the nineteenth century did not have that reputation for erudition they later acquired: it was only after their expulsion in 1882, when they were more or less forced out of secondary education, that they decided to specialise in research and high intellectual standards. In the twentieth century, an increasing number of priests obtained high university honours: but on the whole the teachers of the church schools were less brilliant than those in the *lycées*. Still, they used the universal cramming techniques and prepared for the same examinations. They were as attached to the classics as their lay rivals. In 1852 the Jesuits even decided that Alvarez's *De Institutione Grammatica*, first published in 1572 and one of the most widely used of all Latin grammar books, should be restored as their standard textbook—a reactionary move which was not typical of them. Though the church schools were always more literary than the state ones, partly because they wished to avoid the expense of laboratories, they did not all neglect science. The Jesuit school in the rue des Postes specialised in preparing pupils for the *grandes écoles* and won remarkable successes. The church schools produced their own textbooks, so their teaching had a distinctive flavour, and this meant that they were able to do better for their pupils than the state in certain subjects.

Thus in 1932, a comparative study was made of the *baccalauréat* results of public and private pupils and it showed that, in over-all totals, the state schools got better results: 53 per cent of the state's candidates passed, as opposed to only 33 per cent of candidates from private schools; but the highest pass rates in the philosophy papers were obtained by the church's pupils

[1] E. Durkheim, *L'Évolution pédagogique en France* (1938), 2. 112.

(74 per cent). The interest shown in theological and moral questions throughout their school careers made philosophy easier for them to master. By contrast, in the mathematics papers, the pass rate for the church's candidates was a very feeble 28 per cent.[1] No doubt those who wished to specialise in science changed to a Paris *lycée* in their final year; but generally speaking, the church's pupils were less interested in obtaining the *baccalauréat*, because increasingly more of them came from the business, industrial and agricultural world, where it was by no means indispensable. In 1900 a Jesuit author claimed that less than one-third of the pupils of church schools stayed on to the end of the course (at least in the same school). The church schools produced, according to his estimate, only one-third of the entrants into the Polytechnic, and even only one-quarter or one-fifth of entrants to Saint-Cyr. On the other hand they turned out a fair number of industrialists (particularly in the north of France, for in the south their pupils went more for the liberal professions). Thus between 1850 and 1870 Saint Clement School at Metz turned out 68 priests, 219 army officers, 70 magistrates, 68 engineers and industrialists, 84 businessmen and financiers, 35 lawyers, 5 ambassadors and consuls, 2 prefects, 2 deputies, 2 university professors and 6 journalists.[2] So it may well be that the church schools paradoxically made more of a contribution to the industrial revival of France after 1950 than may appear at first sight, not so much because they discouraged the obsession with civil service careers—which was more influenced by family traditions—nor simply because they served a clientele that produced more children, but because they tried to turn their pupils away from philosophic doubt. Their pupils, as one of them said, had read neither Sartre nor Heidegger.[3] But no one has yet attempted to apportion statistically the responsibility for this new phase in French history as between the two rival educational systems.

There can be no doubt, however, that in the period between the two world wars the church schools experienced a revival of remarkable proportions. There had always been room for

[1] C. Bouglé, *Enquêtes sur le baccalauréat* (1935), 117.

[2] W. Tampé, S J., *Nos anciens élèves* (1900).

[3] Compte Rendu des Journées nationales d'Études, 1953, Union des Frères Enseignants, *La Vocation du Frère Enseignant* (1953), 3.

Catholics in the state system, not only in the mid-nineteenth century when the state schools were Catholic and taught religion, but even later when, in many parts of the country, teachers who did not share the rabid anticlericalism of the politicians continued to behave in the traditional way. It is true that a Catholic boy attending a *lycée* might find himself subjected to ridicule, as happened to Jacques Valdour, whose memoirs of his childhood show that teachers could sometimes be maliciously intolerant. His first impressions of his *lycée*, which he joined at the age of 9, was that the pupils did not seem to like each other and that they detested the teachers. 'Reciprocal hostility seemed to be the law.' The teachers seemed to dislike their work, and disappeared after it; God and religion were never mentioned, except occasionally to be ridiculed. The mathematics teacher would say ironically when someone could not do a sum, 'But even the Ignorantine Friars would be capable of it.' When Valdour misbehaved, he would snap at him, 'This boy is trying to play the fool with me, in his little, hypocritical way. One can see clearly that he has been brought up by the *curés*.' And when a boy made a mistake, saying, 'But sir, I believed . . .': 'I believed,' replied the teacher. 'What does that mean, to believe? Belief is a neurosis. I believe in nothing. To believe is absurd.' The history lessons were a defence of 1789 and a condemnation above all of Napoleon III: 'Never forget his perjury to the republic': his claim to have won seven million votes was a sham: he used voting urns with false bottoms. Valdour says the painful result of his going to a *lycée* was that he found a terrible conflict between what he was taught at school and at home. He had thirty comrades in his class; when they left the *lycée* only one remained a Catholic.[1]

This is an extreme testimony by a Catholic militant, and there were doubtless other reasons why boys lost their faith. The important point is that parents did feel that they were losing control of their offspring when they sent them to state schools. They very seldom conceded that children had traditions and a way of life of their own making, and that their changing fashions could be, at different times, atheist or religious. There was little discussion of just how much difference a Catholic school meant to the future beliefs of its pupils. The Jesuits, for example, gave

[1] Nic [Jacques Valdour], *Le Lycée corrupteur* (1905), 41–54.

very little formal religious instruction—only two periods a week, while there were other Catholic schools in which piety was intense. Even at a *petit séminaire* the general education could be so formal, basing itself on such old-fashioned textbooks, that plenty of scope was left for individual children to develop in their own way. Jean Calvet, who later became dean and rector of the Catholic Institute in Paris, was tormented at his primary school, though it was run by friars, by the humiliation of being the son of a poor peasant, who had to eat sandwiches at mid-day with the other poor ones, while the sons of the grocer, the hairdresser and the notary, who wore high collars and short breeches, went home: there was bitter division between the boys of the *bourg* and those of the farms, and they were always fighting. The lesson Calvet learnt from this Catholic school was the importance of force, because only force saved him and his friends from persecution: 'I have never been able to forget the contempt of which the little peasant comrades of my youth were the victims.' At his *petit séminaire* 'there were no more castes: we were all more or less sons of peasants'. The only aristocracy was that of intelligence: the clever boys were admired and no one was allowed to tease them. The school, however, had very few books, so Calvet was reduced to reading dictionaries for his entertainment. There was a great respect for memorising: whole plays of Racine, whole books of the *Aeneid* were learnt off by heart; and prizes were awarded to boys who could recite without mistakes. They were forbidden to buy any books except an almanac once a year, and the boys learnt that off by heart too, holding a competition amongst themselves as to who could be most accurate. The winner was called the *Bachelier en Almanach*; but one boy outdid the rest by reciting his almanac backwards. In old age Calvet used still to quote bits from it, even advertisements in it: 'Henri Chevaly, prize-winning pharmacist, first class, at Carpentras (Vaucluse), manufactures an embrocation of incomparable virtue.' The boys were taught Catholic doctrine, but left to be pious in their own way.[1] The history of the anticlerical Émile Combes, among many others, showed that this kind of education was no guarantee of orthodoxy in adult life.[2]

[1] Mgr. Jean Calvet, *Mémoires* (1967), 28–43.
[2] For Combes's rebellion against his religious background, see vol. 1, pp. 683–4.

At the other extreme Jaurès's assassin, Raoul Villain, who was a *surveillant* at the Collège Stanislas (one of the best Catholic secondary schools in Paris), illustrates the extreme mysticism into which a boy with an unhappy home background could be led. His father had remarried after his mother's death and neglected him; Villain was too unmethodical to be able to pass the *baccalauréat* and just before the war broke out had abandoned hope of ever getting it; he believed that he had a mission like Joan of Arc to kill Jaurès and that the success of this was dependent on his chastity, which he had scrupulously preserved in order to keep himself fit for his patriotic duty.

The expansion of Catholic education between the two world wars therefore represented, to a certain extent, a desperate and not altogether clearly thought-out attempt by parents to keep control of their children, and it is significant that it occurred when it did. It was above all else the work of parents. The old boys of the Catholic schools began forming associations which did a great deal both to finance expansion and to find jobs for pupils from them. In 1930 the A.P.E.L. (Association des parents d'élèves de l'enseignement libre) began spreading throughout the country, with a journal *École et liberté*, renamed *La Famille éducatrice* in 1947; by 1953 it had 450,000 members.[1] While the number of state secondary schools even fell from 561 to 552, Catholic ones increased from 632 in 1920 to 1,420 in 1936. This was not due to any large benefactions on the Anglo-Saxon model, and the Catholic schools were all of them in constant financial difficulties. They did much of their building by borrowing, often from the banks, and by incurring debts to their builders and suppliers. The schools thus blossomed 'in a spirit of crusade and revenge', and they were perhaps the greatest beneficiaries of inflation. In 1951 Catholics were estimated to have debts, from their educational work in the department of the Vendée alone, to the tune of 100 million francs. By that date they were spending, in the diocese of Paris, 560 m. a year on primary education, 800 m. a year on secondary education and 110 m. on technical schools.[2] The secondary schools were naturally by far the most expensive to build and to run. They were saved from bankruptcy by the Vichy government, which

[1] G. Jacquemart, *Catholicisme* (1956), 4. 235.
[2] Jean Pélissier, *Grandeurs et servitudes de l'enseignement libre* (1951), 51.

in 1941 allowed communes to subsidise private education and
itself undertook to pay three-quarters of the expenses of private
schools, though it calculated the salaries of their teachers at only
60 per cent of the level received by state teachers. In 1945 these
subsidies were withdrawn, but it was obvious by then that,
whatever the ideological objections, the Church was educating
too large a proportion of the country's youth for it to be simply
ignored; and the advent of de Gaulle led to the state paying the
salaries of all approved and qualified teachers, and a proportion
of running expenses (Loi Debré, 1959). As the church schools
increasingly used lay and specialised teachers and as (after 1945)
the clergy moved away from the schools back to pastoral work,
their salary bill grew ceaselessly. It was not surprising that some
people began questioning whether separate church schools were
in fact the best means of advancing the cause of religion, for it
meant cutting Catholics off from contacts where they could hope
to exert influence.[1]

The new wave in Catholic education, which began in the
1920s and 1930s, was, on the whole, more modern and forward-
looking than its first revival of the 1850s had been. The Catholics
rewrote their textbooks. Their schools were expanding so fast
that this was highly profitable, quite apart from anything else.
The Alliance des Maisons d'Éducation Chrétienne, which
brought the headmasters together, had a vigorous publisher in
Joseph de Gigord, who specialised in producing Catholic secondary textbooks, written for the most part by highly qualified
authors, some of them holding appointments in the University.
Many other publishers joined in.[2] Following the pastoral letter
by Archbishop Germain of Toulouse in 1919, urging that the
social conflicts of the nineteenth century should be ended, and
that a new relationship between workers and employers should
be evolved, the headmasters drew up a syllabus of social morals
—which they opposed to that of Durkheim sociology—involving

---

[1] Cercle Jean XXIII, *École Catholique: Aliénation*, ed. by Guy Goureaux *et al.*
(1968), particularly instructive on the diocese of Nantes and the history of its
church schools.

[2] Gigord died in 1947, when his son-in-law took over. The firm is still at 14 rue
Cassette, Paris 6. Other major Catholic publishers included Mame (founded 1767),
Lethielleux (1864), Beauchesne (1851 in Lyon, transferring to Paris in 1895),
Bloud et Gay (1875), Casterman (1780 in Belgium, Paris branch 1857), Desclée de
Brouwer (1877), Letouzy et Ané (1885), Alsatia (Colmar, 1897), Spes (1923),
Seuil (1936), Éditions Ouvrières (1929), La Bonne Presse, etc.

the study of trade unions, wages, the organisation of companies and of labour relations, to be supplemented by practical work through pupil participation in charitable clubs. Abbé Renaud, almoner of the Collège Stanislas, undertook to write a textbook for this, and Gigord offered to publish it.[1] The articles in *L'Enseignement chrétien*, the Catholic headmasters' journal, gave prominence to moral education with a view to encouraging boys to enjoy taking risks, assuming responsibility and showing initiative: parents and teachers should aim at making themselves useless. They denied that schoolboys were overworked, saying their hours were no longer than those of their contemporaries who earned their livings. Far from locking themselves away in the contemplation of ancient authors, they regularly reviewed the latest novels, though it was significant that they condemned Proust as 'a failed genius' and believed that he had attacked homosexuality.[2] The claim that the Catholics were pioneers first in primary education, and then in technical and social education, had much truth in it. The child was no longer seen as an incomplete or evil being, but as an independent and whole personality.[3] Of course, there were many different tendencies among the headmasters: the large and flourishing schools in the cities had the resources to be more original.

How much of their attitudes penetrated to the pupils is difficult to assess, but certainly some fashionable schools left their boys plenty of freedom. At the Catholic boarding-school, Beaucamps, near Lille, run by the Marist order, the sermons in the 1920s were still based on those of Tronson (1622–1700), whose principal book, published in 1690, was reprinted at least fifty-two times in the course of the nineteenth and twentieth centuries. But this traditional approach was counterbalanced by the almoner's catechism class every morning between eight and nine, which in fact consisted of his reading out bits of political, economic or literary news from the paper, or reporting what he had heard on the radio, and discussing it with the boys; but then he had written a book and his ambition was to become a member of the French Academy, for whose members he had a great respect. Holy books were read aloud during breakfast, but

---

[1] *L'Enseignement chrétien* (1930), 26–38.
[2] Ibid. (1931), 39. Cf. Henri Pradel, *Comment donner le goût de l'effort* (1930).
[3] *L'Enseignement chrétien* (1931), 80.

history, travel or adventure ones at lunch—like Marbot's Napoleonic Memoirs.[1] The evolution of the attitudes of Catholics can
be seen in the history of these Marists, who were one of the most
successful teaching orders. Their founders, in the early nineteenth century, were inspired by the view that 'man has only
one thing to do on earth, seek his salvation. All else is illusion
and folly.' But the superior of the order from 1883 to 1907,
Frère Théophane, was above all an administrator—he had
become headmaster of one of their large boarding-schools at the
age of twenty-six—who had other educational interests beyond
improving the religion of the teachers, even though he made use
of a bed of nails as an instrument of penance for himself: he
saved half their schools through the period of anticlericalism.
Frère Diogène (1920–42) not only expanded their already large
boarding-schools, but also built a new one in Buenos Aires for
800 pupils, and one in Syria for 700. In 1940 this order had
10,000 teachers in forty-two countries.[2]

Side by side with these international chains of schools were
purely local ones, which resulted from much humbler local
efforts. In Roanne, where the *lycée* occupied the buildings of the
old Jesuit college, a rival Institution Saint Joseph was founded
in 1901 as a result of two benefactions. One was from the bishop,
whose brother was a wealthy industrialist; the second was from
a cotton wholesale merchant of Lyon who had settled in a
château in the district; and in addition the Superior of the local
convent and the Crédit Foncier provided sizeable loans. They
started with 100 boys in 1903, rising to 150 in 1914, 250 in 1940
and 400 in 1962. Despite constant deficits, and an accumulated
debt of nearly two million francs in 1931, they continued to buy
more property, expand, build new dormitories and supply them
with new furniture and linen. Their philosophy class had an
average of a dozen boys in it between the wars, but the success
rate was exceptional—between 68 and 77 per cent got through
the *baccalauréat*. At first most of the teachers were priests, but in
1918 only seven out of thirty were. They provided a service
designed above all to appeal to the parents who supported
them.[3] This kind of school on the one hand offered teachers the

---

[1] Paul Dehondt, *Beaucamps ou la vie de collège* (Monte Carlo, 1970), 53.
[2] Institut des Petits Frères de Marie, *Nos Supérieurs* (St. Genis-Laval, 1954).
[3] Jean Canard, *L'Institution Saint Joseph de Roanne 1901–61* (Roanne, 1962).

opportunity to provide alternative types of education, stressing in particular the adaptation of methods to suit the individual child and service to the community, and on the other hand to 'enable pupils rejected by the *lycées* to appeal against a premature and precipitate judgement'.[1]

## Privilege and Culture

The effect of secondary education on the relationships between social classes was, throughout this period, a subject of passionate debate and of contradictory interpretations. On the one hand the *lycées* were said to be the democratic instrument which made the rule of merit possible, by allowing intelligent boys to climb the social ladder. The function of secondary education, declared the chairman of the parliamentary inquiry into it in 1895, 'is to create a ruling élite'.[2] On the other hand, however, the *lycées* were denounced as bastions of class privilege, where the bourgeoisie segregated their children and had them stamped with distinctive characteristics, to differentiate them from the vulgar masses. Primary education effectively kept the masses, for which it catered exclusively, inferior to the small minority that enjoyed instead a separate training on its own. The radical party on the whole took the former view: so long as boys could win scholarships and work their way to the top, they believed democracy existed. The socialists, however, protested that the very existence of two kinds of school was divisive and unfair, that a complete education should be available for everybody, and that children should choose careers not on the basis of accident of birth, wealth or schooling, but in accord with their individual temperaments and gifts. The facts did not completely support any of these various assertions about the educational system. The satisfactions and animosities the schools produced were commented on in an atmosphere of much ignorance, prejudice and confusion. Even today, it is not easy to get at the facts, for the statistics

---

[1] P. Gerbod, 'Les Catholiques et l'enseignement secondaire, 1919–39', *Revue d'histoire moderne et contemporaine* (1971), 375–414; Jean Jaouen, *La Formation sociale dans l'enseignement secondaire* (1932). For an example of an old boys' association, see *Les 50 ans 1906–1956 de l'Amicale des anciens du collège St. Joseph Matzenheim* (1956). Memoirs, e.g., in Edward Mortier, *L'Âge enclos dans un collège libre* (1907); Abbé Léon Joly, *Quinze ans à la rue des Postes 1880–95. Souvenirs* (1909).

[2] A. Ribot, *La Réforme de l'enseignement secondaire* (1900), 60.

which would be needed to make defensible generalisations were never properly collected in this period, and what statistics there are remain difficult to use. The generalisations are well worth investigating, however, because they point to forces of great power in this society. Social mobility was a universal and constant preoccupation. The ambitions and the frustrations the schools produced often marked people for the whole of their lives. Quite apart from the knowledge the schools imparted, quite apart from the way they encouraged their pupils to talk and to think, they played a crucial role in the formation of their emotional attitudes, and of the view they had of their place in society.

That secondary education catered for a small minority is the starting-point of every discussion. The proportion of boys aged between 11 and 17 who went to state secondary schools was as follows (%):

| | | | | |
|---|---|---|---|---|
| 1850 | 1·35 | | 1930 | 3·58 |
| 1860 | 1·54 | under 2% | 1939 | 5·44 |
| 1871 | 1·81 | | 1944 | 6·95 |
| | | | 1951 | 8·28 |
| 1881 | 2·35 | | 1955 | 11·26 |
| 1890 | 2·40 | | 1960 | 14·11 |
| 1900 | 2·59 | under 3% | 1964 | 19·65 |
| 1910 | 2·74 | | | |
| 1920 | 2·59 | | | |

These are the statistics for state schools. They therefore need to be, roughly, doubled to include the pupils of private schools. But they then need to be reduced because these schools did not give a full secondary education to all their pupils. Thus in 1843 it was calculated that only one boy in ninety-three in fact received a secondary education; in the 1860s, the amended figure would be under 2 per cent (for both public and private schools). In the course of the second half of the nineteenth century, the number of pupils doubled, but the largest rise occurred in the years 1850–80, and there was not much change in the total between 1880 and 1925. It was only in the 1930s that secondary education began to be an experience for more than a tiny number, and only after the 1960s that it ceased to be the preserve of a minority.[1]

[1] Statistics in Isambert-Jamati, op. cit. 377.

It was perfectly true that most of its pupils were, throughout this period, at least relatively well-to-do, if only for the obvious reason that the poor needed their children's wages simply to survive. Secondary education was, without doubt, a luxury, an investment and a status symbol. But, just as quite poor peasants were often landowners—a very diverse class—so there were many varieties of secondary education and many different types of people were able to get at least a smattering of it. In 1864 the minister of education asked headmasters of state secondary schools to produce a list of the occupations of the parents of their pupils. These showed that the rich were certainly vastly over-represented, but also that the poor formed a far from negligible proportion of the pupils. Thus even the Lycée Bonaparte (later Lycée Condorcet), which was situated in a fashionable quarter of Paris, had nearly one-third of its pupils who were sons of small shopkeepers (250), clerks (50) and teachers (50), almost as many, put together, as the sons of 'property owners and *rentiers*' (395), and as the sons of 'notable merchants' (150), bankers (55) and lawyers (90). It also had fifty sons of army officers, of unspecified rank, fifty artists and musicians, sixty doctors. Altogether therefore it was nowhere like a representative sample of society, but it did have representatives of all but the humblest levels of it. Almost every town had an individual mixture of these different elements, depending on its economic character and on the types of opportunity it offered. Thus the *lycée* of Marseille, for example, had fewer 'property owners' but more people from commerce, shipping and industry. The *lycée* of Lyon, with 852 pupils, had 291 sons of small shopkeepers, 17 workers, 2 peasants, in addition to 209 property owners, 106 merchants, industrialists and bankers, 97 members of the liberal professions, 89 civil servants and 39 soldiers. The small *collèges*, municipal secondary schools in the minor towns, were patronised very largely by the peasantry and some of them had a large falling-off in attendance during harvest time, just like the primary schools. In towns where there was no teacher-training college, there were *lycées* with pupils who became primary teachers. Over half of the pupils of the municipal college of the Meuse between 1850 and 1855 went into agriculture. In Paris, with its large variety of *lycées*, each had a distinctive social character: those on the right bank took only day-boys;

Charlemagne, near the Faubourg Saint-Antoine, was the least snobbish; Saint-Louis specialised in science; Louis-le-Grand and Napoléon (later Henri IV) were more literary; each appealed therefore to a slightly different clientele.[1]

However, with the passage of time, the *lycées'* social composition altered considerably. During the Second Empire they were almost comprehensive schools; not the least significant of their functions was that they also provided 'complementary courses', which were really of a primary nature and designed to prepare children for humbler careers: in some *lycées* as many as a quarter or even a third of the pupils followed these courses, and of course left long before they reached the age for taking the *baccalauréat*. One needs to distinguish between those who meant to stay for the full secondary course and those who did not. The rector of the academy of Douai wrote in 1864: 'There are boys from the countryside whose families "send them to town", as they put it, so that they should learn something more than the village schoolmaster can teach them and so that they should develop a little through contact with children who are better brought up . . . They leave the *lycée* after one or two years to go back to their parents, to help in their farming.' But as the *lycée* became increasingly dominated by the *baccalauréat* and as a greater variety of specialised schools were established, the *lycée* pupils became more homogeneous. The *école primaire supérieure*, the technical school, the 'special' schools were invented to increase the educational opportunities open to the masses but their effect was to segregate the different classes for whom they were individually intended. So the Third Republic was to a considerable extent responsible for increasing social divisions by its nominally egalitarian educational policies. Thus by 1907–8 the Lycée Condorcet had a noticeably different social composition: only 5·58 per cent of its pupils were sons of artisans and shopkeepers; it had no sons of workers; 11·6 per cent were sons of clerks and supervisors, 1·59 were sons of primary teachers—altogether only 20 per cent were now from the lower and lower middle classes.[2]

The growth of the church schools increased the separation of

[1] R. D. Anderson, 'Some Developments in French Secondary Education during the Second Empire' (Oxford D.Phil. thesis, 1967), chapter 7, has analysed the replies of the headmasters to the minister's inquiry.

[2] G. Vincent, 'Les Professeurs du second degré au début du 20ᵉ siècle', *Le Mouvement social* (Apr.–June 1966), 60.

families of different tastes and aspirations. It has been seen that the church schools, though also involving fees, were in no way exclusively aristocratic or bourgeois, but it is clear that many parents with social pretensions preferred to send their children to church schools. The result was that, particularly in the smaller towns, the *lycées* became increasingly dominated by the sons of civil servants. The state catered for its own employees, reverting to the original purpose of the *lycées*, and it helped to

*Social origins of candidates for the* baccalauréat, *1932* (%)

|  |  | Private Schools | State Schools |
|---|---|---|---|
| Occupations favouring state education | Civil servants | 13·69 | 25·23 |
|  | Executives (*employés dirigeants*) | 8·55 | 10·83 |
|  | Clerks | 4·56 | 13·54 |
|  | Workers | 0·95 | 2·27 |
|  | Artisans | 0·76 | 1·95 |
|  | Small shopkeepers | 1·14 | 1·94 |
| Occupations favouring private education | Liberal professions | 19·22 | 14·33 |
|  | Businessmen | 17·68 | 10·83 |
|  | Industrialists | 13·12 | 6·92 |
|  | Property owners and *rentiers* | 10·26 | 1·95 |
|  | Peasants | 2·47 | 1·27 |
|  | Miscellaneous | 7·60 | 8·94 |

Source: C. Bouglé, *Enquêtes sur le baccalauréat. Recherches statistiques sur les origines scolaires et sociales des candidats au baccalauréat dans l'académie de Paris* (1935).

build up a wall around its own small world. Thus in 1932, one-quarter of the state schools' pupils taking the *baccalauréat* were children of civil servants: in Paris only 21·8 per cent were, while in the provinces the proportion was as high as 37 per cent. Whereas in Paris state schools 15 per cent of *baccalauréat* candidates were children of the liberal professions, in the provinces only 10 per cent were. At this final point in the school careers of the pupils, very few members of the working class were left in the secondary system.

The industrial working class entered secondary education in significant numbers only in the late 1930s and during the Second World War. In 1936–7 only 2·6 per cent of pupils entering secondary schools were the children of workers (plus 4·47 per cent who were children of artisans). In 1943–4, 14·4 per cent were children of workers (plus 9·7 per cent children of artisans). The obstacles to the democratisation of the *lycées* were partly financial, but there was also strong reluctance by the workers to penetrate into institutions which they did not regard as their own, and in which they did not feel at ease. This was clearly revealed when fees were abolished. But long before then, it was not just fees that kept the workers out.

*Social origins of pupils entering secondary school* (%)

|  | 1936–7 | 1943–4 |
|---|---|---|
| Liberal professions | 10·6 | 6·9 |
| Heads of industrial and commercial firms | 24·6 | 14·3 |
| Civil servants and soldiers | 28·5 | 24·47 |
| Clerks | 20·3 | 19·2 |
| Artisans | 4·47 | 9·7 |
| Peasants | 1·7 | 8·2 |
| Workers | 2·6 | 14·4 |
| Miscellaneous | 5·8 | 2·8 |

Source: Christiane Peyre, 'L'Origine sociale des élèves de l'enseignement secondaire en France', P. Naville *et al.*, *École et société* (1959), 6–33.

As has been shown, day-boys were offered tuition at a rate within the reach of perhaps half the country, that is all of those who were capable of saving something from their earnings. During the Second Empire, scholarships were still a means of rewarding loyal service to the government more than a form of assistance to bright children; and there were only about 1,300 of them in the 1850s. The ministry had no hesitation in awarding them to well-to-do civil servants in preference to junior ones. By the turn of the century the state was still awarding only 1,000 scholarships annually, but the departments and municipalities raised the total to 5,528. Of these, 1,586 were to boys going on from primary schools to secondary schools. Only about 20 per cent of scholarships were given to sons of peasants and workers. The decisive factor which brought the workers in was not the abolition of fees and the award of scholarships, but, first, the payment of wages (and family allowances) to parents which enabled them to support a family without the children having to go to work and, secondly, the development of attitudes which would encourage children in remaining idle up to their eighteenth year. This is bound up with the question of social aspirations and mobility, with the question, that is, of what people expected from the schools in career terms, how much the schools could advance them, and what difference the schools did in fact make to the jobs their pupils got.

It has been seen[1] that in the middle of the nineteenth century the desire to rise above the station into which one was born was still something of an exception. On the whole jobs were obtained through one's father and his connections; despite the French Revolution, professions and trades still had, to some degree, the character of corporations, in which family tradition and nepotism played an important part. At the same time as democrats talked of careers being open to talent, others (and sometimes democrats too) were worried by the dangers this could produce, and social mobility was still called *déclassement*. Thus the republican Vacherot lamented that when poor children tasted the educational fruits hitherto reserved for the aristocracy 'for the most part they rejected their fathers and made themselves noticed for the harshness and contempt in the ranks of society into which the exhausted hands of their heroic families have raised them'. In the inquiry of 1864, headmasters were asked to give not only the profession of their pupils' fathers, but also the profession which these pupils hoped to enter. In the department of the Seine-Inférieure, one-third of the pupils in the classical forms intended to follow in their fathers' footsteps, but in the 'special', i.e. modern forms, 54 per cent did. The sons of poor people, who predominated in these latter, clearly did not expect too much from the schools; while a classical education was by contrast more often seen as a means by which one could move into the liberal professions or the civil service. Far more statistics about the fate of schoolchildren in their later working life will be needed before firm statements can be made about the country as a whole. But it seems that the schools were not as active agents of social change as they were sometimes said to be.[2]

A survey carried out in the early 1960s showed that even then the family's influence was still more powerful than that of the

---

[1] See vol. 1, chapter 7, on 'The Ambitions of Ordinary Men'.

[2] See Robert Gildea's doctoral thesis on education in the Ille-et-Vilaine (unpublished, Oxford, 1977).

school. Those who went on from school to university were predominantly from backgrounds which favoured this. Thirty years after the introduction of free secondary schooling, only 1 per cent of the sons of agricultural workers went to university, compared to 80 per cent of the sons of members of the liberal professions. The subjects which students chose for their university courses were clearly related to their fathers' profession. Fifteen per cent of sons of the liberal professions and of managers chose medicine, but only 3 to 5 per cent of sons of workers and peasants did: the long training and capital required to set oneself up as a doctor were clear deterrents. The class which chose science in a greater proportion than any other was that of the workers (52·5 per cent); and it was the agricultural workers who chose the faculty of letters most (37 per cent), presumably because it led to teaching jobs. (The daughters of agricultural workers also went in massively for this—65·6 per cent, but letters attracted all girls, even 48·6 per cent of daughters of managers and the liberal professions.) The law faculty was favoured most by the sons and daughters of clerks, aspiring to rise, and by the sons of liberal professions and management, inheriting their parents' firms or training for administrative jobs.[1]

A subtle difference remained between education and culture. The schools' diplomas were certainly highly valued. Positions of importance were controlled by holders of diplomas who insisted on diplomas as essential qualifications for those seeking jobs under them: the proliferation of examinations increasingly made the schools almost indispensable for anyone with ambition. In the 1960s, students of the lower classes obtained distinctions (*mentions*) twice as often as upper-class students. The schools rewarded perseverance, hard work and intelligence. But there were limits to what they could do. To be cultured meant to be more than educated, in the sense that it involved knowledge which had to be acquired outside the school—by going, for example, to the theatre, concerts and museums, by knowing about *avant-garde* art as opposed to the classical art taught in schools. Interest in exotic countries was found to be more frequent as one went up the social scale, as also were

[1] Pierre Bourdieu and J.-C. Passeron, *Les Héritiers, les étudiants et la culture* (1964), 16.

breadth of interest and dilettantism: it required a sense of security to be detached from the school syllabus, and it needed rich parents to enable one to cultivate unusual tastes. Significantly, the cinema was the only extra-curricular interest of which all classes had more or less equal knowledge. The schools sought to give their pupils general culture but, in the most sophisticated forms, they also had aristocratic ambitions beyond their capabilities: their best teachers despised syllabuses and pedantry and exalted what they could not really teach. They could not perform their whole task in a single generation, nor independently of the life-style parents adopted. The schools were on the road that children had to tread in order to acquire culture, but only the beginning of the road. That is why they were both praised as democratic and criticised as bastions of privilege. While opening new horizons for many, they also created privileges for those who passed successfully through them. They never discovered how to console their failures, for they were part of a society that punished stupidity, slowness and lack of competitiveness. They were not able to eliminate the advantages enjoyed by children from cultivated homes; and since they laid such stress on linguistic fluency, the upper classes usually had the advantage, not least in oral examinations. Economic inequality could not be eradicated simply by educational reforms.

But the schools, in the eyes of a great number of people, nevertheless seemed to be the pivot round which all other reforms would have to turn, and their democratisation became a mounting obsession during the twentieth century. Previously literacy had been the great goal; now it was the *école unique*, the comprehensive school. This was the answer to the fact that the primary and secondary systems were largely independent, so that in 1913 only three or four thousand pupils finishing their education in the former continued it in secondary schools. In the years 1880–1930, when the number of pupils in *lycées* was almost static, those in the *écoles primaires supérieures* increased fourfold. The contrast of the two systems thus gradually became more noticeable and the question of whether their existence and rivalry was desirable inevitably became important. However, the debate was initiated not by frustrated workers but by university professors. A group of them calling themselves Les Compagnons de l'université nouvelle, shaken by their experience of near-defeat in 1914–18, declared that this war had shown the failure of the bourgeois élite; they believed that the country must look to the common people, whose virtues had been 'the great revelation of the war', for its revitalisation. They protested that education had hitherto been 'the creed of a sect', proud of enjoying 'spiritual benefits unknown to the vulgar'; that its hero was the intellectual who sought truth in books rather than in life, and whose skill was his ability to imprison life in verbal formulae. Education, they said, produced intellectuals of narrow rationalism, unconstructive critical powers and selfish individualism. It must cease to be dilettante and must yield a more socially useful return, for, in its present form, it produced too much frustration, disillusionment, revolt, and dangerous errors in vocation; it diminished the vigour of the nation without increasing its idealism. Education must contribute to the country's resurrection: its reform was possible now because such a large proportion of the teachers had been killed in the war. It should turn its attention to training producers and industrialists, to rebuilding France's economic life. The schools should be practical and democratic in their objectives; they should be free and they should not insist on teaching Latin to everybody. There should be one school for children of all classes until the age of 13 or 14: the *école unique* required the abolition of the *petites classes*, the preparatory forms of the *lycées* which the snobs used, to avoid the primary schools. After that, the *école prolongée* should prepare children for a profession, but without neglecting to educate the whole personality—the mind, the body and the will. The syllabus should be adapted to the needs of each region; and the habit of teaching in order to produce teachers, of a uniform stamp, should be got rid of. The war on the church schools should be ended: these should receive state subsidies; but totally free education would ensure that parents would not prefer church schools for purely class reasons. The Compagnons condemned the teacher in almost unmeasured terms: 'The harm that these *fakirs* have done to France, without realising it, is great. They have led people to think that the educational system had a life outside that of the nation; they cultivated a

critical disposition among children at the expense of the will
and character which are the supreme faculties; they have
given them a distaste for action and so they have incurred
a heavy responsibility in the crisis we have suffered.' A few
teachers, it is true, had participated in national life, but then
only to go into politics and produce the 'very worst exaggerations'. The Compagnons said they wanted to stop the University being a church and they did not want to create a new
church to replace it; they did not want 'to model people's
consciences'. But they also said, rather contradictorily, that
the divisions of the teachers had made them weak, and that in
the new order the teachers must cast off the control of the
state and become an independent corporation, uniting teachers
—both lay and religious—of primary, secondary, higher and
professional education, in regional groupings. The political
implications of this programme—its anti-anticlericalism, its
opposition to state control, its regionalism and corporatism—
inevitably prevented it from being universally acceptable: the
école unique was not a simple summons to national unity.[1]

It was presented as democratic, but it was more truly meri-
tocratic, in that it wanted secondary education reserved for
'the élite', except that the élite would now be those judged fit
to belong to it, and it would be the teachers who would be
the judges. The école unique became a slogan which concealed
numerous and different aims. François Albert, the radical
minister of education in 1924, saw in it a means of destroying
the church schools. The more extreme left wing, interested in
a more thorough transformation of society, disliked the idea of
the école unique being the preparation for a qualitative selection:
they wanted not to pick out the bright children by this 'suction
device to extract the new spiritual forces from the people and
put them into the service of the bourgeoisie', but rather to
make mass education the basis of every individual finding the
career that suited him best. Some of them considered that the
école unique would by itself be powerless, and that the workers
should build their own educational system, teaching a workers'
culture. The problem of embourgeoisement by education was
never properly tackled by the advocates of the école unique.
The precise effect of the école unique on parental and individual

[1] Les Compagnons, L'Université nouvelle (1918).

freedom also remained confused. Léon Blum, speaking for the socialists, made it clear that they saw it as a 'national and social idea', opposed to 'the family idea': parents should not have the right to prefer church schools to it. It was denied that children would be obliged to adopt the career which the experts in selection and orientation declared suitable for them, but nevertheless the Catholics prophesied the 'seizure by a caste—the teachers— of the entire life of the nation'.[1] The formula *l'école unique* became fashionable, so that people of many persuasions claimed to be its partisans, but interpreted it to suit their own ends. Thus most secondary-school teachers, determined to uphold the superiority of their teaching over all others, paid lip-service to its egalitarian ideals but resisted it in practice, not least because those of them who taught in the junior forms of *lycées* would be reclassified as primary teachers.[2]

## The Influence of Teachers

Many people seem to have hated their schooldays and yet very few disapproved of governments pouring increasing sums of money into the expansion of education. Many people despised teachers as a class and yet they allowed teachers to claim an essential role and a profound influence on the improvement of mankind. To understand these paradoxes, one must examine more closely the social status of the teachers and also the range of activities and ideas which were affected by them. For the teachers were at once disadvantaged inhabitants of a ghetto and upholders of the *status quo* in the world around them: they were unwavering admirers of classical traditions but they were also revolutionary or utopian reformers; they aspired to win acceptance as members of the bourgeoisie and yet they often despised bourgeois values, while continuing to inculcate them at school; they were both the champions of children and their enemies. Their equivocal position on many issues is the explanation of why such different roles have been attributed to them. In Germany in the 1840s, a secondary-school teacher would not have been indulging in a wild fantasy if he hoped to marry a

[1] Marc Dubruel, *Le Règne des pédagogues: l'école unique* (1926).

[2] There is an excellent discussion of education in the interwar period in John E. Talbott, *The Politics of Educational Reform in France 1918-40* (Princeton, 1969).

general's daughter: his salary was equal to that of a councillor of state (fifth class it is true) and if he rose to be a successful university professor he could hope to earn as much as a minister. The French teacher could have no dreams of such wealth, but far more French teachers actually became ministers. The contrast of France and Germany, two countries where education was highly valued but in very different ways, is a useful way of seeing the extent and the limits of the teachers' importance.

The secondary-school teachers who believed that they were shaping not just the minds of their pupils, but perpetuating and perfecting France's peculiar genius, were a small group, and one forgets just how few of them there were until quite recently. In 1840, there were only 670 *professeurs de lycée*. Altogether, including ushers and administrators, there were only 4,500 teachers in the state's secondary schools at that date. The number rose to 7,500 by 1877, 10,000 by 1887 and in 1945 it was still only 17,400. To this one needs to add teachers in private secondary schools. In 1854 there were 7,500 of these, in 1938 13,000. The great explosion in the number of secondary teachers occurred only after 1950, when they more than doubled over fifteen years, so that in 1965 there were altogether 67,000 secondary teachers. But in the last years of the reign of Louis-Philippe the total number of people living who had ever been to a secondary school was still only 80,000. In the nineteenth century, secondary education thus occupied a very small place in society. In 1848 there might be only ten secondary teachers in a whole department; in 1877 only nineteen departments had more than a hundred of them. The majority of these teachers, moreover, had a profound contempt for most of their fellows, because they were even more hierarchical than an army. At least military men got promotion of sorts by seniority, but teachers claimed superiority by virtue of their knowledge and the examinations they had passed to prove it; and they clearly had difficulty in passing examinations.

Theoretically, only *agrégés de l'université*, selected in an annual competition, were considered fit for the dignity of occupying teaching chairs in *lycées*; the more junior forms were supposed to be staffed by *licenciés*, i.e. university graduates. But in the 1840s only 10 per cent of the secondary teachers were *agrégés* (about 360 in all), another 20 per cent were *licenciés*, but over 50 per cent had no more than the *baccalauréat*. At the turn of the century the *agrégés* were still only 1,855 in number and in 1938 only 2,466. In 1966 the *agrégés* were still an élite comprising only 17 per cent of the secondary teaching body, even after a vast increase in the number admitted to their exalted ranks, following the expansion of education. The idea obstinately survived that to teach the senior forms was a task calling for such gifts and such knowledge that enough intelligent men could never be found of an adequate standard. Between 1866 and 1876 under 20 per cent of the 3,500 candidates offering themselves for the *agrégation* were successful. The schools were thus continuously staffed by teachers officially judged to be incompetent. In 1877 only 21 per cent of teachers in the *collèges communaux* were graduates (*licenciés*); in 1909 only 66 per cent were. In 1965 a quarter of all teachers in secondary schools were still unqualified. The Third Republic had conspired to maintain this situation almost as a tradition, while pretending to lament it, but obstinately refusing to increase the number of well-paid teaching posts. Instead it preferred to pay teachers overtime: in 1900 this expenditure amounted to a sum equivalent to the salaries of 270 chairs. The teachers accepted this system, because they wanted more money and because it increased their differentials, though they also complained that they were overworked and that their expectation of life was, as a result, below the national average. Inequality of merit was something they believed in as passionately as the principle of equality for equal merit. How else could they have continued to accept the enormous differences in salary they received for very similar work?

The *agrégés* were the privileged minority among them. During the early Second Empire, when a good Parisian carpenter could earn 1,300 francs a year, the *agrégés* started at 2,200 francs and they could hope to rise to 6,600 francs as senior teachers at the best Paris *lycées*. This latter salary was six times what a teacher in a communal college would earn; while a junior usher might earn even less, under 1,000 francs. Like labourers, teachers were expected to improve their incomes by extra work, and private lessons were therefore a minor industry, exploiting the anxiety of parents keen on getting their children through examinations. A headmaster who knew how to run a boarding-school efficiently and economically might reach 20,000 francs a year; and private schools were sold for large sums, as profitable ventures; but under Napoleon III only 5 per cent of teachers got salaries of over 4,500 francs a year; more than half got between 1,100 and 1,900 francs; while 13 per cent got less than 1,000 francs. In 1900 the salary range still started at 700–2,700 for ushers and rose to 7,500 for *agrégés* in Paris. An *agrégé* in a Paris *lycée* had a maximum salary which was higher than that of a provincial university professor, and it is this sort of person who, disdaining the pretensions of the faculties, gloried in his prestige as teacher of the élite of the élite. Between the world wars, the gaps in salaries between senior and junior teachers diminished very considerably, and between the different types of school. In theory this ought to have made the jealousies between provincials and Parisians, *lycée* teachers and municipal teachers, old and young, certified and unqualified less bitter, but they all continued to receive slightly different slaries which offended quite as much because movement from one category to another was not easy. The Parisian *agrégé* earned the same as a lieutenant-colonel in the army, the provincial one as much as a captain, while the average municipal college teacher got as much as a sub-lieutenant. The trouble of course was that these latter would remain sub-lieutenants all their lives. The dangerous men in this academic army were the captains and a few of the colonels. But these—the *agrégés*—clung tenaciously to their privileges, forming a society which watched over their special interests with fervour, publishing in their bulletin every individual promotion and transfer, so that all should know exactly how much their colleagues were earning.[1] Their power, inevitably, was limited by the fact that they were unable to unite their inferiors behind them. When the secondary teachers got round to forming trade unions, they divided up into four different ones: *lycée* ushers kept separate from municipal college ushers, and *lycée* teachers both from them and from municipal college teachers; and in addition all of them remained aloof from the primary teachers and from the Fédération des Fonctionnaires. Many teachers refused to join unions at all and preferred societies

---

[1] *L'Agrégation. Bulletin officiel de la société des agrégés de l'Université* (Bimonthly) (1938, 22nd year), 245, for debates about salaries.

catering for their individual specialities, between which there always remained rivalry if not contempt: like supporters of rival football teams, classicists despised scientists and modernising believers in pedagogic reforms ridiculed the traditionalists, and they could only with difficulty unite to look down on those who could not play football at all. The *agrégés* were barely on speaking terms with the ushers (*répétiteurs*), condemned to the status of non-commissioned officers; they seldom invited them to their weddings; they thought it right that a *professeur* should have a clean napkin twice a week, but a *répétiteur* only once a week. At the turn of the century, *répétiteurs* were complaining, more loudly now, that barely one *professeur* in twenty ever condescended to shake their hands, and, as for headmasters, it was unheard of for them to take off their hats to salute them. The Normalien in particular, they said, 'believed himself to be of a superior essence, rejoicing in the humiliating position in which he always keeps his subordinate'. There was a class struggle within the teaching profession itself. The pupils were well aware of it and reproduced their quarrels in the play-ground.[1]

But what distinguished the successful teacher was that he was a man on the move. Teaching was often an absorbing passion, a dearly loved profession, but from the social point of view it was often an escape and a step towards something better. The large majority of teachers had parents who were socially inferior to themselves. Artisans, small shopkeepers and clerks produced the largest proportion of teachers—about 40 per cent in 1850, about 33 per cent in 1910. Ten per cent of teachers in 1850 and 14 per cent in 1910 were sons of peasants. About one-fifth or one-quarter of teachers were always the sons of other teachers.[2] Only gradually did the liberal and mana-gerial professions come to regard teaching as an acceptable career: in 1850 and 1910 only one-tenth of the teachers came from such families, but in the 1960s about one-third did. This was the great change stimulated by the creation of a new

[1] G. Vincent, 'Les Professeurs de l'enseignement secondaire dans la société de la belle époque', *Revue d'histoire moderne et contemporaine* (Jan.–Mar. 1966), 49–86.

[2] At one stage, these teachers were more often than not sons of primary teachers, doing one better; but in the 1870s as many as 16 per cent were sons of secondary teachers and only 11·5 per cent sons of primary teachers. In 1960, the proportions were 12 and 11 per cent respectively.

intellectual proletariat endowed with university degrees, fashionable labels but otherwise often useless, except for teaching. Previously, however, three-quarters of secondary teachers came from homes with virtually no traditions of culture, or sometimes even of literacy. The acquisition of culture was the great achievement of their lives, and that is why they were so deeply and so conservatively attached to the study of the classics, which made them what they were. They fought so passionately for the preservation of the old syllabus precisely because it was so new to them.[1]

The teachers were men on the move in another sense too, in that promotion was obtained by transfer to larger schools and more senior forms: they had so many grades to climb that they seldom stayed long in any one place. In the early years of the Third Republic one-third of the teachers and half the ushers were, on average, always new to the schools in which they served, either through appointment or transfer, though the municipal college staffs were more permanent—only one-fifth were moved around each year. They tolerated this even though three-quarters of them were now married (only 42 per cent had been in the 1840s). This meant that they could not build up influence and respect in their localities in the way of doctors and barristers, who seldom moved. They were dependent for their status on their minister and their inspectors, whom they cordially resented. But they could try to force themselves past these hurdles by study, research and examinations. In the July Monarchy, ambition was still moderate, even rare, amongst them. But as the century progressed, they seem to have grown more dissatisfied and restive. They enrolled in the faculties for higher degrees. They increasingly wrote books, abetted by the growing phalanx of publishers and printers. In 1877 the government invited teachers to send in copies of their works for an exhibition: an amazing total of 1,650 works arrived, suggesting that in the preceding decade two-thirds of teachers of senior forms had published something. It is true 70 per cent of these productions were textbooks, and that the rest were lectures at prize-givings, articles in learned periodicals and translations.

[1] Gérard Vincent, 'Les Professeurs du second degré au début du 20ᵉ siècle: essai sur la mobilité sociale et la mobilité géographique', *Le Mouvement social* (Apr.–June 1966), 47–73.

Originality was not their strong point, and they certainly preferred literary criticism to novel writing. They did not therefore make any large contribution to the movement of ideas.
Combes, the radical prime minister who had started as a
teacher, was right when he said in 1899 that the teachers were
'essentially conservatives . . . men who mistrust novelty'. In
the 1870s, about 10 per cent of them were inscribed as students
at the faculties, aiming to better themselves. Each year, about
twenty-five teachers obtained doctorates, the crowning achievement. This was the tiny minority that was successful in climbing out of the schoolroom, and on to a more national or public
stage. The weakness of the profession was that the best in it
moved out of it altogether, on G. B. Shaw's principle that 'those
who can, do; those who cannot, teach'. But this became a
serious problem only after 1945, when the universities expanded
and the agrégés, originally specifically selected for secondary
teaching, invaded the faculties.

It is impossible to say how frustrated teachers were before
then, for lack of sufficiently detailed information about the
silent majority. A sample survey conducted in the early 1960s
is the only source available to answer this question, and its
results cannot be read back into the prewar period; but it is
suggestive. Roughly half the teachers questioned declared
themselves to be satisfied with their profession and half dissatisfied; but 87 per cent of those who had passed the secondary-
school teachers' certificate examination[1] said they were satisfied.
The latter were teachers who had been specifically trained for
their jobs. Women teachers were distinctly more satisfied than
male ones. The agrégés were the most frustrated of all, though
they were also very satisfied with their training and had a
good opinion of themselves. But altogether about a quarter of
teachers said they had become teachers because they wanted to
do something else, whether it was research or some other activity,
political or literary. As many as 59 per cent indeed regretted
that they had been unable to pursue a career in research. When
asked what other jobs they would be willing to do, 62 per cent
aspired to a career in the liberal professions (33 per cent as
doctors, 20 per cent as pharmacists). None wanted to be civil

[1] C.A.P.E.S. (Certificat d'aptitude professionnel de l'enseignement secondaire).

servants, because, as the historian Ch.-V. Langlois (1863–1929) had said in 1905, and as still seemed true, one became a teacher because it provided a decent living straight away, but it also gave one a great deal of liberty or independence. The liberal professions gave more liberty but one needed a private income to survive the early days without clients. That is why, at the turn of the century, four out of the seven senior ushers at the Lycée Montaigne in Paris were doctors of medicine, who lacked the capital to set up in practice. Beyond independence, teachers admired genius. 'Artists' were the occupation they selected as that for which they had the greatest admiration. These were the impractical, uncommercial values they upheld. No wonder, forced as they were to devote their lives to a perpetual routine, that they came at the top of the table for frequency of mental illness and that hypochondria constantly plagued them. Four-fifths of a sample of teachers retiring in 1958–64 were classified as 'psychologically abnormal, obsessional or hyperaesthesic'.[1] It would be wrong, however, to see the teachers of the Third Republic as sad or embittered. Far from it, they were probably on the whole men of enthusiasm, with an almost childish optimism which experience had much difficulty in abating. Francisque Sarcey, a Normalien who escaped into journalism, declared that 'twenty years of teaching kills a man. One goes to bed a wit, and one is amazed to find that one wakes up an old fogy.' But what the teachers felt they lacked in themselves, they made up for by their love of learning and their faith in its saving grace. Though they therefore suffered from the exclusiveness and self-righteousness of converts, their conversion had involved a rebellion against their own background. For all their obsession with never having enough money, they were ultimately not materialists. That is why they were simultaneously a challenge to and a pillar of a society that never lived up to their ideals.

Their place in society was therefore infinitely subtle, difficult both for themselves and for others to define. If one simply considered the monetary rewards they received, one would dismiss them as servants of the bourgeoisie, who sometimes forgot their place, but who were essentially servants. This would be as misleading as any similar judgement on the clergy would

[1] Gérard Vincent, *Les Professeurs du second degré* (1967).

be. If one read novels to discover what contemporaries thought of them, one might reach the conclusion that they were generally regarded as figures of fun, weak, ignorant of the world behind their pedantry, always at the mercy of their superiors, and therefore sometimes rebellious, but basically conscious of their own inferiority, of their modest origins, lacking in social grace and so kept at a distance by the smartest people, forced to make friends only with other teachers—a profession, in short, to be pitied, even though individual members of it very often had admirable qualities like generosity, intelligence and self-sacrifice. This portrait must not be accepted uncritically, because one must remember that novelists were too close to teachers to be impartial observers; they had often escaped from teaching into literature and they were describing in the teachers' lot all that they themselves wanted to avoid. One must add evidence from other sources and try to distinguish between the reputation teachers enjoyed—which contained much inaccurate representation of their situation—the view they had of themselves, and the real influence—less obviously discernible and seldom analysed—which they wielded despite their poverty.

Victor Laprade's book, *Education as Homicide* (1867), blamed the teachers for making the schools a combination of monasteries, barracks and prisons. They ruined the health of children by their obsession with examinations. Their repetitive, mechanical teaching did more harm than good; the whole history of French pedagogy indeed was 'a monument of stupidity and harshness'.[1] The career guides warned that unless one was an *agrégé*, one was condemned to a life of 'modest simplicity', in which moreover one was in danger of suffocating intellectually, so narrowing and oppressive were the conditions of work. The men who innocently went into teaching were those who 'felt some attraction for letters or science, those who had failed to obtain admission to the state's *grandes écoles* [which led to better careers] and those who feared military service'.[2] Victor Duruy himself, who was a teacher and inspector before he became Napoleon III's minister of public instruction, was ambivalent towards the profession. He proclaimed, on taking

---

[1] V. Laprade, *L'Éducation homicide* (1867).
[2] V. Doublet, *Dictionnaire universel des professions* (1858), 303.

office, that the teachers were 'the Great Army of Peace . . . waging war without respite against all evil, against ignorance, against sloth, against the defects of the mind as against the vices of the heart'. They formed, he said, that 'great institution that Napoleon I hurled like a block of granite in the midst of the current of the century, to regularise its flow'—an analogy that in part contradicted the grander metaphor he had previously used. For he also admitted that 'if the French are the wittiest people on earth, it is not always to our teachers that we owe it'. He was well aware of the inertia, apathy and mediocrity that balanced the teachers' virtues and knowledge.[1] At the lower levels of the profession, there was indeed little pretentiousness. As the headmaster of the municipal college of Nantua said in 1861: 'We are rarely crowned with glory; our lives run their course laboriously, monotonously and obscurely in a narrow sphere; our exhausting duties come to an end only when we die. That does not matter . . . To prepare virtuous citizens and new generations of honourable men . . . that is our ambition. It is the love of this modest good that sustains us in our unprofitable careers.'[2]

The paradox was that the teachers seldom believed that they were succeeding in putting the world right. On the contrary, they were always lamenting that it was going to the dogs, that immorality, laziness, materialism were everywhere triumphing. Beauty and truth, as they saw it, were always being trampled on. They were essentially in love with the past, even if their whole lives were devoted to improving the future. They taught admiration for the classical traditions, just as the clergy urged men to turn their minds to the next world: both feared and disliked the present. The teachers' reputation as radicals was unjustified. In 1848 at most only a third of them were republicans, and these were largely concentrated in the *lycées*: the vast majority of municipal colleges had no republican sympathisers in them at all. Teachers were blamed for the spread of socialism, for instilling wild ideas into pupils 'inflamed with erudition and blown up with vanity'; they were told to shave off their beards, a sign of insubordination, by Napoleon III, who however thought his own became him; but only about

[1] P. Gerbod, *La Condition universitaire* (1965), 427, 447.
[2] Ibid. 389.

300 were actually sacked for strictly political reasons by his government. Less drastic persecution affected many more, and the teachers came to have the reputation of being hostile to Bonapartism, but this again is exaggerated: only a minority expressed strong views on the matter. In the early years of the Third Republic, very few teachers joined the freemasons; even fewer were freethinkers when that was a bold thing to be. In 1850 Émile Deschanel had been suspended from his teaching post for participating in politics: the council of the University rejected his view that a teacher could say and write what he pleased outside his class; it laid down that a teacher had 'special obligations' which 'diminish his liberty as a citizen'. This case had been used as a precedent for repressing inconvenient republicans under the empire, but, contrary to what might have been expected, under the Third Republic the secondary teachers' unions repeatedly refused to concern themselves with politics. They were far from all being radicals. They refused to vote an address of encouragement to Combes, drowning the motion with cries of 'No politics'.

One must distinguish between the teachers as a political pressure group—in which capacity they were as strong only as their numbers, which have only recently become large—and the teachers as an influence on children—in which case their ideas are multiplied many times over. But the teachers did not find it easy to modify their pupils' beliefs and behaviour. In the first place, they too often approached the children with hostile prejudices. Though they were infinitely well meaning, the teachers did generally regard their pupils as having evil propensities, a liability to laziness, perpetuating in effect the Catholic doctrine of original sin even when they formally rejected it, because it was artificiality, knowledge and morals that they tried to impose upon them. The teachers did not consider that they were being oppressive, for the acquisition of culture had liberated them: they were only forcing children to be free, in their wake. But it was inevitable that this should have aroused resistance among their pupils. The teachers' ideal was to be monarchs of their classes, even when they preached liberal doctrines. Those in secondary schools were the slowest to adopt 'modern' theories of education. The pupils replied by ragging—a kind of child's sabotage—and by forming what have been termed 'delinquent groups'—a miniature version of trade unions. Above all, they adopted special attitudes and a special language while in school, which lulled the teacher into thinking he had won his victory, so that his demands on them were reduced; but this could be as superficial a subservience as the workers taking off their caps to their employers. The independent culture of secondary-school children was, however, nowhere near as resistant to their teachers as was that of primary children. It is true that older children could sometimes penetrate the mask their teachers wore, realise that they were not monarchs so much as actors, discern the inferiority complex that lay behind the severity and seize on the self-denigration into which teachers lapsed intermittently. Secondary-school children mocked their teachers in an almost institutionalised way: except for the few children who succeeded, most of them resented the humiliations which the teachers' marking system regularly imposed on them; and they practised the war of generations against their teachers, before they took it into the outside world. But the central feature of the teachers' message and role was the belief in the importance of ideas, and secondary pupils did not wholly reject this, partly because they adopted it as an instrument to fight off the teacher's oppression: the most successful ragger was the wittiest one, who could turn the teachers' guns to fire back in their faces. The role of wit and taste was all-important.

The teachers' power came precisely from their modesty. This is what distinguished them from their German counterparts, whom they generally envied for the higher status these enjoyed. German teachers built up elaborate philosophical theories to bolster their self-importance, but this placed them in a fool's paradise. They developed an ideal of *Bildung* and *Kultur* which was far more ambitious than anything French teachers claimed to achieve. German idealism disdained French 'civilisation' which it condemned as frivolous polish, a superficial veneer of good manners. It saw the world as the product of consciousness, it attributed 'objective reality' to its intellectual constructions, it claimed that scholarship was capable of yielding not just knowledge, but also wisdom and virtue, and a whole *Weltanschauung* which was essentially a self-justification. The German academic tradition made its philosophising the highest

L

goal. It cut itself off therefore from the rest of the country, despised the world of industry and commerce and put all its reliance on the state, which it tried to turn into a Kultur-state. In France this mistake was made not by the academics but by the Catholic Church, whose alliance with monarchy proved disastrous for it. Erudition was never valued so highly in France as in Germany, unless it was seasoned with elegance, precisely because French teachers never convinced either themselves or anybody else that they were the salt of the earth. Since the teacher did not have this philosophical justification of his own importance, he aimed to please society more, to make education an ornament more than an initiation, to seek out what was judged tasteful in the world at large and attempt to propagate it, rather than to oppose an alternative, Platonic or mystical ideal of perfection. The French teachers achieved their importance by trying to make themselves more immediately, even if less exaltedly, useful.

They too escaped from their sense of inferiority by cultivating speculation, though to a lesser degree than the Germans. They too lived in their own small world, bolstering their importance by professionalising themselves, by developing 'pedagogy' into a science. Their love of abstraction was also a roundabout way of protesting against new technical and commercial forces that they were unable to cope with. But the vast majority of them did not aspire to being more than intellectual tailors, who dressed up their contemporaries with the ideas and the forms of speech that they thought society valued. The clothes they made were almost always out of date, and in the depths of the provinces sometimes positively archaic; these were the clothes that they had learnt to admire from their teachers and it was by no means the case that society at large did consider them as becoming as the teachers imagined. Their achievement remained important, however, for three reaons. Even if their values were largely rejected by the people who passed through their schools, the forms of speech and of thought they cultivated seem to have had a permanent effect on a not inconsiderable portion of their pupils: so though the pedantic clothes they tailored were hardly ever seen being worn by adults (apart from teachers), they were often kept as underclothes, taken for granted, unmentioned and unnoticed. It is this substratum of life that the teachers were responsible for. In addition, apart from this general effect on the educated classes, the teachers were increasingly important as a force magnifying the virtues of literary and intellectual activity. It will be shown in due course how the writers, in their books, their reviews and their newspapers, blew up their own productions and rivalries into matters of national, even universal, significance. The teachers were a sort of chorus on the sidelines of this world of mutual congratulation and denigration; and they encouraged their older pupils to be spectators if not participants in it. They thus increased the size of the world that revolved around books, though one must always remember that this was only one of many worlds. Finally, the teaching profession was one of the most active vehicles of social ascension in France. The vast majority of its members came of humble backgrounds and it is not surprising that they therefore held examinations, which had recognised their merits, in such esteem. France was therefore a country in which it was relatively easy for poor families to rise, in the space of about three generations, to middle-class respectability, if not wealth; its character was certainly modified by the fact that this social climbing could be achieved simply through book-learning. The main alternative methods of ascension were the army and commerce. Each of these paths was taken by people of different temperament, different family tradition, or from different regions: the teachers (before 1914 at any rate) came very definitely from only some (mainly northern) parts of France. The worlds of education, commerce and the army always remained hostile to one another. But they had a common origin in their ambition, directed towards social ascension. They were three products of the same motivation, and their antipathy for each other should not be allowed to obscure the fact that together they represented a distinct segment in a society which did not always move in the same direction as the rest of France.

# 7. Universities

THE secondary schools were important instruments for the creation of national uniformity. The universities, by contrast, split the nation again. They did this in two ways, by breaking it up into specialist groups, and by enabling students to establish themselves as the leaders of the emergent new class that young people now came to form.

There is no higher education in France, said a work on 'The Ruling Classes' in 1875.[1] This statement was almost true. There were no universities in the nineteenth century until 1896. The twenty-two universities which had existed in 1789 were abolished by the Revolution. Decay and corruption had reduced them to a mere shadow of their original medieval selves.[2] For a large part, it was no longer a university education that they dispensed. The superior faculties of theology, law and medicine nominally provided professional training but their standards had fallen abysmally low, as had the number of students in them. Many professors had abandoned lecturing altogether, and confined themselves to the lucrative task of issuing degrees. On one occasion the students of Bordeaux even sued their professors to compel them to lecture, but their zeal was exceptional; in the faculty of law, less than 2 per cent of the students bothered to attend lectures. Examinations were more a financial than an academic matter, in fact the purchase of a privilege. General education in the humanities and the sciences was provided by the faculty of arts and the degree of master of arts was the normal preliminary for entry to the higher faculties. This M.A., however, was of secondary-school standard; children entered the faculty of arts at the age of 10 or even 9, stayed on till 17 or 18, and confined themselves

[1] Charles Bigot, *Les Classes dirigeantes* (1875), 129–35. Cf. the pessimistic view of Gabriel Hanotaux, *Du choix d'une carrière* (1902), 205-6, 219–20, and Jules Payot, *La Faillite de l'enseignement* (1937), 36–7.

[2] Louis Liard, *L'Enseignement supérieure en France 1789–1889* (1888–94), vol. 1; Stephen d'Irsay, *Histoire des universités françaises et étrangères* (1933–5), vol. 2; F. Ponteil, *Histoire de l'enseignement en France 1789–1964* (1966); and A. Prost, *Histoire de l'enseignement en France 1800–1967* (1968).

largely to the study of Latin. The universities had no connection, therefore, with the important scientific discoveries of the eighteenth century, and they taught virtually nothing about them: sixty years passed before Newton's *Principia* was lectured on in Paris.[1]

During the Revolution and Empire, the idea of universities dealing with the whole of human knowledge was abandoned. Instead specialised schools were founded to provide professional training in separate subjects. The former elements of the universities were fragmented into independent faculties, designed, like the *écoles spéciales*, to provide professional training, though rather less efficiently, because, unlike the schools, they were not residential. The use of the medieval word 'faculty' was confusing. They were no longer faculties, or parts, of universities, for these were abolished. They were faculties only in the sense that they had the right to issue degrees or licences to practise in certain professions, particularly medicine, law and teaching. Each faculty was entirely independent of the others. The situation in the mid-nineteenth century was that sixteen major towns had faculties, but only a few of these towns had the full range, since medicine and theology in particular were taught only in a few places. But all sixteen had at the very least faculties of sciences and letters (the medieval faculties of arts were now thus subdivided into two), because these were essential to the secondary-school system. They not only awarded degrees to school-teachers (the *licence* or teacher's diploma), but also examined for the *baccalauréat* (the school-leaving certificate). The old connection of the faculty of arts with secondary education was thus retained and the faculties of sciences and letters awarded most of their *grades* for work done in *lycées*. The syllabuses for the *baccalauréat* and the *licence* were much the same: *lycée* students sometimes attended university lectures and prospective teachers were principally required to learn how to teach this syllabus rather than to engage in higher studies.[2]

Most faculties were given only four to six professors, who between them had to cover all the subjects. Pluralism flourished:

---

[1] Strasbourg was an exception: the standard was higher and the outlook more international and modern.

[2] A. de Beauchamp and A. Générès, *Recueil des lois et règlements sur l'enseignement supérieur* (1880–1915) is the best source for the legislation on this subject.

at one period the Rector of the Academy of Pau was simultaneously also dean and professor of the faculty and headmaster of the *lycée*. There were few students: the faculty of letters at Caen had only forty-two at one point during the Restoration: twenty-two of them were boys at the *lycée* and twenty students of the faculty of law. Research was almost unknown. The lectures at these faculties were open to the general public and for the most part attracted retired or leisured people. They tended to be rhetorical, elegant popularisations. Guizot, Cousin and Villemain set the standard of the professor as a man of the world rather than a scholar; moreover, they quickly left the university for parliament; and nearly all the professors of Paris got substitutes (*suppléants*) to lecture for them. Professors at the faculties of law were often more interested in their practice at the bar than in their lectures. There was some discussion during the July Monarchy about reducing the number of these isolated small faculties and building up a few great provincial centres of learning, but the need for the state to strengthen its secondary schools against the competition of the Church seemed to make this impossible. Louis-Philippe's ministers confined themselves to creating some more faculties here and there (very few towns had all four faculties). This cost the state little, if anything; higher education paid for itself because of the very substantial income received in examination fees. As late as 1866 the state was spending only 221,000 francs (£9,046) on the faculties—the total budget of 3,800,000 francs was almost balanced by receipts of 3,597,000 francs.[1] When Nancy petitioned for a faculty of law, it was granted one in 1864, on condition that it would compensate the state if any expenditure was involved in the first ten years—and hardly any was.[2] It was the municipalities themselves which, from civic pride, supplied the buildings. Nancy was in fact the first to give its faculties a new building: most towns did not do so till the latter part of the century. Till then, nearly all the faculties had only the most primitive and exiguous accommodation, frequently tucked away in some hidden corner of the city. In

[1] V. Duruy, *Rapport à S.M. l'Empereur sur l'enseignement supérieur 1865–8* (Dec. 1868), xxvii.

[2] Aline Logette, *Histoire de la Faculté de Droit de Nancy, 1768–1864–1914* (Nancy, 1964), 87, 95.

the 1870s the faculty of sciences at the Sorbonne was still housed in a few tiny rooms, formerly used as bedrooms and kitchens by students. An inquiry of 1885 revealed that the scientific equipment in the faculties was almost identical with that of 1847: they had hardly any money to spend. The law faculty of Paris in 1869–70 allocated 1,000 francs (£40) to its library—and took no foreign periodicals at all. Marseille spent nothing on books.[1] The faculty of letters of Clermont-Ferrand in 1855 used up virtually all its budget of 22,286 francs (£891) on paying its five professors 4,000 francs each. In 1876 it still had only seven regular students; in 1894–5 the rector proudly reported 'the imposing figure of seventy-eight students'.[2]

Dissatisfaction with this state of affairs in due course developed. There was little public feeling on the subject before 1945, since popular interest was concentrated on school education. Because school-teachers were regarded with suspicion by conservative governments, the faculties, responsible for the training of teachers, had to be carefully controlled. Fortoul (minister 1851–6) warned faculties against the dangers of too much knowledge. He restricted the syllabus in order to reduce controversy; he transformed the chair of the history of philosophy at the Sorbonne into a safer one of comparative classical grammar. The first man to undertake a serious study of the situation of the faculties was Victor Duruy, whose thorough inquiry, begun in 1865, revealed the appalling physical conditions in which they were working. 'All Paris has been rebuilt,' he wrote; 'the buildings for higher education have alone remained in a state of decay which contrasts painfully with the imposing grandeur of the edifices created for other departments.' Duruy wished to create a genuinely *higher* education, of whose function he gave a revolutionary definition: it should no longer concern itself with preparation for examinations but should teach the methods by which students might learn the sciences which these methods have created. He wanted specialisation, erudition, teaching in small groups, the study of subjects beyond those of the secondary syllabus, and university scholarships. There were already 408 professorial chairs in fifty-three

[1] Louis Liard, *Universités et facultés* (1890), 16–20.
[2] Pierre Janelle, 'Histoire de la Faculté des lettres de Clermont-Ferrand', *Revue d'Auvergne*, vol. 68 (1954). A good article based on archival sources.

faculties: it was not institutions that the country lacked but their right application. However, he despaired of changing the conservative faculties and set up instead, outside them, the École Pratique des Hautes Études, a research institute. Once again the university continued unreformed because progress could be achieved more easily outside it. As it was, Duruy had great difficulty in finding the money to pay even for his small creation. The reform of the faculties was too colossal and expensive a task.

The war of 1870 gave the reform movement a great stimulus. Renan declared that it was the German universities which had won the war. A group of French scholars, meeting at the Collège de France, lamented also that 'there is no higher education in France'. The isolation of the faculties meant they could not treat knowledge as a whole; they concerned themselves with only a limited range of subjects; their teaching was not disinterested, because it was primarily directed at professional examinations, and government control meant they were not free in the pursuit of knowledge. All their lectures could be abolished without altering very much the way in which students studied; they were incapable of stimulating a taste for research because they merely prepared men to be schoolmasters. Reporting their conclusions, Gabriel Monod (who was later to found the *Revue historique*) wrote that the purpose of higher education should be 'on the one hand to maintain the taste for and the tradition of disinterested research, and on the other to create the spiritual unity of the nation by being the centre of its intellectual life'. The first of these aims involved the total transformation of the faculties on the lines of the École Pratique des Hautes Études; the second meant giving them an entirely new place in society, and a very central one. Monod proposed that all secondary and primary teachers should spend three years at a faculty—so bringing unity to the educational system and at the same time giving the faculties real full-time pupils. They should be given scholarships, and the state could in this way compel them to go to provincial universities, rather than to overcrowded Paris. University degrees should be purely academic: entry into the civil service (including the teaching profession) should be by separate examination. Academic study would thus become more disinterested. The faculties should be given more freedom to decide what they would teach, but since they would need greater strength to sustain their increased responsibilities and independence, they should be united into provincial universities. They should absorb the *écoles spéciales*, which would cease to drain off the best pupils. They would need a lot more money, though they could economise somewhat by obtaining *privatim docentes* to give many of the new courses free of charge. Monod's pamphlet is particularly interesting because it raised most of the issues involved in the reorganisation of higher education.[1]

For the first years of the Third Republic, however, attention was taken up by the Catholics' demand for freedom in higher education, that is, the right to establish Catholic faculties. In 1875 the monarchist Assembly passed a law granting this, though in 1880 the republicans withdrew the right to award degrees. The Catholics' success was slight; they attracted few students and could never compete in prestige against the state faculties.[2] The 1875 law required the government to present a bill for the reform of the state faculties within a year—but the ministers did not find a propitious moment to do so. The budget for higher education was indeed substantially increased at this period. It had been 2,876,000 francs in 1847; the Second Empire had raised it to 4,200,000. Waddington in 1877 raised it from 5,100,000 to 7,799,000 and Ferry brought it up to 11,600,000, at which figure it remained for another ten years. This should be compared, however, with the 18 million francs spent on secondary and the 100 million on primary schools. The increased expenditure represented little real change: most of it was used to create eleven small new faculties of the old pattern. It is true that sixty-seven new chairs were created in the already existing faculties, so that for example the faculty of sciences at Lyon, which in 1870 had only seven chairs, had in 1890 ten, plus three 'supplementary courses' and five *conférences* or seminars. These were an innovation borrowed from the École Normale, which had long used seminars as a method of instruction. Keen faculty professors had begun to introduce

---

[1] Gabriel Monod, *De la possibilité d'une réforme de l'enseignement supérieur* (1876).

[2] Mgr J. Calvet, 'L'Institut Catholique de Paris', in L. Halphen *et al.*, *Aspects de l'Université de Paris* (1949); René Aigrain, *Les Universités catholiques* (1935).

them on their own initiative, in order to make contact with serious students, but they remained the exception. Another innovation was the introduction of scholarships for university students: 300 were established in 1877, and another 200 in 1881. These, it should be noted, were respectively for students for the *licence* and the *agrégation*, i.e. for prospective school-masters. But the idea of disinterested study by autonomous faculties was not yet accepted.[1]

The man who did most to stimulate higher education in this period was Louis Liard. A graduate of the École Normale, placed first in the competition for the *agrégation* in philosophy, while still a young lecturer at Bordeaux he became deputy mayor of the city and organised the rebuilding of the faculty. His reputation as an administrator got him appointed rector of the Academy of Caen at thirty-six, and in 1884 he became director of higher education in the ministry, where he re-mained for eighteen years. Even when he moved on to be vice-rector of Paris University (1902–17) he continued to dominate the administration, visiting his old offices every afternoon. In his final years his principal achievement for Paris University lay in the collection of a large number of benefactions from private individuals. He had a strong respect for vested interests and his ideas were never revolutionary. The professors of faculties with whom he had to deal were even more conserva-tive and slow. It took twenty years for his principal reform to be passed into law. In 1883 Jules Ferry had invited the professors to give their opinion on a possible amalgamation of the faculties into provincial universities. Most had been favour-able, though some feared for a loss of their independence. One man—Boutroux, the philosopher—with exceptional foresight thought such a reform would be bound to increase the adminis-trative chores of the professors.[2] The republican politicians felt too weak to surrender any power or control over the state's faculties, at the height of their battle against the Church. In 1885 no more was done than to establish some liaison between faculties in the same town, which were to meet in a *conseil général des facultés* to discuss common problems and to

[1] Paul Gerbod, *La Condition universitaire en France au 19ᵉ siècle* (1965), 568; L. Liard, *Universités et facultés* (1890), 34–56.

[2] *Enquêtes et documents relatifs à l'enseignement supérieur*, vol. 16 (1885), 35.

share a common budget. In 1896 finally they were united and the provincial universities were established.[1]

The new universities were not true copies of the German ideal of the generation of 1870. Dissatisfaction remained, because they were not really independent bodies simply devoted to higher learning. The Rector continued to be the representative of the government, in charge also of primary and secondary education in the region. The faculties continued to be examining bodies for the secondary schools, and the best institutions of higher learning, the *grandes écoles*, remained outside them. The amalgamation was largely superficial and the real unit remained the faculty, to such an extent that Monod in 1900 proposed the abolition of the faculties within the universities—without success, of course. Right up to 1968, professors usually referred to themselves as *professeurs à la faculté* rather than *à l'université*. Ferdinand Lot, the medieval historian and deputy director of the École des Hautes Études, published a vigorous denunciation of the new system in 1905, showing how far the new universities were from rivalling their German counterparts. The Directeur de l'Enseignement Supérieur, overwhelmed by paperwork and personal solicitations, saw only the satisfied Paris professors who had enough money and students, but provincial scholars were very unhappy. Paris could stand comparison with Berlin: it had an income (faculties and *écoles*) of 10 million francs, one-half of the whole higher education budget of 21 million. But the German universities, apart from Berlin, had an income three times as large as that of the French provincial universities (and this excluded very considerable extraordinary expenditure by the Germans). Since the establishment of the French provincial universities, the state had done little for them, and they were in debt. The German professor gave six to eight lectures or classes a week: the French one was still required to give only three. His isolation from the students continued. The gaps in the courses offered by provincial universities were so great as to make it doubtful whether they could be called universities. The

---

[1] Texts of the laws and decrees of the various steps in this reform in *Enquêtes et documents*, vol. 58 (1898), together with extracts from relevant parliamentary debates; E. Lavisse, 'Louis Liard', *Revue internationale de l'enseignement* (1918), vol. 72, 81–99.

traditional domination of the secondary syllabus continued. For example, in five provincial universities the professor of modern history had to teach geography as well; two universities had no professor of German, two had no professor of English, and in Montpellier English and Italian were combined in one chair. The history of the French language was studied more in Germany than in France: 'matters have reached such a stage that it is necessary to know German in order to study French.' There was not even a chair of Provençal in France—a subject better studied in Germany. Slavonic studies, Sanskrit, and oriental philosophy barely existed at all in the provinces. The teaching of economics, sociology and psychology was still rudimentary. The French science faculties were strong in zoology, anatomy and physiology, because they taught these subjects to prospective medical students; and they were also good on anthropology and botany; but the Germans had more than twice as many professors of chemistry. Lot estimated that two hundred more chairs were needed in the provinces. With few exceptions, the old methods of teaching by magisterial lectures continued. *Conférences* or discussion classes were organised for students preparing for the *agrégation*, but here a student would simply read an essay and the professor would say how it ought to be written in order to pass: there was no real discussion of the subject. The attitude was indistinguishable from that in secondary education. The standard of examinations was still absurdly low and to obtain a degree did not require any physical attendance at the university. The French universities had only half the number of students the Germans had.[1]

The war of 1914 postponed reform for a generation. Inflation produced acute financial difficulties in the universities, so that it was not even possible to maintain the standards of 1914. When in 1921 the faculty of sciences of Paris asked for 4·7 million francs it was allocated 800,000—as in 1914. With salaries lagging far behind prices, professors resorted even more to pluralism. Any idea of expanding the universities was shelved for two different reasons. On the one hand, the country's

[1] F. Lot, *De la situation faite à l'enseignement supérieur en France, Cahiers de la Quinzaine*, série 7, 9, 11 (1905); C. Seignobos, *Le Régime de l'enseignement supérieur des lettres* (1904).

economic problems made retrenchment a principal objective of successive governments. The universities were quickly picked on as particularly wasteful institutions, overgrown, overlapping, capable of being pruned without harm; indeed a definite hostility to them developed. On the other hand, reformers declared that the universities were based on outdated principles. A reaction set in against Liard's work—or rather, the demands which his partial reforms had barely satisfied now made themselves heard. The Compagnons de l'Université nouvelle, whose ideas were to dominate the debates on all grades of education from the publication of their articles in 1919 until the Second World War, advocated a totally new system. A number of faculties, they declared, had never really lived except on paper. The dispersal of resources between them was wasteful. The very idea of a faculty was in any case out of date. The aim of making universities encyclopedic should be abandoned and instead the unit in higher education should be the specialised institute, which could combine several linked subjects.[1] Léon Bérard, minister of education in 1922, wished to abolish a considerable number of faculties, to have only five national universities and eight regional ones—the latter being reduced in size and specialising in a few subjects only. The faculties in general should lose their financial autonomy. They should avoid too much theoretical teaching 'expensive for the state and the need for which is not always evident'; the laboratories and libraries of different faculties should be combined to achieve economies. Professors must be made to work harder: 'it is indispensable to put an end to certain habits and traditions and to fix, at all levels, each one's duties so as to safeguard the interests of the students and of the state'.[2] Bérard destroyed any chances of implementing this programme by his unpopular attempt to revive Latin as a predominant subject in secondary education, in the interests, as he claimed, of saving

[1] The Compagnons included Edmond Vermeil, later well known as professor of German history, and a number of secondary-school masters. See J. M. Carré, 'L'Histoire des Compagnons', in *Les Compagnons de l'Université nouvelle* (1920); Les Compagnons: *L'Université nouvelle* (2nd edition, 1919), 2. 147–96. For the place of the Compagnons in the history of education reform, see Luc Decaunes, *Réformes et projets de réforme de l'enseignement français de la Révolution à nos jours 1789–1960* (1962).

[2] Proposals of Léon Bérard, 29 May 1922, in *Revue internationale de l'enseignement* (1923), vol. 77; for his ideas in general see Léon Bérard, *Au service de la pensée française* (1925).

French culture from 'barbaric materialism'. His successor Anatole de Monzie in 1925 again brought up the suggestion of creating specialist universities, instead of expecting them all to cover the whole of knowledge.[1] He had a certain amount of support, but too many political considerations, rivalries and electoral interests were involved, and nothing was done. Attention was concentrated on primary and secondary education. Jean Zay, the most active reforming education minister of the century (1936–9), does not appear to have had a particular interest in the universities—or at least he did not give them a high priority. This was certainly justified from the social point of view which concerned him most—the universities could never be made democratic until the *lycées*, which supplied them with pupils, lost their class character. He said he did not propose to do anything for the universities until he saw how the reforms at the lower levels worked out.[2] The major achievement of the inter-war period was the establishment of the Caisse des Recherches, later the Centre National de la Recherche Scientifique—which, one professor wrote, 'saved French science'. But the C.N.R.S. still left unsolved the problem of making research an integral part of the universities' work, and of freeing more professors from the chores of administration; it had besides difficulty in its early years in obtaining the co-operation of industry and of the different ministries engaged in scientific research. A national programme of scientific research was far from achieved.

In 1939, therefore, the universities were still shackled by the outdated ambitions of Napoleon and still enslaved to the needs of the secondary schools. This can be seen with special force in the syllabuses, for despite the reforming zeal of some critical professors, few basic changes were made in this period. The most static subject of all was probably medicine. Until 1835 doctors trained in Paris went into practice without ever having seen a woman give birth or even without having examined a pregnant woman. There was for long a contempt by doctors for sciences called 'accessory', like chemistry or

[1] A. Audolent, 'Y a-t-il lieu de "spécialiser" et de "moderniser" nos universités provinciales?', *Revue internationale de l'enseignement* (1926), vol. 80; cf. A. de Monzie, *Discours en action* (1927), 193–220.

[2] Jean Zay and Henri Belliot, *La Réforme de l'enseignement* (1938), 93–4; Jean Zay, *Souvenirs et solitude* (1945), 271.

microscopy. It was only in the late nineteenth century that therapeutics aroused the same interest as diagnostics. What professors prided themselves on was the beauty of their diagnosis, rather than its practical consequences. In the early part of the century they went round the wards followed by as many as 200 students each, so few could see the patients that were talked about; later they abandoned all reference to the patients and gave 'magisterial lectures', in which each preached his pet theory. If one was more interested in actual treatment, one went to Germany.[1] Little provision was made for medical research, and laboratories were totally inadequate (Pasteur got more support from the personal benefaction of Napoleon III than from the state). The French could defend this on the ground that they were interested in turning out practical physicians, but they soon fell so far behind advances in the medical sciences that their degrees ceased to be recognised by a number of countries, including the United States. It was only in the late 1950s that universities and hospitals were at last united.[2] This conservatism did not prevent France from producing some of the world's most brilliant physicians and medical scientists; but their influence on students was not always evident.

The faculties of law throughout this period had the largest number of students: they had long been looked upon as a kind of finishing school for gentlemen, as well as providing professional training for many lucrative professions, including the civil service. But they were having increasing difficulty in fulfilling this dual role. They had too many students (their number doubled between 1900 and 1939); their libraries and lecture halls were quite inadequate to accommodate even a fraction of them. In Paris, where there were 14,000 law students in 1920 and 19,000 in 1930, the law library had only 765 seats. The professors were overwhelmed with examinations: one professor reported having read no fewer than 200 theses in one year.[3]

---

[1] Mireille Wirot, *L'Enseignement clinique dans les hôpitaux de Paris entre 1794 et 1848* (1970), 125, 140 ff.; C. D. O'Malley, *The History of Medical Education* (U.C.L.A., 1970).

[2] Abraham Flexner, *Medical Education, a comparative study* (New York, 1925), 15–27, 118, 166, 167, 170; J. L. Crémieux-Brilhac, *L'Éducation nationale* (1965), 183–93; *Enquêtes et documents relatifs à l'enseignement supérieur* (1883–1922), vol. 91.

[3] H. Berthélemy, *L'École de Droit* (1932), 28.

The Paris faculty pressed for higher standards to eliminate the weak, but it failed to lengthen the course from three to four years. The lawyers insisted, however, on dominating social studies and keeping these within their faculty. Their syllabus was from time to time widened to include politics, economics, statistics and administration. As early as 1877 economics was made a compulsory subject for second-year law students—though in the face of much opposition from some lawyers, who in 1889 succeeded in transferring it to the first year. In 1905 the amount of economics taught was doubled, but it always remained a subsidiary subject, without a complete undergraduate course; the standard therefore remained very low, even at the doctoral level. Only in 1960 was a fully independent *licence ès sciences économiques* established.[1]

In 1894 the faculty of letters of Paris complained that its *licence* was still 'expressly and exclusively an attestation of good secondary studies' and expressed the wish that it should become a mark of higher education.[2] Until 1880 the *licence ès lettres* involved no specialisation: it required two dissertations, one in Latin and one in French, and used to be prepared for in the *lycées* with as much success as in the faculties. In 1880 a timid effort was made to add a *partie spéciale* devoted to philosophy, history and languages, but in practice this was neglected and the examinations in these subjects were purely formal, because the candidates' time was absorbed by the *partie commune*, done by everybody, on French and classics. In 1894, when candidates were allowed the option of offering a short thesis in the *partie spéciale* instead of undergoing a written examination, some professors took the opportunity to create seminars for these students, with good results—but the vast majority of candidates continued to opt for the traditional examination. In 1907 the compulsory French and classics were abolished and students were allowed to choose their own subjects. For the first time specialisation at a respectable level became possible, but again in practice the standard remained low: most candidates still read only a few textbooks. A further reform in 1920

[1] M. Lefas, 'La Réforme des études juridiques' in *Les Cahiers de redressement français*, no. 4 (1927). For the failure of earlier reforms see *Enquêtes et documents*, vol. 26 (1888); C. Rist, G. Pirou *et al.*, *L'Enseignement économique* (1937).

[2] *Enquêtes et documents*, vol. 52 (1894), 3.

raised the level a little but the traditional methods continued. History students, for example, could hardly ever read works in foreign languages, and their knowledge of foreign history was elementary. Special classes were sometimes offered by professors but attended by only a tiny minority. The memorising of dogmatic lectures and textbooks remained the students' principal occupation. In 1932 French and classics were once again made compulsory for students wishing to become schoolmasters. The schools spent about half their time on these subjects, up to a quarter of their time on modern languages, but very much less on each of their other arts subjects, philosophy, history and geography. Nevertheless, out of every 100 *licenciés* the universities were producing 26·5 classicists, 17 philosophers, 26 historians and geographers, and 30 modern linguists. Historians, geographers, and philosophers were declared to be lacking in 'culture générale', and compelled to take one paper in French, Greek and Latin. The confusion between teacher training and university education remained a difficult obstacle in the way of improved standards.[1]

The same was true in the science faculties. The university course was in theory distinguished from the school syllabus by far more practical work, but lack of laboratories, overcrowding, and chronic shortage of funds made this impossible in practice. There was even no special allocation for scientific research by the professors, and the acknowledged need for more demonstrators and technicians was not met: indeed, the government talked of economising. There was great variety in the standard of students in the various subjects—which were also taken to very different levels in the schools. But even in mathematics, in which France had a very high international reputation around 1900, the standard fell between the wars, when the reform of the secondary syllabus reduced the amount of time allocated to science. The scientists bitterly complained that far less was spent on higher education than was still allocated to the feeding of horses in the French cavalry in 1927, in the age of the motor car.

This stagnation in university methods was all the more remarkable and unacceptable because it survived into a period

---

[1] Louis Villat, 'L'Agrégation et l'enseignement supérieur', *Revue internationale de l'enseignement* (1930), vol. 34, 19–29.

when the demand for higher education was greater than ever before. The increase in the number of students can be seen from the table:[1]

|  | 1900 | 1910 | 1920 | 1930 | 1939 | 1968 |
|---|---|---|---|---|---|---|
| Students in the Faculty of: | | | | | | |
| Law | 9,709 | 16,915 | 13,948 | 19,585 | 22,470 | 126,000 |
| Letters | 3,476 | 6,363 | 6,355 | 16,928 | 21,339 | 196,000 |
| Sciences | 3,857 | 6,287 | 10,517 | 14,781 | 12,822 | 123,000 |
| Medicine | 8,781 | 9,721 | 11,990 | 16,246 | 16,027 | 98,000 |
| Pharmacy | 3,395 | 1,758 | 2,128 | 5,737 | 6,023 | 20,000 |

The increase in science students, though considerable, was very much less than that of students of letters; in 1939 there were still fewer students of science than of medicine, and law was still the most popular subject. There were more students, that is, but they were of the traditional type. The distribution of resources between the faculties was thus not really challenged by public opinion. The increase moreover was quite slight. The explosion in university education was to come well after the war of 1939–45. In 1939 there were 80,000 university students; in 1955–6 the number was 157,000; in 1965 it was 357,000. The small place held by the universities in the nation's life can be seen even more clearly if the number of professors is compared:[2]

| 1867 | 1878 | 1945 | 1950 | 1960 | 1963 | 1970 |
|---|---|---|---|---|---|---|
| 678 | 942 | 2,090 | 2,853 | 10,967 | 24,798 | 35,679 |

The increase in the number of students was not generally viewed with approval, for though more teachers were required, there was also much talk about graduate unemployment. In 1933, for example, a single post of junior master in Rennes—a perfectly ordinary post—attracted 245 applications.[3] Many professors spoke contemptuously of incompetent students and demanded entrance examinations and a limitation of numbers. 'Those who have not the talent or who have

[1] *Receuil des statistiques scolaires et professionnelles de 1936 à 1942*, published by the Bureau Universitaire de Statistique (1943), 12, 28, 44, 60, 76; *Annuaire statistique 1969* (1971), vol. 76, 104.

[2] Crémieux-Brilhac, op. cit., 375; *Statistique de l'enseignement supérieur* (1878), xliv.

[3] The Rector of Rennes who reported this said the situation had changed by 1937 and unemployment had disappeared. Cf. Walter M. Kotschnig, *Unemployment in the Learned Professions: an International Study of Occupational and Educational Planning* (Oxford, 1937), 114–17.

not acquired the knowledge necessary for receiving higher education, should confine themselves to secondary education.'[1]

This is perhaps why so little was done for the material welfare of the students. The Cité Universitaire in Paris (mainly for foreigners) and that at Lille, built between the wars, were exceptions. Students were expected to look after themselves. Most of them were still supported by their parents; many worked part or even full time to keep themselves; a minority seem to have survived in great poverty. Medical examinations before 1914 revealed that 7 per cent of students were tubercular and 12 per cent syphilitic.[2] Students' unions and associations were still weak. Perhaps the best account of the students' life and attitude can be obtained from the speeches of the young Merleau-Ponty, representing France at an international conference of students in 1938. He protested against the German delegate's view that the universities were too intellectual, that they did not devote enough attention to the students and to their 'affective life'. 'I think', he said, 'that this state of affairs is quite satisfactory, and that the university has nothing to do with their affective life nor even with their individual conduct. It is not a church, nor a school of character, nor even a sanatorium for melancholy students.' His description of Paris university life was interesting. There were no relations between students and professors in most subjects, he said. 'The professor gives his course, assigns grades to the dissertations of the students when they write any, and asks questions in the examinations.' There was a total absence of corporate life or internal cohesion—and so no pressures were exerted. 'Certain currents of thought prevail, inevitably, but each individual is free to revolt against them. The spirit of conformity is practically unknown. Each member of the university feels himself so much a stranger to the others that the attacks directed against it leave him indifferent . . . There are, however, some exceptions. Within the faculty of letters there exist certain rather closely united groups where there is much greater cohesion than in the faculty as a whole. These are groups which are

[1] Société de l'Enseignement Supérieur, *Problèmes d'université* (1938), 216, 226.
[2] Achille Mestre, *Études et étudiants* (1928); Marcelle Risler, 'L'Évolution de la condition des étudiants de la seconde moitié du xixe siècle à 1959', in *Cahiers de Musée Social* (1960), no. 1, 11.

concerned with highly specialised questions and which have a sort of monopoly of their subjects. Here the professors know their students, direct their work, accept their collaboration, and train them to become their successors. Professors and students are bound by very close ties; and these groups are very exclusive. It is not always easy to enter them. But these groups are separated by watertight compartments. They have nothing to do with one another or with the mass of the students. By the narrowness of the aims pursued, by their strictly technical character, they are rather collaborative workshops than genuine communities. The same is true as regards the sciences. In that field the work is less scattered, and a certain unity is maintained by virtue of the predominance of mathematical training. Furthermore, through the necessities of experimental work, a close contact is maintained between professors and students. But here too, I think, we must speak of collaboration rather than community. One only of the branches of the university presents the character of a genuine community: the faculty of medicine. That institution exercises a real monopoly over medicine in France. Not only have all who practise medicine passed through it, but the élite of French doctors is composed of the professors of the faculty. Outside the faculty there is no salvation, either for the doctor or for the patient. Although rivalries between doctors reach a degree of intensity rarely seen elsewhere, and although each student who wishes to succeed must attach himself to a *patron* who will defend him with all his influence against the favourite of another *patron*, the medical community is very coherent and very conscious of its privileges.'[1]

It has been said that Liard's provincial universities were a complete failure.[2] At any rate they did not succeed in winning an influential or highly respected place in the nation's life in this period, and there are several reasons for this. The principal one is that the reform of the universities was tackled in a very piecemeal manner, so that they never became the true apex of the educational system. The scale of values established by Napoleon survived. It was the *lycées* which were considered to

---

[1] League of Nations: International Institute of Intellectual Co-operation (Paris), *Students in search of University* (1938), 125–7.
[2] Georges Gusdorf, *L'Université en question* (1964), 197.

provide *culture générale*, a complete education in itself, rather than a mere preparation. Their top forms, the *classes de philosophie* and *mathématiques spéciales*, and the preparatory classes for candidates for the *grandes écoles*, had very high standards, and worked to a level which could rival that of the *licence*. Some of the teachers in these higher forms, like Alain and Bellesort, provided what was virtually higher education in the *lycée*, and more effectively in their small classes than the professors of the faculties could do with their anonymous audiences. The *licence* remained depressed because it was a professional qualification for an ill-paid and still inferior school-teaching job. The revival of the universities took place long after an active cultural life had already been established in France and had found different ground in which to grow. The intellectual élite, men of letters, the world of the *salons*, continued more or less independent of the universities. The progress of knowledge took place largely outside them too. The most specialised forms of education were entrusted to *grandes écoles*, which became major institutions of higher learning outside the university. It is these very small institutions which produced the country's 'mandarins'.

In the eighteenth century two special schools were founded to train engineers for the Ponts et Chaussées and for the Mines, and others for army and naval officers. In 1794 another was established to train engineers for public works—extended in 1795, as the Polytechnique, to train all kinds of military and civil engineers. In 1795 also the École Normale Supérieure was founded to train senior schoolmasters. As new sciences and new public needs developed, further *grandes écoles* and *écoles d'application* were established to provide even more specialised and advanced education in different forms of engineering and applied science. Important social consequences followed. The *grandes écoles* were entered by competitive examination (unlike the universities, which were open to all who had very elementary paper qualifications) and they offered scholarships, long before the universities did. The École Normale and the Polytechnique particularly came to attract the very best students in the country, and the marked success their graduates had in public life and in industry gave them enormous and increasing prestige. Both were residential and developed a unique *esprit de corps*. The result was that sizeable groups within the ruling class and among the most influential people in the country's economic and intellectual life were graduates of a few institutions. The lawyers had always had a dominant position in politics. Many of them, trained in Paris, knew each other from their student days, when they won oratorical distinction in moots. (The conférence Molé, where Gambetta's generation met, is perhaps the most famous of these.) It would be too simple to say that their position was challenged first by the Normaliens, particularly powerful in the Socialist party, and then by the Polytechniciens, who came to dominate big business. But there is just a little truth in this.

Though originally a teacher training college, the École Normale quickly became, because of the distinction of its professors and its pupils, a leading institution of higher learning. It developed methods of instruction totally different from the dogmatic ex-cathedra lecturing of the faculties. The professors were called *maîtres de conférences*, the discussion class was given more emphasis than the lecture, and private reading in the large library replaced the memorising of textbooks. Unlike the faculties, here the students were in intimate contact with their teachers, and being boarders, living in dormitories and in shared studies, they taught one another too. They had no difficulty in getting the best jobs in the schools and increasingly in the universities also, to such an extent that the school was attacked for abandoning its original function of teacher training and becoming a rival of the Sorbonne. The hostility aroused by their success led to the idea that the Normaliens were moulded into a single type. Zola wrote of them as 'musty pedants . . . filled with the silent impotent envy of bachelors who had failed with women'. The idea that they generally had any one political or religious opinion was misconceived. The school produced men of totally opposed tendencies—Jaurès and Bergson in one year; Herriot but also Mgr Baudrillart, Tardieu, Déat, Giraudoux, Bellesort, Massigli, and Louis Bertrand. Its teachers were equally diverse and never even tried to impose a single dogma. One of its directors, Bersot, called it *un lieu de tolérance*.[1]

[1] Jules Lemaître, 'L'Esprit normalien', in *Le Centenaire de l'École Normale 1795–1895* (1895), 565–71; Alain Payrefitte, *Chroniques de la vie normalienne* (1950),

The École Normale's relations with successive regimes were chequered and its character was considerably modified by successive directors. It was suspect under the Restoration for its liberalism: it did not seem to Bishop Frayssinous to be a repository of the 'sound doctrines, good traditions and useful knowledge which it is called upon to spread among the various classes of society'. By contrast it enjoyed high favour under Louis-Philippe, and no less a man than Cousin became its head. He had a passion for discipline and maintained the full rigour of Napoleonic austerity. The students rose at five and spent long periods in silent study under supervision; only in their third year could they obtain private rooms. 'Dangerous or futile books', said his regulations, 'must not enter the school; the reading of newspapers is forbidden, being irrelevant to the syllabus.' Since there are records of students being punished for spending the morning in bed, the severity of the rules must have been mitigated in practice. However, provided he was obeyed, Cousin was a powerful patron who actively assisted the graduates of the school to the best jobs: he was perhaps the first to give them the consciousness of being an élite, as well as of belonging to an organised clientage. In 1847 the school was moved out of highly insalubrious slums (for it was still an appendage of the Lycée Louis-le-Grand) into new buildings in the rue d'Ulm, which it occupies to this day. But the Second Empire plunged it again into disgrace. For fear of political deviation, it was firmly restricted to training only 'modest teachers, not rhetoricians, more skilled at raising insoluble and dangerous problems than at transmitting useful knowledge'. The tough minister of education Fortoul halted its progress towards becoming an institution of higher learning by ending the specialisation which had gradually developed. The students were confined to learning how to teach the *lycée* syllabus: they had to choose between being teachers of science or teachers of the arts. The specialist philosophy course was abolished as producing only 'vanity and doubt'. Even geometry had now to be taught so as not to inspire 'the pride which

272–3; for brief and bitter sketches of many other graduates Hubert Bourgin, *De Jaurès à Léon Blum: l'École Normale et la politique* (1938). R. J. Smith, 'L'Atmosphère politique à l'E.N.S. à la fin du 19ᵉ siècle', *Revue d'histoire moderne et contemporaine* (Apr.–June 1973), 248–68.

leads to false ideas'; geography should be purely descriptive, so as to 'show man his smallness . . . and lead his thoughts towards the Creator'. The students were not completely cowed, however: a new rule that they should request loans from the library in writing produced a strike, and they abstained from using the library for a year. This governmental hostility led to a catastrophic decline in applications for admission. The second half of Napoleon III's reign was spent undoing the damage, and specialisation was gradually restored. Pasteur, who became head of the science department, did a great deal to get the school recognised as a research establishment: in 1864 he founded the *Annales scientifiques de l'ENS* in which its discoveries were published. His fame even won him an allocation for research assistants. But he did not treat his students as equals: he expected them to be as obedient to constituted authority as he was himself, and he became pretty unpopular. There is a solemn table and statistical analysis, written in his own hand, of punishments imposed in 1858–9: they include castigations 'for having read a novel', 'for having read a newspaper', 'for having introduced a periodical into the school'. On one occasion he threatened to expel anyone caught smoking: seventy-three students handed in their resignation in protest: the matter had to be settled by the minister. When one student refused to attend prayers on the ground that he had been converted to Protestantism, Pasteur refused to accept this unless he produced a certificate from a pastor and he declared that if the student 'had no religion recognised by the state', he would be expelled.[1] Only in 1867 were the students allowed to get up at six instead of five.

It was some time before the arts side made precise erudition its ideal. Nisard (director 1857–67) believed the 'admiration of the classics' to be the best occupation for an educated man and 'French commentary' to be superior to 'German philological explication', taste to be more important than industry. Bersot (director 1871–80) had not completely abandoned his master Cousin's view of philosophy as involving 'adherence to those compromise truths, consecrated both by the faith of centuries and by the spiritual witness of men's conscience'; he approved of inquiry but did not believe it could lead anywhere. However,

[1] Cf. V. Glachant, 'Pasteur disciplinaire', *Revue universitaire*, July 1938.

Fustel de Coulanges (professor of history 1870, director 1880–3) abhorred dilettantism and indifference; he incited his students to engage in controversy, to avoid generalisation, to make detailed studies of small subjects based on original sources. He never spoke to them about their examinations; his lectures did not contain long recitals of facts, but enthusiastic extempore arguments, propounding one or two ideas. He was never known to smile or tell a joke, but his appeal to their intellectual liberty filled them with confidence. His successor, the archaeologist Perrot (1883–1904), tried (unsuccessfully) to make the school a graduate one, admitting only *licenciés*, but he also defended the traditional syllabus, praising even the educational merits of writing Latin verse.

Hostility to the school developed; the faculties protested that it was stealing the best students from them, but not fulfilling its function of giving pedagogic training to secondary teachers. The success of its graduates aroused envy: in the history *agrégation* in 1903, all six of its candidates were successful, but only three out of the forty from the Sorbonne and one out of the thirty from the provincial universities. The spread of socialism in the school, largely through the influence of its librarian Lucien Herr (famous for helping to convert Jaurès), exacerbated the hostility to it. In 1903, as a result of parliamentary pressure, it was made part of the University of Paris; its professors were withdrawn and attached to the Sorbonne; its independent teaching was largely ended; it was turned into a hostel, whose students attended the university lectures; it was to become simply the pedagogical department of the university, and its students were to devote a considerable period (instead of a nominal fortnight as before) to teaching practice in *lycées*. Its budget was drastically cut, and deputies in parliament even demanded its abolition altogether.[1] It had just then reached the peak of its influence: Wallon, the father of the constitution, and at one stage the presidents of both chambers of parliament were graduates of it. Whereas in 1890 it had ten times as many applications as it could admit, by 1914 this ratio was halved. In science, its standing became distinctly inferior to the

[1] C. Bouglé, 'Rapport sur les réformes proposées', *Revue internationale de l'enseignement* (1904), vol. 47, 45–9; G. Monod, 'La Réforme de l'École Normale', *Revue historique* (1904), vol. 84, 79 n.

Polytechnique, and candidates for both schools almost invariably preferred the latter if elected to both: the École Normale was reduced to taking the Polytechnique's rejects. This was very different from the situation in the nineteenth century: in 1864 a man who came top in the entrance examination for the Polytechnique, and second in that for the École Normale, had chosen the latter.

The principal architect of this transformation was the historian Ernest Lavisse (director 1904–19), one of the most influential figures behind the reorganisation of French education during the first half of the Third Republic. He made some changes in almost every arts examination. He wrote history textbooks for every stage of the school and university curricula. He was a close friend of Du Mesnil, Dumont, and Liard (successively directors of higher education at the ministry) and, some said, the man really behind the creation of the provincial universities. He was determined to make the Sorbonne not only eminent but also an active teaching institution with real students—of which the Normaliens would be the nucleus. It was not promotion for Lavisse to be made director; he had held more senior jobs; and he did not even bother to take up his official residence in the school. His unwillingness to supervise it closely was conscious: his temperament and his system both led to a great relaxation of discipline.[1]

The very existence of the school seemed threatened. It was saved partly by the heroism of its students in the war: 50 per cent of them were killed and the school was awarded the Croix de Guerre. The inter-war period was an uneasy one. Lanson (director 1919–27), famous as the author of a standard textbook on French literature which had sold 350,000 copies in its first twenty-seven years, tried to preserve the school's independence within the university. In 1927 a scientist (Vessiot) was appointed director and began the building of new laboratories, though he was unable to prevent the students' meagre scholarships being reduced by a quarter in the national economy drive. Bouglé (director 1935–40), the sociologist and founder of the school's Centre de Documentation Sociale (of which he made

[1] E. Lavisse, *Questions d'enseignement national* (1885); *Études et étudiants* (1890); *A propos de nos écoles* (1895); *Souvenirs* (1912); Inaugural speech on becoming director of the ENS in *Revue internationale d'enseignement* (1904), vol. 48.

Raymond Aron secretary), broadened its relations with the
outside world, encouraged travel abroad, at last introduced
central heating and running water. New life was thus injected
into the school. But it survived also because it moderated its
pretensions. From being a training college, it had developed
the ambition of providing the republic with its ruling class.
'Democracy', wrote its director Perrot in 1895, at the height
of its prestige, 'needs an élite, to represent the only superiority
it recognises, that of the mind. It is up to us to recruit this
élite, or, to speak more modestly, to work to furnish some of the
elements which will constitute it.'[1] Lanson in 1926 still regarded
his task as the 'training of the élite . . . the discovery and education of individuals fit to become leaders'.[2] However, when Herriot wrote on the school in 1932, he was content to speak of it
only as a nursery of wit, intelligence, and liberalism. Extreme
left-wing graduates poured scorn on its 'esprit de corps reminiscent of the seminary and the regiment'.[3]

At the École Polytechnique the idea of forming an élite persisted more strongly. Placed under the ministry of war, this
school, exclusively scientific, was designed to train officers for
the technical corps of the army and engineers for the various
departments of state such as the Mines and the Ponts et Chaussées. The great majority of the graduates used to go into the
army, a tendency strengthened after the war of 1870. The
military law of 1905 which required them to spend one year in
the ranks before entering the school reduced the ardour of some
when they saw the army from the private soldier's viewpoint.
The proportion of soldiers diminished henceforth, probably
even more because other careers appeared more attractive.
In the 1914–18 war, many of the French commanders were
Polytechniciens, including Marshals Fayolle, Foch, Joffre,
Manoury, and General Nivelle. By 1924 only a quarter of the
graduates went into the army; Pétain is said to have excluded
them systematically from the highest posts; so they could maintain that the school had no responsibility for the débâcle of

[1] *Le Centenaire de L'École Normale 1795–1895* (1895), xlv.
[2] G. Lanson, 'L'École Normale Supérieure', in *Revue des Deux Mondes*, 1 Feb.
1926; cf. A. François-Poncet, *G. Lanson* (1958).
[3] E. Herriot, *Nos Grandes Écoles: Normale* (1932), 194–9; Pierre Jeannin, *École
Normale Supérieure, Livre d'Or* (1963), 138.

1940.[1] Increasing numbers went into private companies. Many of the greatest names in the history of industry and applied science are those of Polytechniciens, from Talabot and Citroen to Louis Armand. The school produced only a few politicians—Freycinet, Sadi Carnot, Albert Lebrun, Jules Moch, but its influence in politics has nevertheless been considerable. In the early years it was a seminary of Saint-Simonians and other theorists—Comte, Enfantin, Michel Chevalier, Considérant, Le Play. Its graduates played a leading part in the acquisition of the French empire. Between the wars, the school produced numerous graduates who took an interest in economics and advised successive governments.[2] The Polytechniciens were an important link between government and industry. Their *esprit de corps* was, and is, legendary. The school indeed consciously sought to create this by its military organisation. Its students lived in groups of about eight, for the two years of their course, with one room in which there were eight desks, a bedroom with eight beds, and a bathroom with eight wash-basins. On the wall a time-table told them exactly how they would be spending every minute of the day.[3] Little more than 100 students were recruited annually in the first half of the nineteenth century; and usually between 200 and 250 after 1870. As freshmen they were subjected to initiation ceremonies, sometimes of considerable brutality. A strong respect for the traditions of the school was quickly established and the 'glorification of its past' flourished as 'a respectable rite of the community'. This is not to say all of them were turned into conservatives, even though the school remained military. The students opposed the Restoration and the July Monarchy (the school was closed four times by the government in this period), and played a popular part in the revolutions of 1830 and 1848. In 1855 they refused to shout 'Vive l'Empereur' at the review by Napoleon III, and in 1868 they greeted a visit from the Prince Imperial with stony silence.[4] Since then they have remained politically diverse, though they do not seem to have

[1] J. P. Callot, *Histoire de l'École Polytechnique* (1959), 238; Maurice d'Ocagne, 'L'École Polytechnique', *Revue des Deux Mondes*, 1 June 1926.

[2] See below, chapter 21.

[3] I describe what I saw in 1965 in the buildings put up between the wars: these have since been abandoned and the school has moved to the outskirts of Paris.

[4] G. Pinet, *Histoire de l'École Polytechnique* (1887), 273.

produced any revolutionaries. The social origins of the students may partly explain this. Napoleon had established only thirty scholarships. In 1850 the number of scholarships was made unlimited but dependent on a means test; about a third of the students were given scholarships, and by 1881 one-half were; in 1926 two-thirds were; only in 1930 was the school made entirely free. A considerable proportion thus came from well-to-do families. The idea of the hierarchy of merit dominated the whole course. The students were perpetually examined, usually at short notice, in brief, surprise orals; they were placed in numbered order on entry and graduation. They used the library very little and were taught mainly by lectures. Half the Polytechnique's entrance examination was in mathematics, discouraging the schools from teaching more natural science. Special classes in the best *lycées* prepared able boys for it, but these boys spent two or three years repeating the same narrow syllabus, for it was usual to fail a few times before getting in. It has been claimed that the 'Polytechnic mentality' was in fact acquired in these classes, where lessons, in the 1960s, still lasted from eight in the morning to eight in the evening, after which there was 'homework' to do; and only some did not study on Sundays. Admission to the Polytechnique was based on *surmenage* (overwork), so that by the time the successful candidates were admitted, they were already distinguished by their 'exceptional industriousness, rapidity of reasoning, memory and suppleness of mind'; but by then, they were already exhausted and their 'curiosity' vanished for ever once they had won their place. In the 1960s it was claimed about 60 per cent of them did not worry about the rank they would achieve in their final examination; only a minority continued to be competitive.[1]

Only two small institutions were devoted exclusively to research. The Collège de France had been founded in 1530 with six professors to advance humane studies and the spirit of the Renaissance, for the university, hidebound by its privileges and traditions, already appeared incapable of reform. By 1798 the College had twenty professors; by 1930 it had forty-seven. New chairs were added to advance new sciences; when a chair fell

[1] Michel Ullmann, 'Formations et mentalité polytechniciennes. Causes et conséquences' (mémoire Institut d'Études Politiques, unpublished, 1963).

vacant, it was not necessarily filled with a specialist in the same subject; the professors met to decide freely which subject—and often a new one—was most in need of further research. The College was entirely independent of the university; its professors did not have to hold any degrees; they could lecture on any subject they pleased, without having any examinations in view; they were required only to make their lectures contributions to knowledge, rather than simply popularisations; and these lectures were open free to the general public. The College was served by the most distinguished scholars and it did a great deal to maintain France's prestige in the world of learning. But, in common with the universities, its premises and laboratories were seriously inadequate, and extensions never kept up with its growing needs.[1]

The École Pratique des Hautes Études was founded in 1868 to fulfil two functions which the faculties were neglecting: the pursuit of *higher* learning, and the training of scholars for this by the *practical* co-operation of pupil and teacher in seminars and laboratories, instead of the former simply listening to the lectures of the latter. Originally its principal activity was to have been scientific—the provision of laboratories, but these laboratories never had an independent life, being attached to other establishments such as the Museum, the Collège de France, or the faculties of science. Nothing came of the economic section, because the faculty of law expressed no interest. The section of historical and philological sciences alone developed as an independent body, though at first it had only a corner in the Sorbonne library to meet in. It did a great deal for oriental studies and for linguistics. Gabriel Monod, who had attended seminars at Göttingen, introduced the seminar system into the historical sections, recruiting his first pupils from the École des Chartes and later the École Normale. It was a great innovation for professors and students to sit at the same table and work together on the solution of a problem or the editing of a text. But the directors of studies (as they were called here, there were no professors) usually also had other jobs, for example at the

[1] *Le Collège de France 1530–1930, Livre jubilaire*, by A. Lefranc, P. Langevin *et al.* (1932); M. Croiset, 'Le Collège de France' in E. Durkheim, *La Vie universitaire à Paris* (1918); M. Croiset, 'Le Collège de France' in *Revue des Deux Mondes*, 1 May 1926.

Collège de France or the Sorbonne. A characteristic of many of the institutes and other similar establishments is that they were often simply a group of men, rather than a building, and of men who spent much of their time in other institutions: they were more clubs than schools, and the importance of their publications was out of all proportion to their physical size. In 1886, when the faculties of Catholic theology were abolished, a section of religious sciences was added to the École Pratique. This was again a remarkable novelty, the first body to study all religions, including primitive and oriental ones. The École des Hautes Études demanded no paper qualifications from its students and it had no examinations. In these exceptional conditions, it was able to do work of great interest, but again for only a tiny minority of scholars and only in a few subjects.

The École Libre des Sciences Politiques, established in 1872, under the influence of the defeat by Germany, represented another attempt to remedy the gaps in the faculty system. Émile Boutmy, its founder, intended it to fulfil two functions. *Culture générale* was offered only in the *lycées*: he proposed to provide it at university level, and by the study of modern subjects instead of the classics. This liberal education would be different from the traditional type because it would turn out not 'conversationalists with ornamental minds' but 'competent judges of political questions, capable of solid discussions on these and capable of leading opinion'. He wished, secondly, to train 'an élite . . . formed of men who by their family situation or special aptitudes had the right to aspire to exercise an influence on the masses in politics, in the service of the state, or in big business'.[1] It began with ninety-five pupils paying 70 francs each in fees; by 1882 it had 250; in the 1890s between 300 and 400; by 1938 over 1,750. Over a tenth of these came from other countries. It was indeed unique in its international outlook and its interest in foreign politics and institutions, particularly those of England and the United States. Nearly all its professors worked elsewhere most of the time (they were for long paid for their lectures by the hour), and so it had close links with the outside world of politics, business and the civil service. Two departments were established at first, for diplomatic and administrative

<hr />

[1] Pierre Rain, *L'École Libre des Sciences Politiques* (1963), 13–15; E. d'Eichtal, *L'École Libre des Sciences Politiques* (1932), 73, 77.

studies; later three more were added—economic and financial, economic and social, and general. The most successful was the financial, which in 1932 attracted 42 per cent of the school's students. Leading companies sent trainees to it. Until 1931 anybody could join, no qualifications being required. A large number of students of the faculty of law attended its lectures as supplementary courses. It became highly influential because it was in effect an administrative college, and in time it gained a virtual monopoly of the best civil service jobs. In the period 1901–35, of 117 successful candidates in the competition for entry into the Conseil d'État, 113 were from Sciences Po., 202 out of 211 admissions to the Inspection des Finances, 82 out of 92 to the Cour des Comptes, and 246 out of 280 to the ministry of foreign affairs.[1]

A sizeable proportion of the country's intellectual and technical leaders passed through the institutions of higher learning[2]— it is of course impossible to review them all here—but perhaps for this very reason, their general structure and organisation remained largely unchanged. The *esprit de corps* of their graduates and the conservatism (in professional, as distinct from political, matters) of most of their teachers, preserved their privileged, almost oligarchical, character. They claimed they were democratic because the élite they created was recruited by examination, but there was no real equality of opportunity to pass the examinations. They drew the vast majority of their pupils from the middle classes, because secondary education was not yet freely available to the poor. They offered some scholarships, but very few in proportion to their total numbers. They still made study in Paris an almost indispensable condition—and sign—of success. Their examinations, moreover, were extremely old-fashioned and universally decried for rewarding memory more than anything else. Nevertheless, the institutions were not intolerable, precisely because of their defects. Their limited ambitions allowed freedom, their decadence left room for hope and for leisure. For all their theoretical stress on

[1] Rain, op. cit. 90.

[2] Nicole Delefortrie-Soubeyroux, *Les Dirigeants de l'industrie française* (1961), 57–8; Alain Girard, *La Réussite sociale en France* (1961), *passim*; Pierre Lalumière, *L'Inspection des Finances* (1959), 30, 70; A. Odin, *Genèse des grands hommes: gens de lettres français modernes* (1895).

uniformity, their chaotic disorganisation gave plenty of scope for individuality. Despite them and partly thanks to them, France was able to enjoy a century of cultural achievement as distinguished as any in its history. The significance of the expansion of higher education was not generally appreciated, partly because this expansion was moderate compared to that which took place in the 1960s, partly because the static population meant that there were proportionately fewer young people in the country, and partly because the best students were quickly absorbed by society and given a more or less privileged position. But the universities were already beginning to create a vast new *compagnonage*, and it was no accident that students played a major role in the revolution of 1968.

France, as a nation, was to a large extent created by an effort of will. These seven chapters have shown how politicians and intellectuals tried to make it much more than a conglomeration of neighbours, but also how their ideals were never quite realised. The French did not all come to think alike; the schools did not quite succeed in transforming their pupils. The elaborate hierarchical structure of examinations produced much more mediocrity and parody than anyone had bargained for. There were too many forces, regional, ideological, temperamental, which resisted uniformity. The conflicts of boys and girls, of young and old, of the primary and the secondary mentality, were paradoxically strengthened. To measure the success of the French nationalists, it is necessary to study this resistance further, to look at the parallel development of the non-intellectual sides of life, to assess the strength of other attractions and to investigate the emotional demands of the people out of school. Only then will it be possible to judge the role of the intellectuals in a comprehensive context.[1]

[1] See chapter 23 below.

**M**

# Part II

# 8. Good and Bad Taste

'TASTE', said Littré in his dictionary, 'is a completely spontaneous faculty, which precedes reflection. Everybody
possesses it, but it is different in everybody.' His definition
raises several major puzzles. The first concerns the independence
of the individual. Moralists have traditionally argued that man
has the power to choose between the options facing him, between
good and evil, between the beautiful and the ugly, and that the
pressures around him do not ultimately determine his actions.
In the course of this century, the individual was increasingly
placed in an even more difficult position. On the one hand, he
was assured that the rights of the individual were the Revolution's most sacred conquest and that he was therefore freer than
ever; good and evil no longer had unchallenged sanctions
behind them, they could no longer be easily recognised and
the individual was required to think everything out for himself. On the other hand, he was assured that social and economic
forces were more powerful than he was, or that he belonged
inescapably to a class with identical interests, or that the effect
of democracy was to level everybody down so that they became
increasingly alike. Historians have usually preferred to discuss
these problems as an ideological debate, instead of trying to
investigate the realities alongside the beliefs. But whether people
were in fact becoming more alike, whether there was now more
or less room for whim and temperament, are uncertainties that
need clarification.

This immediately comes up against the question of just how
much history can or should explain. The popularity of biography comes in large measure from its implicit assertion that
individuals have a uniqueness which transcends all the
categorisations that can be made about them, and from its
encouragement of the belief that individuals can make some
impact on the course of events. Historians have moved increasingly away from this position and have preferred to write
about causes, influences, forces and crises. There can be no

doubt that, if they are viewed from a sufficient distance, all individuals can be made to fit into general patterns. But this leaves the reader with two sets of facts which are left unrelated and unreconciled. The history of the individual in the face of the forces that surround him has not been treated at a general level. Yet, after all the determinist influences had been at work, individuals did, equally certainly, behave eccentrically, make random choices, suffer accidents. There is on the one hand the world of the molecules, where combinations of atoms follow regular patterns, and the world of electrons, where apparent chaos rules. History can never produce the biography of every single individual, which would alone allow irrefutable generalisations. What it can try to do, however, is to study more carefully the relationship between the patterns and the chaos, between the universal and the particular.

Taste is a notion whose ambiguity makes it particularly suitable for this. Taste is the assertion of individuality but also the acceptance of standards. Popular taste has the appearance, as Littré claimed, of being instinctive or irrational and it can therefore be looked on as an instance of the resistance of the 'primitive' to what is imposed from above. Like love and anxiety, it is a spanner thrown into the works, which stops the machinery of society from functioning as its principles would have it, even if one can also show that society produces these spanners for its own destruction. Taste in literature and art is just one kind of taste; but it is a valuable starting-point because it is the most articulate kind. However, its significance can only be appreciated if it is placed in a wider context, among other prejudices, interests and amusements.

History is a sieve that picks up only a small portion of the debris of the past. What it salvages is, above all, books and manuscripts. But, as Goethe put it, 'of what has been done and said, only a tiny part has been written; and of what has been written, only a tiny part has been remembered'. What is honoured as literature is a 'fragment of fragments'. In this period there were perhaps thirty writers classified as being of the 'first importance', about whom it is possible to satisfy one's curiosity, and whose works have been minutely studied. There are a few hundred others who have been considered 'significant' and on whom more or less research has been undertaken. But these constitute a sort of ruling class, equivalent to the kings and parliaments of politics. The great mass of writers have been condemned to oblivion. The criteria by which they have been judged are literary; that is to say, 'taste' has decided. But exactly how some writers have become famous, how reputations have been created and broken, which writers were most read in their own day, how popularity has altered, what position writers had in society, how increasing circulation affected them, what influence critics exerted on attitudes to them: these are some of the questions that need to be answered before an adequate appreciation of historical sources is possible. However, it is not easy to supply the answers, because the history of publishing and bookselling is in its infancy, and the history of public opinion on non-political matters, of prejudice and of *idées reçues* is particularly difficult to write. There is a danger of setting up a vicious circle by arguing that literature 'reflects' society and that the answers to these problems can be found in literature itself. It is fashionable to hold that literature is not just beautiful, entertaining or revealing about human nature, but that it is the best form of history. 'Literature', one modern student of it has said, 'is the conscience of society. It expresses the social feelings of a period, at the same time as it analyses them and judges them. Like a seismograph, it registers and amplifies the shocks agitating society—currents of opinion, moods, confused aspirations, discontent, hope.'[1] It is indeed perfectly true that some novelists have left studies of society which are richer and livelier than what historians have written, but their testimony still needs to be subjected to scrutiny in the same way as all other testimony. Because historians have, until recently, avoided the intimate subjects on which novelists have concentrated, literature has been the major source of enlightenment on the deeper motivations, the ambitions, tastes and anxieties of ordinary people. One needs to look at its contribution, however, in the context of all the other material that is available. Authors inevitably express only their own opinions and their own vision: the historian finds their work most valuable as evidence of how one particular individual felt and interpreted the world around him. How 'influential' their

[1] Micheline Tison-Braun, *La Crise de l'humanisme* (1958), 1. ii. And for a more complex theory, Lucien Goldman, *Pour une sociologie du roman* (1964).

attitudes were is something that should not be judged too fast. The relation between author and reader is a complex one and cannot be unravelled in purely literary terms: the fact that literary schools—romantic, realist, symbolist and so on—succeeded each other does not mean that each generation can be given the same blanket label. The claim of novelists to speak for their generation can be dismissed almost out of hand, for one thing that is certain is that no generation spoke with a united voice. France was far too complicated a society to allow· that. What needs investigation is the size of the audience the writer enjoyed, how far his ideas were accepted, but also what other ideas survived in his audience, side by side with his. Clear-cut, coherent attitudes were no more to be found in readers, than they were in writers, and every new study of a writer shows how the labels attached to him are exaggerated simplifications. What one must seek therefore is a way of understanding the incoherence and confusion of taste, which does not falsely diminish that confusion.

The first need is to look at all the books that were published, irrespective of the merits that have been attributed to them. The figures are:[1]

### Number of Books Published (annual titles)

| | | | |
|------|--------|------|--------|
| 1815 | 3,357  | 1915 | 4,274  |
| 1830 | 6,739  | 1917 | 5,054  |
| 1847 | 5,530  | 1920 | 6,315  |
| 1848 | 7,234  | 1924 | 8,864  |
| 1855 | 8,253  | 1925 | 15,054 |
| 1860 | 11,905 | 1926 | 11,095 |
| 1869 | 12,269 | 1930 | 9,176  |
| 1870 | 8,831  | 1935 | 7,964  |
| 1875 | 14,195 | 1939 | 7,505  |
| 1880 | 12,414 | 1945 | 7,291  |
| 1885 | 12,342 | 1948 | 16,020 |
| 1890 | 13,643 | 1950 | 11,849 |
| 1900 | 13,362 | 1955 | 11,793 |
| 1910 | 12,615 | 1960 | 11,827 |
| 1913 | 14,460 | 1970 | 22,935 |

[1] Estivals, *La Statistique bibliographique de la France sous la monarchie au 18e siècle* (1965), 415.

Two facts are immediately striking. Books multiplied before the advent of mass literacy. The most rapid increase in book production took place in the eighteenth century, when it rose fivefold. In the nineteenth century, there were indeed more books than ever before, but the great novelty was the newspaper rather than the book, and it was to the newspaper that the newly educated masses turned. Books cannot be regarded in a simple way either as the immediate expression of democratic public opinion, or as the major influence on people's ideas. Secondly, France does not appear to be as much of a literary nation as its reputation suggests. The exceptional brilliance of French literature and the fame that the country's great writers enjoyed have given the impression that literature mattered more in France. That, paradoxically, may be due to fewer books being published there than in other countries: writers seemed less important when there were more of them. When comparative statistics were collected, France came fairly low on the list of book producers:

*Number of books (titles) published*

|              | 1950   | 1970   |
|--------------|--------|--------|
| France       | 11,849 | 22,935 |
| Japan        | 13,009 | 31,249 |
| German F.R.  | 14,094 | 45,369 |
| U.K.         | 17,072 | 33,441 |

Book production took a new turn after 1950. What characterises the century before that is a relative stability. This seems to have applied to the kinds of books published as well as to their total numbers, at least from 1900, when comparable figures become available:[1]

|      | General | Religion | Philosophy | Science | Medicine | Applied Science |
|------|---------|----------|------------|---------|----------|-----------------|
| 1900 | 40      | 793      | 192        | 286     | 1,347    | 890             |
| 1910 | 40      | 891      | 168        | 350     | 1,229    | 842             |
| 1920 | 39      | 422      | 108        | 178     | 392      | 1,041           |
| 1930 | 80      | 402      | 217        | 781     | 791      | 706             |
| 1938 | 353     | 558      | 238        | 424     | 501      | 1,044           |

[1] Brigitte Levrier, 'Sources bibliographiques et statistiques concernant la production intellectuelle en France et l'exportation 1900–1951', Mémoire présenté à l'Institut National des Techniques de la Documentation, Conservatoire National des Arts-et-Métiers (1952 typescript) (B.N. Q.4666), 9–18.

|  | Social Science | History & Geography | Fine Arts | Literature |
|---|---|---|---|---|
| 1900 | 2,516 | 1,568 | 190 | 2,185 |
| 1910 | 1,985 | 1,894 | 516 | 2,397 |
| 1920 | 867 | 1,205 | 172 | 1,383 |
| 1930 | 735 | 1,765 | 289 | 3,414 |
| 1938 | 1,140 | 1,170 | 411 | 2,297 |

'Literature'—which includes all fiction—represented less than a quarter of the total, but it was the largest single category, and there is no doubt that this was the age of the novel. Literature's lead has been maintained since 1950; for although social science titles had quadrupled by 1970, those of literature had doubled and still remained ahead. What, unfortunately, is not clear, is how many copies of these books were sold, as opposed to how many titles were published. It is only recently that figures have been collected to show that in 1970 literature accounted for roughly half the total copies sold; school books and books for children accounted for nearly a third; scientific books for only about 5 per cent, the social sciences for perhaps 3 per cent, only a little more than religion; art for just over 1 per cent and history and geography for under 0·3 per cent.

Just how many readers of books there were is uncertain. Voltaire claimed that there were 3,000 people in the court and in the city of Paris who determined taste and decided what other people read. What Paris liked was not as decisive as all that. It has been estimated that in 1660 France had about 150,000 readers of books and in 1820 perhaps one million. There are no statistics until the opinion polls got to work. In 1960 they revealed that half the country never read a book, which came as a great shock to the intellectuals. The figures would have been worse but for the enormous growth of education: only 18 per cent of adolescents did not read books, whereas 53 per cent of adults were abstainers. The peasants and workers read least (but some workers, though poor, were avid readers), and reading was far more frequent in large cities than in rural areas and small towns. Another, fuller, survey in 1974 showed that 70 per cent of those interviewed had read at least one book in the course of the year; 8·9 per cent claimed to have read between twenty-five and fifty books and 12·6 per cent over fifty books. These high figures must be related to the doubling of the productivity of the French publishing industry since the last war, and the spread of secondary and higher education. Even so, 27 per cent of homes had no books in them.[1] The position today is that out of the thirty-eight million people aged over fifteen, who may be assumed to be capable of reading books, about five million buy and read books in sufficient quantities to make them true citizens of the republic of letters. Before 1945 half that figure would probably be over-generous.

The failure of the reading public to grow faster was due in part to the high cost of books. At the beginning of the nineteenth century, English octavo books cost 12 or 14 shillings, and duodecimo novels as much as 5 or 6 shillings; but Sir Walter Scott published his *Lady of the Lake* at 42 shillings and sold 20,000 copies all the same. Dickens's *Pickwick* (1837) was cheap at 21 shillings. At the same time in France books were normally published at 7 fr. 50, which was the equivalent of about 6 shillings; but novels were issued in several sparsely printed volumes (fifteen to eighteen lines a page): Alexandre Dumas issued his *Les Mohicans de Paris* (1854) in nineteen volumes, so that the total cost was 142 fr. 50 (nearly £6). This system was encouraged by the *cabinets de lecture*, or public reading-rooms, which was where most people read these novels, and where many volumes meant the book could be more easily shared out. *Cabinets de lecture* began to develop during the Restoration. There were 23 of them in Paris in 1819, 198 in 1845, 183 in 1860, 146 in 1870 and 118 in 1883; and there were probably many more obscure ones omitted in this count. For a subscription of 5 francs a month one had access to a library of between 2,000 and 10,000 volumes. The largest of these *cabinets* in Paris, that of Madame Cardinal, had 160,000 volumes in 1888 (bought by Louvain after 1918 to replace their own library, destroyed by the Germans). For an extra 10 or 20 centimes per volume, a reader could take his book home. Otherwise he read in what was often a congenial social meeting-place, provided also with newspapers and journals.[2] French lending libraries were far less successful, nevertheless, than English ones. Mudie's in New Oxford Street, already in the 1850s had a stock of

---

[1] *Pratiques culturelles des Français* (Dec. 1974).
[2] Claude Pichois, 'Les Cabinets de lecture à Paris pendant la première moitié du XIX$^e$ siècle', *Annales* (1959), 521–34.

960,000 books (only half of them novels); it bought 2,400 copies of the third and fourth volumes of Macaulay's *History of England* and 2,000 of *The Mill on the Floss*. In France the average novel was printed in only a thousand copies.

Books became cheaper owing to two new developments. First, pirated editions appeared in large quantities, printed in Belgium, and selling at low prices. Their success was such (they sold books at about a tenth of their normal price) that the production of pirated books is said to have increased tenfold in the decade 1834–45. Balzac calculated that half a million pirated copies of his works were printed in Belgium, depriving him of as many francs in royalties. Novels began to be serialised in the newspapers from the 1840s, so that they could be read by a far wider public. The *Constitutionel* in 1844–5 increased its readership from 3,000 to 40,000 by serialising Eugène Sue's *Juif errant*. So, in 1838, Gervais Charpentier, then aged thirty-three, replied to this challenge by publishing books at 3 fr. 50, half the normal price, complete in one volume. Michel Lévy went further during the Second Empire and reduced his price to 2 francs; his rival Jacottet went down to 1 franc (about 10*d*.). In 1904 Arthème Fayard published new and illustrated novels at 95 centimes and in 1913 classics at 10 centimes. Nevertheless France failed to bring its prices down as fast as England did, for the sixpenny novel had arrived there by the 1860s. The French, accordingly, were unable to rival the English publishers' mass sales, and there is no record of anything comparable in France to the million-copy edition of Kingsley which Macmillan brought out in 1889.[1]

Regional variations in book reading remained enormous, despite the unification of the country by the railways and despite the fact that by 1882 Hachette had bookstalls at 750 stations. A survey published in 1945 revealed that many departments still spent less than 10 francs per annum per inhabitant on books, and this did not refer simply to the poor provinces of the west and centre. The highest expenditure was in the Seine and Rhône but also Haute-Garonne, Allier, Haute-Savoie and Alpes-Maritimes. Large towns on the whole did not

---

[1] R. D. Altick, *The English Common Reader. A Social History of the Mass Reading Public 1800–1900* (Chicago, 1957). There is no French equivalent of this book, either.

read much (Bordeaux is the main exception). These variations
seem to be due to historical causes, rather than to differences in
industrial or other modern developments. There exists a survey
of bookshops made in 1764, which shows a geographical distribution remarkably similar to that of 1945. Book buying was to
a considerable extent a traditional habit.[1] Tobacco caught on
much more easily, and even today Frenchmen spend more
on smoking than on books. Per head of population they spend on
books only two-thirds of what the Germans and the Dutch do.

Public libraries provided negligible opportunities for reading
novels or modern works. Most public libraries were taken over
from bishops, parlements, monasteries or émigrés and enriched
by the chance bequest of some local scholar. They were run by
erudite products of the École des Chartes, biased towards
medieval studies; their hours of opening suited only those with
plenty of leisure. In 1968 there were still only 700 municipal
libraries in France, that is to say most towns with over 15,000
inhabitants had one. Only in 1945 did the state order the
creation of libraries for small communes, for which it offered an
80 per cent subsidy, but by 1960 only twenty-three departments
had established them and in 1968 only forty-four. Half the
rural population thus had no public library. The number of
books borrowed by Frenchmen from their libraries in 1960 was
still extremely small.

|                                        | France | U.S.A. | G.B. |
|----------------------------------------|--------|--------|------|
| Number of loans per inhabitant per annum | 0·74 | 5·4 | 9·4 |

France's public library position then was thus inferior to that of
England in 1900.[2]

The tastes of French readers must be guessed at, first of all,
from the fragmentary evidence of sales of individual works.
What is at once clear is that many of the works now regarded
as among the most important gems of literature were barely
noticed in their time. Baudelaire's *Fleurs du mal* (1857) sold a

[1] François de Dainville, 'La Géographie du livre en France de 1764 à 1945',
*Le Courrier géographique* (Jan.–Feb. 1951), 43–52.
[2] *La Lecture publique en France. Notes et études documentaires*, No. 3459, 1 Feb. 1968;
C. de Serres de Mesplès, *Les Bibliothèques publiques françaises* (Montpellier, 1933);
J. Hassendorfer, *Les Bibliothèques publiques en France* (1957).

mere 1,300 copies; Verlaine's *Poètes maudits* (1884), 253. The
*Nouvelle Revue française*, which printed works later greatly
admired or successful, started at 120 copies an issue, reaching
about 2,000 by 1914, and Gide's *Nourritures terrestres* (1897)
sold only 500 copies in its first edition. In the early nineteenth
century, a sale of 2,500 copies made a book exceptional, and
only Paul de Kock and Victor Hugo normally reached this
figure. Authors like Eugène Sue, Soulié and Janin sold about
1,500 and Alfred de Musset only 600–900. Constant's *Adolphe*
(1816) sold 2,000 copies. Lamartine was the first person to
break this pattern: his *Méditations* (1820) sold 20,000 in three
years; but Lamennais made the standard for best-sellers wholly
different when his *Paroles d'un croyant* (1834) sold 100,000 copies
in a year. Renan's *Life of Jesus* (1863), after having sold 60,000
copies in five months at 7 fr. 50, reached 130,000 copies in
four years, plus 100,000 copies of an abridged edition.[1]

In 1961 publishers were asked to name the best-sellers of the
century from their records. The *Petit Larousse* came top with
25,000,000 copies sold since 1906. There were only a dozen
books published in this century which had sold over 1,000,000.
These included Saint-Exupéry's *Vol de nuit* (1931), Alain
Fournier's *Le Grand Meaulnes* (1913), Marie-Anne Desmarets's
*Torrents* (1951), Paul Geraldy's poems *Toi et Moi* (1921), a
pious biography of Guy de Fontgalland, published by the
Catholic Bonne Presse, the *Diary of Major Thompson* (1955),
Irwin Shaw's *Le Bal des maudits*, F. G. Slaughter's *That None
Should Die* (1942), the comic strip *Tin Tin*, the *Book of Hymns
and Psalms* and Xavier de Montépin's 1,000-page sentimental
novel (published in 1895) *La Porteuse de pain*. Two of Saint-
Exupéry's other books had very nearly reached a million. Other
great successes were *Le Maître des forges* by Georges Ohnet
(1848–1918), *Cyrano de Bergerac* (1898) by Edmond Rostand
and Closterman's war book, *Le Grand Cirque* (1951) (all over
900,000 copies); Hector Malot's *Sans famille* (1879), Jules
Verne's *Voyage au centre de la terre* (1864), Ginette Mathiot's *Je
sais cuisiner* (1932), Françoise Sagan's *Bonjour Tristesse* (1957)
and Margaret Mitchell's *Gone with the Wind* (1936) (all over
800,000). Camus's most successful book *La Peste* (1947),
Malraux's *La Condition humaine* (1933) and Vercors's *Silence*

*de la mer* (1943), had sold about the same as the comtesse de Ségur's best-seller, *Les Malheurs de Sophie* (1859), Henry Bordeaux's *La Neige sur les pas* (1911) and G. Acremant's *Ces dames aux chapeaux verts* (1934) (over 700,000 copies). Another of the comtesse de Ségur's children's books, *Les Mémoires d'un âne* (1860), the New Testament, D. H. Lawrence's *Lady Chatterley's Lover* (1928), Pierre Benoit's *L'Atlantide* (1919), Bernanos's *Journal d'un curé de campagne* (1936), Victor Margueritte's *La Garçonne* (1922), Louis Hémon's *Maria Chapdelaine* (1916) and Gilbert Cesbron's *Les Saints vont en enfer* (1952) were equal at over 600,000. Gide's most successful work was *La Symphonie pastorale* (1919) (594,000 copies) which was roughly what Zola's *Nana* (1871) and *L'Assommoir* (1876) had each sold, as well as Jacques Prévert's *Paroles* (1947), Barbusse's *Le Feu* (1916) and Armand Carrel's *L'Homme cet inconnu* (1935). Proust's *Du côté de chez Swann* (1913) had reached 449,000, about the same as General de Gaulle's *Memoirs* (1954-9), Radiguet's *Le Diable au corps* (1923), Pagnol's *Marius* (1931) and Maurice Thorez's autobiography *Fils du peuple* (1937). Zola over three-quarters of a century had got half a dozen books at three or four hundred thousand, but Delly and H. Ardel had done as well with several of their books for women.[1] It is unlikely that these names constitute a comprehensive list: it is unlikely such a list could ever be produced, given the disappearance of so many publishers' archives. The success of the different classics of previous centuries has yet to be studied. But this list is useful as showing the wide variety of books that have been popular, and that the accolade of literary merit is only sometimes reflected in popular esteem; on the other hand it should not be assumed that a book was 'influential' simply because many people bought it.

The public's idea of a great writer was largely determined by what they had read as children. When conscripts were asked in 1966 to name five authors, Victor Hugo was mentioned most frequently, followed by La Fontaine, Alexandre Dumas, Molière, Alphonse Daudet, Voltaire, Saint-Exupéry, Racine and Lamartine. Over half the authors mentioned were nineteenth-century ones. The answers of the graduates of secondary

[1] 'Les Bestsellers du siècle', *Bulletin du livre*, 15 Oct. 1961 and 15 June 1962 (nos. 65 and 81).

schools, however, were very different, and showed how general taste lagged about fifty years behind that of the intellectual élite. They talked instead of Descartes, Stendhal, Flaubert (who came very low down in the popular list, perhaps because his books had not yet been made into films), Dostoevsky, Bergson, Proust, Péguy, Kafka and Bernanos.[1] It will be noticed that nearly all these names were French. It is indeed only recently that foreign books have been translated into French in any numbers. In 1913, only 127 translations of foreign books were published (half of them from English). Between the wars, under the influence of such men as Gabriel Marcel, foreign books for the first time appeared in significant quantities: 430 translations in 1929, 834 in 1935 and over 1,000 in 1938, that is reaching 13 per cent of all books (a proportion which has been equalled, but not exceeded since). Only the Spaniards translated more; the French translated several times more books than the English.[2] Translations increased the reading of Shakespeare, but also of Charles Morgan, Enid Blyton and Rex Stout.

The 1966 survey of the reading habits of conscripts showed that the classics interested 40 per cent of teachers and students but only 23 per cent of clerks, 8·6 per cent of workers and 5 per cent of peasants. Teachers and students read novels more than other classes, but detective stories were read most by clerks (57 per cent), workers (52 per cent) and peasants (37 per cent), all of whom however declared (unlike the more educated classes) that they preferred the cinema to books. The proposition that no novel was good unless it had a love story in it was approved by 49 per cent of peasants, 41 per cent of workers, 26 per cent of clerks, 15 per cent of students and 11 per cent of teachers; peasants and workers demanded a happy ending too. Science fiction interested all classes except peasants and teachers.[3]

In 1934 a sixth-form master in one of Paris's best schools analysed the books read by his pupils. Twenty-two per cent

[1] R. Escarpit, *Le Livre et le conscrit* (1966), 85–7.

[2] Julien Cain, *Le Livre français* (1972), 263–79—a mine of statistics and information. Foreign interest in French books is revealed by export statistics for 1971: Canada and Switzerland were by far the most important buyers of them (29 m. francs' worth each). Italy came next (12 m.), and the U.S. after it, but far behind (7 m.). The U.K. imported less (3 m.) than the Netherlands (3·5 m.), Spain (3·7 m.) or Germany (4 m.).—*Bibliographie de la France* (1971), 680–2.

[3] Escarpit, op. cit. 48, 79.

were contemporary novels (the most popular being André Maurois, Claude Farrère, Pierre Benoit and François Mauriac; only one pupil·had read Proust). Eight per cent were novels of the previous generation (particularly Alphonse Daudet, Pierre Loti, Anatole France, Émile Zola and Maupassant). Eighteen per cent were romantic works (Hugo—by far the most widely read—Vigny, Dumas, Chateaubriand, Flaubert, Sand). Four per cent were detective stories, especially Conan Doyle. Eleven per cent were adventure books (Jules Verne, Jack London, H. G. Wells, Kipling). French classics not studied at school accounted for nearly 9 per cent; contemporary English novels 4 per cent, poetry 3 per cent, the theatre 5 per cent, politics and social books 1 per cent, war books 4 per cent, history, literature and music 7 per cent, erotica 1 per cent.[1] Too many conclusions should not be drawn from this one example, but it illustrates again the divergence between popular taste and the judgement of critics and of posterity. The romantics were not necessarily read most during the romantic age. The popularity of the classics survived strongly into periods which supposedly rebelled against them: it would be worth studying the changing fortunes of different authors. At the *Comédie-Française*, Molière remained the most popular playwright—one-seventh of all performances there between 1680 and 1920 being of his plays. That made him three times more popular than Racine. Hugo's *Hernani* was performed only 102 times in its first twenty years 1830–49, but six times as often in the supposedly anti-romantic years 1867–1920. The popularity of men like Scribe and Augier during the Second Empire and Pailleron in the 1870s and 1880s deserves to be remembered.[2]

What the national statistics do not show is that there was more reading at certain periods than at others. The sales figures of one firm suggest that though the total number of titles published may have been fairly constant, the number of copies printed and sold went up in periods of prosperity and that the high point may have been reached in the years 1895–1925. The First World War gave publishing a great stimulus.

[1] Philippe Van Tieghem, professeur de première au lycée St. Louis, 'Ce que lisent nos élèves', *Revue universitaire* (Dec. 1934), 408–15.

[2] A. Joannidès, *La Comédie-Française de 1680 à 1920. Tableau des représentations par auteurs et par pièces* (1921).

The success of books about the war revealed that there was a large market that had still not been exploited. But there was then a crisis, brought about partly by too many publishers trying to take advantage of this, and sales dropped drastically during the 1930s. Fayard, who used to publish novels in the first decade of the twentieth century with first printings of up to 82,000, reduced them to 35,000 in 1924, 20,000 in 1934, 16,500 in 1937 and 12,000 in the 1950s. The overproduction was not disastrous, however, because in the Second World War the demand for books rose to unprecedented levels; almost any book could be sold, if paper could be found to print it, and publishers were able to get rid of all their old, hitherto unsaleable stocks.[1]

A large number of books were published at the expense of their authors. By the middle of the century the cost of both paper and printing had fallen considerably and it was not difficult even for relatively modest people to pay a few hundred francs, as for example Camille Flammarion did in 1862, when he was an unknown boy of nineteen anxious to publicise his views on life in other planets. His book was printed in 500 copies and costs were covered by charging 2 francs a copy.[2] Printing costs were even lower in the provinces, and that explains the proliferation of erudite monographs which in some cases were printed only in 100 or 500 copies.[3] When Proust had difficulty in finding a publisher who would take his book as it stood, he preferred to have it printed at his own expense. Huysmans, Gide and Mauriac also made their débuts in this way. Until 1870, the number of printers was limited by the state, but after that anyone could become one, so their numbers decupled and competition forced prices down to unprecedented levels. It was as a result of ruthless bargaining with printers that publishers like Fayard were able to sell their books so cheaply.

[1] Archives of Librairie Arthème Fayard, registers of sales figures. For the history of publishing in the Second World War, see Comité d'Organisation des Industries, Arts et Commerce du Livre, 'Séances de la commission consultative centrale' (stencilled minutes in B.N. 4° Fw 106 etc.).

[2] C. Flammarion, *Mémoires biographiques et philosophiques d'un astronome* (1911), 214.

[3] For a 300-page book in 18mo the cost of paper, printing and binding was 725 francs for 500 copies and 900 francs for 1,000 copies, in Paris. In the Aube, a book of 156 pages in 12mo cost 340 francs for 500 copies—G. Tillié, *Éditeurs contre auteurs* (n.d. about 1910), 53-4.

The problem of distribution was however more difficult. Much publishing had originally been done by booksellers, who either acted as agents for the authors and printers, charging a commission which was at first only 5 per cent, or sometimes took the financial risks themselves. By 1815 they were charging 33 per cent commission and soon after, when they became just retailers, they demanded 40 per cent. They gained the privilege, moreover, of being simply depositaries for the publishers, able to return unsold copies and obtain a complete refund on them. The result was that the cost of distributing books eventually rose to 51 per cent of the published price.[1] Competition between booksellers led to vigorous price cutting—21 per cent discounts, post free, used to be advertised around 1900; but somehow booksellers managed to survive and in 1974 there were still 1,300 who did nothing but sell books. Because they did not have to pay for their books until about three months after they received them, booksellers were willing to display new books in their windows, and then send them back if no one bought them. This meant that books came in fashion for brief moments and then vanished to be replaced by the next batch; stocks were kept low and getting a book that had been published a year before usually meant writing to the publisher. There was a custom in the early nineteenth century for booksellers to form little committees of clients to decide which books to order from Paris, both for sale and for the *cabinets de lecture* which were often an adjunct to the shop. This was local taste judging Parisian fashion; booksellers then formed a personal opinion on everything they sold; but with the great increase in titles this became more difficult.[2] Booksellers, however, had rivals in door-to-door salesmen. It was in 1875 that Abel Pilon began to sell books on credit and by 1922 twelve firms had followed him, so that there were then 'thousands of salesmen on the roads', using elaborately worked out techniques: a 300-page book, showing them exactly what to do and say, served as their guide.[3] It was largely by this method that Larousse sold 150,000 copies of his

---

[1] Robert Laffont, *Éditeur* (1974), 140, says a book of 320 pages, in 8,000 copies, selling for 23 francs, involves 51·39% in distribution costs, 17% for its manufacturer, 3% for advertising, 6·5% in state taxes, 10% author's royalty, 12·78% for the publisher.          [2] Alfred Humblot, *L'Édition littéraire au 19ᵉ siècle* (1911).

[3] Schwartz, *Guide du courtier en librairie. Conseils pratiques pour la vente et la diffusion du livre* (1922).

many-volumed New Encyclopedia (1928) at 200 francs each, an operation that brought in 30,000,000 francs.[1] The problems of the bookseller were aggravated by the growing practice of remaindering, which was already active in 1840. Firms used to buy up unsaleable books, bind them in gold and sell them, at a 200 per cent profit, but still at only a quarter of the price they originally cost, to schools to be used as prizes. Newspapers bought them up to give away as free gifts to readers who took out long subscriptions. Many readers held back from buying books in the expectation that they could get them as remainders in due course. There were therefore constant complaints about chaos and crisis in the bookselling business.

Nevertheless, there was still plenty of room left for second-hand bookshops. These seem generally to have sold books at five-sevenths of their published price, but one could also (in 1886) buy a forty-seven-volume edition of Voltaire's complete works, bound in calf, for only 30 francs, and five volumes of Montesquieu's works, unbound, for 5 francs.[2] Book collecting was a widespread mania, of the same kind as art collecting but far more active. The *quais* of the Seine in Paris provided a busy hunting-ground for collectors, and revealed the existence of an enormous variety of specialities. The dispersion of monastic and aristocratic libraries fed the market with masses of old works. During the Second Empire one could buy books by weight, for 20 or 30 centimes a kilogramme, at Père Joux's shop on the Quai Conti. Just how far collecting could go was shown by A. M. H. Boulard, a notary who gave up his profession to devote himself to his hobby; when he died in 1825 he left over half a million books, which he had acquired for their appearance rather than their content. Eugène La Senne, by contrast, bought up every book about Paris and its history he could find, and his invaluable collection is now in the Bibliothèque Nationale. After the First World War, many provincials descended on Paris to find replacements for books lost during the war and it was significant that they often tried to reconstitute their libraries exactly as they had been before the Germans destroyed them.[3] These book collectors formed a sort

---

[1] Henri Baillère, *La Crise du livre* (1904), 82.
[2] J. Espagno, *Ouvrages d'occasion, Catalogue* (75 rue Madame, 1886–7).
[3] Charles Dodeman, *Le Journal d'un bouquiniste* (1922).

of loose fraternity; they knew who owned what and where one could find certain kinds of books; the distinction between collector and bookseller was vague, for the specialist booksellers were often erudite experts. On the whole, however, it seems that the lovers of old books despised new books. There were also collectors with a passion for books that completely ignored content, appreciating them only for their extraordinary bindings, luxurious paper, original illustrations and rare first editions. Around 1917 the collecting of modern first editions arrived as a new speciality, and publishers profited from it by printing 'first edition' on their title-pages, and producing some copies of every work on beautiful paper just to satisfy this new market. One wrote in 1929, 'There is such emulation in the world of the bibliophiles, such an appetite for the acquisition of all that is rare, that if a writer enjoying esteem in our day took it into his head to publish his laundry bills in sixty copies on Madagascar paper, I am certain that even if he sold them at 200 francs a copy, he would find they would be over-subscribed twenty times over.'[1]

The public chose from among the mass of works offered to it in this way according to principles which a few perceptive publishers vaguely intuited but which no one fully understood. An opinion poll in 1967 found that roughly one-tenth of books were bought as a result of reading reviews and one-tenth from seeing advertisements.[2] Advertising in newspapers, as will be seen,[3] only sometimes involved payment and more often required good relations with the editors and staff. The publisher Aubanel, for example, kept a list of 500 newspaper book reviewers: 'some are happy that we should prompt the article we would like from them, others will feel offended that we should appear to want to dictate their opinions'.[4] The known venality of the press was perhaps one reason why reviews carried such little weight. They probably mattered more to authors than to buyers, for they were essentially a system for the distribution of mutual esteem among authors. The weakness of advertising, however, led to the increasing reliance on literary prizes as a method of stimulating sales. These were originally

---

[1] Bernard Grasset, *La Chose littéraire* (1929), 172; Baillère, op. cit. 58.
[2] Cain, op. cit. 214–15.  [3] See chapter 11.
[4] Édouard Théodore-Aubanel, *Comment on lance un nouveau livre* (1937).

designed to encourage the publication of certain kinds of book, in the tradition established by the Academies (the Prix Montyon for the book most useful to the improvement of morals, the Prix en l'honneur de la Vierge, for a book or poem on the Virgin Mary, the Prix J.-J. Weiss for the book 'in the purest classical style', the Prix des Français d'Asie for the book that spread love of Asia and the civilising mission of France in Asia, the Prix Jules Favre for a non-fiction book by a woman, the Prix Lucien Graux for a work by an author living in the provinces in praise of the provinces).[1] In 1939 there were at least sixty major literary prizes. The one which probably became most influential, as far as fiction was concerned, was the Prix Goncourt. The judges, however, were inevitably authors themselves; and between the wars, most of the judges of literary prizes were published by either Gallimard or Grasset. One stood little chance of winning the prize unless one's book was published by one of these firms, for a powerful *esprit de corps* developed between authors and their publishers. This prize thus became essentially a subtle method of advertising the works of these major firms. After the Second World War, Gallimard won ten out of the fourteen Goncourt prizes awarded between 1949 and 1962; it and Hachette (which absorbed Grasset) between them carried off 85 per cent of the major literary prizes in the 1960s.[2]

The influence of publishers on taste, exercised in the course of selecting what they brought out and in deciding how large the printing of each book should be, was clearly important, but very little is known about either the personality or policy of these men. The first general characteristic about them was that they were on the whole highly specialised, in the same way that the retail food trade was split up into people who sold only eggs and cheese, or cakes, or smoked meats. In the Second Empire, medical books were published above all by Masson, law books by Hingray, Cotillon and Durand, theatrical plays by Tresse, religious books by Lecoffre and Gaume, books in foreign languages by Klincksieck and Galignani. J. B. M. Baillère (1797–1885), who had started as a specialist in medical publish-

---

[1] E. Théodore-Aubanel, *Cueillons des lauriers. Promenade à travers le jardin des prix littéraires* (1937).

[2] R. Laffont, op. cit.

ing in 1819, expanded into general scientific publishing. But
the leading scientific publishers were Baudry (originally established in Belgium, but moving their main office to Paris in
1863); in 1884 Charles Bérenger, a graduate of the Polytechnic
and the École des Mines, invested in the firm and in 1899
bought it up; by 1925 its catalogue was more than 300 pages
long.[1] The classics became a major specialisation of the Garnier
brothers who had originally started, in 1833, as publishers of
light literature and political books. Some of their pamphlets,
like *La Vérité aux ouvriers, aux paysans et aux soldats* (1848–9),
sold in unprecedented numbers—over half a million copies; they
also acquired fame as the publishers of Proudhon's *La Justice
dans la Révolution* (1858), for which they were sent to prison. It
was then that they moved to the safer realms of the eighteenth-
century classics and also produced a vast collection of Latin
authors in translation, which has remained the steadfast crib for
schoolboys ever since. One of the brothers emigrated to Brazil,
which became their main export market.[2] Armand Colin (b.
1842), the son of a provincial bookseller, set up in 1871 as a
publisher of textbooks for primary education, and made his
fortune out of the best-sellers for the school market like Niel's
reading books, Lavisse's histories, Larive and Fleury's grammar,
Paul Bert's science books, Leyssenne's *Arithmetic*, etc.; he became a leading populariser of knowledge with his Collection
Armand Colin (started in 1921 by Paul Montel). The firm of
Calmann-Lévy was founded during the July Monarchy by
Michel Lévy and his brother Calmann originally to publish
theatrical plays; and it then spread into periodicals (*l'Univers
illustré, le Journal de dimanche,* etc.). Their bookshop stayed open
till ten o'clock at night and became a kind of literary *salon*,
where many of the famous writers of the day met, and the
firm indeed published an extraordinarily large proportion of
the great names of contemporary literature, from Guizot and
Tocqueville to Anatole France, as well as Edgar Poe, Macaulay and Dickens. It is unfortunate that these and other entrepreneurs of literature and learning should have been so neglected
by historians, for, quite apart from their own interesting careers,
they played an important part in winning an audience for

[1] J. Makowsky, *Histoire de l'industrie et du commerce en France* (1926), 3. 194.
[2] Vapereau, *Dictionnaire des contemporains* (6th edition, 1893).

writers. It would be worth investigating to what extent their skill made it possible to publish so many philosophy books for example (a speciality of Felix Alcan), or whether it was the educational system which created the demand for such publications. The precise process by which taste of this kind developed is still very much clouded in obscurity.[1]

There was one section of the community which, to a certain extent, lived its own independent life in the matter of book reading, largely isolated from the literary currents of the time, or rather absorbing only the conservative elements in them. The Catholics had their own bookshops, libraries and publishers. The clergy were, despite their poverty, always passionately interested in books and convinced also that the right kind of book, given to innocent minds, could make a great difference to the development of the ideas of successive generations. They encouraged and disseminated a special kind of literature, the history of which has not been written. They had parish libraries, which may well have been much more numerous than those set up by the state. What those libraries bought can be seen from the catalogues of a bookseller of Arras who has long specialised in supplying them. The books he still offers are extremely cheap, and are very largely by authors totally neglected by literary historians, but they are what generations of pious girls have been brought up on. Much of what the world had judged to be best in the literature of France was, in this period, on the Catholic Church's Index of Prohibited Books. Abbé Louis Bethléem produced a guide to tell the faithful what books they could safely read and what they ought to avoid.[2] This showed that in 1932 most of the 'love stories' if not the complete works of Balzac, Dumas, Flaubert, Stendhal, Zola, E. Sue, Maeterlinck and Anatole France were on the Index, as well as Montesquieu, Rousseau, Bentham, Darwin, Kant and even Taine's *History of English Literature*. The books which were recommended were those of Dickens, Conan Doyle, George Eliot, René Bazin, Henri

---

[1] For other publishers, see A. Parménie and C. Bonnier de la Chapelle, *Histoire d'un éditeur et de ses auteurs: P. J. Hetzel* (1953); J. Mistler, *Le Librairie Hachette de 1826 à nos jours* (1964); J. Debu-Bridel, *Les Éditions de Minuit* (1945); D. Montel and G. Rageot, *Rapport sur l'organisation de la lecture publique, du commerce du livre etc.* (1937); A. Dinar, *Fortune des livres* (1938); A. Rétif, *Pierre Larousse* (1975).

[2] Abbé Louis Bethléem, *Romans à lire et romans à prescrire: essai de classification au point de vue moral des principaux romans et romanciers 1500–1932* (11th edition, 1932).

Bordeaux and above all a host of obscure writers who clearly sold very well because they had this Catholic accolade. The best example of these is probably Paul Féval (1817–87), who was already the author of some 200 books when in 1876 he was converted to Catholicism 'as a result of a reversal of fortune and under the influence of his wife'. He bought his works back from his publishers and corrected them to make them acceptable to Catholics. They were placed by Bethléem 'in the first rank of Christian novels' and forty-five of them were particularly recommended. One reprint of his *Le Chevalier de Lagardère* sold a quarter of a million copies simply between 1900 and 1923.[1] Another example was Zenaïde Fleuriot (1829–90) whose eighty-three books were said to be 'still much read' in 1932, especially by girls, even though 'a certain number of them contain descriptions of worldly parties, whose size and brilliance might disturb country-folk and persons with little education'. Edgar Wallace, though 'morally irreproachable' was considered unsuitable for 'excessively young imaginations'. Catholic readers were thus protected from the disturbance of changes in morals and their taste was preserved as if clocks were kept running at different times in different groups. Catholics, of course, did not ignore what non-believers published, if only because they were keen to refute and attack their enemies, and they could also make good use of the trends in literature that pleased them. Thus Huysmans, who is now remembered chiefly as the author of the immoral *A Rebours*, was nowhere near as successful with that work as with the novels which recounted his conversion to religion. *A Rebours* sold 14,000 copies in his lifetime and another 50,000 copies between 1910 and 1960. But *La Cathédrale* sold 20,000 copies in 1898 and another 169,000 by 1960, and *En route* has sold 90,000 copies.[2] In 1951 there were about 120 Catholic publishers, or at any rate publishers whose activity was mainly directed to satisfying the Catholic market. Bloud et Gay (founded in 1875) were responsible for the series 'Science and Religion' (started in 1897) which had 700 titles by 1950. Desclée de Brouwer (1877) by the same date was publishing nearly a million volumes a year; Mame (established as printers in 1767 and as publishers

[1] Fayard archives.
[2] M. Issacharoff, *J.-K. Huysmans devant la critique en France 1874–1960* (1970), 15.

in 1796) employed about a thousand workers. One should not forget, however, those firms which published Catholic authors in the company of others of a different persuasion, in the way that Fayard published Daniel Rops and Flammarion published Mauriac. The Éditions du Seuil (1936), originally a Catholic house, revived after the war as a much more eclectic one, but one which gave Catholics a new integrated status in the literary world.[1]

Why some books were more successful than others was to a certain extent a mystery.[2] It might be argued that literature involved a constant lottery, in which 99 per cent of manuscripts were rejected and never even drew a ticket. Why some authors became famous and others not was, however, not simply a question of chance. Enough work has not yet been done on the process by which books were selected for publication, launched and sold for it to be possible to generalise about the origins of literary reputations, but a few examples can show some of the forces involved in making reputations. Marcel Proust's career provides evidence of one form of pressure. When he started offering the manuscript of his novel to publishers in 1911, it was 1,500 pages long, and barely legible in places, for he did not have it typed. He did not dare send it to the large respectable firms, for fear that it would be considered too improper. He hoped that the *Nouvelle Revue française*, which was run by authors, would take it, but he had a reputation as a dandy, an amateur, a journalist; people talked about his eccentricities but few knew how hard he had worked on his book. André Gide, for the *N.R.F.*, leafed through the manuscript, and was at once put off by a few phrases which seemed incomprehensible or obscure. It was assumed that the subject of the book was simply the smart society which these puritan authors despised and so they rejected it. The *Mercure de France* rejected it because it was too long. Fasquelle, the publishers of Flaubert and Zola, rejected it because, as they said, 'it was too different from what the public is accustomed to read'. Ollendorff could make no sense of it: 'I may be dense,' he said, 'but

---

[1] A Luchini, *La Production, la distribution et la consommation du livre religieux en France* (1964); *Catholicisme (encyclopédie)* (1952), 3. 1358.

[2] G. Rageot, *Le Succès: auteurs et public* (1906); F. Baldensperger, *La Littérature: création, succès, durée* (1913).

I cannot understand how a man can use up thirty pages to describe the way he turns over and moves about in bed before falling asleep. It makes me want to scream.' So Proust published the novel at his own expense. He was not unhappy about this because it meant at least that he did not have to cut his manuscript. His only sacrifice was that he limited the first instalment to 500 printed pages. After this difficult start, Proust had no further trouble in having the rest of his novel published in the normal commercial way. His experience does not prove that only the well-to-do could get into print. A few years before, an ordinary, almost penniless peasant, Émile Guillaumin, had succeeded in having his autobiography published, after several rejections, on a shared-profits basis. But it does show that an author seeking to get into print came up against the desire of publishers to produce books which accorded with what they considered to be contemporary taste. It does not follow that publishers made taste when they tried to be conformist in this way, for the competition between them, and their own eccentricities, made it impossible for them to agree on what taste was or should be. They were moreover advised by authors who spoke with many different voices. The publisher Grasset claimed that it was the second-rate authors who made most decisions about which novels were published, because they acted as publishers' readers. These men conscientiously and indulgently acted as 'the advocates of acceptable mediocrity': there were so many authors in the republic of letters that mediocrity was inevitably in the majority. The readers judged that a manuscript was no worse than any other. They were inevitably moved by the spirit of camaraderie. This limited their openness but it also allowed beginners with influence to get published, however unusual their ideas or their style. Grasset considered publishers, or at least himself, as the enemy of these mediocre readers, who were too confident that they knew 'what pleases the public'. There were always enough such publishers to enable at least some unorthodox authors to break through.

There were two kinds of author: those who fought hard to get their books noticed and those who waited for their contemporaries, or more usually for posterity, to judge them. Proust was definitely in the first category, a category which could be joined only if one had a lot of friends. Proust was very keen to have his book noticed. So first of all he had it put on sale at one-third of the price needed to make it commercially viable. He then pestered his friends to make the press draw attention to the book. He very ingeniously had one favourable review reproduced not directly, but by writing an article in praise of his reviewer and quoting the review as an illustration of the reviewer's talent in recognising important new works. He got the *Figaro* to reprint this article by adding a headline that *Swann's Way* was dedicated to the *Figaro*'s editor. On one occasion, when he received a notice of his book on page two of a newspaper, he considered this inadequate and made such a fuss that the paper reprinted the notice the next day, word for word, on the front page. He used a female friend to persuade *Le Temps* to publish an extract from the novel, a very unusual thing for such a serious political paper to do. He knew many of the leading writers of the day; his first book of essays had been launched with a preface by Anatole France, partly because Proust was a close friend of the son of France's mistress. *Swann's Way* was accordingly reviewed by his friends who compared him to Shakespeare, Goethe and Dostoevsky. But when he entered the book for the Prix Goncourt, it was not even discussed: his influence did not extend that far. However, in 1919 he did win the prize, largely thanks to hard work on the part of Léon Daudet, father of another of Proust's close friends. This is usually considered the event which made him famous. The controversy it aroused was however probably more important than the prize itself: there was a lot of hostile comment. Proust, in fact, was for long famous only to a relatively small group of people. His association with right-wing and aristocratic circles made him distasteful to many; his work seemed irrelevant in the 1930s when political commitment and guidance were sought from authors. By 1960 the book which Proust had narrowly defeated for the Goncourt prize by six votes to four, Dorgelès's war novel *The Wooden Crosses*, had sold almost 50 per cent more copies than *Swann's Way*. Proust did not enjoy a mass market until after the Second World War, when his book was put into paperback and into the Pléiade edition (1954). In 1956 it had still not made the list of books that sold over 10,000 copies in that year, when Françoise Sagan sold 450,000 copies, Camus 84,000,

Dorgelès 63,000, Sartre 12,000 and Conan Doyle (translated) 20,000. *Swann's Way* seems to have sold about seven times more copies than the other volumes: it is not clear that many people have read the whole work, or that his message has penetrated very far.

What success Proust did have was paradoxically not due to his originality, or to his innovations in literary technique and in analysis of character. The reviewers were much troubled by his unusual style. Souday, who was a famous reviewer of the time, complained that the book was chaotic, terribly boring in parts and loaded with useless digressions which served only to increase its obscurity. What was more significant was that many of those who were favourable were so because they were able to fit him into traditions they could understand: they did not value him for the qualities for which he is now admired. Jacques Rivière, though interested in the psychological side of the book, praised it on the ground that it analysed the emotions in a positivist way, such as Claude Bernard and Auguste Comte would have approved. He said the book was revolutionary, because it knocked down the supremacy of the will, but he insisted that it represented a classical revolution, a reply to the woolliness of romanticism and a triumph for the mind, the logical French intelligence. Rivière did not accept Proust's iconoclastic attitude towards love. Indeed, Proust was interpreted by some so as to appear almost a bastion of moral order. There was one reviewer who praised Proust for showing respect for the family, filial love and understanding of provincial life: he said Proust had written a moral book. Lamartine had suffered the same fate. The poems most appreciated by his admirers in his lifetime are those now considered least original. To say, therefore, that Proust expressed the attitudes of his period is quite unjustifiable. At first Proust was in fact less popular in France than he was abroad, but there too he owed his fame to the adulation of a small clique. In England, his book sold roughly 1,250 copies a year in translation between 1922 and 1959, when Painter's biography publicised his eccentricities and had an immense effect in widening his reputation. Till then, he was read on personal recommendation by a clique of aesthetes. (Proust's greater popularity abroad may have had something to do with the fact that France was the country which was least favourable to Freud's ideas.[1]) Originally a clique could more easily confer *succès d'estime* on an author than large sales, but its power has grown more recently. Thus Proust's admirers have grown into something of a minor industry thanks to the expansion of education. In the 1940s no less than 108 books were published about him. In 1955 he had more books written about him than any other modern French writer. In 1971 alone, another seventeen books and at least seventy-four articles appeared, but by then he was no longer the largest literary industry: Camus, Gide and Teilhard de Chardin each had twenty-three books about them, Beckett and Sartre twenty-two, Claudel nineteen. Proust came sixth after them. Zola still managed to produce twelve, which shows that this academic interest can breed on itself. There are over 2,000 members of the Society of the Friends of Proust (founded 1947), who perpetuate the cult. A large variety of commercial, social, literary and personal factors have thus contributed to making the reputation of this author, a reputation moreover which is constantly changing.

The influence of publishers on what people read was exerted, at its most elementary level, by the number of copies they printed of a book. Balzac and Alexandre Dumas had their books printed and reprinted in the second half of the nineteenth century in roughly equal numbers, as far as the number of titles was concerned, but Balzac's works tended to be produced in small editions of between 500 and 1,000 copies, while Dumas's were considerably larger.[2] A publisher who was very determined could make many people read a certain book. This can be illustrated from the way the publisher Grasset made a bestseller out of a novel written by a boy of seventeen, Raymond Radiguet (1903–23). Radiguet was to begin with a protégé of Cocteau, who liked beautiful boys. Grasset had set up a new literary prize, the Prix Balzac, ostensibly to encourage young authors, but designed no less to attract them to his firm, which kept the right to publish the winning entry and which benefited from the publicity. When he heard about Cocteau's friend, and saw the manuscript, he was convinced he had discovered a genius. He took it upon himself to make sure that Radiguet was

[1] See chapter 17.
[2] Information from Dr. Bellos, who is doing a computerised study of the *Bibliographie de la France*.

recognised as such and that the firm of Grasset should be associated with his fame. He signed a contract by which Radiguet would allow Grasset to publish all his works written within the next ten years, in return for a monthly allowance of 1,500 francs, payable for two years. Before publishing the book, he sent the proofs to forty-one leading critics, asking their opinion, but informing them that his was that nothing like it had been seen since Rimbaud had published his first poems at the same precocious age. This association of Radiguet with Rimbaud became Grasset's slogan, which he repeated endlessly. He, Cocteau and Radiguet together composed a striking blurb which dominated all that the critics wrote about the book. The thirty-odd reviews that appeared in the first month after publication all quoted this blurb either to agree or to refute it. A film was distributed showing Radiguet 'the youngest novelist in France' signing his contract with the great publisher who uncovered the talent of the age. Radiguet was awarded not only the Prix Balzac, on the jury of which Grasset's friends had a majority, but also the Prix du Nouveau Monde, on which Cocteau sat. The book sold 40,000 copies in its first year. This was a remarkable figure for a first novel. It was nothing much compared to what Grasset had achieved with *Maria Chapdelaine* which had sold 160,000 in its first year, but for that he had spent over 100,000 francs on advertising and had distributed over 10,000 free copies to journalists and writers. Grasset argued that the success of a book was decided before it was published. His methods, however, were considered improper and many critics joined in a campaign to condemn the introduction of vulgar processes of common trading into the world of letters. Grasset unrepentantly replied that he could see no reason why 'we should do less for art and faith than Cadum does for its soap'. He prepared an even greater campaign to launch Radiguet's second novel, and got his author deferment of military service, through the influence of a friend on the President of the Republic's staff, to enable Radiguet to correct the proofs. But it is significant that one of Grasset's editors, Daniel Halévy, refused to include this novel in the series which he ran: the independence of literary men was almost automatically reasserted when too much pressure was put on it. A publisher could not repeat such successes too often. Rivals

immediately made similar discoveries of boy geniuses, the
public grew tired of young authors, and the young authors for
their part tried to monopolise the market as they established
themselves and won a following.[1]

Why people had the tastes they professed was therefore no
simple matter. It does not follow that they always read the
books they did because they were able to identify with the
characters in them, or because they found in them an exposition
of the dilemmas of their time: there were other pressures at
work. It is uncertain how exactly authors influenced their
public. The most influential books were probably those which
could be understood in different ways at different times (the
most famous of these is perhaps Rousseau's), so the influence has
not always been what the author intended: authors have
probably been as much misunderstood as influential. Occasionally, an author wins a following while he is still young, and his
admirers, as they become influential, turn him into a hero, but
by then he is often dead. The process by which the tiny minority
of heroes were selected in literature involved a large element of
accident: perhaps that was why increasing numbers bought
lottery tickets to fame by becoming authors. In the seventeenth
century, it is estimated, there were only 300 or 400 authors in
France; in 1876 about 4,000 people declared themselves to be
'men of letters' to the census.[2] In 1960, only 3,500 considered
themselves to be professional enough to be members of the
Society of Men of Letters, though about 40,000 were writers of
some sort.[3] The average annual earnings of those who lived off
writing were then only 4,000 francs.[4] The consolation prizes,
even for the successful, were small. Victor Hugo sold *Les
Misérables* for 240,000 francs, Lamartine got 2 million francs for
his complete works, and Louis Blanc half a million francs for
his history of the Revolution, but it should not be forgotten that
Sainte-Beuve sold his best-selling *Causeries de lundi* for only
2,000 francs a volume (an outright sale of copyright), that
Flaubert got only 400 francs for *Madame Bovary*, that George

---

[1] Gabriel Boillat, *Un Maître de 17 ans: Raymond Radiguet* (Neuchâtel, 1973).
[2] *Statistique de la France, Résultats généraux du dénombrement de 1876* (1878),
198–203.
[3] R. Escarpit, *Le Littéraire et le social* (1970), 140, 145, 155.
[4] M. Mansuy, *Positions et oppositions sur le roman contemporain* (1971), 35.

Sand received the same amount for her first novel. It was estimated in 1899 that the average successful author could not hope, after ten years of success, to earn more than 10,000 francs a year (i.e. £400), which was roughly the same as an obscure member of parliament. At this time most novels made their authors between 500 and 1,000 francs.[1] But authors were compensated, at least so far as their vanity was concerned, by the increasing critical attention they received, from the ever-growing periodical press and university system. The constant debate about merit and significance was, it is true, largely an internal one, within the republic of letters itself, but its growth meant that the republic could be self-sufficient. One should not criticise the critics for awarding the medals to authors whom subsequent generations discarded. Literature was not for most people synonymous with revolution and originality, but with taste, which meant that it had to be acceptable and meaningful to the average intelligent man, who was, moreover, nurtured on the classics. René Doumic, the editor of the *Revue des Deux Mondes*, was called the 'prefect of police of Parisian literature', because he was slow to accept novelty, at least until people got used to it, but he illustrated the inevitable difficulty that change and originality, by their very nature, had to encounter. Every generation criticises its predecessor for its blindness; and every generation also has its own reasons for turning forgotten writers into masters.[2]

### Popular Literature

There was another sort of book that the critics ignored or barely noticed. There was a separate literary world, of books condemned as 'trash', or as 'popular'. To like them could never show good taste; and yet they sold in far larger numbers than books with higher pretensions. They were produced entirely for

[1] Camille Mauclair, 'La Condition matérielle et morale de l'écrivain à Paris', *Nouvelle Revue* (Sept.–Oct. 1899), vol. 120, 26–52; Anon., 'Ce que gagnent les écrivains', *Revue encyclopédique* (1897), 957–8; Bernard Leuilliot, *Victor Hugo publie Les Misérables* (1970), 24–32; A. Bellesort, 'L'Écrivain français d'aujourd'hui', *Revue hebdomadaire* (1926), vol. 2, 147–68.

[2] F. Baldensperger, *La Critique et l'histoire littéraires en France au 19e et au début du 20e siècles* (New York, 1945); cf. Henri Peyre, *Les Générations littéraires* (1948); L. L. Schücking, *The Sociology of Literary Taste* (1944); G. Lanson, 'L'Histoire littéraire et la sociologie', *Revue de métaphysique et de morale* (1904), 621–42.

commercial reasons, not to influence; but the question may be asked whether they reflected interests which the masses already had. There was a long tradition behind 'popular literature'. It never got into libraries or bookshops, and was sold principally by pedlars. The Bibliothèque bleue de Troyes, one of the popular series of this kind that had a wide sale in the eighteenth century, contained, among its 450 titles, about 120 works of piety, about 80 novels, stories and plays, about 40 history books and 50 practical manuals about games etc. This perhaps gives some indication of the interests of the 'popular' audience at this time. There were very few books in this series about science, but many more on the occult; calendars with astrological information were eagerly bought: readers wanted to know what the future held and how to deal with the practical problems that faced them; they needed arithmetical and meteorological tables and medical prescriptions. They bought few books about how to practise trades, because this was learnt orally, not through books. What they turned to books for, rather, was magical formulae. They were centuries out of date compared to what the élite was thinking in Paris. Their books contained much that was copied out of sixteenth-century aristocratic, religious and chivalric works; the travel they read about was not that of the latest geographical discoveries but itineraries for pilgrims and merchants. The history in these books was about Charlemagne, the lives of the nobility and the Crusades, but never about the suffering of the poor, the conflict of bourgeoisie and aristocracy or excessive taxation. The educational works were above all manuals of etiquette, how to write polite letters, and behave as well-brought-up men should; there were no complaints about social discrimination. The Jansenist controversies were completely ignored in the religious books, and Christianity was always presented in an elementary way, with liberal additions of magic. The songs were frequently about saints, about how the good were rewarded; but the majority (60 per cent) were about love and a quarter about the virtues of drink. The stories showed the world divided into three categories, the ruling class, the common people and the outlaws. The masses were usually presented as contemptible while the nobles were praised. There were some anti-conformist heroes, who went around redressing wrongs, and there was an interest in outlaws, but there were no social implications behind this: their misadventures were designed to evoke laughter; the most popular were those full of slang and swear words, puns and burlesque. The adventure story and the romantic hero had not yet arrived. Love-stories were about how to make a conquest of women, how to choose a wife, but they were seldom optimistic: they painted marriage as destructive of passion, women as inconstant and naughty. Crime attracted great interest, being presented as the result of passion men could not control. Death appeared as terrifying, though it was also used to prove that all were ultimately equal, and the clergy were criticised for trying to make money out of men's fears.[1]

This was the basis from which nineteenth-century popular literature developed. In 1852 a government commission was established to examine it, and recommended that two-thirds of it should be prohibited as immoral; what was left should be censored and subject to the prefects' authorisation.[2] There were at this time about 3,000 pedlars who toured the country selling these books, together with pictures, wallets, spectacles, diaries and stationery; they were mainly peasants from the poor regions of the Pyrenees and Gascony, but behind them were several hundred specialist publishers. Altogether they distributed between 10 and 40 million volumes a year. In 1868 the 37 million items they sold consisted of about 10,000,000 almanacs, 1,400,000 books, 6,000,000 pamphlets and 20,000,000 'prospectuses and miscellaneous opuscules'. These enormous figures should not be compared with the figures of book production, even if the latter were available: the earliest statistics of the total number of copies of books printed are for 1959, when 145 million copies appeared; in 1970, 322 million copies were published.[3] One should rather see this mass literature as in some ways a primitive version of the daily and weekly newspapers, whose growth was one of the main causes of its eclipse (much more than censorship); it is in this perspective that one should understand both the rise of the periodical press and also the direction in which most of it went.

[1] Robert Mandrou, *De la culture populaire aux 17ᵉ et 18ᵉ siècles* (1964).
[2] Charles Nisard, *Histoire des livres populaires ou de la littérature de colportage* (1864, 2nd edition).
[3] J. Dumazedier and J. Hassendorfer, *Éléments pour une sociologie comparée de la production, de la diffusion et de l'utilisation du livre* (1962), 17–20; Cain, op. cit. 113.

Already by 1852 novels of the kind which the newspapers were to serialise with such success constituted the largest single category of book; photographs were beginning to compete with the engravings; songs remained numerous. *The Art of Not Getting Bored*, *The Key to Dreams*, *The Catechism of Lovers or the Art of Making Love* and the *Historic Account of the Glories of the French Armies* were typical titles that were and remained popular, though, for example, Charlemagne was replaced by Napoleon as the historical hero. The almanacs, with their hints on health, their Bonapartist propaganda, sermons, funeral orations, model marriage contracts, reports of criminal trials, lives of famous men, models of business letters and novelettes, were carried over almost wholesale into the newspapers. Novels based on medieval stories were still sold in this period, but they were increasingly replaced by a new set, written in the late eighteenth or early nineteenth century, like the works of Madame Daubenton (*Zélie dans le désert*, first published in 1786, and reprinted at least twenty-one times by 1861). The masses were only slowly given new reading matter: story-telling was still to a certain extent a repetitive ritual. But specialists in popular novels had already emerged, the most successful (who can be regarded as the ancestor of the newspaper serial writers) being F. G. Ducray-Duminil (1761–1819), who, imitating Mrs. Radcliffe, specialised in terror stories, and took good care to write in a way that could appeal to children at the same time. It is tempting to argue that the masses, even if they welcomed the useful and edifying books the schools gave them, were already addicted to a very different intellectual diet: they wanted to know about the world, but, quite as much or even more, they seemed to want to escape from it, to identify with criminal heroes who broke all the rules they themselves had to obey in real life, to use literature as an instrument of wish fulfilment, day-dreaming and vicarious emotionalism. The establishment of compulsory education was to some extent an attempt to tear the masses away from what was considered pernicious and demoralising reading. The *instituteurs* were supposed to replace the *colporteurs* (pedlars) and to distribute a new, more wholesome, diet. They were not altogether successful.[1]

However, when one looks in greater detail at the popular

[1] J. J. Darmon, *Le Colportage de librairie en France sous le second empire* (1972).

literature, one becomes less certain that it expressed popular taste against the taste of the educated. Popular literature should not be confused with folklore, though it incorporated elements of it. It was still literature of sorts. The authors who produced the popular books were bourgeois; they were very often journalists who had not made the grade for 'literary' achievement. The masses were thus offered several alternatives by bourgeois writers, and most chose the alternative with the least pretension or which approximated nearest to their own inclinations. The popular novels were as subtly graded in quality as they were in price, according to the audience they were intended for. The 'masses' were not a homogeneous category, and the same novelists did not appeal equally to primary and secondary school graduates. The rise of the detective novel was indeed an acknowledgement that a new audience was developing, which, though it still wanted escapism, also demanded exercise for its intelligence.

Popular novels thus passed through several stages. In the traditional story, the reader often knew how things would end before he had begun: suspense was a new device to compensate for the diminished role of supernatural mystery. In the 1830s, the first popular novels written for newspaper serialisation had (to the extent of about 50 per cent) historical subjects. The crime story was an extension of the eighteenth-century tales about great bandits, but it was given a new twist by the rise of the detective. Crime and violence had always been fascinating. The detective added a new kind of game, which Gaboriau (1835–73) the inventor of Monsieur Lecoq (1868) defined as a battle of wits between author and reader. One year before the first Sherlock Holmes story was published, Henri Cauvain (1847–99) invented a similar hero called *Maximilien Heller* (1886), who was, like Holmes, a drug addict, who had a faithful doctor accompanying him, and who in addition was involved with a character called Dr. Wickson. Increasingly the English detective story was the model on which the French based themselves and indeed a large proportion of the detective stories published were translations from English. Maurice Leblanc (1864–1941) created Arsène Lupin as a French alternative to Holmes, though there was, it was true, a difference: Lupin was a French kind of hero, a weak 'small man' who proved to himself and to his readers that he could over-come his weaknesses: he knew how to resist authority and how to be theatrical about it. Maurice Leblanc was however him-self the son of a well-to-do Rouen shipowner. Gaston Leroux (1867–1927), the creator of Rouletabille (an infant-prodigy newspaper reporter detective) and of Cheri-Bibi, became a writer only after gambling away the million francs he inherited. The pioneer of the endless adventure story, Ponson du Terrail (1829–71), creator of Rocambole, had called himself a viscount. These writers made their heroes mildly anti-social, but they were not aiming to challenge the established order. The fascination with scientific techniques diverted attention from social problems.

But the traditional hero of the popular novels had been a redresser of wrongs, an outlaw who could be admired despite his crimes. Fantômas carried this tradition further, by abandon-ing the convention that good should triumph over evil. Fan-tômas was so rebellious, indeed, that in Russia he has been officially condemned as an enemy of society. The first volume in the Fantômas series (1909) had sold nearly 2,500,000 copies by 1967: between 1909 and 1914, thirty-one more volumes of his adventures were published, and the series continued to be churned out until 1962. Its main author, Marcel Allain (1885–1969) wrote 197 books in all. He used to write a book in ten days (until 1914 in collaboration with Pierre Souvestre: they took it in turns to write alternate chapters). In the five years 1909–14, Allain and Souvestre also produced thirty-five volumes of *Naz-en-lait* and twelve of *Titi-le-Moblot*; in addition Allain worked as a journalist on *Comoedia*, and Souvestre on *L'Auto*; together they also produced a specialised motoring periodical, *La Poids lourd*. They were mass producers of litera-ture. They aimed to give readers what readers wanted. Marcel Allain said that if he did put in philosophical ideas of his own, his readers did not notice, whereas if he made a small mistake about some detail, for example about how a steam-engine was brought to a halt, he would receive 200 letters from train drivers complaining that he had got it wrong. Eugène Sue had also had this communication with his readers.[1] There was far more of it now. The message Marcel Allain got was that his readers did not want complicated psychological explanations,

[1] J. L. Borel, *Eugène Sue* (1962).

and they were not interested in the unconscious. They did accept novels which were essentially irrational, but at the same time they valued accurate documentation of real life. Marcel Allain obtained his material from *faits divers* newspaper stories, which he cut out and collected for use whenever he needed a new twist.[1] Above all, he was a story-teller.

Simenon (1903–   ) appealed to a slightly higher social class. He was the son of a Liège insurance clerk and he wrote mainly about the poor people among whom he had grown up; but his theme was more universal, for he saw life as the problem of being true to one's nature. This involved escaping from the hypocrisy on which respectability was built, freeing oneself from the pressures of family and work which shut one in, but then also coping with a world which was harsh and unfriendly. Simenon's favourite uncle had been a tramp and the tramp was always a hero for him. But he wanted to bring order into this confusing world: in the course of his life he refurbished no less than thirty farms or châteaux to express this side of himself. Simenon believed that every man has a shady part, of which he is more or less ashamed: his books were designed to show the reader that he was not alone, that others suffered the same internal torments, and that one could be lovable, even success-ful, despite them. Simenon identified with the criminal, seeking to restore his self-respect, arguing that no humiliation was more intolerable than that of feeling one was rejected by one's com-munity. His detective was therefore not a policeman but a 'mender of destinies'. His solutions were male ones; he thought paternal love was stronger than maternal love and that many women indeed did not know what maternal love was: he usually showed women as adversaries; he said he preferred to call them 'females'. He was an infinitely careful observer of the humbler sections of society, but also one who tried to explain their behaviour. Before the Maigret series, he had already published over 200 popular novels and over 1,000 short stories, having started at the age of seventeen; between 1932 and 1970 he published another 230 novels; and by 1970 over fifty million copies of his books had been sold, in twenty-seven languages, so that it was estimated that 450 million people had read him.

[1] See Marcel Allain's 'Confessions' in Noel Arnaud, *Entretiens sur la para-littérature* (1970), 79–96.

He was the only French-language crime writer to win international popularity, in Russia as well as the U.S.A.[1]

One may wonder whether the effect of success of this kind
was to subject ever larger parts of the nation to the same addiction, on the assumption that popular literature had previously
been more regionalised. Certainly during the Second Empire,
there was still much popular literature being produced in the
provinces, for local consumption. Aix, Lyon, Toulouse were
important centres of such publishing. The books of Lille have
been studied more particularly: the public library of that city,
though rich in theology, history, science and the arts, had practically no books of 'general utility', only one work by Jules
Simon, only one by Quinet; it ceased to lend books from 1836
to 1872 and visitors in 'blouses or sabots were much disapproved of'. However, a local publisher produced cheap books
at 50 centimes (1859) and these seem to have provided the
inhabitants of Lille with much of their reading matter. Three
thousand copies was the normal size of an edition and some
were reprinted more than ten times. This one publisher,
Lefort, between 1827 and 1866, produced 692 titles, and he
was only one (though the largest) of many others in Lille. He
wrote many of the books himself, but he had a large panel of
equally obscure authors to help him—pious ladies, retired
gentlemen and industrious priests. One of his authors was
Madame Josephine de Gaulle, grandmother of the general.
Many of his books appeared anonymously. They all preached
standard Christian morality: there was little that was local
about them except their place of publication. They had such
titles as *Jules, ou la vertu dans l'indigence*, which pointed out that
starving workers would attain bliss eventually in the next world.[2]
The market for this kind of book did not disappear. Women and
girls always had their own separate intellectual and emotional
diet. What happened was therefore not the imposition of a
uniform national novel, in place of regional variations, but the
continuous discovery of special interests, so that an ever richer
variety of alternatives was placed before readers.

[1] 'Le Roman Feuilleton', special issue of *Europe* (June 1974), with a good bibliography; J. J. Tourteau, *D'Arsène Lupin à San-Antonio. Le roman policier français* (1970);
Regis Messac, *Le Detective Novel et l'influence de la pensée scientifique* (1929).
[2] Pierre Pierrard, *La Vie ouvrière à Lille sous le second empire* (1965), 268–76.

Children's literature was one example. This was a genre that was already well established at the beginning of the nineteenth century: 80 titles for children were published in 1811, and 275 in 1836. Production continued at almost exactly this annual figure for a whole century and it was only after 1945 that it suddenly doubled, reaching 650 titles in 1958.[1] One must, however, beware of attributing too much influence to these books. Madame de Ségur (1799–1874) was one of the most successful of authors for children, but it is doubtful whether this authoritarian Russian-born lady had much effect with her recommendations to sobriety, to acceptance of hierarchy and duty, which have led modern interpreters to accuse her of sado-masochism.[2] Children had an ability to use the stories given to them for their own purposes. Parents, for their part, transformed the significance of works they turned into children's classics. Thus Perrault's Mother Goose stories originally represented a seventeenth-century reaction against classical mythology, which schools had made boring, and a precocious return to folklore: they were not intended for children, but were adopted as such when their mythological significance was forgotten. Grimm's Tales, originally published weighed down with learned footnotes as a contribution to the creation of a German national consciousness, were taken over none the less by French parents, because they seemed to create a separate, fantastic world for their children. La Fontaine's Fables were written as an ironic study of the *ancien régime* and as a general satire on man: Rousseau and Lamartine both condemned them as preaching a hard and cold philosophy; they were made into children's books irrespective of their message.[3]

Taste, good and bad, seems to be the work of time. It can be deflected by fashion, and express itself in the cult of novelty, but this novelty must not be too new. Most best-sellers were books that successive generations got into the habit of reading. This

---

[1] Odile Limousin, 'Essais statistiques sur l'évolution de l'édition du livre pour enfants et l'évolution de la scolarisation de 1800 à 1966', *Bibliographie de la France* (1971), chronique, 699–711.

[2] P. Guérande, *Le Petit Monde de la comtesse de Ségur* (1964).

[3] Marc Soriano, *Guide de la littérature enfantine* (1959); Anne Pellowski, *The World of Children's Literature* (1968); Paul Hazard, *Les Livres, les enfants et les hommes* (1949 edition); M. T. Latzarus, *La Littérature enfantine en France dans la seconde moitié du 19e siècle* (1923).

was particularly the case with children's books, which came to form part of the ritual of growing up. But one can see this also in novels. It usually took time for authors to build up their following; once established they could go on producing virtually the same sort of book over and over again; finally they were raised to the status of masters and adopted as set books by the schools. Before the war Simenon's books were published in relatively small editions; he produced so many titles they added up to large totals; but even so it was only after the Second World War that the really large printings became a regular practice, as his cult spread. Gide, now regarded as the most important novelist of the inter-war period, reached his peak again only after the Second World War.[1] *Le Grand Meaulnes* (1913) sells roughly three times as many copies per year today as it did in all its first twenty years put together, substantial though those early sales were.[2] The popular books which did not establish themselves as literature took a long time to die, just as the medieval romances had. Thus *La Porteuse de pain* (1885) by Xavier de Montépin (1823–1902) still sold 320,000 copies between 1907 and 1923, but sold almost twice that amount again between 1923 and 1956. Paul Féval (1816–87) was still popular enough for him to be reprinted after the Second World War in editions as large as Gide's. But publishers seem to have suddenly tired of reprinting old books, as the dramatic revision of publishers' catalogues in the late Second Empire, and again in the 1950s, indicates. The significance of these breaches has still to be investigated.

Though the normal run of history books sold few copies, history was nevertheless one of the most popular subjects in this period when it was written in a suitable way. The growth of the market can be seen if one remembers that the first volume of Michelet's *History of the Revolution* (1847) was printed in 6,000 copies and that six years later 3,500 copies still remained

---

[1] *La Porte étroite* was published in 1934 in an edition of 26,400. There were four reprints 1935–41, of between 8,250 and 13,200 copies each. But in 1947 it was reprinted in 33,000 copies, and again in 1950 in 44,000 copies. Fayard Archives.

[2] Sales 1913–31 were 59,523; before 1950 it used to sell about 12,000 a year; in the 1970s it has been selling between 160,000 and 200,000 copies a year. G.H., 'Recherches bibliographiques sur Le Grand Meaulnes', *Le Livre et l'estampe* (Brussels, 1972), 9–16.

unsold.[1] Jacques Bainville's *History of France* (1924), printed in 22,000 copies, sold out at once and was reprinted five times in that same year, selling in all 77,000; it continued to be reprinted every year, with particularly large prints in 1941 (40,000) and 1946 (30,000), so that by 1969 it had sold altogether 303,000 copies. Bainville's *Napoléon* (1931) sold 55,000 in its first year and by 1968 had reached 197,700 copies; his *Troisième République* (1935) sold 64,000 by 1941 and 100,000 by 1960. André Maurois's *History of England* (1937) was reprinted seven times in its first year, selling 84,000; by 1940 it had sold 108,000 and by 1951 146,000. Louis Bertrand's *Louis XIV* (1923) sold 75,000 by 1949. Funck Brentano's *Ancien Régime* (1926) printed in 1,100 copies, sold out within three months, was reprinted twice in the same year and had sold 42,000 by 1942. Hitler's *Mein Kampf*, translated in 1938, sold 33,000 in its first year, but altogether only 41,825 by 1942. This was less than Pierre Gaxotte's *Frédéric II* (1938) which sold 44,000 by 1941. Perhaps that was because Gaxotte was considered a better writer; his *French Revolution* (1928) had sold 40,000 in its first year and had reached 124,000 by 1970. Or perhaps the French were more interested in their own history, rather than in foreigners. Maurois showed that England, in the hands of a fluent writer, was a subject of wide appeal, but Firmin Roz's *History of the United States* (1930) had sold only about 25,000 by 1943 and only 41,000 by 1956; Louis Bertrand's *History of Spain* (1932) sold 36,000 by the same date. That was just about what a biography of the Empress Eugénie sold and half of one of the King of Rome and another of St. Augustine. Of course, one way of encouraging people to buy books was to pretend that everybody else was buying them. It was customary to put the number of copies sold on the front cover, for example, 50th thousand. It was generally known in the book trade that this should not be taken literally. Fayard's practice was to give exactly double the real figure, but many firms gave four times the real one, so that 1,000 meant 250. Thus Gustave Lanson's *L'Art de la prose* (1921) was printed in 1,650 copies; by 1936 it

---

[1] However, Michelet's *La Femme* (1859) sold nearly 13,000 copies in its first year and his *Amour* (1858) sold 5,700 in its first year. Information kindly supplied by M. Paul Viallaneix from the unpublished correspondence of Michelet with his publishers.

had sold less than 6,000 but was described as 26th thousand. This gives a useful contrast, to show that learned and literary works, even by famous authors, often appeared in very small editions. The complete theatre of Capus (1921), a popular dramatist in his day, appeared in seven volumes but only 2,200 copies were printed and there was no call for a reprint. Donnay's *Molière* (1922) was published in 1,650 copies and one reprint of the same number was issued four years later.[1]

### The Cinema

What is now remembered of the history of cinema is likewise not what the majority of Frenchmen were aware of at the time. The same clash of artistic and popular taste manifested itself, but in a more serious way, because films were so very much more expensive to produce than books and needed audiences so very much larger to pay for them. When Lumière put on the world's first public film show in the basement of the Grand Café, in the boulevard des Capucines, on 28 December 1895, the films he offered, which lasted only one or two minutes each, were the beginnings of what came to be known as newsreels, though they were then little more than animated picture postcards; but within three weeks he was making a profit of 2,000 francs a day. The cinema was originally popularised by travelling showmen, and it fitted in with the traditional entertainment they offered. Comic films were the most popular and France's first international film star was Max Linder (1883–1925), whom Chaplin was to acknowledge as his master, and who, having made his fortune in France, went on to make another in the U.S.A., before committing suicide, in a classic case of comic's depression. Georges Méliès (1861–1938) was an amateur magician who used the fortune he inherited from his father, a shoe manufacturer, to buy the Théâtre Robert-Houdini; he saw in trick photography a new way of making the magician's art more marvellous still. He also specialised in newsreels and in films reconstituting contemporary events, like the Dreyfus Affair. He produced nearly 500 films before the First World War, but by then his skills had been overtaken by new forms of competition: he ended up selling toys at the Gare Montparnasse.

[1] Figures from Fayard Archives.

In 1908 the action film arrived with the *Adventures of Nick Carter*, followed by the filming of Fantômas (1913) and of an interminable series of popular detective novels. In 1912 Charles Pathé, a butcher's son who had started life as a travelling showman with a gramophone, and who came to be France's leading film magnate, produced *La Femme fatale*, which was to inaugurate an inextinguishable genre. Religious films were highly popular at this time, and several were made of the life of Jesus, until the Pope forbade the cinema to use biblical themes. War films made their appearance in 1914 but were not generally successful: audiences seemed to wish to get away from real life. Cinema receipts in France were now 16,000,000 francs a year, and, a newspaper claimed, films had become the third largest commodity in international trade, after wheat and coal.[1]

For a time, while the novelty of the new art continued to excite wonder, there was little problem about distinguishing between the taste of different kinds of audience. Intellectuals delighted in the cinema's absurdities, its gaffes and its naïveté. The poet Louis Aragon, replying to an inquiry by a newspaper, said 'I like straightforward films where people kill each other and make love. I like films where the actors are beautiful, with magnificent skins that you can see close up . . . films which have neither philosophy nor poetry.'[2] American films, which began invading France in 1915, quickly came to provide the basic fare of the French cinema-goer, partly because they fulfilled these conditions, partly because they were produced in such large numbers, partly because the French film industry failed to organise itself—its magnates found there was more money to be made distributing American films than making French ones. In 1927 Charles Pathé sold his company (in part) to Eastman-Kodak; his main French rival, Léon Gaumont, retired in the following year; and in 1929 Paramount established its European studios in Paris, to turn out versions of its American films in the major European languages.

[1] Jacques Deslandes, *Histoire comparée du cinéma*, vol. 1: 1826–96 (1966), vol. 2: 1896–1906 (1968); Maurice Bardèche and Robert Brasillach, *Histoire du cinéma* (1935); Jean Mitry, *Histoire du cinéma: art et industrie*, 3 vols., up to 1925 (1963–73).

[2] René Clair, *Réflexion faite. Notes pour servir à l'histoire de l'art cinématographique de 1920 à 1950* (1951), 26; and Paul Reboux in 'Histoire du cinéma', *Le Crapouillot*, special issue (Nov. 1932), 11.

However, the lowering of standards, which René Clair was already lamenting in 1925, saying that 'cinema as an art is dying, devoured by its double, the cinema industry', was not an obstacle to inventiveness and originality. The French were the first to treat the cinema as an independent art; in 1920 they established the 'Friends of the Seventh Art' and specialised small cinemas were opened in Paris and elsewhere to allow low-cost films to be shown. There was enough competition among financiers—precisely because there was an element of gambling in film making and the rewards could be high—for backers to be available even for obscure beginners. The film industry was probably the most cosmopolitan of any, in its actors, directors, technical staff and backers; and the extreme right was able to denounce it as an international Jewish conspiracy.[1] René Clair's early talkies, for example, were financed by the German firm Tobis, before he emigrated to England and the U.S.A. That did not prevent the French from developing a very distinctive genre of their own. Clair himself insisted that the general public could not be expected to applaud innovation and experiment until this was already outdated. He saw the cinema as a kind of drug, which opened the mind to new experiences; what mattered was not the script, but the picture; and the spectator should treat it like a dreamer, allowing himself to be carried away by its suggestive powers.[2] Louis Delluc (1890–1924), who was also a novelist, poet and playwright, made films which did not attempt to tell a story, but only to create a mood, and to play on the theme of memory and dream. Marcel Pagnol (1895–1974), by contrast, thought the text was all-important; he loved speech and eloquence; but his films probably owed their power more to the atmosphere they created, even if the Provençal villages he portrayed were studio reconstructions. Jean Epstein (1897–1953) (of Polish origin, but educated in Lyon) tried to use the film as a means of discovering aspects of the world the naked eye did not notice. Abel Gance (b. 1889) carried the absorption in the technical possibilities of the camera to its limits, trying to produce overwhelming effects, as in his *Napoléon* (1927) which was three films in one, simultaneously projected on three contiguous

---

[1] Lucien Rebatet [François Vinneuil], *Les Tribus du cinéma et du théâtre* (1941).
[2] Clair, op. cit. 111–12.

screens. It was a German firm that originally put up the money for this. It was a Polish industrialist who enabled Jean Vigo (1905–34), son of the anarchist Almereyda, to enter film-making as a powerful social satirist and it was a Jewish business-man who financed his masterpiece *Zéro de conduite* (1933), in which children were shown as oppressed by adults in the same way as the masses were exploited by the bourgeoisie. The Catho-lic papers called this film 'the work of an obsessive maniac who expresses his deranged thoughts without art': its showing was prohibited by the censors until after 1945.[1] Originality was not rewarded, but it was not altogether stifled. Jean Renoir (b. 1894), the son of the painter, was able to enter film-making because he inherited 3 million francs, plus a share of the paint-ings. That was not enough to last very long. Of his twenty-five films some did make money, like *On purge Bébé* (1930), based on Feydeau, which he filmed in four days, the script being written in a week and the editing being completed in another week; it brought in over a million francs for an outlay of one-fifth of that amount. But those of his films which are now considered his best work were flops, and *La Règle du jeu* (1935) was also banned. Renoir had no esoteric aims, but even though he cultivated simplicity, he clearly put too much into his films. He was absorbed by the problem of class differences, by the complexity of human motivation, by the fact that 'everyone has his reasons . . . and convincing reasons'. He was fascinated by physical appearance, by everyday sights, and used film to study 'French gestures', helped by the similar study his father and other painters had also made. He tried to 'look at the world and tell what he saw' but with 'naked eyes', putting aside the coloured lenses with which habit screened reality. But this 'demystification', as he called it, was not generally appreciated, at least until after the war. 'Ingenuous-ness', he said, 'is absolutely essential to creation.' That was to offer something too raw. It required the gap of a generation for Frenchmen to be able to look at themselves through his mirror.[2]

---

[1] P. E. Salès Gomès, *Jean Vigo* (1957), one of the few film biographies based on private papers.

[2] Pierre Leprohon, *Renoir* (1967), 121, 127; François Poulle, *Renoir 1938* (1969); Charles W. Brooks, 'Jean Renoir's The Rules of the Game', *French Historical Studies* (Fall, 1971), 264–83, and his forthcoming work on the French cinema in the thirties.

In 1954 a survey of the public's declared preferences in films showed that the most popular kind were historical ones. This probably meant that adventure in exotic surroundings and beautiful costumes, with the large dose of brutality that often appeared in this sort of film, was the kind of mixture that was considered a balanced diet. The order of priorities of what constituted a good film was:

> history 13%, murder mysteries 10%, sentimental comedies 9%, documentaries 9%, comedies with music 7%, operettas 7%, dramatic comedies 6%, adventure films 6%, light comedies 6%, social problems 5%, cartoons 4%, dramas 4%, cloak and dagger 4%, British humour 3%, military comedies 2%, Westerns 2%, war 2%, hellzapoppin 1%, science fiction 1%, horror 1%.[1]

It is uncertain when Westerns first became as unpopular as they were at this period. More people said they hated Westerns than any other kind (22 per cent), immoral films coming next (13 per cent) and war films third (12 per cent). But the artistic merit of films did not seem to be of much concern: though the middle classes read reviews, a sizeable proportion of poorer people declared that they went to the cinema irrespective of what was showing. But the cinema had not captured the public taste as much as it did in other European countries. The average Frenchman saw only nine films a year, compared to the West German who saw twelve, the Italian who saw fifteen and the Englishman who saw twenty-five. The average Frenchman spent ten times more on drink than on films.[2]

The history of book publishing, reading and cinema-going shows some of the difficulties that generalisation about taste encounters. Taste can only be understood if it is seen as the expression of choice made among many conflicting pressures. Its chronology remains imprecise. So one must isolate the different factors at work and examine them in turn.

[1] Dourdin Institute, *A Survey for the French National Cinema Center*, adapted by Jane Palmer White (Sept. 1954).

[2] Ibid. 34. Cf. Thorold Dickinson, *A Discovery of Cinema* (1971); André Malraux, *Esquisse d'une psychologie du cinéma* (1946); Pierre Leprohon, *Cinquante ans de cinéma français 1895-1945* (1954); G. Charensol, *Quarante ans de cinéma 1895-1935* (1935).

# 9. Conformity and Superstition

THE conflict between conformity and individualism must be, to a certain extent, the theme of every modern history, in every country. In France, however, the conflict has involved a great deal of polemic and it has been obscured by value-judgements. The political divisions of the country have dominated discussion of the subject, so that the conflict has been seen in terms of reaction against revolution. This simplification, based on the belief that all divergences can be explained in concordant ways, conceals the fact that there are several meanings to conformity. There is conformity to traditional attitudes and values, but also to fashionable new ideas; there is the conformity that shows the cohesiveness of a society and that which results from insecurity in competitive situations; and there is a great deal of difference between conformity in public, under the pressure of group influences, and conformity in private, in ways of thinking and feeling. This book has, at various stages, shown the powerful efforts made by governments to impose a uniform language, a uniform education, uniform ways of thinking, a centralised government and an egalitarian political system on the country. It has analysed the loyalties and patterns of behaviour that grew up within classes and professions; and it has studied the conventional roles men, women and children played as members of the family. The argument throughout has been that none of these pressures towards conformity were totally successful, that the ideals of the moralists, educationists and politicians were far from being implemented in practice, and that the different affiliations of Frenchmen cut across each other in an infinite variety of permutations.

However, in the middle of the nineteenth century, an outstanding political thinker, Alexis de Tocqueville (1805–59), claimed that Frenchmen were in fact becoming more and more alike, under the influence of two forces which he considered to be almost irresistible: the centralisation of government and the spread of democracy. The United States showed, in his view, how democracy could lead to the tyranny of the majority, which, living 'in perpetual adoration of itself' is hurt by the least reproach, the least criticism. As a result, independence of mind and liberty of discussion are shackled, mediocrity is preferred to genius, peaceful habits are more esteemed than heroic virtues, vice is more tolerated than crime and material prosperity becomes the universal goal. In the United States, there were various obstacles to the majority being omnipotent, but France had far fewer, because centralised government gave the state unlimited power and destroyed the barriers that local initiative, private societies and religious sects could raise against it. If Tocqueville was right, then a history of the century covered by this book should be a description of the social consequences of democracy, in terms of the gradual triumph of conformity. That, however, did not happen, first because the democracy that France adopted did not involve as total a breach with aristocracy as Tocqueville feared, and secondly because centralised government proved less effective against regional variety than it had hoped. One of Tocqueville's most important arguments was that institutions had 'only a secondary influence over men's destiny', that political action and legislation had only limited results and that the character of societies was determined more by 'the notions and sentiments dominant in a people', 'their habits of thought', 'their *mores*'. But he did not fully integrate these beliefs into his major writings. He was ultimately more a politician than a moralist, a failed politician, who had never quite liberated himself from his legitimist heritage. His theory of the tyranny of the majority was the protest of an aristocrat against tendencies he did not like, but which he did not study in sufficient detail; he attributed great importance to intellectuals in influencing public opinion, but he did not go very deeply into the mechanisms of their influence.[1]

Tocqueville's statement that the *mores* and habits of thought of a country are more influential than its institutions needs to be pursued further if the pressures on individuals and the nature of

[1] A. de Tocqueville, *De la démocratie en Amérique* (1951 edition), 1. 256, 265–6, 2. 145; id., *L'Ancien Régime et la Révolution* (1856), Book 2 and chapters 1 and 2 of Book 3; id., *Souvenirs* (1893); A. Redier, *Comme disait Monsieur de Tocqueville* (1925); G. W. Pierson, *Tocqueville and Beaumont in America* (New York, 1938); J. Lively, *The Social and Political Thought of Alexis de Tocqueville* (Oxford, 1962).

conformity are to be properly understood. Rather than study conformity, therefore, as a growing menace, in confrontation with individualism; rather than see these as opposing alternatives, it is best to examine, one by one, the different attitudes to life that were practised or preached. It is common to divide these chronologically, as a series of 'ages' which succeeded and replaced each other. Thus the romantic age lasted until roughly 1848, to be followed by a positivist age until around 1890 when anti-intellectualism followed; finally disillusion and extremism dominated the period between the two world wars. This simplifies the truth too much. No one way of thought was ever supreme at any one time. It only seems to be so when the ideas of a few outstanding writers are allowed to eclipse the great mass of obscure and muddled men. Even if the leading men of letters are accepted as representative of the age in which they lived, they are usually far more complicated than the labels attached to them suggest; to identify them with a certain idea is usually to leave out a great portion of their personality. Historians of ideas and of literature naturally try to extract the originality and unique features of the authors they deal with, but if one is trying to understand behaviour as well as ideas, and to treat the total man and the total society, one needs to see the ideas as a succession of layers, superimposed on each other and continuing to be influential long after they were fashionable. For ideas took time to be accepted and absorbed: they were usually incorporated into a different set of ideas, with more or less superficial reconciliation, and did not totally replace old beliefs. People picked up ideas from many different sources, which were themselves far from coherent. Fashionable people who adopted the vocabulary of new ideas were thus often doubly conformist, in that they also superimposed this verbiage on traditional ways of thinking.

The first layer of conformity that needs to be examined, therefore, is what may be alternatively termed traditional, irrational, pre-literate, or superstitious. Because, by the end of the nineteenth century, France had become a literate country, little mention is made of the civilisation of the spoken word, which existed side by side with that of science, literature and government. Though disdained by these, the spoken word preserved traditions and attitudes which remained influential.

To call this civilisation simply one of the spoken word would, however, be misleading, because much that mattered in it was assumed rather than uttered, and the spoken word, besides, took on new functions when society became literate. Literacy paradoxically made spoken fluency and certain accents a source of power and prestige. But it is important to appreciate the forces that resisted science and rationality.[1]

The contrast between civilisations which are literate and those which are not was first studied by Lucien Lévy-Bruhl (1857–1939), who was a professor of the history of modern philosophy at the Sorbonne, and the author of a whole series of books on the subject of 'primitive' man. Lévy-Bruhl's dramatic suggestion was that mankind was not, intellectually, of one kind and that there was a clear distinction between what he called the primitive mentality and the mentality of modern societies. Basing himself on the discoveries of anthropologists, he argued that the inhabitants of primitive societies had a different logic, or rather were not ruled only by logic: they did not worry about contradictions and they had a different view of causation, because they saw the supernatural active everywhere. Its manifestation inspired fear, and the world, for them, was emotional and mystical, rather than open to cognitive understanding. Whereas modern man kept mysticism and reason in more or less separate compartments, confining the former to religion and children's fairy-tales, primitive people did not even distinguish between dream and reality, or symbols and what they symbolised; they did not draw a clear line between the individual and the collective, between body and soul, regarding their clothes and their footprints, for example, as parts of themselves. In the course of time, Lévy-Bruhl modified these views, and abandoned his original idea of a primitive mentality existing only in primitive societies: in his journal, which was published after his death, he admitted that he had exaggerated the mystical side of primitive life, as well as the rational character of modern thought, and suggested that there were degrees of mysticism, or pre-logical thinking, to be found in both.

These problems attracted the attention of folklorists, whose numbers increased greatly in the 1880s, just as the old illiterate

[1] Cf. Marcel Cohen, *L'Écriture et la psychologie des peuples* (1963).

society was disappearing. The folklorists were, until the last decade, virtually excluded from the universities and almost from respectability. But their work throws much light on the outlook of those whom science and technology failed to dominate. Science, it will be seen, was influential on certain aspects of life only and there was hardly anyone whose views were completely formed by it. The simple distinction between science and superstition, moreover, is a survival of nineteenth-century polemic and is not adequate to describe the dimensions of the conflicts which were set up. Recent research on illiterates entering a literate world has claimed, for example, that a major change is the passage from the world of sound to that of sight; the eye takes on new functions. Time too takes on another meaning, and the nature of freedom alters. The illiterate who used to express his feelings in an extrovert and emotional way, while also accepting subordination of his personal wishes to the interests of his family, is launched on the path of individual ambition, which opens more horizons but requires conscious self-control. The conflict of reason and passion, which the Greeks invented, and which classical Frenchmen continued to believe in, over-simplified human behaviour into a schizophrenic model, which the cult of moderation and the golden mean was supposed to overcome. This dichotomy was a way of keeping society in order, by relegating large portions of activity to inferior status. The precise nature of these inferior activities, however, needs closer study.[1]

One set of beliefs that survived throughout this period was superstition and, in particular, faith in astrology. Unusually precise information about the hopes of those who consulted astrologers is available thanks to some ingenious work by a medical student, L. H. Couderc, in the 1930s. He was training

---

[1] Cf. H. J. Martin, *Le Livre et la société écrite* (1968); Lucien Lévy-Bruhl, *Les Fonctions mentales dans les sociétés inférieures* (1910); id., *La Mentalité primitive* (1922); id., *L'Âme primitive* (1927); id., *Le Surnaturel et la nature dans la mentalité primitive* (1931); id., *La Mythologie primitive* (1935); id., *L'Expérience mystique et les symboles chez les primitifs* (1938); id., *Carnets* (1949); Jean Cazeneuve, *Lévy-Bruhl* (1961), and id., *La Mentalité archaïque* (1961). On the folklorists, cf. Robert J. Theodoratus, *Europe: a selected ethnographic bibliography* (New Haven, 1969); the works of P. Y. Seignolle; Robert Jalby, *Le Folklore du Languedoc* (1971) and other volumes in this series published by Maisonneuve; and Van Gennep, *Bibliography* (1964); J. and C. Fraysse, *Mon Village* (1965). For a comparative study of transition to literacy, M. E. Morgaut, *Cinq années de psychologies africaines* (1962).

to be a psychiatrist and, noting that a very large number of patients in his mental hospital had consulted astrologers, card-readers and clairvoyants, he decided to write his thesis about these. His investigations showed that the popularity of the occult profession was far greater than any scientist, locked up in his own private world, could even imagine; it was far from being the case that only the feeble-minded consulted the astrologers. Science undoubtedly had more prestige than astrology; though some astrologers gave themselves fancy oriental names, many called themselves professors, of imaginary institutes they had created themselves, or entitled themselves *voyante diplômée* or *médium agréé*. Their advertisements were to be found in nearly every newspaper, as well as in literary, scientific and pornographic periodicals, in far greater numbers than those of procurers proposing 'relationships', midwives offering abortions or quacks promising to cure cancer or syphilis by correspondence. What the astrologers held out was 'happiness and success', with the emphasis on love and money. They catered for every class of society, some charging only 5 francs and some 500; the luxury ones had receptionists and waiting-rooms full of respectable-looking people, as serious as any to be found in ministerial antechambers. Couderc answered a large number of the advertisements, of every kind, but received strangely uniform replies, virtually all of them not personal but stencilled and couched in more or less identical terms, almost as though the astrologers all belonged to a trade union. They stated that their fee was 200 francs, or 80 francs, but that they would offer him a special discount price of 40 or 50 francs. If their letter was ignored, they sent others, increasingly threatening but also lowering their fee; they promised to return the fee if the client was dissatisfied, though they seldom carried out their promise. But there was a considerable difference in the kind of function these astrologers performed, despite the uniformity of their epistolary and divining methods. Those who worked by correspondence were interested simply in making money. The card-readers, however, often became confessors and moral guides to their clients. Some 'fakirs' catered for erotic needs: one was convicted for undressing and 'massaging' his clients. Having learnt their skills, Couderc put his own advertisement in the papers, offering his services, and sent out stencilled letters in exactly the same way. He received a vast number of replies, and he was thus able to show what the clients were seeking. Very few of them, he said, were mentally defective: most were of average intelligence and educated, some even highly intelligent; what they had in common most of all was anxiety about the future, difficulty in coping with daily problems, loneliness or exasperation. 'I wish to know', wrote one man, 'how a young girl I love, but with whom I am on bad terms, spends her Sundays, whether she has any flirtatious relationships with anyone else and if so, who; and whether she is chaste.' A woman of sixty wrote: 'I have had many troubles in the course of my life; and these have not been my fault, for I have always been hard-working, thrifty and straightforward, as I think you will see from my handwriting. Now tell me if I ought to get married again. A young man has asked my hand in marriage: should I accept? Is he sincere or acting from self-interest? Please study my handwriting carefully.' Couderc wrote back assuring her that she was a courageous and intelligent woman, so she asked for further guidance: should she buy a certain piece of land? Another of the clients who approached him was a graduate army officer who wrote: 'Could you rid me of a woman obsessed by the idea of marriage; she has a hold on me only because I fear scandal; I cannot escape her. My social situation does not allow me to marry her because she has neither my education nor my culture.' It turned out in further correspondence that she was an Annamite girl he had kept while serving in the Far East and who had followed him back to France. He asked that Couderc should use 'hypnotic suggestion' to get her to leave him alone; but when he discovered that Couderc was in fact a doctor, he broke off the correspondence. The value of the occultists was that they were outsiders to the normal world. One tradesman wrote: 'Can you destroy a business which is competing with mine by annihilating the two women who run it and who are my greatest enemies?' Another correspondent begged for a 'serious car accident' to be arranged for 'a person who does me nothing but harm'. Other frequent requests were for a win on the national lottery, or guidance on how to find a husband. The penal code forbade 'divination, prognostication and the explanation of dreams' (article 479), and in 1896 the Prefect of Police issued an injunction repeating the prohibition, on pain of severe penalties; but the courts held that there was no fraud involved, in that the astrologers sold advice, and their clients knew what they were getting when they bought it.[1]

It was in medicine that superstition survived most noticeably as an alternative to rationality. The choice between scientific and superstitious cures was not always obvious in the nineteenth century: Balzac, for example, showed the qualified doctor Bénassis prescribing snail soup as a cure for tuberculosis; the textbook nursing nuns and amateur healers relied on right up to the Second World War was Dr. Cazin's old *Treatise on Medicinal Plants*;[2] midwives, even if they practised their art in the way the medical experts prescribed, still preserved, into the 1920s, the custom of keeping the dried umbilical cord until the child's seventh birthday; and in 1961 doctors in the Saumurois were still being asked to cut the tongues of new-born babies, 'to facilitate speech'. Non-scientific medicine was by no means all magical. Though bone-setters used hot sweetened wine, or butter, as their disinfectants, charms were not necessarily involved. One particularly skilful amateur doctor, the Auvergnat Pierre Brioude (1831–1905), was originally a cheesemaker but his success both with animals and humans was such that around 1890 he was being visited by twenty-five or thirty patients daily, some coming long distances, and a few even from the Auvergnat community in the U.S.A. He made so much money that his son-in-law was able to start a hotel, which lodged these sick visitors. After his death a statue of him was put up at Nasbinals, paid for mainly by the Auvergnats of Paris. This man was probably an osteopath before his time, but he was also a fervent Catholic, who was considered to have special powers of healing. His kind need to be distinguished on the one hand from sorcerers and on the other from miracle workers.

Sorcerers, said an author of a book on them published in 1910, were to be found in almost every canton of France. In the previous year, their power had been publicised by the arrest of a married couple living in Blois, on the charge of extorting from peasants sums of between 3,000 and 30,000 francs for freeing

[1] Louis-Henri Couderc, *Astrologues, voyantes, cartomanciennes et leur clientèle. Enquête médico-psychologique sur la pratique commerciale de l'occultisme* (Paris medical thesis, 1934).
[2] F. J. Cazin, *Traité des plantes médicinales* (1847, 5th edition, 1886).

them from spells: their services were in such demand that they were rich enough to visit their clients by car and to own three houses. Sorcerers were sometimes people with some physical deformity; nine-tenths of them were said to be shepherds, who lived lonely lives and who were held in suspicion and awe. Blacksmiths, considered to have a special relationship with the devil, tailors and cobblers, held to have a particular influence on women, ambitious children who had unsuccessfully tried to become priests and who had acquired a little learning, midwives and women who prepared the dead for burial, were also among those who dabbled in this field. Often they inherited their secrets from their parents, as others inherited a grocery or a notary's practice; and there was a widespread feeling, at least until 1914, that every village needed a sorcerer.[1]

That diseases could be cured by the miraculous intervention of the saints was a belief which survived independently of other forms of religious practice. This has been strikingly shown by surveys of the cult of 'healing saints' carried out in the 1960s. A questionnaire distributed in the *arrondissement* of Villefranche (Aveyron) revealed that 59 per cent of men and 78 per cent of women had appealed to these saints at some time; only 20 per cent of men and 12 per cent of women had not (the rest were vague). There was no appreciable difference in these proportions as between areas with high and low levels of church attendance, or between rural and industrial regions; indeed the workers of the mining town of Decazeville were very assiduous pilgrims to these saints' shrines, even though only 5 per cent of them attended church. The great majority of rural families in this *arrondissement* went on two or three pilgrimages a year, simply to ensure that the saints would protect their animals against disease; specific illnesses would produce additional visits. The workers of Decazeville were, however, constantly searching for new saints to help them, and they sometimes visited two or three each Sunday, even though they were incapable of reciting a Christian prayer: they demanded to be told, at each shrine, what gestures they had to perform, and were uncomprehending if they were required to show a wider religious faith. Though the old appealed to these saints more often, that was rather because they were more frequently ill, and

[1] Charles Lancelin, *La Sorcellerie des campagnes* (1910).

there were several saints who attracted the appeals of the young, like Saint Blaise, popular among young motor-cyclists with colds.[1] People very seldom appealed to their local village saint for help: physical hardship in getting to a shrine was considered desirable; but villages often created new cults to commemorate local heroes. Thus in the 1960s about 2,000 people a year still visited the grave of the *curé* Guy of Malleville (1758–1840) who had in his lifetime suffered from rheumatism and who has ever since been regarded as offering a cure for that disease. At Orlhonac, between 150 and 200 masses were still being said each year to invoke the intervention of the *curé* Boscredon, a sufferer from diseases of the throat who died in 1857 and who has been valued particularly for curing whooping cough.[2] Parish records reveal that the cult of these saints has remained remarkably constant. In Saint-Privat (Lozère), for example, about 15,000 pilgrims visited the shrine in June 1906, about 20,000 in June 1939, and 15,000 again in June 1958.[3] Some cults fell into decay, but new ones were constantly being invented to replace them. Those that decayed had often specialised in diseases that had vanished. The demand in the 1960s was above all for the treatment of animals' and children's diseases, pains of undefined character, skin diseases and burns, nervous troubles, toothache and indigestion. Saints, of course, could perform other services. Until 1962 the statue of Saint Gondon was kept in the village of Thoureil, for example, for girls to stick nails into, so as to obtain his help in finding them husbands. In the 1939–45 war, the help of religion, more vaguely, was sought at Fontenay-le-Comte, when the threshing-machine stopped working: a visiting teacher was horrified to see that when all efforts to restart it had failed, the mechanic sent for a bottle of holy water and sprinkled it on it. In a national opinion poll in 1965 49 per cent of Frenchmen admitted that if conventional medicine failed to cure them, they would turn to the healers. This was a continuation of the attitude of

[1] 73 per cent of those over 65 who were questioned admitted to having appealed to healing saints, 68 per cent of those between 45 and 65 and 59 per cent of those between 35 and 45.

[2] Monique Bornes, épouse Vernet, 'Les Saints guérisseurs en Bas Rouergue' (Montpellier sociology thesis, troisième cycle, unpublished, 1969).

[3] Frédéric Uhmann, 'Le Culte des saints en Lozère' (Montpellier ethnology thesis, troisième cycle, unpublished, 1969), 156.

peasants who, when science failed them, turned to 'those who had not been spoiled by the primary school'.[1]

The desire to predict the future kept astrology alive also, though a vigorous battle was fought over it. The *Almanach liégeois* or *Almanach Laensberg*, which was one of the best-sellers of the seventeenth and eighteenth centuries, continued to sell in the nineteenth in large numbers. The Catholic Church had not attempted to destroy the beliefs for which it catered, at least not wholly. It combated that part of astrology which claimed that the stars influenced human destiny, but it allowed that they could influence the climate, and so agriculture. Scientists, however, were more determined: in 1800 Lamarck produced an *Annuaire météorologique* to put the facts straight, but it was of course too learned to have any popular effect. A publisher, Veuve Lepetit, issued an almanac entitled *L'Astrologie parisien ou le nouveau Mathieu Laensberg* which argued that the moon had no influence on the weather and still less on health; but it is significant that she kept Laensberg in her title, as too did another publisher, Pagnerre, with his *Le Petit Liégeois* (1837). Faith in the old almanacs survived; and when they began to die out, astrological horoscopes were saved by the new popular press.[2] These in fact became the townsmen's alternative for the more complex beliefs of the peasants. An inquiry in 1963 revealed that 53 per cent of the population regularly read their horoscopes in the press. Another inquiry, in 1968, showed that clerks were the most fervent addicts (68 per cent read the horoscopes in the press regularly or occasionally) with employers and workers not far behind (62 to 63 per cent), but only 44 per cent of peasants were interested. It was claimed in 1954 that France had 30,000 professional fortune tellers, and in 1971 it was calculated that Parisians alone spent 60 million new francs annually to discover their future.[3]

Interest in the occult was often propagated by educated people, who were rebels against the limitations and disappointments

---

[1] Marcelle Bouteiller, *Médecine populaire d'hier et d'aujourd'hui* (1966) with an excellent bibliography. The author was head of the Department of Beliefs at the Musée des Arts et Traditions Populaires. Cf. Pierre Neuville, *Les Meilleurs Guérisseurs de France* (1951).

[2] P. Saintyves, *L'Astrologie populaire étudiée spécialement dans les doctrines et les traditions relatives à l'influence de la lune* (1937).

[3] M. Gauquelin and J. Sadoul, *L'Astrologie hier et aujourd'hui* (1972), 53, 55.

of science. Large tomes, of confused mysticism and erudition, were published to interpret the discoveries of science in an occult sense. Louis Lucas (1816–63) tried to produce a synthesis of alchemy and the new medicine.[1] Dr. Philippe Encausse, finding the teaching of positivism 'too dry for the heart' and the theory of evolution 'comforting only to the successful', founded the 'independent group for esoteric studies', and the 'School of Hermetic Sciences', which attracted quite a few second-rate writers and artists. He sought to keep his approach compatible with Christianity; that is why he resigned from the Theosophical Society, which was interested in eastern mysticism. Interest in the occult has left its mark on several important novelists and poets; it is something that deserves further study in a wider context.

Arnold van Gennep (1873–1957) was the most remarkable and the most original of the many scholars who tried to record and explain the various beliefs and customs which were lumped together as folklore. He had the complicated family background that was almost a model for a certain type of anthropologist: of mixed national origin, his parents divorced when he was six, and his mother remarried twice after that. His stepfather, a doctor, wanted him to follow in that profession, but Van Gennep went off to study sociology, ethnology and languages in Paris; he married a wife without a dowry, so his stepfather cut him off and he was forced to earn his living as a tutor in Russian Poland. He wrote theses on Taboo in Madagascar and Myths in Australia, but he could never get a proper university job: Durkheim, who was the king of French sociology, execrated him. After his return to France in 1901, Van Gennep lived at Bourg-la-Reine, just outside Paris (apart from a six-month experiment raising chickens in the south), keeping himself as a translator, first in the ministry of agriculture and later at the Pelman Institute: he knew most European languages. In his spare time, working regularly till the early hours of the morning, he wrote his *Manual of Contemporary French Folklore* (1943–58) and edited several journals on the same subject. It was only after 1945 that he at last obtained a grant from the C.N.R.S.

---

[1] Louis Lucas, *La Chimie nouvelle* (1854); id., *La Médecine nouvelle* (1862); P. Encausse, *Sciences occultes ou 25 années d'occultisme occidental. Papus, sa vie, son œuvre* (1949).

to complete his masterpiece. He attempted to show that the study of folklore should not be considered as simply the collection of quaint customs for the amusement of antiquarians, nor as a branch of theology concerned with devil worship and heresy. He defined it as the study of 'the popular' and the 'collective beliefs of the masses', contrasting its subject-matter with that of literature, which was concerned with the creation of individuals, and which was usually addressed to an élite audience. He urged that folklore should not confine itself to legends and songs but look also at all ceremonies, games, devices, cults, domestic utensils, all 'institutions and ways of feeling and expressing oneself which differentiated the popular from the superior'. The nineteenth-century folklorists, he said, had been essentially historians or antiquaries; and he thought that sociologists had taken over the historical method: 'The whole of sociology needs to be redone.' He felt more akin with linguists, who understood that language was constantly changing: he called his own method 'biological', meaning that he based himself on observation of the present, but linked this with the evolving lives of his subjects. He respected peasant culture as it was and was scathing of the attempts by scholars to produce erudite theoretical explanations of it. He resisted the definition of folklore as excluding all that is transmitted by writing, because writing sometimes played an important part in the transmission of songs, for example. He appreciated that the distinction between collective and individual creation was a weak one; he was as interested in the folklore of the forces that overthrew old beliefs as he was in these. He urged the study of the folklore of schoolchildren, conscripts and convicts.

The study of folklore, Van Gennep argued, revealed that peasants lived mentally in two worlds, one of which had rules which were officially and formally taught, while the other was governed by custom. They did not make any clear distinction between these, but managed their lives as if each was binding or true; this implied no exclusive commitment to either. Van Gennep collected a vast array of facts to illustrate the survival of customary habits at every stage from birth to death and he made a particular study of rites of passage from one stage to another, which continued side by side with the examination system and the state's official classification. He showed the

recurring themes of birth, rebirth and seasonal change in these
rites of passage; he sought therefore to study man not in terms
of individual psychology, which he considered inadequate, but
as part of nature, of biology. He produced elaborate documentation of superstitious behaviour in pregnancy (the fear of
envies), in infancy (rites to encourage growth, like not cutting
the hair, or leaving fleas in it, and judging health by the
abundance of vermin), in marriage and in death. He showed
how the official education system had done little to destroy the
solidarity of children in face of the school on the one hand and
other generations on the other, how children had kept their
own codes of violence and property, their own language, but
also had strong internal divisions amongst themselves, with
cliques and peer groups. He was one of the first to study
adolescent gangs, to record the depredation they caused and
the battles and brutalities that kept them together. He showed
how when the pharmacy students of Paris marched through
the streets in 1939, burning their overalls behind giant effigies
of a devil and of Julius Caesar, they were unwittingly reproducing almost exactly the symbolism of their predecessors in the
middle ages. Despite his isolation from the university, Van
Gennep had able disciples and collaborators, some of whom
carried out remarkable studies on the lines he laid down; the
Seignolle brothers, for example, analysed the relationship of
urban and rural cultures in the villages just outside Paris,
tracing both the decay and the survival of folkloric beliefs. At
Orly in 1937, parents marrying-off their last daughter still
carried her through the village in a chair, to a bonfire in the
square, where the chair was ritually burnt, to show they had
no daughters left to marry. Orly airport had been opened (as
a military base) at the end of the First World War.[1]

## The Classical Spirit

Respect for the past was not the crucial element in these kinds
of conformity. Conformity based on historical grounds was much

[1] *Bibliographie des œuvres d'Arnold van Gennep*, ed. K. van Gennep (Épernay,
1964); A. van Gennep, *Le Folklore: croyances et coutumes populaires françaises* (1941);
id., *Manuel de folklore français contemporain* (1943–58); C. and J. Seignolle, *Le
Folklore de Hurepoix* (*Seine, Seine-et-Oise, Seine-et-Marne*) (1937), 83. Cf. *Niveaux de
culture et groupes sociaux* (1967), proceedings of a conference held at the École
Normale Supérieure.

more the result of education, which, as has been seen, was not as revolutionary as it was often believed to be. The chapters on education have shown how the schools cultivated an approach to life that took past attitudes as the starting-point of its reasoning. Successive generations of rebels had to fight what could be called the classical spirit, and they had to do this repeatedly because it survived so indestructibly. The minister of education of 1877–9 publicly declared that the ideal that all teachers ought to hold before them was 'the *honnête homme* as the seventeenth century understood him'.[1] The men of the Renaissance and the ancient Greeks continued to be models of conduct in this period. Educated people could probably recite an ode of Horace more easily than verses from the Bible, and Livy and Marcus Aurelius provided them with ideals of virtue as much as the Church. That the revolution of 1789 should have strengthened the cult of antiquity was no temporary aberration, for that cult became even more widespread with the growth of schooling, and with the development of classical erudition, in archaeology, comparative philology and ancient religions. Théophile Gautier (1811–72) read the *Iliad* some thirty times in the original Greek.[2] The Parnassian poets found in antiquity the majesty, grandeur and ideal beauty they could not see in their own day. The classics were admired not only as the source of French civilisation, as containing models of wisdom and simplicity, but also as an escape from the present. Flaubert, that arch-critic of both the romantic and bourgeois minds, read a great deal of Greek. Leconte de Lisle's translation of Homer won many to hellenism. The politicians Herriot and Clemenceau wrote in praise of Greece, the latter regarding Demosthenes as his hero. Barrès's *Voyage de Sparte* (1906), Thibaudet's *Images de Grèce* (1926) show the constant return to the past. Gide records in his Journal how the mere name of Agamemnon in the theatre sufficed to cause tears to flow down his cheeks and how terribly he suffered seeing Sophocles' *Antigone* profaned by the over-clever Cocteau. He, like Cocteau and Giraudoux used Greek themes freely. Giraudoux in 1929 claimed, as a

[1] Agénor Bardoux, in Anon., *L'Église de France et les réformes nécessaires* (1880), 32.
[2] Daniel Mornet, *Histoire de la clarté française* (1929); Pierre Moreau, *Le Classicisme des romantiques* (1932); Harold T. Parker, *The Cult of Antiquity and the French Revolution* (Chicago, 1937).

matter of pride, 'I believe no writer of my age is as impregnated by antiquity as I am'. Claudel in turn has been called 'The most Latin Frenchman since Bossuet': he regarded Virgil as the greatest genius humanity had ever produced.[1] The taste for originality, though a marked feature of the century covered by this book, was combined with a respect for the classical past. Total originality met with considerable resistance among the reading public. The poems of popular authors which were most admired by their contemporaries were those now considered least original.[2]

In 1891 J.-J. Weiss, an acute literary critic, wrote, 'The classical spirit is dead . . . so is classical culture. Around 1869 still, there was hardly any conversation between educated men (*honnêtes gens*)—whether serious or frivolous, learned or worldly —which was not strewn and spangled with Greek or Latin quotations, bits of the Bible, mythological references, aphorisms from ancient history. All these things became with time so usual, so common and so banal that no one bothered asking how they had come into modern conversation. People understood each other in this way with references which summed up a whole series of ideas, sensations and arguments—abbreviations as clear and quick, more substantial and concise than those of stenography. Today these references would sound like Sanskrit. A quarter of a century has sufficed to alter French vocabulary in this way and to modify so considerably the atmosphere in which familiar conversation was made.' J.-J. Weiss was probably accurate about conversation, but the classics, respect for the past, pleasure in identifying oneself with antique models, survived for several generations longer. The widespread fondness for quotations was only a superficial indication of this. What this attitude implied was the assertion of the respectability of the ordinary man, who did as other sensible men before him had done, and who did not claim to greater wisdom than previous generations.

The philosophic doctrine for this attitude had been provided

---

[1] Henri Peyre, *L'Influence des littératures antiques sur la littérature française moderne* (New Haven, 1941). This book has useful suggestions for further research. Cf. Charly Clerc, *Le Génie du paganisme. Essais sur l'inspiration antique dans la littérature française contemporaine* (1926).

[2] Henri Peyre, *Writers and their Critics. A Study of Misunderstanding* (New York, 1944), 92–3.

by Victor Cousin (1792–1867). His book, *Du Vrai, du Beau et du Bien* (1837), was an official textbook not only during the July Monarchy, when he personally dominated the university, but for much of the nineteenth century, when schoolboys studied it on a par with Plato and Descartes. It enjoyed its vogue because it was a true epitome and justification of middle-class common sense. Known as *eclecticism*, Cousin's doctrine sought to combine all that was best in the philosophies of the past. It sought to apply the Orleanist idea of the *juste milieu* to philosophy, to abandon the revolutionary method by which all previous French philosophies had condemned their predecessors, and to practise instead the spirit of conciliation with a view to ending the clash of ideas. It was directed against scepticism, but it also avoided dogmatism. It claimed to be based on experience, but it rejected empiricism. It called its method psychological, by which it meant that it studied human nature, but it took as its guide common-sense beliefs. Instead of showing up the philosophical difficulties which these entail, it accepted them as necessary truths and combined them into a complete moral and aesthetic system. It began with the principle that the great need of the time was for absolute truths. It rapidly established these, refuting the objections of men like Locke and Kant. Since truth was impossible without God, therefore God existed. He necessarily had to be good and the established order was his work. Reason was man's faculty for understanding this and it led directly to truth. Cousin's conclusions soon sounded banal, but he was at first a great innovator himself. He reintroduced into French philosophy Plato—whose works he had translated by an army of pupils, under his own name—and Descartes, discredited by the *philosophes* of the eighteenth century. He travelled in Germany and brought back Kant's morals of duty, which placed the primitive study of ethics in France on an entirely new basis. He made friends with Hegel, and brought back his dialectic; he introduced the philosophical term *Absolute* into France. These influences were to have an important effect on French thought in the future. They gave Cousin himself an enormous prestige in his youth and made him appear the creator of a new morality, 'We have tried too long', he proclaimed, 'to be free with the ethical code of slaves. It is time to inaugurate a philosophy which is, as Plato says, the

philosophy of free men.' 'It is difficult to realise', wrote Jules
Favre, 'what his lectures meant to the young. They gave men
hope, confidence, pride.'[1]

Cousin's great achievement was to abolish doubt. He told
men exactly what they must do and gave the blessing of philosophy to traditional behaviour which waning religious faith
could no longer justify. The most important duty, he said, was
self-discipline, to maintain the rule of reason. Men should show
prudence and moderation in all things, they should improve
their intelligence by education, cultivate their sensibilities, feel
affection for their family, donate to charity, respect property,
justice and the rights of others, and support governments which
guaranteed liberty, which could be none other than the Orleanist constitutional monarchy. They should love art, because that
stimulated an admiration for the ideal, and so for God—art
purified and perfected the soul. The best art was not the purely
representational, nor the religious kind which sought to be
moral by direct means; it was rather that which satisfied
reason, taste, imagination, and sentiment all at once.

His doctrine, which owes much to Plato, came very near
pantheism. The Church attacked Cousin and he, anxious to
please everybody, consequently modified his teachings very
considerably. In later editions, he cut out large sections of the
metaphysical part of his book—precisely those which had won
him his philosophical reputation—and made it largely a work
on morals and aesthetics. He rebaptised his doctrine 'spiritualism'. He abandoned one of his most important achievements,
the setting-up of philosophy as a study totally independent of
theology; and instead increasingly stressed the need for religion; and it is significant that he did this at the very time when
many were beginning to fear the results of free-thinking and
going back to Catholicism. But by allying with the Church just
when it was losing prestige among a new generation of intellectuals, he invited attack from them. In the same way, by concentrating on the philosophical syllabus, he neglected the
study of science, just when this was becoming popular.

Under the July Monarchy it had not been easy to attack
Cousin, for he established an extraordinary ascendancy. He
appointed all the teachers of philosophy in the country, who

[1] Paul Janet, *Victor Cousin et son œuvre* (1885), 158.

were known as his regiment. He used them as the mouthpiece of his doctrine and, in the vacation, they came to pay court to him in his apartment at the Sorbonne. He was a self-made man, the son, like Rousseau, of a watchmaker (some say of a jeweller); his mother had been a washerwoman. His eloquence, which made him more of a preacher than a professor, won him acclaim when he was still in his early twenties. He had a prodigious memory, which as much as anything was the basis of his power. After thirty years he could still recall word for word every reply a man had made in his university examination. He seldom flattered, he never yielded, he was a master of raillery and contempt; he was hardest on those he liked best; he obtained from his pupils terror and admiration; he never forgot their faults or their virtues, he devoted endless trouble to their promotions and transfers, and he kept them intellectually alive by allocating philosophical tasks, translations or commentaries to each one. He convinced men that he was master of every imaginable subject, for he could talk brilliantly about anything. In time, however, the lack of coherence, rigour and precision in his theories became too evident. His disciples modified their doctrines too. But woolly-headed men long continued to think as he did.

Cousin represented the conformity that tried to avoid arguments and to allow some truth to every point of view, without lapsing into scepticism. Respect for the past was encouraged in another form by the leading conservative literary critic during the July Monarchy and the Second Empire, Désiré Nisard (1806–88), who was as important as Cousin, in that he dominated the teaching of literature in almost the same way as Cousin dominated philosophy. Nisard was head of the Division of Science and Letters at the ministry of education and Member of Parliament under Louis-Philippe, professor of Latin eloquence at the Collège de France and then of French eloquence at the Sorbonne; he was elected Member of the French Academy in 1850, against Alfred de Musset; he was inspector-general of higher education under Napoleon III, and Director of the École Normale Supérieure, 1857–67, where he was able to influence a whole generation of schoolmasters. Nisard had made his name as a young man with a *Manifeste contre la littérature facile* (1833), attacking the novel, on the ground that the sole

respectable form of literature was that which could be understood only after study, application and criticism. His doctrine
was formulated in his *Histoire de la littérature française* (1844–61)
in which he asserted that the aim of literature, and the criterion for judging it, was not originality. 'The man of genius
in France is he who says what everybody knows. He is only the
intelligent echo of the crowd. Instead of astonishing us by his
private opinions, he makes us see the inside of ourselves, as
Montaigne says, and he gets us to know ourselves.' Nisard's
view implied that there was no more knowledge to be discovered
about humans; all that was needed was to express that knowledge: that was the function of art. 'Art is the expression of
general truths in perfect language.' Perfect language was
recognisable because it was 'at once clear and intelligible to the
nation (which spoke it) and to the cultivated minds of all
nations'. The truths expressed by art, and the terms it used, were
not liable to change. In this history of French literature, he
sought to study not change—because what changed was
ephemeral—but what was 'constant, essential and immutable
in the French spirit'. French literature was not a reflection of
changing ideas and social conditions: Nisard's view was firmly
anti-sociological. French literature, he confidently asserted,
reached maturity and perfection in the seventeenth century;
the eighteenth century was the beginning of decadence. The
seventeenth century alone gave proper expression to the French
genius—which was for clarity, discipline and practicality. It
differed from that of ancient Greece in that Greece gave too
much time to 'vain curiosity and idle speculations', favouring
liberty, 'which is full of perils and aberrations, rather than
discipline which gives strength'. The best in French literature
was the study of the ideal of life, in all countries and in all
times, but with a practical intention. 'It gives little attention
to pure curiosity and to speculations which do not lead to some
truth which can be put into practice. It removes the gross and
superfluous from reality, to render knowledge of it at once
useful and innocent. . . . In France all that is not knowledge
interesting to the majority and a rule of conduct for men of
goodwill is in grave danger of being irrelevant and inadequate.'
France believed in the supremacy of reason, clarity, simplicity,
precision. Reason should be applied to practical purposes—

art's function was to teach morals, to purge the passions. What it advocated must be plausible, and conforming to common educated opinion.[1]

The complex results of basing oneself on the classical tradition can be seen in the life of Anatole France (1844–1924). He shows that classicism survived so long because it did not frontally oppose the forces which challenged it, but sought to absorb them. As a result, it degenerated into a colourless scepticism. In the case of Anatole France, it produced brilliant wit and fluent style, but this was only a false veneer concealing a profound despair. He shows how wrong it is to equate conformity with complacency, or to assume that conformity is necessarily static. He was undoubtedly one of the most popular authors in the country in the twenty years before 1914. A pamphlet was published entitled *Three Thinkers: Anatole France, Jesus, Pascal*. He was admired both by the cultured élite and by the masses.[2] He was considered the equal of Rabelais, Montaigne and Voltaire. His death was heralded as the end of an epoch and was greeted by an offensive on his memory comparable in violence only to that launched against Victor Hugo on his death.[3] He was one of those authors whose enormous popularity during his lifetime is paid for by almost total oblivion afterwards. Valéry, his successor in the Academy, ridiculed his superficiality. Everybody agreed he had no influence on literature and that he left no school: but he remains important because he reveals many of the problems that conformity created.

Anatole France was an unhappy man: his classicism was not based on contentment. His contemporaries knew very little about him and assumed that he was a gentle, wise old pedant, disabused of illusions but remaining sensitive and kind. It was only after his death, with the publication of more intimate

---

[1] D. Nisard, *Histoire de la littérature française* (4 vols., 1844–61) and *Précis de l'histoire de la littérature française* (1878), *Études de critique littéraire* (1858); obituary in *Modern Language Notes* (1888), 294; E. des Essarts, 'Désiré Nisard', in *La Nouvelle Revue* (1888), vol. 51, 929–36; René Bray, *La Formation de la doctrine classique en France* (1927).

[2] Paul Gisell, 'Sur la popularité d'Anatole France', *Revue mondiale* (1 Nov. 1924), 22–9.

[3] Gaston Picard, 'L'Influence littéraire et sociale d'Anatole France. Enquête', *Revue mondiale* (1 and 15 Dec. 1924), 227–56, 339–66.

reminiscences by his friends, that he was shown up as a tragic and melancholy figure, wounded by life, torn by doubt and appallingly alone; sparkling with intelligence, often smiling but never gay. The explanation was partly personal. He was a self made man (the son of a bookseller), but one whom success could not satisfy. The only passion of his life, he said, was his adoration for his mother; he did not love his wife, whom he soon divorced; he broke off relations with his daughter when she contracted a marriage of which he disapproved. For twenty years he conducted a celebrated liaison with Mme Arman de Caillavet, of whose salon he was the principal ornament; but she was in some ways a substitute-mother, who kept him working hard, to the extent that he had to indulge in ludicrous subterfuges to be able to read light novels. He left her, too, in the end, and spent his final years living with her maid. Anatole France could never escape his childhood and he wrote four autobiographies. His heroes in his books were nearly always orphans, and like himself, unfulfilled ones. He was tormented by his inability to find satisfaction in love, arguing that love is necessarily jealous, seeking an impossible unity and never giving men what they want. So he tried to confine himself to being an observer of life. He said he was in this way typical of the curious, idle, ingenuous Parisians, who were basically still children, whom everything amused. He wrote books though he disliked writing, finding it painful, like a task imposed on a child as a punishment.

'Why are we unhappy?' was the title of one of his articles. The answer went beyond the failure of family life. Anatole France represented disillusionment with knowledge and progress, despair at the discoveries of science—which showed man his insignificance—loneliness after the loss of religious faith, horror at the prospect of society being dominated by 'engineers and electricians', awareness of the mediocrity of life. He was too clever to believe in any ideal. His solution was to seek to embellish life, to render it tolerable by superficial gaiety, humour and beauty. He gave up his youthful enthusiasm for knowledge and change. What men needed, he decided, was imagination and 'enchantment', 'to forget the sad truth', to escape from themselves; he no longer wanted to discover reality but to reorganise it in fantasy, to make it amusing, to conceal its unpleasant aspects. Beyond truth, it was even more important to find hope and consolation; without lies, he said, humanity 'would perish of despair and boredom'. He therefore placed supreme importance on art, but not as a means of innovation. Originality was not necessary to beauty and the function of the artist was not to advance into the unknown. He wrote only 'to give brief amusement to delicate and curious minds'. He addressed himself to 'delicate' people, to the educated public; he could be understood by them only, he said, and his wide popularity was accidental, due to incomprehension. *Délicatesse* was his password. Delicate people must not be disturbed, but their jaded nerves needed refined and sophisticated entertainment. It was in this way that he was a classic. He emulated the clarity and simplicity of seventeenth century prose and the balance and polish of the eighteenth; he was hailed as the final flowering of the classicism of Greece and Rome as well as of that of France; his books were full of Greek myth. He said of himself that he had no pretence to originality: 'All my art is to scribble in the margins of books'. He was genuinely modest, and that was how Gide defined classicism, as opposed to the pride of romanticism.

His humour, and his political tergiversations, were both the result of this. His humour was above all ironic, and irony he himself defined as 'the last phase of disillusion'. One of his most famous fictional characters, Monsieur Bergeret, is told by his wife: 'You laugh at what is not laughable and one never knows if you are joking or if you are serious.' Anatole France spared nothing and no one; but it was not from arrogance: 'Though I have been a mocker in all stages of my life', he wrote, 'I have never made fun of anyone so cruelly as of myself, nor with such delight.' This did not mean that he was incapable of idealism. He supported almost every progressive idea of his day, constantly keeping up with his times. He was a liberal republican under Napoleon III; he was terrified by the Commune, but then became one of the principal supporters of Dreyfus, moved on to socialism and finally ended up, at least in name, a communist. While remaining convinced of the vanity of all human action, he became one of the country's most popular political orators. He wrote his sceptical books in the morning and talked hopefully of a new world at socialist banquets in the evening. He was not insincere: 'our contradictions', he said, 'are not the least true part of ourselves'. It is this complexity that makes him illuminating about conformity. Conformity did not necessarily involve faith. The classicism with which Anatole France was identified was supposed to signify repose and harmony, but this was what he sought, not what he achieved.[1]

Conformity was one of the principal problems that the new subject of sociology tried to study. In France, under the leadership of Émile Durkheim sociology concentrated on the relationship of the individual and the group. It took as the starting-point the view that society was threatened with collapse and needed to be restored by a new discipline and new moral bonds.[2] Durkheim argued that the growth of nations did not increase conformity, but on the contrary stimulated individual diversity: the larger the social group, the more it had to be adaptable to the multiplicity of situations it encountered, and the less it was able to resist individual variations. As a result 'everyone increasingly follows his own path', and the country was 'gradually proceeding to a state of affairs, now almost attained, in which the members of a single social group will no longer have anything in common other than their humanity'. There was nothing stable to 'love and honour in common, apart from man himself'.[3] This should not be taken as an accurate description of French society at the turn of the century, for Durkheim owes his fame not to his powers of observation of the situation around him, but for developing an analytical approach to the study of social phenomena. Durkheim's laments—for that is what they were—represented a longing for closer ties between humans, and for an expansion of the individualism of the eighteenth century, which had essentially

[1] H. M. Chevalier, *The Ironic Temperament. Anatole France and his time* (N.Y. 1932); J. Levaillant, *Les Aventures du scepticisme. Essai sur l'évolution intellectuelle d'Anatole France* (1965); L. B. Walton, *Anatole France and the Greek World* (Durham, North Carolina, 1950).

[2] Raymond Aron, *La Sociologie allemande contemporaine* (1935), 170. Cf. C. Bouglé, *Bilan de la sociologie française* (1935).

[3] E. Durkheim, 'L'Individualisme et les intellectuels', *Revue bleue* (1898), 4th series, vol. 10, 7–13; English translation published by Steven Lukes. Cf. Joan Rowland, 'Durkheim's social theory with special reference to the position of the individual in society' (M.A. London, unpublished thesis, 1948).

been a rebellion against political constraints. Durkheim was the secretary-general of the Bordeaux section of the League of the Rights of Man, a founder of the *Jeunesse laïque* association in that city and a sympathiser of the socialist party. He had inherited the individualist principles of the Revolution. But he was also a philosopher who was uncomfortable with these principles. The supporters of the Revolution hoped, as another philosopher, Charles Renouvier put it, to convert the superstitious, sensual and immoral individuals, who were thus liberated, into rational beings, with the ability and the will to lead moral lives. Philosophers looked on the rabble as barbarians, who needed to be tamed, and on the educated élite who were emerging from them as lost souls, who could not be left simply to their own devices. Durkheim, the son and grandson of rabbis, and trained as a philosopher, was above all a moralist. He was a sociologist because he believed that the functions once performed by common ideas and sentiments were now determined by new social institutions and relationships; and this had transformed the nature of morality. He attacked traditional moralists for regarding the individual as an autonomous entity, depending only on himself, irrespective of the social context in which he found himself. He wished to place the study of morality on a scientific footing. He called himself a rationalist. He was the disciple both of Kant and of Comte. He believed that individual appetites are 'by nature boundless and insatiable: if there is nothing to control them they will not be able to control themselves'. Morality was therefore concerned with imposing social discipline. It was not a means to individual happiness, but to the prevention of anarchy, both in society and within the individual himself. Durkheim, his biographer records, could never experience happiness himself without a feeling of remorse. He believed a free man was one who was victorious over his instincts: self-discipline was a good in itself. Children were like primitive peoples, who needed to be civilised. That is why he devoted so much of his efforts to the study of education, and why the book he wanted to write more than any, but which he never got round to, was on the sociology of morality. His ideal was rational uniformity, in which men would be free, but would nevertheless recognise their duties and act altruistically. But he also saw that sacrifice and disinterestedness could not be understood in purely intellectual terms and he was increasingly interested by religion.[1]

Durkheim shows the problem of conformity growing ever larger, as its social dimensions were revealed. His school, at the same time, illustrates another aspect of conformity, in that it itself represented at once a rebellion, an orthodoxy and a catalyst. Sociology as he developed it was a breakaway from philosophy. His disciples, in the first generation, were like himself, philosophers who opted for a heresy. This was shown in the way they were not particularly attracted by fieldwork, but specialised in general methodology, in defining what constitutes scientific fact and in distinguishing between different kinds of truth. Like the school of Cousin, they obtained much of their impetus from the introduction of foreign ideas. Forty per cent of the books reviewed in Durkheim's periodical, *L'Année sociologique*, were German ones, 21 per cent were English, 12 per cent Italian, and only 26 per cent were French. Just how far Durkheim was absorbed by morals and religion may be seen from the fact that 47 per cent of the references in this periodical were to books concerned with religion, 15 per cent were on law and only 20 per cent on economics.[2] Durkheim was raised to his pre-eminence in French sociology by the admiration of philosophers, particularly those in the École Normale Supérieure. It was the *Revue de métaphysique et morale*, the *Revue philosophique* and the *Revue de synthèse historique* which wrote in praise of the *Année*, and it was educators and moralists like Gustave Belot, and the logician Goblot, who backed Durkheim. Durkheim's sociology was vigorously attacked by that of others who had rival schools, like Worms (who inclined more to law and economics) and the disciples of Le Play (who specialised in empirical monographs and who were politically more right wing). Durkheim gradually established his brand of sociology as the dominant one in the universities of France, so

[1] The indispensable source is Steven Lukes, *Émile Durkheim: his life and work* (1973), which also contains the best bibliography. Cf. in particular, E. Durkheim, *L'Éducation morale* (1938). Also Claude Lévi-Strauss, 'La Sociologie française' in G. Gurvitch and W. E. Moore, *La Sociologie au 20ᵉ siècle* (1947), 513-45.

[2] Yash Nandan, 'Le Maître, les doctrines et le magnum opus: une étude critique et analytique de l'école durkheimienne et de l'Année sociologique' (unpublished thèse de troisième cycle, Paris V, 1974), 129.

that his approach—though much modified by his followers—produced almost a new way of talking.[1]

This was due, in part, to the marriages sociology entered into with other heretics from other subjects. The *Annales* school of history was, to some extent, an offspring of one of these marriages, though Lucien Febvre, in his rebellion against the political historians, found inspiration not only in Durkheim—or rather in his son-in-law Mauss—but also in Vidal de la Blache the geographer, the economist Simiand, and not negligibly, in Michelet also. History was immeasurably broadened as a result, but, as Lucien Febvre said, he felt he was better understood by people in other disciplines than by other historians. The sociological approach (though Febvre's ideas had more to them than this label would suggest) represented an alliance of a generation (or rather of part of one, for traditional history, like traditional philosophy, continued to flourish).[2] What held these rebels together was a common temperament and a similar kind of curiosity, that transcended the apparent divisions of their subjects. Their alliance could be called a new kind of conformity. The study of conformities reduces one to recognising a whole variety of conformities, and conformity emerges as much more than static resistance.[3]

[1] For the rival theory of conformity by imitation, see the works of Gabriel Tarde, especially *Les Lois de l'imitation* (1890) and Jean Milet, *Gabriel Tarde et la philosophie de l'histoire* (1970); A. Matagrin, *La Psychologie sociale de G. Tarde* (1910).

[2] H. D. Mann, *Lucien Febvre* (1971).

[3] T. N. Clark, *Prophets and Patrons: The French University and the Emergence of the Social Sciences* (Cambridge, Mass., 1973). For the psychological problems, e.g. the relationships of detachment, radicalism and introversion, see M. Brewster Smith, J. S. Brunner and R. W. White, *Opinions and Personality* (1956), full of interesting ideas for the historian.

# 10. Fashion and Beauty

*Furniture*

FURNITURE is a particularly valuable indicator of national taste. Everybody needs furniture and everybody in theory has to declare his preferences when buying it. The history of furniture reveals aesthetic ideals in their social context, subject to a whole variety of pressures, of fashion, technical change, snobbishness, economy and practical needs. It is a great misfortune that its development is, nevertheless, one of the most neglected branches of art history, and indeed of every kind of history: there is still an enormous amount to be discovered about the economic history of the industry which played a major part in satisfying the mass demand for comfort and well-being, about the social history of the changes in behaviour which new kinds of homes both produced and reflected, and about the political history of the furniture makers, who had an extraordinary record of revolutionary agitation. The fragments of information at present available make possible only the most tentative generalisations.[1]

Much more has been written about the furniture of the eighteenth century, because pieces of outstandingly skilful craftsmanship were produced then. Many of these are now preserved in museums, and they are readily available for study. The nineteenth century never had the same pride in its taste, perhaps because it made its taste serve other more powerful ideals. The *ancien régime* is generally associated with expensive, elaborate furniture made for kings and aristocrats; the nineteenth century is usually seen as an age of cheap production and banal copying of old styles for a mass market. The contrast is, however, false, and the nineteenth century's achievements have been underestimated because its aims have been misunderstood. To use the same criteria on it as on the *ancien régime* is misleading. It is

---

[1] Jacqueline Viaux, 'Bibliographie du meuble' (unpublished, stencilled, 1966), is the indispensable starting-point—by the librarian of the Musée Forney, which specialises in industrial art.

wrong to assume that all eighteenth-century furniture was as fine, as elegant or as well made as the museum pieces. No one was more scathing of the furniture-making of this period than its most revered craftsman Roubo (1739–91), who lamented even then that there were very few artisans capable of making beautiful furniture. Specialisation was already so advanced in his day that nearly all the people in the trade made only a single part; 'their skill', said Roubo, 'consisted only in a more or less successful routine'. There were few enlightened patrons either: most buyers were 'without taste and without knowledge and, what is worse, without the money to pay for good work; they take what is offered to them, indiscriminately, provided it is cheap, which is the reason for the large amount produced and its poor quality'.[1] Good furniture was very expensive, and all the more so because intermediaries took their cut. It is true that artisans went to the houses of buyers, to receive orders and detailed instructions, and it has been argued that this system was the basis of the high standards and individual design of the age; but professional 'decorators' also played an important role in determining what was produced, and the artisans resented their interference and profiteering as much as they later resented the department stores. The pressure to produce cheaply was always present, except in rare cases. Mercier, writing in 1788, said that three-quarters of the furniture produced in Paris went to buyers from the country, who were given the worst and shoddiest goods. Fraud was rampant; the decorators sold on credit, demanding down payments of 30 per cent—which was the cost of the furniture to them—and pocketing the rest as profit; much furniture was held together by glue and quickly fell apart. The decorator was able to dominate the market, because buyers wanted to furnish whole rooms with complete sets which he put together: the alternative to his shoddy goods was to buy older, more solid furniture, which had stood the test of time, but that was hard to find. The great cabinet-makers flourished thanks to the idea adopted by some sections of the aristocracy and the rich that furniture should be changed almost as frequently as one's clothes. The cult of fashion and novelty provided a great stimulus to the best artisans, as also did the mania for collecting fine objects, which were beautiful even if

[1] J. A. Roubo, *L'Art du menuisier* (1769–72), 2. 366.

they were useless. There were thus two kinds of chairs—those made to sit on, and those which simply decorated a room; and in the best houses, people also had chairs made to measure, to suit their individual dimensions. But though the cult of originality predominated (resulting in the introduction of embellishments based, for example, on Chinese models), buyers were already divided between those who favoured the exotic and the new, and those who were attached to antiques. In 1777 the comte d'Artois himself purchased a reproduction of a piece of furniture by Boulle.[1]

Furniture-making in the nineteenth century continued trends which were already well established. Thus the production of fine pieces, not unworthy of comparison with the more celebrated ones of the eighteenth century, continued in the Second Empire. Second Empire furniture has for long been dismissed as ugly and unoriginal, but it is the cheap copies of the best work which have given the period its bad reputation. Henri Fourdinois (†1887), Napoleon III's principal cabinet-maker, was a craftsman of great ingenuity and skill; thirty-two manuscript order books, with illustrations of every piece he made, survive to show the ingenuity with which he combined borrowing from past designs with original creation. He made furniture not only for the imperial yacht and for the grandees of the regime like Achille Fould, but for many middle-class clients who simply wanted 'armchairs in rose and violet silk'.[2] Napoleon III's chief cabinet-maker, Jean Becker, who was permanently employed to look after the imperial furniture, received a salary of 1,500 francs a month, as much as senior officers. Enough information is beginning to emerge about these artisans to show that there was no uniform fashion, slavishly copied—that is the impression given by the second-rate imitations which followed twenty years later. One of the leading arbiters of Second Empire taste, Aimé Chenavard (b. 1798), had a wild imagination which led him to mix Gothic, Renaissance and Oriental styles; another, M. J. N. Lienard (1810–70), however, was an advocate of greater simplicity. The upholsterers now became rivals of the cabinet-makers, adding skirts to chairs and urging the elaborate use of rich cloths; but the most accepted rule was that each room

[1] Pierre Verlet, *La Maison du 18ᵉ siècle en France: Société, décoration, mobilier* (1966).
[2] Fourdinois MSS. (Forney Library).

should be in a different style: the dining-room Renaissance, the drawing-room eighteenth century, the boudoir and library Empire. A whole variety of new tables, for every kind of purpose, were introduced. There was thus a great deal of inventiveness in this period, and too many rich men to allow the drab monotony which is normally attributed to it.[1]

In selecting from this vast and increasing range of styles the young couple setting up home had to declare their taste almost in the way they had to admit their political opinions. They could follow the conservative programme set out by Charles Blanc, France's director of Fine Arts in 1848 and again in 1870-3. Paradoxically and significantly this gentle brother of the socialist Louis Blanc was, for all his sympathy with the working class, an admirer of the classical tradition in art; Raphael and Ingres were his heroes even if he preached that art should be carried to the masses; he illustrates well how limited the revolutionary elements in republicanism were, and how men with aspirations to modernity and justice retained (as has been shown in the political chapters of this book) many of the values of the *ancien régime*. Charles Blanc's *Grammar of the Decorative Arts* argued that nature, on its own, was not beautiful, because it lacked order, proportion and unity. These were the three qualities one should seek to create in one's home. Order, in particular, was 'the sovereign law of the decorative arts'. The furniture of Louis XVI, he thought, captured the dignity, grace and elegance one should aim for, better than any other. He advocated symmetry, harmony, discretion: decency was an inseparable element of beauty; and taste was 'the delicate appreciation of the relationships between men and things'. One should not seek to follow fashions slavishly, therefore, but rather to reflect one's moral worth in one's surroundings. The love of domestic luxury was a good thing because it encouraged the love of family life. One did not have to be rich to have a graceful home, for grace 'had no need of more than the appearance of richness'. There was nothing wrong with fakes or imitation. That was one reason why wallpaper was such a great invention: it gave if not the equivalent of luxury, at least the mirage of it. All the resources of modern technology should be used freely,

[1] J. Viaux, 'Le mobilier Napoleon III', *Revue de l'ameublement* (Mar. 1965), 191-7, (Apr. 1965), 175-81, (May 1965), 123-9.

because they showed the superiority of art over matter and enabled the humblest material to be given artistic shape. Charles Blanc showed that there were very good reasons why ordinary people should find merit in the banal copying of classical taste, and also why they should have a sense of achievement in doing so successfully. His advice was the counterpart of that of the professors who taught the men of the Third Republic to express their humanitarian principles according to the rules of traditional rhetoric.[1] But Blanc represented only one approach. An alternative was that of the individualistic school, of which an inspector of Fine Arts of the next generation, Henry Havard, was a particularly influential example. His *Grammar of Furnishing* (1884) said that just as it would be ridiculous to wear eighteenth-century clothes, so it was absurd to surround oneself with eighteenth-century furniture. Outside the home, men should respect dominant taste, but inside it they should follow their own and concentrate on pleasing themselves. There were no fixed rules, particularly in the bedroom, where one could do as one liked, and seek comfort above all else. The dining-room should not distract attention away from the main function of eating; it should not be filled with old furniture or decorated excessively, but made light and gay. Old people should sit in Louis XIV chairs if they wished to give expression to the authority they incarnated, and the middle-aged in Louis XVI chairs, but eclecticism in styles was a good rule, and modern furniture was quite in place in intimate sitting-rooms. However, eclecticism should not be exaggerated: the heaping of bibelot upon bibelot was not enough: that was where *taste* came in. It was better to have a single masterpiece than a mass of furniture of doubtful value. 'If people judge our fortune by quantity, it is by our choice that they judge our taste.' Havard shows that ultimately taste was the one thing that no book could teach.[2]

That was one reason why the third alternative, which was the school of modernity, had a certain appeal. In reaction against copying the past and the chaotic mixing of styles, a movement arose to make furniture original in a fuller sense and to give the applied arts in general a higher status. The leaders—Gallé,

[1] Charles Blanc, *Grammaire des arts décoratifs. Décoration intérieur de la maison* (2nd edition, 1882), 10, 22, 135, 146, 337–9.
[2] H. Havard, *L'Art dans la maison. Grammaire de l'ameublement* (1884), 356, 431.

Majorelle, Prouvé, Émile Ruhlmann—were influenced by William Morris. Living mainly in Nancy, they were conscious of trends in German art. They produced unusual jewellery, ceramics, book illustrations, but they met most resistance in furniture, even though they obtained the patronage of Corbin, the young heir of the Magasins Réunis of Nancy. It was only after 1921, when one of their group, Dufrène, became artistic director of the Galeries Lafayette in Paris and another, Francis Jourdain, abandoned painting for business, that their furniture became widely available to the public. The decorative pieces they designed were just as bastardised in mass production as fine pieces of the eighteenth century were in reproduction. The escape from the banal was not easy.[1]

The kind of furniture people bought was ultimately determined as much by the development of the furniture-making industry as by that elusive gift of taste. This industry has almost always been in a state of crisis: furniture is something people can always do without in hard times, and undercutting, by the use of cheaper materials, is a constant temptation and problem. In the depression of 1848, many cabinet-makers emigrated to England in search of work; the war of 1870 and the Commune were again disastrous, 'like an Edict of Nantes', because several thousand German furniture workers left France. The surviving artisans sought refuge not in innovation, but in reducing costs, by dispensing with the services of designers. Duchesne's collection of some 12,000 models of the sixteenth to eighteenth centuries made it unnecessary for manufacturers to find new ones for almost half a century. There was money to be made in reproduction furniture, because the boundary between copying and forging was so uncertain. The ambition of the best artisans was to emulate the great cabinet-makers of the past, to produce work indistinguishable from theirs, to have their pieces exhibited in museums as originals. In the twentieth century there were perhaps only eighty or a hundred top-class cabinet-makers of this kind, and they could make a very good living. André Mailfert, a highly skilled polisher who could fool the experts, set up a veritable forging industry at Annemasse in 1923; it was very

[1] Pierre Olmer, *La Renaissance du mobilier français 1890–1910* (1927); id., *Le Mobilier français d'aujourd'hui 1910–1925* (1926); Francis Jourdain, *Né en 76* (1951), 175–6; Madeleine Prouvé, *Victor Prouvé 1858–1943* (n.d.), 13.

successful; he sold one of his commodes for 1,200,000 francs; and he has unashamedly written about the gullibility and greed of his customers.[1] There was indeed always a certain mystery about reproduction furniture. It was not generally known—and the furniture makers of the Faubourg Saint-Antoine took care to keep the fact quiet—that chairs sold as the product of Parisian artisan skill were manufactured in Liffol-le-Grand (Meuse), a small town of barely 2,000 inhabitants, virtually all of whom made 'antique' chair frames; Paris artisans then polished these to make them more or less indistinguishable from genuine antiques. This industry had been set up in Liffol in 1864 and prospered continuously since then. The Parisian workshops did their best to maintain public interest in antique furniture by organising 'retrospective exhibitions', devoted to whatever period they had particularly large unsold stocks of at the time. The Union Centrale des Arts décoratives, which claimed to be a disinterested body devoted to the applied arts, was for a time controlled by the forgers and the copyists. The export of pseudo-antiques mounted steadily, to reach a peak in 1927–9. The U.S.A. was France's best customer. The U.S.A. played an indispensable part in the history of modern French furniture-making, as it did in that of French painting, replacing the patronage of the old aristocracy. It was possible to sell to it at as much as four times the cost of manufacture; and the Americans were attracted by poor quality furniture also, provided it was skilfully advertised: clever merchants describing themselves as the leading manufacturers and artisans of France made handsome profits from the shoddy goods they unloaded on the other side of the Atlantic. The essential feature of this trade was that the customer never quite knew what he was buying. The investment value of antiques made the buying of old or pseudo-old furniture attractive, whatever one thought of its appearance: prices roughly doubled between 1865 and 1913, though between 1914 and 1939 they rose only 12 per cent. But by 1929 good modern furniture began to appreciate with age (rising by 27 per cent in the next decade). The more the value of money fell, the more did speculation in objects become widespread.[2]

[1] A. Mailfert, *Au pays des antiquaires: Confidences d'un maquilleur professionnel* (new edition, 1959).

[2] Janine Capronnier, *Le Prix des meubles d'époque 1860–1956* (1966), 75, 83.

The paradox about the art that went into making this furniture was that the artist accepted an inferior role. The furniture makers, with few exceptions, were content to remain nameless, and their individual skill—unlike that of painters—was never recognised outside trade circles. This was because the industry was dominated by merchants and intermediaries, who profited from the extreme specialisation and division of labour. In 1938 nearly 90 per cent of furniture makers worked in units of between one and five workers: each process, from that performed by the sawyer, to the finishing by the mirror maker, lacquerer, polisher and *patineur*, was a separate, independent activity. It took a long time for all these specialists to do their little bit on any particular item and they were therefore always short of cash. Merchants hovered around them, buying up their products cheaply, particularly on Fridays and Saturdays when they had to pay their wages and needed ready money; and these merchants usually resold at 40 or even 100 per cent profit. The great department stores carried this even further, by making regular contracts for very low prices, and insisting that their own names be affixed to the furniture. The contact between the artisan and the public, which, as one cabinet-maker said, had given them 'a constant communion of taste, ideas and initiative', was thus destroyed; 'personal originality and professional conscience' vanished when the sole aim was the largest possible turnover. Factories grew up to meet the demands of the *nouveaux riches*, each specialising in a definite type. Caned chairs from the 1880s onwards were made very largely in Halluin (Nord), Neuville-Coppegueule and the Bresle region; plain wooden chairs in Orthez; hotel furniture in washable beech in Montbéliard and modern furniture in Limoges, in a large factory founded in 1890 originally to produce Henri II styles from local walnut. Provincial styles (folkloric, rustic, chests and fourposters) which became popular after the First World War (like regional cooking), thanks to the development of tourism, were produced mainly in Auray (where fifteen factories with over 100 workers each were established) and in Bourg-en-Bresse (which switched from Louis XV to meet the new demands of the antique trade). The most decisive change in production was, however, due not to changed demand, but to the invention of plywood, the first patent for which was taken out in London in 1884 (though a machine to saw wood very thinly had been invented in 1834). Plywood could not be sculpted; it required large square surfaces; and that is what the customer increasingly got; but it was only after 1945 that new habits, the desire to reduce housework, and limitations of space, made people accept simple furniture of this kind with pleasure. Then for the first time furniture ceased to be a major sign of wealth and became just a collection of useful objects.[1]

The intervention of the department stores meant that one could buy cheap reproductions for not much more than plain furniture. Thus in 1878 at the Bon Marché a straightforward 'Victorian' armchair cost 75 francs, or even 59 francs, but one could buy a 'Pompadour' for 95 francs, a 'fauteuil anglais' or a 'polonais' for 85; and a carved Louis XII was only 125 francs.[2] At the Galeries Nancéiennes in 1898 reproduction chairs were often exactly the same price as modern ones: Louis XIII and caned bamboo both cost 12 fr. 75; the cheaper bentwood chair was 6 fr. 50, but the 'old oak François I' chair was only double that. An ordinary, plain 'modern' sideboard was 225 francs, whereas an elaborately carved 'Renaissance' one in 'old oak' was 600 francs, but one could get a variation of this massive piece, with slightly modified decoration, in 'Breton' style, for only 300 francs. Nevertheless the best buy was the 'Henri II' sideboard for only 180 francs.[3] The furniture shops that sprang up in provincial cities in the late nineteenth century ensured that what traces there were of local originality vanished. Louis XIII and above all Louis XV styles had already transformed the general appearance of country furniture by then; the influence of Paris had become all-powerful, even if functional peasant furniture—as opposed to furniture designed for ostentation—continued to be made up to the 1880s by local craftsmen.[4] Bordeaux, which in 1827 had 1,700 furniture makers, came to be dominated by the grand new stores, which relied increasingly on small country artisans producing to firm specifications. Every clerk getting married, it was said here, demanded a full set of Henri II or Louis XV furniture, at rock-bottom prices;

[1] Paule Garenc, *L'Industrie du meuble en France* (1957).
[2] Maison Aristide Boucicault: Au Bon Marché, *Album de l'ameublement* (1878).
[3] Aux Galeries Nancéiennes, *Album de l'ameublement* (1898).
[4] Suzanne Tardieu, *Meubles régionaux datés* (1950). Cf. J. Gauthier, *Le Mobilier des vieilles provinces de France* (1933).

the twenty-five antique shops of the city increasingly commissioned fakes of the styles they were asked for; and that was
what the artisans had to produce. The president of the trade
union of wood sculptors said in 1884 that his members were 'as
skilful today as at any other period, but we are not now allowed
to be original; we are asked for Renaissance, Louis XIV, Louis
XV and Louis XVI; we are being turned into machines by
being forced to copy'. Objects produced for a few hundred
francs—including enamel miniatures, jewellery, porcelain—
were covered in dirt, distributed among foreign antique shops
and resold there for ten times their original cost.[1] The trouble
was that foreigners became just as skilful at faking and they
could do it more cheaply, because they paid lower wages. Old
regional centres like Lyon stopped producing their own designs,
modelling themselves on Parisian styles, because snobbery preferred these.[2] One author put the blame for the decay of quality
on architects, competition among whom led to fierce price-
cutting. Between 1877 and 1897 the number of architects in
Bordeaux, for example, rose from 8 to 121. The obsession with
economy, among patrons who could not quite afford to satisfy
their ambitions, and among public authorities with rising costs,
led to the adoption of contracts by tender, so that frequently the
shoddiest workman got the job. A massive trade developed in
bits of old châteaux, which were pulled apart for use in new
houses: the craftsmen complained that commissions for interesting and original work became even rarer.

The simplification of wallpapers as they became increasingly
popular illustrates this tendency. In the middle of the nineteenth
century, papers were produced which were enormous murals,
often involving thirty different scenes, like 'The Lyon–Saint-
Étienne Railway' (1854) by Paillard (the wallpaper manufacturer who was mayor of Saint-Denis) which still survived in a
café in the 1930s; or, on an even grander scale, Délicourt's
'Hunting in the Forest' (1851) involving 4,000 engravings.
Already in the eighteenth century the poor used to buy small
bits of these and paste them up like pictures; but the introduction of steam machines (1858) turned wallpaper into an

[1] Marius Vachon, *La Crise industrielle et artistique en France et en Europe* (n.d.)
[*c*. 1886].
[2] Marius Vachon, *Les Industries d'art* (Nancy, 1897).

enormous industry—there were over 200 firms producing it by 1889. Much ingenuity was used to imitate silk and other signs of luxury; and some very remarkable papers were printed for the rich, but cheap, elementary repetitive patterns, bearing little resemblance to these sophisticated products, soon drowned the market.[1]

What the people of this period liked in their furniture was thus first of all a symbol of status. The poor had virtually no furniture; even the middle classes took a long time to collect more than bare essentials—a bed, a table and cheap chairs. It was natural that the taste of an age of increasing prosperity, obsessed by social climbing, should have expressed itself in the collection of objects and bric-à-brac, simply to indulge its pleasure in the ownership of property, and that it should have favoured in particular furniture that was solid, impressive and that gave evidence of the hard work and money that had gone into it. Since furniture was above all property, people wanted theirs to look as much like the furniture of the rich as possible. There were alternative ways of gaining status, but when it came to exhibiting one's wealth, it was hard to fool one's neighbours. The people of this period tried hard, nevertheless, to do so; they tried to make their homes—or at least their sitting-rooms—into miniature versions of châteaux. But they favoured the old and the fake-old also because it had the essential quality of property, permanence and investment value. They preferred the styles of Paris, which had as it were received the consecration of the state, to the eccentricities of what local craftsmen had escaped the attractions of the city; and it was only when Paris set the fashion, after 1919, for regional styles that the regions set up industries to produce these. Since competitiveness played such an important role in the exhibition of taste, each class, each profession, each set of people developed minor variations in the way it collected and displayed domestic equipment, but the overriding general uniformity between them testified to the fact that taste, like education, had purposes other than its own satisfaction.

The counterpart of the concern with ostentation was the constraint of economy. This was probably the most important influence on the changing appearance and construction of furni-

[1] H. Clouzot and C. Follot, *Histoire du papier peint en France* (1935); M. Vachon, *Les Arts et les industries du papier 1871–1894* (1894), 205–17.

ture; and one should not judge people's taste too simply on the basis of what they bought. A survey carried out in Britain some years ago revealed that there were almost three times as many people who disliked the furniture they owned as those who were pleased with their purchases. One should not imagine that the furniture produced reflected the taste either of the manufacturers or the artisans who made it; both had to make a living, to cut their costs to the minimum; and the buyer had to buy what he could afford. If there was an increasing preoccupation, it was not with beauty, but with comfort, which was a more easily attainable alternative. The variations in people's idea of beauty have still to be studied, taking into account all these distorting factors. But the sale prices of furniture have hitherto barely been used with the precision that economic historians have learnt to apply to other consumer goods.

### Fashions in Clothes

Taste in clothes seems, at first sight, to have followed very different trends. Whereas in furniture most people continued to admire antique and unchanging styles, in their personal appearance they seemed to demand constant, almost annual, changes. Paris became established as the capital of fashion. This contrast is, however, deceptive. The cult of status dominated clothes exactly as it determined the choice of furniture, though men, it is true, pursued this goal more obviously and openly than women.[1]

The revolution that took place in men's clothes in this period brought about a most unusual and perhaps unique change in the landscape and in human relationships. Virtually all males took to wearing black or dark suits, without decoration, and with differences of cut and cloth so slight as to be barely distinguishable. Men had previously dressed to show their rank, their profession, their pride. Now discretion, modesty and, on the surface, acceptance of equality were what they paraded instead. In 1848 men wore their hair in every conceivable style, and in every length; fifty years later, long hair had virtually vanished and the skill of the male barber was reduced to the handling of clippers that left room for only minute variations.

[1] René Colas, *Bibliographie générale du costume et de la mode* (2 vols., 1933).

The differing speed at which this happened in different parts of the country suggests that this increasing uniformity reflected the gradual triumph of the Parisian principles of fraternity and equality (though perhaps not of liberty). It was only in the period 1880–1900 that the Breton peasants adopted what they called the 'French style'. Previously they had worn distinctive jackets and waistcoats—the *chupen manchek* and the *jilet*—which were decorated and embroidered in a whole variety of ways, so that one could at a glance tell what village, or group of villages, the wearer came from. This was a uniform, but each uniform was shared by only a few hundred people, and the specimens of them that survive—with their elaborate and colourful needle-work patterns—suggest a sense of pride in belonging to the local community, almost as though it was a military regiment.[1] A Breton doctor writing in 1904 said that one could still see these varied costumes at fairs and markets, but one could also recognise the inhabitants of more modernised towns, like those from the canton of Pont-l'Abbé who had in the last fifteen years taken to buttoning up their jackets at the front 'the French way', concealing their embroidered waistcoats, dropping the decoration though keeping a coloured lining, moving steadily, as he put it, towards the monotony and platitude of 'the European-American' style.[2] This style was in fact originally the style of the English country gentleman, which the French aristocratic dandies had imported in the early nineteenth century as a mark of distinction and originality.[3] The theory behind it—developed by Beau Brummell—was that men should seek to impress not by decoration, strong colour or rich materials, but by the perfect fit of their clothes, which should follow the natural line of the body. The arrangement of their neckcloth was the only way they could henceforth allow themselves some scope for fantasy, and the cleanliness of their linen should be the measure of their respectability. It is excessively simple to explain the triumph of this fashion in terms of the progressive democratisation of the western world, for it was first adopted by the most aristocratic of nations. The gentlemen of England wore the same clothes,

---

[1] See the large display in the municipal museum of Rennes.
[2] Dr. C. A. Picquenard, *De l'evolution moderne du chupen et du jilet dans le costume masculin aux environs de Kemper* (Vannes, 1904).
[3] J. Boulenger, *Les Dandys* (1907).

originally, as a kind of caste uniform. To ape them was to pretend that one belonged to this exalted group. The universal black suit denoted not the triumph of democracy, so much as a new form of the search for social distinction.

The remarkable speed with which other classes succeeded in looking like gentlemen was due to the transformation of the tailoring trade by new commercial practices. The French Revolution had not produced an immediate simplification of male clothing: elegant people in 1803 wore three or four waistcoats one on top of the other; in the Restoration 'Polish' trousers, 'Turkish' boots, 'Cossack' waistcoats, short 'English' coats and a profusion of gold buttons were at various stages fashionable. But around 1825 ready-made tailoring shops appeared in Paris and by the end of the Second Empire they had completely altered men's habits in dress. At first these shops simply sold unclaimed bespoke clothes. The poor had always worn the cast-off clothing of the rich: differences in appearance between the classes had been mitigated by this, but the poor perforce mixed the different styles they picked up, so that variety was even greater. But in 1830 the firm of Coutard was founded in the rue Croix des Petits Champs to sell ready-made and bespoke suits at the same price, for cash only, but at a great saving on what ordinary tailors—who always gave long credit—charged. By 1867 this firm employed forty cutters; it dressed the bourgeoisie of every rank, and it exported 3 million francs' worth of suits a year, mainly to South America and Egypt.[1] The Paris department stores, with their mailed catalogues, soon extended this system to the provinces. La Belle Jardinière, founded in 1827 to produce ready-made clothes, moved into a palatial new building on the Pont Neuf in 1866.[2] Charles Blanc in 1875 was still laying it down that clothes should give expression to a man's functions in life, but they were on the contrary increasingly doing just the opposite. Blanc noted that clothes were now being made of materials that would not last long; that was the mark of the new mobile society. He urged that men should cultivate gravity in their appearance, because clothes were a 'moral indication'.[3]

[1] Charles Eck, *Histoire chronologique du vêtement (homme) jadis et aujourd'hui, suivie de l'art de se vêtir au 19ᵉ siècle* (1867).

[2] By 1913 it was employing 10,000 workers. For other men's wear firms see H. Detrois, *Industries de la confection et de la couture* (1913).

[3] Charles Blanc, *L'Art dans la parure et dans le vêtement* (1875), 239, 366.

The appearance of respectability could now be bought very cheaply. Appearances were, of course, deceptive. The president of the Syndicate of Men's Underwear Manufacturers reported in 1908 that 'there are quite a large number of men who demand fancy linen (*linge de fantaisie*) and bring much coquetry into their undergarments'; though the white shirt was most popular, printed coloured ones had recently been increasingly asked for.[1] But these were cravings which men were not allowed to publicise. It could be claimed that the age of the black suit coincided more exactly with the age of sexual inhibitions than with that of democracy. Men had to abandon sartorial provocativeness at the same time as they had to start concealing their marital infidelities. The black suit was what one wore, in particular, to church on Sundays. Men's clothes showed the limitations on eccentricity that were generally accepted; a general conformity was required and obtained; individual whim could manifest itself only in trivial details, and it was nearly always inspired by snobbishness or by wealth.

But why, if the capital of men's fashion was London, was the capital of women's fashion Paris? It had not yet become so in 1850. It is true that at the end of the *ancien régime* Mademoiselle Bertin, dressmaker to Marie-Antoinette, included many foreigners (and particularly Russians, but also the Duchess of Devonshire) among her clients, but fashion had not yet taken on its modern characteristics: she specialised above all in hats and in the garnishing of dresses with ingenious accoutrements.[2] Women's fashions used to move very slowly, partly because making women's clothes, with all their lace and embroidery, took so long that they could not be worn until many months after they were ordered. There was enormous variation in the nature and juxtaposition of colours and ornaments but the basic forms were relatively limited, a single model being made up in different cloths. Dressmakers were frequently given an old dress to copy in a new cloth. It was only in 1850 that the first shop appeared in Paris which both sold cloth and undertook to make it into clothes, but its owner, Madame Roger (of the rue

[1] Georges Dehesdin, *Exposition internationale de Milan, 1906. Section française, groupe 42* (1908), 599.

[2] Pierre de Nouvion and Émile Liez, *Un Ministre des modes sous Louis XVI: Mademoiselle Bertin, marchande de modes de la reine 1747–1813* (1911).

Nationale Saint-Martin), had only one model. Worth, who had arrived in Paris at the age of 20 four years before, noting her success, persuaded his employers, the drapers Gagelin, to follow her lead, but now he gave each cloth a different model and ingeniously invented a whole range of variations that could be added. His originality was much criticised, but by perseverance, and also by making his clothes more comfortable, more in accord with the human shape, he persuaded an increasing number of clients that they should abandon following the standard patterns and seek instead to have a unique dress, suited to their individual personality. These clients were at first largely foreigners: Englishwomen in particular came to Paris to be dressed by this Englishman. Worth's success came from his confidence and powers of persuasion. He introduced new forms of decoration which people disliked, but by persuading enough rich women to wear them, he made them fashionable and then popular. He got the silk manufacturers of Lyon to produce new types and new colours; and he persuaded his most famous customer, the Empress Eugénie, who vigorously resisted all the innovations he recommended, that in wearing these novelties, she was performing a national duty by stimulating the textile trade. The number of silk looms in Lyon did indeed double during the Second Empire. Worth also transformed widows' weeds by introducing alternative types of crêpe, violet and jade. In 1872 he started making clothes out of sculpted and beaten velvet, one of the oldest of Lyon furnishing fabrics: after some years of resistance by his clients who objected to being dressed like furniture, this material became so popular that a vast new industry developed to mass produce it, except that this was done in cotton instead of silk, and velvet dresses thus became a popular fashion. Worth's adoption of new materials and new ornaments did an enormous amount to stimulate business, to develop mechanical lace-making and a gigantic flowers and feathers industry (Paris came to have 800 firms specialising in this). Fashion, as Worth established it, aimed at individuality in clothes; far from meeting a demand for novelty from women, it had to fight against their conservatism. It was only when rich, eccentric women or actresses showed off new styles—and the theatre played an essential role in the popularisation of female fashions—that women imagined that they could become as pretty as them, if only they wore similar clothes. Fashion, as the masses came to understand it, meant imitation, the opposite of individuality.[1] Fashion now had to change constantly, because with the development of a large dressmaking industry, new styles were imitated so quickly that the rich demanded yet further innovation to keep one step ahead; and the poor were offered such parodies of the original styles, in cheap materials, with the grace missing both from cut and colour, that their admiration for the original innovation rapidly flagged. The industry became so competitive with the almost infinite multiplication of cloths, that it was impossible to be sure any longer who took the lead, as between manufacturers and couturiers, in inventing new cloths. A silk manufacturer who accumulated excessive stocks, say, of moiré would be glad to sell it off at a low price to a famous couturier, who would use it to line his coats. This would make moiré 'fashionable' and the factories would start churning it out for all sorts of other purposes. The unpredictability of the market made it difficult to make money in this business, but because there was an element of gambling and indefinable ingenuity involved, it attracted increasing recruits. In 1850 the *Bottin* listed 158 couturiers in Paris; by 1872 there were 684, by 1895 1,636; and these excluded small independent dressmakers. In 1895 six of these firms employed between 400 and 600 workers each, and fifty others around 100 each. France as a whole then had 400,000 workers exclusively employed in making women's clothes.

There was an enormous difference between the sort of garments which were produced at either end of this business. 'Haute couture' meant the production of individual items for particular customers, which cost (at the turn of the century) from 800 to 1,500 francs. Only 37 per cent of its purchasers were French. French inventiveness in clothes design was largely sustained by foreign admiration (as art in general was): it was admired because it was well made, but also because it was foreign. The cost to the couturier in wages for one of these expensive dresses was usually only about 150 francs; but he had to spend a great deal of money on the paraphernalia of luxury, on elegant showrooms in the most expensive parts of Paris, and on well-advertised high living. At this time, the average working dressmaker made

[1] Gaston Worth, *La Couture et la confection des vêtements de femme* (1895).

only 2 francs a day: it was this kind of person who produced the mass of clothes for the French market.[1] But the Germans were more efficient at mass production and imports played an increasing role. The notion that Frenchwomen were universally well dressed or elegant is a myth that cannot be sustained by what is known about price-cutting and savings on quality perpetrated by the producers. For the age in which women still made their own clothes, or had them individually made, was on the point of disappearing by the end of the nineteenth century. There were then still no firms manufacturing women's underwear—that was still hand-made—but the corset industry had become very largely mechanised. In 1848 about 10,000 workers were employed in making corsets; by 1889 that number had doubled; the money spent on corsets rose from 11,000,000 to 55,000,000 francs between 1878 and 1889, which was the period when mechanisation transformed the industry: only a quarter of this sum now went on made-to-measure corsets. In the 1830s a corset cost between 8 and 15 francs (depending on whether it had whalebone in it or not); in the 1850s they were being imported from England at 60 centimes each. In 1839 they were considered dangerous and banned from the Paris Industrial Exhibition, even though 'safe', 'painless' and rubber ones had been invented. But that made no difference and in 1902 the ministry of education vainly forbade schoolgirls to wear them.[2] The mountains of feathers, flowers and fruit—largely manufactured in Paris—that women wore increased enormously as the masses abandoned bonnets and kerchiefs and took to parading in hats. The importance of hats as status symbols became such that neither men nor women dared show themselves in the street without one, and of a kind appropriate to the rank to which they aspired (this was one of the ambivalent contributions of the early Third Republic to visible equality). In the Second Empire the *Code de la mode* said that fashion consisted in 'imprinting the cachet of one's personal fantasy' on the clothes one wore: the problem was to find or make individual ornaments, and to avoid the ruses of manufacturers who produced cloth stiffened

[1] Cf. Henriette Vanier, *La Mode et ses métiers. Frivolités et luttes de classes 1830–70* (1960).
[2] See *Les Dessous élégants* (founded 1901), the organ of the Union of Corset Manufacturers; Dehesdin, op. cit. 525–36.

with glue and made to shine with sugar, which disintegrated in the rain.[1] Women took to wearing ready-made dresses roughly fifty years later than men adopted ready-made suits. By 1930 most Frenchwomen bought their clothes ready made, because these were now available not just in department stores but from a whole host of small shops; manufacturers no longer produced thousands of copies of the same style but limited themselves to a few, and besides they created new styles every week; improvements in dyeing techniques after the First World War made it possible for the colours of expensive cloths to be reproduced for the masses.[2]

It was these technical improvements that made possible the acceleration of fashion, with a new style every season. The new styles were of course very slight amendments, but only a united effort by manufacturers selling something different each year could force women to change their appearance. The top couturiers at first fought against this tendency, before exploiting it. The next great innovator in fashion after Worth, Paul Poiret, reiterated Worth's injunction that women should wear what suited them: he was horrified by the question he was increasingly asked, 'What would next year's fashion be?'. He rose to fame in the employment of Worth's two sons, but they took him on to produce a simple range of clothes. Jean Worth loved making dresses out of rich materials, held together with jewels; his brother Gaston, who looked after the commercial side of the business, argued that with the coming of the twentieth century even princesses sometimes travelled by bus, and they needed appropriate clothes. 'We find ourselves', he said, 'in the situation of a great restaurant, which would prefer to serve only truffles. But we need to create a bar producing fried potatoes.' Poiret, who soon set up on his own to pursue this revolution in his own way, won fame with his kimono-coat, which introduced the Oriental influence into ordinary clothes. In 1903 he declared the abolition of petticoats, then of corsets, then of false hair, then of hats with leaves, flowers, ribbons, fruits and plumes, each decree sounding the death knell of an industry and producing protests and delegations from them. Poiret was not trying to

[1] H. Despaigne, *Le Code de la mode* (1866), 14, 30.
[2] Germaine Deschamps, *La Crise dans les industries du vêtement et de la mode à Paris pendant la période de 1930 à 1937* (1938), 1–20.

'liberate' women: though he revealed their natural shapes more, he put them into sheath dresses in which they could not walk, and he bared their backs so that they froze. He declared that fashion was a 'provocation to good sense'; its function was essentially sexual, and Paris was the leading city in fashion because it allowed the freest development of 'the sensual and voluptuous life'. But he did not expect women to follow his models slavishly: his designs were only 'suggestions' which each woman should adapt to her own personality. Certain of his suggestions were rejected: he insisted (before 1914) that the culotte would inevitably become a dominant fashion, because the scope for varying the skirt had been exhausted; he tried to make women wear really bright colours, but they resisted this. He was the first couturier to tour America, which had always played an essential part in the prosperity of his trade; he was hailed there as the King of Fashion; but he was soon dethroned by the capitalist forces which were transforming the clothes business. He chided American women for lacking imagination and individuality; he deplored their readiness to buy a model exactly as he made it, whereas Frenchwomen would demand it altered and made up in a different colour and cloth. American women, he said, kept their schoolgirl mentality all their lives, so that they looked like a giant orphanage in uniform. Their manufacturers took advantage of this, bought last year's success from Paris and reproduced it *ad nauseam*. Fashion was thus reduced to simple annual changes. The French couturiers saw their creations plagiarised and mutilated; they were reduced to selling their names to be stuck on stockings and handbags and even clothes, in the manufacture of which they had no hand. Poiret's bankruptcy, and his subordination to a group of financiers who knew nothing about fashion, made public the constraints that shackled individual genius. The great depression completed the massacre of the couturiers. After the war, when new alliances between manufacturers and designers developed, the former were in the saddle: Christian Dior was financed by the textile manufacturer Boussac. Dior showed that a single Frenchman could still make women all over the world throw away their old clothes, but this involved the co-operation and self-interest of a vast industry. French supremacy in female fashion was partly a legend, fostered by the women's magazines. Only a small proportion of the designers' fashions penetrated to the masses, and that was through the mediation of capitalists, whose history is still unwritten.[1]

The relationship between ideas of female beauty, fashion and the desire for comfortable clothes also needs careful investigation. It is very difficult to know whether there was an ideal woman in popular taste, or how this evolved, because virtually all evidence about this comes from writers, whose taste is not representative. The courtiers of the eighteenth century seem to have admired majestic women, but the intellectuals found merit in less classical forms, in irregular and rebellious features that hinted at sarcasm and wit. Under the Revolution, grace, innocence, Olympian dignity were all praised with confusing variety. The romantics did not always fall for thin, pale, worried and tubercular women; and it is too simple to say that the mother or matron, mistress of the household, was the type of the rest of the century: it was just that there were far more portraits, in paint and in photography, to unbalance all comparisons. Novelists were surprisingly imprecise in saying what exactly made their heroines beautiful. The two main changes were probably the triumph of the thin over the fat woman, of which the healthy, sporty type of the twentieth century was only one variation, and the prolongation of the years of a woman's life during which she might be considered attractive. Men used to say that woman was God's finest creation, but, like a flower, she was beautiful only for a brief moment (which was when a man married her). They implied, and also wrote, that most women were ugly.[2] Women clearly believed this. At the same time as the masses became obsessed by Paris fashions in clothes, they also began to make increasing use of cosmetics. The playwright Feydeau's father wrote in 1873 that if you took a walk in the Bois de Boulogne, or the Champs Élysées, or even on the Boulevards, you would find that at least half the young women were heavily made up.[3] It was fashionable then to dye your hair

[1] Paul Poiret, *En habillant l'époque* (1930); Lucien François [pseud. of Lucien t'Serstevens], *Comment un nom devient une griffe* (1961); Bernard Roscho, *The Rag Race. How New York and Paris run the breakneck business of dressing American women* (New York, 1963).

[2] Marcel Brunschvig, *La Femme et la beauté* (1929).

[3] Ernest Feydeau, *L'Art de plaire. Études d'hygiène, de goût et de toilettes, dédiées aux jolies femmes de tous les pays du monde* (1873), 113.

colours known as 'egg yolk' and 'cow's tail'. The aristocrats of the eighteenth century wore wigs; the masses at the beginning of the twentieth century built up their heads with false hair similarly, though with less show of artificiality: imports of hair into France were rising at such a speed that they doubled between 1902 and 1906, reaching about a third of a million kilogrammes. 'Institutes of Beauty' now sprang up which undertook to rejuvenate women who feared they were losing their charms.[1] Women, in short, expended more and more effort in trying to be different from what they were, so that the ideal of feminine beauty, far from being an inspiration, was, at least for women, a source of constant anxiety.[2] Their main worry, according to a doctor who ran an advisory service for a women's magazine in the 1880s, was the size of their bust (40 per cent of the letters he received were about this), how best to make themselves up (25 per cent) and how to deal with hair in the wrong place (10 per cent). In this period women were willing to spend large sums at the hairdresser's: 5 francs was the price of an 'ordinary' styling, 15–20 francs for arranging the hair for a ball, with flowers and feathers, 20–30 francs for a *coiffure poudrée*, 30–40 francs for a 'historic' style and 40–50 for a *coiffure de genre pour travestissement*.[3]

The great attraction of fashion was that it diverted attention from the insoluble problems of beauty and provided an easy way —which money could buy—of at any rate approximating outwardly to a simply stated, easily reproduced, ideal of beauty, however temporary that ideal. That was why women bore with the tyrants of fashion, even when they maligned them. Beside the severe prescriptions of traditional dress, these tyrants almost represented freedom. The women who protested, and those who objected to the main burden of fashion being placed upon their sex, had little success. This was partly because the battle was not a straightforward one between comfort or equality and the fashion industry. The great designers were liberators also, in their own way. Even the crinoline represented a liberation when it was invented, because it dispensed with the heavy petticoats,

---

[1] Alfred Capus, *L'Institut de Bequté* (1913).
[2] Henri Lavent, *Le Peuple et la beauté* (1902); Eugène Montfort, *La Beauté moderne* (1902); Émile Bayard, *L'Art de reconnaître la beauté du corps humain* (1926).
[3] A. Coffignon, *Les Coulisses de la mode* (1888), 19, 30.

whose number had progressively increased. Many of the decrees of fashion appeared, at the time, to be improvements and clever ideas. Efforts by women to wear the same clothes as men were repeatedly repressed. The prefect of police, in an ordinance of the Year IX, 'informed that many women dress as men', laid it down that they must get an individual authorisation from him to do so, which would be given only for reasons of health. In 1848, a women's club was formed demanding that the skirt should be replaced by breeches (and that men should do house-work at least three times a week). No one in France, however, followed the American Bloomerists, and it was ultimately sport that enabled women to abandon skirts. But by then trousers had already, after a long struggle, been accepted as a form of female underclothing. They were worn at balls (as the *Moniteur de la mode* reported in 1852) 'to guard against the indiscretions of the waltz and the polka'; the *Conseiller des dames* published a pattern in 1853 for 'ladies who travel'; and *La Lingerie parisienne* (1854) 'at the request of many of our readers' produced a pattern also, defining the *pantalon* as 'a garment women must never be with-out, especially in winter'. The crinoline finally made trousers essential, because when getting through confined spaces, it had to be partially dismantled. *La France élégante* complained in 1857 'Our clothes are becoming like men's: we wear round hats, turned-down collars, musketeer's cuffs; nothing is missing, not even trousers for many of us.' But on this occasion the fashion did not last: the peasants and workers could not afford this fancy style; a doctor said he recognised them by their dirty knees.

One should not too easily associate this fashion with sexual equality, any more than one should assume that short hair 'liberated' women. The first occasion on which women cut their hair short, wearing it *à la Titus*, was during the First Empire; the Eton crop (1927) compelled women to use the services of hairdressers far more often.[1] More important perhaps was the revolution of Coco Chanel (1883–1971) who during the First World War invented a new elegance for the masses by ennobling cheap materials and producing fashionable, unornamented comfortable clothes, originally out of jersey, which no one wanted and which she picked up for a song. In 1921 she naturalised

[1] Laure-Paul Flobert, *La Femme et le costume masculin* (Lille, 1911); Pierre Dufay, *Le Pantalon féminin* (1906).

the Russian peasant's blouse (the *roubaschka*), in 1926–31 she pushed English fashions with a 'resolutely masculine cut'. But she was something of an outsider—an illegitimate daughter of a pedlar, who began as a maid servant until picked up by the garrison officers of Moulins. She then had a series of foreign lovers, all of whom were orphans like herself—Arthur Capel, an Englishman said to be an illegitimate son of Pereire, the second duke of Westminster, the Grand Duke Dmitri and German aristocrats under Vichy. It was only in the 1950s that her styles really caught on, and above all in America. The new fashion of dressing down was thus invented by women and followed later by men.[1] That shows fashion coming full circle—begun as part of the rat race produced by the ending of barriers to social climbing, and taking on a new direction when social climbing ceased to be a major preoccupation.[2] How far people liked what they wore is a different matter.

*Painting*

The painting of this period is, in popular belief, distinguished by the much publicised divorce that took place between public taste and artistic genius. The painters who had the most success-ful careers, like Bouguereau and Meissonier, are now remem-bered only by art historians, while those who are now considered to be among the greatest artists of all time, like Manet and Cézanne, had much trouble selling their works. From Impres-sionism to Cubism, every new school was greeted with almost universal hostility. To be a painter seemed, in most cases, to involve a rebellion against 'bourgeois' society and a condemna-tion of its sentimentality, hypocrisy and materialism. The whole question of the relationship of art and society seems to require consideration in new terms.

However, this contrast of the modern with the good old times is superficial. In the first place, the breach between the artists

[1] Edmonde Charles-Roux, *L'Irrégulière, ou mon itinéraire Chanel* (1974).

[2] For an attempt at a statistical analysis of fashion, see Jane Richardson and A. L. Kroeber, *Three Centuries of Women's Dress Fashions. A Quantitative Analysis* (U.C. Berkeley and L.A. 1940). Cf. Raoul de La Grasserie, *Du rôle psychologique et sociologique du monde et de la mode* (Bologna, 1902, by a judge of Rennes). The standard general history is still James Laver, *Taste and Fashion from the French Revolution to the Present Day* (1937, new edition 1945). Cf. Giselle d'Assailly, *Les 15 révolutions de la mode* (1968).

of this period and their contemporaries appears to be pro-
founder than it was, because of the intervention of a new factor
quite extraneous to art, but which became a most important
influence on attitudes towards art, namely the newspaper. Art
now received more attention than ever before. To this extent,
art—in all its forms—attracted more interest, even if some manifestations of it pleased only a small circle of initiates. The newspapers introduced far greater polemic into the discussion of art
than had ever been seen—as they did into every sphere of
activity; but they should not be taken as accurate reflections of
public opinion.[1] The division of artists into conflicting schools
was to a certain extent a journalistic simplification, and partly
a mystification by artists adopting literary and political techniques. It will be some time before the history of art in this
period can finally be seen in terms which are less clear cut, and
the dramatic battles, into which journalists and critics have tried
to condense it, can be appreciated as only one side and one part
of the story.

The role of art had become more complex in any case, if only
because more people were involved in it. The Salons (the official
annual art exhibitions) of the eighteenth century had generally
exhibited only three or four hundred paintings a year; but
during the first half of the nineteenth century they expanded to
include over 2,000 paintings, and by 1864 they had reached
3,478 a year. The first open Salon, in 1791, at which anybody
who wished could exhibit, without approval from official judges,
showed 794 works; the second one, in 1848, showed 5,180. The
latter figure constituted the production of 1,900 painters. During
the next century, numbers increased still further, though the
break-up of the Salon system makes it difficult to say by how
much. In 1885, 3,851 artists submitted their work to the Salon.[2]
In 1954 (and again in 1962) about 11,500 people declared themselves to the census to be artists;[3] and the Salons (fragmented

[1] See chapter 11.

[2] 1,243 of these artists were successful in having their works exhibited; but note
that 389 of these were foreigners, Americans being most numerous (98), then
Belgians (47), English (34), Germans (31).

[3] 1954: 7,600 painters (2,260 of them women); 2,220 teachers of painting
(equally men and women) and 1,700 sculptors and engravers (of whom 260 were
women). In 1962 only 2,595 of the artists said they earned more than half their
income from art.

into over thirty different ones) now exhibited the work of roughly 4,500 painters. The expansion of painting as a profession occurred about a century later than that of literature (the number of books published, as has been seen, quadrupled in the eighteenth century, trebled in the early nineteenth and then remained roughly steady). Painting therefore grew under the scrutiny of a sister or rival art, which, with unceasing comments and criticisms, made its existence infinitely more complicated.

The audience for painting moreover did not evolve in simple correlation with this expansion. The Salons had quickly become a much-enjoyed popular entertainment, in which all classes partook. In 1884 238,000 people visited the Salon, in 1887 as many as 562,000 in the course of the fifty-five days which Salons usually lasted. The Salons were free on Sundays and roughly half the visitors entered in this way. In 1887, however, there were 8,612 people who paid 5 francs to gain admission on special days (instead of the 1 or 2 francs normally charged) and who might have been the core of the connoisseurs, or the snobs. Such figures should not mislead into conclusions about the popularity of art. Art exhibitions were decidedly less popular than other exhibitions, as was revealed already in 1855: the Paris International Exposition of that year was so arranged that those wishing to see the fine arts in it had to go to a separate building: whereas 4,180,000 visited the industrial sections, only 982,000 visited the fine arts exhibition.[1] These are impressive numbers, but they already show over three-quarters of the visitors refusing to look at the paintings. Moreover, art did not enjoy the same popularity in the provinces as it did in Paris. Not even the largest provincial cities managed to get over 10,000 visitors into any of their art exhibitions in 1887, when—in a single day—the Paris Salon of that year drew in about 50,000. The Moulins Art Exhibition (held in conjunction with the *Concours agricole*) in 1885, included 275 'proprietors' among its subscribers, but also 164 small shop keepers and artisans and 24 clerks. However, when provincial art exhibitions were organised on their own and not as part of some such regional show, they always got a low attendance and were almost exclusively middle-class affairs. After 1918, and more noticeably after 1945, two new

[1] *Exposition universelle de 1867 à Paris: rapports du Jury internationale publiés sous la direction de M. Michel Chevalier* (1868), introduction to vol. 1.

developments altered this situation. The great increase in travel put museums and historical monuments on the holiday itinerary and a new class of person—the idle tourist—came to look at pictures, even though he was very often a person who never set foot in his own local museum. The number of small exhibitions increased, but they came to rely on a restricted, predominantly middle-class clientele, with a strong contingent of leisured house-wives. But despite all the increase in leisure, only 4·4 per cent of French people, questioned in 1974, claimed to paint or sculpt as a hobby—a figure which needs to be compared with the 15·4 per cent who said they played a musical instrument and the 49·4 per cent of men who said photography was a hobby. Art lovers tended to look at pictures much more than actually to paint themselves, whereas music lovers entertained themselves more than they went to concerts. In this survey, 18·6 per cent said they had been to at least one art exhibition that year, but 70 per cent said they had read at least one book, and 51 per cent had been to the cinema, on average thirteen times. Despite their new affluence, almost half the French population, according to this survey, had no pictures or reproductions with pretensions of any kind to art in their homes; about 20 per cent had repro-ductions; about 26 per cent had original paintings by amateurs, which shows a wide distribution of the production of the hobby-ists, 23·5 per cent had posters and 8 per cent had paintings by contemporary professional artists (but this last category were to be found four times more frequently in Paris than in the provinces).[1] Those interested in art were always a minority, and the arrival of unorthodox and 'incomprehensible' art probably did not make all that much difference to the size of this minority: academic art had often demanded erudition and imagination for the deciphering of its allegories and significance. The impor-tant point is that the growth of education did not dramatically increase the audience for art. On the contrary, the effect of mass schooling was that art became part of that rather indefinable 'culture' which the schools did not really impart to their pupils, but for the appreciation of which a great deal of schooling seemed to be required. Culture, and therefore art, was what highly educated people alone knew how to enjoy. Museums

[1] Secrétariat d'État à la Culture, *Pratiques culturelles des Français* (Dec. 1974), 41, 100–13.

(which of course had never been particularly popular) remained the preserve of the highly educated classes. Thus in the 1960s, only 1 per cent of visitors to museums in France were peasants, only 4 per cent workers and 5 per cent artisans and shopkeepers, but 45 per cent were 'upper class'. Forty per cent of those who went to museums had studied Latin, a third had the *baccalauréat*, a quarter had university degrees.[1]

There may at first sight appear to be a contradiction between this monopolisation of art by the most literate classes (whose training was essentially verbal) and the alienation of the masses, who were distinguished precisely by their preference for the pictorial over the literary, but who confined themselves to the illustrated magazines and newspapers. This is a question of definitions. Popular illustrations were not classified as art, any more than popular novels were accepted as literature. Taste implied contempt; refined taste could not, by definition, be shared by the masses. Exclusiveness became an essential feature in the appreciation of art; and no serious effort was made to interest the masses in art, to accompany the compulsory spread of literacy. The attitude of schools towards art went through four different stages. Until 1853 they ignored it. Art was then introduced for the first time into the syllabus of secondary education, under the influence of the philosopher Ravaisson. Basing himself, as he believed, on the doctrines of Leonardo da Vinci, Ravaisson insisted that the schools should not teach rough drawing and should not adopt any hasty methods. The aim of art education was to 'train the eye', to develop taste, to show people how to recognise the ideal in ordinary objects. Children were therefore required to draw the human face, so as to study the different emotions. On the principle that they should move from the simple to the complex, they were asked to draw parts of the face first, like the nose or ear, and only when they had learnt to do these could they proceed to drawing a complete face. They were first given prints and photographs from which to copy their drawings, then bits of antique sculpture, and only when they were well advanced were they allowed to draw the human face directly from nature. This method not surprisingly created too many difficulties, and there were few teachers

---

[1] Pierre Bourdieu and Alain Darbel, *L'Amour de l'art. Les musées d'art européens et leur public* (2nd edition, 1969), 36.

available in any case to implement it.[1] In 1878 it was therefore replaced by a totally different system, known as the 'geometrical method', as opposed to Ravaisson's 'intuitive' one. The inspiration behind the reform was Eugène Guillaume—a painter this time rather than a philosopher—but a painter conscious that he was living in the age of science.[2] He saw drawing as above all a science; the purpose of teaching it was not to stimulate the personality but to enable children to reproduce their models accurately; and it was the mathematics teachers who were required to teach drawing. Nature and landscapes were to be the very last things pupils would be allowed to draw: first they had to learn to draw in two dimensions, then to produce drawings of cones and cubes. Quite often, the pupils were not even allowed to copy real-life cubes, but only photographs or drawings of cubes; but little geometrical objects, made of paper, plaster or wire, were sometimes distributed as the principal equipment for art lessons. Primary schools never got beyond this stage, but more senior children were then allowed to graduate to copying vases and bits of architecture, usually antique. In theory, the drawing of the human head and of animals was to come next, the study of the human figure after that, and landscapes last. There was a mixture therefore of the antique—for most models were plasters of old statues—and of science. The inspectors who implemented this programme said there was a need to develop 'the feeling for art and the ability to experience the emotions that the sensations of sight can procure' but the ability to measure was more important, for science was the basis of modern civilisation. Traditional literary methods were applied to art: the 'dictated drawing' was the equivalent of dictated prose: the teacher drew on the blackboard and the pupil copied. The intuitive method was condemned as anarchic because children had had their exercises corrected individually. Now 'collective teaching' meant everybody in the class did the same thing and marks were given immediately after the class.[3] But geometric art

---

[1] F. Ravaisson, *De l'enseignement du dessin dans les lycées* (1854).

[2] Eugène Guillaume (1822–1905) won the prix de Rome in 1845 with his 'Thésée retrouvant l'épée de son père sur un rocher'. He became a member of the Academy of Fine Arts in 1862, and was appointed Director of Fine Arts by Jules Ferry in 1879.

[3] Eugène Guillaume and Jules Pillet, *L'Enseignement du dessin* (1889); J. J. Pillet and P. Steck, *L'Enseignement du dessin en France dans les établissements universitaires* (Berne and Paris, 1904).

was soon attacked, first by industrialists who complained that it did not produce good draughtsmen—its purely practical aims were not fulfilled—and secondly by educationists, in the name of the teachings of child psychology. The fourth stage, which got going with the reform of 1909, was that of the 'active' method, inspired this time by Gaston Quénioux, professor at the School of Decorative Arts in Paris. He argued that the aim of art education should not be the teaching of technical skill but rather the development of personal impressions: the teacher should give higher marks for sincerity than for exact execution; the child's art must be creative in its own terms; it must be an expression of its joy in life. Quénioux protested against the precedence that French education gave to writing over drawing, saying that drawing came naturally to children, and they should, until the age of nine, be allowed to draw as they pleased. They should not be given antique busts to copy, but should be allowed to draw what they liked. Later, they might be helped to observe, and at the age of fifteen perhaps be allowed to copy great paintings; but art lessons should be not the inculcation of a skill so much as a contribution to the general increase of happiness.[1] One should not imagine that the schools in fact switched from one style of teaching to another, as the official instructions did. There were never enough art teachers; the training programmes for them were rudimentary. One of the men associated with Quénioux in his reform, Pottier, who was a keeper at the Louvre museum, said that he himself had never had any art lessons of any kind at school. Many teachers did not like first the monopolisation of art by the mathematicians, and then the idea that children should be allowed to do what they pleased, in contradiction with the schools' general emphasis on discipline. More investigation is needed, however, of the effects of this teaching, not simply on the receptivity of people at large, but also on painters; for hitherto, only the training of the art schools has attracted the attention of historians.[2]

Art in ordinary schools had two faces. On the one hand, until

---

[1] L. Guébin, *L'Enseignement du dessin* (1908), article by Quénioux 63–89; P. Buisson, *Nouveau dictionnaire de pédagogie et d'instruction primaire* (1911), article by Quénioux under 'Dessin'; Marcel Braunschvig, *L'Art et l'enfant. Essai sur l'éducation esthétique* (1907).

[2] For a link, see Horace Lecoq de Boisbaudran (who was Rodin's teacher), *Coup d'œil sur l'enseignement des Beaux-Arts* (1782).

well into the twentieth century, it was taught in an abstract technical way which may, in a few cases, have prepared pupils for a certain kind of artistic appreciation; but it was perhaps only when freedom was allowed to children in their art lessons that they could begin to approve an art which stressed personal expression before all else. But on the other hand the decoration of schools evolved in a totally separate way and with a different chronology. In the first half of the nineteenth century, there were very few pictures on the walls of schools beyond portraits of the kings of France, 'Amusing Arithmetic' and geographical maps. In the early infant schools, the pictures were kept in a folder and brought out only for the appropriate lessons; they were usually too small for the whole class to see. The break comes with the Paris Exhibition of 1867, which had a remarkable section of teaching materials. The invention of lithography, and the new catchphrase *la leçon des choses*, stimulated publishers to produce a new range of posters for schools. E. Deyrolle began (1871) publishing a successful series on Animals and Industry, trying to represent aspects of nature and of the world, with the stress on accuracy, in colour, and as far as possible in life-size. He argued that children loved to learn about natural science but had difficulty in finding suitable pictures; they must be given colourful pictures which appealed to them and did not tire them. In 1879 Hachette followed with Pictures for Schools, producing six years later a series of a hundred pictures illustrating the history of France, for only 11 fr. 40. Delagrave in 1888 published his *Modern Languages Taught in Pictures*. A government commission was established to organise the artistic decoration of schools, to develop the taste and aesthetic curiosity of children. But a special children's art developed which became too concerned with instilling moral lessons. The first works distributed by the government were *L'Hiver* by Henri Rivière, *Little Red Riding Hood* by Willette and *Alsace* by Moreau-Nélaton. Mademoiselle Dufau then produced a series with titles such as *Love Your Parents*, *Courage is Better than Force*, *Co-operation*, etc. Visual taste always came low in the priorities of the schools, long behind didactic morals. The art teacher was too humble to contribute to the appearance of the classroom. The art lesson was completely divorced from the rest of the school's activities.[1]

[1] J. Pichard, 'Les Images éducatives et leur utilisation dans l'enseignement au

Museums, where people could freely look at works of art, were an essentially modern phenomenon; and in this period they were an inadequate intermediary between art and the public. Until 1789 there were virtually no public museums outside Paris. It was the Revolution which made public the royal collection in the Louvre, and it was Napoleon who in 1801 created the provincial museums, to show works of art for which the Louvre had no room. The state undertook a regular programme of buying both old and new art, to build up these new institutions, which already numbered over 100 in the 1880s and over 700 by 1945. Benefactions and bequests from collectors became an established custom. The state and the municipalities became by far the largest owners of works of art. But the museums were not inspired by any proselytising zeal; they saw their role more as one of conservation than exhibition, and indeed they could exhibit only a small proportion of what they accumulated. Provincial collections grew up on a rather haphazard basis, though two principles influenced them: that the works of painters born in the region, and of representatives, as far as possible, of every school and period, should be included, even if only by a single minor work. The untutored eye would be more likely to be confused rather than inspired by the fragmentary nature of most museums. The salaries offered to the staff were small, so most curators were amateurs, often part-time. It is not surprising that the provincial museums were called, at the turn of the century, 'prisons of art'. There were then museum curators who thought that Meissonier and Brascassat were still alive, and who recorded the dates of Eugène Boudin as 'unknown'. The museum of Vaucouleurs (Meuse), founded in 1893, clothed its replicas of ancient statues in paper underpants. The museum of Besançon was occasionally used as a market-place. Comparatively few people studied the painting exhibited with very great care: in the first decade of the twentieth century, the museum of Dijon sold only forty copies of its catalogue a year, which was perhaps because this was incomplete and out of date, but Grenoble, which also had excellent collections, sold only 125. However, entrance fees varied, ranging from one franc to nothing, to make it possible for large

19ᵉ siècle' (unpublished, Centre Audio-Visuel, 1961); Bibliothèque Nationale, Cabinet des Estampes, files of old pictures used in schools.

numbers to visit museums.[1] The choice available broadened far
beyond traditional painting. In 1818 a Museum of Living
Artists was founded in the Palais du Luxembourg (which moved
to the Orangerie in 1886 and which became the Museum of
Modern Art in 1937).[2] In 1879 Ferry established the Museum
of French Monuments, which came to illustrate the whole
history of sculpture. The Lyonnais industrialist, Émile Guimet,
founded the museum bearing his name, as a centre for the study
of oriental religions, ten years later; and in 1896 Henri Cer-
nuschi, a friend of Gambetta, of Maltese origin, bequeathed
his collection of Chinese art to the nation. The duchesse de
Galliera's collections formed the nucleus of the Museum of
Decorative Arts (1877), and the Museum of Popular Arts and
Traditions (1937) preserved the masterpieces of peasant craftsmanship.[3] How much was spent on museums has not been
properly calculated, though it has been claimed that the Third
Republic's expenditure on acquisitions was roughly one-third
that of London's National Gallery.[4]

It was probably through reproductions that most people discovered painting, and the masses had a well-developed taste for
prints, which went a long way back, but it was a taste for
traditional, well-known and well-liked subjects. In the nineteenth century, print makers were still selling barely modernised
versions of seventeenth-century drawings. *Crédit est mort* which
many cafés still exhibited in 1914 was a print that had hardly
altered since it first appeared in 1720. J. C. Pellerin (1756–1836)
created a highly successful children's print business at Épinal,
which turned out about seventeen million prints during the
Second Empire, many of them making use of traditional
material. The print pedlar, who toured the countryside with
his pictures fastened to a string by clothes-pegs, was an important source of entertainment.[5] But in the second half of the

---

[1] Ministère de l'instruction publique, *Rapport de la commission chargée d'étudier . . .
l'organisation des musées de province* (25 Oct. 1907), by Henry Lapauze (1908).

[2] This exhibited 149 paintings in 1849, 240 in 1875.

[3] *Arts, musées et curiosité en France* (1946) for a list of museums with descriptions;
J. Comyns Carr, *L'Art en France* (1887), a review of museums, by a correspondent
of the *Manchester Guardian*.

[4] Jeanne Laurent, *La République et les Beaux-Arts* (1955), 29.

[5] Musée National des Arts et Traditions Populaires, *Cinq siècles d'imagerie française*
(1973); J. Mistler, *Épinal et l'imagerie populaire* (1961); for comic strips, see F. F.
Empaytaz and J. Peignot, *Les Copains de votre enfance* (1963).

century, the original print came increasingly to be classified as a rare work of art,[1] and the masses turned to the newspapers and to photographic reproductions. A pioneer in the popularisation of these was Adolphe Braun (1811–77), who for long had the exclusive right to reproduce the paintings in the Louvre. He had set up as a photographer in Mulhouse in 1848 and had won a reputation with the photographs of flowers that he published in six albums, originally intending them as models for textile printing; but he then turned to photographing paintings in museums all over Europe, using plates a yard square or more in size. By 1867 he was employing 100 workers. His catalogue of 1896 contained about 20,000 different reproductions, which he sold for 15 francs each (40 × 50 cm). Every year he added a couple of hundred pictures from the Salon, so that in 1907 he was able to offer nearly 9,000 modern works painted over the previous thirty years by over a thousand different artists. His catalogues are probably more representative of what pictures the masses were conscious of, than the catalogues of museums. He offered about 800 different reproductions of Raphael, nearly 400 each of Leonardo, Rubens and Rembrandt, about 300 each of Michelangelo and Holbein, 250 of Dürer and Van Dyck, 200 of Titian. Among the moderns, Corot and Millet were the favourites, with about 150 each, Puvis had 40 paintings and 150 drawings, Paul Baudry about 100, Charles Chaplin (1825–91) about 80, Ingres, David, Bouguereau and Chenavard about 60, Meissonier, Rosa Bonheur and Delacroix about 50, Degas 5, Monet 2, Manet 1. It was the Germans who were the pioneers in the reproduction of the Impressionists: the first illustrated books about them were published in Germany from 1903 onwards, with photographs by the Frenchman Édouard Druet. The popularisation of the Impressionists in France began only in 1926 when Les Albums d'art Druet started coming out (the first was on Cézanne), but this was still in black and white. The firm of Braun—now in its fourth generation, but employing Georges Besson, a friend of many avant-garde painters—began publishing collections of Impressionist pictures between the world wars, but it was only after 1945 that they got round to volumes on Monet and Manet. The public in general were thus not exposed to the

[1] Jean Laran, *Inventaire du fonds français après 1800, Cabinet des Estampes* (1930 ff.) lists the half-million nineteenth-century prints in the Bibliothèque Nationale.

Impressionists until about half a century after they had died.[1]
To what extent these painters appeared on postcards (which
were first produced in the early 1870s) is uncertain. The whole
history of reproduction remains obscure, partly because the
sources are not easily accessible.[2] But it would be worth investigating what painters were most frequently reproduced in the
press. In *L'Illustration*, for example, Cézanne did not appear till
1905; Manet was not mentioned by it before 1883 and it was
only in 1929 that he was given a major article. Bouguereau, by
contrast, was written about in this journal twenty-eight times
between 1853 and 1905, but has had only one mention since
then. Puvis, Rodin, Roll and Paul Thomas were regular names,
but the journal had not, in 1932, yet heard of Seurat or Signac.[3]

Buying reproductions has become an activity, predominantly,
of the educated. A survey, published in 1973, reported that 58
per cent of buyers possessed the *baccalauréat*, and only 7 per cent
of them had got no further than primary school. The Impressionists are now the most popular painters: when asked to name
ten painters, Renoir and Van Gogh are the two most frequently
mentioned, followed by Monet and Picasso. Three-quarters of
the sample could recognise a painting by Renoir and Van Gogh,
but only a third could recognise Rubens, El Greco or Corot, and
only a tenth Poussin or Klee. People, however, have their own
reasons for buying one reproduction rather than another: colour
counts most, and the subject-matter next; great weight is always
placed on harmonisation with furniture, curtains and walls;
some bring cuttings of wallpaper with them. It is only the highly
educated who ignore these considerations, and it is only they
who choose abstract paintings. Nudes are bought for bedrooms
and still lifes for dining-rooms. Relatively uneducated and older
people like landscapes and flowers, and it is for that reason that
they like the Dutch painters and some Impressionists equally.

[1] Éts. Braun et Cⁱᵉ, *Un Siècle de technique* [1948]; Ad. Braun et Cⁱᵉ, *Catalogue
général des reproductions inaltérables au charbon* (1896); id., *Galerie contemporaine* (1905
and 1907). Julius Meier-Graefe, *Manet* (Berlin, 1903), *Cézanne* (Munich, 1910);
Les Albums d'art Druet, *Cézanne* (1926); Éditions Rieder, *Maîtres de l'art moderne*
(1925): 1. Toulouse-Lautrec, 2. William Blake, 3. William Turner.

[2] For the difficulties see Marcel Neveux, *Le Dépôt légal des productions des arts
graphiques* (Paris law thesis, 1934); 'Centenaire de la carte postale 1871–1970',
*Le Vieux Papier* (Nov. 1970), fasc. 238; Jules Adeline, *Les Arts de reproduction vul-
garisés* (n.d.); L. Tarible, *Les Industries graphiques* (5th edition, 1952).

[3] *L'Illustration*, Index 1843–1932.

Middle-aged people with a secondary education, or university graduates who are children of uneducated parents, tend to like the old masters, some moderns such as Utrillo and Vlaminck, but only Buffet among the contemporaries. It is above all the young, highly educated people from cultured backgrounds who like 'modern' painting—beginning with the Post-Impressionists. The decisive factor seems to be not education as such, nor wealth, but the tastes acquired in childhood, and here the influence of mothers has been shown to be noticeably greater than that of fathers. It is the cultured mother who passes on taste for *avant-garde* art.[1] Another psychologist, investigating the taste of French and American children, found no significant difference according to the social origins of parents; children as a whole preferred realistic painting, but American children, who received a free kind of art education, were noticeably less inclined than French ones to reject abstract painting as they grew older. The French working class, it is true, continued to value realism in painting in adult life, as well as technique and colour; whereas educated people gave purely subjective replies, which merely affirmed that they liked or disliked a painting, they preferred to talk about expressiveness and atmosphere rather than about subject-matter.[2] It is obvious therefore that it is quite impossible to talk about the taste of a period, without explaining whether one is referring to the taste of *avant-garde*, traditional or Sunday painters, to a particular generation, class or group, to a particular region, to museum visitors or the readers of the popular newspapers. Attempts to make Impressionism, for example, a reflection of economic or social changes, or, even more boldly, of contemporaneous philosophical trends, are completely misleading and simplistic.[3]

The popular visual art of the nineteenth century was photography, just as that of the twentieth was to be the cinema. This had a profound effect on attitudes towards painting, as well as on the character of painting itself. In the first place, the increase in the output of paintings was nothing compared with the proliferation of photographs. It was said that in 1849, in Paris alone, 100,000 daguerreotype portraits were taken; another

---

[1] Yvonne Bernard, *Psycho-sociologie du goût en matière de peinture* (1973).
[2] Robert Francès, *Psychologie de l'esthétique* (1968), 87, 127.
[3] A. Hauser, *A Social History of Art* (1951) is an appalling example.

source claims that in 1847 half a million photographic plates were sold there. In 1850 Marseille had four or five miniature painters, two of whom had some reputation for artistry, and they did roughly fifty portraits a year each. A few years later the city had nearly fifty photographers, each of whom produced on average about a thousand portraits. The miniaturists had barely kept themselves alive with their work. The photographers made a handsome income; and soon every sizeable town boasted one or more photographers. A photographic portrait in the 1840s cost about 15 francs, and sometimes as much as 100 francs; but in the 1850s the invention of a new method and a new format (the 'visiting-card' portrait, 6 × 9 cm) brought the price down to 20 francs for a set of twelve portraits; in the 1860s every worker could afford the 2 francs that was asked. The leader in the popularisation of the photograph, Disderi, quickly made an enormous fortune, though the competition he stimulated eventually ruined him and he died as poor as he had begun, a beach photographer at Nice. Disderi's motto was: 'One must seek the greatest beauty that the subject is capable of.' His idea of beauty was distinctly banal, but it was for that reason popular. Nadar, the exotic journalist and balloonist whom poverty diverted into photography, showed that portraits of high artistic quality were possible, and these early photographs remain unsurpassed, partly because many of the first photographers were often also painters.[1] The first victim of the camera was the miniaturist painter, who virtually disappeared between 1850 and 1890, when a reaction against the vulgarity of the photograph gave him a new lease of life. Many miniaturists became photographers, or they coloured photographs or painted portraits over photographs. The invention of the camera did not mean that the demand for painting was reduced, but rather that most people demanded that painting should be as accurate as photography. The quasi-photographic paintings of the second half of the nineteenth century are the result. Some painters even prided themselves on producing works which were almost indistinguishable from photographs. Portrait painting was revolutionised, because

[1] Gisèle Freund, *La Photographie en France au 19ᵉ siècle* (1936); Félix Tournachon Nadar, *Quand j'étais photographe* (1900); Disderi, *Esthétique de la photographie* (1862); Secrétan, *Prix courants de tous les articles de photographie* (May 1859), shows camera prices then starting at 200 francs, going up to 2,000; daguerreotypes cost 195–480 francs.

many painters made increasing use of photographs, instead of relying on sketches. No less a master than Ingres took the lead in this new technique. In the 1860s methods were invented to enable photographs to be projected directly on to canvas, so that the artist could paint over them. Manet relied on photographs for the figures in the *Execution of the Emperor Maximilian*, which is therefore an accurate historical document, whatever symbolism or significance may be read into it. Photography thus for a time accentuated the traditional character of painting, in encouraging it to be even more erudite and accurate; but it also produced new kinds of painting. Corot in 1848 suddenly adopted a blurred style which seems to have been associated with his discovery of coated-glass photography, which created the same effect. Impressionism coincided with the advent of the snapshot, which had already produced the same sort of hazy images, and the same kind of composition, with randomly distributed figures, cut by the frame. The development of the fast shutter, allowing objects in motion to be captured as they never had been before, 'proved the painters wrong' by showing, for example, that a horse at the gallop had all four legs off the ground. No one had painted it like that before. The painter Meissonier, who was a maniac for accuracy, held a party in honour of the photographer who made this discovery; and Degas translated the new knowledge of motion into painting, inspired probably more by photography than by Japanese prints. It is true there were artists like Rodin who said that galloping horses seem to be motionless in photographs and that only painters, even if they were anatomically wrong, could make them look as though they were galloping. Painters resented the pretensions of photographers to the status of artists, and they generally concealed their use of photography. With the Post-Impressionists, a reaction set in against photography, and all painting that resembled it, and painting turned, in a more radical way than ever before, from the simple representation or imitation of nature. But 1888 was the year of the appearance of the Kodak camera; and in 1900 it was estimated that 17 per cent of the people admitted to the Paris Universal Exhibition carried portable cameras. That could mean as many as 50,000 people carrying cameras in Paris in a single day. So, though superficially it might seem that a break now occurred between everyman's photographic art, which was essentially representative, and the art of the painter, who concerned himself with images as such, for their own sake, one could see both developments as showing the same concern with individual creativity. The distinction is rather between those who liked to make their own pictures and the vast majority for whom pictures were simply a source of information.

It is customary to be scathing about the enormous industry of pornographic photography that arose as early as the 1840s but anyone wishing to understand the emotional and imaginative responses to higher art cannot ignore the appeal of the non-intellectual, visual experiences this afforded. Photography and painting were not as much rivals as they might at first appear to have been. 'What we see, and how we see it, depends on the arts that have influenced us', said Oscar Wilde. The relationship between these two visual forms brings out the very important changes that took place in what people did see.[1] Photography showed people things they had never seen before. Indeed the development of optical science in general should be regarded as an important instrument of greater equality between men. About 15 to 20 per cent of Europeans are short-sighted and about 50 per cent long-sighted. Until efficient spectacles were generally worn by these, the world looked very different. Just how different can be judged from the work of numerous painters whose visual defects are known about. Impressionism has been called 'the triumphant exploitation of myopic vision', a condition which of course affects perception of colour as well as outline. Cézanne, Monet, Renoir, Pissarro, Degas can all be shown to owe some of their eccentricities to myopia, or cataract, or corneal ulcers. A recent survey of masters and pupils at the School of Fine Arts in Paris revealed that 48 per cent of them were myopic, which is almost three times more than the national average.[2]

The diversity and richness of French art in this period was stimulated by the existence of patrons with many different motives and tastes. The seventeenth-century diarist John Evelyn

---

[1] Aaron Scharf, *Art and Photography* (1968) is a highly intelligent guide to this problem.

[2] Patrick Trevor-Roper, *The World through Blunted Sight. An Enquiry into the Influence of Defective Vision on Art and Character* (1970).

was struck by the fact that in the Holland of his time perfectly ordinary farmers bought paintings for two or three hundred pounds. In nineteenth-century France, the buyers of pictures had long ceased to be simply kings, aristocrats and very wealthy men. Paintings had become an essential decoration for every home with pretensions. 'Every rich family', wrote a connoisseur describing the collections of Bordeaux in 1893, 'is necessarily obliged to possess a gallery of pictures, and this for two compelling reasons: first, from a natural taste for modern luxury, and, secondly, because *fortune oblige*.'[1] Snobbishness was certainly important, as well as the desire to make a sound investment. The royal and aristocratic collections were copied by the millionaires, Rothschild leading the way. The department store owner Cognacq-Jay seems to have bought pictures without any particular love of art, and painters offering him their works were normally sent away to speak to an assistant he employed for the purpose. Some people were collectors by inheritance, preserving and building up bequests from relatives and ancestors, in the same way as they looked after all their other property. An inquiry carried out in the 1960s among French collectors found all these extraneous motives still surviving: some saw in collecting simply a pastime, some found in pictures a substitute for friends and a cure for loneliness; some saw in it a way of purchasing prestige, especially when the source of their wealth was not a subject of particular pride. Those with a taste for erudition, or with a desire to lead fashion, preferred obscure or unpopular artists; those who sought the approval of conformist circles, and who simply wanted to decorate their homes with a painting of whose value they could be sure, chose from the artists who won prizes at the official Salons. Local loyalties played their part: in Flanders it was said painters were supported by patrons with the same zeal as the football clubs were by not very different kinds of benefactors; provincial painters who made good in Paris could usually count on buyers in their native regions. But it was rare for anyone to admit that financial or social considerations were predominant; and many indeed developed a collector's mania and an obsession with art which defied any explanation in terms of self-interest. Some were able to describe

[1] Georges de Sonneville, *Collections et collectionneurs bordelais* (Bordeaux, 1893), 1–7.

their love of art only with the language of romantic passion; their zeal was stimulated precisely because the search for good pictures was as hard as that for the perfectly beautiful woman.

Just how much people were willing to invest in painting can be seen from the collection of Secrétan, an industrialist who, within the space of fifteen years, built up the most important private collection in France, as it was described in 1879 when he went bankrupt and it was sold by auction, for 6 million francs. Over half of this sum was paid for French paintings. Secrétan was a great admirer of the Salon's favourite, Meissonier, and had twenty-three of his works; he also had seven paintings by Troyon, five by Diaz, four by Corot, one by Courbet, Millet's *Angélus*, as well as four Rembrandts, two Rubens, one Velasquez, four Frans Hals and many other Dutch and Flemish works.[1] The art sales of this period show, among the owners of important collections, some solid well-to-do middle-class men, like Armand Bertin, the editor of the *Journal des Débats*, or Jules Claye, a printer who favoured Troyon, Géricault and Français. There were also people who had had a chance to pick up masterpieces cheaply, like Collot, director of the Paris Mint, who returned from Bonaparte's 1799 campaign in Italy laden with a Leonardo and various other old masters.[2] In the 1860s, it was said that there were sometimes up to three art auctions a day in Paris; leading industrialists and politicians attended the important ones; there was constant movement in these treasures.[3] Provincial art collectors were a distinct group in their communities. They were not rivals of the great Paris collectors, for they could not afford Paris prices. A favourite practice of theirs was to form local art societies (there were 368 of these in 1885) and organise local exhibitions, at which they would run lotteries. Sometimes the lottery tickets would cost only 25 centimes and in such cases 15,000 might be sold (at Agen in 1886) or even 60,000 (as in Cherbourg in the same year); more usually they were 10 francs —one-tenth of what they cost in Paris. For its exhibition of 1885, the Society of Arts of Bordeaux bought forty-two of the entries, which it resold by lottery in this way; private individuals bought

[1] *Catalogue de tableaux anciens et modernes . . . formant la célèbre collection de M. E. Secrétan* (1889); prices realised in *Larousse du XIXᵉ siècle*, second supplement (1890), 1. 830.

[2] Charles Blanc, *Le Trésor de la curiosité* (1857), a major source for art prices.

[3] Ivan Golovine, *Manuel du marchand de tableaux* (1862), 124.

a further seventy-one; on average prices were between 500 and 650 francs. Only occasionally were really high prices paid, and this by rich foreigners, as in the Nice exhibitions of that year, where two Bouguereaus went for 25,000 francs each.[1]

Bordeaux in 1893 had about thirty private collections of paintings sizeable enough to attract public attention. Dr. Azam, for example, had about 200 mainly Dutch and Flemish paintings, which his uncle, who had been a merchant trading with Holland, had collected since the 1830s. Fourestier had inherited a collection of old masters, again mainly Dutch and Flemish, from his uncle, a senior tax official, but had added modern works by Salon painters like Armand Leleux and Jean-Paul Laurens. Bourges, a member of the chamber of commerce, had thirty paintings by Eugène Boudin, many more by Bordeaux painters and others by Swedish and Norwegian artists, acquired in the course of his business dealings in Scandinavia. There were collectors infatuated with the work of a single artist. Thus Degas found a passionate admirer in Friedmann, who bought virtually nothing else; Auguste Pellerin bought seventeen Manets and then over a hundred Cézannes. Renand at one time had forty Corots.[2] Friendship was sometimes the basis of their patronage: the marine engineer Gustave Caillebotte, whom Monet met boating on the Seine, whom he taught to paint and with whom he became very close, bought large numbers of Impressionist paintings, which he subsequently bequeathed to the state, from admiration, but also from a desire to help painters he liked personally.[3] Painters were among the most important collectors of paintings, as too were those who came most into contact with them—auctioneers, colour merchants, and dealers. Writers who backed artistic movements with sympathetic criticism helped to create little cliques of admirers who gave material encouragement. The publisher Georges Charpentier, for example (whose father Gervais, founder of the firm, had been a supporter,

[1] Raymonde Moulin, 'Les Expositions des Beaux-Arts en province 1885-7' (unpublished thesis Paris, 1967, in the Sorbonne library), 246.

[2] Jean Dauberville, La Bataille de l'impressionisme, suivi de En encadrant le siècle, par Jean Dauberville (1967), 516. Cf. La Collection Oscar Schmitz (1936), describing the patronage of the Impressionists by the Swiss cotton merchant of Le Havre (1861–1933).

[3] Cf. Maurice Rheims, Art on the Market: Thirty-five Centuries of Collecting and Collectors from Midas to Paul Getty (1961).

of the romantics), was a Maecenas to the Impressionists, as Renoir's paintings of his family commemorate.[1] In 1956, still, the marquis de Chasseloup-Laubat had a painter installed in his château as a permanent guest, almost as blind as Degas and working in a similar style, with his studio in the stables. This was continuing the tradition of hospitality to art that had enabled the animal painter Brascassat (1804–67) to establish himself, supported by the civil servant-engineer-painter Théodore Richard, who was president of the Society of Fine Arts of Bordeaux. Brascassat, when he became famous, used to go round the country staying with aristocrats, painting portraits of their prize cattle.[2] Bouguereau got his start in life decorating the walls of houses bought by rising financiers like Bartholoni and Pereire. But these kinds of domestic commissions became increasingly rare.

As in seventeenth-century Italy, the patrons of contemporary art were often people outside the traditional ruling class, with tastes unshackled by the prevalent conventions.[3] Thus the Fauves sold their paintings to odd men like King Milan of Serbia and the restaurant owner Bauchy (whose Café des Variétés was decorated also with the still cheap works of Cézanne and Van Gogh). But they relied ultimately on a handful of faithful admirers. The socialist deputy Marcel Sembat (whose wife had studied painting with Gustave Moreau) was one of their regular buyers: he bequeathed his collection of their works to the state, which refused it—as it had once refused Caillebotte's bequest of Impressionists. (It was the socialist curator of the museum of Grenoble who rescued Sembat's collection, so that Grenoble was the first French Museum to exhibit the Fauves.) The Americans Leo and Gertrude Stein and Dr. Barnes, the inventor of the antiseptic Argyrol, were important patrons not only to the Fauves, but to many of their contemporaries. Barnes finally accumulated about 120 Cézannes, 200 Renoirs, 95 Picassos and 100 Matisses. Two Russian merchants, Morozov and Shchukin, similarly bought in large quantities and the vast collections of modern French paintings in the Soviet Union are

[1] Michel Robida, *Le Salon Charpentier et les Impressionistes* (1958).
[2] C. Marionneau, *Brascassat, sa vie et son œuvre* (1872).
[3] F. Haskell, *Patrons and Painters. A Study in the Relations between Italian Art and Society in the Age of the Baroque* (1963) is full of stimulating ideas; id., *Rediscoveries in Art* (1976), published since this book went to press, is indispensable.

the results of their enthusiasm and generosity in Paris.[1] The owners of Cézanne paintings just before the First World War included writers like Octave Mirbeau and Zola, dealers like Bernheim and Vollard, but also many foreigners, in Berlin, Hamburg, Budapest, Moscow and the U.S.A.[2] One of the reasons why French art acquired an international reputation and influence was perhaps because an important section of it was rather neglected in France itself, picked up by foreigners.

In 1938 Britain was the largest importer of French paintings, followed by the U.S.A., as these figures show:[3]

| | |
|---|---|
| Britain | 317 |
| U.S.A. | 270 |
| Netherlands | 82 |
| Belgium and Luxembourg | 51 |
| Sweden | 49 |
| Other countries | 88 |

By 1953 the U.S.A. had overtaken Britain and by 1963 Switzerland had also. The export of French paintings to England still awaits proper investigation, but a certain amount is known about exports to the U.S.A. The great American collectors enthusiastically patronised the most successful contemporary French painters. Bouguereau, Gérome, Meissonier, Troyon and Rosa Bonheur were to be found in almost every collection by the middle of the nineteenth century; scenes from domestic life and landscapes with interesting figures were preferred to grand historical themes. In 1849 Goupil and Vibert founded the International Art Union in New York to stimulate this taste and for the rest of the century the 'academic' painters continued to please the Americans. Collectors in Boston and New England, however, repeatedly took the lead in introducing more controversial artists. From 1850 Quincy Adams Shaw began buying the Barbizon school and by 1870 he had twenty-five Millets. The French dealer De Vose established himself in Providence (Rhode Island), and in 1852 organised the first exhibition in the U.S.A. of Corot, who failed to make much headway in England, but who became such a success in America that a vast number

---

[1] J. P. Crespelle, *The Fauves* (c. 1962), 344–7.
[2] J. Meier-Graefe, *Paul Cézanne* (Munich, 1913).
[3] Figures of exports in thousands New Francs.

of forgeries of his paintings, as well as pastiches by his pupils amiably signed by him, were profitably exported there. The French, of course, had to compete with the Düsseldorf school and the modern Dutch school, and American taste extended very broadly, to all periods and over all kinds of artistic objects. But the French had special advocates in the American painters who came to study in France and who spread the fame of the younger generation; and there were some American collectors with special links with France, like Henry Walters of the Atlantic Coast Line Co. Durand-Ruel's exhibition of the Impressionists in New York in 1885 attracted sympathetic interest; by the 1890s every picture Monet could produce was readily sold in America for 4–6,000 francs; in 1922 the Chicago Art Institute received a large bequest of Impressionists and in 1929 the Havemeyer donation added 36 Degas, 20 Courbets, 9 Corots, 8 Manets, 8 Monets and 5 Cézannes to the collections of the Metropolitan Art Museum. The Impressionists became museum masters in the U.S.A. well before they reached that status in France. (In England sales of the Impressionists were slower: of the two main collectors, Sir Hugh Lane started buying in 1905 and Samuel Courtauld in 1922. In Russia, Shchukin had begun his collection in the 1890s.) Cézanne, the Fauves and the Cubists owed their introduction into the U.S.A. above all to the Armory Show organised by American painters in 1913. But there were individual collectors, like Adolph Lewisohn, who bought modern paintings ahead even of these fashions, with great independence and sureness of taste.[1]

There were 104 picture dealers in Paris in 1861; in 1958 there were 275 (and another 70 in the rest of the country). These figures, however, represent only a proportion of the many middlemen, painters' widows, unemployed artists, women of leisure, and crooks who lived on the fringes of the art world, profiting from the passions of collectors, the poverty of painters and each other's gambling instincts. Art was a merchandise but one clothed in secrecy and mystery, because its price was so difficult to fix, and because its relationship with commerce was so ambivalent. Art had long been an international merchandise, whose value was usually increased by export; and dealers had

[1] René Brimo, L'Évolution du goût aux États-Unis d'après l'histoire des collections (1938).

become essential already in the seventeenth century. But because of the increase in the number of pictures and because the vast majority of them were no longer commissioned, dealers now had a larger role as bankers, stockists and promoters. Rembrandt had sold his paintings to a dealer for what was virtually a salary. This system was now much developed by Durand-Ruel (1831–1922), who introduced a new element by seeking a monopoly of the production of the artists he patronised, building up large stocks first of the Barbizon school and then of the Impressionists. In 1866 he bought seventy paintings by Théodore Rousseau; in 1872 he visited Manet and bought all the paintings he had —twenty-three of them, for 35,000 francs. He worked hard to spread his taste among collectors, by holding exhibitions, starting art journals and opening a branch office in New York (1886). Behind Durand-Ruel was the banker Feder, of the Catholic Union nationale, but it crashed in 1882, and Durand-Ruel was at times on the verge of bankruptcy himself. He had too many rivals for him to be able to profit fully from his efforts.[1] The American dealer Sueton, who had collected 120 Monets, was only one of the army of middlemen who were combing Europe for rare objects to sell in the United States, exports to which had become very considerable since the 1840s. It was Kahnweiler (b. 1884), the Cubists' art dealer, who perfected Durand-Ruel's monopoly methods: he undertook to buy all the paintings of Juan Gris and also of Picasso at a fixed price according to size; but he had a contempt for art criticism and for mass opinion, and never spent a penny on advertising. The ultimate factor in a dealer's success was how long he could afford to wait. The one who probably waited longest was Nathan Wildenstein (1851–1934) whose motto was *Savoir Attendre*. Wildenstein was originally an Alsatian textile merchant; he turned to picture dealing by chance, and came to specialise in old masters and particularly eighteenth-century paintings, whose popularity in around 1900 he helped to create. Under his son Georges (1892–1963) the firm expanded to cover the Impressionists. Their stocks in New York (they opened their gallery on Fifth Avenue in 1902) consisted at one time of some 2,000 paintings, including 8 Rembrandts, 79 Fragonards, 20 Renoirs and 250 Picassos. Dealers, however, did not create

[1] Mrs. Linda Whiteley is writing a doctoral thesis at Oxford on Durand-Ruel.

taste; their influence spread only slowly; economic conditions and changing fashions could destroy their work. After the First World War, for example, the Barbizon school, which had steadily increased in value, collapsed (with a few exceptions); and no propaganda could attenuate the effects of the great depression. The provinces continued to provide a steady market for traditional painting, particularly in cities like Lyon and Marseille which had their own favourite local schools. There can be no doubt, however, that dealers did create reputations: a good example is that of Villon, whose paintings sold very cheaply until 1942 when Louis Carré became his propagandist, organised twenty-seven exhibitions for him all over the world in the space of sixteen years, and his price increased more than a thousandfold. But one should not glamorise these dealers too much into prophets of future taste. Paul Rosenberg said modestly in 1948: 'I made a fortune by mistake, because all my life I had to keep pictures I could not sell, by Picasso, Braque and Juan Gris, which all of a sudden became priceless.' Le Barc de Boutteville, who was one of the main dealers of the Nabis, cared little about what he sold, and often expressed amazement at the strange pictures that passed through his hands. Tostain, who advertised in the *Figaro* in 1858 that he always had 4,000 paintings in stock, to suit all tastes, at 20 francs for four, framed, English spoken, was perhaps not unrepresentative. Ambroise Vollard at his death was said to have over 700 Rouaults, and hundreds of Impressionists, but he also owned the complete works of painters like Iturino who have never been heard of since; and he was heartily disliked by many of the young painters, who complained that he used his exhibitions of their works to attract clients interested in established names; he had a filthy shop, and himself wore threadbare clothes and broken shoes. Berthe Weil, who sold many of the Fauves, began as a second-hand dealer, and though she eventually had three galleries, she never made much money out of her flair. Other dealers who supported the Fauves were Soulié, a former clown, and Druet, who originally ran a bistro patronised by painters, and then took up photography.[1] Nevertheless, the dealers often

[1] A. Vollard, *Souvenirs d'un marchand de tableaux* (1948); Gustave Cogniot, *Les Indépendants 1884–1920* (3rd edition, n.d.), 29–30; D. H. Kahnweiler, *Confessions esthétiques* (1963); Rheims, op. cit. 105; Crespelle, op. cit. 336.

did have both faith in their protégés and a feeling for art, which has influenced the history of painting.

The influence of art critics on taste is more difficult to assess. Monet wrote in 1883 that 'nothing can be achieved nowadays without the press'; he cared nothing for what it said, but 'it is from the commercial point of view that one must look at it . . . for even intelligent connoisseurs are sensitive to the least noise made by the newspapers'. But an art critic had already written in 1859 that 'criticism has little power today and it is seldom that anyone listens'.[1] The press was certainly important in the process of selection of fashionable painters, particularly as the number of painters increased, but it is possible that those it condemned benefited as much from their publicity as their favourites. It tended to discuss painters more than painting, and it is not clear that it aroused interest in the arts among those who cared nothing for them. The critics to whom it opened its columns met with hostility from an early stage, and not only among complete philistines. A professor of the Paris faculty of letters published a satirical commentary on their style in 1861, suggesting that those who felt lost at exhibitions could acquire the vocabulary and mannerisms of connoisseurs in a couple of hours.[2] The profession of art critic was a comparatively recent one, begun in the eighteenth century and developing fully only with the growth of the Salon and the press in the nineteenth. There were about a hundred art critics under Napoleon III and nearly 350 in 1961; in 1899 they formed themselves into a trade union. Most of them were part-time writers, journalists, academics, novelists, failed painters, and leisured civil servants. Because of that, they could be expected to reflect what was said at the Salons; but by developing their own jargon, fancy phrases and platitudes, which their pretentious readers aped with more or less success, they attempted to make the appreciation of art more complex; they may have explained things to some people, but they also turned others away with insults about their bad taste. The most fashionable critics, writing for the newspapers with large circulations, seldom formed taste, but rather

[1] M. H. Dumesnil, *Le Salon de 1859* (1859), quoted Joseph C. Sloane, *French Painting between the Past and the Present. Artists, Critics and Traditions from 1848 to 1870* (Princeton, 1951), 33 n.

[2] Nicolas Martin, *Le Parfait Connaisseur, ou l'art de devenir un critique d'art en deux heures, imité de l'allemand* (1861).

embroidered around the orthodoxies familiar to their readers, confirming prejudices that already existed, but backing them up with moral considerations and seeking to show how the style they approved was the inevitable one. The critics who wrote for small journals often played a different role. They sought to vindicate the claims of new painters and new styles to public attention, and sometimes set themselves up as interpreters or even guides of new work. The paper battles of the critics consolidated factions and friendships and exacerbated disputes. It is above all to the critics that the division of painters into schools, with opprobrious titles, is due. In the process, aesthetic theories were developed which sometimes stimulated the artists to whom they were attributed, but just as frequently left them indifferent or protesting that their aims were being over-simplified, over-clarified. The categorisations the critics popularised gave their world a framework which did not accurately contain the variety within it, but which was nevertheless influential as a myth that neither painters nor public could escape. The critics who are now most esteemed are those who were, in their day, considered the most biased and the least learned. Certainly, Baudelaire's knowledge of art history was superficial; Zola was only twenty-six years old, and his experience was limited to advertising for Hachette the publisher, when he launched his unmeasured praise of Manet; Apollinaire, as Braque said, could not even recognise a Leonardo when he saw one; he knew nothing of painting, but he loved originality, change, fantasy and the painters with whom he associated; his advocacy of a succession of new artistic schools was the product of a temperament. The enthusiasms of Baudelaire and Zola did not last; they were each seeking more than what the painters offered; and they ended by condemning the modern art which they had helped create. What critics of this kind did was to bring new theories and words from other disciplines, like philosophy, or mysticism or science, to add the same kind of weight to new painting styles that morals gave to the academic painters. In course of time— it often took as much as thirty years—the critics of the provinces absorbed their doctrines. Thus it was only around the 1880s that realism was accepted and indeed espoused by provincial critics, whose articles then reproduced almost word for word what Thoré had written a generation before in Paris. They resisted innovation, at least till it had become familiar and had moderated its eccentricities. They liked to understand what the painters were trying to do, and it is a measure of the failure of the Parisian critics that their provincial colleagues took so long to get their message. The difficulty new painters had in being accepted came in some measure from the fact that these critics insisted on painters speaking the language of ordinary men: the Impressionists were rejected by provincial critics because, as *Le Dauphiné* put it in 1886, they had something wrong with their eyes: they could not see 'the sights commonly visible to humans, to you and to me'.[1]

Critics thus on the one hand formulated the resistance of the public to the painters' claim to an independent and original view of the world. On the other hand some of them helped the public to build a bridge between their ordinary perceptions and those of painters, and to extend the range of their sensibilities. Baudelaire held up as the ideal the art lover who was 'partial, passionate and political, amusing and poetic', who can analyse and translate the shock of pleasure he experiences in front of a picture, and whose imagination is capable of penetrating beneath the surface, to perceive hidden analogies between the different arts. He urged the painter to interpret the age he lived in to itself, to be the philosopher of modernity. He made temperament—or individuality—the crucial quality that a painter needed.[2] This was to make art the preserve of the happy few. Zola, who repeated Baudelaire's injunction when he said 'a work of art is a corner of nature viewed through a temperament', added however that the public's reactions were as important as the picture. He wanted the artist to 'conquer the crowd' by the force of his genius, though without making any concessions.[3] These two critics set up a debate on the status of art which was never resolved.

One constant and decisive factor in the world of art was the artists' determination to win independence and recognition of themselves as a superior creative profession. All these economic

[1] *Le Dauphiné* (12 Aug. 1886) quoted in R. Moulin, *Lex Expositions* (1967), 216. Cf. L. Venturi, *History of Art Criticism* (New York, new edition 1964).
[2] Charles Baudelaire, *The Painter of Modern Life and other Essays* (1964, English translation).
[3] E. Zola, *Salons* (ed. F. W. J. Hemmings) (1959).

and social pressures upon them had to battle with the way they wanted to see themselves, with their ambition for a kind of life which involved much more than selling their pictures. Their whole history, indeed, had been dominated by a remarkably steady determination in the same direction; though each successive victory also brought with it unexpected difficulties, which tied them up in new knots. In the middle ages, they set themselves up as a guild, and this protected them against their principal employer in those days, the Church, but this also had the effect of cutting them off from another corporation, the University. The fine arts and letters as a result remained separate for many centuries, and artists were weakened by their isolation. The guild in course of time became oppressive and the king set up an Academy of Fine Arts as a rival to it, in which his court painters could work free of its restrictions; but though this body gave an élite of artists the benefits and prestige of royal protection, it soon got embogged in rules it formulated in the hope of strengthening and safeguarding that prestige. In the eighteenth century a division was established between the fine arts and the applied arts; this appeared to the court painters as a great triumph; but the long-term result was to isolate painters still further, this time from industry and science. Many people who might have become good artisans were condemned to remaining bad and embittered painters. To make itself more respectable, the Academy laid down rules about what art should be, which inevitably caused almost every generation to rebel against it. Internal feuds were built into the art world's institutions. When the Academy was revived after its temporary abolition at the Revolution, it had lost much of its power, but it retained and strengthened its hold on art education. The academicians were professors at the School of Fine Arts, and artists continued to be divided into pupils, *agréés* and academicians, preserving the old apprentice, journeyman and master division. But this was a system which could no longer work in modern conditions. There were now too many students and the chances of becoming an academician became increasingly remote. In the seventeenth century one could hope to be elected to the Academy while still in one's twenties. In the nineteenth century the average age of new members was 53. The competition for the prix de Rome, the top annual scholarship which set a painter on the path of success, dominated the training of young painters; the near-inevitability of failing weighed them down into a feeling of helplessness, which they concealed behind the bohemian *joie de vivre* they cultivated—a façade of assumed frivolity that covered up insecurity and brutality. The relationship of master and student collapsed when the former could no longer guarantee jobs to his disciples; and the Renaissance and Baroque practice of working together as collaborators had died under the assaults of individualism. Courbet's studio, where there was no teaching, marked the crisis of the system, as also did the other independent studios—which the Impressionists were to attend. Many students not unnaturally responded to the crisis by opting out of a rat race they could not win, and that was the basis of independent art.

However, the belief that the revolutions in artistic style of this period were essentially rebellions against the Academy is mistaken. The idea that there was academic art on the one hand and progressive or modern art on the other—represented by that famous succession of groups whose -isms summarise the art history of this century—is a misleading simplification. It is true that the Academy saw itself as the guardian of doctrines evolved in the seventeenth and eighteenth centuries. These were that the subject-matter of art had to be selected with great discrimination, that only 'noble' themes should be painted, that these were to be found above all in classical or Christian history, that the human figure expressed ideal beauty best, and that it should be presented in ideal form, in traditionally admired poses, that harmonious composition and accurate drawing should prove the painter's skill. The Academy tried to make painting appeal to the intellect: a work of art should translate 'a profound thought or an ingenious idea'. Poussin had said that those who painted 'mean subjects take refuge in them because of the meanness of their talents'. A painter had to be a moralist, to point out what was worthy of admiration. That is why academic art was identified with 'grand' pictures, depicting 'battles, heroic actions and divine things'.[1] That, too, is why such pains were taken to fill paintings with accurate historical and mythological detail. Erudition raised the painter to a much higher level than a decorator. Meissonier declared that if he were not a painter, he

[1] Sloane, op. cit. 16 n.

would wish to be a historian. Copying old paintings was an essential part of the artist's training, which maintained reverence for the skills and the methods of the old masters. These doctrines, whatever might be thought of them aesthetically, were defensible if art was seen as a servant of the state, and if the state's duty was seen as the preservation of order and morals. The state was by far the most important patron of the arts, and it commissioned 'grand' art, which was both impressive and edifying. Historical painting was much encouraged by King Louis-Philippe for the decoration of the palace of Versailles, and in the 1830s such paintings formed the bulk of state commissions. In the 1840s about 85 per cent of the state's purchases were of religious paintings and in the 1850s about 45 per cent.[1] In all, between 1851 and 1860, the state bought about 2,000 pictures. These were by no means all different pictures, for favourites were ordered in many copies: at least thirty-two churches, for example, were sent copies of Prud'hon's *Christ en Croix* and thirty-two others of his *Assomption de la Vierge*. Only about one-sixth (319 in all) of the state's purchases were originals; but the difference between an original and a copy was not all that great. The painters who were commissioned to do an original painting were told what to paint—for example the thirty local saints, commissioned to satisfy the requests of *curés*, and the portraits of the Holy Family, commissioned from nineteen different artists. One of the Second Republic's most grandiose ideas had been to establish a Museum of Copies in Paris, which would reproduce the best paintings of the whole world, and in 1851 four painters were dispatched to copy the works in the National Gallery in London.[2] Under the Third Republic, the decoration of town halls and public buildings, raised up in great numbers, continued the demand for moralising works, with a new 'social' element added to them.

The Academy, however, did not monopolise the patronage of the state, and it is not true that the 'modern' painters were totally rejected and, as it were, thrown into opposition. Between 'academic' and 'modern' art, there was a middle ground of 'official' art which attempted a reconciliation between them.

[1] Pierre Angrand, *Monsieur Ingres et son époque* (1967), 165.
[2] Id., 'L'État mécène, période autoritaire du second empire 1851-60', *Gazette des Beaux-Arts* (1968), vol. 71, 303-48.

Delacroix, who was long rejected by the Academy and not elected to it until he was an old man, nevertheless received important commissions from the state. The Barbizon painters, though they broke the academic rules, included the king's son, the duc d'Orléans, and the prime minister, Casimir Périer, among their first patrons. The Second Empire favoured watered-down versions of their style, and then watered-down realism, which was what a large number of middle-of-the-road painters were producing. The extreme innovators had difficulties, but they soon attracted moderate imitators, who made them respectable by marrying moderation with their eccentricity. Delaroche made romanticism acceptable, and later the highly esteemed Bastien-Lepage adopted the lighter palette and looser style of the Impressionists—these men seemed, in their day, to be the protagonists of modernity. As Henry Houssaye said in 1882: 'Impressionism earns every form of sarcasm when it takes the names Manet, Monet, Renoir, Caillebotte, Degas, [but] every honour when it is called Bastien-Lepage, Duez, Gervex, Danton, Gœneutte, Butin, Mangeant, Jean Béraud or Dagnan-Bouveret.' The real innovators in any case were not permanently ostracised. Manet was eventually given a medal under the Third Republic, and Millet's work was bought by the state in the 1870s. It was the same in politics: the electorate was frightened by the extreme Reds, except in certain traditionally extreme circles, and it was the moderate radical-socialists who were admitted to apply their ideals of social justice in suitably diluted form; it was fifty years after their death that the utopians became heroes. In art, the division between apparently opposing sides was really almost as false as it was in politics. On a personal level, many academic and Impressionist painters were friends; the Impressionists had a great admiration for some 'official' painters, like Puvis de Chavannes; and on the other hand they did not get on too well with others who were more 'modern': Manet was hated by Courbet. The invention of labels to characterise and categorise painters confused the issues enormously. The more artistic rebellions of the century are examined, the more their debt to and their links with the art of their predecessors is seen to be crucially important. Thus it used to be thought that Manet, who spent many years as a pupil of Couture, hated all that Couture stood for, and that the rise of Impressionism

Q

could be epitomised in the clash of their contrasting doctrines. But now that Couture's painting and teaching have been more carefully examined, it has been discovered that, in his day, Couture was seen as the antithesis of academic ideals: he urged his pupils to ignore the intellectualist attitude of the Academy and to concentrate on pictorial technique, on purity of colour, on spontaneity and self-expression. 'Produce with a fresh mind and a hearty spirit whatever you feel like doing', he used to say. He had a little group of loyal admirers around him, but he was 'so violently attacked', as he himself said, that he gave up teaching. The battle the Impressionists fought was not a new one: Couture's happens to be less famous. Couture was a product of the Academy, but one who had narrowly missed success: he had been runner-up in the prix de Rome competition. How different would he have been if he had won? Couture, in denouncing 'serious painting', was himself repeating the iconoclasm of Delacroix, who ended up in the Academy.

The Academy should not be seen as the enemy of good painting because of these quarrels. Its rules were not as absolute as they were in theory, and it in fact encouraged tendencies with which its theory conflicted. Thus landscape painting was, according to its teaching, an inferior form of art; but in 1817 it was made part of the academic syllabus for students; it was the academician Valenciennes who wrote the first textbook on landscape painting, which was recommended by Pissarro to his son some fifty years later; and most academicians of the nineteenth century painted landscapes. Gleyre, in whose studio several Impressionists studied, emphasised landscape painting, and Couture took his pupils on field trips to paint from nature. The rigid hierarchy of subject-matter had been greatly attenuated in the face of the romantic sensibility in both artists and public. Again, the Academy laid enormous theoretical stress on perfect finish as an ideal, on line as opposed to colour, and indeed it did not allow its pupils to paint at all until they had mastered drawing. It criticised the romantics for producing mere sketches, which it condemned as being morally as well as artistically inferior, as a dishonest way of reducing the amount of labour put into pictures, and of increasing output. Nevertheless it did establish a special competition for compositional sketches, which had a great influence on the development of painting. The cult of copying old masters was modernised by doing more sketches of them, thus combining veneration for the past with the cultivation of originality. The sketch, which the romantics had valued for its expressiveness and spontaneity, was gradually seen as a valid work of art, and not simply as a preparation. When applied to landscape painting, it led to the shift of interest from the objects painted to the study of light and the representation and juxtaposition of colour. It was from this basis that the Impressionists developed the idea of the outdoor sketch, produced in a few hours, as a self-sufficient work of art. What used to be condemned as amateurism was now raised to a new status; and this opened up great possibilities for genuinely amateur painters too. It was not a pure coincidence that amateur painting now suddenly became a popular hobby and that long, academic training no longer seemed essential—as the flood of Teach Yourself Painting books testified. In 1872 there were already twenty art schools for girls in Paris.[1]

What emerged from these conflicts was the triumph of self-expression as the artist's main preoccupation and this was at the root of the new styles from the romantics onwards. This culmination of the artists' struggle for independence marked a very important transformation in the criteria of taste. The Academy had in theory set out clear ideas about what good painting was, and the artist's function, if its doctrine was rigorously interpreted, was simply to approximate to that ideal. But the Academy also believed in originality. Its interpretation of originality was, however, aristocratic; it considered that only some people were original and the vast majority were definitely not so; to be original was to be a member of a superior élite. Now a democratic view of originality challenged this. As early as 1819 Alexandre Lenoir in a paper on this subject declared, 'Originality belongs to every human being and to every genre. It is independent of talent.' During the Second Empire Viollet

---

[1] Horace Lecoq de Boisbaubran, *Coup d'œil sur l'enseignement des Beaux-Arts* (1872) 69 ff.; J. de La Rochenoir, *La Couleur et le dessin appris seul* (1857); R. de Lasalle, *L'Aquarelle en six leçons* (1856); Mme Veuve Cavé, *L'Aquarelle sans maître* (1856); J. P. Thénot, *Le Pastel appris sans maître* (1856); Victori, *Tout le monde artiste. Procédé pour faire de jolies peintures sans avoir la moindre notion de dessin* (1898); Camille Bellanger, *Le Peintre; Traité usuel de peinture à l'usage de tous le monde* (1898); Madame Bourdox-Sody, *Nouveau Procédé de l'art de peindre, sans maître et sans notions du dessin* (1882).

le Duc added that originality was 'the most important of qualities'.[1] The sketch, the artist's impression, constituted the expression of this originality. Once again, however, this victory for the
artist had a high price: his relationship with the community
was altered. On the one hand this new doctrine meant that
everybody could be an artist: to be an artist no longer meant to
cut oneself off. But now everybody was entitled to his opinion,
and the shift of emphasis from communication with the public
to self-exploration meant that the artist became a more isolated
and lonely figure than he had ever been. The proliferation of
sects and groups was partly a compensation for this, but the
labels artists adopted have never been enough to explain them
or to summarise their individual ambitions. 'Good taste', as a
result, became more elusive than ever; it no longer followed
from membership of the ruling class or polite society.

Already in 1848 French art, as illustrated in the Paris Salon
of that year, which was open to all artists without restriction,
was declared to be 'distinguished by such a variety of styles that
no one looking at it would believe in the existence of a French
school.' There were already different avenues to success and
different markets for the specialisations into which artists divided
themselves. The controversies which raged about the merits of
particular individuals and particular styles show that there was
never any unanimity of judgement. Though grand historical
and religious art was held in the highest esteem, in the sense that
success in it led to official honours, the majority of private buyers
wanted pictures of scenes from daily life, and it was these that
fetched the highest prices. For long, the painters who were most
successful financially were those who managed to combine the
lofty idealism of the former with the anecdotal relevance of the
latter. The Impressionists were derided for eliminating the intellectual content from art; they were condemned as 'materialists'
by Catholics, as 'democratic' by the royalists, as 'mad' by the
*Figaro*, the organ of well-to-do men of the world.[2] But their
crime was more one of exaggeration than of innovation, more
in the way they made their statements than in what they said.
If one takes Bouguereau (1825–1905) as the representative of

[1] Albert Boime, *The Academy and French Painting in the Nineteenth Century* (1971),
important.

[2] Jacques Lethève, *Impressionistes et symbolistes devant la presse* (1959), 23, 73, 76.

the successful academic painter, one sees that, though he was an artist as sincere as any 'modern', he was more modest, willing to adapt his work to satisfy convention, without any sacrifice of his integrity. Bouguereau's passion was the study of nature; he would spend hours admiring and meditating about a passing cloud or a wild flower. He believed in the importance of the artist's personality as an equal source of inspiration, in so far as composition was concerned. One was born an artist, according to him, because an artist was 'a special kind of creature with a special sensitivity, that of seeing form and colour, spontaneously and together, in perfect harmony'. The skills of the painter had to be learnt by practice and hard work, and he himself did almost nothing but work. His enormous fees led people to accuse him of painting only to make money, but he denied this, and indeed he lived very modestly and avoided fashionable society, having only a few painters as friends. Far from instilling any doctrines into his pupils, he urged them to follow their natural bent, to find their originality by individual research and by the development of their special gifts. He thought that there was no point in trying to produce painters on the model of those of the Renaissance, with encyclopedic knowledge. He was himself uninterested by philosophy, or politics, or literature; he cared nothing for theories about painting and disliked analysing it too much. He knew a lot about mythology, but though his paintings were often of mythological or classical subjects, they were not primarily or essentially about their ostensible subjects, the gods and goddesses. He painted, above all, beautiful women with beautiful skins, and it was only afterwards that he found titles for them, labelling them Venus, or Magdalen, or 'La Rêverie'. The long conversations he had with his wife about these titles are said to have been full of humour. He aimed at simplicity in his allegories, addressing himself to 'all intelligences and imaginations'. His painting came to be considered too perfect, but his sketches show he had more to him than technical mastery. He has been in eclipse for nearly a century but a recent exhibition of his work in New York indicates that he is on the way back into fashion.[1]

It will be a long time and will need a great deal of research before Bouguereau's contemporaries—whose work is nowadays

[1] Marius Vachon, *W. Bouguereau* (1900).

dismissed contemptuously as *art pompier*—are properly understood. The richness of their legacy was shown in a striking way when the paintings which were in the Luxembourg Museum (the Museum of Living Artists) in 1874 were, in 1974, brought out of their cellars and exhibited once again. It is no longer possible to maintain that it was only the 'modern', as opposed to the academic painters, who expressed 'modernity'. Gérome (1823–1903), who came to be seen as the incarnation of reaction in art, was nevertheless a representative figure, even if, or rather precisely because, his eroticism was clothed in erudite epigrams. Meissonier's precision was a source of endless interest to his contemporaries. Adolphe Leleux (1812–91) and Gustave Brion (1824–77) recorded the folkloric aspects of provincial life in a way that went beyond the suburban horizons of most Parisian painters, while Jules Breton (1827–1906), regarded as the leading landscape painter of his day, sought to defend dignity and grandeur in rural existence. François Bonhommé (1809–81) was one of the increasingly numerous painters of industry and machines. Charles Chaplin (1825–91) produced pictures that people liked to put in their bedrooms and boudoirs. J. J. Henner (1829–1905) and Jules Lefebvre (1836–1911) specialised in female nudes, with great success. Fromentin (1820–76) was famous for his subtle colours: his rose-greys and delicate mauves were copied by many admirers. Gleyre's (1806–74) remarkable studies of light should not be overlooked because they were outdone by his pupils Renoir, Monet and Whistler. Ernest Hébert (1817–1908) was condemned by Baudelaire for trying to please his public, but he deserves to be remembered, perhaps, because he was so successful in doing this. Bastien-Lepage created a new synthesis of styles which was for a time regarded as the vanguard of modernity; and it is not irrelevant, if one wants a comprehensive notion of what modernity was, to remember that he was also a great expert on music-hall songs.[1]

What painters represented, in social or political terms, cannot be easily stated. It is tempting to identify art which was revolutionary in its technique or new in the treatment of its subject-matter with revolutionary ideas in general, but the connection is not always there. J. F. Millet (1814–75), for example, is

[1] Cf. Francis Jourdain, 'L'Art officiel de Jules Grévy à Albert Lebrun', *Le Point* (Apr. 1949), with numerous reproductions.

celebrated as the painter of the peasantry, whom he depicted without sentimentality. He was therefore regarded by some as a demagogic socialist, by others as teaching that 'art should confine itself to copying servilely ignoble models'. Who would want to hang a picture of a dirty, sweating, gloomy labourer on his wall? But Millet ultimately emerged from the traditional near-starvation of the unrecognised painter to become a very successful painter, and that was because, despite the boldness of his art, he stood only partly on the side of modernity. He painted real life, but he commented on his work with learned citations from old authors; his paintings could variously be given biblical or contemporary titles. His peasants could appeal to romantics like George Sand, for they contained idealisation as well as sadness. He said that he painted peasants because they were the section of society he knew best. He was indeed the son of a peasant, but he had formed a liaison with a Breton servant-girl, who bore him four children, and he preferred to break with his parents rather than reveal either her or their existence. The peasants in his pictures were thus partly nostalgic symbols of the way of life he had abandoned, as well as being partly illustrations of biblical and classical pastoral life, which greatly interested him. He did not in fact either like or even get to know the peasants among whom he lived in Barbizon: he considered them narrow-minded, insensitive to the charms of nature. Millet mocked the idea of labour being a source of happiness, and that was one reason why he worried the critics; but he said he did not paint the joyful side of life, because he had never seen it. The only happiness he knew was rest, calm, silence—the opposite of work. He was deeply conscious of the pain that life involved. He painted peasants beaten down by hard labour because the sight of pain was what moved him most. His view of the world was sad, he admitted, but he drew no conclusions from this. He was no philosopher, he said; he had no desire to suppress unhappiness nor to find a formula to make men stoical or indifferent towards it. As an artist, he believed his function was to express what he saw, to give things their true character. The subtlety of all this could not be readily appreciated by his critics, by his admirers or his detractors. He made his reputation eventually, though it was foreigners—Belgians—who recognised his power first.[1]

[1] Étienne Moreau-Nélaton, *Millet raconté par lui-même* (1921); R. L. Herbert,

The link between politics and painting can perhaps be established more firmly in the case of Gustave Courbet (1819–77), but Courbet was not only a socialist: he was also a narcissist, doing self-portraits over and over again. What irritated his critics was that he did not make it altogether clear what message he was conveying. He declared that art should have a social purpose, but also that it could not be taught, for it was strictly individual, and the result of individual inspiration.[1] There were equally painters who identified themselves with new radical ideas, with a religious outlook or with the technical changes of their times, but also others who rejected all such relationships. Impressionism was not the application to art of the optical discoveries of Chevreuil, but when the painters of this school learnt of these, some of them found a justification in them. Pissarro and Seurat declared that art, which sought harmony, should use science to find it.[2] Renoir on the other hand, who was very attached to his status as an artisan, deplored rationalism as 'incompatible with any conception of art', and attacked the 'mania for false perfection that is tending to make the unadorned cleanness of the engineer the ideal'. He had no use for politics either. To exhibit side by side with 'the Jew Pissarro' and Gauguin was to be 'revolutionary' and 'at my age, I do not want to be revolutionary: the public does not like what smells of politics'.[3] Puvis de Chavannes, whose father had been a mine engineer, likewise had a horror of machines: he had nightmares after a visit to the Exhibition of 1889 and exclaimed: 'What will become of us artists in the face of this invasion of engineers and mechanics?'[4] For him painting was about painting: 'I am an

'Millet Revisited', *Burlington Magazine* (Apr. 1962), 294–305; L. Le Poittevin, *J. F. Millet, portraitiste* (1971).

[1] For the links of art, politics and society, see the ingenious and stimulating work of Timothy J. Clark, *The Absolute Bourgeois: Artists and Politics in France 1848–51* (1973) and *Image of the People: Gustave Courbet and the 1848 Revolution* (1973).

[2] J. Rewald, *The History of Impressionism* (New York, new edition 1961) and *The History of Post-Impressionism* (New York, 2nd edition 1962); L. Venturi, *Les Archives de l'Impressionisme* (1939); Pierre Francastel, *Art et technique au 19ᵉ et 20ᵉ siècles* (1956).

[3] Sven Lörgren, *The Genesis of Modernism. Seurat, Gauguin, van Gogh and French Symbolism in the 1880s* (Stockholm, 1959), 81; cf. also Jean Renoir, *Renoir my father* (1962).

[4] Maurice Vachon, *Puvis de Chavannes* (1895), 62; cf. Jon Whiteley, *Puvis de Chavannes* (forthcoming).

ignoramus,' he said. 'I know nothing about philosophy, history or science. I busy myself only with my own profession.'[1]

Art was so inventive in these years neither because of politics nor because of science—though both of these affected it—but because artists were able to paint with more independence than ever before and because their right to individuality was turned into the basic principle of their work. This meant that art became, more than anything, the means by which they expressed their feelings and their attitudes. Courbet proclaimed their independence in his typically flamboyant way, saying 'I too am a government'. Van Gogh used his painting as a means of spiritual salvation and emotional release: he called it 'the lightning-conductor of my illness'; it was the logical extension of his restless and tortured years as a missionary.[2] That meant also that art became a more searching investigation into the nature of reality. With the Impressionists, this involved the study of appearance and the fleeting moment. For the Symbolists, it was more ambitious: Moreau thought he had a 'synoptic message' and would reveal 'the truth underlying all myth and all religion in his paintings'. Cézanne, for his part, said he could not paint a landscape until he had studied its geological structure. Gauguin turned away from civilisation in order to rejuvenate it, through a new vision. Distortion became a vitally important element in painting, because it enabled the artist to express his own interpretation: inaccuracy could reveal, as Van Gogh said, truth that was more real than literal truth. Cubism was thus 'an art of realism', which enabled more information to be included than traditional methods allowed, though it also required more effort from the spectator to reconstruct the subject-matter; it was a more intellectual approach, showing the world not as it appeared to be, but as the painter knew it to be. It was significant that it was a socialist member of parliament, J. L. Breton, who in 1912 denounced the Cubists as 'obviously anti-artistic and anti-national' and demanded that they should not be allowed to exhibit in the Salon d'Automne.[3] But Cubism was

---

[1] P. Jullian and A. Bowness, *French Symbolist Painters* (catalogue of the exhibition at the Hayward Gallery, 1972), 17.

[2] Meyer Schapiro, *Vincent van Gogh* (1951), 96; cf. Jean Leymarie, *Van Gogh* (1951).

[3] John Golding, *Cubism. A history and an analysis 1907–1914* (2nd edition, 1969) is the best guide; cf. Christopher Gray, *Cubist Aesthetic Theories* (Baltimore, 1953) for philosophical links.

also a stage in the process by which the object ceased to be of interest: abstract art allowed the painter to construct his own world. Delaunay made colour, on its own, his preoccupation. The Paris exhibition 'Art d'Aujourd'hui' in 1925 declared in its manifesto: 'the purpose of this new technique [is] to relieve art of the weight of reality, which is essentially anti-lyrical. Mankind needs an escape from reality.'[1] Matisse said that the colours he chose for his paintings had no explanation in any scientific theory: they were designed to express his emotions, not the object on which they were based. His goal was to reorganise and simplify his perceptions so as to produce harmony, equilibrium, tranquillity, which was what he was trying to find in life, and he hoped that the tired businessman would obtain calm and relaxation—without intellectual effort—from looking at his pictures.[2]

Artists were not necessarily the best persons to explain what they were doing, but the critics who grouped them into schools performed an equally suspect task.[3] A potted history of each -ism would give a false account of the development of art. A whole string of biographies—and there would need to be a very large number of them—would not be adequate either, but it would, perhaps, stress that the art of this period found, as Rodin said, beauty in everything.[4]

### Music

'Music is, without a possibility of contradiction, the most popular of all the arts.' So wrote one of the ministry of education's experts in 1889. Musicians, said the newspaper Le Monde in 1964, are the poor relations of the arts.[5] Both statements were true. Together they show how wrong it is to judge French taste by its reputation, how false an indication of popular values is given by state support for officially favoured manifestations of

[1] M. Semphor, *Abstract Painting* (1964), 92.

[2] Henri Matisse, *Écrits et propos sur l'art* (1972), 50. Cf. C. E. Gauss, *The Aesthetic Theories of French Artists, 1855 to the present* (Baltimore, 1949); Marcel Brion, *L'Œil, l'esprit et la main du peintre* (1966).

[3] Cf. Rudolf Arnheim, *Art and Visual Perception* (1954).

[4] Auguste Rodin, *L'Art. Entretiens réunis par Paul Gsell* (1924), 217. Cf. Alan Bowness, *Rodin: sculptures and drawings* (Hayward Gallery exhibition, 1970).

[5] A. Cornet, *L'Enseignement du chant* (1889); *Le Monde* (7–11 Aug. 1962).

them, and how necessary it is to distinguish, in studying attitudes and loyalties, between different groups in society.

The taste for music was not inculcated at school. When primary schools were reorganised in 1833, even singing was not made a compulsory part of the syllabus, and there were indeed, at that time, no song books specifically for children. It is true women teachers (but not men) were required in 1836 to study singing, but between 1851 and 1866 this was defined as religious chanting. The law of 1850 placed singing in schools at the very end of the optional subjects, together with gymnastics. Only in the 1880s was an effort to stimulate it made, but the results seem to have been negligible and, despite a further reform in 1922, there could be no disputing the statement made in 1941 that 'musical education has failed to find a place in the school'. However, in the eastern part of France, under German influence, the situation was different: in the 1820s it was said that there was a piano in every school in Alsace and the schoolteachers, who were frequently organists, were often skilful musicians. The city of Paris also showed great, and exceptional, interest in the teaching of music. In 1819 it appointed L. G. Bocquillon (1781–1842) director of singing in its schools. He (having adopted the more German-sounding pseudonym of Wilhem) used the mutual system of teaching (by which older pupils taught younger ones) to make up for the lack of teachers; but despite the efforts of his successors Gounod (1818–93), Jules Pasdeloup (1819–87) and François Bazin (1816–78) Paris had during the Second Empire only fifty music teachers for all its schools, who gave three hours to each school, and they were paid roughly half of what drawing masters got. France was way behind Germany in producing songs for children, and indeed the first successful song book for schools was an adaptation by two Alsatians of German ones with moralising lyrics, 'Let us chase away sorrow', 'Life is good', 'Be happy'.[1]

The proselytes in the cause of music had much more success outside the schools, particularly in the formation of choral societies. During the July Monarchy Wilhem brought together his best pupils into a choir of 1,200 voices, called the Orphéon;

---

[1] M. Delcasso and M. Gross, *Recueil de morceaux de chant à une, deux et trois voix à l'usage des écoles normales et des écoles primaires* (first published 1856, reprinted 11 times by 1870).

within a few decades similar societies had blossomed all over France. Paris took the lead with its Athéniens de Montmartre and its Carlovingiens (who became the Montagnards in 1848 and the Tyroliens in 1852). By 1868 there were 3,243 choral societies in France, with 147,000 members. In 1859 Eugène Delaporte, organist of Sens Cathedral and one of the leaders of this movement, took 3,000 singers to the Crystal Palace for an international competition. The government gave its backing, since the idea was to 'moralise the worker' and bring about a 'fusion of youth', but this support only resulted in a split of the movement into three. In Paris, the choirs were composed mainly of workers and clerks; but in the provinces the bourgeoisie, civil servants and clergymen also took part. The singers were praised as model citizens who were quick to lose their provincial accents and to wear smarter clothes; the railways gave them reduced fares and they travelled widely to take part in competitions. There were also politically inspired, left-wing societies. In the 1840s the choral societies used to parade through the streets of Toulouse singing, but the police later forbade this; so they took to giving concerts, which high society patronised. Individual groups, like the forty Chanteurs Montagnards des Hautes-Pyrénées, or the Chanteurs Béarnais, toured the whole of Europe giving concerts in the 1840s. A large number of composers arose to produce songs and music for them. Villages increasingly participated in competitions held in towns, but a new fragmentation soon appeared. Military music became a rival of the *orphéons*, and in many places it grew so popular that it replaced the choirs.[1] Francisque Sarcey claimed that these societies existed more to encourage drinking than singing, and people commented that few of the members could read music; much effort was put into inventing easier ways of teaching it. It seems that the choirs reached the peak of their popularity towards the end of the Second Empire. Never before has there been so much singing in France, it was said; 'France has become at least as musical as Germany; melomania has invaded us on

---

[1] Ch. Poirson, *Guide manuel de l'orphéoniste* (1868); P. Marcel, *L'Art du chant en France* (1900); 'De la musique dans les campagnes', *Journal d'Amiens* (20–1 July, 29–30 Aug. 1864); Édouard Garnier, 'La Musique de chambre', in *La Phare de la Loire* (8 Dec. 1868, Nantes); F. G. Hainl, *De la musique à Lyon depuis 1713 jusqu'à 1852* (Lyon, 1852); Oscar Comettant, *Les Musiciens, les philosophes et les gaietés de la musique en chiffres* (1870).

all sides.'[1] The obstacle to further development seems to have been that they sang songs which never won popularity; perhaps they were dominated by bad composers; at their competitions, they had to sing the songs of the unknown Kucken and Schwahal. There was a gap therefore between their activities and the vulgar ditties and patriotic and revolutionary hymns that the workers and peasants liked. When the Vichy regime regrouped these choirs into its Jeunesses Musicales de France in 1941, it collected only 130,000 members.[2]

The experience of the choral societies is important because it shows the transition from music as a constituent part of a religious or social ritual to music as a recreation and as an end in itself. In the eighteenth century music was used largely as a background for conversation, for theatrical performances, for religious or military ceremonies. The romantics gave it a totally different significance when they claimed that its function was to plumb the secrets of the universe and the deepest emotions of man: composers emphasised the expression of their own feelings and music was now expected to produce private ecstasies, reveries, essentially personal and egocentric sensations. At the same time the number of musical instruments multiplied and public performances became increasingly grandiose spectacles. In the seventeenth century, the orchestra in the Opéra had about twenty members; by 1860 it had increased to eighty-four and Meyerbeer caused a sensation by using a hundred players for his Africaine. In the Second Empire it was still common for fashionable people to arrive at the Opéra during the second act, to watch the pretty ballet girls, to meet and be seen by their friends, rather than to listen to the music, at most to be amazed by the richness and splendour of the costumes and the settings —which was what Meyerbeer was particularly good at. But the interest in Italian music, stimulated by Rossini, created a circle of passionate devotees who gave the Théâtre italien a totally different atmosphere. The Concerts of the Conservatoire (started in 1828) were attended by an even more refined audience, who were more silent than churchgoers and who indeed seemed to look on the concert hall as a sort of temple.

[1] J. M. Bailbé, Le Roman et la musique en France sous la monarchie de juillet (1969), 105.
[2] Bernard Gavoty, Les Français sont-ils musiciens? (1950), 165, 168.

In due course, therefore, there developed a breach between serious and popular music; and music lovers adopted the characteristics of initiates. At first this was not apparent. Pasdeloup started his popular Sunday concerts in Napoleon III's reign with the aim of introducing the workers to the symphonies of Haydn, Mozart, Beethoven and Mendelssohn, who were barely known; but when Lamoureux founded his orchestra (1881) he requested his audience to avoid giving marks of approval or disapproval until the performance was over. Concerts, and particularly opera, used to be noisy affairs, as theatres were too. The presence of the claque, who applauded or hissed at the order of the leader, could make them almost like public meetings. The claque was difficult to eradicate, because it was not the theatres which hired it; on the contrary it was the *chef de claque* who paid the theatre, which of course needed the money. He sometimes described himself as an 'entrepreneur of theatrical success'. He visited impresarios, composers, authors, actors and singers and promised them applause in return for a fee; he then bought blocks of seats, which helped ensure a full house. He could become so powerful that even major artists were forced to give him regular protection money. Auguste, *chef de claque* at the Opéra, made so much out of his profession that he retired with an income of 20,000 francs a year. When Queen Victoria went to the Opéra during her visit to Paris in 1855, the whole of the pit was occupied by the claque, and they all wore full evening dress to ensure that their applause was appreciated. Usually the claque at the Opéra-Comique consisted of fifty people on ordinary days, but as many as 300 on first nights.[1]

The changes that occurred in the financial bases of music-making produced an increasing specialisation of audiences and of performers. In the eighteenth century, the main patrons of musicians were the court and the very rich. Now these ceased to keep private musicians. The opera, the theatres and the churches, which at first provided the general public with the bulk of their musical fare, were in the course of the eighteenth century supplemented by professional concerts—like the Concerts Spirituels of Paris which already specialised in German music and at which the world's greatest instrumentalists appeared,

[1] Auguste Laget, *Le Chant et les chanteurs* (Paris and Toulouse, 1874), 332.

or the Concerts des Amateurs, held in a Masonic lodge, which went in for 'progressive' music. The difficulty of finding an audience in this period is illustrated by Mozart's getting only 176 subscribers for his series of subscription concerts in Vienna in 1784. But by the Second Empire Parisians had a very large choice. In 1866, for example, they could take their pick from the Opéra's performances of *Don Juan*, *La Trouvère*, *Robert le Diable*, *Giselle*, Halévy's *La Juive*, Weckerlin's *Paix*, *Chante et Grandeur* and the first performance of *Le Roi d'Yvetot* by Massa Petipa and Labarre. The Opéra-Comique put on five new operas, including Gounod's *La Colombe* and Victor Massé's *Fior d'Aliza*, based on the novel by Lamartine. The Théâtre italien had Verdi and Donizetti as well as six new operas by other Italian composers. The Théâtre lyrique had eight new operas including a new version of *Don Juan*. Offenbach offered six new operas at the Bouffes Parisiennes (one of them by himself); and the Fantaisies Parisiennes had about a dozen operas by young composers. There were in addition about ten 'non-lyrical' theatres which put on operettas. The Conservatoire gave eleven concerts, of its usual repertory, though it added three works to it this year. Pasdeloup gave twenty-four popular concerts of Haydn, Meyerbeer, Weber and Liszt. The Philharmonic Society of Paris, started in 1865, played modern music, while the Société des concerts de chant classique, in its seventh year, performedthe choral works of dead composers only. Weckerlin's Société Ste Cécile, in its second year, gave six concerts of music by himself and others. Deledicque, first violinist of the Théâtre italien, also ran a Société des Symphonistes, in its sixth year; Lalo and Saint Saens played for the Société de musique de chambre; the Société de quattuors, in its sixteenth year, devoted itself exclusively to the last works of Beethoven. Various composers and virtuosi gave personal concerts in addition; while the musical schools held numerous competitions. The provinces of course usually had to make do with local talent, but at least ten new French operas were performed in the provinces this year.[1] It will be noticed that opera still dominated the musical scene at this time, as it had done a century before, and that the concert societies were largely new; music was still a social event, combined with other forms of entertainment and attracting

[1] *Almanach de la musique* (1867).

an audience of very mixed tastes and origins. A lot of money could be made from the spectacular shows and opera singers in particular received very large fees. Naudin, the greatest tenor of his day, was paid 110,000 francs in 1865 to sing in Meyer-beer's *Africaine*, which was about six times as much as the country's leading tenor got thirty years before. The new director of the Opéra, appointed in 1866, received a salary of 100,000 francs, which made him one of the highest paid men in the country. The status of singers was accordingly transformed. France's most famous tenor in the eighteenth century, Garat (†1823), had been cut off by his family for becoming a singer: now singers were lionised, and even took to writing their memoirs. The discovery of the American market increased the rewards still further: the company of the Théâtre italien toured the U.S.A. in 1891 and came home with a million dollars' profit.[1]

By the twentieth century all this had changed. The symphony concert replaced the opera as the major attraction. The distribution of the musical events in Paris was as follows:

|                    | 1924–5 season | 1938–9 season |
| ------------------ | ------------- | ------------- |
| Symphony concerts  | 451           | 321           |
| Piano recitals     | 296           | 121           |
| Chamber music      | 142           | 125           |
| Miscellaneous      | 921           | 452           |

In 1913 there had been in all only about 700 concerts of all kinds in Paris; in the 1920s this figure more than doubled to as much as 1,880; but in the 1930s it fell sharply, and was only 1,009 in 1938–9. What happened was that an increasing number of groups were formed to play different kinds of music, beginning with the Société Nationale de Musique (1871) to perform the works of new French composers, the Concerts Calonne (1873) to spread the taste for the symphony, and especially Berlioz, who was then more famous abroad than in France, and the Concerts Lamoureux (1882) to advance the cult of Wagner. In the prosperity of the 1920s small sects could flourish; in the depression they collapsed; in 1945–6 about 85 per cent of

[1] Victor Maurel, *Dix ans de carrière 1887–1897* (1897), 151–2, 246; A. Laget, op. cit. 45–7.

recitals given in Paris lost money. There was increasing difficulty in finding audiences for new works. In Angers, with a population of 80,000 just before the Second World War, there were only about 400 regular patrons of the local concerts, but the attendance doubled for Bach, Beethoven and Wagner and quadrupled for the *Damnation of Faust*. In Lyon, with a population of 600,000 at the same time, older traditions survived, for there was an Opéra, which performed five times a week, but its audience (there were 1,500 seats) was directly proportionate to the classicism of its repertoire; and the Lyon Philharmonic Association gave ten subscription concerts a year, to, on average, an audience of 800. The result of music being an increasingly specialist activity, with a small circle of increasingly erudite listeners, was that composers lost their social function as general organisers of entertainment, and became isolated figures, without regular contact with either performers or audience; and their music showed less concern with popularity. Debussy began by saying that 'music must humbly seek to give pleasure' but later despaired of art being appreciated by the masses; his work became more abstract and he declared 'One can no more order the crowds to love beauty than one can ask them to walk on their hands'.[1]

In 1780 Paris was a major international centre of musical publishing: it had forty-four firms specialising in this. That was the time when European and especially German firms were beginning to develop, and these soon outstripped their French rivals. There are now only some twenty-three publishers of classical music, and seven or eight of them produce three-quarters of the total output. The demand for sheet music barely justifies even this number, for editions are often limited to a few hundred copies and they may take fifty years or more to sell out. Georges Auric's Three Impromptus for piano, published in 1946 in 500 copies, had sold only 330 by 1962; and this was typical.[2] How long the bourgeois cult of the piano as a necessary symbol of respectability lasted and how many pianos were produced to enable idle daughters to acquire the accomplishments of a lady, would be worth calculating, for it would help to establish the

---

[1] Bernard Gavoty, *Les Français sont-ils musiciens?* (1950), 50, 136.

[2] Alicia de Schwarzer, 'Certains aspects de la sociologie de la musique en France 1960–70' (unpublished mémoire, École Pratique des Hautes Études, 1972).

size of the musical constituency. Pleyel started making pianos under the Restoration and by 1890 had produced 100,000;[1] he was one of many. Today, 8·2 per cent of the French population own pianos (but one-quarter of the managerial class have them). The guitar (12·9 per cent) and wind instruments (12·7 per cent) are more popular.[2] But the French have almost completely ceased to make musical instruments. In 1969 only about 13,000 new pianos were bought (compared to about 220,000 in the U.S.A.).[3]

Music has clearly been transformed by the radio. Already in 1939 there were about 1,500 shops selling radios, compared to about 160 selling pianos.[4] In the 1940s the radio stations interpreted popular taste, or popular needs, by broadcasting (hours per annum):

| | | |
|---|---|---|
| 1,622 | hours of | light music |
| 1,555 | ,, | songs (variety and folkloric) |
| 1,369 | ,, | symphonic music |
| 942 | ,, | chamber music |
| 916 | ,, | dance and jazz music |
| 463 | ,, | opera |
| 229 | ,, | operetta |
| 61 | ,, | religious music |

Opera has fallen low after the supremacy it enjoyed a century ago. The present-day opera-goers constitute only 2·6 per cent of the population, compared with 6·9 per cent who go to symphony concerts, 5·8 per cent who go to the ballet, 4·4 per cent who go to operettas and 6·5 per cent who go to jazz or pop concerts; though it is true that opera-goers tend to be fanatics, and attend twice as often as other music lovers. The effect of broadcasting on musical taste has still not been worked out.[5] But broadcasting and gramophone music have undoubtedly increased the amount of music, and the breadth of choice, available. This is all the more true because the old music teacher,

[1] Oscar Comettant, *Histoire de cent mille pianos et d'une salle de concert* (1890); L. E. Gratia, *Les Instruments de musique du 20ᵉ siècle* (1931).

[2] *Pratiques culturelles des Français* (1974).

[3] Elizabeth Lion, 'L'Offre et la demande de musique. Essai d'analyse économique' (unpublished mémoire, École Pratique des Hautes Études 1970), 94–6.

[4] *Annuaire O.G.M. (ex-Musique-Adresses) du commerce et de l'industrie de musique, radio, phono* (1939).

[5] Cf. Paul Beaud and Alfred Willener, *Musique et vie quotidienne* (1973), 12.

who was once a not unimportant part of bourgeois households, has become a much rarer figure. In 1921 there were 14,105 teachers of music and singing in France; in 1936 there were 10,305; in 1946 6,941. There were in addition about 12,000 musicians, 6,000 singers and 700 composers between the wars. Their numbers have fallen too, but the most dramatic loss has been that of the singers, who were down to under 3,000 in 1962.[1] The effect of new technology has been a great centralisation (and, accordingly, 56 per cent of musicians live in Paris). The same famous artists reach an enormous audience, and the obscure provincial teacher cannot compete with them. Music, more than ever, has become an individual experience and the meaning given to it probably varies more than ever before.[2]

It is impossible to write a satisfactory history of musical taste in France, first of all because so many of its composers have fallen into complete oblivion, and only a few names, surviving from this period, have been heard by the present generation.[3] The paradox that needs to be explained is why German and Italian music was so popular, why (as Romain Rolland said, with much exaggeration) all great French composers were foreigners, but why at the same time a distinctly French kind of music—distinguished by a characteristic lightness—continued to be produced and to remain immediately recognisable. French painting soon became international: French music did not.

This chapter has suggested that ideas of beauty were moving in two opposing directions simultaneously: the increasing individualism of artists was paralleled by strong pressures, on the side of their public, in favour of conformist taste. These pressures can be understood more clearly if one looks at the newspapers, which acted as the intermediaries between the two.

[1] Schwarzer, op. cit. 30–6.

[2] R. Francès, *La Perception de la musique* (1958); A. Silbermann, *La Musique, le radio et l'auditeur* (1955); id., *Introduction à une sociologie de la musique* (1955).

[3] André Coenroy, *La Musique et le peuple en France* (1941), for an inquiry into the most popular songs of that period, p. 76. Henry Raynor, *A Social History of Music* (1972) unfortunately stops in the early nineteenth century.

# 11. Newspapers and Corruption

THE press, more than anything else, created reputations. Reputation, said Balzac, is a crowned prostitute; it has to be bought. There is a great deal to learn about the frustrations of France by looking at who was keen to buy reputation and who was willing to be bought. The press brought information to the masses, but a lot of bargaining took place between the journalists and the people as to the kind of information they were willing to pay for. This was an age of education, but the people seemed to demand relaxation and entertainment instead: what one witnesses in the history of the press is the clash of Parisian culture and primitive taste. The press, finally, was an astonishing world in itself, attracting strange, deluded and disillusioned men; and their adventures are worth investigation even if their impact on the masses was not as great as they believed it to be.

The character of the press was shaped by three forces—the journalists, the newspaper owners, and the readers, whose interests and aspirations were far from coinciding. One cannot talk simply of the former exercising an influence on, or leading, the latter, nor can one accept the view that the press expressed the opinions and attitudes of its readers, mirroring 'public opinion'. Each of the pressures in the newspaper world was itself infinitely complex and varied.

### *Journalists*

No clear image of the French journalist is possible, because he had too many faces. To begin with, the journalist, born (in a professional sense) in the eighteenth century, had an ambiguous and dubious origin. In his most primitive form, he was a news-seller, who wandered around Paris, picking up and repeating whatever gossip he could find: the Tuileries and Luxembourg gardens were his favourite haunt; in different parts of these, scientists, economists, literary men met to hear and discuss the latest events. Montesquieu was contemptuous of these *nouvellistes*: 'they are useless to the state,' he wrote, 'but they believe themselves to be important because they discuss magnificent projects and deal with great interests. The basis of their conversation is a frivolous and ridiculous curiosity; there are no offices too secret for them not to be able to penetrate into; they refuse to be ignorant of anything . . . all that they lack is good sense.'[1] But one of these news-sellers was revealed in 1774 to have been a former royal counsellor and intendant's subdelegate, who found it worth while to remain in the business for twenty years, employing fifty copyists and pedlars, and having 280 subscribers to the manuscript service he provided: among his clients were the archbishop of Paris and several dukes. However, the printed newspaper had serious obstacles to its rise. The king employed no less than 121 censors in 1763, and he gave a monopoly to the *Gazette de France* and the *Journal des savants*: all those wishing to compete with these had to buy their permission and a licence; and even foreign papers entering the country had to pay them a fee. Manuscript newspapers were theoretically altogether forbidden, under pain of flogging. But such was the demand for news, and such were the profits to be made, that this new challenge to serious literature grew rapidly. The great minds of the eighteenth century were divided in their attitude towards this development: on the one hand their principles favoured free speech and the freedom to publish, but on the other hand they had a profound contempt for the low quality of those who sought to profit from this freedom. Voltaire said journalism was discredited by the 'multitude of papers which mutually competing and greedy booksellers have published and which obscure writers fill with incorrect extracts, stupidities and lies . . . to the extent that there has developed a public trade in praise and criticism'. Diderot remarked, 'People discovered that it was easier to write a review of a good book than to write a decent line of prose of one's own, and many sterile minds have therefore applied themselves to this.' Newspapers, he said, were invented 'for the solace of those who are either too busy or too lazy to read whole books. They are a means of satisfying

[1] Montesquieu, *Lettres persanes* (1719), Letter 130; F. Funck-Brentano, *Les Nouvellistes* (1905).

curiosity and giving learning at a small cost.' Rousseau thought journalism a labourer's task, and a periodical 'an ephemeral work, without merit and without utility, which cultivated men avoid and despise and which serves only to give women and fools vanity without instruction: its fate is to shine in the morning at the toilette and to die in the evening in a cupboard'. But already in 1749 the marquis d'Argenson was attributing 'the great ferment among the people' to their reading newspapers. This was too prophetic an explanation, for most newspapers sold only 300 to 500 copies an issue under the *ancien régime*, and the *Gazette de France* itself never had more than 12,260 subscribers. These small sales were enough, however, to make journalism a profitable business. The editor of *Le Patriote français*, with only 5,000 subscribers (1790), earned 6,000 livres a year and the publisher made 24,000.[1] Newspapers were expensive, a luxury product. In the 1830s a subscription to most papers cost about a tenth of a worker's wages.

Journalists became much more ambitious and much more dangerous as a result of the French Revolution. The complete freedom temporarily won by the press meant that 500 new papers were published between 1789 and 1792. Not only were many of the most distinguished leaders of the Revolution, from Mirabeau to Marat, active in journalism, but almost every group started a paper, and seemed to acquire influence from it. The press became a political tool as never before. The Revolution established the tradition by which, in 1830 and in 1848, journalists played leading roles in overthrowing governments. The freedom of the press became a major political issue. But precisely because the number of newspapers multiplied greatly in the course of the nineteenth century, the quality and functions of journalists became much more varied; their position became much more ambiguous; the contrast between what they actually achieved and the pretensions they put forward was accentuated.

Émile de Girardin (1806–81), perhaps the most influential figure in the history of the modern French press, illustrates well the heights journalists aspired to. He was the illegitimate son of a distinguished noble general by the beautiful Madame

[1] C. Bellanger *et al.*, *Histoire générale de la presse française*, vol. 1 (*des origines à 1814*) (1969), 159, 439.

Dupuy (whom Greuze painted, as *The Girl with the Dove*, in the Wallace Collection), but both father and mother found his existence inconvenient, gave him a fake birth certificate in the name of Émile Delamothe, sent him away to be brought up by strangers, and neglected to have him educated. When he grew up his father saw him once a month, gave him lunch in his gardener's cottage, refusing to let him into his house. Girardin grew up obsessed, as he said, by 'the triple longing for a name, the affection of a father and the love of a mother'. At the age of twenty-one he published his autobiography, a plea for the rights of bastards, affirming his determination to 'draw upon him the eyes of the masses and so revenge himself for having been abandoned . . . to win an honourable situation which I shall owe to no one but myself, a situation in the world which will be so brilliant that I shall hear people say: Though without family and without fortune, he surmounted the obstacles which condemned him to obscurity: he succeeded in overcoming his misfortune, and having no name, he made himself a reputation'. His parents would then come running to him, and he would not repulse them. The way to become famous, he said, was not to help people, but to flatter the passions of the masses. Merit was useless unless backed up by money and he had to become rich too.[1] He achieved these aims with extraordinary rapidity. At eighteen, another beautiful lady, Madame de Sesonnes (painted by Ingres), taking a liking to him, got him a job in the civil service; a few years later he was appointed assistant inspector of Fine Arts, but this was unpaid; so he abandoned the safe paths of bureaucracy to make himself a living in journalism and literature. He founded a newspaper called *The Thief*, which, without hypocrisy, made clear that it provided summaries of other newspapers. He raised 500 francs, just enough to print the first issue, but instead of paying the printer, he used the whole sum to advertise the paper and this brought in several thousand francs in subscriptions: very soon his paper was giving him an income of 50,000 francs net. At twenty-three, he established *La Mode* (1829), as a paper for the fashionable world, which he had illustrated by Gavarni, and for which he obtained contributions from a host of writers who were soon to reach the front rank of literature—Balzac among

[1] E. de Girardin, *Émile* (1828).

them. Two years later, his *Journal of Useful Knowledge* (1831) obtained 132,000 subscribers within a year, yielding an income of 200,000 francs. It issued an *Almanach de France* in 1,300,000 copies, with the motto 'Health, Prosperity and Knowledge'. This was Girardin's programme. He presented himself as a pioneer of mass education, through mass journalism, and he sought to educate the people in every aspect of life. His *Musée des familles*, *La Musée rustique* and a host of other periodicals made him one of the most important publishers of his day. In 1834 he was elected to parliament (falsely declaring himself older than he was so as to qualify: he had endless trouble with his birth certificates). He crowned his achievement in 1836 by founding *La Presse*, a daily newspaper costing 40 francs a year, instead of the 80 francs which was normal at the time; he proposed to make advertisements pay the difference. This inaugurated a revolution in newspaper production, beginning the steady fall in the price asked of the reader, and increasing dependence on advertising. Like most revolutions, other people had the same idea at the same time, and a rival paper, *Le Siècle*, was founded on the same basis simultaneously, and it was in fact somewhat more successful. But Girardin was as remarkable a journalist as he was an entrepreneur; he wrote his paper as well as managing it; and unlike the masters of *Le Siècle*, he saw in *La Presse* a stepping-stone to higher things.

He was a member of parliament for much of his life, under successive regimes. He had no particular preference as between them, making his programme simply Liberty. He consistently fought on behalf of anybody who suffered at the hands of governments, pressing for the release of political prisoners, demanding amnesties. 'What is the State?', he asked. 'Everything. What should it be? Nothing.' He had vague ideas about abolishing centralised government, partly echoing the ideas of Proudhon; but he never joined any party. Independence was his watchword; 'an idea every day' was what he offered in his paper. He had a universally recognised genius for journalistic strategy, in the sense that he was a brilliant polemicist, a master of controversy, whose articles, always written in short sentences, bursting with striking formulae, kept him continuously in the public eye. But all this made him incapable of obtaining political power, which was the unfulfilled ambition of his life.

He regularly supported compromise policies and compromise politicians: he was a 'progressive conservative' under Louis-Philippe, which pleased neither conservatives nor progressives. He played a decisive role in persuading Louis-Philippe to abdicate, but got him to proclaim a regency, which never materialised. He supported the Provisional Government of 1848, but soon fell foul of it, and was arrested by General Cavaignac. He took up the cause of Louis Napoleon, the first major paper to do so; but he was cruelly disappointed when the latter failed to give him the ministerial portfolio he longed for. He then became the most active supporter of Émile Ollivier's liberal Empire, but again failed to have a post offered to him. He never concealed that active participation in government was what he wanted. He had quickly lost his illusions about the power of the press; its scribblings, he said, were condemned to immediate oblivion; 'the so-called tyrants of opinion were really only busy-body flies', living on the surface of events. The time for discussions was over, what he wanted was action, and that was the function of government, not journalism. The great men of the day, he declared, were 'Garibaldi and Kossuth, not Proudhon or Girardin'. But because he held himself aloof from all parties, because he appeared a speculator as well as a journalist, because he was haughty and cold, he never got beyond the fringes of politics. Émile Ollivier said he 'had neither the wide knowledge of Proudhon, nor his skill as a writer, nor his integrity, but he equalled him in his passion and his hard work and he appeared more practical because he was more pedestrian'. His unashamed advocacy of material well-being, industrialism and *Universal Prosperity* (the title of another of his periodicals) made him a crank in a political world which placed more emphasis on grand rhetoric and principle. His newspaper empire expanded considerably during the Third Republic and he died worth well over eight million francs, but in old age he lamented to Villemessant, the editor of the *Figaro*, 'I have everything and yet I have nothing'. His was perhaps an ambition that could not be satisfied.[1]

[1] Maurice Reclus, *Émile de Girardin* (1934); E. de Girardin, *L'Abolition de l'autorité par la simplification du gouvernement* (1851), *L'Abolition de la misère par l'élévation des salaires* (1850), *L'Impôt* (1852), *La Liberté* (1857), *Le Désarmement européen* (1859), *Pensées et maximes* (1867), *L'homme et la femme* (1872), etc.

This combination of business and politics that characterised the press can be seen in another important journalist of the Second Empire, Adolphe Guéroult (1810–72). The son of a textile manufacturer, whose old-established family business collapsed in 1814, Guéroult was converted to Saint-Simonianism while a law student. He abandoned himself, as he wrote to a friend, 'without reservation to the influence' of the leader of the sect, Enfantin, but 'there was always a part of me, the best part perhaps, which remained outside the affection I bore him and . . . which always resisted him'. Guéroult had a muddled political life and a muddled private life. He fell in love with a leader of the women's rights movement, Pauline Roland, who refused to marry him, but decided to have an illegitimate child by him; then just before the child was born she left him for another man, by whom she had four other children, before leaving him to marry someone else. Guéroult in time got over this and married another girl whom he met at a Saint-Simonian club. But he had some difficulty in deciding what to do with his life. On the one hand, he had his political convictions; on the other his love of music 'which is art *par excellence*, the most popular, the most powerful, the most inspired of all arts', which led him to specialise for a time as a music critic; but there was also his desire for a career and a conventional family life. He was much abused when he took a job on the conservative *Journal des Débats* and then accepted appointment by Guizot's reactionary government as French consul in Mexico, and then (because he could not stand the food there) in Moldavia. He did not resign at the revolution of 1848, saying he had a family to support, and it was only when he was sacked the following year that he returned to journalism. He now made a name for himself with articles attacking the Catholic Church, and in favour of industrial expansion and material prosperity; he denounced, like Girardin, the fear of the useful and the comfortable. The capitalist Millaud offered him the editorship of *La Presse* (1858), though requiring an undated letter of resignation before he started, just in case things went wrong. This was a pro-government paper, but Guéroult accepted its political line, though he added anticlerical and pro-Italian touches of his own. In 1859 the emperor's radical cousin, Prince Jérôme Napoléon, started up a new paper for Guéroult with the help of a printer, a banker and probably with secret funds from Piedmont. In *L'Opinion nationale* Guéroult was able to give free rein to his advocacy of nationalism (the unification of Italy and Germany), anticlericalism, and the reorganisation of Europe into a federation. In 1863 he was elected to parliament for Paris, showing the leading role that newspapers were playing at that time in political life. But Guéroult's publication of a series of articles by Champfleury on the seedy side of fashionable life 'La Mascarade de la vie parisienne' was considered indecent; his chief assistant and two other journalists employed by him were dishonest; the paper failed to win a mass circulation despite the considerable skill with which it was written; it appealed, apparently, as a police inspector reported, to 'second-class railway travellers' (at a time when there were three classes). Guéroult's friendship with Prince Napoléon made him suspect to the republican opposition he was supposed also to be friends with; and in 1867 he (and the editors of four other papers) was accused publicly of being in the pay of the Italian and Prussian governments. The investigation into the charge was never completed, but his name was sullied; he lost his parliamentary seat in 1869, returning to a paper whose circulation had been halved by his preoccupation with politics and by internal feuds. After the revolution of 1870 he rallied to the republic, saying he was willing to serve all governments, because something of value could be drawn from each, whatever its politics. Guéroult was a very active partisan of the rights of the press, a sober, courteous, persevering man. He looked the 'very archetype of the bourgeois, a mixture of blooming health, malice and complacency'. He bequeathed his paper to his son as a family business; another son became an inspector of finances and *trésorier payeur général*; a third was an engineer.[1] The biography of Guéroult illustrated how journalism acquired a dubious reputation, despite the talent that went into it, and how its influence was therefore equivocal, despite its occasional political and commercial triumphs.

One can see the same in the career of the colourful, amazing, but equally ambivalent Henri Rochefort (1831–1913), who

[1] Bernard Coste, 'Adolphe Guéroult et l'Opinion nationale' (doctoral thesis, unpublished, in the library of the Paris Faculty of Law, 1968).

made his fortune by whipping up journalistic polemic to unprecedented heights of violence, audacity and wit. He was the son of the marquis de Rochefort-Luçay, a ruined aristocrat who had become a successful vaudevillist; he was one of the very rare people who abandoned, instead of adopting, a title. His mother 'generally saw everything as gloomy': he was himself sad, nervous and rebellious at school; his family condemned him as stupid; he seems always to have been a lonely man, who said 'adults have not always liked me, though children have'. He had a constant feud with his father and allowed him to die in poverty; and his own elder son committed suicide. A fellow journalist wrote of him: 'Every time I saw Rochefort . . . I always found him frantic to escape from a formidable bore, suggesting both a permanent anxiety of mind and very violent stomach pains. He sought pleasure in every form, tracked down all the emotional thrills. He gambled at roulette, at the races, at cards, in the stock-market; suppers, girls, theatre and journalism. The dominant feature of his character was vanity and what vanity . . .'[1] Rochefort denied this, saying he neither smoked, drank nor gambled; but he certainly seems to have had difficulties with women, for all his three marriages ended in divorce or separation and he had three illegitimate children. There can be no doubt that he was one of the sharpest wits of his generation; his journalism was an unending show of brilliant and dangerous fireworks, that found many lesser imitators. But it was rather by accident that he found his way into the newspaper world. He began as a clerk in the patent department of the Paris Hôtel de Ville, and then in the department of architecture, where his colleague was Drumont, father of another journalistic incendiary. His job left him with plenty of leisure to cultivate his interest in art, or more precisely in art dealing and restoration, which he learnt about from another ruined aristocrat, who kept himself by restoring old paintings for those who were still rich. This was a time when people like Dr. Lacaze, another of Rochefort's friends, who left his collection to the Louvre, could buy up a Frans Hals for 300 francs, because the dealers were so ignorant: Rochefort mocked them in a series of articles for Le Charivari, reprinted as a book

[1] Quoted in R. L. Williams, *Henri Rochefort, Prince of the Gutter Press* (New York, 1966), 130.

entitled *The Mysteries of the Sale Rooms*, saying they attributed a head of Christ inscribed with the words Salvator Mundi to 'the painter of the Bolognese school, Salvator Mundi'. But it was the time also when these antiquarian art lovers painted extra objects on to the paintings they discovered, saying they needed improvement. Rochefort earned his first 100 francs from writing by producing a novel for Mirecourt, who churned them out like a factory. He tried his hand also at vaudeville, following in his father's footsteps, and altogether produced eighteen light comedies. He started journalism as a theatre critic; when he lost his civil service job, he joined *Le Nain jaune* at 100 francs a week, moved to the *Figaro*, where he was so successful that in 1868 its editor raised the money to set up a separate paper for him, *La Lanterne*, to do the things the *Figaro* dared not do itself. The editor, Villemessant, liked Rochefort because, as he said, he was the only journalist in his employ who was not trying to write so as to get elected to the French Academy: 'Tease and make them laugh' was his advice and Rochefort had followed it. He fought lots of duels, including one with the cousin of the emperor, Prince Achille Murat, and that gave him his fame. *La Lanterne* which he now brought out, writing it almost entirely himself, sold 100,000 copies of its first issue, which alone gave the investors behind it their money back. Its first sentence was 'France has 36 million subjects, not counting the subjects of discontent', and that was typical of the bitter jokes Rochefort produced inexhaustibly. His readers were entranced not only by his outrageous humour and his pitiless satire, but also by the boldness of his attacks, and none could tell what retribution each issue would bring from the government and from the people he insulted. He was a kind of stunt man who was funny as well as frightening. He helped to stir up the largest demonstration against the Second Empire in 1870; he was exiled to New Caledonia for his part in the Commune; he escaped dramatically; he got elected to parliament in 1885 where he was a violent anti-Semite and Boulangist, until he was exiled again. But he had created a style of satirical and rebellious journalism so successful that, even without him, his paper earned enough to send to him in London 242,000 francs a year. The journalists who tried to ape him, lacking his humour and reproducing only his violence, made the French press one of the most vituperative in the world. That politics so often confused opposition with insult, and mistook words for deeds, owed much to the tradition he helped establish.[1]

One could certainly make a lot of money out of journalism. In the middle of the nineteenth century, when a good worker or successful artisan could earn 1,000 francs a year, a poor weaver half of that, a sub-prefect three times as much and the rector of an Academy around 7,000 francs, there were famous journalists whose earnings were among the highest in France. Zola as a young man had earned 6,000 francs a year but by 1867 was getting about 10,000. Théophile Gauthier is said to have earned 20,000 francs over twenty years from his books and his plays, but 100,000 in fifteen years from his journalism. La Gueronnière, editor of the government-backed *La France*, got 20,000 a year, and that also is what Prévost-Paradol, once a professor on a pittance, earned by supplementing his French journalism with articles for the London *Times*. When Edmond About ran the *Dix-neuvième Siècle* his salary shot up to 30,000, five times what he had started with on the *Opinion nationale*. Villemessant, the phoney aristocrat who made the *Figaro* the record of the frivolities of the idle rich, said that he had been accused of raising the price of the journalist and that he was proud of it: he poached his authors from other papers, doubling their salaries. But it was in the new popular press that the largest sums were to be obtained: the master of sensation journalism, Léo Lespès, made as much as 40,000 francs. Even Jules Vallès, though he never got over his rage with society, reached 24,000 francs.[2] A newspaper could not only finance a popular politician, but keep him in some style, as Gambetta discovered. Gambetta was a very poor man when he entered political life, but *La République française*, with a sale of only 18,000 in 1873, made enough profits to keep him, and even to buy itself a house in the rue de la Chaussée d'Antin, where Gambetta was given a free flat. In 1876 Gambetta was such a power in politics, it was decided to launch a popular daily under his aegis. A Swiss businessman, Dubochet, president of the Eastern Railway Company and of the Gas Company, offered to put up the money

[1] Henri Rochefort, *Les Aventures de ma vie* (5 vols., 1896); Williams, op. cit.

[2] Pierre Denoyer and Jean Morienval, 'La Condition sociale du journaliste française', *Études de presse* (15 Jan. 1952), 10–20, and Bellanger, op. cit. 2. 343.

needed, though he was completely uninterested by politics and only wanted a good investment. Gambetta refused his offer; instead, he got an Alsatian industrialist of republican sympathies, Scheurer-Kestner, to write 129 letters to suitable capitalists, from whom 300,000 francs were raised. Gambetta was given shares in the new company worth 300,000 francs too, though he contributed only his name. It does not appear that he even contributed his pen, or his managerial skill, for he limited himself to having the ideas for the major articles and it was his Achates Spuller who wrote them. By the time he was prime minister, therefore, journalism had given him financial independence. Of course, it was a fragile one, depending on his political popularity. After his death, the paper had financial difficulties and a new set of businessmen came to its rescue, under Joseph Reinach's leadership; in 1893 a third set took it over, to back another rising star, Jules Méline, in his anti-free-trade campaign. Journalism could be highly profitable for some people.

But these were the top names, and they were exceptions. The majority of journalists earned only a tiny fraction of these salaries. Brazier (1783–1838), who later kept himself by writing over 200 vaudevilles, started as a collector of 'the little misfortunes of Paris', and he was paid three francs for each misfortune published. Victor Considérant's Fourierist paper, *La Démocratie pacifique* (1843–51) paid its staff daily according to its receipts—usually between three and five francs—little more than a carpenter could earn—and when it was out of funds, they contented themselves drinking sugared water spiced with rum. When Jules Vallès was at the beginning of his career and wrote for the *Journal de la cordonnerie*, he was paid with a gift of a pair of shoes. In 1893 Aristide Briand started on *La Lanterne* at 250 francs a month; after five years he reached 1,000 francs a month. The rewards of the majority of journalists were very modest indeed, and between the wars, when inflation struck, they were even worse. Between 1914 and 1925, while the cost of living rose fourfold, the wages of journalists rose on average between two and two and a half times. A reporter in 1925 earned more or less the same wage as a primary school master; a *secrétaire de redaction* started at the same level as a junior secondary teacher; an editor might not earn very much more, though a successful one could earn several times as much. There was nothing unusual in the French situation: the wages of the reporters and the printers on English provincial papers were also roughly the same.[1] Paris reporters might earn twice as much as provincial ones, but they had a higher cost of living to bear. Their poverty was unchanged in 1950, when reporters were still on the same level as *instituteurs*; they bitterly complained that they earned less than sewer workers, but then there was intense competition for very few jobs. Even in 1970, there were still only 12,000 journalists in France (at a time when there were 65,000 doctors). Theirs moreover was the only profession—apart from banking—for which no prior professional qualifications were required.

Balzac had the most profound contempt for journalists and left scathing portraits of them in his *Illusions perdues*. Theirs was an occupation, he said, from which it was no more possible to emerge pure than it was when one went to a brothel. During the Second Empire, there was general agreement that they enjoyed, as a class, little prestige. They were condemned as bohemians, who were redeemed only by their wit. They were placed on the same level as actors 'whom people both despise and envy'. They were, to some degree, even performing bears, in that, to attract publicity, they made a habit of fighting duels; a room for fencing practice was often provided next to that in which they wrote their copy; and one of the leading experts on duels, who tried to continue them into the twentieth century, was Paul de Cassagnac, the Bonapartist editor. Everyone knew that the violence of their polemic was a mask, that the insults they hurled at each other through their papers were a game, simply serving as an entertainment for the bourgeois. There were very few journalists, as there were bankers, notaries and priests, who had made themselves notorious as criminals, and yet, as one provincial journalist wrote, 'There are few professions which are the object of more widespread discredit.'[2] The reporter, said Larousse's Encyclopedia in 1875, was an 'inferior writer', whose legs were more important than his style, and who 'is in general rather poorly

[1] Bureau International du Travail, *Les Conditions de travail et de vie des journalistes* (Geneva, 1928), 147–9.

[2] Anatole Willox, *Le Journalisme en province* (new ed. 1887), 130.

thought of by serious people who regret seeing news taking on exaggerated importance, expelling the serious article from newspapers. He is generally held in little esteem by those who read him with the greatest assiduity.' But Larousse conceded that he was nevertheless a useful person, however despicable 'the intimate dramas and the loves of fashionable *cocottes*' about which he collected information, because, if the press was to survive, these stories were needed to win the readership of 'the indifferent part of the public'.[1] Barbey d'Aurevilly, in his study of *Journalists and Polemicists* (1895), said journalism 'diminished the faculties, when it did not kill them, after having depraved them'. It destroyed budding writers by giving them bad habits, frivolity, inconstancy, party passion, false judgement and worst of all it made them fool themselves, so as to be able to fool their readers better. They were dominated by the search for pretty formulae, but though they aimed to be amusing, their vehicle, and the instrument of their success, was always the banal idea. He was not sure whom he hated more, the frustrated rebel, whose opinions were no more than the expression of hurt pride, or the pompous editorialist looking at the world through drawn curtains, or the gossip writers, unable to distinguish what was important, or to make any judgements at all. The spoilt child of journalism was the young man of wit, who made his appearance during the Second Empire, and who at least could make fun of the world, to leaven the doctrinaire sententiousness so many papers still adopted, but he was regarded as being on the fringes of the profession.[2] A professor of medicine, in a work on *The Influence of Journalism on the Health of the Body and of the Mind* (1871), classified journalists as 'jealous, ambitious for popularity, and infatuated with themselves; they excite themselves by wrintig, taking the risk of overstepping boundaries as the drinker who drinks thoughtlessly and befuddles himself in despite of the stupor that threatens him'. The violence of their language did not mean they were brave, as they imagined themselves to be, but that they lived in a state of 'pathological excitement and hot fever'.

---

[1] *Grande Encyclopédie Larousse* (1875), s.v. Reporter.

[2] J. Barbey d'Aurevilly, *Les Œuvres et les hommes. Journalistes et polémistes, chroniqueurs et pamphletaires* (1895), 20, 204, 231–2, 342. For examples of this light journalism, see Louis Duchemin, *Durand et Cie, scènes de la vie parisienne* (1878).

R

They were dangerous people, because they spread their nervousness to their readers.[1] They were dangerous people also, as one of them pointed out, because they had it in their power to harm those who got on the wrong side of them, and that is what saved them from being completely ostracised by good society. By fighting against each other and by their fake duels, they had won attention as entertainers, but they had also lost in dignity. There would always be more respect for authors of books than for the mere journalist: 'The job of journalist is suitable only for vagabonds and men without any means of support.' It could be a perfectly honourable occupation, though one in which ambition was out of place. What brought it so low was 'advertising, camaraderie and blackmail', using newspapers to advance the cause of their friends, writing reviews and praising artists and actors corruptly.[2]

By the twentieth century, however, the power of the journalist had become too obvious for these moral doubts to matter too much, just as the *nouveau riche* financier was eventually welcomed into the aristocratic society that had once disdained him. In 1910 it was said that 'whereas twenty years ago a bourgeois would have had scruples about finding himself in the company of a journalist in a *salon* of high society, now the journalist is everywhere respected and it is to him that one almost always turns to obtain a favour, knowing very well that he has his own ways of getting at influential personages'.[3] Too many famous men of letters had dabbled in journalism; too many journalists had become politicians and ministers; too many people in the liberal professions earned supplementary income from part-time journalistic activities: in 1930, indeed, a professor of literature—it is true not a representative one— wrote that it was time that it was realised that newspapers were not the enemy of literature, but one of the forms of literature, the form that the general public loved best, and 'the most vigorous of all literary genres'.[4] It also now appeared as one of

---

[1] I. Druhen, *De l'influence du journalisme sur la santé du corps et de l'esprit* (Besançon, 1871), 20–1.

[2] N. Fourgeaud-Lagrèze, *La Petite Presse en province* (Ribérac, 1869), 12, 19, 38.

[3] Alexandre Guérin, *Comment on devient journaliste* (1910), 19. Cf. René Perlat, *Le Journalisme poitevin* (Poitiers, 1898).

[4] Léon Levrault, professeur au lycée Condorcet, *Le Journalisme* (1930), 7–10. But cf. N. Nikoladzé, *La Presse de la décadence. Observations d'un journaliste étranger* (1875).

the most exciting of occupations, having attractions for young people which were frequently compared to those of sport. The hunt for news, and the race to be first with the news, was an exhilarating adventure. The reporter who was sent off to some distant country sometimes won the prestige of an explorer, record breaker and fighter for just causes. It is true that the first reporter to carry out one of these grand assignments, involving travelling round the world in sixty-three days, came back so worn out, that he immediately accepted a job as a provincial librarian. But the generation that grew up just before the 1914 war, which thirsted for adventure and found it in sport or war, also revelled in the opportunities provided by the popular press; and it was a job that girls could enter also. Geneviève Tabouis, one of the most successful of these girls, loved the power: 'With his pen and his notebook the journalist is the censor and the equal of the greatest people in the world.'[1] Paul Bodin made the hero of his novel about a journalist say he had chosen the profession because 'I discovered in it the privileges of our function: we are witnesses and spectators but we can, whenever we wish, mix with the actors. We choose the moment when their passions can be made public. We join the participants in events; though we are barely noticed, even the greatest of these send us away only with extreme prudence: the journalist is one of the powers of the modern world.'[2] The fact that they might write rotten prose, or even make imbecile mistakes revealing crass ignorance (and one of them published a curious collection of these)[3] no longer mattered much. The new breed of reporter did not always take his job all that seriously: he might start as a sports writer and move on to every speciality in turn, but he would continue to praise the sporting spirit as the key to good journalism.[4] Sometimes he burnt himself out in constant, restless travel, like Albert Londres (1884–1932), one of the most famous of the early 'grands reporters'. The grandson of a pedlar, he claimed that he became a journalist in order to lead the same kind of wandering existence. His ideal was always to live out of a suitcase, to feel that he would be

[1] Christian Brincourt and Michel Leblanc, *Les Reporters* (1970), 347.

[2] Paul Bodin, *De notre envoyé spécial* (c. 1950), quoted in *Études de presse* (15 Oct. 1951), 325.

[3] Marcel Schwob, *Mœurs des diurnales. Traité de journalisme* (1926).

[4] Renée Pierre-Gosset, *Cochon de métier* (1950).

moving soon. 'I am not a weak man', he wrote, 'but an unquiet one.' He liked doing only three or four large articles a year, so he was often broke; he sometimes went without meals; he had no interest in luxurious living. He made his name with an investigation of conditions in the prisons of Cayenne; he got intense pleasure when the articles were printed as a book. Another of his great successes was *The Road to Buenos Aires* about the white slave trade. He wrote in the style of a popular novelist, but at forty-five he decided he would stop writing fast and would compose 'like a writer'. When he was accused of having an insufficiently formed style, he went out and bought a textbook on *The Art of Composition*. He was apparently a manic depressive, greatly dependent on the encouragement of his editor. He was a great believer in Justice, but had no definite political or religious ideas. He was drowned in a shipwreck at the height of his powers.[1]

The variety of characters that were attracted by journalism may be seen from the case of Eugène Lautier (1867–1935) who joined *Le Temps* at the age of eighteen and stayed with it for thirty-five years, becoming its pontiff on internal politics. He was a large fat man, a bachelor with an enormous appetite, whose favourite saying was 'I am never wrong'. His infuriating, genuine self-confidence went with an inexhaustible ambition for honour and power. At *Le Temps* he came to know everybody who mattered in politics, finance and literature; he helped to create the idea that the journalists on his paper were a power in the world; and when a former member of its staff, Tardieu, became prime minister, Lautier hitched himself on as under-secretary for Fine Arts. He was certain that he had the makings of a statesman: but he was only briefly a deputy for the corrupt constituency of Guyana. He knew all about political intrigue, but he offended too many people as a result. Because he had only his journalism to base himself on, he failed as a politician. He is a curious example of the frustrations of a certain kind of journalist.[2]

---

[1] Florise Londres, *Mon père* (1934); Paul Mousset, *Albert Londres: l'aventure du grand reportage* (1972); Albert Londres, *Aubagne* (1923), *Le Chemin de Buenos Aires* (1927), *Pêcheurs de perles* (1931).

[1] Victor Goedorp, *Figures du Temps* (1943), 9–58. For other attitudes to the press, see Henri Béranger, 'Les Responsabilités de la presse', *Revue bleue* (4–25 Dec. 1897), quoting leading public figures.

Jules Vallès, a journalist who had other talents too, when accused of vanity, replied 'One does not become a man of letters from modesty'. Vanity was no doubt common among journalists, as it was in many of the liberal professions, and the journalist Edmond Texier (1816–87) was also probably right that 'it is sometimes because you have a cruel father who, when you were young, had a coat made for you out of his old breeches, that you are driven to write elegies'.[1] But journalism was to many people a job much like any other, which they not infrequently entered because their fathers had worked in it before them, or because they simply longed to escape from the civil service or teaching. The memoirs of some provincial journalists are, contrary to Vallès's dictum, very much the work of modest men. Arsène Thévenot, editor of *Le Vosgien*, recorded that 'in 1883, as a result of a reverse of fortune, I was obliged to seek my living from my pen'.[2] J. M. Villefranche, editor of the *Journal de l'Ain* (circulation 2,200), who spent fourteen years on the paper, attacking its anticlerical rival (circulation 1,600), said that there were two kinds of journalists, those who were convinced and those who were sceptics, willing to write to order: the latter were far more numerous. Despite the status in local politics that his editorship gave him, he valued his obscure poems and novels more highly than his daily polemic; and in his memoirs, of which he realistically had only 300 copies printed, he said 'One writes for the papers to earn a living or to serve truth, but neither is valued as much as a book, in the eyes of posterity.'[3] Likewise, Edmund Claris, though he went quite far in Parisian journalism, had no illusions. The son of the editor of the obscure *Dépêche de Paris*, he entered journalism as an adolescent, with a series of articles on the week's suicides for an ephemeral illustrated periodical, *L'Œuvre sociale*; he worked part-time as a research assistant to historians, while also

---

[1] Firmin Maillard, *La Cité des intellectuels: scènes cruelles et plaisantes de la vie littéraire des gens de lettres au 19ᵉ siècle* (3rd edition 1905).

[2] Arsène Thévenot, *Souvenirs d'un journaliste 1883–9* (Arcis-sur-Aube, 1901).

[3] J. M. Villefranche, *Photographies contemporaines. Souvenirs et menus propos d'un vieux journaliste* (Bourg, 1890), 271:

> On écrit journaux pour vivre
> Ou pour servir la vérité
> Mais aucun d'eux ne vaut un livre
> Auprès de la posterité.

selling 'news in brief' items to *Le Matin*. He then at last got a job with a regular salary on *La Petite République*, where he defended the rights of Algerians, trade unionists and madmen, and helped to start a shop, 'The Hundred Thousand Overcoats', whose profits were designed to save the paper from bankruptcy. He had friends in the art world of the Latin Quarter, so he became an art critic, and at the same time he published a serial novel and edited the speeches of Jaurès. He had to turn his hand to whatever task presented itself. Though a socialist, in 1909 he became the editor of *Le Radical*, but after obtaining a contract which stipulated that he should not be obliged to follow the radical party line slavishly: the owner of the paper was not too much of a radical either, for he employed a priest as tutor to his children. But after a quarrel, Claris moved on to *Le Journal*, where, because he was not paid much, he was allowed to have lunch daily for only five francs at Maxim's Restaurant, which tended to be empty at lunch time, and which his employer partly owned. From his socialist days, Claris had many friends who were now becoming ministers, like Viviani and Briand, and these gave him an entrée into the government offices; when Millerand became prime minister, Claris, who had long known him, became his assistant *chef de cabinet*. But all the while he kept on several other jobs, because pay was low: he worked for a news agency Agence-Radio, for *La France d'Outre Mer*, and for various provincial papers. He knew Clemenceau and Mandel, too, from his youth, so he was never short of news; but he never got more than a modest living from journalism; despite his experience and his contacts, he had to take work wherever he could find it.[1]

Journalists were ultimately wage earners with no security, at the mercy of arbitrary proprietors; many did not even have regular wages, but got paid by the line, and sometimes a small retainer. Some associated themselves with barristers, to whom they brought cases for a commission. They had to pick up what earnings they could, and they competed in a profession in which, it was said, there were six times as many people as were needed.[2] At the extremities of the journalistic world were a host of amateur part-timers, whom the professionals looked on

[1] Edmond Claris, *Souvenirs de soixante ans de journalisme 1895–1955* (1958).
[2] Paul Pottier, *Professions et métiers: Les Journalistes* (n.d., about 1907).

as interlopers, but the professionals were too individualistic to be able to organise themselves effectually.[1] They began forming unions in the 1870s, but Catholics, republicans, specialists each formed separate associations.[2] The National Union of Journalists was founded only in 1918 and by 1939 still had only 2,750 members. It spent about ten years negotiating for a collective contract for journalists, but in vain. However, in 1935 it succeeded in getting a law passed[3] which gave the journalist a professional status, entitled him to an official press card, annual holidays, compensation for dismissal, even when the journalist left his job for reasons of conscience following 'a notable change in the character or orientation of his paper or periodical, if this change creates for the employee a situation which endangers his honour, his reputation or, in a general way, his moral interests'. This was an important first step in the process which was to lead journalists, after the 1939–45 war, to strike against their employers and even in some cases to take over the running of the papers they worked on. But the exceptional power that the journalists of *Le Monde* and *Le Figaro* have won remains an exception, and the capitalist newspaper owners remain supreme. Even though they were temporarily dislodged by the Resistance in 1944, they have returned virtually omnipotent.[4]

### Advertising

The power of capital behind the press was one of the great obstacles that stood in the way of journalism becoming an independent and influential profession. In 1836 Émile de Girardin, the pioneer of a cheap press for the masses based on advertising, killed, in a duel, Armand Carrel, who represented the identification of journalism with politics, and whose newspaper indeed had played a decisive part in overthrowing King Louis-Philippe in 1830. This duel has, rather fancifully, been taken as symbolising the victory of the new press—a commercial, profit-making industry—over the old doctrinaire press, devoted

[1] Robert de Jouvenel, *Le Journalisme en vingt leçons* (1920); Georges Bourdon, *Le Journalisme d'aujourd'hui* (1931); Joseph Folliet, *Tu seras journaliste* (1961).
[2] Syndicat des journalistes français, *80 ans, 1886–1966* (1966), for a brief history.
[3] Law of 29 March 1935. See F. Terron, 'L'Évolution du droit de la presse de 1881 à 1940', in Bellenger *et al.*, *Histoire générale de la presse française*, vol. 3 (1972), 42–4.        [4] Jean Schwoebel, *La Presse, le pouvoir et l'argent* (1968).

mainly to party polemic, and justifying itself not on financial grounds but as an essential part of democratic government. No such victory was ever won, both because purely political newspapers have survived—even if they have usually been on the verge of financial collapse—and also because the commercial press was not in any case properly established. Girardin hoped to get most of the income for his paper from advertising but he did not entirely succeed. Advertising developed very slowly in this period and never attained anything like the proportions it reached in the U.S.A., Germany or even England. Even in 1970, after a decade during which expenditure on advertising had risen by between 8 and 15 per cent per annum, the annual amount spent in France was still only 80 francs per inhabitant, compared to 150 francs in the United Kingdom, 220 francs in Germany and 419 francs in the U.S.A.[1] This has had a profound effect on the character of the French press, and indeed on French life.

It has been seen how in politics, bureaucracy and industry, favouritism and personal recommendation remained of great importance.[2] Though careers were gradually opened to talent, no one believed that success in open examinations was enough to enable a man to get on in the world; and most politicians realised they had to be of personal service to individual electors to secure their votes, however attractive their programme was. The same kind of attitude prevented the rise of advertising. In 1848 Girardin assured his readers that there was nothing to be ashamed of if one advertised in a newspaper: in England at any rate 'people no longer blush' when they place advertisements.[3] But the tradition of mutual exchange of services was not eradicated. In the first French newspaper, Renaudot's *Gazette* (founded in 1631), advertisers did not pay anything, but simply gave the publisher a few copies of the object they advertised. Publisher and advertiser were considered to be in league, and with time advertising did indeed develop into something of a conspiracy, because so much trouble was taken to conceal its true character from the consumer. During the French Revolution, some newspapers offered their readers space not simply to advertise goods, but to publish their

[1] Bernard Voyenne, *L'Information en France* (1972), 59.
[2] See vol. 1, ch. 7.          [3] *La Presse*, 3 Oct. 1848.

opinions on any subject they pleased. In the course of the nineteenth century, this system was standardised so that newspapers came to offer four different kinds of advertising space. First was what was known as the 'English advertisement', which was an advertisement which did not pretend to be anything else. These were generally grouped on the fourth or back page and were the cheapest of all. But they were not very popular, precisely because they were cheap. Girardin tried to develop the 'small ad.', arguing that he would prefer to have a vast number of these than a few displayed ones; but in 1845, when the London *Times* was publishing about 1,500 advertisements a day, the most successful French papers were still unable to find more than forty or fifty each. More expensive than the open advertisement on the fourth page was the *réclame* on the third page, which usually cost two-thirds more, or a *faits divers* news item on the second page, which cost another 30 per cent, and most expensive of all was an article on the front page. These were known as 'editorial publicity', as opposed to 'advertisements': their purpose was to convey information about a product but without letting the reader know that he was reading an advertisement, until the last line. Sometimes, especially in articles or *chroniques*, the advertisement was totally camouflaged: a recommendation of a particular share would appear to result from an independent and objective assessment of the stock-market, and a review of a book would apparently have only the values of literature in mind. Villemessant, editor of the *Figaro* during the Second Empire, declared himself to be satisfied with an issue of his paper only when every single line in it had been paid for in this way.

One reason why the advertisement invaded the whole paper was the way advertising agencies developed. Newspapers were generally established with inadequate capital; because they needed income at once, they often started by farming their back page out to an agency. The pattern was set very early on by the *Société générale des annonces* founded in 1845 by Charles Duveyrier (1803–66), an enterprising Saint-Simonian, who had been in turn a missionary of his sect to England and Belgium, and a journalist—until he was sentenced to a year's imprisonment for outraging morals in an article on women; but a revolution had then made him Inspector-General of Prisons, and between times he was also a playwright and a businessman. He offered the three leading Paris papers 300,000 francs per annum each, plus half of his profits, in return for control of their advertising; and he offered the public an advertisement in all three papers, which together had 60,000 subscribers, at only 6 francs a line. Over 200 shopkeepers all over Paris were appointed sub-agents to collect advertisements. Havas, who had taken over Duveyrier's firm, became overwhelmingly powerful by amalgamating with two other leading agencies. Havas also owned (as will be seen) a news information service. His expanded agency now offered provincial newspapers a free news service by telegraph, in return for the right to insert advertisements free of change. Since this enabled provincial papers to do without their own Paris correspondents, the scheme was attractive and successful. But the growth of this formidable advertising monopoly (or near-monopoly) left the newspapers with a fixed income from advertisements (and in the case of those who exchanged advertisements for news, no income at all). Having lost control of their back pages, they therefore attempted to raise more revenue by selling space in the rest of the paper, and they did this by in effect becoming advertising agencies themselves, offering to write advertisements and pass them off as news. But another middleman now arose in the form of rival agencies which offered to put clients in contact with newspapers willing to sell themselves in this way. These agencies differed from British or American ones in that they did not charge their clients the cost of the advertisements they advised, and add 10 per cent for their services. Competition between them was not based on the quality of the advice or service they offered, but solely on price. They obtained discounts from the newspapers for whom they secured advertisements; the advice they gave was usually determined by the amount of money they could make from the deal themselves. Since throughout this period the newspapers refused to allow audited circulation figures, it was impossible to have objective criteria on which to base advertising policy; and, of course, this made it possible for a whole host of papers to appear, whose aim was simply prostitutional, to sell space and articles at the highest possible price. Advertising agencies tended to have a group of assorted papers, a few well-known ones and other obscurer ones, with whom they had arrangements, and they usually tried to sell their clients package deals—an advertisement in seven different papers, for example, for what they claimed cost little more than a single advertisement in one high-circulation daily. This uncertainty as to what press advertisements really cost resulted in a general belief that they were expensive, more expensive than in other countries, and this was often adduced as the reason for the failure of this activity to grow in the same way as it did abroad. In fact in 1911 it was calculated that a square centimetre of advertising space, per 100,000 copies, cost 91 centimes in the U.S.A., 68 centimes in England and only 54 centimes in France. It is true that the French price was impossible to state accurately, both because circulation figures were unreliable and because rates varied, as much as fivefold, depending on where the advertisement was placed. Large advertisements were proportionately much cheaper in France than small ones; enormous discounts encouraged clients to take half or whole pages, and the newspapers got little profit. It was true that advertising in provincial newspapers was expensive if done from Paris, for the Paris agencies often charged two or three times the rates payable in the provinces itself. In this industry, as in the retail food trade, the middlemen inflated costs in a quite disproportionate way. They asked a different price from every client, and the clients not surprisingly sought alternative avenues.[1]

Only certain sorts of people advertised in the press. In 1938 advertising space was distributed as follows:

| | |
|---|---|
| Pharmaceutical products | 29·87 per cent |
| Department stores | 17·46 |
| Food | 8·85 |
| Furniture | 7·28 |
| Household goods (produits d'entretien) | 5·43 |
| Cars | 5·18 |
| Alcoholic drinks | 4·35 |
| Soaps and cosmetics | 4·20 |
| Clothes | 3·30 |
| Miscellaneous | 14·08[2] |

[1] Émile Mermet, avocat, *La Publicité en France. Guide manuel* (4th edition, 1880), by one of the first advertising consultants; Henri Vathelet, *La Publicité dans le journalisme* (doctoral thesis, Paris, 1911), 67–89.

[2] Claude Bellenger, 'La Publicité dans la presse en 1938 et en 1951', *Études*

The most striking omission is industry and finance. The great failure of the press was its inability to obtain public advertising from the wealthiest firms and indeed from most sections of business in general. There were several reasons for this. Really large firms with expansionist ambitions preferred to buy up newspapers, or to obtain secret support from newspapers. Usually they did not see newspapers as a means of increasing demand in the general public, but rather as a way of stimulating public contracts and influencing politics. For purely trade purposes, they tended to advertise in trade journals, which accordingly flourished in very large numbers and which were often no more than collections of advertisements. There were a few manufacturers who believed in general advertising, of whom perhaps the most famous was Menier the chocolate a manufacturer, who had discovered—when he temporarily stopped advertising—that it really did pay; but Menier was also something of an eccentric and not the usual kind of businessman. Advertising by foreign manufacturers—like the Belgian Esders clothes chain, or Scott's Emulsion—did not compensate for the general wariness towards the papers. Even the department stores, who used press advertising so much, seem to have done so with some reluctance and from fear of blackmail. When one of them once stopped advertising, the newspapers replied by announcing that the store was stricken by the plague, imported with its Oriental carpets: it was forced to resume. Firms usually preferred to pay the newspapers to keep quiet about them rather than to parade their wares. Thus the suicide of the head of one firm was passed over in complete silence, and marked only by the fact that advertising by the firm suddenly filled the papers. The Société des Bains de Mer de Monaco was said to have spent large sums getting the papers to praise the merits of the south coast and to avoid mentioning the disasters caused by gambling in its casinos. But generally, apart from certain trades, businessmen looked on advertising as an extra expense, which would reduce profits and raise prices.

Press advertising was discredited because it was indeed used

de presse (Spring 1953), 37–40. In 1951 pharmaceutics were temporarily down to 8 per cent because of legislation limiting their advertising, clothes were up to 14·50, food to 16·88, cosmetics and soaps to 6·22.

most noticeably by dubious businesses and by obvious charlatans. Among the regular advertisers were usurers, into whose
hands no sensible man would entrust himself, small contractors, seeking domestic outworkers at exploitative wages, estate
agents, particularly those selling small shops, cafés and hotels
—where the advertisement was usually a way of extorting a
high advance fee from the seller, much larger than the actual
cost of the advertisement. Attentive readers could see that
advertisements were not infrequently a form of blackmail: press
campaigns in support of noble causes, for the extirpation of
various vices, turned out to be simply methods of forcing people
to advertise, as when Les Nouvelles waged an attack on a casino
on the outskirts of Paris, and then suddenly stopped, sporting
instead advertisements for the casino. The result was that in
1938 only 41 per cent of advertising expenditure went to the
press, compared to about 50 per cent in Britain and 80 per cent
in the U.S.A.

Perhaps it was because newspapers were a favourite place for
advertisements by charlatans offering every kind of medical
cure and elixir that the pharmaceutical industry was forced to
compete with them and advertise in the papers too. Pharmacists were originally forbidden to advertise, by the rules of the
College of Pharmacy founded in 1801; members of the society of
Pharmacists of the Seine, founded in 1819, likewise had to give an
undertaking not to advertise—though some broke this rule. But
a Pharmacists' Congress in 1867 voted to allow advertising and
from that time on the pharmacists were leaders among the
newspaper advertisers.[1] This decision marked the triumph of
the pharmaceutical industry, manufacturing patent drugs, or
'secret remedies' as some people still called them, over the
individual local pharmacist, who made up prescriptions to the
doctor's order. In the period 1900–14 these firms were said to
be spending about thirteen or fourteen million francs annually
on press advertisements, which appeared to be an enormous
amount.[2] When radio stations started to take advertisements,
one-half of these were pharmaceutical.[3] It did not enhance the

[1] Eugène Guitard, Deux siècles de presse au service de la pharmacie (1913).
[2] 'La publicité pharmaceutique', special issue of Le Courrier graphique (May 1938), no. 15.
[3] René Mante, La Publicité pharmaceutique au point de vue de la déontologie et de l'hygiène publique (Paris medical thesis, 1939).

prestige of the media that they were willing to accept advertisements which were, strictly speaking, illegal, for the law forbade 'secret remedies'.

Another source of revenue for the press was the theatre, though in a more roundabout way, which again reflected little credit on either party, and in the end brought in comparatively little actual cash. The announcement of the titles and times of plays was inserted in most papers free of charge, or rather in return for some free tickets, but the *chronique des théâtres* was paid for by the theatres though it purported to be an independent gossip column. The great literary figures whom the major newspapers employed as theatre critics had a free hand to write what they pleased, and the papers paid them large sums for their articles; but many minor journalists were in the pay of the theatres, and used by them to announce that every play was a great success, so as to attract more custom. There was no safer way to ensure that one got one's own play put on if one was a playwright, than if one was also a theatre critic at the same time, with a regular column in a paper. So, for example, Henri Rochefort discovered, when, in his early twenties he had a play accepted: he was incensed to discover that it was put on only to placate *La Presse théâtral*, the journal for which he worked. The same principles applied also in book reviews. Publishers were among the first people to use newspapers for advertising. Originally they simply gave two free copies of the book they wanted advertised: one went to the editor and the other to the reviewer, who wrote his article free. In time, stronger inducements became necessary. In 1845 a Paris artisan with literary pretensions and Maratist sympathies, Constant Hilbey, published a revealing account of his attempts to have his work recognised by the press. He sent a play he had written to the newspapers but it was ignored. He went to the offices of *La Presse* to protest, but he was assured that 'one must either pay, or else be a friend of one of the staff' to be noticed. So he paid to have a verse inserted in the paper, as a sample, and he negotiated to have a review printed; but difficulties arose about the price: they were willing to give him only one and a half columns for a hundred francs, but he demanded a longer article. The editor, Granier de Cassagnac (a well-known author of historical works, and a Bonapartist member of the legislature throughout the Second Empire), heard about the dispute, agreed to write the review himself, and refused any money, though he asked instead for 'a present'—and he later sent a clerk to suggest a silver teapot costing 200 francs. However, he put off writing it and in the end sent word that Hilbey should write it himself. When Hilbey asked what he should say, Cassagnac replied, 'Please yourself: say, for example, that the first edition is sold out.' In the end Cassagnac wrote the article and Hilbey, who had refused to pay anything until he had seen it, was pleased and gave him silver cutlery for four, with which Cassagnac declared himself very satisfied. While all this negotiation was in progress, Hilbey had inserted a note, for 6 francs, in *La Presse*, to prepare the readers: 'People may say that this century is not interested in poetry, but a new printing of the poems of the young tailor M. Constant Hilbey has just appeared . . .' When the review was published, a journalist from another paper, *La Patrie*, wrote to Hilbey offering to publish extracts of his work in an anthology he was bringing out, and indeed to manage all his publicity. Hilbey agreed to pay him forty francs to write an article about him in *La Patrie*. This process of buying reviews kept Hilbey busy for some time, until, for a bribe of 800 francs, he got a promise from the director of the Odéon Theatre to give his play twenty-five performances; but the director, having taken the money, dropped the play after only a few showings, demanding a further fifty francs for each night. Hilbey tried to insert a (paid) article denouncing this, but no paper would take it, fearing a libel suit. Hilbey's lawyer, the famous republican Emmanuel Arago, advised him against making a fuss, because no author could afford to offend the press.[1]

As the number of books published continued to increase, and as critics formed higher views of their status, their attention had to be won less by money and more by connections. George Sand wrote to the journalist Guéroult saying she was publishing a book and needed his assistance: would he come to lunch?[2] Marcel Proust got a favourable review written by a friend

---

[1] Constantin Hilbey, ouvrier, *Vénalité des journaux. Révélations accompagnées de preuves* (1845).

[2] B. Coste, 'Adolphe Guéroult' (law thesis, unpublished, in the library of the Faculté de Droit, Paris, 1968), 21.

reprinted in several papers, by putting pressure on his connections in the literary world. No money seems to have changed
hands in these cases, but the Catholic writer Fonsegrive
claimed in 1903 that when, for example, the *Figaro* published
a review of a novel by its critic Albert Wolf, this would cost the
author or publisher at least 2,000 francs, half of which went to
the newspaper and half to Wolf. Fonsegrive published a book
on *How to read a Newspaper*, to enable the reader to distinguish
between advertisement and independent comment, but he
concluded that it was precisely the papers which claimed to be
most impartial, to be purely literary or simply to give news, who
should be the most suspect. 'One is never sure, except when an
article appears over the signature of a few names, and they are
very few indeed, that one is not reading an advertisement, a
piece of advocacy for which the paper has been paid and often
for which both the author and the paper have been paid. An
article which appears completely objective, even if it deals with
nothing but chemistry or geography, serves to prepare, in the
following issue or even in another column of the paper, the
launching of some industrial company or some exotic mining
enterprise.'[1] The gossip columns of the newspapers, which were
supposed to meet the demand of readers anxious for more entertainment and less dull politics, were also frequently a new way
of making money. When a paper reported the famous or not so
famous people seen at the theatre, this enabled it to get paid
by the decorators and costumiers it mentioned; the mention of
the tradesmen involved, particularly when accompanied by a
flattering epithet, was a sure sign of money changing hands.
Thus it came out in court that Arthur Meyer, the *Figaro's*
colourful editor, had paid his florist's bill of 4,000 francs by
mentioning her in his reports of society parties. Gossip about
actors was often paid for, or at least recompensed with free
tickets. The reporting of sports was another case of commercial
forces making it worth while, as much as a concession to
readers' interests.

This petty corruption is difficult if not impossible to prove,
and no accurate assessment of its extent can be made. But more
substantial evidence does exist about corruption on a larger
scale. A very considerable proportion of the advertising obtained

[1] G. Fonsegrive, *Comment lire les journaux* (1903), 22.

by the press appeared in the form of apparently independent stock-market commentary. There was so much of this that it had a major influence on the solvency of the press, and indeed a number of secret institutions grew up to organise the distribution of this financial advertising. Very early on, the papers farmed out their financial page, as they had farmed out their back, small-ads. page. Banks and financial institutions wishing to raise money from the public were thus able to insert articles in praise of themselves, in return for a subsidy to the paper. The man who had first got this going on an organised scale was Jules Mirès, who bought the *Journal des chemins de fer* in 1848 for the express purpose of getting banks and companies to pay him to boost the shares they were trying to sell. In the course of the Second Empire, he obtained control of five more similar papers; backed by the Péreires, his ambition was to create a Saint-Simonian *omnium*, which would be master of all financial advertising in the country. This was a time when the value of shares on the stock-market increased threefold, and until the crash of 1882, the press took full advantage of the competition for the investments of the small saver. Girardin and a few other press magnates formed a National Bank which acted, in effect, as a financial advertising agency. Soubeyran, the Bonapartist Governor of the Crédit Foncier, was particularly effective in manipulating the financial columns of many newspapers, with a view to raising the value of stocks he dealt in; when he launched his Discount Bank in 1878, he allocated almost 10,000 shares to journalists so as to win their complaisance; by 1880 he was said to have obtained control of the financial pages of no less than sixty-four papers.[1] In the 1880s specialised advertising agencies grew up to exploit this lucrative game, and to share with the newspapers the profits which were to be made by hoodwinking gullible provincials. Batiau (publicity agent for the Crédit Lyonnais and the Crédit Foncier), Gustave Laffont (publicity agent for Rothschild), Alphonse Lenoir (connected with the Havas agency) were unknown to most readers, but they played a highly important role in the newspaper world. Lenoir, for example, was not simply a financial agent: as a police report had it, 'When individual ministers or even a whole cabinet needed the help of newspapers in some

[1] M. B. Palmer, *Some Aspects of the French Press* (Oxford D.Phil. thesis, 1973), 45.

matter or other, for some parliamentary vote for which public opinion had to be prepared, it was Lenoir who undertook to visit the newspapers and to distribute special subsidies to them. When the papers waged campaigns either against important financiers or against famous individuals, like the Reinach family for example, or against members of the government, it was Lenoir who was very often asked to arrange the matter and end the campaign, when the campaign was inconvenient to those who were the object of it.'[1] In 1909 Léon Rénier (1857–1950), one of the directors of the Havas agency, tried to consolidate all the financial advertising in the country into a monopoly and he was, indeed, for a time, the distributor of largess to the major Paris papers—half a million francs a year, or more, to the *Petit Parisien*, the *Petit Journal* and *Le Journal* for example, down to a mere 10,000 francs for the royalist *Action française* and the Bonapartist *Autorité*; and in addition he was master of the financial advertisements of eighty provincial newspapers. It was not inappropriate, considering his influence, that Rénier was made a Grand Cross of the Legion of Honour in the decorations list of 1929, which promoted only one other person to this exalted rank—Bergson. These financial agents certainly became rich men, since they exacted large commissions from the banks for their services; and it became accepted practice that no bank could even consider raising money without bribing the press. Occasionally, the details of individual bribes would be made public in some scandal. Thus it was revealed that over the years 1875–90, the Crédit Foncier spent sixty million francs a year on press subsidies, twenty-two million paid directly and thirty-eight million through various intermediaries. In 1887–9, during the Boulangist crisis, the money seems to have been paid to ministers, who used it to encourage the press to defend the republic. The Panama Canal Company gave about twelve million francs to the press to boost its shares. The most fully documented instance of bribery is that carried out by the Russian government. To assist it to raise its loans in France—of over five milliard francs during the period 1889 to 1904—it distributed at first between

---

[1] A.N. F(7.) 13969, quoted by P. Albert, in *Histoire générale de la presse française*, ed. C. Bellanger *et al.*, vol. 3 (1972), 265. New light on the inter-war period by J. N. Jeanneney, in *Revue française de science politique* (1975), 717–38.

70,000 and 110,000 francs a year, but when the Russo-Japanese war and the revolution of 1905 made raising money much harder, its subsidy was increased to two million francs. It employed as its Paris agent Raffalovitch, grand officer of the Legion of Honour, corresponding member of the Institute of France, a prolific writer on economics with a high reputation. Raffalovitch's correspondence with the Russian government, preserved in the archives opened up by the Soviets, was published by L'Humanité in 1923–4, and showed that a large number of highly respectable journalists accepted and solicited bribes, as a condition for writing articles in favour of Russia. They included Leroy-Beaulieu, a distinguished economist, who demanded and got 4,000 roubles a year as a subsidy for his journal L'Économiste français. Hébrard, owner of Le Temps, supposedly a dignified independent, conservative daily, had, as Raffalovitch reported, 'mad pretensions' demanding 10,000 francs, but his circulation figures were too low and he was given much less. The secretary of the journalists' trade union seems likewise to have sold his support, suddenly shifting from pro-German to anti-German articles. The Association of Paris Stockbrokers passed an official motion refusing to handle Russian loans unless the Russian government placed 200,000 francs a month 'at the disposal of the press' for the duration of the Russo-Japanese war. Blackmail was not practised only by journalists.[1] Nor was Russia a lone victim. The Turkish government, for example, had to spend three million francs in 1914 on publicity to raise a loan on the Paris market; over two million of this sum was distributed to the press through Léon Rénier, who kept 490,000 francs out of it as his commission. During the 1914–18 war, the Germans distributed large sums to a number of French newspapers, who were not deterred from accepting even though these bribes now involved treason. Le Journal, which had one of the largest sales in Paris, received ten million francs through the German ambassador in the U.S.A., or rather it got five and a half million, because the intermediary, Bolo Pacha, a Marseille businessman, kept the rest as his commission. The editor of Le Journal was tried but narrowly acquitted by a majority vote; the owner of the paper—Pierre Lenoir,

---

[1] A. Raffalovitch, L'Abominable vénalité de la presse, d'après les documents des archives russes 1897–1917 (1931), vii–xvi, 28, 38–9, 57–8, 64, etc.

playboy son of the leading advertising agent of the previous generation, Alphonse Lenoir—was convicted and executed, as too was Bolo Pacha. The left-wing *Bonnet rouge*, which had a daily sale of around 50,000, had before the war been encouraged in its pacifist line by regular subsidies from Caillaux. In 1916 it accepted money from the union of manufacturers of alcoholic drinks to assist its campaign against the temperance leagues; it got a further 45,000 francs from Cinzano, 60,000 francs from Martini-Rossi and 200,000 francs from other similar firms. Its editor, Almereyda, either committed suicide or died of drug addiction; its manager, Duval, who had received subsidies from the German ambassador in Switzerland, was executed for treason. It is by no means clear that the Germans got much in exchange for their bribes; one could claim that the newspapers simply used them as a milch-cow; but secret subsidies came to be regarded by all except a very few papers as a normal source of revenue. Between the two world wars several newly created countries were added to the list of the major powers which continued as benefactors of the French press.

The French government, far from disapproving of this bribery, took an active part in it, in the hope of deriving short-term political advantages itself. There had always been pro-government papers which owed their existence to ministerial benevolence: secret funds were always available to help a few newspapers; prefects had the power to give their favourite the monopoly of official advertisements; and individual ministers had often had their own papers to support them. Grévy had *La Paix*, Freycinet *Le Télégraphe*, Jules Ferry *L'Estafette*; Waldeck-Rousseau, who was rich, spent, just in the years 1882–4, no less than 135,000 francs on *La Réforme de Paris* and *L'Opinion*. Governments always wanted the news presented in a way that suited them and the press kept up the illusion that it was doing them a favour by publishing it. Ministerial press offices began to appear in a rudimentary form in the 1920s, but the idea of favouritism in the distribution of news remained, so that in the 1930s it was a regular practice for the main ministries to give the journalists they dealt with monthly 'envelopes'. The journalists became unofficial civil servants— but they also got 'envelopes' from banks and businesses. Jean Luchaire, editor of *Notre temps* (founded in 1927), said in 1946 at his trial for collaboration with the Germans: 'Before the war political newspapers and journals could not exist without subsidies. They had the choice of getting them from abroad, or from capitalist firms. The source that was least bad was the state.' He gave details of the sums he had received from a whole succession of French foreign ministers, which he combined with a regular income from the Germans, who, in addition, bought 4,000 copies of each issue. Blum in 1936 created a special department to consolidate and control the allocation of state advertising: this naturally went mainly to sympathetic papers, but not entirely. Some newspapers were set up simply to collect subsidies from anyone willing to pay, and the way to attract attention was to wage violent campaigns against likely benefactors. It is surprising what totally insignificant papers, with tiny circulations, were able to pick up by this method. It was the same method that non-political papers, as for example *Gil Blas* (founded 1879), used against prostitutes, gambling houses and men of fashion: Maupassant, who worked on this journal, which was at once scurrilous and served by famous literary figures, left a fictionalised account of it in his novel *Bel-Ami*.[1]

A more vigorous advertising industry might perhaps have saved the French press from this corruption, even if it created other problems, but there was a rival to the press which needs to be mentioned briefly, because it took a lot of advertising income which might otherwise have gone to the press. This was the poster, in which the French claimed to lead the world. Certainly advertising agencies tended to recommend posters in preference to press announcements, because they were much cheaper and lasted longer. Newspapers themselves, after all, were often posted up on walls before they became cheap enough for almost everyone to buy. In 1950 there were about 200 firms specialising in poster advertising, and controlling about two million square metres of hoardings on which to place them. Posters had the added attraction that they were often artistic. Perhaps the press should have shown itself more appreciative of the power of the artist.[2]

---

[1] Pierre Albert, in C. Bellanger *et al.*, *Histoire générale de la presse française*, vol. 3 (1972), 249–50, 259–75, 380, 432, 435 n., 439–40, 487–9, 493, 496–509, 529.
[2] Pigier, *Cours pratique de publicité* (2nd edition, 1928), 33; B. de Plas and H. Verdier, *La Publicité* (1951), 11.

## The Press Magnates

The press magnates were not all that different from the journalists. At first, they included successful journalists who turned out also to have great skill at financial manipulation, and Girardin is the best example of one who was both a journalist and a newspaper tycoon. With time, it is true, they were increasingly financiers or industrialists who dabbled in journalism. The first example of this latter kind was Moïse (alias Polydore) Millaud. He was a man of great originality, in the sense that he was responsible for the major change which took place in the character of the press during the Second Empire: the foundation of a newspaper which was sold not to subscribers but on a daily basis and at a lower price—5 centimes, equivalent to an English halfpenny—than any paper in the world had yet reached. Millaud was a member of a group of Bordeaux Jews who were behind a whole series of radical changes carried out under the Second Empire. The Péreire brothers were the most famous of these, because their democratisation of banking, and their leadership in railway building, were combined with Saint-Simonian sympathies. Jules Mirès was another member of the group; though usually remembered as a speculator, because his schemes collapsed in the end, he had, as has been shown, a most important place in the history of advertising. Millaud, about whom personally little is known, was associated with Mirès in his advertising adventures, from which they had made eight million francs between them. Millaud then went on to establish *Le Petit Journal* (1863), a totally new kind of daily newspaper. It was specifically designed for the masses and not for those interested in politics. It would be non-political also because in this way it would not have to deposit any caution money (which could be as much as 50,000 francs), nor pay stamp duty (6 centimes a copy): it would be distributed not by post but by the paper's own criers, and Millaud employed 1,200 of these. It distinguished itself from other papers by starting out with no intention of influencing its readers, or of leading opinion: its editor, Henri Escoffier, was given the mission of 'expressing what everyone is thinking', and assured that he must be 'bold enough to appear stupid'. 'Do not try to impress, or to achieve *tours de force*,' Millaud told his reporters. 'You should spend your time in buses, in trains, in theatres, in the street. Find out what the average man is thinking. Then let yourself be guided by this. At the same time keep up with all the latest discoveries, all the latest inventions. Publicise all the knowledge that gets buried away in the serious "heavies" . . . Your job is to report what most men are thinking and to speak of everything as if you know far more about it than anybody else.' He invented 'Timothy Trimm' to give expression, in a personal way, to these banal opinions—daily articles, written at first by Leo Lespès, who said 'I teach things I know nothing about' and who became one of the highest-paid journalists in Paris. Millaud signed on Ponson du Terrail, and other famous novelists, to produce a daily serial, providing 'the excitement that the masses love'. He made sensationalism the criterion of what the paper included. He advertised his paper's stories with brilliant use of suspense, printing mysterious posters, for example, saying simply 'Monsieur Lecocq, who is this Monsieur Lecocq?'. Eventually a poster revealed: 'Monsieur Lecocq, the great, the brilliant, the famous, the learned Cop, Monsieur Lecocq, Monsieur Lecocq by Émile Gaboriau, the popular author. It is *Le Petit Journal* that will recount the exploits of Monsieur Lecocq.' This 'mouthpiece of all who work, save and progress, the supporter of all who seek to become capitalists but also the defender of existing property-owners', as it called itself, attained an unprecedented circulation of 582,000 in 1880, four times that of its nearest rival and more than a quarter of all the Paris dailies put together. Millaud, however, did not reap the rewards of his ingenuity. He died in 1871, leaving his firm heavily in debt to the printer Marinoni, who had invented the machines which provided the technical basis of this newspaper revolution. The heavy investment needed was not covered by the profits. *Le Petit Journal* was bought up, bankrupt, by a trio of newspaper magnates—Marinoni, Girardin and Jenty, owner of *La France*—who planned to expand into a giant press consortium, with provincial offshoots.[1] Concentration of newspaper ownership was, however, very slow to come to France. Agreements between the major dailies were attempted from 1916 onwards, but they were repeatedly

[1] Michael B. Palmer, 'Some Aspects of the French Press 1860–90' (Oxford D.Phil. thesis, 1973), 78–128, shortly to be published.

broken. Monopolies were achieved only in the news agency (Havas) and distribution (Hachette) sides of the business.

No single paper was ever able to obtain a dominant position. One of the characteristics of journalism was that papers existed in rival pairs almost from necessity, like political parties for whom an enemy was as important as a programme. At the turn of the century there were still fifty dailies in Paris alone, though five-sixths of their total circulation was provided by five major papers. *Le Petit Journal*, abandoning its political neutrality and becoming fiercely polemical under Ernest Judet, found its rival in *Le Petit Parisien*. This latter paper has been the subject of a doctoral thesis which has made public a wealth of detail about the profitability and management of newspapers, which is quite unique in French press history. The reason this has come about is that the paper, the property of the Dupuy family, was closed down in 1944, accused of collaboration; it was bought up by Émile Amaury, a former advertising tycoon, who owns *Le Parisien libéré*. Normally, newspaper archives are either lost with every change of ownership or concealed from historians by the descendants of their proprietors, for fear of scandalous revelations. In this case, however, Amaury had nothing to lose by allowing his daughter—but no one else—to use the archives he bought, to obtain her doctorate. She has shown that between 1880 and 1914 *Le Petit Parisien* distributed sixty-eight million francs to its shareholders, and a declining but not negligible amount thereafter, as the difficulties of the Paris press increased.[1] From 1909 Charles Dupuy owned 53 per cent of the shares, but he had already obtained a stake in the paper in the early 1880s. Charles Dupuy, in contrast to Millaud, had very little originality about him; he repeated and developed the methods of *Le Petit Journal* and he was very handsomely rewarded for his perseverance, but personally he was a singularly unmemorable character. He was prime minister of France but has been totally forgotten. He was one of those hard-working, self-made businessmen who helped the Third Republic to appear to be a meritocracy, but who, by founding a vigorous dynasty of plutocrats,

[1] 41 m. francs 1929–27, 49 m. 1928–32, no profits distributed 1936–44. Dividends accounted for 80·5 per cent of profits, the rest being reinvested. Profits represented 30 per cent on turnover 1890–1900, and 23–30 per cent in 1914.

gave the lie to its pretence that it was democratic. Dupuy was descended from a line of humble serge weavers; his father was a well-to-do village shopkeeper; he himself married the daughter of an artisan. He began life as a solicitor's clerk, rose to be a tipstaff (*huissier*), made so many contacts that his firm became one of the most successful in Paris, with 25,000 cases a year; finally in 1882 he abandoned law and became a 'business consultant'. So when *Le Petit Parisien*, founded in 1876 by a radical politician, and soon on the verge of bankruptcy, came to him for advice he was able first to arrange a banker's loan, and then to offer it accommodation in a building which his mortgage work placed at his disposal. In this way he became its principal shareholder, though he only gradually obtained a majority holding. The profits came in quickly however; he bought a château; he got himself elected as a senator. With Lourdes in his constituency, he had to play a careful role between defending the rights of pilgrims and supporting the republicans' anticlericalism. In his paper, he similarly succeeded in offending as few people as possible: that was essential to achieve a mass circulation. *Le Petit Parisien* had a sale of 1,453,000 in 1914 and in 1916 had the largest sale hitherto reached in any country: 2,183,000. It played down the Panama scandal, was prudently reserved about the Dreyfus Affair, approved the republic's foreign policy, and was always a reliable supporter of the establishment. It saw itself as unifying the country. 'To read one's newspaper', it declared in an editorial on 13 October 1893, 'is to live the universal life, the life of the whole capital, of all the town, of all France, the life of all nations . . . The worker, with the earnings of a few minutes [for the paper cost only a *sou*] buys his paper, and he sees all, and he knows all: his mind surveys the whole universe. It is thus that in a great country like France, the same thought, at one and the same time, animates the whole population . . . It is the newspaper which establishes this sublime communion of souls across distances . . . It is *par excellence* the instrument of discussion from which enlightenment emerges . . . It teaches men to reflect and to judge.' In fact, though its success was founded on an impressive distribution network—which rose from 330 sales depots in 1881 to 23,000 in 1939, and which gave wholesalers a discount of 30 per cent, and sellers 20 per cent, buying back unsold copies—it failed to penetrate into either the extreme east or west of France, or into the south. In 1921 40 per cent of its sales were bought within fifty kilometres of Paris. It was unable to meet the challenge of the rising provincial dailies and in vain tried to set up a regional offshoot in the west: its *Ouest-Journal* (1931) lost seven million francs and had to close down in 1936. As a result, in the inter-war period, its circulation fell from one and a half million to half a million. On Charles Dupuy's death, the control of the paper passed to his son Jacques-Paul Dupuy, who succeeded him also as a senator for the Hautes-Pyrénées, while sharing ownership with his other children, Pierre Dupuy, deputy for the Gironde, and Marie, who married François Arago, vice-president of the Chamber of Deputies. This family illustrates well the interconnections of politics, money and the press. But its income was derived from newspaper selling in the strictest sense. Advertising revenue accounted for only between 7 and 10 per cent of profits before 1914, and never more than 25 per cent (1928). *Le Petit Parisien* was a family business which steered clear of involvements with other financial interests; it manufactured its own paper; it did not farm out its advertising columns; it made minimal use of Hachette's distribution service. What distinguished it was its exceptionally sound commercial sense. In 1925, it was the first paper to establish a radio station: it was always alive to the opportunities around it. Perhaps the one important mistake it made was to take its cult of independence too far, rejecting co-operation with the other Paris dailies, so that they all, by their rivalry, destroyed themselves.[1]

A rather different approach to newspaper ownership can be illustrated from the case of *Le Matin*. This was founded in 1884 by an American, Sam Chamberlain, backed by two English financiers; but it was rapidly sold to Alfred Edwards, the son of a rich Levantine, who pretended to be English, though he had a French passport. Edwards was quite genuinely a journalist, who had tried to make *Le Matin* essentially a *news*paper. He had

---

[1] Francine Amaury, *Histoire du plus grand quotidien de la troisième république: Le Petit Parisien 1876–1944* (1972), 271–2, 366, 511, 1326, a very rich source of information; Micheline Dupuy, *Un Homme, un journal: Jean Dupuy 1844–1919* (1959), a more personal, much briefer biography.

leaders written in turn by politicians from different parties. But he used the paper above all as an instrument of blackmail, making much more money from this activity than from the proceeds of sales. He collected 200,000 francs from the Panama Canal Company, but then he got tired of the game and sold to a banker and advertising agent, Henry Poidatz, and another profiteer of Panama, Maurice Bunau-Varilla (1897). Bunau-Varilla, who ran *Le Matin* for forty-five years, was one of the most remarkable personalities of the French press. He was an Auvergnat, originally called Varillat, but he had changed his name to make it sound more exotic and vaguely South American. He was an actor taken in by the role he assumed. Having made a fortune by dubious means, he longed to be considered the disinterested defender of noble causes, the benefactor of his country—to purge the magistracy of corruption, to speed up the slow bureaucracy, to clear the streets of orange peel, to purify milk, to eliminate pornography from the theatre—and he could never see the hypocrisy that underlay the press campaigns he was constantly waging. He was an acute businessman: he increased the circulation of *Le Matin* more than tenfold, raising it to 1,610,000 copies in 1916 and keeping it at around a million for several years; but he wanted the credit for himself. 'What the state cannot do, *Le Matin* can,' he said. His conceit verged on megalomania. He treated his journalists like servants, paying them very well, but demanding obsequious obedience to his every command: he made them write under pseudonyms to prevent their having any false notions about their importance. 'At *Le Matin*', he told them, 'there are no journalists, only employees.' One of these employees, F. I. Mouthon, has left a vivid description of their relationship. Mouthon joined the paper as a greenhorn graduate of the Catholic faculty of Lyon, an enthusiastic Christian socialist, happy to accept a low starting wage because he saw journalism as a cause. Bunau-Varilla summoned him to his office one day and said gravely 'The King of Belgium has committed suicide. (Pause) He has committed moral suicide. He has abandoned his wife and children to live in infamous concubinage. He has given himself up to trafficking in rubber, ivory and white slaves. This royal scandal can no longer be allowed to weigh on the conscience of Europe and it is the duty of *Le Matin*, the defender of all noble causes, to bring about its end.' Varilla, who had large shareholdings in the Belgian Congo, asked Mouthon to go and collect anything he could discover that might embarrass the king. They published 'The Memoirs of Leopold II which might be authentic'. Bunau-Varilla waged another of his 'moral' campaigns against absinthe: he called a public meeting of 5,000 scientists and sociologists to discuss this scourge but suddenly his campaign ceased. The reason was that the National Federation of Paris Wine Merchants replied by plastering the walls of the city with a counter-attack, and their own shops with posters saying 'Here *Le Matin* is no longer taken'. In four months *Le Matin* lost 95,000 readers. Bunau-Varilla relented and gave the wine sellers 25,000 francs in 'damages'. That interest group was too powerful for him, but it was very reluctantly that he acknowledged that anyone could stand in his way. Once one of his reporters extracted some correspondence from a house in which a crime had occurred and *Le Matin* published it. He and the reporter were prosecuted for theft of the correspondence. Bunau-Varilla asked the minister of justice to sack the officials responsible for the prosecution. The minister, Chaumié, refused. *Le Matin* waged a campaign against him. Chaumié sued it. It replied by sending reporters to collect all possible scandal against him, to discover whether a piano teacher in his constituency owed his Legion of Honour to the fact that he was a friend of Mme Chaumié; every case of favouritism, every female friend of Chaumié's was investigated; every juryman was visited. *Le Matin* published its discoveries in the name of morality, in the interests of eliminating corruption and favouritism. 'My paper', said Bunau-Varilla, 'is, one may say, without limits. What it wants, it accomplishes; and it never wants anything but good things, useful to the greatest number.' All the while, Bunau-Varilla was involved, together with his associate Poidatz, in several of the most shady speculations of his day. He represents the flamboyant, mad-dictator type of press magnate.[1]

Between the wars it was far less easy to make money out of newspapers, at least in Paris; and newspapers now tended to attract millionaires whose aim was not so much to increase their

---

[1] F. I. Mouthon, *De bluff au chantage. Les Grandes Campagnes du Matin. Comment on fait l'opinion en France* (n.d.).

wealth as to win power and influence. François Coty (1874–1934), born François Spoturno, had made an enormous fortune out of his perfumes, thanks largely to America's appreciation of them, but he formed the view that his destiny was to go much farther. In 1922 he bought *Le Figaro* and spent eighty-five millions on it over the next eleven years; he raised its circulation from 20,000 to 50,000, though by making it the organ of his personal opinions, he lost its traditional audience and sales sunk in 1932 to 10,000. At the same time, he subsidised half a dozen extremist papers, including the *Action française* (to which he gave over five million francs), Cassagnac's Bonapartist *Autorité* and *Le Flambeau*, the organ of the Croix de Feu. In 1926 he founded a new daily of his own, *L'Ami du peuple*. He fixed its price at about half that charged by other papers, so all the press turned against him; Havas refused to sell him news and Hachette to distribute his paper. Coty sued them and won ten million francs in damages. By 1930, *L'Ami du peuple* was printing one million copies, even though it was full of long articles of polemic, had few pictures and no serial novel. Coty was appealing to the small man, holding himself up as the enemy of the state, the capitalists and every possible bogy man. But he could not go on subsidising losses for ever, particularly after his divorce in 1929 forced him to settle 425 million francs on his former wife; his press empire had virtually collapsed by the time of his death in 1934. Coty's megalomania had increased with the years; because he was a Corsican, he claimed to be descended from the Bonapartes. He had bought himself a seat in the Senate, but his election having been declared invalid, he had borne the Republic a bitter grudge ever after; and the communists in particular were his *bête noire*. Never before, perhaps, had so many millions been spent on printing newspapers to satisfy the neuroses of a single individual.[1]

The inexorable grip of the capitalists on the press, even the left-wing press, was revealed in the disillusioning career of Henri Dumay. He was the man who organised two major left-wing publications, *Le Progrès civique* (1919), a serious weekly which he ran in co-operation with left-wing leaders like Ferdinand Buisson, the historian Alphonse Aulard and Pierre

[1] Alfred Kupferman, 'François Coty' (unpublished Paris thesis, 1965).

Renaudel, and *Le Quotidien* (1922), which had the distinction of being largely owned by its readers. But Henri Dumay was an advertising agent by profession. He had been in charge of publicity for Barnum's Circus in the U.S.A. and Buffalo Bill's tour of Europe; he had joined Dupuy's *Petit Parisien* and launched *Nos loisirs* for his group; but he then quarrelled with his employer, was sacked, extracted an enormous golden handshake and went into parliament instead (1919). *Le Progrès civique*, which he founded, was so successful (50,000 copies) that he decided to found his own daily, and he invited his readers to subscribe shares of 100 francs to raise the money for 'an honest paper for honest people'. Twenty-five thousand readers sent in between 200 and 500 francs each. *Le Quotidien*, thanks to the enthusiasm of its readers, was able to overcome the obstacles placed in its way by the consortium of the five main dailies and by Hachette's distribution network and by 1925 it had 385,000 readers. It became the main organ of the Cartel, in whose electoral victory of 1924 it was considered to have played an important part. The leading politicians of the left wrote for it and it became a political power to be reckoned with. But in 1927 it emerged that Dumay had tricked his readers: the shares held by him and his friends, worth 1,600,000 francs, had ten votes each, while those of ordinary shareholders, who had subscribed 9,900,000 francs, had only one each. Behind the democratic, co-operative façade, Dumay was master of the paper, and he had used it to extract (unknown to his readers, but in the typical traditions of advertising in this period) subsidies from the railways, the Gas Company and the Bank of France, to mitigate his attacks; he had farmed out his financial columns to an adventuress, Marthe Hanau, and kept a large commission for himself on the deal. When his financial empire collapsed, it all came out. Dumay had in addition secretly sold half his shares to a right-wing politician, the cognac distiller Hennessy; as his paper's circulation declined, he appealed for help to the very people he was attacking.[1] *Le Quotidien* ended up an organ of the right. *L'Œuvre* (1915), its principal radical rival, with a circulation of between 125,000 and 274,000, was also owned by Hennessy. The left wing indeed

---

[1] René de Livois, *Histoire de la presse française* (Lausanne, 1965), 2.463; and Albert in Bellanger, op. cit. 570-1.

had a great deal of difficulty in supporting a daily, and the socialists most of all. Their *Populaire* (1920) collapsed in 1924, was revived in 1927 but regularly made a loss, and the proportion of unsold copies sometimes reached 30 per cent. In the provinces, too, many obscure local journals were preferred to it by the faithful, for it was much more a doctrinal than a news paper. But that a political party could run a paper efficiently was shown by the Communists, who made a commercial success of *L'Humanité* (1904), raising its circulation to 300,000 in 1936 and even adding an evening paper, *Le Soir*, in 1937. A whole host of periodicals for women, children, peasants, etc. made the communist press a counterpart to that of the Catholics—all with the minimum of advertising.[1]

The most successful press magnate was probably the only one who liked journalism for its own sake, as a profession and a skill. Jean Prouvost (1885–    ) was a textile manufacturer. His grandfather had founded a wool-combing factory which became the largest in France. Prouvost expanded his inheritance by marrying a rich cousin, modernised his equipment with the proceeds of war compensation, modelling himself on American and British examples, and opening up subsidiaries in New York and Czechoslovakia. But though he successfully transformed his business into one of international importance he had since boyhood longed to be a journalist, and in the U.S.A. he admired above all the press magnates. The key to his success in journalism was that he had no axe to grind, and no professional training to fix him in any tradition: he always took the viewpoint of the reader, stressing the market above all. His main idea was that 'a newspaper must do all it can to obtain the largest possible circulation. Once it has this, no one can do anything against it, because it has the power. Advertisers will be obliged in the end, despite boycotts, to bring it their advertisements, whatever price it asks. Then, its investment will be paid off and profits could be considerable.' This straightforward commercial approach, with no illusions about educational missions or political apostolates, was rare at this level. No one would believe that he had no ulterior purpose, and they wondered what game he was playing when he refused

[1] Claude Estier, *La Gauche hebdomadaire 1914–62* (1962); 'Les Problèmes financiers de *l'Humanité* 1920–39', *Revue d'histoire moderne et contemporaine* (Oct. 1973).

subsidies from foreign embassies and decorations from the government. His purpose was to sell a new product, for which he was sure there was a demand: 'people are no longer content to know, they want to see'. *Paris Soir* came out in 1931 with no less than nine photographs on its front page alone. The stress on pictures was combined with exceptional coverage of sport, a final edition with two extra pages of horseracing results, easily inserted and numerous small advertisements and a daily horoscope. But it combined its gift for sensational reporting with serious articles by famous people; its staff included not only Pierre Lazareff, who had entered journalism at fourteen and who was a master of the popular style, and not only the crime reporter Georges Simenon, but also graduates of the École Normale, like the historian Georges Perreux. It saw the commercial advantages to be derived from independence, when the rest of the press was largely corrupt. By 1939 it had a sale of 1,800,000, which was more than the two leading Paris morning dailies put together; and its success was multiplied by the magazine *Match* (1938), modelled on the American *Life*, which had a sale of 1,400,000 within a year, and *Marie-Claire* (1937), for women, which sold a million. It had all the capital it needed thanks to the backing not only of Prouvost's own fortune, but also the Beghin sugar and paper firm. Jean Prouvost became minister of information in 1940.[1]

It is inevitable that the press magnates of Paris should be most famous, but to concentrate on them is to form a distorted picture of the French press in general. For the provincial press was extremely active; in terms of readership, provincial dailies already had in 1939 as many readers as the Paris dailies; but the variety of provincial papers was so great that, apart from a few local monographs, historians have been unable to get far beyond compiling long catalogues, and doing that has proved difficult enough. In 1884 there were in the provinces 258 dailies, 363 papers which appeared two, three or four times a week and 601 weekly journals. In 1914 there were still 240 dailies; in 1938 there were 175 dailies and 1,160 weekly or semi-weeklies.[2]

---

[1] Raymond Barrillon, *Le Cas Paris-Soir* (1959); Pierre Lazareff, *Dernière édition* (n.d., memoirs published in New York during the 1939–45 war).

[2] The readership of the provincial daily press was in 1868 25 per cent of the

Local papers were originally essentially advertising sheets; they could be profitable even with small circulations, and so they expanded to accommodate the ambitions of local printers, politicians and men of letters. They thrived on local gossip, on the reporting of local events and the announcement of property sales—all of which were extremely popular; and they enabled men with a relatively small amount of capital to acquire local importance. Almost every member of parliament, actual or prospective, thought he needed a local paper in order to succeed, and some papers were little more than electoral posters. Thus the department of Pas-de-Calais, with a population of one million, had 692 local papers between 1865 and 1944. Two-thirds of these lasted less than two years, but there were times when it had seventy papers existing simultaneously. Every interest liked to have one, so that there was even a *British Continental Mercury* for the British colony and a *Narodowiec* for the Poles.[1] Local pride kept some periodicals going, in small towns, with circulations of well under a thousand, sometimes even only 300. But some local papers blossomed to become successful and influential on a regional scale. The Catholic *Ouest-Éclair* (Rennes) and the radical *Dépêche de Toulouse* are perhaps the best known, but in 1939 there were nineteen regional daily papers with circulations of over 100,000 copies each.[2] These papers became the focus of local political life and controversy, and the slanging matches between rival ones in the same town were an endless source of entertainment and anxiety. But one must distinguish between the small town paper, which had to be very careful not to offend anyone and to record every celebration, and the political rag, which was designed to be just that, an incitement to frenzy, the local advertising weekly, which was essentially a money-spinner, and finally the regional dailies, which won their popularity by

total readership of French dailies, 35 per cent in 1914, 50 per cent in 1939, 62 per cent in 1969—Pierre Albert, *Documents pour l'histoire de la presse de province dans la seconde moitié du 19e siècle* (roneoed, n.d., about 1973), 3.

[1] G. Bellard, *Pas-de-Calais: Bibliographie de la presse française politique et d'information générale 1865–1944* (1968). This is volume 62 of a series, published by the Bibliothèque Nationale, each volume covering one department.

[2] The other major ones were *La Petite Gironde* (Bordeaux), *L'Écho du Nord* (Lille), *Le Progrès de Lyon*, *Le Réveil du Nord* (Lille), *Le Petit Dauphinois* (Grenoble), all selling over 200,000 copies a day. For a list, see Albert in Bellanger, op. cit. 604–5. Henri Lerner is writing a thesis on the *Dépêche de Toulouse*.

doing what the Paris mass circulation dailies did, providing sensational news, but adding the local news too—a combination that proved irresistible.[1]

However, the variety of French newspapers concealed a common source of information, particularly for foreign news. The Havas News Agency made it possible for these newspapers to survive. As Balzac said, 'Every paper places its own colour, white, green, red or blue, on the news that is sent to it by Monsieur Havas, Jack of all trades to the press. [From the point of view of foreign news] there is only one newspaper, written by him, and all newspapers draw from its source.' In 1832 Havas, a former newspaper owner and son of a government book censor, founded an agency which summarised the news taken from foreign papers. By 1852 Havas had 200 subscribers among provincial newspapers. In the course of the Second Empire he made agreements with similar agencies in other countries (notably Reuter in England and Wolff in Germany), and later with Associated Press, for a mutual exchange of news, which made it possible for them to share the world between them, with Havas covering South America, the Balkans and the French Empire. Havas was not the only news agency in France, and Reuter's rivals, Dalziel, established an agency in Paris in 1891 which, in alliance with some right-wing papers, for a time posed a serious threat. Havas had well-established connections with all the French ministries, which provided it with news in return for giving publicity to information the government wanted to make known. At the turn of the century, Havas was able to provide a provincial newspaper with 1,760 lines of text daily for an annual subscription of around 10,000 francs. Foreign news was something French newspapers were for long weak on; they depended on occasional articles, and selected

---

[1] Raymond Manevy, *L'Évolution des formules de présentation de la presse quotidienne* (1956). The classic on the local press is Jacques Kayser, *La Presse de province sous la troisième république* (1958). On the non-political press, see N. Fourgeaud-Lagrèze, *La Petite Presse en province* (Ribérac, 1869). For a general survey, André Demaison, *Lex Voix de la France. La Presse de province au 20ᵉ siècle* (1932). For examples, see Paul Mansire, 'La Presse en Seine-Inférieure sous la troisième république 1871 à 1939', in *Études de presse* (1955), no. 12, vol. 7, which describes the *Dépêche de Rouen*, for which Alain wrote. It had a circulation of only 25,000, as compared with the 75,000 of the *Journal de Rouen*. Also André Parrain, *La Presse dans le Puy-de-Dôme de 1870 à 1914* (Clermont-Ferrand, 1972).

their news arbitrarily. Some newspapers made a speciality of it, and the obscure *Messager du Midi* of Montpellier, for example, was very well informed about Italian affairs in the 1859 war. *Le Temps* had some notable foreign correspondents, like Clemenceau, Louis Blanc and André Tardieu. *Le Matin*, under Edwards, gave a new stimulus to interest in foreign news. Havas was able to benefit from this and his became a highly profitable business. The family was bought out in 1879 for seven million francs, by a group of forty subscribers, mainly bankers. The agency's prosperity increased steadily until the 1914 war, but after that, because of increasing costs, it was kept going largely by its advertising side, and eventually it could no longer pay its way: Radio Luxembourg, which it owned, was still too insignificant to make good the loss. In 1938 the French foreign office gave it a subsidy; in 1940 its news service was nationalised as the Office Français d'Information, and so it continued to turn out its 40,000 words a day. After the war, it was succeeded by the Agence France-Presse, founded as a rival during the Resistance; in 1957 the problem of monopoly was at last resolved by placing this agency under the management of a board representing the country's newspaper editors.[1]

But there was a slightly different ending to the story of the other great monopoly behind the French press, the Messageries Hachette, the French equivalent of England's W. H. Smith. Hachette had obtained the exclusive right to open kiosks to sell books and newspapers on railway stations in 1852–5 and it kept the concession, except for a partial interruption in 1896–1905, until the Second World War. The business took some time to get established, and the kiosks were at first staffed by the wives or widows of railway employees, but as from 1865 newspapers became more important than books, in terms of turnover. The number of stalls reached 442 in 1874 and around 1,100 at the turn of the century, when newspaper sales accounted for about four-fifths of their business. There were a few newspapers which avoided using Hachette's services, but it required enormous resources to do so, and Hachette was in a position to place serious obstacles in the way of new papers which threatened the equilibrium it supported. The war of 1939–45

[1] Pierre Frédérix, *Un Siècle de chasse aux nouvelles. De l'Agence d'Information Havas à l'Agence France-Presse 1935–1957* (1959).

put an end to its stranglehold: in 1947 a new distribution system was set up, in which a co-operative of all newspapers had a 51 per cent shareholding, and Hachette 49 per cent. But Hachette has compensated by not only expanding its book-publishing activities, but also by buying control of several major newspapers and journals, from *France-Soir* to *Mickey* and *Elle*. It remains a major force in the newspaper world.[1]

### Newspaper Readers

The final force in the making of the press was the reader, first because newspapers often claimed to be speaking on behalf of public opinion, and to be reflecting their readers' wishes, and secondly because the frantic competition to increase sales meant that the reader's demands had to be discovered and met. However, what readers thought is, and was, very difficult to ascertain. Only very general ideas are possible, for example, as to who these readers were: no paper seemed to have any accurate analysis of its readership. Not all sections of the community were newspaper readers. In 1858, the Paris dailies sold only about 235,000 copies; newspapers, at that date, were clearly still an interest of a small minority. By 1870 the rapid expansion of popular dailies raised the sales figure to one million, and by 1880 to two million. In 1910 the figure was up to five million and in 1939 to six million. To this one should add the provincial press. In 1868, the provincial political papers had 343,700 subscribers—though many of these papers appeared only twice or three times a week; they reached one million by about 1885, four million by 1914 and six million by 1939. So in 1939 there was a total sale of twelve million copies. Since the war, this total figure has remained roughly constant, the only change being that the provincial press has made headway against the Paris press and captured two-thirds instead of half the sales. This means that the French read far less newspapers than many other countries, indeed only half the number of papers the British read. In 1956, UNESCO's statistics placed France twenty-third in world rank for the number of copies sold per head of population.

[1] Jean Mistler, *La Librairie Hachette de 1826 à nos jours* (1964).

### Comparative Newspaper Sales 1956

| | Number of dailies | Total print copies (millions) | Copies per 1,000 inhabitants |
|---|---|---|---|
| Great Britain | 114 | 29·1 | 570 |
| U.S.A. | 1,765 | 55 | 339 |
| France | 137 | 10·6 | 246 |
| West Germany | 598 | 12·5 | 254 |
| Italy | 107 | 5 | 107 |

In 1955, 75 per cent of the population of France (or at least of a representative sample) said they read a paper every day, and only 12 per cent said they never read one. But 24 per cent of people over sixty-five never read a daily paper, nor did 17 per cent of peasants, nor 15 per cent of people in small towns with under 5,000 inhabitants. In one province, only 51 per cent of agricultural labourers read a paper daily, as compared with 90 per cent of members of the liberal professions. Twice as many women as men did not read papers. It is clear therefore that newspapers have been a predominantly urban and masculine interest. This comes out strikingly in the way people answered the question of how far they felt deprived by the disappearance of newspapers as a result of a strike for a month in 1947. Fifty-seven per cent replied that they felt no deprivation, but their answers differed markedly according to the size of the towns in which they lived. Only 32 per cent of Parisians felt no deprivation: the figures rose steadily as the size of town fell, reaching 78 per cent in villages of under 2,000 inhabitants.[1] It is probable that the majority of the peasantry did not read papers regularly till after the First World War.[2] A more detailed and carefully phrased questionnaire revealed in 1965 that only 53 per cent of those questioned had read all the last six issues of the paper they regularly took. This finding needs to be balanced against the fact that newspapers were passed around: 23 per cent said they gave their newspaper to someone else, outside the family.[3] On the other

[1] No deprivation: Paris 32%; but 44% in cities over 100,000; 46% in towns of 40,000–100,000; 52% in towns of 20,000–40,000; 64% in towns of 2,000–20,000 and 78% in villages of under 2,000.

[2] *Sondages. Revue française de l'opinion publique* (1955), n. 3, 'La Presse, le public et l'opinion', 31–3.

[3] Groupement des grands régionaux, *Enquête par sondage sur l'audience de dix grands quotidiens régionaux* (1965), 29.

hand, newspapers were clearly not read with uniform attention: on average people spent thirty-eight minutes a day on their papers in 1947, about an hour in 1949 and 1954, about fifty minutes in 1965. Nor did all subjects attract the attention of readers. The earliest sociological investigation of readers' interests, made by the *Petit Parisien* in 1938, showed that its readers looked at the illustrations first (68 per cent); 65 per cent said they were most interested by the *faits divers* (human interest stories) and pictures, 55 per cent by general news, 37 per cent by the serial novel, 27 per cent by the *contes*, and only a tiny fraction by politics. In the north and in Normandy, the serial novel came unashamedly at the top of the list.[1]

It is not clear, indeed, just how important a part newspapers played in disseminating news: the generalisation that they made democracy possible by educating the country politically, and spreading the message of the politicians, needs qualification. Some people no doubt did absorb what they read about Paris politics, but when in 1954 the sample of newspaper readers were asked how they heard of the fall of Mendès France from power, only 20 per cent said they got it from the newspapers: 28 per cent said from conversation and 49 per cent from the radio. The role of gossip and the café may well have been larger before the age of the radio. It is certainly significant that when this sample was asked what they thought was wrong with the press, the criticism which was voiced most frequently was that newspapers had too many pages. The inquiry of 1965 is most instructive about how different sections of the population responded to the varied content of newspapers. This was a survey carried out in the provinces, to determine the character of the readers of regional newspapers, but by that time of course there were more of these than Parisian papers. It showed the following order of priorities in what interested readers most:

| | |
|---|---|
| Local news | 86% |
| News of France and the world | 62 |
| Comic strips | 39 |
| Radio programme timetables | 34 |
| Small advertisements | 33 |
| Local sport | 31 |
| Women's page | 30 |

[1] Francine Amaury, *Le Petit Parisien 1876–1944* (1972), 1.290.

| | |
|---|---|
| National sport | 29% |
| Serial novel | 23 |
| Social, economic and financial | 19 |
| Agricultural news | 18 |
| Horse-racing | 15 |
| Travel | 14 |
| Camping | 7 |

There was a surprising uniformity in these answers as between the different regions—except that, among the readers of the *Dernières Nouvelles d'Alsace*, 67 per cent were most interested by the small ads. and only 7 per cent in horse-racing. But men and women differed very much in their attitude to sport— 50 per cent of men were interested but only 10 per cent of women. The serial was read by twice as many women as men, while horse-racing interested 21 per cent of men but only 10 per cent of women. Rural readers were less interested in national and international news (51 to 56 per cent) than were the upper classes and liberal professions (79 per cent). Peasants were less interested in sports than other classes; clerks and workers were very keen on horse-racing.

It was not easy for the press to satisfy the wishes of its readers, even if it could discover them accurately, because it had to reconcile those wishes with several other pressures—the desire of newspaper owners to further their own political ambitions, the need to win advertisers, the expense of buying news. Since one of the well-established rules of press management was that readers tended to remain loyal to their papers from habit, the scope for innovation was limited; new methods tended to be tried out by new papers, and they were not always universally copied even if they were successful. To satisfy the desire for illustrations, *Excelsior* (1910) was created, full of photographs (backed by the arms-dealer Basil Zaharoff), but it was not a great success; photographs were not exactly what the masses wanted and it was only later discovered that drawings were preferred—comic-strip cartoons. This suggested that the old *images d'Épinal* which had provided just this, and which used to be sold by pedlars, still had a faithful following: the old style had become outdated, it illustrated mainly old and traditional stories, so it came to be read mainly by children, but when revived as comic strips in newspapers, it was instantly popular, and it contributed considerably to the success of *Paris-Soir*. In 1974 the comic strip was even admitted into the sober pages of *Le Monde*, a paper which has no photographs at all. Behind the reader of popular newspapers, who tended to be regarded as the newly educated offspring of the Third Republic's schools, there clearly lurked the old superstitious peasant, who could always spare a copper for an almanac with frightening stories and prophecies of future catastrophes. But it was not a discovery of his ghoulish tastes that led the newspapers to devote so much space to crime stories, but rather a perpetuation of the tradition of obsession with the marvellous and the unusual, which the old almanacs had long catered for. The popular newspapers which began to develop their *faits divers* rubrics from the 1860s, took over from where the *canards* left off. The *canard* was a flysheet, much used in the first half of the century, to distribute sensational news; it told stories about visions of the Virgin, fantastic animals, national disasters, the ravages caused by passion, gambling and debauchery, the perils of travelling, the return of prodigal sons and missing persons, and every kind of crime. They were very much in the medieval tradition, appealing to the love of the marvellous. A typical title would be: *Horrible details of the misfortunes occasioned by rabid animals.* Journalists out of work used to invent these stories, for the *canard* was a way of printing money. One story, for example, about a woman shipwrecked in the Pacific, captured by a monster with whom she lived until rescued, published in 1849, was the subject of no less than fifty-two different editions. Larousse said the *canard* was designed to discover just how far the reader's credulity would stretch; but what was important about these stories was that they were interesting, rather than that they were true.[1] It became immediately clear that newspaper readers, beyond the small circles who were personally involved in politics and administration, were keener to have this kind of entertainment from the press, rather than an education in democracy. *Le Petit Journal* was able to boost its circulation by over 200,000 in a few weeks by giving predominant attention to the *affaire Tropmann*, involving sensational multiple murders. The selection of the news that was printed was, however, far from being an automatic process, in which

[1] J. P. Séguin, *Nouvelles à sensation. Canards du 19ᵉ siècle* (1959), 157.

journalists simply applied a formula.[1] There was roughly one suicide in France (in 1970) every hour, but it was the journalist who selected the very small number which were in fact reported. The attitude of local and national papers differed: the larger the circulation of a paper, the less did it matter where things happened, provided they were odd enough; and that is one reason why international news was for long so sketchy and arbitrary. But the local paper felt it had to concentrate on giving the news about people whom readers knew, even if there was very little new to report. Thus the *Sud-Ouest* of La Rochelle thought it proper to print this item: 'In the rue Grade, Monsieur X's car collided with Madame Y's dog. The dog was unhurt. The car sustained no damage.' The increasing popularity of the regional newspaper suggests that this kind of local news was highly valued. Simone de Beauvoir recalled how when she and Sartre were teachers in a provincial *lycée* 'we had few friends, almost no social life. It was partly to palliate this lack that we developed an ardent taste for the human-interest stories in the newspapers.' It was in the same way that she frequently bought *Detective* (founded 1928, circulation 250,000), a fiction magazine which had the added advantage that, in its early days at any rate, it made a practice of attacking the police and the establishment.[2] Newspapers, like novels, did not provide simply an aid to escapism, for they were also an aid to a different kind of participation in life. Politics was a means by which some people found a role for themselves in the world around them, but it did not appeal to every temperament: the newspaper provided, through its *faits divers*, both alternative subjects of conversation, of a less abstract or distant nature, and also opportunities for readers to exercise their imaginations and give vent to their emotions in less systematic ways than politics required.[3] They also helped to reconcile the contradictions which people's hypocrisy created. They worked on the assumption that people liked reading about vice, but that they were also ashamed of doing so: and the popular newspaper provided a combined package, which contained both vice and

[1] On the process by which news is selected, see Edward J. Epstein, *News from Nowhere* (New York, 1973).

[2] Simone de Beauvoir, *La Force de l'âge* (1960), 131.

[3] Georges Auclair, *Le 'Mana' quotidien. Structures et fonctions des faits divers* (1970), 33.

moralising united. Thus *Le Journal*, at the turn of the century, always adopted a puritan and austere tone: it was fond of lamenting that the world was going to the dogs; it complained, for example, that girls were no longer what they used to be, but had become 'flirtatious, brazen and easy-going to the point of impertinence, saying things which would make a monkey blush' (24 April 1895), but it simultaneously published short stories which were full of pornography, sexual perversion, adultery and violence.[1] *Le Journal* had literary pretensions and gave much space to literature, aiming to attract the middle classes, but though it never printed any manifestos saying so, it obviously believed that its readers both aspired to culture and were bored by it, that their cultural, intellectual life was only one side of them and that eroticism and sadism were in no way extinguished by this. That is why it also gave them plenty of xenophobia, nationalism, anti-Semitism and scandals. It seems that the press, as it gradually shed its concentration on politics, was accurately responding to a demand from its readers which obsession with politics had temporarily masked. These newspapers tried to be accurate reflections of the conflicting aspirations and anxieties of their readers.

In 1902, the distribution of space in newspapers as between different subjects was as follows.

|  | Paris newspapers | Provincial newspapers |
|---|---|---|
| Home news | 13·05 | 19·55 |
| Literature | 9·95 | 14·35 |
| Crime | 8·80 | 8·75 |
| Internal politics | 7·15 | 5·75 |
| Foreign news | 8·35 | 4·35 |
| Theatre and other 'spectacles' | 6·45 | 2·55 |
| Arts | 4·50 | 2·95 |
| Useful literature | 3·90 | 4·0 |
| Sports | 3·20 | 2·80 |
| Moral and charitable works | 2·65 | 4·65 |
| Science | 1·85 | 2·0 |
| Foreign politics | 1·8 | 1·2 |
| Travel | 0·8 | 0·55 |
| Advertisements (appearing as such) | 23·9 | 27·95 |
| ,, (disguised) | 3·6 | 1·1 |

[1] Patrick Dumont, *La Petite Bourgeoisie vue à travers les contes quotidiens du Journal 1894–5* (1973), 21.

These statistics[1] are averages, but as such they show that if the interests of readers at the turn of the century bore any relation to those which readers admitted to fifty years later, newspapers still gave readers what they did not want. The amount of space devoted to crime was in 1902: 670 lines daily in *Le Petit Parisien*, 500 in the *Figaro*, 310 in *Le Petit Journal*, 160 in *Le Matin* and 40 in *Le Temps*; 330 in *L'Écho du Nord* of Lille but only 75 in *La Dépêche de Toulouse*. By contrast, in 1937, *Paris-Soir* had established its fame by giving no less than 1,250 lines to crime; *Le Petit Parisien* had gone up to 1,110, *Le Petit Journal* to 775; most papers indeed had almost exactly doubled their ration. But papers were now 8,000 lines long as opposed to 3,200, so the proportion devoted to crime did not actually increase. It is wrong to talk of an increasing demoralisation of the public by the press. One should not contrast the popular press with the political press of the July Monarchy. The popular press was an industrialised version of the old almanacs and *canards*: if it did innovate, it was probably in the direction of forcing a lot of facts, of a new kind, down its readers' throats.

What did change somewhat was the freedom the press enjoyed. During the Second Empire, and indeed till 1881, political commentary had been strictly controlled, with a severity which was only slightly less than that of the *ancien régime*. But instead of employing censors to read papers before they were published, the Second Empire distributed punishment for wrongdoing after the event: the threat of this, combined with a system of official warnings and culminating in the closing down of the paper altogether, was fairly successful in restraining the press.[2] The prefects, who were the principal instruments of this repression, carried their censorship well beyond politics, in that criticism of any kind could be seen as a threat to the established order. Thus the prefect of the Côtes-du-Nord, for example, ruled that 'polemic about artificial fertilisers causes indecision among buyers' and he warned newspapers against exciting discontent in any form. As a journalist said on the publication of Renan's *Life of Jesus*: 'One can

---

[1] H. de Noussanne, *Ce que vaut la presse quotidienne française* (1902).
[2] For the history of press legislation, see Irene Collins, *Government and Newspaper Press in France 1814–81* (Oxford, 1959).

no longer attack anybody except Christ.' This was one reason why non-political journalism developed so rapidly in this period: whereas political papers had to give the government a large sum as caution money for their good behaviour, non-political papers were freer—and much comment on public life was therefore rephrased in allegorical or satirical language. The censors were always on the look-out for political references, as Victorien Sardou discovered in 1863 when in one of his plays he was unwise enough to insert a tirade against blonde women. Four censors summoned him to say that could not be allowed: did he not know that the empress was blonde. And, added another of them, so too was Madame Walewska (the emperor's cousin).[1]

The abolition of censorship in 1881 gave the press a free rein, almost untrammelled even by libel laws. The freedom was not total, for what really allowed anyone to say almost what he pleased was the feebleness of sanctions. Thus after 1881 there were still several kinds of offence journalists could commit. The law of libel, as far as private citizens were concerned, was far-reaching. The courts ruled that a report of a rumour that a certain mayor had wrongly allowed some people in his village to pay less taxes than they should have done was a libel (1884); they held it was libellous to accuse someone of sorcery (1909), or even to assert that a doctor held philosophical and religious opinions contrary to the beliefs of the majority of the inhabitants of his locality (1905). The law assumed that there was an intention to libel, unless the defendant proved the contrary. There were even more stringent rules about attacking members of the civil service or government—an offence known as *outrage*. It was an outrage to accuse these depositaries of authority of whistling (1903), of making obscene gestures, or to call the government a collection of bandits and the judges a group of thieves (1910). It was still seditious to shout 'Vive le roi' (1909), and anarchist propaganda was nominally forbidden by the law of 1894. It was possible for a newspaper to be prosecuted for spreading false news or corrupting morals, though the courts varied in their attitudes: in 1908 an advertisement of a brothel, under the guise of a massage parlour, was held to be innocent, but in 1928 it was not. However, all these

[1] Roger Bellet, *Presse et journalisme sous le Second Empire* (1967), 16.

threats held over the press were mitigated by three factors. First, the reluctance of juries to convict meant that prosecutions were infrequent, though libel litigation was far more active than is realised. Secondly, there was the right of reply, which was preferred as a means of settling disputes. The law required newspapers to give persons it had mentioned the right of reply; and this reply must be published in the same place and in the same characters as the article which provoked it; though if the reply was longer than the original article, the writer of the reply had to pay for the extra space at advertisement rates. Civil servants had the 'right of rectification', and this right allowed them twice as much space as the libellous passage. However, thirdly, the theory of provocation modified this right. It was held that a person who stood for election to public office provoked criticism and so had less right to protection against libel: the divulging of defamatory facts about him, designed to enlighten the voters, was therefore legitimate. The question of whether this principle of provocation applied to literature was long controversial. Some held that the mere fact of publishing something invited people to criticise it and so literary or artistic criticism should not be liable to the right of reply. When in 1897 Jules Lemaitre wrote a totally damning review of a play by Dubout, a banker of Boulogne-sur-Mer, which had been put on at the Comédie-Française, the appeal court forced the *Revue des Deux Mondes* to publish Dubout's reply, arguing that whatever the principle of provocation, Lemaitre had written in 'a moment of malice' and that the play had in fact been enthusiastically applauded by the audience. Again, in 1923, when Dunoyer said in the *Revue universelle* that Nordmann's book on Einstein was a 'scandal' and its success 'incomprehensible', the court ordered the review to publish a reply, judging that Dunoyer had, in jealousy, gone beyond just criticism. All this meant that the papers could get away with a great deal, and if their victims protested, that only served to add vivacity to the polemic.[1]

The extent of this liberty can be seen in the way the press dealt with crime. In France, as elsewhere, the reporter rose up as a rival to the policeman, searching for criminals, or missing

[1] Marcel Hoursiangou, *Le Journaliste en France. Conditions économiques et juridiques de son activité* (Bordeaux law thesis, 1936), 113–214.

persons, at least when there was a sensational aspect to the story; but in France the press was probably freer in its hostility to the police, and that added to its popularity. In the case of the *curé* of Châtenay, for example, who disappeared in 1905, the papers attacked the police violently for failing to find him; they cried murder, offered large rewards for information, and stimulated a shower of anonymous letters in which neighbours accused each other of the crime. In the end the poor *curé* was discovered in Brussels, where he had gone, as he hoped, to live in peace with his mistress. The fact that a case was *sub judice* seldom worried the press, which published full details of sensational trials and of relevant documents, even when the law forbade it. The *Figaro* in 1899, for example, illegally published full reports of the Dreyfus trial in the court of cassation: it was fined 500 francs, and it then continued to publish them. The press regularly revealed every intimate fact about accused persons, so that people wrongly accused nevertheless seldom escaped unscathed. It reported verdicts with approval or disapproval, passing its own sentence on the judge and on the accused. Judges and barristers quickly saw that it was necessary to keep on good terms with journalists, who distributed praise or blame to them, or were totally silent about them, in proportion to the amount of co-operation they received: journalists said they had no need to seek out information, they got it without asking; leaks were common; court officials allowed the press to look at their files; they were all on terms of *tutoiement*. A law of 1849 forbade the press to publish details of charges before the public trial; another forbade it to publish facts about private life (11 May 1868, article 11); but in vain. The press waged a war against the secret inquisitorial procedure of French law, in the name of the liberty of the press and of the individual, but without much success, and perhaps in the process it damaged the lives of many individuals whom it tried in its own columns. Its hypocrisy was revealed in the way it treated public executions, whose immorality it attacked, but to which it devoted a great deal of space. In 1909 scenes of appalling savagery occurred at an execution at Béthune, which the press had publicised, to which it sent an army of reporters, and which photographers captured for the cinema. On three successive days *Le Petit Journal* devoted seven columns on its front page and three on its second page to the execution, publishing eight photographs of it. The conclusion of a legal commentator on the relations of the press and the law was that 'the judiciary has been not only defeated in its duel with the press, but it has completely capitulated. The press reported almost exactly what it liked between 1881 and 1940 and prosecutions were rare.'[1]

## Smaller Worlds

Books about the press have tended to be above all about the political press, but this gives a very incomplete view of the activities of journalists, the vast majority of whom were not political. In 1881, for example, 1,343 periodicals were published in Paris. Of these only seventy-one were political. A far larger number were financial (209), medical (97), general illustrated papers (88) or fashion magazines (81). These statistics give one a curious hierarchy of the interests of newspaper readers. During the next fifty years financial journals increased slightly in number, and it was only in 1930 that they were outnumbered by political journals (252 against 281).[2] The medical press more than doubled (236), so that it remained very important. Literature had remarkably few journals devoted exclusively to it: in 1881 only 30, in 1900 only 46, in 1930 73. But at the turn of the century an additional category of 'political and literary reviews' suddenly blossomed into importance: at these three dates there were respectively 46, 188, and 161 of these in Paris alone. What gave the impression of intense literary activity was the large number of little ephemeral literary reviews: from 1914 to 1939 no less than 269, which lasted for less than ten issues, are recorded.[3] By the 1930s there were more journals devoted to photography than to the fine arts, and almost four times as many devoted to sports. Though religion had been nominally defeated by the anticlericals, it still found

[1] Georges O. Junosza-Zdrojewski, *Le Crime et la presse* (1943).
[2] On the financial press, see above, page 521; and also J. Gascuel and R. Sedillot, *Comment lire un journal économique et financier* (1957, 2nd edition 1960), and Francine Batailler *et al.*, *Analyses de presse* (1963), part 3, 'Sociologie de lecteurs de la presse économique et financière', 177–232. These deal with the 1950s and 1960s; there is room for an interesting historical study of this subject.
[3] Richard L. Admussen, *Les Petites Revues littéraires 1914–1939. Répertoire descriptif* (St. Louis, Missouri, and Paris, 1970).

readers for its very numerous journals, with their own independent parochial distribution system. A rough list of the Parisian press, arranged by subject, may give an indication of the variety of preoccupations in the capital, which belie any generalisation about France as devoted to literature, or the arts, or free thought, or politics. (The list is illustrative rather than exhaustive; there are many difficulties in classifying newspapers.)

*The Press in 1881, 1901 and 1930[1]*

|  | Paris 1881 | Paris 1901 | Paris 1930 | Provincial 1930 |
|---|---|---|---|---|
| Politics | 71 | 178 | 281 | ? |
| Political economy | 3 | 40 | 85 | 11 |
| Administration | 28 | 35 | 65 | 2 |
| Diplomacy | 6 | 10 | 12 | .. |
| Colonial | .. | 46 | 71 | 6 |
| Military | 17 | 41 | 75 | 27 |
| Naval | 8 | 11 | 32 | 9 |
| Literature | 30 | 46 | 73 | .. |
| Literary and political reviews | 46 | 188 | 161 | 28 |
| Fine Arts | 19 | 45 | 43 | .. |
| Photography | 5 | 28 | 45 | |
| Music | 14 | 37 | 46 | 2 |
| Theatre | 13 | 37 | 32 | 8 |
| Architecture | 26 | 14 | 31 | 3 |
| Humour | .. | 26 | 34 | 7 |
| Sports | 21 | 46 | 219 | 45 |
| Catholic | 61 | 83 | 108 | 40 |
| Protestant | 24 | 22 | 30 | 22 |
| Jewish | 2 | 3 | 8 | .. |
| Freemason | .. | 4 | ? | .. |
| Financial | 209 | 219 | 252 | 15 |
| Professional, industrial and commercial | ? | ? | 243 | .. |
| Technology | 38 | .. | .. | .. |
| Industry | 27 | 44 | 67 | 20 |
| Metallurgy | .. | 12 | 29 | 3 |
| Mines | 5 | 6 | 12 | 11 |
| Petrol | .. | .. | 8 | .. |
| Electricity and radio | .. | .. | 56 | .. |
| Gas and electricity | .. | 25 | .. | .. |
| Gas | .. | .. | 7 | .. |
| Printing | .. | 14 | 20 | .. |
| Science | 41 | 89 | 103 | .. |
| Sugar | .. | 3 | 4 | .. |

[1] Based on the *Annuaire de la presse française* (1882, 1901 and 1930).

|  | Paris 1881 | Paris 1901 | Paris 1930 | Provincial 1930 |
|---|---|---|---|---|
| Motor cars and cycles | .. | 22 | ? | .. |
| Textiles | .. | 9 | 8 | 6 |
| Transport | .. | .. | 25 | .. |
| Public works | .. | 23 | 34 | 2 |
| Commerce | 32 | 56 | 96 | 17 |
| Agriculture | 34 | 70 | 121 | 148 |
| Insurance | 18 | 25 | 35 | .. |
| Fashion | 81 | 127 | 166 | 4 |
| Feminist | ? | 17 | 18 | .. |
| Illustrated | 88 | 130 | 109 | 33 |
| Stenography | .. | 16 | 20 | .. |
| Medicine | 97 | 219 | 236 | 26 |
| Pharmacy | 9 | 9 | 11 | 5 |
| Jurisprudence | 61 | 98 | 122 | 14 |
| Education | 38 | 50 | 85 | 7 |

The history of medical journalism shows how one section of
the country used the press to develop its sense of community.
It is a subject so extensive that it will require a whole team of
researchers to reveal its full variety and the richness of the
talents that expressed themselves through it. Doctors in
France were—as indeed they still are in most developing countries—intellectual leaders, whose contribution to man's view
of himself has never been adequately assessed; they were often
men with leisure, whose hobbies were more literary and artistic
than those of businessmen or landowners. The first French
newspaper was started by a doctor in 1631; the first French
medical journal followed soon after, in 1679, founded by
Nicolas de Blégny, a surgeon, who was also a seller of drugs,
author of books on venereal diseases, manager of a clinic and
of a bathing establishment, publisher of the Paris directory
which later became the *Bottin*, and, inevitably, an enemy of
the Paris faculty of medicine: he got his doctorate from the
faculty at Caen and collaborated with a graduate of Montpellier to produce the *Journal des nouvelles découvertes en médecine*.
By 1848 another eighty-one medical journals had been started
in Paris alone, to which one should add twelve more on popular
medicine, seventeen on magnetism, fourteen on specialised
branches of medicine, and thirty-two provincial journals. Between 1848 and 1867 another fifty-seven medical journals had

been founded.[1] In 1950 it was calculated that there were about 300 medical journals, excluding trade union organs and publications for private circulation.[2] Many journals originally began as a means of propagating the views of a particular doctor, famous or eccentric: thus the controversial Dr. Broussais (1772–1838) had his *Annales de la médecine physiologique*, which lasted from 1822 to 1884, and which, to begin with, published one of his faculty lectures each week. Daily medical newspapers were even founded, mainly by students. *La Lancette française*, founded in 1828 and renamed *La Gazette des hôpitaux* in 1850, appeared three times a week. The *Moniteur des hôpitaux* (1852–6) published the lectures of Claude Bernard, and to cater for Spanish students in Paris, there was even a *Gaceta medica clinica de los hospitales de Paris* (1850–4). Dr. Amédée Latour founded *L'Union médical* in 1845 as the first periodical designed to defend the pecuniary and professional interests of doctors. Some medical men had journalistic gifts and they were able to use them; Dr. Charles Bouchard, founder of *La Gazette hebdomadaire de médecine et de chirurgie* (1859), had a career which was as much journalistic as medical. Writing was often a consolation for obscure country doctors who had not won the fame they had dreamt of: as one wrote: 'Medical journals, when they are not the organ of a *camarilla*, fulfil a role which allows us to participate, even the least important among us, in the great movement of contemporary thought and scientific creation. They offer a *chair*, to which all may accede and from which they can make themselves heard. . . . They are thus a *compensatory chair* for those who will never enter any post, for those whom seem condemned to silence, even though their minds and hearts boil with activity.'[3] There was always room for doctors to produce humorous magazines, or journals devoted to gastronomy, and there was even a periodical devoted exclusively to advising doctors on investment in the stock-market—and it was said that its recommendations always produced a noticeable movement in share price.

[1] Dr. Achille Chéreau, *Essai sur les origines du journalisme médical français suivi de sa bibliographie* (1867).
[2] Marcel Lhopiteau, 'Contribution à l'histoire des journaux médicaux' (Paris medical thesis, 1950, unpublished, in the library of the Faculty of Medicine, Paris).
[3] *Bulletin mensuel de l'Association professionelle des journalistes médicaux français* (March 1932), 3.

As medicine became more specialised, an increasing number of journals appeared devoted to new sciences, like the *Archives d'opthalmologie* (1883), the *Revue neurologique* (1893), or *La Médecine infantile* (1894). These were very substantial publications, each issue being longer than an average book. The *Annales des maladies vénériennes* (1906) was 400 pages long in its first issue, but 950 pages by the 1930s. The development of the social services added a further crop, as too did colonial and military medicine, and even the history of medicine had four journals devoted to it.[1] This meant that an increasing number of doctors became involved in part-time editorial duties, and publication was a normal part of the professional lives of even more. The *Journal de pharmacie et de chimie* (1809), which was already producing over 1,100 pages a year, and 1,500 by 1910, had been founded quite humbly by a group of six people to help pharmacists 'perfect themselves in their art', which was necessary if 'they wanted to be distinguished by public esteem', but as the different branches of these sciences became more specialised, it needed twenty-one people to run it.[2] Many of these were professors, but an independent profession of medical journalists also arose, who formed their own association. In 1933 it had 114 members, but they were more powerful than this figure might suggest. At least, the pharmaceutical industry realised that they could have a considerable influence on the habits and expenditure of their contemporaries; and it accordingly gave regular subsidies to the medical journalists' pension fund, which was maintained very largely by these gifts, rather than by the subscriptions of the journalists themselves. The mineral-water firms of Vichy and Évian were also important benefactors. This made sure that the medical press was not unfriendly to them, or to new pharmaceutical products placed on the market.[3] It is clear that in medical journalism, as in all other forms of journalism, periodicals were sometimes started with the express intention of blackmailing manufacturers into adver-

[1] 'La Presse et l'édition médicale', special issue of *Le Courrier graphique* (Dec. 1938), especially 65–71.
[2] Émile Bourquelot, *Le Centenaire du Journal de pharmacie et de chimie 1809–1909* (1910), 24.
[3] *Bulletin mensuel de l'association professionelle des journalistes médicaux français* (there are copies of this rare publication, for 1932–5, in the library of the Faculty of Medicine, Paris).

tising in them. It became essential to collect an editorial board of distinguished practitioners to ensure that pharmaceutical firms and clinics dared not refuse to advertise in a new journal. Masson, which published about sixty medical journals, derived its strength partly from the advertising arrangements it was able to make. But there was no monopoly in this field. There was a great deal of local journalism by doctors, which survived on a strictly provincial readership. Thus Montpellier—admittedly the most important medical faculty after Paris but still only a small town—had forty different medical journals in the period 1791–1958. The proceedings of the faculty were the basis of these, but individual professors published separate journals to publicise their lectures and their theories. In 1840 a *Gazette médicale de Montpellier* was founded, which lasted fifteen years, to attack the professors of the faculty, edited by a doctor who could not get a job in it. The *Gazette hebdomadaire des sciences médicales de Montpellier* (1879–92) was run by a group of local professors to defend the Montpellier brand of medicine against 'the threat of asphyxia caused by the foundation of new rival faculties'. The *Languedoc médical*, started in 1912, became the basis of a family business, passed from father to son, and complemented by *Le Journal des sages-femmes de la Provence* (1924–32). In the 1930s, Montpellier was still producing two medical journals and in 1952 a third was added.[1] This proliferation of literature naturally encouraged the establishment of still more journals to summarise it, so that doctors could keep up with new discoveries. From the 1870s, some periodicals made a point of trying to review foreign discoveries too, but with varying success. It is noteworthy that the major indexes to world-wide research in medicine are published in the U.S.A. and in Germany: there is no French one; and certain discoveries, like penicillin, took some time to be publicised in France.[2] The most successful journals for the popularisation of medical knowledge, perhaps because they were usually started by doctors who were more interested in commerce than in medicine, often repeated, year after year, the same old remedies. The *Journal de la santé* (1893), which

[1] Louis Dulieu, 'Le Journalisme médical montpellérien' in *Montpellier médical* (July–Aug. 1958), 3rd series, vol. 54, no. 1, 28–38.
[2] Lhopiteau, op. cit. 78.

claimed a weekly circulation of 35,000 copies, gave subscribers the right to fifty-two free consultations a year, but it was crammed mainly with advertising and indeed charged the highest advertising rates of any periodical. In 1929, by contrast, the *Droit de guérir* was started to 'defend the interests of the sick' against doctors; it managed to sell almost as many copies.[1]

Women's magazines form another important category about which very little is known. It is too early to say what role they played in shaping the interests and the outlook of women, but there can be no doubt that by the end of the nineteenth century, and even more in the course of the period 1930–60, they provided women with reading matter which consolidated their status as a separate caste. Already in 1774 the *Journal des dames* was complaining about the hard lot of the unmarried mother; and in 1832 the *Journal des femmes* was founded as a paper run and written exclusively by women, but feminism was the cause of a tiny minority and the successful women's papers were those which concerned themselves with women's more immediate preoccupations.[2] *La Mode illustrée*, founded in 1860, lasted till 1937 and contributed substantially to the profits of the printer Firmin Didot who owned it. He had the good fortune to find an editor of outstanding ability in Emmeline Raymond, the daughter of a Belgian officer in the service of Austria and of a French mother who had established a school in Romania. Such was Madame Raymond's success that when she retired in 1902, after forty-two years as editor, her successor adopted her name, to guarantee that continuity would be ensured. Madame Raymond was a writer of considerable talent who had firm opinions which she could state forcibly in clear and straightforward language. Her achievement was to make her journal a link between Paris and the middle and petty bourgeoisie of the provinces, in a way that made her readers imagine that she was their personal friend and adviser, as her voluminous correspondence testified. On her retirement, the journal invited readers to say why they read the paper and

[1] The *Annuaire de la presse française* gives curious details about the medical press and the advertisements it carries. Cf., e.g., *L'Actualité thérapeutique* (1890), distributed free, *La Semaine médicale* (1881), *Maman* (1929), etc.

[2] Evelyne Sullerot, *Histoire de la presse féminine en France des origines à 1848* (1966). Continuations of this work are still awaited.

their letters revealed that there were many women who had bought it regularly for thirty or forty years, keeping it in bound volumes on their shelves, treating it as a guide to the practical and even moral problems of life. The journal, as they saw it, preached that it was 'woman's mission to occupy herself with the material and moral well-being of others', to create a home that was always harmonious, gentle and pretty, to achieve this by strict economy, making as many as possible of the things needed in the home herself. From the start La Mode illustrée insisted that wealth and elegance were totally different, and that one did not have to be rich to be worthy of respect; it rejected fashions which were too 'operatic', and instead told readers how to remake their old dresses to bring them up to date. It offered them patterns to make their clothes from, detailed instructions on how to produce the thousand knick-nacks that the bourgeois household contained, but it was an 'enemy of all exaggerations'. One reader wrote appreciatively of its understanding that 'we want to dress not luxuriously but with good taste and simply, that is to say in conformity with the rank we occupy'. Another said its moral advice 'frightened and infuriated me', because Madame Raymond seemed 'to know me so well, and I recognised all my faults'. A third approved its ambition to make women see that 'excellence lies in *not* being dazzling or brilliant', and congratulated it on 'trying to make us humble and hard-working women'. But it was not a paper that talked down to its readers. Madame Raymond's numerous books contained a great deal of solid information, common sense and shrewd knowledge of the world. Advertising, of course, assumed an increasing role in the paper, but this also enabled it to double in size (to sixteen pages a week) and include articles on women's careers, child rearing and literature, as well as cooking and gardening, and at the turn of the century it sold 100,000 copies a week.[1]

The connection between the fashion magazines and the fashion industry has still to be investigated; the financial bases of the increasing number of titles remains obscure.[2]

[1] La Mode illustrée (see in particular the prospectus of 1860 and the special issue of 1902); Le Livre d'or de La Mode illustrée (1904); Mme Emmeline Raymond, Autobiographie d'une inconnue (1888).

[2] Henriette Vanier, La Mode et ses métiers. Frivolité et luttes de classes 1830–70 (1960) is mainly about the clothing industry and its workers. Cf. Les Dessous

There were a few publishing firms which seemed to specialise in the market from an early date, like that owned by François Tedesco, who published *La Femme chez elle, Journal des ouvrages des dames, Mademoiselle, Ma poupée, Mon aiguille*; or that of the Catholic senator Huon de Penanster, who bought *Le Petit Écho de la mode* in 1879, when it was selling 5,000 copies, raised its circulation to over 100,000 by 1893, and up to a million by 1923, so founding the prosperity of his family, which still owned this paper in the 1960s. However, the expansion of the mass-circulation women's magazine (in which Cino del Duca's publishing group is now supreme) came only in the 1950s, though the basis for it had been laid between the wars by a few outstandingly successful magazines. Most of them were, significantly, Catholic. *Marie-Claire* (1937) was edited by Marcelle Auclair, who had been educated in a South American convent; *Confidences*, which reached half a million copies within a year of its launching, was based on letters from readers, as though it was supplementing or replacing the confessional.[1]

Children's magazines were also numerous, starting as early as the 1830s. They were given a great impetus by the publishers Hachette and Hetzel under Napoleon III, with Jules Verne as an outstanding contributor; they were modernised first under the influence of *L'Épatant* (1908) and then with *Le Journal de Mickey* (1937) which popularised the comic. These magazines were, however, read very largely by the middle classes, and they reflected the values and morals of the middle classes. In 1958, 38 per cent of children's papers were still published by political, religious or educational institutions. As a result, their commercial efficiency was not great; *La Semaine de Suzette* regularly had around half its print left unsold, and even *Mickey* had 18 per cent unsold. This meant, also, that the ownership of the children's press was less concentrated than, for example, in England. In 1970 the weekly sale of children's papers in France was only two million, whereas in England, with roughly an equal population, it was nine and a half million.[2] It seems

*élégants* (founded 1901) as an example of a fashion magazine devoted entirely to corsets and underwear, and full of advertisements.

[1] Evelyne Sullerot, *La Presse féminine* (1963) is mainly an account of the 1950s.

[2] Dominique Prieur and Alain Chahin, 'La Presse enfantine en Grande Bretagne et en France. Étude économique' (unpublished D.E.S. mémoire, in the Faculty of Law Library, Paris, 1970).

likely that French children read the adult press more than papers written specially for them.[1] Children were being gradually turned into a distinct class, but though they were provided with a separate opium to keep their minds off the realities of the adult world, it is probable that it had little effect upon them.

The use of the press as a new advertising instrument by industry can be seen most clearly from the astounding growth of newspapers devoted exclusively to sport. The first such paper was *Le Sport*, founded in 1854, but this was subtitled 'journal des gens du monde': it was a paper for the idle rich, concentrating on horse-racing. However, it found a surprisingly wide audience and it had added swimming, boxing, wrestling, billiards, tennis, cock-fighting and travel to its coverage by the time it collapsed in 1893. By then new developments had changed the situation. In 1869 the cycle manufacturer Fabre founded *Le Vélocipède*, partly to refute the attacks of doctors who were saying that cycling was unhealthy because it tired the legs while leaving the rest of the body 'in dangerous immobility', and partly to reply to *Le Cocher français* which denounced cycling as mad. In 1876 the president of the Nautical Club of France founded *La Revue des sports* and several more journals quickly followed, sustained by plentiful specialised advertising: *La Bicyclette* (founded 1892 and soon selling 20,000 copies a week) had as many as seventeen of its forty-two pages filled with advertisements—all but two of them about cycles. *Les Sports athlétiques* (1890), started by the founder of the Olympics, Pierre de Coubertin, was sustained by railway advertisements. The profits to be made were such that in 1891 a daily devoted exclusively to sports, *Le Vélo*, was launched and within a few years it had a sale of 80,000, considerably more than many respected political dailies. This paper was backed by the car and cycle manufacturer Darracq. In 1900 Adolphe Clément, a rival cycle manufacturer, in association with a number of leaders of the motor-car industry—the comte de Dion, Édouard Michelin, the baron de Zuylen de Nyevelt (president of the Automobile Club de France) and the comte de Chasseloup-Laubat—started another daily, *L'Auto-Vélo*.

[1] Béatrice de Buffevent, *Qu'attendent de leurs journaux les 11–14 ans?* (1963); Elisabeth Gérin, *Tout sur la presse enfantine* (Bonne Presse, 1958).

There was bitter competition between these two dailies: the latter was forced to change its name to *L'Auto* following a court case brought against it by *Le Vélo*. But *L'Auto* had a remarkable man as its editor in Henri Desgrange (1865–1940), who had started life as a notary's clerk, became a fanatical cyclist and world champion, got appointed publicity manager to the Clément Cycle Company, and opened a new velodrome in the Parc de Prince. *Le Vélo* refused to report the races held there. *L'Auto* appointed 542 correspondents in France and abroad and sent in addition special reporters to every big meeting. *Le Vélo* was slower with the news, but it replied to the challenge by giving reductions of between one-third and one-half on its advertising rates to firms which undertook not to advertise in any other sporting journal. *L'Auto* was unable to rise much above 20,000 until in 1903 Desgranges had the brilliant idea of organising the Tour de France cycling race, with a prize of 20,000 francs. His paper's circulation at once more than doubled and its fortune was made: in July 1914 it sold 320,000 copies a day, in July 1923 495,000, in July 1933 730,000 (the July figures, during the Tour de France, were at least 50 per cent higher than the average sale). *Le Vélo* long refused to mention this race.

Newspapers gradually realised how they too could benefit from having a sports page: in 1914 political dailies usually gave a quarter of a page to sport, and conceded a whole page only around 1930. Their weakness was that they paid attention mainly to the great races, ignoring the amateurs, and this is what allowed the specialist papers to survive. *Paris-Soir* was the first general daily to exploit sport with real commercial acumen: in 1939 it employed no less than eighteen sports reporters and it sent as many to cover the Tour de France as *L'Auto* did. It made sport sound more dramatic, emotional, sensational; it regularly gave sport a whole page, and three pages on Monday. As a result *L'Auto*'s circulation had fallen to 200,000 by the beginning of the war: its attempt to stave off disaster by adding general news failed; and at the end of the war it was closed down as part of the general collaborationist purge. *Élans* was founded in 1946 with the express intention of ending the influence of *L'Auto*, which, it claimed, had deliberately, for commercial reasons, given more publicity to certain sports, like cycling and motor-car racing, to the neglect of football. But *Élans* failed, and so too did *Sports* (1946), started with similar intentions by the communist party. *L'Auto* re-emerged as *L'Équipe*, making good its earlier shortcomings by publishing a weekly supplement, *France-Football*, which at once obtained a circulation of 140,000. The *Dépêche du Midi* of Toulouse replied by publishing a weekly devoted to rugby, *Midi olympique*; and the communist party renewed its attack with *Miroir-Sprint* and a host of other *Miroirs* devoted to individual sports, which kept up the attack on *L'Équipe* as the cause of all France's sporting troubles. *L'Équipe* continued to prefer professional sports, but football, which now surpassed cycling in popularity, had become professional too. The rivalry of the sporting press gives a good reflection of the complex motivations behind recreation; divisions were far more intricate than this brief account may suggest: in 1958 there were at least 231 periodicals devoted to sport with a total sale of 1,457,000 per issue. This was so even though the main Paris newspapers devoted 14·7 per cent of their space to sport, as compared with 9·9 per cent to general news, 8·9 to internal politics and 8·8 to foreign politics;[1] and the provincial press was even more lavish, for on Mondays some of them gave as many as five pages to sport. What this signified in terms of the interests and attitudes of their readers will need separate attention. But the press certainly co-operated in developing a sub-culture of entertainment and relaxation.

Religion, too, had a formidable collection of periodicals to support it. Nearly all of them were consistently moralising, in the sense that they made a practice of relating ephemeral events to the teachings of the Church; and yet the question of just how influential they were is not easy to answer. The most famous Catholic papers had very small readerships. *L'Univers*, started in 1833 by Abbé Migne, who was the editor also of a Catholic encyclopedia in 171 volumes, was taken over in 1843 by Louis Veuillot (1813–83), one of the most pungent and talked-about journalists of the century; but its circulation was only 4,700 in 1845 and around 7,000 in the 1870s. This is a good example of a newspaper which was essentially the organ of an individual, who had style, firmly held ideas and a determination to express them. Veuillot was considered to express the views of the

[1] Figures for 1947. Édouard Seidler, *Le Sport et la presse* (1964).

backwoods clergy who read him, but he hardly represented the Church's official line. His paper had perhaps received some financial help from the Vatican, but it was really an independent and profitable family business, which Veuillot handed over to his brother Eugène in his old age. Similarly *La Croix* was founded in 1880 by Vincent Bailly, who was the son of Emmanuel Bailly who had helped start *L'Univers* in the 1830s and who had succeeded Migne as its editor. *La Croix* was maintained as a polemical paper by the Assumptionist Order, vigorously attacking the republic until it was expelled from France; it was then kept going by a Catholic industrialist, Paul Feron-Vrau, till 1914, but it subsequently came under the control of two able editors, Abbé Bertoye and Professor Jean Giraud. The political line of the paper was always vigorous, though it changed from support of liberal Catholicism to advocacy of the Action Française. Its circulation varied between 150,000 and 180,000, which it achieved thanks to the support of a unique distribution system (run by parish workers), low costs (by having nuns print it) and very loyal subscribers (it had the lowest rate of unsold copies of any paper). But it was too serious a paper to be able to compete with the mass-circulation dailies, even though it showed considerable business acumen and sensitivity to its readers' demands. In 1960 it came second only to *Le Monde* in the amount of space it gave to foreign and economic news, but second only to *Paris-Jour* for the space occupied by photographs. At that date it sold a larger proportion of its copies in the provinces than any other daily (81 per cent, as opposed to *Le Monde*'s 44 per cent): but it was not a great commercial success. Its advertising income in 1960 was the same as that of the communist *L'Humanité*, about a quarter of that of *Le Monde* and one-twentieth of that of *Le Figaro*.[1] Its more popular Sunday editions sold roughly twice as many copies, and regional editions widened its impact.

What, however, was most impressive about the Catholic press was the way it catered for every taste, every level of intelligence, every type of reader; instead of trying to please everybody with one large daily, it produced numerous specialised journals. For purely religious purposes, the *Petit Messager du Cœur de Marie*

[1] J. and P. Godfrin, *Une Centrale de la presse catholique. La Maison de la Bonne Presse et ses publications* (1965), 161.

(1875) (with a circulation of 39,000 in 1936) kept up the zeal of the followers of the Virgin Mary; *Le Petit Bulletin de la croisade eucharistique* (1916) sold 300,000 copies monthly; and there were a host of other similar ones for different fraternities. The clergy had *L'Ami du clergé* (1878), which sold 6,000 at the turn of the century and 25,000 in the 1930s, and which had the virtue of being particularly cheap, but also *L'Ouvrier de la Moisson* (1927, 3,600 sales), *Les Annales des Prêtres adorateurs* (1888, 8,500 copies), etc. More intellectual Catholics could read the Jesuits' *Études* (1856, whose circulation rose from 3,000 to 13,000), or *La Vie intellectuelle* or *Sept* published by the Dominicans; and Abbé Bethléem's *La Revue des lectures* (20,000 copies, 128 pages monthly) gave advice on what books to read and what to avoid. There were special magazines for different professions, like *Le Postier catholique* (1922, 4,500 copies), others for pharmacists, for teachers, for soldiers, one even for people in hospital, *L'Ami des malades* (1928, 10,000 copies). There were at least thirteen educational journals, but also many others specially written for the young, like *La Semaine de Suzette* for the very young, *Les Veillées des chaumières* for older girls (this one, established in 1877, sold 200,000): every age group was catered for, and every class: *Noël* for the children of the bourgeoisie, *Bernadette* for poorer ones. Advice on entertainments was available in *Nos spectacles*, *Nos chansons*, *Choisir*, etc. *Le Sel* (1932) provided a humorous paper to rival those which might be too dirty for pious readers. All these journals were successful because they catered for definite groups of people, most of whom were organised to buy them. But the Catholic press, like the left-wing press, was suspicious of advertising and did not rely on it. Seventy-five per cent of the advertising revenue of La Bonne Presse, which was by far the largest Catholic publisher of periodicals, came from one daily paper, *Le Pèlerin* (1872), originally founded for pilgrims to La Salette, but quickly transformed into a successful popular family paper.[1] The Catholics converted no one with all this vast output. Their journals were read by the faithful; they were indeed a mark of solidarity. This is clearly seen from the wide regional variations in their sales. They were most successful in the west and least so in the Paris region.

[1] Anon., *Les Revues catholiques françaises à l'exposition internationale de la presse catholique au Vatican en 1936* (1936).

## The Catholic Press in 1936[1]

| | | | | | | | |
|---|---|---|---|---|---|---|---|
| North | 10 dailies and 31 weeklies. | | | Sale 668,000 | for a population of | 5,200,000 |
| East | 29 | ,, | 49 | ,, | ,, 536,000 | ,, | 3,900,000 |
| South-East | 5 | ,, | 37 | ,, | ,, 596,000 | ,, | 8,117,000 |
| South | 1 | ,, | 14 | ,, | ,, 124,000 | ,, | 2,160,000 |
| South-west | 6 | ,, | 25 | ,, | ,, 304,000 | ,, | 4,240,000 |
| West | 7 | ,, | 49 | ,, | ,, 942,000 | ,, | 6,730,000 |
| Centre including Paris | 4 | ,, | 30 | ,, | ,, 315,000 | ,, | 19,759,000 |

It would be quite wrong to imagine that this was in any way a unified Catholic press empire. The French press was character-ised by extreme fragmentation and, apart from a few combines, each journal was individual, representing the eccentricities and ambitions of writers, businessmen, politicians and men of leisure of very different kinds. One can see this, for example, in the history of *Le Nouvelliste de Lyon*, which in the early Third Republic was the most successful Catholic regional daily. It was founded in 1879—when there were already several well-estab-lished dailies in Lyon—by a group of fifty-one Catholics of the city. Twenty-nine of these were members of the Catholic Asso-ciation of Employers of Lyon, each of whom subscribed between 500 and 2,500 francs; thirty-seven of them were old boys of the fashionable Jesuit boarding-school of Mongré. There were no professional journalists or politicians among them. The main organiser, Joseph Rambaud (1849–1919), was an industrialist and landowner, who in his spare time taught at the Catholic Faculty at Lyon and was the author of a textbook on economics —which he hoped would replace that of Gide—designed to show economic development as the accomplishment of the divine will. Rambaud, who went to church every day, was a conserva-tive Catholic, a disciple of Bishop Pie and of Le Play but an enemy of the Social Catholics, whose reliance on the state he disapproved of. Within a year, his paper had a circulation of 40,000, at a time when in Paris the respectable *Journal des Débats* sold only 6,500 and the *Figaro* 97,000. In 1886 the paper bought out the printer, so great were its profits. It had started

[1] Based on Paul Verschave, *La Situation de la presse catholique en France en 1936* (1936).

with only 125,000 francs of capital; within ten years the value of its shares had almost trebled; by 1899 it was paying a dividend of 30 francs on each 100-franc share, and it owned buildings and reserves worth over a million francs. The paper took the view that religion was the answer to all problems, but that was not why it was successful. Despite its high principles, it borrowed the methods of the popular press and gave a lot of space to sensational news, 'sad and violent dramas'. Rambaud acknowledged that this was wrong, but explained that charity must 'bend to the needs and weaknesses of those it wished to serve'; he personally would prefer to print serious articles, but to do so in a popular paper would be egoism, which was the opposite of charity and love. He drew the line only at rape, adultery and seduction, which were never mentioned.[1]

This was a paper in which the shareholders allowed one man to make money for them unhindered, while also defending a cause they held dear, but when control was shared by a number of people, Catholic papers were just as liable to be torn by internal rows and rivalries as those of any other persuasion. The *Ouest-Éclair*, for example, was started by two radical priests in Rennes at the turn of the century, with the help of four local dignitaries, barristers and merchants, each of whom invested a sizeable part of his savings in the enterprise. They soon had trouble with the bishop, who disapproved of their democratic tendencies, and with their professional editor, who was an unpractical bohemian, with no head for business. The paper established itself not because of its religious character but on the contrary because the priests who started it discovered that its rivals failed to give enough news about prices at local fairs and practical, local information of that kind. This was the gap they filled. Endless personal and doctrinal bickering, however, left the paper unstable, until the politician Louis Loucheur and the Havas news agency gave it the capital it needed for expansion.[2] The *abbé*-journalists who entered this fray had no illusions about the press. They realised that newspapers were essentially businesses. As one of them wrote, with resignation or complacency,

---

[1] Louis de Vancelles, *'Le Nouvelliste de Lyon' et la défense religieuse 1879–1889* (Lyon, 1971), 85, 212.

[2] Paul Delourme, *Trente-cinq années de politique religieuse ou l'histoire de l'Ouest-Éclair* (1936).

| North | 10 dailies and 31 weeklies. Sale 668,000 for a population of 5,200,000 |
|---|---|

'Everything in the newspaper world is venal, even silence; everything in it is bought, everything has to be paid for.' It was impossible to resist the offers of printers and paper merchants, and of advertisers who made sure that even when a murder was reported, the article ended with the assurance that it would not have happened if the victim had used the soap made by X, or the umbrella of Y and Co. The press, said one *abbé*, was accused of engaging in blackmail, and he could not deny it; it was forced to do so; but the public was a willing accomplice of the game.[1] In religious life, as in so many other aspects of life, the press was one way by which people obtained a sense of belonging to a group, easier to identify with than the nation as a whole; but the question of who was fooling whom was left unanswered.

All these newspapers and periodicals were dependent on the printing industry, whose efficiency, or at least whose cheap rates, made it possible for almost anyone who was determined to get himself before the public eye to do so. This is an industry, however, about which virtually nothing is known. The emphasis in the study of typographical history has been almost exclusively antiquarian: much more is known about the eighteenth and earlier centuries than about the modern period. There are some books about individual firms but they are mainly commemorative; a fair amount has been written about the new kinds of printing machines, but little about the men who exploited them. Printing workers were among the most sophisticated members of the proletariat; their employers, who were often former workers, were, one suspects, additionally endowed with shrewd business sense. Printing had been a regulated corporation under the *ancien régime*, and until 1870 there were only a limited number of printers who were allowed to practise. The *brevets*, or government licences, were family property, or could be sold, like notary's *études*, so dynasties of printers were common; but their prosperity depended on how many new *brevets* the government issued. The July Monarchy was generous with them, but there was then still plenty of work to go round. But when the Third Republic ended all restrictions, many workers set up on their own and competition forced down prices. There remained

---

[1] Abbé P. Fesch, *Les Souvenirs d'un abbé journaliste* (1898), 218–34. Cf. Georges Hourdin, *La Presse catholique* (1957).

an important distinction between the small printer and the large firms equipped with expensive machines.[1] The former were often antiquaries interested in local history, typography and bibliography, like Adolphe Grange, deputy librarian of Dijon, who in 1861 bought a local printing works, on which he printed the *Journal de la Côte d'Or*, until, persecuted because he gave it a republican slant, he sold out to become one of the authors of Larousse's *Grand Dictionnaire du dix-neuvième siècle*.[2] The firm of Caillard of Narbonne, established in 1790, was handed down from father to son until 1920, when the last descendant gave up printing and devoted himself exclusively to bookselling.[3] There were many printers who were one-man businesses, or employed only a couple of workers; some were part-time, printing when there was work. The small town of Valence (population about 20,000) had eight printers at the turn of the century; and that sort of number meant that the town could publish, in the course of the previous fifty years, eight Catholic journals, seven Protestant ones, twenty-five political ones, fifteen financial, commercial and advertising papers, ten artistic and literary journals, ten humorous ones, one educational one and eleven miscellaneous reviews.[4] Bordeaux in 1852 (population 180,000) had eighteen printers, forty-two lithographers, twenty-eight booksellers. Here there were opportunities for the growth of larger firms, as the history of the Gounouilhou family showed. They were Protestants, artisan armourers and watchmakers, but a member of the family was apprenticed to a printer, married his daughter and in 1851 bought the firm of Faye-LaCourt, which went back to the seventeenth century, and had valuable contracts as printers to the archbishop, the courts, the faculties and various learned societies. Gounouilhou continued to print for the archbishop but he also printed a Bonapartist journal established in Bordeaux by a Paris speculator, Delamarre. This paper, however, lost money, so Gounouilhou bought it from its owner for a song. He replaced

[1] Georges Dangon, 'Sociologie du maître imprimeur', *Le Courrier graphique* (Dec. 1936), 3–12, (Jan. 1937), 3–10.
[2] Clément Janin, *Les Imprimeurs et les libraires dans la Côte d'Or* (Dijon, 1883), 90–4.
[3] H. Malet, *Les Imprimeurs de Narbonne 1491–1966* (Narbonne, 1966); cf. Émile Pasquier, *Imprimeurs et libraires de l'Anjou* (Angers, 1932).
[4] Léon Emblard, 'Les Imprimeurs et les journaux à Valence', *Bulletin de la Société départementale d'archéologie et de statistique de la Drôme* (Valence, 1902), vol. 36, 49–56.

its editor (who went off to become a restaurant manager instead)[1]
by his brother-in-law André Lavertujon. The paper, *La Gironde*,
became, under his direction, the organ of the republican party.
It was very much a family business: Lavertujon wrote it,
Gounouilhou printed it, Gounouilhou's wife managed the
finances and other relatives did other jobs. Their politics lost
them the privilege of printing official advertisements, which the
firm had long enjoyed, but the profitability of the newspaper
cancelled that out: in five years its circulation rose from 300 to
14,000. With the proclamation of the republic, Lavertujon was
summoned to Paris to be editor of its *Journal officiel* and he
later became an ambassador; his assistant was appointed to a
prefecture; another of its journalists became Resident-General
in Tunis. *La Gironde*, and its evening edition, *La Petite Gironde*,
became the establishment papers of Bordeaux. By 1900 the
Gounouilhou firm was employing 337 people, and was an important publisher, with its *Gironde maritime et commerciale*, *Gironde
littéraire et scientifique*, *Gironde illustré*, *Gironde du dimanche*, *Écho du
Palais*, and not least *Véloce-Sports* (1885). The firm was taken
over by Jules Chapon, a journalist on *La Gironde* who married
the boss's daughter, and by their son after him.[2] Printers had
an important influence on the press. They were often the decisive factor in determining whether a particular town had its
own newspaper, though many, and often elusive, forces must be
investigated to explain the erratic birth and irregular life of
newspapers.[3] The economic basis of the French newspaper
industry is still very obscure.

Any historical study of the press must inevitably be unsatisfactory because there is no way of measuring the influence it has
had. In the past, it has simply been taken for granted that the
press was an important force in politics; and historians still
quote newspapers as expressions of public opinion, no doubt

[1] This was Jules d'Auriol, who ran Les Dîners de Paris, a large restaurant
founded by the press magnate Émile de Girardin. D'Auriol then married the
widow of the founder of the Bouillons Duval restaurant chain and died a millionaire.

[2] G. Bouchon, *Histoire d'une imprimerie bordelaise. Les Imprimeries G. Gounouilhou*
(Bordeaux, 1901).

[3] Georges Auclair, 'Conditions d'existence d'une presse quotidienne départementale: le cas de La Rochelle', *Revue française de sociologie* (Oct.–Dec. 1962),
415–31.

because they can find no alternative source for discovering this. The French have not, to this day, investigated the question of the influence of the press in any systematic way. One is therefore forced to turn to American studies, of which there have been a very large number. Their general conclusion has been that the press has had the effect much more of reinforcing existing opinions than of changing them, that minor changes in attitude have occasionally followed from reading the press, but that conversions are rare. People expose themselves to the press selectively, choosing papers which are in accord with their existing views; they avoid exposure to information they do not like and if they come into contact with this, they tend either to distort it, so as to make it fit in with their existing views, or they remember only acceptable parts of it. The press can be effective in matters in which its audience has no previous opinions, but the information it conveys often acts as a vaccination, which renders the audience immune to any further opinions. It is true that some people are more persuadable than others, and in particular people under conflicting pressures, with unstable convictions, are open to persuasion; but such people often prefer escapist literature to reasoned argument. It seems to have been clearly established that personal conversation or contact is most effective as an instrument of persuasion, that the radio is less so, and that the printed medium is least so. The crucial role of 'opinion leaders' and of small groups in creating opinion is stressed, and these tend, on the whole, to work towards reinforcement of traditional views rather than towards change.[1]

The few investigations of detailed incidents in which the press was involved seem to confirm this. In the presidential election of 1848, 190 newspapers supported Cavaignac and only 103 were in favour of Louis Napoleon, but Napoleon nevertheless obtained nearly four times more votes. The influence of the press on this occasion seems to have been virtually negligible; that of clubs, by contrast, was probably considerably greater.[2] In the second half of the nineteenth century, the radicals waged a very vigorous campaign against the Church, using, as one of their main instruments, press propaganda; but investigations of voting behaviour in individual villages show that their invasion by

---

[1] Joseph T. Klapper, *The Effects of Mass Communication* (Glencoe, Illinois, 1960).
[2] A. J. Tudesq, *L'Élection présidentielle de L. N. Bonaparte* (1965), 145–98.

anticlerical newspapers had virtually no effect.[1] It is quite true that a press campaign directed against Blum's minister of the interior, Roger Salengro, led to his committing suicide in 1936, but that represents a different kind of power—there can be no doubt that the press was able to attack individuals, and sometimes with tragic results, but it does not follow that anyone but its victim was worried by this. The press was very active in propagating anti-Semitism, but it is by no means clear that it did more than give expression in writing to what people were saying in any case; if anything, it may well have been counterproductive, in that it made the prejudice it supported appear all the more unjust, so encouraging the left wing to rally to the defence of a minority which it had hitherto generally disliked.

The most important role of the press was probably to shape the news, and so to modify the way issues were discussed. The press, almost inevitably, presented the news in a sensational, partisan, simplified manner. This was quite separate a matter from the bribery and corruption of which the press was guilty, when it deliberately concealed the truth. Once the press had developed the way it did, with the ultimate emphasis always being on securing the highest possible circulation, journalists were almost automatically the victims of a technical pressure, of the rules of a game which required them, impossibly, to reconcile conflicting demands of professionalism, truth and popularity. Newspapers became obsessed with being first with the news, and their rivalry concentrated their attention, therefore, on the ephemeral and the personal. The press was particularly important in revealing scandals, in creating political crises, and the Dreyfus Affair is the most famous illustration of its power. This was much more a crisis induced and sustained by the press than the result of popular concern. There is no doubt, too, that, as a result of the rise of the newspaper industry, the country knew far more about itself than it had ever done before, but the fragmentary, episodic nature of the information passed on through the press was such that, if the press did make any permanent impact, it may well have been more to confuse than to enlighten. The newspapers were frequently, indeed usually, critics of government, in a constant relationship of envy and hate towards it, but they were also major supporters of the

[1] G. Cholvy, *La Géographie religieuse de l'Hérault* (1968).

centralising mission and inculcation of uniform behaviour that all governments sought. The progress of this uniformity suggests they contributed to the victory, or at any rate were on the winning side; but the rise of the regional newspapers showed that the local interests and traditional superstitions of the masses were not eliminated. The press was nominally on the side of education, or at least saw itself as one of the instruments of the spread of science and knowledge, but, under pressure from its readers, it also did a great deal to give a new status to sport, relaxation and entertainment. It is partly due to the press, and not simply to politicians—though they were often the same thing—that French politics was seen as the struggle of irreconcilable animosities; the press flattered prejudice and feared to disturb its readers in their habits; it therefore helped to give those animosities a greater reality, preventing people from seeing them in their true light. It was thus ultimately a highly conservative force; it did not encourage its readers to tear themselves away from the past.

There was a good reason for this. The press was not free; it had not, in this period, won its independence, even if the laws hollowly proclaimed the freedom of the press. It failed to find a formula which would allow journalists to write without irresistible pressures weighing upon them, or newspapers to be published profitably without accepting financial servitude. Even today, this formula has not been found. The French press is in a continual state of economic crisis. About half its total revenue is obtained from state subsidies, given indirectly in the form of preferential prices for materials, postal charges, rail freight, etc. This has not altered the traditions of the press, which continues to attack and criticise the government that succours it. The French press is, in some ways, the equivalent of the British institution of Her Majesty's Opposition. But though a few newspapers have secured editorial independence, the press as a whole is very much in the hands of large capitalist combines, whose concentration has increased steadily since 1914–18 and much more since 1945. The blatant corruption of pre-war days has been ended, but less obvious pressures survive, and no doubt inevitably.[1] The very considerable talent, and sometimes even genius, that was expended in the service of this profession almost

[1] M. Mottin, *Histoire politique de la presse 1944–9* (1949).

always ended in frustration; but on the other hand the exceptionally large amount of imagination and wit that went into it
added spice and excitement to many lives. Despite its corruption, the press did a great deal to reveal corruption, injustice
and stupidity in government and society; because there were so
many newspapers in rivalry, it remained immensely active as a
defender of the rights of the individual, and of liberal values
which it did not always practise itself. Thanks to it, the smoke-
screens manufactured by verbose politicians were sometimes
dissipated, even if they were more often taken seriously. It was
a major factor in liberating literary style from archaic rules,
though in seeking to reflect the popular style, it often lost sight
of elegance.[1] It did a great deal to undermine the faith that the
illiterate originally had in the printed word. It showed up, in
short, the resistance of taste, or at least popular taste, against
intellect.[2] The press probably did a considerable amount to
create fashions, which came and went; and it is in this sense that
it created reputations, even if these lasted only for short periods.
It was perhaps most powerful in times of national or social crisis,
but conversely, it was disgust with its brain-washing propaganda
campaigns during the First World War that turned so many
people against it. If it is true that opinion is created mainly
by small groups mutually sustaining themselves, and by personal influences, then the press should be seen as the mouthpiece of certain cliques, reinforcing rather than creating loyalties.
But it is impossible, in the present state of knowledge, to be
too precise about the elusive problem of how ideas were
transmitted and how tastes changed.

[1] On journalistic style, see Criticus, *Le Style au microscope* (*grands journalistes*)
(1953); Charles Bruneau, *La Langue du journal* (1958).

[2] On problems of class and readership see C. A. Tuffal, 'Étude de la presse
quotidienne parisienne. Le rapport entre informateurs et informés' (unpublished
Toulouse political science doctoral thesis, 1966).

# 12. Science and Comfort

At the end of the eighteenth century, there was probably a greater concentration of famous scientists in Paris than in any other city in the world. In 1900 the idea of French scientific supremacy had clearly become an illusion, even if many people still clung to it, and in 1960 only 6 per cent of the French population thought that France could still hope for leadership in this domain.[1] The paradox is that when France did have more scientists than anyone else, the country was taken over by lawyers and soldiers, and men of letters portrayed France to foreigners as being devoted above all to the arts; but when French scientific achievements were clearly lagging well behind those of America and Russia, the technocrats were able to capture power and the whole direction of the economy was altered towards the attainment of essentially materialistic goals. It will be seen that there is of course no paradox, and that the triumph of the technocrats should not cause surprise. It is important to study the role of science in French life precisely because the scientists were for long relatively silent, while literary writers, who did not share their ideals, created dark smoke-screens around the whole subject. Under the cover of this, a division of France between artistic and materialistic ideals was concealed, though it was a subtle, overlapping and un-acknowledged division. However, the reason why American ideals, of prosperity before all else, could become the creed of the post-1945 era was that they had silently penetrated into sections of most classes. A trained élite was already available to lead the new order that emerged from the collapse of France.

In the eighteenth century, the study of science was a common hobby among educated men of leisure. It was carried on in much the same way as collecting paintings was, as an alternative or a complement to this. A list has been compiled of nearly 500 people known to have had *cabinets d'histoire naturelle*—aristocrats,

[1] Jean Meynaud, *Les Savants dans la vie internationale. Éléments pour un auto-portrait* (Lausanne, 1962), 14.

priests, actors, collectors of taxes, doctors, factory inspectors, and the duc d'Orléans's chief cook. Lamarck said that the purpose of these was very often to 'provide a show and perhaps to give an idea of the wealth or luxury of the owner'; and they were certainly fashionable among people who knew little mathematics or mechanics, but who satisfied their taste for collecting by accumulating hoards of minerals, plants and animals, and classifying them into species.[1] The division between science and the arts had not occurred. The most popular books of the age were not only Voltaire and Rousseau but also Buffon's *Natural History* (in forty-four volumes, 1749–1804) and Abbé Pluché's *Spectacles of Nature* (1732, in eight volumes).[2] Most scientists, including those who made discoveries of international importance, had other jobs, like Lavoisier (1743–94), who laid the foundations of modern chemistry but who was also a senior tax-collecting official and was guillotined as such in the Terror. Scientists were closely associated therefore with public affairs. Napoleon made Laplace (1749–1827), the leading mathematician of the age, minister of the interior; on his expedition to Egypt, he took with him a large group of brilliant scientists, whose researches remain as the most impressive monument of the war. This was almost to be expected, because scientific discovery was seen as an integral part of progress and of military power. The great Encyclopedia of the eighteenth century was produced jointly by the philosopher, playwright and art critic Diderot and the mathematician d'Alembert, author of an important *Treatise on Dynamics* (1743). The prestige of French science was such therefore that Frederick II, the king of Prussia, modelled his Berlin Academy on the French Academy of Sciences and successively invited three Frenchmen—Maupertuis, d'Alembert and Condorcet—to direct it. Science was so fashionable in Paris high society that a *grande dame*, the marquise de Chatelet, undertook the translation of Newton's *Principia*. There were few branches of science to which France did not make major and fundamental contributions in the century 1750–1850.

[1] René Taton, Charles Bedel et al., *Enseignement et diffusion des sciences en France au 18ᵉ siècle* (1964), 669.
[2] D. Mornet, 'Les Enseignements des bibliothèques privées 1750–1780', *Revue d'histoire littéraire de la France* (1910), 449–96.

Scientists produced such a profound transformation in men's view of themselves that they had every right to expect a dominant role in society. Their discoveries led to more radical changes than the theories of philosophers because the implications could be demonstrated in such dramatic and convincing ways. Politicians might preach an end to resignation—the dominant attitude that Christianity had fostered—but scientists could show that it was possible to change one's environment, to alter what seemed to be rigid decrees of nature, to travel at unprecedented speeds. Politicians might blame the nation's misfortunes on human error and argue that man could put an end to his miseries, but it was scientists who proved that disease was not a punishment from heaven, but the work of germs, and they showed that they could destroy them. Optimism took on a new strength when the mass of people were, in consequence, able to live twice and three times as long as they had previously done. The claim that God had created the world at a particular time was challenged in such a way that the very basis of religious authority seemed to be undermined; scepticism on the one hand, determinism on the other, were given a wide popularity. The idea that men existed in order to fulfil some divine purpose, that they were different in kind from animals, or indeed from ordinary matter, was so weakened that both government and morals had to turn in new directions. The physical well-being of the masses assumed a much higher priority than it had ever done. Science set up a new pattern of attitudes, in which the possibility of change was an essential element.

However, though in the early nineteenth century the Saint-Simonians suggested that scientists should take over government, this did not come about. The explanation is to be found, first of all, in the very conditions that scientific progress created, which paradoxically limited the ability of scientists to seize the full implications of their work, or to convey these to the public. Specialisation reached a turning-point around the middle of the nineteenth century, after which not only did laymen become incapable of understanding what the scientists were doing, but the scientists themselves branched off into separate disciplines, with only the gifted few being able to keep up in more than one. It is too simple to say that, as a result, two cultures developed. That was a slower process, particularly in France, where the

tradition of science as part of culture survived, where leading
scientists continue to be elected to the French Academy—a body
that epitomises the union of literature, the arts and all forms of
public service in the defence of style and taste—and where a
smattering of philosophy and of rhetoric were required accomplishments from all educated people, as piano playing was from
well-brought-up girls. But precisely because scientists continued
to mix, to a certain extent, with men of letters, they grew increasingly modest about their capacity to philosophise about
their work, and they were profoundly influenced by the positivist theories that the men of letters developed for them. The
essence of positivism was that people should not draw metaphysical conclusions from their observations and should confine
themselves to studying observable facts. French science took on
characteristics which were the opposite of those found in other
fields of endeavour. It grew frightened of general theories, even
of working hypotheses, and scorned the Germans for making so
much use of these, even though they were sometimes highly
fruitful.[1] The basis of its early success was the advanced state
of mathematical teaching in France, and this mathematical bias
was long preserved. The result was that French scientists favoured mathematical research more than investigations of industrial applications. They were of course not unique in despising,
or being ignorant about, the work of engineers—Rutherford was
too—but because the best scientific research was concentrated
in Paris and in a few non-university institutions—the faculties
of science for long remaining essentially teacher training establishments—a serious gap grew up between scientists and the rest
of the world. The scientists were themselves largely to blame for
their growing impotence, because they cherished their independence so much. Condorcet had argued that the scientific community deserved a privileged position in the state but had
insisted that it should receive no money from it, so as to be
completely autonomous. The result was that throughout the
nineteenth century scientific research was carried on with very
limited financial resources, and in 1933 Jean Perrin was still
able to say that the allocation of money for research in the
university was 'an irregularity' which the government consented

[1] Maurice Caullery, *La Science française depuis le 17ᵉ siècle* (1933, 2nd edition 1948),
198.

not to notice. The government could hardly be blamed, because most of the scientists behaved like artists, absorbing themselves in their researches oblivious of the practical consequences.[1] Whereas in Germany industry quickly took charge of scientific research and forced it to devote time to technological applications, there was less contact in France. It was claimed in 1914 that 'unfortunately there is a very widespread prejudice [among French industrialists] today that it is in every one's interest to retard the progress of science, so as to preserve more easily one's advantages over one's competitors'. This was perhaps an exaggeration, and there were instances of grants from industry to assist scientific research, but they were of small sums. The Conservatoire des Arts et Métiers, moreover, which was founded (1794) to copy its German equivalent, developed in a totally different way and avoided research on subjects of general utility.[2]

It is incorrect, however, to ascribe the relative decline of French science from the heights it reached around 1800 to financial or institutional causes, to suggest, that is, that science became a minor interest of the country, to which little value was attached. The whole question of the 'decline' of French science is, to begin with, confusing. A sociologist has counted the number of papers published on medical science in the nineteenth century, and has shown that France led in 'productivity' up to 1840, when it was overtaken by Britain; in 1850 it was overtaken also by Germany, and in 1890 by the U.S.A. This should not be surprising. In 1800 France was still the most populous nation in the western world, and probably the richest; the latest view of the economists is that though Britain is supposed to have been the pioneer of the Industrial Revolution, statistics prove that French industrial production in the eighteenth century was greater than that of Britain. These dates simply reflect France's changing international situation as its population ceased to grow.[3] The real question is whether France

[1] J. J. Salomon, *Science et Politique* (1970), 60–5.

[2] Henry Le Chatelier, *Les Encouragements à la recherche scientifique*, Mémoires et documents du Musée social (1914), 58–88.

[3] J. Ben-David, 'Scientific Productivity and Academic Organisation in 19th century Medicine', reprinted in B. Barber and W. Hirsch, *The Sociology of Science* (New York, 1962), 305–28; T. J. Markovitch, 'L'Évolution industrielle de la France', *Revue d'histoire économique et sociale* (1975), 266–88; P. K. O'Brien, *Two Paths to the 20th Century* (1977).

came to place less emphasis or value on science. The answer is not clear, because of the war of words between arts and sciences and between religion and science. But if one considers what happened, as opposed to what was said, and if one ceases to give special attention to the opinions of literary men, simply because they were artistically eminent, the decline of science can be seen to have been a withdrawal into discreet obscurity rather than a collapse into insignificance. Science continued to have its admirers and its adepts, but they kept to themselves more. This did not mean that science became less important in society, but only that society was more fragmented, and the results of scientific activity were experienced more than they were written about. A great deal has been made of the influence of the École Normale Supérieure as a nursery of writers and politicians; a certain amount has been said about the crucial positions that graduates of the Polytechnic came to occupy; but very little has been written about the École Centrale and the schools of applied science. Yet France was the world's pioneer in the organisation of technical education.[1] However it did not expand this into a mass system, but kept it within the bounds set by the demands of industry. The results were nevertheless very considerable. The first calculation of the number of scientists and engineers trained at university level was made only in 1950, but the figure then was 137,000, to which should be added 145,000 'technicians'.[2] This army of over a quarter of a million people was, comparatively speaking, small. Even though the proportion of science degrees in all university degrees rose between 1950 and 1959 from 29 to 42 per cent, France in 1959 still had less than. half the number of science graduates, per head of population, than the U.S.A. had. But the French scientists were a more cohesive and united group, even with something of the characteristics of a caste. The École Centrale was to the industrialists of France what Oxford and Cambridge were to the ruling class of England, but even more so. In the nineteenth century, about

[1] F. B. Artz, *The Development of Technical Education in France 1500–1850* (Cambridge, Mass., 1966).

[2] 24,000 natural scientists, 95,000 engineers, 18,000 agricultural engineers, of whom 53 per cent worked in industry, 40 per cent in services (mainly teaching and administration) and 7 per cent in agriculture. O.E.C.D., *Resources of Scientific and Technical Personnel in the O.E.C.D. Area* (1963), 147, 69; O.E.C.D., *Shortages and Surpluses of Highly Qualified Scientists and Engineers in Western Europe* (1955), 52.

80 per cent of its students came from bourgeois families, and mainly from those running industry. Between 1831 and 1900, seven Japys, seven Peugeots and seven Dollfusses were educated at the École Centrale. There was much intermarriage between the families of its graduates; it had a very strong old boys' association which virtually dominated recruitment into technical and management posts in industry. But the graduates of the École Centrale on the whole kept out of politics, unlike the Polytechniciens, and contented themselves with supremacy in a limited world.[1] The Polytechniciens, and the graduates of the schools of applied science, of course had their own *esprit de corps*, which, however, was more tied up with control of the state administration.[2] There were rivalries and jealousies between all these sub-groups, but together they did have a recognisable individuality. Because they were so comfortably ensconced in one sector of the economy, they took care not to draw too much attention to their privileges, and they adopted a system of live and let live towards the rest of society. The consequence was that, as an eminent biologist has put it, science won its place in the practice but not in the hearts of society at large.[3] Science and ethics remained separate. But that is not to say that science's place was inferior.

The history of France's scientists and engineers has not yet been written. The attention of historians of science has been concentrated on the period around 1800, because this is considered France's golden age in scientific achievement. But the French were the first to make science a professional career and the results of that deserve study.[4] The achievements of French scientists were far from negligible, even against the competition of larger countries. Jean Perrin, Louis de Broglie and Frédéric Joliot, for example, played a decisive role in the development of nuclear physics. French science continued to be distinguished by important discoveries, even if they were not often applied for purposes of mass production. In 1930 France was still the second

[1] Michel Bouille, 'Enseignement technique et idéologies au 19ᵉ siècle' (unpublished thesis, École Pratique des Hautes Études, 1972).

[2] J. C. Thoenig, *L'Ère des technocrates. Le cas des ponts et chaussées* (1973).

[3] Jacques Monod, *Chance and Necessity. An Essay in the Natural Philosophy of Modern Biology* (1972), 158.

[4] M. Crosland, 'The Development of a Professional Career in Science in France', *Minerva* (Spring 1975), 38–57.

largest exporter of patents in the world after the United States; though by 1938 it had dropped into fourth place, after the U.S., Britain and Germany.[1] The activity of French engineers abroad made highly important contributions to the economic development of many of the smaller European countries. At present, it is possible only to illustrate the problem of the relationship between science and society by taking the cases of a few notable individuals, on whom there is something approaching adequate information.

The way scientists could be extremely bold in their own specialities, but nevertheless very modest in drawing any general conclusions from their work, for the guidance of general conduct, can be seen in Claude Bernard (1813–78). He placed physiology on a new footing by chasing vitalism out of it—the old notion that a mysterious vital force ruled the body, making it radically different from the inorganic world. Bernard showed how the body produced the energy it used, how digestion worked, how the blood supply to different parts was regulated; he destroyed the view that the body was simply a bundle of organs, each with separate and appropriate functions, and instead argued that it was one chemical and physical mechanism, whose activities were interrelated and subordinate to its over-all physiological needs. Life was thus defined mechanistically as the maintenance of the equilibrium of the body. Bernard's *Introduction to the study of experimental medicine* (1865) defined the principles that should guide the research worker, emphasising experiment, methodical doubt and the avoidance of unjustified system building. Bernard thus made the physiology of man as precise and exact a science as physics or chemistry. But he firmly refused to draw general conclusions about the world from his particular discoveries. He insisted that man had three faculties—believing, reasoning and experimenting—and that these produced three distinct disciplines—religion, philosophy and science. His fundamental idea was that the limits of each of these must be strictly observed, and that progress could be measured in terms of their more exact delimitation. The rule of reason would make man a monster. All men—even scientists

[1] Harry W. Paul, 'The Issue of Decline in 19th Century French Science', *French Historical Studies* (Spring 1972), 416–50, is a valuable critique of Robert Gilpin, *France in the Age of the Scientific State* (Princeton, 1968), 35.

—needed metaphysics and religion, and their problem was simply how to reconcile their ideas. Science itself was in any case only a provisional belief, and it did not exclude the search for first or final causes, though it never reached them. Ignorance was the lot of man; progress in science was not linked to the progress of humanity; the determinism he saw in phenomena did not affect the liberty man's thought and actions enjoyed. Claude Bernard, the son of a wine-growing peasant, educated by his village priest and by the Jesuits, died in the faith of his boyhood, asserting his belief in the immortality of the soul. Science did not solve his personal problems: 'Science absorbs and consumes me', he said. 'I ask no more if it helps me to forget.' His wife and daughters protested against his refusing to be an ordinary medical practitioner and contributed to the anti-vivisection societies which harassed him; and it was a Russian, Madame Raffalovitch, who sustained his confidence. Despite the modesty of his conclusions, he was held up as the champion of a new attitude to knowledge and his *Introduction* became a textbook in the schools. In their enthusiasm, his positivist popularisers omitted to point out how much he disagreed with them.[1]

Pasteur (1822–95) is another example of scientific genius united with the most conservative political and social ideas. Pasteur's views—outside his laboratory—may indeed be taken as typically representative of the average man of his time. He was a scholarship boy, the son of a tanner who had been a sergeant-major under Napoleon I, and Pasteur inherited an admiration for the emperor. The educational system, said Pasteur, should be based on the principle of the cult of great men. He had a profound faith in hard work as the means of rising in the world, and when he had a cerebral haemorrhage at the age of forty-six, from too much of it, he read Samuel Smiles's *Self-Help* during his convalescence. *Laboremus* was his motto. Another of his favourite books was Joseph Droz's *The Art of Being Happy*, in which he found confirmation for his view that life consisted of 'will-power, work and success', success

[1] C. Bernard, *La Science expérimentale* (1878); C. Bernard, *Philosophie*. Manuscrit inédit présenté par Jacques Chevalier (1937); Joseph Schiller, *Claude Bernard et les problèmes scientifiques de son temps* (1967); Reino Virtanen, *Claude Bernard and his place in the history of ideas* (Lincoln, Nebraska U.P., 1960).

being a 'brilliant and happy career'. He married the daughter of the Rector of the Academy where he was a professor; he replied to her protests against his dedication with the assurance that he was leading her to eternal fame. But there was no greed or selfishness in him. When Napoleon III asked him why he did not try to profit personally from his discoveries and their important industrial applications, he replied that he thought this would take up too much time and would impair his spirit of invention; besides 'in France scientists would consider that they would be demeaning themselves by trying to make money'. He had no philosophical ideas, and he said that 'my philosophy is one of the heart, not of the mind'. He had read very little philosophy, and thought scientists should avoid being influenced by it, since it might make them *hommes de système*; but, he added, 'I admire them all, our great philosophers'. He made a clear distinction between himself as a scientist, basing himself on observation, experiment and reason in his search for truth, and himself as 'a man of feeling, of tradition, faith or doubt, a man of sentiment, a man who cries for his dead children, who cannot, alas, prove that he will see them again, but who believes and hopes this, who does not want to die as a vibrio dies, who tells himself that the strength in him will transform itself. The two domains are distinct and woe to him who wants to make them infringe on each other in the present very imperfect state of human knowledge.' In his work, therefore, he found 'the sole distraction from such great sorrows'. He saw no affinity between the revolution he was carrying out in science and the political agitations of his time. He was strictly authoritarian in his dealings with students, and passionately patriotic. The influence he exercised was therefore totally at variance with his ambitions. He became France's most famous scientist, because the practical results of his research were so dramatic. He showed that diseases formerly attributed to some inner failing were due to infection by microbes—a new word and a new idea, which placed life at the mercy of new, almost invisible beings. He developed 'pasteurisation' as a defence against them, and vaccines also. His work on fermentation had a profound effect on the methods of making beer, wine and vinegar; but it also destroyed the notion of spontaneous generation. However, he did not like the broader generalisations that were developed from this. He was an example of a scientist who undermined, without seeking to, the religious and philosophical principles of his society, who showed how research could increase the well-being of his fellow men more efficaciously than political agitation. He held science up as the instrument of 'wealth and prosperity', but showed also that its discoveries could not solve emotional or moral problems. He gave prestige to materialist solutions despite himself.[1]

Marcellin Berthelot (1827–1907), the pioneer of chemical synthesis, gave detailed expression to the hopes science raised in this direction. In his fantasy on *The Year 2000* (written in 1897) he prophesied that chemistry would by then make agriculture and mining unnecessary; food would be eaten in the form of small synthetic pills; industry would be powered by inexhaustible energy from the sun and from the heat of the earth, reached by wells five kilometres deep; air transport would replace all other forms. Man would become gentler and more moral because he would cease to feed himself by carnage and the destruction of living creatures. The world would become an immense and beautiful garden. Everything would be all set to 'realise the dreams of socialism'. But he admitted two difficulties. There would be less work to do, but idleness was bad. This was surmountable: since labour was the source of all virtue, people would work harder than ever all the same, because they would get the full rewards of their efforts. Nevertheless, the condition for this transformation was still 'the discovery of a spiritual chemistry, which will change man's moral nature'. He had no method for finding this.[2] Science thus held out the prospect of all the conditions of bliss, though never bliss itself. Berthelot, having written thirty volumes and about 1,500 articles, which showed above all that organic matter was subject to the same chemical laws as inorganic, went into politics as a radical, as though with the pretension, as his enemies put it, of annexing science to his party's electoral programme. The results were disquieting. As minister of education, he defended censorship of the theatre and maintained the ban on a play based on Zola's *Germinal*. As minister of foreign affairs his ineptitude was held up as disproving the claim that scientists had a contribution to

---

[1] *Discours de réception de M. Louis Pasteur* (1882); R. Vallery-Radot, *La Vie de Pasteur* (1900).

[2] M. Berthelot, *Science et morale* (1897), 508–15.

make to the maintenance of peace. Outside his own subject, Berthelot was a conservative. He was for long a staunch enemy of the atomic theory and prevented it being fully admitted into the school syllabus until the 1890s, in the same way as Claude Bernard and many others remained sceptical about Pasteur's theory of microbes. The disputes among scientists—the long and violent battles in the Academy of Medicine on the subject of contagious diseases were the most celebrated—encouraged a section of the lay public to resist the new doctrines. And even the scientists themselves did not seem to find full satisfaction in what they preached. Berthelot confessed he was often sad: 'I do not know . . . how to deal with life as it is and to produce harmony from all its parts.' His research involved a constant struggle against doubts; and only intense intellectual work gave him 'moral peace'. Privately, he admitted that the belief in progress was perhaps an illusion and his unhappy conclusion was that 'We must drain the cup to its dregs, because, outside that, there is only worry and absence of dignity'.[1]

As scientists gradually transformed more and more aspects of daily life, they increasingly came to be seen as benefactors of mankind and as national heroes. A new kind of hagiography developed, which praised them for their genius and disinterested devotion to their work, in the same way as medieval saints had been extolled for their piety and asceticism. Marie Curie (1867–1934), the discoverer of radium and popular above all because that promised a cure for cancer, was hailed as 'a lay saint of science'. A large number of biographies have been written of her, most of them simple and edifying ones for children, which built up a whole legend around her name. She was presented as a pure, altruistic woman of supreme intellectual gifts, working for the benefit of her fellows, 'giving all and taking nothing . . . gentle, stubborn, timid and curious', refusing wealth, enduring honours with indifference, uncorrupted by fame. All this was not far from the truth, but no nuance or reservation was allowed to modify the picture of perfection. She was raised to heroic status not only because her research contributed to the transformation of the very notion of 'matter' and the inauguration of new methods in medicine, but partly also because she was a woman. One should not conclude that scientists were more open-minded in their attitude to women and willing to admit them to a share in their work. Marie Curie was helped by the fact that she was of Polish origin and foreign girls could do things in France which French girls, watched over by parents with pretensions, could not: a sizeable proportion of the first female university students were for that reason foreign. Many more women exercised power in the worlds of commerce and industry than in the scientific community. But Marie Curie was the first woman to reach the very peaks of achievement in the field of discovery, and she owes her popular fame in good measure to that. In scientific circles, she was treated less generously. Her life was dogged by the sordid rivalry and competitiveness which was an inescapable part of the academic, as of other worlds. She herself took great pains to ensure that she should personally get all the credit that was due to her; she carefully distinguished between what she and her husband had each achieved. Her relationship with her fellow scientist Rutherford, for example, was friendly, but behind her back Rutherford complained of her 'constitutional unwillingness to do anything that might directly or indirectly assist any worker in radioactivity outside her own laboratory . . . it is a great pity that some people are so darn sensitive about criticism and the Madame apparently has the idea that anyone associated with her laboratory is a sort of holy person'. He had doubts about just how great a scientist she was, and there is still disagreement as to whether she deserved to be the only person to be awarded the Nobel Prize twice. Harvard University at any rate refused to give her an honorary degree, its physicists protesting that 'since her husband died in 1906, Madame Curie has done nothing of great importance'. But after his death, she revealed very considerable gifts as an administrator of research, a status to which so many scientists were raised by success. She had the good fortune to be discovered by an American journalist who arranged for her to tour the U.S.A. and who organised a campaign to raise money and buy equipment and materials for her. She showed herself to be an unusually determined and successful fund-raiser, only occasionally giving way to complaints that she was being exhibited 'like a wild animal', or resorting to putting her arm in a sling to save her from constant handshaking. The institute founded in her honour—like that founded in Pasteur's—was, significantly, financed by international rather than French benefactions. By American standards both were of course mean and tiny establishments, but they were very important in that they enabled a few more scientists to devote themselves purely and simply to research. Marie Curie's own life, indeed, was totally absorbed by research. She had no interest in politics, or even in feminism. Her private life, though affectionate, was efficiently organised so as not to interfere with her work. She shows how many scientists created closed worlds around them in which they moved untroubled by external events. She came of a family of doctors and teachers. She married a scientist who was the son and grandson of doctors. Her daughter became a scientist and married a scientist. It was not surprising that some people became suspicious of such charmed magician's circles, and that when Marie Curie, in her widowhood, had an affair with another famous scientist, Langevin, the newspapers, which saw scientists as dangerous people, should ruthlessly and mercilessly make her private life public, so as to discredit them as morally outrageous also. Langevin fought a duel with the editor of the anti-Semitic magazine which published his private correspondence with her ('The Sorbonne Scandals'). This editor, significantly, had been Langevin's fellow student at the École Normale and then a teacher of philosophy until sacked for political extremism. The scientists frequently had the same origins as their enemies, but they sometimes cut themselves off in later life, and they were then treated like a medieval heretical sect.[1]

Marie Curie's distinguished family shows, however, how complex the reality was behind the appearance. Her husband Pierre Curie (1859–1906) was indeed the son of a Protestant who had close associations with the radicals of 1848, and all his political sympathies were on the left, but he believed that men were 'powerless to change the social order and would probably do more harm than good if they tried to interfere with "inevitable evolution"'. To concentrate on science was safer; every

[1] Robert Reid, *Marie Curie* (1974); Eve Curie, *Madame Curie* (1939); P. Bignard, *Paul Langevin* (1969); Maria Sklodowska-Curie, *Centenary Lectures* (Vienna, 1968), 13–23, 125–35; Marie and Irène Curie, *Correspondance 1905–1934* (1974).

discovery at least would remain acquired knowledge. In his youth he wore only blue shirts, so as to look like a workman, but he was too gentle and modest to seek to influence political events. Their son-in-law Frédéric Joliot (1900–58), later known as Joliot-Curie, was, similarly, the son of a Communard, but one who had done well enough in business to be able to devote himself to shooting and fishing, a passion which, he argued, was not cruel or incompatible with his hatred of violence, because it was a survival of man's natural method of searching for food. Joliot-Curie's mother (a Protestant, daughter of Napoleon III's sauce-cook) was also very republican. He was active in left-wing political demonstrations from his earliest youth; in the 1930s he was a leading member of the Committee of Anti-Fascist Intellectuals and in 1942, when Langevin's son-in-law, Jacques Solomon, a brilliant young scientist, was shot by the Nazis, he joined the communist party. He complained that he was, as a result, ostracised as a class traitor: 'I was born into a middle-class family; I received a good education; I have been successful; I am comfortably off; in their eyes [those of the middle class] I have no excuse. . . . They could have forgiven me any error, any crime, but not that of being a communist.' But the belief that he was totally opposed to the society he lived in simply showed how the divisions in that society were misconceived and confused. Joliot-Curie said, 'I am a communist because I am a patriot.' His radicalism or communism was not the expression of a carefully thought-out plan of subversion. He frequently insisted that he was not an intellectual, being too fond of working with his own hands for that. If he could choose his life freely, he would like to be a professional fisherman. He said he was surprised to find himself classified as an intellectual and it had been an effort to learn to be one. He always found it difficult to write, partly because he could not concentrate and partly because 'expressing my ideas to other people risks committing other people. It is a great responsibility [whereas] preparing fishing nets makes immediate sense to me, it concerns only me. . . .' His politics were essentially instinctive, and also the product of mistrust of political thinkers: 'There is one word I never like to hear used in my presence', he said, 'and that is philosophy.' His breach with the blasé writers and cynical profiteers of the capitalist system reflected a time-lag that had developed between scientific research and the world of letters. Scientists were achieving such rapid and stimulating advances in knowledge that, as far as their work was concerned, they could not help being optimistic, and they carried forward something of the youthful naïvety of the eighteenth century, with which moralists, endlessly rotating around the same insoluble problems, had become disabused. The temperaments of science and arts specialists failed to coincide, paradoxically, because the arts men were trying to become more scientific while the scientists, for all their methodological rigour, increasingly saw themselves as poetic creators. Henri Poincaré the mathematician had had, it is true, a profound contempt for the 'metaphysical' studies of his brother Raymond, who became president of the republic, saying that 'science should alone rule our actions'. This was the simple form that the quarrel assumed on a banal level. But Joliot-Curie insisted that the qualities needed for fundamental research in science were 'close to those which favour artistic creation: a sure grasp of basic techniques and solid craftsmanship (Van Gogh was not an inspired dauber—he had learned his craft meticulously) at the service of a creative imagination and intuition'. As director of the Centre National de la Recherche Scientifique, he abolished the distinction between pure and applied science but he was very concerned that the researcher's independence and personality should not be stifled by the pressures of a society that had moved from the artisan to the industrial stage: 'one cannot do original work in chains', he wrote. The value of science, for him, was that it enabled man to understand himself better, in the sense that it showed him that he was a creature still in extreme youth; it banished superstition and the fear of invisible forces; it gave its researchers a sense of collective effort, and ultimately therefore he was hopeful that science would do more good than harm. This was a confident declaration of faith by the man whose discovery of nuclear chain reactions was, as he realised, potentially as dangerous (and beneficial) as Marie Curie's discovery of radium. His stormy career showed that the gaps in understanding between scientists and the rest of the community continued to increase. The scientists were partly responsible for that gap, because most of them ceased to be able to communicate with laymen. Laymen got too involved in quarrels about the philosophical and religious consequences of scientific discoveries to understand what scientists were like in temperament and imagination. Indeed so little has been written about the scientists of this period, that it is too early even to attempt a description of them.[1] When Léon Blum appointed Marie Curie's daughter, Irène Joliot-Curie, as the first under-secretary for scientific research, the identification of science with left-wing ideals seemed complete, but it is by no means certain that the majority of scientists were socialists. It is very probable that they were to be found in all parties, and there was certainly a significant number of Catholic ones. The divisions of politics, religion and science did not coincide.[2]

The chief characteristic of the scientist, wrote the biologist Charles Richet in 1923, is that he does not try to apply his work in practice. He is above all disinterested, seeking truth for its own sake, and treating science as a religion. He lectures as little as possible, because he much prefers research. All this 'places him apart in our venal society'. Whereas British and American scientists were 'men of the world' who knew how to play their part in public affairs, the French were different. The scientists of Paris nearly all lived isolated in the Latin Quarter, but did not form a united community. There were watertight partitions separating their family from their laboratory lives and 'we rarely know whether a colleague is married'. What emotional energies they spared from their labours they devoted to mutual criticism and to jealousy, becoming enemies of all those who disagreed with their theories. The advice that Richet gave his pupils was: 'Never think about the possible practical consequences of your discoveries'. The result was that other people had to do this thinking for them.[3]

The simplification of the issues involved in scientific discovery was largely left to people on the fringes of the scientific world or

[1] Pierre Bignard, *Frédéric Joliot-Curie. The Man and his Theories* (1961, English translation 1965), 70, 81–2, 141, 157. Cf. Liam Hudson, *Contrary Imaginations* (1966), a psychological study of the difference between arts and science specialists based on interviews with English schoolboys.

[2] Dr. Louis Fleury, *Science et religion* (1868); François Russo S.J., *Pensée scientifique et foi chrétienne* (1953).

[3] Charles Richet, *The Natural History of a Savant* (1923, translated into English 1927 by Sir Oliver Lodge).

even wholly outside it. These were of three kinds. First there were professional popularisers; secondly the philosophers; and thirdly the moralists. Each deserves separate examination.

Few of the great scientific names of this period wrote for the general public. Professional popularisers did this work for them; a vast number of popular scientific periodicals was published, increasing rapidly during the Second Empire. Historians of science have not got round to reading them and assessing the accuracy or bias of the picture they painted; but these popularisers were interesting men. Some were simply journalists who specialised in science because there was a demand for articles on the subject. Such a man, for example, was S. H. Berthoud (b. 1804), famous for his scientific column in *Le Pays* and, later, in *La Patrie*. He was also a novelist, a playwright, a historian, an organiser of adult education, and a collector of children's toys, of which he founded a museum. He was one of those highly prolific writers now totally forgotten, whose works ranged from treatises on the problems of marriage to histories of *Man over the last five thousand years* (1865) and whose *Village Botany* (1862) and *Scientific Fantasies* (1861–2) combined wonder at modern miracles with dour Protestant moralising. Another populariser was Victor Meunier (1817–1903), a Fourierist, who wrote the scientific articles for the republican papers of the Second Empire. He predicted in 1865 that 'before long the popularity of the sciences will not yield to that of letters', books about science would be read like novels and people would attend lectures on it in the same way as they went to the theatre.[1] This was an admission that science had still not reached that position, even in the eyes of those who were most enthusiastic about it. But journalists like Meunier helped to make it more exciting by the battles they waged in the press in favour of or against the theories scientists put forward: the scientific journalists of different persuasions attacked each other with great verve, so that the political diatribe between newspapers was matched by constant polemic about the latest discoveries in geology or zoology.[2] Meunier claimed that each subject was a fief of some specialist, who established dogmas and stopped his opponents from obtaining

[1] V. Meunier, *La Science et les savants en 1865* (1865), premier trimestre, 212.

[2] For disputes about evolution, for example, see R. E. Stebbins, 'French Reactions to Darwin' (Minnesota Ph.D. thesis, unpublished, 1965).

jobs; he revealed a lot about the sordid politics of science.[1] The most widely read populariser of the Second Empire was, however, probably the Abbé Moigno (1804–84), a Jesuit, whose weeklies, *Cosmos* and *Les Mondes*, provided very solid summaries of the latest experiments and theories. Moigno knew twelve languages and had travelled all over Europe to report on scientific advances. He was a serious mathematician in his youth; he then devoted himself to reconciling science and religion. He argued that the threat of irreligion was still capable of being snuffed out, for whereas the national subscription to raise a memorial to Voltaire had collected only 30,000 francs, that to celebrate Pius IX's jubilee had produced ten times as much. His work on the *Splendours of faith, showing the perfect accord of revelation and science* (in five volumes, 1883) collected the testimony of many leading scientists to support this view.[2]

Under the Third Republic, the most widely read populariser may perhaps have been Camille Flammarion (1842–1925), whose *Popular Astronomy* (1879) was for long a best-seller. He was entirely self-taught. Had his father, a well-to-do peasant, not been ruined by an unsuccessful business venture, he would have stayed on at school and become a priest. Instead he came to Paris and got a job in the Paris Observatory (while his father started a new life in Nadar's photographic studio). He was horrified to find that his scientific colleagues were pious, unimaginative civil servants, who felt no sense of wonder at the mysteries of the universe; for them astronomy 'was simply a table of logarithms'; they did their mathematical calculations, but all of them were dissatisfied with their jobs and looking for better ones. Flammarion at once rebelled against this specialised view of science, which, he said, was purely mechanical and ignored life. At the age of nineteen, he published his *Plurality of Inhabited Worlds* (1862) which sold 41,000 copies and was in addition translated into Arabic, Chinese, Czech, Danish, English, German, Italian, Polish, Portuguese, Spanish, Swedish and Turkish. Flammarion's fame abroad was probably even greater and he received many foreign decorations. The impact his book

---

[1] V. Meunier, *Essais scientifiques* (1857), esp. vol. 1, 'L'Apostolat scientifique'.

[2] Abbé Moigno, *Les Splendeurs de la foi* (1883), 1. 35, 3. 1446–59; *Cosmos: Revue encyclopédique hebdomadaire des progrès des sciences* (1852–63); cf. *La Science populaire* (1883–4) edited by a royalist.

created may be judged from the remark made by Napoleon III, that the thing that had struck him most in it was the engraving showing the comparative sizes of the earth and the sun: 'Is this possible?' he asked. 'How insignificant we are! It is better not to think about it; it makes us invisible; it is enough to destroy us.' The empress refused to believe it. At the end of his long life, Flammarion noted that despite his efforts 'the general ignorance about astronomy is really stupefying' and he gave examples of the absurd questions famous people had asked him. Meunier's prophecy that science would be the most popular subject was not fulfilled. Flammarion said that it had been overtaken by pornography. He declared himself surprised by 'the general indifference of the inhabitants of the earth' to its mysteries, and to the question of what life meant; men, busy with their little jobs or pleasures, were no different from snails. For him, understanding everything was a passion, reading an obsession (he accumulated a library of 10,000 volumes); 'thinking and loving' were the essential parts of life. The astronomer Le Verrier (who discovered Neptune) sacked Flammarion, telling him he was a poet not a scientist, and Flammarion admitted that for him astronomy was 'the poetry of life'. He was dominated throughout by 'the conviction that there is no death', or rather he was determined to prove this. He lost his Christian faith but he became a leading advocate of spiritism: he greatly admired Allan Kardec (author of *The Book of Spirits*) and was invited to succeed him as president of the Société Spirite. He combined these interests with the presidency of the Paris branch of the republican Ligue de l'Enseignement. He wrote seven books criticising Catholicism but also positivism. He was firmly 'anti-materialist' and published a 'Declaration of the Rights of the Soul'. He was an unorthodox, enthusiastic, generous optimist who illustrates well the confused views that amateurs who interested themselves in science formed. Most professional scientists were suspicious of him: the popularised version of their work that he produced in his many publications was far from being an accurate reflection of what they believed. But Flammarion was representative because there were so many different strands in him. He fell in love with Victor Hugo's niece when he was fifteen; he courted her for ten years and finally persuaded her to leave her husband. They lived together for many years and were married only much later, after the husband's death, spending their honeymoon in a balloon. When she reached the age of sixty—she was ten years older than him—he fell in love with a young girl, one of the many admiring women who attended his lectures, and established a *ménage à trois* with all parties consenting. But he said not a word about this in his memoirs, which are an important source for scientific speculation outside the laboratories.[1]

These memoirs show how people did not simply transfer from religion to science. They emphasise that credulity was not the monopoly of those who rejected scientific method. This credulity needs to be remembered: one can illustrate it with the story of the forgery scandal in which Flammarion was marginally involved and which tore the Academy of Sciences in 1867-9. The inventor of modern geometry, Michel Chasles, professor at the Polytechnic and the Sorbonne, Copley medallist of the Royal Society of London, presented a paper to the Academy arguing that Pascal had discovered the law of gravity before Newton. He produced letters from Pascal to Boyle proving this. Many Academicians were convinced. The astronomer Le Verrier denounced the letters as forgeries. The chemists examined them and declared them to be at any rate very old. Chasles supported their authenticity by yet more letters. It turned out that he had accumulated a collection of 27,320 autographs, by some 660 famous people, from Thales, Pythagoras, Cleopatra and Julius Caesar downwards, including 2,000 by Galileo. The world of science was shaken by the totally new light this placed on the history of discovery, showing in particular that France had played a much larger part than hitherto realised. Chasles resisted all the arguments attacking their authenticity for two years, until the forger was finally unmasked.[2] Great scientists made fools of themselves often enough for their opponents to be able to refuse to believe them even when they were right.

Philosophical reflection on science attempted to give it a much more precise significance than these popularisers achieved.

[1] Hilaire Cuny, *Camille Flammarion et l'astronomie populaire* (1964); C. Flammarion, *Mémoires biographiques et philosophiques d'un astronome* (1911).

[2] Henri Bordier and Émile Mabille, *Une Fabrique de faux autographes ou récit de l'affaire Vrain Lucas* (1870).

There were three thinkers in particular who took the lead in this effort of interpretation, Comte, Taine and Renan. Auguste Comte (1798–1857) came to be regarded, by people of almost all parties, and with the virtually official agreement of the university, as possibly the most important thinker of the nineteenth century. It was said of him, during the Second Empire, that he 'inaugurated a new mental regime for humanity'; and in 1925 it was still argued that Comte 'really founded a new conception of human life'.[1] A leading anthology on political thought in the nineteenth century, published in 1924, gave him more space than anyone else.[2] Men like Gambetta and Ferry acknowledged themselves to bᵣ his disciples. Through him, therefore, the influence of science may appear to extend over the whole thinking of society and the Third Republic may almost seem to be, as some people claimed, the offspring of science. But this is a superficial impression. Comte was indeed a scientist, a pupil and later examiner in mathematics at the Polytechnic, a popular lecturer on astronomy; and he did have quite exceptionally wide knowledge of the different sciences of his day. No man was better qualified to interpret them. Comte, however, declared that no existing science, not even mathematics, was capable of producing a synthesis to guide mankind, either on the intellectual plane or, still less, on the plane of daily conduct. He undertook his researches indeed precisely because he found his own scientific knowledge so emotionally unsatisfying. The importance of Comte was that he extracted from science a methodology for tackling human problems. He argued that all knowledge passed through three chronological phases, the theological or fictional phase, the metaphysical or abstract phase and the scientific or positive phase. Men, in other words, have employed three different ways of thinking: first interpreting what they saw in terms of divine intervention, seeking the primary causes and ultimate purpose of things and finding them in supernatural forces; and secondly, replacing theology by philosophy, they explained behaviour in abstract terms. The third, positive attitude, which was just beginning to penetrate the natural sciences, involved the renunciation of the possibility

[1] E. Littré, *Auguste Comte et la philosophie positive* (1864, 2nd edition), 32; D. Mornet, *Histoire générale de la littérature française* (1925), 204.

[2] Bayet and André, *Écrivains politiques du 19ᵉ siècle* (1924).

of discovering the origin or purpose of the universe and confined itself to the study of observable phenomena only, and to the establishment of regular relationships between them. Societies were theological in their infantile or primitive state, metaphysical in their youth (which was what France was) and finally positive in their prime.

Positivism meant a concern with the real as opposed to the chimerical. It meant a search for the useful—for knowledge was worthwhile only if it led to the improvement of individual or collective life, and not simply to the satisfaction of sterile curiosity. It involved also a search for both certitude and precision (though accepting that knowledge was always relative), the establishment of harmony between individuals, their fellows and their environment, and above all a determination to organise rather than to criticise. What Comte reproached the liberalism that had emerged from the Revolution for was intellectual anarchy, which he found intolerable. The natural sciences could not cure this themselves, but the creation of a new science, which he first called social physics and then sociology, could do so, by applying the methods of science to politics. Comte's major book began with a long review of scientific knowledge. He argued that a scientific background was an essential training for politicians, but government was an independent science, in the study of which they then needed to specialise. Comte arranged the different sciences in hierarchic order with sociology as the supreme science. His method was the distillation of all human knowledge, which it arranged in an order that revealed both the unity and the connections between the parts; it allowed those who applied the method to see the significance of every problem, because it taught them to identify what kind of problem it was. He believed that politics could be made into a science with fixed laws, based on the observation of human behaviour in the past and capable of predicting the future, in general terms. Historical study should be its basis, but history seen in terms of civilisations. Though he understood the growth of specialisation, he argued for an inter-disciplinary social science saying that it should not blindly copy the natural sciences: its fragmentation into isolated subjects would render it sterile.[1] Comte's immense erudition, his grasp

[1] A. Comte, *Cours de philosophie positive* (1830–42, 1894 edition), 4. 282.

of a vast range of problems, his ability to sustain his argument through a mass of detail, throwing off innumerable insights as he went along, could not fail to make a profound impression on his readers. His clearly was a quite exceptionally powerful intellect, and those who could keep up with him shared, to some extent, in the ecstatic feeling that he was indeed opening up a new way of understanding.

Comte was a typical intellectual, critical of the society around him, proposing radical reforms for it, but finding it difficult to agree with other intellectuals, feeling that his genius was unappreciated by them or by the establishment he was attacking, proposing a higher status for the intellectual élite but full of contempt for that which existed around him. He was a man who both loved his work and found it unsatisfying. He was able to illuminate the problems he tackled with great clarity but he was obsessed by illusions where his own person was concerned. He could, at times, be infinitely gentle in his relationships but he generally had great difficulty in living harmoniously with others. He never succeeded in getting a proper job, and his part-time employment at the Polytechnic was terminated; he was forced to live off the charity of a few admirers, notably some English benefactors whom J. S. Mill rallied round him. When he descended into the political arena, he did grave damage to his reputation.

Comte's second major work, *The System of Positive Politics* (four volumes, 1851-4), claimed to apply the principle of positivism to the organisation of society; but his bitter experience of life modified the conclusions he drew. Intelligence, he now decided, was not enough. He remained enough of an intellectual to insist that traditional revolutions, which overturned political institutions, did not achieve much in practice and that what was needed was a revolution of the mind, in people's ideas. The great need was to make people see that egoism was an unsatisfactory basis for conduct, and that it should be replaced by the idea of service to others, by living for others. However, one could not convert the masses to altruism by argument: it had to be a question of emotion, not of intelligence. Comte, rather to the amazement of his intellectual disciples, concluded that what was needed was a new religion, which he called the religion of humanity to indicate that it aimed at binding the world together in mutual love. He insisted that ritual and feasts were things man could not do without and proposed elaborate institutions to provide them. Family life must be strengthened, to lay the basis for a new emotional security. The aim of politics should not therefore be equality, but the acceptance of the facts of life, and the adaptation of institutions to them. Inequality of wealth and of intelligence should be recognised as inescapable. Government should be by those most fitted for the task, not because Comte favoured the dictatorship of intellectuals, but because he believed there should be a specialisation of functions. The masses knew what they wanted, and no one had the right to speak for them. But the formulation of plans for bringing about their wishes should be left to 'publicists' and the execution of these plans to a government. 'Sociocracy' was therefore not democracy, but, rather, the end of democracy. Science could not tolerate the chaos of individualism; liberty, equality and fraternity could not be accepted as a satisfactory motto and Comte proposed instead Order and Progress.[1]

The result of Comte's arguments was that science ended up by proposing something very similar to the Catholicism it sought to dethrone. One might wonder why Comte did not simply become converted to Catholicism, for whose organisation he had great admiration. The answer seems to have been largely personal, in the sense that Comte had a personal antipathy for Christ, whom he hated as an impostor or adventurer, 'a mixture of hypocrisy and charisma'. He regarded Christianity as muddled, incomplete, mystical, even if it was the precursor of the true religion, which was the scientific religion of humanity. He looked forward to preaching the doctrine of positivism himself from the pulpit of Notre-Dame. He thus made positivism anti-religious, but also aroused hostility because he wanted a church of his own. He placed a great emphasis on the role of women in the development of altruism, arguing that they understood affection far better than men, but he took this to the point of insisting that they should therefore remain at home, to devote all their energies to being mothers. Comte was so certain of the importance of family love because he had never enjoyed it: he broke with his own father (a tax-office clerk) in early life and refused to see him again; he decided his marriage was the

[1] A. Comte, *Système de politique positive* (1854), vol. 4, appendix p. 5.

greatest misfortune of his life and he finally left his wife, declaring that she was 'despotic and incapable of being disciplined, having a false notion of the necessary condition of her sex in the human economy'; only in later life did he finally fall in love, with a divorcée who died eighteen months later: it was she who, he said, taught him the value of 'the influence of feminine sentiment on masculine activity'.

Comte considered himself superior to Bacon and Leibniz, but not to Descartes. His self-confidence, and his personal eccentricities, have produced strong reactions against his claims. There could be no denying that he was, like all original thinkers, greatly indebted to others who had come before him, and notably Condorcet and Montesquieu. Renan, who had his own debts to Comte, denounced him nevertheless for saying 'in bad French what all scientific minds in the past two hundred years had seen as clearly as he'. A historian has described him as combining 'many of the worst and weakest aspects, often in exacerbated form, of the eighteenth century *esprit de système*, Kantian phenomenalism, the Hegelian coherence theory of truth, scientism and garbled scientific method, pseudo-romantic evangelical sentimentality and totalitarian notions of social engineering'.[1] It is certainly true that positivism, as he formulated it, was capable of creating difficulties not very different from those he wished to remedy. He became an advocate of 'cerebral hygiene', which meant that he stopped reading almost entirely, distracting himself only with opera and some poetry. His science therefore remained the science of the 1820s. His ideas on science have, apparently, been influential on the development of biology; but he reduced psychology to phrenology, and he downgraded geometry in his hierarchy because he was at war with the geometricians of the Polytechnic.[2]

Comte's followers fell into two distinct schools. The orthodox positivists, who accepted the whole of his work, founded churches and practised his religion. They were led at first by Laffitte, a man with remarkable gifts for lucid exposition who did much to make the master's doctrines more intelligible. Not surprisingly these men, who accepted Comte's politics, moved to the right of the Republic and a third of their ruling committee were

[1] W. M. Simon, *European Positivism in the Nineteenth Century* (Ithaca, 1963), 46.
[2] See *Bulletin de la société française de philosophie* (1958), special issue on Comte, 15.

members of Action Française in the early twentieth century. Since the Second World War the Church of Humanity in Paris has been maintained by donations from Brazil, where positivism has found its main refuge. The more important section of Comte's heirs, however, were those who rejected his politics. Émile Littré (1801–81), the author of the famous dictionary, was their leader, again a man with a clear style, who popularised an expurgated condensation of Comte's writings. Littré became a highly influential figure in the Third Republic. He was a senator and editor of an important journal, *La Philosophie positive* (1867–83), which greatly broadened the appeal of positivism, precisely because it did not make it into an organised movement or sect. He saw positivism as simultaneously revolutionary, conservative and socialist—just the kind of broad and vague ideal to appeal to radical republicans sobered by the acquisition of power. He kept it firmly parliamentarian and disowned Comte's later opinions as an aberration. But his election to the French Academy in 1871 led to the resignation of Bishop Dupanloup, who saw in it a triumph of anticlericalism. The significance of science was confused by political animosities.[1]

Just how limited faith in science was, and just how complex and muddled its votaries were, may be illustrated from the life of Ernest Renan (1823–92), the author of the *Life of Jesus* and the *Future of Science*; he was the champion of the 'progressive ideas' of the second half of the nineteenth century, and in him were reflected also a large number of common opinions. His ideas were called 'the most contagious of his time.' 'There is no example in literary history', it has been said, 'of a man—not even Voltaire—who so occupied the attention of not only the educated but of the whole public.' But Renan was well aware that he was a confused man. 'I am a romantic protesting against romanticism, a utopian preaching down-to-earth politics, an idealist vainly giving himself much trouble to appear bourgeois, a tissue of contradictions.'[2] Renan, for all his intellectual inde-

[1] H. Gouhier, *La Jeunesse d'Auguste Comte* (3 vols., 1933), excellent; E. Littré, *Auguste Comte et la philosophie positive* (2nd edition, 1864), for Littré's interpretation; T. Chiappini, *Les Idées politiques d'Auguste Comte* (Paris thesis, 1913); Stanislas Aquarone, *The Life and Works of Émile Littré* (Leyden, 1958); E. Littré, *Conservation, révolution, positivisme* (1852); D. G. Charlton, *Positivist Thought in France during the Second Empire* (Oxford, 1959); Pierre Arnaud, *La Pensée d'A. Comte* (1969).

[2] E. Renan, *Souvenirs d'enfance et de jeunesse*, ed. Jean Pommier (1959), 51.

pendence, never lost the characteristics imprinted on him by his background. He had been destined for the priesthood but did not take orders, partly because the study of exegesis made him doubt the reliability of the Bible but partly also because he was too cold towards the Church, too sceptical, more interested in truth than in prayer. The worldly religion he was taught in his Paris seminary had nothing in common with that of Brittany, where Catholicism was mixed up with mythology and superstition—interests which continued with him all his life. He was a Breton and he attributed to this his lack of interest in the practical side of life, his taste for dreaming about ideal worlds, which he regarded as the inevitable lot of an isolated population. The classical education he received gave him a lifelong obsession with antiquity and an admiration for Greek values which conflicted with his Christianity; but it also left him time to read the romantic poets of his own day and to cultivate enthusiasm: he voted for Lamartine in 1848. He did not feel he belonged to any one class: he despised the bourgeoisie ('the rule of businessmen, industrialists, workers—the most selfish of classes—Jews, Englishmen of the old school, Germans of the new school') but he also sought to reassure it; he considered himself a son of the people and thought that was why he could understand Christ, who shared this popular origin with him; in practice, however, he lived a thoroughly bourgeois life. Because he had been so chaste in his youth, he found merit in libertinage at an age when other men took to frowning upon it. The way he lived and what he preached conflicted; he was incapable of sincerity in conversation; he lived uneasily with his opinions. He sought a compromise between science and Christianity, scepticism and faith, liberalism and tradition, optimism and pessimism.

His hesitations and confusions may be illustrated from three of his most important books. His *Future of Science* was regarded as a manifesto of confidence in science as man's necessary instrument in the search for truth and happiness. He wrote this book in 1848 and published it only in 1890. It shows how ideas about science could remain static for half a century, how his notion of it was an eighteenth-century one, and how equivocal he was about it. 'The triumph of science', he said, 'is in reality the triumph of idealism.' In 1848 he wrote 'Science alone can give man vital truths, without which life would be insupportable and society impossible.' In his preface of 1890 he was much more cautious: 'No one knows, in the social order, where the good is to be found . . . Science preserves man from error rather than telling him the truth; but it is something to be certain that one is not a dupe.'[1] His philosophy of history was that man had passed through the ages of faith and criticism and was now moving on to that of synthesis: he did not seek to jettison the past; he respected superstition and feeling. He could never get away from traditional vocabulary: he believed in God, the soul and immortality, though he used these words in the most diverse and often pagan senses.[2] He was not keen on the realist novel, saying that since reality was unpleasant enough, there was no point in representing it in fiction. His favourite novelist remained George Sand.

Renan's *Life of Jesus* (1863) won the reputation of being the first major attack on Christ's divinity, based upon the fruits of modern biblical scholarship. It made an impact which, it was said by a contemporary newspaper, could be compared only to Luther. It argued that the Scriptures should be studied critically, like all the ancient writings, that they were full of inaccuracies, and in effect history mixed with fiction; miracles could no longer be accepted. Christ was only a man, though the greatness of his work could justify his being called metaphorically a god. Renan claimed in his preface that his book was the result of great labours; in fact he wrote it rapidly in a Lebanese hut, with only five or six books at hand, inspired by a sudden vision and by the atmosphere of Nazareth. His long dissertation on the historical value of the Scriptures he thought up and wrote afterwards, and it was not the result of personal research but of reading other books. He was much influenced by certain German Protestant theologians and by the views of the Protestant circle into which his marriage with Cornélie, the sister of the painter Ary Scheffer, introduced him: these looked on Christ not as a god but as a superior man in whom religious feeling reached its highest form and whose essentially moral preaching was quite different from the dogmatism and ritualism of the Catholic Church. Ary Scheffer's painting *The Temptation of Christ* to a certain extent served him as a model. His book was more a work of art than

[1] E. Renan, *L'Avenir de la science* in *Œuvres complètes*, vol. 2 (1949), 726–7, 758.
[2] Jean Pommier, *La Pensée religieuse de Renan* (1925) has a good analysis.

of science. His notes show him to have been moved by impressions rather than by logical arguments; he wrote brief notes summarising his feelings, which he later combined when he had a 'general sensation'. His Jesus was really an idealised self-portrait—not a Galilean but a nineteenth-century Frenchman. One can recognise Renan himself in his view of Christ as a man who 'had risen from the ranks of the people, of a family of artisans', among a population given to 'ethereal dreams and a sort of poetic mysticism' (reminiscent of Brittany). Jesus, said Renan, was (like himself) a great master of irony and eloquence who appeared to submit to the established powers outwardly, though really derisive of them: he replied to questions with 'the fine raillery of a man of the world combined with divine goodness'. He was a 'delicious moralist' and a 'revolutionary in the highest degree', who proclaimed 'the rights of man and of the freedom of conscience'.[1]

However, even on this question of the rights of man, Renan did not hold consistent views. In his *Intellectual Reform of France* (1871) he attacked democracy as the cause of his country's defeat, and urged the re-establishment of monarchy and the rule of an élite, as the solution for its decadence. Renan had the misfortune of being repeatedly let down by the ideals he cherished. After Christianity came the Germans, whom he had worshipped as the representatives of modernity and science. That is partly why by the end of his life Renan became the embodiment of scepticism, though he was not simply that. 'Renanism' meant a mixture of seriousness and mockery, unctuousness and blasphemy. He was held to be responsible for the dilettantism of the last years of the century—a dilettantism which his pupil Anatole France carried to the point of nihilism. The evocative and dramatic power of his style helped greatly to popularise his teaching. He became a hero to every party—which is perhaps a decisive mark of his importance. Combes unveiled his statue in 1903 in an emotional speech; Clemenceau in 1917 said, 'I do not show deference to many but I do to him, for he made us what we are'. His anticlericalism however was

---

[1] Prosper Alfaric, *Les Manuscrits de la* Vie de Jésus *d'Ernest Renan* (Publications de la Faculté des lettres de l'université de Strasbourg, fascicule 90, 1939), introduction; P. M. J. Lagrange, *La Vie de Jésus d'après Renan* (1923). See also the preface to the 13th edition of the *Vie de Jésus*.

only one side of him. Barrès and Maurras looked on his *Reform*
as a key work in the movement for national regeneration. Sorel
praised him for having seen that the salvation of the world
would come from the proletariat. Bourget praised him for his
monarchism, forgetting what he said also on the other side. His
forty volumes, 24,000 pages long, are a monument that points
in every direction, revealing that if this was the age of science,
it was equally the age of uncertainty.[1]

The man who most successfully showed how science could be
a guide in everyday conduct, in morals and in art, was Hippolyte Taine (1828–93). Taine was probably the most talented
writer among the so-called positivists: he wrote about the most
difficult and dry subjects with an astonishing vivacity: he had
a gift for making abstract ideas clear and even dramatic; he
illustrated his arguments with vivid and varied examples. He
was interested in contemporary literature and art (in a way in
which Renan was not) and so he won a strong following among
a wide circle of young writers. Anatole France recalled how
around 1870 'the thought of his powerful mind inspired in us
an ardent enthusiasm, a sort of religion, for what I would call
the dynamic cult of life'.[2] Taine gained his ascendancy because
he was first of all a brilliant demolisher of the doctrines of the
past, in a way that liberated and excited the men who read him.
His book on *The French philosophers of the nineteenth century* (1857)
can be compared in importance with Renan's *Life of Jesus*, as
the popularisation of an intellectual attitude. In it Taine ridiculed the reigning philosophers of his day with a measured wit
and vigour that were profoundly effective. Taine was the enemy
of the classical view of man—the universal type with a clearly
defined character which was to be found in whatever time or
place he lived. This, he argued, made impossible the accurate
study of man, based on observation. Taine equally castigated
the romantic way of life ('The taste for general terms, the loss
of precision in style, the forgetting of analysis . . . the passion
to see without proof . . . the theatre and novels accepted as
manuals of science . . . every poet explaining man and the world

---

[1] H. W. Wardman, *Ernest Renan* (1964); Henriette Psichari, *Renan d'après lui-
même* (1937).
[2] Victor Giraud, *Essai sur Taine: son œuvre et son influence* (Fribourg, 1901), 138,
quoting from *Le Temps* of 7 Mar. 1893.

and in addition, claiming to be the saviour of humanity', a constant buzzing of metaphysical dreams and God transformed into an interior decorator, employed to make life more agreeable). Above all Taine vilipended the eclecticism of Cousin, whom he described as 'the most admirable tragedian of the century', an orator not a philosopher, whose work was admirably elegant but totally devoid of genuine thought or inquiry. Cousin, said Taine, was interested in maintaining order rather than in finding the truth; he took the need to preserve existing morality as the basis of his arguments, and deduced that God existed because morality needed him; art was justifiable only if it expressed moral beauty. The success of Cousin, he argued, was due to the country's exhaustion with the critical spirit of the eighteenth century, its determination to restore some sort of agreement, its having greater interest in morals than in science, but also its continuing to cherish a taste for abstract words and empty phraseology.

Taine had good reason to be so bitter in his invective. His career had been almost ruined by his rebellion as a student against eclecticism. His prospects had been brilliant. Born the son of a solicitor, the grandson of a sub-prefect, he had been called by his teacher, the philosopher Vacherot, 'the most hardworking and distinguished student I have known at the École Normale Supérieure. [He had] prodigious learning for his age; an ardour and avidity for knowledge the like of which I have never seen.'[1] But he did not succeed at the school because he would not accept the orthodox doctrines; he was sent to a junior post in Nevers, though he eventually made the grade by writing a thesis on the inoffensive subject of La Fontaine. It was only some ten years later that he obtained a job as examiner for Saint-Cyr—involving three months' travel and the rest of the year free; in 1866 he succeeded Viollet-le-Duc as lecturer in the history of art at the École des Beaux-Arts, where he remained for twenty years. Taine all his life felt himself torn between the vocation of artist and philosopher. A semi-autobiographical novel he wrote shows how he worked hard as a boy because of an overwhelming sense of isolation. He read Stendhal's *Le Rouge et le noir* over thirty times, and identified himself with the

[1] Sholom J. Kahn, *Science and Aesthetic Judgement. A Study in Taine's Critical Method* (1953), 13.

explanation of Julien Sorel: 'He could not please: he was too different.' In science, he found, as he said, 'an alibi. In the east, they have opium and dreams. We have science. It is a slow and intelligent suicide.'[1] 'Science is an anchor which holds man.'[2] He did not seek happiness: 'We shall reach truth, not calm . . . The more I enter real life, the more it displeases me.'[3]

Taine argued that 'all states of the human soul are products having their causes and their laws, and that the whole future of history consists in the search for these causes and these laws. The assimilation of historical and psychological researches to physiological and chemical researches, that is my object and my principal idea.' Man must be studied as an individual and in nations, in the same way as plants and animals were; the methods of science must be applied to all human activity. Taine summarised these methods in two striking formulae. First, all things could be explained in terms of their *race*, their *milieu* and their *moment*; that is to say, a plant owed its peculiar characteristics to its being a certain species, to the environment in which it grew and to the time in which it existed; and human activity could be analysed in the same way. Secondly, the accumulation of these details should be crowned by the discovery of the *qualité maîtresse*, the principal quality of the object studied, in which all its characteristics were summarised and from which all the facts about it followed. The impact Taine made was due to the simplicity of this method and to the consistency with which he illustrated its application to different forms of human behaviour. He applied it to history in his *Origins of Contemporary France* (1875–93). He showed how societies should be looked at in the same way as trees, the product of a long history and therefore not capable of radical or rapid change. The culprit of French history was, to him, classicism resurrected in the revolutionary spirit and in Jacobinism: its inflexible logic, he said, 'installed in narrow minds which cannot hold two ideas at the same time, . . . became a cold or furious monomania, determined on the destruction of the past which it curses and the establishment of a millennium it seeks; all this in the name of an imaginary contract, at once anarchic and despotic, which

[1] H. Taine, *Étienne Mayran* (1910), 35.
[2] Id., *Vie et correspondance* (1901–7), 1. 83.
[3] Id., *Histoire de la littérature anglaise* (1863).

lets loose insurrection and justifies dictatorship; all this to end up with a contradictory social order resembling now a fanatics' Bacchanalia and now a Spartan convent'.[1] As a result Taine became an admirer of English politics, an advocate of conservatism, decentralisation, and a two-tier voting system to limit the influence of the ignorant. His historical conclusions, reached by supposedly scientific methods, were immediately attacked by the Sorbonne professor, Aulard, who pointed out innumerable errors of fact, the neglect of everything that did not fit in with his theories, and above all a tendency to make vast generalisations based on preconceived ideas: Taine, Aulard claimed, was just another romantic, in the school of Michelet, loving the picturesque and abnormal and capable of appalling bias. The only difference was that unlike Michelet, Taine, under the influence of the horrors of the Commune, called the masses of the Revolution 'an epileptic and scrofulous rabble', 'a grimacing, bloody and lewd monkey'.[2] Positivism was thus once again reactionary.

Taine applied his method to literature in his *History of English Literature* (1864–9), the introduction to which was a concise summary of his doctrine. He argued that literature provided the best material for writing 'moral history' and for discovering the 'psychological laws on which events depend'. His ultimate aim was to discover, through literature, 'the psychology of the nation'. His conclusions were therefore inevitably the opposite of Renan's, in that the importance of individual genius and initiative was minimised, and great general laws stressed instead. Taine is a precursor of the sociology of literature, even though he was never quite able to achieve what he set out to do. He is important also in the history of art criticism, his views on which were given in his *Philosophie de l'art* (1865–9). He saw one ideal as supreme in each period—the beautiful young athlete in Greece, the Christian knight or pious monk in the middle ages, the perfect courtier in the seventeenth century, Faust or Werther in the romantic age. Artists gave expression to this ideal, which was responsible for producing harmony between the different arts in any one period. The moral climate of an age caused art

[1] H. Taine, *Les Origines de la France contemporaine* (24th edition, 1902), 2. 76.
[2] A. Aulard, *Taine, historien de la révolution française* (1907); L. Halphen, *L'Histoire en France depuis cent ans* (1914), 100–3.

that was in keeping with it to succeed and the rest to die, in the same way as climate and geography caused plants to survive. The value of a work of art depended on the faithfulness with which it gave expression to this climate; for example, if it represented the essence of romanticism it was more important than if it reflected only a superficial and temporary fashion; it was most successful if its various parts harmonised to produce a coherent effect. This theory was based partly on Taine's idea of the *qualité maîtresse*, but also on a study of what works in the past were great. It was a historical approach, seeking to be impartial, in that it refused to judge; but it was much more ambitious in simplification, seeking to explain everything in a formula.

Taine did much to make positivism, understood in a wide sense, attractive and prestigious. He gave his disciples the illusion that their judgements were scientific; he taught them how to proceed further, beyond his own researches. His most famous comment, 'that vice and virtue are products like vitriol and sugar', gave him the reputation of being a complete materialist. Though he was a materialist, an atheist and a pessimist, he also respected the individual in a way his philosophy did not allow and he believed in the values of humanism and Christianity. He influenced men of all parties; and it was largely through him that the ideas of positivism entered literature. When Barrès and Bourget in their novels wished to describe the positivism they were rebelling against, it was Taine they used to incarnate it, even though they both owed a great deal to him. However, while his teaching gave faith to some, it also inhibited a lot of human emotions. 'Taine taught us', wrote the philosopher Boutroux, 'that science is not made to satisfy our desires, nor to oppose them, but to find and show the truth.'[1] This, as Taine realised, was not enough to console his generation.

Just as there was a considerable difference between the truth as scientists saw it and the simplifications that the popularisers

---

[1] 'Quelques opinions sur l'œuvre de H. Taine', Enquête, *La Revue blanche* (15 Aug. 1897), 263–95; André Cresson, *Hippolyte Taine. Sa vie, son œuvre, avec un esquisse de sa philosophie* (1951), a useful summary; André Chevrillon, *Taine, la formation de sa pensée* (1932); R. Gibaudan, *Les Idées sociales de Taine* (1928); Maxime Leroy, *Taine* (1933); Alvin A. Eustis, *Hippolyte Taine and the Classical Genius* (California U.P., 1951); P. G. Castex, *La Critique d'art en France au XIXᵉ siècle: Taine et Fromentin* (Cours de la Sorbonne, 1964).

spread among the public, so there was also a discrepancy between the intentions of the popularisers and the message that the public absorbed. This can be seen particularly in the novels of Jules Verne (1828–1905) which became not only standard reading for virtually all French children who read books, but also an international best-seller: in 1953 UNESCO placed him fourth as the world's most translated author, after Stalin, Lenin and Simenon. Verne's books were deliberately written to take advantage of the interest in the wonders of science and they had a strong didactic element, aiming to convey information as well as to appeal to the century's sense of adventure. Verne transformed the fairy-tale into science fiction and in the place of the traditional excursions into mythology, animal fantasy and folklore substituted stories which could give their readers the feeling that they had it in their power to transform the world. It is, however, only in a simple reading that Verne appears to be the optimistic herald of a new age. Unlike his successor in the genre, H. G. Wells, Jules Verne was a conservative, who hated the Communards, the Dreyfusards and the suffragettes. He was not by training a scientist, but a lawyer and stockbroker, who escaped into playwriting before becoming a novelist; he wrote surrounded by encyclopedias, for he had hardly travelled at all and his only participation in the world around him was a period of service as municipal councillor of Amiens, where he lived a quiet bourgeois life. Jules Verne did believe that knowledge of science was important and that science would bring more comfort to daily life, but his optimism was romantic, and therefore of a kind that could go sour, as it did. He was a utopian of the 1848 vintage, so that he was ultimately more concerned with moral than with material progress. He came to the conclusion indeed that every invention contained within it a germ of evil, that technology could not solve man's spiritual contradictions, and that despite the undoubted power that machines gave him over objects, they left him as helpless as before in the face of the uncontrollable forces around him. The omnipotence of 'accident' was thus one major theme of his works, and there was much ambivalence in his attitude to the virtues and ideals of his society. His heroes were usually either orphans or bastards, men without family or name, escaping from the normal world, in search of mysterious places or unknown islands, fighting against monstrous forces, seeking to unravel impenetrable enigmas. Beneath his bourgeois exterior, Verne thought of himself as an orphan and an outcast, and his life was dominated by rebellion against his father, whose solicitor's practice he had refused to continue. 'I am not what you would call a civilised man,' he wrote. 'I have broken with the whole of society.' His books reflect his aggressive attitude to men in general, and even more towards women, who very rarely appear at all in them. His marriage broke down; a nephew shot him and made him lame; he was, increasingly, a recluse.[1] It is curious, and typical of the unpredictable influence of authors—which is so often like a shot that misfires in the wrong direction—that the product of Verne's tormented imagination should have been taken as symbolic of confidence and hope and recommended to children. But then that is only further evidence that one should not too readily assume that literature reflects its age, or that its message is understood.

It was Émile Zola (1840–1902) who did most to publicise the introduction of scientific methods into novel-writing. In *Le Roman expérimentale* (1880) he called the novel naturalist rather than realist to give it the suggestion of a natural science. He claimed he was applying the theories of Claude Bernard's *Médecine expérimentale* to literature. Zola developed the view that all things were interesting: 'the first man he comes across will do as a hero: examine him and you are sure to find a straightforward plot'. He took over Flaubert's principle of scientific detachment: 'A novelist . . . has no right to give his opinion about the things of the world . . . The author is not a moralist but an anatomist who confines himself to stating what he finds inside the human corpse . . . He believes that his own emotion would interfere with that of his characters.' Zola was particularly interested by the effect of heredity and environment on human conduct. He was influenced in this by Lucas's *Traité philosophique et physiologique de l'hérédité* (1847–50) and by the theories of Taine. He believed that man's life was determined

[1] Jean Chesneau, *Une Lecture politique de Jules Verne* (1971); Simone Vierne, *Jules Verne et le roman initiatique* (1973); Marcel Moré, *Le Très Curieux Jules Verne* (1960) and *Nouvelles Explorations de Jules Verne* (1963). Cf. Robert Fath, *L'Influence de la science sur la littérature française dans la seconde moitié du 19ᵉ siècle* (Lausanne, 1901) and J. J. Bridenne, *La Littérature française d'imagination scientifique* (1950).

by his physical constitution, which he received mainly from his parents, according to the laws of heredity. Physical defects were carried on from generation to generation, often accentuated, so that people almost inevitably became alcoholics, cretins and prostitutes. He accordingly wrote a series of twenty connected books, *Les Rougon-Macquart* (1871–93), tracing the history of a single family through many situations, designed to illustrate these theories. Each book portrayed a different social class or a different aspect of life, so that the whole presented a comprehensive portrait of French society in what appeared to be a factual way. Far from deifying his heroes, he stressed their animality. He did not go in for careful psychological analysis but painted with large brush-strokes, showing the supremacy of insuperable natural forces. He excelled in describing crowds, because he sought powerful effects and he found the greatest violence and passions in masses. The terrible effects of drink, poverty, hard toil and the struggle for wealth and power were shown to be inexorable, with tremendous force. He sought to be impartial, on the whole, revealing vice everywhere, among workers and the rich classes, so that, despite his liberal sympathies, some of his books, especially *L'Assommoir*, were criticised by the socialists for giving an unduly black picture of the workers. Others criticised him for his inaccuracy. He made considerable efforts to collect material on which to base his supposedly factual studies but, given that he wrote on average a book a year, his knowledge was inevitably superficial. His study of mining life in *Germinal* was based only on a week spent at Anzin, and on about three books on miners' diseases and conditions. Research was not the inspiration of his writings: he did it only after he had worked out a story.

Zola did not have the temperament of a scientist. He was the son of a Venetian immigrant, an orphan at six; he failed his *baccalauréat*. He had a romantic passion to be recognised as a leader: 'all that matters is to stir the crowd'. But he always led an isolated life, and in journalism and novel-writing he obtained the illusion of contact with men. He longed for popularity. He adopted causes that drew attention to himself: he felt he existed with a real identity, above all, when he was the object of attacks. He led a blameless life but filled his books with sexual excess. He was a hypochondriac, superstitious and melancholic. There is much that is artificial in his books, and his opinions often seem to be shallow or poses. He wrote in praise of Fourierism (*Le Travail*), of science (*Dr. Pascal*), of Dreyfus; he attacked the Church (*Lourdes* and *Rome*) and was placed on the Index. After the birth of his illegitimate children late in life, by a girl twenty-eight years younger than himself, he lost most of his misanthropy (*Fécondité*). His life represents an attempt to cast off illusions— because dreaming had led him nowhere—and an acceptance of things as they were, a willingness to leave them as they were and to confine himself to describing them. But there was some conflict between this attitude, which goes with his 'scientific' impartiality, and the faith he also had in progress. He cannot be taken as a reliable source about his times. Ultimately he was popular for the same reasons as the romantics were popular: the power of his imagination, which endowed reality with 'a sort of brutal poetry and symbolic grandeur'.[1]

Science thus failed to make as much impact on men's minds as it did on their practical lives. The scientists were unable to find in it an adequate guide to conduct. They did not, in this period, dare to claim superiority in fields outside their own, and indeed retreated into a specialisation which limited their influence. They thus strengthened the cellular nature of this society. The writers who tried to interpret science made great claims on its behalf, and put its message into some striking formulae, but they were all ambivalent in their attitude to it, for their enthusiasm usually concealed anxieties for which science had no effective remedies. The hopes placed in science were far from being fulfilled, and not even in the material sense. This latter aspect, the physical changes wrought by science, needs to be examined now.

## Comfort

The consequences of scientific and technical advances on the daily lives of Frenchmen is not a subject that has received much attention. The history of science is generally written from the

[1] F. W. J. Hemmings, *Zola* (Oxford, 1953); I. M. Frandon, *La Pensée politique de Zola* (1959); R. Ternois, *Zola et son temps* (1961); H. Mitterand, *Zola journaliste* (1962); Guy Robert, *E. Zola* (1952) and *La Terre d'E. Zola* (1952); E. M. Grant, *Zola's Germinal* (1970); D. Baguley, *Fécondité d'E. Zola* (Toronto, 1973).

point of view of the scientist, or as part of the development of knowledge. The consumer, however, has yet to find a historian. Science viewed from the receiving end had a different appearance: what was important in the realm of theory took decades, or even centuries, to make an impact, and it has been seen how difficult people found it to reorganise their mental habits to take account of new theories. The immediate result of technical improvements, however, was greater productivity, more goods on the market and eventually more money to buy them with. A new kind of consumer was therefore created, with far more choice than he had ever had. How he exercised that choice can throw light on the question of how much importance he placed on different aspects of his life. Did the consumer society have its origins in this period?[1]

The masses could get a sight of the latest advances in technology and the practical results of science in the international exhibitions, which were events of great importance in several different ways. The exhibitions were voluntarily attended by more people than went to any other attraction or entertainment that was organised in this period. That of 1862 was visited by 6,200,000, that of 1867 by 9,000,000, that of 1878 by 16,000,000, that of 1889 by 39,000,000 and that of 1900 by 50,000,000. The exhibitions brought the industrial portion of the nation out of its traditional secretiveness and enabled it both to boast of its achievements and to receive public acknowledgement of the value that people placed on them, despite all the attacks on profiteering and chimney smoke. They drowned, even if only while they lasted, the pessimistic complaints of the poets and moralists in exclamations of awe and self-congratulation; and the delight in technical progress that they stimulated should not be overlooked simply because there were few great writers who echoed it.

Industrial exhibitions had first started in 1798, which was an important date, because for the first time industrialists received honours hitherto reserved for the fine arts; in 1801 when a second one was held, the artists refused an invitation to exhibit together with industrialists; in later years they agreed provided they had a special section. In 1798 only 110 manufacturers

[1] For the complicated question of rising living standards, see J. Fourastié, *Machinisme et bien-être* (1962).

showed their wares; at the seventh exhibition in 1827 there were 1,600; by 1878 there were 52,000 exhibitors, of whom half were French. Those who were admitted to exhibit, moreover, represented only a fraction of those who were anxious to (one-fifth in 1867). A great attraction was not only the orders that businesses could expect, but also the honour of medals and decorations, which constitute a kind of nobility peculiar to the nineteenth century; it is only recently that labels listing prizes won at international exhibitions have been replaced by advertising slogans as proof of a product's merit. Admission as an exhibitor gave one a very good chance of getting a medal: in 1844 there were 3,960 exhibitors and 3,253 prizes. The large manufacturers dominated the selection process and got most of the honours.[1] Successful manufacturers were increasingly recognised as the equals of any other profession. In 1819 the king awarded the Legion of Honour to twenty-three of them and made two of them barons. In 1849 fifty-one exhibitors were given the Legion of Honour.[2] Contempt for the 'mechanical arts' no doubt continued in some quarters, but manufacturers began to enjoy an increasing sense of pride, rationalising their activities with the defence that 'work is the greatest moraliser in the world'. Technology had its own morality also.

One of the uses of the exhibitions was that they made it possible to take stock of the relationship between inventiveness and public demand, and to discover, if not what the public would buy, at least what aroused its curiosity most. In the 1839 exhibition, French heavy industry occupied a very minor part, and it was Belgium which impressed most in this field: France distinguished itself in perfumery, jewellery, craftwork, music— 'noisy music is the veritable mania of the century' wrote an official observer. The problems for which visitors came seeking solutions were things like inefficient heating ('smoke is one of the curses of our homes') and better lighting (Thillorier, inventor of the 'hydrostatic lamp', sold hundreds of thousands of them).[3] In 1849 a gold medal went to the inventor of a calculating machine, which no one bought, and to Sax, the inventor of the

[1] A. Chirac, *Lettres d'un Marseillais sur l'exposition universelle de 1867 à Paris* (1868).

[2] Achille de Colmont, *Histoire des expositions des produits de l'industrie française* (1855), 56, 317.

[3] J. B. A. M. Jobard, *Industrie française. Rapport sur l'exposition française de 1839* (1841), 1. 3, 2. 95.

Saxophone, which no one played. In 1855, there were 128 exhibitors of agricultural machines, but the report on them declared they were thirty years behind England and there was comparatively little interest in these. 'France', it said, 'is, by taste, military, artistic, literary'; it was forcing itself to become industrial and commercial; but it had still not got round to applying science to agriculture.[1] More excitement was roused by central-heating systems and by metal beds, now considered to have 'reached perfection'. Above all, it was the enormous reduction in prices of articles of daily use, which were once luxuries, and which now came within the reach of the masses, that seemed important. Industrialisation meant, more than anything else, cheaper goods. Textiles led the way in this. Shawls, for example (which were to the nineteenth century what pullovers became for the twentieth) used to cost as much as 450 francs for the best 'cashmere' quality—a labourer's annual wage. By the middle of the century Reims had taken up the manufacture of Scottish tartan shawls which were sold for only 8–12 francs and 'Kabyl' ones for 14–25 francs. Sizes had to be diminished and the number of colours used reduced from six to three, but these cheap parodies of luxury now became the pride of every working woman. French manufacturers exploited these opportunities with varying speed, because it took some time for traditional tastes to be abandoned and new standards to be accepted. Thus in 1867 the peasants were said to be resisting the wool–cotton mixtures of poor quality which manufacturers thought ought to be the material for the clothes of the masses. Peasants wanted clothes that lasted. It was the better-off fashion-conscious buyers who took the lead in preferring clothes of poor quality, which they could change frequently. The workers followed them, demanding clothes that appeared to be fashionable. So because the demand for 'cheap' clothes was so great, prices remained relatively high, despite the fall in the cost of raw materials. One could buy pure wool cloth for only 1 fr. 40 a metre in Périgueux but there was very little of it; in Sedan there were some wool mixtures at 3 francs a metre; but 9 francs was still considered a low price. English goods were both cheaper and of better quality.

Mass production thus roused ambivalent feelings from its earliest stages; and it did not at once become possible to enjoy

[1] Colmont, op. cit. 368.

its benefits. The mass production of shoes, for example, still involved only shoes with the uppers screwed or nailed on; American machine-sewn shoes were a novelty, inspected with great curiosity, though vulcanisation brought the price of rubber boots down by 40 per cent in the 1860s. Wooden clogs were then in the process of disappearing in the towns, but they were being replaced by galoshes with wooden soles, because these were still one-third of the price even of mass-produced leather shoes. Cheap products for household and kitchen use had been a major theme of the 1855 exhibition, and that of 1867 laid particular stress on 'objects for the improvement of the physical and moral condition of the masses', but only one-third of the space allocated to this was taken up. Some cheap crockery and cutlery was shown but the iron furniture exhibited met with almost universal disapproval from the workers who saw it: they insisted that furniture must be varnished and ornamented. One trouble was that the large gap between wholesale and retail prices prevented these goods from being really cheap, and the gap increased as the object was cheaper. The most successful article of cheap mass production in this period was perhaps the sewing machine, which was down to 300 francs. By contrast a mechanical drill, which could have appealed to the male population as that did to women, cost twice as much as a piano. The section of the exhibition in which workers could show things they had made themselves significantly contained almost nothing but *objets d'art*, for use by the rich. Despite the curiosity aroused by the typewriters, phonographs and rubber tyres, and despite the emphasis on machines in the propaganda about the exhibition, these occupied only 4,600 square metres of space, compared to 2,500 given to textiles, 3,000 to furniture and domestic goods, 3,100 to art and 769 to 'objects for the improvement of the masses'.[1]

The exhibition of 1900 was the most magnificent that had ever been staged, but it brought to a head the tensions that had revealed themselves in earlier ones. This was symbolised by the difficulty the organisers had in deciding what its theme should

---

[1] *Exposition universelle de 1867 à Paris. Rapports du jury international publiés sous la direction de M. Michel Chevalier* (1868), esp. volumes 1 and 18; C. A. Oppermann, *Visites d'un ingénieur à l'exposition universelle de 1867* (1867), 16–18, 141, 189, 446; Jules Mesnard, *Les Merveilles de l'Exposition de 1867* (1868), I. 39.

be. In 1889, the Eiffel tower, the electrically illuminated fountains, the huge Gallery of Machines had paid unreserved homage to modernisation, and the protest signed by many writers
and artists, like Dumas, Maupassant, Bouguereau and Meissonier, against the 'ridiculous tower dominating Paris like a
gigantic black factory chimney . . . a dishonour to the city' did
not prevent Eiffel, who had the rights to the profits from it for
twenty years, from becoming a very rich man, for the crowds
were enthralled. In 1900, however, the theme chosen was retrospective and whimsical: at the front gate a statue of 'La Parisienne' in a tight skirt and hat of the latest style symbolised Paris
as a centre of fashion, and the major exhibition was one of Old
Paris. France's particular contribution was nationalist rather
than scientific, with expensive reconstructions of an Algerian
and an Indo-Chinese village, to show off colonial might. It was
the Germans who made the most profound impression from the
technological point of view, with their huge dynamos and whole
factories producing synthetic chemicals. The French had organised the exhibits in order of the importance they had, in the
French view, for the development of mankind: they placed
education first (but its pavilion in fact attracted very few
visitors) and art second (but only a few large paintings held the
attention of the crowds). All this was too serious: the exhibition
was treated as an entertainment by most. There was now too
much to see and many people declared themselves overwhelmed.
A frequent tendency was for people to go and look only at the
exhibits of objects in their own specialities. France felt itself
humiliated by the industrial superiority of other nations—some
talked of 1900 as an 'industrial Sedan' and reacted by losing all
enthusiasm for exhibitions of this kind. The next one, held in
1937, was dedicated to 'Arts and Technology' and the emphasis
was as much on the former as the latter. The French pavilion
contained virtually no heavy industry. There was, however, a
section on folklore, which expressed a revived interest in the
artisan idea, and in traditional feasts, given greater meaning
by the new concern about leisure.[1] All this should not be

[1] Richard D. Mandell, *Paris 1900. The Great World's Fair* (Toronto, 1967);
Georges Gerault, *Les Expositions universelles envisagées au point de vue de leurs résultats
économiques* (1902); G. de Wailly, *A Travers l'exposition de 1900* (1899–1900). The
industrial exhibitions deserve further study and the sources available are large.
Régine de Plinval-Salgues, 'Bibliographie analytique des expositions industrielles

interpreted as showing the 'bankruptcy of science'—a slogan popularised by the literary critic Brunetière in the 1890s. What it shows is the parting of the ways between science and literature. The hold of science—and of the attitudes that it fostered—on the imagination of the majority was not diminished. The intellectuals took fright because they could not control the monster they had helped to create, but the monster was more attractive than they realised.

Science was attractive because it offered the masses comfort, mobility, and health. These were precisely the demands the utopian philosophers had made in the eighteenth century. The scientists brought their demands to fulfilment, but the intellectuals were appalled by the unforeseen consequences that came with them. Material improvements had been intended as a basis for spiritual and artistic growth; but the majority took the means to be the end. That was the source of the antagonism of the 'two cultures'. Moreover, science seemed to bring more obvious benefits than democracy or education. Education, worst of all, became for most people an instrument for improving the level of their earnings rather than a cultural experience. The benefits of democracy were forgotten once they had become an accepted and therefore unnoticed part of everyday life: freedom from arbitrary arrest, for example, increasingly appeared no longer as the triumph of a political creed, but as natural as breathing the air. Science's offerings, which seemed to be the antithesis of Christian abnegation, austerity and resignation, presented the ordinary man with an opportunity to rearrange his attitude to life and to reassess his hierarchy of values. He had to decide whether he preferred ambition or tranquillity, immediate or deferred rewards. The road to wisdom and perfection remained very difficult, despite the enormous efforts of priests, teachers and politicians to point the way, but the ordinary man now had the option of forgetting or postponing these superior goals and

et commerciales en France depuis l'origine jusqu'à 1867' (unpublished mémoire, Institut National des Techniques de Documentation, 1960) lists 1,020 items. See also Colette Famy, 'Bibliographie analytique de l'exposition universelle tenue à Paris en 1878' (unpublished, I.N.T.D., 1962) and Colette Signat, 'Bibliographie analytique des documents publiés à l'occasion de l'Exposition Universelle de 1900 à Paris' (unpublished, I.N.T.D., 1959), which contains a useful guide to the 48 volumes of the *Rapport du jury international* (1902–6).

of contenting himself with more attainable material ends. The unresolved problem is whether science supplied him with the objects and facilities he wanted, or whether, by inventing them, it created needs he had never felt and expectations that became compulsive. This is a problem that will never be resolved, because there is very little evidence about what ordinary people wanted until the public opinion poll arrived (which in France, was in the 1940s), and even then the question asked often forced a certain kind of answer.

By the 1940s, the preoccupation with comfort was certainly overwhelming, though what is even more interesting is that it was still not universal. An inquiry held in 1955 revealed, for example, that one-third of the working class had no desire for what was to become the symbol of affluence, the washing machine, and a further one-fifth philosophically accepted that they would never own one; only one-third hoped to obtain one, and only 13 per cent actually had one. It was not just the workers who felt this way: about 30 per cent of both clerks and managers also had no desire for a washing machine. A fifth of the workers (and a tenth of other classes) had no desire for a bathroom or running hot water; there was even 1 per cent which saw no need for running cold water. The country was thus still divided into four groups, those who enjoyed modern comforts, in varying degrees, those who desired them, those who were indifferent, or who even disliked them, and finally those who were so resigned to never having them that they had no opinion on the matter. Despite the primitive and crowded conditions in which, as will be seen, many lived, only 54 per cent declared that they considered their homes insufficiently comfortable, only 43 per cent complained of not having enough rooms and only one-third thought the buildings they lived in were too old. The ideal of a more leisured life had still not overcome the preoccupation with earning money for basic necessities: only about 5 per cent thought a working week of 35 hours or less was desirable; about half favoured 40 hours, but a third accepted 45 hours or more; 3 per cent were willing to work 50 hours or more.[1] The 'materialism' of this society therefore needs to be qualified, both by the fact that not everyone was obsessed by the same dream, and also by the fact that the options were

[1] *Sondages* (1956), no. 2, 13–32.

irrelevant to many, who were too busy simply surviving to have any choice.

A more detailed inquiry, carried out in Toulouse in 1936–8, showed that the decisive factor in determining how people spent their wages was not simply the size of their pay-packet, nor simply the class or occupation they belonged to. Among workers and clerks earning roughly the same amount, the former spent more on food, while the latter were frequently undernourished and contented themselves with cheaper and preserved foods. However, workers who had recently come out of agriculture put up with worse housing and economised in their eating habits more than those who were long-established townsmen. What mattered, therefore, was how long a worker had been in his class. Once he had accepted the limitation of his prospects, he became keener to spend his money on immediate enjoyment, like food and amusements. It was the worker who reached his maximum earnings quickly who set the pace in consumer expenditure. Already in the 1890s, it was the younger miners at Carmaux who saw fashionable clothes as a necessity. Workers in Toulouse, at any rate in the 1930s, did not use their money to imitate the bourgeoisie: they still wore galoshes in winter and espadrilles in summer, and when they got more money, they simply bought more of these rather than leather shoes. They preferred to use any increase in wages to move to more expensive housing, 'less from a desire for comfort than from a sense of conformity'. The richest workers doubled their expenditure on amusements, but the richest clerks trebled their expenditure on cultural pursuits. There was thus a definite division among Frenchmen between those who had distant ideals, for which they were willing to save (and it was often the poorest workers who, proportionately, saved most in Toulouse) and those who lived in the present. It was not a division of class but of hope.[1]

There were clearly things people wanted that science could not provide, or failed to, and this led to a modification in demand. One can see this in the history of people's attitude to housing, the most basic of needs after food. In 1954, exactly 50 per cent of a sample of people questioned said that what they felt the lack of most was clothes, while 30 per cent said improved

[1] Henry Delpech, *Recherches sur le niveau de vie et les habitudes de consommation, Toulouse 1936–8* (1938), 70–2, 261, 303.

housing was their main need, and 17 per cent more food.[1] This stress on clothes may perhaps be dated from around 1890, which is when building ceased to be the country's main activity after agriculture, and when it was overtaken by textiles.[2] It was in the eighteenth and nineteenth centuries that the French equipped themselves with their houses, which meant that when modern comforts became available in the second half of the latter century, it was an adaptation, rather than complete renewal, of housing that was the inevitable choice, because too much had already been invested in old houses. In 1946, the average age of houses in Normandy was 137 years, in the Paris region and the north-east of France about 120 years, in Brittany and the centre between 95 and 104 years. The rapid increase in population had made much building necessary between 1750 and 1850. When that pressure ceased, new building became a largely urban phenomenon. The peasants had a clear order of priorities: when they had money to spare, they put it first into buying land, next into improving their farm buildings and only last into constructing new houses for themselves.[3] The result was that the modernisation of rural housing was a slow process; and only certain changes were seen as urgent. The first was separation of the humans from the animals. In 1885–94, when a large-scale survey of living conditions was carried out, there were still peasants, in the Aveyron for example, who lived side by side with their animals, separated only by a partition, in rudimentary hovels with a single window. The way to escape was to build an additional storey: 'the peasant rises in the social hierarchy when he puts the twenty or thirty steps of a staircase between his bed and the many inconveniences of the ground floor, open to the dust, the mud, the foul smells, the coming and going of passers-by and of animals.' Many peasants, as in the Orne and Quercy, built two-storey houses from vanity, but could not adapt themselves to the change and continued to live downstairs. In 1856 60 per cent of French houses were bungalows; by 1911 only 48 per cent were; only 1·2 per cent had four or

[1] M. de Clinchamps, *Enquête sur les tendances de la consommation des salariés urbains. Vous gagnez 20% de plus. Qu'en faites vous?* (1955), 31.

[2] M. Lévy-Leboyer, 'Croissance économique en France au 19ᵉ siècle', *Annales* (July–Aug. 1968), 806.

[3] J. P. Bardet, P. Chaunu et al., *Le Bâtiment: enquête d'histoire économique 14–19ᵉ siècles* (1971), 1–120.

more storeys.[1] The next stage was to make houses more solid. In 1856 about one-fifth of them were thatched. These were mainly in the north—84 per cent of houses in the Manche were thatched, and 62 per cent in Calvados. But by then tiles were already cheaper; thatch began to disappear and by 1941 it was found on only 4 per cent of houses (15 per cent in Normandy). Uniformity of appearance had been impossible until the mid-nineteenth century, because of the cost of transporting building materials (the price of a cubic metre of stone was increased by 80 per cent when carried a mere 21 kilometres). Now the very substantial regional variations in style were progressively modi-fied into a more national uniformity. Imitation of a new kind set in: one village virtually rebuilt itself in brick, following the erection of a brick railway station in it. Traditional methods of basic construction, apart from minor improvements, continued. Science made little difference, except in the cities.

Improved sanitation was not regarded as an urgency, for in 1954 only 27 per cent of homes had indoor w.c.s, and only 10 per cent had baths or central heating.[2] Government investi-gators complained about the extremely elementary provisions for sanitation in the 1880s but reported that 'what is filth to the townsman is manure to the countryman . . . which delights his eye too much for him to worry about its smell'. But at that period townsmen did not have standards that were very differ-ent: 'Even in the finest palaces, we could denounce staircases and corridors, serving the major public administrations, where the most distressing revelations are perpetually inflicted on those whose business takes them there.'[3] Hygiene was imposed by government regulations, rather than voluntarily adopted; and these regulations were one of the major sources of the increased uniformity in the layout of houses. That is not to say, however, that cleanliness was a modern innovation. Housewives in many parts of the country were famous for the meticulous care they

[1] J. P. Bardet, op. cit. 60; *Statistique des familles et des habitations en 1911* (1918).

[2] CORDES (Commissariat général du plan, Comité d'organisation des re-cherches appliquées sur le développement économique et social), *Recherche com-parative internationale sur les critères de choix entre les modes marchands et non marchands de satisfaction des besoins* (Puteaux, Feb. 1973), 2.25.

[3] Ministère de l'instruction publique, *Enquête sur les conditions de l'habitation en France. Les maisons-type*, vol. 1 (1894), introduction by A. de Foville. In 1906 two-thirds of French houses still had no w.c.s (indoor or outdoor).

lavished on their homes, but what they cleaned and polished changed with time.[1] The crucial factor was the theory of germs, which created new taboos about what could be touched and what was dangerous. This theory was no doubt assisted by increasing individualism which also made people keep their distance more. But just how slow these ideas were to gain hold may be seen from the crowding people were willing to tolerate. The government's criterion (in 1911) was that every person ought to have one room: less than that was 'insufficient' and two people to a room was 'overcrowded'. At that date, a third or a half of the population (depending on which statistics one believes) lacked adequate accommodation by this criterion; in the towns, and particularly the growing industrial towns, the proportion was even higher. In Paris, 2 per cent of families even had six or more people living in one room. Privacy for the individual was a national goal, but it was not attained till the 1960s, when, after the enormous building programme of the post-war years, there were at last as many rooms as people. In the previous century, it is true, the country's stock of houses did rise a little more than its population:

*Number of houses in France*

| 1847 | 7 | million |
|------|------|------|
| 1870 | 8¼ | ,, |
| 1890 | 9 | ,, |
| 1914 | 9½ | ,, |
| 1920 | 9¼ | ,, |
| 1939 | 9¾ | ,, |

But that meant that the accommodation available in the towns, where most of the new population went, became increasingly inadequate.

It is not at all clear how far the development of housing in this century satisfied the wishes of the majority. It is true peasants had more and more space as their numbers fell, but that did not necessarily imply greater comfort. In 1937 only one-third of rural communes had running water, and even fewer had drains.[2] Opinion was still divided as to whether drains

---

[1] Dr. R. Martial, in *L'Hygiène sociale* (25 Jan. 1933), shows that cleanliness did not increase in constant progression.

[2] *Enquête sur l'habitation rurale en France* (1939), 33.

were worth having, and it was only in some parts of the country that they were adopted. The townsmen, for their part, had drains forced upon them. The policy inaugurated by the Second Empire was that the slums the city workers lived in should be demolished and that they should be replaced by blocks of flats, or terraces of small houses in the suburbs. The workers made it plain that they did not like this 'improvement'. 'They attach the highest price' (they said in 1867) 'to the continuous spectacle presented by the boulevards, the public gardens and the main streets of a large town; they find in this a source of enjoyment that costs nothing'; and they preferred to live in an attic in the centre of town, rather than be segregated into estates.[1] It was argued by some that the ideal, at this period, was the detached house. Occasionally this was made available to workers at prices they could afford. Thus the firm of Japy built three-bedroomed detached houses which they sold to their employees for 2,000 francs (£80), payable over eleven years. That however was unusually cheap, and included a subsidy and land at provincial prices. The cité Jouffroy-Renault, erected in Clichy, a northern suburb of Paris, by a philanthropic widow in the 1860s, more typically offered two up and two down accommodation for 4,800 francs. The cost of buying these over fifteen years, including mortgage interest at 5½ per cent, was 381 francs a month, which was more than a worker could afford. These therefore became lower-middle-class estates. Most city workers had to be content with rented flats; some even preferred these because it made it easier for them to move; but the 'modern' blocks put up by Napoleon III in Paris were contemptuously derided by them as 'prison blocks'. When the Co-operative Housing Society experimented with buildings held up by steel frame supports, they complained that their walls were too flimsy, and, in any case, what was supposed to be a cheap substitute turned out to be 50 per cent more expensive. So too did Napoleon III's concrete buildings. Experiment in building techniques was thus constantly resisted, because in building modernity did not also mean greater cheapness, though this may have been a vicious circle. Modern conveniences, as the manufacturers themselves admitted, were so simplified and skimped for mass consumption that they gave much trouble; plumbing was often defective and

[1] *Exposition universelle de 1867 à Paris. Rapports* (1868), vol. 13, 892.

there were drains on the market which were not even water-tight.[1] Speculative building often created houses which were less attractive than those they replaced; and because building costs continued to increase, good, cheap housing for the masses never quite materialised. The laws of 1894 and 1908, codified in 1922 and 1928, by which low-interest government loans were given to encourage *habitations à bon marché*, had only a limited effect. Between 1925 and 1939 about 2,400,000 buildings were put up but only a quarter of a million of these were H.B.M.s. These H.B.M.s moreover were put on the market at rents which the workers considered excessive. They were usually of two or three rooms, with a w.c., but a bathroom was still, in the inter-war period, not considered necessary for workers. Rents were controlled as from 1914: landlords stopped carrying out repairs, with the result that the number of homes declared unfit for human habitation rose from 150,000 in 1911 to 2,800,000 in 1939.[2] Mortgages were difficult to obtain (apart from schemes sponsored by companies for their employees) and were usually for less than half the price of the house.[3]

It was only after the Second World War that the provision of housing was accepted as an urgent national priority. The annual rate of building in the 1960s was almost exactly ten times higher than that in the period 1920–39. In 1968, as a result, France had almost twice as many houses as it did in 1939 (18¼ million). In the process, the proportion of people owning their homes has probably fallen. In the 1880s, 61·3 per cent of houses were occupied by their owners (56·3 per cent by the owner alone and 5 per cent by the owner and tenants jointly). In Paris the proportion was only 29·7 per cent; in rural communes it was 66·6 per cent; in Corsica it was 85 per cent, in the Puy-de-Dôme 83 per cent, but in Brittany only 38 per cent.[4] The full figures for more recent times are not quite comparable, but they suggest that, out of the 14 million 'non-agricultural' houses in 1967,

[1] *Exposition internationale des industries et du travail de Turin* (1911), groupe XII, classes 62 à 70: 'La Ville moderne: rapport général' (n.d.), 119–22.
[2] A. Sauvy, *Histoire économique de la France entre les deux guerres*, vol. 3 (1972), chapter on 'Le logement', 99.
[3] Société des Nations, Services d'Études Économiques, *L'Habitation urbaine et rurale* (Geneva, Aug. 1939), 77–99.
[4] A. de Foville, *Enquête* (1894), op. cit. i. xliii. A. Pinard, *La Consommation, le bien-être et le luxe* (1918), 91, claims that in 1918 79 per cent of homes were owner occupied.

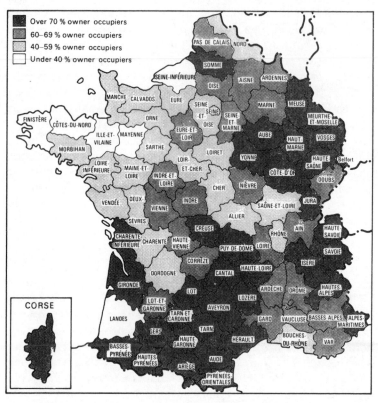

Map 2. Owner Occupiers (1894). Based on A. de Foville, *Enquête sur les conditions de l'habitation en France* (1894), 1. xliv.

42 per cent were owner occupied; if one excludes those with mortgages, the figure would be about 30 per cent.[1] This shows that home ownership was psychologically but not economically very attractive. One of the main reasons why more houses were not built was that rents were very low; a loan to buy a little house in the 1880s would cost at the very least twice as much as the rent.

The acquisition of material possessions often involved borrowing. The amount people borrowed is a partial indication of the extent to which they preferred immediate to deferred pleasures. In the United States in 1935-6, almost one-quarter of the population were involved in purchasing by instalments; about a third of the purchases were of furniture; but cars accounted for 59 per cent of the total debt. There was, however, even in the United States, an enormous amount of regional variation in the use of this method; it was most common in the cities of the north central part of the country.[2] Very little is known about indebtedness in France, but preliminary researches indicate that there were, similarly, enormous variations from region to region;[3] and the complex interplay of psychology and economics in this has still to be unravelled. The poor, of course, had always bought their food on credit, but what was new was the extension of their interest into consumer goods. A thesis on the subject, written in 1904, observed that 'the taste for comfort, the desire to rise or to appear to rise in the social hierarchy' had launched many humble people into debt and a whole new section of business had sprung up to cater for them. Bakers and grocers were expensive because their customers expected credit; co-operators had little success because they refused it (whereas English co-operators in the nineteenth century often gave credit). French retailers of food, drink and pharmaceutical goods used to offer credit even if it was not asked for. It was a way of increasing sales and of investing their money; they put up their prices by about 20 per cent as a result. But their credit system was based on whim and mutual confidence and it

[1] CORDES, op. cit. 2.22.
[2] Blanche Bernstein, *The Pattern of Consumer Debt 1935–6. A Statistical Analysis* (New York, 1940), 19, 35–6.
[3] M. Philippe Vigier is supervising some research on this subject.

involved no written contracts. The development of purchase by instalments, with regular payments, was invented, or rather developed into a national institution, by Georges Dufayel (1855–1916) who claimed to have the largest instalment business in the world. It all started humbly in 1850 when Crespin, a peasant's son, came to Paris and set up as a photographer, offering twenty portraits for 1 franc, the balance—20 francs—being repayable over several months. He grew prosperous, employed door-to-door salesmen to advertise his services and soon expanded into furniture and clothes. For 25 francs a subscriber had the right to buy 100 francs' worth of goods at a selection of shops. But because Crespin charged 40 or even 50 per cent commission to the shops, they put up their prices accordingly and the scheme was discredited. Crespin's widow associated one of their employees, Dufayel, in the business in the early 1870s, and it was from then that it became important. By 1900 Dufayel had 2,400,000 clients and by 1904 nearly 3,500,000. His system was based on the co-operation of concierges, who answered inquiries about the credit-worthiness of clients, and on inspectors (800 in Paris) who each looked after a few streets, from which they collected repayments. There were 400 shops (including the Samaritaine) from which the clients could buy goods with Dufayel's tokens (on which he made 18 per cent commission); but he then opened his own luxurious stores in the rue de Clignancourt and the Boulevard Barbes, which sold every kind of goods except clothes and food, but including cars; and he had branches in all the large towns. Dufayel defended himself by claiming that he was helping the workers to acquire the comforts of life while preventing them from falling into the hands of usurers. Shopkeepers replied by setting up rival credit companies, especially in the north of France (e.g. the Crédit Lillois, 1885). The department stores of Paris replied by a greater use of advertising, which was an alternative method of increasing sales, or, in the case of the Samaritaine, by establishing, in 1913, its own credit company, La Semeuse. Dufayel, who was, almost typically, a great art collector, also founded an insurance company on the instalment principle and a seaside resort at Sainte-Adresse. His shops were shut down in 1940.[1]

[1] Ch. Couture, *Des différents combinaisons de vente à crédit dans leurs rapports avec*

The motor car did a great deal to spread the habit of instalment purchase. In the U.S.A. in the 1930s, at least 60 per cent of cars were bought on credit. In France, only 3 per cent were in 1926, but by 1937 35 per cent were. Just as it was General Motors which developed this in the U.S.A. by setting up a finance house, so in France Citroen, Renault and Peugeot in turn started to lend people money to buy their cars (1923–8). Many independent firms joined in to participate in the profitable business of hire-purchase, because already by 1937 70 per cent of new cars sold involved a part-exchange and 50 per cent of cars were already being resold within two years.[1] At that date, it was claimed that 45,000 second-hand cars were sold every month, to the accompaniment of a vast amount of deception and usury.[2] The manufacturers insisted that theirs was not a luxury article, but a useful one, which stimulated business, expanded markets, increased incomes. Only 15 per cent of purchasers said they bought cars simply for pleasure. But there were those who protested that the car had created needs that had never before existed. Since the price of a new car was twice a worker's annual wage, borrowing was necessary. Borrowing was generally something new for the bourgeoisie, which had hitherto liked to pay cash. It was the rich and the poor who used to buy on credit. The spread of their habit was to a considerable extent the work of women—leaders of change in this too: in 1906 it was said that 80 per cent of instalment buying was by women. Peasants, and bachelors, abstained.[3] But in 1954, an inquiry into the spending habits of townspeople found that only 43 per cent of them had bought goods on the instalment system. Only 11 per cent of them owned cars at that date, but of those who did not, only 44 per cent wanted one. Likewise, only one-tenth of those who did not own bicycles said they would like to have one.[4] One should not exaggerate the pressure for ownership of material luxuries, or even of labour-saving devices. Michel Chevalier, in

la petite épargne (Paris law thesis, 1904); cf. G. Dufayel, Indicateur Dufayel (1901–4), his estate agency's publication, in 28 volumes.

[1] A. C. Dedé, Traité pratique de la vente à crédit des automobiles (1937) (by an employee of Peugeot), 59, 63.

[2] Léonce Daries, Autos d'occasion. Piraterie moderne! (Toulouse, 1937).

[3] Jean Boucher, De la vente à tempérament des meubles corporels au point de vue économique (Paris law thesis, 1906), 138.

[4] Clinchamps, op. cit. 44–5, 68. Forty-seven per cent owned bicycles.

1851, had claimed, as all the Saint-Simonians did, that 'the desire for comfort, an ardent desire which has almost become a passion, has penetrated society in all its parts and there is no class which is not profoundly affected by it'.[1] He also said that the ordinary French artisan was already more comfortable than King Agamemnon had been. That perhaps was one reason why the desire for greater comfort was not as universal as he thought. Another was that prices rose constantly, and even if wages rose faster in certain periods, the poor had great difficulty in adjusting to these changes. They ate more and better food, but when the price of this rose, they felt deprived of what had become necessities, and the struggle to live was not eased. In 1912, there were angry demonstrations by housewives in many parts of the country because the price of butter and eggs had temporarily gone up: they behaved almost as they had done in the middle ages, when threatened by famine.[2] The growth of consumers' associations against *la vie chère* showed many people on the defensive, rather than profiting from abundance.[3]

The difficulties of adaptation may be seen also in people's attitude towards medicine. Better health was one of the most important benefits science offered, and it will be seen that, most noticeably of all, it gave longer life.[4] The longer people lived, however, the more they had need of medicine, particularly in old age. Thus the number of hospital patients increased threefold between 1870 and 1936, when a million and a quarter people received treatment.[5] General practitioners, too, received more visits; in the department of the Indre-et-Loire in 1900 doctors on average gave only sixty-two consultations a month and paid 250 domiciliary visits; in 1936 their average consultations were 180 a month, though their domiciliary visits remained virtually unchanged at 264. The increase since then has been

[1] M. Chevalier, *La Science mise à la portée de toutes les intelligences. Le désir de bien-être est légitime; il peut obtenir satisfaction; mais sous quelles conditions?*, Inaugural lecture at the Collège de France (1851), 7.

[2] Émile Watelet, *Les Récents Troubles du Nord de la France au point de vue historique et économique* (1912).

[3] A. Lemonnier, *La Ligue des consommateurs* (1910); M. Deslandres, *Pour la reconstitution de la Ligue sociale d'acheteurs* (1931).          [4] See chapter 19.

[5] Number of persons treated in hospitals: 1873 410,000; 1883 448,000; 1893 571,000; 1903 642,000; 1912 775,000; 1923 768,000; 1927 913,000; 1930 1,100,000; 1933 1,153,000; 1936 1,235,000. *Annuaire statistique* (1939), 42.

only in the order of 16 per cent.[1] The explanation is partly that the standard of health people expected rose, and they could afford to look after themselves more, but also that new diseases replaced those that medicine cured. Tuberculosis, from which Frenchmen suffered more than any other nation in Europe, apart from Austria and Hungary, began to decline around 1910, and by 1936 its victims had been reduced by about two-sevenths. Death from typhoid was halved between 1890 and 1908. Smallpox, after a final epidemic in 1907, declined and became insignificant after 1927. Between 1906 and 1930, death from whooping-cough was halved and typhoid reduced by two-thirds. But diphtheria was barely diminished, deaths attributed to cancer rose by a third between 1906 and 1927, and those to heart disease rose by one-fifth in the 1920s.[2] Not only was the French death rate, in the inter-war period, higher than that of most European countries, but in certain regions, afflicted by tuberculosis and alcoholism, it was very much higher. Equality in legal rights may have been achieved, but not equality in the face of death: the death rate was 80 per cent higher in the working-class fourteenth *arrondissement* of Paris than in the wealthy eighth *arrondissement*.[3] In 1930, tuberculosis was killing about 100,000 people a year, but the sanatoriums and hospitals set up to deal with this had only 12,628 beds. Venereal disease, it was estimated, was killing about 80,000 people a year, as well as causing 40,000 abortions and 20,000 stillbirths, despite the 532 dispensaries set up since the First World War in virtually every large town. (When the schoolchildren of the department of the Aisne were medically examined only 51 per cent were declared to be in good health, 25 per cent had signs of tuberculosis and 3·75 per cent suffered from hereditary syphilis.) Six per cent of French deaths were from cancer, but in Paris the rate was 13·3 per cent.[4] Cancer moreover struck in a mysterious manner, affecting women more than men, cancer of the uterus and the breast being the most common forms.[5] Epidemics, such

[1] Jean Paul Mercat, 'Évolution de la médecine de campagne en Indre-et-Loire de 1900 à nos jours' (unpublished medical thesis, Tours, 1970), 95.
[2] *Annuaire statistique* (1939), 36*. The figures for heart disease in the 1930s are incomplete.    [3] P. Guillaume, *La Population de Bordeaux au 19ᵉ siècle* (1972).
[4] A. Landry, *L'Hygiène publique en France* (1930), 15, 44, 89, 116.
[5] M. D. Grmek, 'Préliminaires d'une étude historique des maladies', *Annales* (Nov.–Dec. 1969), 1473–83, shows the gaps in our knowledge of this subject. A

[continued on p. 634]

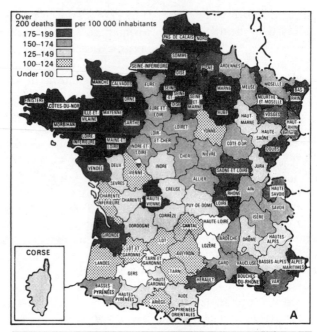

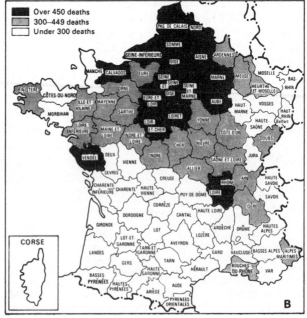

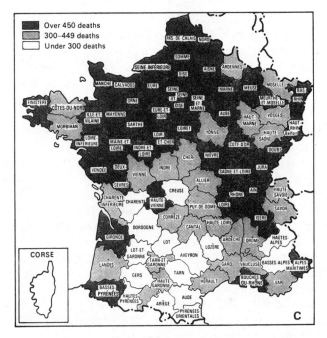

Map 3.
Deaths from Tuberculosis and Cancer
(1913–33).

A. Tuberculosis in 1913.
B. Cancer in 1913.
C. Cancer in 1933.

Based on *Enquête sur l'habitation rurale en France* (1939), I. 59–69.

as the typhoid which affected several thousand people in Lyon in 1928, could still strike. Viruses replaced microbes as soon as the latter seemed to be in the process of being defeated. Occupational diseases remained a grave and neglected hazard (one-fifth of porcelain workers, for example, suffered from silicosis still in the 1950s). Infant mortality was not fully controlled, and yet, as the proportion of old people increased, their illnesses added new problems. Conquest of the environment brought with it subjection to dangers of a new kind. Industrial accidents increased fourfold between 1900 and 1930, and came to involve over 1 million people a year. In 1930 855 people were killed in railway accidents and 1,506 injured, and railways were just beginning to become safer when motor cars replaced them as a new and much more frequent cause of death.[1]

The transition from a traditional to a scientific attitude towards medicine had only partially taken place at the end of this period. Different groups turned to medicine with very different enthusiasm. Peasants spent much less on health than other people: in 1950 their expenditure was roughly half of the average and in 1960 just under three-quarters. Women in 1960 spent about 50 per cent more than men; people over sixty (and children under two years) spent three or four times as much as people in their teens and twenties.[2] The consumption of pharmaceutical products regularly rose in the years 1950–65 at the rate of nearly 10 per cent per annum. This represented partly increased prosperity, but partly also increased costs and the spread of subsidised medicine. There are no comparable figures to enable one to trace expenditure in the pre-war era, but it is clear that people have recently been more willing to classify themselves as ill. In 1938 insured people were ill for an average of 5·08 days a year and in 1950 for 9·36 days a year.[3] It was only

good comparative study, lacking for France, is Monroe Lerner and O. W. Anderson, *Health Progress in the U.S. 1900–1960* (1963). For regional variations see R. Morot, *Pathologie régionale de la France* (1958), 2. 63, 333, 375; Louis Spillmann and Jacques Parisot, *Guérir est bien, prévenir est mieux. L'effort réalisé en hygiène et en médecine sociales dans le département de Meurthe-et-Moselle* (1925), 179.

[1] *Annuaire statistique* (1939), 199*.

[2] Les Cahiers de l'industrie pharmaceutique, no. 5, *La Consommation pharmaceutique dans les pays du marché commun* (1969), 12, and id., no. 1, *Le Développement de la consommation pharmaceutique* (1967), 15.

[3] Henri Péquignot and J. P. Étienne, *Éléments de politique et d'administration sanitaires* (1954), 25.

in 1902 that smallpox vaccination was at last made compulsory, a victory over mistrust of new-fangled ideas that took three-quarters of a century of agitation to bring about. It was only during the First World War that serious sanitary regulations began to be implemented, and only in 1919 that a law on occupational diseases was passed. It was only in 1922 that a ministry of hygiene was established, but it was part of the ministry of labour until 1930 and in 1939 it still had no technical resources of its own, employing only two doctors and having to rely on the good-will of local authorities. In 1920 one-third of the country's departments did not have the inspectors of hygiene established by a law of 1902; and it was only in 1945 that the compulsory medical inspection of babies and schoolchildren at last made possible an efficient preventive service. The obligatory treatment of venereal disease was introduced only in November 1939. Health thus remained very largely a private matter. In 1951, at a Catholic congress on the subject, a bishop reiterated the traditional view that 'health, though a precious thing, is not the supreme good. Illness, which harms the body, can be profitable to the soul.' A Christian's life did not belong to himself, but to God, and suffering could be beneficial and sanctifying.[1] Even in the 1960s the average Frenchman's view of illness was still not altogether that held by his doctor. Though the microbe had been popularised as the great enemy, it was still more common for people to talk of the causes of disease in a more general and traditional way, as the result of 'poisoning' (intoxication), and to blame their environment, city life, stresses of various kinds, noise and unnatural tinned food for their troubles. Death, it is true, was no longer seen as an imminent threat—death was talked of much less—and this was indeed a great change; but exhaustion, which replaced it as the prime complaint, largely transformed health into a battle between the individual and society, rather than something capable of being ensured by science.[2]

Though an important break occurred in the First World War, principally in attitudes to surgery, for this was the first war in which more soldiers were killed by guns than by infection, the really decisive change in the use of medicine occurred in the

[1] Santé et société. Les Découvertes biologiques et la médecine sociale au service de l'homme, 38e Semaine Sociale de France (1951), 12–17.
[2] Claudine Herzlich, Santé et maladie. Analyse d'une représentation sociale (1969).

1960s. Many important new drugs were discovered in the inter-war period, but they were not much used in the country at large until much later. Thus in Montluçon hospital the drug used for blood pressure was, until 1963, still the traditional alkaloid Rauwolfia Serpentina. It was only in that decade that medica-tion was drastically revised and put on a more scientific basis.[1] What characterised the use of drugs before then was a faith in simple remedies, and their application, almost as cure-alls, to a large range of troubles. Thus quinine (invented in 1820) was in turn prescribed for almost all infectious diseases, colds, skin troubles, anaemia and neuralgia, and a century later the factory at Nogent-sur-Marne that had been founded to manufacture it was producing $1\frac{1}{2}$ million kilogrammes a year.[2] Potassium iodide was the universal panacea for the diseases of middle age—bad digestion, high blood pressure, heart trouble, obesity. Fashion changed the emphasis in the use of particular drugs, and intro-duced new ones, but loyalties died hard. In the late nineteenth century 'there was practically no dining-table on which iron did not find its place—in the form of Bland, or Blancard, or Vallet pills—the girl taking them for her paleness, her mother for her stomach pains and the father for his breathlessness. . . . Anaemia was the universal illness' and so iron was prescribed not just for neurasthenia but also for tuberculosis, renal complaints and arthritis, though after 1900 it lost popularity. Bicarbonate of soda was in 1913 still widely and indiscriminately used for all nutritional and infectious diseases, from diabetes to bronchitis. Belladonna, which used to be a cure for eye troubles and consti-pation, among other things, is an example of the drug that has best survived disillusionment; it continues to be sold as a cure for colds.[3] The full history of the consumption of pharmaceutical products has still to be written.[4]

[1] A. M. Batissat-Champomier, 'Évolution de la consommation de quelques médicaments au centre hospitalier de Montluçon' (unpublished pharmacy thesis, Clermont-Ferrand, 1969), 31–3.

[2] Anon. [Jacques Makowsky], *Histoire de l'industrie et du commerce en France* (1926), 3. 96.

[3] H. Huchard and Ch. Fiessinger, *La Thérapeutique en vingt médicaments* (1913, 3rd edition); Ernest Léonhart, *La Thérapeutique médicale à Strasbourg de 1800 à 1870. Évolution des tendances médicales et résultats pratiques* (Strasbourg medical thesis, 1925).

[4] W. Breckon, *The Drug Makers* (1972), 32, gives the following comparative table of consumption of pharmaceuticals for 1967, in millions of dollars: U.S.A. 3,108, Japan 1,156, France 843, Italy 755, West Germany 716, U.K. 421, Spain 357, Brazil 271, Sweden 112. Cf. also G. E. Trease, *Pharmacy in History* (1964).

Fast travel was another new possibility of this age and a new enticement to expenditure. However, new methods of transport did not destroy the old ones. Throughout this period the number of horses remained virtually constant: about three million farm horses and about one million carriage horses. The number of unmechanised carriages in the 1930s was identical with what it was in 1890.[1] But to these were gradually added first the railways:

### Kilometres of Railways

| | |
|---|---|
| 1850 | 3,083 |
| 1860 | 9,525 |
| 1870 | 17,929 |
| 1880 | 26,198 |
| 1890 | 36,894 |
| 1900 | 43,059 |
| 1910 | 49,628 |

Then the trams arrived:

### Kilometres of Tramways

| | |
|---|---|
| 1870 | 24 |
| 1880 | 411 |
| 1890 | 1,085 |
| 1900 | 4,231 |
| 1910 | 8,690 |
| 1913 | 10,236 |

(But only about one-third of these were passenger trams.) Next came the bicycles:

### Number of Bicycles

| | |
|---|---|
| 1900 | 981,000 |
| 1914 | 3,552,000 |
| 1920 | 4,398,000 |
| 1930 | 6,820,000 |
| 1938 | 8,788,000 |

to which should be added 51,000 motor bicycles in 1920 and over half a million in 1933.

[1] 1891: 1,389,000 carriages; 1913: 1,733,000; 1925: 1,653,000; 1934: 1,352,000. The only change in the animal population was that the number of mules was one-third of what it had been and that of donkeys one-half. Mules fell from 316,000 to 108,000; donkeys from 380,000 to 185,000 (1852–1938).

Finally the motor car:

### Number of Motor Cars

|      | Passenger | Goods   |
| ---- | --------- | ------- |
| 1900 | 3,000     | ..      |
| 1910 | 54,000    | ..      |
| 1920 | 135,000   | 73,000  |
| 1930 | 1,109,000 | 411,000 |
| 1933 | 1,397,000 | 458,000 |
| 1939 | 1,831,000 | ?       |
| 1955 | 2,472,000 | ?       |

In addition, communication by telephone spread at roughly the same pace as the car:

### Telephone Subscribers

| 1890 | 16,000    |
| ---- | --------- |
| 1900 | 70,000    |
| 1910 | 210,000   |
| 1913 | 310,000   |
| 1920 | 439,000   |
| 1930 | 1,113,000 |
| 1938 | 1,590,000 |

The history of this century could be written around the rise of the railway, which dominated economic life as much as any other single invention. The stimulus it gave to the growth of industry and to the unification of the country, the new relationships it set up between men, and between men and their environment, the transformation it wrought in the landscape and in architecture, make it an influence of crucial importance. Life could almost be said to have come to centre round the railway station more than it did round any other single building, probably more than the church or the town hall. Unfortunately the construction of the railways, the speculation and disputes this aroused, has attracted more attention than the social consequences that followed. In France, only the Northern Railway has been the subject of study thorough enough to reveal the reactions of the public to the new opportunities placed before them. It is not typical, but it shows that under the Second Empire people travelled very largely only when they had to. Some provincials paid a visit to Paris for some special occasion, like the Exhibitions, but on the whole this remained a unique experience. The increase in traffic was due largely to the growth of the suburbs—the commuter to the cities already becoming important—and also to the Sunday trip of the townsman into the suburbs. Already in the early 1870s, 77 per cent of the travellers from the Gare du Nord travelled to suburban destinations. After them, the most numerous category of travellers were businessmen, and international business travel was not insignificant. Gradually, the attraction of Paris as a shopping centre for provincials, to which wives liked to make trips, began to assert itself. In the reverse direction, the introduction of cheap excursion fares 'filled the trains with [Parisian] men and women who had not seen their native province for many years and whose return created a veritable sensation' in their villages. The railways thus strengthened family relations which difficulties of transport had weakened. Railway fares only became really cheap in the period 1883–1913, when they were on average 40 per cent lower than in the previous two decades. The great innovation was the introduction of cheaper return fares for families (1891) and workers' season tickets (1883). The railways, by their policies on fares, created new habits. Commuting from suburbs became possible for all classes, even though commercially the low fares were not justifiable. The railways were already losing money on suburban traffic from as early as 1895, but by doing so they transformed the country's working habits and the location of industry. They set in motion new patterns of leisure by running cheap trains to the seaside. The great increase in traffic between 1883 and 1913 was not in first-class passengers, who remained at virtually the same level, but above all in third-class ones. By the turn of the century, railway travel was not only a banal aspect of life, but it had been so much integrated into working-class habits that only a small proportion of them now travelled at full fare.[1] In 1910 37 per cent of travellers were season ticket holders, which meant over a quarter of a million commuters on the Northern Railway. The result was that when the motor car began to compete with the railway after the First World War, the railways could make no further headway, and since public opinion, government policy and trade union activity made it impossible for them to raise fares

[1] In 1887–91 46·5 per cent of tickets were paid at full fare, in 1909–13 21·8 per cent—the rest benefited from various reductions.

or to keep down the numbers or wages of their staff, they were already heading for insolvency: they had become a social service.[1] The railways had created new needs and had set up patterns of both work and leisure which depended on them. Their staff enjoyed security of employment, and pensions comparable to the civil service. Working on the railways was as attractive as working for the state. This was wholly appropriate, because the country had come to expect services from the railways, in the same way as they took it for granted that the roads would be kept in repair and the schools would provide free learning. Rather oddly, however, no one claimed the 'right to travel' or that the railways should be free also. It would have been a logical conclusion; but that it was not seen as such shows how equality of opportunity applied to very strictly limited fields and freedom in most things was still available only to those who had the money to buy it.

This was even more obvious in the case of the motor car. The history of the motor car provides instructive indications of how Frenchmen viewed and responded to technical modernisation in its most advanced form. The automobile industry refuted the generalisation that the French were too traditional to be capable of rapid economic growth. Between 1890 and 1904 France led the world in the production of motor cars, and until 1930 it made more cars than any other country in Europe. Between 1923 and 1938, when the U.S.A. increased its production of cars by only 20 per cent, France increased its by 180 per cent. But the paradox of this is that the French had not developed a cheap popular car by the Second World War, as every other country had. They clung to artisan methods and luxury standards longer than most. Firms like Dion-Bouton (founded by the marquis de Dion, who built a steam tricycle in 1883), Delaunay-Belleville (founded in 1903, and making 'cars that last'), Rochet-Schneider (1893), Delage (1905), Panhard-Levassor—and there were altogether 155 different manufacturers in France by 1914—have remained famous for their individualist skills. Renault, it is true, got near to mass production. This firm was established in 1899 by Louis Renault, the son of a draper and button manufacturer, after failing to pass the entrance examination into the École

[1] François Caron, *Histoire de l'exploitation d'un grand réseau. La Compagnie du chemin de fer du Nord 1846–1937* (1973).

Centrale. He expanded rapidly because he made his cars very largely out of components manufactured by others and because he (or rather his brother Fernand) quickly adopted a very active export policy, with selling outlets all over the world. He specialised at first in taxis and by 1909 two-thirds of the 3,000 taxis in Paris and half of London's 2,400 taxis were Renaults. Instead of reducing prices, he increased sales. He was very much alive to developments in the U.S.A., which he visited in 1911, and he was quick to introduce Taylorisation, but only partially. His prices long remained higher than those of his foreign competitors, and in 1927 it was calculated that whereas it took American firms 70 working days to produce a car, it took the French 300 days. It was only around 1925 that the price of French cars began to drop, long after the dramatic drop started by Ford, whose model T cost almost a third in 1916 of what it had cost in 1909.[1] Renault had the highest ambitions. In 1919 he said that he hoped France would become the 'economic centre of the universe'. But, as one of his collaborators rather unfairly said, his financial skills were those of a peasant. When the great depression struck, he had not overreached himself and he survived the crisis, unlike Citroen, who was the real practitioner of mass production in France, making only one or two models. In 1933–5 the three main car manufacturers in France, Renault, Citroen and Peugeot, were all thinking of launching a cheap popular car, to be sold at about two-thirds or less of the price then current, but partly because of the difficulties created by the depression, and partly because of the resistance of their salesmen, who had got used to dealing with wealthy customers and who argued that the demand was for more powerful cars rather than cheaper ones, the idea was abandoned. The car manufacturers preferred to maximise profits rather than turnover. Renault, despite his genius at seizing commercial opportunities, remained at heart a very conservative employer, anxious to resist the workers' demands and to fight the communists, and his collaboration with the Vichy regime led to the nationalisation of his firm at the Liberation.[2]

[1] The price of a 12 CV in 1913 was 12,000 francs, when the maximum annual salary of an *instituteur* was 2,500 francs and that of a Conseiller d'État 16,000 francs.

[2] Patrick Fridenson, *Histoire des Usines Renault*, vol. 1: *1898–1939* (1972), one of the best histories of a business, with a good guide to the considerable literature on the subject.

There gradually grew up two distinct markets for cars, the new and the second-hand. The very early cars did not last long. Of those built between 1898 and 1908, only 48 per cent were still on the road after seven years and virtually none after fourteen. Of those built between 1908 and 1914, 78 per cent were still working after seven years, and of those built between the wars, 83 per cent survived more than seven years. In 1927 the cutting of the road tax by half for cars of over nine years of age further encouraged people not to throw these away. The result was that in 1930 52 per cent of car sales were of second-hand cars and 68 per cent in 1935. The interesting fact about the people who bought cars was that they were not just the richest. Two-thirds of car owners in 1932 lived in villages or small provincial towns. There were many merchants and doctors among them, but also well-to-do peasants. The car appealed above all to the rural notables, for whom railways had not fully catered, and whom the car freed from their isolation. The middle classes of the cities found the expense of the car less necessary. The idea that every man needed a car, wherever he lived, had certainly not yet established itself; it was in any case an impossible idea, because most people were far too poor even to think about it. An economist calculated the number of families, at various periods, who had an income large enough to run a car, and found that at no time between 1900 and 1952 were there more than about 20 per cent more possible car owners, on this criterion, than actual car owners. Cars were still so expensive that people almost had to choose between having a car and having a child: there is a striking concordance between the map showing areas of low birth-rates and that of car ownership, as there is also with the map showing areas where least new houses were built. Most significantly, perhaps, it was areas with high divorce rates that bought most cars. These relationships were clearly in existence in 1938; it was not until the 1950s that they disappeared, and it was only then that the car established itself as an object whose ownership no longer implied such drastic choices.[1]

The world of the car had by then expanded in two ways.

[1] Janine Morice, *La Demande d'automobiles en France* (1957); Ho-Thoï-Sang, 'Le Marché des voitures de tourisme en France depuis la fin de la guerre' (Toulouse economics thesis, 1958, unpublished).

First there was a growing number of people working in the industry, not only in the factories but also in the garages, which now established themselves in every little town, side by side with and as essential as the pharmacists.[1] Secondly, there was increasing reliance on public road transport, particularly in rural areas. In a rural department like the Puy-de-Dôme, for example, in 1913 cars carried under a tenth of the goods but about a quarter of the passengers on the roads; by 1928 cars carried 25 per cent more goods than horse-drawn carriages but over ten times as many passengers as still used horses. Bus company lines here increased fivefold in the years 1923-9. In the country as a whole, cars and buses were by 1934 transporting as many passengers as the railways, though only one-sixth of the goods that railways carried.[2] The Bordeaux regional bus companies were then carrying 4 million passengers a year. The bus manufacturers encouraged the proliferation of bus services by selling their vehicles on credit, so that there were many bus services run by individuals, with no capital and vague time-tables. Though the speed limit was 50 k.p.h., it was frequently broken, because the bus companies competed against each other in speeding, encouraged by the passengers.[3] It was ironic that the car industry, which began in such a romantic way with characters like Bollée, the bellfounder of Le Mans, who christened his steam car for twelve passengers 'L'Obéissante' (1873),[4] should have developed into the tensest and most inflammable part of the economy, but it was perhaps not inappropriate that the workers in it should have played a leading part in the crucial confrontations of 1936 and 1968.[5] The manufacture of cars would come to symbolise the choice that had been made for the masses by economic forces, by which they sacrificed a third of their day in wholly unenjoyable factory work, in return for greater freedom, during another third of the day, to give themselves up to the enjoyment of leisure. This segregation of work and play had not

[1] See H. M. Astruc, *L'Automobile à la portée de tous* (*ouvrage de vulgarisation*) (1920, 6oth edition 1938).

[2] Maurice Wolkowitch, *L'Économie régionale des transports dans le Centre et le Centre-Ouest de la France* (1960), 188 ff.

[3] André Clavier, *Étude économique des autobus régionaux desservant Bordeaux* (Bordeaux thesis, 1936), 54.

[4] Cf. J. P. Peugeot, *Le Film de l'automobile* (n.d., about 1958).

[5] Pierre Naville *et al.*, *L'État entrepreneur. Le cas de la régie Renault* (1972), on problems of labour relations.

yet come about fully in 1945. But that was perhaps to be the most important consequence of the growth of industry and of the technical ingenuity it produced.

The corollary of this was that life became both cheaper and more expensive—cheaper in the sense that the wages of the working class rose very considerably, but more expensive also in the sense that there were far more goods to buy. It is not possible to draw up a balance-sheet of profit and loss, because the history of income and expenditure of different classes has not yet been fully written, and precisely which goods and services were bought most and by whom is not known. What is clear, however, is that for the majority of the nation, food still constituted the major item of expenditure (between 50 and 60 per cent in 1945). Real wages rose for most people, but so too did the additional demands on them: for transport, furniture, newspapers, entertainment and health. Life involved many more opportunities, but the advantages created by industrial progress were distributed in a very unequal way. More food was clearly what the increased prosperity went into first. The consumption of wheat and grain per inhabitant rose by about 50 per cent, 1830–70. That of potatoes almost doubled 1840–1940, and in this period the consumption of sugar increased sevenfold, that of coffee ninefold, and that of cocoa by more than fifty times. People next bought more clothes: the consumption of cotton per inhabitant rose fourfold and that of wool doubled. However, the prices of different goods fluctuated in a way that pushed expenditure in unexpected directions. The price of cigarettes remained steady (1891–1915), and so in real terms they became cheaper; the cost of sending a letter was halved (1849–1907), so was the price of sugar (1875–1909) and ink (1904–14). Gas cost 50 per cent less (1880–1907), clinical thermometers fell 60 per cent (1904–9) and crockery fell by about a third (1907–14); taxi fares fell 3 per cent (1901–14). On the other hand doctors' fees went up by 50 per cent (1900–14) and then decupled between the wars. The price of a man's haircut rose 36 per cent (1900–14), that of waterproof raincoats by 25 per cent (1899–1914). The price of eggs rose by a third (1875–1914) and then increased ninefold between the wars. The conveniences that made up the comfortable life were increasingly expensive: the price of cookers rose twelvefold (1906–39); when electric irons replaced stove-heated ones (about 1930) they cost three times as much; the price of a mattress was ten times as much in 1939 as in 1914. The money wages of provincial labourers did indeed increase by about eighteen times (1910–39), but those of civil service engineers by only seven times. The real purchasing power of the engineers thus fell between the wars by over a third—and many middle-class people found themselves in the same plight—whereas the workers became considerably richer: the primary-school teacher did best of all, doubling his real income (1914–49). A redistribution of wealth was taking place independently of the policies of governments. The effects of science and technology were thus profoundly revolutionary but in a chaotic way: the kind of life they made possible involved just as much accident and inequality as that which it replaced. It was certainly not the expression of democratic choice, and the scientists had very little idea of the implications of their work.[1]

[1] The difficulty of generalising about prices can be seen from Rémy Alasseur, J. Fourastié, et al., *Documents pour l'élaboration d'indices du coût de la vie en France de 1910 à 1965*. The following table should therefore be read with reservations.

|  | Real wages | Industrial prices | Food prices |
| --- | --- | --- | --- |
| 1840 | 78·5 | 57·0 | 73·1 |
| 1850 | 87·9 | 51·5 | 52·2 |
| 1860 | 84·9 | 65·0 | 69·8 |
| 1870 | 91·6 | 55·7 | 73·1 |
| 1880 | 114·7 | 46·1 | 73·1 |
| 1890 | 129·5 | 40·7 | 56·6 |
| 1900 | 136·6 | 43·2 | 51·1 |
| 1910 | 144·6 | 45·4 | 59·9 |
| 1920 | 97·3 | 266·4 | 292·5 |
| 1930 | 144·2 | 268·2 | 364·4 |
| 1938/9 | 155·9 | 338·5 | 449·5 |
| 1952 | 100·0 |  |  |

Based on J. Singer-Kerel, *Le Coût de la vie à Paris de 1840 à 1954* (1961), 104, and tables.

# 13. Happiness and Humour

IN 1776 the American Declaration of Independence held it to be self-evident that the pursuit of happiness was one of the inalienable rights of man. In 1789 the French Revolution proclaimed, as the American one had done, the importance of liberty and equality, but it did not mention happiness, only fraternity. This is a very significant difference. American history could perhaps be written in terms of that country's search for happiness, from the time when Josiah Quincy, Jr. and Jefferson described this as the main object of society to F. D. Roosevelt's second inaugural address, when he asked, 'Have we reached the goal of our vision? Have we found our happy valley?' Happiness was most visibly made America's ideal in its advertising: one historian counted 257 faces in a single issue of an American weekly magazine, and of these no less than 178 were smiling or laughing, 14 singing and 3 smiling through their tears: the rest were not smiling for a variety of reasons, such as that they were asleep, or 'Arabs or other obvious outsiders'.[1] Laughter has not always met with equal approval elsewhere. Lord Chesterfield wrote that it was a 'low and unbecoming thing', a characteristic of folly and ill manners; it was the way in which the mob express 'their silly joy in silly things', and he denied that he had ever laughed himself a single time since adulthood. That did not stop the English winning fame for their sense of humour, though Taine commented that this was based in melancholy and that 'the man who jests in England is seldom kindly, and never happy'. Happiness and humour require separate attention; but before humour is examined, it is worth seeing why happiness has held such an ambiguous place in French life.

In the eighteenth century, the French were as keen on happiness as the Americans. On the theoretical and literary levels, indeed, they could probably claim to have been the world's experts on it, for they then, suddenly, published about two hundred treatises on the subject. In the process, however, they

[1] Howard Mumford Jones, *The Pursuit of Happiness* (Cambridge, Mass., 1953), 132. Cf. V. J. McGill, *The Idea of Happiness* (New York, 1967).

discovered, or rediscovered, many of the complications that happiness involves; and their longing for it was therefore balanced by vigorous arguments about its nature and much uncertainty about how it could be achieved. Neither Boudier de Villemert's *Apology for Frivolity* (1750), nor the Jesuit Sarasa's often reprinted *Art of Tranquillising Oneself* (1664) nor Paradis de Moncrif's *Essays on the Necessity and the Means of Pleasing People* (1738), nor any single work can be looked to for a summary of accepted opinion, because this was in constant evolution. All that was agreed was that everybody, without exception, wanted to be happy, but the solutions that were offered to the problems that this posed were either incomplete, or unsatisfactory even to those who thought them up, or compromises which involved a large measure of self-deception. The eighteenth century was not as straightforwardly optimistic as is often believed, and it bequeathed doubts as well as hopes. Thus the strict Christian view that happiness should not be sought in this world, and could not be enjoyed here—except perhaps for the hope of attaining it in the next world—was vigorously reiterated, as it would continue to be in the nineteenth century too. The steady flow of young women into convents showed that renunciation was practised as well as believed. But there were also Christian authors, like Le Maître de Claville, from whose best-selling *Treatise on True Merit* (1734) even Rousseau borrowed, who tried to reconcile the search for personal salvation with the 'enjoyment of innocent pleasures' and who held up the attainable ideal of the Christian gentleman, finding satisfaction in marital bliss and honourable entertainments. There were thus a large variety of attitudes, even within the Church itself, towards happiness.

The challenge of the *philosophes* consisted of three propositions which apparently completely negated the Christian view. They argued that there was a science of happiness, which could be deduced from an objective study of man and the laws governing both his emotions and the world around him. Happiness, for them, was no longer something reserved for an élite, but was attainable by all, because their science considered the universal man, and their teachings were not concerned, as the rules of society were, simply with polite courtiers. Above all, they saw happiness as no longer to be won by individuals in isolation, seeking their personal salvation, but as necessarily a social achievement, depending on the way society was organised, and involving the harmonisation of human relationships. However, when they began to work out the implications of these new rules, as they did in their Encyclopedia and, in greater detail, in Levesque de Pouilly's *Theory of Agreeable Sentiments* (1736), they did not, on many points, contradict Christianity's teaching, though they left out all reference to it. Man, they said, was a machine; if his faculties were used properly, 'agreeable sensations' would result. This meant that mere contemplation was not enough, and the exercise of all sides of the personality was desirable. However, they restricted their praise of pleasure by reviving traditional views about the different value of different pleasures, insisting on moderation and the golden mean in their enjoyment, and above all proclaiming that there was a providential plan which naturally harmonised the diversity of life. So, though morals required man to do nothing which did not make him happy, happiness ended up as not much different from virtue. The ideal of the egocentric saint was replaced by the public-spirited man, seeking the good of his fellow beings, but this did not really substitute a dynamic attitude in the place of Christian resignation. Voltaire illustrated the uncertainties that remained when, in his stories *Zadig* and *Candide*, he showed life as tragic, because the search for happiness was subject to the most absurd effects of chance and of human folly; man was torn 'between the convulsions of anxiety and the lethargy of boredom'. Voltaire ended up with only a moderate optimism, advising sadly that we should 'cultivate our gardens', because boredom was easier to bear; work was the way to avoid thinking, abstention from involvement with the world was the way to reduce suffering. Fontenelle, similarly, argued that man's troubles all came from uncontrolled imaginations; that the way to happiness was therefore to enjoy what one possessed, to know oneself as one really was, to adjust oneself to one's situation, putting aside distracting dreams and phobias, seeking above all repose—cold and boring though that might be. Montesquieu was an advocate of a judicious balancing of human inclinations, to avoid the dangers of exaggerated emotions, for he was particularly conscious of the variety and inconstancy of the individual personality. Helvétius worried about the 'ravages and crimes' of ambition, though he was very much aware of its pleasures. There were many tirades

against the ill-effects of money and business, and that was partly
why the pastoral life away from the cities, quiet study and gentle
friendship, avoiding passion, were so frequently vaunted. The
fear of suffering was thus still as strong as, if not stronger than,
the hope for better things and the desire to enjoy life to the full.

In the seventeenth century, glory had been held up as something to aim for. Praise for it diminished notably now, many
people declaring that it was incompatible with happiness; but
there was disagreement about this. Vauvenargues still advocated glory, which involved action, courage, ambition, and
Diderot saw applause and praise as man's best stimulant. In the
seventeenth century, again, love had seldom been studied in
relation to happiness, but it now became 'the great affair of life'.
Love was declared to open a new way to self-fulfilment. However, it was now scrutinised in such detail, analysed so coldly,
that it emerged full of paradoxes as well as endowed with new
attractions. The links of love with vanity, self-love and anxiety
were revealed, and much effort was put into freeing it from the
myths surrounding it; at the same time, it was idealised in new
ways; it was identified with virtue; and a hierarchy of its manifestations was elaborated, so that only its 'pure', 'delicate', and
'true' forms were declared acceptable. Some people nevertheless
were bold enough now to sing the praises of its purely sexual
side, but the eighteenth century generally was of course not as
immoral as its reputation. The materialist physician La Mettrie
did indeed argue that the pleasures of the body were the only
ones that mattered and that happiness should be sought in them
without troubling oneself about problems of good and evil; but
though this was how his doctrine was generally understood, and
why it was almost universally rejected, he himself made careful
distinctions, as far as his own pleasures were concerned, between
'vulgar' and 'estimable' ones. There were advocates of sheer
frivolity, even of libertinage, which was indeed part of the education of young men of most classes, but their attitudes were
complicated by the restraints of both conscience and propriety,
which were seldom wholly absent.

The erotic challenge to Christianity was paralleled by the
economic one, but it was not reinforced by it. The commercial
middle classes who devoted themselves to the accumulation of
wealth seemed to be rejecting not only the idea of the vanity of

the things of this world, but also idealism, love and sentiment. However, they were seldom content simply to enjoy their material goods; they wanted esteem also, public recognition of their merit. On the one hand, therefore, they claimed that their economic achievements benefited the whole state, for they were creators of prosperity, and on the other hand they prided themselves on practising most if not all the Christian virtues; they fortified themselves by being models of approved behaviour in their domestic and moral lives, making use of their ill-gotten gains with Christian modesty, seeking to win on all fronts. There was uncertainty, after all, as to whether poverty was a condition of virtue. Rochefort, in his *Critical History of the Opinions of the Philosophers on Happiness* (1778), argued that wealth provided the means which could bring happiness, but that it also destroyed its owner's aptitude to be happy. The philosophers with economic interests justified and praised wealth, as the sign and condition of progress; and the traditional Christian view that, individually, the poor man was the most content, gave way to doubts, as in the works of the abbé Trublet: he thought that there were probably more happy than unhappy people in the world, because there were more poor people, but he wondered whether he would have a different opinion if he knew more poor people, particularly since, when he congratulated them on their gaiety, he was told that they sang at work not because they were happy, but in order to diminish their sorrows and to forget the pain of their labour.

The situation at the end of the eighteenth century therefore was that there was no clear view of how to cope with the conflicts of the heart and the mind, of selfishness and generosity, of natural instincts and the search for virtue, of the desire for repose and the fear of boredom, of the problem of satisfying all these hopes and of finding happiness also. Making money, education, improved hygiene and medicine were put forward as short cuts to general well-being, but the philosophers could not point out obvious cases to prove that their magic cures worked. So meanwhile the aristocracy continued to content themselves with *politeness* as a less exalted way of smoothing human relations and of satisfying the desire to be loved. For them conversation was the prime instrument for the attainment of their goal of making as many friends as possible, or at least not offending too many people. They also believed that society held the key to happiness, but they concentrated on adapting themselves to it, instead of seeking to change it.[1]

In the nineteenth century, adapting oneself was perhaps the most common attitude, partly because it was the easiest course and partly because it incorporated copying the behaviour of one's social superiors, with all the flattering consequences that involved. The counterpart of ambition was imitation. If one confines oneself to what philosophers said about happiness, one is bound to get the impression that this was a complex ideal, never actually achieved, always elusive, even if the formulae for capturing it are simplicity itself. If one turns to other kinds of writers, and particularly novelists and poets, one is faced with the problem of deducing what the average was from the study of exceptional cases; the novelists of this period were personally, on the whole, not particularly happy people: their idealisation of life, or their sombre picture of its difficulties, leave it uncertain whether anybody was happy at all. It is much easier to find records of the pathological, of violence, crime and disaster, than of quiet and contented lives.

### Friendship

One can best get an idea of the way changing social conditions bore upon the problem of being happy, for the ordinary man, by looking at the history of friendship. In the chapters on politics, attention has been drawn to the contrast between regions in which family and clan loyalties remained powerful and those where they were replaced by friendship; and it was suggested that it was in these latter regions that advanced republican ideas were most actively propagated. It is often said that in primitive societies all relationships are dominated by family and kin, and the world is divided into the clan on the one hand and strangers on the other, the latter generally being regarded as the enemy. There is very little room in this situation for neutral, intermediary or emotional relationships. France in the nineteenth century had long passed this simple state, but people were still not entirely free to choose their friends where they

[1] Robert Mauzi, *L'Idée du bonheur dans la littérature et la pensée françaises a u 18 siècle* (1960).

pleased, and the idea of friendship, indeed, could only develop slowly against this traditional background. To their obligations to their families, people gradually added obligations to their neighbours and to those with whom they worked: the workshop, the factory, the fraternity, societies, clubs and cafés gradually extended their contacts. The romantic idea was that a man should have free choice in those with whom he associated, and it praised emotional attachments as superior to others which were in various ways imposed; but this was an ideal, to which different classes and different regions were attracted in different degrees. The preference for friends one had chosen oneself over family and social commitments implied that the individual had become self-conscious in a new way, aware more of the peculiarities of his personality than of the status that membership of his family gave him; and it involved experiencing loneliness and the sense of solitude. None of these circumstances came equally to all classes, or at the same time.

This emerged very clearly in a study of the different social relationships of workers, clerks and engineers, residing in Paris, in a middle-sized town and a small town in 1954–5. There were then powerful obstacles still to the formation of friendships. Sexual differences were the most important. Eighty per cent of the sample said that friendship with a person of the opposite sex was possible but only half of them actually had such a friend. Well-to-do professional people were the pioneers in breaking down this barrier—almost twice as many engineers as workers had friends of the opposite sex—while clerks were the most suspicious of such relationships, partly because they saw women as economic rivals.[1] Class was the next barrier. About half of all friends were of the same social class. Workers and clerks kept pretty much apart from each other, for only 15 per cent of workers admitted to having clerks as friends, and only 15 per cent of clerks had workers for friends. Friendships between rich and poor were of course rarer still: only 2 per cent of engineers had workers for friends. This is confirmed by what is known about intermarriage between social classes. About 45 per cent of French people in this period were still marrying within their own social class. This stability varied however with different

---

[1] 62 per cent of engineers had a female friend, 35 per cent of workers and 26 per cent of clerks.

groups. Thus 64 per cent of peasants married other peasants, 49 per cent of workers married workers, but only 26 per cent of clerks married clerks, and the most ambiguous people were middle management, of whom only 10 per cent married within their own ranks.[1] By now class, or occupation, was not decisive, though it was important: the effect of the Third Republic's work had been to make education even more important: two-thirds of couples were of the same educational level. But though workers and clerks often had the same education and were of roughly the same educational level, they seldom became friends: when they did, it was usually a sign that the worker was treading the path of *embourgeoisement*. This crossing of barriers occurred most frequently in modern industries and in large cities. Miners had far more friends from among their own class than workers in the petroleum industry.[2]

It emerges that friendship did not mean the same thing to the various people who were questioned about it. Workers stressed the reciprocity and the exchange of services as a major element in their view of it; many of them indeed refused to distinguish between *camaraderie* and *amitié*; and manual workers seldom used the word *amitié* at all, preferring to talk about *copains*, mates. Workers liked to form a group of friends, and to have them all

[1] The details are to be found in A. Girard, *Le Choix du conjoint* (1964), and can be summarised as follows:

| Profession of wife's father | Profession of the husband | | | | | | |
|---|---|---|---|---|---|---|---|
| | Agric. worker | Peasant | Worker | Artisan | Clerk | Middle manage-ment | Senior management and liberal professions |
| Agric. worker | 35 | 27 | 24 | 8 | 6 | .. | .. |
| Peasant | 5 | 64 | 14 | 8 | 5 | 1 | 3 |
| Worker | 4 | 17 | 49 | 13 | 12 | 2 | 3 |
| Artisan | 1 | 21 | 22 | 34 | 10 | 4 | 8 |
| Clerk | 4 | 16 | 32 | 14 | 26 | 3 | 5 |
| Middle manage-ment | .. | 12 | 21 | 19 | 21 | 10 | 17 |
| Senior manage-ment and liberal professions | 1 | 12 | 13 | 18 | 15 | 5 | 36 |

Elizabeth Glass, *Getting Married: Women and Marriage in Parisian Society in the Later Nineteenth Century* (forthcoming) shows that in 1865, roughly 40 per cent of Parisians in her sample married members of their own social group.

[2] Miners 68 per cent, petroleum workers 39 per cent.

meeting together; they saw friendship as a collective sentiment. In rural areas, *amitié* was used very broadly to mean simply concord or harmony, as in the statement 'There is more *amitié* in this village than the next', meaning more solidarity. Friendship for the workers was thus often closely related to the traditional neighbourly mutual aid, practised most actively in slum quarters. The element of personal choice was limited. The engineers by contrast romanticised friendship much more, making it a kind of substitute for the support of which their escape from community life had deprived them. They saw friendship as more of a personal interchange, in which each friend was valued for unique qualities, so that it was less common for them all to be brought together. This kind of friendship was essentially urban and the product of new classes without traditional organisations. Friendship was still a rare thing. Fifty per cent of all those questioned admitted to having only between two and four friends; 10 per cent said they had no friends at all. The clerks were the loneliest of all, for one-quarter of them said they had no friends. The engineers cultivated friendship most, having twice as many friends as the workers. Three-quarters of the engineers said they often discussed their intimate preoccupations with at least one friend, and only 5 per cent of them never did, but only about half of the workers admitted to these personal discussions and the clerks were even more chary of them: 21 per cent of the clerks indeed never discussed their private affairs with friends. The engineers very seldom broke up their friendships as a result of rows, which the workers did much more often.[1] Almost half of friendships were ended by change of residence and almost a quarter by marriage. The engineers not only formed friendships more, but also broke them more, perhaps because they moved around most. There was obviously a close link between the need for friendship and the sense of isolation; the idealisation of friendship was the work of those who both disliked isolation and feared to show that they suffered from it. The hierarchy of values into which friendship fitted was revealed by what these people said about how it stood in relation to their other commitments. Family still came first, and only a minority would sacrifice it to friendship; work also came high,

---

[1] Engineers break up because of rows 2 per cent, workers 16 per cent, clerks 10 per cent.

in most cases even higher than family, implying that the need to earn a living, or ambition, were dominant incentives. Political and religious opinions came considerably lower, and 65 per cent said they had friendships with people of diametrically opposed views. This should not be surprising, for though friendship claimed to unite like minds, it seldom did; people have more often sought in friends qualities they admire, rather than those they possess, or some combination of their image of themselves and the ideal they would like to be; and it is only the more confident, those with most self-esteem, who attribute to their friends characteristics they have themselves. Friendship thus did not replace the old ties of neighbourhood and kin in a simple way, for it involved a meeting of ideals rather than of solidly based obligations; it represented a desire for a new security but also for self-transcendence; it was on the fringes of reality and fantasy.[1]

'Sociability' has recently been revealed as one of the key factors in the growth of republicanism.[2] The urban aspect of sociability is certainly emphasised when it is regarded from the political point of view. But, as the chapter on regionalism has suggested, sociability in the south of France had a different significance from what it had elsewhere, and the idea needs to be clarified, for nuances mattered a great deal in something so subtle. The variations of sociability as between classes and professional groups, and the effect of social mobility upon it, need to be borne in mind. There is a need, that is, for much more investigation of the history of sociability. The history of affection between husbands and wives must, moreover, be regarded as closely related to this, for the growth of friendship between husband and wife probably reduced their reliance on support from other members of their families. This is suggested by the way widows were treated. By the Napoleonic Code, widows had very small claims to their late husbands' estates, and it was only in 1891 that a law gave the usufruct of one-half of his property if they had no children and one-quarter if they had. Until then, marriage was often a financial alliance which ended with the death of either partner, and both sides kept as their principal

---

[1] Jean Maisonneuve, *Psycho-sociologie des affinités* (Paris doctoral thesis, 1966).
[2] M. Agulhon, *La République au village* (1970), an essential work for the understanding of modern French society.

heirs their own families. It was the poor, who had least to lose, and whose family ties were least complicated by economic ties, who were the keenest on introducing clauses into marriage contracts providing generously for their surviving partners; it was people with fewest other relationships for whom marriage thus came to mean most in emotional terms. Small shopkeepers very frequently bequeathed their businesses to their spouses, but this was rarer among the rich.[1] The capacity for friendship involved certain preconditions, and it was the same with the capacity for happiness.

It is clear therefore that it would be futile to trace the history of happiness as though this had a constant meaning, but that does not mean that the question of whether people became more or less happy in this period is a frivolous one. The answer must be sought, however, on several levels. Historians have hitherto tended to concentrate on those factors which *should* have made people happier, notably the increase in material possessions and the improvement in physical health. These are very far from negligible; but the conclusions to which they lead are incomplete in themselves, because they do not prove anything about the state of mind of those who have become richer or healthier. Another approach is to consider the manifestations of happiness—joy, revelry and celebration—and work from them to the social relationships with which they were linked. Perhaps the best phenomenon to analyse for this purpose is dancing.

## Dancing

Paintings of traditional dancing immediately pose an apparently puzzling problem. Adolphe Leleux (1812–91), a prolific painter of folkloric scenes, has left a most instructive picture of *A Marriage in Brittany* (1863), which was exhibited in the Second Empire's museum of modern art, the Luxembourg. The peasants are shown dancing, but the expressions on their faces give no sign of merriment or joy. There is an explanation of this. There are two opposing sides of happiness, the kind which comes from security, acceptance and conformity, and that which represents liberation from the constraints of daily life. Breton dancing

---

[1] Elizabeth Glass, *Getting Married: Women and Marriage in Parisian Society* (forthcoming), part three.

allows one to see the meaning of this, for though it was not typical of France as a whole, it has the advantage that there was a great deal of it, and it survived long enough for folklorists and ethno-musicologists to record its steps and rituals before it became simply a tourist attraction. Its history to very recent times may be traced, in particular, from a detailed description of Breton dancing compiled on the basis of interviews with old people in 375 villages during the years 1945–60.[1] Many of the informants who were then questioned spoke about the dancing of their youth with exceptional emotion, recalling how people would walk many miles to participate in a dance, arriving all covered in sweat, but at once joining in. 'When I was very young,' said one, 'during the harvesting of the beet, I could barely lift up my overflowing basket; but if I thought about the dance and remembered a tune, I would raise it without effort and I would dance with my load.' An old woman of eighty uttered the proverb: 'Dancing keeps a man standing.' 'Once upon a time,' said a third, 'when one had black thoughts or when one did not feel well, one said, "Let's go and dance the ronde".'

This traditional dancing, which survived up to around 1900 in the Morlaix and Plouaret regions, to around 1914 in northern Finistère and to about 1945 in southern Finistère, was the expression above all of group consciousness, in which bodily movement and gesture, without speech, was the language used to assert the cohesion of the community. Dancing was a collective activity, in which all classes and, most noticeably, all age groups participated. It had little erotic content and most of the old dances could be performed perfectly well by people of the same sex, and many were. It was not done for men to dance frequently with the same women (except for recently engaged couples); and though there were different ways of holding one's partner, the variations were mainly designed to limit contact: if a girl did not like her partner, she would still dance with him, but perhaps hold on to him with a handkerchief rather than by hand, and that is what priests who danced at the weddings of their relatives did. The young never had separate dances in Brittany (though they did in other parts of France). The old

[1] Jean Michel Guilcher, *La Tradition populaire de danse en Basse Bretagne* (Chambéry, 1963, doctoral thesis).

Breton dances were a reflection of the compulsory neighbourliness which was a prime feature of village life. The inhabitants of a village were linked by a common childhood, by much work in common, by frequent use of help from outside the family for the accomplishment of the larger agricultural tasks. Work in the fields, like harvesting, and work at home, like spinning, was often done on a team basis, in which the help of neighbours was sought and subsequently returned. This social aspect made it possible to turn the most back-breaking forms of labour into feasts, so that, for example, the potato harvest was looked forward to by the young, who would find out when each hamlet was planning it, and would come from neighbouring villages to participate in the dancing and games which were the reward of toil. People recalling their youth spoke with great pleasure of these gatherings, the amusements of which had led them to forget the hard labour involved; no task was so exhausting that at least the young did not end the day dancing. Those who sought the help of their neighbours had to provide entertainment afterwards, and much effort was put into ensuring that the pleasure would be greater than the pain.

An example of the way work and feasting were combined was the *renderie*. When a farmer wanted to weave a large amount of cloth, he asked the help of the village girls, to spin enough thread for the weaver; or rather, he asked nine young men, who each had to find nine girls to spin, and a competition was set up between them. The young men attended the competition too; the winning girl won a handkerchief as a prize and her boy friend some tobacco; they then all ate together and danced for half the night. These gatherings were very popular and as many as four or five hundred people might come to join in. They required as much preparation as weddings, which were the other principal form of collective demonstration. Weddings were designed to show off the extent and power of the families involved, but understanding family in the broadest sense, as though it were a Roman clan. Average weddings mustered between two and three hundred guests but attendances of one or two thousand were not rare, and even larger ones are recorded. The religious ceremony would be followed by a dance of honour which, as late as 1935, was still being observed as itself 'a sort of sacred ceremony generally marked by much gravity and dignity'; it was performed in the village square, started off by the bride, alone, until all joined in, including the very old, so that the relatives of the two families were solemnly united. In this region, which was very poor, festivities of this kind stood out all the more by their contrast. No one was completely left out: it was customary to invite the village's poorest inhabitants to weddings, for example, and the couple would dance with them. There were dances even at the *pardons*, the Breton pilgrimages to honour saints, particularly when the clergy did not control them. There were dances after fairs, dances to raise funds for good causes, 'magic dances' and 'marriage dances', the one in Penzé openly having as its function to find marriage partners; but what they all had in common was the staid concentration of the participants. A visitor to Brittany in the 1820s remarked: 'They dance with gravity; the women lower their eyes and the men are serious; no one would guess that they were enjoying themselves.'[1] That was because Breton dances were not designed to give expression to any dramatic idea, or to show off an individual's skill. In a prolonged feast, it is true, the gravity might give way to frenzy, when the dancers were carried away by the atmosphere they had created: most stood between 'the serene joy of the balanced dance and the mad joy of collective excitement'; but all of them were essentially public manifestations of collective security. There was a place in them for all the inhabitants. The dances enabled the community metaphorically to stroke its children, and children to bask in its protection. There was very little change therefore in the steps used. The peasants who participated were not concerned with imitating the aristocracy, and indeed there was only one Parisian dance, out of the thousands the capital invented, which was borrowed by the Bretons, and that only after it had been popular in the towns for over a century. It was only at the very end of the nineteenth century that the rural areas began dancing *la chaîne des dames* or *la chaîne anglaise*, which had then been current in Paris *salons* for about 150 years. It was only when both the authority of tradition and the economic organisation of society began to change that imitation of the towns took a hold. The new kinds of dance allowed the triumph of the individual, or the couple, and they took a hold at the same time as intimate

[1] Boucher de Perthes, *Chants armoricains ou souvenirs de Basse Bretagne* (1831), 187.

friendship, previously described, developed. Dancing competitions were an innovation, beginning only in the late nineteenth century. Till then, dancers simply had to conform; obedience to ritual was the price they paid for security. There were, it is true, some dances, like the *danse du rôti*, which took place during the wedding feast, after a lot of food and drink had been consumed, and which allowed people to show off their strength; but, in general, individual exhibitionism was avoided, particularly in the dance of honour after weddings, where everything was absolutely regulated by strict rules. The idea of pleasing one's partner in a dance, of having personal relations during it, of talking during a dance, was the result of a different conception of happiness.

This can be seen in the way the towns danced, or at least the way Paris danced, for the amusements of the capital are those which are best documented. One needs to distinguish three different kinds of dancing here in the nineteenth century: official, private and public balls. For originally dancing in the towns, like most things, was regulated by the government. Before the Revolution, indeed, the Opéra had a sort of monopoly of public dancing. In 1715 Louis XV authorised public dancing three times a week at the Opéra, dancing, that is, in which anyone could participate by paying an entrance fee. These dances were still very popular under Louis-Philippe and Napoleon III: the Opéra's parterre and orchestra pit were covered with a movable floor after performances for the purpose, and whole families would attend, for these dances were originally a family entertainment. Private family dances, to celebrate marriages, betrothals and feasts, and government balls, with several thousand guests, resembled the dancing of the Breton villagers in the sense that as well as being an amusement, they were also very much concerned with who belonged and who did not; inviting the right people was half the labour, and receiving invitations was a sign of one's acceptance by officialdom or by a particular section of society. The gatherings of small groups multiplied as more small groups were formed by the city's growing population. However, the rituals they enacted were now vigorously challenged by new dances and new forms of organisation.

The traditional *salon* dance was essentially a ballet, with complicated and varied steps, and with the quadrille, for example, requiring as many as sixteen couples. Long practice and rehearsal were needed for them, and dancing lessons were part of a gentleman's education as much as fencing lessons were. The dancing masters were however much more than teachers of a sport, for they taught their pupils also how to walk and salute properly, how to enter a room, how to give grace and harmony to every movement of the body. George Sand's dancing master, the polite and solemn Monsieur Abraham, was still dancing and still teaching in his eighties, and gave her the same precepts that he had given Marie Antoinette. The dances which expressed the fashionable ideals of elegance and decorum were the gavotte— an elaborate ballet for two, with a set choreography though with plenty of scope for the exhibition of individual grace and originality—and the minuet, which had started as a stage ballet and had then been popularised by the court. These were still being danced in the 1830s, but by then the standard *salon* dance had become the *contredanse*, dominant from the First to the Second Empire. This, renamed the *quadrille*, represented, as people then thought, a gayer and freer movement, even though it involved five different figures, each with different steps; but these were gradually all reduced to a simplified, uniform shuffling backwards and forwards. The great complaint from every new generation was that *salon* dancing was boring; and in the nineteenth century there were repeated changes of fashion, in an attempt to introduce more varied emotions into them. The waltz represented one of these attempted revolutions. In 1820 it was forbidden at court; in 1857 Flaubert was prosecuted for describing a waltz without concealing its sexual overtones. The waltz had in fact been introduced into France in 1787, in the theatre; a form of it may have existed in seventeenth-century Provence; but it was welcomed in the nineteenth century as a sentimental and romantic import from Germany. Originally, under Napoleon I, it was danced, as old prints show, with couples holding both hands, or sometimes holding round the waist, and they moved without turning; only in 1819 did Weber's *Invitation* give it its modern form. This was shocking, but innovations of this kind were constantly being introduced, so that the shock was forgotten under the impact of new audacities. In 1832 the 'Saint-Simonian galop' modified the quadrille, by allowing a change of partners. The cotillion, invented in the

1820s, and particularly popular in the early Third Republic, added the clapping of hands and the beating of a drum by the leader of the dance, whom everyone had to copy: it was much used as an ending for balls. The carillon, which had stamping as well as clapping, making a great deal of noise, enjoyed a vogue, until it became a favourite with the children. Another great revolution was that created by the polka, brought to France from Prague in 1844 and instantly copied after its performance on the stage. It made the fortune of its teacher, the Hungarian dancing master Cellarius of the rue Vivienne. 'One needs to have spent the winter of that year in Paris to have a real idea of the dancing revolution that broke like an insurrection in all the *salons*, to understand to what point young and old, mothers and daughters, magistrates and barristers, doctors and students, gave themselves up to the most passionate polkaic *ébats*. Everything was called a polka, from brands of men's and women's clothing to dishes and puddings served in the most sumptuous dinners . . . Boys used to go home from school dancing the polka through the streets, singing the original Bohemian song.'[1]

Fashion took different directions. Sometimes, as in 1830, it meant dancing negligently, shuffling, removing and replacing one's gloves instead of executing a particular step; but this led to dances losing their vitality and becoming unacceptable to the young. So, alternatively, more energetic or rhythmic ways of performing traditional dances were introduced, as for example the Boston, which was a kind of waltz, but less a step than a way of dancing, that could be applied equally to the polka and the quadrille. 'Bostonner' meant to advance or retreat or turn as one pleased, varying one's movements as much as possible, and sliding more than jumping. This became the rage after 1874; and a few years later the old quadrille, rejected as too staid, was replaced by the 'American quadrille', which was more amusing. Innovations were almost invariably foreign, which was the excuse or justification of their break with propriety. In 1892 the Two-Step arrived, in 1894 the Berlin; then the Tango, which was supposed to have been brought by gipsies from China through Spain to Argentina, and at the turn of the century

---

[1] G. Desrats, *Dictionnaire de la danse, historique, théorique, pratique et bibliographique* (1895), 293. Desrats, himself an erudite dancing master, was the son of a famous dancing master, a contemporary of Cellarius.

tango was the word used to describe every exotic dance that was introduced.

There was a constant conflict, therefore, in Parisian dancing. The Revolution, which ended the regulation of public balls, had let loose a dancing mania, as revealed by the 400 and more dancing places listed in the *Almanach des spectacles* for 1791. The revolution of 1830 coincided with the invention of the *can-can*, which was seen as the last straw by civilised society. Voltaire had said that dancing could be considered an art, because it was subject to rules. The *can-can*, as one dancing master said, was 'an epileptic dance, a delirium tremens, which is to proper dancing what slang is to the French language . . . it is subjected to no musical law, it is the result of the dancer's character as well as of his suppleness or his agility'. It was declared to be obscene, and it probably became increasingly so: at least those who remembered it in its early days complained in their old age that it had become dirty, and had never been so originally.[1] But it is from the 1830s that the conflict of taught and untaught dancing developed; the *bals publics* were abandoned by the bourgeoisie, and it was there that the livelier new steps were danced, becoming, in the eyes of the traditionalists, 'orgies and veritable saturnalia'.

But there was a wide variety of public balls. Though these represented liberation from one tradition, they were so popular that they were captured by impresarios who organised them into a new industry, so that the dancers were now victims of a more elusive regimentation. *Bals publics* were organised to meet every taste. Some indeed were specifically designed to revive the family atmosphere that they once had: the Jardin d'Hiver, near the Champs Élysées, which flourished during the Second Empire, was such a one; it also organised 'poetic and national concerts' to popularise the music of the masters, with singers from the Opéra and the Opéra comique. In the rue des Anglais, which was only six metres wide, flanked by rotting houses, there was a shop with the sign 'Dancing for the Family: calm guaranteed, complete propriety required'; and it attracted considerable numbers of Auvergnat families to its accordion music. By

---

[1] F. de Mesnil, *Histoire de la danse à travers les âges* (1905), v; Charles Narrey, *Ce que l'on dit pendant une contredanse* (1863); Pierre Veron, *Paris s'amuse* (1861); Auguste Vitu, *Les Bals d'hiver* (1851).

contrast the Bal Bullier was an example of a small, dirty, smoke-filled hall, which was stifling but renowned for its 'devilish' atmosphere: it was a family business, the third Bullier inheriting it from the son of the founder in 1882. The Folies-Robert in the Boulevard Rochechouart was founded by Gilles Robert, who had been in turn a ropemaker, a locksmith, a steamboat mechanic, a railway worker and assistant to Monsieur Salvart 'teacher of dancing and of good manners'. He had supplemented his income by teaching dancing in the evenings, until he was picked up by an English major who mistook him for a ballerina and who took dancing lessons from him at a guinea an hour. With the capital accumulated from all these sources, he opened his dance hall in 1856 and made enough of a success of it to have his biography written by a former student agitator.[1] The Salle Rivoli, once known as the Dame Blanche and then l'Astic, was where the boys of the nearby Lycée Charlemagne used to go on Sundays to smoke a cigarette and where famous painters went to seek their models among the exotic girls who came from the Jewish quarter close by. The Grand-Saint-Martin in Belleville, founded in 1800 by Dunoyez (one of whose brothers became a general while another owned most of Paris's taxis), had a different clientele, because it stayed open later than all its rivals.[2] The Élysée Montmartre ball, from the beginning of the nineteenth century, had catered for Parisians who came out of the city on Sundays to amuse themselves under the trees: in 1860 a hall of 1,000 square metres was built by the Serres family, which retained its ownership for several generations—another of the new professional organisers of mass entertainment. La Reine Blanche, a dance hall dating back to around 1850, rebuilt as the Moulin Rouge in 1885, had a reputation as a very gay and amusing place.[3] The Bals Incohérents (1885–98) required compulsory disguise. The Bals du Courrier français, organised by Jules Roques in the same period, after his conviction for publishing pornography, had a different theme each year—pastoral (1890), mystical (1891), transvestite (1892), pagan (1894). The Bal des Quat'z'Arts was the annual carnival of the arts students.

[1] Tony Fanfan [pseud. of Antonio Watripon], *Paris qui danse. Étude, types et mœurs* (1861), 28–35.

[2] Manuscript notes on *bals publics*, with numerous press cuttings, by G. Desrats, in B.N. 8° Z. Le Senne.5544.

[3] André Warnod, *Bals, cafés, cabarets* (1913, 5th edition), 97.

In 1892 it forbade 'formal dress, workers' overalls, bourgeois suits and bathing costumes': the students processed through the streets with four naked models till the early hours, for which they were prosecuted as a result of complaints from the League Against Licence in the Streets. Every year they thought up a new joke.[1]

The war of 1914–18 seems to have had the same effect on dancing as the French Revolution: it greatly increased its popularity, though the Gay Twenties represented relaxation from the austerities of the war rather than enthusiasm of a new kind. In 1921 the Academy of Paris Dancing Teachers issued a statement deploring the 'exotic fantasies executed to the sound of savage music', where each danced according to his whim; they attributed this decay of art to unnamed foreign influences; and they announced that they would refuse to teach the shimmy 'because it resembles too closely St. Vitus's dance and other chronic infirmities'. The headmistress of one of Paris's girls' *lycées* protested that the craze for dancing was producing a 'lowering of the intellectual level' among her pupils: she admitted she knew little about modern dancing but had by accident seen some briefly: she urged the revival of the minuet and gavotte and the dances of ancient Greece. Mgr. Baudrillart, one of the leading Catholic intellectuals, complained that these new dances were 'a direct preparation for the sexual act'. Dr. Bernard, a leading gynaecologist, warned that they brought on dangerous illnesses, like metritis and cystitis in women and impotence in men. Paul Bourget went to visit a dance hall 'for research purposes' and declared that he was horrified by the coarseness and impropriety. The Germans were accused of encouraging the multiplication of dance halls so that they could peddle cocaine in them. The *Revue philosophique* published an article classifying 'the new Argentinian dances' as 'manifestations of satyriasis'. Madame Lefort, a well-known dancing teacher, proclaimed the importance of maintaining the French tradition, of banishing cheek-to-cheek dancing; and if the new steps could not be banned, they could at least be purified: she herself gave lessons in which the shimmy was turned into 'an honest foxtrot and a sort of hygienic and sporting promenade'. The government, however, refused to take action. The Prefect

[1] Georges Pillement, *Paris en fête* (1972), 366 ff.

Y

of the Seine said that personally he found dancing good exercise and he always felt much better the morning after.[1]

But these complaints showed that considerable sections of the bourgeoisie feared and disliked celebrations which broke down too many barriers. Only some people enjoyed themselves in this way. How many is not clear, but in 1962 an opinion poll found that dancing was the favourite pastime of only 13 per cent of young people between sixteen and twenty-four. By then giving dancing parties was a minority, middle-class practice: 68 per cent of these adolescents had never given one; the *lycée* school-boys claimed to go to between eleven and forty a year, while working-class boys very seldom went.[2] The process by which dancing changed its significance and lost its universal appeal still needs to be studied, as too does the system of influences by which modern steps were introduced and copied. One parti-cular problem is how the middle classes ceased to ape the aristocracy and preferred to borrow from foreigners or from the 'demi monde' of which their parents disapproved so strongly. Another is to trace the movement for the revival of traditional dances, complete with dressing up in *ancien régime* clothes, which started as early as the 1880s.

### Roles and Etiquette

The attitude of a middle class towards pleasure is always ambivalent, because those who have a social position to safe-guard can seldom afford to ignore the consequences of even their most insignificant actions. In France the ambition to rise in the social scale was not only a very common preoccu-pation but also one within the grasp of most people, so happi-ness, for many, must have meant simply the fulfilment of this ambition. Ambition implied self-control and the renunciation of immediate pleasures; and it usually meant imitating those whose status and manners one admired most. This explains the enormous sales of etiquette books, which are therefore a most instructive source of information: they are the comple-ment of the career books studied in the chapter on Ambition,[3]

[1] José Germain, *Danseront-elles? Enquête sur les danses modernes* (n.d., about 1923).
[2] Agnes Villadary, *Fête et vie quotidienne* (1968), 151, quoting J. Duquesne, *Les 16–24 ans, ce qu'ils font, ce qu'ils pensent* (1962).
[3] Vol. 1, 87–113.

except that they were written mainly for women, as the career books were written mainly for men. These etiquette books are perhaps a more reliable indication of female fantasies than novels, in that they deal with all those details of daily life which have no dramatic interest but which absorbed the attention of women; they summarise the advice of the women's magazines and enunciate the philosophy which lay behind the endless articles about crocheting and embroidery; they were meant for the women about whom novelists did not write. What is particularly impressive about them is that they—or at least the most successful ones—seldom held out any false hopes. They did not promise happiness to those who carried out their precepts, but only an approximation of it; they urged that women should obtain satisfaction, or contentment, from the observance of rules as a kind of substitute for the bliss that existed only in fairy-tales.

The etiquette books were also much more than that, for they dealt with the general problem of how to conduct one's life, what goals and principles to give it, and not just with how to hold a fork. For about three centuries before this period, the same standard work, *La Civilité puérile et honnête*, based on Erasmus, and endlessly reprinted in various guises, had been given to children, both as a guide to good manners and as a reading text, and the generation of the second Empire had been brought up on it.[1] In 1865 Madame Emmeline Raymond, editor of *La Mode illustrée*, attempted to rewrite it, to bring it up to date at last and to make it a guide for the adult and not just the child.[2] Her book makes clear that old-fashioned politeness was already collapsing and that the rules of good behaviour were far from static. She, however, urged her readers to resist the movement towards informality. She sought to rehabilitate decorum by showing that every one of its rules had a moral basis. She complained that in France, supposedly the land of chivalry, men rushed to the food at parties, and ate it all up, mercilessly, leaving the ladies hungry; and equally women, who

---

[1] Catalogued in the 'anonymous' index of the Bibliothèque Nationale under Civilité; cf. Mathurin Cordier's and J. B. de La Salle's versions of it and *Le Crapouillot*, no. 19 (1952), issue on Les Bonnes manières; Michelle Calais, 'Répertoire bibliographique des manuels de savoir-vivre en France' (I.N.T.D. mémoire, unpublished, 1970).

[2] Madame Emmeline Raymond, *La Civilité non puérile mais honnête* (1865, 3rd edition 1867).

were supposed to be coquettish, were not infrequently arrogant, over-confident, adopting a military bearing and talking in peremptory tones, quite contrary to traditional ideals. The great culprit, she said was the cult of personality, which was the germ of all defects. 'The personality, a mixture of vanity and egoism, incites us to try and substitute on all occasions our own tastes and our own habits for those of other people.' It produced the desire to dominate and to get one's own way, and gave caprice an almost sacred character. This was an astute appreciation of the growing clash of individualism and established usage. The new generation was happy to go on teaching the old rules to their children, but they no longer wished to obey them themselves. The contrast of children's education and adults' behaviour was being accentuated, with portentous results. Madame Raymond said it was not surprising that 'many young people think politeness is an old bore, from which it is absolutely necessary to free oneself, so as to prove that one has a great brain, incapable of subordinating itself to these futile rules'. She urged women to make themselves the guardians of the chivalric tradition, for as soon as their vanity asserted itself, as soon as they aspired to become reformers, their power would diminish: they would be asserting their will to dominate, their own superiority and so their contempt for others. Women should never contradict. That did not mean they should have no opinions of their own, but that they should make it their overriding aim to please others, to soften the asperities of life, to forget about themselves and to devote themselves to others. They should not cultivate timidity, for that was only fear of being ridiculed, which betrayed excessive concern with oneself. They should obtain their happiness from helping others, and from constantly working to improve themselves morally. Many of the laws of *savoir-vivre* that she enumerated were, as she said, designed to repress women's passions, tastes and opinions. That was a good thing. Happiness for her was repression and self-chastisement.

The Baronne Staffe (*née* Soyer) was perhaps the most succesful of all writers of books on good manners in this period. Her *Usages du monde* (1887) reached its 131st edition within ten years and was still being reprinted between the wars.[1] She, too,

---

[1] Baronne Staffe, *Usages du monde. Règles de savoir-vivre dans la société moderne* (1887).

insisted that 'the more a woman is a woman, the more men like her'. A woman who attempted to go outside her sphere would be in danger of losing her grace and her happiness; she should aim to live in the shade rather than in the bright lights, in the home rather than in the big world; with her children rather than among men. In the opinion of the Baronne Staffe, what women wanted above all was to be loved. She assured them that to achieve this they needed neither exceptional beauty, nor great intelligence, nor even extraordinary virtue: they could acquire the qualities needed, and the first step was to submit. Dependence on their menfolk was a sign of grace. By always being tactful, affectionate, kind, gentle and gay even when they did not feel it, they would create happiness around them. All sensible women knew that 'complete happiness does not exist'; they should not have impossible dreams, or at least they should repress these if they did. A little coquetry was allowed and even necessary in a woman, for it showed a legitimate desire to please others, but 'do not seek dangerous consolations, even in your thoughts. Resign yourself. Lose yourself completely in your children.' But Baronne Staffe was not entirely a conservative. She had no use for 'silly prudery', nor for girls with angelic airs, constantly fainting. She urged her readers to keep their weight down, to avoid being dominated by fashion, to beware of going to seed at forty. Her ideal was, as she said, *la vie douce*. The ideal woman smiled, but seldom laughed, first because laughing made her ugly, and secondly because life was too tough for there to be anything to laugh about. There can be no doubt that this philosophy had many adherents.[1]

Madame Louise d'Alq (1840–1901), another women's magazine editor, sold 100,000 copies of her guide to the art of living because, as she wrote, she did not give her own opinions but simply described what happened in the world; and her description certainly suggested that the Baronne Staffe's ideas were widely held. Madame d'Alq however also revealed the obstacles these ideas encountered. The readers of her magazines, she reported, were wholly absorbed, as adolescent girls, in pleasing men. At eighteen, they wanted to be either actresses, so that they could wear beautiful clothes and be admired in them, or

[1] See also Baronne Staffe, *Mes secrets* (1896) and *Indications pratiques pour réussir dans le monde, dans la vie* (1906).

else nuns, because they were too timid to leave their convent schools. Many of them looked forward to marriage as an Eden full of delirious joys, or at least something that gave them greater freedom. But observation of the world as it was showed that women who were loved for their appearance had a very fragile happiness; that being married involved hard work running a home and carrying out numerous duties; that being able to afford beautiful clothes was a pleasure ruined by competition to outdo one's neighbours, which was why hats were piled higher and higher with plumes, ribbons and flowers; that friends were difficult to come by, and one had to accept any that offered themselves, particularly when they came from a class above one's own and flattered one's vanity; when one became a parent, one might well be abandoned by one's children; and when one grew old, the young generation would treat one in an odious and cruel way, pushing and insulting old women though always ready to help a pretty girl. Madame d'Alq was rather uncertain about what her readers ought to do. She herself had dealt with a 'reversal of fortune' by taking up writing, and her motto was 'work is the key to independence', but she had obviously found it a tough life producing her thirty volumes and she warned women against competing in a man's world. 'I make so bold as to affirm', she wrote, 'that a woman who has a sensitive husband has nothing further to ask in the way of happiness in this world.' Happiness could never be perfect, but a good husband would at least diminish the clouds which were inevitable. A woman should preserve her influence over him by her virtues, her sacrifices and her weakness, so that he would always see that her happiness was dependent on him. This might seem, she agreed, a rather humdrum prospect compared to the bright lights and applause that girls dreamed of, but even an ordinary husband who loved you was preferable to the trials of a personal ambition; and if his passion for you waned, at least you could do your best to keep his esteem. Madame d'Alq urged women to find esteem, indeed, wherever they could: they should go to church even if they were not believers, since it might raise them in the opinion of others; they should bear with men who smoked and even pretend to like the smell of tobacco, be willing to talk about stocks and shares and sport, so as to be attractive to the opposite sex. They should put

aside all thoughts of changing the world: 'let us criticise nothing; let us simply conform to the customs of the country we live
in.' Women should take great care whom they spoke to, for
every town was divided into coteries, and if one associated with
an inferior one, one would be rejected by the others. It was
true that modern society was supposed to be equal, and everybody could think they were as good as everybody else. But this
egalitarianism was riddled with jealousies, vanity and envy;
everybody wanted to be *distingué* and they claimed that talent
was an adequate substitute for wealth; but Madame d'Alq had
been forced to agree that the right though difficult course was
to know one's place and to accept that a hierarchy did exist.
The solution was to keep one's distance, and to do so in one's
family also. Familiarity was undesirable either between men
and women or between husband and wife. The sexual barrier
must preserve modesty on one side and respect on the other;
demonstrations of affection between father and daughter were
wrong. Women were allowed to make friends among themselves, but their rivalry and passion for malicious gossip made
their company difficult also. One can see now why politeness
was so highly prized. It alone made social relations possible; it
enabled people to please each other, to win affection or respect,
and it was something which one could learn.[1]

Fear of suffering remained stronger than the desire for pleasure among many conservatives right to the end of this period.
A provincial guide to good behaviour published in 1936 started
off by saying that young women were totally different from
what they were thirty years before, but it nevertheless repeated
the most restrictive traditional advice to them: 'Good taste
consists in remaining unnoticed, not in drawing attention to
oneself.' Fashion in clothes should be followed so as not to
appear eccentric, but all its exaggerations should be avoided.
This book had a section on careers for girls, but it still warned
about the dangers of shaking hands too readily with young men,
of excessive liberty in dancing, of seeing pornographic plays or

[1] Armand Bourgeois, *Conférence sur Madame Louise d'Alq et ses œuvres* (1901);
Madame Louise d'Alq, *Le Nouveau Savoir-vivre universel*: 3 volumes (i) *Le Savoir-
vivre en toutes les circonstances de la vie*, (ii) *La Science du monde*, (iii) *Les Usages et
coutumes de chaque profession* (1881, new edition); id., *Essais pour l'éducation du sens
moral. La Science de la vie. La vie intime* (n.d., about 1895); *Les Causeries familières*
(1880–95); *Paris charmant: Journal illustré des modes parisiennes* (1878–93).

films.[1] Another guide published in 1942, and reaching its fifth edition in 1954, was all about duty, about how to behave respectfully towards one's superiors, and firmly towards one's inferiors, for 'equality is rare'. One should make friends only with those whose families are honest, with the same education and the same beliefs.[2] The Association for Christian Marriage laid it down that once a person got married, his pleasures should be family, not individual, ones; but it did not hold out the prospect of much happiness, for it saw marriage as a way of 'suffering together'.[3]

A moral guide written for policemen, by a policeman, took the same view, but it went into rather more interesting detail on the particular torments and pleasures of this profession. In all times, it said, policemen have been ridiculed, and there was no policeman who did not dream of seeing his sons reach a social status higher than his own. The way to save oneself from mockery was to have good manners, and the way to advance one's children's careers was to give them a good education. 'Happiness, therefore, is to be found in the simple, quiet and regular life of the family home.' The first step to it was to keep clean: the Romans used to have daily baths but 'in France people bathe much less': to wash one's face every morning, to shave at least every time one went on duty, was recommended. One should spit 'as little as possible and then discreetly into one's handkerchief'; one should not scratch one's head or pick one's nose. Meal times should be the hour for relaxation and good humour, and gaiety assisted the digestion, but this gaiety should not degenerate into misplaced or malicious jokes; good food and good wine predisposed one to tell saucy stories, 'which might overstep the limits allowed by good education, if one does not take care'. One should not be so vulgar as to wear one's napkin tucked into one's collar, though in a restaurant one was permitted to use it to wipe one's plate if one suspected the plate was dirty; but nowhere should one throw bits of food one had not eaten under the table. Policemen were not in a position to lead a social life, to visit people outside their profession, so they should

---

[1] Germaine Charpentier, *La Jeune Fille moderne. Guide de convenances et de politesse* (Strasbourg, 1936).

[2] M. M. Laloyaux, *Savoir-vivre. Politesse, éducation* (1942, 5th edition 1954), 50–1, 119.

[3] André Bragade, *Le Bonheur en famille, pourquoi pas?* (1934).

concentrate on being on good terms with their colleagues. A good education made this easier; but to live on good terms with one's colleagues did not mean being on intimate terms with them. 'I will go further: experience has shown that the most serious discord occurs between families which have been most friendly. Avoid competitive vanity—a piece of advice for wives in particular.' A policeman must take especial care not to expose himself to ridicule, or to a loss of dignity. Good manners forbade him 'to show his joy by loud laughter or noisy clapping of hands'. He must avoid using slang or obscene language, particularly with his superiors; he must answer the telephone not with 'What is the matter? What are you saying?' but 'To whom have I the honour of speaking? Yes sir, no sir'. It was not laid down how he ought to treat his inferiors, but at any rate as far as superiors were concerned—and his world was very much a hierarchical one—he should not presume to try to shake hands with a person occupying a rank in society higher than his own.[1] Happiness thus involved balancing self-esteem and resignation, obtaining pleasure from behaving in a way one thought distinguished, and possibly giving vent to the emotions that remained only by actions which would not damage one's public reputation. Respectability was of course maintained only with the support of hypocrisy. As has been shown, marital bliss was closely associated with prostitution, and likewise prudery depended on an enormous pornographic industry. The least-chronicled aspect of the Third Republic's granting complete freedom to the press was its unleashing of a vast number of pornographic publications.[2] Happiness through respectability could ally equally well with religious morals or lay ideologies; it reconciled the satisfactions of self-control with the stimulus of limited ambition. Its weakness, of course, was that it could not appeal for very long to those who had no real chance of ever obtaining its rewards.

There were more pictures than books about happiness. Pictures were also concerned with the respectable and the proper, but by their very nature they commented on a finite moment of human experience, while books were freer to make qualifications and reservations. Novels were much more often about the

[1] Col. N. . ., *Conseils d'un ancien à un jeune gendarme* (10th edition, 1949).
[2] See volume 1, 303–14.

conflict and the difficulties of life, even if they had happy endings, so one probably gets a more direct appreciation of how people enjoyed themselves by looking at them doing so in paintings. The simple pleasures and beauty of children, dancing, couples in love, satisfaction in work well done, relaxing in the sun, looking at flowers and pretty scenery—these were ever-popular subjects for paintings.[1] By contrast the country's great authors had little to say to it about happiness. The members of the French Academy and similar celebrities who were questioned on the subject in 1898 gave gloomy replies. Melchior de Vogüé answered briefly that he had no experience of happiness, never having discovered its secret, and so could not advise anybody. Barthélemy Saint-Hilaire read out the preface he had written forty years ago to his edition of Aristotle's *Morals*, saying that men should not seek happiness, but only duty, though happiness might follow from that. The comte d'Haussonville, a specialist on social problems, was uncertain whether happiness increased or diminished with the standard of living, but he was inclined to believe it was something we dreamt about, or imagined had once existed or would exist some day, but which one never actually reached. Édouard Drumont, the panegyrist of nationalism, thought happiness was very rare: 'as soon as you get to know people intimately, you are astonished to see the sadness that is at the bottom of most lives'. Several people, including Alexandre Dumas, quoted Tolstoy's *Cruel Pleasures* as embodying their opinions. Victor Cherbuliez, the playwright, said happiness was a gift of the gods: so what was needed was books not on how to be happy, but how to do without happiness. This was the view also of the scientist Berthelot, who claimed that happiness 'depends upon our physiological constitution more than on our will'; the search for it was therefore futile.[2]

The tired old men, however, gave only part of the message of literature and learning. There were always talented writers to offer, if not a key to happiness, at least a guide to the conduct of life, and the inspiration of their ideas, even when these bordered on pessimism, gave meaning and sometimes purpose

---

[1] *Les Peinture. témoins de leurs temps*, volume iv: *Le Bonheur*. Exhibition at the Musée Galliera, March–May 1955 (B.N. 8°.V. 61463(4)).

[2] Victorin Vidal, *L'Art d'être heureux. Études morales* (1898), 338–66.

to many people's lives.[1] But the discussion of happiness itself was seldom to be found in them, at least in any direct way. It was left to secondary writers to put their teaching and the conventional wisdom of the age into simple formulae. A vast and increasing number of books were published on the subject of how to be happy. The masses who bought them must have believed, despite the warnings of their leaders, that the elusive prize could be captured. And they were encouraged in this belief by the teaching of the schools. This was one way in which the lay republic and the Church did differ. The state's schools promised rewards in this life for good behaviour. Jules Payot, one of their leading educational theorists and administrators, who ended up as a university rector, wrote a particularly interesting summary of their hopes, entitled *The Conquest of Happiness*. He believed that the application of intelligence to life could lead to happiness, with all the certainty that scientific method guaranteed. Ignorance was the cause of unhappiness. He agreed that there was a great deal of evil, but for 'reasons of mental hygiene' it was best not to think about it, and to rise above it by the contemplation of beauty. Péguy said that at the age of forty he discovered the terrible truth that no one was happy; but Payot replied that one should repress such thoughts, which might disturb the serenity one should aim for. Men had lost the consolations of religion, but in compensation they had been freed from the fear of evil spirits. Death should no longer be taken into consideration in planning one's life; it should be regarded simply as the rest, like sleep, which came at the end— a desirable end, since death allowed constant renewal. Modern man was emerging from centuries of violence and was at last recognising the value of co-operation and spiritual values: he was on the point of emerging from a barbaric childhood, and the reward would be happiness.

There were nine conditions, said Payot, that were required for this. The first was good health, and that ruled out debauchery. Most people thought pleasure meant 'having a good time', which meant stupid, vulgar, exhausting amusement, but these left only sadness and emptiness behind them. 'The miserable literature of anaemic townsmen' encouraged this, but it was the open-air life that was best. Happiness in one's work was the

[1] See chapters 12 and 16.

second condition. Most people in factories hated their work; intellectuals encouraged them in this hate, partly to win leadership of political movements, but also quite sincerely, because for intellectuals physical labour was hell itself. But even the humblest could find creative satisfaction in their work: that is what should be encouraged, and it would need better education to show people how. Understanding was the key to the third condition also, the enjoyment of moral liberty, because that meant understanding oneself and one's desires. Good sense could help people tackle the fourth problem, which was loneliness, 'the supreme unhappiness', but an active social life, which was how most people countered this, was only a source of new servitudes: better be content with a few good friends. Money was not very important, its only value being to reduce insecurity. Power was demoralising; Payot was scathing about politicians, as ambitious parasites, but he was rather vague about who should take their place, beyond saying that politicians should be those who were 'naturally gifted' for government: this was the doctrine of each man to the task he was fit for. Payot was more interested in the family as a source of bliss. The only escape from boredom was to discover the poetry of daily life. One should get rid of domestic servants, because running a home was a pleasure to be enjoyed. Love of nature was the final consolation. And to put all this into practice, one needed to cultivate the mind, for happiness was ultimately a question of good sense and clear thinking. Though Payot favoured greater social justice, he thought happiness could be won by the mind triumphing over material adversities; and the poor peasant could be as happy as any man, enjoying the beauty of the fields, loving his wife and children, reading fine books; wealth was indeed more an obstacle to than an aid to happiness. Happiness should not be judged by appearances, and it was not true that only the wicked succeeded, for one could not be happy except with a clear conscience.[1] Payot, for all his criticism of intellectuals, represented the view of those whose main assets were education and will-power, a view that hovered between a desire to improve the world and an inclination to avoid contact with it. There was always an element of bitterness in this view, despite its apparent complacency. But it was a

[1] Jules Payot, *La Conquête du bonheur* (1921) and *La Morale à l'école* (1907), 242–3.

natural view for those for whom the acquisition of knowledge had been a constantly thrilling and rewarding experience; it was a view held not only by teachers and educated men, but also by the autodidacts and all those who regretted not having had a better education. Faith in knowledge as the key to happiness may not have been universal among some cynical writers, but it was extremely widespread in the middle and lower ranks of the literate.

The effect of social change upon this, and upon traditional views of happiness, often produced uncertain and confused behaviour. Thus aristocratic politeness got a new lease of life in some quarters, precisely because birth and wealth became such unstable criteria of respectability after 1914–18. Since one's origins or background mattered less, one's behaviour counted for more and etiquette books by the aristocracy were both sneered at and much read. Some aristocrats, for their part, attempted to modernise their doctrines. The duc de Lévis Mirepoix and the comte Félix de Vogüé, for example, offered aristocratic politeness in 1937 as 'the armour' that Frenchmen could use in their search for 'distinction' and social success. They argued that distinction manifested itself above all in conversation, which they held up as an 'intellectual dance'.[1] Others, by contrast, found a new pleasure in *Sweeping Out Old Customs*, which was the title of a rival book. According to it, it was now (1930) increasingly fashionable for people to reveal themselves to each other in the nude; there was nothing wrong with husband and wife carrying out their ablutions together, after having done their Swedish exercises. 'If I had a son, I would be proud if he took walks with a volume of Kant or Bergson in his pocket, but also if he carried a contraceptive in his wallet.' The relations between the sexes had changed and conjugal subjection could not be expected. Nevertheless the author advises girls to pretend to be silly and submissive, because that made life easier. There is a repeated emphasis here on pretence as a valid modern principle. People should pretend to treat workers as equals, because that would ensure the workers did their job more efficiently; a handshake would go down better than a tip, which might now be considered offensive; though with lazy workers

---

[1] Duc de Lévis Mirepoix and comte Félix de Vogüé, *La Politesse, son rôle, ses usages* (1937).

only an authoritarian tone was any use. He advised against wearing monocles, which made one look cold, but was in favour of gloves, which could give men an air of elegance; and for all his modernity, he still wore a cotton bonnet at night, to protect himself from draughts. The combination of freeing oneself from some traditional restraints and clinging to others, was a very common feature.[1]

An aristocrat suggested in 1948 that it was probably the workers and peasants who now had the strictest codes of behaviour.[2] This might have much truth in it, though it is, as always, difficult to generalise too broadly about them. Certainly in the middle classes there remained a strong phalanx among the older generation who made a virtue of deploring all change.[3] Catholics continued to be worried by pleasure, though to different degrees in different parts of the country;[4] but in the 1930s, and still more after the Second World War, some Catholic intellectuals attempted to reconcile happiness with Christianity—through the medium, above all, of sport, the open-air life and healthy living.[5] However, one of the commonest attitudes to happiness was possibly that which was dominated by superstition, as is shown in the advice given by Marcelle Auclair, editor of the supposedly very modern women's magazine *Marie-Claire* (founded 1937). She was a Catholic (though a divorced one) but her attitude to life was a mishmash of faith in God, astrology, fate, intuition and will-power. Her very successful guide to happiness was full of quotations from Christian authors and the life of St. Thérèse, but also of anecdotes about coincidences in her own life, which, she argued, confirmed her philosophy. It is a most interesting book, because it seems to reproduce so accurately the conversations that millions of people must have had. It illustrates how new ideas were simply added on to old ones, without bothering about contradictions. Marcelle Auclair once obtained five kilogrammes of coffee during the war, when it was scarce; she over-generously gave it all away to friends.

[1] Paul Reboux, *Pour balayer les vieux usages. Le Nouveau Savoir-vivre* (1930, reprinted with almost no alterations in 1948).
[2] Marc de Saligny, *Précis de nouveaux usages* (1948), 11.
[3] Giselle d'Assailly and Jean Baudry, *Savoir vivre tous les jours* (Maine, 1951).
[4] Theodore Zeldin, *Conflicts in French Society* (1971), chapter on Confession, sin and pleasure.
[5] René Rémond, *Oui au bonheur.* Semaine des intellectuels catholiques (1970).

Then, out of the blue, a reader of her magazine, who knew nothing about this, sent her a present of exactly that amount of coffee. 'From that moment I had an unshakeable faith in the great principles which govern the world and which we know so inadequately.' She escaped injury in the war because she had a presentiment that a certain place was dangerous and lo! it was bombed. Her advice was to adapt oneself to conditions around one—'revolt is a very bad mental attitude'—and to avoid letting misfortune depress one: there is always an angel, a friendly hand or one's intuition to help one out.[1]

Péguy wrote that a happy man is a guilty man. All the forms of happiness that have been discussed so far have involved compromise or repression, and an awareness of guilt was an inseparable part of them. The attempts to get rid of guilt were not successful. Those who came nearest to achieving this were those who sought to simplify life by forgetting about its ultimate purpose and concentrating on the diminution of discomfort. The accumulation of wealth and of material goods was, in many people's minds, equated with happiness. To those who had very little experience of wealth, it opened up new worlds of enjoyment, as well as new worlds of desire. Zola's *Au bonheur des Dames* (1883), describing the temptations created by the new department stores, revealed the disturbing effects of this change; and the historian Rolande Trempé has shown, in her study of the miners of Carmaux, how the chain effect was created, of greater expectations and greater desire for material goods developing as their standard of living rose. The most profound change in the factors involved in happiness that took place in this period was without doubt the increasing prosperity of the country, or at least the decline of destitution, which meant that more people were raised above the starvation level, and became capable of having priorities and choosing between alternatives. As both government and science claimed to be able to do more, so more was expected of them: Freud argued from this that the sum total of unhappiness had therefore increased, because men felt more frustrated when they saw science carry out such marvels in the physical world while it was seemingly incapable of making equally rapid progress in the spiritual and emotional spheres.

[1] Marcelle Auclair, *La Pratique du bonheur* (1956) and *Le Bonheur est en vous* (n.d.)

Certainly ill health may well have become more intolerable when there was more prospect of its being cured.

At any rate, in 1949 an international opinion poll revealed that one-third of Frenchmen considered themselves 'not very happy', which was the highest proportion in any country: the next highest was only 12 per cent in the Netherlands. France had the largest proportion of people who said they had difficulty in sleeping; only one-tenth admitted to being 'very happy', compared with half of all Australians and a quarter of Britons.[1] These statistics, for what they are worth, do not support the theory that industrialisation or prosperity produce unhappiness. Dissatisfaction with the social order does not necessarily imply unhappiness, as the magazine *Express* showed in 1969, when it asked people aged between fifteen and twenty-five whether they were happy: 35 per cent said very, 54 per cent said quite, and only 9 per cent said not.[2] It is impossible to be certain about the relationship between these replies and the events of May 1968, or indeed about the value of these answers in general. But it has been plausibly argued—with reference to France in the 1970s— that the majority of French people are happy but that they dare not admit it. Happiness has not become—as it may be in Australia, for example—a condition that it is considered proper to flaunt. In France, it has been claimed, the only kind of pleasure one is allowed to talk about is food, just as the English confine themselves to talking about the weather or gardening.[3] France's religious, social and literary traditions may well have kept happiness under the cloud of guilt; and before 1945 that cloud was doubtless larger. Perhaps that is why the French were, in that earlier period, associated more with pleasure than with happiness—with gay times rather than with deep satisfaction with life. This may well be a condition that favours the flowering of literature and art, and militates against devotion to economic expansion.[4]

[1] G. Rotvand, *L'Imprévisible Monsieur Durand* (1956), 95.
[2] Christiane Collange, *Madame et le bonheur* (1972), 27.
[3] Ibid. 90.
[4] Abbé Raoul Pradal, *Le Bonheur, fin dernière de l'homme. Étude historique et critique.* Thèse de doctorat en philosophie presentée à la faculté catholique de Lyon (Montpellier, 1908); François Mauriac, *Souffrances et bonheur du chrétien* (1931); André Maurois, *Cours de bonheur conjugal* (1951); Victor Hugo, *L'Art d'être grand-père*, in *Œuvres complètes* (1914), 8. 621 ff.

## Sport

It has been shown in another chapter how complex people's attitude to comfort was, and how relatively limited the increases in it were. But comfort and prosperity at any rate provided politicians with an easy method of measuring happiness. Increases not only in wage rates but also in productivity and trade came to constitute a new barometer. Economic science could thus claim to hold the key to the fulfilment of man's desires.

At the same time, however, the search for happiness seemed to involve turning away from work, to sport. Rousseau had observed that one of the effects of the civilisation of his time was that it transformed the happy child into 'a severe and irritable man'. Sport was one of the ways that perpetuated childhood, though it showed in the process that childhood was not as carefree as Rousseau imagined. Sport was also a result of a new relationship between work and leisure. It is sometimes argued that sport developed when people came to have more leisure, with the reduction in working hours and the invention of the weekend; but sport in fact developed before the laws reducing working hours; and the working classes were in any case the last to participate in the modern organised sports. People may well have had as much leisure in the middle ages as they do now; there were once nearly a hundred holy and feast days a year; free Saturdays are new, but previously workers used to take Mondays off, to recover from their Sunday orgies. The unique feature of the nineteenth century was that the adoption of factory methods made employers demand long hours from their workers, so that machines should never be idle; people probably worked harder in the early phase of industrialisation than they had ever done before, and certainly more regularly. One should see the growth of sport for the masses not as the cult of more free time but as a reaction against the lack of it; if they could no longer play when they pleased, they had to organise it after work. Sport, though it brought new rituals with it, was also a reaction against older rituals: the traditional village and religious festivals provided similar scope for relaxation, but they were governed by rules and everybody had to participate; the new sports enabled people to assert the individuality of their taste and their aptitudes. They brought about a new distinction between work and play. Sport institutionalised play into an apparently separate activity, and work was therefore looked at as more of a chore. This created a false dichotomy. In reality work and play were and continued to be intermingled. Peasants and workers had learnt to alleviate the severity of their toil by developing the social aspects of it into a form of play, and by compensating for routine with camaraderie; it was probably only in the early phases of industrialisation that workers failed to extract enjoyment from their factories, however dreary these were. But the more sport and leisure were distinguished as being dedicated to happiness, the more were the demands on satisfaction from work increased. It was professional people, and the clerks of the growing tertiary sector, who complained most about boredom, as they did about overwork, and they therefore played an especially active role in the growth of sport. Sport was thus much more than a way of filling in time: it represented both a continuation of the tradition of festivity and a search for liberation from it.[1]

A great deal was written about sports in this period, nearly all of it with a moral purpose. Many organisers of sport certainly believed that sport was a way of stimulating national prowess, improving health, taming violence and disciplining youth. These ideals did not preoccupy most of those who actually played games. A history in terms of these ideals would largely overlook the element of totally disinterested enjoyment that motivated most participants. Sports clubs had two sides to them. Their leaders included many who liked power, who were fond of organising, who wanted to receive recognition and decorations from the state for their public service, and who believed sport was a public service. The mass of members, however, were there to amuse themselves, to make use of the social amenities they offered, to drink and talk as much as to do physical exercises.

Sports seem to play a larger role in society in this century because improvements in communication meant that regional, national and international competitions were developed, and because sports were now organised in societies and federations;

[1] Alasdair Clayre, *Work and Play* (1974); M. R. Marrus, *The Rise of Leisure in Industrial Society* (Forums in History pamphlet, 1974), and his forthcoming book on 'The Emergence of Leisure in France'.

the whole appeared much larger than its parts. But many sports continued on traditional lines, and despite the centralisation of the country, most sports continued to be concentrated in certain regions only. Cock-fighting, for example, was a speciality of the department of the Nord. It had existed there for many centuries; it had been prohibited as cruel (and also, no doubt, as encouraging dangerous meetings) in 1852; but the growth of the cities led to its expansion none the less. In the first decade of the twentieth century, several new cockpits were built in Lille and Roubaix and in a single week in February 1904, 300 cocks were killed in that region. Roubaix in 1892 had twenty-five cock-fighting clubs; and in 1907 ninety-six societies, watched by 10,000 spectators, competed for several days. The municipality of Douai even subsidised cock-fighting, which attracted people from all classes. Gambling on the cocks was a widespread passion; breeding cocks was a form of luxury, like horse-breeding, which gave prestige to middle-class businessmen with money to spare. The north continued with this violent sport oblivious of the changes in the rest of France.[1]

The south, for its part, remained faithful to bullfighting. This again was an old French sport, though the French version did not involve killing the bull, but rather performing acrobatic feats around it. In the mid-nineteenth century, however, the Spanish *corrida* was introduced, and in the 1890s arenas were built in several southern towns. This sport again was prohibited by law (at least killing the bulls was illegal), but in 1896 prosecutions, claiming that 376 bulls had been killed in that year, showed that the law was easily defied. Fifty-five newspapers devoted to bullfighting were published in France between 1887 and 1914. But this sport failed to become a major interest despite all the efforts of commercial entertainment organisers, because it was made too expensive. It had been popular as a sideshow at local festivals when it had still been informal; but the builders of arenas recouped their expenses by charging admission fees too high for the masses. The one arena in Paris, opened in 1889, collapsed because it charged 6 francs for admission.

By contrast hunting, which was an expensive sport, prospered

[1] Richard Holt, 'Sports in France 1871–1914' (unpublished Oxford D.Phil. thesis, 1977).

precisely for that reason. It was run by noblemen and as one of them said, maintaining it was 'like rebuilding the Bastille'. Families gave themselves up to it with passion, like the four generations of the du Joncherays, the third of whom (who died in 1927) claimed to have killed 1,373 stags. Baron Jacques de Vezins, who kept sixteen horses and 120 dogs in the 1880s, was particularly famous for his record-breaking feats, but he was only one of many similar aristocrats. There were then seventy-three major hunts with over forty hounds each, plus several hundred small ones. In 1912 it was estimated that about 70 million francs were spent annually on this sport, even though it was largely confined to the west and to the Île de France, and had to combat a great deal of litigation from protesting small peasant proprietors. It brought social prestige and constantly attracted recruits from the *nouveaux riches*. Napoleon III revived it as a court pastime and President Fallières took it up also, showing that republicanism was not incompatible with enjoyment of *ancien régime* pleasures.

Shooting was another traditional sport that grew enormously in this period. In 1844 there were about 10,000 shooting permits, in 1854 76,000; in 1899 430,000; in 1922 one million and in 1924 one and a half million.[1] These are official figures, which may however indicate that the repression of unlicensed shooting was gradually more successful. But now clubs and syndicates proliferated to enable townsmen to participate: they could charge over 2,000 francs for a season, though fees of as little as 300 francs (with very doubtful supply of game) did exist. It may be, however, that fishing was the most popular of this kind of sport. In Annecy in the 1960s it was found that 26 per cent of the population engaged in fishing (when only 13 per cent engaged in team sports).[2] This was a good example of rural pursuits surviving urbanisation.

Sport, at the end of the nineteenth century, was made out to be something peculiarly English, but France in fact had a sporting tradition which was just as remarkable, even if the townsmen had forgotten it.[3] Sir Robert Dallington, visiting

---

[1] J. J. Verzier, *La Chasse. Son organisation technique, juridique, économique et sociale* (Lyon thesis, 1926), 14; Comte de Chabot, *La Chasse à travers les âges* (1898).
[2] J. Dumazedier and A. Ripert, *Le Loisir et la ville* (1966), 1011.
[3] J. J. Jusserand, *Les Sports et les jeux d'exercise dans l'ancienne France* (1901).

France under Henri IV, was astonished to find that the *jeu de paume*, which later developed into tennis (etym. *tenez*), was played more in France than in the whole of the rest of Christendom; 'the players are more numerous here', he wrote, 'than the drunkards are in England.' France exported tennis to England in the fourteenth century, and reimported it as an English game in the 1890s. *Hoquet*, likewise, was an old Breton game, played with great violence, but when it was reintroduced as an English game and modified into hockey, by the schoolboys of Paris in 1898, it attracted a totally new kind of player; and the Bretons did not recognise it, though it became popular in Anjou. In fencing, the French had developed a national style of elegance, agility and silence, and had specialised in the foil, but in the second half of the nineteenth century this gave way to a greater popularity of sword fencing; there was however still great rivalry between the sword, foil and sabre, as the fencing federation (formed in 1906) discovered. *Boules*, which in 1945 had over 5,000 associations and 150,000 officially licensed players, had ancient origins, but seems to have become popular only in recent times. The *boule de fort* variety played in the west, very similar to English bowls, and requiring a carefully prepared pitch, started only around 1850; the southern variety *pétanque* and the Lyonnais *boules* seem to have become important only after 1919, and to have spread very rapidly; they were essentially an alternative to immobile drinking in cafés, and often continued to be played near cafés. In the 1960s, 25 per cent of the population of Annecy said they played it.

Rugby, again, was related to *la soule*, *choule barette* and *mellé* which were played all over northern and western France from the twelfth century onwards, with a ball usually twice the size of the modern one, of wood or leather, filled with hay, moss, bran or air. It used to be played in the fields between two parishes, each of which tried to keep the ball in its own camp. Victory went to the side that could get it to their church door. Teams could be of any size, from ten to as many as a thousand; the games could last half a day; and all forms of violence were allowed. '*La soule*', wrote Souvestre describing it in Brittany in the early nineteenth century, 'is not an ordinary amusement but a heated and dramatic game in which the players fight, strangle each other and smash each other's heads . . . a game that allows one to kill an enemy without losing one's right to Easter communion, provided one takes care to strike as though by accident. . . . Blood flows . . . a sort of frenetic drunkenness seizes the players, the instincts of wild beasts seem to be aroused in the hearts of men, the thirst for murder seizes their throats, drives them on and blinds them.' (Compared to it, American football was child's play.) Edicts forbidding it had been issued in the eighteenth century; one showed that women participated, sometimes with the married challenging the unmarried. *Soule* had fallen into decay when rugby was introduced into France. This was a game with much stricter rules, but it attracted the same kind of parish loyalties, except that now it was larger towns that played it. Rugby was introduced into France by the English—by the Havre Athletic Club of English residents in 1872—and the first Anglo-French match was played in the Bois de Boulogne in 1877. An English schoolboy introduced it into the Lycée Montaigne in Bordeaux, and a pupil of that school who moved to the Lycée of Bayonne introduced it there. Clubs grew up in the small towns of the south-west in the first decade of the twentieth century. The Scottish player Alfred Russell, who later became captain of the Glasgow Academicals, came to Bayonne to learn French and translated E. G. Nicholls's book *The Modern Rugby Game* into French. A player of Bayonne went to study business in Wales and in 1910 brought back the Penarth Football Club to play in Bayonne. One of their players, H. O. Roe, decided to settle there and under his influence the Bayonne club developed the Welsh style, with much more hand-passing.[1] In the regional competitions, the success of this team, which now claimed that its style was 'Basque', as opposed to the 'Catalan' style of its rivals in Perpignan, was associated with a passionate fervour for Basque traditions, the Basque beret and red-striped clothes. The Paris team meanwhile was captained by the Scotsman Jack Muir, but though in 1914 crowds of up to 30,000 gathered to watch rugby games in the Parc des Princes, the sport was most popular in the south-west. In 1921 Béziers's ground was invaded by enthusiasts six hours before the national final was due to be held there. In 1924 there were 891 clubs. But there was little progress beyond that; rugby

---

[1] Claude Duhan, *Histoire de l'aviron bayonnais. Tome 1. L'Époque héroïque 1904–14* (Bayonne, 1968), 44–95.

remained a regional interest; and was overtaken by association football.[1]

In 1914 the Anglo-French football matches at Gentilly drew only 800 spectators but in 1919 the Football Federation was founded and Henri Jooris, a rich businessman of Lille, who was president of the Olympique Lillois and the Lions de Flandres, provided the financial backing. The small town of Sète established the best team in the country by an astute policy of buying and selling players. Professionalism raised standards and increased interest. In 1931 France beat both Germany and England. By 1943 there were 7,000 clubs and about 300,000 registered players, of whom about 300 were professionals.[2] This is a small enough figure, but it is treble that of 1939 and about eight times that of 1935. The great growth of football, as of so many other sports, took place above all under the Vichy government, which gave them encouragement as the Third Republic had never done. The unique feature of French sport was that it developed very largely outside the schools, or at any rate schoolboys who were interested had to form or join private clubs to participate. Sport was an alternative to school, except in the few progressive establishments, like the Collège de Normandie, which existed to copy English methods. That was perhaps why regionalism showed itself so strongly. The Anglomania which was at the origin of much upper-class sport affected only small groups in the senior classes of the best schools. Sport was still something that the rationalist school system could not comprehend. It was the Catholics who were keenest to develop sport among young people, because they laid so much stress on 'moral' qualities, and particularly after 1905 they saw in sport a way of attracting young people into their leisure organisations. The state abstained from allocating any credits to sporting clubs, so it was the national union of students which autonomously took on the federation of school and university sport: the teachers kept largely clear of it, partly because they considered it beneath them, partly because they feared responsibility for accidents, and partly because they were reluctant to run activities over which they did not have full hierarchical control.

[1] Georges Pastre, *Histoire générale du rugby* (Toulouse, 1968), i. 208; id., *Rugby, capital Béziers* (1972).

[2] Gaston Bénac, *Champions dans la coulisse* (Toulouse, 1944).

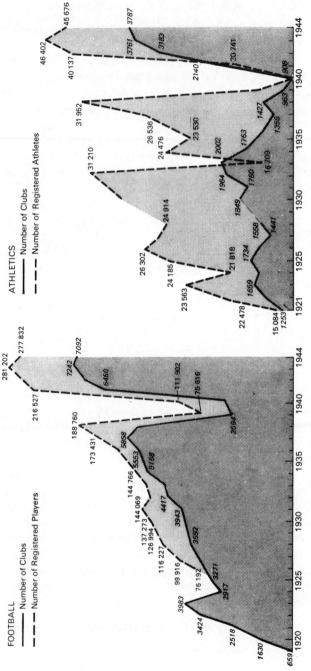

Graph. Football and Athletics (1919–44). Based on *Encyclopédie générale des sports* (1946), 33, 398.

What the state did approve of was gymnastics, because this had a clear didactic purpose. Gymnastics was made an optional subject in primary schools in 1850 and a compulsory one in 1869, and a part of the secondary syllabus in 1853, but this was purely on paper. Local authorities found the idea baffling: the general council of the Nièvre warned that children would lose their respect for teachers who 'engaged in exercises where the dignity of man can suffer cruel failures'. However, the defeat of 1870 transformed gymnastics into a patriotic duty and in 1880 four and a half hours a week of it were prescribed in every school. Numerous gymnastics societies were formed and by 1914 these had over half a million members. The idea was that the nation would be trained to beat the Germans with their own methods. These societies were noisily jingoist, their organisation military, their aim to teach discipline and movements in unison on the German model, rather than the individual agility that the Swedish school advocated. Membership was limited to French citizens. Both traditional sports and athletics were frowned on here, because these lost sight of the main purpose. But in practice the gymnastics societies were largely taken over by lower-middle-class people—shop workers, clerks and artisans—who used them for social purposes, and who spent most of their funds on dinners and excursions. The most military thing they liked doing was marching through the streets on festivals, dressed up and playing music, but there was probably more traditionalism than nationalism in this revelry. These clubs got official subsidies, and were one more way of milking the state. The proportion of non-practising members was soon far higher than those who actually did gymnastics: 'L'Ancienne Lorraine', in Paris, had only 91 active members out of 479. However, the shooting clubs which were often associated with this gymnastic movement were popular and led to successful national competitions, in a different town every year, from 1886; there were 3,500 such clubs in 1945.

Probably the most popular sport in France was cycling. No doubt the fact that bicycles were utilitarian as well as amusing made them popular, but in no other country has cycling as a competitive sport continued to attract so much public interest, even after the advent of the motor car. There are several factors that explain this. Cycling was the first sport that had a manufacturing industry behind it, and the cycle manufacturers showed great enterprise in stimulating racing and providing the finance to make this into a major national sport. Secondly, a specialised press developed which was exceptionally skilful at arousing interest, thanks to a number of remarkable journalists, notably Henri Desgranges, editor of *l'Auto* (combining car and cycle racing). As has been seen, he started the Tour de France to promote its sales, and made this into a national institution in the summer months. The press joined in to make heroes of the cycling champions, who should be compared to the stars of the music hall: men of humble origin who made good, like Edmond Jacquelin, the baker from Ménilmontant, champion of France in 1896, whose success made him so rich that he travelled around in a carriage with top hat and white gloves and had a box at the Comédie-Française, but who, like so many music-hall artists, died poor (1929) after a retirement spent in vain speculations: his invention of a street-cleaning tricycle was unsuccessful and his cycle-racing track became valuable—it was expropriated for a quarter of a million francs—too late, after his death. Just how much money could be made out of cycling was shown by Charles Terront (b. 1857) the son of a railway worker who had started life as a messenger boy for the Agence Havas, and who turned professional in the late 1870s. In 1895 he earned 6,000 francs by riding in sixty-five races, of which he won fifty-five. He retired in due course to become a cycle retailer and manufacturer. Another popular hero was Georges Paillard (b. 1904) champion of France six times 1928–34, who reached a speed of 137 k.p.h. Behind them were a new race of trainers and managers, like Paul Ruinart, who started in this profession in 1900 and claimed to have trained a hundred champions and to have made fifteen of them millionaires. Many cycle-shop owners and café keepers started up clubs to increase their custom. In 1898 there were twenty-two firms hiring bicycles in Bordeaux alone. Cycle racing was thus an industry as well as a sport, but it had the advantage that it was associated with cheap travel, easy movement, tourism, the discovery of the countryside and a new kind of holiday. By the time the car had become a more widespread means of transport, cycling had established an impregnable tradition.

Horse-racing started, like cycling, as a rich man's sport, but in its case, popularisation came from its success in opening up quite exceptional new opportunities for gambling. The state used to organise lotteries during the *ancien régime*, with great success. In 1789 it employed about a thousand people on this task but it made about 12 million *livres* out of it, at a time when the national budget was only three times that amount. However, because the system was full of abuses, it was abolished by the Revolution, but it was soon re-established, simply to bring more money in. During the Restoration some 50 million francs were staked annually, but in 1836 the state lottery was once again abolished, this time on the ground that it was immoral.[1] Though many lotteries were subsequently organised for specific purposes, as for the benefit of the singers of the Opéra (1859) and all sorts of other good causes, it was not till 1933 that the national lottery was re-established, to become an indispensable institution.[2] Horse-racing appealed to gambling instincts, but its attractions were more sophisticated, and it could be indulged with varying degrees of participation. The state had looked upon it with favour, because the improvement of breeding seemed to be a national and military interest; and it had fixed the rules and organised its beginnings. Already before the Revolution racing had been attacked for 'bringing confusion to fortunes and making the workers desert their workshops' but Napoleon I nevertheless revived it in 1805 and Louis-Philippe established the French Stud Book in 1833. In 1866 Napoleon III gave up control of racing (as he gave up control of the Artists' Salons) to the three leading societies then in existence, which specialised in flat racing, steeplechasing and trotting respectively. The aristocracy and the financial and industrial magnates put a lot of money into horse-racing, which they continued to dominate. The Jockey Club (founded in 1833) was probably the most exclusive club in Paris.[3] By 1845 there were over fifty provincial societies organising races and by the 1950s about 400, so horse-racing became not a weekly, but a daily event. In 1973 it was said that there were altogether 2,500 racehorse owners in France.[4]

[1] Jean Lénnet, *Les Loteries d'état en France au 18ᵉ et 19ᵉ siècles* (1963).
[2] Marcel Charpaux, *La Loterie créatrice* (1943).
[3] J. A. Roy, *Histoire du Jockey Club de Paris* (1958).
[4] Guy de la Brosse, *La France au galop* (1973), 74; cf. R. Longrigg, *The History of Horse Racing* (1972).

Under the Second Empire, gambling was organised by some 200 bookmakers shouting their prices at the Paris courses, on the English model. A favourite method was *poules*, drawing a horse's name out of a hat, so that it was pure chance whether one won. The courts repeatedly forbade all this, and in 1887 Goblet, the minister of the interior, enforced the prohibition, declaring that betting was 'a principle of demoralisation'. Takings at the racecourses fell dramatically and it looked as though the sport would collapse. It was at last realised that betting was an indispensable part of its attraction. So in 1891 a law established the Pari-Mutuel, which collected all the money staked and distributed it to those choosing the winning horse, with a small amount being retained as a subsidy for the societies organising the races and for various charitable works.[1] Bookmakers were officially abolished in 1905 but survived all the same. However, the horse-racing societies leased their rights to two firms, Oller and Chauvin, who ran the new system. In 1930 the Pari-Mutuel Urbain was established to organise betting off the courses, with agents all over the country. The stakes rose as follows:

| 1892 | 169 million francs staked | | |
|---|---|---|---|
| 1913 | 395 | ,, | ,, | ,, |
| 1920 | 1,324 | ,, | ,, | ,, |
| 1930 | 1,844 | ,, | ,, | ,, |
| 1938 | 2,567 | ,, | ,, | ,, |

The betting habit was unevenly distributed. In 1950 Paris led the field with 11·24 francs staked per annum per head of population, while rural departments like the Cantal, Aveyron, Lozère and Creuse staked nothing at all. By 1965 the Alpes-Maritimes were in the lead, with 208 francs staked per annum, followed by the Bouches-du-Rhône and Paris third: the north and south of France (including Corsica) were keenest, while the Creuse still showed least interest, with only 13 francs a head. Between 1951 and 1970 the amount staked on horses rose fourteenfold. It was the press that turned this (like cycling) into a national pastime.[2]

[1] At first the subsidy was for the assistance publique, then for hospital building (2 per cent), for supplying towns with drinkable water (1903, 1 per cent), for repairing war-devastation (1919, 1 per cent).

[2] E. G. Sabatier, *Chevaux, courses et jeu. Histoire des courses et du pari-mutuel* (1972); L. F. Gabolde, *Les Sociétés de courses* (1937); G. de Contades, *Les Courses de chevaux en France 1651–1890* (1892).

In 1925 Jean Prévost wrote, of *The Pleasures of Sport*, that 'The Greeks trained to adapt themselves to their civilisation. We train to withstand ours.'[1] This was only partly true, or at any rate it betrayed a peculiarly narrow definition of civilisation that intellectuals favoured. Intellectuals considered their function to be the classification of values, to show what the priorities among different activities should be, and they not surprisingly always placed contemplation and thought as the 'purest'. There was therefore a breach between the intellectualism the schools tried to instil and the physical pleasures sport cultivated. Jingoist gymnastics did not bridge this gulf. Sport was the object of much derisory contempt. The educational system allowed intellectually gifted children to reach the very top without playing games of any kind. However, the intellectual whose main physical movement was to smoke cigarettes was only one type among several. In its early days the cycling and motoring paper *L'Auto* used to have articles by Clemenceau, Tristan Bernard and Franc Nohain. The development by the sporting press of its own popular style soon cut it off from the intellectuals, but there were many writers and academics who nevertheless continued to have a foot in both camps. The development of sport in France in fact owed a great deal to university students and senior schoolboys, acting in rebellion against the routine of their curricula. The nationalist movement of the end of the nineteenth century and the conservative reaction of the pre-1914 generation brought a new emphasis on physical prowess. Thus the science-fiction writer J. H. Rosny, one of the founders of the Association of Sporting Writers, and long-jump champion of the world in his youth, did morning exercises throughout his long life, saying physical fitness gave him a greater sense of security, which affected even his intellectual work: he wrote that the bicycle was one of the greatest inventions in history, comparable to fire, writing and printing. Thibaudet pointed out that novelists had been so absorbed by the passionate and voluptuous side of the human body that they had forgotten the other aspects of physical energy, and sport was producing an ethic of its own as

[1] Quoted in Eugen Weber, 'Gymnastics and Sports in Fin de Siècle France', *American Historical Review* (Feb. 1971), 70–98, an important article by the first professional historian to study the subject in France. See also his forthcoming work on the Tour de France.

worthy as that of eroticism. Paul Adam wrote a book on *The Morals of Sport* to attempt to spell this out. Marcel Berger, the dramatist, who was an *agrégé des lettres*, had been a school discus-throwing champion, and published an explanation of what some still considered an eccentricity: *Why I am a Sportsman*. The poet Tristan Bernard became Director of the Vélodrome de la Seine. Raymond Boisset, another *agrégé des lettres* and 400-metre record holder, wrote on the *Spirit of Sport* giving an inside view of the Olympic Games. Henri Chabrol, one of France's most famous football centre forwards, and author of *Youth of the World*, was another *agrégé*, as too was Georges Magnane, a leading sprinter, who also boxed, did judo and studied at Oxford: his novel *Bête à concours* was an attack on 'degenerate students' who simply worked for examinations, while his *Les Hommes forts* praised the new kind of all-rounder. Joseph Jolinon, author of *Le Joueur de balle*, which became a classic of sporting literature, had the manuscript rejected by five publishers before it was accepted: he had been responsible for introducing football into the Catholic University of Lille in 1908. Pierre MacOrlan, in *La Clique du Café Brébis* (1919), described the failure of a schoolboy to receive approval from his parents for his successes on the sports field; he suggested that during their games children vaguely realised that they were at least temporarily no longer under the control of their parents, that girls preferred men 'who knew how to win a liberty that they did not desire for themselves', and that the emotions that sports aroused would produce a new way of writing books and of reading them. Paul Valéry was a keen cyclist, swimmer and rowing man who regretted that his generation had underestimated sport, which required the same qualities of effort, discipline, style, simplicity, that intellectual work did. Jean Giraudoux attacked the view that strong men were necessarily stupid and criticised the professors who praised the Greek hero of the open air only in theory, refusing to copy him in practice. Sport, he said, was 'the art by which man liberates himself from himself', that is, from the burden of an unwieldy, neglected body. 'Every human with a dull, bent or obese body is in some sense a beggar.' The sportsman, contrary to his reputation, was not dominated by his body, but knew its capacities, and so was capable of being more honest with himself.[1] Louis

---

[1] J. Giraudoux, *Sans pouvoirs* (1946); *Le Sport* (1928).

Hémon's *Battling Malone* (1925) defended boxing against puritans, who, he said, tried to ignore that life involved constant battles. The Prix Goncourt was awarded in 1939 to Philippe Henriat for his novel praising sport, *Les Enfants gâtés*. The conservative novelist Georges Duhamel, who attacked spectator sports, particularly as they had developed in America, took care to add that he was not hostile to sport itself: 'I have walked across half of Europe with a haversack on my back. I can, like any reasonable man, swim, ride a bicycle, drive a car, wield a racket and even row. I have for years used fencing as an exercise. I do not disdain physical exercise: I love it, I recommend it, I often long for it as part of a studious retirement.'[1] Pierre Loti was devoted to gymnastics, which he saw, like love, travel and books, as one defence against death that terrified him.[2]

Sport brought out the interest in physical pleasures which had always been important but which moralists had either neglected or attacked. There was a close link between these pleasures and the erotic joys that most novelists concentrated on; but it was a link that was barely realised in this period, and on the whole the advocates of happiness in its physical aspects divided themselves into two hostile camps, who condemned each other for, respectively, brutality and degeneracy. The sexual changes of the post-1945 period could take place only when that antagonism was resolved; and already some people had seen that it could be. But organised sport still played too small a role in French life for it to be possible for it to be understood outside its own circles. In 1946, a government official estimated that barely 10 per cent of young people between fourteen and twenty were involved in the sporting organisations then existing, and that street life, the cinema, dancing, and the café were more popular interests among them.[3] The importance of sport in the liberation of women—physically, sartorially and morally—has often been stressed, but it had not affected more than a small minority of women in this period. In 1893 only about 1 per cent

[1] G. Duhamel, *Scènes de la vie future* (1930).

[2] Cf. M. Maeterlinck, *L'Intelligence des fleurs* (1907); Raymond Pouilliart and J. Willens, *Le Sport et les lettres. Le Sport dans la littérature française 1919–25* (Louvain, 1953) and G. Pronteau, *Anthologie des textes sportifs de la littérature* (1948).

[3] Georges Denis (ed.), *Encyclopédie générale des sports et sociétés sportives en France* (1946), 22–3. This massive work is the best source for statistics on every kind of sport.

of cyclists were women: they were so noticeable precisely because they were so rare. The male sports associations were
originally hostile to female sports; and the women who played
football or rugby, and even those who cycled, were attacked by
the press as pursuing excessively violent activities. Women held
their first athletics championships in 1915, and challenged the
women of England in football in 1920, but it was only during
the Second World War that women's sports obtained anything
like widespread participation.[1] In the 1960s roughly one-half of
the French population took no part in sport and had no interest
in it.[2]

### Humour

What made people happy, and what made them laugh, was not
necessarily the same thing.

The idea of happiness implied a particular way of looking at
the world; and it is clear that not everyone was searching for it,
at least not with the deliberation it required. Happiness, as it
was understood by the people who gave advice about it, normally involved on the one hand thrift and on the other hierarchy.
It had to be accumulated gradually, saving up immediate enjoyment for the future, exactly like money. Some forms of pleasure
were regarded as better than others, in the same way as the
society of this time was composed of classes of unequal merit.
The affinity between happiness and capitalism was especially
striking in the views of those who held that happiness consisted
in doing one's duty, for there the criterion of efficiency was
decisive. Janet, professor at the Sorbonne, one of the leading
popularisers of this moral view, defined happiness as 'the harmonious and durable deployment of all our faculties in the order
of their excellence'; happiness was therefore not pleasure, nor
primarily a matter of feeling—let alone sensuality—but a problem of organisation.[3] Its attractions were most evident to those
people who were interested in rising in the social scale; it was
one form of ambition. It is clear, however, that many people

---

[1] M. T. Eyquem, *La Femme et le sport* (1944). For sport during the Vichy regime,
see André Frahier, *Sport et vie rurale* (1943); but for the inadequacy of facilities for
sport see M. Joffet, *Les Études et les réalisations sportives de la ville de Paris* (1943).

[2] Richard Holt, 'Sports in France 1871–1914' (Oxford unpublished D.Phil.
thesis, 1977) is the fullest general historical study.

[3] Pierre Janet, *Philosophie du bonheur* (9th edition, 1898), 20.

either did not think in this way or did so only intermittently. If one looks at this question from the perspective of those who were too poor or too miserable to entertain such hopes, and who were not primarily concerned with what other people thought about them, one sees that temporary relief from pain was the limit of their aspirations. Side by side with the long-term search for happiness, there was the more casual approach to life, aiming not at permanent contentment, but at momentary fun, not at married bliss, but at sexual gratification, and accepting even fleeting pleasure as a good in itself. This can be seen in the history of laughing, of eating and of drinking.

The creation of an American nation is said to have produced a people all of whom could laugh at the same joke. France had not reached that stage in this period. Laughter was not always approved of, nor as universal as might be assumed. It was impossible to conceive Christ laughing, wrote the author of a treatise on laughter, and in a perfect world laughter would be forbidden. There were both aesthetic and moral objections to it. On the first count, it was ugly, as proved by the general practice of covering one's mouth when one laughed; it was aesthetically undesirable also because it turned attention to the imperfect aspects of life, to what was ridiculous, instead of to the beautiful; and there was inevitably something inferior in an act for which no training was required. Morally, laughter contained too many elements of malice, rivalry and envy. Besides, 'the right to laughter does not belong to inferiors vis-à-vis their superiors'; laughter was dangerous as well as silly; it encouraged superficiality, and often obscenity too.[1] So laughter was repressed in the same way as sex was, and it is not accidental that people laughed about sex as much as about anything else. And yet France claimed to be a gay nation, the land of *gauloiserie*, of Rabelais and Molière, mistress of all the frivolous arts. These apparent contradictions need to be disentangled.

The barriers of propriety and of social pretension meant that there were at least three different forms of laughter—popular, middle-class and intellectual—in which Frenchmen shared in varying degrees. The poor did not have a totally different sense of humour from the rich, for the rich might enjoy jokes which

[1] Louis Philibert (avocat à la cour d'appel de Paris), *Le Rire: Essai littéraire, moral et psychologique* (1883), 450, 455.

Z

pleased the poor; but there certainly were class and cultural conditions on what made people laugh. Thus the peasantry of the mid-nineteenth century had a ritualistic humour, which centred around two particular institutions. The *veillée* was the evening meeting of villagers, at which they pursued their indoor tasks, the women spinning or sewing, the men making or mending tools, while at the same time stories were told and, on special occasions, games played and celebratory meals eaten. What amused people most at these *veillées* was the repetition of stories and folk-tales that everybody knew but nevertheless enjoyed hearing over and over again. Repartee consisted not in verbal fireworks but in recognising the appropriate proverb for different situations. The most popular jokes were practical ones, and brutality was not always absent from them. In party games, dressing up was a particular favourite, with the sexes swopping clothes or the poor pretending to be rich, or putting on soldiers' uniform or that of different trades; and disguised in this way, people would go round the village visiting; but the arrival of the 60-watt electric bulb helped to put an end to this, by making it too obvious. Mimes were another entertainment, particularly of weddings, with grotesque mothers-in-law as a principal source of laughter. Singing and card-playing (especially tarots) were popular, but dancing had to be controlled, so as not to frighten the animals. Until the end of the nineteenth century, these *veillées* were essentially village institutions, often attended by twenty or even forty people, and it was only in the twentieth century that they became meetings confined to family and friends, meetings that is in the realm of leisure, as opposed to the combination of work and pleasure that they used to be; but *veillées* held in stables were still to be found as late as 1940.[1]

These home-made amusements were supplemented by another institution, that of travelling entertainers, whose visits broke up the working day. There were troupes of actors, who put on historical or sentimental playlets, or pantomimes; there were magicians, clowns, acrobats and fortune-tellers; and later magic lanterns and travelling cinemas arrived. To this should be added the visits of the snake hunter, the frog catcher, the song merchant, the seller of holy statues, and on an even more practical

[1] Suzanne Tardieu, *La Vie domestique dans le mâconnais rural préindustriel* (1964), 140 ff.; Émile Violet, *Les Joies et les peines des gens de la terre* (Mâcon, 1946).

level, those of artisans of every kind of trade like glaziers, knife sharpeners, cobblers and grocers, and not least the smugglers— the most important being the match-sellers (who sold contraband matches, much cheaper than the state monopoly ones). Visiting tradesmen would very often be asked to stay to a meal. The variety would not be diminished by the fact that all the transactions were totally predictable, or even that the villagers would sometimes know the plays put on for them by heart, from having seen them so often. Novelty was not always a requirement of entertainment. On the contrary, much peasant fun simply involved finding opportunities for the uttering of old saws, which were a regular signal for laughter: more often than not, this meant spotting faults in one's neighbours or deviations from normality, like a man being cuckolded by his wife, or having his fly-buttons undone ('It is Saturday, his shop is open').

With time, the café took on an increasing role in social life. By the turn of the century Paris had 27,000 of them and France as a whole 413,000. This period marked the apogee of their importance, for their numbers have progressively declined since: in 1960 Paris was down to only 11,000. The cafés were to the late nineteenth century what the *salons* had been to the eighteenth, but a democratisation of them. The peculiar brand of sociability they encouraged lasted till the age of broadcasting, which provided a less personal entertainment and made it easier for people to stay at home.

The café concert was one of the inventions of the nineteenth century which added most to the gaiety and sociability of Paris. Dances and open-air concerts, which were increasingly numerous in the first half of the century, were only occasional events, but the café concert was an institution which made entertainment much more regularly, and casually, available. In 1865 the government restriction on the use of theatrical costume outside the few licensed theatres was removed, and the humble performers at the café concerts, who had hitherto been compelled to appear only in ordinary clothes, were henceforth given free rein for their talents. The casual approach was nevertheless preserved: what distinguished the café concert from the theatre was that there was no formality involved; one came when one pleased, in shirt sleeves or overalls if one liked; one ate and drank as one watched the show; one shouted applause, abuse and comments freely; one was always incited to join in the singing. Originally, ordinary cafés simply put on a little show in a corner, sometimes by professionals working for paltry fees, but as often by local amateurs. Maurice Chevalier, who later became France's leading music-hall singer, started his career in the very humble café concerts of the Parisian suburb where he grew up; it was because he admired the performers at the Palais du Travail, a small café in the rue de Belleville to which his mother (the widow of a drunken housepainter) took him every Sunday as a boy, that he chose the profession he did. His first performances were at the Café des Trois Lions and the Concert du Commerce, where workers, prostitutes and idle *déclassés* on tiny incomes went for their relaxation.[1] What they got had no pretensions to art, but it made sense to them. The songs were above all about landlords and concierges, mothers-in-law, creditors, bureaucrats, love, drink and duped spouses; dirty jokes were an essential ingredient, while references to recent political events or crimes were also much appreciated. The performers had to make themselves heard over the din of drinking and conversation, the cries of the flower sellers and the pedlars of sweets and other trifles; and they had to put up with smoking, which was allowed here (as it was not in the theatres).[2] Such was the popularity of these entertainments that speculators came in to expand and profit from them, so that they gradually turned into music halls, before finally ending up as cinemas. The entertainment industry remained small scale, however, seldom going beyond family firms, so the variety remained, and every pocket continued to be catered for.

At the top end of the scale was the Eldorado, which had the same importance in the history of French entertainment as Canterbury Hall had in that of London. Built in 1858 in the Boulevard de Strasbourg, aiming at something of the grandeur and solemnity of the theatres, embellished in due course with electric lights, it was the palace of variety, where the most famous performers were to be seen. Across the road, its rival the Scala, stinking of dirty lavatories and the violent perfumes of the performers, was frequented by a much lower class of person, and it was much noisier, though in the twentieth century it outdid

---

[1] Maurice Chevalier, *Ma route et mes chansons* (1946), 29.
[2] André Chadourne, *Les Cafés-Concerts* (3rd edition, 1889), 13, 163.

the Eldorado and was considered by far the superior of the two. The Moulin Rouge, immortalised by Toulouse Lautrec, was built in 1889, a large ballroom with tables in the gallery where one could drink while watching the show; and there was a large garden with fine trees outside where one could take the air in summer, watching the girls show off their black-stockinged legs and their petticoats, as they took rides on the donkeys. The owner, Joseph Oller (1839–1922), was a remarkable impresario, who also founded Le Nouveau Cirque, Le Jardin de Paris, Les Fantaisies Oller, Les Montagnes russes, L'Olympia, two horse-racing courses and the Rochechouart swimming pool: he was an inventive entertainer, but one who always got bored with every enterprise he brought to fruition. The Folies Bergère was originally the Café du Sommier élastique founded in 1869 to produce vaudevilles and concerts; when this went bankrupt in 1889, it was bought up by the Allemand family, owners of the Scala, who put the husband of their niece, Édouard Marchand, in charge of it. It was he who raised it to European fame, travelling all over the continent to recruit artists for his shows. On his death in 1901 it was taken over by the Isola brothers, who showed how the ambitions of these impresarios were growing. The Isolas made a fortune out of the Folies Bergère but then left it to take over the Opéra-Comique, where they proceeded to lose their money in their search for culture. But individual singers and comics also set up on their own. The best-known was perhaps Mayol, a smooth, charming, romantic singer, who was very popular even though the fact that he was a homosexual was said to have limited his audience: his Concerts Mayol became a major and long-lasting music hall. The Chat Noir in Montmartre has been written about more frequently, because poets and painters frequented it, but it quickly lost its genuine character and became a night spot for the bourgeoisie. The landlord, Rodolphe Salis, used to put on a masquerade of politeness, treating every client as a prince and addressing everyone by a title. Aristide Bruant (1851–1925), who was one of the performers there, moved out to set up his own establishment Le Mirliton, which used a gimmick of exactly the opposite kind: he insulted every client who entered, and served every drink with abuse: the delighted audience was taught the routine of greeting every woman who came in with a chorus of cries: 'O how pale she is'.

In 1900 there were perhaps 150 café concerts in Paris, but since their history has not been investigated, it is impossible to make more than a guess at the precise importance of their role in the life of the city, in the same way, for example, as it is possible to give statistics about the music-hall takings in New York. (There, in 1911, 700,000 people, that is 16 per cent of the total population, each week attended some forty 'low price' theatres whose takings were 315,000 dollars, compared to only 190,000 dollars a week earned by the theatres proper.)[1]

Inevitably, what survives of these café concerts is only a few photographs and drawings of the acrobats, magicians, comedians and musicians who performed in them. The only written records are of the songs. It is through them that one can try to get an idea of the sense of humour that prevailed in these audiences; one is helped also by the memories of the entertainers who sang the songs. The picture is blurred by the fact that a song-writing industry sprang up to cater for this market. This was concentrated in a little street between the Faubourg Saint-Martin and the Faubourg Saint-Denis (the centre of the café-concert world), the passage de l'Industrie, now renamed the rue Gustave Groublier, after one of the most successful of these writers. Aristide Bruant's songs give only an imperfect, or partial, idea of what was popular. He is famous because he was also an author and publisher, and that is a major reason why his songs survive and are easy to find. He ran a magazine, *Le Mirliton*, in which he printed his songs. Bruant shows how a song writer deliberately sought out themes to appeal to his audience. He was by birth a bourgeois but his father's death forced him to earn a living, as a jeweller, and then as a clerk in the Northern Railway. In his spare time he learnt music and frequented the cafés. At first he was horrified by the triviality and grossness of working-class slang, but in time he came to savour its richness and humour. He collected popular jokes and turned them into songs. He got part-time engagements in small cafés as his talents became known. He was probably more amusing and light-hearted in these early days: later, he specialised in laments on the sad lives of the down-and-outs of the slums, and biting satires on those 'who can eat and drink when

[1] Albert F. McLean, *American Vaudeville as Ritual* (University of Kentucky Press, 1965), 46.

they wish'. He became more and more of a showman; in his own café he always wore the boots and red shirt which were his trade-mark. He made a lot of money out of his singing and at fifty bought a farm in his native province, where he retired to write novels, journalism and a dictionary of slang. A gramophone record of his singing was made in 1924 when, at the age of seventy-three, he staged a come-back at the Empire theatre in the avenue de Wagram. From it and from his published songs, one can savour some of his boisterous pugnacity, which places him in the line of Pierre Dupont and Béranger, whose tunes were hummed as widely in the mid-nineteenth century. Though Bruant composed his songs from elements he found in the working-class and déclassé circles he frequented, there was a considerable element of art and artificiality in the finished product.[1]

The taste for dirty songs and dirty jokes, though much more difficult to document, can be illustrated from the life of Joseph Pujol (1857–1945) who is also quite revealing about the sort of people who were successful entertainers in this period. Pujol's speciality was farting. His performance at the Moulin Rouge produced, as Yvette Guilbert the popular singer recorded in her memoirs, 'the longest spasms of laughter, the most hysterical attacks of hilarity' ever seen in Paris. Nurses had to be employed to carry away the women in the audience whose laughter split their corsets and reduced them to agony or collapse. 'Le Pétomane', richly dressed in red and black silk, with a William II haircut and moustache, explained to the audience in a sober and serious way that he was endowed with unusual anal gifts, and that he would give imitations of a young girl, a mother-in-law, and a bride before her wedding night and on the morning after; culminating in the fart of the dressmaker, which lasted ten seconds and imitated the tearing of cloth. He inserted a hose into his anus and puffed at a cigarette attached to the end, and then played the flute with it. So popular was he that he built a theatre of his own, the Pompadour (1895), where he added imitations of birds and animals to his show, as well as a performance of black magic by his sister. So when Sarah Bernhardt was taking 8,000 francs at the box office, and Lucien Guitry 6,500, the Pétomane reached as much as 20,000 on a Sunday. He went

[1] A. Zévaès, *Aristide Bruant* (1943); *Le Mirliton* (1885–94); A. Bruant, *Dans la rue* (1889–95).

on tours abroad, being a particular success in Cairo, but he was forbidden to perform in Madrid and had to change to a clowning act at the last moment. He was the son of a stonemason who was also something of a sculptor, whose works are exhibited in the Museum of Marseille. He himself started life as a baker, but his family moved into show business; one brother became a peripatetic actor, ran a little theatre in Paris and also a lottery, but worked as a baker in bad times; his sister was a regular café-concert performer. He had ten children, who became either singers, comedians and jazz musicians or else bakers, potato-chips sellers or wine merchants. After the Great War, Pujol returned to baking and set up a biscuit and slimming-bread factory in Toulon which still survives in the hands of his descendants.[1] The cohesion of the entertainment world can be seen from the subsequent history of this family. One of Pujol's sons was apprenticed as a mechanic, but alternated between that trade and show business; his son, Marcel Pujol, was the famous Marseille cycling champion.

The stars of this comedy world were generally of humble origin, and they owed their success to their ability to perfect some trait in working-class life. 'Thérèsa' (born in 1837 as Emma Valadon) was one of the first of these stars. Originally a dressmaker, she became famous as the chief singer of the newly opened Eldorado. She earned the unprecedentedly large fee of 200 francs a month. The Alcazar then offered her 300 francs a month, provided she changed to comic songs; and eventually her salary rose to 233 francs a day. Her earnings were not the least amazing thing about her; connoisseurs doubted her talent, but she grew from a thin stripling to a large and heavily jowled matron, and crowned her achievement by publishing her memoirs, just as she fell out of favour.[2] She was perhaps more than anything a symbol of the myth of success, an example of how a humble girl could suddenly rise to riches, and she became someone with whom the poor could identify, in wishful thought. It is true she soon alienated them by her brashness and arrogance: that was one reason why stars rose

---

[1] Jean Nohain and F. Caradex, *Le Pétomane 1857–1945. Sa vie, son œuvre* (1967).

[2] Emma Valadon, dit Thérèsa, *Mémoires de Thérèsa de l'Alcazar, écrits par elle-même* (1865, reprinted six times); Albéric Menetière, *Les Étoiles du café concert* (1870).

and waned so fast. A more talented performer was Paulus (Paul Habans), who was the inventor of the practice of dancing while one sang: he won his fame for romping jollity with his song *Les Pompiers de Nanterre*, which he performed surrounded by actors dressed up as sailors and dancing a quadrille around him. In 1878 he moved from the Eldorado to the Scala, where he earned 150 francs a day; he later appeared at several shows in different parts of Paris in the same evening, travelling in his own carriage. He made a display of his prosperity, changed clothes for every song, bought a magnificent house in Neuilly, toured throughout Europe and the U.S.A., became the owner of the Eldorado of Nice, the Alhambra of Marseille, the Bataclan of Paris and a vineyard, the Clos Paulus, in his native Bordelais. His haircut 'à la Titus' was imitated by every aspiring actor. But he was eventually overwhelmed by his speculations and broken by his divorce: in 1906 a charity performance was given to raise money for him and he died a ruined man two years later. Paulus used to sing his songs in a stentorian voice. Inevitably the next star did the opposite: Polin sang his in a whisper, waving a handkerchief before his face as though to conceal his embarrassment at the dirty jokes he made. He was for long the leading male star of the Scala and the Ambassadeurs, and had his own magazine, *Paris qui chante*. Another star of the Scala was Fragson (real name Pot) who specialised in songs about the English, accompanying himself at the piano. He had worked in London as a boy; his command of two languages made him one of the early international performers; his inseparable attachment to his father, who accompanied him everywhere, was one of the oddities which won him indulgent affection; his death in 1913 —shot by his father, who became jealous when Fragson showed too much interest in a mistress—was a contribution to the aura of legend and gossip that was already surrounding these popular heroes. Dranem, who was made an officer of the Legion of Honour, was not only a great sad-comic, in enormous shoes, ill-fitting clothes and an American sailor's hat on his bald head —singing with his eyes shut, without a gesture—but also a hard worker in the cause of the growing number of unemployed and ruined entertainers; and his many marriages provided plenty of gossip to publicise him. There were a whole variety of genres: Sulbac (born 1860) specialised in peasant roles; he appeared dressed as one, uttering farming monologues in pseudo-patois and singing songs explaining what was happening in his village. Baldy played the debauched beau; Moricey was a sort of epileptic clown.[1]

Nakedness on the stage came early, though it is not certain exactly when. By the 1890s, however, there were already thirty strip-tease shows in Paris. The critic Francisque Sarcey described Mademoiselle Cavelli, the star of the Alcazar d'Été, 'doffing her hat, her dress, her petticoats, her corset, her pretty white and pink underwear, with a decent interval between each stage of her undressing to allow the spectators to recover their sang-froid'. Hugo, who was for twenty years *maître d'hôtel* at Maxim's restaurant, recalled that this did not take place only on the stage: at a dinner given by a newspaper magnate in his restaurant, with fifty guests, a pretty young blonde, completely naked, was brought in and sat in the middle of the table; after it was over, she got up and went round to collect her tips from the guests. The Concert Mayol began putting on strip shows only in 1934. In the following year a fan dancer, Joan Warner, was prosecuted, at the instigation of the National Alliance against Depopulation, and fined fifty francs, after a three-week trial, but another court ruled that advertisements of naked girls outside strip clubs were not an outrage to morals, provided the pubic hair was concealed. It was only after the Second World War that, under the management of Alain Bernardin, who considered himself an apostle of 'visual education', stripping laid claim to being an art and that Rita Renoir, one of its most famous practitioners, defended it as a valuable ritual ceremony.[2] But photographs of music halls in the interwar period show a large proportion of the girls naked from the waist up, and the clothes of female singers were always provocative, far ahead of current fashions.

Popular entertainment of this kind made people laugh for several different reasons. On the one hand it lyricised, romanticised daily life, taking the small talk of ordinary people and giving it brilliance by skilful mimicry and presentation. The

[1] Jacques Charles, *Cent ans de music hall* (Geneva and Paris, 1956); id., *Caf'Conc* (1966).

[2] Jean Charvil, *Histoire et sociologie du strip-tease* (1969); Denys Chevalier, *Métaphysique du strip-tease* (1960).

performers who came from the same background as the audience, and who neither talked down nor preached at them, concentrated on pleasing without pretension or tension. But there was also another kind of laughter which was to be found here, created by the reversal of roles and situations, and by the public flouting of decency. These café concerts were places where the respectable values of family life could be momentarily mocked. This is why the history of humour is such an important adjunct to every other kind of history. It shows the reverse side of respectable institutions, and shows that the burdens these institutions imposed were borne only because they were not always taken seriously, or at least because outlets were available where relief from their weight could be found. The endless jokes about mothers-in-law were one of the essential pillars of this society. Here, the battle between Vulgarity and Distinction, as one commentator put it, was regularly won by the former, for the crowds nearly always came down on the side of 'trivial jesting and coarse farce' rather than of beautiful singing.[1]

Between the wars, the French music hall was dominated by Maurice Chevalier and Mistinguett. The contrasting approaches of these two stars—who were for ten years the symbol of the romantic couple until they separated, estranged by their intellectual and temperamental differences—illustrate the complexities concealed behind the happy masks. Chevalier and Mistinguett were both great successes because of their charm— he was the handsome, dandy, relaxed young man, who never seemed to take either himself or life too seriously, who sang catchy songs as though simply to please himself, and who always tried to exude gaiety and good humour; she never claimed to have a pretty face, but she made herself attractive by her exuberance, vitality and impishness, and by the skill with which she moved and showed off her body (she insured her legs for half a million francs). Both of them came from very humble backgrounds, and knew how to flirt with the public even when they became very rich. Chevalier, however, had a passion for learning, he was always trying to improve his style, move with the times, expand his horizons. He came to embody many of the petty bourgeois ambitions of his countrymen; his songs were mildly philosophical and moralistic, subtly mixing old saws with

[1] Menetière, op. cit. 35.

a surface optimism, designed to forget rather than to deny sorrow. In old age he became an author and wrote his memoirs in nine volumes. He needed the consolations of philosophy, because he always feared, and exaggerated, the jealousy he aroused among his fellow entertainers; and despite all the invitations he received to dine with the most celebrated people of his age—kings, ministers, industrialists and men of letters— he was never at ease except with members of his own profession and with the working class from which he came. His mother and his job were his two anchors of security. He could not get on with Mistinguett because he found her too capricious, and a challenge to his independence. She said that he loved playing the role of gentleman, while she liked being the urchin, but that was misleading. Mistinguett said of herself that she was a practical woman. 'God created us to be happy . . . I insist on being happy', but 'speeding along the boulevards in big American cars at all hours of the night, dancing until dawn—that was my idea of living'. She bought du Barry's château in Bougival and had a lavish villa in Antibes. She had the reputation of being selfish, mean and a hard worker. She lived for the moment. 'Chevalier's presence', she said of their ten years together, 'never brought me very much, but his absence has dominated the rest of my life. . . . I loved him too much to want to understand him.' The performances and the private lives of these two popular heroes were more than just distractions for their countrymen: they expressed widespread aspirations and equally widespread frustrations.[1]

Popular humour can be studied more precisely in the theatre, both because the texts survive and because more elaborate jokes, appealing to a wider range of sensibilities, were offered here. The dramatic classics always had to fight against shallow, humorous entertainments which were put on by theatres seeking quick commercial rewards. Voltaire used to complain that 'the masses are not happy if one offers them jokes which appeal only to the intelligence: they want to laugh loudly'; he grumbled

[1] Maurice Chevalier, *Ma route et mes chansons* (1946), 216; id., *Londres, Hollywood, Paris* (1946), 15; id., *Temps gris* (1948), 17, 130–2, 157, 196, 204; id., *Par çi, par là* (1950), 9, 25; *Y a tant d'amour* (1952), 7–11; id., *Artisan de France* (1957); André Rivollet, *Maurice Chevalier, De Ménilmontant au Casino de Paris* (1927), 239, 247; Mistinguett, Memoirs, translated as *Mistinguett, Queen of the Paris Night* (1954), 135, 143, 163.

that the farces of Dancourt and Legrand had accustomed them to low and scurrilous comedy 'so that gradually the public has developed the prejudice that one-act plays must be farces full of dirt, and not noble comedies in which morals are respected'.[1] In the early seventeenth century there had been little difference in theatrical taste between the masses and the court, neither of them noted for sophistication or refinement, but from 1630 a new theatre audience developed, which was to be the counterpart of the *salons*, and which demanded higher forms of art. The Parisian populace, however, with time showed an interest in these plays also, and their presence in the pit—standing room only before the nineteenth century—was an important influence on dramatists. Voltaire used to hire a claque to make them clap and laugh; their approval was indispensable for the success of a play. The distinction between serious and popular drama was therefore not complete, and this meant that a play attracted wide attention, beyond the limits of a single class. When in 1791 the liberty of the theatre was established, forty-five new theatres sprang up in Paris: Napoleon ended this liberty in 1806 and allowed only eight theatres in the capital; but when liberty was restored in 1864, they multiplied once again and there were fifty-eight by 1875. Each tended to specialise in a particular genre. The Palais-Royal put on gay humour (and the plays of Labiche); the Gymnase went in for vaudevilles, Scribe and then realist plays—it was fashionable and literary; the Vaudeville was bourgeois, while Les Variétés and Les Funambules were more working class. A play put on at the Comédie-Française for thirty performances would be seen by 25,000 people. At the end of the eighteenth century, this major theatre had an annual audience of 170,000. The theatre was therefore an indication of popular taste, and an element in life as important as newspapers or novels.

Humorous plays had always been popular and the traditions of the medieval travelling players, variously called the Joyful Companies, the Fools, the Idiots, and the Scholars—whose favourite character was the naïve man getting into scrapes—were continued. The early modern comedies were never worried by fears of repeating themselves: stock types like the libidinous

[1] John Lloyd, *Paris Theatre Audiences in the Seventeenth and Eighteenth Centuries* (Oxford, 1957), 190.

old man and the naughty servant constantly reappeared, and always to receive their due chastisement or reward at the end. Humour was not taken seriously until Molière raised it to unprecedented heights and defended it as a dignified art, with a moral purpose; but because he introduced far greater depth and art into it, comedy for two centuries after his death was dominated by him and, with few exceptions, mediocre imitations of his genius became the rule: the public contented itself with noting how well the laws of drama were observed. But then, as a reaction against the five-act play, the *vaudeville* and the *revue* developed. The vaudeville was originally a happy song, and it then became a light comedy play, based around an amusing intrigue, with singing to some well-known tune. It developed into 'comic opera', and vaudeville became the branch of it without music. The revue paid less attention to plot and more to topicality: never aiming to last more than thirty or forty shows at most, it was, from about 1830 onwards, a popular form of satire. The Coignard brothers used to produce one every year under Louis-Philippe, at the Théâtre de la Porte Saint-Martin, one of the most successful being *1841 and 1941*, which made fun of all new inventions and the railways in particular; their *Îles Marquises* about a machine into which whole live sheep are inserted, to emerge at the other end transformed into ready-made overcoats and cutlets, was found so amusing that it was revived for the Exhibition of 1867. During the Second Republic there were a large number of reviews about politics, like *The Members of Parliament on Holiday* and *Property is Theft*; under Napoleon III, politics was forbidden, so writers turned their sarcasm on to every other aspect of life. *La Revue des Deux Mondes*, by Clairville and Abraham Dreyfus (1875), made fun of the press and the literary world, in a style that foreshadowed the tendency of authors and comics to talk increasingly about their own worlds, with jokes that outsiders could barely understand; but this revue had an amusing idea as its base: a provincial *pâtissier* bequeathed a sum to the *Revue des Deux Mondes* to award a prize for the best literary work of the year: the editor, accompanied by a woman reporter, go on a tour of the opera and theatres, which gave opportunities for a whole series of parodies of the shows and actors of the day. The decisive factor in the success of the revues was the skill of the performers; few of the texts were published. The vaudeville is therefore easier for posterity to appreciate, though it has barely been investigated. Jules Janin, writing in 1832, claimed there were 168 vaudevillists in his day. But the author who dominated this genre was Scribe (1791–1861). He specialised in perfect plots, where everything worked out in the end, with an unexpected explanation. He is important as the incarnation of anti-romanticism; he had a wild success and earned several million francs by attacking romanticism, just when romanticism was most fashionable: his play *La Camaraderie* (1836) mocked the mutual praise that the romantics gave each other.[1] Under the Third Republic Victorien Sardou (1831–1908) continued Scribe's methods, with the stress above all on intrigue, so that human characterisation was largely forgotten. Feydeau (1862–1921) represented the farcical culmination of this entertainment. He raised vaudeville to the level of higher mathematics, taking logic to its limits and fantasy to absurdity. His farces were, in effect, alternatives to detective stories, or to crossword puzzles, but with the clock-work inevitability of the action made ridiculous by merciless exaggeration. This kind of play was performed at a fast rhythm, with a liberal use of stereotyped gestures, so that it bordered on pantomime, and indeed it is said that some of Feydeau's farces produced so much laughter that the final scenes were played as pantomimes, because the actors could not make themselves heard above the din. Feydeau, who descended from an *ancien régime* marquis, was the son of the author of *Fanny*, condemned by the Archbishop of Paris for impropriety. He said he became a writer from laziness; he started writing plays at the age of seven, producing such pride in his parents that he was let off homework; his first play was put on when he was twenty-one. He then gambled his considerable royalties on the stock exchange, losing several million francs, and had to go on writing in order to pay his debts. He was reduced to living in a single room at the Hôtel Terminus St Lazare, and to drinking Vittel cassis at the café Napolitain, his favourite haunt. Despite the industrialisation of entertainment, the insecurity of the theatre somehow survived.[2]

[1] Maurice Descotes, *Le Public de théâtre et son histoire* (1964), 287–90.

[2] Marcel Achard *et al.*, 'La Question Feydeau', *Cahiers Renaud-Barrault* (Dec. 1960), no. 32, special issue. Cf. Henri Beaulieu, *Les Théâtres du Boulevard du Crime 1752–1862* (1905); Jacques de Plunkett, *160 ans de théâtre. Fantômes et souvenirs de la Porte Saint Martin* (1946).

Feydeau's farces were capable of repetition because they were based on absurd situations, with no realism to go out of date; and they provided great opportunities for actors. Labiche (1815–88) was more richly amusing but he wrote for his time, and his favourite subject, the problem of arranging marriages, of passionate interest to men on the make during the Second Empire, was presented in too simple a way to survive. Labiche had no desire to do more than make people laugh; he was extremely modest about his work, and consented only reluctantly to the publication of his collected plays. He wrote about 175 in all; in 1856 he had as many as eight performed: after 1860 he was, with Offenbach, the acknowledged master of the humorous theatre. But in 1877 he stopped writing, having invested his earnings in a 900 hectare farm, and preferring to devote his time to his new role as village mayor. His history is a success story dreamt of by many young men about town. He was the son of a syrup manufacturer; he wrote funny plays because he liked laughing and because he had no serious ambitions. He mocked the bourgeoisie, and they flocked to see themselves mocked; Labiche was a mild satirist, whose humour was like a vaccination, which ultimately reinforced the complacency of his audience.[1] But the passages in his plays which, according to contemporary accounts, drew the loudest laughter, now often seem insignificant, because the gestures and style of the performers were all important. Labiche was fortunate in having the amiable Geoffroy as one of his main actors, whose interpretations ensured that the plays came across not as satires on the audience, but as jokes at the expense of their neighbours. Labiche's characters, particularly his female ones, were unremarkable when they were not dull: it was the scrapes they got into that were amusing. Labiche catered therefore for a public which had developed certain habits of laughter; certain kinds of jokes were always successful. The joke which dominated all others was the ridiculousness of the bourgeoisie—an essential counterpart to the rule of the bourgeoisie that is supposed to have been established in this period. That is another reason why his humour appears either dated or formalistic. It is important to bear in mind that side by side with the liberal and progressive

[1] Philippe Soupault, *Eugène Labiche* (1964). See in particular his *Perrichon* and *Le Chapeau de paille d'Italie.*

developments of this century, which tend to monopolise the attention of history, there was also a vast body of third-rate plays and farces, which produced endless laughter by repeating jokes about things like *avant-garde* painting, Wagner, and the equality of the sexes.[1]

A more biting and sadder kind of humour was presented in the plays of Courteline.[2] Here humour consisted in the expression of the dreams and animosities of the petty bourgeoisie, but from the point of view of those of them who had not succeeded in life, and had little hope of doing so. What Courteline wrote about was the reverse side of ambition. He made laziness and failure tolerable. Courteline, again, came from modest stock and from a family of entertainers: his grandfather had a tobacco shop; his father was a banker's clerk who wrote many successful comic operas, libretti for Offenbach and amusing accounts of criminal trials for the *Gazette des tribunaux*. It was a family that was steadily rising into the lower middle class, but Courteline found the pressures to continue this rise unbearable. He was sent to a good school, which only filled him with a lasting horror of education and of the repressive, monotonous methods of schools. He looked back on his childhood with pain, saying schools 'brand children, like a red-hot iron, with a melancholy which time can never heal'. He was put into business (as a clerk in the firm of Bouillons Duval) but he lasted only a few weeks. Military service roused bitter resentment at the severity of the discipline, the constant punishments and the futile tasks: he got himself certified ill and spent six months convalescing from the ordeal. Finally his father set him up as a junior civil servant, at 100 francs a month, in the ministry of religions: this was a secure job, even if the wage was no more than a labourer's. Courteline could not bear it. He hated work. He much preferred sitting in cafés, watching the world go by, at most playing cards. To his father's fury, he had no desire to make a success of life; he used to absent himself from his office for extraordinarily long periods, but with impunity, because his boss liked to patronise the arts and also valued having a journalist on his staff, who could protect him against attacks in the press (this was the period when the ministry of religions was in the thick of its

[1] Cf. Félix Gaiffe, *Le Rire et la scène française* (1931).
[2] Real name Georges Moinaux (1858–1929).

battle against the Church; the boss was none other than Dumay, one of the main architects of the disestablishment of the Church). Finally, Courteline gave half his salary to an unemployed friend, who went to the office to do his work for him, carefully forging his signature. He was free now to devote himself to journalism and playwriting, which he had taken up at a young age to supplement his meagre salary, but also to fulfil his deeper ambition to be a travelling actor. He toured France with the Tournet Baret, a repertory company founded in 1889 by Charles Baret, a pharmacist's son (another social misfit).[1] He gave little talks before the performance of his plays, and he took parts in them; he wanted to be a complete man of the theatre. He alternated between a quiet sedentary life, centring round his café—'it is less difficult to change one's religion than one's café' he said—and restless travel: he went on tours of Belgium and Holland, accompanied by Zipette, the pornographic photographer. He lived with an actress by whom he had children, but he could not bear children and sent them away to their grandparents. He was both obsessed by women and despised them, treating them as 'instruments of pleasure'. He visited brothels and slept with many of the actresses who appeared in his plays, but he was always dissatisfied with sex: though he constantly wrote about this, he entitled a chapter in his *Philosophy* (a collection of maxims he published in old age)[2] 'Things of little importance: love, women etc.'. He quarrelled endlessly with all his women, but he eventually married his mistress on her death-bed, and then indeed married another. Quarrelling was an essential part of life for him: he loved making scenes in his café when he got the wrong change; he was violently angry when he was contradicted and always insisted on having the last word: he had a passion for practical jokes but was furious when he was a victim of one. He was a mass of contradictions and clarity of thought was never his strong point: he was anticlerical, but he solemnly took off his hat when a religious procession passed; he mocked medicine but was always consulting doctors; he called himself 'a bohemian whose bourgeois background

---

[1] The Tournet Baret has survived to the present day, being continued under the management of Janvier, the son of one of the principal performers of Courteline's plays.

[2] *La Philosophie de Georges Courteline* (1917).

bothers him and makes him go to bed too early'. He was made miserable by an inferiority complex, which the enormous success of his plays never diminished. He declared that he had no imaginative gifts: he was only 'a sculptor of umbrella handles'. This was probably what lay at the bottom of his horror of work. At forty-seven, just when he was reaching the apogee of his fame, he stopped writing, saying he hated working and he could afford to stop. He spent the rest of his life in provincial retirement, going daily to his café, playing bridge, gossiping with his cronies. The world, he said, was divided into two classes of people, with totally distinct mentalities: those who went to cafés and those who did not.[1]

The humour of Courteline's plays made game of all these dissatisfactions. It was humour for a definite class of people—nearly all his characters were from the middle and lower bourgeoisie—and it made fun of their plight by showing up the contradictions they had to cope with, and the absurd situations from which they could not escape. The plays were about civil servants, soldiers, lawyers, journalists, actors, cab-drivers and bus conductors faced by the problems of the big world and by the frustrations of their own inadequacies; they were a tirade against stupidity, selfishness, laziness, pride, irritability and dishonesty, but they pointed no moral. Courteline had no solutions. He held out no hopes, because in his own life he had found the business of growing up infinitely painful. His constant refrain was a lament for his lost youth and a curse on advancing age. 'I loved my youth madly,' he said. 'I loved it with passion, like a mistress for whom one would kill oneself.' The motto he asked to be put on his tombstone was: 'I was born to remain young'. He denied that every age had its pleasure, saying youth alone had any. So his life was dedicated to *s'en foutre*, as he said, to mock and forget. The characters in his plays were overwhelmingly unsympathetic: only sixteen out of 275 male ones, it has been calculated, and only two out of the 65 female ones could be said to be likeable.[2] Courteline felt deeply insecure about the loyalties around him: he never tired of 're-reading the letters from mistresses who have deceived me and friends who have

[1] Pierre Bornecque, 'La Vie de Georges Courteline' (unpublished doctoral thesis, Montpellier, 1968).

[2] Pierre Bornecque, *Le Théâtre de Georges Courteline* (1969), 453-4.

betrayed me'. He wrote a great deal about betrayal, and about the problems of gratitude and obligation. Monsieur Badin 'the clerk who did not want to go to his office', but who lived in terror of losing his job, was presented as a funny character, but only because his dilemma was so real to both Courteline and his audience. Courteline was not a revolutionary, but his humour fits into the broad category of humour that is protest if not revolution, and is an armchair substitute for real insurrection.

The manufacturing of humour by professional entertainers increased enormously in this period, and nowhere was the increase more pronounced than in humorous journalism. The growth of printed humour was on a hitherto unprecedented scale. It could perhaps be argued that this humour was an answer to the greater stresses and complexities of life, and that sharpened sensibilities, which laid people more open to frustration, also included a developing appreciation of the ridiculous; but, in the present state of knowledge, such a view could not be easily substantiated. The humorous press, rather oddly, is one of the least studied aspects of literature and art. Most of the caricaturists of this period are little more than names, and the ideas behind their activities are difficult to discover. It was in 1830 that journals devoted entirely to caricature first made their appearance. Of course there had previously been a considerable production of humorous prints, which continued, but the publication of humorous journals greatly widened the scope and the impact of caricature. Charles Philipon (1800–62) was the organiser of this development.[1] He was interested first in making money, and secondly in attacking the government in a new way. *La Caricature* (1830) and *Le Charivari* (1832) were above all republican papers, ridiculing King Louis-Philippe, and Philipon was sent to prison for his famous caricature turning the king into a pear; but at the same time ridicule was poured on a vast variety of subjects—the latest hairstyles, plays, inventions, fashions, as well as soldiers, barristers, prostitutes and the inevitable 'bourgeois'. Philipon's achievement was to bring together some twenty artists and to give them a regular supply of ideas. After 1835 *Le Charivari* became, for a time, a daily and it was for this paper that Daumier created Robert Macaire, the

---

[1] Edwin de T. Bechtel, *Freedom of the Press and l'Association Mensuelle. Philipon versus Louis-Philippe* (New York, 1952); J. Prinet and A. Dilasser, *Nadar* (1966).

incarnation of the modern speculator, and that Grandville produced his fantastic transformations of humans into animals, and his enormously detailed studies of political demonstrations. Caricature became such an important political weapon that every party came to have its own funny paper: the monarchists had *Le Triboulet* (1878–93), the Bonapartists *Le Droit du peuple* (1885–6), the Boulangists *La Diane*, the republicans *La Lune* (1865–8) and *L'Éclipse* (1868–1919). It does not seem that everybody found the same things funny, for almost every occupation and every interest came to have a humorous paper, both with jokes which appealed to it and as an instrument of attack against its enemies. Soldiers had *La Vie militaire* (1883), sportsmen had *Le Centaure* (1866); tenants had *L'Anti-Concierge* (1881–2); the beer industry had *Le Bon Bock* (1865) to denigrate the Germans; advertisers had *Le Comique-Annonces* (1885); bankers had *L'Éclat du rire* (1877) and *La Vie de la Bourse* (1882). Parisians of Provençal origin had *Le Tartarin* (1884). The most famous paper to combine both political satire and jokes which only the initiated could understand was *Le Canard enchaîné* (founded 1915); it has made itself into something of a national institution, incarnating the resistance of the small man to authority and conformity, while clinging tenaciously to such prejudices as anti-militarism, anticlericalism, respect for education: the *instituteur* was always sacred to it.[1]

During the Second Empire political journalism was restricted, and so a great deal of energy was switched instead to newspapers that would entertain. *La Vie parisienne*, founded in 1863 and lasting till 1949, had as its original sub-title 'the elegant life, topics of the day, fantasies, travel, theatre, music, fine arts, sport and fashion'; it attempted to provide mild relaxation for those with too much leisure: it won a firm foothold by being very well informed on women's fashions and on Paris gossip in general, but it attracted male readers by dealing with these subjects in a titillating way. Its most successful issues were reprinted as mild pornography, but just mild enough to escape prosecution. When in 1890 a rival paper was brought to trial, its defence lawyer complained that the supposedly respectable *Vie parisienne*, catering for well-to-do society, was no better: its speciality, he said,

[1] F. Batailler *et al.*, *Analyses de presse* (1963), section on 'L'Idéologie du *Canard enchaîné*', 91–176.

was to show how women put on their stockings, 'in which all positions are shown, with plenty of indiscreet glimpses and it is not always the garter which marks the boundary limiting the sight offered to the spectator'. It would have a page of cartoons on 'how women take their baths, in baths which seem to be made of crystal; a page on how to put on a blouse, which arouses no preoccupation other than the desire to remove it from them'. There were infinite and subtle gradations in the scatological press. One of the papers that often got into trouble with the law, but which was also one of the most distinguished artistically (with Willette, Forain and Louis Legrand drawing for it), was *Le Courrier français* (1884–1913). It was read because its staff seemed to be 'at once boldly *avant-garde* and worryingly and scandalously paradoxical'. It was backed financially by the Geraudel pharmaceutical firm, and advised its readers to buy the pastilles of that name before they opened the paper. *L'Événement parisien* (1880–2), which was perhaps one of the most pornographic, was also one of the most successful; its highly profitable sale of 150,000 copies made the fines and convictions easy to bear.[1]

Professional humorists were very often bitter satirists, but it would be wrong to deduce that, generally speaking, French humour was always acid. Superficially, it is possible to argue that, in so far as there was such a thing as specifically French humour, it was more often than not biting and an instrument of attack. This would fit in with Coleridge's criticism of the humour of Voltaire, as being devoid of the pathos that gives humour its magic charm, and Carlyle's comment that Voltaire's laughter represented gaiety of the head, not of the heart, showing contempt but not sympathy; it would suggest that, because of a more turbulent political and social development, France did not experience the same transformation of humour that occurred in England at the turn of the eighteenth and nineteenth centuries, when the satirical tradition of the Restoration gave way to a more amiable sense of fun, in which eccentrics were presented as objects of delight and love, and the picturesque and the incongruous were portrayed with affection, not with

[1] Philippe Jones, 'La Presse satirique illustrée entre 1860 et 1890', *Études de presse* (1956), vol. 8, no. 14, 7–116. Cf. 'Les Journaux pornographiques', anonymous article in *Annuaire de la presse française* (1881), 91–119.

irony.[1] This argument would have it that England's complacency and stability in the nineteenth century were reflected in its humour, though after 1918, when that social background vanished, a more tough-minded style returned. But the bitterness of professional French humorists, such as it was, perhaps reflected the different social status of the artist and writer in France. Humour and caricature were low genres, which seldom led to honours or official recognition, and those who earned their living in this way were professional nonconformists. The angry humorists have attracted more attention from posterity, partly because they had more to say and said it with greater force; but this should not lead one to neglect the not inconsiderable number of happy humorists. Side by side with the gay paintings of the Impressionists, for example, there were successful caricaturists like Linder, Morlon, Numa, Guirard and Vernier who specialised in showing the joys of existence and the exuberance to be found in ordinary life. There is no bitterness and much ingenious fun in the cartoons of Albert Robida (1848–1926). He was an artist of great modesty, who lived quietly in Le Vésinet with his seven children; the son of a carpenter, his father had tried to make a notary's clerk of him, but Robida's inventive imagination turned instead to science fiction and to fantasy, which was always innocent.[2] Alphonse Allais (1855–1905) was his counterpart in prose. The son of a pharmacist, trained as a pharmacist, he gave up his career just before his final examinations and took up the café life, spending his time moving from one to another, and doing all his writing on their little tables, with endless drinks to help him along. He made fun of everything, pushing every situation to absurdity, using his scientific knowledge to imagine extraordinary inventions to cure common troubles. He proposed, for example, the nationalisation of the umbrella-making industry, so that umbrellas could be made in different sizes, with a view to diminishing the frequency with which they collided in the street; he stood for parliament with a programme advocating the abolition of the tax on bicycles, the re-establishment of licence in the streets so as to increase France's dwindling population, and the

---

[1] S. M. Tave, *The Amiable Humorist. A Study in the Comic Theory and Criticism of the Eighteenth and early Nineteenth Centuries* (Chicago, 1960).

[2] A. Robida, *La Vie éléctrique* (1895); id., *Le XIX^e siècle* (1888).

suppression of bureaucracy and the School of Fine Arts. He called his humour literature for the commercial traveller. It enabled him to earn 20,000 francs a year, buy his furniture in England and have a magnificent bathroom with constant hot water. It is true his gaiety was ambiguous, tarnished by a marriage to a pretty girl much younger than himself and ending in near-bankruptcy. Not everyone thought he was funny, even though he laughed so much. Madame Waldeck-Rousseau refused to use her influence to get him decorated, saying she found him stupid.[1]

Matthew Arnold claimed that what was attractive about French frivolity was that it took as its base 'the average sensual man', accepting the wishes of the flesh as part of life and so producing a much more relaxed kind of fun than the Englishman's doubts and repressions allowed. That France was a Catholic country and that puritanism had never won complete supremacy in it were certainly important factors, and perhaps comparisons with Irish humour would be more useful than with that of England or the U.S.A.[2] The vitality of the Rabelaisian tradition of gross humour was certainly emphasised by the extraordinary success of Gabriel Chevalier's *Clochemerle* (1936), a story about a urinal. There was no malice here but only laughter at what people had in common. The book has no individual characters, but only types, who give pleasure because everyone can recognise them as true. This was the laughter of sociability overcoming shyness and prudery.[3]

However, it is true that there was often great sadness behind much humour. The transformation of gaiety into gloom by the intellectual can be seen rather strikingly in the history of pantomime. Pierrot and Harlequin were originally happy characters, in a simple way, but the romantics turned them into philosophical commentators on the tragedy of life. The intellectuals discovered pantomime in the 1830s, when J. G. Deburau who used to play Pierrot at the working-class Théâtre des Funambules was turned into a fashionable hero by Charles Nodier and

---

[1] Anatole Jakovsky, *Alphonse Allais* (1955); *Tout Allais* (1964), a reprint of his works, in ten volumes.

[2] Francis Halkett, 'The Frivolous French', *The Atlantic Monthly* (Boston, June 1926), 726–33.

[3] Gabriel Chevalier, *Clochemerle* (1936); Marcel Tetel, *Étude sur le comique de Rabelais* (Florence, 1964).

Jules Janin. Deburau was a great change from the stock situations and stock types of the theatre of the time; he became a
symbol of the pure working class, and was seen as the creator
of fantasies that could distract one from the ugly realities of life.
Formerly the heroes of pantomime were Harlequin and Colum-
bine, young lovers who eventually triumphed over all obstacles.
Now Pierrot, who was always the victim, deceived and punished, took on the central role, and as Deburau became more
famous, he made Pierrot vicious also, hitting back and getting
his way too. In the 1880s, the macabre side of the clown was
greatly accentuated, to the point that he sometimes wore black.[1]

Daumier was one of those who portrayed these clowns as sad,
because he saw behind them the insecure, despised, wandering
artist, with whom he sympathised and identified. It is, however,
very difficult to characterise Daumier's work as a whole by any
simple formula, for though (at the last count) no less than 340
books and articles have been written about him, Daumier left
very few explicit indications of his aims or ideas. In the early
part of his career he was given his subject-matter by Philipon,
who also provided the legends to go under the cartoons, or
employed witty young men to write them for a small fee.
Daumier was a republican, but he also nourished frustrated
ambitions to be a painter; he was a caricaturist mainly to earn
his living and was always hoping he could concentrate on
grander forms of art. He was the son of a glazier, and like his
father he was an artisan who produced for the market. He
was not verbally fluent, but a quiet, contemplative and steady
worker, whose interest was probably above all in visual observation and the expressive recording of life around him. His most
revealing remark—one of the few he made—was 'It is necessary
to be a man of one's time'. His contemporary, Champfleury,
who knew him well, argued that caricature was 'the expression
of the intimate sentiments of the people'; it was cruel, because
it reflected the feelings of revolt of a people in a state of revolt;
and it was significant only in periods of revolution. A great deal
of Daumier's work was a satire on the bourgeoisie, but it was not

---

[1] V. J. Rubin, 'Clowns in Nineteenth Century French Literature: Buffoons,
Pierrots and Saltimbanques' (unpublished Ph.D. thesis, Berkeley, California, 1970);
F. Haskell, 'The Sad Clown: some notes on a nineteenth century myth', in
U. Finke, *French Nineteenth Century Painting and Literature* (Manchester, 1972), 2–16.

always angry, for his good nature and his interest in character and physiognomy for its own sake survived his political commitment. He saw laughter as one answer to the problems of life, by which 'good humour and mental serenity' could be preserved.[1]

Forain was another caricaturist who was inspired by irritation with injustice and pity for its victims: 'on top', he said, 'there is neurosis; at the bottom, there is hunger.' But with him, again, the pictorial interest was uppermost: he drew his men and women first, gave them expressions 'and it is only when they are there, in front of me, that I ask what they have got to say —I question them and they reply'.[2] He showed that caricature need not be funny. Willette, whose art appeared to breathe disillusionment and regret, insisted however that people attributed excessively complex intentions to him. He was fond of drawing Pierrot, but that was not symbolic: 'it is above all by his clothes that Pierrot attracted me. I needed a personage sufficiently general to express all human passions through his movements. I did not want to put him into ordinary clothes: Pierrot's were the clothes of the poet.'[3]

There are definite limitations to what one can deduce from caricature.[4] Not that caricature in prose is much simpler. Alphonse Daudet's *Tartarin*, for example, has survived as a portrayal of the joviality of the Provençals. Daudet himself described his book as a *galéjade*—the Provençal word for a burst of mocking laughter. Tartarin was however a self-portrait, giving expression to Daudet's hesitation between heroic ambitions and cowardly fears, inflated to comic proportions. His book raises the question of whether there was more laughter in the south than the north: certainly their laughter was not entirely of the same kind.[5]

[1] Champfleury [J. F. F. Husson], *Histoire de la caricature moderne* (2nd edition, 1865), x, 170, 175; K. E. Maison, *Honoré Daumier, Catalogue raisonné* (1968); Oliver W. Larkin, *Daumier, Man of his Time* (1967); Arsène Alexandre, *Honoré Daumier* (1888), 199; and for a clever and well-argued political interpretation, T. J. Clark, *The Absolute Bourgeois* (1973), 99–123. On the ambiguity of the ridiculing of the bourgeoisie see Edith Melcher, *The Life and Times of Henry Monnier 1799–1827* (Cambridge, Mass., 1950).
[2] Adolphe Brisson, *Nos humoristes* (1900), 44.
[3] Ibid. 152; and Paul Gaultier, *Le Rire et la caricature* (1906), ch. 3.
[4] Jacques Lethève, *La Caricature et la presse sous la troisième république* (1961); J. Grand Carteret, *Les Mœurs et la caricature en France* (n.d.); and Raoul Deberdt, *La Caricature et l'humour français au 19ᵉ siècle* (n.d.) are valuable starting-points.
[5] Murray Sachs, *The Career of Alphonse Daudet* (Cambridge, Mass., 1965).

The most famous analyst of laughter in this period, Bergson, rightly stressed that laughter was a social art, involving complicity with others who laughed also: the larger the audience, the more laughter there was. He argued that the person who was laughed at was essentially unsociable: he was funny because he failed to adapt to circumstances around him, or because he acted automatically (as in absent-mindedness) without taking others into account; laughter was therefore above all a penalty meted out by society to those who took liberties against it, who were nonconformists or failures. It was designed to humiliate; it was a form of vengeance and was incompatible with compassion or emotion. He concluded therefore that comic situations were essentially creations of the intelligence.[1] There was always a strong element of this kind of humour in France, which reinforced the critical and combative characteristics of the society. But that is not the most significant function that humour performed. In other hands, humour was an instrument of detachment from the world, not a reinforcement of ties; it was therefore an emotional even more than an intellectual reaction. One can see this in Proust, for example, who certainly uses humour with fiercely satirical purpose on a large variety of subjects, but his humour is so universal, including even death, love and the author himself in its scope, that it emerges as a method by which Proust can take up a detached view of himself. 'Gaiety', wrote Proust, 'is a fundamental element in all things.' He showed how every action, every statement, however serious in appearance, could be shown to be funny, if only two people—in this case the author and his reader—conspired to declare it to be so: and he showed this by simply reporting such statements with a serious face.[2] Paul Valéry, who said 'anxiety is my real profession', was a southerner with a great admiration for gaiety and vivacity, who made humour the logical outcome of Descartes's universal doubt; he saved himself from madness by treating life not only as a drama but also as a game, making himself a spectator as well as an actor.[3]

The balance of this society was probably preserved by these

[1] H. Bergson, *Le Rire. Essai sur la signification du comique* (1900).

[2] Maya Slater, 'The Humour in the Works of Marcel Proust' (unpublished Oxford D.Phil. thesis, 1970).

[3] Paul Gifford, 'L'Humour chez Paul Valéry' (unpublished doctoral thesis, Toulouse-Mirail, 1971).

different kinds of humour, and not least by the fact that there were such a variety of them. Every serious political proclamation, every achievement of science and industry, needs to be seen also from the point of view of the jokes that were made about it. It is unfortunate that the jokes were recorded so much less frequently, and that they have been studied so much less by historians. The search for humour should not be regarded, however, simply as an evasion of, or escape from, the realities of life; it was also a positive attempt to create joy and pleasure around everyday events, as well as a rebellion against the restrictions of morality and prudence. As such, it deserves to have its achievements recorded quite as much as the more long-term efforts of the legislators and educators, whose success was perhaps not as great.

# 14. Eating and Drinking

EATING and drinking loomed large in the Frenchman's idea of the good life. No study of his sense of values can be complete without explaining the high priority he accorded both to the pleasures of the table and to discussion of those pleasures. But France's international renown as the home of good food was acquired only at the beginning of the nineteenth century, and what was understood by French cooking then was not the same as what it came to mean in the twentieth century. French food has a history which in some ways parallels that of the country's political development. There were the great cooks, and the philosophers of gastronomy, who created the ideals and theorised about the restaurant, originally representing a democratic advance but soon revealed as surrounded by privilege and profiteering. There was the clash of Jacobin centralisation—the efforts to create a French national style of cooking—and regional individuality. And there were the sordid realities which were allowed to survive while the leaders of fashion set the pace, like the adulteration of ingredients, the near-starvation of the poor, and the ever-rising toll of alcoholism.

In the nineteenth century, the vast majority of Frenchmen ate food which was very different from what the gastronomes were concocting in Paris. Peasant cooking was dominated first of all by the method of heating. The cauldron hanging from a hook in the fireplace was almost universal until the mid-nineteenth century. Inventories of furniture and effects, drawn up in connection with the distribution of property after death, show that the break in heating methods came at this time. In the Mâconnais, cauldrons disappear between 1850 and 1870, but they survived much longer in other parts of France, and in Normandy —though it was supposedly open to the influence of Paris—they were still to be found after the Second World War. Food used to be eaten with pocket knives, which each man brought with him, and spoons: there are few references to cutlery sets in poor households till the very end of the century. This meant that peasant cooking involved, above all, slow boiling. The basic dish was soup, made generally of vegetables, given bulk by the addition of chunks of old bread. Among the very poor, this soup would contain mainly salted water, and not all that much salt either, since it took a long time for people to get over the habits acquired under the *ancien régime*, when salt was taxed and expensive. The addition of pork fat transformed the soup into a luxury. In order to save fuel, enough soup would often be cooked for several meals; very little would be thrown away, and very confused tastes would develop as new ingredients were constantly added. The other basic food was porridge (*bouillie*), obtained by boiling grain or flour—often maize or buckwheat—in water or milk: this survived until the end of the nineteenth century, and much longer as a dish for evening meals and for children. As soon as one emerged from absolute poverty, one tried to keep a pig: the peasants usually killed one or two a year. Its main function was to produce fat, which immediately raised the level of cooking, but it was also eaten with spinach, potatoes and chestnuts; sausages were made from the entrails and the blood. Butcher's meat was the next step up: the principal way of cooking it was again boiling or stewing, or else *en daube*, i.e. in a pot called a *daubière*, placed between two layers of embers. But it is impossible to talk about peasant cooking once one has risen to this level of prosperity, for its essential characteristic was that it relied on local produce and local traditions. Thus in the Mâconnais, of which a particularly detailed study has been made, rabbits did not enter the peasant cook's repertoire till the end of the nineteenth century, whereas they were much used in other regions. The isolation of regions from each other meant that some villages would rely a great deal on fish, while others hardly knew this food; chickens were much eaten in the southwest, but only for feasts in the Mâconnais, and that only after 1870, for most of them were sold off to raise cash. The fact that a region produced a certain food did not mean that the peasants necessarily ate it, at least not until they had reached some prosperity. The Mâconnais had lots of mushrooms, but they began to be eaten only around 1900, and even today a certain dislike of them persists. Though chestnuts were much valued and eaten, other nuts were kept for making oil.

It is generally believed that the south of France has traditionally used olive oil for its cooking and the north butter, but this is a recent development. Quite apart from the fact that the basis of most cooking, first of all, was water and not oil, there was far more variety in the kinds of oil used than this simple division suggests, depending both on the province and on the social hierarchy within it. Thus the Morbihan was a major producer of butter, but until the twentieth century it exported it all. Nut-oil was widely used all over France until 1900, and in Touraine until 1920; it was valued for lighting as well as cooking. In the Vosges, pork fat was long used instead of butter, to spread on bread. This was connected with the way milk was treated: it was seldom drunk, except by the sick, but more often turned into soft cheese, whey and buttermilk, because of the difficulty of preserving it. In the west, butter was preserved by salting, but in many other regions by melting it—in which form it was treated as precious and used with parsimony. The peasants tended to eat fresh cheese themselves, to which spices or garlic might be added, but to set aside more elaborate cheeses for sale to the towns: even goat's cheese, when fermented in vine leaves, was treated as an export. In the Mâconnais, to use butter in cooking was a sign of one's rise in the social scale: colza-oil, nut-oil and pork fat were more common. Fresh fruit and vegetables were not a particular feature of peasant food. One reason was that peasants tended to eat only what they grew themselves; the habit of buying vegetables developed slowly and variety in salads, for example, came late. Another reason was that these foods tended to be kept for preserving. Dried vegetables, like beans and lentils, were popular; fruit was seldom eaten raw, more usually being turned into compotes and jams. Because sugar was expensive, beetroot was often used instead; but honey was an alternative: the *arrondissement* of Clamecy, it was recorded in 1832, had 2,540 beehives.

However, all this was a supplement to the single most important food—bread. In the Nivernais, peasants spent between one-third and one-half of their budgets on it, but this varied from region to region, as did the composition of the bread. Apart from the complication that most flour was severely adulterated, sometimes with noxious substances, so that not everyone knew what he was eating, some regions, like the Nivernais, mixed their flour—from equal parts of wheat, barley and rye—while others, like the Morvan, ate only rye bread. Townsmen were not complimentary about the skill of peasants' baking, and noted that their bread was kept for long periods, degenerating into an almost solid lump. In Nevers in 1860 the best-quality bread comprised only one-tenth of the total sold; by 1900 it was one-third; there were many gradations in the bread available. The quality of flour improved only gradually, from around 1880; bakers were notorious for their frauds and short weight and made large profits. Peasant bread, as it is now esteemed, is a recent invention, not a traditional food; the old bread was seldom wholesome or pure. It tasted different also because there has been a great change in the amount of salt added to bread: in the eighteenth century hardly any salt was used; in the nineteenth, there was a great increase, to 3 per cent, the highest proportion in Europe; since the Second World War, the proportion has fallen to 1·2 to 1·5 per cent, though in rainy years it is raised to as much as 2·5 per cent, depending on the condition of the wheat.[1]

In so far as peasants' cooking was influenced by ideas from outside, in the nineteenth century it conformed to the medieval school of thought. This had as its principle to mix many ingredients, without much attention to quantities—which medieval recipe books seldom specified—and to add spices as liberally as possible. Spices were esteemed, first, because they were a way of preserving food, secondly because they were considered to have medicinal properties, and lastly as a way of showing off one's wealth, because they were expensive. Many different spices were not often found in French peasant kitchens before 1900, but individual spices—and herbs—were used liberally when they were available. The medieval gastronome used to show his knowledge by guessing correctly what a dish was made of, and this guessing used to be a favourite entertainment at meals. So the peasants were not encouraged either by culinary science, or by their poverty, to depart from the rather indiscriminate mixture of ingredients and flavours. Peasant cooking, said a recipe book produced in 1867 under the auspices of the ministry of agriculture, was either insipid or too spiced: it was primitive, traditional and monotonous.[2] Just how different peasant and

---

[1] J. J. Hemardinquer, *Pour une histoire de l'alimentation* (1970); Suzanne Tardieu, *La Vie domestique dans le Mâconnais rural pré-industriel* (1964), 92–138.
[2] Madame Marceline Michaux, *La Cuisine de la ferme* (1867).

Parisian cooking could be may be seen by comparing the recipe for cabbage soup given by Madame Michaux, the author of this book, with that in *Le Cuisinier impérial* by one of the new generation of master cooks, Viard. In the peasant version, a cabbage was simply boiled with a leek and a clove of garlic, and a drop of butter was put in at the end. In Viard's version for the rich, two cabbages were boiled, then carefully dried and finally allowed to cook over slices of veal covered with bacon fat, together with carrots, onions and mushrooms. This required both time and money, but peasants had little leisure for elaborate preparations and observers of their methods commented on their adherence to recipes requiring the minimum of effort. What created bourgeois cooking was the almost limitless application that came to be given to it and the lavish use of more varied ingredients. In the peasant cook-book, vegetable recipes occupied over one-third of the space; in Viard's manual, they were allocated less than 5 per cent, for much more impressive dishes could be created with meat, fish and fowl. Most peasant cooking was probably not even wholesome: there were numerous comments about their 'poisonous' and fetid soups. When it came to cooking potatoes, they seem often to have been guilty of overboiling, whereas Viard suggested a whole range of imaginative and ingenious recipes. He proposed ten different ways of cooking artichokes, whereas the peasant book records only five. Greater variety was the mark of the new style: Viard's book, first published in 1806, had doubled in size by the time it reached its thirty-first edition in 1873, its range of soups rising from 74 to 134 different recipes.[1]

The long survival of the peasant style was shown in an inquiry carried out in the 1950s. This revealed two distinct types of meal still coexisting in France. In traditional regions like the Morbihan, soup was eaten at all meals, and this was above all vegetable soup, involving slow boiling in water. Soup was the staple diet not only of peasants but of many workers who retained peasant traditions: in Saint-Étienne, for example, 49·6 per cent of households still had soup for breakfast in the early 1950s. Modernisation meant the abandonment of this soup—

[1] A. Viard, *Le Cuisinier impérial, ou l'art de faire la cuisine et la pâtisserie pour toutes les fortunes, avec différents recettes d'office et de fruits confits, et la manière de servir une table depuis 20 jusqu'à 60 couverts* (1806); 31st edition 1873 is *Le Cuisinier national*.

A a

which in wealthier families used to be accompanied by eggs, cheese, *charcuterie*, and wine or cider—in favour of the small breakfast of coffee and rolls. Soup next began disappearing from the townsman's midday meal—only one-third of the poor of Marseille, for example, still ate soup for lunch in 1950. But soup has survived most tenaciously at supper, which as the major family meal, respected older traditions more. One of the most important changes in popular methods of cooking came largely after 1919, when instead of boiling meat and putting fats in their soup, the poor began to roast and grill meat, garnishing it with butter. The greater use of butcher's meat was another innovation of the towns—between two-thirds and 90 per cent of urban households ate more of it in 1950 than pork, fowl and rabbit, whereas only 50 per cent of peasants did so. Peasants in general consumed about 300 more calories than townsmen, but that was largely because they ate more bread; the fall in consumption of this once staple diet was the final indication of modernisation, but bread ceased to be the basis of the peasant's diet only in the twentieth century.[1]

The traditional generalisation that the rich ate more meat than the poor needs qualification. In 1850 Paris consumed 62 kilogrammes of butcher's meat per inhabitant per annum, Rennes 60, Bordeaux 53, Strasbourg 44, Toulouse 38, and Caen 28; and if pork is added, the figures go from 72 kilogrammes in Paris to 33 in Caen. This does not seem to have any direct correlation with the prosperity or social composition of these towns: thus the predominantly working-class town of Saint-Étienne consumed 49 kilogrammes of butcher's meat, while Dijon, with a large bourgeois element, ate only 42. The same variation existed in drinking habits. Bordeaux came top of the table, drinking 196 litres of wine per head per annum, Caen came bottom with only 12, while Paris was in the middle with 113. If cider, beer and other alcoholic drinks are added, Rennes came top with 440, Caen second with 245 and Brest bottom with 80. Dijon, a leading wine centre, consumed much more beer than wine.[2] The explanation of these variations lies in local

---

[1] J. Claudian and Y. Soville, 'Composition des repas et urbanisation' in J.J. Hemardinquer, op. cit. 174–87; Cf. R. Mandrou, *Introduction à la France moderne 1500–1640* (1961), which has some instructive pages on food in this period.
[2] Mandrou, op. cit.; and cf. Armand Husson, *Les Consommations de Paris* (1856).

and family traditions, which resisted the spread of uniformity very strongly.

Mademoiselle Léontine, a cook writing in 1856, lamented that most people were very unwilling to alter their eating habits and were generally satisfied simply when their stomachs were full. Most people had confused notions of what was wholesome and what was not: the result was that 'half the population is constantly ill'.[1] The digestive process was, by this date, understood by doctors, but the value of different foods was still largely a matter of guesswork. In so far as any rules about diet were accepted, the main one was that different temperaments required different foods. The problem for those who got beyond the level of satiating their hunger was how to reconcile the preservation of their health with the titillation of their palates. A traditional approach to this was to go from one extreme to another, and alternate between relative abstinence and overeating.[2] Popular cook-books with pretensions to science tried to develop different habits: they warned those with sanguine temperaments to avoid strong flavours (e.g. lemon, tomato, onion) but to eat lots of vegetables. The lymphatic were urged to keep off sweet things, even fruit; the nervous to beware of tea. Sexual exhaustion should be remedied by concentrated broths, intellectual exhaustion by coffee. But delicate women would be damaged by coffee and indeed were in danger from a large number of foods. Apart from all the differences that age, sex, temperament, climate and profession imposed, there was the problem of what was 'digestible' and what was not—pork, for example, was considered less digestible than beef. As late as 1913, a doctor recorded that pre-scientific superstitions about diet flourished unabated. Babies were still being purged for every trouble, including bronchitis. Women were addicts of every kind of indigestion and constipation pill offered in the advertisement columns of the newspapers. A very frequent complaint was 'the dislocated stomach', and many quacks made a fortune 'resetting' stomachs. There were phobias about a whole variety of foods, from spinach and sorrel to chocolate. Obsession with digestion led some to take laxatives daily, or even daily

[1] Mademoiselle Léontine, *La Cuisine hygiénique, confortable et économique, à l'usage de toutes les classes de la société* (new edition, 1856).
[2] L. M. Lombard, *Le Cuisinier et le médecin . . . ou l'art de conserver ou de rétablir sa santé par une alimentation convenable* (1855).

enemas.[1] Some people claimed that the peasant had none of these troubles and was the model of good health, but others described his food as disgusting, on the verge of being poisonous, and far from nutritious: 'One should not be surprised by the slowness, the laziness and the inertia of these poor devils.'[2]

What is now known as the French style of cooking was created largely in the nineteenth century by the efforts of four different sets of people, who reinforced each other's ambitions by their discussions, comparisons and competition. These were the professional male cooks, the restaurant-keepers, the gastronomes and the female cooks employed in the domestic service of the bourgeoisie. The development of the profession of cook took on new proportions in the nineteenth century. Every history of cooks mentions Vatel, who committed suicide in 1602 because he could not face the humiliation of not having two roasts he had planned for a banquet ready in time; there were doubtless many skilled cooks before the nineteenth century, who produced magnificent meals. But their pride in their work was now given a new range under the leadership of Antoine Carême (1784–1833). Carême was a man of letters and an architect as well as a cook. He raised cooking to the level of a supreme art, claiming that it was 'the most ancient of the arts and the art which has rendered the most important services to civil life'. It should be a science too, embodying knowledge of agriculture, chemistry and pharmacy; but to have full scope it had to be treated as a form of showmanship and advertising. Carême worked for the Tsar of Russia and for Talleyrand but he was fully happy only when he finally became cook to Baron Rothschild in Paris. Here he was allowed to spend as much money as he wished, which he said was 'the only way to stimulate the genius of cooks jealous of their reputation, for what use is talent if it lacks the money necessary to procure provisions of the highest quality?' Carême developed, in these conditions, what might be called ideal cooking, unlimited by considerations of economy; but though his menus could be attempted only by princes and millionaires, his style was highly influential, because he carried out several fundamental changes in the methods of preparing food. First,

[1] Dr. A. Mollière, *Les Préjugés en diététique et dans les maladies des voies digestives* (1913). [2] Lombard, op. cit. 114.

he greatly reduced the use of herbs and spices: 'modern cooking', he wrote, 'must know how to extract the nutritive juices from foods by rational cooking.' Secondly, he limited the mixture of different types of food: in grand dinners it used to be common to serve fish, for example, surrounded by sweetbreads, pigeons, cocks' crests and kidneys: Carême mixed like with like, surrounding fish only with other fish. Thirdly, he transformed the decoration of food, making great use of skewers to create elaborate mountains of food, harmonising with the complicated silver and crystal plates they were served on; and he developed new ways of garnishing principal dishes to heighten their effect. This reflected the grandiose ideas he expressed in his architecture, which was his hobby. Carême argued that once the value of cooking of this kind was appreciated, cooks would be recognised as men of great importance: they should not stay in the kitchen but come out to the dining-room to supervise the eating; they were in fact doctors, with far more influence on their employers' well-being than the charlatans who posed as doctors (though the dietetical textbook he relied on was a very old-fashioned work of 1709).[1] A cook, as Carême conceived him, was 'a god on earth'. There were no limits to Carême's arrogance or self-confidence: he despised Cambacérès, the archchancellor of Napoleon's Empire, because he insisted on leftovers being used and would not give Carême his best wines to cook with; he was sorry for Napoleon's cook, who had to serve him the very simple foods he demanded. He advised humbler people who could not reproduce his recipes not to attempt simplified versions of them, but to put all their money into creating one grand dish: 'better give two great dinners than four mediocre ones'. His literary masterpiece (and he warned readers that unless they read it in its entirety 'they will largely lose the benefit of this fruit of long meditations', this 'most laborious work that any expert on cooking has ever undertaken') contained 500 soup and 500 fish recipes. Though he was confident that French food was the best in the world, he did not disdain *potage de choux à la paysanne russe*, or *bortsch*, or English turtle soup, though he embellished them appropriately.[2]

[1] Lémery, *Dictionnaire des aliments* (1709).
[2] Antoine Carême, *L'Art de la cuisine française au 19ᵉ siècle. Traité élémentaire et pratique suivi de dissertations culinaires et gastronomiques utiles au progrès de cet art* (1833).

Carême was venerated as the greatest of French cooks, but aspects of his teaching had different results. His stress on sumptuousness made the French cooking that followed his lead notable above all for its richness, and particularly for its sauces: it became the style adopted almost universally by embassies and later by grand palace hotels, where ostentation was all-important. The *sauce espagnole*, which, despite its name, was the basis of this French style, required, to be made properly, bacon fat, ham, fowl, veal, hare and partridge: it was clearly beyond the means of the ordinary small family. Carême's style was ostentatious also in its presentation, and this side of him was considerably exaggerated during the Second Empire. Urbain Dubois, who was one of the most famous cooks of this period (chef to the king of Prussia for a time), published illustrated books showing the most elaborate and amazing architectural arrangements of food, differing from Carême in that many colourful uneatable objects were added as ornaments.[1] But this system, which aimed to produce 'magnificent spectacles' had the serious disadvantage that the food was usually cold when it came to be eaten, since it was the practice to put these monuments on the table well before they were consumed. *Service à la française* meant that a meal was divided, like a play, into three acts—the first consisted of *potages*, *relevés* and *entrées*, the second of *rôtis* and *entremets* and the third of *desserts*—and that the food was brought on to the table not individually, but in these three stages. The enormous menus of this period—which in a dinner given by Talleyrand once contained no less than forty-eight *entrées*—were an indication not of what everybody would eat, but of the choice from which the diners would select. Thus in a dinner for thirty people, Carême would serve only half a dozen birds: not everyone would get a piece; but there would be many alternatives placed on the table at the same time. *Hors d'œuvres*, in this system, were designed to fill in the gaps, for those who were unable to get enough of the main courses. The table would be cleared after the *entrées*, and the various roasts and *entremets* would then be brought in all together. The snag of this buffet-like method was not only that the food got cold, but also that it was difficult to

---

[1] Urbain Dubois and Émile Bernard, *La Cuisine classique. Études pratiques, raisonnées et démonstratives de l'école française appliquée au service à la russe* (1864); Urbain Dubois, *Cuisine artistique. Études de l'école moderne* (2nd edition, 1882).

share out equitably; and from the middle of the nineteenth century therefore *service à la russe* was increasingly adopted, which meant that the food was cut up in the kitchen and each diner was offered a portion by the waiters. This led to a great diminution of the number of dishes that had to be cooked, but it was only around 1890 that this Russian method became more or less universal. The old 'costly prodigality, more suited to dazzle than to satisfy' was thus moderated. 'Extravagant super-abundance', said Dubois, should be avoided and meals should be 'rich and luxurious without excess'—though he made up for this by fantastic arrangements of the fewer courses that were served.

Escoffier, however, who was perhaps the most influential cook of the Third Republic, altered the character of the meal once again. Writing at the beginning of the twentieth century, he said that Carême and Dubois, though great cooks, had catered for an age that had passed, and what had suited the Second Empire 'when life was easy and the future assured' was no longer appropriate when people were in a hurry, and demanded, above all else, rapid service. He discarded the plinths, skewers, tampons and borders that had been used to build up dishes into artistic constructions, as well as the complicated garnishings. He invented new equipment and new methods for simplified presentation; he removed most of the uneatable ornaments, and he compensated by increasing the savour and nutritional value of the food, making it lighter and 'more easily digestible by weakened stomachs'. 'My success', he said, 'comes from the fact that my best dishes were created for ladies.' It was only around the turn of the century indeed that it became respectable or fashionable for ladies to be taken to restaurants. But Escoffier's recipes were also drawn up with unprecedented accuracy, every ingredient being carefully measured. 'Cooking,' he said, 'without ceasing to be an art, will become a science', leaving nothing to chance. He was not opposed to the tradition of grand meals, which were 'both a ceremony and a feast' but he quoted Carême's maxim that in cooking the only principle was to satisfy the person one served. Modern taste no longer accepted the *sauce espagnole*, 'whose richness amazes our parsimonious eye'; sauces had, in the last quarter of the nineteenth century, reached a stage of exaggeration with the result that they drowned the aroma of the foods they were served with, and everything came to taste much the same. Escoffier was not deterred from devoting sixty-seven pages of his book to sauces, but he also made much more use of *fumets*, the lighter juices of the meat and fish he served. He reproduced many of the old-fashioned ornate recipes, and he was a skilled sculptor in sugar and ice: *pêche Melba*, which he invented, was originally called *pêche au cygne*, because the peaches and vanilla ice-cream came served between the wings of a swan made of ice (representing the swan in *Lohengrin*, in which Melba had been singing); it was only later that he added raspberry *purée* to create the present *pêche Melba*. But Escoffier was not only a chef: he was also an associate of César Ritz and his collaborator in organising the enormous new hotels that now sprang up all over Europe. These provided a new venue for the international aristocracy and set up a new pattern in entertaining and eating. Escoffier spent much of his life at the Savoy and Carlton Hotels in London, ruling over eighty cooks. He was an apostle of efficiency and saw that cooking methods had to be adapted to meet the changed demands placed upon them by large and rich clienteles. He established principles of teamwork, so that whereas previously an order for 'deux œufs sur le plat Meyerbeer' would take a cook fifteen minutes to prepare, now the eggs were cooked by the *entremettier*, the kidney was grilled by the *rôtisseur* and the truffle sauce prepared by the *saucier*: the order could thus be fulfilled in a few minutes. Escoffier's ideas were influential not only in his own or other large hotels, but throughout the profession, for he wrote frequently in the press, notably in the periodical *L'Art culinaire*. His ideas, however, did not always triumph. Thus he lamented the rise of *hors d'œuvres* into a regular course, saying that these were only a method of keeping a client waiting in a restaurant. *Hors d'œuvres*, it is true, had greatly altered in the course of the century. Originally they had been prepared by a special cook, the *officier*, in a separate kitchen, which had also been in charge of making sweets and decorating the table.[1] The kitchen obtained command over them only in the second half of the nineteenth century, and that is partly why they became mainly cold dishes. Soups likewise were transformed in the course of the

---

[1] Étienne, *officier* at the British Embassy in Paris in the mid-nineteenth century was one of the most influential, and one of the last.

century, from very substantial dishes, which were almost a meal in themselves, to mere exciters of the appetite. The result of all these changes was that grand French cooking was substantially different in 1939 from what it had been in 1850.[1] This is not to say, however, that French cooking was uniform in any one period, for the ideas of these famous chefs never obtained complete sway. Thus while Escoffier was preaching greater simplicity, others simultaneously continued and developed the complicated style. The recipe for *lièvre à la royale*, in a cook-book by one of his contemporaries, was ten pages long, with *foie gras*, truffles, cognac and many condiments added, so that the taste of the hare virtually vanished.[2] In the 1920s one of the most famous and expensive restaurants in Paris was Prosper Montagné's in the rue de l'Échelle, where the food served was based on worship of Carême, whose manuscript notes in the Talleyrand archives the chef studied in order to achieve perfection. The spiritual descendants of Napoleon III's cook Jules Gouffée (1807–77), who was later chef to the Jockey Club, and who carried decoration and ostentation to its limits, found refuge in the international hotels, where cooking had to be more French than it was in France: the rivalry of restaurants encouraged fantastic mixtures and, as one chef put it, 'a paroxysm of amalgams'.[3] On the other hand, simple and rapid cooking obviously did not start with Escoffier, the popularisation of whose work might lead one to forget that he was a master of *haute cuisine* none the less. The pressure for quickly prepared meals had a strong popular base. The great recipe books were far outnumbered by humbler ones of limited pretensions which stressed economy above all: the most successful of these continued to be reprinted in disregard of changing fashion.[4] The

[1] A. Escoffier, avec la collaboration de Philéas Gilbert et Émile Fetu, *Le Guide culinaire* (1912, 3rd edition, containing over 5,000 recipes, and dedicated to Urbain Dubois and Émile Bernard); E. Herbodeau and P. Thalamas, *Georges Auguste Escoffier* (1955).

[2] *Gastronomie pratique d'Ali Bab* (1907). Ali Bab was the pseudonym of an engineer Babinski, brother of the famous psychiatrist.

[3] E. Darenne, secretary-general of the Academy of Cuisine, *La Cuisine française et étrangère* (26 May 1883); Mourier, thesis on 'La Cuisine naturelle et la cuisine composée', ibid. 63.

[4] The most popular recipe book of the early nineteenth century was said to be L. E. Audot, *La Cuisinière de la campagne et de la ville* (1818, 10th edition 1832, 41 reprints 1833–1900). The author was a publisher, not a cook. Other long-lasting books were *Le Cuisinier gascon*, first published 1740, and reaching its 29th edition

introduction of gas, which was a great aid to all forms of cooking, also encouraged fast cooking, particularly since the gas companies organised lessons and issued recipes stressing this advantage. The mass restaurant trade simplified dishes not on principle, but to increase profits:[1] one *restaurateur*'s encyclopedia abbreviated its 3,250 recipes into one or two lines each, so that all its wisdom could be carried in the pocket.[2] In 1930 a book of 'Ten-minute Recipes' claimed that there was a great demand for these from students, working girls, shop assistants, artists, scholars, poets, men of action and lazy people; Napoleon himself had after all prided himself on the speed with which he got through his food. It recommended making soups out of powdered extracts, some of which were terrible but others, it said, excellent.[3] Tinned food, in the use of which the army were pioneers, was welcomed by the official organ of professional cooks as the solution to the problem of cheap catering for the masses: the peasants of course had long experience of preserving food. When in 1878 tinned beef was imported from the U.S.A. for the first time, in a period of high meat prices, it was approved because it was 40 per cent cheaper than European meat.[4] But though France played a leading role in the discovery of methods of preserving and refrigerating, the French canning industry did not develop to take full advantage of this new knowledge. Appert, who established a food-preserving factory at Massy, outside Paris, in 1804, died in poverty. In 1847 Martin de Lignac began manufacturing concentrated milk, and in 1854 desiccated beef. Charles Tellier founded a food-freezing factory at Auteuil in 1874 and two years later built the first French refrigerator-ship. But it was England which became master of the meat-carrying trade from South America. At the turn of the century, the French canning industry produced 120 million tins a year, but of these, 80 million were of sardines, and the French

in 1896, and *La Cuisinière bourgeoise*, first published in 1746, 22nd edition 1866. For the twentieth century, see in particular the works of Mademoiselle Rose, published by Flammarion.

[1] *La Cuisine française et étrangère* (30 Nov. 1893), 155. In 1894 Paris had 140,000 gas cookers. Ibid., 25 Oct. 1894.

[2] P. Dagouret, *Petite Encyclopédie du restaurateur* (8th edition, 1923).

[3] Édouard de Pomiane, *La Cuisine en dix minutes. Ou l'adaptation au rhythme moderne* (1830), 14, 74.

[4] *La Cuisine française et étrangère* (25 Sept. 1893), 'Les Conserves alimentaires'.

themselves consumed only about 15 per cent of their sardine tins, exporting the rest. The French canning industry was thus about one-sixth the size of that of the U.S.A. In 1899 a commission was established to investigate the frequent cases of food-poisoning occurring in the army—a principal consumer of tins —which may suggest that hygiene was not a strong point. But there is no evidence to support the view that the French did not eat tinned food because they despised it as inferior; it may well be that they would have got into the habit if there had been more available, at reasonable prices. One may guess that either food producers preferred to stick to traditional methods of adulteration, which were well developed, in order to reduce the cost of food, rather than embark on the expensive investment that canning required, or else that profits in the retail grocery trade were so high that there was little inducement to try new methods; or finally that the preserving of food by the housewife in the home was an established alternative. Escoffier was a great believer in the value of tinned tomatoes, but it took him about fifteen years to persuade French manufacturers to produce them.[1]

France's reputation for good cooking owes a great deal to the growth of its restaurants. The first Parisian restaurant with à la carte menus was Beauvilliers's, in the galerie de Valois, founded in 1782, but restaurants began to multiply and flourish above all during the Revolution. There were less than fifty of them in Paris in 1789, but nearly 3,000 by 1820. The chefs of the aristocracy, thrown out of work, set up public eating places, and it was *Chez Méot* (formerly the prince de Condé's cook) that the leaders of the Revolution drafted the constitution of 1793. Many luxury artisans, such as goldsmiths and jewellers, whose businesses collapsed, took up cooking also. In a period when food was scarce and expensive, restaurants were the answer for those who could afford high prices. Méot's had the reputation of always being full of contractors and speculators newly enriched by dubious methods, who now ate like kings. 'The Jacobins, who abolished decorum and suspended politeness and courtesy, made indulgence in good food fashionable', wrote Madame de Genlis.

[1] See the advice on the importance of stocking-up with tins of preserves in *Le Gourmet. Journal des intérêts gastronomiques* (28 Feb. 1858), 2; Herbodeau and Thalamas, *Escoffier* (1955), 101–3.

Whole streets of Paris filled up with restaurants of varying quality, and already in 1800 Paris seemed transformed by them. Les Trois Frères Provençaux, where Barras and Bonaparte used to dine, and which all the generals of the empire came to patronise, saw its takings rise to as much as 15,000 francs a day. Its fame, and that of other major restaurants of the time, became international and it was to them that the Russian officers who entered France in 1814 immediately hastened. Hunger during the Revolution, which has absorbed the attention of historians, went hand in hand with unequalled culinary abundance for the rich. Under the Restoration, the luxurious restaurants reached even greater heights of splendour and profitability. Lord Hertford was able to rent out the ground floor of his Paris house to a *restaurateur* for 12,000 francs a year. By 1848 restaurants were changing hands for as much as 320,000 francs. It was said during the Second Empire that it needed less than five years for a restaurant-keeper to recoup his investment and make a fortune sufficient to enable him to retire. The chef of the Café Anglais was then paid 25,000 francs a year; its owner was a member of a *conseil général*, living a leisured life on a country estate. The Café Riche was one of the most magnificent creations of Napoleon III's reign, a veritable palace, with a cellar worth 200,000 francs. In the 1870s, many of the famous old restaurants, like the Trois Frères Provençaux and Philippe's, disappeared, to make way for new ones which were to acquire equal celebrity, like Lapérouse. In parallel with the restaurants there grew up a large number of public caterers, who sold meals to take away, or served them in their clients' own homes. The most successful was Chevet, who used to supply roses to Marie Antoinette until arrested in the Revolution: he then took to making cakes and other foods which he and some of his seventeen children sold on the street: his became the best food shop in Paris. In 1869 the fourth Chevet succeeded to the headship of a firm which had an international clientele, supplying weddings in St. Petersburg and exporting to America. When Maxim's came to be founded in 1890, the restaurant trade was important enough for Lebaudy, the sugar manufacturer, to give it financial backing. These were places where the menu might well contain 200 different items; and where prices were purposely kept high to make them the exclusive preserve of the rich.

What distinguished Paris also, however, was the vast choice of restaurants for every pocket, as eating out became increasingly common. In the Latin quarter, it was possible to eat well for less than a franc at Flicoteaux, where the table-cloths were changed only once a week, or at Viot's, where 600 students ate daily, paying thirty centimes for meat dishes, fifteen centimes for vegetables and fifteen for wine—all the prices being standard.[1] In the rue Molière, Chez Dufour provided a five-course meal with wine and as much bread as you liked for 1 fr. 80. The artists and painters of the Second Empire used to go out to rural Montparnasse to eat wholesome, unpretentious food Chez la mère Saguet; an alternative outing would be to Jouanne's in Batignolles, which specialised in *tripes à la mode de Caen*. There were already innumerable *bistrots* serving meals of indifferent quality but in a gay and informal atmosphere, as well as more discreet ones to which ageing gentlemen could take their actress friends. In 1840–5 Les Bouillons hollandais toured the city in vans, offering cheap but wholesome soup, to cater for the very poor, who ate in the streets. In 1855 an improved version of this came with the establishment of the Bouillons Duval in the rue de la Monnaie, which within a decade had a dozen branches. Duval was a butcher, who originally served broth and beef only, of good quality, but he soon became famous for the new standards he introduced into mass catering. His restaurants had large rooms, clean marble tables, rapid service by well-dressed waitresses, but very low fixed prices for each item, and one paid the cashier as one left.[2] In 1860 two fashionable English restaurants were founded, Hill's in the Boulevard des Capucines and Peter's, off the rue Richelieu, to serve English food and beer; but the demand for this seems to have been limited, for in 1926 only three 'Anglo-American' restaurants were listed in a gastronomic guide of Paris, side by side with eleven Italian ones, eight Russian, four Jewish and one 'Hindu'.[3] Already during the Second Empire the business lunch was an established institution; and so of course was 'political gastronomy', by which

[1] See Jules P. Vatel, *Mémoires d'un garçon d'hôtel* (1892) for a description of a restaurant in the rue Monsieur le Prince frequented by Courbet and Vallès.

[2] See the biography of Pierre-Louis Duval (1811–70) in *Larousse du dix-neuvième siècle*.

[3] Edouard Dulac, *Le Tour de France gastronomique. Guide du touriste gourmand* (1926).

political meetings were held in the form of banquets. The fashion spread, for banquets were popular with every kind of organisation, society, industry and corporation; publicity dinners to launch new ventures, or theatrical plays, were very numerous already in the 1840s.[1] Banqueting was carried to its absolute extreme when in 1900 the President of the Republic gave one for all the mayors of France and 22,695 of them attended: tables 7 kilometres long were laid out under tents in the Tuileries gardens, and the manager of the famous catering firm of Potel and Chabot drove around them in a car to supervise while his *maîtres d'hôtel* did their duty on bicycles.[2] It should not be thought that the food at these dinners, or at Parisian restaurants in general, was always, or even usually, good. Complaints about the tricks and frauds of *restaurateurs* arose from the very beginning: they were after all an extension of the food trade, which was notorious for dishonest adulteration. A *Manuel de gastronomie* in the 1890s already listed 927 restaurants with pretensions and an author of that decade counted 1,400.[3] Good food was to be found in a small minority of these. Already in 1858 Théodore de Banville, in an article on restaurants, complained that the poets, artists and authors of the capital 'have only one dream: to eat something other than that eternal lamb cutlet and that eternal uncooked beefsteak, to which they are condemned by the cruelty of the Parisian *restaurateur.* . . . The basis of his cooking is a brown sauce, mixed with flour, which, if one is to judge by its execrable taste, must combine the most dangerous ingredients and the most frightful poisons. Everybody is terrified of this brown sauce, but the *restaurateur* spares no intrigue, prayers or violence to force you to eat it', serving it with every dish. Roast meat was seldom freshly cooked, and usually reheated from the day before; 'madeira sauce' had no connection with that wine.[4] The esteem that French cooking enjoyed was due to the masterpieces of an élite of cooks, and to the skill of a fairly limited number of practitioners of the second class, in the same way that French literature or art was far from being

[1] Eugène Briffault, *Paris à table* (1846), 75.
[2] André Castelot, *L'Histoire à table* (1972), 1. 82.
[3] Chatillon-Pléssis, *La Vie à table à la fin du 19ᵉ siècle. Théorie pratique et historique de gastronomie moderne* (1894).
[4] Théodore de Banville, 'Les Restaurateurs', *Le Gourmet. Journal des intérêts gastronomiques* (18 July 1858), 1–2.

universally, or even generally, of high quality. But what made France a paradise for gastronomes was the respect that good cooking, like good literature, received, the constant concern over standards and the excited discussions about recipes and quality. The professional cooks of France were very interesting men, and it is surprising that their careers and ideas have not received attention. They were much concerned about their status in society, which was indeed ambiguous. 'Because of the art we practise,' wrote Philéas Gilbert, a famous cook who also managed to write for thirty-two different journals, 'we have a right to respect and consideration from all, because cooking can and must march hand in hand with the liberal arts. But it seems that cooks are, through prejudice, avoided and regarded as mercenaries.'[1] They demanded that they should be recognised as scientists; and they sought to develop their professional training so as to raise their status. The Academy of Cooking was founded in 1883. Membership involved the presentation of a 'thesis', which often embodied remarkable historical researches. Fondness for scholarship and writing was indeed a frequent characteristic of these cooks; they liked lecturing and attending each other's lectures; and they were exceptionally well travelled also. The propaganda they spread in favour of France was not negligible. They claimed that by 1900 there were about 10,000 of them distributed abroad throughout the world, mainly working for the ruling classes, so that they were in influential positions. The export of cooks perhaps came second only to the export of books. Cooks generally came from humble stock. Auguste Colombié, for example (born 1845), was apprenticed to a Toulouse *pâtissier* at the age of twelve. His reading of Carême's treatise on cake-making filled him with ambition to follow in the footsteps of the master, whose account of his early poverty showed that this was a career open to talent. Colombié spent his meagre savings buying books, and after doing his Tour de France, he founded a Society for the Study of Cooking, and a school of cooking in Paris, which lent books and organised lectures. Six hundred cooks attended his first lecture. He offered three levels of instruction: popular, bourgeois and grand cooking. He published a periodical to publicise his ideas. He became

---

[1] Philéas Gilbert in *L'Art culinaire: Revue bimenseulle, organe spécial de la société des cuisiniers français et de l'école professionnelle de cuisine* (1883), 23.

chef to the Prince of Hatzfeld-Wildenbourg, who gave him long vacations to allow him to write his books, of which he produced at least three. He was a brilliant lecturer, pouring out aphorisms, quotations and anecdotes in a colourful southern accent.[1] Cooks admired erudition and historical research; they often had a wide curiosity; they tended to move frequently from job to job, and sometimes from country to country, from Russia to America. Though proud of their native style of cooking, they had a surprisingly wide knowledge of foreign methods, and their journals were always publishing articles about culinary experiences all over the world, neglecting neither Colombia nor Korea. They generally worked their way up from an apprenticeship in a *pâtisserie* (skill in this field was considered, since Carême set the fashion, the first necessary accomplishment); the successful ones obtained jobs in the houses of the aristocracy and the rich, the best of them preferring financiers and foreign noblemen as employers; they would spend several seasons in large hotels, in Vichy, for example, or in London clubs; and they often ended their days reasonably well off as restaurant-owners, or as managers of food factories. Their families intermarried, so that the restaurants of Paris formed a community which was more than professional. They had a high opinion of their importance. One of them publicly complained in 1907 that doctors had developed a tendency to interfere in the cook's domain, giving complicated advice about what to eat and what not to eat. 'All this is nonsense.' Cooking was the 'patrimony of cooks. We have created and embellished it, we made it interesting and appetising and we therefore think we must defend it against encroachment.' Doctors should be consulted only by the sick: the hungry should turn to the cooks.[2] Escoffier wrote: 'Good cooking is the foundation of true happiness.' Unfortunately, it is by no means clear that they themselves always obtained this reward from the practice of their art. Their conditions of work were a subject of constant complaint: their health suffered from the badly ventilated kitchens they cooked in; many of them seem to have drunk more than they ate, partly to counteract perspiration, and alcoholism was frequent. Young cooks complained that they

were seldom taught anything by the chefs, who demanded submissive obedience from their juniors; the chefs protested that
their skills were not allowed full scope, owing to the thrift of the
bourgeoisie and to the commercialisation of restaurants. Cooks
were not well enough organised to obtain holidays, but they
were frequently unemployed, seasonal engagements being common, and they were fleeced by the employment exchanges which
charged exorbitant fees for finding them work (as high as 20 per
cent of their wages).[1] The whole profession, moreover, rested on
a foundation of appallingly exploited waiters and kitchen hands,
whose tribulations were graphically recorded in George Orwell's
*Down and Out in Paris and London* (1933).[2]

The cooks were backed up and encouraged by a new class of
men, the gastronomes. Brillat-Savarin (1755–1826) is usually
regarded as the first and greatest of these, but he was not in all
ways their model and he received severe criticism from many
cooks, which shows that gastronomy was no simple science.
Brillat-Savarin's *Physiologie du goût* (1826) was important because
it provided a justification of concern about food, but written
with wit and style, so that it acquired the *cachet* of a literary
masterpiece. It claimed that the discovery of a new dish gave
more happiness to mankind than that of a new star; cooking
was not just a branch of knowledge, but governed life itself; it
should have an Academy, which would study subjects like the
different species of thirst, the theory of frying, the influence of
eating habits on sociability and conjugal harmony. Not everyone
could be a gastronome—'a physical and organic predestination'
was needed—but men of letters, doctors, the clergy and above
all financiers were particularly gifted for the enjoyment of food.
Englishmen could be seen in restaurants 'stuffing themselves
with double helpings of meat, ordering the most expensive
dishes, drinking the most famous wines and not always leaving
without help': but that was not what eating was about. Carême
criticised Brillat-Savarin for being a bore, witty only in his
writings, and not fulfilling Carême's condition of being a host

---

[1] J. Barberet, 'Les Cuisiniers', in *Le Travail en France: monographies professionnels*,
vol. 6 (1889), 15–285.

[2] For the waiters, see Union syndicale et mutuelle des restaurateurs et limo-
nadiers du département de la Seine, fondée le 14 janvier 1876, *Annuaire de l'exercice
1890–91* (1892), which gives biographies, and describes their fight for the right to
wear moustaches.

himself: he was a bachelor, in old-fashioned clothes, a mere theorist. Their contemporary Grimod de la Reynière, who published the *Almanach des gourmands*, provided an alternative approach: he was a very hearty eater, as though permanently suffering from tapeworm; his guests were required to drink a minimum of eighteen cups of coffee; he enjoyed not delicate refinement but food showing fantasy or burlesque and accompanied by macabre jokes.[1] This tradition was continued by people who had competitions as to who could eat most, and was symbolised by Balzac's comte de Montriveau who used to eat ten dozen oysters every day. Its survival could be seen during the Second Empire at Philippe's restaurant in the rue Montorgueil where on Saturdays eighteen diners were privileged to eat an enormous meal from six in the evening to midnight, followed by a second meal from midnight to six a.m., and a third one from six a.m. to midday on Sunday—each consisting of some ten courses and as many wines: they ate, that is to say, for a whole day.[2] Dr. Véron (1798–1867) was perhaps the last of the hosts who virtually kept an open table. He had made his fortune as the manufacturer of a cough mixture, the pâte Regnauld, as a newspaper owner and as director of the Opéra. His cook Sophie produced amazing meals, which went on almost like a permanent film-show, with people getting up from the table when they wished, and Véron himself often leaving first for the Opéra.[3]

One of the characteristics of gastronomy was that its followers nearly always lamented that taste was decaying and that good food was becoming increasingly rare. One of the very first journals devoted to it, *La Gastronomie* (1839), reported that people were already saying interest in food was no longer as great as during the First Empire, though it refuted this by showing that whereas in 1800 there were only three shops in Paris providing cooked food and delicacies, there were now forty, ten of which had very high reputations. This paper, which had a circulation of 2,000, organised tastings and excursions, and reported where specially remarkable ingredients could be found. It laid down that one should never talk politics at table:

---

[1] Maurice des Ombiaux, *La Physiologie du goût de Brillat-Savarin* (1937); Jean Armand-Laroche, *Brillat-Savarin et la médecine* (medical thesis, Paris, 1931).

[2] Jean Paul Aron, *Le Mangeur du 19ᵉ siècle* (1973), 83.

[3] Joseph d'Arcay, *La Salle à manger du Docteur Véron* (1858).

the conversation should always be light, so as not to distract from the main interest, which was the food: 'in a dinner of knowledgeable people, the arrival of the soup is followed by a silence'. What talk there was should be mainly about the food. 'If one eats eggs, one does not omit to recall that Louis XV liked them a lot and maintained that a well-cooked egg was the best of all foods.'[1] At the end of the century, another theoretician laid it down that 'until the third course, there should be no talk about anything except what one was eating, what one has eaten and what one will eat'. But 'after one has eaten well, one has a duty to make witty conversation'.[2] This kind of gastronomy was not in keeping with another tradition of sociability, for it was considered best, when one was eating seriously, to exclude women, so as not to be distracted by the needs of politeness. Perhaps that is why bachelors were the leaders of this cult; and they did turn out to be, as Brillat-Savarin anticipated, mainly authors or men on the fringes of the literary world, civil servants and doctors. Among the most famous were such men as Charles Monselet (1825–88) a club-footed bachelor, drama critic, author of vaudevilles and of *La Cuisinière pratique*, who was an advocate of experiment and novelty, attacking cooks for being slaves of routine: why were rats not eaten, he asked, while pigs were? (In fact the coopers of Bordeaux did not scorn them, treating them as delicacies, cut in half, grilled and seasoned with herbs.) Why were salads so limited, ignoring the vast possibilities of flowers? (Salads, wrote the Goncourt brothers, probably divided men more than politics.)[3] Baron Brisse (1813–76), another bachelor, was probably the first man to have a regular cookery column in a daily newspaper: his recipes became famous as *The 365 Menus*. But it was Curnonsky (1862–1956) who did more than anyone to broaden interest in gastronomy and to institutionalise it as a national pastime. Maurice Sailland (he adopted the pseudonym Cur-Non-Sky at the suggestion of the humorist Alphonse Allais) was an orphan bachelor journalist of enormous size and weight, who had originally moved on the fringes of the

---

[1] *La Gastronomie. Revue de l'art culinaire ancien et moderne* (6 Oct., 3 Nov. and 8 Dec. 1839, 6 Feb. 1840).

[2] Chatillon-Pléssis, *La Vie à table à la fin du 19ᵉ siècle* (1894), 12.

[3] Charles Monselet, *Lettres gourmandes. Manuel de l'homme à table* (1877). Cf. Léon de Fos, *Gastronomiana* (1870), also a bachelor, formerly in the Forests Administration.

music-hall world, as secretary of the Bataclan. In 1907 he invented Bibendum for Michelin's motor-car tyre advertisements, and it was he who brought together the automobile, tourist and catering industries for their common benefit. In that same year *Les Lundis de Michelin* first appeared in *Le Journal*, showing the pleasures to be derived from motoring. Curnonsky toured France by car himself and wrote twenty-eight volumes of *La France gastronomique* over a period of about as many years. In 1933 he condensed this into a single volume, *Le Trésor gastronomique de France*. He spared no effort to track down a noteworthy cook, travelling all the way to Castelnaudary, for example, to eat a perfect *cassoulet*, not hesitating to wait the fourteen hours necessary for the dish to be prepared for him in exactly the right way. In 1927 he was elected Prince of Gastronomes in a national ballot organised by a newspaper; he created the Academy of Gastronomes, with forty members, to set the standards. By now, good eating was being taken seriously by an ever-growing body of people, who organised themselves into clubs to cultivate the art. Dining clubs are to be found in the early nineteenth century, but they now proliferated as never before. They were particularly influential now because they attracted many of the rich, articulate and powerful men from industry, politics and the professions—those, that is to say, who indulged in the new amusement of motoring, and who therefore gave the provincial hotel and restaurant trade a vastly increased clientele. The Academy of Gastronomes thus included the prime minister André Tardieu, Fernand Payen, president of the corporation of barristers, the author Maurice Maeterlinck, the mayor of Dijon, the secretary-general of the Opéra and a doctor from the Institut Pasteur. The Club des Cents, founded in 1912, admission to which was limited to those who had driven at least 4,000 kilometres by car, included the heads of the country's major firms and leading civil servants. There were dining clubs for barristers (Le Fin Palais, 1927), for singers, song writers and publishers (Le Pot au Feu de la Chanson, 1930), for doctors (Les Esculapes Gourmands, 1934), and for golfers (organised by the periodical *Le Golf*, 1921).

Regional cooking took on a new importance as a result. The impression the gastronomes spread was that there was a vast variety of remarkable dishes to be found all over France like a neglected treasure. There were indeed a number of provincial specialities which found new admirers, but quite as many were the creations of skilful cooks rather than genuinely traditional. The Parisian cooks had counterparts in the provinces, though these have not been so well recorded. Lyon certainly owed its high reputation to the efforts of its restaurants, established simultaneously with those of Paris (and dominated, rather exceptionally, by a number of celebrated women, like la Mère Guy, la Mère Fillioux and la Mère Brazier), as well as to its dining clubs, which flourished early in the nineteenth century, and to its prosperous bourgeoisie, who provided the patronage necessary for the rise of devoted local cooks.[1] In general, however, popular provincial cook-books, though they used different ingredients, seldom made anything very elaborate out of these. *Le Cuisinier gascon*, for example, first published in 1740 and reaching its twenty-ninth edition in 1896, was an essentially simple book of recipes, with modest claims, not seeking to do more than teach peasant girls who went into domestic service rudimentary rules. Some of the originality of provincial cooking came from the return to simpler methods, to the long slow stewing peasants used to employ, but with rather better ingredients than peasants had generally been able to afford.[2] Southerners exiled in Paris did much to propagate the taste for the dishes of Provence: during the Second Empire Creste and Roudiel's food shop in the rue de Turbigo 'Aux Produits du Midi' kept them supplied with the necessary ingredients. However, it was only towards the end of the nineteenth century that the tomato, for example, ceased to be a rarity in the northern half of the country.[3] It needed not only a revolution in transport, but also in market gardening, before the dishes of the provinces could be properly copied. The ministry of education distributed a cook-book, with recipes arranged by province, to schools in the first decade of the twentieth century: this, it was claimed,

[1] Mathieu Varille, *La Cuisine lyonnaise* (Lyon, 1928).

[2] Hugues Lapaire, *La Cuisine berrichonne* (1925), who however notes that interest in the cooking and dialect of Berry was, outside Berry, strongest in Germany: a German professor published a book on cake-making in Roman Gaul. Cf. Pierre Dupin, *Les Secrets de la cuisine comtoise* (1927); Maurice Beguin, *La Cuisine en Poitou* (Niort, 1932, by the Archivist of the Deux Sèvres).

[3] Cf. Marius Morard, *Les Secrets de la cuisine dévoilés* (Marseille, 1886) for southern cooking.

was the first book of its kind.[1] Madame Léon Daudet also wrote a book drawing attention to regional specialities, which spread the vogue. How exactly these new products and new methods were used has not been the subject of much research, however: the new history of the provinces of France, recently published in many volumes, is, strangely, almost silent about cooking. The exotic products probably came first and the re-creation of traditional recipes may well have been partly a romantic reaction against their rather inexpert use. Already in 1854 Gravier's grocery shop in Nevers was selling Roquefort, gruyère and Dutch cheese, raisins, figs, almonds, dates, oranges, sardines and anchovies. The incorporation of these luxuries into the national diet required the advent of prosperity: the list stresses the great difference between the food of the poor and the rich. On the other hand, the *canuts* of Lyon were famous for the vast amount of time and effort they spent on improving simple ingredients. These ingredients, moreover, were once much more varied than they have since become. Thus mid-nineteenth-century cookbooks often devoted much space to discussing the innumerable varieties of fruit and vegetables. As production for the towns became an increasing concern of the peasants, standardisation made rapid strides and the fifty different types of pear once available, for example, gave way to just two or three principal varieties. Regional cooking thus had to be resurrected, like regional dialects, when the economic basis for it had been partly undermined.

Cooking had its parties, just like politics. Curnonsky once produced an analysis of their programmes. The extreme right were patrons of the grand, complicated learned style, requiring a brilliant chef and first-class materials: theirs was 'diplomats' food', though they often got only 'palace hotel food', which was a parody of it. The right favoured traditional cooking on wood fires and by slow methods, preferring the produce of their own gardens and the style of their own cooks, who had been in the family for thirty years; and they drew on cellars stocked with pre-phylloxera wine. Then there was bourgeois or regionalised

[1] Edmond Richardin, *L'Art de bien manger* (n.d., about 1904); Curnonsky and Austin de Croze, *Le Trésor gastronomique de France. Répertoire complet des spécialités gourmandes des trente deux provinces françaises* (1933); Elizabeth David, *French Provincial Cooking* (2nd edition, 1965).

cooking, occupying the middle ground; its adepts were willing
to admit that one could dine well in a restaurant and they welcomed the development of good hotels. The left wing believed
in simple and quick cooking, being satisfied with an omelette,
a slice of ham, or an *entrecôte*; they did not object to tins and
sometimes indeed argued that tinned beans were as good as
fresh ones; they liked eating in little *bistrots*, and enjoyed the
'country style' and 'amusing' local wines. The extreme left,
finally, were the innovators and the worried, the searchers for
new sensations, for fantastic and exotic experiences; they liked
colonial and foreign dishes; they had their saints and their
martyrs.[1] All these parties have made contributions to what is
known as French cooking. The temptation is to identify the
national style with that of the middle group, the solid, careful
bourgeois style, whose rules seem as well established as those of
classical literary prose. There are arguments both in favour and
against this. On the one hand the bourgeoisie did as much for
the raising and maintenance of high standards as either the great
cooks or the restaurants did. A description of achievements in
cooking which limited itself to the public sector would be very
incomplete. The best food in Paris, said a knowledgeable guide
in 1846, is to be eaten in the homes of the well-to-do bourgeoisie.
The grand restaurant cooks despised female cooks, but that was
partly professional jealousy, for the humble but highly skilful
women in private service 'whom tradition still designates by the
name of cordons bleus' were often very remarkable in their own
way. 'It is impossible to bring more care, more delicacy, more
taste and more intelligence than they apply to the selection and
the preparation of food. A good Paris *cuisinière*, to whom an
appropriate liberty of action is left, has talents which can compete with those of the illustrious chefs, the only reservation being
with regard to the great dishes of the table, the office and
dessert.' They did not produce great architectural constructions;
they were not allowed the luxury and extravagance of the
masters; they avoided the 'monstrous foreign puddings', and
they were slow to adopt new methods; but they laid great stress
both on quality and on cleanliness. Bourgeois cooking involved
co-operation between these cooks and the mistress of the household; and as one descended to lower levels of prosperity, even

[1] Curnonsky, *Souvenirs* (1958), 235.

more effort was applied, particularly in shopping. This guide of 1846 contrasts this kind of cooking with the 'outrageously simple' lunches served in canteens, the even worse food provided in factories and schools, and the hastily prepared and hastily eaten meals of small shopkeepers.[1] The cook-books used by the bourgeoisie certainly required ample leisure and full-time application; and those who ate the food prepared by their women cooks seem to have spent about two hours doing justice to each meal.[2] Good food was held to be one of the bases of the stable family life. When cooking came to be taught in schools from the 1880s, this was one subject where traditional virtues were significantly perpetuated. Thus one successful domestic science textbook pointed out the dangers of over-rich sauces, but insisted nevertheless that everybody should know how to prepare them and that no dinner was complete without them; the serving of appetising food, its artistic preparation and display were held up as one of the most important duties of every housewife.[3] It may be that lay schools stressed the scientific principles of nutrition rather more, and that Catholic ones were more traditionalist, more interested in encouraging food that was sensually enjoyable; but it is likely that bourgeois girls learnt more from their mothers, the schools being most influential on the poorer classes.[4] However, the attitude of the bourgeoisie to food was not uniform, as a study of the budgets of 547 bourgeois households, between 1873 and 1953, has revealed. The most important conclusion of this detailed investigation of income and expenditure is that the main characteristic of their behaviour was its astonishing diversity. This is what argues most strongly against the view that bourgeois cooking should be regarded as typically French. Only some of the bourgeoisie gave a high priority to eating. On average, throughout these years, the families studied spent between 21·5 and 25 per cent of their incomes on food; but the variations which produce these

---

[1] Eugène Briffault, *Paris à table* (1846), 53–64.

[2] Anon., *La Cuisinière bourgeoise* (1st edition 1746, 22nd edition 1866, published in Lyon, Avignon, Besançon, Montbéliard, etc.) is a good indication of this style.

[3] Madame M. Sage, *L'Enseignement ménager* (3rd edition, 1909), 268–77.

[4] Mesdames G. Rudler and A. Saint-Paul, *L'Enseignement ménager* (1910, 12th edition 1933), as an example of the scientific approach; for the private schools' approach see *Le Cordon bleu* (1897) and C. Driessens, *Alphabet de la ménagère* (1891, 2nd edition, 1900).

averages were very wide. Four-fifths of the families can be contained within the range of 14 and 34 per cent, but there were those who spent only 10 per cent on food. Engels's law that people spend a smaller proportion of their total income on food as they grow richer was not confirmed by this study. There was the case of one household, consisting of husband, wife and teenage daughter, who spent only 17·5 per cent of their income on food, but this turns out to be a very large sum indeed, for they were rich. A complicating factor is the proportion of the food budget spent on drink: this accounted, in most cases, for between one-tenth and one-third of the food budget, but a not inconsiderable proportion spent over a third and one even 49·6 per cent (though this was probably a case of a cellar being laid down). There is no link between how much was spent on wine and how much on food, except that expenditure on drink has fallen very considerably, from an average of 17·3 per cent of the food budget at the end of the nineteenth century to only 7 or 8 per cent in 1945–53, with expenditure over 10 per cent becoming very rare. There were equally wide variations in spending on different items of food: expenditure on bread varied between 3 and 16 per cent, meat between 17 and 40, cheese between 1 and 7; vegetables represented 6 to 8 per cent before 1914, and then went up to 10 to 12 per cent. It cannot be said that food was always an overriding preoccupation. Expenditure on clothes varied from 3 to 18 per cent, and in over one-third of these families, the men spent more on clothes than the women.[1] The bourgeoisie was certainly not representative of the country as a whole in what they ate. Baron Brisse's *365 Menus*, if they were an accurate reflection of their tastes in Paris during the Second Empire, show, for example, that they ate proportionately less pork and chicken than the peasants. Thus pork appeared in these menus only twenty-four times, mainly in the form of *charcuterie*, compared to 139 beef dishes and 102 mutton ones. Leg of mutton was the most frequent meat dish, occurring thirty-two times. Fish was eaten almost every day (363 times). More game (168) than fowl (139) was consumed, but chicken accounted for only half of the fowl. Vegetables were also eaten much less by the bourgeoisie than the peasantry, as the number of dishes using them shows: potatoes 62, beans 38, artichokes

[1] Marguerite Perrot, *Le Mode de vie des familles bourgeoises 1873–1953* (1961).

and asparagus 27, spinach 26, green peas 24, turnips 23, mushrooms 19, cauliflower 18, celery 17, sorrel 15, dried peas 14, lettuce and onions 13, tomato and cucumber 7, rice 75, Italian pasta 63. The potato invaded the bourgeois menu only in the years 1840–60, and cheese became a regular course only in the second half of the nineteenth century; fruit also used to be scarce, a pear in 1850 costing twice as much as a slice of Roquefort.[1] The services available to those wanting a good meal also changed. Thus whereas in 1851 Paris had one *pâtisserie* for every 2,640 inhabitants, by 1900 there was only one for every 9,000 (the number of shops falling from 402 to 294, while the population more than doubled). This was because about half of the city's 1,880 bakeries had taken to making cakes also: but it is likely that the standard of their cakes was not as high as that of the specialists, who moreover had produced not just sweet cakes but a whole variety of pastries.[2] There was thus, in the course of this century, a considerable change in the diet of the bourgeoisie. The number of people who could afford to eat what they liked increased only slowly and was never very large.

One of the great problems in the history of cooking is why England, which was a richer country than France and had a vastly richer aristocracy capable of spending without limit to obtain the best food, did not develop as sophisticated or as varied a style of cooking as France did. England's prosperity may in fact have been excessive: ample supplies of good meat may have made skilful preparation unnecessary—which was certainly what happened in the U.S.A. England also preferred to devote its attention more to the elaboration of sweet dishes; it consumed three times more sugar than France. The cooks of France complained that the French did not give large dinners and parties, and did not employ grand male cooks so much; but the English, precisely because they were rich enough to entertain at home, therefore ate out less, and there were far fewer restaurants in England as a result. The restaurant was an essential cause of France's competitiveness in cooking. But it would be wrong to contrast English and French cooking too

---

[1] J. P. Aron, *Essai sur la sensibilité alimentaire à Paris au 19ᵉ siècle* (1967), 85–117.

[2] A. Charabot, *La Pâtisserie à travers les âges. Résumé historique de la communauté des pâtissiers* (Meulan, S. & O., 1904); E. Darenne, *Histoire des métiers de l'alimentation* (Meulan, 1904), 162.

sharply in this period. The English were interested by good food, as the very large number of cook-books published shows.[1] French books were translated into English from as early as 1725;[2] and the English aristocracy employed a large number of French cooks. One must compare like with like: the best food in England was not inferior to the best in France. But when the English aristocracy lost their predominance, the grand style of life vanished with it. In France, by contrast, the tastes of the aristocracy were spread by their cooks who opened restaurants, and upper- rather than lower-class ideals became the most widespread in matters of food. The prosperous English worker kept his tastes even when he moved into the middle class; but the French peasant who ended up as a bourgeois sought to become, at least in his eating habits, a minor seigneur. The French have also put much more effort into propaganda about their food and they exported a very large number of cooks, whereas the English sent abroad more colonists, missionaries and administrators.

Another way that Frenchmen made themselves happy, or less unhappy, was by drinking. Wine, said Taine, is the people's philosopher. The part wine played in life was indeed as considerable and as complex as that of political or social ideas. Wine was held to be responsible for 'that part of the national character which was most admirable—cordiality, frankness in human relations, good humour, the gift for conversation and delicacy of taste'. Albert Lebrun, President of the Republic, declared in 1934 that 'wine does not only confer health and vigour. It also has soothing properties which both ensure the rational equilibrium of the organism and create a predisposition to harmony among men. In addition, it can, in difficult times, pour confidence and hope into our hesitating hearts.'[3] Wine, however, was drunk in very different ways in the course of this period, and the cult surrounding it went through interestingly changing fashions.[4]

[1] A. W. Oxford, *English Cookery Books to the Year 1850* (1913).

[2] Noel Chomel's *Dictionnaire oeconomique* translated 1725; *The French Family Cook* (1793); A. B. Beauvilliers, *The Art of French Cooking* (French edition 1814, English translation 1824); *La Cuisinière de la campagne et de la ville*, the French best-seller, translated as *French Domestic Cookery* (1846).

[3] M. L. Laval, *Le Vin dans l'histoire de France* (1935), ii, 87.

[4] For the economic history of wine production and the outlook of the wine-growers, see vol. 1. 165–70.

The French were not always a nation of wine drinkers. Wine used to be a luxury, which only the well-to-do could afford; the peasants had to be content at most with *piquette*; and in the late eighteenth century the town worker still had relatively few bars where he could go to quench his thirst. The upper classes used to produce wine mainly for their own consumption. Tariff barriers between provinces, as well as problems of transport, made the exchange of wine between different regions rare or difficult, so that the very rich who wanted something special tended to drink imported wines from Spain or Portugal for preference. The wines of the Beaune region were an exception: they won a high reputation in Paris, but perhaps even more in the Netherlands. Bordeaux wines were better known in England than in Paris, until Louis XIV was converted to them on medical grounds, but it was not until the Second Empire that they received their present-day classification into graded *crus*. While they rose in esteem, the wines of the Île-de-France and of Orléans, on which Paris had hitherto relied, lost their reputation. The choices open to wine drinkers and the number of wine drinkers changed drastically in the eighteenth and nineteenth centuries. The rise of democracy was paralleled by a vast increase in the production of wine, so that people got the right to vote and to drink roughly simultaneously. This was due to the expansion of the production of *vin ordinaire*, mainly from the south. Between 1840 and 1875, the amount of wine produced in France roughly doubled. Then the phylloxera crisis, which led to the replanting of most vineyards with American plants, both changed the taste of wine and, by reducing supplies for a decade to less than their level in 1840, forced people who had acquired new tastes either to drink foreign wine or to take to other forms of alcohol: and it is in this period that spirit drinking made enormous gains. The building of the railways meant that cheap wine could be carried cheaply to every part of the country, but it meant also that wines could be mixed and blended in new ways, and turned effectively into an industrial product.

A guide to wine drinking published in 1865 recommended that sherry or dry madeira should be served after the soup; between the first and the second course madeira, cognac, rum or vermouth were suitable; bordeaux or burgundy could be served indifferently with any food, but the plainer varieties should be served first and the better ones later in the meal; champagne should come with the dessert.[1] The 'oenological education' of the country was only effected gradually. The 'wine connoisseur' is a modern creature. Originally, it was considered acceptable to drink red or white wine indiscriminately, and the best wines were drunk to the accompaniment of the vegetables. This was now condemned, by a new kind of author, as 'rudimentary and unmethodical'. Dogmatic rules developed as to what was proper, though there were disagreements. Thus in the 1920s, it was recommended, by Paul de Cassagnac, who was not only the leading Bonapartist journalist in France, but also an expert both on duelling and on drinking, that fish should be accompanied by sauterne, which could also be used at the end of the meal for dessert and cheese; bordeaux and burgundy should not be served at the same meal; bordeaux should be decanted but burgundy should not, though others declared that it should.[2] These rules were perhaps the necessary counterpart to the unprecedented variety of options that were now available. But it was difficult for them to have permanent validity, because the conditions of wine production changed so frequently. Thus burgundy which was once the supreme French wine was badly hit by the phylloxera crisis and never fully recovered: none of the new vintages, it was said, ever equalled the Musigny 1869 or the Chambertin 1865. Burgundy was one of the wine-producing regions where land ownership was most divided. Thus Chambertin wine was produced from only 27 hectares (67 acres) and these were divided between twenty-five owners; Clos Vougeot came from 50 hectares divided among thirty-eight owners. This meant that no owner could produce his own wine. The situation was completely different from that in the Bordeaux region, where the estates were large enough to allow independent vintages to be manufactured by individual owners: Château d'Yquem was an estate of 148 hectares, with 90 hectares of vine, yielding on average 125 casks (of nearly a thousand litres each); Château Margaux had 90 hectares of vine producing 275 casks of the best quality. The result was that in Burgundy, wine was made above all by wholesale merchants, and

---

[1] L. Maurial, *L'Art de boire, connaître et acheter le vin et toutes les boissons. Guide vinicole du producteur, du commerçant et du consommateur* (1865, 2nd edition).

[2] Paul de Cassagnac, *Les Vins de France* (1927), 45.

the reputations of different wines depended as much on their names as on the regions they purported to come from. Now the law on labels and trade-marks in the nineteenth century was designed to protect the producer rather than the consumer, and it was only in 1919 that a law was passed requiring that wine had to come from the region specified on its label. The effect of this was, paradoxically, disastrous. It meant that any wine produced, say, in the commune of Pommard, was allowed to call itself that. However, Pommard originally was a high-class wine; inferior grades were not marketed under that name. Now they had a right to be; and the peasants exploited this new situation by growing as much wine as they could, even on the poorest soil which had never been used for this purpose, and selling it, quite legally, with an expensive-sounding label. But Pommard, as it was once known, had not been made exclusively from vines of that village: Chassagne's wines, for instance, were incorporated in it. Because some names had become famous, neighbouring villages had sold their wine under these famous labels: thus Morey wine, which was just as good as Chambertin, used to be sold under the latter name: but this could no longer be.[1] Bordeaux wine, for its part, had seldom contained only locally produced wine; and it was considered that it was improved, that its bitterness was diminished, by the addition, for example, of Ermitage or Roussillon wine. There were regions, like the Gaillac in the Tarn, which produced wine almost solely for the purpose of selling it to the Bordeaux producers, for mixing.[2] The alcoholic content of some fine wines was too low (little above eight degrees) for the taste of northern France, and it needed to be reinforced. The quality of wine, besides, varied each year, but the consumer demanded that it should always taste the same: this required very skilled blending. A wine merchant writing in 1903 said that only 10 per cent of wines, at most, were not mixtures.[3] Connoisseurship therefore had to battle against these charges and these frauds, and it was in some way an answer to the challenge thrown to the consumer. Some

[1] On the legislation, see Joseph Giraud, *La Vigne et le vin en Franche Comté. Les Vignobles comtois devant le problème des appellations d'origine* (Besançon, 1939).

[2] J. L. Riol, *Le Vignoble de Gaillac depuis ses origines jusqu'à nos jours et l'emploi de ses vins à Bordeaux* (1913), 262.

[3] P. Maigne, *Nouveau Manuel complet du sommelier et du marchand de vins*. New edition by Raymond Brunet (1903), 400.

experts declared that one could only tell the difference between years, not between vineyards of the same type. Their battle with the producers was certainly an unequal one, particularly because of the way the wine trade developed, which placed further complications in the path of the consumer.

Most wine was of poor quality, and this was increasingly the case as mass production, aiming above all at quantity, spread in the south; improvements in techniques of manufacture failed to keep up with this. It used to be the practice for peasants to drink the worst wine themselves and sell only the best, which could fetch a decent price. Thus in the mid-nineteenth century there was a whole range of unknown wines, described as 'disagreeable' and 'bad', which were produced in considerable quantities but consumed locally. The most important development of this century was the rise of the wholesale wine merchant, who barely existed in the eighteenth century, and the enormous multiplication of retail wine merchants. In 1790 Paris had only 4,300 *cabarets*; but the Revolution allowed anyone to open one and their numbers quickly increased. Though restrictions were reimposed, the number of bars and shops selling wine rose as follows:

| | | | |
|------|---------|------|----------|
| 1830 | 282,000 | 1913 | 483,000 |
| 1865 | 351,000 | 1922 | 452,000[2] |
| 1900 | 435,000[1] | 1937 | 509,000 |
| 1901 | 464,000[1] | 1953 | 439,000 |

This meant that France came to have in 1937 on average one bar for every 81 inhabitants, and in 1953 one for every 97 inhabitants. This compared with one for 225 in Italy, 273 in Germany, and 425 in England (1953).[3] The great jump in the number of bars came after 1880 when the decree of 1851, which had required the prefect's authorisation to open a bar, was rescinded: within a decade, the number of bars in Paris rose by 37 per cent. The general averages conceal great variations: thus in the Nord, there was one bar per 46 inhabitants already in 1890, which could mean, in some communes, two for every three adult men. The wine-producing regions had, for obvious reasons, far fewer—but even so the Gers still had one for every

---

[1] Paris is not included in the statistics until 1901.
[2] Alsace Lorraine included.
[3] S. Ledermann, *Alcool, Alcoolisme, alcoolisation* (1956), 78.

187 inhabitants at that same date (comparing with one for 580 in Boston). The result of this proliferation was impossible competition between the bars, and profits could only be made by adulterating and diluting the wine. There was a great difference therefore between the wine bought from the grower (which was seldom done now) and from the retailer. Adding water was perfectly legal, and until 1919, so was mixing wines. Wholesalers used to do the mixing—or some of it—in the presence of the retailers, usually so as to produce a wine with an alcohol content five degrees higher than that which it was proposed to sell to the consumer. The retailer could then add 20 per cent of water, and still serve wine above the legal minimum of 10°. However, since growers often also added water, before sending their wine to the wholesaler, the customer may sometimes have drunk as much water as wine. Adding water was harmless—indeed it was very common for people to dilute even good wines in the nineteenth century, the prohibition on this by the connoisseurs being quite recent. Gambetta defended this kind of dilution as 'honest fraud'. Wine from the south of France was often 15° strong, and when it arrived in Paris up to one-third of it was frequently water when it was sold in bars, at 10°. The bar-keepers almost had to do this, because it greatly reduced the taxes they paid, raising their profits by about 25 per cent. The customers used to joke about this 'baptism' to which wine was subject, with only the state being the loser. More serious, however, was the addition of alcohol, sugar, chalk, and a whole variety of chemicals and colorants, some of which had a defensible place in the making of wine, but some were positively noxious. It was no easy matter spotting the fraud, though many ingenious methods were tried by amateur analysts. When in 1880 the municipal laboratories of Paris tested 300 samples of wine bought at random in local bars, they found 225 of them to be seriously adulterated, fifty slightly so, and only twenty-five to be pure. It was ironical that bar-keepers, who tended to be radical or boulangist or advanced in politics, should have based their leadership on regular commercial fraud.[1]

High-class wine, with recognised *appellations*, formed only about one-tenth of the wine consumed. France consumed more

---

[1] Adrien Berget, *Les Vins de France . . . Manuel du consommateur* (1900); J. Barberet, *Les Débitants de boisson* (monographies professionnelles, vol. 7) (1890).

alcohol than any other country in the world. In 1950–4 France consumed 30 litres of pure alcohol per adult, which was accounted for by 200 litres of wine, 25 litres of beer and 3·8 litres of spirits (expressed in terms of litres of pure alcohol). This was double its nearest rival as the table shows.

*Consumption of Alcohol per adult, 1950–4*[1]

|  | Litres of pure alcohol | Consumed as | | |
|---|---|---|---|---|
|  |  | Litres of wine | Litres of beer | Litres of spirits (pure alcohol) |
| France | 30 | 200 | 25 | 3·8 |
| Italy | 14·2 | 130 | 4·5 | 1·1 |
| U.S.A. | 8·8 | 5 | 100 | 3·3 |
| Great Britain | 8·5 | 1·5 | 137 | 0·8 |
| West Germany | 5·1 | 12 | 66 | 1·6 |
| Sweden | 5·1 | 2 | 36 | 3·6 |

The national average again concealed the fact that in Brittany the average annual consumption of pure alcohol per male adult was between 54 and 70 litres (but only 21 to 31 litres in Provence). The really hard drinkers constituted 7 per cent of the population—30 per cent in Brittany, and 3 to 4 per cent in Provence; they drank one-quarter of all the alcohol consumed in the country. By themselves, they would have been unable to resist legislation to stop them, but they were protected by one of the most powerful lobbies in the country, that of the *bouilleurs de cru*. These were the people who took advantage of the law that though alcohol sales were taxed, ordinary individuals who made spirits for their own use were exempt. Their numbers increased sixfold in the course of this period:

| *Bouilleurs de cru* in 1877 | 490,000 |
|---|---|
| 1890 | 550,000 |
| 1900 | 930,000 |
| 1920 | 1,730,000 |
| 1925 | 2,640,000 |
| 1934 | 3,100,000 |
| 1951 | 3,100,000 |
| 1955 | 2,490,000 |

[1] Ledermann, op. cit. 68–9.

B b

The result was that they became too united a force for the politicians to offend: in twenty-three departments, half the electors were *bouilleurs*, and in twenty-four others, one-third were.

Absinthe, which thus became a popular drink, was, of course, only one way of forgetting one's troubles. This century also developed rather more elaborate ways—if not to forget, then at least to cope—as people began analysing their troubles with a more minute curiosity. It is these troubles or anxieties that will now be examined.

# Part III

# 15. Private Lives

PRIVATE lives have, on the whole, been an area into which historians have not penetrated, and certainly not systematically. This is due partly to tradition, to a convention inherited from public figures who have mutually conceded each other immunity outside the arena of politics and war. It has been only poets and novelists who have enjoyed baring their souls and their emotional troubles and it is mainly concerning them therefore that the rule of silence is broken. But the silence has been due also to a genuine lack of interest by historians in individuals as such, or at least to a preference for grander, less limited themes. That does not mean that historians have not written about individuals, but rather that they have subordinated such writing to other purposes. This was particularly the case in France. Any approach to a study of private lives must first explain what people's attitude to the subject was, since the facts about them can be seen only through this veil that envelops them. There is no book about biography in France in this period, but it is important to investigate its prestige and its function in the writing of this period. Secondly, one needs to discover the relationship between biography and the way character and personality were interpreted. What, in other words, were the psychological assumptions that biographers made, and how did the development of scientific and medical knowledge alter views about motivation and behaviour? Psychology in the mid-nineteenth century was still largely a branch of philosophy, and philosophy—or at least the 'philosophical approach'—was the principal enemy of biography.

## Biography

The number of biographies written in the nineteenth century was quite enormous. If one opens the *Bibliographie de la France*, say for the year 1856, one finds that of the sixty-four pages listing historical works, biography takes up ten, more than local history, which has nine, and twice as much as foreign history, which has four. It is not worth trying to make these very rough statistics more precise, because the titles indicate very different things. The vast majority of publications—and particularly biographies—were only short pamphlets. A historian who examined 400 biographies of bishops of the *ancien régime* found only about ten to be really substantial.[1] But some idea of the accumulating mass of biographies—whatever their quality—can be obtained from looking at the *Catalogue de l'histoire de France*. In 1865 this contained 21,027 individual biographies of persons involved in the French Revolution alone. By 1940 this number had increased to 71,716.[2] This leaves aside the collective biographies, in which the nineteenth century was particularly prolific, produced by men like Michaud, Hoefer, Vapereau and Larousse.

A count has been made simply of the biographical dictionaries devoted to contemporaries. The nineteenth century produced no less than 200 of these, to which should be added another eighty-one begun but never finished. This contrasts with only fifty-two produced in the first sixty-one years of the twentieth century. These figures refer to general dictionaries only, and exclude the large number of specialised regional and professional ones, and the ones devoted to historical figures.[3] These biographical dictionaries, though enormous, were nevertheless surprisingly modest in their pretensions. They were obviously as much financial speculations as contributions to knowledge. Plagiarism was one of their principal methods. Levot, author, with forty collaborators, of the *Biographie bretonne* (1852), did not presume to claim for biography a place more exalted than that of 'History's younger sister'. Rochas, author of the *Biographie du Dauphiné* (1856), saw his function as to collect information 'disdained by the gravity of history'. None of these compilers seems to have developed any independent philosophy to justify his activity. The Court

[1] M. Peronnet, 'Pour un renouveau des études biographiques: approches méthodiques', *Actes du 91ᵉ Congrès des sociétés savantes, Rennes 1966*, ancien régime et révolution (1969), 7–17. This article limits itself to proposing the compilation of biographical index cards.

[2] G. Walter, *Répertoire de l'histoire de la Révolution française. Travaux publiés de 1800 à 1940* (1941), preface.

[3] J. Auffray, 'Bibliographie des recueils biographiques de contemporains au 19ᵉ et 20ᵉ siècles en France', Mémoire pour l'Institut National des Techniques de la Documentation, unpublished, 1963.

of Paris, in its judgement in the lawsuit between two of the most famous compilers of biographical dictionaries, Michaud and Hoefer, in which the former accused the latter of plagiarism, ruled that Michaud had shown no 'unity of thought or of doctrine', and that his work gave no evidence of 'over-all supervision or direction'.[1] Dr. Hoefer did not even claim that he was showing that a man's life could have an interest of its own: he said that his main innovation was that he was remedying the defect attributed to other dictionaries of biography, that they gave too much space to obscurities. He said that he aimed to proportion 'the length of his articles to the importance of the personality, as exactly as possible'. He accepted, that is, the criterion imposed by the general historians.

This timidity of biographers was explained by the firmness with which the most esteemed authors spurned their activities, when they laid down what was and what was not worthy of study in the past. Thus Victor Cousin (who, one tends to forget, did not die till 1867) affirmed that a nation was not an accidental collection of individuals: it could not be 'a veritable People except on condition that it expressed an idea that, by passing through all the elements of which the People's internal life was composed, gave it a special character'. The proper subject of history was the idea, not the individual, who was nothing without it. 'The individual by himself is a miserable and petty fact . . . Humanity has not got the time and cannot bother to concern itself with individuals who are nothing but individuals.' It was interested only in great men, who incarnated the idea of their time. But the great man was only one who succeeded and who was recognised as such by his contemporaries. This severely limited the scope of biography. In any case, in studying great men, one should not concern oneself with their private lives, with what, i.e., was particular about them. The private lives of the great, as memoirs revealed, were perfectly common, like those of all ordinary men, and were not worthy of the true historian. 'The philosophy of history is a classical muse; it seeks out in the great man that which makes him great, and the rest it leaves to memoirs and biography.'[2]

[1] *Bibliographie de la France* (19 Mar. 1853), 118.

[2] Victor Cousin, *Introduction à l'histoire de la philosophie* (4th edition, 1861), 10ᵉ leçon. Cf., for the development of biography in England, from the eighteenth-century 'character' to the nineteenth-century 'compilation', and for theories about

Guizot took a similar view. 'It matters little to us', he said, 'to know what Constantine's face was like, or what the precise date of his birth was; we do not need to discover what particular motives, what personal sentiments influenced his decisions and his conduct on this or that occasion, nor to be informed about all the details of his wars and his victories against Maxentius or Licinius: these circumstances concern only the monarch and the monarch is dead.' History should be concerned with large and general questions only, such as the results of Constantine's conversion, his administration and his political principles. There were, for Guizot, two parts to the past. One was dead, and was not worth resurrecting: this included all personal accidents. Only the other, the dominating ideas, because of the influence they had on nations and whole centuries, were the proper subject-matter of history. Besides, it was futile to try to penetrate the private motivations of individuals, which were too complicated, obscure and mysterious to understand. 'Man can barely know himself and he is never more than guessed about by others. The most simple person would have a thousand secrets to reveal to us, which we never suspected, if he tried to paint himself.' This perhaps was an honest explanation of why historians did not examine biography: they had no real theory for interpreting the lives of individuals. In his study of Sir Robert Peel (1850), Guizot gave only 8 out of 354 pages to the first twenty-one years of Peel's life. In his books on the English Revolution, his main concern was to collect documents rather than fathom the characters of the contenders. At most he saw them as examples of types, Ludlow as the archetype of the spirit of faction, Fairfax was that of the disinterested dupe, and so on. When it came to writing his own memoirs, however, he claimed to want to tell his 'personal and intimate history, what I thought, felt and wanted', and to describe 'our internal life in our actions'. But that was the function of memoirs, not history.[1]

It is not surprising to find, therefore, that Bishop Dupanloup, the 'dignity of history', Joseph W. Reed, Jr., *English Biography in the Early 19th Century* (Yale U.P., 1966).

[1] F. Guizot, *Mémoires pour servir à l'histoire de mon temps*, vol. 1 (1858), 388–95, 3–4; id., *Études biographiques sur la révolution de l'Angleterre* (1851), 51, 99, 214. Cf. Barante, *La Vie politique de M. Royer-Collard* (1861), which covers the first 22 years of his life in one page.

in his manual on the teaching of history, should have classified biography, with chronology, as that elementary part of history which was most suitable to be taught to children. He considered it to involve little more than the memorising of genealogical and chronological tables.[1] Despite this condemnation, there was nevertheless a great deal of curiosity about and interest in biography. The views of men like Cousin did not go unchallenged. One of his former pupils, professor of philosophy at Bordeaux, wrote a book to contradict him on this very question, protesting against the ruling that only great, representative and successful men should be studied. This would make it impossible to concern oneself with rebels, with innovators who were unrecognised by their own generation; private lives, moreover, were as much part of such men as anything else, and were deserving of investigation if only to ensure that history did not hold people up to admiration who were unworthy of it.[2] Sainte-Beuve was probably the most illustrious of the opponents of the 'high and philosophical method', as he called it, which linked a man so closely to his epoch and background that all was foreseen and inevitable in his career. Sainte-Beuve claimed that at any rate artists and poets who did not represent a whole epoch should not have their lives complicated from the start by 'too vast a philosophical apparatus'; it was enough 'to confine oneself, at first, to the private character and domestic liaisons, and to follow the individual closely in his interior destiny, and only then, when one knew him well, to bring him into broad daylight and to confront him with his century'. In his biography of Proudhon, for example, he declares his aim to be 'to show the man as he was, to draw out his moral qualities, the core of his sincerity, the form of his talent, in short his personality'.[3]

The biographer Levot was another who protested against the 'abusive extension' given to the philosophy of history. The

[1] Mgr Dupanloup, *Conseils aux jeunes gens sur l'étude de l'histoire* (1872), 49.

[2] C. A. Sainte-Beuve, *Proudhon* (1872), 12; A. G. Lehmann, 'Sainte-Beuve and the Historical Movement', in *The French Mind, Studies in Honour of Gustave Rudler* (Oxford, 1952), 256–72; J. Bourdeau, 'La Psychologie et la philosophie de Sainte-Beuve', *Séances et travaux de l'académie des sciences morales et politiques* (17 Dec. 1904), 354–74.

[3] Ladevi-Roche, *Variétés philosophiques* (1867), 1. 84–5.

individual, he insisted, could only rarely be regarded as the 'personification of the various passions that are active around him. By more or less idealising characters and by creating types, writers have too frequently condensed disparate or irreconcilable things into a single humanity, and the real man has disappeared to give way to a conventional man.'[1] First, there was the approach of the 'philosophers of history', who were concerned to show general trends and the large forces that dominated mankind. Mignet had been the principal initiator and exponent of this attitude.[2] Secondly, there were the romantics, who were sometimes interested in other people's emotions as well as in their own. Michelet gave considerable thought to the problem of biography: he agreed with Rousseau that Plutarch 'excelled by using those very details into which we no longer dare enter'; but when he embarked on his national history he was really more interested in penetrating the 'interior of the national soul' than in going deeply into that of any particular individual.[3] The romantic hero usually got lost as the personification of an abstraction. Renan cloaked this approach in a new scientific garb, but his best-selling *Life of Jesus* was basically a self-portrait, with a thin veneer of scholarship placed over it.[4] Taine's view that political doctrines were the result more of a special kind of sensibility than of pure intelligence meant that he was keen to study the heart as much as the mind. 'Political or religious fanaticism,' he wrote, 'whatever the theological or philosophical channel along which it flows, always has as its principal source an avid need, a secret passion, an accumulation of profound and powerful desires to which theory gives an outlet.' His application of psychology to history of course also led to very broad generalisations about what individuals typified, and usually presented a static view of them, in that they tended to remain under the domination of the same psychological state all their lives.[5]

[1] P. Levot, *Biographie bretonne* (1852), avant-propos.

[2] Y. Knibiehler, *Naissance des sciences humaines: Mignet et l'histoire philosophique au 19e siècle* (1973).

[3] On Michelet, see below, pp. 799–801.

[4] P. Alfaric, *Les Manuscrits de la vie de Jésus d'Ernest Renan* (1909).

[5] H. Taine, 'La Psychologie des Jacobins', *Revue des Deux Mondes* (1881), 44. 536–59; id., *De l'intelligence* (1870), 1. 7–9; Paul Lacombe, *La Psychologie des individus et des sociétés chez Taine* (1906).

The uncertainties and hesitations of biographers may be illustrated by some instances. Gaston Boissier, professor at the Collège de France, made something of a name for himself with his study of the public and private life of Cicero. He thought the latter worth investigating, even though he came to the conclusion that 'The feelings which are the basis of human nature have not changed and they always produce more or less the same consequences.' But at the same time Ernest Bersot, director of the École Normale, was moralising that 'There are details of our lives which occur behind the scenes: I demand, in the name of decency, that they should be left there.'[1] Napoleon III's *Histoire de Jules César* shows best of all the variety of contradictory attitudes towards biography, which he —as one could expect—tried somehow to reconcile. On the one hand he said that the aim of biographers should be to discover 'the predominant idea that makes a man act in the way he does', but on the other hand he insisted that great men were simply the instruments of Providence and it was wrong to explain the actions of 'superior men' by 'mean motives', egoism or cunning. On the one hand he wished history to teach moral lessons, to inspire love of justice and progress, but on the other hand he also paid lip-service to erudition. It is no wonder that his 'portrait' of Caesar is so brief and superficial.[2]

The bulk of biographical writing during the Second Empire was monumental, that is, it served to commemorate and extol the virtues of the dead. The largest proportion of biographies were *éloges*. This genre was not necessarily the antithesis of analytical biography. A. L. Thomas (1732–85), whose *Essai sur les éloges* was still regarded as the best guide on how to write these essays, had provided extremely acute and subtle precepts, which, if they had been followed, would have produced historically very interesting results. But since *éloges* were the speciality of Academicians, who were restrained by their *esprit de corps*, they did not emphasise criticism. One function of the *éloge* was to defend the choice the particular academy had made in electing the dead man as a member, proving, as Vicq d'Azyr of the Academy of Medicine had said, that they

---

[1] G. Boissier, 'Ciceron', *Revue des Deux Mondes* (1865), 56. 73; E. Bersot, *Études et pensées* (1882), 'De la médecine en littérature', written in 1860, 102–33.
[2] Napoleon III, *Histoire de Jules César* (1865), preface and 1. 410.

had chosen 'only persons, praise of whom the public could applaud'. The *éloge* had the moral purpose of holding up good examples to stimulate virtue, which was the function of history too, as some saw it. The *éloge* was also considered as a source of 'materials for history', a recording by friends of facts which would be lost unless enshrined in this way. The vast mass of these *éloges* would repay study, for it was not all simply secular hagiography. Some specialists made very interesting contributions; and there was a continuing debate about what ought and what ought not to be said about the dead.[1]

The clergy were probably the largest single category of whom biographies were written—followed by soldiers. Now hagiography, like the *éloge*, had a long tradition behind it. But this laid stress not on showing up the individuality of the subject, but rather on showing the virtue he represented. It was common to claim that the hero possessed all his future qualities and his vocation at birth. Hagiography was thus a discourse on virtue more than a biography. Great precision of detail was not infrequently attempted, and massive documentation collected in the tradition established by the Bollandists, but the aim was to edify rather than to explain.[2]

The main exception, in this period, to this attitude was that of Lavisse, who wrote two books on the early life of Frederick the Great, exceptionally lively and readable ones too. Lavisse concentrated on the struggle between Frederick and his father, which he saw as reflecting the struggle of opposing forces in society, from the fusion of which Prussia emerged. His subtle analysis stressed the influence of Frederick's mother who 'on every single point thought differently' from his father; and of Frederick's tutors, who gave him ideas directly contrary to those of his father; but he concludes that the rebellion of the young Frederick was really only a protest against excessive paternal demands, and that the resemblance of father and son,

---

[1] A. L. Thomas, *Œuvres* (new edition, 1773), 'Essai sur les éloges'; cf. the *éloges* by François Arago (1854), Flourens, Dubois d'Amiens, Mignet, etc. For the survival of these ideas, Georges Picot, *Études d'histoire contemporaine* (1907), ix, and Henri Dumeril, 'Éloge des éloges', *Mémoires de l'Académie des sciences, inscriptions et belles lettres de Toulouse* (1912), 131–48.

[2] René Aigrain, *L'Hagiographie, ses sources, ses méthodes, son histoire* (1953) and compare the works of Mgr Paul Guérin, *Les Petits Bollandistes* (1st edition 1858–60, 6th edition 1866–9), and Mgr Crosnier, *Hagiologie nivernaise* (Nevers, 1858).

which the son always tried to conceal, made itself evident as soon as he succeeded to the throne. This was in effect an intellectual as well as a political biography, based on the view that 'our philosophy always obeys our instincts'. But neither Lavisse nor his pupils developed these ideas.[1] It was André Maurois, a novelist, who became the country's most successful biographer, and it was popularised, fictionalised, superficial biography that was most favoured. The large quantities of this kind of writing that were published led to stern expressions of disapproval and contempt from those who regarded themselves as the guardians of the nation's good taste. In 1927 the *Revue des Deux Mondes* had an article complaining that the new reading public was demanding 'pure biography', meaning biography which served no purpose beyond satisfying idle curiosity about the doings of famous people, skimming on the surface of things, recounting amusing anecdotes. The author argued that this was a sign of the country's general decadence. 'Tired epochs have, in common with young epochs, the taste for fables. The essay, the maxim, and direct reasoning which demand meditation and the exercise of the understanding are reserved for vigorous periods.' The cinema was derided as a manifestation of this corrupting taste for a rapid succession of images. In Ancient Greece (which, for such men, was still the model) everybody who went to the theatre knew the plot of the play, and what mattered was the skill with which it was developed, and how character, passion and ideas were portrayed. Nowadays, by contrast, it was information unknown to the reader that was valued, revelations of scandals, so that most biography was reduced to stories of passion. This was acceptable to many readers because they themselves had experience only of passion, and they had done nothing that mattered beyond their own lives. For this classical critic, the theatre and the novel were acceptable forms of art, because 'they had their laws'. But biography 'is a more uncertain genre'. His conclusion was that its worth was determined ultimately by the qualities of the author: the best biographers would therefore be poets or literary critics, who could make out of the biography either a poetic creation, or an essay in philosophy or morals. 'The painter

[1] E. Lavisse, *La Jeunesse du grand Frédéric* (1888), 47, and *Le Grand Frédéric avant l'avènement* (1893), ix.

matters more than the model.' Historians could continue to devote themselves to laboriously collecting the facts, but only they were modest enough to place the hero in the forefront, for that meant that they themselves, as authors, would be forgotten.[1]

This is not to say that polemical biography was not also very much in demand. The success of men like Eugène de Mirecourt, whose hundred little volumes on *Les Contemporains* set unbreakable standards in scurrility and inaccuracy, may be linked with the new opportunities being opened up by the popular press.[2] Biography as a serious art was probably discredited by the sensationalism and anecdote-collecting to which journalists usually reduced it. It is not surprising therefore that few professional historians thought biography worthy of their attention, and remarkably few doctoral theses have been written about individuals. Even in very recent times, now that this tacit taboo has lost its force, historians who have written biographies have felt it necessary to apologise and justify their eccentricity, and all the more so because, now that class and economic forces are fashionable, the individual is held to 'make history' even less than before.[3]

### Psychology

Biographers were faced by a whole variety of psychological ideas, which they had to choose between when they embarked on their task. The most academically respectable method of discovering the springs of human action continued to be introspection. Psychology was in the mid-nineteenth century above all a branch of philosophy, and so it was a theoretical study, whose principal activity was to classify and define human faculties and passions. The leading expert then was probably Adolphe Garnier (Tocqueville's successor at the Académie des sciences morales et politiques), whose *Treatise on the Faculties of the Soul* was highly esteemed as a 'complete survey, a vast

---

[1] André Chaumeix, 'Le Goût des biographies', *Revue des Deux Mondes* (1 Dec. 1927), 698–708.

[2] Alexis Giraud, *Monsieur Eugène de Mirecourt* (1856); for an example, E. de Mirecourt, *Fabrique de romans: Maison Alexandre Dumas et compagnie* (1845).

[3] See the prefaces to P. Guiral, *Prévost-Paradol* (1955) and P. Sorlin, *Waldeck-Rousseau* (1966).

compendium of the behaviour of the soul'. Its principal originality was that it increased the number of faculties; but it was still very much an abstract exercise, since it offered no means of discovering which faculties were predominant in any particular person, in what proportions and why. Thus Garnier states that the instinct for power represents a desire for intellectual pleasure, and fortunately nature distributes this desire very unevenly, so that only some people have a strong desire to dominate while most have an inclination for submission and docility. Otherwise, society would be impossible. Heads of state, with a taste for domination and talents necessary to exercise it, are thus a natural phenomenon, explicable not in personal terms, but by the foresight of Providence. Garnier concluded that human nature was in any case so complicated that it was difficult for men to judge each other: his study had led him only to 'the dogma of indulgence and mutual charity'. Professor Paul Janet, who belonged to the same school, accepted that psychology was 'condemned, for a long time to come, to being simply a descriptive science'.[1] The type of biography that followed logically from this kind of psychology was one which attributed individuals to particular predetermined categories in a more or less random fashion. The constant arguments about how many faculties there were and what their exact nature was, however, made this kind of psychology, as the Premier Président de la Cour d'appel de Paris was to put it, 'a clever game or pedantic fantasy', of little use to practical men: its uncertainties discredited any pretensions it had to being a science, and all the more so because it gave little help in understanding the problems of ordinary behaviour.[2] Nevertheless, this is what was taught in the schools.

More popular was the theory of temperaments, which of course originates, like that of the faculties, in ancient Greek ideas. It is too readily assumed that this brand of psychology was no longer acceptable in the age of positivism; but Littré and Robin, the positivists who in 1855 revised Nysten's standard *Dictionary of Medicine*, wrote that 'the doctrine of temperaments is no longer accepted, now that it has been recognised that it is

---

[1] A. Garnier, *Traité des facultés de l'âme* (3rd edition, 1872), with a preface by Paul Janet; id., *La Psychologie et la phrénologie comparées* (1839).
[2] Alphonse Gilardin, *Considérations sur les divers systèmes de psychologie* (1883), 1–2.

due to particular variations in the brain that inclinations or affections, passions, intellectual faculties and moral qualities must be attributed'. But it was only the humours which were completely discredited; and the theory of temperaments was modified rather than overthrown. Littré and Robin still thought it significant to talk of the sanguine temperament, attributed now to men with large blood vessels, and the nervous temperament, which meant an irritable nervous system. Michel Lévy, Napoleon III's medical consultant and sometime president of the Academy of Medicine, still kept, in the fifth edition of his standard *Traité d'hygiène* (1869), the theory of temperaments as his preliminary explanation of human character and disease. He said that there was disagreement about its formulation, but 'only truth survives the test of time and we want no other testimony in favour of the doctrine of temperaments than this universal agreement about it'. Its strength was that it was easily capable of being adapted to suit the changing and almost equally vague ideas of the new science. Thus Professor Becquerel, in his treatise on hygiene, was satisfied that by renaming them the vascular, nervous and muscular temperaments, the theory accorded perfectly with modern discoveries. The *Moniteur des hôpitaux* ran a series in 1857 on the temperaments, in very conservative form, illustrating the bilious type from the medical history of Napoleon, and sub-categories like 'obstinate dogmatics' from that of Bossuet. These examples were regularly copied in the textbooks.[1]

Claude Bernard[2] himself—the physiologist who was famous as the exponent of the experimental method—was believed to have given his support to the theory of temperaments when he published an article on the physiology of the heart. In this he went out of his way to insist that 'the sentimental role that has in all ages been attributed to the heart' was not disproved by modern discoveries and was not 'purely arbitrary fiction':

---

[1] P. H. Nysten, *Dictionnaire de médecine* (10th edition, 1855), 1240–1, 156; Michel Lévy, *Traité d'hygiène publique et privée* (1844, 5th edition 1869), 46–71; A. Becquerel, *Traité élémentaire d'hygiène privée et publique* (1851, 3rd edition 1864), 77–88. Contrast F. V. Raspail, *Manuel annuaire de la santé* (e.g. 1879), which while condemning temperaments, recommends camphor and blood baths. Armand de Fleury (de Mansle), 'Du type bilieux', *Le Moniteur des hôpitaux* (4 Apr. 1857), 321–5.

[2] On Bernard, see above, pp. 581–2.

science was not destroying the ideas of art and poetry.[1] As late as 1895 the philosopher Fouillée revised the temperament theory in the light of that of evolution, but using protoplasm to replace the humours. Fouillée argued that the sanguine temperament 'long admitted and whose reality it is impossible to doubt' was caused by a highly oxygenated blood supply, and that it produced all the usual traits of character, in the description of which he invoked a host of traditional authorities.[2] Dr. Michel Lévy's chapter on temperaments, originally written in 1851, was reproduced in the textbook of Bouchardat, professor at the Paris medical faculty, published in 1881; but Bouchardat, who was an expert on nutrition, added a new twist by incorporating his discoveries, while keeping the basic framework. Thus he concluded that the English, who ate a lot of meat, were therefore energetic and 'keen on work', whereas the Chinese, who did not, were therefore 'weak and timid'.[3] As racial theories came to acquire great favour, the temperament theory was given a new lease of life by being united with it. Fouillée's book was hailed as an important contribution because it skilfully combined the two.[4] Nor were these ideas confined to specialist circles. Charles Letourneau, one of the most successful popularisers of science, was writing in favour of the theory of four temperaments in 1878, saying that the microscope had revealed differences in the blood between sanguine and bilious people.[5] When applied to biography, the temperaments of course produced a static psychology, even though considerable thought was given to how they could be modified.

Perhaps the greatest change that occurred in nineteenth-century popular psychology was the transfer of the source of the emotions from the stomach to the brain. This created a new determinism but also new uncertainties, because knowledge of the brain was still pretty elementary. The first important breakthrough in its dissection was made by Gall (1758–1828, a naturalised Frenchman of German origin), who instead of

---

[1] Claude Bernard, 'Étude sur la physiologie du cœur', *Revue des Deux Mondes* (1 Mar. 1865), 236–52.

[2] A. Fouillée, *Tempérament et caractère, selon les individus, les sexes et les races* (1895).

[3] A. Bouchardat, *Traité d'hygiène publique et privée basée sur l'étiologie* (1881), 25–9, 215.     [4] *Mercure de France* (Feb. 1896), review of Fouillée's book.

[5] Charles Letourneau, *Physiologie des passions* (1878, 2nd edition), 350–9.

cutting through it in a symmetrical and arbitrary way, pulled it apart, into its natural sections. It was a simple step to attribute to each of these independent functions. Phrenology offered a coherent and clear explanation of behaviour, and it carried all the more conviction because it was based on the work of a man who was universally recognised (for his anatomical work) as one of the greatest scientists of the day. A history of phrenology has collected abundant documentation to show that this enjoyed great prestige under the July Monarchy, even if it lost it under Napoleon III. A lot of distinguished people nevertheless still remained faithful to it. In 1865 there was a vigorous debate about phrenology in the Academy of Medicine. The discoveries of Dr. Broca, who had made the first genuine localisation in the brain shortly before, were used as additional support by the phrenologists, even though Broca's conclusions did not accord with Gall's, but at least they seemed to suggest that the basic idea of localisation was tenable and promising.[1] The great attraction of phrenology was that it was simple to understand. As developed by men like Broussais, it produced a psychology of common sense in plain language. Instead of subtleties and abstractions, it offered a series of twenty-seven human characteristics (later increased), whose importance in any particular individual could be physically discovered by simple examination. The inexplicable, and the element of pure chance, thus seemed removed from psychology. In the popular view, phrenology appeared to be scientific and based on observation: if thirty musicians were got together, they would all be found to have the same bump. Talent could thus be linked with physique. Gall did not mean to be as determinist as his simpler followers interpreted him. For him, the bumps simply denoted predispositions or potentialities, and the individual remained free to choose between them. He insisted that criminals should not be regarded as irresponsible. But all the same his theory was much misinterpreted, and was condemned not only for being arbitrary in its attribution of qualities, but above all for being atheist.[2]

[1] Jules Soury, *Le Système nerveux central, structure et fonctions: histoire critique des théories et des doctrines* (1899) places Broca's work in its context.

[2] G. Lanteri-Laura, *Histoire de la phrénologie* (1970) has a good bibliography. For physiognomy, and the related theory of 'cineseologie', see Prof. P. Gratiolet, *De la physionomie et des mouvements d'expression* (1865).

It might have been thought that the positivists would have produced a new psychology for the modern world. But, by their own admission, they did not. Littré lamented that this was a great gap in their doctrine. In his *Cours de philosophie positive*, Comte had based himself on Gall, on whom he wrote a brilliant chapter hailing him as the man who had shown the right approach. The metaphysical unity of the personality must be abandoned, and psychology must become a branch of cérebral anatomy. But then in the *Système de politique positive* he forgot all this and invented an arbitrary 'positive classification of the eighteen internal functions of the brain'. The originality of this was that it made the emotional faculties most important and most numerous. Both Comte's theories were anathema to Littré, the first because it kept so much of Gall, whom Littré considered old-fashioned, and the second because it was anti-intellectual and subjective. Littré had nothing to propose instead. But Dr. Audiffrent, one of Comte's religious disciples and his link with the medical world, wrote a book at the end of the Second Empire to make good the defect. This was not simply traditionalist: it amalgamated the ideas of the Montpellier school, Gall, Bichat and Broussais with the theory of temperaments, declared that the world was heading for nervous collapse, that 'névrosisme' was developing into an epidemic because of the lack of any generally accepted beliefs; that physical illness was simply a symptom of this inability of the mind to offer any resistance. This was—despite many interesting ideas— too much a political programme and a universal condemnation to be widely accepted.[1]

A great new body of detailed observation of human behaviour and emotion was meanwhile becoming available through the work of the psychiatrists. The law of 1838 on lunatic asylums, for all its defects, had provided a great stimulus to the development of this new specialisation, and much research and publication of an original kind followed, which has been unjustly neglected. It is too often assumed that between Pinel (1745–1826)

---

[1] A. Comte, *Cours de philosophie positive* (2nd edition, 1864), vol. 3, 45th lesson, 530–89; id., *Système de politique positive* (1851–3), 1. 724–5; E. Littré, *Auguste Comte et la philosophie positive* (1863), 677; G. Audiffrent, *Des maladies du cerveau et de l'innervation d'après Auguste Comte* (1875, enlarged edition of the 1869 book); Dr. Eugène Bourdet, *Des maladies du caractère: hygiène, morale et philosophie* (1858); cf. Charles Robin, *L'Instruction et l'éducation* (1877).

and Esquirol (1772–1840) on the one hand and Charcot (1825–93)[1] on the other, there was not much that was happening. In fact the ideas of Esquirol were quickly challenged in many respects by his pupils, devoted though they were to him, and a succession of methodological innovations were attempted to penetrate the causes of mental disturbances. Reacting against his 'moral' approach, some of his pupils devoted themselves to the autopsy of the brain, seeking physical lesions to explain abnormal behaviour—as was already fashionable in Germany. Others studied all the organs of the body, believing that the malfunctioning of any one could be responsible for mental troubles. Others, seeing, as Esquirol had done, the difficulty of making definite attributions of this kind, returned to the study of normal psychology; and finally, in reaction against all of these, some advocated the clinical approach, the most distinguished of whom was J. P. Falret. His method could be called the historical method, because he urged doctors to go beyond the facts of the case as they were presented to them: 'Instead of writing one's observations at the dictation of the lunatics, instead of making oneself the secretary of these sick people and simply noting down the most striking facts noticed by all those who have dealings with them, one should penetrate more deeply into the intimacy of their intellectual and moral characters; one should study the general dispositions of their minds and hearts, which are the basis of these predominant ideas or sentiments; one should go into the past of these lunatics, follow their affection in its development, from the most distant origin to the present.' He stressed the need to study all moral and physical symptoms in their chronological order, and he pointed out that 'negative facts', what they did not do, were as important as what they did do.[2]

From the layman's point of view, the discoveries of these psychiatrists which were of particular interest were those concerning mental troubles to be found, in various degrees of mildness, among the 'normal' population as a whole, as well as in the asylums. Thus there were new ideas about melancholy. The theory that it was caused by atrabile no longer stood. The melancholic temperament survived in traditional circles.

[1] On Charcot, see below, pp. 857–62.
[2] J. P. Falret, *Des maladies mentales et des asiles d'aliénés* (1864), xv–xvi.

Esquirol had tried to make the concept more precise, renaming it *lypémanie*, but he had regarded it as caused by a defect of the intellectual faculties, brought on by moral causes—though noting also the influence of heredity, temperament, puberty and the menopause. The important development came in 1854 when almost simultaneously Baillarger and Falret discovered the link between melancholy and mania. Baillarger called this form of melancholy *folie à double forme*; Falret named it *folie circulaire*. The discovery had a surprising result. Whereas, as separate troubles, melancholy and mania had each been considered curable, this new manic-depressive form was declared to be almost never curable or even capable of durable amelioration. Heredity was considered to be its principal cause, though traumatic experiences and physical diseases like syphilis could contribute to starting it. The only hope of a cure was to change it into either pure mania or pure melancholy, which could then be treated. Baillarger thus tried to get rid of manic symptoms by prolonged bleeding. Michéa used massive doses of stupefying drugs. There was still disagreement as to whether melancholy was a symptom of other troubles, or a morbid entity in itself. Provincial doctors, combining the various theories, became even more puzzled, declaring it to be 'the disease of an epoch, a family, a temperament', and felt more helpless than ever. The most significant result of the new discovery was that it confirmed melancholy as a highly serious disease, which should be treated in an asylum.[1]

In 1852 the *délire des persécutions* was isolated by Professor Charles Lasègue. His findings were the subject of an article in a medical journal, but they became known also to the new generation of medical students through his lectures and through those of Dr. Legrand du Saulle, who in 1871 published an impressive book containing their combined observations. They calculated that about one-sixth of patients in mental hospitals had this form of trouble. All the usual causes were invoked to explain it, but it was interesting to the world outside the asylums that Legrand du Saulle considered that illegitimate

---

[1] Dr. Antoine Ritti, *Traité clinique de la folie à double forme* (1883); Dr. Michéa, *Du traitement de la lypémanie ou folie mélancolique* (1860); *Bulletin de l'Académie de Médecine* (31 Jan. and 14 Feb. 1854); E. Du Vivier, *De la mélancolie* (1864); Dr. P. F. Gachet, *Étude sur la mélancolie* (Montpellier, 1858).

birth was probably one of the most frequent factors responsible for it. He laid a lot of stress on unsatisfactory relations between parents and children, leading to lack of confidence developing in the latter. There was also a certain amount of discussion about the effects of political and social revolutions as causes of insanity. The statistics were not very convincing, particularly because life became too chaotic—for the asylums as well as for everybody else—for comparable figures to be produced. But interesting case studies are available of the delusions of legitimists on the one hand and advanced radicals on the other who were locked up because their nostalgia or their ambitions appeared excessive; and the reactions of at least some people to the German invasion and occupation can be seen in this same kind of source.[1]

It was during the Second Empire also that hysteria ceased to be regarded as being produced by troubles of the uterus, or as being exclusively a female complaint. Charcot's work on this subject has caused the revolutionary work of an immediate predecessor, Dr. P. Briquet, to be forgotten. Briquet's book on hysteria, published in 1859, with detailed observations on 396 cases and much statistical analysis, argued that it was a nervous, not a physical complaint, produced by women's peculiar 'mode of sensibility', but that men could suffer from it too. Heredity played a major role in its transmission: so that whereas there was one hysteric to every sixty-six normal inhabitants, in hysterical families there was one hysteric in every four. He dismissed the idea that sexual continence had anything to do with it; and suggested instead that it was hysterical mothers who passed it on to their daughters. Marriage could no longer be recommended as the cure. Legrand du Saulle, who also wrote a book on hysteria, estimated that there were 50,000 hysterics in Paris alone: he urged that they should be studied no longer as isolated cases, but with reference to their social background. Shoplifting from the department stores by

---

[1] Charles Lasègue, 'Le Délire de persécutions', first published in the *Archives générales de médecine* (1852), reprinted in his *Études médicales* (1884), 1. 545–66; H. Legrand du Saulle, *Le Délire des persécutions* (1871); C. A. Claude, *De la folie causée par les pertes séminales* (Paris medical thesis, 1849); Dr. L. Lunier, *De l'influence des grandes commotions politiques et sociales sur le développement des maladies mentales* (1874); Paul Schiff, 'L'Évolution des idées sur la folie de persécution', *L'Hygiène mentale* (1935), 1–56.

otherwise respectable women was one of the new fashions of the Second Empire which was explained by hysteria.[1] Hallucination was an especially controversial subject, because doctors were bold enough to apply it to the supposedly normal world. Among the important works on it, was a long and thorough study by Dr. L. F. Calmeil, who was head of the Charenton Asylum for most of the Second Empire, of mass hallucination and 'great epidemics of delirium' between the fifteenth and eighteenth centuries. This was both a history of ideas about madness and an investigation of the pathological elements in many historical movements of the *ancien régime*. There was a great scandal when Dr. Lelut argued that psychology could study not just the mental troubles of the poor (and of course patients in the asylums were mainly poor), but also the great men of history, that it was possible, as he said, to apply psychology to history. He claimed that Socrates, Pascal and Luther suffered from pathological states of hallucination. The politician Eugène Pelletan replied that ordinary men could perhaps have mental eclipses of this kind, but he refused to accept that the great could be diagnosed in this way. 'We are willing to abandon the body of Pascal to the doctors' autopsy, but we do not abandon his intelligence to them . . . Illness, which among the vulgar is but a collapse or failure of one or more organs, is, among great men, seeking new ideas, only a natural predisposition to the sublime.' The Société médico-psychologique had long debates on hallucinations in 1856 which showed that the doctors were much divided about them. Dr. Brierre de Boismont, who particularly specialised in them, refused to allow medical science to destroy historical reputations: 'We cannot but feel profoundly saddened by the efforts being made to bring down from their pedestals the most noble personifications of human genius.' He accordingly invented a special theory for the great creative minds which enabled him to call their hallucinations 'intuitions'.[2]

---

[1] Dr. P. Briquet, *Traité clinique et thérapeutique de l'hystérie* (1859); Dr. H. Legrand du Saulle, *Les Hystériques* (1883), 3, 450. On the later history of hysteria, see below, p. 857.

[2] L. F. Calmeil, *De la folie* (2 vols., 1845); L. F. Lelut, *Du démon de Socrate, spécimen d'une application de la science psychologique à celle de l'histoire* (1838, new edition 1856), 45–6; *Annales médico-psychologiques* (1856), 126, 193, 300, 434; A. Brierre de Boismont, *Des hallucinations* (3rd edition, 1862); id., *Études médico-psychologiques sur les hommes célèbres* (1869).

This raised the question of who was mad and who was not. It was a matter of urgent concern because a new category of madness, *la folie lucide* or *manie raisonnante*, began to be written about, suggesting that people who appeared quite normal might in fact be mad. Dr. Ulysse Trélat, better known perhaps for his political role, was specially interested by this in his capacity as a psychiatrist at the Salpêtrière. He argued that this kind of disturbance revealed itself mainly in private life, within the intimacy of marriage, and that the way to learn about it was to talk to the families of patients more than with the patients themselves. This made some people protest that the experts were now arrogating to themselves the right to pronounce anybody mad, though he behaved perfectly normally to the outside world. The great increase in the admissions to the asylums seemed to lend substance to these fears.[1]

One may relate attitudes to madness to new attitudes to pain, which the discovery of analgesics and anaesthesia in the early nineteenth century encouraged. When in 1847 the Academy of Sciences discussed the subject, the famous physiologist Magendie asked 'What interest can the Academy of Sciences have in whether people suffer more or less?'[2] But now things changed. It took some time for chloroform, which was independently discovered by chemists in the U.S.A., France and Germany in 1831, to be widely used, for between 1855 and 1875 the amount prescribed in Paris hospitals only doubled. In the same period however, the amount of ether used trebled; in 1869 chloral was introduced, and by 1875 they were already using more of it than of chloroform. The consumption of bromides rose from only 3 kilogrammes in 1855 to 730 kilogrammes in 1875;[3] and of morphine from a quarter of a kilogramme in 1855 to over 10 kilogrammes in 1875. In addition the traditional pain-killers continued to be employed, especially opium (about 150 kilogrammes a year throughout this period). Though alcoholism was making rapid progress, doctors vastly

---

[1] Dr. U. Trélat, *La Folie lucide, étudiée et considérée au point de vue de la famille et de la société* (1861); Dr. Campagne, *La Manie raisonnante* (1869); Dr. H. Thulie, *La Manie raisonnante du Dr Campagne* (1870); *Statistique des asiles d'aliénés 1854–60* (1865), xvii.

[2] Victor Robinson, *Victory over Pain. A History of Anaesthesia* (New York, 1946), 162; M. A. Armstrong-Davison, *The Evolution of Anaesthesia* (Altrincham, 1965), 135.

[3] Cf. Dr. Georges Huette, *Histoire thérapeutique du bromure de potassium* (1878).

increased their use of alcohol and wine as a treatment of fever and as a tranquilliser: in 1855–75 the consumption of alcohol in Paris hospitals rose from 1,270 to 37,578 litres and that of red wine from 17,000 to 163,000 litres—though the number of their patients remained the same. It is symbolic that Napoleon III stuffed himself with drugs to kill the pain of his diseased kidneys. The Second Empire witnessed an enormous increase in drug-taking as well as a recourse to the asylums.[1]

The practical consequences of the new attitudes may be illustrated from a double murder committed in Marseille in 1853. The illiterate peasant, aged twenty-three, who was responsible, was an epileptic. Esquirol had laid it down that epilepsy led sooner or later to madness; and the psychiatrists who examined the criminal accordingly certified him as mad and incurably so. But the peasant appears to have committed the crime because he was highly superstitious, believed in witchcraft and had become convinced that his epilepsy was caused by a spell cast upon him. Not far from him lived a widow of seventy and her grandson aged seventeen who had received some primary education and who used to copy from religious books, which the epileptic interpreted as signifying that he had supernatural powers. When asked why he murdered them, it was he who volunteered the explanation: 'I was mad'.[2] The court accepted the medical explanation and seems to have given no weight to the social one. It is in such cases—which form an almost inexhaustible source, still untapped, in the criminal archives—that one can see particularly clearly how people opted between alternative interpretations of human behaviour.

What is striking in all this psychological writing is the emphasis given to heredity. Dr. Prosper Lucas's book on the subject became famous but Zola greatly simplified Lucas in making him popular. Lucas did not claim that heredity was the decisive factor in either behaviour or illness. On the contrary he argued that nature acted through two principles:

[1] Prof. Ch. Lasègue, *Études médicales* (1884), chapter on 'La Thérapeutique jugée par les chiffres', 492–542, reprinted from *Archives générales de la médecine* (1877); for later developments, cf. A. Martinet, *Thérapeutique clinique* (2nd edition, 1923), 151–202, on medicines for nervous troubles.

[2] H. Aubanel, 'Rapports médico-légaux sur deux aliénés accusés de meurtre', *Annales médico-psychologiques* (1856), 191–248.

imitation, which meant heredity, and creation, which he rather confusingly called *innéité*, meaning that certain qualities were innate to an individual as opposed to inherited from his family. But there was much controversy as to what characteristics could be inherited, and what accounted for the differences between individuals in the same family. One school attributed these to the uterine experiences of the baby, under the nutritional and emotional influence of the mother. Another school stressed the state of mind of the couple at the time of coitus and many books were published advising parents on how to procreate children with desirable qualities. The third school, which claimed that education and example could have an overriding influence, thus had to battle against considerable opposition. These disagreements were of course politically and socially important. When Dr. Moreau de Tours developed his theory that 'psycho-cerebral vitality is essentially innate', that the taste for work, for example, could not be inculcated, that genius was to a certain extent a variation of madness, which was largely hereditary, he by implication attacked the whole philosophy of meritocracy. He was aware of this and said that his opponents exalted the value of education only because they had reached their positions in the world through education. The conflict of the doctors and the educators was never an obvious or open one, because they were never clearly separated; but the educational philosophy of the republicans needs to be seen in this context. When Paul Bert (a physiologist who became Gambetta's minister of education) claimed that the men who had control of education could reshape the world, he was arguing in the face of a contrary opinion, that man was threatened with degeneration. Statistics were produced to show that crime was rising in precisely those areas with most education. The case for education was not clear cut.[1]

The question arose therefore of just how much free will was left by psychology, how determined was the course of history, how much individuals could do to alter their own characters, and education to modify the destiny of nations. This was an old controversy, but what was notable about its conduct during the

[1] Dr. Prosper Lucas, *Traité philosophique et physiologique de l'hérédité* (1847–50); Dr. J. Moreau (de Tours), *La Psychologie morbide dans ses rapports avec la philosophie de l'histoire* (1859), 1–13 and appendix.

Second Empire was the moderation of the determinists, who did all they could to leave some room for free will, and the vigour of the partisans of free will in defending their case. The question was complicate.i by the uncertainty as to what will was. It may be recalled that for Balzac it was a 'nervous fluid' or 'the soul-substance in the blood', or, after his conversion to magnetism, a form of electricity.[1] Since it was believed that people had only a limited quantity of this fluid, its use in any one direction, to develop any one faculty or skill, meant that other parts of the character might atrophy. That was one reason why it was believed that intellectuals, who used their brains excessively, were liable to have a host of compensating defects: cerebral effort was considered dangerous.[2] Some people claimed that will was something you either did or did not have, but since this had disturbing moral implications, alternative doctrines were available: first that will could be cultivated by moral influences, as physical exercise could strengthen the muscles of the body, and secondly that its apparent limitations were due to social causes, which could be altered. Thus a feminist argued that women had just as much will-power (potentially) as men, but were restrained from using it by convention, habit and repression. The idea that certain forms of anti-social behaviour were caused by repression of instincts was already current. Those who, against the partisans of heredity, believed in the infinite perfectibility of man, and in the power of education to eradicate laziness and drunkenness, appealed, for their part, to comparative anthropology, which they thought could show how different peoples had approached nearer that goal.[3]

The contrast between the relatively static nature of the biographical art and the rapidly changing views of human

[1] Moïse Le Yaouanc, *Nosographie de l'humanité balzacienne* (1959), 131.
[2] See e.g. the classic works of Réveillé-Parise.
[3] Mlle J. Marchef-Girard, *Des facultés humaines et de leur développement par l'éducation* (1865); cf. C. Sedillot (prof. de médecine, Nancy), *Du relèvement de la France* (1874); P. Foissac, *De l'influence des climats sur l'homme* (1867); Dr. Cerise, *Des fonctions et des maladies nerveuses dans leurs rapports avec l'éducation sociale et privée, morale et physique* (1842). For later ideas, see J. F. Richard, 'La Découverte du fait des différences individuelles comme obstacle dans les premières expériences de mesure en psychologie', *Douzième congrès international d'histoire des sciences, colloques, textes des rapports* (1968), 369–82; and M. Reuchlin, 'La Psychologie différentielle au xixe siècle', ibid. 383–400.

personality developed by the psychiatrists—who, during the Second Empire, were almost as revolutionary as the financiers and industrialists were in the economic sphere—has an important significance. There were, it is clear, strong forces which inhibited the development of biography as a major historical activity: first there was the preoccupation with *histoire philosophique*, and the desire to deal only with very general subjects; and secondly, there was the strong tradition which saw biography as a means of praising the dead. It is true that against this, a number of writers urged that individuals should be studied for their own sake, in the greatest possible detail, but they did not always carry out their own precepts, being caught up in the advocacy of more general causes. Biography thus remained on the whole a minor genre.

The fact that it was a genre of its own was perhaps another reason why it did not get caught up in the investigation of the mind and the emotions which the psychologists were pursuing so actively. Biography had its own rules, its own purposes and its own preoccupations. It was therefore largely to the novelists that the task of taking up the suggestions of the psychologists was left. This has a social significance which deserves to be stressed. The more organised a particular form of writing was, the less likely was it to be influenced by other forms. Biographers and psychologists thus on the whole worked side by side in separate worlds. There were occasions when these barriers were broken, but whenever this happened, there were usually hesitations and always loud protests. No simple influence by psychology on biography was possible in any case, because the psychologists were so divided in their views.

It might be maintained therefore that the best biographers of this early period were often not those who were ostensibly engaged in the genre, but rather the psychiatrists and the medico-legal experts. Their reports of cases are extremely impressive. They often reveal very exceptional ability, clarity of mind and powers of exposition. These doctors deserve to be regarded as important witnesses of their age: they have left a mass of biographical material which still awaits investigation. Historians today rightly lament that they cannot get the poor in the past to speak, that evidence about the most numerous class is exiguous in the extreme. Police reports have often been used, despite their obvious, but not insuperable, defects. Medical reports also have their faults, but they contain information about aspects of life—personal and domestic in particular—which historians are now coming increasingly to value. Succeeding chapters will examine one of these aspects, anxiety, and attempt to show that it has a history which is no less important because it was played out in obscurity.

People willing to talk about their private lives were above all of two kinds. First, there were the novelists and other writers who were fascinated by emotion and by themselves. Their evidence will be examined in the following chapter. The second type, which will be considered after that, were odd, sick and mad people. This chapter has tried to show that their behaviour should not be immediately classified as completely abnormal. 'The philosopher', wrote Esquirol in his classic work on *Mental Illnesses* (1844), 'will find in an asylum the same ideas, errors, passions and misfortunes as in the world, but in more marked forms and in more lively colour, because man is found there in all his nakedness, because he does not dissimulate his thought, because he does not give to his passions the charm that seduces nor to his vices the appearances that deceive.'[1] The number of people who were declared to be insane rose about fifteenfold during the period covered by this book:

### Number of Madmen treated[2]

| | | | |
|------|--------|------|---------|
| 1838 | 8,390  | 1910 | 98,477  |
| 1844 | 16,000 | 1920 | 92,541  |
| 1864 | 34,919 | 1930 | 119,154 |
| 1871 | 49,589 | 1940 | 150,265 |
| 1880 | 63,600 | 1945 | 62,786  |
| 1890 | 73,641 | 1950 | 85,659  |
| 1900 | 87,428 | 1970 | 262,060 |

It was in the Second Empire that this rise was most rapid. When the first major law on the insane was passed in 1838,

[1] J. E. D. Esquirol, *Les Maladies mentales* (1844) is one of the most interesting social commentaries of the period. Cf. T. Owsianik, *De la conception de l'aliéné* (Paris medical thesis, 1941).

[2] Jacques Prévault, *L'Échec du système 'administratif' d'internement des aliénés* (1955), 37. For 1970, patients treated in psychiatric hospitals.

there were under 10,000 people so classified. By 1871 there were about 50,000. To this should be added 'madmen living at home', a difficult category to be accurate about. Altogether this makes two per 1,000 insane in 1861. In the Second Empire, 17 per cent of those who went to asylums spent less than a month there, and 26 per cent between one and six months. So over a generation, the number of people who had been classified as mentally ill, however briefly, must have been very considerable.[1] As the numbers continued to increase during the Third Republic, they reached the point when there were eight times more people suffering from mental illnesses than from tuberculosis.

Of course, not everyone in an asylum was mad. In the U.S.A. (which had twice as many people so classified, proportionately to its population, as France) it has been argued that the increase in mental illness should not be attributed to the increased strains of life, because the major portion of the increase was due to people over fifty going into asylums: it was a problem of ageing.[2] It is not clear whether the same could be argued of France, and similar studies have not been carried out there, but it was certainly the case that the asylums contained many sane old people, because it was easier to get into an asylum than into an old people's home. A critic of the asylum system claimed in 1955 that about 60 per cent of the inmates of asylums should not have been there.[3] Stories about people being wrongly locked up are never easy to check and the publicity given to a few cases of obvious injustice may perhaps give a false impression.[4] But the law in France established two methods for locking people up: they could either be sent to asylums by the medical authorities, or they could go as voluntary patients: but a voluntary patient was not necessarily one who himself volunteered to enter an asylum; anyone, whether a relative or not, had the right to request that another person should be confined to an asylum, and if the prefect and the

[1] *Statistique des asiles d'aliénés, 1854–60* (1865).
[2] George Rosen, *Madness in Society* (1968); H. Goldhamer and A. Marshal, *Psychosis and Civilisation* (1953). For the old, see below, p. 975.
[3] Prévault, op. cit. 136.
[4] This is the view taken for England by W. L. Parry-Jones, *The Trade in Lunacy. A Study of Private Madhouses in England in the Eighteenth and Nineteenth Centuries* (1972), 290.

doctors gave their consent, then he became a 'voluntary' patient, destined to remain there indefinitely. This allowed plenty of scope for people to get rid of their enemies. The case that particularly deserves to be recorded is that concerning Colonel Picard, head of the army's historical department, who had a feud with Jean Lemoine, librarian at the ministry of war. Lemoine, for his part, had a feud with his wife over their inheritance from her mother. Picard used this to get the wife to apply for the voluntary internment of Lemoine, who was accordingly locked up for eleven years, until he was let out following a press campaign run by the Abbé Trochu: in 1925 Lemoine (shades of the Dreyfus Affair!) was restored to his post in the ministry of war and his wife was condemned to pay him damages.[1] Jules Vallès is famous for having been locked up at his father's instigation for being unorthodox. At the time, there were better-known cases, like Napoleon III's minister Billault's locking up a barrister of Limoges who was black-mailing him over some compromising letters.[2] In 1920 Veuve Becker, daughter of the founder of the Bazaar de l'Hotel de Ville, was seized at the instigation of her sons-in-law and forcibly sent to a lunatic asylum, as a way of stopping her remarrying. How one fared in an asylum depended on how much money one had. Those who paid for their keep had their rooms cleaned by those who did not. Some asylums, in the 1930s, were still likened to barracks, and some inmates still slept on the floor.[3] But there were private asylums with several different classes of comfort, and the very rich, by paying six times more than those at the lowest rate, could get a private chalet.[4]

In the Second Empire, a calculation was made showing that, proportionately to their total numbers, soldiers went to asylums most often, followed by members of the liberal professions.[5] A doctor's study in the same period showed that these classes came fairly low for the frequency with which they committed suicide;

---

[1] J. Lemoine, *Les Dessous d'un internement arbitraire* (1937).

[2] N. Blayau, *Billault* (1969), 386–7 shows how difficult it is to be certain about the rights and wrongs of such cases.

[3] Th. Simon, *L'Aliéné, l'asile, l'infirmier* (Cahors, 1937); Georges Imann, *Voyage au pays des déments* (1934), 82; but cf. Henry Bonnet, *L'Aliéné devant lui-même* (1866).

[4] See advertisements in *L'Aliéniste français* (1934) for Villa Lunier à Blois, founded by Dr. Lunier in 1860; and the 'chambre meublée avec luxe' at the Château de Suresne clinic, founded by Magnan.

[5] *Statistiques des institutions d'assistance* (1854–60), xxix.

it was artisans, by contrast, who committed suicide most.[1] In the 1850s, men and women went into asylums in roughly equal numbers, but women increasingly outnumbered men there, especially after 1920.[2] The growth in the population of the asylums did not, however, make the country a safer place. In 1932, 94 people were murdered by 'lunatics' and 116 gravely injured.[3] All this raises difficult problems which have still to be elucidated. Public opinion remained throughly confused about them. But the causes given by the asylums to explain why their inmates collapsed—'intellectual overwork', 'domestic sorrows', 'loss of fortune', 'loss of a person dear to them', 'frustrated ambition', 'remorse', 'damaged honour', 'jealousy', 'pride', 'nostalgia', 'excessive religiosity', drink, the menopause, poverty, disease, etc.—provide an almost complete catalogue of the private stresses and sorrows of ordinary living that is the subject of the following chapters.

[1] A. Brierre de Boismont, *Du suicide* (1856), 91.
[2] E. Toulouse, R. Dupouy and M. Moine, 'Statistique de la psychopathie', *Annales médico-psychologiques* (1930), 2. 390–404.
[3] Henri Claude, *Psychiatrie médico-légale* (2nd edition, 1944), 81.

# 16. Individualism and the Emotions

FOR most of this period, France was distinguished among nations for the personal freedom enjoyed by the individual and for a considerable amount of mutual tolerance. 'The notion that a resident in France', wrote a British journalist in 1898, 'is the prey of constant official vexation is exaggerated, and there is no country where under normal circumstances life can be enjoyed more tranquilly.'[1] Private liberty was one of the most fundamental features of this society, as was the variety of thought and action that has attracted admiration ever since. This liberty was a recent acquisition, however, and needs explanation, because though France had had its Revolution, the institutions and many of the administrative methods of the *ancien régime* had not been shaken off. There were three reasons why the power of the centralised government no longer seriously threatened the individual. The first was that the administrative system was not as efficient in practice as its formidable organisation and size should have made it. A succession of revolutions had filled it with men of opposing opinions and traditions; vested interests had entrenched themselves at the local level; it was too large and too slow to move effectively. Secondly, it was held in check by parliament and by a multitude of pressure groups, which were diverse enough to ensure that most people had some kind of support against authority. The political system was so complex that it became self-defeating, and though reform was its avowed purpose, the control, limitation and diffusion of power became its main function. But perhaps the most important reason was that the rights of the individual were established as a dominant creed, thanks largely to the continuous efforts of a whole succession of writers, journalists and polemicists. Writers and intellectuals were, inevitably, infinitely divided, but the right to give and hold their opinion was what they all valued very highly.

[1] J. E. C. Bodley, *France* (revised edition, 1899), 104.

They were far from agreed that tolerance was a good thing, and most of them indeed attacked their enemies with great violence—the bitter struggle between clericals and free-thinkers disposes of any suggestion that this was a genuinely tolerant century—but liberals of different kinds were in a majority among them and France was on the whole a free country, because the individual's dignity was respected.

This was the conclusion of many centuries of argument. The idea that the individual is an autonomous entity, with a right to act by his own judgement, subjecting authority to independent and critical assessment, was enunciated by various writers, by Luther and by Kant before being taken up by the *philosophes*. The right to privacy, 'liberty of tastes and pursuits, of framing the plan of our life to suit our own character', had deep roots in Christian mysticism before being glorified by the Renaissance, the American and French Revolutions, Benjamin Constant and J. S. Mill. The declaration of the rights of man of 1791 was the culmination of a battle of many centuries to defend the dignity of the individual against claims that the public good should always have priority over him. It is inaccurate to see individual liberty as simply a conquest of the Revolution. The cult of reason, of which the Revolution was one expression, had established itself as a French tradition before then. And the full implications of individualism were only drawn out after it.[1]

It was the romantic movement that finally entrenched the independence of the individual in an unassailable way, by greatly expanding the idea of what an individual was. The romantics were writers, and it was the influence of writers therefore that must explain the greatly increased sense of individuality that developed in this period. From the point of view of literary history, romanticism flourished mainly in the early nineteenth century, but its teachings were incorporated into virtually all subsequent thought. Any account of the way people have thought and felt since then must give an important place to them. Romanticism was more than an episode. It left a permanent sediment above the classicism or conformism described in a previous chapter. It constituted an important layer in popular mentality.

Romanticism was not an organised movement with a

[1] Steven Lukes, *Individualism* (1973).

coherent doctrine. It was revolutionary, in the sense that it involved the overflowing of all boundaries, as Kierkegaard defined it; but it overflowed them in different ways. Maurras and Pierre Lasserre at the turn of the century argued that romanticism was the literary or moral counterpart of the great revolution of 1789, that both came from Rousseau. Others, like Taine, have argued on the contrary that the Revolution was the product of the classical, rationalist tradition. The romantic poets and writers were looked on by the bourgeoisie as revolutionaries, if only because they dressed and behaved to flout respectable conventions. In 1871 Thiers said 'The romantics, c'est la Commune'. The romantics were first of all liberators of forms of expression and communication. They began as pioneers of the emancipation of literature from the rules and styles established by classical authors. They rejected the view that only certain words, poetic forms and subjects were proper in art. They addressed their writings to all men, not simply to the educated, and they took an interest in the sufferings of the masses. They sought inspiration no longer just from Greece and Rome, but from the Celtic, Germanic, medieval and oriental worlds. They drew material for their art from every class of society. They were revolutionaries also in the sense that they refused to allow their conduct to be determined by the sole guide of reason, and even less by prudence. They were declared enemies of the bourgeoisie, whom they vituperated as grocers and philistines; they abhorred compromise, materialism, sobriety, thrift. Their hero was the artist who flouted society and who by his special powers offered men a new faith or new experiences. The nineteenth century, said Stendhal, 'has a thirst for strong emotions'. The romantics rehabilitated the passions, cultivated sensibility, gave free rein to the imagination. They praised love and gave themselves up to it with lyricism. They sought less to understand reality than to idealise it, so that they quickly got confused in their fantasies and had difficulty in distinguishing their dreams from reality. They replaced self-control by caprice. They developed a new kind of morality. The good and the beautiful were confused in a new way: the value of an individual was determined by the nobility of the sentiments he expressed, the elegance or grandeur of his emotions, irrespective of what he actually achieved. Originality thus acquired a moral value. The criterion by which beauty was judged was revolutionised. What mattered now was not the reflection of a preordained ideal, but the impression or emotion the reader or spectator felt. The artist sought to establish a personal relationship with his audience, and since both could change with time, so his art would change. There was thus often great diversity in the production of artists—which did not favour the founding of any coherent school. But it led, because the romantics were concerned with finding an echo in the masses, or with being themselves echoes of the masses' frustrated, unspoken aspirations, to a stress on harmony, music and colour as a means of reaching a wide audience, to the use of incantation, aiming at winning through the heart, without necessarily passing through the mind.

The romantics were unhappy. Their dreams could not be realised; they disliked the world as it was, their passions consumed and tormented them; they saw themselves in tragic roles. Their founders were 'ardent, pale, nervous', as Alfred de Musset described them in his *Confessions d'un enfant du siècle* (1835), born during the wars of the empire, the children of anxious mothers and absent fathers, doomed to a *mal de siècle*, which he attributed to the collapse of the old world, a nostalgia for its glory, an inability to rebuild it, an uncertainty about the future, doubt, paralysis of the will. 'For thirty years', wrote Taine, 'every young man was a little Hamlet, disgusted with everything, not knowing what to desire, believe or do, discouraged, doubting, bitter, having a need for happiness, looking to the toes of his boots to see if by chance he might not find there the system of the world, juggling with the words God, Nature, Humanity, Ideal, Synthesis. . . . Men were sceptical, idealists, mystics, Indian, pagan, Christian, humanitarian, Manichaean, in stanzas and in verses. . . . Except in the first two centuries of our era, never has there been so strong and continuous a buzzing of metaphysical dreams.'[1] The romantics were often interested in improving the world, but there was also an element of escapism in their outlook. They were constantly searching for new pleasures, exotic countries; they tired of Paris and longed for the East, but they were more excited

[1] H. Taine, *Les Philosophes français du dix-neuvième siècle* (1857), 292–3.

by the camels of the Holy Land than by the wonders of modern science. They gave themselves up to fantastic mental adventures. Berlioz longed to be a brigand in Sicily and 'see magnificent crimes'. Flaubert as a schoolboy slept with a dagger under his pillow. Madame Lafargue, who can be taken as an example of an 'ordinary woman', wrote in her memoirs: 'I habituated my intelligence to poetise the most minute details of life and I preserved it with infinite solicitude from all vulgar or trivial contact. I added to the mistake of embellishing reality so as to render it pleasant to my imagination, the even greater error of feeling the love of the beautiful perhaps more than the love of the good, of carrying out more easily excesses in duty than the duties themselves, of preferring in all the impossible to the possible.' Public prosecutors complained that fictional criminals were becoming popular heroes; that young romantics came to the courts wearing 'the contemptuous smile of an unrecognised superiority', victims of a 'fatal mixture of unbridled egoism and powerless pride, of sombre melancholy and active energy which leads to despair or revolt, suicide or crime'.[1]

Romanticism was far from being of one type. In appearance there were the hirsute bohemians but also the elegant dandies; what they had in common was their desire to be different from the ordinary bourgeois. The romantics proclaimed the rights of fantasy and originality against conventional social morality; they appear as individualists. But they were also advocates of social conscience and pioneers of social reform. They quickly abandoned the theory of art for art's sake, to replace it by one of social art. Some looked back to Christianity and to the middle ages; others were utopian and builders of new religions, but all disapproved of the present. The qualities they stressed, such as passion, or love of liberty, were not peculiar to them, but eternal characteristics of man, and this is why romanticism is difficult to define; but they gave a new prestige to these qualities and greatly expanded their significance. They did much to widen the sympathies and horizons of men, even if they also clouded their outlook and obscured their view.[2]

[1] Louis Maigron, *Le Romantisme et les mœurs* (1910), 381, 384.
[2] Roger Picard, *Le Romantisme social* (New York, 1944); H. G. Schenk, *The Mind of the European Romantics* (1967); Jacques Barzun, *Classic, Romantic and Modern*

To document the effect of romanticism on conduct one must look in detail at biographies. When Rousseau said: 'I am made unlike anyone I have ever met . . . I am like no one in the whole world' he was, by implication, denying the subjection of the individual to class and family; he was making the revolutionary statement that a man had a right to be different from his father. The whole history of France could be presented in terms of that rebellion. But to see how romanticism worked in practice, as well as how it developed, one should look at the lives of some of its principal advocates. This approach has the advantage of showing at the same time how the generalisations about romanticism need to be modified every time one particular individual's experiences are analysed, and also of showing in more precise detail the ambivalence of romanticism on the subject of the individual. Just as conformism was not conservatism, so individualism did not necessarily involve either originality or egoism. Here, some of the varied aspects and problems of individualism will be illustrated from the biographies of seven writers who have left particularly instructive accounts of their personal rebellions.

Jules Michelet (1798–1874), author of a *History of France* in seventeen volumes and a *History of the Revolution* in seven more, throws light on the complex relations between individualism, emotion and sociability. Michelet was an intensely lonely and an intensely emotional man. 'My childhood had no feasts.' It was in the study of history that he found the means of escaping from his intolerable solitude, while yet remaining alone. That is why he was able to put so much into his work and to give it such new dimensions. He made history the crowning science, claiming as much for it as Comte was simultaneously claiming for sociology. He did a great deal of research in archives; he interviewed survivors of the Revolution; he took an interest in all aspects and particularly the social aspects of history, with a stress on the lives of ordinary people; and he adopted a highly imaginative interpretation of his facts, which he sought not to report but to relive, as an

(1962, revised edition of book originally published in 1943); P. Van Tieghem, *Le Romantisme français* (1966) and *Le Romantisme dans la littérature européenne* (1948); M. Levaillant, *Problèmes du romantisme* (special number of the *Revue des sciences humaines*, 1951).

'integral resurrection of the past'. He used a poetical style, full of emotion, passion and colourful imagery. The writing of his books was an intense experience for him—he was ill when his heroes died, he was in ecstasy when the Bastille was taken, he fulminated uncontrollably against the men he disliked and was lyrical in praise of the liberal ideas he championed. Not only the individuals of the past were real for him, but he gave life to collective entities, like the provinces of France, the different social groups, and above all 'the people'. His books were a hymn in praise of the people, whom he saw personified with a clearly defined character and with an independent soul.

Michelet was proud of being a man of the people—the only important romantic writer who genuinely was and who could therefore feel a fraternal rather than an outsider's sympathy for them. His father had been a printer, his mother was of peasant stock. He deliberately clung to his artisan origins; even though he rose very rapidly to the top of the academic hierarchy, becoming professor at the Collège de France at forty. He denounced embourgeoisement: 'Those who rise [in the social hierarchy] lose by it . . . they become mixed, bastard, they lose the originality of their class without gaining that of another.' In the masses he saw a 'new, living, rejuvenating sap', less culture perhaps but more 'vital warmth'. This desire to 'plunge into the living sea of the people' fitted in with Michelet's fear of loneliness. Their life was made up of 'work and family', which meant co-operation with their fellows. Sociability was the way to progress. Michelet rebelled with terror against the pure theories of individualism. Man, he insisted, was a social being and history was the supreme science because it studied him as such. He found support for his views in Vico, whom he translated; in the Scottish philosophers and in Lamennais he found proof of the common sense of the people as equal in value to the theories of philosophers; in Rousseau he discovered the general will. From these and others (Maistre, Voltaire) he developed what he considered his crowning idea, that each nation has a real personality, a collective being, endowed with a will and intelligence. Patriotism was one of the highest virtues, it ought to be a dogma and a legend, 'the first gospel of the people'.

Another virtue closely linked with it was love, from which he expected the emancipation of man. The evil of his time was 'paralysis of the heart' which causes 'unsociability'. Michelet had a desperate craving for affection, for complete union with his wives and mistresses; few men have recorded so carefully, and been so torn by, their need for sexual satisfaction and also their search for spiritual communion with women. Michelet's ideal of love was that his wife would be at once his mistress, his daughter, his sister and his mother. That is why he wrote not only books about history, but also others on women and on love. Love in the family, co-operative association in work, love of the fatherland—the creation of a great 'amitié de France'—were his goals. Michelet thus placed his hopes in sentiment and a return to traditional, partly Christian virtues. He deplored industrialisation which, he thought, caused men to 'co-operate without loving each other, to act and live together without knowing each other'. He wanted France to stick to artisan production, so as to safeguard good taste and the dignity of the worker. He urged the bourgeoisie to marry peasant girls or they would decay like the old nobility. He denounced as vain the ambitious who sought jobs in the civil service or in commerce, which were corrupt. He urged the poor not to get rich, not to aspire to enter the bourgeoisie but to be themselves, to keep their popular instincts. This was their best chance of originality. The people did indeed need a hero to guide and enlighten them, but this hero only gave them a voice: Michelet's real hero was the people as a mass. Michelet founded, as he said, 'a religious philosophy of the people'. Individualism, in him, can be seen already to have met emotional difficulties because of its social implications.[1]

The individualist could claim to be unique, and yet claim to understand ordinary people better than they could themselves. Victor Hugo (1802–85) tried to be the kind of hero Michelet described, giving expression to the ideas of his century. 'Every

---

[1] The complete works of Michelet are in the process of being brought out in an excellent new edition, with full introductions and notes, by Paul Viallaneix; six volumes, out of the twenty projected, have appeared since 1971. See also Paul Viallaneix, *La Voie royale: essai sur l'idée du peuple dans l'œuvre de Michelet* (1959); G. Monod, *La Vie et la pensée de Jules Michelet* (1923); Jeanne Calo, *La Création de la femme chez Michelet* (1975); J. Cornuz, *Jules Michelet, un aspect de la pensée religieuse au 19ᵉ siècle* (Geneva, 1955).

true poet', he wrote, 'independently of the thoughts which come to him from his own system and those which come to him from the eternal truth, must contain the sum of the ideas of his time.' He believed he was 'the voice of Humanity',[1] and he was indeed probably the most widely read poet of this period. It is important to know what link he established with his readers. Many commentators, in the years following his death, acknowledged, despite their hostility to him, that he did achieve this aim of being the representative of his readers. Paul Lafargue explained this by saying that 'Victor Hugo clothed the ideas and sentiments supplied to him by the bourgeois in a stunning phraseology calculated to strike the ear and provoke bewilderment, in a grandiloquent verbiage, harmoniously rhythmic and rhymed, bristling with startling, dazzling antitheses and flashy epithets. He was, after Chateaubriand, the greatest window-dresser of the words and images of the century.' Taine called Hugo 'a national guard in delirium'.[2] His *Misérables* was hailed as 'the gospel of the nineteenth century [because] everybody understood it'. Only when he published *L'Homme qui rit*, with its monstrous symbolism, did he admit that 'a separation has taken place between my contemporaries and myself'.[3]

Hugo aimed at producing a popular literature. 'Hitherto', he wrote, 'there has only been literature for the educated. In France especially . . . to be a poet meant almost to be a mandarin. Not all words had a right to be written . . . Imagine botany declaring to some vegetable that it did not exist . . . Civilisation has now grown up and needs a literature of the people.'[4] Hugo deliberately avoided Greek and Roman subjects. His greatest achievement was to democratise poetry by using ordinary language, to enrich it enormously by introducing into it every type of word, sound, image, to make verse as free as prose, apart from a few rules, like hiatus and rhyme. Everything in nature was a fit subject for art, which should concern itself not just with the sublime, but with the grotesque too. Rules and fixed taste were obstacles to genius. It

---

[1] Jacques Roos, *Les Idées philosophiques de Victor Hugo* (1958), 7.
[2] Tristan Legay, *Victor Hugo jugé par son siècle* (1902), 565, 567.
[3] J. B. Barrère, *Hugo, l'homme et l'œuvre* (1952), 191-2.
[4] V. Hugo, *William Shakespeare* (1864, 2nd edition 1867), 257-8.

is not the beautiful but the characteristic that the artist should capture. Hugo had the imagination of a visionary and he used this to create a dazzling world—to evoke splendours in picturesque and moving detail, of countries and places he had never seen. He imagined emperors and sultans, monsters and phantoms, crowds and battles, the East and the middle ages with dithyrambic intensity. He was no profound thinker and he wrote above all about the universal commonplace feelings: love of children, the home, the fatherland, nature, compassion for the poor, sorrow, pleasure in life and hope for progress mixed with a nostalgia for the past. But he succeeded in dressing up these ideas in highly emotional and richly coloured language. Today it might be complained that his verse is static, with words leading only to yet more words, repeating the same things in varying forms, with no development in ideas. However he continued to fill his readers with the same excitement that the repetitive beat of pop music did for a later generation, because he carried imagination to the point of paroxysm. His gift for the epic form gave his writing greater power still. The world he created has been compared to that mixture of the miraculous and the real recorded by Homer.

Hugo was popular partly because he was in sympathy with a primitive facet of the century which is too often forgotten by those who stress industrialisation and scientific progress as its principal characteristics. Hugo believed in the survival of the dead, their frequent intervention in the present world and the successive migrations of the soul. There was an invisible world, not in the sky, but mixed up in the same space as the material world. Hugo communicated with the dead—he had talks at séances with Socrates, Christ, Luther, Shakespeare, Byron and the lion of Androcles. He had visions and presentiments which often terrified him. But he was not just a dabbler in spiritualism and the occult. He believed he was a prophet, called by God, and the founder of a new religion, to succeed Druidism and Christianity. His teaching was that there was no hell. God had created the world with an element of evil, and history was the struggle between good and evil. But all men (and all things, for even stones had souls) had a right to forgiveness. This was democracy and progress brought into religion; it was also the peasant's primitive pre-Christian mentality justified. It was not by reason that truth could be found. Science and the intelligence could observe facts, but they could study only the superficial, evanescent phenomena. The imagination on the other hand created art and attained the infinite and the absolute. Intuition was the means to achieve supreme knowledge; certainty came from sentiment, i.e. from mysticism. Science dealt with the relative, art with the definitive. The poet must replace the priest as man's guide, with three particular functions: to explain the past, to civilise the present (by preaching veneration for age, compassion for women, the cult of natural affections, raising human dignity), and to predict the future. His audience must be the masses, who had 'the instinct for the ideal'.

Victor Hugo established himself as a romantic poet in his twenties, under the Restoration, but it was the works he wrote during the Second Empire, particularly *Les Châtiments* (1853), *Les Contemplations* (1856) and *Les Misérables* (1862), which won him his greatest popularity. These revealed that romanticism was very much alive at a time when new literary and scientific movements were making themselves felt. Hugo was the son of a general of the Napoleonic army, and he began as a social climber; he wrote official poetry for Louis XVIII; he was made a peer by Louis-Philippe and was friends with the heir to the throne. But as he became increasingly aware of his social role, he gradually moved towards republicanism. He was still right-wing in 1848, but his hostility to Louis Napoleon led to his being exiled in 1851, and he spent nearly twenty years in Jersey attacking *Napoléon le petit*. He returned in 1870 to become the grand old man of the Third Republic, Senator of the department of the Seine. He came to represent devotion to art, to politics, to social progress, to one's family, to one's mistress and not least to oneself. He showed how individualism could turn into megalomania, but also how it remained attached to primitive traditions, and how it could cultivate both dedication and generosity.

Romantics could not stand still: individualists were free to try every elixir. How they moved from creed to creed, building up their individuality, like bees in search of honey, can be seen in the life of Sainte-Beuve (1804–69), probably France's most admired literary critic. In his youth he was a disciple of the ideologues, a student of medicine, and he disapproved of romanticism because of its mysticism and early royalism. But he was drawn to it by the charm of Hugo, with whom he was great friends until he fell in love with Hugo's wife. His novels *Joseph Delorme* (1829) and *Volupté* (1834) are important (partly autobiographical) descriptions of the romantic mind. Michelet congratulated Sainte-Beuve on the latter work, as successfully portraying the 'moral psychology of our epoch'. Sainte-Beuve defined romanticism as 'disgust with life, inaction, abuse of dreaming, a proud sentiment of isolation, a feeling that one was misjudged, a contempt for the world and for well-worn tracks, a belief that they are unworthy of one, a view of oneself as the most unhappy of men and yet a love for one's sorrow; the last stage of this evil would be suicide'. He described his own life as a 'slow and profound suicide . . . an inconceivable chaos with monstrous imaginings, vivid reminiscences, criminal fantasies, great abortive thoughts, wise prudence followed by foolish actions, transports of piety after blasphemy . . . and, at the base, despair'. Sainte-Beuve never recovered from this; he never became gay. He turned to Saint-Simonianism in his search for a faith but it did not change the character of his life. He complained to Enfantin, 'Why, in helping me to understand so many things, have you not taught me to *love life*? . . . Sick of the end of the old world and of the beginning of this one, sick you found me, sick you have left me.' Intellectual satisfactions were inadequate: 'I live by the heart . . . the need of love and friendship, that is the basis of my life.' His repeated efforts to find love were unsuccessful: he ended by visiting prostitutes.

He found only slight consolation in his search for knowledge. As a literary critic he pioneered the biographical method, judging works no longer against a precise ideal of taste or morals but as the products of individual lives. He founded what he called 'the natural history of the mind', seeking to show the growth of genius as though it were a plant. He even believed that minds could be grouped into types, as scientists classified the objects they studied—though he never actually attempted to do this. He claimed, that is, to be scientific. This illustrates well how it is impossible to differentiate scientists and romantics. His science came from the ideologues; he was opposed to Taine's scientific criticism. He cannot be classified simply in his politics either: he admired in turn Hugo, Enfantin, Lamennais, Molé and finally Jérôme Napoléon. He became increasingly conservative as he mixed with the great, and he borrowed his ideas almost like a chameleon. The romantics were particularly responsive to changing times, which is another reason why their school is so diverse. Sainte-Beuve stood at the crossroads between individualism, socialism and scientism. The one constant in his life—which was a major legacy of romanticism—was emotional dissatisfaction and restlessness.[1]

The result of this was that romantics could be disillusioned even before they set off on their enthusiastic adventures. Gustave Flaubert (1821–80) is essential reading for anyone who wants to understand this bankruptcy of romanticism and the origins of modern forms of anxiety. Flaubert was not very successful in his own lifetime, and in fact made only about £1,000 from his writings. He was appreciated mainly by a small group of distinguished realist novelists who acknowledged him as their master and who recognised his quite exceptionally brilliant literary craftmanship. He was nevertheless a most acute analyst of his age, and his own life, as revealed by his correspondence, shows in poignant detail the torments contemporary attitudes produced. Flaubert grew up as a romantic; he knew *René* by heart; he was determined to be a writer from an early age and he devoted his whole life to literature. 'I was born', he said, 'with little faith in happiness. When I was very young, I had a complete presentiment of life. It was like a nauseous smell of cooking escaping from a vent. You don't need to eat it to know that it will make you sick.' At sixteen he fell in love with a married woman eleven years older than himself and this remained the great passion of his life (and the inspiration of his *Éducation sentimentale*). He was afraid of life, as he himself admitted: he chose as his ideal woman one so remote that he could not hope to win her. He was unable to enjoy any other love; his spasmodic affair with the poetess Louise Colet consisted in a series of rejections by him. He feared happiness because he expected it to involve

[1] André Billy, *Sainte-Beuve. Sa vie et son temps* (1952); Maxime Leroy, *La Pensée de Sainte-Beuve* (1940); Marcel Proust, *Contre Sainte-Beuve* (reprinted 1954).

pain and ultimately despair. He had the romantics' sense of destiny, believing he was chosen for misfortune, but, even more than the romantics, he thought unhappiness was part of the general human destiny. He hated mankind; he despised and mocked it. He despised bourgeois conventionality, the platitudes of conversation, the hypocrisy of politicians; he saw moral degradation everywhere. 'How tired I am of the ignoble workman, the inept bourgeois, the stupid peasant and the odious priest.' He assiduously collected examples of human stupidity from which he compiled a *Dictionnaire des idées reçues*. He delighted in the discomfiture of the pompous, in the showing-up of false pretensions, in the denigration of all that was respectable. Mockery was his defence against the world. He laughed at everything, but with a bitterness which showed how this masked other emotions; and he was surprised when he found 'nowadays I laugh at things no one laughs at any more'. 'A gendarme', he declared, for example, 'is essentially ludicrous; I cannot look at one without laughing. It is grotesque and inexplicable—the effect this pillar of society has on me, like public prosecutors, justices of any kind and professors of literature.' Disenchantment to him was inevitable; his answer was to seek not happiness but detachment. He shows how romanticism turned into scientific realism not because of the adoption of a new intellectual doctrine, but from lassitude. Flaubert sought satisfaction from the observation of life, but his ultimate aim was not to draw conclusions about mankind, not to establish laws about its behaviour, not to prescribe means for its improvement. He was convinced there was no solution to the human problem; there was not even a problem; the world had to be accepted as it was. He had no ideals in politics. 'The whole dream of democracy', he wrote, 'is to raise the proletarian to the level of stupidity attained by the bourgeois . . . The great moral of this reign will be to show that universal suffrage is as stupid as the divine right of kings, though slightly less odious.' He was not even patriotic. 'I am as much a Chinaman as a Frenchman, and I derive not the slightest pleasure from our victories over the Arabs.' He abandoned the search for experience at the outset of his life; he spent it brooding about emotions he had felt in his youth. He is a good example of the obstinate survival of youthful

ideas for many years after they had been thought up—a characteristic very frequently encountered with politicians in this
period. He denied that he found a goal in the search for
beauty: 'Art', he wrote, 'is perhaps no more serious than skittles.'
But he toiled at his writing with a devotion hardly ever
equalled. He spent days seeking the right word; he rewrote
endlessly; he observed with a fanatical search for accuracy;
he could spend a whole day, for example, looking at the
countryside through coloured glasses, in order to be able to
write one sentence describing such a situation; he claimed to
have read 1,500 books as research for *Bouvard et Pécuchet*.

Flaubert was a universal demoraliser. 'If ever I take an
active part in the world it will be as a thinker and demoraliser.'
It was just that *Madame Bovary* should have been incriminated,
for it was a dangerous work. The public prosecutor, in accusing
Flaubert of writing an immoral book, was right, even though he
was unable to put his finger on what exactly was dangerous
about it. His arguments are an interesting definition, in any
case, of the scandalous. When Emma goes waltzing with her
lover, her dress touches his trousers; 'their legs entered each
into the other, he lowered his eyes upon her; she looked up at
him . . .' 'I do know well that people waltz more or less in this
manner,' said the prosecutor, 'but that does not make it moral.'
He found the descriptions of Madame Bovary's beauty lascivious, provocative; no attempt was made to describe her intelligence. The story of her adultery lapsed into glorification of it;
marriage was painted as being full of platitudes but adultery
as being nothing but poetry. However, the public prosecutor
should have argued that Flaubert was not only undermining society but removing all hope from it. He not only described adultery, but showed how it gave no happiness, any
more than did marriage, or love or any activity at all. He showed
the monotony of passion, which at least the romantics had
believed in, the hypocrisy of religion, the dangers of thinking.[1]
Persigny complained that Flaubert had no ideal. At the end of
the book Emma Bovary's husband pathetically declares, 'It is the
fault of destiny'. This book is a brilliant study of the romantic
attitude—and particularly of that aspect of it which has now
acquired the name of Bovaryisme—the inability to distinguish

[1] 'Il ne faut pas toucher aux idoles'—Flaubert says, but he does.

between illusion and reality. It was more than description. 'Madame Bovary, c'est moi.'

In *L'Éducation sentimentale*, Flaubert was again partly auto-biographical: 'I wish to write the moral—or rather sentimen-tal—history of the men of my generation.' He saw it might alternatively have been called *Les Fruits secs*; it is again a book about failure. The hero was devoted to passion: he was en-thusiastic about *Werther, René, Lélia*; he believed that 'love is the pasture and, as it were, the atmosphere for genius'. He loved luxury, women and the life of Paris with its 'amorous effluvium and intellectual emanations'. But he was sad; he had no will-power. 'Action for certain men is all the more impracticable as the desire for it is strong. Distrust of them-selves embarrasses them, fear of displeasing terrifies them; besides, profound affections are like respectable women: they are frightened of being discovered and they pass through life with downcast eyes.' So the men in Flaubert's books spend their lives metaphorically chasing butterflies; one who sought power is dismissed from his prefecture and is in turn an organiser of colonisation in Algeria, secretary to a pasha, manager of a newspaper, advertising agent and finally legal assistant in an industrial company. Another gets involved in turn in Fourier-ism, homoeopathy, table-turning, Gothic art and finally photo-graphy. *Bouvard et Pécuchet* (1881), Flaubert's funniest book, was called by René de Gourmont 'the archive in which pos-terity will clearly read the hopes and disappointments of a century'.[1] This is a caricature of two petty bourgeois who give themselves up to studying every science in turn, but repeatedly meet disaster and failure. Flaubert declared the book had 'immense significance'; some critics have said it was the culmination of his work. It was an attack on human imbecility and on the absurd consequences of progress, but Flaubert took some pains to make it difficult to see what his point was beyond this: he enigmatically wrote in the preface that its purpose was to praise tradition and order, so that it would be unclear whom he was making fun of. 'I wish to produce such an impression of lassitude and boredom, that in reading the book people could think it was written by an idiot.' Voltaire's

---

[1] D. L. Demorest, *A Travers les plans, manuscrits et dossiers de Bouvard et Pécuchet* (1931), 154.

conclusion, 'cultivate your garden', was also Flaubert's. The romantic Flaubert ended by preaching something not very different from the classicist Anatole France.[1]

When individualists reached this kind of despair, they sometimes tried to exorcise the pain by renouncing their independence. This was shown most strikingly by Bourget and Barrès. The novels of Paul Bourget (1852–1935) are largely forgotten today. They cannot be read for pleasure, which is perhaps not surprising, for he believed that the trouble with the world was that it sought pleasure. But his novels were acclaimed by a wide and loyal audience in his own day; he wrote no less than seventy-three volumes. He edified a whole generation seeking moral guidance and in the prefaces to his works of fiction he made clear exactly what the moral of each story was. His celebrated *Le Disciple* (1890) was the manifesto of a new code of behaviour. In subsequent works, he specialised in stories about the domestic problems of the bourgeoisie. He devoted himself above all to defending the middle-class family as an institution. He attacked divorce, adultery, irreligion, democracy. He praised the cult of ancestors, the respect of family tradition and property, moderation in social ambition. Yet Bourget began life as a literary critic of rare perception; he was in his youth a positivist and a pupil of Taine. His career is worth examining, because it shows how the worship of science failed to satisfy him, and men like him, and how the Catholic reaction of the end of the century was born. Hitherto the problem was why writers lost their religious faith; now it was why an increasing number returned to it.

Bourget claimed that he remained a positivist all his life. One of the sources of strength in his writing was that he did not deny all value to scientific investigation, but only defined its limits, and incorporated it into a wider philosophy of life. Bourget was thus not so much disillusioned with science, as emotionally unsatisfied by it. He did not abandon positivism for Christianity but combined them. The result was perhaps unorthodox but no more so than his early adherence to positivism was superficial. He made his name with a collection of essays on the psychology of his generation, which turned the positivist

[1] Philip Spencer, *Flaubert* (1952); R. Dumesnil, *Gustave Flaubert* (1932); B. F. Bart, *Madame Bovary and the Critics* (New York, 1966).

method against its creators.[1] Bourget had a very unhappy childhood. It was dominated on the one hand by the loss of his mother when he was five—a loss to which he attributed his permanent inability to love or to be loved, and which may possibly explain his admiration for family life, which he was never to experience. On the other hand, he felt himself to be a child without roots, whose parents came from different parts of the country, whose father, a professor, carried him around France as he was transferred from post to post. He lived with books; he read the whole of Shakespeare, Scott, Dickens and George Sand before he was ten; then all the romantics and positivists in adolescence. This reading filled him with an 'irremediable despair'. The collapse of France in 1871 gave him a desire for action, but the determinism of the positivists discouraged him in advance. The Commune, after a short period of enthusiasm, terrified him and in 1890 he still recalled with horror the fusillade of May 1871. His trouble, he decided, was that 'there was a complete divorce between our intelligence and our sensibility'. Most young men of his generation were equally torn, and his essays were an attempt to lay bare the causes of their anxieties, to be a document, as he said, for future historians studying the moral life of the second half of the century. The essays were a brilliant attack on five leading writers who had, he said, formed the outlook of his generation. They were effective because they attributed one principal characteristic to each author, as his *idée maîtresse*, in the manner of Taine, studying above all mentality and attitudes, rather than biography or events. He used the latest methods of science to show the bankruptcy of all the intellectual system-building and emotional adventures of the century. He argued that literature had become one of the principal influences in life, now that traditional and local influences had diminished. Baudelaire had spread 'decadence' among young men—which was a state in which individuals were 'unfit for the tasks of ordinary life'. Renan had made dilettantism fashionable, 'a state of the mind, at once very intelligent and very voluptuous, which inclines us in turn towards various forms of hope and leads us to lend ourselves to all these forms without giving ourselves up to any one . . . It transformed scepticism into

[1] P. Bourget, *Essais de psychologie contemporaine* (1885).

an instrument of pleasure.' The result was that 'thirty volte-faces, in politics, literature, religion and general thought have cast into the current of ideas all sorts of formulae of taste, aesthetics and belief'. Flaubert preached a virtual nihilism, that 'every human effort ended in failure', that ambition was useless because its fulfilment did not yield the expected pleasure. Taine argued that wisdom was to be found in the acceptance of what was inevitable and that man, far from being good, was 'carnivorous'. Stendhal's hero is a man at war with society; his conclusion is pessimistic, a desire for death. These five masters of modern times, Bourget concludes, are thus all tired of life. They could not offer hope. In his subsequent books, Bourget applied the same method. In reaction against the realist novel, he wrote psychological analyses not of manners and events but of the state of the soul. He became 'an analyst of the disorders of the heart', a student of the revived *mal de siècle*. He had no talent for description; he could remember visual impressions only with difficulty; but he was fascinated by emotions and obsessed by memories of his own. Though he could occasionally invent dramatic twists and surprising end-ings for his novels, they always remained moral essays rather than stories.

The severest criticism Bourget levelled against the authors whose writings had dominated his youth was that they had deprived him of all sense of identity.[1] This is what he tried to regain through his writings, and this is why he was attracted increasingly by traditional values, roots and patriotism. His interest in psychology made him feel the overwhelming im-importance of the unconscious: this, more than anything, he later said, was what made him a traditionalist.[2] His long investigation of the moral ills of France—and their study, he thought, was the principal business of literature—led him to the conclusion that the conservative doctrines in which Balzac, Le Play and Taine had ended were the only ones which could serve as a remedy. In *Le Disciple* he told the story of a fervent disciple of positivism who comes to a tragic end. This book caused a considerable stir: 20,000 copies were sold in six weeks,

[1] Lettre Autobiographique, printed as an appendix to V. Giraud, *Paul Bourget* (1934), 195.
[2] V. Giraud, op. cit. 107, quoting letter in *Revue des revues* (1 May 1904).

Anatole France and Brunetière led a violent controversy on its moral message, a controversy which was in some ways a rehearsal of the Dreyfus Affair. Taine accused Bourget of caricaturing his teaching, but he admitted sadly: 'Taste has changed, my generation is finished.' Bourget again aroused a furore with his novel *L'Étape* (1902) which argued that class differences and heredity were so fundamental that it was impossible for people to *bruler l'étape*, to skip a rung in the ladder, without grave danger; the doctrine of personal merit was false.

What Bourget had wanted originally was hope, and a cure for the doubts of his generation. 'Who will give us back the divine virtue of joy in work and hope in struggle . . . Men do not need leaders who make them doubt.' He did not quite achieve his aims. He learnt to hate a great deal in modern society, to castigate the *machiavellian Italian* Gambetta, the *abominable* Ferry, the *hideous error* of having a republic, the *stupid* Declaration of the Rights of Man and *ignoble* democracy. But he never succeeded in getting beyond agnosticism, even when he preached Christianity: the absolute for him was the unknowable; he never quite found faith. His conclusion was that 'the laws of human life, discovered by the purely realistic observation of facts, are identical with the laws promulgated by the Revelation'.[1] Too much reading had been the bane of his youth; too much thinking was as dangerous as incautious use of noxious chemicals, so he ended up as a critic chastising criticism, while still believing criticism had its uses. He reconciled science and religion because he could not be entirely happy with either alone.[2]

Maurice Barrès (1862–1923) was even more significant, because the philosophy he offered was not that of a disillusioned middle-aged man, preaching to his juniors, but that of a young man spontaneously rebelling against his elders, and acknowledged by many of his contemporaries as their representative. He rebelled first of all against his school: he hated its 'vie de ménagerie'. He was humiliated by two years of German occupation after the Franco-Prussian War. He was frustrated by the contrast between the romantic ideals he found in Walter

---

[1] Charles Baussan, *De Frédéric Le Play à Paul Bourget* (1935), 177–8.
[2] Michel Mansuy, *Un Moderne: Paul Bourget* (Besançon, 1960).

Scott, Balzac and Fenimore Cooper and the mediocrity of his life. He was incensed by the doctrines he was taught. His philosophy teacher Burdeau (a disciple of Ferry, a brilliant graduate of the École Normale Supérieure, who soon after entered parliament and later became president of the Chamber of Deputies) represented the successful modern man approved of by the previous generation: he was a good speaker, well read, self-made, had fought in the war. But Barrès saw him as his enemy because he preached the fashionable Kantian philosophy, universally applicable, which Barrès regarded as hostile to individual whim, and because he sought to cut his pupils from their roots, from their families and provinces, and drive them to seek success in Paris, in a standard mould. Barrès did at first follow his master's teaching and at twenty-one went to Paris. There, however, he published *Sous l'œil des barbares* (1892) which stated his hostility to society and his belief that the world was barbarous and brutish to sensitive men like himself, but he offered no positive answer to what could be done about this. Paul Bourget gave the book a long review and Barrès became famous. The Latin Quarter in 1889 elected him *Prince des Jeunes* and member of parliament—where he sat on the extreme left as a Boulangist, symbolising protest. *Le Culte du moi* (1888–91) defined his position. This trilogy was both a portrait of the new type of young man becoming increasingly numerous, as he said, and of which he was the representative, and a guide to this new type. He aspired to winning their attention by accurately describing their difficulties and by offering them, at last, a solution. 'Our malaise', he wrote, 'comes from our living in a social order inspired by the dead and in no way chosen by us. The dead are poisoning us.' Let the young cast off these shackles. 'Let each one of us satisfy his ego and humanity will be a beautiful forest, beautiful because everything, trees, plants and animals, will develop and rise according to their nature.' Abandon guilt, which is the enemy of love and of enthusiasm. Seek every kind of experience, use up your youthful energy. He summarised his creed in three formulae: 'First Principle: We are never so happy as when we are in a state of exaltation. Second Principle: The pleasure of exaltation is much increased·if it is analysed.' Even humiliating emotions, if analysed, can become voluptuous. 'Conclusion: We must feel as much as possible and analyse as much as possible.' This meant cultivating the ego, freeing it from the influence of the barbarians, from German metaphysics and Latin compartmentalisation. He quoted Ignatius Loyola, Benjamin Constant and Sainte-Beuve as models of this art. 'The religious orders created a hygiene of the soul, seeking to love God perfectly. A similar hygiene will lead us to the adoration of the ego. It will be a laboratory of enthusiasm.' But what should young men be enthusiastic about, apart from themselves? Barrès had nothing to offer as yet in these first books. 'Dear modern life,' he wrote, 'so ill at ease with its hereditary formulae and prejudices, let us live it with ardour, and hell! it will certainly end by working out for itself a new moral code and new duties.'

The cult of the self, on its own, was not enough. Barrès found the ego too ephemeral an object for adoration, he wanted to worship something eternal; and so he came to see the ego as part of a larger whole. 'I saw that I was only an instant in a long culture, a gesture among a thousand others of a force that preceded me and which will survive me. I became conscious of the essential of my ego, of the element of eternity of which I have custody.' The cult of the ego thus turned into the cult of his native province, and of the French nation. His rebellion against the dead ended with a worship of the dead. He decided the ego had no permanent reality on its own, that it was the product of tradition, past forces, the nation. 'To save ourselves from a sterile anarchy, we wish to bind ourselves to our land and our dead.' Analysis and introspection, which he had urged in his youth, now failed to satisfy him. Intelligence was only 'a small thing on the surface of ourselves'. So Barrès became a nationalist, and one of the principal writers responsible for its revival in this period. He now said that men's thoughts were not their own, but the result of racial and hereditary influence: 'our fathers and our ancestors speak through us'. Nationalism meant the acceptance of this influence of the past, but also it was a means of discovering the best in each individual, for it was this eternal voice that was the best in him. In 1894 Barrès founded *La Cocarde* to preach this doctrine, coupled with anti-Semitism. His *Roman de l'énergie nationale* (1897–1902), of which *Les Déracinés*, perhaps the most famous of his works, is the first volume, spread the message in half-fictional, half-autobiographical form. He was a founder member of the Ligue de la Patrie Française (1899). In 1906 his respectability was acknowledged by his election to the French Academy. From that date to his death he sat continuously in parliament, a member of the party of order now, but not fully a member of the right wing, and he refused to join Maurras. In his *Les Diverses Familles spirituelles de la France*, he accepted them all. 'Each group', he said, 'leaves too much outside it.'

But nationalism, again, was not enough for him. It 'lacks the dimension of infinity'. So he moved towards Catholicism. His campaign for the preservation of churches after the Separation (*La Grande Pitié des églises de France*, 1914) was one stage in this; his *Colline inspirée* (1913) marked his acceptance of certain aspects of Catholicism. But he never obtained faith; he died before he was sixty and his conversion was never completed. Already in 1909, however, he was preaching an ideal very different from that of his youth. 'Lead a Christian life. Have faith. Take the Sacraments . . . I do not know whether religion is true, but I love it.' Barrès's life was thus a continual flight from abstract ideals and a search for a creed that would appeal to the heart. He could not find any ideal in the future, and so he returned to the past he had once abhorred, with a nihilism as complete as that which he had denounced in his youth. He became obsessed by death, and it is only in death that he ultimately found the peace and conciliation he sought. His traditionalism and rationalism were the cult of the dead. Gide with some justice complained: 'Graves, graves, everywhere and always. To bear wreaths of flowers to graves—it is really only that.'

Barrès was greatly admired in his time and his *Déracinés* has been called one of the ten greatest social novels of the nineteenth century. Its style, with its 'brilliant lyricism, its melody of abrupt beginnings and slow development, its movement, sudden stops and prolonged pauses', has been likened to a combination of geometry and music and the nearest thing in literature to Wagner. The position Barrès held in French society has been well summarised by Léon Blum: 'He was for me, as for most of my friends, not only a master but a guide. We formed a school around him, almost a court . . . To a coldly sceptical society, Barrès brought a philosophy charged with provocative metaphysics and poetry, quivering with pride and domination. A whole generation, reduced and conquered by him, breathed this intoxicating mixture of conquering activity, philosophy and sensuality. It thought it had discovered its master, its model and its leader.' Maurras wrote, 'He was one of the greatest influences, the essential transformer of young intellectual opinion in 1900 and 1914.' For that very reason, and also because the part he chose was rejected by many of his early followers, he was bitterly attacked by the succeeding generation. Gide denounced him as the most evil of educators: all that is marked by his influence is moribund, dead, because he had a taste for death. A few months before Barrès died, a public mock trial of him was held, presided over by André Breton, in which he was accused of damaging the security of the mind. Tristan Tzara gave evidence that 'Barrès is the greatest scoundrel Europe has produced since Napoleon'.[1]

*Proust*

The analysis of the individual was raised to a new plane by Marcel Proust (1871–1922). His work was for long appreciated by a much smaller audience than was that, for example, of Barrès or Bourget. It was only after the Second World War that he came to be acknowledged as one of France's most original and profound authors. An inquiry by the *Figaro* in 1947, asking people whether he had influenced them, drew largely non-committal answers. But three years later there were twenty theses being written about him in the Sorbonne alone, and the flood of publications about him has not abated since then.[2] Frenchmen did not immediately recognise them-

[1] A. Zarach, *Bibliographie barrèsienne 1881–1948* (1951); P. de Boisdeffre, *Barrès parmi nous* (1952); J. M. Domenach, *Barrès par lui-même* (1954); J. Vier, *M. Barrès et le culte du moi* (1958); Z. Sternhell, *M. Barrès et le nationalisme française* (1972); R. Soucy, *Fascism in France: the case of M. Barrès* (Berkeley, California, 1972, controversial); M. Davanture, 'La Jeunesse de M. Barrès 1862–1888' (unpublished Paris thesis, 1975, 2 vols.).

[2] For opinion on him in 1923, R. Fernandez (ed.), 'Hommage à Marcel Proust', *Les Cahiers Marcel Proust*, no. 1 (1927); D. W. Alden, *Marcel Proust and his French Critics* (Los Angeles, 1940); Germaine Brée, 'New Trends in Proust Criticism',

selves in Proust, who must therefore be seen as a precursor rather than as the leader of a generation, as offering explanations before most people had formulated the problems.

Proust's whole life was dominated by his unsatisfactory relationship with his parents. He was the son of a successful doctor and a talented and well-to-do mother; he won high honours as a schoolboy; but though as a young man he published a book of essays and verse (1896), which was a flop, he seemed incapable of doing anything with his life. At the age of thirty-five he withdrew from the world as a neurotic invalid. He spent the rest of his life working out the cause of his troubles and reflecting on his relatively brief experience of society. His conclusions represented an important advance on those offered by his predecessors, but they were also much more complex. Whereas Barrès and Bourget urged men to prop themselves up with the aid of traditional institutions, declaring individualism to be too painful to sustain, Proust argued that this suffering held the key to the solution of the human dilemma. Suffering produced detachment, which in turn made self-knowledge possible. Suffering also produced sympathy for others and that was essential if one was to understand other people too. But Proust had no universal formula for explaining human motivation. On the contrary, he believed that the most fundamental characteristic of men was their instability— like a kaleidoscope—so that prediction of their actions was impossible. His method was to analyse them under the microscope and to reveal the many different sides of their personalities; he saw them changing constantly with time; he excelled in showing the contradictions in them, and the gap between behaviour and intention. The appearance of continuity and cohesion in character was purely superficial: it was partly the result of individuals assuming roles, and partly of those around them creating fixed stereotypes to give them a semblance of stability. The psychiatrist Ribot had recently identified dissociation of the personality as a disease.[1] Proust

*Symposium* (Syracuse Univ.) (May 1951), vol. 5, no. 1, 62–71; C. B. Osburn, *The Present State of French Studies* (Metuchen, N.J., 1971), 825–36. For the publishing history of Proust, see above, chapter 8. Cf. also G. D. Lindner, *Marcel Proust, Reviews and estimates in English* (Stanford, 1942).

[1] T. Ribot, *Les Maladies de la personnalité* (1885).

argued that it was in fact normal. Ribot thought man's identity came simply from his body. Proust saw much more in individuals; he was fascinated by the sound of their names, by their handwriting, by their every mannerism; but he believed that it was virtually impossible for one person to know another. All that could be hoped for was to know oneself. Proust was a solipsist, for whom man 'is a being who cannot come out of himself, who cannot know others except in himself, and who, if he denies this, lies'.

It took him a long time to accept loneliness and to turn it from an inescapable fact into the basis of a philosophy, for Proust felt a profound need for affection. At the age of seven he had his first presentiment that love and happiness were impossible, when he begged his mother for a goodnight kiss and realised that by asking for it, he had ruined its savour; there could be no consolation for the fact that he could not have enough affection from her. At fourteen he wrote that his greatest misery was to be separated from his mother; guilt, remorse, and a highly developed sensitivity made it impossible for him to resolve the problems of living independently of her, and it was only in late middle age, when he gave his parents' furniture away to a brothel, that he at last resolved his longing for revenge on them. At school, he demanded 'a tyrannical and total affection' from his fellow pupils; as an adult he was distinguished by 'beautiful manners', exquisite politeness and a readiness to flatter which verged on fawning. He quickly lost hope of obtaining satisfaction in love for women, deciding that the desire for possession was both absurd and painful, that jealousy was its necessary corollary, that in any case what one loved was a creation of one's own imagination, and the consciousness of the disparity between this ideal and the reality was more painful still. Love was a poison, bound to create suffering. One could not make a bad choice, because every choice was bad. Later, he found the answer in seeing the suffering love caused as the stimulus that was needed to re-examine oneself and one's motives. But meanwhile he was made to feel even more alone by the realisation, or the decision, that he was a homosexual, and so an outcast, forced into deceit, reduced, after a succession of unsuccessful attempts to combine love and friendship with his equals, to abandon the belief that friendship was a possibility either. His love-affairs with young men of the working class, and his resort to male brothels culminated in his having himself beaten there, and sticking pins into rats, in an effort to come to terms with the haunting image of his parents. Proust became the first famous author to write openly about homosexuality (though Binet-Valmer's novel *Lucien* (1910) and Achille Essebac's *Dédé* (1901) had prepared the way). He defended it against the opprobrium the Church and moralists had laid upon it, but he asserted that it was an incurable malady, and Gide, who was the first author to make public profession of his own homosexuality, attacked Proust for talking of it as deviation, instead of as 'Greek love'. It is wrong to see in homosexuality the basic explanation of Proust's dilemmas. Proust was not entirely in either camp, just as he was not entirely a Jew, that other race of outcasts whose lot tormented him. It was precisely because he stood on so many boundaries that he was able to be so perceptive.[1]

Proust had a strong belief in the importance of heredity. At one stage, he thought he could assuage his desire by being accepted into the most exclusive social circles of Paris. He imagined the aristocracy were able to transcend the limitations of the individual because they were so firmly anchored in the past. It was not quite snobbishness that attracted him to such people; he had no illusions about their stupidity, their inability to appreciate intellectual or artistic worth, even when he was carried away by the suggestiveness and euphony of their historic titles. Proust did come from a family that was only on the first step of the ladder to social respectability; his grandfather had been a grocer, his uncle was a draper who had made his fortune in Algeria; his father had been a scholarship boy, who had risen to be a professor of medicine but who lacked artistic taste; his mother—who was artistic—was the daughter of a Jewish stockbroker and niece of a button manufacturer. Proust in his novel idealised the hostesses and *salons* he frequented. The aristocratic families involved were, like him, on the fringes of their class and so very much more concerned

[1] Eugène Montfort, 'L'Homosexualité dans la littérature', an inquiry in *Les Marges* (1926, 176–215); Dr. Robert Soupault, *Marcel Proust du côté de la médecine* (1967); L. Lesage, *Marcel Proust and his Literary Friends* (Urbana, Ill., 1958), 89.

with their status (like the Belgian banker, ennobled during the Restoration, on whose descendant the duc de Guermantes was modelled) or else people with titles who had married into money (like Boni de Castellane, who married the American heiress Anna Gould, and on whom Saint-Loup was based). Proust for a time felt he lacked family traditions and admired the aristocracy who, he believed, were, on account of their ancestry, more than isolated individuals. He also admired professional men who derived substance and stability from their work, like the doctor Cottard in his novel, who was in his social life a pretentious imbecile, but who nevertheless was a 'great clinician', with a 'mysterious gift' for healing. Within a few years, however, this idol also lost its glitter and the Dreyfus Affair completed his disillusionment. Proust nevertheless remained ambiguous in his attitude to class also. He believed that society would become even more hierarchical as it became outwardly more democratic. He did not entirely dissociate himself from the view that the members of each class were doomed to remain in the one into which they were born, and that no communication between classes was really possible: class was a prison, just as individual isolation was; he both mocked and praised those who were typical representatives of their class.

Humour was one of the methods he perfected to cope with the problems of the world. When all his hopes of salvation through external forces faded, he was thrown back on himself. He did not see a solution in any positive action, for all action seemed to him either ridiculous or mean. Life could be either lived, or dreamt, and he thought those who dreamt it did better. There are only two pages in his book when he expresses confidence in the future. He turned rather to the past, and to introspection. He was no longer afraid of his loneliness, for he now found his own 'passionate conversations' with himself to be what he valued most.[1] The key to reality was to be found in memory, which held together the isolated fragments of men's existence; not in intelligence, which was only a source of confusion, providing pretexts for eluding the duties that instinct dictated. It was not deliberate memory therefore that mattered, but involuntary memory, unsullied by intelligence, which

[1] M. Proust, *Le Temps retrouvé* (Livre de poche, 1954), 251, 234.

revived parts of one's former self that one had thought dead. In this way one was freed from the domination of time; one glimpsed eternity; the fear of death vanished, because one realised that parts of one were always dying. Proust at last found his vocation, to be an artist, whose function was to translate these visions, to express the truths he had in himself. The artist provided the links between isolated individuals. It no longer mattered that men were alone, once they realised that reality was unique for each one of them. They should not take the behaviour they saw around them as indications of reality, because it was superficial, and needed to be interpreted, as symbols of what lay behind. He was not in favour of esotericism; he insisted that intelligence had its uses; and the artist must use it to clarify what seemed to be obscure. The real world, however, was only partly in the objects surrounding one: it was even more in oneself. The artist therefore led the fullest kind of life, even though he was isolated; literature was the most fulfilling activity, because it enabled men to see beyond the limits of their own vision; books were like spectacles, designed to help the reader see better, and if the reader recognised in himself what the author was describing, then that was truth. What made life worth living, then, was to be an artist who could illuminate the darkness that surrounded all men. The suffering that artistic sensitivity involved was worth bearing, because it was through suffering that one was driven to make the effort from which the discovery of truth could follow. Proust's solution was not self-realisation, but withdrawal, reflection and understanding. He did not aim to offer hope, still less happiness, for he was too conscious of unhappiness everywhere, and 'happy years are wasted years', because they prevented one from knowing oneself. What he felt he could achieve was to 'bring harmony to scattered spirits and peace to troubled hearts'. He believed his method had the power of reconciliation in it, and the victim of internal conflicts himself, this was what seemed most urgent. His detachment, however, had no limits, and he could see the flaws in his own solutions. It was in that way, as much as through art, that he found his liberation.[1]

[1] M. Proust, *A la recherche du temps perdu* (1913–27). Among the several hundred books about Proust and the many thousands of articles, the following are useful

This sample of novelists and moralists, inevitably a small sample, gives some indication of the internal turmoils of individualism as well as of its inextinguishable attractions. The pains caused by individual freedom need to be recorded as much as the principles that made it possible. How ordinary people coped with them, when not sustained by philosophic or religious ideas, or even when they were, may be seen by looking at those who ended up in the consulting rooms of the growing number of doctors treating nervous troubles.

introductory guides: G. Painter, *Marcel Proust, a biography* (2 vols., 1961–5); Jacques Rivière, *Quelques progrès dans l'étude du cœur humain* (1924); Arnaud Dandieu, *Marcel Proust, sa révélation psychologique* (1930); Dr. Charles Blondel, *La Psychographie de Marcel Proust* (1932); Milton Hindus, *The Proustian Vision* (1954); Jacques Nathan, *La Morale de Proust* (1953); E. Czoniczer, *Quelques antécédents de 'A la recherche du temps perdu'* (1957); J. J. Zéphir, *La Personnalité humaine dans l'œuvre de Marcel Proust* (1959); Floris Delattre, 'Bergson et Proust', *Les Études bergsonniennes* (1948), vol. i, 1–127. See also pp. 852–3. For new attitudes to intimacy, cf. Lion Murard and Patrick Zylberman, *Le Petit Travailleur infatigable* (1976).

# 17. Worry, Boredom and Hysteria

THE age of fear is as good a label for this century as the age of progress: both labels reveal one side of it. For though there were unprecedented material transformations, it did not follow that there was also increasing hope in all spheres of life, let alone increasing happiness. Opportunities widened in this period, knowledge of the world's workings grew enormously and people, to a considerable extent, became accustomed to coping with far more change. That better things were coming from all this was frequently repeated but perhaps not as often as is assumed: perhaps the optimists talked loudest. For at the same time the whole notion of what constituted an improvement was always a matter of debate and uncertainty. Happiness remained an elusive and controversial ideal. Anxiety, by contrast, may well have increased (though not necessarily in all groups) in the sense that traditional supports of behaviour were weakened, that people were left facing a larger world and a vastly greater range of problems, with far less certainty as to how they should treat them, and often with sharpened sensibilities. To understand this society, one must study it not just in the achievements of its members, but in their loneliness too. One must look into the history, in other words, of personal anxiety—the way people worried, what frightened them and what hurt them.

But this is uncharted territory. It is true that there is no lack of information about the triumphs of science over the great physical scourges of mankind, like smallpox, cholera, tuberculosis and puerperal fever, which were gradually subjugated in this period, though there is still scope for a vast amount of research in this subject. But medical history is inevitably written largely from the point of view of the progress of knowledge; it tells more about the doctor than the patient; and it is more concerned with general demographic results than with the details of how individuals bore their sufferings. This negative side of medical history—the way people reacted to disease, the way they faced pain and death—is far less documented, but it brings out a factor that was crucial in determining people's general attitude to life. The history of mental illness, which has recently attracted considerable attention, can provide clues as to how the strains of existence were met or not met, though again the evidence is twisted by the succession of psychological theories through which it was seen—and it is too often presented as a social problem concerning only a minority. The history of the mental troubles of the vast majority of the population, who were not mad but who had their own—not unrelated—anguish to deal with, falls between two stools, outside the scope of medical history. But it can help to provide the context of obsessions and fears into which all other preoccupations—about work, family, friends and politics—had to fit.

These intimate fears were seldom written down and there is little hint of them in the sources historians generally concentrate on. They come out, however, for example, in the Catholic confessional.[1] One can find traces of them also in doctors' case histories; this is a still untapped source, through which one can eavesdrop on accounts of pain, guilt and an immense amount of suffering. The very same people who, at other times, were busy making money, or protesting vigorously about class repression, the high cost of living, the policies of governments, or any of the other causes historians have recorded, in the privacy of the consulting room give the impression of an overwhelming preoccupation with very different and far less grandiose problems, but ones that generated terror, fury and deep despondency. Their worries were sometimes worries about the human condition itself, but these too have their history, for the unchanging problems of life and death did not always meet with the same response and there was more to them than a variation in the balance of resignation or acceptance.

The diseases people imagined they suffered from are a useful introduction to this, because they reveal imagination and attitude as well as reaction to pain. Hypochondria has the advantage that it blows up into exaggerated forms the

[1] Theodore Zeldin, *Conflicts in French Society* (1970), chapter on 'Confession, Sin and Pleasure'.

kinds of worries that tormented people. And in this period, the advance of medicine introduced severe complications in the way disease was perceived, at the same time as it reduced the incidence of disease. The popularisation of medical knowledge added a whole new dimension to consciousness. In this intermediary stage, between the supremacy of religious and superstitious ideas on the one hand and scientific confidence on the other, a vast number of dangerous possibilities were added to the mere business of existence. As the doctors' nosographies were expanded, many pains were endowed with more terrifying names, and first germs and then viruses invaded a universe previously inhabited only by simple humours and demons. Thus, there had once been an easily understandable explanation of hypochondria: it had been a disturbance of the hypochonder, which caused vapours to rise from the stomach and liver and endocrine gland. Some doctors regarded this as a physical trouble, like Tissot,[1] who attributed it to disturbances in the 'nervous fibres' and 'nervous fluid', or Broussais, who linked it with gastro-enteritis. But in the eighteenth century Sauvages had argued that hypochondria was due to 'excessive self-love, attachment to life and to the pleasures it procures', and that it was therefore an intellectual trouble. In the middle of the nineteenth century these different views continued to be held simultaneously, so there was no generally accepted way of dealing with it. Doctors who received the most varied confessions labelled them as hypochondria when they could find no other explanation. Dr. Michéa, who was one of the national experts on hypochondria at the beginning of this period, stated that hypochondria occurred twice as often among men as among women, and most of all in the liberal professions; it was one of the results of education; the reading of medical books by laymen was both a cause and a symptom of it. But retired soldiers also suffered from it, as though the fear of death only worried them after they had ceased to be confronted with it directly. It may indeed be that as serious dangers to life diminished, men had more leisure to think about less immediate ones, and worry, inevitably, was the principal element in this condition.

[1] S. A. Tissot (1728–97), famous for his best-sellers *L'Onanisme* (1760) and *L'Avis au peuple sur sa santé* (1761).

D d

Four case histories of hypochondria, related by Dr. Michéa, show how the imagination of patients expanded. There was the case of 'an intelligent man of thirty-seven', for whom timidity had been a lifelong problem. He had given up his intention of becoming a notary for fear of 'succumbing under the yoke'. At eighteen he had suffered palpitations of the heart, which gave him a fixed conviction that he had a mortal disease: the doctors he consulted could suggest no remedy. He was overwhelmed by the notion that he was powerless; all work, even reading, became painful; 'the sense of not being like other men towards my wife has always dominated me', he said, though he had one son. After twenty years of suffering, he turned to homoeopathy, and declared himself cured. The obscurity of this case is typical: only a fraction of the truth ever got out and disease was very much a mystery. Book learning could not solve this problem. Many laymen studied medicine—and a flow of medical books catered for them; some later became doctors, because of worry about their own health.[1] A second case illustrates, however, how frightening this new medical knowledge could be. A man, recounting his troubles to his doctor, complained that at thirteen he suffered from 'premature erections' at the sight of a girl. This led him to masturbate; at eighteen he 'obtained a rendez-vous' with a woman to whom he was much attached but 'I experienced so much agitation that it was impossible for me to profit from it'. He was more fortunate the next year, but he then found he had gonorrhoea with inflammation of the testicles. His health deteriorated and he suffered liver and stomach pains. He gave up his plans for a military career and became a medical student instead; but, he said, the cold and humidity of Paris and the sedentary nature of his occupation worsened his condition. He diagnosed that he had a kidney stone, and determined to have an operation; the surgeon he

[1] For example, F. V. Raspail, *Manuel-Annuaire de la santé* (40th edition, 1885); Dr. Jules Massé, *La Médecine des accidents* (9th edition, 1869); Dr. Alexis Belliol, *Le Guide des malades* (10th edition, 1845); Louis Riond, *La Médecine populaire* (5th edition, 1849); Abbé David, *Petit Manuel médical à l'usage des familles, des maisons d'éducation et des établissements de bienfaisances, mis à la portée des ouvriers et des habitants de la campagne* (3rd edition, 1862); E. Barrier, *Médecine des pauvres* (5th edition, 1892). There were over one hundred works classified as 'popular medicine' published between 1846 and 1875.

approached recommended baths instead, which calmed him down. But his hard work for his examinations 'spoilt his digestion and produced frequent ejaculation of sperm'. He had noises in his ears and fainting fits and feared apoplexy. By the time he graduated, he suspected he also had heart trouble and tuberculosis. He returned to the security of his native province, but there he caught syphilis; he treated himself with mercury pills, which 'completed the ruin of his health', and, by producing flatulence, forced him to lead a solitary life. He interpreted this last trouble as being caused by chronic gastritis, which he treated by living on a diet of milk for eighteen months. The work of the once-celebrated German Wichmann then revealed the true cause of his ailments to him as loss of sperm.[1] He learnt the book by heart in his enthusiasm. He cut his sphincters, and had his prostate cauterised to stop the loss. At that point he declared himself cured, sleep and appetite returned and 'my erections had an energy I had never seen before'. That was his own conclusion. Modern readers will immediately interpret his troubles according to doctrines now fashionable, but in his own time this man, a respectable physician in the eyes of his neighbours, had only taken to extremes the spirit of scientific curiosity and the search for explanations. This was the reverse side of progress. When Flaubert satirised it in *Bouvard et Pécuchet*, he was pointing to genuine and painful dilemmas. And children were particularly vulnerable, as witness a third case, of an eighteen-year-old shop assistant who went to see Dr. Michéa. He admitted to having masturbated since the age of fifteen, until he developed acne: his workmates mocked him for his disfigurement, saying it was masturbation that caused the acne. He read Tissot's book on *Onanism*, which led him to feeling all sorts of other symptoms that Tissot said followed from the evil practice. The boy was convinced his brain was 'going dry'. So he gave up masturbation in favour of women, but he almost at once caught gonorrhoea. Though he was quickly cured, he remained convinced that 'a venereal element' survived in his blood, which would eventually produce terrible sufferings. A whole succession of pains, vomiting and fainting followed. He imagined that he was going blind, that he had tuberculosis, that he was

[1] J. E. Wichmann, *De Pollutione diurna* (1791).

going to die. A doctor attributed his troubles to loss of sperm and cauterised his ureter seven times. He felt better after this, despite the appalling pain of the operations, but he was still worried. Dr. Michéa, when consulted, prescribed cold baths and complete abstinence from both women and masturbation; he insisted on his spending at least three-quarters of an hour each day immersed in the Seine; and he claimed this effected his cure.

Finally, worry about the mysteries of disease and death may be illustrated by the case of the Parisian butcher, aged thirty-eight, of generally sanguine temperament, who suffered only from haemorrhoids, until he began to worry that he had a tumour in his stomach, because his father had died of one at forty-two. Every pain he felt, he now interpreted as a warning. He told his family he was dying and constantly lamented that it was sad one so young should pass away. One day, Dr. Michéa was summoned to find him vomiting, with a violent stomach ache, terrified that his moment had come. Dr. Michéa appeased him by placing twenty leeches on his anus and an opium plaster on his stomach and giving him orangeade to drink. Henceforth the man lived on 'calming potions'.[1] Dr. Michéa believed that the basic trouble was materialism and the decline of religion. In his private clinic, he made his patients go daily to chapel, with excellent results, he said. But to his outpatients he gave tranquillising drugs, which, as has been seen, were one of the less discussed alternatives to religion.[2] These various cases show that the history of both science and religion needs to be complemented by that of imagination. The terrors this inspired was another of the important forces that influenced behaviour.

### Nervousness

As medical views changed, so worry about one's health, with all that that implied about one's personality and one's functioning, became absorbed into the more general category of nervousness. This was, around 1850, again very much one of the mysteries of life, because opinions on it were also in a

---

[1] Dr. C. F. Michéa, *Traité pratique, dogmatique et critique de l'hypochondrie* (1845).

[2] Id., *Le Matérialisme refuté à l'aide d'arguments empruntés à l'histoire naturelle, à la physiologie et à la médecine* (1850); see above, 784–5.

state of flux. In the course of the next century a whole host of novel explanations of nervousness were offered; its manifestations were renamed and subdivided with increasing complexity, so that it appeared to grow into a problem that more and more people felt touched by. Since nervous diseases were, of course, no modern invention, the mid-nineteenth century preserved the heritage of the ancient world in its view of them. Nervousness had been explained simply, though vaguely, by the Greeks (whose statements were still reproduced respectfully in the French medical textbooks) as the result of man being endowed with 'passions'. One of the most popular guides to self-knowledge was still the treatise entitled *The Physiology of the Passions* by J. L. Alibert, who had been physician to Louis XVIII.[1] Passion was the cause of misery, when it was not controlled, and the cure for this therefore lay in self-mastery. This doctrine could easily be absorbed into Christian language: will-power was the answer to temptation. But the issue was complicated by the association of the different passions with states of the body, brought about by people's differing constitution and temperament, and by the different conditions in which they lived. Thus melancholy was brought on more directly by an excess of black bile, and choler by too much yellow bile; but it was all a vicious circle, because sorrows 'dried the body', 'consumed the spirits', exhausted the warmth and moisture of the body, and so brought about further troubles; blood-letting and purges got rid of 'the humours'. The ambiguity of the condition was shown by Cicero translating the Greek word melancholia as *furor*. Plato had made frenzy a divine gift. Aristotle had combined melancholy and frenzy to produce the idea of the gifted melancholic, so that the same physical condition could produce both madness and genius. Thus whereas the medieval Christian tradition regarded melancholia as a trial, sent from God, to be conquered by will, the Aristotelian and Renaissance view was that melancholy could be a condition of creativity, and that it was implied in the ideal of the speculative life. One of the main hazards of intellectual activity thus became nervous disease; civilisation itself seemed to bring gloom in the wake

[1] J. L. Alibert, *Physiologie des passions ou nouvelle doctrine des sentimens moraux* (2nd edition, 1827).

of its victories. The educated man sought inspiration in his own independent thinking, but only too often collapsed into despair between his moments of ecstatic self-affirmation.[1] The whole notion of depression was still very obscure in the mid-nineteenth century. Dr. Du Vivier, a Paris factory inspector and member of the commission on insalubrious lodgings, writing in 1864, declared that it was uncertain whether melancholy was induced by 'an alteration of the intellectual faculties' or by the 'predominance of the liver': 'the precise seat of its cause is hidden from us.'[2] Dr. Lelut, member of the Academy of Moral and Political Sciences, confessed also that man's nature was 'indeterminable' and the 'seat of his passions', which people variously placed either in the 'nervous viscerae or plexus', or in the spinal cord, or in the brain, was really a mystery. Nevertheless, Dr. Lelut insisted that happiness could not be predetermined or accidental, for in that case life would be intolerable. In a treatise on equality, officially commissioned by his academy during the revolution of 1848, he assured his compatriots that all had an equal hope of becoming happy. Some, it is true, had to do disagreeable work, but they were generally not intelligent, so did not mind it. Habit, moreover, could 'soften or annihilate even the most poignant privations' just as it could render luxury insipid. Happiness, he argued, was a habit, or produced by it; inequalities in happiness resulted from people doing work which was not in conformity with the habits they had acquired in childhood. People who did not fit into the harmonious designs of Providence had no cause for despair: education (rather than the redistribution of wealth) would train them for a better life.[3] In such ways, the difficulties of the melancholic enigma were either denied or explained away.

The popularity of novelists came, to a certain degree, from the fact that, even if they could not explain all this,

[1] Jean Starobinski, *Histoire du traitement de la mélancolie des origines à 1900* (Basle 1960, Acta Psychosomatica, no. 3); Raymond Klibansky *et al.*, *Saturn and Melancholy* (1964) for the ancient and Renaissance doctrines; Lawrence Babb, *The Elizabethan Malady. A Study of Melancholia in English Literature from 1580 to 1642* (East Lansing, 1951), on the early problems of intellectuals.

[2] E. Du Vivier, *De la mélancolie* (1864), 65.

[3] L. F. Lelut, *Petit Traité de l'égalité* (2nd edition, 1858), 53, 73, 88, 90; id., *Physiologie de la pensée: recherches critiques des rapports du corps à l'esprit* (2nd edition, 1862), 1. 375, 2. 196.

they did at any rate give it a central place in their description of life. Balzac's world, for example, is one in which the great enemies of health were not physical troubles but strong emotions, unsatisfied or injured passions. His characters frequently died of grief or became ill from a variety of mental causes. Worry was thus not just a side-effect or an inconvenience, but one of the principal torments of life, and what was most frightening about it was that it was an epidemic on the increase, and that intelligence and greater wealth, far from being a safeguard against it, as they were against physical disease, usually brought it on in severer form. Balzac saw man as having a certain amount of energy, a sort of moral capital, which was easily and quickly lost by excessive activity, and above all intellectual activity. He makes his old doctor say in *Ecce Homo*: 'I am convinced that the length of life is determined by the force that the individual can oppose to thought . . . Men who, despite the use of their brain, have arrived at a great age, would have lived three times as long if they had not used this homicidal force.' This was in accord with contemporary medical doctrine: education was a form of suicide. Dr. Broussais's treatise on physiology (1822) had a chapter entitled 'How the exercise of the intellect, the emotions and the passions causes illnesses'.[1] Balzac also stressed the suffering that resulted from hereditary traits of character, from the vicissitudes of sexual life, from the unbalanced ordering of people's activity. Women were exhausted by menstruation and childbirth; they were more emotional, but they also needed emotion and, relatively speaking, they bore its trials better. These inner troubles, in Balzac's view, were much more important than natural catastrophes like war and fire, and he criticised painters for simply depicting the superficial contexts of life. Another of his ideas, which was also widespread, was that social relations had noxious effects: he planned to write a 'pathology of social life', to show how men's stock of strength was diminished by too much expense of effort, indeed, of any kind. The division of labour was in particular disastrous; individual professions had their special ailments, and accentuated any disequilibrium

[1] F. J. V. Broussais, *Traité de physiologie appliquée à la pathologie* (1822–3), I. 276; S. Tissot, *De la santé des gens de lettres* (1768, new edition 1859); E. Brunaud, *De l'hygiène des gens de lettres* (1819).

that existed in those who specialised. Dr. Cabanis (physician to Mirabeau and Condorcet) had said that 'sensibility is like a fluid whose total quantity is fixed: every time it throws itself in greater abundance into one of its channels, it proportionately diminishes in its centre'. Worry thus brought on additional troubles; it culminated in complete exhaustion—a view which was to survive in a more scientifically sophisticated form.[1]

'Nervous disease' was a subject that aroused increasing attention in the eighteenth century; in the early nineteenth 'neurosis' was the new term for it, coined by Pinel. But when in 1836 the Academy of Medicine offered a prize for the best essay on 'the influence of physical and moral education on the production of overexcitement in the nervous system and the illnesses which are the consequences of this overexcitement', the winner, Dr. Cerise, was not able to offer any clear explanation. He contented himself with satirising the absurdities in all theories that had hitherto been offered, and in particular those of the materialists Dr. Cabanis and Dr. Raspail, who believed that thought was 'secreted by the brain as bile is by the liver'.[2] The study of the mind by doctors involved the invasion of a theological preserve, for the mind, traditionally, was inseparable from the soul, which was the concern of priests. The doctors were conscious of this and for a long time a considerable proportion of them, being conformist Christians, moved rather hesitatingly in this domain. Their invasion, however, had the important result that mental troubles were henceforth studied as illnesses rather than as the inevitable consequence of being human. In 1843 Cerise, together with Baillarger, founded the Medico-Psychological Society whose *Annales* were to contain a great deal of the writing on this subject. The specialists increasingly concentrated on the obviously mad; the expansion of lunatic asylums gave them the material on which they worked; and their natural inclination was to make those who showed any symptoms which could be linked with madness to come into the asylum, if only for short stays. Dr. Baillarger gave melancholy the status of a morbid entity, thus transforming traditional views of it. For about

[1] P. J. G. Cabanis, *Rapports du physique et moral* (3rd edition, 1815), 1. 121.
[2] Dr. Cerise, *Des fonctions et des maladies nerveuses dans leurs rapports avec l'éducation sociale et privée, morale et physique* (1842), 331.

fifty years, his influence continued to be felt, even though the enormously wide definition of melancholy that he gave gradually fell apart, as his successors isolated different diseases from it. Despite all the lip-service paid to the virtues of the clinical approach, stressing observation, the old nosological method survived, in that to find a 'new disease', with a new label, became the ambition of the psychiatrists. Whereas the Church had developed a doctrine for the vast majority, and had exiled the mad as sub-human, the doctors based their theories on the aberrations of their most bizarre patients and left the majority to see their emotional problems as pale reflections of major diseases. The eighteenth-century age of reason may have refused to acknowledge the existence of the human rights of mad people, but the nineteenth-century age of science turned the old-fashioned passions into sources of illness instead of accepting them as the inevitable condition of humanity. When people worried, therefore, or were deeply depressed, they now expected a medical name for their condition, and they got it, though it altered from time to time; when too many people thought they suffered from it, then something more esoteric was needed.

Thus in 1860 Dr. Bouchut, professor at the faculty of medicine in Paris, invented *névrosisme* to describe the condition of people who had nothing physically wrong with them, whose hypochonders and whose uteruses functioned normally, but who were mentally tormented.[1] This was designed to replace all those vague old-fashioned terms like the 'vapours', 'nervous overexcitement' and 'nervous fever'; but it did not have much success, even though it was elaborately subdivided, because there was little perception behind it; it was nothing but a new word, which did nothing new to help those who suffered from it. At the same time as Dr. Bouchut put forward his new theory, however, Dr. Morel developed a more serious threat to the peace of mind of those who felt that theirs was troubled. His theory of 'degeneration' was that madness represented the decay of man from the form originally created by God, as a result of social or physical influences. The main damage was being caused by alcohol (and opium in the East), but

[1] E. Bouchut, *De l'état aigu et chronique du névrosisme appelé névropathie aiguë cérébropneumo-gastrique* . . . (1860).

industrialisation was also doing harm. Madness was thus not a sign of a primitive mind but on the contrary of collapse, and that is why most madness was incurable. It was increasing and would inevitably continue to do so, unless there was an improvement in moral standards. Meanwhile, vast numbers of people had a hereditary predisposition to it, and the asylums contained only a small minority of those who succumbed. The hereditary fault was usually so ingrained that it could be eliminated only by racial interbreeding, with primitive people who were not yet affected; the most degenerate Frenchmen, meanwhile, should be discouraged from intermarrying.[1] This theory was profoundly influential partly because it fitted in so well with traditional prejudices and Christian doctrines about hereditary influences and moral decay, so that science seemed to be confirming people's gloomiest fears, and partly because it was taken up and developed by Valentin Magnan (1835–1916), one of the most respected of the psychiatrists of the turn of the century.

Magnan, who came from Roussillon (as Pinel, Esquirol and J. P. Falret did also), spent forty-five years living in the St. Anne asylum, looking after his patients with a total devotion that made him eschew all social life, and take only an occasional and very brief seaside holiday. He was an exceptionally gentle, sympathetic, smiling man, who could gain the confidence of his patients and converse even with the most agitatedly mad ones. He was much struck by the influence of alcohol on madness and at the end of his life he calculated that out of the 113,000 cases treated by him, 27 per cent of the male patients had had alcoholic delirium; and if he added also those for whom alcohol was only one of the causes of their troubles, the percentage was 47 (and 20 per cent for women). He saw alcoholism, however, as part of the general problem of hereditary disease, leading to progressive degeneration. He accordingly produced a new nosology of mental illness, which made 'chronic delirium' or 'the delirium of degenerates' into a vast central category. The characteristic of this was that it was progressive: it started with a period of

---

[1] B. A. Morel, médecin en chef de l'Asile des Aliénés de Saint-Yon (Seine-Inf.), *Traité des dégénérescences physiques, intellectuelles et morales de l'espèce humaine et des causes qui produisent ces variétés de maladies* (1857).

incubation, in which only mild symptoms like suspicion, disquiet, preoccupation were visible. The second phase was one of persecution mania, and hallucinations. The third was megalomania and disordered ambition. Finally came 'madness'. This was an easily understandable theory, into which individual cases could easily be made to fit and it acquired considerable popularity. A whole new class of 'degenerates' was thus created. Magnan specified that this could include highly intelligent men, whom he labelled 'superior degenerates', who had 'exuberant imaginations' and 'anomalies in judgement and reflection' combining 'remarkable talents with total lack of certain aptitudes'. Every year he published studies of individual troubles like kleptomania and pyromania, showing the hereditary element in them; he was the first to extend this to sexual perversions, his publications setting off a whole series of research monographs on this subject.[1]

In Magnan's time, the sort of person who might be classified in this way was 'Mademoiselle Lef . . .'. Her father, an intelligent and sober man, had died of pneumonia; her mother had become an alcoholic at the menopause; her brother had died of tuberculosis. She looked after her widowed mother until she was left alone at the age of twenty-eight. She lived in a room by herself and had no social life. At thirty-seven she stopped working in a factory to set up a little business of her own. One of the residents in her block then began to court her; she refused him, and all sorts of troubles followed. The man began spreading rumours that she was the mistress of her former employer; the concierge who 'gossiped all day' repeated these rumours everywhere, embellishing them until she was said to have illegitimate children. She complained to the commissaire de police that she was being slandered. Her obsession with her concierge grew into a persecution mania and she was put into an asylum, protesting her sanity, but developing wild hallucinations as people mocked her. It was up to the doctors to decide when such a person 'whose intelligence seemed intact and who carries out his habitual occupations'

[1] Dr. Paul Sérieux, *V. Magnan, sa vie et son œuvre* (1921); V. Magnan, *Leçons cliniques sur les maladies mentales: le délire chronique* (1890); V. Magnan, *De l'alcoolisme, des diverses formes du délire alcoolique et de leur traitement* (1874); cf. Dr. M. Legrain, *Hérédité et alcoolisme. Étude psychologique et clinique sur les dégénérés buveurs et les familles d'ivrognes* (1889)—case studies by a pupil.

moved from the incubatory to the hallucinatory stage: the decisive factor was often the discovery that he had mad parents, which indicated that there was a disease in germ.[1]

The idea of degeneracy ceased to be so fashionable in the twentieth century, but it still had its adherents. Dupré and Delmas produced a revised version of it under the name of 'constitutional' madness.[2] Kraepelin's dementia praecox was imported from Germany; it carried the implication that hallucinations and delusions were a progressive trouble, leading irreversibly to complete madness; paranoia replaced 'persecution mania' and became a subvariety of dementia praecox. During the First World War, therefore, the psychiatrists found themselves in a difficult position when asked to assess the contribution of the war to the mental troubles suffered by vast numbers of soldiers: they were usually generous, saying that the war was the factor that stimulated madness, even if there were predisposing and hereditary causes of it; but one military psychiatric centre, for example, classified no less than 46 per cent of its patients as 'constitutional psychopaths', 9 per cent as 'organic psychopaths', 11 per cent as neurasthenic, 7 per cent as hysterics; it succeeded in curing about a quarter, it discharged another quarter from the army, it sent a third quarter to convalesce and the rest 'ran away'.[3] These statistics are, of course, ambiguous, for, as two other psychiatrists involved said, 'The whole mental pathology of the modern army is vitiated by the question of alcoholism'.[4]

After the war dementia praecox was often used with great severity in child psychology. Children who misbehaved in various ways were labelled as doomed to madness. The case books of two practitioners in this field contain histories like that of 'André M.', who had been an excellent and normal pupil at the Collège Rollin, until at the age of sixteen he stopped working and insisted on leaving. His father put him into

[1] V. Magnan, Le Délire chronique (1890), 349.

[2] F. Achille-Delmas and Maurice Boll, La Personnalité humaine: son analyse (1922), 40–55; Laignel Lavastine, André Barbé and Delmas, La Pratique psychiatrique à l'usage des étudiants et des praticiens (2nd edition, 1929), 350.

[3] M. A. J. M. Levrault, Étude historique et statistique sur le fonctionnement pendant la guerre du centre de psychiatrie de la 18e région (Bordeaux medical thesis, 1921). For case studies see Fribourg-Blanc and Gauthier, La Pratique psychiatrique dans l'armée (1935).

[4] A. Porot and A. Hesnard, Psychiatrie de guerre (1919), 49.

commerce, but he gave up that job, for no apparent reason. He was put successively into Félix Potin, the Northern Railway (where his father was chief clerk), the Comptoir d'escompte, but he always left after a few months; he sometimes did not come home for a week, keeping himself by miscellaneous jobs, for example, selling gramophones. Finally in 1926 at the age of nineteen, he refused to work any more. His mother demanded a mental examination, complaining also that he was no longer affectionate to his family. He was put in hospital as a schizophrenic, which was a new development from dementia praecox, advanced by the Swiss Bleuler (1857–1939), whose ideas had been imported into the clinic of professor Claude: this boy was duly sent there.[1] Another rebellious child, 'Aline', the object of a sexual assault at the age of thirteen, became violent, uncontrollable and 'ready to go off with any man who invited her in the street'; she became hostile to her family and complained that her mother was persecuting her. Her doctor diagnosed dementia praecox and she was interned at the age of eighteen. The availability of new diagnoses clearly put a new weapon in the hands of those who would not tolerate the rebelliousness of the young.[2]

The family was thus not simply the pillar of respectability, as moralists claimed, but also a source of anxiety, alcoholism, illness and even madness. Respectability, indeed, was the means by which these difficulties were concealed and the family's dirty linen kept out of public sight. Even if one abandoned the theories of heredity, one was still left with those of environment. It was long recognised that people could suffer all these troubles through the effect of those around them, as a result of demands made on them by those closest to them, and in reaction to parental influence. 'Isolation', or removing nervous patients from their homes, was valued by Esquirol and much used by Charcot. The latter, for example, was once consulted by a Russian Jew, who brought his son, aged thirteen, 'very impressionable and nervous but without any special characteristics', all the way to Paris for treatment. The boy had convulsions every day at five o'clock in the afternoon: the father, who was passionately fond of him, waited

---

[1] E. Bleuler, *La Schizophrénie* (1926).
[2] Dr. A. Rodiet and Dr. G. Heuyer, *La Folie au 20ᵉ siècle. Étude médico-sociale* (1931), 102, 108.

anxiously for these, watch in hand. Charcot told the father to leave the child alone; he sent him away and after two weeks on his own the child was cured.[1] It was in a development of this tradition that, in 1932, Lacan made a vigorous attack on the family as a source of paranoia: the best condition for its cure was the death of the patient's parents. Lacan argued that there had been too much attention paid to the symptoms of paranoiac crises and not enough to the internal history of the patient's feelings and the influence of his surroundings on him.

'Hallucinations' were now seen as more than a morbid aberration. The poet Paul Valéry said that there was a growing class of people suffering from them—the 'delirious professions': 'I give this name to all those trades whose principal instrument is the opinion that one has of oneself, and whose raw material is the opinion that others have of one. The people who exercise it, vowed to being eternally candidates, are necessarily always afflicted by a certain megalomania which a certain persecution mania ceaselessly crosses and torments.' They were men who wanted to achieve what no one else had done; they both ignored the existence of others and demanded their approval. The writing and teaching professions, said Lacan, were full of paranoia.[2] The progress of civilisation, said the anarchist Charles Albert, was inevitably increasing paranoia, because it exalted self-esteem and the subjective interpretation of social incidents. The reverse side of the sense of personal dignity that democracy cultivated was a greatly increased capacity to be hurt. 'What are today only superficial scratches may tomorrow become profound wounds. A day will come when we shall suffer from the least lack of consideration as cruelly as we now suffer from violent injustice. Social friction is undoubtedly diminishing, but our skin is becoming more delicate.'[3]

If the idea of the individual as a fixed entity, born with definite characteristics, was abandoned, then he became, as Dr. René Laforgue argued in 1941, no longer comparable to a house, built brick by brick, but constantly changing, aban-

[1] Œuvres complètes de J. M. Charcot, ed. Babinski (1890), 3. 92–6.

[2] Jacques Lacan, De la psychose paranoïque dans ses rapports avec la personnalité (medical thesis, 1932), 282–3.

[3] Quoted from L'Effort libre (Jan. 1914) by Paul Schiff, L'Évolution des idées sur la folie de persécution (republished from L'Hygiène mentale) (1935), 18. Cf. P. Sérieux and J. Capgras, Les Folies raisonnantes. Le délire d'interprétation (1909).

doning parts of himself all the time and acquiring new features; and the personality's mobility exposed it to far greater strains of adaptation. Success in a competitive society was no guarantee of serenity. Laforgue quoted examples of patients who came complaining that they could not stand the strain of success.[1] Even the much-lauded virtue of thrift, that basis of social ascension and so the basis of French society, was seen as a cause of 'incurable morbidity'. The Frenchman, wrote the author of a monograph on the psychology of avarice, was peculiarly subject to this pathological exaltation of thrift; 'he is haunted by the spectre of ruin because in our old country ruin is terrible, much more terrible than in a new country like America . . . He who falls is pitilessly stepped on and crushed . . . In France, ruin is shame, social excommunication . . .'[2] The asylums contained many people who could not bear the burden of having transgressed the rules of society, and outside them melancholics, suffering from remorse, must have easily outnumbered the convicts in prisons who had had the misfortune to be caught. Case histories of the disastrous effects of commercial failure could easily be multiplied, and of marital failures also. 'Mme Pauline Ta . . .', a baker's wife, aged thirty-seven, admitted into an asylum in 1893, was typical: she had two daughters and was perfectly healthy until she committed adultery with her brother-in-law. Her remorse made her spend whole days crying, exhausted, hearing voices telling her that she would burn in hell, feeling that everybody knew and was watching her. She finally confessed to her husband, who forgave her, and to all her neighbours; but 'seeing that she was ill', he took her to the asylum to recover.[3]

For much of the nineteenth century, anxiety and melancholy were characteristics one was born with; they were a sign of one's temperament or of one's ancestry. The explanation of their origin corresponded fairly accurately to the attitude that conservatives had towards the social status they occupied, which was generally seen as inevitably unequal: only exceptional individual effort and outstanding moral qualities could change things. But this was too pessimistic for many people, and so, as

[1] R. Laforgue, *Psychopathologie de l'échec* (1941).
[2] J. Rogues de Fursac, *L'Avarice. Essai de psychologie morbide* (1911), 144-5.
[3] J. Roubinovitch and Édouard Toulouse, *La Mélancolie* (1897), 269.

an alternative to neurosis and degeneration, there appeared neurasthenia. This was an American import, though it effectively only systematised ideas that had been in the air in Europe for a long time. The word was invented (or rather launched) in 1869 by Dr. George M. Beard of New York, to describe what he called the most frequent, most interesting and most neglected nervous disease of modern times. Neurasthenia meant nervous exhaustion. 'If a patient complains of general malaise, debility of all the functions, poor appetite, abiding weakness in the back and spine, fugitive neuralgic pains, hysteria, insomnia, hypochondriasis, disinclination for consecutive manual labor, severe and weakening attacks of sick headache, and other analogous symptoms, and at the same time gives no evidence of anaemia or any organic disease, we have reason to suspect . . . that we are dealing with a typical case of neurasthenia.' Beard believed he had discovered a peculiarly American disease, produced by the stresses of modern life. Freud later identified this American peculiarity as the 'undue suppression of sexual life'. But the success of the idea in Europe can be seen from the fact that by 1894 a bibliography of neurasthenia ran to no fewer than fourteen pages; and though Beard's *Nervous Exhaustion* was translated into French only in 1895, there had already been several books on it dating from 1881.[1] The other American influence was that of Silas Weir Mitchell (1829–1914), the inventor of the 'rest cure', whose highly acceptable answer to what he called the inability or the indisposition of Americans to play, was a series of fashionable homes where women patients in particular were put in bed, forbidden movement of any kind, massaged in order to avoid atrophy, overfed with copious meals, so that their weight was raised by as much as fifty or even seventy pounds in six weeks.[2]

[1] Significantly Beard's work was translated under the title *La Neurasthénie sexuelle* (1895). Cf. his *Stimulants and Narcotics, medically, philosophically and morally considered* (New York, 1871). Dr. Léon Bouveret, *La Neurasthénie, épuisement nerveux* (1890); Dr. F. Levillain, *La Neurasthénie* (1891); id., *Neurasthénie et arthritisme* (1893); *Essais de neurologie clinique: neurasthénie de Beard et états neurasthéniformes* (1896).

[2] S. W. Mitchell, *Wear and Tear* (1871); *Fat and Blood* (1877); *The Nervous System especially of Women* (1871). Cf. J. K. Hall, *One Hundred Years of American Psychiatry* (1944), 213. Weir Mitchell is only the most famous of the advocates of the rest cure, partly because of his literary talents: he also wrote poetry and novels. Others involved were Samuel J. Jackson and Playfair.

In France neurasthenia was popularised, among others, by two Paris professors, G. Ballet and A. Proust, the father of the novelist.[1] What is striking about their work, undertaken at the turn of the century, is that it shows their patients complaining about those very same things that Balzac had inveighed against, but which were now dignified as causes of neurasthenia. Many patients attributed the vague but distressing physical symptoms described by Beard, to intellectual overwork. Parents worried about the dangerous effects of the long hours of homework done by the pupils at *lycées*. They quoted a German investigator who found that 30 per cent of a sample of 588 middle-class secondary schoolboys had neurasthenic symptoms such as languor, sadness, paleness, palpitation, headaches and sleepiness but also insomnia; the proportion was only 8 per cent in the junior classes but 89 per cent in the top class. Dr. Proust denied that hard work could do anyone any harm: a few days' rest could put any ill effects right: it was rather the poor hygienic conditions in boarding-schools, lack of fresh air, no physical exercise and the habit of masturbation which caused the trouble.

But many adults complained of the same symptoms. Dr. Proust, echoing the general consensus, blamed the competitiveness of life, and 'moral preoccupations, more common and above all felt more deeply in certain social classes'. This meant 'the fear of failure', and worry about one's profession and about passing examinations. Social life 'which left little leisure for rest and for the calm and comforting distractions of the home', overcopious meals, overheated rooms, staying up too late, inadequate and irregular sleep, intoxication, 'the preoccupation with the search for pleasure and the satisfaction of the least elevated and least noble desires'—all this weakened the nerves; and what finally knocked people out was 'the vexations of pride resulting from the inability to realise the fantasies of vanity', and moral (rather than intellectual) overwork, caused by sorrows, disappointments, remorse, anxiety, 'depressive passions'. There were two main types of neurasthenic: the one who complained of headaches, stomach pains and indeed pains everywhere, lamenting that he was tired,

[1] Dr. Robert Le Masle, *Le Professeur Adrien Proust 1834–1903* (1936) is a biography, which however makes no mention of this.

weak and could no longer do any work, but who could not
give very precise details; and the one who looked perfectly
healthy and active, and who gave a fluent account of his
troubles, insisting that the doctor should pay attention to
every one of them, to the point even of bringing a written list
of them with him. Three-quarters complained of headaches—
not so much of pain, however, as of pressure, fullness, constric-
tion, what Charcot called the 'neurasthenic hat'. Tiredness
when waking up in the morning was also a frequent symptom,
as well as 'cerebral depression', weakening of the will, loss of
concentration. A few had 'genital neurasthenia', but they were
'degenerates', suffering from congenital debilities, exacerbated
by masturbation and sometimes excessive sexual intercourse.
'It is clear', said Dr. Proust dismissively, 'that organic lesions
and functional troubles of the genital organs have no specific
action on the nervous centres', though he added that very
little was known about the chemistry of the nerves. Nevertheless, the cure for neurasthenics was self-evident: it required
the strengthening of the physique, by means of exercise. French
schools were not even capable of supplying this in their gymnastics classes, because their exercises were too complicated
and produced nervous exhaustion: they required pupils to
use their heads too much. Old-fashioned French games like
ball and leapfrog, and skipping for girls, were best. Then what
these people needed was confidence: they should be encouraged
and praised in public, and criticised very gently and tactfully;
they should be given only tasks within their capacities. Most
neurasthenics had inherited 'excessive emotivity': this must be
fought, for example, by avoiding telling children terrifying or
fantastic stories. Most children, who were troubled profoundly
by the awakening of sexual desire, masturbated in an exaggerated way and were frequently nervously exhausted by this.
Their attention should be turned away from sex. The very
ideals of life, however, needed to be altered if neurasthenia was
to be diminished. The businessman thought only of money;
work had been turned into an end in itself. War had been
replaced by equally exhausting obsessions. 'It is time to move
on to the gospel of relaxation.' The strains in life, according
to Dr. Proust, came between the ages of twenty and fifty.
Occasionally he had seen a 'precocious neurasthenic', usually

an adolescent boy who had grown too tall too' quickly and who was therefore excessively fragile, 'yielding to the least shock'. Men suffered more than women from neurasthenia, because they had more pressure on them at work; but 40 per cent of them had some hereditary predisposition to it. He had seen little neurasthenia among the working class, which was perhaps explained by the kind of clientele he had, though he attributed it to their not having to use their brains.[1]

But a country doctor in the west of France, in a work published in 1906, reporting on sixteen years of practice, challenged this view. Formerly, he said, it had been thought that neurasthenia was an exclusively urban phenomenon, produced by too many parties, theatres etc., while the peasant was supposed to be satisfied with the little he had. Dr. Terrien claimed that on the contrary there was probably more mental trouble among the peasants than in the towns. For one thing, the peasant normally drank five or six litres of wine a day, and when he got drunk he made love—most conceptions were the result of drunkenness; for another, the peasant was superstitious, his children were overexcited by terrifying stories and sorcery was a constant worry; and not least, peasants were more liable to contract consanguine marriages. 'Psychoneurosis', far from diminishing, was increasing noticeably among the peasants, but it took on different forms. The men were generally hysterical when they were troubled, while the women were neurasthenic. This was because the men normally left it to the women to worry. The peasants had the same symptoms as the townsmen, but they consulted a wider variety of people to cure them, sorcerers as well as doctors. They were terrified of incurability, of death and of madness, as, of course, the townsmen were too. Dr. Terrien published some fifty case studies showing how different forms of anxiety stopped the peasants working and drove them to despair as deep as that of the most refined intellectuals.[2]

It was easy to draw facile conclusions about nervous exhaustion being related to a decadent civilisation; the epidemic of it in America was quoted against this to show that a young nation could suffer from it as well as a satiated one like

[1] A. Proust and G. Ballet, *L'Hygiène du neurasthénique* (1897).
[2] Dr. Terrien, *L'Hystérie et la neurasthénie chez le paysan* (Angers, 1906).

France. The reasons why the theory appealed to doctors were not above suspicion: just as they had at the beginning of the century replaced the chaining of lunatics by incarcerating them in asylums, so at the end of it they completed the abolition of strait jackets by keeping their patients constantly motionless in bed, on the ground that they must have complete rest. Dubois of Berne attacked this, saying that these patients were not really tired, or at least that there was no exhaustion of their nervous system; what was at fault was their defective upbringing; self-control was the answer.[1] His view received a certain amount of support and some people argued that these complaints of tiredness should be ignored, that such people thought too much about themselves.[2] A. Deschamps, in his *Energy Illnesses*, tried to reconcile the opposing views by saying that some really were tired, while the others were obsessed by being tired, and he built up a whole new collection of illnesses for which rest was the cure.[3] But the psychiatrist who examined this subject in the most detailed way was Pierre Janet (1859–1947), one of the most brilliant students of mental troubles in this period, a remarkably fluent and productive writer also, and for a time France's alternative to Freud. He deserves to be better known.

### Fear, Tension and Exhaustion

The richness of Janet's view of human character and anxiety came from a combination of several distinct interests. He was trained as a philosopher and was the nephew of Paul Janet, professor of philosophy at the Sorbonne. His uncle was more a moralist than a metaphysician and encouraged him to study medicine at the same time: he got his colleague Dastre, the professor of physiology at the Sorbonne, to admit him into his laboratory. Pierre Janet, at the age of eighteen, was deeply religious, and indeed said that he always retained his mystical tendencies though he 'succeeded in controlling them'. He was also always fond of the natural sciences, especially botany, and his herbarium, which he increased every year, was a

[1] Dr. Paul Dubois, Professor of Neuropathology at Berne, *Self Control and how to achieve it* (*L'Éducation de soi-même*) (New York, 1910).

[2] Déjérine and Gankler, *Les Psychoneuroses* (1911).

[3] Cf. Dr. P. E. Lévy, *L'Éducation rationnelle de la volonté* (1898, 12th ed. 1925.)

passionate hobby all his life: it was from this interest, he said, that he acquired his love of dissection, precise observation and classification, which found their expression in his very detailed medical case histories. It was his desire to resolve the conflict between religion and science that led him to specialise in psychology, which was then still a branch of philosophy. When he was appointed the philosophy teacher at the *lycée* of Le Havre at the age of twenty-two, he undertook a thesis on hallucination. In due course, he went to work with Charcot and wrote a treatise on hysteria, stressing in particular the mental aspects of it, for he believed that Charcot was too much· of a physiologist. Janet became interested in the role of suggestion and auto-suggestion in hysteria and formed a preliminary theory that suggestibility was the result of the weakening of the individual's functions of resistance and synthesis. This led him to study the causes of this weakening, which became the central area of his research. One factor he stressed at first was trauma, the influence of one or more events in a person's past life which had produced a violent emotion and so had absorbed a great deal of energy. He moved on to study various other depressive neuroses, phobias, obsessions, which had hitherto been described independently: he sought to discover what was common to them.[1] He gave the name of *psychasthenia* to a broad range of neuroses characterised by feelings of inadequacy or of emptiness, which he saw at the root of them. These feelings could be explained by exhaustion, whose mechanism he now described in a theory of psychological energy and tension.

Janet's theory owed a good deal to his also being a philosopher. He drew his inspiration from what used to be known as 'functional psychology', which was a revival and expansion of 'faculty psychology'. In the early nineteenth century the philosopher Maine de Biran had put forward a theory of the ego as one force, and passive functions as another, capable of operating independently of the ego. Maine de Biran's friend, Dr. A. A. Royer-Collard (brother of the politician) wrote an article on him in volume 2 of the *Annales médico-psychologiques*, which introduced his influence into medicine. Jouffroy, another philosopher, had developed Maine de Biran's views into a

[1] Autobiography in Carl Murchison, *A History of Psychology in Autobiography* (Worcester, Mass., 1930), 1. 123–33.

theory that man had a number of faculties or capacities, that his aim should be to exploit the energies in them, but draining the lower tendencies for the benefit of the higher ones. Janet acknowledged his indebtedness to these thinkers in his theory that mental life had two aspects—the automatic, self-preserving one, and the synthesising and creative one. A weakening in the latter allowed the former to gain the upper hand and so made mental illness possible. Hysterics were prime examples of people who failed to achieve a synthesis of their thoughts and acts; but the split between the automatic and the synthetic was more commonly apparent in dreams. Janet, however, broke away from a number of psychological schools which were more fashionable in his day, like those of Wundt (1832–1920) who sought to discover a chemistry of the mind, and who significantly also talked in terms of a 'creative synthesis' being established among the atoms: in the U.S.A., E. B. Titchener (1867–1927) gave a version of this theory the name of 'structuralism'. Janet was also a heretical rebel against Charcot, whose attempts to find anatomical localisations for nervous troubles he considered off the point. He criticised psychology for having reacted in too extreme a fashion against the charge that it was metaphysics: it had therefore tried to turn itself into physiology; but Janet insisted it must study behaviour; he welcomed the new tendency towards this shown by William James, Baldwin and Bergson, though he rejected J. B. Watson's behaviourism as being concerned simply with external acts, to the neglect of beliefs and thought processes.

Janet's methods can be seen from the case of Marie, a girl who was blind in one eye. Janet got Marie, under hypnosis, to relive her experiences at the age of six when she had gone blind. She had then had to sleep with a child who had eczema on the left side of its face; Marie had developed a similar rash and had gone blind in her left eye. Janet cured her by suggesting to her, under hypnosis, as she relived this event, that the child next to her was healthy; he got her to stroke the child without fear and all the symptoms of the illness then disappeared. Janet aimed to change feelings by suggestion: he offered not abreaction therapy, but integration therapy, getting his patients to incorporate vague memories into the continuity of their personality. He was more interested in the will than in the unconscious. Personality was for him 'a work that we carry out socially to distinguish ourselves one from the other, and in order to assume a role more or less distinct from that of our neighbours'. The idea goes back to Maine de Biran who had had to wage an exhausting battle to overcome his own apathy and depression, and who had seen will-power as the very essence of the ego. Janet refined this, distinguishing energy and tension. He divided activity into nine hierarchically ordered states, rising from the automatic reflex to higher ones in which experience was put to use, finally reaching the creative stage. Energy was needed to produce these activities and to move from the more elementary to the higher levels, but the curing of exhaustion was by itself not enough. The more elevated or complicated an act was, the more energy it required. But in addition 'tension'—or moral energy—was needed to co-ordinate the whole personality.[1] What handicapped most people was not tiredness so much as the inability to rest. Thus trouble often started around the age of twelve to fourteen, and the majority of neuroses began between seventeen and nineteen, usually unnoticed, but explained by the fact that moving into adulthood involved great outlays of physical effort and also enormous moral adaptations. Suddenly all the problems of life—love, work, social relations, religion—were posed simultaneously and the efforts to solve them could easily cause 'fear of life'. Then making friends, passing examinations, could easily increase timidity; even holidays could worsen this, because they involved readaptation, as also did travel. 'Professional occupations are such an evident cause of mental troubles that a special class of professional psychoses have often been admitted.' Women had additional worries from the running of their households and could go into deep depressions when faced with having to order a menu or choose a servant. 'Family life, the reciprocal adaptation of people who live together in the same house' could also be a very important cause of stress.

The importance of Janet's theory was that it tried to explain not only madness and extreme mental collapse, but the strains of everyday life. Accordingly, in the case histories of his

[1] Björn Sjövall, *Psychology of Tension. An Analysis of Pierre Janet's concept of 'tension psychologique' together with an historical aspect* (Stockholm, 1967).

patients, one can see how this strain affected ordinary people. Janet did not try to divide them into distinct categories, because he said 'mental illnesses in our day are not means of classifying illnesses, but stratagems to distinguish the rival psychiatric schools'.[1] At the root of all the different types of melancholy and depression he saw fear, of one kind or another: fear was the word he heard most frequently. Some feared death itself, and were tormented by obsessions which always involved catastrophe. Above all, many worried about the need to act, to take decisions. Some therefore did the opposite of what was expected of them. 'Hermine', a woman of forty, depressed by the death of her two sons in the 1914–18 war, sought consolation in religion and in charitable work, but felt strangely drawn to committing immoral acts: when she prayed at the tomb of her son, she felt she was undressing him; she came to Janet demanding to be watched in order to avoid committing a scandal. 'José' loved his mother but also wanted to kick her and 'this idea', he said, 'makes me mad'. Freud's theory was that it was repressed desire that produced anxiety. Durkheim, giving a sociological interpretation, argued that 'anomie', lack of integration in society, found its extreme expression in suicide. Janet, on the contrary, saw suicide as the expression of the fear of action: to die was a way of stopping action, of getting people to behave towards one as they behave towards the dead. Depression was therefore the opposite of resignation; it was egoism of a special kind, carrying personal defence to extremes. It came naturally with physical weakness, produced by hard work or emotional stress; and it could persist in the way that infectious diseases sometimes continued long after the disappearance of the microbe responsible. It was associated with a feeling of inadequacy or emptiness. The problem therefore was to recover enough energy to overcome this, so as to be able to cope with reality. A whole variety of obsessions concealed this problem, often in the most roundabout way. Janet quoted many cases of people who came to him obsessed that they were too fat or too thin, that they blushed, that they were ugly, that they got writer's cramp. Many women worried about the possibility that they might kill their children, young girls

[1] P. Janet, *De l'angoisse à l'extase. Études sur les croyances et les sentiments* (1928), 2. 302.

had visions of male sexual organs, or felt pushed by Satan to masturbate when preparing for the confession, 'to stop me being saved'. Boys of fifteen ran away from home and travelled aimlessly around the country, hesitating to break completely, however, writing to friends for advice and ultimately returning shamefacedly when they had no money left. 'Byl', a girl of twenty-one, had long refused to go out, being obsessed with the thought that she was ugly. Suddenly she married her gardener, to the horror of her parents, stopped washing her hands in order to place herself on the same level as him, finding expression at last for her self-hate. Ambition, apparently so prevalent in society, found its counterpart in shame: while politicians praised individualism, people worried about every oddity in their appearance, about how they walked, how they stood; while moralists urged virtuous living, virtuous people imagined the most wicked things they could think of. It was often a sense of inadequacy that led people to be conscientious to the utmost limits; precisely because they felt they always did things badly, they forced themselves to read books to the very end, to do homework with great care, and ambition sometimes had its source in this.

Some patients talked of fear; others of anxiety or disquiet, lack of security; others of timidity. Timidity attracted much attention,[1] and doctors heard a lot about it from people seeking reassurance at all hours of the day, or searching for guidance and direction. Wives complained that their husbands did not understand them, and sometimes gave themselves up to lovers who were intellectually their inferiors, but who satisfied their desire to be dominated; some men were so timid that they never spoke to their servants except through the intermediary of their wives, for fear of not being obeyed. One housewife, 'Qi', aged thirty-five, who was obsessed by a desire to cut her hair, to wear it loose, to be called by her pet name Nanette, lamented: 'A child is loved for its pranks, for its good little heart, for its prettiness, and what is it asked for in return? To love you, nothing else. I like that, but I cannot tell that to my husband; he would not understand me. I would like to be a child again, to have a father or mother who would hold me

---

[1] See a review in L. Dugas, *La Timidité, étude psychologique et morale* (7th edition, 1921).

on their knees, who would caress my hair . . . but no, I am Madame, mother of a family, I must look after my home, be serious, think all on my own. Oh what a life!' Inability to adapt themselves to the real world made some quite similar people become highly authoritarian, which was just another way of avoiding having clashes with others, obtaining submissiveness instead of offering it. Janet believed that these feelings of inadequacy were partly hereditary and partly the result of early education, which involved humiliations and frustrations, instilled fear of vices like laziness, stimulated self-deprecation and a demand for love and direction, but also partly the result of 'genital auto-intoxication', because three-quarters of these neuroses started in puberty. 'Nothing was more common than genital phobias,' said Janet: 'they often play an important role in people's lives, to the great distress particularly of young couples.'

The most interesting of Janet's cases are those of people who went about their daily lives in what was apparently a normal way, and only their close relatives or their doctor knew of the terrors that tormented them. Thus one could have taken a cab in Paris driven by 'Gaq', aged thirty-four, who seemed full of confidence taking his fares to all parts of the city, but who, once out of his driving seat, was a terrified pedestrian, refusing to cross roads and clinging to the walls. His father had been an alcoholic who died in delirium. 'Gaq' had always been timid, but two events had brought him down: first he had fallen in the street once when he was drunk, and then his fiancée had died shortly before their wedding day. His confidence disappeared at home, though he could still do his job. 'Bal', likewise, was a primary-school teacher, but one who worried endlessly about her work, and increasingly not just about the morrow or the day after, but even about her husband's health in ten years' time. She worried about religion and death; she lost her faith and that made her worry more. She came to see her doctor, however, only because of stomach pains, which alternated with her worries and distracted her from them. People indeed worried when they did not worry. Thus 'Af', a man of twenty-eight, had always suffered from tiredness, indigestion, insomnia and headaches and was indeed a typical neurasthenic; but his really serious troubles started on a day when a neighbour's wife was killed by her husband, who then committed suicide. 'Af' was the first to find the bodies; he was totally unaffected by the sight; he reported it to the concierge and spent the rest of the day without giving it another thought. But the following morning he read in the *Petit Journal* an extremely vivid account of the crime, in which the anguish of the couple and their appalling wounds were described in highly dramatic style. 'Af' was deeply moved, and horrified that he had been unable to notice anything appalling in the sight itself. This was a typical situation, said Janet. He was one of those who were much more moved by literature and art than by real life. There were women, for example, who never cried in real life, but poured out tears in the theatre: the ablest of them became writers, because they found fiction easier to feel about: real life was too complicated.

Just how many difficulties a simple life could present, and how frightening its ordinary accidents could be, may be seen from the case of 'Ku', aged thirty-seven, of peasant stock and the daughter of an authoritarian and demanding mother. 'Ku' since childhood had had a craving for affection; she used to do everything she could to win a smile; she was always amiable, hated offending people, and was deeply hurt if her friendliness was not reciprocated. When she was criticised by the local park-keeper for allowing her dog to walk on the flower-beds, she made her husband move house rather than chance meeting the park-keeper again. She had a terror of conflict, typical, said Janet, of a class of people who sought situations where everything could be foreseen, where there were never any crises— which they sought to avoid, alternatively by being authoritarian or by being nice and humble. 'Ku' managed in her new house for eighteen months, until another event ruined her life. A young student living across the road was arrested for 'outraging decency, having performed an improper pantomime from his window'. He summoned all his neighbours to his trial to attest the innocence of his gestures. A policeman came to see 'Ku', when, as it happened, her husband was out. She was deeply distressed, did not know what to say, but murmured that she had seen nothing reprehensible. As a result the prosecution was abandoned. But the incident tormented her ever after, because she could not decide whether to reveal the visit of the

policeman to her husband; if she admitted that she had defended the young man, would not her husband think she was
in league with him? Perhaps, indeed, she was in love with the
student: she got worried every time she saw a round hat and
a brown overcoat in the street, such as he wore. The neighbours
would certainly become hostile to her if her feelings were
known; her husband would abandon her: how could she persuade him to move again, this time perhaps to America?
After three months of silence, the poor woman confessed
all to her husband, to her concierge and her neighbours: she
was hypnotised, injected with morphine and finally carried
away to hospital—an extreme illustration of a probably not
uncommon situation.

One of Janet's most prized cases was called 'Jean'; he
combined in himself almost every symptom of a 'psychasthenic'.
He was aged thirty-two in 1903 and was described as the son of
a very distinguished man: one is tempted to guess his identity.
Jean was said to have always been timid, so that at eighteen he
was still taken to his *lycée* and brought back by a servant. He
used to be paralysed by the least difficulty. He attributed all
his troubles to his having masturbated from the age of fifteen,
which on one occasion led to a terrifying experience, when
ejaculation was accompanied by the feeling that he was going to
die. At nineteen he amazed his confessor by revealing his
complete ignorance of the facts of sex: he was taught some
elementary ones, but these tempted him instead of reassuring
him and all sorts of obsessions, manias and allergies followed.
Every action worried him because of the prospect that it might
lead to disease: he refused to read out a few lines from a book
for Janet, saying it might make him catch meningitis. He was
obsessed by his childhood maid, who produced erotic sensations
in him; he was a hypochondriac; he measured the temperature
of the water he used, counted his heartbeats, had a mania for
precision, and an astonishing memory for figures and dates.
His most remarkable characteristic was an extraordinary habit
of associating ideas in a most complicated way, as when he said
that he had a pain in his stomach because (1) he ate bread
(2) which came from the baker (3) who was recommended
to his mother by a gentleman (4) whose wife died (5) on
the anniversary of the day (6) on which his obsession

relative to his maid began. He was able to analyse his troubles with great finesse, but every action involved endless preparation, forethought and hesitation. Janet said it would take a whole year to recount all his symptoms. The odd thing is that this man Jean was exactly the same age as Marcel Proust —there is a strange similarity between them.[1]

Janet's solution for exhaustion was to tell his patients to pull themselves together. He did not do this directly, and used infinite tact and much imagination to bring it about, but ultimately he was in the tradition of the moralists who thought that it was up to the individual to master himself by the exercise of will. The difference was that he did not use moral injunctions but treated the will almost as a machine, with the psychiatrist discovering why it was not functioning properly, which parts were damaged and how its activity could be restored. It was in this sense that he called his method analytical psychology, which aimed at discovering what behavioural traits distinguished one individual from another. Freud was to distinguish his method by turning the label round into psychoanalysis.[2] Janet's analysis was directed not to freeing his patients from their past, but to getting them to admit it as part of their experience and to work out an acceptable personality by means that were ultimately rational. He admitted that he studied the abnormal only because it was easier: 'nothing is more complicated', he said, 'than a normal man'.[3] His ideas were to be developed—in combination with those of others—by Jean-Paul Sartre, who stressed the role of the will even more, claiming not only that emotional behaviour was an organised system, but that the passions which composed it were not involuntary. To will to love and to love were one and the same thing. Emotion became with Sartre conscious self-deception.[4] It thus becomes very much the concern of the historian.

[1] P. Janet, Les Obsessions et la psychasthénie (1903), 2. 341–51, and passim.

[2] Carl Murchison, Psychologies of 1930 (Worcester, Mass., 1930) contains an article by Janet on his 'analytical psychology'.

[3] For a popularisation of 'will therapy', see Dr. E. Toulouse, Comment former un esprit (1908); for a traditional Catholic version, A. Chaillot, Leçons pratiques de psychologie et de logique spécialement rédigées pour les pensionnats de demoiselles (1867), 55–6; cf. G. Villey-Desméserets, Contribution à l'étude des doctrines en médecine mentale (Paris medical thesis, 1924).

[4] Joseph P. Fell, Emotion in the Thought of Sartre (New York, 1965).

## Boredom

The strains of living were compounded under the influence of fashion. The spread of education itself, while producing unlimited optimism amongst some, probably the majority, also stimulated the deepest gloom in those who claimed the greatest refinement of taste. Numerous writers described the nineteenth century as the age of *ennui*; 'the sadness of modern times' was deplored by the Goncourt brothers; Paul Bourget defined 'modern man as an animal who is miserable'; Baudelaire, whose poem *Spleen* was to strike chords of sympathy in many successive generations, summarised his outlook (1857) as 'an immense discouragement, an insupportable sensation of isolation, a perpetual fear of a vague misfortune, a complete lack of confidence in my abilities, a total absence of desires, an impossibility of finding an amusement of any kind'.[1] Barbey d'Aurevilly wrote: 'I believe that tiredness and unhappiness decide almost everything in the lives of men.' Melancholy was known as the English malady in the seventeenth century: French writers used a foreign vocabulary to describe it: *morbidezze*, *schwärmerisch* and above all spleen. Diderot in 1760 had talked of '*le spleen* or the English vapours' and in 1844 the *Encyclopedia of Men of the World* defined spleen as 'formerly little known in France but now spreading only too much amongst us—a morbid affection . . . originating from 'foggy England', characterised by 'a profound disgust for life, a continual sadness and an incurable apathy which, little by little, leads to despair and often ends with suicide'.

The romantics made *ennui* a fashionable literary pose among many of those who read their works. Flaubert, in his *Dictionary of Received Ideas*, defined it as a sign of 'distinction of the heart and elevation of the spirit'.[2] It degenerated at its extremes into what Baudelaire called 'the stupid melancholy of young women'. In the founders of the cult, it had highly complicated origins; it was produced partly by family troubles, and several romantics claimed they had inherited it from their mothers, but it was cherished also as a divine gift which could be turned to

---

[1] C. Baudelaire, *Œuvres complètes. Correspondance générale*, ed. J. Crepet (1947), 2. 108.
[2] *Dictionnaire des idées reçues* (1881), s.v. Mélancolie.

aesthetic ends and it was accepted as a kind of martyrdom. Chateaubriand interpreted it as the result of being over-whelmed by the distance that separated his hopes and what life in fact offered, but it was more than frustrated hope, for he and his successors, led by Sainte-Beuve, added to this feeling introspection and self-analysis. Melancholy could thus turn into self-obsession; and it came to be valued as a form of spiritual life, a rejection of materialism. It did not necessarily imply self-hate, though it sometimes involved it. But the end result of this literary fashion was that suffering was adopted as a way of life, even when it was simultaneously idealised and ridiculed (as it was, for example, by Flaubert).

One needs to distinguish between this elitist cult, which later found a philosophical justification in Schopenhauer and fitted in with a whole tradition of decadence, and forms of *ennui* which verged on boredom, and were the mark of people who had too much time on their hands. The development of activities to fill the growing amount of leisure was of course not simply an expression of *joie de vivre*.[1] On the contrary, the frenzy with which they were pursued was seen as a sign of deeper dissatisfactions. Lamartine had complained during the July Monarchy that 'France is getting bored'; and quite apart from the aesthetes, there were more and more people who talked of being bored, in a less sophisticated way than they. 'Sunday boredom', for example, was one of the most painful discoveries of the nineteenth century. A magazine short story published in 1861 begins: 'It was Sunday, the feast day of spleen in Paris . . . It was Sunday and it was raining torrentially.' Alphonse Daudet complained of 'that terrible day of rest of these poor people'. The upper classes, who had most resources to combat boredom, probably suffered most: as a gossip writer of the *salons* wrote in 1866: 'Paris, and especially the Faubourg Saint-Germain, has a host of bored people who seek out every means of spending their evenings at parties, for boredom shared seems easier to bear than solitary boredom.'[2] In 1855 a *Revue anecdotique* was founded, designed, as its prospectus announced, to act as 'a specific against boredom and spleen'. In the sixteenth century, Rabelais used the word

[1] See chapter 13.
[2] Mme Ancelot, *Un Salon de Paris, 1824 à 1864* (1866), 239.

*ennui* to mean simply loneliness: in the nineteenth century this timeless feeling might well have been sharper, but it was certainly expanded. There was thus the loneliness and boredom of provincial life, which became an object of increasing ridicule with the growth of towns. Not that towns diminished boredom, for the loneliness of towns was another complaint: the distractions they offered stimulated the need for yet more distraction. Artists interpreted the mania for money-making as a sign of boredom, as well as being boring in itself; the enthusiasm for progress was seen as the product of dissatisfaction with the present, of vulgar American materialism and loss of religious faith. Renan, the ambiguous apostle of scientific progress, warned that 'improvements in the mechanical arts can go hand in hand with a great moral and intellectual depression'.[1] Maxime Du Camp decried photography as marking the triumph of boredom over art. Flaubert enjoyed himself chronicling the absurdities into which frustration and an incoherent search for novelty led the soulless partisans of good causes, the 'fetid mediocracy' with its 'utilitarian poetry' and its 'economic vomit'.

Too much credence should not be given to the accusations that France was losing the capacity to enjoy itself. What is more significant is the repetitiveness with which every generation marvelled uncomprehendingly at the way its successors chose to seek out amusement. The Goncourt brothers claimed that 'the great pleasures of the masses are collective joys. As the individual rises from the masses and distinguishes himself from them, he has a greater need of pleasures which are personal and made for himself alone.' This was to make education and social mobility factors which vastly complicated the problem of enjoyment. It is certainly possible that they brought pressures to bear which altered the character of laughter. Zola declared: 'It is not thus that people used to laugh, when they could still laugh. Today, joy is a spasm, gaiety is a form of madness that knocks one down.' The Goncourts claimed indeed that the coldness of youth was the peculiar mark of the second half of the nineteenth century; good old-fashioned joviality was disappearing. A newspaper, writing on 'the young men of today' in

---

[1] E. Renan, *Œuvres complètes* (1948), 2. 249, article on 'La Poésie de l'Exposition' first published in the *Journal des Débats*, 27 Nov. 1855.

1859, castigated them for being too serious, sententious, 'scholarship boys'. The condemnation of the scientists as bores does not mean that they were bored, but it did mean that radically different notions about what was interesting were developing, and people had increasing trouble in finding congenial companions.[1]

## Hysteria

The way people reacted to these strains varied with time. One of the most interesting was hysterical behaviour. This, of course, is a disease as old as man, but France in this period has a significant place in its history. To see this, one must look at the work of Charcot, who is, besides, interesting for several other reasons.

J. M. Charcot (1825–93) was not only one of the dominating figures of French medicine in the early Third Republic but also one of the most influential men of his time, because of the new attitudes to behaviour that he popularised. He was a product of the petite bourgeoisie of Paris: his father was a coach builder and his brother took over the family business; he himself married the daughter of Laurent Richard, a well-known tailor. He was adopted first by the Bonapartists, when Achille Fould, the banker and finance minister, made him his family doctor, and then by the republicans, when Gambetta had a special chair created for him in the diseases of the nervous system. Charcot came to be a consultant to royalty from all over the world, and his lectures to his medical students were regularly invaded by writers, actors, journalists and fashionable society in general. Charcot's performances were almost theatrical, not because he was a great orator, but because of his immense stress on the visual effect of his lectures on his audience. He wrote out his lectures in full but then memorised them, and devoted his energy to getting the best effect from the patients he exhibited: he would go from one to the other showing how they all suffered from the same disease, pointing out unexpected similarities in posture, gait, deformity and clinical manifestations. He was one of the first to use projection equipment in medical lectures; he employed photographers and artists to make a

[1] Guy Sagnes, *L'Ennui dans la littérature française de Flaubert à Laforgue, 1848–1884* (1969).

record of his patients, and to produce some remarkable portrait studies of behaviour in distress and anxiety, which deserve to be better known as a grim analysis of his generation.[1] Charcot was, as Freud said, above all a man with a visual sense. He was indeed an artist in his spare time, painting mainly on porcelain and enamel, and also sketching and doing caricatures. He travelled throughout Europe to look at pictures, but his enthusiasms, which started with ancient Greece and came down to Flemish and Dutch painting, seem to have stopped short with Delacroix: he had no interest in the Impressionists. He published a book on *Demoniacs in Art*, with numerous illustrations of epileptics, ecstatics, and other 'possessed' people taken from all centuries, to prove that 'hysteria is in no way, as some claim, a sickness typical of our century'. One of his assistants who did the drawings for his lectures, was simultaneously professor of creative anatomy at the School of Fine Arts as well as being a member of the Academy of Medicine. But Charcot considered himself not so much an artist as a seer. He was a generally silent man, who seemed shy of human contact and disdained banal expressions of politeness; by contrast, he had a passionate affection for animals, to whom he talked and whom he caressed freely; at table he would play with his pet monkey or with his many dogs. He was a great enemy of fox-hunting and vivisection. He refused invitations to the theatre or to dinner, though he occasionally went to the circus. He hardly ever took any physical exercise. His sociability expressed itself only at the dinner and reception he held at home on Tuesdays, when he held court to admiring visitors and amazed them with the brilliance of his conversation. His house was furnished in medieval and Renaissance style; his study was dark, with stained-glass windows. It was here that he saw his patients when he became famous, for he abandoned the practice of going round his wards and had the patients brought to his home from the hospital, one by one. An assistant reported what happened: 'He would seat himself near a table and immediately call for the patient who was to be studied. The patient was then completely undressed. The intern would read a clinical summary of the case, while the master listened

[1] Bourneville and Regnard, *Iconographie photographique de la Salpêtrière* (3 vols., 1873–80).

attentively. Then there was a long silence, during which Charcot looked, kept looking at the patient while tapping his hand on the table. His assistants, standing close together, waited anxiously for a word of enlightenment. Charcot continued to remain silent. After a while he would request the patient to make a movement; he would induce him to speak; he would ask that his reflexes be examined and that his sensory responses be tested. And then again silence, the mysterious silence of Charcot. Finally, he would call for a second patient, examine him like the first one, call for a third patient and always without a word, silently make comparisons between them. This type of meticulous clinical scrutiny, particularly of the visual type, was at the root of all Charcot's discoveries.' When asked to explain his diagnoses, however, Charcot would reply 'I cannot tell you why, but I know it is this disease, I can sense it.'[1]

In the popular view, Charcot's importance was that he was the first man to recognise the role of the emotions in the production of hysteria. This was of course not true, but his predecessors who had seen this had written only weighty monographs for their own profession, and it was Charcot who popularised the notion and indeed thus made hysteria a new kind of almost fashionable nervous disease. Though he stressed psychic factors, he applied the same procedures of analysis to hysteria as he did to organic physical illness: but he established hysteria as an autonomous trouble, separate from any physical causes.[2] Despite Charcot's disclaimer that hysteria was nothing special to his own time, the *Encyclopaedia Britannica* of 1910 declared that 'hysterical fits in their fully developed form are rarely seen in England, though common in France'; and after the waning of Charcot's influence, they were seldom seen in France either. Charcot invented *grande hystérie*, whose symptoms and manifestations he described in enormous detail; he subdivided it into four stages of progressive development, and above all he discovered the *stigmata* by which one could recognise a hysterical person before any crisis occurred. *Grande*

[1] Georges Guillain, *J. M. Charcot 1825–1893, His Life and Work* (English translation, 1959), 52–3; A. R. G. Owen, *Hysteria, Hypnosis and Healing. The Work of J. M. Charcot* (1971).

[2] Cf. Mme G. Abricosoff, *L'Hystérie au 17ᵉ et 18ᵉ siècles* (1897), by a pupil of Charcot.

*hystérie* was a terrifying performance, resembling an epileptic fit, with fainting, convulsions, and paralysis. Charcot's achievement was to show that all these various symptoms, hitherto studied separately, were all one, and that they followed a predictable pattern. Dr. Briquet in 1859 had described the symptoms with equal care: he had declared that far from being inexplicable, they obeyed clear laws: but he had not formulated these laws. Charcot gave the disease a perfectly homogeneous and apparently powerful theoretical framework.

Everybody is agreed that Charcot was a great doctor, but on hysteria he was in important ways wrong. That he was able to get away with it for so long reveals a great deal about the organisation of the medical profession. Once Charcot had invented his theory, hordes of disciples began writing theses illustrating it in detail and applying it to different parts of the body, and to different groups of people. An immovable vested interest in the disease was the result. Loyalty to Charcot was intense, to a degree remarkable even in a profession ruled by clique, where every doctor knew who his *patron* was. Medical theses always began with fawning expressions of thanks to 'venerated teachers'; Lacan's thesis on paranoia, for example, had no less than eight pages of dedication. Gilles de la Tourette, the professor who codified Charcot's teaching on hysteria into a textbook in three large volumes, worshipped him 'as a God', says his biographer, and his textbook indeed over and over again points out the genius of the great master, seldom mentioning him without an epithet of praise. Long after faults in the theory had been pointed out, respected professors insisted on clinging to it; Gilles de la Tourette himself never abandoned it. (He was a special case, however: following the loss of a son, and after being shot in the head by one of the lunatics in his asylum, he devoted himself to his work of codification with a fury which some considered to be 'ambitious mania'; and he seems to have gone completely mad in old age.)[1]

The attack on Charcot was launched from Nancy, where an obscure professor who was interested in hypnotism pointed out that all the symptoms Charcot considered to be peculiar to hysteria were capable of being reproduced by hypnotic suggestion: there were no symptoms which could not be so

[1] P. Le Gendre, *Gilles de la Tourette, 1857–1904* (n.d.).

reproduced and indeed also cured by suggestion: no hysteric patient's heart stopped beating. Charcot's followers replied that it was the mark of a hysteric that he could be hypnotised: this became a new sign of it. It meant that the category of hysteria was widened enormously; but whereas Charcot's critic Berrheim had had a vast experience of hypnotism, Charcot had never once hypnotised anybody. He investigated hypnotism as a cure, but it was his assistants who did the hypnotising for him; and since they used to rehearse before the great man arrived, the behaviour of the patients not surprisingly took on predictable forms. Now it so happened that, as a result of an administrative reorganisation, epileptics and hysterics—i.e. all those with occasional attacks—had been segregated from the rest of the madwomen of La Salpêtrière into a separate wing, placed under Charcot's direction. The hysterics therefore tended to copy the epileptics' crises.[1] Charcot was well aware of the problem of simulation, but though he invented various lie detectors, he still got what the patients thought he wanted: a few of them put on magnificent performances of incredible violence and drama and their fascinating poses remain recorded in drawings which, incidentally, show how theatricality was generally accepted then as a common form of behaviour. Charcot's scientific efforts to locate the areas of the body most associated with hysteria resulted in his discovering that the region of the ovaries was the key one: pressure on it could start a hysterical crisis and stronger pressure on it would stop it. The breasts could sometimes also be massaged in a similar way and with similar results. In men, it was the testicles that were pressed. Special 'ovarian belts' were made to enable women prone to hysteria to control themselves. But there were several different elements in Charcot's theory, and in his later years he became interested in traumatic experiences as the cause of hysteria, with auto-suggestion prolonging the effect of the shock; this was very different from the emphasis he placed on hereditary predisposition to hysteria, which made him an advocate of the constitutional or inborn nature of nervous disease at a time when Pasteur was demonstrating the environmental and

---

[1] For a detailed description, see Dr. Paul Richer, *Études cliniques sur l'hystéro-épilepsie ou grande hystérie* (1881), with interesting pictures.

infective origins of other diseases.[1] Eventually one of Charcot's disciples, Babinski, cut the Gordian knot by renaming hysteria pithiatism (meaning curable by suggestion); the bitter controversy only gradually died down.[2]

Hysterical behaviour was far from always taking the grandiose forms that some of the prima donnas of the Saltpêtrière hospital gave it; but, in humbler manifestations, it was frequently an outlet for the anxieties of ordinary people. Thus, for example, Jean-Baptiste Tissier, a house painter, who had hitherto enjoyed good health except for some lead poisoning and who was one of the rioters in the insurrection of June 1848, reacted to his arrest by an attack of hysteria, with convulsions, suffocation, headache and local anaesthesia. Then he took to drink, and two years later, after a 'debauching party' he had another attack, and was taken to hospital—where he was quickly cured with electric shocks, sulphur baths and opium. Émile Laroche, a twenty-nine-year-old cook, had no complaints (except for loss of sperm 'even though he made considerable use of women') when in 1849 a friend of his died of cholera in his arms. This resulted in his having hysterical convulsions almost daily for three months, lasting ten to fifteen minutes each. He sought no treatment, but took ether 'which he abused'. Ernest Langlois, a twenty-five-year-old baker, normal in every respect except that he was very romantic, cried easily and was always very moved when he went to the theatre, went into convulsions after a quarrel with his mistress, and then again three years later, after an operation to his ear. On the second occasion, he was kept in hospital for sixteen days, while his loss of the sense of touch, his pains and his low pulse rate were treated. These cases were recorded to show that men could be hysterical and that no sexual, let alone uterine, trouble was needed to spark it off. But the statistics accumulated by Dr. Briquet suggested that women had hysteria twenty times more often than men. Dr. Briquet claimed indeed that half of all women were hysterical or 'very impressionable', though only one-fifth of all women actually had attacks of convulsions in their full

---

[1] Œuvres complètes de J. M. Charcot. Leçons sur les maladies du système nerveux, vol. 3 (1890), 114; N. Baruk, Psychiatrie médicale, physiologique et expérimentale (1938), 322–5.

[2] Auguste Tournay, La Vie de Joseph Babinski (Amsterdam, 1967).

form. About 20 per cent of hysterics were children, 40 per cent were aged between twelve and eighteen, and there were almost none after the age of forty. Almost half of the servant girls who came for treatment to his hospital for venereal diseases were hysterical—partly because they were young, and partly because of the difficulties of their lives and of the illicit unions they were involved in; over half of Paris's prostitutes were likewise hysterical. In some cases, being hysterical became a way of life, and poor girls spent many years incurable in hospital, serving as specimens for the doctors. An example was Celina Tonnelle, an illegitimate girl who had been in trouble all her life and finally ended up in hospital at the age of twenty-two when her illegitimate baby died. Léontine Bellard, likewise, had been abandoned by her mother at the age of eight, to which she reacted with her first attack of hysterical convulsions. Marriage at seventeen cured her, but six years later the hysterics returned when her sister died: she was taken to hospital: powerful electric shocks under chloroform rapidly cured her.[1] But hysteria also came to be the 'waste-paper basket into which all inexplicable nervous symptoms' were thrown. Princess Marie Bonaparte, for example, hated the worship of Napoleon that her family forced upon her; at fifteen she began taking an interest in men, but, as she said, 'since hysteria was fashionable', her disapproving grandmother who brought her up, declared her to be hysterical, summoned Charcot's successor to come and examine her, and he recommended that she be sent to a convent.[2] A more curious brand of hysteria was diagnosed for one Albert D——, born in 1858, who at the age of twelve left his job in the gas factory of Bordeaux and ran away from home. He was brought back, but kept on running away, travelling in due course all over France, Germany, Algeria and even Russia, whence, however, he was expelled under suspicion of being a nihilist. Charcot's pupil Pitres, dean of the medical faculty of Bordeaux, declared that this man was neither an eccentric who enjoyed travelling, because in his 'normal' state he lamented with accents of profound distress the troubles that his travels caused his family (he had gone off once just before his wedding day); nor a madman, because when hypnotised he recounted the details of his adventures with remarkable precision; nor an epileptic, as the doctors said he was, because his 'crises of deambulation' were preceded by 'premonitory symptoms' like sadness, headaches, poor sleep, buzzing in the ears and an obsessive desire to visit some town. His trouble was *vigilambulisme hystérique à forme ambulatoire*—or, in other words, hysterical double-personality.[1]

Hysteria was not always treated with indulgence. Another Salpêtrière psychiatrist, Jules Falret (son of J. P. Falret, also a psychiatrist, who discovered the depressive cycle), denounced hysteria as 'nothing but perpetual falsehood'. Hysterical people 'affect airs of piety and devotion and let themselves be taken for saints while at the same time secretly abandoning themselves to the most shameful actions, and at home, before their husbands and children, making the most violent scenes in which they employ the coarsest and often most obscene language and give themselves up to most disorderly actions'.[2] So, in contrast to the sedatives that some doctors prescribed, and to the vaginal camphor pommade that Dr. Raspail sold (saying hysteria was caused by an insect), a few angrier doctors cauterised the clitoris and considered operations to remove it altogether, and the ovaries too, when patients declared they had an irresistible 'need to overturn furniture and to utter strident cries'.

On occasion, hysteria ceased to be a domestic drama and became a problem of public order, when it assumed mass proportions and whole factories and villages were affected. Conservative writers claimed that the French Revolution itself was nothing but neurosis and hysteria: doctors saw a medieval obsessional fear at the root of it, and sadism as the explanation of its massacres.[3] In 1848 at least one factory experienced mass hysteria, starting with one woman and spreading to 115.

---

[1] Dr. Gilles de la Tourette, *Traité clinique et thérapeutique de l'hystérie d'après l'enseignement de la Salpêtrière* (1895), vol. 2, part 1, 353; J. M. Charcot, *Clinique des maladies du système nerveux* (1893), 2. 168–76.

[2] Quoted in Ilza Veith, *Hysteria, The History of a Disease* (Chicago, 1965), 211, which stresses the international context and the sexual aspects of hysteria.

[3] Dr. Cabanès and Dr. L. Nass, *La Névrose révolutionnaire* (1906), 5–12; Dr. L. Nass, *Essais de pathologie historique: le Siège de Paris et la Commune* (1914).

In 1861 forty girls at a school in Montmartre went wild in convulsions. The most interesting and best-documented case is that of the village of Morzine in Haute-Savoie 'and everybody knows', wrote the doctor who went to investigate it, 'how common hysteria is in Savoy'. This was a village of 2,000 souls, with 90 per cent illiteracy, deep piety and much superstition, where people 'lied in good faith, so that they ended by believing their own lies as they believed those of others'. In the sixteenth century, sorcerers had been very numerous, and in the nineteenth century the young men who migrated seasonally to search for work regularly came back with magic books, as their most precious booty from the civilised world. In 1857 this village declared itself possessed by demons. It started with a child, who had been badly cut on her leg, going into hysterics, and even more so when it would not heal, saying that the devil was responsible for the wound. The hysteria spread to other children, many women and some men, but half the hysterics were aged between seventeen and twenty-two. The explanation of the villagers was very definitely that the spasms, convulsions and pains they suffered from were due to possession by demons: the municipal council unanimously voted a resolution saying that *natural* remedies were of no use. It was decided that the person responsible might be a former priest who had quarrelled with many in the parish: a band of villagers went fully armed at dead of night to a chapel he had built, where they killed and eviscerated a dog, to the accompaniment of cabalistic curses. It was all in vain, and the village grew increasingly depressed as people feared that they, or their families, would be attacked next. The Parisian spiritualists were fascinated by this case, but the most detailed report suggests that hysteria, in the guise of demonic possession, was adopted as a means of giving expression to family rebelliousness and social deviance. The girls who went into hysterics (and they were the largest group) did so whenever anything unpleasant was said, whenever they suffered any pain, or whenever religion was mentioned. They shouted that they were not mad but damned devils, that they despised medicine, that they should be sent priests to cure them, though when priests came, they insulted them, saying they wanted holy men. They threw furniture around, rolled on the floor, beat themselves, but claimed after their attack that they could remember nothing of this. They refused to eat, but drank a lot of coffee, and demanded good food, butcher's meat and baker's bread. When out of their trances, their main pleasure was to congregate among themselves, playing cards and inciting one another against their parents. One girl entered into the power of the demons after her father had told her to go to bed early: she was hysterical for a whole hour until her normal bedtime, when she went to sleep as usual. Next day she joined the hysterical gang. Another girl began her 'crises' by calling the *curé* a dirty dog to his face. One father cured his daughter by grabbing her by the hair, brandishing an axe and swearing to kill her if her 'crisis' did not stop; and it did. Another cured his by throwing her into an oven, pretending he would roast her alive; another by promising her a new dress. But one father was struck such a blow by his daughter in one of her fits that he never recovered; he stopped eating, saying the devil prevented him, and he died three months later. In the end, the troops were brought in, the most serious hysterics expelled to distant hospitals, and the threat of imprisonment held out as a penalty for hysteria. Sunday mass, which used to be constantly punctuated by hysterical attacks, was, after three years, at last said uninterrupted again. It is curious, however, that the doctor who organised this cure never mentioned indiscipline and always talked of it as an 'illness'.[1] The relationship of hysteria and possession by evil spirits aroused much interest particularly as Charcot's stigmata so closely resembled the diabolic stigmata that medieval inquisitors used to identify sorcerers.[2]

## Freud and Sex

It did not need Freud to make the French worry about sex. On the contrary, it might be argued that they became interested in obscure, unconscious and invisible sexual problems only when

---

[1] Dr. A. Constans, *Relation sur une épidémie d'hystéro-démonopathie en 1861* (2nd edition, 1863); cf. Joseph Tissot, *Les Possédées de Morzine* (1865) and A. Vigouroux, *La Contagion mentale* (1905).

[2] Dr. Henri Cesbron, *Histoire critique de l'hystérie* (1909), 123–54; Joseph de Tonquédec, *Les Maladies nerveuses ou mentales et les manifestations diaboliques* (1938), by the official exorcist of the diocese of Paris; Dr. Jean Camus, *Isolement et psychothérapie, traitement de l'hystérie et de la neurasthénie* (1904).

their directly physical troubles in this connection ceased to be overwhelming. Venereal disease, until it became more easily curable—which only happened in the twentieth century— caused an enormous amount of anxiety, quite apart from the physical suffering it produced. It has been suggested that perhaps 15 per cent of deaths around 1900 were from syphilis, and that half of those who had the disease caught it in adolescence.[1] Syphilis was a subject on which, between 1840 and 1875, no less than 180 books were published, excluding obscure theses, innumerable articles, works on other sexual illnesses, like the even more widespread gonorrhoea, and putting aside the vast literature on female diseases. The sale of these works was very considerable. One unremarkable treatise on diseases of the sexual organs written for 'men of the world' sold 7,000 copies each year between 1853 and 1862; a guide to the *Hygiene and Physiology of Marriage* went through 172 editions between 1848 and 1883.[2] Those who did not have syphilis did not seem much less worried than those who did, for it was a constant menace, with terrifying implications of incurability and ultimate madness and paralysis. At a time when a qualified doctor could warn patients that even constipation could produce lunacy itself, let alone nervous trouble or poisoning of the body,[3] the sexual act was seen as surrounded by innumerable dangers;[4] the use of contraceptives was supposed to produce all sorts of additional irritations, quite apart from the guilt feelings that moralists tried to instil about it: a young man complained to his doctor that contraceptives made him 'confused as though he had committed infanticide'.[5] Coitus interruptus was blamed as the cause of the 'multiple neuroses and bizarre affections that women suffered from', because they found it unsatisfying.[6] Impotence and sterility were much more worrying when their mechanism was barely understood; loss

[1] See vol. 1, 304.
[2] Dr. Émile Jozan, *Traité pratique des maladies des voies urinaires et des organes générateurs . . . spécialement destiné aux gens du monde* (9th edition, 1862); A. Debay, *Hygiène et physiologie du mariage* (1848).
[3] Dr. Félix Bremond, *Les Préjugés en médecine et en hygiène* (1892), 82.
[4] For example, Dr. Louis Seraine, *De la santé des gens mariés* (1865, 2nd edition), 68.
[5] Dr. L. Bergeret, *Des fraudes dans l'accomplissement des fonctions génératrices. Causes, dangers et inconvénients* (18th edition, 1910), 101.
[6] Dr. Antonin Bossu, *Lois et mystères des fonctions de reproduction* (n.d.), 307.

of virility was something that was constantly held up as a danger to young people who masturbated, or who engaged in debauchery; and the terror this inspired can be seen from the varied potions and gadgets placed on the market, apparently with commercial success, to restore virility; massaging, douches, ether, dried Spanish flies, electrical and magnetic shocks, acupuncture, hellebore and strychnine were just some of the remedies people willingly submitted to.[1] A leading authority laid it down that sexual aberrations were 'fatally incurable' when they were produced by both physical and psychic causes, almost so when they were purely psychological in origin, and capable of cure only when they were simply physical.[2]

France was one of the countries which was least sympathetic to the doctrines of Freud, as he himself noted; and the reasons for this are revealing. Freud had close links with France; he had studied under Charcot and had translated some of his writings into German; he had visited Nancy to learn about developments in the use of hypnosis there; and French work on hysteria and hypnosis was a principal starting-point of Freud's thought. The result however was that Freud was looked on in France as a renegade pupil, or more precisely as an outdated one, who continued to develop ideas which had long been discredited in France. The bitterness occasioned by the disputes of Charcot and his rivals meant that Freud had to overcome almost insurmountable prejudices and personal animosities. The people who took up his ideas tended therefore at first to come from outside Paris and outside the top rank of psychiatrists, for these latter had theories of their own. Janet and Freud had a lot of views or attitudes in common; Janet was interested in 'psychological analysis', 'mental systems', 'mental disinfection' and 'contraction of the conscience', which in Freud's language were respectively psycho-analysis, complex, catharsis and repression. But Janet was by temperament the very opposite of Freud, cheerful, optimistic, giving the impression, even in extreme old age, of effortless activity and wide interests; and he considered that Freud was creating a

[1] Dr. Félix Rouband, *Traité de l'impuissance et de la stérilité* (1855), 216, 230.

[2] Dr. Paul Moreau de Tours, *Des aberrations du sens générique* (1887, 4th edition), 287. Cf. Dr. Alexandre Paris, *Folie des femmes enceintes, de nouvelles accouchées et des nourrices* (1897).

closed dogma and carrying his arguments to extremes. Janet said some very harsh things about Freud, which rankled ever after, notably at the London International Congress of 1913: Freud's disciple and biographer Ernest Jones criticised Janet for judging psycho-analysis without even trying it: Janet replied that he had not tried it precisely because he did not believe in interpreting the statements of patients 'to fit a dogma that had been fixed in advance', instead of seeking to find the truth. Janet objected to excessive weight being given to sex and to traumatic memories, though he considered them important, and he thought Freud was promising too much: he was himself very modest about the effects of his psycho-therapy, noting that most cures were inevitably temporary and relapses all too frequent; a long process of re-education was needed to rebuild the personality of the psychasthenic. Nevertheless, Janet knew about Freud's work long before most of his contemporaries; and in his writings he frequently showed his interest in them, though seldom in an enthusiastic way.

The first study of Freud in France was an article on his theory of dreams, published in 1911; in the same year a doctor at Poitiers made him known to general practitioners with a series of articles in the *Gazette des hôpitaux*; and a couple of medical textbooks made references to him. But the first book on psycho-analysis to be published in France appeared in 1914, just before the war, and it passed largely unnoticed. Its authors were Régis, professor of psychiatry at Bordeaux, and Angelo Hesnard, who was the enthusiast behind the project. Hesnard (1886–1969) came from outside the ruling hierarchy of professors. He was the son of an impoverished civil servant; he had joined the navy in order to get a medical education on the cheap and he was now a naval doctor at Bordeaux. His brother Oswald was an *agrégé* in German and founder of the French Institute in Berlin; there he had learnt about Freud from medical friends and, persuaded by Angelo, he was to undertake the first French translation of Freud.[1] Hesnard and Régis were sharply critical of Freud, at the same time as they were fascinated by his ideas. Freud's theory 'had a philosophical allure so manifest that it has justly been likened to certain

[1] He later became rector of the Academy of Grenoble and interpreter to Briand in his conversations with Stresemann.

doctrines of psychological metaphysics'. It was a harmonious theory which would 'satisfy the dilettante, by freeing him from the need to engage in detailed researches, the patient accumulation of small facts, which is the current coin of medical methods'. It was 'purely hypothetical and completely unprovable', and Kraepelin was right to call it 'metapsychiatry'. Its ideas on sex had drawn most attention to it and had aroused most criticism. Hesnard and Régis applauded Freud for dealing with sexual problems; they agreed they were important: 'Obsessional people instinctively choose sexual things to motivate their inadequacies, because sexuality is, in the present state of our civilisation, the most mysterious aspect of the human personality and because it represents the most suitable material out of which to create symbols of their inability to act and to think like normal people; in absolutely the same way as they choose certain social, metaphysical and above all religious questions to express the constitutional debility of their affections. . . That sexual troubles are the rule among neurotics is indubitable, but that the former are the cause of the latter, we cannot admit.' They argued that though sexual troubles could cause some of the symptoms of neurosis, they were themselves effects of more general troubles. The frequency of sexual obsessions among neurotics was 'a matter of civilisation and milieu'; and it was just one instance of obsession with what was forbidden; if society forbade gastronomic satisfactions or making money, they might well be obsessed by digestion or gold. Hesnard and Régis claimed neurotics of this kind were 'totally different' from sexual perverts: these had instincts which were impossible to alter, they were like criminals, marked men, with damage if not to their intelligence at any rate to their effectivity; they were incapable of love, which is what, on the contrary, tormented neurotics. 'It is imprudent to admit, from a social point of view, that we are all potentially incestuous or homosexuals.' 'Pan-sexualism' was, however, the only original idea they attributed to Freud. They quoted French precursors for his theories of transference, trauma, the unconscious, dreams, etc. They concluded therefore that Freud's work represented an advance in only a very slight sense, because basically he was a delayed survivor of the old German psychological tradition of the early nineteenth century, of Stahl and Heinroth, which saw the conflict of morality and reason as the cause of madness.[1]

Hesnard nevertheless remained one of the most important commentators on Freud in France for a whole generation, being a fluent and popular writer. His interest was, however, more in the non-medical side of Freud, in his views on symbolism, art and religion; he was always convinced that psycho-analysis would open up great changes in morals. He never underwent analysis himself and so remained somewhat outside the charmed circle; he was keen to put Freud to work in the educational sphere, believing that it was in the bringing-up of children that guilt and repression were cultivated and the seeds of much of human unhappiness produced. He urged the Freudians to abandon 'their isolation into small closed cliques'. But his *Morals without Sin* (1954) was placed on the Index by the Catholic Church. By then, Hesnard, who loved new ideas, had become interested in Marxism, in phenomenology and in linguistics. He replaced the libido by love, which he interpreted as joy in life. He turned Freudianism into a humanistic gospel, which the psycho-analysts could not recognise, stressing man's ability for infinite sympathy as the link that must draw him into harmonious living.[2] Hesnard illustrates how the French assimilated a foreign theory by incorporating it into their own traditions, taking what suited them, and remodelling it in their own image.

The early popular reactions to Freud hesitated between castigating him for being a bad pupil of Charcot and insulting him for being a foreigner. A doctor who published a book on Freud in 1925 said that it was France's 'delicacy and critical sense' that had made most of its medical men turn away from him. Sexual relations were very different in France and Germany: in Germany 'they are not discreet and intimate as in France; they are cynically displayed in all forms, to the point that perverts have their official journals and meetings'; 'German towns were the only ones to have erotic films shown publicly . . . virgin girls were a much rarer exception in Germany than in France'. That is why Freud was obsessed by sex

[1] E. Régis and A. Hesnard, *La Psychoanalyse des névroses et des psychoses* (1914), 321–8, 341.

[2] 'Hommage au docteur A. Hesnard', *L'Évolution psychiatrique* (Jan.–June 1971), 301–75.

and why also his teachings were most successful in the English-speaking world with its narrow puritanism. France was a Catholic country and the confession 'provided an outlet for perverse thoughts'.[1] In 1934, when a journalist asked a variety of medical men for their views of Freud, reactions had changed only slightly. The director of the lunatic asylum of Toulouse, Professor Maurice Dide, for example, repeated that 'Freudism belongs to the past'; it was based on the study of the abnormal and was no more reliable than Charcot's now-ridiculed stigmata; it had besides never cured anything but hysteria. Its only value was that it had made possible the posing of problems about sex with less hypocrisy. Dr. A. Marie, a leading Paris psychiatrist, agreed that Freud had performed a useful service, in that 'pan-sexualism was a salutary reaction against people whose psychological puritanism caused them to forget and be silent about the important role of sex', but he considered him 'the victim of a verbal construction and of a narrowly exclusive ideology'; the repression of the libido could not be accepted until it was proved by biochemical and anatomical analyses. There was some disagreement, however, as to just how much of a liberating force Freud was. Some doctors insisted that this puritanism was not universal, that the Catholic Church had long been aware of sexual problems and that confessors had been psycho-analysts in their own way. So, while one emancipationist woman doctor hailed Freud for 'helping to liberate humanity from its prejudices', the novelist Jeanne Boujassy protested that his doctrines were 'extremely humiliating: one can no longer go to a fashionable doctor now without feeling immediately scrutinised and undressed to the very depths of one's soul by his inquiries'. Another female novelist, Renée Dunan, was enthusiastic about Freud, as she was also about nudism, but she said he was having no influence on France's way of life or on the literary world: 'no one knows about him except André Gide and me'. The critic Ernest Seillière declared, 'The views of Freud apply above all to the Jews, his co-religionists, who were particularly disposed to a congenital libidinous pan-sexualism by ethnic fatality.' Freud clearly aroused strong feelings: one professor murmured that 'the attitude of his zealots was as disquieting as their rudimentary

[1] Dr. J. Lammonier, *Le Freudisme* (1925), 7–9, 167.

knowledge of biology'. Princess Marie Bonaparte summed it up by saying that the French liked clarity, taste and common sense too much to accept him, but the English were willing to face up to the truth.[1]

It was she who organised the small band of Freudian analysts in Paris. She was the daughter of Prince Roland Bonaparte, a noteworthy explorer and ethnographer, who had added wealth as well as learning to the family's distinctions by marrying Mademoiselle Blanc, daughter of the organiser of the gaming-houses of Monte Carlo, and who then set up a foundation to finance scientific research. Marie herself married Prince George of Greece, whose hobby was collecting snuff-boxes. She was a highly intelligent and energetic woman, who had gone to Vienna to be psycho-analysed by Freud and who then regarded herself as the authentic mouthpiece of his doctrines. In 1926 she founded the Psychoanalytical Society of Paris, with a handful of members; but divisions soon appeared within their small ranks. Some accused her of demanding 'rigorous conformity' from them, and using their meetings 'as simply an excuse for quoting Freudian texts'. In the 1950s the movement split, with one faction remaining loyal to the Freudian International and another claiming independence. In the next decade Lacan, who tried to develop psycho-analysis into the study of language, in turn seceded and founded a dissident *École freudienne*. A number of foreigners participated in the early dissemination of Freud's teaching, and it was above all through Switzerland and through Swiss disciples like Saussure that his works reached France, published by the Éditions du Mont Blanc of Geneva. But even the French university system found a niche for the Freudians. One of the leading Paris professors of psychiatry, H. Claude, the only one to remain faithful to Charcot's organodynamic theory and a pupil of Charcot's successor Raymond, gave teaching appointments to a number of them—to Saussure and Odie from Lausanne, to Madame Sokolnicka, who had no medical qualifications but who was one of the earliest analysts to practise in Paris, but above all to Dr. R. Laforgue, who became one of the major popularisers of Freudianism in readily

[1] P. Vigné d'Octon, *La Vie et l'amour: les doctrines freudiennes et la psychanalyse* (1934).

understandable language.[1] It was only in the late 1950s that a wider range of French doctors, mainly young ones, began to take a serious interest in Freud.

So when in 1961 a sociologist published a report on the attitude of public opinion to psycho-analysis, it emerged that Freud was still considered by the average Frenchman as being above all the theorist of pan-sexualism. Public opinion, in other words, still identified Freud with the first phase of his work, carried out before 1920; it knew virtually nothing of the new directions his researches had taken after that; and there was thus a clear gap between the popular interest in Freud which came after the 1939–45 war on the one hand, and the attitudes of the professional psychiatrists and the leading intellectuals on the other, who were at this very time trying to develop notably different psychological theories on the basis of Freud's researches. The vast majority of the people questioned in this survey thought that psycho-analysis was similar to the confession and to hypnotism. Some 51 per cent of middle-class parents questioned said that they would allow psycho-analysis to be used on their children, and 70 per cent thought it could with profit be used on criminals. Between 58 and 64 per cent thought it helped people, between 9 and 15 per cent thought it did not, 27 per cent did not know. The striking fact was that this large support for it came from the working classes and the least-educated sections of the community. Twice as high a proportion of workers as of intellectuals thought psycho-analysis could cure people. This was not simply because the communists condemned it as charlatanism, for at the same time the right wing dismissed it as a theory of sexuality. Freud became acceptable through popularisation by the mass-circulation press: those who accepted him had not read him. But perhaps he had touched on an aspect of life that meant more than a little to them.[2]

These are just some of the ways that anxiety expressed itself.

[1] A. Hesnard and R. Laforgue, 'Aperçu historique du mouvement psychiatrique en France', in L'Évolution psychiatrique (1925), 1. 11–26; A. Hesnard, De Freud à Lacan (1970). Claude himself had other interests: see H. Claude and P. Rubenovitch, Thérapeutiques biologiques des affections morales (1940).

[2] Serge Moscovici, La Psychanalyse. Son image et son public. Étude sur la représentation sociale de la psychanalyse (1961), 119–21, 138, 421.

How people coped with anxiety is more complicated still. One needs to look at various forms of evasion, like the development of leisure activities, whioh were not simply an expression of *joie de vivre*, and at different types of palliatives, like drug-taking and alcoholism, which reflected more than a rising standard of living. One must not forget the more elusive readjustments of behaviour, which are virtually impossible to document, like attitudes towards loss of temper. Above all, one must realise that rationalism was, in some small part, a reaction and a defence against emotionalism. But the history of emotion has still to be established as a branch of scholarship.[1]

[1] Judith Devlin has started a doctoral thesis at Oxford on 'Fear in Nineteenth Century France'.

# 18. Hierarchy and Violence

## The Army

FRANCE was an artistic, intellectual, agricultural country, but also a militaristic one. In 1848 it appointed a poet to head its government in a time of crisis and in 1870 it chose a historian to rescue it from the Prussians, but it turned to military leaders more often. The tradition of Napoleon, as the soldier who would save the nation, was continued by General Cavaignac in 1848, by Marshal MacMahon in 1873, by General Boulanger in 1888, by Marshal Pétain in 1940 and then by General de Gaulle. In none of these cases, however, was military government established. The relationship between army and society in France was curious. Even when the country became republican, the prestige of the army was almost as high as it was in despotic monarchies which based themselves on force. France managed to be the apostle of fraternity but also chauvinistic, egalitarian but also accepting a hierarchical military organisation, a parliamentary democracy but one proud of its military virtues. The army united the nation in war but divided it in peace. To be a soldier was a patriotic act, but patriotism was not always fashionable, and to be a soldier could also mean cutting oneself off from society. The army had its own set of values, but it was also regarded as one of the most important instruments of social climbing and also of national unification. These contradictions are important, and they are explicable.[1]

One of the main reasons why the army was the object of so much controversy and violent emotion was that its character changed considerably over time and its significance was therefore difficult to appreciate clearly. The army inherited some of the aura of its *ancien régime* origins. It was associated with the arbitrary discipline that the Revolution had overthrown, with the nobleman's claim to the right to command,

---

[1] État-major de l'Armée de terre, Service Historique, *Guide bibliographique sommaire d'histoire militaire et coloniale française* (1969) is the fullest bibliography.

with the idea that war was an aristocratic hobby. Famine, pestilence and war used to be the poor man's terror; the press-gang, and then conscription, were the state's most serious attacks on his independence. In the eighteenth century, a soldier was something of a social outcast, often escaping from his village because he had transgressed its moral code, or because he was discontented or disinherited. A large proportion of the army came from the newly annexed provinces of the east of France. The army gave its recruits a sense of belonging; patriotism gave them a sense of mission; *esprit de corps* enabled pride to replace the reputation they used to have of being brutal, lazy and immoral. The army at this time did not have any of the reactionary characteristics which were later associated with it: it was not noted for blind discipline; insubordination and mutinies were not rare; it was not completely devoted to throne and altar, or at any rate it was noted for anticlericalism; and it was not yet isolated in barracks, but was allowed to take civil employment and long leaves in its spare time. The retired soldier came back to his village a non-conformist, speaking French, widely travelled, having lost the taste for hard work but self-confident and capable of dealing with authority and civil servants.[1] There were still notices outside public parks saying 'No dogs, prostitutes, servants or soldiers' and the peasants resisted conscription to the revolutionary and Napoleonic armies with bitter determination.[2] In 1798 the government succeeded in enrolling only one-quarter of the men it summoned to arms; in 1811 no less than 66,000 men were arrested as deserters; but gradually Napoleon increased the success rate of conscription from two-thirds to nine-tenths, and by 1830 conscription was finally accepted, with only 2 per cent defaulting. Two per cent was the proportion of defaulters in 1902 and 1910 also—equivalent to two army corps—but the state had gradually made military service an essential part of national life.[3]

It was successful because it introduced universal conscription slowly. In 1848 only one-quarter of the army consisted of

[1] André Corvisier, *L'Armée française de la fin du 17ᵉ siècle au ministère de Choiseul. Le Soldat* (1964); cf. Richard Cobb, *Les Armées révolutionnaires* (1963), 724–32.
[2] Marcel Baldet, *La Vie quotidienne dans les armées de Napoléon* (1964), 13.
[3] Joseph Vidal, *Histoire et statistique de l'insoumission* (Paris law thesis, 1913).

conscripts. Another quarter were substitutes, for until 1873 the law allowed those called up to pay someone else to perform their service for them and there were always poor people, or soldiers who had served their term and had nowhere to go, who were willing to sell themselves in this way.[1] (Forty per cent of the *remplaçants* were former soldiers.) The remaining half of the army were volunteers. It was thus an essentially professional army, even though ostensibly based on conscription. It was still so small that it had no use for all the conscripts who were theoretically obliged to serve in it. Thus in 1847, 304,000 young men were summoned to draw lots as to who should be called up; 144,000 drawing 'good numbers' were set free. The remainder were then examined medically, and 48 per cent of them were exempted either as unfit, or because they were priests, teachers or students. So only 64,000 had to serve; but a quarter of these were placed in reserve and were not troubled any further. Military service was thus a misfortune that befell only a small proportion of young men, and money could save those who were determined and could afford (between 800 and 1,200 francs) to avoid it.[2]

The army, however, had definite attractions for those who did join it. Almost exactly half of the volunteers were of middle-class origin, about a third workers and a fifth peasants. One third of recruits were illiterate, and anybody who could read and write was immediately considered a potential officer. Under Louis-Philippe one-third of officer commissions were reserved for N.C.O.s but by 1848 three-quarters of the officers had risen from the ranks (80 per cent in the infantry, but 35 per cent in the cavalry). Becoming an officer was considered a natural continuation of non-commissioned rank, but though it was thus easy to become an officer, promotion was very slow after that. One had to wait for vacancies to occur in one's regiment, so there was a considerable element of chance in the matter, but generally a N.C.O. who became a sub-lieutenant at the age of thirty would be promoted a lieutenant at about thirty-seven and a captain at forty-five. He would be unlikely to go further. The army was thus an excellent way of making

[1] Bernard Schnapper, *Le Remplacement militaire en France* (1968).

[2] W. Zaniewicki, 'L'Armée française en 1848' (unpublished troisième cycle thesis, in the Sorbonne library, 1966).

good socially, provided one's ambitions were distinctly limited. A sub-lieutenant was paid only 1,350 to 1,500 francs a year (not much more than a primary-school master), a captain 2,000–2,400. One could not easily get married on such pay and the army was to a considerable extent a society of bachelors —not unlike the Church—enjoying a certain prestige and comfort by sacrificing family life. For the more determined, however, there were two ways of moving up faster. One was to go to the military cadet schools, but that cost about 12,000 francs. Another was to join the colonial army, and seek distinction in the conquest of Algeria; but that involved cutting oneself off from the home country for long periods: that is why the 'Africans' were such a special kind of freemasonry. The colonial army was outside the life of the nation, but the ordinary one was not. There were not enough barracks to lodge its soldiers and these lived as paying guests in the attics of small garrison towns, taking on odd jobs when off duty. In 1848 the army was distinguished by no special political leanings. Its votes in elections showed it was as divided as the nation.[1]

Two new factors altered this situation. First, governments used the army for political repression. In the June days of 1848 and in the Commune, the army spilt the blood of its fellow-countrymen, in civil wars of unforgettable poignancy. Napoleon III destroyed parliamentary government in 1851 with the help of the army and was identified with military rule. Troops came to be regularly used in the breaking of workers' strikes. Secondly, the army became the refuge, in the course of the second half of the nineteenth century, of the aristocracy, who compensated for their expulsion from public office by reviving their traditions of military service. Under the Restoration, the aristocracy used the army as a kind of finishing school; its youth took commissions for a few years as an alternative to a university education; but by the end of the Second Empire they were turning to the army for a life's career. In the early Third Republic, the number of candidates for Saint-Cyr almost trebled; and the proportion of noble names in the officer lists rose enormously. The army therefore came to be considered a danger to the republic, a relic of the *ancien régime* and a bastion of clericalism. Anti-militarism developed in

[1] Raoul Girardet, *La Société militaire dans la France contemporaine 1815–1939* (1953).

close association with socialism. But though the army's character became politically controversial, there were very few who wanted to abolish armies altogether.

All parties placed great hopes on the army for the moral regeneration of the country. The republicans saw in it a way of ending class barriers. Military service forced all young men to mix socially, to undergo the same experiences and to become conscious that their membership of the national community overrode all their petty private interests. The army now took on a new educational character. It ceased to be simply a source of employment for eccentric paupers and fashionable aristocrats. Because it was under attack, it had to defend its discipline and its authoritarianism, and in doing so, it came to reformulate its ideals in a way that gave militarism a new meaning. Sly intellectuals and sarcastic radicals liked to claim that soldiers were stupid, fit only to do what they were told. Renan said that army service was a sure way of losing one's *esprit de finesse*; Clemenceau declared that 'war is too serious a matter to be confided to military men'. But the pacifist movement had been seriously crippled by the disaster of 1870. The idea, enunciated by Condorcet, that war was the instrument of kings to preserve their tyranny, and that it would end when kings were overthrown, lapsed into irrelevance. The Saint-Simonian theory that industry was the enemy of war and that industrialists were bound to replace soldiers as the leaders of society, obtained little support even from industrialists. The suggestion that armies should be put to useful work, building railways and canals to increase national prosperity, and that only thus could service in them be reconciled with democracy, was never followed up.[1] The army was able to draw on a powerful chauvinistic tradition, which gave it something of a sacred function. Even Anatole France had written that 'military virtues have given birth to the whole of civilisation. Abolish them and the whole of society will crumble.' Victor Cousin, the oracle of banality, pronounced that 'a battle is nothing but the struggle of truth and falsehood' and war was

---

[1] See e.g. Captain Ferdinand Durand, *Des tendances pacifiques de la société européenne et du rôle des armées dans l'avenir* (1841, 2nd edition 1844); C. Pecqueur, *Des armées dans leur rapport avec l'industrie, la morale et la liberté, ou les devoirs civiques des militaires* (1842).

therefore 'the terrible but necessary instrument of civilisation'.[1] Popularised science was drawn on to prove that struggle was the essence of life and that force was synonymous with virtue.[2] War was defended by liberals as 'the supreme recourse of the oppressed' and there was a vast literature in praise of military virtues. Captain Danrit's thirty-odd volumes of science fiction urging the need for preparedness against the 'yellow and black menaces' were much read.[3] Army life was held up as the breeding ground not just of patriotism, but of friendship, courage, energy, gaiety, honour, tenacity and dedication to the highest ideals.[4] The distinction between military and civil life was accentuated, so as to counteract the looser morals and manners which were held to be the cause of all France's troubles. Discipline became a military fetish. The army tried to divest itself of its old easy-going ways. Loyalty was demanded no longer to individual officers but to 'the flag', to the principle of 'order'. The chaotic bravura the Algerian army had fostered gave way to passive obedience and the rigid implementation of regulations. Intellectual qualities were discredited and a new formalism developed which was very different from the traditional French military ethos to which it confusedly believed it was dedicated. In Napoleon I's army, a general who had lost his nerve in the battle of Marengo was booed by his troops in the review he held afterwards, and he never showed his face again before them. Such a thing could no longer happen in 1900.

The *N.C.O.'s Manual* illustrates the army's changing values, and the new functions it sought to assume. 'Discipline', said the edition of 1893, 'will be the soldier's religion. . . . The regiment is the school of subordination, of the virile spirit, of male pride. . . . Soldiers resolved to die can always save their honour.' By 1913 the introduction to the manual, dealing with the army's moral role, had grown from two to thirteen pages. The army, it said, developed not only the spirit of patriotism and sacrifice, but also of solidarity and camaraderie; 'though instituted to defend the country against its foreign enemies, it also had the

---

[1] Maurice Lelong, O.P., *Célébration de l'art militaire* (1962), an interesting anthology.　　　　　　　　　　　　　　[2] J. Izoulet, *La Cité moderne* (1895).

[3] Capt. E. A. C. Driant, alias Danrit, *La Guerre fatale* (1903), *L'Invasion jaune* (1909), *L'Invasion noire* (1913), etc. Biography by G. Jollivet, *Le Colonel Driant* (1918).

[4] General Thoumas, *Le Livre du soldat. Vertus guerrières* (1891).

task of instilling respect for the government of the republic and for property, and ensuring the execution of the laws voted by parliament'. It was also 'the school where man learns to live in society, where the citizen is formed,' where different classes got to know each other. The friendships of the regiment, it declared, were the most lasting, but it warned the N.C.O. not to be 'too familiar with his subordinates: he must neither joke, play, drink nor feast with them'.[1]

This rhetoric should not be taken at its face value. The image of stiffness and rigid hierarchy that army propagandists cultivated was not an accurate reflection of what was actually happening. The hostility between militarists and anti-militarists was partly the result of each side exaggerating its position and misinterpreting the realities. Though on the theoretical plane the army came to stand for principles which could not easily be reconciled with those of the Third Republic, or at least with isolated elements of the Jacobin tradition in it, in practice its way of life was much more complex and varied. The influence it exerted on the conscripts that passed through it was not what the manuals prescribed. Though so much was written about the reactionary dangers of the military, there was very little study of the actual effect of national service, of the results of the 'schooling' function of the army. One can, however, learn more about what the army really meant to people—as opposed to what they said about it in their political disputes—by looking at it from this point of view.

In real life, the officer was not a walking automaton, blindly implementing the rules, as playwrights like Courteline, who had a passionate hatred of the army, portrayed him. The first thing officer cadets were taught when they arrived at Saint-Cyr was how to salute and what the gradations of hierarchy were. They were constantly classified in exact order of subordination according to the marks they received; they were taught precisely how to make their beds and every minute rule of discipline and custom. But as the captain in charge of the class of 1863 said, there were two distinct beings in him, the man and the captain. 'If you address yourself to the man, he will try to be as helpful as he can. But if you address the captain,

---

[1] *Le Livre du gradé à l'usage des élèves caporaux, caporaux et sous officiers d'infanterie* (Toulouse, 1893), 8, and *Le Livre du gradé d'infanterie* (1913), 11.

it is different. The captain knows only the regulations, he moves only according to the regulations, he lives only by the regulations.' The cadets soon discovered how to catch him when he was a man and their life was far more entertaining than the rules foresaw. The smell of boot polish in the dormitories was often drowned by that of perfume, and 'the fashionable cadets had cosmetic kits far more elaborate than many girls'. There were artists of every kind among them, and they spent much time drawing, sculpting, engraving, playing music or writing poetry. It was true that the richer ones hired the music rooms simply in order to have somewhere to smoke and chat at their ease, that those who spent their afternoons off in museums sometimes did so simply to keep warm, that the school library was little frequented and that intellectual activity was not encouraged—the swots used to retire to the infirmary for a few days before examinations—but the cultural life of the army officer was not as narrow as his enemies claimed, though it was not in general bookish.[1] The army was too large an institution, too subdivided into relatively independent units, and too diverse in its recruitment, to make a uniform type of officer possible. The military schools were not as influential as was imagined. They imparted factual knowledge more than a way of life, and groups of individuals within them created styles of behaviour and established links of devotion more powerful than the official programmes. Patronage, and friendship that grew within its networks, was very important. That was why the Staff College, to which the ablest officers went, necessarily allowed so much tolerance towards the diversity of military doctrine. Here, before 1914, while Colonel Pétain taught the importance of fire-power, Colonel de Grandmaison preached all-out offensive: there was almost as much doctrinal disagreement in the army as in the university, and there were similar personal animosities. There were seven different cadet schools—Saint-Cyr, Saint-Maixent, the Polytechnic, Fontainebleau, Versailles, Vincennes and Saumur—and they each had their own traditions, and slightly different social

<hr>

[1] A. Teller, *Souvenirs de Saint-Cyr* (*Esquisses de la vie militaire en France*) (1886, 11th edition), i. 99–114, 147–8. P. de Pardiellan [pseud. of Lt.-Col. P. G. A. Veling], *Grains d'officiers. Scènes de la vie dans les écoles militaires en France, en Russie, en Allemagne et en Autriche* (1895).

mixtures. French officers did not form a distinct caste, as the Germans were supposed to.[1]

At one extreme, there were the depressed and ageing junior officers, risen from the ranks, dedicated to routine because they had no prospect before them but the retirement they dreaded. At the other extreme there were highly intelligent men who chose a military career because they believed it gave more scope for personal fulfilment and public service than corrupt politics or the static civil service; and indeed in the colonial army such men were able to govern empires with far greater power than civilians enjoyed. Ernest Psichari set out the arguments and the emotions behind this kind of choice in an influential book, *L'Appel des armes* (1913), which explained why he had abandoned philosophy for military service. Lyautey, whose famous article on the 'Social Role of the Officer' became the inspiration of several generations of soldiers and whose career proved that the army could offer as much scope for action and influence as any other profession, typified one kind of ideal. In between these extremes, there were the rivalries of the many varieties of officer, whose different experience and origins gave them barely compatible attitudes. Marshal Juin, the son of a retired soldier who became a lighthouse keeper in Algeria, said he joined the army not because of any taste for the life of the barracks, nor indeed because he felt any desire for revenge against Germany—England was the enemy for him after Fashoda—but because the army offered him a scholarship. In the army, he found a contrast between the smoothly shaven, white-gloved, brilliantly polished officer and the hirsute, bearded one, who liked to fight his battles naked to the waist, wearing espadrilles.[2] There was then the new kind of officer who saw himself as a technician and who frightened the older generation with his talk of ballistics and topography; the arrival of a young sub-lieutenant in a regiment, instead of provoking genial reminiscences from the old officers and admiration for the new sartorial fashions, roused a sense of insecurity; lieutenants now seemed uncontrollable and were therefore given petty duties which sergeants had once per-

[1] General Debeney, *La Guerre et les hommes. Réflexions d'après-guerre* (1937), 9–16, 231–8.
[2] Marshal Juin, *Je suis soldat* (1960), 26.

formed.[1] On the other hand there was the reservist who broke down the distinctions between civil and military life, and who inspired horror in the old professionals. The First World War created a gulf between those who had served in it and those who were despised as mere novices and theorists of war. The officers promoted during the First World War 'were fully informed on points of detail but had no general view of their task. They could command, but they could not instruct the soldier.'[2] The increasing number of bureaucratic administrators added new tensions. It was not surprising that the army's defeat in 1940 was not accepted as an inevitable collapse and that bitter internecine recriminations at once tore it apart. Only a small proportion of the army actually had a chance to fight the enemy, and it felt as betrayed by those who remained in the rear as by the politicians.

Throughout this period, therefore, to be an army officer was to occupy an uncertain social position, to be subject to ideological tensions and to continual pressure for modernisation and reorganisation. The country could not decide what kind of army it wanted: some officers reacted to the insecurity this created for them either by grasping at traditional values, or by entrenching themselves in hierarchical routine. But these were reactions which concealed much diversity. Partly because it suffered repeated defeats—in 1870, in 1914, in 1940—and partly because it was so attacked by the left, the army felt it was not appreciated by public opinion, and rather than incarnate the common denominator of French democracy, it withdrew into its own world, cultivating virtues special to itself. Instead of seeing itself as a branch of industrial and technological advance, it confined itself to the cult of individual prowess. The army's endless difficulties should be seen as a particularly well-documented instance of the hesitations of Frenchmen in general before democratic and scientific change, and of the obstacles that stood in the way both of understanding that change and of adapting to it. Alfred de Vigny's statement that the army 'sought its soul everywhere and could not find it' always remained true. The officers were themselves the most

[1] Marcel Souriau, *De la baïonnette à l'épée* (1934), 96–110.
[2] General Tanant, 'Les Officiers de la guerre', *Revue des Deux Mondes* (1 Mar. 1926).

serious and constant critics of the army, in its organisation and its methods, and it was their disputes which provided the basis for the unending political debates about the army.

That the army was only reflecting national difficulties can be seen from the slowness with which parliament itself modernised it.[1] In 1848, as has been seen, the army was still essentially a professional one, even though some people were conscripted into it. Napoleon III, instructed by the astonishing defeat of Austria by Prussia in 1856, determined to increase the size of his forces by making universal conscription a reality; but he met with almost universal opposition and the law of reorganisation passed in 1868 simply instituted a reserve militia which remained a largely paper organisation. After the catastrophic defeat of 1871, public opinion could no longer resist the arguments for universal service, but the law of 1873, while adopting it in theory, allowed the old system to survive. The main reason why this happened was that Thiers—who was proud of his knowledge of military history—was a firm believer in the superiority of professional armies, and he was able to carry the day because a larger army would require more money, which parliament was unwilling to raise. So though five years' military service for everybody was what the new law prescribed, financial constraints prevented this from being implemented. Some men were called up for five years, but let out after four years, while others were simply given basic training for six months (later increased to nine and then twelve months). The system of buying a replacement was abolished, but equality was still not achieved. Those who wished to ensure that they would not fall into the five-year category could volunteer just before their call-up. They then served a definite term of one year only. This was in fact a piece of class favouritism, because the volunteer had to pay 1,500 francs to cover the cost of his clothing and equipment. In fact, only some 6,000 people a year took advantage of this system, but it became a symbol of the undemocratic character of the army—as too did the exemption of priests and schoolmasters. Only in 1905 were these variations abandoned and two years' service for all instituted.[2] The size of the peacetime army in 1872 was half a

---

[1] J. Monteilhet, *Les Institutions militaires de la France 1814–1924* (1926).

[2] Payment for the students' one-year volunteer system was abolished in 1889.

million; in 1900 it was 600,000; and the law of 1913 raised it to over 800,000. Had a war been declared in 1872 only 1,250,000 could have been mobilised, but by 1914 this figure had been raised to over 3,500,000.[1] Between 1800 and 1814, only 1,600,000 Frenchmen had served in Napoleon's army. In the four years of the First World War, 8,400,000 were mobilised. It was only gradually that the full militarisation of the nation was achieved. But this still did not mean that the military experience of Frenchmen attained an egalitarian uniformity, any more than did their educational experience at school.

Young conscripts sometimes found their first year of service a terrible strain. On arrival they might be expected to sleep four in one bed, and if there were still not enough beds, they might have to sleep on the floor. Their work was fixed for them in a programme that covered twelve hours a day, so that they barely had time to wash or keep their clothes clean. They exercised in all weathers. What struck them most painfully was the discipline, the foul language of the N.C.O.s, the mania about polish, the endless parades, the arbitrary punishments. A conscript, writing in 1894, complained that a trivial offence like arriving late for a class, or borrowing a colleague's arms for parade, would be punished with two days' detention, mislaying an item of equipment with four days', impoliteness to a superior with fifteen days'.[2] There were some who complained that the food was disgusting, and indeed the government seems to have budgeted for only one franc a day to feed and clothe a soldier, but to boys from really poor origins, like Marc Bonnefoy, who joined up in 1859 when he failed to gain admission into a teacher training college, meat and white bread every day were a marvellous treat: conversation in his company centred around food and how they could get hold of wine to complete it.[3] Once the initial training had been accomplished, however, the conscript's main problem was boredom: 'after the first year', wrote a captain who had served during the Second Empire, 'the soldier of the period spent three-quarters of his

[1] Richard D. Challener, *The French Theory of the Nation in Arms 1866–1939* (New York, 1955), 47.

[2] Victor Monmillion, *Trois ans au régiment* (1894), 132.

[3] Marc Bonnefoy, *Souvenirs d'un simple soldat en campagne, 1859* (n.d., about 1871), 21–5.

time in complete physical and intellectual idleness'.[1] That used
to be one of the attractions of military life; but as soldiering
came to be taken more seriously and as bureaucracy expanded,
spare time was increasingly filled in with futile administrative
chores and exercises of doubtful value.

In the process, the rigour of discipline increased, though in
the course of the twentieth century it was relaxed again.
Discipline had been fairly loose in the army of the *ancien régime*,
even if punishments were savage. Complaints against 'the
spirit of independence and insubordination' and laments that
'authority no longer exists' were already being made in 1775;
insubordination was doubtless far more frequent than it was
a century later, despite the advent of democracy. However, the
army increasingly differentiated itself from society by building
up rules and regulations which defined with growing precision
the rights and privileges of every rank. The main achievement
of the first half of the century was to give predominance to
promotion by seniority, and the punctual execution of the rules
therefore grew into a fetish. A Russian general argued that
France was defeated in 1870 partly because of the complicated
disciplinary rules it had evolved, which inculcated 'an inveterate habit of blind and inert subordination, erected into
an absolute principle and having the force of law at all levels
of the hierarchy'. It used to be considered improper to talk
about promotion, but this now became a principal topic of
conversation among officers, who therefore concentrated on
the maintenance of appearances, on standing up straight and
carrying out the regulations precisely.[2] The obsession with
saluting correctly, dressing in exactly the right way, went hand
in hand with an increasing stress on differences in rank and
condemnation of excessive familiarity between them.[3] The
regulations gave the soldier no rights to time off: leave was a
rare concession. N.C.O.s decorated with the Legion of Honour
could return to barracks at 1 a.m., other N.C.O.s and decorated
soldiers had to be back by 11 p.m., but the ordinary soldier

---

[1] Capt. Pringent, *Les Permissions dans l'armée. Leur influence sur l'instruction, la
discipline et l'esprit militaire* (1896), 7.

[2] A. Lambert, *Étude sur l'état moral de l'armée française et de l'armée allemande en
1870* (1908), 13, 42.

[3] Capt. Édouard Gillon, *Le Nouveau Soldat du service obligatoire* (1873), 53. Cf.
Capt. d'Arbeux, *L'Officier contemporain: la démocratisation de l'armée 1899–1910* (1911).

was confined after 9 p.m. However, under pressure from electors and influential parents, the army became more lenient at the end of the century in the granting of leave, and soon weekends, public holidays, harvest time and family feasts were accepted as an excuse for absence. A new pattern developed, of soldiers being busy during the week and then going home on Sunday, returning exhausted in the early hours. The old officers complained that all the discipline instilled during the week was forgotten in the riotous, noisy and often drunken behaviour on leave days.[1]

Having first tried to drill independence out of the conscript, the army, in its new regulations of 1905, began appealing to his spirit of initiative. But at that date, there was little possibility of his profiting morally from his military service, and even after it, the 'often brutalising and sometimes revolting life' the army offered, 'duty rendered painful by unintelligent and malicious N.C.O.s', could hardly inspire patriotism. 'There is perhaps no place where ideas of liberty, initiative, responsibility, dignity and duty are more ignored, more outrageously flouted than in the barracks.'[2] A general writing in 1901 admitted that the efforts of some idealist officers to win the affection of their troops had had little result: 'the soldiers do not like their officers, they only fear them'. Too many officers still thought that their task was to snarl, to criticise, to appear to be constantly in a state of fury.[3] However, with the spread of antimilitarism and communism, it became clear that simply punishing soldiers for singing the Internationale would not help the army's effectiveness. A new school of thought urged the application of 'psychological' techniques to win over the unruly conscript, or to get him discredited by his own peers. Orders would be badly executed, it was now said, only if they were badly given; conscripts should no longer be discouraged as soon as they arrived by being boringly forced to memorise the names of different parts of the rifle and a multitude of orders and prohibitions, but shown that a soldier's life could be fun.[4] Already in the first decade of the twentieth century the

---

[1] Capt. Pringent, op. cit.

[2] *Vers une armée démocratique. Trois réunions militaires* (1907, Au Sillon).

[3] Gen. Cremer, *Éducation du soldat et principalement du fantassin* (1911) (written in 1901).

[4] Lt. Vaillant, *L'Âme du soldat. Essai de psychologie militaire pratique* (1910), 9, 35.

officers had yielded to the soldiers' hatred of drill and had greatly
reduced it.[1] After the First World War, it appeared that the
whole notion of military authority was in crisis: 'too many
young officers doubt their right to command'. The army began
to have a more modest view of its role, and to fall on to the
defensive against society. 'The army', wrote an officer in 1919,
'does not demand to be the sole élite. But it must be one of the
élites, and officially recognised and treated as such.'[2] Some
officers now took to shaking hands with their men, though most
stuck to the old ways. Some of those who had risen out of the
ranks during the war were uncertain of their status, feeling,
as one said, 'like *nouveaux riches*'.[3] 'Prussian-style' discipline was
discredited. It was now said that it was impossible to 'radically
transform the mentality' of conscripts who served so briefly,
so all that should be aimed at was their 'adaptation'; but even
this should take account of the peculiar character of Frenchmen. Frenchmen liked talking, so officers should let them talk
and should make speeches back. They were democratic, and
so it was no use trying to get obedience by being dignified,
contemptuous or haughty.[4] Soldiers who persistently rejected
discipline were now therefore treated more leniently, classified
as 'unadapted' or 'degenerate', and declared unfit for military
service. But this influence of psychology was slight: little more
than a thousand men were freed in this way each year. Most
recalcitrant conscripts were declared perfectly sane but 'fond
of liberty' or 'fond of drink', and punished for it.[5]

Those who expressed the hope that the army would instil
discipline into the nation were countered by others who accused
the army of being a major instrument of demoralisation, of
instilling more bad habits than it cured. It is impossible to
decide between these arguments, neither of which could be
proved. It is even uncertain whether the army did anything
to alter the hygienic habits of the nation. The army's sanitary
arrangements were very slow to change. A parliamentary

[1] Capt. Jibé, *L'Armée nouvelle. Ce qu'elle pense, ce qu'elle veut* (1905), 296.
[2] Capt. M., *La Crise de l'autorité et l'armée future*, reprinted from *Études* (20 Oct.
1919).
[3] Marcel Souriau, *De la baïonnette à l'épée* (1934), 110.
[4] General A. J. Tanant, *La Discipline dans les armées françaises* (1938), 232, 334;
id., *L'Officier de France* (1938), 30, 156–9, 195.
[5] Capt. Ch. Pont, *Les Indisciplinés dans l'armée (normaux et anormaux)* (1912), 203.

inquiry of 1914 revealed that the barracks built after 1885 had no drainage system, and were even less satisfactory than the older ones because, owing to financial stringency, they crammed too many soldiers into too small a space. The older barracks usually had small rooms with eight or ten beds in each; the new ones had between twenty and eighty beds in each dormitory and as the size of the army increased, beds were placed so close that there was no room at all between them. Refectories were abolished in most barracks to be turned into dormitories, and it was there that the soldiers had to eat. There were not enough clothes to go round: in 1913 every conscript was issued with one new pair of shoes but these were not to be worn except for inspections; he also got one pair of old, unwearable shoes and one half-worn pair. There were only 24,000 hospital beds for the whole army and only 1,518 doctors.[1] It is probable that the army did more to cure venereal disease than to spread it.[2] In 1869 19 per cent of soldiers in hospital were there for venereal disease; but during the First World War a very active campaign greatly reduced this scourge.[3] The evidence however is somewhat contradictory as to whether the cause of cleanliness, as opposed to that of polish, was advanced. An official manual was in 1926 still warning recruits never to wash their feet in water, but only to grease them, never to divest themselves of their flannel vests and to beware of draughts, not to sleep with their boots on and to spit only into spittoons.[4]

The hopes that the army would unite the nation spiritually and destroy or diminish class divisions, were equally overoptimistic. The army was a democratic institution in the sense that it gave poor people the opportunity to rise in the social

[1] Lachaud, député, *Enquête sur les moyens propres à améliorer les conditions matérielles d'existence et d'hygiène de l'armée. Rapport* (Annexe au p.v. de la séance du 23 mars 1914, Chambre des députés), 432, 516.

[2] *Statistique médicale de l'armée 1869* (1872) claims the incidence of V.D. was halved in the second year of military service. This series, published annually, is an important source which has been little used hitherto.

[3] Philippe Avon, *Contribution à l'histoire des maladies vénériennes dans l'armée française* (Lyon medical and pharmaceutical thesis, 1968), 28, 44; cf. Sigisbert Cassin, *Contribution à l'étude des perversions sexuelles et des maladies vénériennes au cours de la vie de campagne* (Paris medical thesis, 1964), showing 8 per cent homosexuality in one unit.

[4] Lt. T. Zuccarelli, *Comment on se débrouille au régiment. Livre moral et technique du jeune soldat* (5th edition, 1926), 14, 18–19.

scale, but that made it all the more attached to hierarchical distinctions and susceptible to the charms of wealth and birth. It was the last institution to maintain elaborate controls on the marriage of its members. Until the very end of the nineteenth century, even an N.C.O. could not get married unless his bride had a dowry of at least 5,000 francs, or an annual income of 250 francs, but her earnings could not be included. For officers, long inquiries were set in motion to ensure not only that their prospective brides had adequate dowries, but that these were securely invested; full details of their shares and mortgages were required and only state and railway bonds were acceptable; real property which yielded no income was disregarded; if they had siblings, similar details had to be provided about them, so that the position after the parents' death could be guaranteed; a report from the gendarmerie had to be provided to attest their good character.[1] The paradox was that the levels of income required were pathetically small: the officer was a poor man, even if he was obsessed by these monetary considerations. It was not surprising therefore that conscripts from well-to-do families were, in the nineteenth century, treated with more consideration than poor ones. When René Vallery-Radot, of good bourgeois stock, was called up just after the Franco-Prussian war, his hair was cut off and he was set to work at 6 a.m. like everybody else, but the colonel and lieutenants addressed him gently and he was segregated from the masses, together with other bourgeois 'volunteers'. He was allowed to keep his flannel waistcoat, his own shirts and socks. The sergeant amused him by shouting defensively, 'It's me what gives the orders. Well, what's got into you, why are you looking at me like that? Am I not speaking French?'[2]

The attitudes of the N.C.O.s were one major factor in the maintenance of class divisions. They were, as one of them described them in 1882, the 'military bohemians'.[3] They had made the army their life, or at least they dared not leave it when their seven-year term was up, because they had nowhere

[1] Capt. E. Renault, *Du mariage des militaires* (1895).
[2] René Vallery-Radot, *Journal d'un volontaire d'un an au 10e de ligne* (1874), 37.
[3] F. M. J. Dutreuil de Rhins, *La Bohème militaire ou de l'avenir des sous-officiers de l'armée* (Saint-Étienne, 1882).

else to go. They thought a lot about promotion, but they seldom got it. Like artists who never painted the masterpiece they dreamed of and who never won appreciation, the N.C.O.s could barely live off their pay, contracted debts and then joined up for a further term in order to get the 1,000 francs' bounty this brought. If they managed to become sub-lieutenants, they considered themselves worse off than daily labourers, because of the obligations a commission brought. If they retired at forty-five or fifty, they were fit for nothing else, and were as old as civilians of sixty. Some consoled themselves in café life, some in artistic hobbies; later some were to find distraction in sport; few could afford marriage. However, until 1914, the N.C.O.s enjoyed a certain autonomy. The officers kept to themselves, were seldom seen and the adjutants were left in charge. Corporals used to have wide powers of punishment, which required a captain's confirmation only after the reforms of 1905–13. The N.C.O.s were firm believers in hierarchy; discipline restrained them from criticising their officers; but they reflected national attitudes enough to respect a titled officer no more, and no less, than they respected an officer who could ride a horse well. Those who accepted their own limitations looked on the sergeants preparing for entry to Saint-Maixent (with a view to winning commissions) as their intellectual superiors even if they were junior in rank. There were many who did not want to become officers, because they did not feel at home in the officers' world ('it would involve making love to the châtelaine instead of the farmer's wife'). They were content to be instructors, with no pretensions to being educators. They were proud of being masters in their own sphere and relished their power to give or refuse leave. Those who had no academic qualifications enjoyed showing intellectual soldiers their place, to make it clear that intellect was not enough. However, this segregation of ranks was somewhat diminished between the wars, and a certain resentment built up against subalterns who thought they could do the N.C.O.'s job better. The army called this new relationship 'team-work'. A conscript army meant that most officers had to participate in the training of soldiers, rather than leave this task to specialists. There was therefore more contact between different ranks, but not necessarily more social mixing.

The First World War provided those sections of the community which felt unappreciated with a chance to prove their worth. The aristocracy, in particular, saw in it a chance to revive their tradition of military prowess; many of them joined the air force and their bravery was noted; but many ordinary people were equally brave. This equality in the face of danger is said to have ended what remained of the peasants' humility towards the aristocracy, but the change was probably not so fundamental. The relation of peasant and noble was tied up with economic factors which reappeared as soon as they were demobilised; what was probably more important was that the peasant often found himself richer after the war, and the nobleman poorer. The clergy likewise made a reputation for themselves by their spirit of martyrdom and their disregard of danger and death: they won respect on an individual basis but the anticlerical quarrels were too firmly built into the political system to vanish as a result. The intellectuals, for their part, did not emerge as natural leaders in this war. The ordinary soldier showed considerable suspicion of intellectual superiority, and it was the intellectuals who were impressed by the qualities of endurance and humour that the uneducated masses showed. The level of conversation was not generally raised by their presence in the trenches: rather they came down to that of their fellows. They discovered that if they wanted to maintain good relations they had, as one of them put it, to return to the fold, to abandon their aloofness. The war brought to the surface forces in favour of greater egalitarianism, but it also showed that they were by no means all-powerful. There was bitter animosity against those who obtained jobs away from the danger of war. Nevertheless men from the industrial and commercial worlds were largely ill at ease in the army, and many did their best to escape quickly from the front, either back to industry, or into commissions, or into safe jobs in the rear. Those who fought as officers at the front established a tacit pact with their soldiers, by which they got complete obedience in battle, but then withdrew into a sort of reciprocal indifference or broad mutual tolerance. They did not generally make friends with the workers and 'after the storm, these four years of confraternity in arms did not prevent them from resuming their respective places in civil life, each on opposite sides of the barricade'.[1] Two psychologists who studied the effects of the war on individual soldiers claimed that the worker likewise was not basically changed as a result of his military experience. 'Despite the wall that for four years isolated the soldier from his original surroundings, despite his continual impregnation in a new and persistent atmosphere, every *poilu*, with his opinions, attitudes and speech superficially modified, preserved intact his fundamental characteristics.' It was generally city workers, and more especially wine sellers and small shopkeepers, who established themselves as leaders in the little groups of which the army was composed. They gave expression to the spirit of opposition to authority and to the sense of egalitarianism that the soldier felt, which balanced his obedience; their ability to be witty at the expense of the army, to find ways of getting round regulations, but also to work with others, created much of the sense of solidarity that made the co-operation of people of different backgrounds possible. However, 79 per cent of the soldiers at the front were peasants. The war experienced by the peasants and by the rest of society was not entirely the same one. The peasants seem to have borne their war with patient resignation. They were said to have remained as suspicious, egoistical, independent and solitary as ever. They were more respectful of authority than the workers were, but whereas the workers ultimately gave way, the peasants could be obstinate with unshakeable serenity. The peasants consoled themselves with the deep satisfactions they derived from the small items of property they collected and above all from their meals, 'bringing food out of his pockets in every moment of leisure and eating it slowly, religiously, with voluptuousness and concentration'. Soldiers, of whatever class, thus sheltered themselves from the horrors that surrounded them by developing automatic reactions to it, a professional behaviour, escaping with irony, hobbies or physical pleasures whenever they could. Emotion was gradually mastered by distraction and humour.[2]

Few people thought better of the army after 1919 simply because they had served in it. At Saint-Cyr, the first piece of

---

[1] Dr. Louis Huot and Dr. Paul Voivenel, *La Psychologie du soldat* (1918), 44.

[2] Jacques Meyer, *La Vie quotidienne des soldats pendant la grande guerre* (1966). For the more general consequences of the First World War, see chapter 23.

advice young cadets were given was to wear civilian clothes whenever they went into certain districts of Paris, to avoid incidents. 'Among the masses, we were considered the enemy, *les payots*. In bourgeois circles, we were considered imbeciles.' And since officers' pay fell drastically with inflation, some even took on night work as taxi drivers to keep their families and some ate only one meal a day.[1]

There was an obvious lack of concordance between public attitudes to war and state expenditure on it. The army and navy were by far the most expensive items in the budgets, which shows that though politicians talked a great deal about educational and social reform, their priorities were not really altered.[2]

*Budget Expenditure (in million francs)*

|  | 1852 | 1872 | 1891 | 1910 | 1913 | 1930 |
|---|---|---|---|---|---|---|
| Military | 461 | 712 | 1120 | 1520 | 1787 | 15110 |
| Education | 19 | 34 | 194 | 279 | 309 | 3790 |
| Social Services | — | — | — | 93 | 204 | 2140 |
| Public Works | 63 | 109 | 244 | 268 | 269 | 5180 |
| Fine Arts | — | 6 | 8 | 20 | ? | ? |
| Public Debt Interest | 274 | 1075 | 1127 | 1121 | 1165 | 27000 |
| Total | 1525 | 2735 | 3304 | 4265 | 4800 | 61710 |

Now France was of course not unusual in utilising its taxes above all for defence; but the figures illustrate that the nature of its political system made comparatively little difference. Having won universal suffrage and control over their own destinies, the French people exerted no real pressure to diminish this expenditure. Pacifism was preached only by small minorities, and without much practical effect. The reason was that, despite the attractions of peace, force was not discredited. Despite all the hardships of the Napoleonic wars, and all the opposition to the dictatorship they involved, the victories won in those years very quickly turned into a glorious legend, which even liberals like Thiers admired. After the Revolution of 1848, when a new age of fraternity was expected, the republic was strongly

[1] Robert Darcy, *Oraison funèbre pour la vieille armée* (1947), 49–51.

[2] See *Annuaire statistique* (1878 ff.) for budget summaries, but these involve many complications. Cf. Pierre Baudin, *L'Argent de la France* (1914) on some aspects of this; M. Block and Guillaumin, *Annuaire de l'économie politique et de la statistique pour 1857*, 50–1.

attracted by the idea of a war of liberation.[1] Napoleon III, who had an acute understanding of public opinion, at once launched into a series of wars, though he took care to keep them short. His victories in the Crimea and Italy undoubtedly increased his prestige. A writer like Flaubert could protest that these triumphs left him completely cold, but he did so precisely because they excited nearly everyone else. The way the war of 1870 was declared shows how even those who most sincerely desired to put an end to violence in international relations could not escape their atavistic sense of honour, which overrode their utopianism. Émile Ollivier, who was head of the government in that year, was a man of genuinely cosmopolitan culture, passionately fond of Italy, where he frequently travelled, a great admirer of Wagner, husband of the daughter of Liszt, well read in the literature of all Europe, and a firm believer that all peoples have the right to decide their own fate without interference from their neighbours. He rejected the idea of the balance of power as a defensible principle of foreign policy; he insisted that the 'true principle of foreign policy is the principle of non-intervention, precisely because it is the policy of peace'; he denounced all plans for the territorial aggrandisement of France, saying that he wanted his country to be influential 'because it is loved and not because it is feared'; and he looked forward to a Confederation of Europe 'in the manner of the U.S.A.'. But when he was faced with the ambitions of Bismarck, exceptions to his policy of peace revealed themselves. 'The honour of France' had to be preserved and if it was slighted, war was necessary to avenge it. A war was legitimate, he also said, 'when it is desired by a whole nation'. For all his idealism, in the end he gave way to 'popular pressure', or what he judged to be that: his democratic system contained a basic and unavoidable contradiction.[2] For all his pacifism, he also believed that governments should be 'firm'. Militarism was sustained by a much deeper and wider tradition that associated virility with physical strength or brutality.

[1] L. C. Jennings, *France and Europe in 1848* (Oxford, 1973).

[2] Theodore Zeldin, *Émile Ollivier and the Liberal Empire of Napoleon III* (Oxford, 1963), 168–84. On public opinion on the army in this period cf. J. Casevitz, *Une Loi manquée: la Loi Niel 1866–8* (n.d., about 1960) and Gordon Wright, 'Public Opinion and Conscription in France 1866–70', *Journal of Modern History* (Mar. 1942), 26–45.

A peasant who served in the 1914–18 war recorded that when he left home, his mother expressed satisfaction despite her sorrow at his departure, saying 'When one has not been a soldier, one is not a man'.[1] This tradition ultimately overrode all that the economists wrote about war being disastrous for prosperity.[2] The war of 1870–1 was economically disastrous, but after that of 1914–18 it was realised that, if one survived the carnage, one could also make extremely large profits from it.

Under the Second Empire the republicans, having been repressed by Napoleon III's troops, abandoned their original bellicosity, attacked militarism and the 'military spirit' and demanded the suppression of permanent armies. The League for Peace and Liberty, which published a journal called *The United States of Europe* (1867), had as one of its principal organisers Ferdinand Buisson, whom Ferry later appointed director of primary education. Only defensive wars, using the *levée en masse*, were now acceptable. But after 1870 the recovery of Alsace and Lorraine became an essential aim of the republicans, who never quite resolved the contradiction in which this placed them. On the one hand they encouraged military training, even in schools, but on the other they were suspicious of the army, or at least of professional soldiers. One strand of republicanism poured scorn on the 'bandits' whom history had glorified for their barbaric conquests, but another was intensely patriotic, and urged the people to keep their eyes fixed on the frontiers of the lost provinces.[3] It is difficult to be sure how public opinion in general, as opposed to the politicians, felt on this issue; the rhetorical platitudes should not be too easily accepted as expressions of genuine consensus. The hesitations of military reform reflected a wider uncertainty.

In the Third Republic the main advocates of pacifism and anti-militarism were the socialists, who maintained that the army was simply a tool used by the capitalists to keep the proletariat under their yoke; no war was worth fighting, it would only increase the suffering of the masses and involve them in issues which were of no real concern to them. If a war did break

---

[1] J. L. Talmard, *Pages de guerre d'un paysan 1914–18* (Lyon, 1971), 10.
[2] E. Silberner, *The Problem of War in Nineteenth Century Economic Thought* (Princeton, 1946).
[3] Georges Goyau, *L'Idée de patrie et l'humanitarisme 1866–1901* (1903); H. Contamine, *La Revanche 1870–1914* (1957).

out, the workers should declare a general strike and paralyse the state before it could cause any trouble. But though socialist congresses continued to repeat these principles, there were two difficulties: first, that a general strike had little chance of being effective, because French workers were barely unionised; and secondly that the problem of self-defence against invasion was not tackled. It was only Jaurès who finally developed these woolly ideas into a practical programme. He accepted patriotism, provided it was not offensive; and he accepted the need for a policy of defence. He wrote a major work urging the creation of a 'New Army' which he hoped would be a new instrument of national cohesion.[1] Instead of a professional army, which he regarded as inevitably an instrument of aggressive wars, he urged the formation of a citizen army, for which everybody would be trained from the age of thirteen, but which would involve only six months of actual conscript service. Such an army, he thought—and he had the support of a number of officer theoreticians—would be far more formidable than a much smaller professional one. The flaw in this reasoning was the expectation that 'the nation in arms' would necessarily be pacifist. In 1914, at any rate, there was almost no resistance to general mobilisation, and even the socialists found themselves reluctantly and agonisingly compelled to abandon their opposition to the idea of using force.[2] After the war, Léon Blum wrote that the old idea of honour was finally abandoned and that Frenchmen no longer felt the need to fight, in the way they used to, rather than face dishonour.[3] There was some truth in this, but even the socialist party remained divided in its attitude to war.[4] Blum recognised that despite the desire not to repeat the widespread mistake of 1914, 'a dangerous fatalism is in the process of re-establishing itself in the public mind'.[5] The idea of a professional army was abandoned at the very time when Colonel de Gaulle was arguing that technical developments had made any other kind useless, because highly trained technicians were needed to man the new engines of war: the outcome of any struggle, he claimed, would be

[1] Jean Jaurès, *L'Armée nouvelle* (1911, reprinted 1915 and 1932).
[2] Actes du Colloque, *Jaurès et la nation* (Toulouse University, 1965); H. Goldberg, *The Life of Jean Jaurès* (1968), 385-9, 417-74.
[3] Léon Blum, *Les Problèmes de la paix* (1931), 206.
[4] Richard Gombin, *Les Socialistes et la guerre* (1970).        [5] Ibid. viii.

decided by their skill in the first few weeks.[1] Nevertheless military service was reduced to one year and Jaurès's idea of a defensive army was virtually adopted as official policy. The result was that in 1940 France was incapable of meeting the challenge from Germany other than defensively.

In 1914–18, there was no serious threat to the idea of national loyalty in war: the army mutinies of 1917 affected only 30–40,000 men and only 629 soldiers were found guilty in the subsequent courts martial; at no stage did the mutineers stop fighting the enemy; the revolt was against incompetent leadership, not against the war itself.[2] In 1940–4 the idea of collaboration with Germany in the interests of peace was, as will be seen, quite widely accepted as an inevitable necessity, and in some cases even with enthusiasm. But that did not mean that there was a general disillusionment with violence as a political instrument. On the contrary, violence now became more frequent and more brutal than it had ever been in this period. In the wars of 1854–6 and 1859, there was virtually no anger among the soldiers against their enemies. In 1870, there was very little until the Prussians occupied the country; only then, under Gambetta's leadership, did the war, as a German officer noted, 'gradually acquire a hideous character' and atrocities reminiscent of the Thirty Years War were perpetrated, particularly by the volunteer *francs-tireurs*.[3] In 1914–18 for the first time the government applied itself to stimulating hatred of the *Boche* in a propaganda campaign which, however, was more noticeable in print than in conversation. There were some soldiers who derived deep satisfaction from killing Germans, but there were not many who still believed that to die for one's country was the highest good. On the whole, prisoners of war were treated decently and the most common comment on them was that 'they are men like us', *pauvres bougres*.[4] It was only in 1939 that the principle of 'honour' as the basis of war was replaced by hatred of the enemy. Only then were nationalism and violence finally married, though it was a marriage that immediately aroused revulsion.

[1] Charles de Gaulle, *Vers l'armée de métier* (1934).
[2] Guy Pedroncini, *Les Mutineries de 1917* (1967), 308–12.
[3] M. Howard, *The Franco-Prussian War* (1961), 380.
[4] J. Meyer, *La Vie quotidienne des soldats pendant la grande guerre* (1966), 272.

This is a paradoxical conclusion. At the beginning of this period the professional soldier had thought little of death, had accepted the idea of killing others and of being killed himself as simply part of the lot he had chosen. He fought duels on the most trivial pretexts, and it was only in 1857 that, for the first time, an officer was reduced to the ranks for killing another in a duel—though he was recommissioned a year later and ended up a general. Till then, thirty days' detention would have been a more usual reprimand.[1] In the conquest of Algeria, French officers showed themselves capable of extreme cruelty towards their enemies. But as peace descended on Europe, the officer became more and more a bureaucrat and organiser, and as weapons became more complicated, he was increasingly a technician. He ceased to glorify violence and regarded himself essentially as a guardian of peace. But at the same time war became an increasingly murderous business.

The army was indeed united by *esprit de corps* and there undoubtedly was a 'military type' of individual, who could be instantly recognised. This should not cause one to forget that the army was also a microcosm of society at large and, as such, infinitely varied beneath its uniform appearance. It was no accident that Marshal MacMahon, who became the first president of the Third Republic, had hesitated in his youth between becoming a priest or a soldier.[2] There was a great deal in common between these two apparently opposed professions: both were based on a sense of dedication and service to the community and both tended to adopt conservative attitudes. But it should not be surprising, either, that Marshal de Saint-Arnaud, who helped Louis Napoleon carry out the *coup d'état* of 1851, and who therefore has the reputation of a brutal reactionary, should have been an opera singer in his youth, an able musician and a master of four foreign languages. Saint-Arnaud turned to the army as bankrupt authors have turned to novel writing. He had spent his early manhood dissolutely, moving from job to job, falling increasingly into debt. He found in the conquest of Algeria an opportunity to make good, and to restore his fortune. He had nothing to lose: he exhibited extraordinary courage in battle and within

[1] P. Chalmin, *L'Officier français de 1815 à 1870* (1957), 63.
[2] J. Silvestre de Sacy, *Le Maréchal de MacMahon, duc de Magenta 1808–93* (1960).

fourteen years he had risen from the rank of lieutenant to that of general.[1] His was a career that had once been common, under Napoleon I; and under Napoleon III it was still possible for a trooper like Bazaine to become a marshal. Most generals, under the Third Republic, had careers indistinguishable, in the regularity of their promotion and in the obscurity of their services, from those of civil servants, but the army did offer opportunities for very diverse talents. General André, who is remembered for assisting Combes to purge the army of clericals, was a distinguished scientist, who had been top graduate of his year at the Polytechnic, and later its director; he had assisted Littré in the preparation of his dictionary and had many contacts with the scientific and university world.[2]

Eminence in the army could therefore be a qualification for political power, even in the bourgeois Third Republic; generals liked to make names for themselves also as authors, and they were often elected to the French Academy. Philippe Pétain, who had only just scraped into Saint-Cyr (403rd out of 412 admitted), had by the age of fifty-eight reached the rank of colonel and would have retired into oblivion but for the war of 1914. His promotion had been prevented not so much by a lack of distinction—many dull men were promoted above him—nor by his easy morals and his lifelong devotion to women, which made him conclude, in extreme old age, that 'sex and food are the only things that matter', but because he refused to see war as any longer a heroic matter, in which *furia francese* could override all obstacles. He had argued that the experience of 1870-1 had shown that an enemy with superior fire power could not be made to retreat by a heroic offensive, and that far more attention should therefore be given to teaching accurate shooting and to protecting soldiers against enemy guns. When traditional French methods failed in 1914-16, Pétain was given the chance to prove that he was right, and he became the most popular of all generals, because he was regarded as caring about the survival and welfare of his troops. There was in fact nothing specially sentimental in his theory: he was simply adapting old doctrines in the light of technical

[1] Quatrelles l'Épine, *Le Maréchal de Saint-Arnaud* (1929), 1. 39, 107.
[2] Anon., *Les Généraux de l'armée française* (1904) gives the careers of nearly 500 generals then living.

changes. That did not mean that adaptability was what always distinguished him. From 1920 to 1936 he was the dominant influence in defence policy, and throughout that time he continued to reiterate his old ideas, formulated at the end of the nineteenth century, failing to appreciate the revolutionary changes created by the tank and regarding the air force only as an instrument of defence. It was left to a radical politician (Daladier, minister of defence 1936–40) to take the initiative in ordering more tanks; but though France (with England) had more tanks than Germany in 1940, its army was still not trained to use them. Pétain's ambitions inflated as he got older. He arranged for subordinates to write books and articles under his name, giving them an individual stamp by a meticulous correction of style. His breach with Charles de Gaulle dates from 1934, when de Gaulle, who was one of the bright young admirers he employed for this purpose, broke the rules and insisted on claiming personal credit for what he had written: their political estrangement began as an authors' quarrel. Pétain came to believe that as Europe was taken over by military dictatorships, he was better suited than politicians to deal with them; he claimed to be above politics, but did nothing to dissuade the right-wing press from seeing in him the dictator the country needed to end the chaos caused by the politicians. In 1935 *Le Petit Journal* organised a referendum amongst its readers asking them whom they would best like as a dictator. Pétain came top with 38,000 votes, Laval second with 31,000 and Doumergue, the caretaker prime minister, third with 23,000. Pétain's advent to power in 1940 was the result of a long-organised campaign, which he did nothing to discourage. It was later said that he was essentially an actor, who adopted the role of the severe, fatherly old man with calculated ambition.[1]

In Charles de Gaulle, the notion of military service as the highest form of dedication to the country found its fullest and most extraordinary expression. De Gaulle was quickly spotted as an officer of exceptional character and intellect. He was selected to lecture at the Army Staff College while still very

[1] On Pétain's Vichy regime, see below, chapter 22. Cf. Richard Griffiths, *Marshal Pétain* (1970), 173; Henri Amouroux, *Pétain avant Vichy* (1967); D. B. Ralston, *The Army of the Republic: the Place of the Military in the Political Evolution of France 1871–1914* (Cambridge, Mass., 1967); Judith M. Hughes, *To the Maginot Line, The Politics of French Military Preparation in the 1920s* (Cambridge, Mass., 1971).

young, but his superior there, though describing him as brilliant and talented, commented that he 'unfortunately mars these indisputable qualities by his excessive self-confidence, unwillingness to listen to the opinions of others, and his attitude of a king in exile'.[1] This was in 1923. De Gaulle had early decided that 'nothing great can be done without great men, and they are great because they have willed greatness'. He could 'see no other reason for life save to make [his] mark on events'.[2] The most noble cause was to give glory to France, which he regarded not as simply a nation, or a race, but a person, in the way Michelet had done, and he liked to talk of *notre dame la France*. The French army, he said, was 'one of the greatest things in the world'. He had an overriding sense of his own mission and of his own uniqueness. If Pétain took to acting the role of an elder statesman, de Gaulle cultivated his own individuality, so as to become 'destiny's instrument', with a consciousness that leadership was a form of artistry. Neither of them had any original ideas in politics; both had been mildly influenced by the Action Française; but de Gaulle was an intellectual as well as a soldier; he filled his military lectures with quotations from Bergson, Comte, Goethe and Tolstoy; he was acutely aware that power depended on 'charisma', and that 'prestige cannot come without mystery'. Instead of seeking popularity by charm, he distinguished himself by his aloofness. He was concerned not with happiness—which he dismissed as a frivolous ideal—but with distant goals of grandeur and honour. He raised soldiering into an almost religious activity. But if people came to see a national saviour in him, as they did also in Pétain, it was because these soldiers were both outsiders to the political system, rather than because they were soldiers; they were men who refused to compromise, rather than representatives of the army. So the national movements of which they became the head were neither of them militarist.[3]

The history of the army provides a warning against the dangers of 'influence' as a historical idea. It is easy to assert that, because universal military service was established, this had

---

[1] J. R. Tournoux, *Pétain and de Gaulle* (1966) (French original 1964), 46.
[2] C. de Gaulle, *Le Fil de l'épée* (1932).
[3] Stanley Hoffmann, *Decline or Renewal? France since the 1930s* (1974), especially 187–280; A. Werth, *De Gaulle* (1965).

an important effect on the nation; but influence of this kind is very difficult to prove. The army was too complex a body to leave a distinct imprint on those who passed through it. On the contrary, the interest of the army to the historian is rather that it acts as a magnifying lens revealing aspects of national problems, and of personal tensions, more clearly than they can be seen in civil society. Hierarchy and violence were essential features of life in this period, not just of the army. The army helps to show their character. The army, like the criminal courts, enables one to get a glimpse of these forces at work. It shows how Frenchmen had not co-ordinated every side of their behaviour. It is indeed their contradictions that make up their character.

## Crime

How safe was one, and how safe did one feel, when one walked alone at night in Paris in this period? How many people thought it wise to own a fire-arm? How likely was a man to come to blows if he had an argument with a stranger, or with his wife? So much was talked about reason and frater-nity, that one needs to ask also what place violence still had in this society, what were the acceptable limits of cruelty, and to what extent there was agreement about what was right and what was wrong in the use of force between persons, and in dis-putes over property. Was the popularity of crime and detective stories a compensation for an increasing docility of manners?

   In the late eighteenth century, Sebastian Mercier wrote that 'the streets of Paris are as safe at night as they are in the day-time, apart from a few accidents'. But he added that 'all the scandalous offences and all the crimes, which could frighten people and suggest lack of vigilance by those appointed to guard the security of the capital, are hushed up'. There were thus very few court trials for murder; but in four months in 1785, no less than forty-two bodies were fished out of the Seine, and only three were identified. People were thus able to feel safe, because crime was not widely reported; they were probably not as safe as they thought.[1] A century later a senior police official

---

[1] E. Petrovitch, 'Recherches sur la criminalité à Paris dans la seconde moitié du 18ᵉ siècle', *Cahiers des Annales*, no. 33 (1971), 187–261; cf. R. Cobb, *The Police and the People* (1970).

showed that precisely the opposite situation prevailed. In the month of October 1880, no less than 143 nocturnal attacks were reported by the Paris press. So worried did people become that in 1882 Paris cafés were for a time forbidden to stay open beyond 12.30 at night.[1] In 1911 the conseil général of the Seine passed a motion complaining that armed crimes were becoming so frequent that 'to carry a revolver is becoming a habit; men, women and young people carry this arm in the same way as they carry a purse or a bunch of keys'. Between 1880 and 1907 indeed prosecutions for illegally carrying fire-arms increased tenfold, to over 3,000 a year.[2] However, the police claimed that public opinion was quite simply being unduly alarmed by the sensationalism of the press. Of those 143 nocturnal attacks, it said, over a half, on investigation, proved to have been invented by husbands coming home with empty purses and excusing themselves to their wives with dramatic stories. It was quite safe to walk in the streets at night, at least in central Paris. It was only on the external boulevards, in the slummy outskirts of the city, round Clichy, Saint-Ouen, Pantin and Aubervilliers, that it was dangerous, and most of the victims, who were often cab drivers, waiters or bus conductors coming home late, had courted trouble, because they were not sober. Professional criminals haunted these areas, often pretending to be drunk, starting brawls with genuine drunks and then robbing them; by working in groups they had little difficulty in avoiding the police. Because so much more was expected of the police, because there were more offences of which one could be guilty, and because there was now a press to report every incident, people talked constantly about increasing crime rates.

It is uncertain what the truth behind the statistics was, for criminal statistics are notoriously difficult to interpret; changes in the law make comparisons between different periods impossible. What seems to have happened was that the number of people accused of crimes (rather than misdemeanours) fell constantly, and between 1865 and 1927 they fell by more than half:

---

[1] L. Puibaraud, *Les Malfaiteurs de profession* (1893), 12.

[2] Edmond Debruille, *Le Port des armes dites prohibées* (Lille law thesis, 1912), 70, 65; Paul Renard, *Les Armes au point de vue pénal* (Paris law thesis, 1911).

*Numbers accused of crimes*

| 1851 | 7,071 people, i.e. | 19·7 per 100,000 inhabitants |
|------|------|------|
| 1865 | 4,154 ,, | 10·9 ,, |
| 1874 | 5,228 ,, | 14·3 ,, |
| 1900 | 3,278 ,, | 8·4 ,, |
| 1921 | 3,541 ,, | 9·4 ,, |
| 1927 | 1,844 ,, | 4·5 ,, |
| 1940 | 714 ,, | 1·8 ,, |
| 1946 | 1,834 ,, | 4·5 ,, |

This fall, however, is largely to be explained by the leniency of juries; the police increasingly tended to charge people with misdemeanours rather than crimes, in order that they could be tried by judges instead. Altogether the number of people convicted of misdemeanours rose from 237 to 375 per 100,000 inhabitants between 1835 and 1847, and to 444 in 1868. After having thus almost doubled, the figures settled down to a remarkably constant level for the next century. Apart from the two World Wars, the total number of convictions was generally between 490 and 610 per 100,000 inhabitants. This meant that in the course of this century, the total number of offences against the law did increase considerably.

The character of crime, however, altered significantly in these years, so that these total figures conceal much change. In the early 1830s, an average of 135,000 people were charged each year with stealing from forests; in 1835 the state embarked on a policy of settlement out of court, so that in 1855 there were only 75,000 such prosecutions; in 1859 a law gave people the right to settle out of court and these offences greatly diminished. On the other hand the offence of drunkenness, invented in 1873, produced 4,000 accusations in the following year and over 60,000 in 1880 (but this was only one-third of the number of similar prosecutions in England). In 1850, theft was the main offence with which people were charged, but by 1860 fraud had overtaken it. Between 1830 and 1880, thefts rose by 238 per cent, frauds by 323 per cent and 'abuse of confidence' by 630 per cent.[1]

[1] André Davidovitch, 'Criminalité et repression en France depuis un siècle 1851–1952', *Revue française de sociologie* (Jan.–Mar. 1961), 30–49; Michelle Perrot, 'Délinquance et système pénitentiaire en France au 19e siècle', *Annales* (Jan.–Feb. 1975), 67–92.

The criminal statistics give a limited and confusing picture of the dangers of crime. What was probably more influential on public opinion was the growth of the idea of new classes of criminals, who could be seen as concrete and frightening threats. Attention was diverted from the normal violence of ordinary people by the rise of uncontrollable minorities who flouted the very rules of society. In the eighteenth century, there was no idea of criminals in the permanent sense, as a distinct group of people. Much crime was the result of family disputes, and the stronger family ties were, the larger the proportion of murders and assaults that took place within the family.[1] In the course of the nineteenth century, women, who used to play an important part in the violent settlement of disputes of family honour and property, gradually withdrew into a more passive, or at any rate verbal, role: the percentage of prosecutions against women fell by 28 per cent. Women were no longer as dangerous as they had once been, and as they occasionally still were in war and revolution (when their crime rate roughly doubled). Instead there were two new bogies—'the criminal class' and youth.

Balzac in his *Code for Honest Men* warned that 'Thieves form a republic with its own laws, manners . . . and language. Theft is a profession . . .' He estimated that in Paris, with a population of 120,000, there were no less than 10,000 thieves. This was not surprising, he said, because every morning about 20,000 people woke up in Paris not knowing where their next meal was coming from. He pointed out that the garrison of Paris consisted of exactly 20,000 soldiers—and the forces of order and violence thus just held each other in check.[2] During the July Monarchy, crime was considered to be closely associated with poverty and the hordes of immigrants into the slums, suburbs and industrial towns arose as a growing menace.[3] Then elementary applications of anthropology and psychology were invoked to argue that criminals formed a distinct physical type, mentally deficient and physically marked, more brutal

[1] Nicole Castan, 'La criminalité familiale dans le ressort du parlement de Toulouse 1690–1730', *Cahiers des annales* (1971), no. 33, 91–107.

[2] Louis Chevalier, *Classes laborieuses et classes dangereuses à Paris pendant la première moitié du 19ᵉ siècle* (1958), 59–60.

[3] H. A. Frégier, *Des classes dangereuses de la population dans les grandes villes* (1840).

than normal.[1] The theories of the Italian criminologist Lombroso gained credence because they fitted in with French belief in degeneration, the accumulative influence of heredity, alcohol and disease.[2] The criminologist Quetelet argued that people were more violent in the hot south than in the north, but another criminologist, Tarde, pointed out that the difference in behaviour could also be explained by the different degree of urbanisation. Society was therefore held to be to blame for crime, which was increasingly seen as the result of social factors. Durkheim said that crime was a 'normal' rather than a pathological phenomenon, produced by the transformations brought about by the division of labour, which were dissolving old moral ties and leaving individuals without adequate support.[3] Tarde claimed that the majority of murderers and thieves had been abandoned by their parents during childhood, had learnt the criminal way of life on the streets and had found in crime a trade, which they practised in gangs.[4] The question arose therefore of whether criminals were really responsible for their acts and whether society was right to punish them. Public opinion was divided on this. In the nineteenth century juries were very indulgent and tended to acquit as though they felt that only good fortune or accident had saved them from facing trial themselves; but, just when the criminologists were developing theories of diminished responsibility, juries became much more severe and the rate of acquittals fell from 31 to 8.9 per cent between 1901 and 1952. Legal reformers and public opinion were seldom quite in step. The percentage of sentences of over one year's imprisonment fell continuously during the nineteenth century and remained roughly steady till the Second World War. They then climbed back almost to the same rate as during the Second Empire. The outcries against crime were thus largely independent of the real variations in its incidence.

The government, for its part, tied to solve the problem of the criminal class by two different policies. On the one hand it tried to expel hardened criminals from the country; on the

[1] Dr. Charles Perrier, *Les Criminels* (1900).       [2] See chapter 17.

[3] E. Durkheim's articles on crime, published in the *Année sociologique* between 1896 and 1912, are reprinted in *Journal sociologique* (1969).

[4] G. Tarde, *Études pénales et sociales* (1891), *Philosophie pénale* (1890), *La Criminalité comparée* (1890).

other hand, it reduced the length of prison sentences, so that the total number of convicts seemed smaller. France persisted in the policy of transportation of criminals almost throughout this period. In 1854 it stopped building new prisons and passed a law for the transportation to New Caledonia and Guyana of criminals sentenced to hard labour, just when Britain abandoned transportation to Australia. Recidivists were thus systematically got rid of (40 per cent of those coming before the courts were recidivists between 1870 and 1914, but only between 20 and 30 per cent in the interwar years). As a result, the number of convicts in metropolitan prisons fell from nearly 50,000 in 1850 to under 20,000 in 1940. Conditions in the colonies were appallingly inhumane, as Albert Londres's sensational book *Au bagne* (1923) revealed, but it was only in 1938 that transportation was abolished. The apparent decline of the criminal class was, however, due not just to transportation but also to the courts imposing shorter sentences and to the liberation of convicts by amnesties, conditional discharges (instituted in 1885) and suspended sentences (1891). The number of people who were sentenced to imprisonment in fact trebled during the nineteenth century (from 40,000 to 120,000 a year).[1]

Progress thus did not make men more law-abiding, or more reasonable. The crime rates contradicted the faith in education that was the basis of this society. The real crime rates were of course much higher than the statistics suggested. Criminologists pointed out the existence of the 'dark figure of crime', offences not known to the police, and one has estimated that this may be several times higher than the official figure. The proportion of people guilty of an offence against the law undoubtedly increased dramatically, as the number of regulations that could be broken mounted, and public opinion considered infractions of many of them—like tax avoidance and motoring offences—to be venial. Society did not therefore become more honest either. An Italian criminologist, Poletti, argued that the crime rates should be compared with the development of business activity, and he worked out that the increased opportunities for crime were in fact not quite matched by the rise in the crime rates.

[1] Jacques Léauté, *Criminologie et science pénitentiaire* (1972), 698 and *passim*—an excellent general guide.

Attitudes to crime were so emotional because its cause was so uncertain. It was never satisfactorily proved that crime was produced by any of the major trends of this period. Thus though many criminals were alcoholics, there was no direct correlation between crime and the increase in alcohol consumption. Dechristianisation had no effect on crime rates. Victor Hugo had declared that one needed only to open schools in order to close the prisons, but the spread of education made no difference, and the effect of the mass media has not been proved. Drug addiction was also an independent phenomenon. In the 1920s there was a great increase in it: Paris is said to have had 80,000 cocaine addicts in 1924, but these were not otherwise criminals. The consumption of drugs fell drastically after that (80 kilogrammes of heroin was the official estimate in 1939, 12 kg in 1950) without obvious results. After analysing all the evidence, one criminologist recently concluded: 'Criminals are probably not subject to influences different from those which affect non-criminals.' What remained mysterious was the particular combination of factors, shared by criminals and by others, which somehow became an explosive mixture in the former.[1] The trouble with all investigations of these is that they have been based on criminals who have been caught. It is uncertain whether the roughly constant figures of crime meant simply that the police, with their fixed numbers, could deal only with a constant number of cases, or whether crime did reach some kind of saturation point. Thus since 1900 there has been a steady annual murder rate, or at any rate between four and fourteen convicted murderers per million inhabitants. The suicide rate—which is independent of police action—has been similarly steady since 1890. Crime thus had its own laws, which remained impenetrable to the community at large, part of the mystery of human nature. The ministry of justice in 1871 claimed that 28 per cent of crimes of personal violence were due to 'accidental quarrels', 25 per cent to 'hate against individuals', 17 per cent to domestic dissensions, 13 per cent to 'cupidity', 9 per cent to adultery and debauchery, 4 per cent to hatred of the police and 3 per cent to fights in drinking-shops and to gambling. These were causes which could hardly be dealt with by legislation. Human nature did not seem to

[1] Ibid. 410.

be improving. There was no less violence as the country became more educated and more prosperous; at least, more people were accused of violence. In 1846 15,742 people were brought before the courts for 'coups et blessures volontaires'; by 1934 there were 44,942.[1]

The idea of the criminal class was a confused one. It certainly had a basis in truth. France did have its professional gangsters who, in the nineteenth century, showed remarkable cohesion: they formed a number of private militias, membership of which lasted for many years. Later, however, the 'bands' became only temporary alliances, formed from the 'underworld' which was, in the twentieth century, a much looser phenomenon. Already in the 1880s there used to be large teams of burglars specialising in the complete removal of property from unoccupied houses. There were still 'anarchist' gangs after that movement had lost its political importance; in 1912 robberies of banks by men armed with revolvers and explosives and escaping in motor cars became a new form of terror. The motivations of these criminals were a cause of much puzzlement. A journalist who wrote the biographies of one gang of seven showed them to be individualists, vegetarians, fond of reading, quoting Schopenhauer, playing Chopin and doing Swedish exercises, completely contemptuous of the institutions they were robbing.[2] On a humbler level and in smaller groups were the pickpockets, busy in department stores and at the fashionable resorts like Deauville (on which English pickpockets used to descend in large numbers, for a three months' season); there were the professional beggars (often they used to hire babies so as to make their plight appear sadder); in 1892 one man was revealed to have in his employ fifteen children, each of whom earned him thirty francs a day by begging; the young florists on the boulevards were similarly organised, partly as beggars and partly as prostitutes, by prosperous entrepreneurs. But on 1 January and 14 July, the professionals of Paris were swamped by all the maimed and sick from fifty miles around, and even from Brittany—which specialised in diseases of the skin—coming in

[1] Léauté, op. cit. 289.
[2] Émile Michon, *Un Peu de l'âme des bandits. Étude de psychologie criminelle* (n.d., about 1914).

cheap excursion trains, knowing they could earn as much as fifty francs in a day. Beggars were, by tradition, particularly frightening, because superstitition endowed them with evil powers; though the terrifying beggar hordes of the *ancien régime* had vanished, there were still a large number who survived on regular alms, obtained by ambiguous pressure. There was the corporation of dog thieves, with their market on the boulevard de l'Hôpital, who were said to exercise one of the most lucrative illegal professions, and to have a flourishing export trade to England. There were the usurers lending at 25 per cent per day (the barrow boys and women selling garlic, onions, apples and raw herring along the pavements of the rue Saint-Antoine were enslaved by them, borrowing 20 sous in the morning to buy their goods and having to repay 25 in the evening). There was a whole world specialising in confidence tricks, fake marriage bureaux, false employment agencies. Though forgery was punished by hard labour for life, and four or five gangs were convicted every year, it was endlessly popular and one per cent of French silver coins were estimated to be counterfeit; a forger was even discovered inside a prison, using prison cutlery. Crime was a way of life for such people, but all efforts to explain why they had chosen it, or to associate criminality with particular social or psychological circumstances, were unconvincing. In Germany, between the wars, theft and economic depression were shown to go hand in hand; but in France the opposite was proved, as though there was less theft when there was less around to steal. The widely held belief that the poor working class was the most prone to crime was false; peasants, or at least agricultural workers, probably had a higher crime rate, though it was often when they wandered from the land that they got into trouble. In proportion to their total numbers, however, the liberal professions were even more criminal. Crime should rightly have been associated less with urbanisation as such than with travel and movement: in 1877 only eight out of every 100,000 people who still lived in their place of birth were brought before assize courts, but twenty-nine out of every 100,000 who had moved to another department, while no less than forty-one out of 100,000 foreigners suffered the same fate.[1] In 1952

[1] H. Joly, *La France criminelle* (1888), 56, 7.

North African immigrants were arrested and charged roughly one and a half times more frequently than French inhabitants of Paris, but this did not make them, or foreigners and migrants in general, anything like the blacks of the U.S.A., who were prosecuted three times as often as whites.

Juvenile crime was a particular source of concern. Minors constituted between 15 and 18 per cent of persons brought to court.[1] It was established as early as 1831 by Quetelet that the tendency to crime started early, reached its height at the age of twenty-five and then gradually diminished. The law, however, never quite caught up with the implications of this fact. Its principle was, first of all, that minors were not responsible for their offences unless they knowingly intended to do wrong (acting with 'discernment').[2] This distinction between wicked and unfortunate children was a symptom of the law's hesitation between severity towards nascent evil and faith that education could reform the wayward. The apostles of education gradually won the day, on the theoretical plane, but the tradition of severity survived in practice. In 1906 the age of penal minority was raised from 16 to 18; in 1912 all children under thirteen were declared irresponsible and in 1945 this was raised to eighteen years and the question of *discernement* ceased to be asked. Originally children were sent to the same prisons as adults, but there was increasing hesitation about sending them to prison or punishing them at all. Thus the rate of convictions of minors under sixteen rose between 1840 and 1855 but then fell steadily. In 1854 11,026 minors between eight and sixteen were convicted; a century later only 7,066 were. The increase in juvenile crime concerned the sixteen- to twenty-year-olds. In 1831 only some 7,000 of these were convicted, in 1854 27,000, and in 1893 37,000; there was a great fall in convictions in the 1930s ,but during the Second World War a vast increase to unprecedented heights, to be equalled only in the late 1960s, when the figure rose to 47,000.

The problem seemed to be that of the adolescent.[3] It was

[1] Y. Y. Chen, *Études statistiques sur la criminalité en France de 1895 à 1930* (Paris thesis, 1937), 41.

[2] Gustave Mabille, *De la question de discernement relative aux mineurs de seize ans* (1898, Paris doctoral thesis).

[3] Maurice Levade, *La Délinquance des jeunes en France 1825–1968* (1972, 2 volumes of graphs and tables); Jacques Siméon, 'L'Évolution de la criminalité juvénile

established in the 1960s that one-third of juvenile recidivists were orphans: whether the proportion was even higher in the nineteenth century is unknown, but quite likely. The courts had only two rather blunt instruments to meet this situation. The law of 5 August 1850 ordered that convicted children should be detained separately from adults and above all that 'moral, religious and professional education' should be the principal purpose of their detention. Children would not be deported but instead would be sent to 'penitentiary colonies' within France. This law was put into effect very unequally and imperfectly. Fifty years later there were still articles of it which had not been applied. France then had twenty-nine 'colonies' with 6,000 children in them: England had 203 comparable reformatories with 22,000. The French 'colonies' had originally been philanthropic ventures designed to transform young criminals from the slums by rearing them in pastoral surroundings, but compulsory agricultural labour did not instil love of work, and the countryside became more than ever horrible to the children who were forcibly sent there. The 'colonies' became increasingly military in their discipline, and they were twice as expensive as English reformatories because of the superfluity of bureaucrats.[1] They made virtually no contribution to solving the problem of young offenders, beyond isolating them—or rather a few of them—just as adult offenders were isolated in Guyana.[2] The second instrument was the use of private charitable societies to act as guardians for young offenders. The law of 22 July 1912 greatly enlarged the role of these societies, which were the French alternative to a state probation service. They were not particularly successful, and some of them were disguised employment agencies, which exploited the children confided to their care.[3]

The proportion of crimes reported which were followed by prosecution steadily diminished. In 1851–5, only one-third of

depuis 100 ans', in *La Prévention des infractions contre la vie humaine et l'intégrité de la personne*, edited by A. Besson and M. Ancel (1956), 2. 1–32.

[1] Maurice Langlois, *Les Mineurs de l'article 66 du code pénal et la loi du 5 août 1850 (comparaison avec les régimes belge et anglais)* (Paris law thesis, 1898), 131.

[2] Henri Gaillac, *Les Maisons de correction 1830–1945* (1971); Prosper Compans, *De l'exécution de la peine appliquée aux jeunes délinquants* (Paris law thesis, 1896); H. and F. Joubret, *L'Enfance dite coupable* (1946).

[3] H. Donnedieu de Vabres, *La Justice pénale aujourd'hui* (1948), 65–6.

reported crimes led to no action, but by 1940 the proportion had risen to two-thirds. The police were more successful with misdemeanours,[1] but when allowance is made for acquittals, the over-all proportion of offences going unpunished was still two-thirds. Apart from exceptional periods like the early Second Empire, when the number of policemen was increased and their activity stimulated, or periods like 1870–1, when police control greatly deteriorated, a remarkable stability was established in the ratio between the police's rate of prosecution and the extent of crime, as though it was accepted that the police should be undermanned just enough to give the world of crime a sporting chance. This was one measure of the public's sense of security, or of its ambivalent attitude to crime.

Attitudes to violence were complex in this period and the common, optimistic view, that men were beginning to treat each other more gently, was not entirely accurate. On the one hand, it is true, the rights of man were acknowledged in the prohibition of corporal punishment, for criminals as for schoolchildren. This was indeed a great change, even if the prohibition was not rigidly enforced. The rights of man could of course work in the totally opposite direction, as the Revolutionary Terror revealed; the massacres of June 1848, the Commune in 1871 and the Liberation in 1944–5 showed that the French were still as capable of tearing each other to pieces as in the seventeenth century. Torture ceased to be used by the judiciary, as it had been until finally abolished by Louis XVI in 1788, but the capacity for it was not eradicated. In the Second World War, the French had their own torture brigades, copying the methods of the Gestapo, specialising in immersing their victims in cold baths until they nearly drowned; and in the Algerian war brutality reached new levels of refinement.[2] In the nineteenth century, the one thing the French police were not accused of was torturing their prisoners, though it was claimed between the two World Wars that they had a 'room for spontaneous confessions' in the Palais de Justice, the screams from which could be heard four storeys away. Torture now took on new forms, the most effective of which was soli-

---

[1] 58·5 per cent of misdemeanours reported were tried in 1851 (194,000 people involved) but 31 per cent in 1946–60 (269,000 accused).

[2] Pierre Vidal-Naquet, *La Torture dans la république 1954–62* (1972).

tary confinement; since the cells could be dark and window-less, the food reduced to a minimum, there were instances of suspects emerging from this ordeal, after a year or more, virtually destroyed. In 1897 a law forbade solitary confinement for more than ten days, but that was something an examining judge could impose on a suspect without any formal conviction. A standard textbook of police practice, published in 1945, informed policemen that though the law forbade torture, in the sense of violence to the body, there were legitimate forms of it, such as long questioning, forcing suspects to sit in a chair night and day, and depriving them of sleep.[1]

On the other hand, there were forms of violence that large sections of public opinion approved or condoned. The *crime of passion* aroused fascinated and ultimately sympathetic awe. It was at bottom the traditional right to honour and revenge, but given a new twist by the influence of romanticism. Since the jury that tried this kind of crime was asked not just whether the accused had indeed committed it but also whether he was *culpable*, there was ample opportunity for public opinion to express itself. This was a domain in which literature could perhaps claim to have influenced values: Alexandre Dumas is said to have appeared at assize courts, standing behind the presiding judge, as though to ensure that the rights of passion, exalted to the point that they gave the right to kill, should be recognised. Murder thus did not inspire horror if it was committed in the name of the 'right to love', and the phrase 'I shall kill him and I shall be acquitted' became an expletive of daily conversation. Because of the clemency of juries, crimes of passion increased in this period, taking on an almost standard uniformity: the criminal who immediately surrendered to the police, avowing his deed, confessing all his private troubles, invoking uncontrollable emotions, regretting them and weeping over them, had a good chance of acquittal. Thus the actress Marie Bière who in 1879 shot a lover determined to break with her was acquitted after only a few minutes' deliberation: she had won sympathy by relating his cruelty to her—his trying

---

[1] Raymond Aron, *Histoire et dialectique de la violence* (1973); M. Amiot and J. Onimus, *La Violence dans le monde actuel* (Nice, 1968); A. Mellor, *La Torture. Son histoire, son abolition, sa réapparition au 20ᵉ siècle* (new edition, 1961), quoting L. Lambert, *Traité théorique et pratique de police judiciaire* (1945), 209.

to force her to abort their child, his refusal to recognise her—
and by admitting the lies she told him so as to have another
child by him, when this first one died, declaring 'All mothers
will understand me'. The poet Clovis Hugues was in 1878
acquitted of murdering a journalist, whom he shot in a duel
to vindicate his wife's honour. His wife, five years later, shot
another man who had insulted her; his death was slow and
horribly agonising, but in court she declared that she had
suffered even more than he, because of his slanders, and she
was acquitted. The vendetta survived in Corsica despite all the
principles of French law. A certain Antoine Bonelli, condemned
to death several times for various murders in the course of
family quarrels, took to the hills and avoided justice for about
forty years; when he tired of this life, he gave himself up (1892),
was acquitted by a jury and spent his old age as a legendary
testimony of traditional rights of honour. Between the wars,
however, attitudes became somewhat less lenient. Thus in
1934 a prostitute called Nini was given two years' imprisonment for killing her lover, Causeret, the prefect of the Bouches-
du-Rhône. She was a remarkable woman: when plying her
trade in a cheap hotel in the rue des Archives, she had been
visited by the best-selling novelist Pierre Decourcelle, in
search of material for his books. He advised her to change her
name to Germaine d'Anglemont and to move to the more
fashionable quarter of the Champs-Élysées. There indeed
she quickly made her fortune, receiving journalists, ministers
and politicians, becoming engaged to a Bavarian prince, but
going off with a Polish ambassador, then becoming mistress
to the president of Mexico and the prime minister of Yugo-
slavia as well as a spy for the Deuxième Bureau during the
First World War. Finally she ended up as mistress to this
prefect, whom she shot when he tried to abandon her. She
illustrates how, when private lives were made public in the
lawcourts, juries hastened to declare that they should not be
subject to the ordinary rules. In that sense the right to privacy,
even carried to the extreme of murder, was a passionately
held principle.[1]

But only certain forms of violence were condoned. The law

[1] Dr. Hélie Courtis, *Étude médico-légale des crimes passionnels* (Toulouse, 1910);
Maurice Garçon, *Histoire de la justice sous la troisième république* (1957), 3. 105–35.

indeed made a specific distinction between murders committed on impulse and those involving premeditation: it singled out poisoning as a method of murder that aggravated the seriousness of the crime. Poisoning reached its peak in 1836–40, when the courts judged on average forty-one cases a year: the numbers then declined steadily to eighteen a year by the early 1870s. Poisoning used to be the speciality of the upper classes; it now became the crime of illiterates. Men used to be the more frequent offenders until 1847; since then women have been responsible for 70 per cent of cases. Once the death penalty ceased to be mandatory for it in 1832, juries had no hesitation in convicting, though curiosity about the crime was as great as abhorrence of it. Madame Lafarge, sentenced to hard labour for life, wrote her memoirs and retained her fame for a whole generation.[1] What juries would not forgive was the calculating cupidity that was often behind these crimes. They were indulgent, however, towards sexual offences: out of 592 people accused of these in 1888, 174 were acquitted and 194 were accorded extenuating circumstances, so that only a small number suffered the full rigour of the law. Juries tended to be severe only when a child was given venereal disease by an assault; they were not worried by the moral implications. Cases of rape usually revealed so much violence within the families of the victims, that it was the parents' demeanour at the trial that was often decisive: the honest workman who pleaded that he had done his best to raise his daughter honourably and now a lascivious man had ruined her reputation, could get a conviction against a rapist by appealing to the emotions of the jurors, as one parent to another. There was much subtlety therefore in public attitudes to crime. The feeling that some people could not expect protection from violence was widespread. Juries were merciless to tyrannical or arrogant people; they were easily won over by pretty women, distinction of one sort or another, and appeals to their emotions.[2] Able barristers could sway them from one extreme to another, so that there was inevitably much inconsistency in the way crime was punished. Fashions in forensic oratory introduced several extraneous elements into judgments. The classical style,

---

[1] Raoul Sautter, *Étude sur le crime d'empoisonnement* (Paris law thesis, 1896).
[2] Bérard des Glajeux, *Souvenirs d'un président d'assises 1880–1890* (1892), 2. 128–33.

in which verbal elegance predominated, could involve speeches lasting several days, to which judges listened as they might to the reading of good verse; the romantic style, which not infrequently meant the barrister ended his peroration weeping profusely, made trials into melodramatic theatrical performances. Frédéric Lenté, who defended Wilson, President Grévy's son-in-law accused of corruption, spoke in a voice smothered by sobs and on finishing 'covered his face with his pale hands and wept'.[1] The 'modern' style, introduced around 1890 by Henri-Robert, brief, logical, simplified, might have transformed the judicial process if it had been universally adopted, but vestiges of the older traditions survived.

Physical violence within the family probably diminished, but it is difficult to generalise about violence in ordinary life, because sensitivity to pain increased very unevenly in this period and the idea of what constituted violence must have changed. Before the introduction of anaesthetics in the mid-nineteenth century, surgeons performed amputations which were stoically borne. The use of analgesics spread only gradually to the poor. It was when men feared pain that cruelty was seen as a vice. Other values could excuse cruelty: the capacity to be cruel was a sign of manliness, and, as *Poil de Carotte* showed, parents could feel virtuous if they made their children suffer. It was said that women led the movement against cruelty to animals, as a consolation for the brutality they endured from men; there was certainly much wanton cruelty to oppose. Maupassant, for example, was proud of his walking-stick, with which, he said, he had killed at least twenty dogs. Flaubert, in *Bouvard et Pécuchet*, describes a man boiling a cat alive, explaining that there could be no objection to this since the cat belonged to him. The penal code concerned itself indeed with the protection of animals only in so far as they were one type of property. In 1850 a law, sponsored by and named after General de Grammont, for the first time made cruelty to animals an offence, but only if the cruelty was public, 'abusive', and the animal domestic; punishment of an animal's refusal to obey was exempted. It was almost impossible to secure prosecutions under this law, and another law of 1898, which ended the need for the cruelty to be public, was useless because no

[1] Henri-Robert, *Le Palais et la ville. Souvenirs* (1930), 103.

sanctions were imposed. Societies for the Protection of Animals grew up, but they were unable to institute prosecutions themselves, because they had suffered no direct damage; only in 1929 did court decisions allow them more scope. So though the Third Republic made love of animals one of the commandments it tried to instil into children, the idea that animals could suffer, or that there was anything wrong with obtaining pleasure from their suffering, was by no means universal. Games in which turkeys were made to dance on red-hot platforms; or in which spectators hurled stones at pigeons placed in boxes, their heads stuck out to receive the blows; brutality in slaughter-houses, where for example sheep's eyes were gouged out before they were killed; these practices were ac-accepted by many, and seemed appalling at first only to rather eccentric, over-sensitive people. Cruelty remained one form of voluptuousness; and some sports, as has been seen, were a way of giving a new significance, new purposes and new controls to older rituals of violence.[1]

Perhaps that is why *ancien régime* traditions of severity towards accused persons continued to be tolerated. France had thirty times as many judges as England, because some of its judges were also investigating and prosecuting officials. Though judges had security of tenure (occasionally waived, as in 1883), they were divided into many categories, and their struggle for promotion made them susceptible to political and other influences. In 1930 an English county court judge (the lowest paid in the country) drew a salary higher than that of the First President of the Court of Cassation, the most senior in France.[2] French judges were officials more than independent arbiters. That is one reason why barristers were so often political figures, defending individuals against the state: judges were not chosen from among the most successful barristers, but were civil servants, who had opted for state service in their youth.[3]

[1] René Guyon, *La Cruauté* (1927); Léonce de Cazenove, *Considérations sur les sociétés protectrices des animaux* (Lyon, 1865); Dr. Ph. Maréchal, *L'Évolution de l'opinion publique sur les courses de taureaux* (1907); Pierre Giberne, *La Protection juridique des animaux* (Montpellier law thesis, Nîmes, 1931), 91; Bernard Jen, *Le Sport, la mort, la violence* (1972); 'Comprendre l'agressivité', special issue of *Revue internationale des sciences sociales* (UNESCO) (1971), vol. 23, no. 1.
[2] R. C. K. Ensor, *Courts and Judges in France, Germany and England* (Oxford, 1933).
[3] Paul Lallemand, *Le Recrutement des juges* (Paris law thesis, 1936).

Until 1898 an accused person was entirely at the mercy of the examining magistrate (the *juge d'instruction*) who could arrest him and keep him in custody while he collected evidence against him. The proportion of accused who were kept in gaol before trial greatly diminished in the course of the twentieth century, but on the other hand the length of time those who were detained spent there increased very markedly: in 1901 only 7·4 per cent of those held in provisional custody spent more than a month in prison before trial, but between the two wars 16 to 25 per cent did, while in the 1950s and 1960s 40 to 50 per cent did. Only after 1898 was the accused entitled to legal aid from the moment of his arrest (as opposed to having the right to it at his trial). Severe limitations on the right to cross-examine meant that trials were simply occasions for speeches by witnesses and advocates. The depositions of the police, if properly drawn up, were accepted as irrefutable evidence of fact.[1] Justice depended therefore a great deal on the judges.

But one should not criticise this system simply because it was not based on habeas corpus and was so different from the Anglo-Saxon model. Frenchmen were protected in their liberties by the very complexities of their judicial system. Rivalry between the officials was one guarantee: if the *parquet* started a case, the *juge d'instruction* would often try to pull it to pieces simply as a matter of pride. Many officials needed to reach agreement before a man was accused.[2] It is true that repeated attempts to reform criminal procedure were not successful in this period.[3] The individual, however, was increasingly able to sue the state for its misdeeds before the Conseil d'État, and in the course of the twentieth century this power was greatly expanded as a result of that court's growing will to be independent. In the 1870s an average of 1,253 cases against civil servants were referred to the Conseil d'État each year. By 1913 this figure had almost trebled to 4,275.[4] The individual

---

[1] A. L. Wright, 'French Criminal Procedure', *Law Quarterly Review* (1928), vol. 44, 324–43; (1929), vol. 45, 92–117.

[2] C. J. Hamson, 'The Prosecution of the accused. English and French legal methods', *Criminal Law Review* (1955), 272–82.

[3] René Daud and H. P. de Vries, *The French Legal System* (New York, 1958).

[4] Joseph Barthélemy, *Le Gouvernement de la France. Tableau des institutions politiques, administratives et judiciaires de la France contemporaine* (1939), 215–17.

was also protected by the freedom of the press, though this was a double-edged weapon. Newspapers made it possible for the discussion of crime to be a favourite popular pastime; the obsession with its sensational aspects often led to pressure being exerted on juries and judges which, in England for example, would be regarded as gross contempt of court. France retained the death penalty and it was only in 1939 that public executions were finally abolished. It is true that since 1848 these were held at dawn to minimise the danger of disturbance, and that the scaffold was abolished in 1870; but there were still occasions on which executions took place before large crowds—like that of the murderer Momble in Paris in 1869, carried out with medieval publicity. The guillotine ceased to be used in 1905 while parliament considered its abolition, but it was brought back into service in 1909 when the debates had no result, and the first occasion of its revived use—at Béthune—was the scene of appalling savagery in the crowds, whose interest had been aroused by the press, which photographed and filmed the whole proceedings.[1]

So much was talked about reason, and so much faith was put in it, that violence remained largely incomprehensible. The attitude towards it was always to blame it on one thing or another. Perhaps the punishments imposed contributed to its growth. When Durkheim argued that violence and crime were inevitable, normal features of society, most people found this impossible to accept. The main interest of criminal history to the general historian is perhaps that it shows that the variety of human nature is beyond analysis and beyond reform. Why, of two people with identical backgrounds, one should become a murderer, or engage in petty fraud, and the other obey the law, or succeed in evading detection, cannot be explained by any valid generalisation. That, ultimately, may account for the popularity of crime fiction, which, better than the law, freed improbability from the constraints of reason.

## The Colonies

The extent to which hierarchy and violence were elements in the French civilisation of this period (accepted, tolerated, or

[1] G. O. Junosza-Zdrojewski, *Le Crime et la presse* (1943), 183.

ignored) may be gauged from a look at the colonies. Their history has, until very recently, been presented largely as a glorious epic, because their historians were usually emotionally involved in them; the oppression and inequality which colonial administrators imposed on millions of foreigners was not the aspect that attracted particular attention.[1] The contradictions between the liberties and values Frenchmen believed themselves to be fighting for at home and the tyranny they imposed on those they conquered were for long not generally seen as such, partly because colonial life formed a separate world, which most people largely ignored, and partly because the abuses of colonial life simply magnified features of French society, which Frenchmen had learnt to live with. The countries conquered by the French were offered various blends of three different kinds of inequality, all of which existed in embryo in France: military hierarchy, capitalist exploitation and the inequality that came from political corruption and favouritism.[2]

The colonies were, first of all, the creation of the French army and navy. Between the Napoleonic wars and the First World War, it was in the colonies that soldiers got most of their experience of battle and a chance to put their ideas into practice. It was mainly there that military reputations were made and promotion won. A whole edifice of self-esteem was built on the histories of the glory won in subduing various colonial peoples. The colonial wars provided many people with deep satisfactions. It was seldom pointed out how inefficiently and barbarically the subjugation was achieved, or at what expense the glory was bought. A great European power, with a formidable military tradition, able to draw on a population of over thirty million, took fifteen years to reduce four million Algerians to subjection. The war of the Algerian conquest was horrific in its violence. The army's principle was to kill and destroy every

---

[1] For a critique of historical writing on the colonies, see J. C. Vatin, *L'Algérie politique: histoire et société* (1974), 17–80.

[2] [René Couret] *Guide bibliographique sommaire d'histoire militaire et coloniale française* (Service historique, ministère des armées, 1969), 315–483; S. H. Roberts, *The History of French Colonial Policy 1870–1925* (1929); J. Ganiage, *L'Expansion coloniale de la France sous la troisième république 1871–1914* (1968); Henri Brunschwig, *French Colonialism 1871–1914, Myths and Realities* (1966, French original 1960); C. A. Julien, *Les Techniciens de la colonisation* (1946), 55–156; R. Delavignette and C. A. Julien, *Les Constructeurs de la France d'outre-mer* (1946).

obstacle in its path. It raised this into a technique known as the *razzia*, involving the systematic sacking and burning of village after village. There was not so much fighting as devastation, and the reward for the soldiers was not just promotion but booty. The army was a cobweb of cliques and clans, each of which sought to build up its power over the natives, to extort presents for protection, to get rich as fast as possible. Tocqueville, who visited Algeria in 1841, reported (even though he approved the method of razzias) that it was carried so far that 'we are now making war in a way that is much more barbarous than that the Arabs themselves use'. Because the French could not defeat the Arabs militarily, they reduced them by famine and destruction. After the First World War Marshal Lyautey used more tact and sometimes succeeded in obtaining submission with only a show of force, but his methods still included starving the tribesmen by driving them out of their pastures, machine-gunning any who tried to work in the fields, and finally burning their villages.

However, the army did not preach repression as a system of government. The empire was conquered by soldiers (or in the case of Indo-China, by the navy), and so for long the military had a dominant influence on the way the natives were treated. Their prime aim was to keep the colonies under their own control. They were the opponents therefore not only of the natives but also of the Frenchmen who came to settle or to make money in the wake of the conquest; and as a result, they often set themselves up as the defenders of the natives against exploitation by the colonists. Marshal Bugeaud, the conqueror of Algeria, who started this tradition, was able to give it force because in his day there were still as many soldiers as colonists in the province: in 1846 there were 104,000 of the former and 109,000 of the latter. Bugeaud had a profound contempt for the civilian colonists, whom he considered to be the dregs of French society: he tried to protect the Arabs against their depredations, and to use the army instead to develop the country, turning it in effect into a great public-works organisation, building roads and clearing land. Bugeaud was of peasant origin and he appreciated that Arab peasants loved their soil: he was their ally against the city speculators. He respected tradition and so maintained the Arab system of taxation. The army thus emerged not only as conquerors of the natives but also as their protectors against the capitalists and the middlemen who tried to exploit them too. Once the natives stopped fighting, the army became the advocate of paternalism. The colonies provided scope for it to express its belief in hierarchy. This often involved respect for the traditional organisation of native societies, but on the condition that they accepted an inferior status.

Napoleon III, while persecuting his political enemies in France, also set himself up as the protector of the Arabs, but he had a somewhat different vision of their future. He was influenced by Ismail Urbain, the son of a Marseille merchant and a Guyanese, who, conscious of his illegitimacy as well as of his coloured skin, devoted his life to championing oppressed people against racial discrimination. Urbain, who became a Muslim and married an Algerian Muslim girl, published a manifesto with the motto 'Algeria for the Algerians' (1861). Napoleon was convinced by it and so inaugurated a policy which took as its basis that there should be 'perfect equality between the Europeans and the natives'; he declared himself to be Emperor of the Arabs as well as of the French; and looked forward to coexistence between the races, on the principle of the Arabs concentrating on agriculture while the Europeans confined themselves to industry, mines, public works and the introduction of new crops. Free concessions of land would no longer be given to European settlers; the Arabs' right to their property was to be officially recognised for the first time; the Arab chiefs were to be treated with courtesy and respect. But though Napoleon's liking for the Arabs was as genuine as his dislike for the French colonists, what he was offering Algeria was not so much equality as capitalist exploitation. The state would no longer confiscate the land, but it would use private financiers to develop the country. The guarantee of Arab property turned out to be disruptive, because it allowed the transfer of communal property into private ownership; and the Europeans were able to buy up the land cheaply. The Arabs were given only very limited political rights. The legacy of the Second Empire was that it became possible to turn the Arabs from landowners into labourers, as they increasingly fell into debt to the Europeans and were forced or persuaded to sell up. Economic inequalities were thus vastly increased. The colonies were to provide golden opportunities for profiteering at the expense of the natives.[1]

Comparatively few Frenchmen went abroad as colonists, but they nevertheless managed to acquire formidable power, both over the natives and *vis-à-vis* the government of Paris. This was no accident, for it followed from the way the political system worked. The colonists came into their own with the Third Republic. This was at once shown by the way the Algerian rebellion of 1871 was quashed: 70 per cent of the wealth of the 800,000 Muslims involved was confiscated. The impoverishment of the native population now ceased to encounter any barriers. The land laws were so applied that the natives' rights were turned topsy-turvy and colonists were able to buy, in the space of fourteen years, 377 million hectares of land for only 37 million francs. The forests, which in 1851 the government had declared to be state property, had French law applied to them, so that the natives lost their valuable forest rights; collective fines for numerous offences in forest areas were imposed on tribes, which were soon ruined by them; the forests came to yield a larger income from fines than from timber. Parts of the forests were sold, under pressure, to the colonists, for between 1 and 3 per cent of their value. The French took over the Arab taxation system but gradually increased the amounts levied so that the land tax in Algeria came to be about three times higher than that imposed on mainland France. One of the reasons for this was that the corrupt system of collection meant that a great deal disappeared into the hands of officials. French rule for the Arabs brought an effective increase in taxation of 50 per cent between 1860 and 1890: they did not even have the satisfaction of feeling that this made them the equal of Frenchmen, entitled to the same benefits, for they got very little in return and yet they paid special taxes additional to those, paid by Europeans. They had no control over how this money was spent, for they did not have a vote in parliamentary elections, nor enjoy the right to stand for parliament. They had, it is true, representatives on municipal councils: but until 1884 these were

[1] C. A. Julien, *Histoire de l'Algérie contemporaine: la conquête et les débuts de la colonisation 1827–71* (1964) contains the best bibliography for this period, and is itself the best book on it.

appointed by the government and after that only 50,000 of the 4,500,000 Muslims were allowed to participate in municipal elections, and they moreover were entitled to elect only one-quarter of the councillors. Until 1919 these Muslim councillors were not even allowed to vote to choose the mayor. In 1870 Émile Ollivier had proposed to give the Muslims parliamentary representation in Paris, but his republican opponent Jules Faure protested in horror against the 'appearance in this house of a Native'. The republican municipal law of 1884, which was the basis of French municipal liberties, in Algeria had the effect of disenfranchising the Arabs still further.

This could hardly be justified on the grounds of education for the Algerians had been literate in roughly the same proportion as the French when they were first conquered. If they were more illiterate after that, it was largely the doing of the French, for the war disrupted the education of a whole generation and then, when Ferry's compulsory primary education law was passed, its effect in Algeria was to hand over the control of the state village schools to the white colonists, who had no wish to enforce obligatory attendance on the Muslims. As a result in 1889 there were only 10,000 Muslim children in these schools, which was under 2 per cent of those who should have attended. Ferry's legislation simply damaged the Arab Koranic schools. Though liberty of religion was proclaimed, the conquest meant the confiscation of religious endowments, and though Catholic priests were paid salaries by the state, only 78 out of 1,494 mosques were accepted as eligible for state support. The religious fraternities were increasingly regarded as dangerous secret societies and attempts were even made to stop pilgrimages to Mecca. The Arabs were entitled to become full French citizens, but only on condition that they abandoned their adherence to Muslim law: no more than a few hundred did so. They were not allowed to maintain their own judicial system. Napoleon III had restored the power of the *cadis*, who had been dispossessed of their jurisdiction in the conquest, but the first work of the Third Republic was to replace them by French *juges de paix*. These posts were the most junior in the French legal service and were generally given to young men of poor families, who could not afford to start their careers as unpaid assistant judges in France (for judges began in an unpaid capacity). They generally stayed only for a few years, and seldom knew Arabic. Thus though Muslim law was recognised, the judges were ignorant of it. In criminal law, the principle of the separation of judicial and administrative power was overridden: the civil service had power to fine and imprison Muslims (until 1928). The gradual extension of the civil territory and the withdrawal of power from the army did not give the Muslims the rights of French civilians: it merely subjected them to the arbitrary rule of the civil service. The French were more favourable to the Kabyls, about whom they created fanciful myths. This was largely because, in reply to Napoleon's glorification of Arab chivalry, the colonists attempted to strengthen their position by a policy of dividing the natives: they declared that the Arabs were an inferior race, while the Kabyls were less religious, less fanatical and therefore capable of accepting French civilisation. The result was that the Kabyls were taxed less and given more schooling. To the Kabyls, this seemed simply a more vigorous attack on their institutions, and the effort to separate Berbers from Arabs was totally unsuccessful.[1]

The imposition of such an oppressive regime was made possible by the skill with which the colonists exploited the French political system. Under Napoleon III, the colonists had been enemies of the government, but that had got them nowhere. Algeria became, however, a nursery of republicanism. It provided safe seats for republicans, and many eminent politicians thus became defenders of the colonists who elected them: Sadi Carnot, Albert Grévy, Spuller, Constans, Paul Bert all represented Algeria. Above all Gambetta became the patron of a succession of local politicians, who through him obtained considerable power in Paris and were thus able to build up their influence in Algeria. Life in Algeria was always intensely political, even more than in the South of France, and it was dominated by personal considerations and organised in clienteles. The man who developed the most successful system was Eugène Étienne (1844–1921), a close friend of Gambetta,

[1] C. R. Ageron, *Les Algériens musulmans et la France 1871–1969* (2 vols., 1968); Vincent Confer, *France and Algeria: The Problem of Civil and Political Reform 1870–1920* (Syracuse U.P., 1966); R. Le Tourneau, *Évolution politique de l'Afrique du Nord musulmane 1920–61* (1962); J. Berque, *Le Maghreb entre deux guerres* (1962); Y. Turin, *Affrontements culturels dans l'Algérie coloniale: écoles, médecines, religion 1830–80* (1971).

as warm and charming as him, always friendly, a florid orator and a master of both political and business negotiations. Étienne, thanks to his boyhood friendship with another influential politician, Rouvier, became under-secretary of state for Algeria (1887 and 1889–92), long enough to fill the Paris administration with well-disposed civil servants. He established a tradition that Algerian affairs should be left to the Algerian deputies, on the tit-for-tat principle. A colonial group was organised in parliament not out of opposition deputies but out of the regular supporters of all governments. The senate, particularly, cemented the link between republican loyalty and colonial interests. Important colonial laws were thus passed through the Paris parliament with only a few dozen members present or voting. The minister of the colonies, when he was not a representative of the colonists, accepted a secondary role: Clemenceau's nominee, for example, took on the portfolio (1906) announcing that he would follow the advice of 'my eminent friend Monsieur Étienne'. In France, the advocates of the colonies were organised into a series of interrelated pressure groups—the Committee for French Africa, for Madagascar, for Morocco, for Indo-China etc.—which were able to exercise great influence by obtaining key positions in the colonies and even by being left to draw up their own instructions when appointed to negotiate with foreign governments.[1]

The colonies were supposed to be outposts of French civilisation, but they developed a civilisation of their own, though it was a long time before the home country realised this. The people who went to Algeria wanted to get away from France. They were not concerned with spreading the gospel of the French Revolution but with having an easier life. They were probably the least intellectual and religious part of the nation. Their pleasures were above all physical: they were devotees of swimming and sun-bathing, of hunting and of dancing. When Gide visited them at the beginning of the twentieth century, they struck him as 'a new race, proud, voluptuous, vigorous', emphasising practicality, money-making, building. Camus, who was born in Algeria, said the Europeans in it

[1] On the colonial party see C. M. Andrew's articles in the *Historical Journal* (1971 and 1974) and the *Transactions of the Royal Historical Society* (1976) (and for the diplomatic angle, his *Théophile Delcassé and the Making of the Entente Cordiale* (1968)).

were 'a people who had placed all their goods in this world'. These were not Frenchmen seeking security, but gamblers for higher stakes. They were almost as different from Frenchmen as the Americans were from Englishmen, and not least because there were soon more people of non-French origin among the settlers in Algeria than there were Frenchmen. These were mostly Spaniards and Italians, who were quickly granted naturalisation. French nationality was for them above all a guarantee of privilege. Algerians even spoke their own kind of French.[1] It was mainly to Algeria that the French went out as settlers, with the intention of working the soil, though once there they quickly gathered in the towns: in 1954 only one-tenth of them were farmers. Algerians of French and European origin included a sizeable proletariat amongst them, and these were, not surprisingly, passionately attached to the status that distinguished them from almost equally poor Muslims.[2]

The administrators sent out to govern the empire were, as the Governor of Senegal wrote in 1879, largely 'lost children of the mother country', 'persons who if not compromised at home were at least incapable of making a livelihood there'. Until 1912 no educational qualifications, not even the *baccalauréat*, were required of them, and a career in the colonies had none of the prestige that it did in England. An *École Coloniale* was founded in 1885 to train administrators, but by 1914 it was responsible for only one-fifth of those serving. Recruitment continued to be based on favouritism and accident. It was only after 1920 that appointments to the Colonial Corps were restricted to graduates of this school, and only after 1926, when Georges Hardy was put in charge of it, that its standard began to rise; it was only in the 1930s that the colonial school could in any way be considered comparable to the other *grandes écoles*. For long the best graduates chose to go to Indo-China, where promotion was said to be quicker and the climate better; the worst were sent to Africa—as was, for example, Félix Éboué who came one before last in his examinations. For most of this period these graduates constituted a small élite. The majority of administrators were junior officials promoted from the ranks to highly

[1] A. Lanly, *Le Français d'Afrique du Nord* (1962).
[2] Marc Baroli, *La Vie quotidienne des Français en Algérie 1830–1914* (1967). Cf. Albert Memmi, *Portrait du colonisé, précédé du portrait du colonisateur* (1966).

responsible positions, despite their acknowledged unsuitability and inadequacy.

These men were allowed to rule the colonies with the minimum of control, either from Paris or from their local governors. Individual initiative was raised into a cult which made the kind of policy actually implemented depend above all on the person on the spot. Gallieni abolished slavery in Madagascar, but his subordinates virtually perpetuated it by developing a system of labour dues. Most administrators kept their superiors ignorant of what they were doing: 'When I am on an expedition', wrote one, 'my first concern is to cut the telegraph line.' Maurice Delafosse, who ended his career as a governor, said that he was unable to keep up with the stream of regulations and circulars he received, so he just forgot about them, 'leaving it to chance to guide me'. Another governor claimed that in his thirty years in the colonial administration, he never even received an instruction from the ministry of colonies, whose function he saw only as 'to receive our requests and transform them into decrees'. Until 1919, there were practically no officials in the ministry of colonies who had ever been in the colonies. The Colonial Corps was kept distinct from the domestic civil service until 1942; it received far fewer honours and decorations than any other section of the bureaucracy (in 1910 it still got no more medals of the Legion of Honour than it had in 1887, though its size had increased twentyfold). Far lower standards of behaviour and of honesty were tolerated: embezzlers, drunkards, rapists were simply transferred to other colonies when they became too inconvenient. It is against this background that the minority of outstandingly able or eloquent governors should be seen.[1]

Marshal Lyautey (1854–1934) was the most famous of these. His career and policies became the inspiration of the idealistic administrators, who saw their role as one of education rather than simply of power or exploitation. Lyautey's most important achievement was the building-up of the Moroccan protectorate as the most attractive part of the French empire, for settlers as

---

[1] Robert Delavignette, *Les Vrais Chefs de l'empire* (1939); William B. Cohen, *Rulers of Empire. The French Colonial Service in Africa* (Stanford, 1971); D. C. Rigollot, 'L'École Coloniale 1885–1939' (unpublished mémoire, Paris School of Political Sciences, 1970).

well as capitalists. What he did is particularly noteworthy, because his work represented a revised version of French colonial methods. He took it as his basic assumption that the Algerian experiment had been a failure. He tried to cut off Morocco from Algeria, to treat it as a completely separate world, forbidding even the importation of all Arabic newspapers. His declared aim was to make a love match between Morocco and France. To many admirers, he gave the impression that he was successful, first because he was indeed a man of quite outstanding gifts and secondly because he was an incomparable propagandist and charmer. He became the hero and the model for young people seeking to dedicate themselves to a noble cause in a practical way, and not content simply to express themselves by writing novels. Lyautey was the epitome of the man of action, constantly on the move, sleeping only five hours a day, finding everything he encountered interesting, praising hard work and overwork, working too fast, and moved by an undisguised passion for power. The basis of his restlessness was not boredom but, as he himself said, 'moral solitude', which was what he feared most. Action for him, therefore, involved pleasing people; its reward was to be loved as well as to be admired. He needed an *entourage* of ardent followers and he won their devotion not only by his charm but also by the stimulus that his doctrine of individual initiative gave them. He allowed them power to prove themselves as 'chiefs'. He demanded not blind 'soldierly' obedience, but 'team-work' and 'service'. He was an enemy of bureaucracy, *paperasse*, regulations and precedents. He was not interested in the party squabbles of the homeland and lamented that it was so sectarian; and he made friends with people of all parties. He had originally been a monarchist, and always remained one by inclination, but he abandoned legitimism as too narrow. He found in the colonies an opportunity to reconcile his ideas with service of his country: he could spread the principles he favoured more easily in the 'underdeveloped' world. However, instead of trying to stop the clock, he sought to effect a new combination of tradition and modernity. What he despised about France was its bourgeois virtues. He wanted to give new life to the idea of aristocracy by marrying it with capitalism, socially responsible but definitely inegalitarian. Though brought up and dying as a Catholic, he had no illusions about the Church's powers. He was able to attract disciples of many kinds because he was also a man of immensely wide reading and a fluent writer, who liked to patronise the arts, to have poets reading their verses and musicians giving concerts to him in his desert camps. He liked doing things on a grand scale and those who served with him felt that they too were kings, or lords.

This ideal, much-publicised vision of benevolent government made it very difficult for the French to see what they were doing in practice in Morocco. There can be no doubt that French rule did introduce security to the country. Their Roman roads made it possible for people to travel freely as well as safely. Their establishment of markets by the side of their forts stimulated commerce. Ports, railways and public works provided new opportunities for employment. Lyautey claimed that he was seeking the 'common denominator' of France, the policies everybody could agree on, but these great building projects were rather a deceptive façade. Lyautey kept Morocco a protectorate rather than making it a colony, but that was partly to prevent the ministry of the colonies from inter-fering with him, and as resident-general he was in fact almost an absolute monarch. He treated the sultan and the tribal chiefs with great respect; he forbade the Catholic Church to proselytise; and he preserved the traditional organs of government. He thought he owed his success to the fact that he was respectful of monarchy, aristocracy and religion. In practice he gave French backing for the preservation of tradi-tional corruption, while undermining the traditional economy that had sustained it. Thus he used the *caids* as administrators, tax-collectors and judges, under the supervision and 'guidance' of a French official. The *caids* in 1945 were still nearly all illiterate. They bought their jobs and recouped themselves by extortion, bribery and a commission on the taxes they levied; when the French finally did pay them salaries, these were still too low to alter their habits. The most famous of them, the pasha of Marrakesh, El Glaoui, used his position to obtain a monopoly of the main industries in the city, including its 27,000 prostitutes, all of whom had to pay him a percentage of their earnings; and every new development involved payment of bribes to him and his subordinates. In 1938 his income was said to be nine million francs a year, and his debts, which his power made it unnecessary to repay, stood at eighty-four million. The effect of the French occupation was to increase inequality, and to stimulate the development of a proletariat. But by allying themselves with the so-called aristocracy, the French alienated the middle classes, for whom they did very little. Even by 1940, only 3 per cent of Moroccan children were attending school. Lyautey established five different kinds of school, one for each social category, so that everybody would in theory be trained for the station in life into which he was born: but the finances for implementing an educational programme did not materialise, many of the European settlers being hostile to it. Even the Moroccan notables did not like sending their children to the school for notables Lyautey established, and they paid poor children to act as substitutes for their own. As late as 1952, there were only twenty-five Moroccan doctors (and fourteen of these were Moroccan Jews); in 1958 there were still only 1,500 Moroccans who had had a secondary education. In 1952 the European settlers had an average income of about 1,040 U.S. dollars, compared to the average of 715 dollars for the inhabitants of France. The average income in the U.S.A. was then 1,850 dollars, and that was almost exactly what Morocco's European settlers engaged in agriculture made. The natives' average income was 170 dollars (and in the traditional rural sector it was only 90 dollars). Morocco was the country to which Frenchmen went to live at a far higher standard than they could at home. Many, of course, never made their fortunes. Land was not given away free, as it had been in Algeria; many settlers had inadequate resources and some lived off public assistance.

But only some 7 per cent of the Europeans were farmers. About a quarter were civil servants. Despite Lyautey's attacks on the bureaucratic spirit, Morocco became a veritable breeding ground for the bureaucrats. In 1953 three times as many Frenchmen were employed to govern Morocco as Englishmen were used to rule India, with forty times the population. These civil servants, it was generally agreed, were incapable of resisting the pressure of the rich settlers, so virtually no social legislation was enforced which might be an obstacle to the freedom of the capitalist entrepreneurs. In 1930 there were only two inspectors to watch over the labour regulations. The settlers accepted administrative rule of the country, with a limitation of political rights, because they got a free hand for economic enterprise. Capital was freely provided by the large banks and firms in France. Morocco became an outpost of the most advanced sector of French capitalism. When the Popular Front disrupted their idyll, the local employers turned to corporatism, and became fervent supporters of Marshal Pétain. Until the 1950s, the idea that Morocco might want independence was regarded, even by liberals, as a distant and barely practical possibility.[1]

What France offered its colonies was thus, ultimately, a certain amount of prosperity, but this distillation of its civilising mission into material improvements was not as attractive as it imagined. It simply replaced one form of feudalism by another, and created needs which could not be satisfied within the imperial scheme of things. Thus in Indo-China, France's engineers did carry out one of their most impressive feats, comparable to the excavation of the Suez Canal, when they drained and reclaimed the Mekong Delta, and increased the area of cultivable land from 215,000 to 2,200,000 hectares (1869–1930). But here again they were unable to control its economic development. Frenchmen showed no interest in farming this land and by 1931 they owned under 15 per cent of it. The land was bought up by native and Chinese entrepreneurs, who put tenants on it, in return for up to 70 per cent of the crops they produced. The largest landowner in this region was a money lender, who by 1957 had accumulated 28,000 hectares. Agricultural wages did indeed quadruple between 1898 and 1930 and to that extent the French could claim to have raised living standards, but by also improving medical care, they helped to cause the population to treble in the same period. In 1930 the land available for colonisation

[1] H. Lyautey, *Paroles d'action* (1927); G. Hardy, *Portrait de Lyautey* (1949); Robin Bidwell, *Morocco under Colonial Rule: French Administration of Tribal Areas 1912–56* (1973); L. Cerych, *Européens et Marocains 1930–1956: sociologie d'une décolonisation* (Bruges, 1964); René Gallissot, *Le Patronat européen au Maroc 1931–42* (Rabat, 1964); Hervé Bleuchot, *Les Libéraux français au Maroc 1947–55* (Aix, 1973); Alan Scham, *Lyautey in Morocco. Protectorate Administration 1912–25* (U. of California Press, 1970); E. Gellner and C. Micaud, *Arabs and Berbers* (1973); G. Spillmann, *Du protectorat à l'indépendance: Maroc 1912–55* (1967).

was exhausted, but the population doubled again between 1931 and the early 1960s. Wages accordingly fell back to the level at which they had started; agricultural yields did not increase; and the conditions for revolution—land hunger and famine—were established.[1] French rule had benefited a small minority, much more than the masses. Those who acted as middlemen between the French and the natives made enormous profits, as too did some of the businessmen who controlled the country's export trade. Even the minority converted to Catholicism participated in the revolt against the French, and the French did not succeed in creating a sense of community above the traditional rivalries. The irony of it was that the exploitation was of so little benefit to the French state: France spent far more on administering or defending its empire than it collected from it in taxes.[2]

What went on in the colonies, and what was said about them in Paris, was so different that the doctrinal debates about the colonial system need to be seen as a reflection of tensions and anxieties in France, rather than as designed to provide administrators with guidelines for actual behaviour in the field. The colonies were not established as a result of any conscious policy. When the French sent their first expedition to Algeria in 1830, they had no intention of founding a colony; and it was only after much indecision that the naval engagements in Cochin-China were backed up by the government and used to lay the foundations of an eastern empire. France was a European power, absorbed above all by its rivalry with Germany. Colonies began to matter to it when military defeat in Europe caused it to worry about its diminishing prestige, when it saw the other great powers expanding overseas and felt the need to keep up, or lose its status as their equal. It was nationalism that was the prime basis of the interest in the colonies that gradually grew up; it was the clashes with England that raised this interest into a question of national honour, and when Germany became a colonial rival too, as it did in Morocco, then the colonies became a matter of life and death. But for

[1] Robert L. Sansom, *The Economics of Insurgency in the Mekong Delta of Vietnam* (Cambridge, Mass., 1970), 18–52.

[2] Nguyen Van Phong, *La Société vietnamienne de 1882 à 1902* (1971); C. Robequain, *The Economic Development of French Indo-China* (1944); D. J. Duncanson, *Government and Revolution in Vietnam* (1968), 72–139.

long there were many who feared that colonial adventures would only waste French resources, distracting attention from Alsace and Lorraine, which remained the main concern of nationalists. France did not have a surplus population that wished to emigrate. There was no economic pressure for colonial expansion, or for the capture of new markets for industry. In 1900 less than 10 per cent of French trade was with the colonies, and less than 5 per cent of its investments abroad went there. The tenfold expansion of the French empire between 1870 and 1900, so that it had a population of fifty million and an area of 9,500,000 square kilometres, represented not a concerted national effort but the achievement of a number of minorities. People excluded from political life, rebels against prevailing conformities, and eccentrics dissatisfied with or ill at ease in the normal occupations of life found an outlet for their energies in the colonies. That is why there was so much idealistic talk about colonies: colonists were dreamers and adventurers inspired by hope which seldom had a sound basis in reality. Thus the soldiers and sailors who laid the foundations of the empire were rebels against the bureaucratisation of military careers, against the boredom of the long years of peace and the slow promotion that went with it: they found in colonial life a way of transforming the significance of military life, of restoring it to a more dominant position, such as it had once held, and indeed of increasing its influence, to include not just the defence of territory, but also the government of men. The army found a new source of self-respect in the belief that it was serving the community in a more positive way, and new opportunities to win admiration, to fulfil the ambition to be heroes rather than symbols of routine and regulation. Likewise the Catholics who flocked to the colonies as missionaries found there the chance to preach and put into practice their faith, to which the home country was becoming increasingly unsympathetic. In its early stages, colonisation was also a dream of the socialists, particularly the Saint-Simonians and the Fourierists, who saw in it a chance to build a new society, and to bring about a union of east and west. The explorers and the armchair travellers who followed their exploits in the geographical societies (which had 9,500 members in 1881) were partly romantics but also businessmen, merchants, engineers and scientists for whom the colonies could open up exciting new opportunities of achievement and research. It is not surprising that there were so many aristocrats involved in the empire, nor therefore that the empire should have perpetuated some of the characteristics of the *ancien régime* whose disappearance they lamented. But what is equally significant is that the men who showed an interest in the empire came also from every other section of society. The political divisions prevalent in France were laid aside when they went abroad. The colonies effected new alliances between formerly opposed types. They provided an alternative society, in which many old European debates seemed irrelevant.

In course of time, as more people were affected by them, the colonies became more generally important. Between the wars, trade with the colonies increased to one-third of all external trade. The colonial armies made a significant contribution to France's war effort in 1914–18 (and even more in 1939–45). To be hostile to the empire increasingly meant to be anti-patriotic. Only the communist party, indeed, came out fully against imperialism, at least until 1936, when even it changed its tune. That meant that to defend the colonies was to fight the Bolshevik conspiracy to undermine western civilisation. The socialist party favoured the ultimate granting of independence to the colonies, but in this period, it did not think that the time had yet come: it was for a reform of colonial administrative methods (and in 1936–7 vainly attempted to introduce some), but it still believed that France's civilisation was superior to that of the peoples it had the mission of guiding. The radical party, having found in the colonies an important source of patronage, reformulated its doctrines to make imperialism an expression no longer of nationalism, but of solidarity, replacing the right of conquest by the right and duty of the powerful to help the weak, and fitting the colonial ideal into its general preaching of international co-operation. The Catholics for their part began changing the emphasis from conversion to ensuring the general well-being of the colonial peoples. The challenge of the iniquities perpetrated in the colonies, and of the nationalist movements that were rising in them, was met by the growth of a new doctrine of trusteeship and community, to which nearly all parties adhered. Even so,

however, the colonies did not become a matter of prime concern for the majority of the nation. In an inquiry held early
in 1939, only 40 per cent of those questioned said that they
believed France should go to war rather than give up any of
its colonies, whereas 44 per cent thought not. Paradoxically,
it was during the war of 1939–45 that the empire came to be
more generally regarded as an essential part of France, when
the legacy of contempt and maltreatment had already built
up to formidable proportions. It was the slowness with which
France took stock of the realities in the empire, and the time-
lag in its emotional involvement, that made it unable ever to
meet the demands of nationalist movements, moderate though,
for a long time, these were.[1]

The long debate about whether France should pursue a
policy of 'assimilation' or 'association' was largely a theoretical
one, for the assimilation was in practice degraded into bureaucratic uniformity rather than involving any real equality, and
association, though supposed to mean indirect rule and the
maintenance of indigenous cultures, was in practice difficult
to distinguish from direct rule, for native chiefs were made to
do what the French told them to do. The theory simply distracted politicians from appreciating the realities in the
colonies themselves.[2] Assimilation might have been attractive
if it had ever been practised. One can see this from the diaries
left by Mouloud Feraoun, an Algerian primary-school teacher
and novelist (writing in French), who was killed by the colonists in 1962. He wished to be a Frenchman. 'I express myself
in French,' he said; 'I was made what I am in a French
school. . . . But when I say that I am French, I give myself a
label that all Frenchmen refuse me.' He once exclaimed angrily
to a colonial civil servant: 'I am more French than you, you
miserable, narrow-minded little Vichyite.' It was with deep
reluctance that he became a nationalist: he had nothing but
contempt for those who suddenly rediscovered their Muslim
faith and sought to re-create an Algerian identity. But he had
to reach the conclusion that force must be used to overthrow

[1] Raoul Girardet, *L'Idée coloniale en France 1871–1962* (1972).

[2] Raymond F. Betts, *Assimilation and Association in French Colonial Theory 1890–
1914* (Columbia U.P., 1961); and for a good study of what happened, Martin A.
Klein, *Islam and Imperialism in Senegal. Sine-Saloum 1847–1914* (Stanford, 1968),
based almost entirely on the archives.

the French, even though he abhorred it; French troops raided his village, they showed more respect to the son of his concierge, who was of European descent than, to himself, the headmaster. The presence of France was an affront to human dignity, and the declaration of the rights of man had to be upheld against its inventors. Faraoun wished to be a citizen of the world and he was as horrified by the nationalism he had to adopt, as he was by that of Guy Mollet, who claimed to be a disciple of Karl Marx. He consoled himself with the hope that once the French were defeated, they would at last treat the Muslims as equals, and the two races could live together not in harmony perhaps but at least with dignity.[1]

The history of Léopold Senghor (born 1906) likewise shows how the theory of assimilation was undermined by the very culture into which Africans were supposed to be drawn. Senghor was the son of a Catholic groundnut merchant, but his mother was the daughter of a pagan cattle herder. He was educated in a missionary school, then in a *lycée*, and ended up an *agrégé*, teaching French grammar in a *lycée* in Tours. He tried to become an *évolué* (the privileged status accorded to the small minority that were offered full assimilation) but he always felt torn between his French and his African ties, between his father's and his mother's families. He was fashionable enough, in French terms, to be a royalist in the 1930s. He was deeply influenced by Barrès's doctrine of the need for roots and by Gide's urging that it was through stressing one's uniqueness that one arrived at universality. It was the ethnologists of Paris who opened up his appreciation of Negro culture and it was the surrealists who encouraged him to justify and defend African irrationalism or emotion against French logic. 'France', he wrote, 'opened me to self-knowledge . . . and revealed to me the values of my ancestral civilisation.' His answer to assimilation was that the Africans should assimilate, rather than be assimilated, but it was a symbiosis of African and European values that he sought to create in his concept of 'negritude'. He rejected French colonialism with a concept which had strong French elements in it and which he developed in highly polished French prose and verse.[2]

[1] Mouloud Feraoun, *Journal 1955–62* (1962).
[2] J. L. Hymans, *Léopold Sedar Senghor, An Intellectual Biography* (Edinburgh, 1971).

Senghor's Catholic background is important. The French culture that was propagated abroad was not just the culture of the republic, but also that of traditional, Catholic France. So it was a confused or ambiguous message that was transmitted. Whether France would have won more influence abroad had it abstained from colonial conquest is, however, uncertain. Thus though Egypt, for example, was taken over politically by England in 1882, French missionary schools continued to flourish there and in 1942 55 per cent of the well-to-do Egyptians attending foreign schools in that country chose these French schools. But whereas until 1882 most Egyptians going abroad for their education went to France, British rule at once changed this and henceforth the vast majority went to study in England. French could become the language of polite society, but the jobs and careers that political control offered were ultimately more important.[1]

What the colonies rejected was a corruption of ideals; but that also was largely what they inherited. France exported its national pride in its most arrogant form, undiluted by its universalism and its capacity for self-doubt; it was a similar national pride which rose up to expel it from its colonies. It exported materialism more than its spiritual concerns. The legacy of this century of tutelage did not reflect the values France could have transmitted.[2]

*Servants*

The status of servants was another indication of attitudes to hierarchy and of the progress of equality. They formed a large and important group, though their character changed. A servant in ancient usage was above all a farm-hand, lodging with his master. In this general sense, the total number of servants fell:

|      | Men     | Women     |
| ---- | ------- | --------- |
| 1866 | 892,000 | 1,311,000 |
| 1896 | 160,000 | 703,000   |

[1] Raoul Makarius, *La Jeunesse intellectuelle d'Égypte* (The Hague, 1960), 82; Anouar Abdel-Malek, *La Formation de l'idéologie nationale de l'Égypte 1805–1892* (Paris thesis, 1969), 76; and cf. S. Longrigg, *Syria and Lebanon under French Mandate* (1958).

[2] André Nouschi, *La Naissance du nationalisme algérien 1914–54* (1962); David C. Gordon, *The Passing of French Algeria* (1966); C. Micaud, *Tunisia, the Politics of Modernisation* (1964); R. von Albertini, *Decolonisation* (New York, 1971).

However, domestic servants increased as the urban middle classes grew in prosperity and as the peasants migrated to the towns:

Domestic Servants

| | |
|---|---|
| 1891 | 683,000 |
| 1906 | 840,000 |
| 1911 | 940,000 |

Paris in 1866 had 100,000 servants, but by 1906 it had 206,000, which was 11 per cent of its population; and in Paris there were then five times more female than male servants. The principle of the career open to talent meant not just equality but also that every successful man wanted to have a servant to show off his status. Thus in the 1890s virtually all barristers, doctors and magistrates kept servants, 71 per cent of pharmacists, 44 per cent of dentists, 12 per cent of midwives, 44 per cent of scientists, men of letters and journalists, 61 per cent of architects and engineers, 20 per cent of artists and 26 per cent of retired *rentiers*.[1]

The French Revolution had attempted to abolish domestic servants as a class, at least in their traditional form, and it sought to give them a new name, *officieux*; but Napoleon's Civil Code reaffirmed their subordination, by laying down that in a dispute about wages, the master was to be believed by the courts simply on his word: it gave the master the right to dismiss servants without the customary eight days' notice in cases of drunkenness, theft, insolence or misbehaviour. It is true it allowed the servant to leave without notice if he was insulted, or refused his wages, but the master had the right to search his baggage before he left, and a crime committed by a servant against his master was held to be aggravated because it involved a breach of trust. A servant could be dismissed without compensation if he fell ill (unless it was of a contagious disease caught from his master) or when he was too old to be of further use.[2] In 1875 a Paris court condemned a lady to pay 2,000 francs damages for having falsely accused her maid of stealing her jewels; after six weeks in police custody the maid's innocence

[1] Viviane Léon, épouse Ayme, 'La Domesticité féminine à Paris de 1890 à 1914' (unpublished mémoire de maîtrise, Nanterre, 1973).

[2] *Manuel des bons domestiques. Droits et devoirs des maîtres et des domestiques* (1896), 8° R 13245.

was proved and she successfully sued her mistress; but a case two years later showed that if an accusation was made against a servant in good faith and not 'maliciously or lightly', there was no redress against it. It was only in 1923 that the 1898 law on accident insurance for industrial workers was applied to them (but governesses, companions and secretaries were still excluded).[1]

The legal inferiority of servants was however less of a worry to them than the way they were treated in their daily lives. Moralists liked to look back to a golden age when servants respected their masters and masters treated them as members of the family. At the end of the nineteenth century, there were indeed still rural employers in traditional regions like Brittany who made little distinction between their children and their servants, who had maids sleeping in the same room as their mistress, and who used to say, not 'Go and work', but 'Let's go and work'. In Tréguier and Cornouailles servants used to call their masters uncle and aunt.[2] There is no doubt that some servants, who worked all their lives in the same family and who had brought up the children, had a respected role which they valued. But already in the eighteenth century there were complaints from both sides which showed that these idealised relations were always the exception. In the nineteenth century there were increasing laments that 'reciprocal confidence barely exists any more'. The Agricultural Inquiry of 1866 noted 'a certain enmity'. In 1867 a play, *Ces Scélérates de bonnes*, showed masters already despairing of their ability to control their servants: it showed a maid, when interviewed by her prospective employers, submitting them to long questioning on exactly what her duties would be, on how much free time she would have, when she would have to get up in the morning, and adding that she drank only Bordeaux wine: the master replied by asking, 'Do you know Greek? Do you know astronomy? Can you paint in oils? Then I am afraid you are no use to us.' This was a verbatim reproduction of the experience of an American author in Paris.

---

[1] Adrien Sachet, *Maîtres de maison et domestiques sous le régime de la législation sur les accidents du travail. Commentaire de la loi du 2 août 1923* (1924).

[2] Jean Choleau, *Condition actuelle des serviteurs ruraux bretons, domestiques à gages et journaliers agricoles* (1907), 94.

The Salon of 1864 showed a painting by Marchal of an Alsatian Servants' Fair, where they could be hired in the traditional way, but these had almost vanished by the end of the century, when there was much talk of a 'crisis' in the servant situation. Too many people wanted servants now. They were much harder to find, particularly *bonnes à tout faire*. Though their wages increased considerably as a result, they had new grievances. The employment agencies, trying to profit from the shortage, were said to extract no less than two million francs a year in fees from servants in Paris alone.[1] The growth of the practice of segregating them on the sixth floor of apartment blocks gave them a sense of being outcasts, but also encouraged them to become more aware of their exploitation, to demand improvements, and to move on to better jobs. A newspaper (*Le Larbin*) appeared specifically for domestic servants, edited by a cook. A Declaration of the Rights of Servants demanded that employers should cease to expect more than the performance of duties for which they paid.[2]

But employers also demanded respect. A servant was socially and educationally inferior, even if he did have the vote, and employers used servants to assert their superiority, either by ostentation, by showing that they could avoid menial tasks, or by trampling on their servants' dignity. One servant, in his memoirs, argued that employers were not worthy of the respect they demanded: maids were seduced by their masters and sacked when they became pregnant, so that they often became prostitutes; Balzac had shown wives, anxious to liberate themselves from their husbands' sexual demands, choosing pretty maids as substitutes; Eugène Sue had complained: 'Nothing is more frequent than this corruption more or less imposed by the master on the servant.' Employers confided their worries to their servants, so 'the vices of Monsieur and the coldnesses of Madame' drained away respect. This servant described his successive employers with great wit.[3] Others had a different way of getting their own back: they compensated for their low wages by stealing. It was a favourite complaint

---

[1] Jean-Pierre, *Maîtres et serviteurs. La crise du service domestique* (1904).
[2] Emmanuel Chauvet, *Les Domestiques* (Caen, 1896).
[3] *Maîtres et domestiques fin de siècle* par un cuisinier philosophe, ancien gendarme (dix ans de service militaire) devenu domestique de 1875 à 1897 (1898), 8° Li(5)439.

that servants were often thieves; and there was constant squabbling about property. The servants, however, profited from their masters by a tacit bargain with other poor people who served the well-to-do: in the Paris markets, there were two prices, one for masters and one for servants, and other tradesmen also generally gave servants a 5 per cent commission on sales. The concierges were brought into the racket, to overlook other forms of peculation, by being given a share of the remains of the food from the master's table.[1] In this way, servants were able to save considerable sums of money, and that was ultimately the reason why most of them had chosen this kind of work: it was the easiest avenue by which poor peasants could rise into the petty bourgeoisie. Only a minority of servants married. When they did, they married late, and they very often had only one child. Men servants frequently married women servants, but there were more of the latter and these were often successful in using their savings to marry up the social scale. A sample survey of nineteenth-century Versailles has shown 16 per cent of them marrying artisans, 8 per cent marrying shopkeepers and 4 per cent clerks. Another of Lyon in the 1870s showed only about one-tenth of servants making domestic service a lifetime career. Servants were increasingly literate, because service was one way of learning to read and to acquire manners; they were noted for spending a lot of money on clothes, and Balzac said that a cook could dress as well as her mistress.[2] Domestic service declined when alternative professions arose for poor girls to make their way in the world, with the expansion of shops, offices and factories. The hierarchic character of domestic service survived because servants were often imbued with the same obsession with status that tormented their masters: they maintained inequalities amongst themselves—as between valet, cook, chambermaid and scullery maid—and they tried to extract respect from their inferiors, using almost identical brutality. The *Moniteur des gens de maison*, their trade union paper, wrote in 1907: 'They accept social inequalities as one of the consequences of human

[1] Bouniceau-Gesmon, juge d'instruction à Paris, *Domestiques et maîtres. Question sociale* (1896).
[2] Theresa M. McBride, 'Social Mobility for the Lower Classes: Domestic Servants in France', *Journal of Social History* (Fall 1974), 63–75.

existence and they firmly believe that it is above all by faithful duty that they can improve the general lot.'

Fourier, and Vacherot during the Second Empire, had suggested that menial work should be done by children. But that class was rising to independence even faster than the working class. Moralists like Adolphe Garnier and Jules Barni thought, in that same period, that the answer lay in converting domestic service into piece work, so that there should not be anything degrading about it. But in 1925 Madame Moll-Weiss, founder of the *École des Mères*, while urging the mistress to treat her servant with consideration, acknowledged that there was often 'hateful hostility' between them and they just could not understand each other's point of view.[1]

Mutual incomprehension is what all four sections of this chapter have been about. This should not be surprising. The next chapter will show that even in their attitudes to the most basic problems of life, Frenchmen were deeply divided, though in a different way.

[1] Augusta Moll-Weiss, *Madame et sa bonne* (1925).

# 19. Birth and Death

THE French worried obsessively and increasingly about the slow rate at which their population increased. At least that is the impression one gets from the vast literature that poured out on this subject. These hundred years, when birth-control was adopted in France on a scale hitherto unprecedented and never to be repeated, appear to stand out as a crisis, when Frenchmen became neurotic about their virility and about their capacity to survive as a great power. Their decadence could be measured at every census. But despite the warnings of the population experts, the exhortations of moralists and even the financial inducements held out by governments, the country as a whole steadfastly continued to produce fewer and fewer children, and to act in apparently complete disregard of the opinions of its leaders. The demographic history of France is therefore very revealing not only about the attitudes of individuals towards the most basic facts of life and the status of the family, but also about the clash between their interests and the nationalist aspirations of the politicians. This conflict and contrast between the ambitions of different sections of the community, and the way they could ignore each other, makes the problems of population much more than an exercise in statistics. The reasons why Frenchmen had small families but also deplored them are worth investigating.

The word demography was invented by a Frenchman, Achille Guillard, in 1855.[1] The French have long been highly regarded as exponents of this science; the Institut National d'Études Démographiques, founded in 1942–5, has been the source of a very large body of research; no one can study historical demography without examining the theoretical and empirical contributions of French scholars to it; and even now, when population problems have been attracting a vast amount

---

[1] Achille Guillard, *Éléments de statistique humaine, ou démographie comparée* (1855); for his other interests, see id., *Biographie de J. Jacotot, fondateur de la méthode d'émancipation intellectuelle* (1860). But the word statistics was first used in its modern sense in eighteenth-century Germany.

of attention all over the world, Frenchmen continue to play a leading role in their discussion (as they do not, for example, in economics, or most of the natural sciences). However, this should not blind one to the many obstacles which none the less stood in the way of the French knowing the facts about their own population. Officially, French population statistics are available from 1801. But no uniform method of collecting data was prescribed in that year and it was a long time before truly comparable series became available. Only in 1836 were the prefects' estimates replaced by actual counting of heads; only in 1876 did each inhabitant have his particulars inscribed on a separate card; only in 1881 was the actual population present on the day of the census recorded, as opposed to the 'legal' population supposedly existing in *habitual* places of residence. The first complete census of industrial and professional activity was made in 1896; the analysis of families dates from 1906. The census of 1901 was the first to satisfy the experts, but subsequent ones have been criticised, and anomalies appear when these are compared with statistics produced for other purposes, as for example those in agriculture. Part of the explanation is that the Statistical Office had a very small staff; it had to use unpaid assistants in the provinces; and it was only after the Second World War that the collection and analysis of statistics became fully professional.

However, the deficiencies of French statistics could not obscure the most striking fact which became obvious in the mid-nineteenth century, that France was, from the numerical point of view, losing the predominant position it had hitherto held in Europe. In 1800 France had 28 million inhabitants. Great Britain and Ireland together had only 16 million. All the German states put together totalled 22 million, and those of Italy 18 million. But by 1860 the Austrian empire had caught up with France; in 1870 the new German empire had five million more inhabitants than the new Third Republic; in 1900 Britain overtook France and in 1933 even Italy did. So France now came at the bottom of the European league, in fifth place (Russia always leading). Thus in the years 1800–1940 Germany's population quadrupled and Britain's tripled, but France's rose by only 50 per cent. Moreover, this small increase

in the French population—of 13 million odd—was not achieved
by natural increase: on the contrary, the rate of reproduction
produced a loss of five millions; and the war of 1914 was
responsible for a loss of a further three millions. It was simply

*Population of European nations, in millions*

|                  | 1789 | 1815 | 1860 | 1871 | 1910 | 1920 | 1939 |
|------------------|------|------|------|------|------|------|------|
| France           | 26   | 30   | 37·4 | 36·1 | 39·6 | 39·2 | 41·9 |
| Great Britain    | 16   | 20   | 29   | 32   | 45   | 44   | 47·5 |
| Austrian Empire  | 27   | 29   | 36   | 36   | 51   | —    | —    |
| Prussia          | 6    | 10   | 18   | —    | —    | —    | —    |
| Germany          | —    | —    | —    | 41   | 65   | 59   | 80   |
| Italy            | —    | —    | 23   | 27   | 35   | 38   | 44   |
| Russia           | 30   | 48   | 67   | 80   | 142  | 120  | 170  |

the increase in people's longevity, accounting for an increase
of 16 millions, and the immigration of 5 millions, which
explained the rise. All European nations experienced a check
to their population growth in this period, but the decline in the
French birth-rate began almost a century before that of its
rivals, around 1760, so that the accumulative effect was felt
much longer and more noticeably: the decline in England and
Germany started only around 1875–80, that in Italy (and the
U.S.A.) around 1885. The French regularly produced fewer
babies, proportionately to their population:

*Births per 1,000 inhabitants*

|           | France | England | Germany |
|-----------|--------|---------|---------|
| 1841–50   | 27·4   | 32·6    | 36·1    |
| 1891–1900 | 22·2   | 29·9    | 36·1    |
| 1938      | 14·6   | 19·1    | 19·7    |

Historians regularly use these and similar statistics to
show that France was losing its hegemony in Europe and to
imply that there was therefore some moral or economic decadence at work to explain what they always see as a silent
defeat. Both of these common generalisations, however, need
to be looked at more carefully. International comparisons are
fruitful only if one is clear about the criterion one is adopting:
to argue that power comes simply from numbers is to use

military and economic criteria: a large nation wins battles and produces more machinery, but it will be realised by now that France did not wholly accept these ambitions. The fall in its population was indeed a challenge to the idea that these were the principal aims of life. To argue that France was decadent because it produced few children is to adopt the theories of a relatively small minority of conservative propagandists, whose motives need to be examined more carefully. It is too easy to assume that the criticisms these theorists made of their countrymen were empirical observations of fact, and to quote them as impartial judgements above contradiction. Nearly everything written about the French population in these years has looked on its development as manifesting some weakness or aberration: the assumption has nearly always been that because other nations were increasing in size, France ought to have been increasing also. It is worth seeing first, therefore, just who it was who led the lamentations.

In the eighteenth century, French economists had become generally hostile to the traditional belief that the increase of a nation's population was a good thing. Instead of regarding the poor simply as material to supply the state with soldiers and taxes for its own glory, they argued that humanitarian considerations should determine population policy. They asked that the rights and interests of the poor should not be overlooked. They wanted the increase in prosperity to benefit the individual, rather than to be used as a stimulus to make the poor have more children. Some people said that population depended on the amount of work available, so that the way to increase the population was to increase manufacturing. But others replied that no nation could really be improved by having large masses of miserable industrial workers. Malthus, who suggested that men would not automatically gain from technical progress and that the poor would improve their lot by reducing the number of children they had, was widely approved. There was distinct hostility to filling France with smoky factories. In 1847 the head of the state census office, Legoyt, wrote that those countries which had the most rapidly increasing populations, like England, Prussia and Saxony, 'were precisely those where pauperism makes the most redoubtable progress'. It was believed that there was a limit to the amount of food the land could produce, that to rely on imports would be dangerous, that only advances in agronomic science could be looked to for greater productivity, and that meanwhile the stimulation of the birth-rate was wrong. Under Louis-Philippe, ministers and prefects advised the poor to limit their families: in 1866, during debates held on the subject by the Academy of Medicine, the anthropologist Broca insisted that the number of births was 'a false criticism of the prosperity of a population'. France, said Legoyt in 1867, was a 'grown-up country, arrived at maturity': it should concentrate on improving the lot of its existing population.[1] While its population was increasing rapidly, a reaction thus set in against the nationalist attitude that this was an end in itself. At first, no alarm was felt when it was seen that the increase was slowing down, and many indeed applauded.

The first complaint that France was losing its dominant position among the great powers was made in 1849 in a book which went through four editions in a year. C. M. Raudot's *The Decadence of France* claimed that the country was heading for ruin, citing as proof the decline in the height of army recruits. Writers on demographic history who quote him omit to discover who he was—a legitimist public prosecutor who had resigned in 1830 from loyalty to Charles X, and who had written in praise of *France Before the Revolution* (1841).[2] A very considerable proportion of the advocates of a larger population were indeed admirers of a vanished golden age, in which they imagined large families had lived in harmony, ruled benevolently by aged patriarchs. A constant underlying assumption in the debates on this subject was that family life, like religion, was indispensable for the preservation of a hierarchical organisation of society. It is true that this link was by no means always present, nor always in a simple form. Thus Léonce de Lavergne, whose article in the *Revue des Deux Mondes* in 1857 made the facts about the country's declining population known to the majority of educated people interested in public affairs, was a friend of Guizot, an Orleanist politician

[1] J. J. Spengler, *French Predecessors of Malthus. A Study in Eighteenth Century Wage and Population Theory* (Durham, N.C., 1942), 365; id., *France Faces Depopulation* (Durham, N.C., 1938), 111–17.

[2] C. M. Raudot, *De la décadence de la France* (1849); A. Motheré, *Réponse à l'ouvrage de M. Raudot* (1850).

who accepted the republic only in the 1870s. He declared himself to be a 'faithful disciple of Malthus', but he quite correctly said that Malthus was not opposed to increasing population provided it could be achieved without poverty increasing. Lavergne was a great admirer of England and of its agricultural revolution: it was eighteenth-century England, before its industrialisation, that he held up as an ideal; and he urged France to increase its population by improving its agricultural productivity.[1] But the most important source of conservative populationist thought was Frédéric Le Play (1806-82).

## Le Play

He has many different claims to notice, and not only because several generations of leaders of the *familles nombreuses* movement owed much to his influence. He was an outstanding sociologist, engineer, traveller, propagandist and also a very curious man. His private and public careers reveal in a striking way the options, and the difficulties, facing men in their attitudes to the family within the context of modern civilisation.

Superficially Le Play appears to be a representative figure of the Second Empire—that much-simplified, easily labelled regime: a scientist, graduate of the Polytechnic, organiser of the International Exhibitions, professor and senator, standing for authority and material progress, but typically divided between religion and science. In reality he was a sensitive, worried man, searching for stability in a world which depressed him but which he studied minutely and indefatigably for the key to happiness. He was trained as a mining engineer, winning the highest marks ever awarded by the École des Mines, but in 1830 he suffered severe burns and permanent scarring following a laboratory accident: 'one of the decisive events of my career. . . . Eighteen months of physical and moral torture produced a transformation in me.' He made a vow to devote at least half of his time to studying society and the family, and to discovering why there was so much animosity and strife in them. For the next fifteen years he spent six months earning his living as an industrial consultant, manager and professor and

---

[1] A. Armengaud, 'Léonce de Lavergne ou un malthusien populationniste', *Annales de démographie historique* (1968), 29-36.

six months travelling. He covered altogether 175,000 miles, visiting almost every country in Europe, comparing the degree of harmony to be found in different situations, analysing the relationship between technical and social change and investigating above all the organisation of the family in varying situations. He thus developed a new methodology of social study. Whereas the Saint-Simonians, with whom he grew up and among whom he numbered several close friends (Jean Reynaud was often his travelling companion; his son married Michel Chevalier's daughter,[1]), believed that a totally new order must be invented to replace the present intolerable situation, Le Play, breaking away from them, advocated comparative and historical approaches. Foreign countries should be studied for actual examples of possible alternatives; and the past must be looked on not as something to be escaped from, but as a source of wisdom. Denying that progress was infinite and inevitable, he preferred a cyclical view of history, seeing decadence and resurgence alternating; and he thought that the merits of the French past could often be observed surviving in foreign societies untouched by modernisation. He embarked on a gigantic compilation of facts about the different types of families existing in Europe, from Norway to Portugal, arranged according to the amount of 'stability' he detected in them. He wrote monographs on over 300 families, interviewing each for between a week and a month, and using eight languages in the process. The central core of these monographs consisted in a budget, showing the minutest details of income and expenditure, from which, he argued, all else could be deduced, but he added information about the biographies, religious beliefs and social contacts of his subjects. Even if exception may be taken to the way Le Play presented his material, these monographs remain a unique and irreplaceable source for social historians. Le Play's methods prefigure those of social anthropologists: 'The time is not far distant,' he wrote, 'when the fact that an author has not moved out of his study will be sufficient refutation of his theory.' But sociologists have criticised his monographs; Durkheim, who was interested in more abstract argument, dismissed him as of little importance; and

---

[1] Through Michel Chevalier, he was related to Paul Leroy-Beaulieu, Émile Flourens and Émile Pereire.

he seldom figures among the great names of social science. The explanation of this can be found partly in the inaccuracies and inadequacies of his work, but even more in the political implications he drew from it, which condemned him as a reactionary, a 'reincarnation of Bonald', as Sainte-Beuve called him.

There have been over 160 studies (in books or articles) of him, but these have been almost exclusively by admirers praising him and there is still no full biography available.[1] But one needs to do more than categorise him as a reactionary if one is to understand the origins and significance of his nostalgia. There is probably an almost Proustian story behind it, though more research will be needed before any definite explanation can be offered. Le Play's life was devoted to the search for 'happiness' and 'social peace', by which he meant individual contentment, the absence of anxiety and antagonisms, and satisfaction with the organisation of society. It was this psychological, unquantifiable, element in his ideal that first set the sociologists against him. He believed that social peace could be established by three methods: restoring religious belief, increasing the power of the father and legislating to make the 'seduction' of women more difficult. This kind of brief summary is what usually condemns him, but there was an interesting theory and history behind it. Le Play was no orthodox Catholic and, until just before he died, probably not a practising one either. The religion he was interested in was that of the Old Testament, not that of Christ. It may have been coincidental that strong paternal authority should have been one of the principal panaceas of a man whose father died when he was only six. He at any rate attributed his breaking-away from his Saint-Simonian friends to his having been born in the country (Honfleur, where his father had been a customs official), and to having been sent away to Paris on his father's death, to live with an uncle: 'ever since I have always found the sight of towns distasteful'. His schooling was 'a torment the memory of which has never left me'; later his years at the Polytechnic were 'suffocating'. He longed to return to the fishermen he had played with as a child, whose primitive husbandry,

---

[1] The nearest approach is M. Z. Brooke, *Le Play: engineer and social scientist* (1970), which provides a useful introductory survey in 140 pages.

living off natural resources, ever remained his ideal. His uncle was a royalist with a group of counter-revolutionary friends, who filled the boy with horrific stories of the Terror, but also with the moral that it was the corruption of the upper classes and their abandonment of religion that had brought catastrophe to the monarchy. These opinions, he himself noted, revived in him in later life, after having been temporarily obscured by the teaching of the schools. What his relations with his mother, who sent him away, were, and how they relate to his obsession about seduction, is not known, nor what feelings of guilt made him place such stress on the virtues of obedience.

But he based his philosophy on a staunch reaffirmation of original sin. Children were ignorant and vicious, an endless barbarian invasion against which society must guard itself. The spirit of rebellion starts in very infancy, respect for parents is not natural, and needs to be inculcated by chastisement, to show children their weakness; but even that is not enough to quell them, so 'the fear of God and the counsels of reason' must be summoned in support. Le Play argued for the restoration of religion, making the practice of the Ten Commandments the first basis of happiness. He thought this restoration would be possible if the upper classes set the example in their own private lives, and made religion fashionable again, if the clergy improved their morals and ceased to interfere in politics (it was mainly this that had turned people against them). 'The counsels of reason' meant that the father should have the right to dispose freely of his property, to cut off disobedient children, contrary to the Napoleonic Code. The most vigorous nations— Russia and England—were those in which, he claimed, paternal authority was strongest. The French, by compelling a more or less equal distribution of inheritance between children, gave most the prospect of a tiny property, so that modest ambitions prevailed and the need to show individual initiative was reduced. Le Play's ideal family was what he called the stem family (la famille souche), meaning that the family property was transmitted intact from the father to one son, while the other children left the stem to make their own fortunes and to establish stem families of their own. This he contrasted with, on the one hand, the unstable family, which was the

commonest type in France, where the property was divided
up between the children, who dispersed rootless, and, on the
other hand, the patriarchal family, in which many generations
lived together: he saw many virtues in this last form, but
conceded that it was capable of becoming too hostile to innovation. The restoration of paternal authority could be easily
secured, he thought, simply by changing the inheritance laws,
and this became the main demand of his followers.

That such a change would offend the French worship of
equality he denied, because, he said, 'France is of all the
European nations, the least keen on equality', as was proved by
the mania for decorations, and the maintenance of class and
other distinctions. France could borrow a lot from England,
and particularly 'the just equilibrium it maintained between
classes', its religion moderated by tolerance, its hunger for
riches balanced by Christian renunciation, hard work balanced
by Sunday rest, and temperance societies which spread 'moral
influences'. The English loved their past: the French must
learn to do the same. The English had preserved an aristocracy
which lived on its ancestral estates, set an example of morality
and maintained a clergy to ensure obedience to the Ten
Commandments. But Le Play found many faults in England
too, and above all its *laissez-faire* industrialisation, which gave
no kind of security to the workers, and he was no supporter of
aristocracies as such. The people who held the key to the
restoration of social peace were what he called the 'social
authorities'—men residing on their own lands, who won general
respect for their wisdom and morals, who 'found in the traditions of their family the origin of the happiness they enjoy
and the source of the good they spread around them. Their
constant preoccupation is to work for the two fundamental
needs of humanity, social peace, obtainable by regulating their
thoughts and actions according to the prescriptions of the
Decalogue, and the enjoyment of daily bread, by subjecting all
the members of the community to the obligation to work.'
Le Play had searched all Europe for these benevolent patriarchs:
far from modelling them on the English aristocracy, he turned
up examples of them everywhere, in the Norwegian fjords and
the hills of Saxony, Switzerland and the Basque country. His
ideal society was essentially rural, and he wanted industry to

make provision for its workers to have a balanced range of
occupations which freed them from the dangers of unemployment. Though an engineer, he was opposed to technology
providing the model for social planning. He complained that
'the French today are an urban people, as the Gauls and the
Romans were. They must become once again a rural people, as
the Franks were and as the Anglo-Saxons still are.' The great
enemies, therefore, were the bourgeoisie who had despoiled the
countryside and corrupted the masses. More specifically, he
attacked the *lettrés*, who in the eighteenth century had started
the 'universal of contempt for all human and divine authority,
the destruction of all forms of respect and the creation of
insatiable appetites'—all based on hostility towards the past.
Custom, not theories or laws, must be the guide to action.
Royalist decentralisation was no use, because too many de-
centralisers were bourgeois, who would only oppress the rural
populations even more if given power: rural and urban areas
should have separate governments; the parish was the only
real unit; the authority of the 'Voltairian mayor and *instituteur*' must be replaced by that of heads of families. Regulations
must be replaced by rites. The family must be given its autonomy.[1] And to crown all this, chastity, on which he laid great
store as the basis of family morality, must be enforced by placing
the responsibility for its violation entirely on the male; there
must be no truce with the idea that seduction involved consent
by the woman; the family system could not be preserved without
chastity and rigid distinctions in sexual roles.

Le Play does not appear to have been able to implement all
these ideas in his own life. He preached against Malthusianism
but had only one son; he opposed boarding-schools, but sent
his son to one; he extolled the beneficent rule of patriarchs,
but he admitted his grandchildren into his presence only once
a week, when he silently and briefly distributed sweets to them.
But it should not be thought that his ideas were purely theoretical and out of touch with reality. Le Play found numerous—
if odd—examples of patriarchal and stem families in France
and the traditions he wished to restore were far from being
completely dead. A precursor, in some ways, of Maurras, he
was like him an outsider among the conservatives, and his

[1] Charles de Ribbe, *Le Play, d'après sa correspondance* (1884), 403-13.

tragedy was that he was taken up only by the conservatives, when he believed he was appealing beyond the political parties or religious denominations, to what he considered to be universal family values, truths inescapably following from the human condition. Le Play's influence was limited by his refusal to avoid drawing all the implications from his investigations. Montalembert declared that *The Social Reform of France* was 'the most original, useful, courageous and in every respect the most powerful book of this century. It does not have as much eloquence as the illustrious Tocqueville, but much more practical perspicacity and above all moral courage . . . [because it] combated the majority of the dominant prejudices of its time and of France.' Le Play, for his part, thought Tocqueville had produced 'probably the first political and social work of our time', but ended by condemning Tocqueville as a sophist and a coward, because 'he could not see where to go' and did not really dare say what he believed. Le Play himself may well have said too much.[1]

### The Myth of the Only Child

It will be seen in due course how the populationist movement reflected these kinds of anxiety, how Le Play was influential as their most systematic exponent, and also how the movement was always very much a minority one. In this subject, one is always dealing with minorities, for though there are broad national trends, these do not result from everybody following more or less the same pattern of behaviour, but are the average produced by adding up quite a wide diversity of situations. This simple fact was too often overlooked because the propagandists were concerned mainly with national totals. The general condemnations also make the simple error that people knew how many children they wanted and procreated accordingly. But French sociologists have recently shown, through opinion polls and inquiries, just how large the gap between belief and actions can be. Public knowledge of demographic

[1] F. Le Play, *Les Ouvriers européens* (2nd edition, 1879), vol. 1 contains autobiographical information, preface, 17–48 and 395–438; id., *L'Organisation du travail* (1870); id., *L'Organisation de la famille* (1871); id., *La Réforme sociale* (5th edition, 1874); Ferdinand Aubertin, *Frédéric Le Play, d'après lui-même* (1906). For a full bibliography see M. Z. Brooke, op. cit. 142–64.

trends, even in the 1950s and 1960s, when these were constantly discussed, was extraordinarily inaccurate; the ideal family size was considerably higher than the average size; and worries about unemployment, overpopulation and housing remained vigorous even while people did produce more children. In 1947 73 per cent of the country appeared to want the population to rise, but by 1965 only 29 per cent did; the proportion in favour of its remaining stationary rose from 23 to 66: and this was during a period of dramatic economic growth. The attitudes of different classes varied considerably: in 1965 15 per cent of the liberal professions and industrial managers were in favour of having larger families, but only 7 per cent of artisans and retailers were, and only 2 per cent of peasants.[1] Another inquiry carried out in the 1960s in Lyon questioned mothers before and after their child was born, as to whether the child was wanted. Fifty-four per cent said, before its birth, that it was wanted, and 60 per cent gave the same answer after birth. When these replies were averaged out, and broken down according to the number of children the mother already had, the replies were:[2]

85 per cent of those whose first child it was said they wanted it
64 „ „         „     „   second      „   „   „     „     „
35 „ „         „     „   third or fourth „ „   „     „
10 „ „         „     „   fifth or more   „   „   „     „

These examples may be enough to show how dangerous it is to generalise about broad national trends, and to attribute rational or conscious explanations to them.

In 1906, 11·5 per cent of couples had no children, 42·4 per cent had one or two children, 25·3 per cent had three or four, but 20·8 per cent have five or more. The slogan that France was a nation of only sons was false. Half its families failed to reproduce themselves, but the other half amply succeeded. The proportion of couples with one child (21·1 per cent) was almost exactly equal to that of couples with five or more children. This meant, however, that a relatively small group of mothers produced quite a sizeable section of the nation's

[1] Henri Bastide and Alain Girard, 'Les Tendances démographique en France et les attitudes de la population', *Population* (Jan.–Feb. 1966), 9–50.

[2] H. Pigeaud, 'Attitudes devant la maternité. Une enquête à Lyon', *Population* (Mar.–Apr. 1966), 231–72.

children, as can be seen by looking, for example, at the history of the half-million women born in 1881. Twenty-eight per cent of these died before reaching the age of fifteen. Twelve per cent died unmarried; 6 per cent were still alive but spinsters in 1931; only 54 per cent married. Sixty per cent of these married women had either no children, or one or two children, which altogether accounted for 25·6 per cent of the descendants of this generation of 1881. Only 6·3 per cent of the married women bore seven or more children, but they accounted for 20·9 per cent of all the children. The rare couples who had ten or more children produced almost as many children (7·2 per cent of the total) as the large number of couples who had only one child (8·5 per cent). This kind of statistic meant that the Frenchmen of 1880 were themselves descended from only about 10 or 12 per cent of Frenchmen who had lived in 1789.[1] The concentration of the reproductive function is even more marked when one compares fertility in different regions. The most prolific regions of France used to be Brittany, the Massif Central, Corsica, the Nord and Pas-de-Calais. In the course of this period the economically declining parts of France had a drastic fall in their birth-rates, while the urban regions increased theirs. The department of Calvados which in 1906 had the lowest fertility had the highest in 1953. The regional variations became so pronounced that some departments had birth-rates twice as high as others: in 1938, the department of Manche had 210 live births per 10,000 inhabitants, Morbihan and Pas-de-Calais 197, while Bouches-du-Rhône had 102, Corsica and Alpes-Maritimes had 108, and Ariège 113. The southern coast of France stood in direct

[1] P. Vincent, 'Les Familles nombreuses', *Population* (1946), vol. 1, 148–54; A. Landry, *Traité de démographie* (1949), 366. The increase in the size of small families may be seen from the following comparison (per 1,000):

| Families with | 1906 | 1931 |
|---|---|---|
| 0 children | 115 | 121 |
| 1 child | 211 | 264 |
| 2 children | 213 | 236 |
| 3 ,, | 150 | 147 |
| 4 ,, | 103 | 87 |
| 5 ,, | 68 | 52 |
| 6 ,, | 47 | 34 |
| 7 ,, | 32 | 21 |
| 8 ,, | 22 | 15 |
| 9 ,, | 15 | 10 |
| 10 or more | 24 | 16 |

contrast to the north and west: Brittany's population density was, in 1939, twice as high as that in the rest of France's countryside, making it resemble an industrialised region; but at the same date the birth-rate of Lot-et-Garonne was less than half of what it had been a century before. Such enormous variations were something new, for during the Second Empire the ten most prolific departments had been widely distributed over the country.[1] But the histories of different departments themselves contain very striking internal variations: thus within Tarn-et-Garonne, one canton's birth-rate fell by about 60 per cent (1800–1930), from 32·6 to 13·6 per 1,000, while another only a few miles away dropped by half that amount, from 26·2 to 18·4, which meant that the latter, after having had a birth-rate below the national average, came to have one considerably above it. Brittany, despite its reputation for fertility, had widely differing birth-rates in the interior, on the coast and in the towns.

Conservatives tried to explain both the decline in the birth-rate and the regional variations in terms of religious practice. They claimed that the Church's motto 'Increase and multiply', and its opposition to birth-control, made it a powerful force in favour of large families. The north and west, where birth-rates declined far less rapidly than elsewhere, were outstandingly pious. But this kind of correlation was flimsy if not definitely inaccurate. There were other regions, like the Garonne, which had been no less religious, but which had reduced their fertility drastically. On detailed investigation, departments like the Hérault have been found to have had small families equally in religious and in anticlerical communes.[2] It is true that occasionally statistics could be found to show that the pupils of church secondary schools came from families with twice as many children as the average, and that monks and nuns came from families with three times as many children as the average;[3] but this is not enough to make religious belief the determining factor in fertility. The anticlericals were

---

[1] The most prolific departments in the 1860s were Haut-Rhin, Finistère, Bas-Rhin, Nord, Pyrénées-Orientales, Aveyron, Loire, Lozère, Corrèze, Haute-Vienne. The most prolific ones in 1938 were Manche, Morbihan, Pas-de-Calais, Mayenne, Vendée, Calvados, Sarthe, Ille-et-Vilaine, Moselle, Seine-Inférieure.

[2] G. Cholvy, *Géographie religieuse de l'Hérault contemporain* (1968), 325–7.

[3] A. Cauchois, *Démographie de la Seine-Inférieure* (Rouen, 1929).

vociferous in arguing that in any case the Catholic Church's admiration for celibacy, chastity and continence made its influence ambiguous. Certainly it was not always in pious areas that it preached its sexual code most vigorously. There were, occasionally, regions noted for anticlericalism which stood out also as exceptionally prolific; and the decline in religious belief was not necessarily accompanied by a fall in the birthrate. As one *curé* of Finistère (which was by no means all pious) said of his parishioners, 'These unhappy people have lost all their religion, but they have not lost their *esprit de famille*.'[1] But of course this was not a century in which 'dechristianisation' was either uniform or universal; and there were other forms of supernatural belief which were far from declining. A taboo on marriages in the month of May, 'the month of the Virgin Mary', which affected only a few departments in the Vendée and Touraine in 1810, spread to 15 departments in 1837, and to 43 departments by the 1930s, and came to affect an increasing proportion of marriages in them. The avoidance of November, 'the month of the dead', by marrying couples started in the Creuse in the 1870s, spread to neighbouring departments in the next twenty years and then into the south, so that by 1945 in most southern departments this new custom was observed by over 20 per cent, and in three (Creuse, Haute-Vienne and Dordogne) by over 80 per cent.[2] The relationship between religious belief, folk superstitions and fertility was too complicated to make a simple generalisation possible, but that did not stop people from asserting firmly that a revival of Christianity would put matters right. The permanent feature of discussions about demographic trends is that they provided excellent opportunities for everyone to mount his favourite hobby-horse. One learns as much about these—about the commonest platitudes on what was going to the dogs— from these discussions as about demography.

The reverse side of the lament about irreligion was the condemnation of materialism and greed. To have few children,

[1] L. Naudeau, *La France se regarde: le problème de la natalité* (1931), 27, 215; Paul Leroy-Beaulieu, *La Question de la population* (1913), 395. Even the distinguished economist A. Sauvy still attributes the falling birth-rate to the decline of religion: in H. Bergues, *La Prévention des naissances* (1960), 389.

[2] J. Bourgeois-Pichat, 'Le Mariage, coutume saisonnière', *Population* (Oct.– Dec. 1946), 623–42.

it was argued, was to be selfish, because it involved ignoring the interests of the state; and emancipation from feudalism and traditional constraints meant that people were becoming more selfish. Translated into liberal terms, people were wanting to better themselves, to rise in the social hierarchy, to ensure that their children had a better life than they themselves had had. They therefore began to have smaller families as soon as children ceased to be a source of wealth—as they had been when they went to work at an early age. Now that the state was forbidding them to work, compelling them to go to school, but leaving the expense of their upkeep to their parents, they had become a source of poverty: the larger families were now the poorest, in terms of what each member enjoyed in consumable goods. The satisfactions to be drawn from children had to be altered to emotional ones; and since immediate returns ceased to be provided by children, there had to be more concentration on returns in the form of prestige and social climbing. The man who worked this out into a theory was Arsène Dumont (1849–1902), a most interesting student of demography whose monographs on eighty different communes enabled him to base his generalisations on an impressive mass of facts. His works failed to win him the professorship at the School of Anthropology he had set his heart on: he had decided, when embarking on his research, to commit suicide if he did not get it—which he duly did. He invented the phrase 'social capillarity' in 1890 to define what was widely considered the basic cause of depopulation—the desire to enjoy a higher standard of living, with more luxury, elegance, pleasure and justice: it was not quite the same thing as ambition, which he thought implied desire for power through political influence or wealth. Dumont attacked the economists for trying to explain demographic behaviour in terms of the subsistence and employment available: economists 'observed the contingent and proclaimed it necessary'. He claimed that the age of sociology had arrived to replace these simplistic explanations, and that it would transform political understanding in the same way as physiology was transforming medicine. The birth-rate, he said, stood in inverse ratio to the strength of the desire to climb socially. A strong family organisation could diminish 'social capillarity' but a strong centralised state increased it. Power was passing more and more to the civil service, entry into which was becoming an almost universal aim, or at any rate the attractions of the fashions and ideals of Paris were becoming universal. The more egalitarian and homogeneous a country became in its customs, tastes and aspirations, the fiercer would competition between its members be. The rise of individualism intensified people's feelings of isolation and inadequacy, so that they alternated between ambition and melancholy, obsessed by what others thought of them, craving for honour, esteem, knowledge or wealth as compensations. The small family was the inevitable result. Only the industrial working class, which had no hope of rising, did not care and so remained fertile.[1] The economists told men simply to produce more, consume more, accumulate more and it was their advice that was bringing about these catastrophic results. The sociologists, by contrast, should give Frenchmen a national aim, so that the individual would not take his own private concerns as being the ultimate purpose of life, but would see himself as part of a movement of successive generations towards greater beauty, virtue, knowledge, courage. But sociology, of course, never succeeded in propagating any such positive values.[2]

Dumont laid it down as a principle that individuals had families of the size favoured not by their own class, but by the class to which they hoped to belong. In 1908 a newspaper published a list of 445 names, generally regarded as the most celebrated and influential in Paris. Between them, these had only 575 children. One hundred and seventy-seven of these celebrities had no children, 106 had one child and 88 had two children. The great statesmen of the Third Republic included an extraordinarily large proportion who were childless— Thiers, Ferry, Gambetta, Spuller, Challemel-Lacour, Goblet, Floquet, Waldeck-Rousseau. It appears to be an established fact that the merchant-aristocracy of Geneva first set the example of having few children as early as the seventeenth century, and that the French aristocracy, followed by the upper

---

[1] On the expense of bringing up children, see G. de Molinari, *La Viriculture* (1897).

[2] Arsène Dumont, *Dépopulation et civilisation; Étude démographie* (1890); cf. id., *Natalité et démocratie* (1898) and *La Morale basée sur la démographie* (1901).

bourgeoisie, adopted the same pattern in the eighteenth century. In the nineteenth century, the lower middle class and the peasantry followed suit. The variations in fecundity among different classes were very considerable. Thus in 1911 (the year which has the best statistics on this subject), every 100 artists had on average 139 children, journalists and concierges 141, but miners had 289 and metal workers 253.

*Comparative fecundity per 100 families in different professions (1911)*

|  | Total | Employers | Clerks etc. | Manual workers |
|---|---|---|---|---|
| Fishermen | 256 | .. | .. | .. |
| Agriculture | 230 | 228 | .. | 238 |
| Mines | 280 | 244 | .. | 282 |
| Industry | 216 | 209 | 186 | 222 |
| Transport | 198 | 225 | 178 | 203 |
| Commerce | 174 | 183 | 155 | 212 |
| Liberal professions | 163 | 165 | 161 | .. |
| Domestic servants | 159 | .. | .. | .. |
| Civil service | 185 | .. | 165 | 208 |
| Total | 213 | 216 | 165 | 223 |

In industry, the fecundity of different grades varied thus:

| Labourers | 237 |
|---|---|
| Semi-skilled workers | 218 |
| Foremen | 215 |
| Employers and artisans | 209 |
| Clerks | 174 |

A survey carried out by Bertillon with a sample of 3,472 *instituteurs* and road-menders (examples of the lowest-paid civil servants) revealed that they had an average of 1·15 and 1·04 children respectively. Another statistic showed that manual workers in state service had fewer children as their wages rose.[1] But these national figures about professional variations are shown to be averages with little reality in them when they are broken down by departments. Thus fishermen in the Nord had families 142 per cent larger than fishermen in the Gironde and there were regions where civil servants had

[1] Landry, op. cit. 166; Henry Clément, *La Dépopulation en France* (1910), 118. Cf. Philip Ogden, *Marriage Patterns and Population Mobility: A Study in Rural France* (Oxford School of Geography Research Papers, no. 7, 1973, duplicated).

the largest number of children second only to fishermen. A favourite assertion was that the richer you became, the fewer children you had: this was never based on any facts, since incomes were not revealed in this period, but it seemed that though the richer classes set the pattern of smaller families, they also abandoned the practices with which they were associated just when the poorer classes were beginning to copy them. Thus in 1858 half of French dukes had one or two children; in 1878 two-thirds of them had reduced their families to this size; but by 1898 they had already reverted to larger families and only 48 per cent had one or two children, while in 1938 only 40 per cent had that number. In 1938, people with noble titles in general had significantly more children than those without them.[1]

But the idea that comfort, or the desire for it, stimulated sterility had a wide currency. A Swedish statistician produced maps in 1886 to show that those departments in France which had the largest number of savings accounts and of fire in-surance policies also had the lowest birth-rates.[2] It was on the basis of such arguments that the responsibility for the declin-ing birth-rate was placed on the law of property. Peasants, interviewed by journalists, professors and doctors, were quoted as saying that their main aim in limiting their progeny was to avoid the division of the plot of land they had laboriously accumulated: their hope was to have a sole heir, who would marry a sole heiress and so continue the process of building up an estate. This may well have been a motive among many, but it must have been associated with other ones, for there were all sorts of alternative ways of avoiding the division of one's land, and there were, as has been seen, far fewer landowners than people imagined.

Prosperity, it was claimed, was even leading to physical degeneration. Dr. Maurel produced statistics to show that the population of the Haute-Garonne had fallen in direct correla-tion with the rise in the amount of food consumed, which was why the towns, which had started 'overeating' earliest, had been the leaders in having small families. He argued that

---

[1] Worked out from the *Almanach Gotha* and the *Bottin mondain*.

[2] J. V. Tallqvist, *Recherches statistiques sur la tendance à une moindre fécondité des mariages* (Helsingfors thesis, 1886).

'overeating' caused 'arthritis', which he considered to be a hereditary disease as destructive as syphilis, except that it got worse with each generation, attacking the first one at around the age of fifty, the second at around thirty-five or forty and the third in youth; intermarriage exacerbated it, while reverses of fortune retarded it. He included many symptoms under the heading of arthritis, not just gout, but all sorts of affections of the circulatory, respiratory and nervous systems, culminating in the reproductive organs becoming sterile. His theory should not be dismissed as medically absurd, because there can be no doubt that it reflected worries people had and actual or fashionable symptoms for which they wanted to find explanations. He claimed that overeating was partly due to a new custom, which led people to think it right to eat till their appetite was satiated, whereas formerly it was an accepted rule that you rose from table while still feeling hungry. Parents now made children eat more than they wanted. Maurel estimated that about one-third of the population was affected by 'arthritism', and so only partially fertile; birth-control he considered was used by only about 50 per cent of couples.[1]

## The Causes of Death

There can be no doubt, however, that hygiene had a decisive influence on demographic trends. The expectation of life at birth rose as follows:[2]

|         | Men | Women |         | Men | Women |
|---------|-----|-------|---------|-----|-------|
| 1817–31 | 38  | 40    | 1928–33 | 54  | 59    |
| 1861–5  | 39  | 40    | 1933–8  | 55  | 61    |
| 1877–81 | 40  | 43    | 1946–9  | 61  | 67    |
| 1898–1903 | 45 | 49   | 1952–6  | 65  | 71    |
| 1908–13 | 48  | 52    | 1960–4  | 67  | 74    |
| 1920–3  | 52  | 55    |         |     |       |

The significance of this table is threefold. First, the greatest and most rapid rise has occurred only since the Second World War: in the nineteenth century, the expectation of life increased

---

[1] Dr. E. Maurel, *De la dépopulation de la France. Étude sur la natalité* (1896), 240–1.
[2] G. Calot, 'L'Évolution de la situation démographique française', *Population* (July–Aug. 1967), 629–92 and Landry, op. cit. 232.

by only about eight years; in the forty years 1900–39, by about eleven years, but between 1939 and 1964 by thirteen years. However, secondly, the expectation of life for those who survived the hazards of childhood hardly changed at all: in 1861 people aged twenty could expect another 41·40 years of life; in 1903 they could still expect only 42·81 years; though in 1933 they could hope for 45·38. The death-rate of males over fifty remained absolutely fixed between 1817 and 1936; and that of males between thirty-two and fifty fell hardly at all. Thirdly, infant mortality fell in France more slowly than in other countries. In the mid-nineteenth century, about 65 per cent of children could hope to survive to the age of twenty; in England it was the same; in Holland only 60 per cent. But by 1930, the proportion in Holland had grown to 91 per cent, in England to 87 per cent but in France to only 85 per cent. These differences were not extraordinary, for though France was considerably behind Holland and Sweden, it was more or less on a par with England and Germany, and well ahead of Italy.

However, for a country which produced so few children the death-rate was catastrophic, and was all the more disturbing because it could be attributed to clearly remediable facts. Infant mortality was particularly worrying because certain types of children were killed off at rates which suggested almost mass extermination. The French practice of sending infants out to wet-nurses was, from one point of view, conducive to a higher population, because it allowed women both to breed and to stay at work, but on the other hand it was claimed that the mortality rate of these *nourrissons* in the 1870s was 51 per cent—at a time when infants brought up by mothers died only at the rate of 19 per cent. Two contiguous communes of the Gironde, one of which used wet-nurses and one of which did not, had a death-rate before the age of one of 87 and 13 per cent respectively.[1] The *nourrices*, it was claimed, were killing 100,000 children a year.[2] The death-rate of illegitimate children in their first year was even higher, reaching as much as 92 per cent in the Loire-Inférieure; the death-rate of

---

[1] Dr. Brochard, *Des causes de la dépopulation en France et les moyens d'y remédier* (Lyon, 1873).
[2] Edmond Desfossé, *Décroissance de la population en France: causes, remède* (1869).

foundling and other children in the state's care (148,000 of them in 1862, of whom 76,520 were aged under one year) was 56 per cent.[1] Infant mortality fell as follows (deaths in first year per 1,000 live births):[2]

| | | | |
|---|---|---|---|
| 1806–10 | 187 | 1931–5 | 73 |
| 1861–5 | 179 | 1938 | 65 |
| 1881–5 | 167 | 1950 | 47 |
| 1909–13 | 126 | 1960 | 23 |
| 1921–5 | 95 | 1965 | 18 |
| 1926–30 | 89 | | |

But these averages conceal considerable difference between male and female mortality, for in 1938 the figures were 73 for boys but 57 for girls; the illegitimate rate at the same time was 105; and the regional variations extended from 52 in parts of Central France to 105 in Brittany.

France was much in advance of the poor countries of the Balkans and the Mediterranean but well behind more hygienic ones in the north.[3] Then Frenchmen in the 1930s had almost twice as high a chance of dying of tuberculosis as other Europeans, and for every one who died of it, there were probably about seven others suffering from the disease. The male death-rate between the ages of twenty-five and forty-five was much higher also because of alcoholism. The decline in the death-rate of different age groups was uneven. Thus between 1856 and 1937 infant mortality was reduced by two-thirds, that of children by 80 per cent, that of young men from twenty-five to thirty-five by only a half, that of men between fifty-five and sixty-four by less than a quarter, while men over eighty had a higher death-rate in 1935 than in 1856. The result of these combined changes was that the balance between the different age groups altered drastically between 1851 and 1936. There used to be 361 children and adolescents under twenty years of age in every thousand inhabitants: but this fell to 302—i.e.

---

[1] Dr. Brochard, *La Vérité sur les enfants trouvés* (1876), 51.

[2] M. Huber, *La Population de la France* (1943), 187; and Calot, art. cit. 641.

[3] Infant mortality under one year, per 1,000 live births, 1937–9:

| | | | |
|---|---|---|---|
| Romania | 179 | Germany | 61 |
| Poland | 138 | England | 54 |
| Italy | 107 | U.S.A. | 50 |
| Austria | 82 | Netherlands | 36 |

by 16 per cent. There used to be 102 old people over sixty years of age in every thousand, and they increased to 147, i.e. by 45 per cent. Fewer young people, many more old people, accentuated the sense of a vanishing population; even though very similar trends could be observed in neighbouring countries, France in 1936 had a larger population of old people than anywhere else in the world.

*Age groups in 1936 (per 1,000)*

|         | Under 20 years | 20–39 | 40–59 | Over 60 |
|---------|----------------|-------|-------|---------|
| Japan   | 465            | 289   | 172   | 74      |
| Italy   | 379            | 315   | 197   | 109     |
| U.S.A.  | 367            | 317   | 225   | 91      |
| Germany | 305            | 341   | 235   | 119     |
| France  | 302            | 311   | 240   | 147     |
| England | 301            | 323   | 247   | 129     |

## Birth-control

There are no certain facts about the extent to which various methods of birth-control were used during this period. An inquiry in Lyon in the 1960s revealed that 64 per cent of mothers questioned said that they had used contraceptives (in Grenoble the figure was 69 per cent). The most favoured method was coitus interruptus (about 50 per cent, and 61 per cent in Grenoble); about 5 per cent used the condom, and about 12 to 16 per cent used the Ogino and temperature methods.[1] At the turn of the century, the anthropologist Jacques Bertillon wrote to 500 doctors in four selected departments of France to ask them the same question about their patients' use of contraception, and they gave the same answer. In the countryside, ninety doctors reported that coitus interruptus was 'very frequent', five said douches were much used, four mentioned the condom, two abortion and one sponge and pessary. In towns, douches were relatively more frequent, in the proportion of six to fifteen attributed to coitus interruptus, but everywhere the condom was little used.[2] It is clear that

[1] H. Pigeaud, 'Attitudes devant la maternité', *Population* (Mar.–Apr. 1966), 241–57.

[2] Jacques Bertillon, *La Dépopulation de la France* (1911), 99.

Frenchmen did not wait for technological innovations and mass manufacture of rubber goods. It is significant that though Dr. Condom, who invented the contraceptive named after him, was a Frenchman, his product was referred to as a *lettre anglaise*, while the English, who used them much more, referred to them as French letters. The problem is why and how these different practices were introduced into love-making.

There are two alternative ways of finding the answer. As has already been suggested, certain changes in people's view of their own interest caused them to reduce their progeny and one can see this as proof of the triumph of enlightenment and forethought over fatalism, as a sign of changing values, of greater interest in education, of a stronger desire for comfort, for the accumulation of wealth, which could be handed over to one's children, of a new view of how to attain immortality. The fact that the death-rate diminished might have reduced people's desire to react against its ravages. These are all factors so imponderable that no amount of quotation from literary, medical or sociological commentaries will ever make it possible to be certain about the relative weight which should be assigned to them. But it is also worth looking at the problem from the point of view of women. They may well have taken more initiative and had more influence than male writers have conceded to them. The desire to have children, which in recent times is considered to be stronger among women, may previously have been much more of a preoccupation among men, intent on preserving their property. Motherhood was considered to involve some risk, even if the statistics did not support this.[1] So many infants died, Madame de Sévigné had said, that there was little pleasure in giving birth to them. She is the woman whose letters are frequently quoted to show the hesitations of French women towards maternity in the seventeenth century. She urged her daughter to keep her husband at a distance, and congratulated her on her success at avoiding pregnancy; she gave the impression that one of the marks of a good husband was that he was not importunate in his demands

[1] The statistics on deaths in childbirth are unsatisfactory. In Paris in 1884, 386 women were registered as having died, when 63,840 children were born. But there is nothing for the rest of the country. In the U.S.A. at the same time, out of 100 deaths of women aged between 20 and 30, 18 were in childbirth and 6 from diseases of the breast or uterus. Levasseur, *La Population française* (1889-92).

for sexual gratification—or, presumably, went elsewhere for these. Père Féline's *Catechism for Married Couples*, published in 1782 and reprinted in 1880, stated that the fall in the birth-rate was due to wives complaining of the great pain motherhood involved, and to husbands becoming increasingly attentive to their wives' wishes.[1] Mgr Bouvier in the 1840s likewise gave as a reason for smaller families the greater concern of husbands for the health and happiness of their wives. It is interesting that in 1969 an inquiry into explanations of family size showed that women with few children stressed above all considerations of their own health, though many also expressed an unwillingness to give up work to have children.[2]

France was long remarkable for the large proportion of its female population in employment: about 28 per cent of the active population were women in 1866, 30 in 1872, 37 in 1906 and that was the figure it remained at. The second half of the nineteenth century was thus the period when the number of women who went out to work increased most rapidly.[3] It was also the period when the ideal of female beauty changed, as Zola observed, from the plump, large-thighed, heavy-breasted mother to a more boyish, sylphlike form. Breast-feeding was a challenge to male sexuality, because it was considered dangerous to copulate when a woman was still breast-feeding. Galien had argued that sexual intercourse induced menstruation and made the milk bitter; and this idea still flourished. Zola describes in his *Fécondité* the prohibition on copulation imposed on husbands for nine months during pregnancy and for fifteen months thereafter. The use of wet-nurses was a victory for the husband, but then the couple were terrified lest the nurse engaged in sexual activity, from which she was rigorously prohibited.[4]

Rather than see a gradual change in women's attitudes, as evolutionists always like to imagine, one should appreciate that an identical situation might be differently interpreted at different times and in different circumstances: breast-feeding

---

[1] Père Féline, *Catéchisme des gens mariés* (1782).

[2] Louis Roussel, 'Les Mobiles de la limitation des naissances dans les mariages de un ou deux enfants', *Population* (1969), 309–30.

[3] J. Toutain, *La Population de la France de 1700 à 1959* (1963), 152.

[4] E. and F. van de Walle, 'Allaitement, stérilité et conception', *Population* (July–Oct. 1972), 685–701.

could be a sign of a greater prestige for motherhood, but also a defence against it. It should not be forgotten that this was a period when medical ideas on reproduction were changing and surprisingly large problems long remained cloaked in mystery. In the 1850s debates were still active among doctors as to whether it was the father or the mother who produced the germ from which the child developed. The conflicting theories of Hippocrates and Aristotle, as embroidered by Buffon and Descartes, still divided them, so that some called themselves 'seminists', some 'ovarists', and other animalculists' depending on which sex they imagined was decisive, and on how they explained the physiology of copulation. The modern view of menstruation was first advanced by a German only in 1835 and by a Frenchman in 1847, but it was slow to gain ground; and experts continued to say that conception could occur only in the first eight days after it.[1] Impotence and sterility were the subject of many theories, and the extraordinary stories people told their doctors about their sexual difficulties, and the extraordinary remedies prescribed to cure them, show that the idea that people now felt masters of their destiny, able to control birth and postpone death, was far from the truth. The physical properties of the sexual organs had in 1850 still not been fully understood, the mechanism of erection was still being argued about. One doctor, for example, invented a 'mechanical flagellator' to cure impotence, another a special chair incorporating an 'aromatic fumigator', to be sat upon before jumping into bed.[2] One of the greatest sources of inhibition was the worry created by masturbation, which was for long widely considered to induce sterility, and vast numbers of guilty and impotent people poured out confessions on this subject to their medical advisers. It may well be that as education and medical attention spread, these worries also did. A *Medical Guide for Marriage*, published in 1868, records how many men feared that their misdemeanours as children, or their debauchery as young men, had rendered them permanently sterile. A large number, it said, suffered from loss of sperm at every excitement. Premature ejaculation caused much de-

---

[1] Dr. F. A. Pouchet, *Théorie positive de la fécondation* (1847).

[2] Dr. Félix Roubaud, *Traité de l'impuissance et de la stérilité* (1855); Lallemand and Civiale, *Traité pratique des maladies des organes génito-urinaires* (1850).

pression, and women were sometimes found to be virgins years after marriage. Copulation with prostitutes made many men expect the same kind of ecstasy in their wives, and they were disappointed not to find it; wives for their part were lucky if they did not develop a disgust for sex after the exaggerated activity young husbands believed it was their duty to engage in. New fashions in education, which encouraged girls to be 'impressionable and delicate', often filled them with horror for intercourse. Above all, 'our experience, based on innumerable cases, allows us to affirm that the troubles of many couples come not from any real incapacity, but from ignorance of physiological laws'.[1] Among some people, ignorance may well have increased with 'refinement'. There is still a great deal to be discovered about the history of love.[2]

## Old Age and Death

Old people like to look back to happier, more ordered times when old age was respected, when the problem of senile parents did not exist, because their children venerated them. There is little evidence that this situation ever existed. Anthropological research has revealed that respect for the aged is not normal in primitive societies, that though the old are sometimes regarded as repositories of knowledge and mediators with the supernatural, the respect they are accorded is usually due to some special asset, and it is rarely continued when they fall into decrepitude. The old are generally saved by their property rights. But there are peoples who kill them off or even bury them while still alive.[3] In France respect for old age has long been ambivalent and by no means to be relied on. There is an old-established literary tradition mocking old age as ridiculous, ugly and stupid. Montaigne at the age of thirty-five was already lamenting that he was slowing down and he could see no sign that he was getting any wiser. Molière

[1] J. L. Curtis, *Guide médical du mariage* (1868), 46, 50, 78, 93; id., *De la virilité* (56th edition, 1856).

[2] See the new insights in J. L. Flandrin, *Les Amours paysannes: amour et sexualité dans les campagnes de l'ancienne France* (1970), which shows how much can be learnt from demographic statistics (but this book is mainly about the eighteenth century) and E. Shorter, 'Différences de classe et sentiment depuis 1750', *Annales* (July–Aug. 1974).

[3] Leo W. Simmons, *The Role of the Aged in Primitive Society* (Yale U.P., 1945).

made fun of old men as suspicious, avaricious, pusillanimous, grumbling and silly. Parricide was rare: in 1855, for example, four cases of it were recorded; but the report of the official commission investigating the state of agriculture in 1866–70 warned landowners not to divide their property up between their children while they were still alive, because 'the father of a family, once he has surrended his goods, is deprived of all authority. He passes into a state of being despised, rejected by his children, thrown out of the homes of each of them, sent from one to the other with a pension which is often not paid, or promised a house which is not given him.' A newspaper inquiry in 1885 told the same story of the neglect to which old parents were subjected. Zola, in his study of the peasantry (*La Terre*), has left a forceful picture of the terrible clashes that could occur between generations. In the 1960s, statistics established that two-thirds of old people received no help from their children.[1]

The concern with the plight of the aged is not the result of changed treatment, but of three new factors. First, the veil of hypocrisy has been drawn aside, and a new sensibility has made people aware of a situation which has always existed. Secondly, there are now more old people: between 1851 and 1972 the number of those over sixty-five doubled:[2]

*Percentage of population over 65*

| 1851 | 6·7 |
| 1901 | 8·5 |
| 1936 | 10·0 |
| 1954 | 11·5 |
| 1974 | 13·2 |

Thirdly, and not least, old people became more vocal about their plight, and their attitudes also changed. The old became a national problem when they began to unite, to see themselves as a class apart, in the same way as the young asserted their own individuality.

The number of books written about the old increased steadily in this period, but for long they simply repeated advice culled from ancient Greek and other traditional sources. They advised the old to preserve themselves by abstaining from the more

[1] S. de Beauvoir, *La Vieillesse* (1970), 17, 189, 209, 254.

[2] From 2,317,000 to 5,184,000—whereas the population as a whole increased by only one-fifth.

violent pleasures of life, by following the principle of moderation in all things, and by accepting their limitations with
resignation. They attacked modern civilisation and its evils
as sources of the tension and illnesses which reduced the length
of life.[1] These grim warnings continued to be repeated into the
inter-war period. But there were also some doctors who rose
up to protest against the idea of old age being inevitably marked
by decay. The creation of large hospitals, and notably the
Salpêtrière in Paris, which had geriatric wards for between
two and three thousand people, provided opportunities for
closer examination of their peculiar troubles. Dr. Durand-
Fardel wrote in 1854, on the basis of fifteen years of such
research, that it was not one's years that made one old, but
how one functioned: fresh air and exercise could keep one going
efficiently beyond the normal limits. But he still recommended
fifteen leeches on the anus to avert strokes, which he saw as
the worst, mysterious threat to the old, and daily purges to keep
the bowels moving.[2] In the 1860s Dr. Charcot's lectures on the
diseases of old people argued that old age as such was not a
disease, and that each organ deteriorated or ceased to function
largely independently: only a few illnesses were specifically
attributable to old age.[3] In the 1870s Dr. Brown-Sequard
claimed he had succeeded in revitalising himself with solutions
of macerated animal testicles. Hope for women came somewhat
later. In 1923 a woman doctor could still write that those past
the menopause had to accept their situation as inevitable, but
in the 1930s hormonal treatment began to be prescribed.[4]
These new ideas affected a small minority. A recent inquiry
among adults revealed that one-fifth of them thought old
age began before fifty-five. (Another fifth said it started after
sixty-five: one-third placed it between fifty-five and sixty-five
and one-third did not know.)[5] The boundaries of old age have

[1] Dr. Guyétant, L'Âge de retour et la vieillesse. Conseils au gens du monde (1870);
Vicomte de Lapasse, Essai sur la conservation de la vie (1860); Dr. P. Foissac, La
Longévité humaine (1873); Dr. B. Lunel, Dictionnaire de la conservation de l'homme.
Encylopédie de la santé . . . (1857).

[2] M. Durand-Fardel, Traité clinique et pratique des maladies des vieillards (1854),
xi, 285-7, 325.

[3] J. M. Charcot, Leçons cliniques sur les maladies des vieillards (1866-7).

[4] Peter N. Stearns, Aging in French Culture (1976), a pioneering historical survey.

[5] William Grossin, 'Les Temps de la vie quotidienne' (unpublished doctoral
psychology thesis, Paris V, 1972), 453.

not been pushed back in general opinion, mainly because for
the working classes physical impairment means unemployment,
and most managers have come to accept the view, probably
pioneered by the Americans, that full efficiency at work cannot
be expected after the age of fifty.[1]

But the growth in numbers of those who could afford to
retire, or were forced to retire, created a new justification of
old age as a period of independence that came as the reward
of work.[2] Civil servants were the leaders in this movement,
followed by the industrial and commercial middle classes (but
excluding members of the liberal professions, who continued to
work well beyond sixty-five). At the turn of the century, only a
third of workers had retired by the age of sixty-five, compared
to two-thirds of the employees of banking and commerce and
95 per cent of state officials. Special journals began appearing
between the wars to cater for this new class, either as organs to
defend their rights (*Le Cri du retraité*), or to teach them how to
enjoy themselves (*La Vieillesse heureuse*). This latter journal
reported on youth sports and urged the old to develop similar
activities. This illustrates how old and young simultaneously
sought to create a way of life for themselves which was independent of that of adults. This does not mean that the old
wanted to be segregated into old people's homes: on the
contrary, inquiries in the 1950s showed that 80 per cent did
not wish to go into these. But exactly the same proportion also
took the view that they would rather not live with their children
and indeed only a very small minority did live with their
children (mainly in the country). In 1954, 30 per cent of
people over sixty lived alone, 40 per cent lived in couples and
24 per cent in households of more than two members.[3] The
idea of retirement as a Third Age was still very much a utopia
in the distant future. Most people did not have adequate
cultural or financial resources to profit from their leisure.
Retirement, more often than not, meant 'social death', with-

[1] W. A. Achenbaum, 'The Obsolescence of Old Age in America 1865–1914',
*Journal of Social History* (1974), 48–62.

[2] In 1954 74 per cent of men and 37·2 per cent of women were still at work at
the age of 60; at the age of 70, 33·5 per cent of men and 12 per cent of women
were still at work.

[3] [Pierre Laroque], *Politique de la vieillesse*, rapport de la commission d'étude
des problèmes de la vieillesse (1962), 112.

drawal from contact with the world. Pensions and assistance from social workers, the solution offered by the mid-twentieth century, was not enough, because it concentrated exclusively on the old, ignoring the problem of preparation for retirement.[1]

Just how slowly ideas on this subject came to be formulated, and to move beyond the tradition of charity, can be seen from the development of the insurance industry. Until 1818, life insurance was forbidden by law, on the ground that it was immoral to place a value on something so sacred as life, but also because the state wanted to have a monopoly for its own *tontine* system, which was a form of lottery. This system, however, went out of fashion during the Second Empire, as interest shifted from insurance against death to endowment policies: a mixture of the two, introduced in 1857, became, as from 1895, the most common form of insurance. Insurance companies for long appeared as tainted by fraud, on the part of the speculators who profited from them or the customers who tried to cheat them: of those which mushroomed under Louis-Philippe, only four survived the revolution of 1848, and a sensational poisoning case in 1864, in which Dr. Couty de La Pommerais was accused of killing his wife in order to benefit from an insurance policy worth over half a million francs, made the possibilities of insurance better known, but in a dubious way. In 1874 there were probably about 121,000 people insured. The rise of the insurance business took place only between the wars. In 1942 3,300,000 life insurance policies were in force, and 115,000 people were employed selling and administering insurance. But the proportion of the national income invested in insurance represented only one-half of the amount invested in Britain and a little over one-quarter of that invested in the U.S.A.[2]

This must be linked up with attitudes to death. The current view is that death is a subject people have increasingly become unwilling to talk about, that it has indeed succeeded sex as the most important taboo aspect of human existence. In the middle

[1] Anne-Marie Guillemard, *La Retraite, une mort sociale. Sociologie des conduites en situation de retraite* (1972).

[2] I. Tournan, *L'Assurance sur la vie en France au 19ᵉ siècle* (Paris law thesis, 1906), 73, 180; Jacques Deschamps, *Cent trente ans d'une industrie: bilan des assurances privées en France* (Versailles, 1946), 29; P. J. Richard, *Histoire des institutions d'assurance en France* (1956), for new trends after 1945; Raoul Ménard, *De l'assurance sur la vie: son rôle économique et sociale dans la vie moderne* (Poitiers law thesis, 1908).

ages, it has been argued, people knew how to die calmly and without fear; death was accepted as an integral part of experience, met by all ages; funerals were social events and cemeteries were used also for sports. Praying for the dead was a minor religious industry. But then death became more individual, until mourning itself was frowned on, so that there was no way left to express grief: people tried to forget about death, and the aged were sent to hospitals to die in isolation from society.[1] More research is needed before this general contrast of the present and the past can be made less schematic, for the fragmentary evidence available on the period of transition does not fit easily into either stereotype. A doctor who in 1842 published his observations on some 1,000 deaths he had witnessed recorded that there were indeed ideal deaths, by the old criterion, in which the victim had prepared himself for death all his life and was ready for it, expected it to happen at six in the evening, which was when his father had died, had the church bells rung to help him obtain forgiveness of his sins, and took leave of his family very movingly. But this doctor also recorded a labourer going into delirium at the thought of hell, when told the priest had been sent for: his teeth chattered and he wept profusely and begged for pardon, repeating endlessly 'My God, do not damn me.' The majority of poor people however, were, he said, totally indifferent to the admonitions of the priest and expressed interest only in food: there were those who would also tolerate painful surgery in complete silence if promised a meal at the end of it. There were men who died worrying obsessively about the details of their business affairs, or dominated by jealous thoughts concerning their wives. It was impossible to predict how people would behave in dying: 'the approach of death is the beginning of a new way of thinking and of hoping for all'; ideas on the subject were full of contradictions.[2]

Certainly in Normandy, it is known that fraternities to organise burials survived, even if they fell from 550 in 1843 to a mere 100 at the present day. These fraternities had a vigorous

[1] Philippe Ariès, *Western Attitudes towards Death* (Baltimore, 1974); M. Vovelle, *Mourir autrefois* (1970); Geoffrey Gorer, *Death, Grief and Mourning in Contemporary Britain* (1965).

[2] H. Lauvergne, *De l'agonie et de la mort dans toutes les classes de la société* (1842), I. x, 2. 142–50.

life in the nineteenth century, with increasingly codified and elaborate rules. The fines for those who made mistakes, like 'for allowing the straw in one's clogs to fall out', or for 'dropping the body because of drunkenness', show that funerals sometimes remained boisterous affairs.[1] Whether the Association of the Good Death, founded in 1859, achieved anything in perpetuating or spreading Catholic attitudes is not known.[2] Anticlericals were not necessarily freed from the emotions that believers felt. Thus Roger Martin du Gard (1881–1958), who never had any religious beliefs and whose novel *Jean Barois* became a symbol of the triumph of free thought, was all his life terrified by death and obsessed by the thought of it. It was only after having slaved away for twenty years on his major work, *Les Thibault* (1922–40) that he at last felt he would be ready to accept death, because he had created a monument that would ensure his immortality.[3] At another extreme, the romantic attitude involved curiosity about death and even longing for death, resulting from despair with life, or longing for love too absolute to be found in this world.[4] Suicide was something people thought about increasingly as they grew older; its incidence rose steadily with age.[5]

An inquiry by a psychologist in the late 1960s suggests that France has been left with a variety of attitudes, rather than with one 'modern' one. Worrying about death seems to be related not just to religious belief but also to boredom: those who said they were never bored, seldom thought about death. There were clear differences therefore between different professions: thus teachers said they were bored far less often than workers, or wine-growers for example. For them, old age was something

[1] *La Sociologie de la mort.* Special issue of *Archives de sciences sociale des religions,* no. 39 (Jan.–June 1975), 83.

[2] Al. Lefebvre, S.J., *La Science de bien mourir, manuel de l'Association de la Bonne Mort* (1864).

[3] Melvin Gallant, *Le Thème de la mort chez Roger Martin du Gard* (1971). Cf. Louis Bourdeau, *Le Problème de la mort. Les solutions imaginaires et la science positive* (3rd edition, 1900) and L. Leblois, *Mort et immortalité. Trois lettres à un rationaliste* (2nd edition, Strasbourg, 1866).

[4] Malaka Gourdin Servenière (*née* Sedky), 'Sentiment et problème de la mort chez les prosateurs et les penseurs français de la première moitié du 19e siècle' (unpublished doctorat ès lettres, Sorbonne, 1973); N. J. Popa, *Le Thème et le sentiment de la mort chez Gérard de Nerval 1808–55* (1925).

[5] E. Durkheim, *Le Suicide* (1897); J. D. Douglas, *The Social Meaning of Suicide* (Princeton, 1967).

they thought of as arriving late. Altogether, 36 per cent of this sample never thought of death, 31 per cent rarely, 17 per cent quite often, 9 per cent often and 7 per cent very often. This had little connection with belief in afterlife, which itself was not always related to religious belief. Thus a public opinion poll in 1947 found that 58 per cent of those questioned said they believed in an afterlife, while another in 1968 found the figure had fallen to 35 per cent, but in the meantime those who said they believed in God rose from 66 to 73 per cent.[1]

These hints are enough to show that the relationship between attitudes to death and behaviour in life, if it is ever worked out with greater precision, is unlikely to be a simple one, which can be stated by reference to a single, or even a few, social variables. They suggest, as do also the statistics on population and family, that several fundamentally opposed forms of behaviour co-existed. France was not all one in the way it tackled birth, death, or anything else.

[1] William Grossin, 'Les Temps de la vie quotidienne' (unpublished thesis, Paris V, 1972), 455, 457, 471. For other statistics on religious belief, see below, p. 1028.

# 20. Religion and Anticlericalism

TWENTY years ago it would have been possible to argue that the anxieties from which people suffered in this period were directly connected with the decline of religious belief. It is now clear that this was not the case, first because it is by no means certain that religious belief did decline, secondly because religion now came to offer new consolations, and thirdly because the Church was itself torn by anxieties of its own. What the ecclesiastical history of this century shows above all is a crisis of communication: churchmen and free-thinkers were so carried away by the bitterness of their disagreements that they became incapable of understanding each other, and hopelessly confused as to what their quarrels were about. The country split into two, but that split concealed a whole plurality of beliefs and temperaments which it cut across in a most misleading way. The dispute about religion was a genuine dispute of fundamental importance but, at the same time as it created new attitudes to life, it also became a major obstacle to self-knowledge and to perception of the complexities of human motivation. Simply to recount the anticlerical battles in terms of the persecution, the legislation and the insults is to miss at least half of what was going on.[1]

In 1961 85 per cent of French people declared themselves to be believing Catholics: 34 per cent claimed to practise regularly; only 6 per cent stated they had no religion. These findings show that lip-service was still being paid, as it was in the century covered by this book, to the idea that France was a Catholic country. The Church itself, however, had no illusions. It realised that its contact with the 85 per cent was often confined to only three occasions: baptism, marriage and burial. Its statisticians stated that the figure of 34 per cent of regular church-goers was in reality 26 per cent. Two-thirds of

---

[1] A. Dansette, *Histoire religieuse de la France contemporaine* (1849–51); J. McManners, *Church and State in France 1870–1914* (1972); C. Langlois and J. M. Mayeur, 'Sur l'histoire religieuse de l'époque contemporaine', *Revue historique* (Oct.–Dec. 1974), 433–44.

these church-goers moreover were women; the majority of them were middle class; only between 2 and 10 per cent at most of the working class practised regularly; the very rich and the very poor on the whole kept away. The majority of church-goers were not wage earners but children and old people. Most children were taught their Catechism, but between a quarter and a half among the bourgeoisie, and between half and 80 per cent among the working class, abandoned all regular practice immediately after their first communion. Attendance at church varied enormously in different regions of the country; some rural areas had almost totally empty churches; in Paris 15 per cent went to church; in Strasbourg 39 per cent.[1] But these figures do not represent a decline of faith.

Under the *ancien régime* attendance at church was legally compulsory, but it was not in practice enforced. The myth that France was pious and Catholic before the Revolution was invented by modern conservatives idealising the middle ages. In the eighteenth century there was little militant abstention from religion, but only a small and unorganised minority was fervently devout. Most people went to church, but by no means every Sunday; nearly everybody took Easter communion, but though faith was sincere it was frequently passive, induced by social pressure or combined with appalling ignorance of the doctrines of the Church and with much superstition. In church, behaviour was not infrequently rowdy and inattentive. Brittany, then as now, was one of the most religious parts of the country, but as has been seen its religion incorporated considerable elements of pre-Christian origin, and rituals that made it original, which was perhaps why it resisted both Protestant heresy and modern materialism.[2] The study of the different varieties of Catholicism in France, and their relation with local traditions, is still in its infancy; but it is clear that in certain regions the marriage between them was not successful, so that once the pressure for religious conformity was lifted by the revolution of 1789 and then again by that of 1830, the divorce, often latent, became public.

The diocese of Orléans—about which there is detailed information, thanks to the minute inquiries of Dupanloup, its

[1] Philippe Alméras, *Les Catholiques français* (1963), 9–14.
[2] G. Le Bras, *Études de sociologie religieuse* (1955).

bishop under the Second Empire—was by 1850 openly heathen. In its most religious archdeaconry, only 2 per cent of the men took Easter communion, 11·6 per cent of the women, 21·9 per cent of the boys and 56 per cent of the girls—in all 10·6 of the population. In some villages attendance at Easter was 0·5 per cent for men, and 5 to 7 per cent for women. One *curé* wrote contemptuously of his flock: 'They have certain habits, which have nothing to do with religion. They recite the formulae of prayer, but they do not pray; they attend Mass, but they never listen; they believe in a God whom they fashion themselves; they pray to God fervently when they are ill, when they believe they are bewitched, when their animals are sick; they ask God for temporal goods but never for spiritual ones. They pray for the dead but only from habit and custom; and among the prayers for the dead they prefer those which give most glory to the living.' Another wrote 'Faith is lacking in almost every heart; people believe in religion only by a kind of habit.' The regions of highest religiosity in this diocese were not ones of genuine piety: they were regions with high illegitimate birth-rates, exceptional drunkenness, strong superstition. The men who attended church resented the preaching, and made a deafening noise during the services, spitting, slamming doors, coughing and shuffling.[1]

The latest archival investigations reveal that religious practice in some regions continued at virtually unchanged levels between 1850 and 1900, despite the anticlerical battles: in the Romorantin district of the diocese of Blois, for example, the proportion of men taking Easter communion remained at around one-third. In other regions (e.g. Chartres) the proportion fell from 3·8 per cent in 1868 to 1·3 per cent around 1900, but returned to 3·4 per cent in the 1930s and reached 8·3 in 1959.[2] The quality of religion differed so much from region to region and from epoch to epoch that it is virtually impossible to trace the progress of belief as a constant factor: fervent piety, popular religiosity and superstition, conformist attendance at church,

[1] Christianne Marcilhacy, *Le Diocèse d'Orleans au milieu du dix-neuvième siècle* (1964), 302–95.
[2] F. Boulard, 'Aspects de la pratique religieuse en France de 1802 à 1939', *Revue d'histoire de l'église de France* (1973), vol. 59, 269–311; F. Boulard, 'La "Déchristianisation" de Paris', *Archives de sociologie des religions* (1971), vol. 31, 69–98.

membership of charitable, social and militant church organisations each have their own history. It is because there is no easy method of distinguishing between these that there has been so much confused argument, and that so many different factors have been blamed for the supposed decline of faith. France is not unique in this respect: Victorian England was far less dominated by the established church than popular novels pretended, and in 1851 a nation-wide census revealed that almost half of those free to attend church did not go.[1] But the absence in France of nonconformist churches (which provided religion without clericalism) has meant that the anticlerical battles have been greatly exacerbated, and the issues have therefore got more muddled. In particular this has meant that Catholicism has been seen as essentially medieval and irreligion as a modern liberation from it, which vastly oversimplifies the problem.

The Church did indeed repeatedly attack modern civilisation, progress, industrialisation, capitalism, socialism, urbanisation and virtually every new phenomenon, as sources of temptation, degradation and immorality. In the nineteenth century, papal encyclicals spelt out these anathemas in a form that showed no desire for compromise of any kind. People who believed in modernity and progress had every reason to think that the Church had no room for them. But in practice the split between religion and free thought was not one of the backward rural parts of the country against the new towns. Religion survived in Brittany, which was economically backward, but also in Alsace and Lorraine, which were the very opposite. The contrast between town and country, from the point of view of religious practice, was sometimes less marked than the contrast between two towns, like, for example, Béziers and Montpellier. New industrial towns were not necessarily irreligious; far from it. What seems to have been more decisive was, first, the religious character of the region in which the town stood, and secondly, the type of immigrants it attracted. Different areas have had distinct personalities which have not been totally effaced by demographic movement. Migrants have sometimes taken their faith with them to the towns, and they have not always been rebels trying to escape

[1] John D. Gay, *The Geography of Religion in England* (1971), 55.

social constraints. Religious practice could be at an above average level in towns, and on occasion the most religious groups in a town were those whose families had been there longest.[1] Of course, peasants who brought to the towns a view of God as a power to be placated, so as to avoid natural disasters and to obtain good harvests, often came to find alternative methods of advancing their interests and alternative superstitions, in towns where church attendance was not an established practice. Poor industrial workers did indeed often have no religious life at all, and they were not surprisingly regarded by the upper classes as barbarians.[2] The religious sects for the poor that flourished in England and the U.S.A. had no counterpart in France. But this does not mean that the working class as a whole was always irreligious. Apart from local traditions, its beliefs differed from occupation to occupation. The old artisan corporations had had a religious side to them and the workers' funeral clubs showed that they valued the last rites, if not all the teaching of the Church. Non-religious funerals were a well-established custom in the 20th *arrondissement* of Paris before the anticlerical campaigns, but they became no more frequent as a result of these and remained in a minority.

*Percentage of non-religious funerals in Paris*

|       | Paris | 13th *Arrondissement* | 16th *Arrondissement* | 20th *Arrondissement* |
|-------|-------|-----------------------|-----------------------|-----------------------|
| 1884  | 23    | 25                    | 6                     | 41                    |
| 1913  | 33    | 31                    | 13                    | 38                    |

The propaganda of the political classes thus had only a limited influence on the behaviour of the masses. This has been illustrated rather strikingly by a detailed study of the effects of lay schooling and the anticlerical press in the diocese of Montpellier. The establishment of state primary schools made virtually no difference to church attendance and the villages where radical newspapers were bought were not made anticlerical by them: there has been a steady continuity in religious

[1] E. Pin, *Pratique religieuse et classes sociales dans une paroisse urbaine, Saint-Pothin à Lyon* (1956).
[2] F. A. Isambert, *Christianisme et classe ouvrière* (1961).

affiliation, despite all the agitation.[1] This diocese is geographically very diverse, and historically different parts of it have built up different traditions towards religion; but it is not the economically most developed areas which have rejected Catholicism. A doctor writing a 'medico-psychological' study of its beliefs in 1868 noted that it was precisely the most advanced areas which were most superstitious, and superstition and religious practice did not always go together.[2] So though it is true that the middle classes today go to church more than the working classes, this does not mean that there are not regions where substantial numbers of workers are religious.[3] Nor was it always the towns which led in 'dechristianisation': Marseille, for example, was in the eighteenth century considerably more devout than many parts of the surrounding countryside.[4] The history of middle-class religiosity is still only a matter of rough conjecture: it is customary to say that irreligion became fashionable in the late eighteenth century, but that the well-to-do returned to the Church in the course of the nineteenth century, frightened by the chaos produced by their revolution, and still more in the twentieth century, when Catholicism ceased to involve monarchism; but the detailed evidence to justify such generalisations is fragmentary: the piety of the rich has been of less interest to sociologists than the problem of winning the masses to the Church.

A study has been made of the time elapsing between birth and baptism in Marseille between 1806 and 1958. The professions of the parents, known until 1871, show that farmers were most religious, if one takes as one's criterion baptism within three days of birth, while doctors, industrialists, merchants and sailors were least so. This is the nearest that anyone has come to providing a statistical comparison of class behaviour, but the criterion is unfortunately not really indicative of belief. Until 1830 75 per cent of infants were baptised within

[1] Gérard Cholvy, *Géographie religieuse de l'Hérault contemporain* (1968).
[2] Gérard Cholvy, 'Religion et société au 19ᵉ siècle. Le diocèse de Montpellier' (Paris doctoral thesis, unpublished, 1972); Dr. Calixte Cavalier, *Étude médico-psychologique sur la croyance aux sortilèges à l'époque actuelle* (Montpellier, 1868).
[3] See figures for 1965, by profession, in F. Boulard and Jean Rémy, *Pratique religieuse urbaine et régions culturelles* (1968), 96.
[4] Michel Vovelle, *Piété bourgeoise et déchristianisation en Provence au 18ᵉ siècle* (1973).

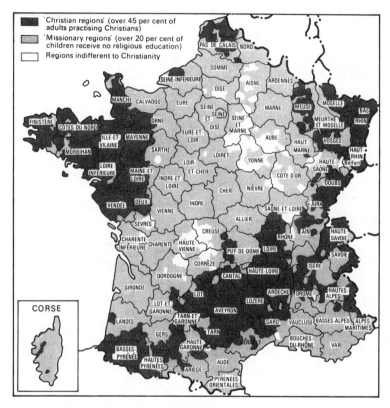

Map 4. Religious Practice (1947). Based on F. Boulard, *Essor ou déclin du clergé français* (1950).

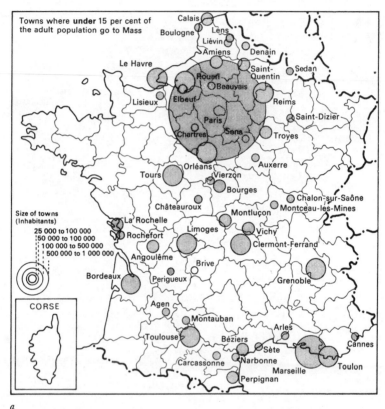

Towns where **under** 15 per cent of
the adult population go to Mass

Size of towns
(Inhabitants)
25 000 to 100 000
50 000 to 100 000
100 000 to 500 000
500 000 to 1 000 000

CORSE

Calais
Boulogne
Lens
Liévin
Amiens
Denain
Le Havre
Saint-Quentin
Sedan
Rouen
Beauvais
Lisieux
Elbeuf
Reims
Saint-Dizier
Paris
Chartres
Sens
Troyes
Orléans
Auxerre
Tours
Vierzon
Bourges
Châteauroux
Chalon-sur-Saône
Montceau-les-Mines
Montluçon
La Rochelle
Rochefort
Limoges
Vichy
Clermont-Ferrand
Angoulême
Brive
Bordeaux
Périgueux
Grenoble
Agen
Montauban
Arles
Toulouse
Béziers
Cannes
Sète
Carcassonne
Narbonne
Marseille
Toulon
Perpignan

a

Maps 5a and b. Religion in the Towns (1960s). Based on F. Boulard and
J. Rémy, *Pratique religieuse urbaine et régions culturelles* (1968).

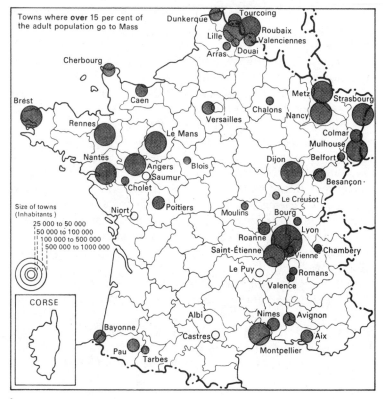

Towns where **over** 15 per cent of the adult population go to Mass

Dunkerque
Tourcoing
Roubaix
Lille
Valenciennes
Arras
Douai
Cherbourg
Metz
Caen
Strasbourg
Chalons
Brest
Nancy
Rennes
Versailles
Le Mans
Colmar
Mulhouse
Nantes
Angers
Blois
Dijon
Belfort
Saumur
Besançon
Cholet
Le Creusot
Niort
Poitiers
Moulins
Bourg
Size of towns
(Inhabitants )
Roanne
Lyon
25 000 to 50 000
50 000 to 100 000
Saint-Étienne
Vienne
Chambery
100 000 to 500 000
500 000 to 1 000 000
Le Puy
Romans
Valence
CORSE
Albi
Nimes
Avignon
Bayonne
Castres
Aix
Pau
Montpellier
Tarbes

b

three days. There was a significant fall to 70 per cent in 1831–3 and this percentage remained constant during the July Monarchy. By 1870, however, it had fallen to 30 per cent; a further important fall occurred after the Commune; and by 1958 the figure was 0·52 per cent.[1] This suggests that political events had immediate repercussions in religious behaviour, but too much cannot be read into these figures, because they are complicated by the fall in infant mortality which made hasty baptism less important. Politics by itself cannot provide an adequate explanation of attitudes to the Church. Thus 'dechristianisation' in Provence has been traced to the middle of the eighteenth century, and to a wide variety of factors, well before the Revolution. The revolution of 1830 revealed a lot of anticlericalism, but it was followed nevertheless by a considerable revival of interest in religion. The identification of the clergy with the monarchist cause in the nineteenth century and their increasingly active role in politics, however, so confused attitudes to religion, that contemporaries could no longer make sense of the very complex relationships that resulted. It remains very difficult to see clearly through the polemic, quite apart from the fact that probably no historian can be totally impartial in approaching the subject.[2]

Thus one of the main peculiarities of this period was that the Church was more popular among women than among men. This is usually looked on negatively, as implying that the Church was not strong enough to hold the allegiance of men. It could, on the contrary, be appreciated positively as one of the most important ways by which women began to liberate themselves from the domination of men. The Church, of course, never thought of itself as doing any such thing, for it was dedicated to the patriarchal family. But in a world in which the male reigned supreme, the Church in fact provided a haven where women were treated as equals, and given opportunities to lead lives independent of their menfolk, organising and participating in exclusively feminine charities and societies. The anticlericals protested loudly against this, claiming that

[1] F. L. Charpin, *Pratique religieuse et formation d'une grande ville. Le geste du baptême et sa signification en sociologie religieuse: Marseille 1806–1950* (1964).

[2] Cf. René Rémond, 'Recherche d'une méthode d'analyse historique de la déchristianisation depuis le milieu du 19e siècle', *Colloque d'histoire religieuse*, Lyon, October 1963 (Grenoble, 1963), 123–54.

the clergy were using weak-minded women to spread their own reactionary influence. Michelet, for example, argued that, through the confessional, priests were invading the privacy of the home, making the wife spy on her husband and using children against their parents. Michelet claimed that he—and the republican anticlericals in general—were keen to make wives into true companions, but he also made clear that this was to be achieved by the husband instructing his wife and moulding her to conform to his ideal. Michelet talks of confessors 'seducing' wives, 'flagellating' them with 'spiritual rods', arrogating the right to visit them when they pleased, insisting that they confess details of their private lives which they would never dream of mentioning to their husbands; the result was that the husband lost control of his own household and 'the home became uninhabitable'.[1] There was a strong element of jealousy in Michelet's attack on the Church, which he accentuated precisely when his mistress, on her death-bed, turned to her confessor, rather than to him.[2] He claimed he wished to strengthen the 'religion of the home' against the religion of the Church. But, as the abbé Laurichesse replied, the Church provided women with consolation to enable them to bear the sexual and other demands made upon them by men and the subordinate role they had to accept: it enabled them to 'obtain spiritual vengeance while being dependent'; it gave them 'an inner life' and 'an asylum against all the oppression from outside'. In this way it strengthened marriage.[3] There were perceptive women who agreed with this abbé, saying that women went to confession because husbands could not understand their wives; husbands blamed wives for frigidity without seeing that they were themselves the cause of it.[4] The building-up of separate male and female preserves in social life was a reflection of this mutual incomprehension. Anticlericalism was, to a certain extent, a confused reaction to this problem of relations between the sexes; female religiosity could be an emotional escape from it.

[1] J. Michelet, *Le Prêtre, la femme et la famille* (1845, 1875 reprint), 267, 307.

[2] Jean Pommier, 'Les Idées de Michelet et de Renan sur la confession en 1845', *Journal de psychologie normale et pathologique* (July–Oct. 1936), 520–2.

[3] Abbé A. M. Laurichesse, *Études philosophiques et morales sur la confession* (1864–5).

[4] Adèle Esquiros, *L'Amour* (1860); see above, vol. 1. 233–4.

There was a great thirst for religion in 1848. Neither republicanism nor socialism was originally hostile to Christianity. But the French Catholic church proved incapable of providing the teaching, the solace or the example that idealistic people asked of it, because the political battles it had engaged in, and the harrowing persecution it had undergone, had left it too aggressive, too frightened, too uncertain of its mission in a changing world. This century was therefore one in which the interests of the Church as an institution and the cause of religion as an attitude to life drifted apart. France was apparently divided by its religious disputes into two camps. But the mentalities to be found in each camp were not as totally opposed as the militants, blinded by anger, believed. Each camp was obsessed by the need to defend itself, and the desire to attack its rival. Clericalism and anticlericalism became probably the most fundamental cause of division among Frenchmen. But it led to another division being forgotten, which was more fundamentally religious: the division between those who were preoccupied by the problems of death, guilt, conscience, the distinction of the valuable from the trivial and the place of the individual in the universe, and those who were not. It is quite wrong to assume that those who attended mass on Sunday represented the religious part of the nation. If one adopts the (over-simple) criterion that it is incompatible to be both religious and materialist, then a good portion of the Sunday communicants should probably not be classified among the religious, whereas not a few of the anticlerical *instituteurs* should. The battles fought about the organisation and power of the Church were a different problem.

### The parish clergy

The parish clergy of the Catholic Church were, in this period, in a phase of development which made them singularly incapable of providing a leadership that would be widely acceptable. In the course of the seventeenth and eighteenth centuries, their condition had been much improved: they were no longer ignorant feudal servants, but of middle-class origin, sometimes aristocrats. They received an up-to-date training, which made them, as some have argued, the most efficient clergy in Europe. They held an influential place in society not only because of their numbers (there were altogether 200,000 priests in France) but also because of their intellectual activity: in Périgord, out of the forty subscribers to the *Encyclopédie*, twenty-four were *curés*. There were already areas where they met with resistance; and there were certainly black sheep among them. But in the revolution of 1789 they took a leading part in the movement for the abolition of privilege. The Revolution, however, had three results which destroyed most of the fruits of the Counter-Reformation and had a disastrous effect on the clergy's action. First, it split them into two, and a large portion of them became irreconcilable enemies of the liberal cause. Secondly, it turned them into civil servants, paid by the state and subject to a far more rigorous discipline from their bishops: by losing their independence, they became involved in the variations of governmental policy. Thirdly, it drove many into exile, and it was half a century before every parish had a priest again: the Church ceased to be a universal institution. The status of the priest fell accordingly: henceforth he was usually of peasant origin, often a poor boy who saw in the Church a way of obtaining a free education and a secure life, and who sacrificed marriage to obtain it. (In the twentieth century, it was the sons of shopkeepers, artisans and clerks who became priests: these classes provided 55 to 60 per cent of the priests in 1950.) The clergy thus suffered from ambitions and anxieties which did not make them the natural guides of society.

The education they received encouraged them to withdraw into a ghetto, where they could be safe from the pressures of the world.[1] They were trained, first, at *petits séminaires*, which were distinguished by the determination with which these sought to cut off children from the pleasures of the world and to 'instil principles into them'. Prayers before and after every lesson, recreation, meal and exercise; daily mass with communion, and ardent worship of the Virgin, gave the pupils a special stamp. It was only in 1938, in an attempt to modernise the seminaries, that Abbé R. Ducasse, a teacher at the seminary of Montréjean, founded a paper, *Servir*, to urge an end of this dissociation of the budding cleric from the

[1] Joseph Rogé, *Le Simple Prêtre* (1965).

layman and the introduction of more modern methods. But as late as 1955 seminaries could still be found issuing exit passes on which it was specified that the exit must be *en famille* and that a promenade with anyone except a member of the boy's family was forbidden. At the end of this schooling, the boys went on to spend five years at the *grand séminaire* (one year of philosophy and four of theology). At the turn of the century, three-quarters of the eighty-four *grands séminaires* taught no science or mathematics; ecclesiastical history was only a recent addition, and considered of secondary importance; there was very little critical study of the Bible, and no effort was made to introduce the pupils to the modern world. The middle ages were held up as the ideal period of Christianity. The theological textbooks, largely renewed in the course of the Second Empire and then kept till 1940, were still based on ancient models; there was virtually no study of original texts or of modern philosophy. Latin was used as the teaching language.

The methods were no different from those of primary schools. The students' function was to prove to their teacher that they had learnt their textbook. The teacher would ask three or four questions in Latin and they would do their best to answer in the same language. He would then read out a few pages from a textbook, translate them into French, and under guise of commentary, repeat the message in several different ways. Occasionally he would dictate a few sentences to the students. They would go away to précis the pages of the textbook they had just studied, copy into their notebooks the dictation of the professor and prepare the next lesson. Questions were not invited; objections were treated as signs of pride and indocility. In some seminaries there were no tables in the classrooms; the students sat with their books on their knees. The ideal was to put every fact into a pigeon-hole, to memorise all definitions, with the dates or articles of the canon law, to label all heresies in red.[1] It was only in the 1940s that group study was developed or pedagogy (with reference to the catechism) taught.

[1] Émile Baudaire, 'La Formation intellectuelle du clergé de France au dix-neuvième siècle', *Annales de philosophie chrétienne*, 3rd series, vol. 5 (1904–5), 153–69, 267–307; J. Hogan, *Les Études du clergé* (Rome and Paris, 1901)—by a former teacher at Saint-Sulpice who emigrated to America.

The *grands séminaires* were boarding establishments, like the state's *grandes écoles*, but with far more severe discipline. No loud talking was allowed, no singing in the students' cells; silence and solitude were the rule; no one was allowed to knock on a student's door without the Director's permission, and the student then answered not 'Enter', but 'Open', for the visitor had to remain outside the cell. Permanent friends in games or conversation were discouraged; the student was required to mix with the first group he met, but these had to be of not less than three and not more than five students. The directors joined the students in their recreations; when they went for walks, it was in single file. Only after 1945 was this abolished and the compulsory wearing of cassocks ended. In this system, discipline and conformity were more highly esteemed than the development of character and the acquisition of knowledge; memory was cultivated at the expense of reason; obedience at the expense of responsibility; routine and prejudice were inculcated in the name of tradition. A former seminarist recalled how he was forbidden to keep up his hobbies of painting and English, on the ground that they were useless or dangerous for a priest; intellectually, he said, the effect of the seminary was to castrate him. He did only four or five written exercises a year: the education was almost entirely oral. The conflicts of theology and science were concealed from him; in his study of the Bible, he was even forbidden to read certain parts of it, until he was considered ready for them.[1] For many years he read the Bible on his knees, 'a posture not designed to encourage criticism'.[2]

The seminarists dealt with the problem of chastity very efficiently from their own point of view, but with disastrous effects for the relations of their graduates with their flocks. The system of close surveillance and active delation (Combes's *fiches* were regarded as typical of a former seminarist) meant that the weak-willed were soon weeded out; there was none of the homosexuality that flourished in the *lycées*. The seminarists were to become merciless censors of contemporary morals.[3] However, their own lives in their parishes were not always

[1] For example, Genesis 19, 29, 30, 38.
[2] Albert Houtin, *Une Vie de prêtre. Mon expérience 1867–1912* (1926).
[3] Abbé Dolonne, *Le Clergé et le célibat* (n.d., about 1900).

blameless and they were charged with hypocrisy. Today a third of pious church-goers doubt the chastity of their *curés*. Half of the people questioned in an opinion poll gave disappointment in love as their explanation of why men became priests.[1] The young priest certainly often emerged from his seminary hostile to the society he aimed to serve and isolated in it. As a result, he spent much of his time defending the rights of the Church against encroachment, rather than seeking to proselytise. He tended to confine his attentions to those who came to him. He condemned the rest for materialism, egoism and licence, without trying to understand.[2] As late as 1945, *curés* were still indiscriminately accusing progress, prosperity, communications and industry of causing dechristianisation, anathematising the desire for profit in work and pleasure afterwards. They were even then classing dances and cinemas as 'facile or immoral pleasures'. One of the Church's leading pastoral experts reported that 'many *curés* have seen dancing as the principal instrument of dechristianisation between the two wars'.[3] They fulminated against abortions, realising there were about a million of these a year but not trying to comprehend the reason for them; they advocated large families in the face of an almost universal desire for their limitation; they inveighed against sexual licence and observed with horror that young men carried around photographs of their naked girl friends.[4]

It was not only the relics of Jansenist influence but also pressure from the self-righteous faithful that made many *curés* unwilling to admit former sinners to communion, to give them only conditional absolution and to impose exaggerated penances. (The movement for frequent, i.e. weekly, communions only got going after 1898.) Such was the bitterness of their struggle with their enemies, that they usually preferred to be content with their few faithful, to live in a closed, fortified world. One of them acknowledged that, as a result, religion became 'a religion of fear, consisting in defences.

[1] Julien Potel, *Le Clergé français* (1967), 239–50.
[2] Abbé Lagoutte, curé du bourg d'Hem, *Du prêtre et de la société présente* (1868) is a good example.
[3] F. Boulard, *Problèmes missionnaires de la France rurale* (1945), 168.
[4] H. Godin and Y. Daniel, *La France, pays de mission?* (1943) has many instructive quotations from *curés* and laymen.

One would say that God was He who prevents men from being happy.'[1] Certainly, the Judgement of God, hell, sacrilege and sin haunted them. To examine one's conscience and to confess therefore seemed the essence of Christian life. In the mid-nineteenth century at least they were often little less ignorant than their flocks: the archives show them writing in bad French, with many mistakes; some were even unable to fill in a questionnaire and asked the local schoolmaster to help them. They were suspicious of meetings, markets, fairs, libraries and newspapers; they saw their function to be the saving of their parishes from the contagion of change.[2] Preaching was one of their weakest points: there were few sermons in the ordinary village church in the nineteenth century: 'the continual movement of people in our vast church', wrote one *curé*, 'does not allow one to go into the pulpit'. When sermons were preached they were based on classical models, with limited relevance. After 1914, these thirty-minute lectures were often abandoned for short extempore outbursts of spiritual fervour distributed throughout the service. Attacks on freemasonry and the enemies of God were for long the favourite subject of sermons. But by the turn of the century priests began talking of Christians as the élite; soon they urged frequent communion; and after the war their concern became grace, predestination and the mystic body of Christ.

There were learned *curés* just as there were ignorant ones. Some had exceptional records for erudition and pastoral zeal, in the organisation of charities and of religious fraternities. In the mid-nineteenth century, the model *curé* was J. M. Vianney of Ars, made famous in numerous biographies.[3] He sanctified himself by penitence and self-renunciation, overcame the persecution of demons to build chapels and orphanages, organise pilgrimages, multiply services, abolish dances and cabarets, obtain Sunday observance and leave a cult of himself behind him when he died. In 1858, the last year of his life, over 100,000 people came to his village, attracted by his fervent preaching. He was simply the best-known of a vast number of priests whose human qualities gave them similar

---

[1] Boulard, op. cit. 66.
[2] C. Marcilhacy, *Le Diocèse d'Orléans* . . . (1964), 247–58.
[3] For example, Abbé Alfred Monnin, *Le Curé d'Ars* (1861).

prestige, and whose influence was exerted more obscurely on their communities.[1] The priests did not emerge in a uniform mould from their training. There were those amongst them who wished to marry religion with popular aspirations. At the end of the nineteenth century, there were some remarkable priests who emerged as advocates of social Catholicism.[2] There were 700 priests who met at Reims in 1896, to demand a reform of clerical education, an acceptance of democracy and a new missionary attitude towards the people.[3] There was the modernist movement, which attempted to reconcile the teachings of the Church with recent discoveries, and which according to some won the support of 1,500 priests, and according to others of 15,000; but it was vigorously suppressed by a series of papal decrees and encyclicals. Its adherents were evicted from positions of influence, a rigid censorship was established in reaction against them and a 'veritable terror' of 'ecclesiastical Combisme', lasting till 1914, stamped them out. In the interwar years there was a revived interest in mysticism which deepened, but sometimes also narrowed, the outlook of many clergy. Only after 1943 did the idea of the *curé* as a missionary in an almost pagan country begin to be formulated.[4]

Most parish priests were not encouraged by their circumstances to adapt themselves to change. Isolation was one of their chief problems, isolation both from society and from each other: 'always alone, everywhere', one of them wrote pathetically. Their bishops seldom summoned them to meetings and visited them perhaps once a year, and in the nineteenth century sometimes only once every four or five years. They were required to attend retreats every few years, and they had their seminary old boys' reunions. In 1882 the Union Apostolique des Prêtres Séculiers du Sacré Cœur was founded, issuing a monthly bulletin, and several other similar ones, with dinners and meetings, to increase their opportunities for contact; after the war came the association of Prêtres Anciens Combattants and in 1931 the Automobile Club Saint Christophe.

---

[1] P. Pierrard, *Le Prêtre français* (1969) is a good guide.

[2] Cf. J. M. Mayeur, *L'Abbé Lemire* (1969).

[3] R. Rémond, *Les Congrès ecclésiastiques de Bourges et de Reims* (1964).

[4] See Georges Fonsegrive, *Lettres d'un curé de campagne* (1894); Henri Bolo, *Ce que sera le prêtre du vingtième siècle* (1908); Cardinal Mercier, *La Vie intérieure* (n.d.); Chanoine R. Cardaliaguet, *Mon curé chez lui* (1926).

The bishop of Besançon suggested in 1907 that parish priests should be turned into a religious order; and since then proposals for some sort of communal life have been repeated. It was realised too that their education needed to be made more intellectual: energetic bishops tried to found schools of advanced study and to train seminary professors, whose standard was far inferior to that of the state's *normaliens*; but these efforts had little success.[1]

The world of the parish priests changed considerably in this century. In the parish of Deville near Rouen in 1875, for example, the *curé* had to assist him, in ministering to a population of 4,500, one *vicaire*, two beadles, one sacristan, one organist and one pew attendant—and only the last two were part-time. (Four employees was quite normal, but some parishes had as many as ten.) On great feasts there was lavish decoration of the church and elaborate processions. The world of the church embraced two schools run by the Brothers of the Christian Doctrine and the Nuns of Providence. There was a fraternity of Christian mothers, a Congregation of the Children of Mary, a Maternal Society (i.e. organisations for women and girls only). By 1954 the population of this town had risen to 8,000. The *curé* now had a second *vicaire* with an auxiliary chapel, but all the minor employees had gone, for the low wages offered no longer attracted anybody, and at important marriages or burials itinerant chanters had to be hired. The Sunday services lost their liturgical splendour; the processions of the Holy Sacrament no longer followed their traditional lengthy route, though pilgrimages to Lourdes compensated. The boys' church school was closed down in 1906. On the other hand religious life became active in innumerable societies—Action Catholique, Jeunesse Ouvrière, Jeunesse Catholique, Cercle Saint-Pierre, Ligue Patriotique, with its annual pilgrimage to Lisieux, a Union Paroissiale for men, with varied lectures, a dispensary run by three nuns, a holiday camp for a hundred children every year and 160 outings for the aged.[2] It was this transformation of the Church from a state institution

[1] Abbé Garilhe, *Le Clergé séculier français au dix-neuvième siècle* (1899), 31–43; Anon., *L'Église de France et les réformes nécessaires. Le clergé séculier* (1880), a vigorous and informed attack.

[2] Robert Eude, 'Histoire religieuse du diocèse de Rouen au 19ᵉ siècle', *Études normandes* no. 14 (1955, first trimestre), 165–96.

into a vigorous complex of private societies that was to give it new life.

In 1814 there were 29,076 churches in use. In 1830 there were 36,000, in 1848 39,000 and in 1869 42,000. The Second Empire marked the peak of the Church's physical presence. Between 1830 and 1869 the total number of priests rose by 39 per cent, whereas the population increased by only 17 per cent. In 1870 there were 56,500 priests compared with 31,870 in 1810 and 42,486 in 1950. Napoleon III's government spent twice as much on its religious budget as it did on education; and it allowed the Church freedom to argue its case at a time when every other section of the community was controlled by censorship. However, the Church did not profit from this opportunity as much as it might have done. The clergy were distributed in inverse proportion to where they were needed. Because the system of recruitment was diocesan, bishops jealously guarded the independence of their seminaries, whose graduates were mainly local children and nearly always made to serve in the same diocese. The more a region became irreligious, therefore, the fewer clergy it got, because it naturally found fewer candidates. Thus whereas the religious diocese of Rennes had 19·2 priests for every 10,000 inhabitants in 1904 and 17·3 in 1946, that of more pagan Limoges had only 8·6 and 5·8, and Mende only 3·5 and 3·7. One diocese could therefore have five times as many priests as another.[1] The Church failed to provide for the growing towns. In Paris in 1956 it was calculated that four times more priests were needed to bring it up to the national average: in the suburbs 26,000 people were expected to share each church.[2] All these calculations, moreover, assume that the parish priests were able-bodied; but in 1948 35 per cent of them were over sixty; in the diocese of Carcassonne 50 per cent were over sixty, and in Ajaccio 60 per cent. The towns got more than their fair share of these old men, for the traditional hierarchy of promotion was from *vicaire* in the countryside to *vicaire* in a town, then *curé* in a suburb and finally *curé* in a town. But the income of the priest varied in proportion to the piety of his flock. Until 1905 the average priest's salary placed him on roughly the same

[1] F. Boulard, *Essor ou déclin du clergé français?* (1950), 40, 78–9.
[2] Yvan Daniel, *L'Équipement paroissial d'un diocèse urbain: Paris 1802–1956* (1957).

level as the village postman.[1] Donations, fees and the hire of pews could often amount to more than this salary. In order to keep alive, the priest had to say as many private masses as possible; but the more actively pious his congregation, the less time he had to give to evangelising those who never came to church. After 1905, priests became wholly dependent on the support of the faithful, and this further accentuated their inequality. Some continued to live in the most pathetic poverty, in crumbling presbyteries.[2]

Paradoxically, however, their professional insecurity, which had plagued them in the nineteenth century, was ended in 1910. Only the *curés de canton* (about 3,425) had enjoyed permanent tenure. The rest were liable to be dismissed or transferred at will by the bishop; and some bishops in the nineteenth century made great use of their power. One changed round every single priest in his diocese. This was a source of bitter humiliation to the parish clergy, for before the Revolution they had all enjoyed security of tenure; their diminished status was due to Napoleon's wish to increase his control of them. Many clergy were very conscious that they had come to occupy a role in society inferior to that which they had had under the *ancien régime*. 'The *curé*'s authority over the people', wrote two disgruntled ones already in 1839, 'is dependent almost entirely on his personal qualities. Some individuals are still respected: the order no longer is.'[3] This partly explains why they had to fight so aggressively to maintain their prestige against the upstart *instituteurs* and mayors. It explains also why some of them made such extravagant claims for religion and refused to compromise with the new society in which they were offered so inferior a place.[4] It is no wonder that they became fervent supporters of papal omnipotence, and that

[1] N. M. Le Senne, *Condition civile et politique des prêtres* (1847), 201–3. Most priests earned between 800 and 1,000 francs, though the first-class *curé* (a tenth of the total) got 1,500–1,600 francs. The *vicaire* got 350 francs, plus a supplement from parish or municipal funds, of 300 to 500 francs (but in the diocese of Orléans in the Second Empire only a fifth of communes paid this supplement).

[2] See the begging letters and descriptions of decaying churches in Guy de Pierrefeu, *Le Clergé fin-de-siècle* (n.d., about 1895).

[3] C. and A. Allignol, *De l'état actuel du clergé en France, et en particulier des curés ruraux appelés desservans* (1839), ix.

[4] For example, Abbé A. Martin, curé du Brusquet (Basses-Alpes), *Le Prêtre devant le siècle* (Guincourt, Ardennes, 1858), 91.

they received their reward in 1910 when the Pope gave back to the *desservants* their security of tenure.

## Bishops

The inadequacies of the parish priests may be partly attributed to the often unsatisfactory leadership they received from their bishops. The Church, indeed, was prevented from formulating a coherent policy. The minister of religions gave the bishops no pastoral orders. The bishops were forbidden to meet to co-ordinate their policies, first by the Concordat and, after the Separation, by the Pope. It was only in 1919 that the archbishops began holding meetings twice a year, and only in 1947 that an assembly of all bishops was called: but neither had any power to legislate. In the nineteenth century the bishops were selected by governments anxious to obtain supporters for their regimes. After 1905 the Pope, who was no less keen to secure the subservience of bishops, made appointments which were sometimes just as eccentric. Only two new sees were created in this whole period (Marseille and Lille) bringing the total to eighty-seven; the general idea was that each department should have its bishop (though seven did not and four had more than one). On average a diocese had about half a million inhabitants but the variations were as enormous as they were in the parishes: the Paris diocese came to have over five million souls, while the smallest, Saint-Jean-de-Maurienne, had only 47,000. Before the Revolution, bishops had been limited in their activity by their cathedral chapters, by their provincial parlements and by numerous lay and ecclesiastical rivals, but after it they became almost absolute, arbitrary sovereigns of their sees, with greatly augmented powers of appointment and decision. The accidents of health combined to vary the kind of administration they provided, for they were seldom appointed before they were fifty years old; they did not retire; and some lasted for thirty or forty years, on occasion leaving their dioceses in complete disarray. There were saints among them, scholars, bureaucrats, preachers, evangelisers, aristocrats, mediocrities, sycophants and recluses; the individual character of each had a profound effect on the way the Church met the changes before it. In the early years of the Third Republic 12 per cent of bishops were noblemen, 33 per cent bourgeois or substantial peasant landowners and 53 per cent of humble origin; in the middle of the twentieth century they came largely from the middle class or petite bourgeoisie; only 10 per cent were sons of workers.[1]

It is impossible to make generalisations about so diverse a collection of men over a whole century. The vigorous Archbishop Donnet, for example, who built 310 churches and 400 presbyteries in his forty years at Bordeaux (1837–82), had little in common with the muddler Fonteneau, Bishop of Agen (1874–84) and of Albi (1884–99) who was absorbed by family worries and accumulated debts totalling 800,000 francs.[2] However, the attitude of bishops in the face of material progress, of increasing agnosticism and of anticlericalism was for most of this century generally conservative. At what was perhaps the most crucial period in the Church's history, the early years of the Third Republic, when it made itself the irreconcilable enemy of modern society, there were indeed a few bishops who had no aspiration to clerical domination. Maret, the most distinguished of these, professor of theology at the Sorbonne since 1841, bishop *in partibus*, and a friend of Victor Cousin, argued that to condemn the Revolution would be to cut the Church off from national life and to destroy its power to combat the evils it admittedly contained. In his major work *Philosophie et religion* (1856), he sought to reconcile human reason and divine revelation; and he urged that state and Church should coexist in a free union, with the former recognising its incompetence in religious matters and the latter renouncing all claim to domination. However, the very large majority of bishops demanded a privileged position for the Church in society, not just freedom to propagate its doctrines. Bishop Dupanloup of Orléans, senator under Napoleon III and a deputy after his fall, the leader of the moderate wing among them, was willing to compromise with modern ideas, and he claimed to accept all modern liberties, but he excluded as intolerable liberty of worship and liberty of the

---

[1] Jacques Gadille, *La Pensée et l'action politiques des évêques français au début de la Troisième République 1870–1883* (1967), i. 27; P. Alméras, op. cit. 122.

[2] R. P. Lecanuet. *La Vie de l'église sous Léon XIII* (1930), chapters 1 and 2.

press. He thought the state should recognise that it would collapse without religion, that it should back the Church's work and suppress its enemies. He linked Atheism and the Social Peril (the title of one of his many forceful pamphlets, 1866), warning the bourgeoisie that it would lose its property—in support of which he quoted the seventh and eighth Commandments—and its privileges, in which he ardently believed. He praised hierarchy and élites, authority, obedience and respect, *laissez-faire* mitigated by private charity, the prohibition of strikes, so that he was a total opponent of republicanism and even more of socialism. Bishop Pie of Poitiers (1815–80), the main spokesman of the less moderate bishops—slightly fewer in number than Dupanloup's followers, but including most of the cardinals and archbishops—frankly and vehemently condemned the French Revolution in its entirety as being dramatically opposed to Christianity. The exercise of reason, he insisted, must be subordinate to the teaching of the Church. The state must implement the divine law, and though he denied that his aim was theocracy, he looked back nostalgically to the thirteenth century, when princes sometimes agreed to be simply the secular arm of the Church. Theology was the crowning science which absorbed all levels of human activity. It was the duty of liberals to realise this and rectify their false ideas.[1] But there were still other bishops who were even more reactionary than he, the neo-ultramontanes who were without qualification keen to return to the thirteenth century. It took a long time for the ambitions of the episcopacy to become more moderate.

The way individual bishops tackled their task in their dioceses will illustrate the resources and energy of some, and the limitations of imagination in others. The diocese of Nantes was an example of a religious area in which the damage of the Revolution was quickly repaired. In 1848 there was very widespread attendance at church. Two active bishops during the later years of the Restoration and during the July Monarchy maintained close links with their clergy by visits, correspondence and frequent meetings. Precisely because it was a pious diocese, Nantes lost more during the Revolution: in 1814

---

[1] For Bishop Pie, see Austin Gough, 'Bishop Pie's campaign against the Nineteenth Century', in T. Zeldin, *Conflicts in French Society* (1970), 94–168.

it had only one-third of the priests it had in the *ancien régime*; but these gaps were quickly filled. Missions were frequently used to stimulate zeal. Over a million francs were collected in gifts and legacies between 1802 and 1850, but then the diocese had lost ninety million from the sale of its lands at the Revolution.[1] This was a diocese capable of being saved, and it was saved. But in the diocese of Toulouse irreligion was becoming increasingly vocal. Around 1830 young people frantically applauded all hostile references to the Church in the theatre and attacked religious processions. Archbishop d'Astros (1830–51) was well aware of the progress of 'dechristianisation'; the state of his diocese, he said, caused him 'terror'. But he attributed it simply to the perversity of his enemies—to whom he refused the least particle of good faith in their errors—and to the 'false doctrines' of the eighteenth-century *philosophes*. He feared innovation above all else and condemned the liberal theologian-politician Lamennais largely because of this. His answer to the challenge of his times was to repeat the need for faith and prayer. There was no question for him of rethinking the Church's apologetics or dogma. His remedy was Sunday observance, the proselytisation of the Protestants, the distribution of 'good books', the spread of religious education, the extension of charity and the limitation of civil marriages. He pointed out to the authorities that religion was essential to safeguard 'the integrity of public and private morals', though he judiciously kept out of politics. Around 1841 he began to take note of the social problem but only to urge charity. 'It is permissible to improve one's condition,' he wrote, 'but provided a Christian moderation is used in this aim.' He condemned 'the passion for lucre so alive in our time' and took the conservative side in the debate within the Church on usury; his instructions were obscure or equivocal on this subject, in which the French church generally was less perceptive than that in Italy and Germany. Archbishop d'Astros always insisted on the *curé* being made president of any new charitable society that was formed and on the inclusion of religious practice among its activities. This excessive zeal turned the working class away: one of his major blunders was to lose, by

---

[1] Marius Faugeras, *Le Diocèse de Nantes sous la monarchie censitaire, 1813–1848* (Fontenay-le-Comte, 1964).

this policy, the friendly societies which were beginning to form. He saw religion as the protector of the *status quo*; it rightly 'repressed passions'; it could not compromise with a society built outside it 'with no basis but pleasure'. He seems to have carefully followed the precepts of Abelly's guide to episcopal conduct, first published in 1668, and reprinted in 1837, which made the maintenance of faith the bishop's principal task: this book might perhaps once have been good advice, but it was barely adequate in the nineteenth century.[1]

Dupanloup, bishop of Orléans from 1849 to 1878, was faced by an exceptionally unchristian diocese. This illegitimate child, brought up by a tailor but then patronised by the families of the aristocratic friends he made in his *petit séminaire*, was perplexed and frightened by the social aspirations of the masses. He saw his task to be to provide them with religious leadership, to contain them. But he made the conquest of the notables his first concern, and he had considerable success, for he was charming and tactful. However, the result was that Catholicism was made to appear a bourgeois religion, and one tainted by nostalgia for the *ancien régime*. Though Dupanloup frequented the Paris *salons*, wrote numerous books and was a member of the French Academy, he did not have the intellectual equipment or curiosity to appeal to the intellectuals and to the new generation of students. He was suspicious of science; though learned in the classics, he was far from being so in theology; his library contained no nineteenth-century books except Chateaubriand's. (Many bishops indeed seem not to have read the books they condemned: another episcopal member of the French Academy, Perraud, bishop of Autun 1874–1906, is said to have avoided reading anything less than fifty years old.) Dupanloup wrote a rival *Life of Jesus* in reply to Renan's, but it was a feeble scissors-and-paste collection of quotations with no attempt at serious exegesis. The religion he offered was above all 'socially useful': it consoled, it preached resignation. The policy he followed with regard to the poor was to conciliate them by charity, to attract them to church by accentuating the spectacular element in services, by having rich ornamentation and pompous processions. He demanded

[1] Paul Droulers, S.J., *Action pastorale et problèmes sociaux sous la monarchie de juillte chez Mgr d'Astros, archevêque de Toulouse* (1954).

obedience, not participation, except in singing, which he encouraged as an incentive to piety. He rebuilt or repaired churches, presbyteries and schools on a large scale, to last his diocese for half a century. He was a boring writer and a poor orator, but he had brilliant gifts as a teacher and he did much to improve the catechism. Whereas previously the children had to answer 'Yes, Sir' or 'No, Sir' to leading questions, he rephrased and simplified the catechism so that they had to learn complete sentences by heart. He did a lot to reduce the ignorance of his clergy, though the ideal he held up to them was a medieval one of asceticism, piety and withdrawal; he castigated them for reading newspapers or even for looking 'imprudently at certain pictures, engravings and statues'; he ordered them to abstain from smoking and to read only religious books. He increased the number of clergy by 24 per cent and used them with a clear sense of strategy, concentrating his best priests in the towns where they could meet the gravest challenges and where they would not be disheartened by rural isolation. He ruled them almost like an army, moving 70 per cent of them to new parishes in his first eight years. After consulting them in synods upon his arrival, he held only one more in thirty years, though it is true a few idiosyncratic clergy remained insubordinate and his cathedral chapter waged a constant war against him, even to the extent of publishing an attack on his administration. Dupanloup was bewildered by the age in which he lived: the last few years of his life, in the 1870s, with its still further diminished church attendance, clearly showed the failure of his approach.[1]

Just how slow things were in changing may be illustrated from the career of Petit de Julleville, bishop of Dijon 1927–36 and archbishop of Rouen 1936–48. On being told by the nuncio of his appointment, he protested his unsuitability on the ground that he had no private income. He then asked the nuncio for advice on how best to perform his new duties: he was told to shave off his beard. Petit de Julleville was the son of a university professor; and he had himself been an energetic headmaster of a church school. He gave much weight to intellectual success—though he never wrote anything of

[1] C. Marcilhacy, *Le Diocèse d'Orléans sous l'épiscopat de Mgr Dupanloup, 1849–1878* (1962). Cf. A. Gough's forthcoming book on the Second Empire clergy.

importance. He was particularly active in trying to reform the catechism, but he had to drop his proposals after a third of his episcopal colleagues ignored them and another third opposed them. He did a lot of visiting, even though for much of his time as archbishop he was too old to walk unaided. But his control over his clergy was erratic: parish priests ignored his letters with impunity, or forgot to meet him when he announced a visit. Petit de Julleville urged his clergy to keep up with modern ideas but he also warned them that youth's exclusive interest 'in today and tomorrow' was 'childish'; he forbade the clergy to *tutoyer* their parishioners, which would be carrying friendliness too far; he insisted on boys wearing ties and jackets at dinner, even in his holiday camps. His own reading was largely in the classics of the seventeenth and eighteenth centuries (including Rousseau), the nineteenth-century historians and religious authors. He was a man of considerable distinction but by now the traditional episcopal organisation was no longer the decisive influence on the religious life of the country. Petit de Julleville was one of the first bishops to urge his clergy to co-operate with the Action Catholique, and he was right to see in this the new hope of the Church.[1]

## Monks and Nuns

The first sign of the changing nature of piety and the new outlets for it was the phenomenal expansion of the monastic orders in the nineteenth century. In 1848 there were still only 3,000 monks; but already in 1861 there were 17,676, in 1877 30,286; in 1901 37,000. There was a slight fall in numbers after the expulsions of 1902–14 but by 1946 the numbers were back at 29,500. These figures were lower than those of the *ancien régime* (about 70,000) but the sudden increase after 1850 made the presence of the monks powerfully felt. Of nuns, however, there were soon far more than there had ever been before. In 1789 there were about 35,000 of them, but by 1877 there were about 128,000, a figure which remained more or less constant (125,000 in 1900; 120,000 in 1960). However, in

---

[1] Mgr de La Serre, *Le Cardinal Petit de Julleville* (1955); cf. André Deroo, *L'Épiscopat français dans la mêlée de son temps, 1930–1954* (1955), a collection of official doctrinal pronouncements.

1900 only some 1,800 men and 4,000 women of these were in contemplative orders. The rest took an active part in providing social services: they taught, it was said, two million children, tended 200,000 sick people, brought up 100,000 orphans.[1] The anticlericals estimated their wealth at a milliard francs; they themselves admitted to about half or a third of that amount.[2] What frightened their enemies was their rapid growth. As against this milliard in 1900, it was said, they had owned only fifty-three million in 1850: the threat of mortmain was menacing France again as in 1789. This was not so. Most of the wealth of these congregations was in houses they inhabited: they claimed they owned only 23,000 hectares, compared for example with the 4,816,000 hectares which were common land in France.[3]

Far less is known about these monks and nuns than about the secular clergy; few historians have examined their archives; no sociologist has studied their lives and organisation.[4] The most controversial among the male orders were the Jesuits. They were expelled or attacked over and over again (1764, 1828, 1843, 1880, 1901) on the grounds that they were politically dangerous, but they returned or survived under one guise or another. There were not many of them—3,085 in 1900—but they ran twenty-nine secondary schools which attracted the sons of the aristocracy and conservative bourgeoisie—9,000 boys at a time—and won them brilliant academic successes. The very close contact between pupils and teachers was said to leave a permanent mark on their products. They were much sought after as confessors. They produced some of Paris's most celebrated preachers like Ravignan and Félix and itinerant ones like Pierre Chaignon, who devoted himself to missions directed at the secular clergy. The Jesuits had a great talent for adapting themselves to changing times, and they exerted far greater influence than their numbers would suggest: they set up religious associations, the Apostolat de la prière and the Association de la Sainte Famille, which had a vast membership; they acted as almoners to numerous lay

[1] Mgr Baunard, *Un Siècle de l'église de France 1800–1900* (1912), 150.
[2] Henri Brisson, *La Congrégation* (1902), 416–17; cf. 304.
[3] Père du Lac; S.J., *Jésuites* (1901), 185.
[4] Leo Moulin, *Le Monde vivant des religieux* (1964) claims to be the first book on monks by a sociologist but it is only a very general survey.

organisations; and they fathered several religious orders, since they could not expand themselves.[1]

Their methods were discretion itself compared to those of the Assumptionists, who soon supplied the anticlericals with far more ammunition. They were one of the many new orders founded in the nineteenth century. Emmanuel d'Alzon, born in 1810, was the son of a legitimist deputy of the Restoration, and great-nephew of the vicar-general of Nîmes, who appointed him a canon at twenty-four and whom he succeeded in 1837. He set out at once to capture the young. Already in 1840 he wrote, 'I am more or less master of all the children of Nîmes, from twelve to fifteen, and with time I can hope to extend my influence to the adults.' He founded a secondary school, with the help of agrégés whom he had converted. He gave the boys a smarter uniform than the state schools, with a military hat; he led them on long marches to the sound of clarions; he devoted great expense to the celebration of religious feasts; he used frequent communion to save boys from temptation; he produced great emulation among them in pious exercises; he encouraged them to join the charitable societies, like that of St. Vincent de Paul; he got the older ones to lecture soldiers and apprentices; and by his 'inflammatory exhortations' filled them with absolute devotion to the Church and the Pope. In 1845 he took monastic vows, and slowly built up the Assumptionist Order with the explicit aim of fighting Protestantism (important in Nîmes), Voltairianism and the French Revolution. The Assumptionists had aims highly relevant to modern society and a determination to make use of all the resources of modern propaganda to achieve them. D'Alzon slept only five hours a day; he was nervous, suffering from 'terrible migraines and nervous diseases'; he left a corresponence of 50,000 letters, and made about 5,000 public speeches, as remarkable for their histrionics as for their passion. He knew how to make religion an all-absorbing obssession for his converts, and filled them with his own vigorous missionary zeal. He loved crowds; he wanted mass conversions. In 1872 he founded the Œuvre de Notre Dame de Salut, assisted by his successor Picard, to save France by public prayer and by the

[1] Joseph Burnichon, La Compagnie de Jésus en France: histoire d'un siècle 1814–1914 (4 vols., 1914–22).

moralisation of the working masses; he distributed millions
of tracts in favour of a day of public prayer, which he established as an annual event. In the following year he collected
1,600,000 signatures from Christian mothers in favour of
sabbatarian legislation. He inaugurated national pilgrimages to
Rome, Lourdes and La Salette, which were major financial and
organisation feats, as well as occasions for remarkable mass
hysteria. He established close co-operation with a parallel
female order, whose founder, Mlle Milleret de Breu, took a
vow of obedience to him. The Assumptionist Order itself
was never very large: there were only eighty monks at d'Alzon's
death in 1880; about 700 in 1923; and 1,264 in 1937; but like
the Jesuits, it made its impact through its innumerable rami-
fications. He established many subsidiary lay societies, through
which the pious could convert, assist, educate and provide
employment for different classes. He was always aware of the
need to modernise his methods and to increase the appeal of
Catholicism to the young. Shortly before his death he wrote,
'We must capture the young, but the young want new forms.
In our part of the world we have now only old methods like
the Conférences de Saint Vincent de Paul and the Catholic
committees. So we must establish new societies, we must have
associations for Catholic youth . . . with two aims, the moral
and religious improvement of the young, and leadership for
social action.' He was keen to fight revolutionary propaganda
with its own methods, and laid the foundations of the great
press empire which made the Assumptionists famous and an
immense national force. Their press campaigns against the
republic led to their expulsion in 1900; they disbanded among
their numerous foreign missions. But in 1924 they took over the
parish of Javel in which the Citröen factories stood. In 1945
they optimistically sent a priest to Moscow—who was promptly
transferred to Siberia.[1]

However, the Assumptionists represented only one type of
nineteenth-century monk and by no means the most common
type. By 1877 there were 116 different male congregations.
The Benedictine monastery of Solesmes, refounded in 1833,
sought to re-create the medieval ideal, giving particular

[1] Anon. (official history), *Les Religieux de l'Assomption* (Bonne Presse, 1963);
Jean Monval, *Les Assomptionistes* (1939).

emphasis to liturgy and reviving plain-chant. The Dominicans distinguished themselves through the writings of Lacordaire and in the mid-twentieth century by their publishing house, Les Éditions du Cerf, which brought out the principal books urging a missionary revival in France, as well as learned biblical studies; their political weekly *Sept* was a significant liberal Catholic journal.[1] New orders devoted themselves to the worship of the Virgin and of the Sacred Heart and the Holy Eucharist. The oblates of Mary Immaculate, founded to revive the faith in Marseille, ran parishes, pilgrimages and some seminaries but directed most of their efforts to foreign missions. This was a field in which there was great activity. The Pères Blancs, founded by Cardinal Lavigerie when he was bishop of Algiers (1869), concentrated on North Africa; but many orders were active both in France and abroad: this enabled them, as it turned out, to find easy refuge when they were expelled, and to return in due course. There was great variety in the organisation of these orders: the Pères Blancs, for instance, took only the vow of obedience: they were never alone, but moved in groups of at least three; each had free use of his private fortune and of the fees he received for mass. The Brothers of the Christian Doctrine, by contrast, were schoolmasters, and highly influential as such in France.[2]

The male orders were nearly always responsible directly to the Pope and independent of the bishops, so that there was a certain amount of resentment against them for drawing off the wealth and potential ordinands of the parishes. The female orders, on the other hand, were part of the diocesan organisation; a far smaller proportion of them had pretensions to national stature. Some consisted of no more than perhaps a dozen members: even in the 1960s there were only four orders with over 2,000 members. One may quote as examples

[1] A. Coutrot, *Un Courant de la pensée catholique, l'hebdomadaire Sept, 1934-7* (1961).

[2] Élie Marie, *Histoire des instituts religieux et missionnaires* (1930); Mgr Landrieux, *La Leçon du passé. Nos congrégations, nos écoles* (1926); Camille de Rochemonteix, S.J., *Les Congrégations non reconnues en France 1789–1881* (Cairo, 1901); H. Marc-Bonnet, *Histoire des ordres religieux* (1968); Mgr Théas, *Livre d'or des congrégations françaises, 1939–45* (1948); A. Belanger, S.J., *Les Méconnus. Ce que sont les religieux, ce qu'ils font, à quoi ils servent* (1901); Édouard Schneider, *Les Grandes Ordres monastiques et instituts religieux* (1917 ff.), a series of volumes, of unequal value, see e.g. Paul Lesourd, *Les Pères Blancs du Cardinal Lavigerie* (1935).

the Filles de la Croix de Casseneuil, founded in 1858 by the *curé* of this parish to educate poor girls; in 1877 they had fourteen members. The Servantes de Marie de Blois (1854) were started by an ordinary domestic, to help other domestics find work and to offer them asylum when ill or old—they dealt with between 100 and 150 cases a year. The Sœurs de la Charité, however, founded in 1662 and authorised by the French government in 1811, had 140 branches in 1877: they ran hospitals, asylums, poor houses, schools, orphanages, adult education classes and workshops. They lived off the produce of these workshops and of the orphanages and off their salaries as teachers. The Sœurs des Prisons, of whom there were about 400 in the 1930s, were founded by a few women under Louis-Philippe, without any private resources. The lay republic removed them from the prisons, which were put on a more professional footing, but it still found a use for them in looking after delinquent and abandoned children; individuals with broken homes brought them others; state subsidies and private fees provided the finances. They helped also in detention centres for prostitutes. All the sisters had a vote in electing the General Chapter of the order, which in turn elected a Superior for six years at a time.[1] These are just a few examples of the many social services performed by nuns. About two-thirds of French nuns were engaged in hospital or other social services and one-third in education (in 1960). It is no wonder the lay republic could not expel them *en masse*.[2]

### Catholic Lay Organisations

Side by side with these full-time propagandists of the faith, the Church was assisted by a much larger army of charitable organisations. There was enormous scope for them, since the Napoleonic system of assistance left public charity to the discretion of each commune: the majority of communes had very limited resources; the large towns had a disproportionately large share of very poor people. (In 1829 one in twelve of the Paris population were classed as 'indigent', in 1856 one in

[1] Jeanne Ancelet-Hustache, *Les Sœurs des Prisons* (1933).
[2] See notices on numerous orders in Émile Keller, *Les Congrégations religieuses en France. Leurs œuvres et leurs services* (1880).

sixteen, in 1880 one in eighteen.)[1] The state system, which
was itself partly kept going by the cheap labour of nuns (very
unequally distributed over the country), counted on being
supplemented by private enterprise; and private charity
increased considerably in the second half of this period. In
1897 2,700 charitable organisations were counted in Paris
alone; in 1904 3,150; in 1912 6,930 (of which 1,330 were
public and 5,600 private); in 1921 9,065. These figures are
unsatisfactory and imprecise but they suggest a vast and
growing activity.[2]

Not all these organisations, by any means, were religious.
For example the Fondation Émile Zola assisted 'debilitated
wet-nurses'; the French Academy administered awards of
1,000 francs to 'poor but well brought up spinsters, of irregular
birth'.[3] The number of neutral organisations was impressive,
but the majority seem to have had religious affiliations. They
covered every stage of life, infancy, apprenticeship, maternity,
illness, old age; there were some that catered for leisure and
others that provided work. The Société de Saint Vincent de
Paul was one of the most successful. Founded in 1833 by a
group of students led by Frédéric Ozanam, its purpose was as
much the salvation of the souls of these students as that of those
they assisted. The society's principal activity was visiting the
poor and sick, distributing alms to them, with the idea that this
practical work would keep students pious more effectively than
church preaching. The society's meetings were preceded and
ended by prayers, but it was decided not to hold these meetings
in churches, so as to avoid anticlerical opposition. The society
spread so rapidly that by 1852 it had branches in every diocese,
usually founded by old student members returning to their
provinces. The principal branch in each diocese then set up
further local branches, sometimes as many as fifty. Napoleon
III grew alarmed by its strength, fearing it might be used for
organising Catholic opposition on the political level: in 1861
he dissolved its central council. Only some 600 branches
survived the isolation of the next decade but the growth was

[1] Émile Chevalier, De l'assistance dans les campagnes (1889), 4, 27, 122; Ferdinand
Dreyfus, L'Assistance sous la seconde république, 1848–1851 (1907), 18, 25.
[2] Office central des Œuvres de Bienfaisance: Paris charitable, bienfaisant et social
(1921), xxxvi.
[3] Ibid. 39, 45.

resumed after 1870, so that by 1903 there were 1,526 branches, and in 1933 1,670, with nearly 25,000 members. Though visiting was their basic activity, they did much more: they supplied the poor with soup kitchens, cheap food, old clothes, help with rent, warm public rooms in winter, cheap housing, employment agencies, free medical and legal advice, holiday camps, old people's homes, catechist teaching, orphanages, apprenticeships, adult classes, clubs, allotments, libraries and pilgrimages. They had a subsidiary organisation, the Œuvre de saint Régis, which got unmarried couples to regularise their unions in church, at the rate, in Paris, of about 2,000 or 2,500 a year in the 1880s, and 250 to 400 in the 1930s.[1] However, the attitude of the almost exclusively middle-class members of this society was paternalistic and traditional. They were not concerned with curing the causes of poverty. They voted to ignore Leo XIII's social encyclical, *Rerum Novarum*; they even thought state legislation on workers' pensions should proceed 'prudently'.[2]

In organisations like this, enthusiastic Catholic laymen could give practical expression to their religion, but it is doubtful whether they converted many of the people they assisted; their significance lies in what they did to stimulate the zeal of donors. The Social Catholic movement, however, attempted to go beyond this and to win back the masses. It was based on an urgent feeling that the tragedy of the nineteenth century was that the Church had 'lost' the working classes and that entirely new methods were needed to win them back. *Laissez-faire* capitalism, it was argued, contradicted Christianity; and Social Catholicism sought to create alternative forms of social relations and economic organisation. It proposed various solutions. In 1848 Buchez attempted to reconcile Catholicism with the French Revolution, by using the universal panacea of that period, 'association', but only a few bishops were favourable, and the failure of the Second Republic discredited this movement.[3] Under the shock of the Commune, two aristocrats, Albert de Mun and René de la Tour du Pin, founded a Catholic club to establish contact with the workers, the Œuvre des

---

[1] Katherine Lynch is writing a doctoral thesis on this subject at Harvard.
[2] Société de Saint Vincent de Paul, *Livre du centenaire* (1933).
[3] J. B. Duroselle, *Les Débuts du catholicisme social en France, 1822–1870* (1951).

Cercles. This had something in common with the Society of St. Vincent de Paul, but it was organised on a more military basis. It was run by 'councils of war' and 'directors'. By 1878 there were about 10,000 such leaders distributed over the country— in effect the provincial nobility and notables. On joining they all denounced the French Revolution and accepted the Papal Syllabus. They attracted only about 35,000 workers into their clubs, whose aim was to keep these men out of trouble in their leisure hours by supplying them with games, food, club rooms, religious services and feasts to celebrate every possible saint's day, with prizes being awarded for frequent attendance. Their libraries contained practically no modern books except Chateaubriand. This military phase collapsed after 1879, under the combined hostility of the republican government, which forbade officers and civil servants to join, and of the Church, which disliked its non-diocesan organisation.

An attempt was then made to christianise the workers by reviving the medieval corporations and by getting paternalistic employers to take on only Christian workers. The theory for this was supplied by La Tour du Pin, ostensibly a disciple of Le Play and even more of the comte de Chambord, but really a traditional aristocrat brought up to believe in the duty of the feudal lord to his serfs; as he himself said, he had been indoctrinated by his own parents 'to the point of being unable to receive any new imprint'. The political leadership was provided by de Mun, who tried to form a Catholic Party, but he was stopped by the Pope, so that he had to devote himself to rather isolated parliamentary agitation for social legislation. The most practical impulse came from Léon Harmel (1827–1915), a textile manufacturer in Champagne, at once a mystic who conversed with the Sacred Heart and an untiring organiser and enthusiastic propagandist of social responsibility among the employer class. In his own factory he was known by everybody as Le Bon Père, and he was willing not only to provide social benefits for his workers but to discuss management problems with them. He converted perhaps a dozen other employers, but on the whole he found Catholic employers too frightened by the prospect of having to share any power at all with their men or even of holding discussions with them. The socially conscious Catholic employers tended simply to put up crucifixes and religious statues in their workshops, to begin the day with prayers, recited in unison by the workers, and to keep nuns around to 'maintain order and good spirits'. They were willing to offer charity, but they feared to talk of justice, rights or state intervention. The idea of the Christian corporation conflicted with the fact that most workers were not Christian, and men like de Mun could not reconcile themselves to admitting pagans.[1] When Père Ludovic de Besse founded a bank to provide cheap loans to workers, without religious tests, and relying on Jewish financial support, he was scorned. The Catholic social movement failed to obtain much success before 1914 because it underestimated the extent of irreligion, because it preached outdated medieval ideas and because it was able to convert only very few employers from *laissez-faire* capitalism. In the 1890s Harmel tried to go further. He launched a Democratic Christian movement, exclusively working-class, but it collapsed likewise from lack of adequate leaders, from the hostility of the conservative Catholics, and perhaps most of all from the fact that a profound change of attitude by the Church was needed before the workers would be attracted to it.[2]

The *Sillon* movement, led by Marc Sangnier, went further towards democracy. He wrote, 'Our primary aim is not to increase the wages of the workers, nor even to get a little garden for each one in which they can relax on Sundays. It is not simply a question of giving the workers roots in beautiful little gardens, and offering them little houses while their boss rubs his hands and says: now my workers will be good and docile because they have a pretty toy. No, citizens must be themselves responsible for what they do.' He urged a reorganization of industry, the abolition of its monarchical system of management, an end to purely mechanical work which destroyed human dignity, and the encouragement of co-operatives for production and consumption as a first step. But Sangnier was no theorist, and no rival to Marx; he read very

[1] H. Rollet, *L'Action sociale des catholiques en France* (1947–58); Robert Talmy, *L'Association catholique des Patrons du Nord 1884–1895* (Lille, 1962).

[2] Georges Guitton, *Léon Harmel* (1925); J. R. and G. Rémy, *L'Abbé Lemire* (1929); Georges Hoog, *Histoire du catholicisme social en France, 1871–1931* (new edition, 1946); Maurice Montuclard, *Conscience religieuse et démocratie: la deuxième démocratie chrétienne en France, 1891–1902* (1965).

little; he worked out his ideas as he went along. His success came from his physical beauty, his gift for inspiring affection and almost hero-worship in the young. First names only were used in his organisation, which was held together mainly by emotional bonds. He was a brilliant propagandist, orator, and organiser. He formed a Young Guard to act as stewards at his meetings, of men whom he initiated with mystical ceremonial in the crypt of Montmartre, like Crusaders, except that they were dressed in modern gymnasts' clothes. In his discussion groups, he chose delicate topics which added excitement to the proceedings. But he was too narcissistic, too emotional and too tyrannical to produce a movement which could last. He could not tolerate rivals and so trained no leaders. His appeal was essentially to adolescents, and worship of him was a major element of the *Sillon*. He was carried away into political ambitions, formed a party, democratic rather than Catholic, and stood for parliament, though he got in only in 1919–24. Already, however, in 1908 thirty bishops and in 1910 the Pope himself condemned him, for ignoring the ecclesiastical hierarchy and too precipitately seeking to overthrow the traditional bases of society. At this time the Church was not generally ready for modernisation. To extirpate the modernist heresy an oath abjuring its tendencies was required after 1910 of every priest, involving the signing of a document twenty-six pages long specifying them in detail. The French clergy submitted to this without any of the protests which arose in Germany. Only with the election of Benedict XV in 1914 did this repression in the French church come to an end; but though relatively brief, it was enough to alienate many intelligent laymen.

The acceptance by the Church of democracy was an essential prerequisite to its regaining its influence in the twentieth century. This acceptance came only slowly and partially in the 1930s. In 1926 the Pope announced his condemnation of the Action Française but eleven out of the seventeen cardinals and archbishops were favourable to Maurras, and a very sizeable proportion of the clergy. It was many years before the conservatives appointed to the episcopacy died off. The majority of Catholics still remained right-wing. General de Castelnau's Fédération Nationale Catholique, founded in 1924 to oppose the laic plans of the Cartel des Gauches, had 1,800,000 members within two years. A large number supported the Italians in Ethiopia and Franco in Spain, being more conscious of the dangers of communism than those of fascism. The official teaching of the Church on temporal matters became, it is true, increasingly cautious, and abstention from party politics ' was firmly demanded. However, its approved guide to social behaviour could not be accepted by men of the left. This condemned socialism as materialistic; it argued that men liked being governed; that they needed a leader; that authority came from God, not from the people. Though it recognised the 'substantial equality of human beings', inequalities in 'acquired or justly inherited situations' were legitimate; it accepted the 'inequality of classes', which it hoped would be attenuated by 'friendly accord'. It admitted that wealth was badly distributed but asked no more than that wages should be adequate to maintain life—and particularly family life. The workers should better themselves by saving, which would enable them to acquire property. Profit-sharing was a good thing; private enterprise was preferable to state intervention; corporate activity was best of all. The Church now at last said that all forms of government were acceptable, and that Catholics should accept the government of the day, whatever its complexion. It even allowed resistance to government 'in extreme cases'. But 'simple individuals' should not presume to decide on this by themselves. The Church no longer preached the acceptance of the *status quo*, but its ideal of 'harmony' was rather tame. It warned the young not to engage too hastily in political activity, which required a lot of experience. This book of guidance, with its scholastic tone, its innumerable scissors-and-paste quotations, and its search for carefully guarded definitions, meant that the Church was still hesitant in its attitude to modern problems.[1] Every attempt to found a democratic Catholic party failed, to some extent because the hierarchy opposed or discouraged it, but even more because the mass of the faithful could not be drawn from their traditional attachments. The failures of Jacques Piou and Marc Sangnier were repeated between the wars with the Parti Démocratique

---

[1] D. Lallement, professor à l'Institut Catholique de Paris, *Principes catholiques d'action civique* (approuvé par l'assemblée des cardinaux et archevêques de France) (1935).

Populaire, which never mustered more than fifteen deputies. It was significant that one member of this party, Georges Bidault, owed his defeat in 1936 partly to the opposition of the Fédération National Catholique.

However, in the 1930s an increasing number of Catholic intellectuals began urging a new attitude which was to transform the situation completely. Emmanuel Mounier ran his journal *Esprit* as a meeting-place for believers and unbelievers and he supported the Popular Front. Jacques Maritain's *Humanisme intégrale* (1936) argued that Catholics could participate in politics without compromising the Church by their commitments. Mauriac took a stand on the Spanish Civil War which showed that Catholics did not necessarily subordinate their political judgement to religious considerations. The Dominican journal *Sept* favoured collaboration with the Marxist parties. During the war, the journal *Témoignage chrétien* showed the resistance of Catholics to totalitarianism and racism. The Vichy regime, to a certain extent, marked the triumph of the Church's traditional aims: the encouragement of the family and of corporations, the recall of the religious congregations and the subsidies to church schools. Most of the bishops supported Pétain, though with diminishing enthusiasm. But the war was far from discrediting the Church. There were also some bishops who were imprisoned or deported by the Nazis. Above all, the important part played by Catholics in the Resistance finally restored them to a central position in public life. In the 1944 election the Mouvement Républicain Populaire won 24 per cent of the votes. Though not a church party, it was dominated by Christian Democrats, and had Marc Sangnier as its honorary president. The post-war Church of France would be as different from that of the Third Republic, and as rejuvenated, as the expansionist post-war economy.

What distinguished the new Church was the active role of the laity, in what was known as Action Catholique. To be a Catholic in 1840 usually meant simply acceptance of a position within a large hierarchical organisation, of which the clergy were the leaders and prophets, so that the layman's function in it was the passive one of attending church, and, at most, giving it alms to distribute to the poor. By 1940 this was no longer so. Membership was much more like membership of a society, like freemasonry. One had to take positive measures to join and it was not just a question of keeping up one's subscription; one became a proselytiser, and, at least in theory, one's way of life reflected one's religious beliefs; to a certain extent one opted out of normal society; one almost became a rebel by being pious. The Catholics now had that enthusiasm that the free-thinkers had shown a century before. Action Catholique, the generic term used to cover the activity of Catholic laymen, began in a series of youth movements. The Association Catholique de la Jeunesse Française was founded as early as 1886 by Albert de Mun, as a student movement, guided by Jesuit almoners, devoted to piety, study of the new role of the Church, and social action. In 1891 it had 5,000 members, in 1904 70,000, in 1914 140,000. It was essentially bourgeois; it expected its members to have enough education to participate in its 'study groups', and for long it was conservative politically. But it became most active in rural areas, where it gave birth to a new élite, founding and leading mutual benefit societies for farmers. In 1927 a similar organisation was founded for workers, the Jeunesse Ouvrière Chrétienne (J.O.C.), which had 65,000 members by 1937. Different movements for different social classes now became the rule, in the belief that the old idea of the upper class converting the poor was hopeless and should be replaced by 'conversion of like by like'. The Jeunesse Agricole Chrétienne, founded in 1929, had 35,000 members by 1935; the Jeunesse Étudiante Chrétienne, founded in 1930, 10,000 members; the Jeunesse Maritime Chrétienne (1932, 7,000 members). The Jeunesse Indépendante Chrétienne, for the bourgeoisie, was founded in 1936. Parallel organisations for women followed. In addition, the Scouts (founded 1920, 55,000 members in 1936) kept Catholic boys separate from the lay Éclaireurs. Pope Pius XI encouraged these movements; a central secretariat in charge of Action Catholique was established in Paris to co-ordinate its efforts; each diocese was required to have commissions (half lay, half clerical) to advise the bishop on pious, educational, charitable and press institutions; and efforts were made to co-ordinate the curés' parochial work with that of these independent organisations. These arrangements were not successful in this period. The organisations were too vigorous and independent to be co-ordinated by the hierarchy; some, like the workers and agriculturalists, were so keen to get mass class support that they were lax about the religious practices of their members; and the older parish clergy for their part were slow to accept this lay interference. This new enthusiasm of the Catholics brought about a fragmentation of attitudes and policies over a considerably wider range than had existed before. The power of the Church was not directly strengthened, but its stability was, and indirectly, because Catholics now had a wider range of options open to them, they were able to participate more fully in the life of the nation.[1]

### Anticlericalism

It was thus only at the very end of this period that the Catholic Church, as a body, began to accept that it could not fulfil its ambition to be universal. Tradition left it with more status than a sect, but its hopes of dominating every aspect of life were now abandoned. Once it acknowledged society to be pluralistic, it was able to respond much more effectively to the demands of its adherents. The conclusion, therefore, is not that there was less religion in the mid-twentieth century than in the *ancien régime*, but that what had previously been spread rather thinly, and often very superficially, over the masses, was now concentrated in smaller numbers, who were more positively interested and satisfied by it. These numbers were probably fewer than they would have been had not the anticlerical campaigns been so bitter, for the enemies of the Church had by no means all been enemies of religion. Religion was discredited quite as much by its supporters as by its own qualities, or by its inability to appeal to all temperaments. Just how powerful the animosities created were may be seen from the fact that as late as 1960 no less than ten and a half million people signed

---

[1] Charles Molette, *L'Association Catholique de la Jeunesse Française, 1886–1907* (doctorat ès lettres, 1968); Mgr Guerry, *Action Catholique* (1936); Raymond Laurent, *Le Parti démocrate populaire* (1965); Aline Controt and F. Dreyfus, *Les Forces religieuses dans la société française* (1965), with good bibliographies; René Rémond, *Les Catholiques, le communisme et les crises 1929–39* (1960); M. P. Fogarty, *Christian Democracy in Western Europe, 1820–1953* (1957); William Bosworth, *Catholicism and Crisis in Modern France* (Princeton, 1962); A. Achard, *Cinquante ans de J.A.C.F.* (1953); Michel Darbon, *Le Conflit entre la droite et la gauche dans le catholicisme français, 1830–1953* (1953).

an anticlerical petition protesting against state subsidies being given to church schools (which meant about half the country's voters). Many of these, even so, still used the church for baptism, marriage and burial. It is important to be clear about the nature and extent of their anticlericalism.[1]

Anticlericalism was, first of all, political. It was originally a protest much less against religious belief than against the political pretensions of the Church. In 1789 and again in 1848 the Church co-operated in revolutions which destroyed privilege, but on both occasions it quickly abandoned the popular cause, and emerged on the winning, reactionary side. It was rewarded with a reinforcement of its position: Napoleon I made the clergy into civil servants, paid by the state; and Napoleon III allowed them to develop an immensely expanded educational system. It may be argued, with hindsight, that this was an option that was beneficial to the Church only in the short term. The alternative was for it to reform itself thoroughly, in keeping with the new aspirations of the century, as the early socialists demanded of it, to revive the stress on love, rather than fear, in its message. Socialism and Christianity were very close in 1848. But the Church was too deeply instilled with the medieval idea that it should have charge of the souls of all men, that the government of lay and spiritual matters was inextricable, and that the state should lend its authority to the Church to ensure that religious principles were obeyed. The clergy were too depressed to opt for a policy of sacrifice. They were panic-stricken by the changes around them, and exaggerated their demands precisely because they suffered from a sense of inferiority. The failure of their occasional efforts at compromise confirmed them in their determination to resist with obstinacy, and to hurl anathemas at their enemies. As in every war, each side claimed the other had started it; but by the nineteenth century the war had gone on long enough for it to have a hereditary tradition, and that is why it is still not extinct. However, it was a war the Church could not win, using the strategy it adopted, for it had never really converted the masses to Christianity. It sometimes had

[1] For general histories, see R. Rémond, *L'Anticléricalisme en France* (1976); Alex Mellor, *Histoire de l'anticléricalisme français* (1966); G. Weill, *Histoire de l'idée laïque en France* (1925); L. Caperan, *Histoire contemporaine de la laïcité* (1960).

governments on its side, but this merely saddled it with all the animosity governments aroused, for reasons independent of religion. As in all wars, also, second-rate polemicists exacerbated the quarrel with arguments of exactly the same level as those which suggested, for example, that Frenchmen could never live in peace with Englishmen or with Germans, and these arguments gave a very misleading indication of the doubts of thoughtful men on both sides.

Renan said that the Catholic Church had never been tolerant, never would be and indeed could not be tolerant. The *coup d'état* of 1851 was perhaps a decisive date in its modern history, because, for a whole decade, having been given the chance by Napoleon III's government, it embarked on a policy of persecution of its enemies which destroyed most of the sympathy that liberals and republicans may have had for it. Proudhon, whose book on *Justice* was condemned in the courts for 'offending religious morals', complained that 'the tyranny of priests' was worse than ever now: 'their avowed plan is to kill science, to snuff out all liberty and all enlightenment. Their anger increases in proportion to their power.'[1] Louis Veuillot, in the *Univers*, delighted in taking Catholic claims to their extremes, condemning all forms of liberty deriving from the French Revolution, demanding the ending of freedom of the press, insisting that toleration was a menace and lamenting that Luther had not been burnt, for he had caused the damnation of millions of souls. The open alliance of Catholic bishops and priests with the legitimist party, their support of the most absolutist theories and their active participation in parliamentary elections, in the end frightened even the Bonapartist government. By staking all on the restoration of the monarchy, they became the political enemies of the majority of the nation, and they united quite disparate forces against them.[2] For a whole century, Catholicism and democracy seemed incompatible, and the bishops' loyalty to Action Française between the wars confirmed this. When the question of the republic's existence was finally settled, that of education

---

[1] P. J. Proudhon, *Correspondance* (1875), 6. 110.
[2] J. Maurain, *La Politique ecclésiastique du second empire* (1930) is the best guide for this period; G. Weill, 'L'Anticléricalisme sous le second empire', *Revue des études napoléoniennes* (July–Aug. 1915), 56–84.

remained to perpetuate the division: now the Church claimed that it was entitled to freedom to educate Catholic children in its own way; but the left rejected this, as divisive. In 1952, an inquiry among practising Catholics revealed that only 8 per cent of them voted for the left wing (5 per cent socialist, 2 per cent radical, 1 per cent communist).[1] Politics thus made people increasingly reject religion—or in occasional reactions, adopt it—for reasons which were not inherently religious. The socialists originally condemned anticlericalism as a bourgeois quarrel, which simply distracted the workers from the class struggle, and Veuillot had indeed said that he was a clerical precisely because he was of humble birth, instinctively opposed to the bourgeois liberals; but the revolutionary and egalitarian aspects of Christianity were lost sight of by the Church in this period.[2] It was only around the time of the Second World War that some Catholic divines began to be attracted or fascinated by Marxism.[3] On certain issues, they were not as opposed as their political stances suggested. Anticlericalism, however, had left a legacy which made it impossible for them to admit any agreement. Its effect was to perpetuate mistrust long after the causes for it had altered; it made French divisions historical as much as actual. Anticlericalism indeed had often developed as a rationalisation of divisions within villages, started off by the clash of personality and the struggle for power, and then solemnised by principles when *curé* and *instituteur* symbolically assumed the leadership of the two parties. From this point of view anticlericalism fulfilled a political need: it provided a means by which the two-party system was effectively established in France, because everybody had to be either for or against the clergy. But, as with the division of Englishmen into Whig and Tory, the principles were not always what divided them most.[4]

Anticlericalism got mixed up with free thought and the quarrel widened into one of science against religion. The

[1] A. Coutrot and F. Dreyfus, *Les Forces religieuses dans la société française* (1965), 195.

[2] 'L'Église et le monde ouvrier en France', special issue of *Le Mouvement social* (Oct.–Dec. 1966).

[3] 'Les Chrétiens et le monde communiste', special issue of *Christianisme social* (Jan. 1959).

[4] See Roger Magraw, 'Popular Anticlericalism in the Isère 1852–70', in T. Zeldin, *Conflicts in French Society* (1970), 169–227.

number of atheists in France may have been even smaller than the number of pious believers. In 1952 only 8 per cent of a sample survey said that the existence of God was improbable and only 5 per cent that there was definitely no God, though when divided according to sex, 24 per cent of men and 9 per cent of women declared themselves to be agnostics or atheists.[1] There was, however, certainly more positive disbelief of religion in France than in either the U.S.A. or Britain.[2] Why should the French, who saw less of the wonders of science than the Americans or the British, have been more convinced that science had disproved religion? Perhaps for that very reason, but perhaps also they were not convinced by science as might be supposed. Science did of course lead some people to doubt the accuracy of the Bible, to reject miracles and revelation and to declare religion to be a conspiracy to keep the masses obedient. Violent polemics did break out in which science and religion attacked each other. But France also had a strong movement of 'concordism' which aimed to show that there was no real conflict. There were plenty of Catholics who used scientific discoveries to support their faith, or who simply put the two in separate compartments of their minds. What was perhaps peculiar to France was that there was a whole combination of grievances against the Church, and therefore much more radical argument. The cause of science was eagerly seized on, as a result, by the enemies of Christianity. Positivism, for example, was often raised up as a new flag by people who had previously been atheists or anticlericals. Until someone analyses all the histories of loss of faith that can be found, it will be impossible to say what factors were most influential; but it is probable that the influence of parents and of friends was important: the hereditary origin of beliefs and the example that schoolboys and students set each other (rather than the doctrines taught by priests or teachers) are frequently referred to. Science may have convinced above all those who were ready to be convinced.[3] The early free-thinking philosophers

[1] G. Rotvand, L'Imprévisible Monsieur Durand (1956), 199.

[2] A less precise international survey in 1947 showed 95 per cent of Americans, 84 per cent of Britons and 66 per cent of Frenchmen admit to belief in God. Ibid.

[3] Alfred Verlière, Guide du libre penseur (1869); Charles Charpillet, Conflit du catholicisme et de la civilisation moderne (1864); J. B. Cloet, L'Arsenal catholique . . . réponses aux objections (1857); Dr. Jean Grange, La Prêtrophobie. De ses causes et de ses

believed that their independence of mind was too difficult for the masses to attain: they considered themselves to be an intellectual élite (not unlike the pious Christians who thought God had picked them out). They were generally profoundly interested by religion, tormented by uncertainty, and sometimes heretics more than unbelievers. The attitude of such men differed from that of the simply cynical, or of the wits who poured scorn on religion in what they believed to be the tradition of Voltaire, or of M. Homais, the village pharmacist, who had no doubts at all and derived considerable satisfaction from his position as the local philosopher. The party of Voltaire, when it comes to be analysed, will be seen to have infinite variations in it. Perhaps that, ultimately, is why religion was able to withstand its onslaughts.[1]

Anticlericalism had a paradoxical relationship with morality. The regions in which it was most active were often ones where the monastic orders had had large estates under the *ancien régime*, where the presence of the Church had been felt particularly strongly and where, above all, Jansenism had been most widespread. The Jansenists had made Catholicism a much more demanding, ascetic and rigorous doctrine, insisting on the basic corruption of man, who was held to be capable of salvation only through severe self-discipline and only if God chose him out specially, by grace; they maintained that only the most holy were worthy of receiving communion and only after submitting to severe penances; absolution should be given by the priest only when the habit of sin was thoroughly

---

*remèdes* (1871); Abbé Isoard, *Le Clergé et la science moderne* (1864); A. F. F. Roselly de Lorgues, *Le Christ devant le siècle ou nouveaux témoignages des sciences en faveur du catholicisme* (1835, 18th edition 1856); François Russo, S.J., *Pensée scientifique et foi chrétienne* (1953); W. C. Dampier-Whetham, *A History of Science and its Relations with Philosophy and Religion* (Cambridge, 1931); Dr. Louis Fleury, *Science et religion* (1868); C. C. Gillespie, *Genesis and Geology* (Harvard U.P., 1951); M. Ladevi-Roche, *Le Positivisme au tribunal de la science* (1867); E. Boutroux, *Science et religion dans la philosophie contemporaine* (1911); F. L. Baumer, *Religion and the Rise of Scepticism* (New York, 1960).

[1] L. A. Prévost-Paradol, *De l'impiété systématique* (1855); Anon. [Guynemer], *Dictionnaire des incrédules* (1869); E. Vacherot, *La Religion* (1869); J. F. Nourisson, *Voltaire et le voltairianisme* (1896); Robert van der Elst, *La Popularité de Voltaire* (1897); Eugène Dufeuille, *L'Anticléricalisme avant et pendant notre république* (1911); Marcel Thiébaut, *Edmond About* (1936); Marcel Mery, *La Critique du christianisme chez Renouvier* (1952); Albert Bayet, *Histoire de la libre pensée* (1959); Keith Thomas, *Religion and the Decline of Magic* (1971).

destroyed. Jansenism was much more than this—it was also a source of individualism and of a certain kind of egalitarianism —but its moral rigorism undoubtedly had the effect of turning people away from church. It set up traditions of anticlericalism, and it was by no means a mere memory in the nineteenth century, for there were still Jansenist journals under Louis-Philippe and Napoleon III and the last Jansenist order, the Brothers of St. Antoine at Mandé, did not collapse till 1888.[1] There were regions, like Lorraine, where Jansenism did not produce a hostile reaction, but in others, like the diocese of Nevers (which became highly anticlerical), the clergy refused absolution and communion so systematically, and demanded penance and contrition over many weeks before yielding, that resentment built up against them. The confessional was an important cause of disaffection, because some clergy used it in a vain attempt to control sexual behaviour. They looked on desire for sensual pleasures as the main source of evil and they demanded that sexual intercourse should seek, as far as possible, only the procreation of children. 'The secret of love', as one priest wrote, 'is in the art of self-restraint.' Confession was seen as 'repressing' sensualism and showing men that life was essentially a painful business: 'without pain, there would be no Church'. This was at a time when people were trying to reduce the size of their families. The confessors not only condemned contraception and coitus interruptus, but urged wives to resist it. The Church, in its effort to uphold the traditional large family, thus made itself a threat to harmony in the family. The anticlericals attacked the clergy for talking about sexual matters, for asking detailed questions about what went on between husband and wife, and they denounced the confessors' manuals as books of pornography, which only put dirty ideas into innocent minds. Anticlericalism was thus two-pronged: on the one hand the masses adopted it because religion interfered too much in their lives—Proudhon said 'their instinct tells them that the only thing that stops them being happy and rich is theology'—but on the other hand the anticlericals' leaders were almost as puritan

[1] La Revue ecclésiastique (1838–48); L'Observateur catholique (1855–64); Augustin Gazier, Histoire générale du mouvement janséniste depuis ses origines jusqu'à nos jours (1922); Pierre Ordioni, La Survivance des idées gallicanes et jansénistes en Auxerrois de 1760 à nos jours (Auxerre, 1933).

as the Jansenists and were very far from wanting to open the doors to sensuality or materialism. The leaders and the masses were therefore at cross purposes, and once the anticlerical battle was won, the theory of anticlericalism had to be overthrown in its turn. If one compares the moral textbooks produced by the advocates of the 'lay school' with the Catholic catechisms one quickly sees that all they were quarrelling with the Church about was the theoretical question of whether morals were of divine origin or whether they were self-imposed and how they should be taught, but the precepts of conduct were virtually identical. The Jesuits were singled out by the anticlericals as the most dangerous enemies of the people, but it was precisely the Jesuits who did most to adapt Catholic dogma to changing times and who urged moderation on confessors. Anticlericals attacked the clergy for dogmatism but they were themselves keen to preserve the social order, and Marion, professor at the Sorbonne and one of their main moral philosophers, warned teachers that children must not be allowed to grow up into dangerous 'little reasoners': 'great circumspection should be used in the choice of occasions given to the child to use his judgement'.[1]

Anticlericalism, frequently, was the product of divergencies of temperament. Sociologists who have tried to explain it have been driven, after showing why it flourished in one village rather than another, to assert that each had a 'character' which was ultimately beyond explanation. Historians who have investigated why particular individuals became anticlericals have, after going through all the intellectual arguments, often felt that personal accidents were as important: thus Voltaire emerges as the son and younger brother of Jansenists, against whose severity and fanaticism he rebelled.[2] Anticlericalism

[1] Louis Bailly, *Theologia dogmatica et moralis ad usum seminarium* (1789, reprinted twenty times 1804–52), the leading Jansenist moral textbook; P. Bert, *La Morale des jésuites* (1880), which is based on P. Gury's textbook of morals; Ch. Bellet, *Le Manuel de M. Paul Bert, ses erreurs et ses falsifications* . . . (Tours, 1882); R. R. Palmer, *Catholics and Unbelievers in 18th Century France* (Princeton, 1939); J. J. Gaume, *Manuel des confesseurs* (9th edition, 1865); Le Curé X, *Les Mystères du confessional par Mgr Bouvier* (n.d.); Abbé D. Léger, *Le Guide du jeune prêtre au tribunal de la pénitence* (1864); G. Belot, *Questions de morale* (1900); R. Allier, *Morale religieuse et morale laïque* (1914); T. Zeldin, *Conflicts in French Society* (1970), chapter on 'Confession, sin and pleasure'.
[2] René Pomeau, *La Religion de Voltaire* (1956); cf. Abbé Berseaux, *La*

was irresistible to inveterate enemies of authority and it was natural that it should have been embraced by the radical party of the *small man*.[1] Once people had taken sides, there was almost nothing they would not believe about the wickedness of their enemies: the Jesuits were accused of inventing instruments of torture to apply to the genitals of their recalcitrant pupils, while the freemasons were very seriously seen by Catholics as communing with the devil. In one of the greatest hoaxes of the century, a third-rate journalist, Léo Taxil, made a living exploiting this credulity, inventing absurd stories which the most respectable Catholics believed, until he revealed that it was all invention.[2]

Anticlericals certainly liked to get together and Freemasonry became their favourite society. Because the freemasons shrouded their activities in secrecy, all sorts of accusations could be made against them: anticlericalism was therefore associated with revolutionary conspiracies and backstairs political intrigue, and attacked as being in league with Jewish and Protestant influences; the subject has proved of inexhaustible fascination and in 1925 a bibliography listed no less than 54,000 titles of works on it. The Vichy regime confiscated the freemasons' archives in its desire to expose their machinations, but they only made it clear, at last, that there was nothing very dramatic to reveal. Freemasonry was not originally anti-religious: in the eighteenth century, priests had been members. Both Napoleons had given it semi-official status, so as to keep it under control. But under the Second Empire many lodges were infiltrated by republicans, and they, in 1877, won the movement over to free thought by ending the homage it had hitherto paid to the 'Grand Architect of the Universe'. In due course, nearly all lodges became affiliated to the radical party. The number of freemasons rose from about 10,000 in 1802 to 20,000 in 1889, 32,000 in 1908, 40,000 in 1926 and about 60,000 in 1936. This was the result of a conscious policy of democratisation. In the eighteenth century there were two kinds of freemasons: members of the upper class and middle-class

---

*Voltairomanie* (Laneuveville devant Nancy, 1865) and Mgr de Ségur, *Les Ennemis des curés. Ce qu'ils sont, ce qu'ils disent* (1875).

[1] E. Faguet, *L'Anticléricalisme* (1906) for a largely psychological interpretation.
[2] E. Weber, *Satan franc-maçon* (1964).

men who liked to ape them, to call each other chevalier and wear honorific regalia. In the course of the nineteenth century, the social composition was increasingly widened; in 1880, reduced initiation fees were offered to soldiers and *instituteurs*; and in the twentieth century policemen and workers from the Confédération Générale du Travail were recruited. Freemasonry appealed first of all to people who liked mystic ritual, esoteric symbolism and fancy uniforms, and to those who liked to have somewhere to discuss ideas and meet like-minded friends. Increasingly however it became an organisation which politicians used for electoral purposes and which civil servants joined in order to further their chances of promotion, which hotel-keepers found useful as a way of enlarging their clientele and where businessmen could make deals and find jobs for their sons. 'Fraternal groups' were set up in the prefecture of police, in journalism, in the gas and electricity industries, in medicine and education. Since most radical politicians belonged to it, and since for a long time its leader was vice-president of the Senate, it was believed that it ran the country, as well as being the principal source of materialistic and anticlerical propaganda. This was a vast exaggeration: certainly it lent its aid to the anticlerical campaigns, but it was hardly responsible for initiating them. Its intellectual level sank rapidly, and though it passed resolutions calling for such reforms as the introduction of income tax, it was perhaps most important as a social club, membership of which was seen as a way of getting on in the world, and in which one also got immediate advantages, such as ten per cent discounts in shops owned by freemasons. It organised a certain amount of charity, but even more mutual insurance.

In 1904 a great fuss was made because the lodges had been asked to collect information about the political affiliations of army officers, with a view to thwarting the promotion of right-wing ones. The enemies of the freemasons, who organised themselves into Anti-Masonic Leagues, replied by publishing lists of freemasons, as a kind of repertoire of dangerous men. Every parliamentary and judicial scandal inevitably involved freemasons and this added fuel to the polemic. However, at the provincial level, the masonic lodges were pretty insignificant. The lodge of Saint-Brioude (Haute-Loire) had only forty-four members in 1911, half of them civil servants, thirteen of them merchants, six *cafetiers* and two barristers. In Laval (Mayenne) the lodge was a small republican club seeking to depose the sitting conservative members of parliament, and occasionally falling apart from disagreements, as it did over the Boulanger Affair; its members were above all *instituteurs*, led by the inspector of primary schools. There was considerable variation in the atmosphere of different lodges: some emphasised ritual, some were musical, some favoured playing cards and dominoes; but all of them loved holding banquets 'resembling sessions of the Convention' with their speeches and toasts. Freemasonry was divided between the Grand Lodge and the Grand Orient (the former, unlike the latter, was on the side of the workers in industrial disputes and admitted worker members), and there were three other minor varieties. The interest in politics palled in due course and after 1945 it was largely expelled. The Grand Master of the National Lodge said in 1972: 'It is time that Frenchmen got into the habit of talking about things other than politics.'[1]

Anticlericalism was, to a certain extent, France's alternative to England's Nonconformist churches. It was no accident that Protestants took a leading part in the anticlerical movement. Protestantism had been largely stamped out by the combined persecution of Church and monarchy, and its revenge was therefore twofold. Protestants entered the civil service in a proportion which may well have been considerably larger than the 2 per cent or less of the total population that they formed. In 1900 there were probably less than 650,000 of them; when Alsace and Lorraine were recovered in 1919, there were perhaps 800,000. If they had had a proportionate share of state posts, they would have had no more than one or two prefects, and ten deputies at most. In 1899, however, there were said to be about ten Protestant prefects and over 100 members

---

[1] A. Lantoine, *Histoire de la franc-maçonnerie française*: vol. 3, *La Franc-Maçonnerie dans l'État* (1935); A. Lantoine, *Les Sociétés secrètes actuelles en Europe et en Amérique* (1940); M. J. Headings, *French Freemasonry under the Third Republic* (Baltimore, 1949); A. Mellor, *La Vie quotidienne de la franc-maçonnerie française du 18ᵉ siècle à nos jours* (1973); E. Gautheron, *Les Loges maçonniques dans la Haute-Loire 1744–1937* (Le Puy, 1937); André Bouton and Marius Lepage, *Histoire de la franc-maçonnerie dans la Mayenne 1756–1951* (Le Mans, 1951); D. Ligou, *Frédéric Desmons et la franc-maçonnerie sous la 3ᵉ république* (1966); Raymond A. Dior, 'La Franc-Maçonnerie', *Le Crapouillot* (Sept. 1938); Paul Nourrisson, *Le Club des Jacobins sous la 3ᵉ république* (1900); Jean Marquès-Rivière, *Les Grands Secrets de la franc-maçonnerie* (1935).

of parliament.[1] In 1924 Gaston Doumergue became the first Protestant president of the republic. A Protestant, Louis Méjan, was one of the principal architects of the law of the separation of Church and state; and many of the politicians responsible for wresting education out of the hands of the Catholics were Protestants. The Protestants seemed to be capturing the state, using it to attack the Catholic Church from above, while at the same time undermining it from below by whipping up the anticlerical movement to unprecedented levels. This is how it seemed to the Catholics. In fact it was only a small minority of Protestants who were involved in active politics, and these formed a heretical group within the community. Protestants were very far from having a united attitude on any subject, even on religion. They were not only divided between Calvinists and Lutherans (as well as a few thousand Methodists, Baptists, Derbyites etc. produced by English proselytisation) but they were also geographically differentiated between the two main regions, the south and the east. In the 1890s, one-quarter of all Protestants lived in the department of Gard. In this period, Protestantism was still predominantly rural, even though there were sizeable communities in Paris and some other cities. The southerners were the descendants of the Camisards, who had fought a guerrilla war against the monarchy in the eighteenth century, and rebellion was a family tradition. But by the end of this period the mountainous regions, to which they had withdrawn, became depopulated, and the influx into the civil service and the liberal professions transformed Protestantism into a nation-wide phenomenon, with a few representatives in most regions. The Protestants thus seemed to be powerful for different and changing reasons. There were however quietists as well as activists among them, Dreyfusards as well as anti-Dreyfusards; they were the inspiration of the Co-operative movement, but they also had notable industrialists and bankers who linked them with capitalism; and in the interwar years, some supported the communist party. They could never present a united front, because their modern history was one of constant internal dispute; but there were enough of them prominent in left-wing politics, and there was enough hostility towards them among the Catholic clergy—

[1] Ernest Renauld, *Le Péril protestant* (1899); id., *La Conquête protestante* (1900).

who became far more vigorous in areas with Protestant communities—for anticlericalism to be seen as a continuation of the wars of religion.[1]

Anticlericalism was, finally, connected with anti-Semitism because Catholics took a leading role in the stirring up of hate against the Jews. Anti-Semitism was not a central problem in France until the end of the nineteenth century. The traditional animosity of the Church towards the Jews was echoed in the vague hostility that the French generally felt for the Jewish minority among them, but there were very few Frenchmen who ever came into contact with Jews: in 1840 there were still only 70,000 Jews in France, two-thirds of whom lived in Alsace. Catholic journalists like Louis Veuillot could thus inveigh against Jews during the Second Empire while revealing extraordinary misapprehensions and ignorance about them. The emancipation of the Jews by the Revolution had made them legally equal, but socially they were still apart. However, the successes that, as a result, some of them were able to obtain in French life soon caused this emancipation to back-fire on them. Rothschild became the symbol of capitalism and it was the socialists who were therefore the first pioneers of anti-Semitism in its modern form. It was the Fourierist Toussenel who published the first major anti-Semitic book of the nineteenth century. The idea that all Jews were wealthy was of course a myth, and as late as 1870, over 60 per cent of them were said to have died paupers. It was no contradiction that, even if Fourierist socialism was anti-Semitic, the Saint-Simonian variety should have had Jews among its most celebrated adherents. For what distinguished the educated Jews in France was their relegation of their Judaism into a purely religious peculiarity and their desire to turn themselves in all other respects into fully-fledged Frenchmen. Many of them saw themselves as symbols of the liberal principles of the French Revolution, and in gratitude their patriotism, as the Grand Rabbi of Paris said, was of 'an extraordinary fervour'. Darmesteter, the director of the École Pratique des Hautes Études,

---

[1] Émile G. Léonard, *Le Protestant français* (1953) and id., *Histoire générale du protestantisme*, vol. 3 (1964) which has a large bibliography. Cf. also Jean Seguy, *Les Sectes protestantes dans la France contemporaine* (1956).

argued that the French Revolution was the fulfilment of the Jewish ideas of justice and progress. By the end of the nineteenth century, assimilation even became the official doctrine of the organised Jewish community.

But because Jews therefore sided with the cause of liberalism, they came to be seen as increasingly dangerous enemies by reactionaries. There were two Jews in the government set up by the revolution of 1848: the barrister Isaac Crémieux, who became minister of justice, and the banker Goudchaux, who was minister of finance. Crémieux was minister again after the overthrow of Napoleon III and used the opportunity to give full French citizenship to the Jews of Algeria—which became one of the bastions of anti-Semitism.[1] The Reinach family was closely associated with Gambetta. Alfred Naquet, the professor of chemistry responsible for the law allowing divorce (1886) and therefore bitterly hated by Catholics, sat on the extreme left; the fact that he had married a Catholic and ceased practising as a Jew did not stop all the animosity this issue raised being directed against the Jews. The admission of Jews into the freemason lodges stimulated the belief that they were involved in a massive conspiracy against the Church. Brilliant examination successes in the state schools, the instrument of Jewish assimilation, exacerbated jealousy.

But what is interesting about the rise of organised anti-Semitism is that it had relatively little to do with the development of the Jewish community. Anti-Semitism was an expression of the ignorance of the modern world that the Church suffered from in the mid-nineteenth century rather than of close observation of it. The anti-Semitic work that the aristocrat Gougenot des Mousseaux (commander of the Order of Pius IX) published in 1869 was inspired by the belief that Jews were cabbalistic worshippers of Satan.[2] The first newspaper devoted specifically to attacking the Jews, *L'Anti-sémitisme* (1882), was founded by a priest, a canon of Angoulême and Poitiers, where there were virtually no Jews at all. The best-seller that turned anti-Semitism into a national movement, *La France juive* (1886), which sold 100,000 copies in its

[1] See chapter 18 for the situation in Algeria.
[2] H. R. Gougenot des Mousseaux, *Le Juif, le judaïsme et la judaïsation des peuples chrétiens* (1869).

first year, was the work of a young journalist, Édouard Drumont, who had tried his hand at historical novels, playwriting
and gossip collecting, and who produced not a work of observation, but a mass of falsehoods, many of them plagiarised
from previous works. He claimed there were half a million
Jews in France, though official statistics registered only 68,000
(plus 44,000 in Algeria). But by combining political polemic
(for one of the main targets was Gambetta, who Drumont
said was really a Wurtemberger Jew called Gamberlé) with
amazing would-you-believe-it stories, he provided an explanation of why the world was going to the dogs. His book was
eagerly bought by Catholics. In 1895 Drumont's newspaper
*La Libre Parole* organised a competition for an essay on how
best Jewish power in France could be annihilated; the two
prizewinners were Catholic priests, as were two of the runners-
up. Drumont was also a palmist and spiritualist, always
carrying a mandrake root with him. His own credulity was
more than matched by that of his followers. No Jew bothered
to answer him.

The Dreyfus Affair ranged the Jews more firmly than ever on
the side of the liberal republic, and therefore against its enemies, the monarchists and the clergy. The Jews deliberately
tried to move the issue away from that of anti-Semitism to the
more general one of toleration and respect for the individual.
But the Jews were now also becoming recognisable as a foreign
minority, as successive waves of immigration swelled their
numbers, above all in Paris. In 1870 there were 24,000 Jews
there. The Alsatians raised this number to 40,000 by 1881.
The Russians then arrived, followed after 1919 by other East
Europeans, so that by 1930 there were 150,000. The vast
majority went into the clothing trade and set up separate
quarters in Paris. Many of them could not speak French,
many of them did not want to be assimilated and stressed
their separateness, to the dismay of the old-established Jews. A
few hundred joined the communist party, and so strengthened
the impression that they were a danger to the established order.
The old or French Jews, anxious to dissociate themselves,
formed a Jewish patriotic organisation, and even allied with
right-wing patriotic organisations, including the Croix de
Feu. This did not prevent the followers of Maurras from making

anti-Semitism a basic part of their teaching, and under Vichy the Jews were finally excommunicated from membership of the nation. It was only the extreme nature of their persecution that at last aroused the conscience of the Catholics, and it was only under Vichy that a section of the clergy at last came out publicly against anti-Semitism.[1]

The history of religious practice and dispute in this period reveals most strikingly how people with broadly similar outlooks could, as a result of disagreement on secondary issues, become enemies so violent that they became quite incapable of understanding or sympathising with each other. Anger, and traditions of animosity, thus prevented the reassessment of differences with changing times; and political divisions became more historical than real. In nineteenth-century France Catholicism was largely a religion of aggression and of incomprehension, with too many enemies to allow its charity to be fruitful. Though it preached resignation, it did not practise it: it was a religion of anxiety. In the twentieth century, it gradually and increasingly altered its outlook so that it came to appeal to a different sort of person: the longing for national uniformity gave way to a much more individualistic emphasis, which was not all that far removed from what the founding fathers of the Revolution had envisaged. Catholicism became, indeed, a refuge from the pressures of mass civilisation, just as it had once itself been a source of pressure for conformity. That it took centuries of warfare to effect this transformation was due partly to successive governments exploiting it to further their own quest for power. Church and state were inseparable when both believed it was their function to control what men thought. Neither ever succeeded. But when they stopped their persecutions, and the infinite variation in ideas was allowed free expression, there were new pressures upon them. It is uncertain just how far the battle for free thought was won.

[1] B. Blumenkranz, *Bibliographie des Juifs en France* (1974); Robert F. Byrnes, *Antisemitism in Modern France* (Rutgers U.P., 1950); Michael R. Marrus, *The Politics of Assimilation. A Study of the French Jewish Community at the time of the Dreyfus Affair* (Oxford, 1971); Pierre Pierrard, *Juifs et Catholiques français 1886–1945* (1970); David H. Weinberg, *Les Juifs à Paris de 1933 à 1939* (1974); Pierre Aubert, *Milieux juifs de la France contemporaine à travers leurs écrivains* (1957).

# 21. Technocracy

THE year 1914 is usually held to mark the beginning of a new era of anxiety. It quickly became a commonplace to contrast the stability of the pre-war years with the chaos that the war inaugurated, and that the Peace of Versailles could not halt. This book has tried to show that the myth of the good old days should not be taken seriously, for the nineteenth century any more than for any other age. That century was very far from being either stable or simple to live in. It is true that it did diminish insecurity in one very important way. For the first time in history, famine ceased to be a threat: on the whole Frenchmen no longer needed to fear death by starvation. But men became more mobile, both physically and socially; the many new opportunities before them complicated the choices they had to make and created tensions as severe as have been experienced before or since. The nineteenth century may, for the sake of schematic convenience, be said to have been dedicated to progress, but it was also frightened by it and quarrelled endlessly about it. It was, quite as much, a century of doubt. Far from living contentedly in the long warm summers that survivors of it liked to remember, it was worried about the future in a very fundamental way, precisely because resignation was not one of its characteristics. One could buy state bonds that yielded regular interest, but one was also obsessed by the need to save, economising on today's pleasures to fend off the dangers of tomorrow and old age. There were no long wars, but there were numerous short ones and the size of armies grew relentlessly.

1914 has been seen as a break in history largely for the wrong reasons. The inter-war years are, at present, rather in the same state as the Second Empire was for some fifty years after its collapse. The reign of Napoleon III could not be judged fairly after the humiliation of 1870: it was almost universally condemned as a failure, an aberration, a contradiction of all the high values that decent men should cherish; the emperor was derided as a fool and it seemed inexplicable that a civilised country like France should have submitted itself to his tyranny, fought in his quixotic wars and participated in the fawning adulation of his pompous rhetoric and of his upstart henchmen. It was only when both those who had lived through his reign and those who based their lives on the rejection of the errors of his generation were dead that the Second Empire could be regarded with detachment. It is only just beginning to be possible to adopt the same attitude to the years since 1914. The diplomatic and military historians have, as usual, been the first to clarify the outlines. The capture of the archives of the Third Reich has, by a curious quirk, illuminated the tergiversations of the Vichy regime, so that it is better known than the twenty years preceding it, but the history of inter-war France remains far less documented than that of Germany in the same period. The memoirs of generals and politicians have been fairly numerous but the French national archives have only recently been (partially) opened to historians. There have therefore been comparatively few doctoral theses that go beyond the study of foreign or party policy. One of the most remarkable of these, by J. N. Jeanneney, submitted in 1975, has shown what a vast array of polemical accusations and misconceptions need to be discarded before even the basic events can be established.[1] It was only in 1965–75, with the publication of Sauvy's four-volume economic history of the inter-war years, that the statistics of the period began to be subjected to critical reappraisal.[2] So it is only gradually that the perspective that regards these years as ones of exceptional chaos and failure will recede and allow the changes that took place in them to be seen in a less negative way, and with some sense of what was permanent and what was superficial.

The period 1914–45 was one of anxiety to those who lived through it not least because they did not know where it was leading. A great many people behaved, even after the war of 1914 and even during the German occupation of 1940–4, as though nothing fundamental had changed. The politicians of these years were most of them men who had picked up their

---

[1] J. N. Jeanneney, *François Wendel en République. L'Argent et le pouvoir 1914–40* (Nanterre doctorat d'état, defended in 1975, published in 1976).

[2] Alfred Sauvy, *Histoire économique de la France entre les deux guerres* (4 vols., 1965–75).

ideas before 1914. The price of success in the war was that the old leaders survived and the war could therefore be interpreted as no more than a severe illness or stroke, suffered by a middle-aged man, but one which was overcome: the republic was able to devote its remaining days to trying to regain the vigour of its youth. The battles of the politicians, the rise and fall of ministries, tell one about day-to-day preoccupations, but that is only one level of history.

At another level, one can see three major changes occurring in these years which transcend the bitter quarrels, which were abetted by politicians of almost all parties, and which place the details of events in a different light. The capitalist system, first of all, received a fatal blow in 1914, at least in the form in which it had existed in the nineteenth century. Its death throes may be regarded as a central theme of the next thirty years. After that, the economy was run on radically different lines and the state, which hitherto had limited its interventions to a comparatively small segment of life, emerged vastly more active, and very much transformed. The rise of an expansionist France in the 1950s, based on a 'mixed economy' and welfare benefits, cannot be understood without going back to these years. The peace of 1919, by returning Alsace and Lorraine, made France a great economic power. From this point of view, one could see the years 1871–1914 as in some sense an interlude. After 1919 the traditions of the Second Empire, stressing material prosperity, were revived. The full fruits of France's revenge were not immediately seen, because the country's expansion was held back by lack of labour and by a muddled fiscal policy. But the rapid development of new industries and the considerable prosperity of the 1920s showed that a path had been opened up. The great Wall Street crash and all the disasters that followed should not cause the promise of the 1920s to be confused with the gloom of the 1930s. Moreover, just as the First World War made Frenchmen say that they would never fight again, so the economic calamities that followed it made them determined not to suffer unemployment again. The end of insecurity in employment—or at least the establishment of insurance and compensation for unemployment—was worked out in these years, and greatly increased the role of the state in the economy. The constitution of 1946 accordingly laid it down that 'everyone has the duty to work and the right to have a job'. This represented the fulfilment of the demand for the Right to Work that the utopians of 1848 had dreamed of. It took a century to bring about; it was probably one of the most important achievements of universal suffrage; it was the state that undertook to guarantee it.

Paradoxically, however (and this is the second transformation that occurred in the period of the World Wars), the state became the supreme guide and director of the nation at the very moment when, from the international point of view, it lost its power of independent action. France had a population of only 40 million, in a world of 2,000 million. It was no longer able to defend itself on its own. Its foreign policy was dominated henceforth by a desperate search for alliances to compensate for its weakness, and by a very gradual realisation that it would have to find security, and a guarantee of its freedom, by co-operating with the rival nations it feared. It discovered that its economic problems, which hitherto it had palliated by customs protection, could not be solved by independent action, but was unable to accept this blow to its pride. The fierce reassertion of French values was the swansong of nationalism.

These were such revolutionary changes that it was difficult for people to adapt to them quickly, or indeed to comprehend them. They stimulated a dual reaction: an effort to ignore or stop change, or, alternatively, vigorous debate about the implications. These years were thus, thirdly, ones of intense intellectual activity, such as had not been witnessed since the early nineteenth century, when socialism was being concocted. However, thanks to the growth of education, intellectuals were far more numerous, and they occupied a less peripheral position in society. They now took a direct part in politics, as they had not hitherto done, and these were critical years in the history of their influence. The results of their activities were indecisive. They were not obviously successful, and they discredited each other also by their profound internal divisions; but they nevertheless continued to be as vocal and as self-confident in the guidance they claimed to offer to the country. This concealed the fact that they had lost their bid for power. A breach between intellectuals and technocrats—a breach which did not exist in the days of Saint-Simon—appeared in these years. It was the technocrats who established themselves in the positions of real power, in the civil service and in the management of industry, while the intellectuals deceived themselves with verbal roles in political parties. The outcome would become apparent only in the 1960s.

In 1914 the state was already the country's largest single employer, and its activities had already gone beyond administration into direct industrial and commercial enterprise. Since 1674 tobacco had been a state monopoly but the trade in tobacco was not carried out by state officials: a 'mixed' compromise between state and private enterprise had already been adopted, whereby the retailers were private individuals, enjoying privileges, but not paid by the state. In 1889 the state took on the direct manufacture of matches and the provision of telephones (which had hitherto been run by both the state and a private company) and in 1908 the state bought the bankrupt Western Railway. The radicals were attracted by this extension of state activity, despite their attachment to private property, because they hoped the profits would obviate the need for higher taxation, and because they valued the patronage that went with it. Unfortunately for them, the state did not make much profit: it was claimed that the state's profits from the manufacture of tobacco were only half of what England raised from its taxes on tobacco. In 1914 the state was engaged in the following business activities (the turnover, in millions of francs, is given in brackets):

Military catering and clothing manufacture (564), post office (362), shipbuilding (216), munition and cannon manufacture (188), building roads and ports, restoring old monuments etc. (175), tobacco and match manufacture (140), gunpowder (77), savings banks (62), aeroplanes (49), horse-breeding (38), insurance (27), forestry (27), porcelain making at Sèvres (17), map making (1·6), newspapers (1·5).[1]

Much of this was in competition with private industry.

But the war of 1914 extended the sphere of state activity to the control of the economy as a whole. Freedom of commerce was limited, in that the state tried to fix prices, limit profits, requisition and share out essential products. Labour was

[1] Adolphe Delemer, *Le Bilan de l'étatisme* (1922), 14.

allocated to industries by the selective release of soldiers from the front. Agricultural land left uncultivated could be requisitioned.[1] Food rationing and the granting of allowances to soldiers' families placed the whole population in much more direct subordination to the state. The state did not nationalise the war factories, however, nor did it institute industrial mobilisation for civilian industry (as Germany did). It worked through the capitalist system. Even for the import of raw materials, it preferred to get the businessmen concerned to combine into consortia which were given official status, but were run as private companies. The history of these consortia, of which there were fifty by the end of the war, provided a most instructive lesson. On the one hand, some hitherto conventional politicians came to think that the extension of state control over the economy should be retained and developed in peace time. The minister of commerce from 1915 to 1919, Étienne Clémentel (notary and mayor of Riom, an amateur opera librettist, playwright and artist) was galvanised by the delights of power and the revelation of chaos that office gave him into urging the establishment of a state department for economic planning: it would 'indicate to industrialists and businessmen . . . the general plan by which their efforts should be directed, so that the actions of individuals would help rather than hinder the interests of the state. A nation, like a business or an industry, must have an economic programme, a plan of action. Until now, nothing like this has ever been done in France.' Traditional methods, like customs regulations, no longer sufficed: 'government and industry must form an alliance to search for raw materials at the lowest possible cost, to plan for the intensive exploitation of all our natural resources and to determine the price of articles which must be manufactured by methods of mass production'. He considered that industry should form regional consultative groups, so that the state could negotiate with it on an adequate geographical basis. His experience of obtaining raw materials in war-time convinced him that international co-operation would be necessary to regulate trade and credit in peace-time and he urged the formation of an 'economic union of all free peoples' (meaning Western Europe and the U.S.A.). Jean Monnet, who forty years later organised

[1] Law of 6 October 1916.

the European Economic Community, was on Clémentel's staff. The roots of the Common Market and of the French state planning system go back to these experiences.

Not surprisingly, however, the war of 1914–18 did more to discredit than to encourage immediate action in this direction. The practical difficulties of mixed economic control were more obvious than its advantages. The effect of the consortia was to destroy many middlemen, but it also provided the businessmen whom the state enrolled into them with undreamed of opportunities for profiteering, even though the consortia were ostensibly designed to control this. The profits of importers involved in the consortia were limited by law to 6 per cent. The consumer did not obtain all the benefit from this, for the state kept prices high enough to rake in very sizeable profits itself: it was the largest profiteer, for example, in the Vegetable Fats consortium, from which it made 16,000,000 francs, and in the Petrol Consortium, which yielded it 25,000,000 francs' profit in a mere nine months. In addition, however, businessmen in the consortia were able, by the astute manipulation of privileges, to make a great deal of money also, as for example Rocca of Marseille did out of agricultural oil-cake. Industrialists quickly became skilful at exploiting government regulations, which therefore had to be constantly altered. Some used government institutions to break their rivals: thus the National Dye Company was set up with state assistance, by a group of industrialists and bankers, to challenge the Saint-Gobain Company, which for its part used the war to extract subsidies from the government, enabling it to re-equip at very little cost to itself. One armaments manufacturer, Louis Loucheur, got himself appointed minister of armaments and then, after the war, minister of industrial reconstruction. This did not guarantee industry against excessive state interference, but on the contrary increased it, for Loucheur quickly turned from poacher into gamekeeper, and did much to increase state control; but his activity showed how biased such control could be, benefiting some firms and harming others. A considerable number of businessmen entered the war ministries: this set up precedents for the interpenetration of government and industry, but also revealed its dangers when private interests were involved.[1]

[1] Jean Galtier-Boissière, *Histoire de la grande guerre 1914–18* (1959), 293; Albert

The proliferation of regulations and officials did little, in the end, to prevent vast profits being made, in a perfectly legal way, out of the war. The Aciéries de France's profits rose from 2,743,000 francs in 1913 to 11,000,000 in 1915; those of the Chambon-Feugerolles Steel Company from one to ten million. An investment company was formed which offered subscribers a return of their capital through dividends within six months and profits greater than the capital every six months. Manufacturers of shells, at least at the beginning of the war, were able to make profits of between 50 and 75 per cent. But it was not only Renault, making tanks, or Boussac, selling the state cloth for its aeroplanes, who did well. The milkmen were able to buy supplies at 17 centimes from farmers and sell them in Paris for up to 60 centimes, and greengrocers to sell Rhône peaches for *fifty* times what they had paid for them. Of course, it was not only the French state which could be exploited: the British and American armies made the fortune of tradesmen wherever they went (notably Rouen and Tours). But the French state's economic activities were publicly discredited by some notable scandals, which distracted attention from its less dramatic but ultimately more important innovations. The expenditure of 203,000,000 francs on setting up an arsenal at Roanne, which never manufactured more than 15,000,000 francs' worth of armaments, showed how the state could plunge into an appallingly expensive mess of mismanagement and interministerial rivalry, beneficial only to the contractors who fed it with useless equipment. The plan to introduce profit-sharing and productivity bonuses, and to run the arsenal with a board of directors consisting both of bureaucrats and of private industrialists indicated, however, the direction that state intervention would ultimately take. There were occasions when the state did benefit the consumer in an easily visible form, as for example when it produced the National Shoe (a simple form of footwear, at half the normal price, to counter the shortage of shoes), but the manufacturers whom it commissioned to make this were reluctant to co-operate, and the comparatively small numbers that were produced quickly got into the hands of black-market profiteers. There were more examples of failure

Aftalion, *L'Industrie textile en France pendant la guerre* (1925), 113–14; G. Perreux, *La Vie quotidienne pendant la grande guerre* (1966), 169–76.

than of success. The symbol of all this planning was perhaps the scheme making schoolchildren collect horse-chestnuts as a substitute for cattle fodder, which produced only great rotting piles at village halls, with no one to take them away.[1]

The state's new role during the war was not the result of any doctrinal or political inspiration, but gradually adopted by force of circumstance, and implemented by conservative politicians. Its whole interventionist apparatus was dismantled after the war, but again a series of crises led to the revival of parts of it and the invention of new forms. The growth of the state's power was, with only a few exceptions, not due to socialist ministries or even to socialist pressure, which is one reason why the political history of these years is so misleading. The political parties were not the forces behind the gradual transformation of the country's economic organisation that took place between the wars. It was under a conservative government that the law of 9 September 1919 laid it down that in future all concessions of mining rights to private companies should involve a share of all profits earned being paid to the state, with a share being reserved also to the workers. It was the same government which in 1919–20 decided that the state should use the ships it had bought in the war, or obtained in reparations, to start a state merchant navy. But this was mismanaged so scandalously that it was disbanded in 1921, at a loss of some 300,000,000 francs.[2] Before the war, the state had given subsidies to encourage shipbuilding; it had distributed over 600,000,000 francs between 1881 and 1914, but France had nevertheless fallen from second to fifth place among the world's merchant navies; and until 1902 these subsidies were given preferentially for the construction of sailing boats, in the belief that there was still a great commercial future for them. After the war, however, the state demanded more than prestige in return. In 1920 it turned the Compagnie des Messageries Maritimes into a mixed company, whose

---

[1] J. F. Godfrey, 'Bureaucracy, Industry and Politics in France during the First World War' (unpublished doctoral thesis, Oxford, 1975); G. Olphe Gaillard, *Histoire économique et financière de la guerre 1914–18* (1923); Raymond Guildhon, *Les Consortiums en France pendant la guerre* (1924); M. Veissière, *Les Transformations du commerce français pendant et après la guerre* (1921).

[2] M. Roubion, *La Flotte d'état en France* (Paris thesis, 1923); L. Roux, *La Marine marchande française* (Paris thesis, 1923).

losses would be guaranteed by the state, but which would yield 80 per cent of its profits to the state, if it made any. In 1933 the state took over the Compagnie générale transatlantique (founded by the Saint-Simonian Péreire in 1861) which, carried away by its prosperity in the 1920s, had committed itself too optimistically in new ventures rendered ruinous by the Great Crash. The *Île de France* (1927), on which the most famous people in the world crossed the Atlantic, was a magnificent ship, but it now lost money, as did also the company's tourist and hotel subsidiaries, premature heralds of an industry stifled by the depression. The state became the majority shareholder, but in co-operation with the private shareholders who still nominated to one-third of the seats on the board. The state subsidy system, which made possible the *Normandie* (1935, the largest and fastest ship ever built), was thus, in part, rationalised; and the state ensured, in return, that the company paid wages approved by it and by the trade unions.[1] The law of 1922 organising the country's electricity distribution system provided that the state should pay for the strategically important network, but that the cost of the remaining lines should be shared roughly equally between it and private industry; the concessions to companies, however, would be for a limited period and would revert to the state. The basis of a nationalised industry was thus laid down very early. The state discovered that it could get very considerable control over industry and very sizeable profits from it without actually having to buy more than a minority share in it, and this is what it set about doing. Thus the Compagnie française des pétroles was set up between 1924 and 1931 with the state buying only 35 per cent of the shares, but getting 40 per cent of the votes on the board and the additional right to nominate two government commissioners to sit on it, with a power of veto on its decisions. The state got a larger share of the company's profits than its contribution warranted (following the precedent set by the law on mining concessions) and it also had a right to buy up to 80 per cent of the company's petrol if it so desired.[2]

[1] Edmond Lanier, *Compagnie générale transatlantique* (1962); R. Matignon, *La Compagnie générale transatlantique depuis la guerre* (Bordeaux thesis, 1937); G. Fabry, *De l'intervention directe de l'État dans les compagnies de navigation maritime* (Paris thesis, 1934).

[2] Edgar Faure, *La Politique française du pétrole* (Paris law thesis, 1938); Jean Rondot, *La Compagnie française des pétroles* (1962).

Long before the formal nationalisation of the railways, the state had virtually turned them into a public service, by forcing its own tariff policy on the companies, which meant that the state cheapened certain forms of transport, effectively lowering the price of certain goods and stimulating the growth of commuter suburbs. The railways had of course been built partly with the aid of government grants or guarantees, and the state was expecting to recover ownership of all the lines between 1950 and 1960. It already enjoyed free transport on the railways for its own employees and the army. In the inter-war years, however, it made the railways into a formal model of a 'mixed economy' company. In 1921 a Conseil Supérieur des Chemins de Fer was established to unify the policies of the seven railway companies and to share out operating losses between them; in 1933 the government obtained the right to nominate two of the directors in each company; and finally in 1937 the Société Nationale des Chemins de Fer was founded which established a single national system. But this represented neither confiscation of the companies' assets (which the socialists, and notably Jules Moch, advocated on the ground that they had failed to provide adequate services), nor buying them out (which would have cost the state a vast amount, and would have freed the companies of their debts to the state), but a compromise. The SNCF was a private company, in which the state was given 51 per cent of the shares. The companies remained in existence as shareholders of remaining stock. The thirty-three directors of the SNCF were to include twelve representatives of the state, twelve of the companies, four of the staff, three *ex officio* and two 'eminent' men nominated by the government. The employees of the railway thus did not become civil servants, but it was planned that the companies would gradually be bought out and that the state would acquire full control in 1982.[1]

In 1934 a law on road transport ensured that lorries should not compete too freely against the railways: the carriers were subjected to state control and required to reach an agreement with the railways to share the available traffic while the railways

---

[1] G. Pirou and M. Byé, *Les Cadres de la vie économique*, vol. 3: *les transports* (1942), 41–62; P. Espaillac, *La Réorganisation du régime des chemins de fer français* (Toulouse thesis, 1939); J. Laffitte, *La SNCF* (Paris thesis, 1939).

were to close their smaller, unprofitable lines.[1] In under-populated regions, however, bus companies had since 1908 received subsidies, which in 1930 ran at 6,500,000 francs a year. Competition from cars was influenced by the taxes on them and, even more, on petrol (nearly 60 per cent of the price of which consisted of taxes), but the car industry, thanks to its prosperity, was the most notable example of old-fashioned private enterprise among the new industries.

Air transport had started in the same way: there were eleven companies in 1920 and the service between Paris and London was provided by three different rivals. But the principle of state subsidy quickly entered the air industry and in the 1920s three-quarters of the income of the five companies that survived this competition came to be provided by the state. As a result, they were amalgamated in 1933 as Air-France, in which the state was allocated a 25 per cent share. The state did not prohibit other private companies from flying, but it undertook to subsidise only Air-France. In 1940 there were still five independent air companies, but all of them had a special relationship with the state. Air Bleu was saved by a contract to carry the country's internal mail. Air Afrique was founded in 1933 as an experiment in full state ownership. Air-France-Transatlantique (1937) was established jointly by Air-France and the Compagnie générale transatlantique. Air-Malgache (1937) was set up by the government of Madagascar. Aéro-Maritime was the only really independent and unsubsidised firm, owned by shipping interests, but it was subject to government supervision of its route to West Africa. Commercial aviation illustrates well the many varieties of 'mixed economy' evolved in these years. The Vichy regime tried to codify these with a view to strengthening the state's control.[2] This was the prelude to full-scale nationalisation which took place in 1945.

It is interesting that the economist who made himself the theorist of these changes, Brocard of Nancy, saw this increase in state activity as only a function of the state's duty to encourage the development of industry, and as only carrying out one step in the transition from a local to an international economy.[3]

[1] Eugène Harter, *Les Chemins de fer français devant la concurrence de l'automobile* (Aix thesis, 1936). [2] Statut de l'aviation marchande, 19 September 1941. [3] L. Brocard, *Les Conditions générales de l'activité économique* (1934).

There is no evidence, however, that there was any coherent plan behind the successive *ad hoc* arrangements made with individual firms and industries. Many state take-overs were unwilling ones, designed to avert a crisis, as those of the Alsace-Lorraine and B.N.C. banks in 1930. Only rarely did the state seek complete ownership: the Alsace Potash Mines, ceded by the Germans, were an exception, and an exception also in the sense that they made large profits. The state was generally saddled with the ailing or experimental part of the economy. The nationalisation of the armaments industry in 1936 was, it is true, aimed at ending the profiteering of the 'death merchants'. The vast increase in municipal services was also largely inspired by socialist doctrines, for the socialists had a far greater hold on the country at a local level. Hitherto the Conseil d'État had opposed the efforts of town councils to take on tasks which private enterprise had carried out, but these legal barriers were broken down between the wars, and municipal transport, swimming baths, wash-houses, and even cinemas and groceries, were set up. Industry and commerce were still largely in private hands in 1939, but the state intervened far more than ever before and public control was extending to actual management in many spheres. The nationalisations of 1944–6 were thus not revolutionary.[1]

Private property no longer enjoyed the sacred status it had had in the nineteenth century. The Declaration of the Rights of Man proclaimed it to be inviolable. The state, since then, considered it to be one of its main functions to protect private property, and individuals seemed to make the accumulation of private property one of the main purposes of their lives. That public interest could override the inviolability of property was acknowledged in the law of 1841 which allowed expropriation for urban development, but the assumption still was that the individual had rights of paramount importance and the juries set up to assess compensation were composed of ordinary local people who were very generous in the sums they awarded. The courts limited expropriation to what was strictly necessary: a house had either to be positively and irremediably insalubrious[2] or actually in the path of a new street

---

[1] B. Chenot, *Les Entreprises nationalisées* (1956).
[2] Law of 13 April 1850.

for it to be possible to expropriate and demolish it. In 1918, however, a new law allowed whole zones to be expropriated, the amount of compensation was considerably limited, and the state began levying a capital appreciation tax on surrounding properties which benefited from works constructed by it.[1] Before the war, the landlord of a house could rent and evict as he pleased. Now tenants were exonerated from carrying out their contracts with him, they were given security of tenure and their rents were fixed by law, at levels far lower than had hitherto prevailed. Even tenants of furnished accommodation were given protection, provided they were permanent residents and declared that they could find nowhere else to go. Only 'luxury houses' were exempted.[2]

Increasingly large portions of people's private wealth were demanded in taxation. The land tax, which had been 3·2 per cent in 1890, rose to 12 per cent in 1920 and 16 per cent by 1939. The tax on industrial profits, which had been inaugurated in 1917 at 4·5 per cent, rose to 9·6 per cent in 1924 and 15 per cent in 1927. The tax on dividends, begun in 1872 at 3 per cent, reached 10 per cent in 1920, 18 per cent in 1926 and finally could in some cases be as high as 36 per cent. When one sold property in the nineteenth century one had to pay the state a tax of 5·5 per cent; in 1905 this was raised to 7 per cent, in 1920 to 10 per cent, and by 1939 it was 14·6 per cent. The inheritance of property was no longer principally a family matter, for the state made itself part-heir of every estate, and by the Second World War its share could be as high as 25 per cent when the property devolved to a child, but when it went to very distant relatives the state could receive as much as 80 per cent.[3] In 1913 the share of the national income collected in taxation was 8 per cent, but in the inter-war period it was between 12 and 15 per cent.[4] There were of course loud protests against this. The increase in taxation did not represent a greater sense of community. On the contrary, the effect of

[1] Jean Nory, *Le Droit de propriété et l'intérêt général* (Lille thesis, 1923); Auguste Étienne, *La Notion d'expropriation: son évolution* (Montpellier thesis, Nîmes, 1926); Louis Boudet, *De l'expropriation conditionnelle* (Toulouse thesis, 1926).
[2] Paul Muselli, *Du Conflit entre propriétaires et locataires et de sa réglementation dans la législation et la jurisprudence actuelle* (Aix thesis, 1928).
[3] Camille Roser, *La Fiscalité française devant l'opinion publique* (1940), 67–72.
[4] A. Sauvy, op. cit., vol. 4 (1975), 100.

the increase was to stimulate ingenuity among taxpayers in avoiding their obligations. The high rates were tolerated because they remained largely theoretical. In 1937 only 1,652,537 people in fact paid income tax, even though the country had 11,000,000 electors. Most of these taxpayers had been declared by their employers and so could not avoid paying; the self-employed got away more lightly: only one-half of the liberal professions paid income tax. The extreme complexity of the tax laws and the very unequal way in which they distributed the burden produced an almost universäl feeling that the taxes were unfair and avoidance of them justifiable.[1] However, direct taxation was still much lower in France than in the rest of Europe.[2]

The important innovation of this period was the taxation of companies. This took two forms. In 1917 the turnover tax was invented, and transformed in 1936 into the production tax (which differed in that it was levied only once on each product). This is the ancestor of the value-added tax which was to become so popular with governments in the next generation. The second way in which money was levied from businesses was through the taxation of profits and dividends. The tax on dividends in 1913 had represented only 3 per cent of all the taxes levied by the state but by 1938 provided it with one-eighth of its income. By 1930 the capitalist had to pay 15 per cent tax on his dividends, and then 18 per cent income tax, plus duties when he bought or sold his shares, and altogether he could expect to keep no more than about 60 per cent of his income. Dividends moreover failed to keep up with the cost of living. In the chemical industry between 1913 and 1930, the changing distribution of income may be seen from this table:

| | |
|---|---|
| Wages rose from | 46·98 to 56·79% |
| Taxes rose from | 6·23 to 18·27% |
| Dividends fell from | 47·77 to 24·92% |

This, of course, did not mean that capitalists necessarily became poorer, for all sorts of stratagems were invented to conceal profits. It was in this period that businesses began to spend

[1] François Pietri, *Justice et injustice fiscale* (1933).
[2] It accounted for about one-sixth of all taxation in 1913, and about one-fifth in 1938.

lavishly on luxurious offices, with desks covered in morocco leather, standing on fine oriental carpets. Profits were used to set up subsidiary companies, yielding rich fees to the directors. In the 1920s about a thousand firms issued multiple-vote shares which turned them into family fiefs.[1] But all this meant that saving, which had been the foundation of nineteenth-century economics, was no longer possible in the old, simple way.

By far the heavist tax of all, and the greatest obstacle to saving, was, however, inflation. Between 1913 and 1948, wholesale prices rose 105 times, and the price of gold 174 times. As against the dollar, the franc was worth in 1939 about one-seventh of what it had been in 1913.[2] Nothing like this had been known since the Revolution of 1789, whose soon-worthless paper money (*assignats*) had left a profound mistrust of all alternatives to gold. The effect of inflation now was rather more complex, because it was difficult to understand what was happening, and the same people could both benefit and lose by it. The first cause of inflation was government borrowing to pay for the First World War, but the press generally attributed inflation to foreign speculators. Successive governments showed themselves equally bewildered, and took totally opposed measures to cure the trouble, even though they were the main beneficiaries. Devaluation, deflation, reflation, confidence, stabilisation, the destruction of the *Mur d'Argent* (the mysterious financiers who seemed to be capable of deciding whether the state should be bankrupted or not) were formulae that economists applied like desperate doctors dabbling in miracle cures. Thought on the matter was dominated by a desire to return to the good old days, when exchange rates were stable, and prices remained fixed for years on end—or so it (falsely) seemed in retrospect. In 1925 a subscription was opened to save the country by voluntary contributions, as though the state was an old man come on bad times, and in need of charity. Virtually no one saw that the state had never been so rich.

[1] Jacques Launey, *L'Évolution comparative des charges de l'industrie française* (Paris thesis, 1931), 249, 337; Désiré Dhamelincourt, *L'Accroissement des charges fiscales en France depuis la guerre 1914–18* (Lille thesis, 1939), 271.

[2] 1913 = 5·18 francs to the dollar; 1921 13·49; 1922 12·33; 1923 16·58; 1924 19·32; 1925 21·23; 1926 31·44; 1927–32 25·50; 1933 20·57; 1934 15·22; 1935 15·15; 1936 16·70; 1937 25·14; 1938 34·95; 1939 39·83; 1940–3 43·80; 1944 44·80; 1946–7 119·10; 1948 308·47. See André Bisson, *L'Inflation française 1914–1952* (1953).

In 1914 it was in debt to the tune of one year of national income. It had paid for the war by borrowing and so in 1921 its debt was two and a half times the national income. But inflation reduced this back to the 1914 level by 1929. It did not have to resort to any drastic socialist measures like capital levies but this in effect was what inflation achieved. Between 1914 and 1929 the state made a profit of about 1,000 million francs, which meant the transfer to it of three years and four months of national income at 1929 levels. The share of private incomes in the national income fell by about one-half. The state held its expenditure steady and indeed slightly reduced it between 1930 and 1935, but it was then able to increase it by almost 60 per cent in the years 1935–8.

Despite inflation, the national income rose between the wars by 0·9 per cent per annum on average, that is 20 per cent in all. Inflation was a disaster only to some people. The real earnings of labourers were 46 per cent higher in 1939 than in 1914. People with mortgages, once obsequious debtors, were turned into property owners. Though the state did best out of inflation, its gains were obscured by the fact that senior civil servants, by contrast, had their real earnings cut by 34 per cent. The worst losers of all were those who had lent the state money, the *rentiers*. They did even worse with their foreign investments, which were in some cases (notably Russian ones) complete losses. Shareholders in French companies lost about 43 per cent in the 1930s alone. Because prices were rising, investment had to become more speculative, with a view to capital appreciation rather than dividend income, and the speculation inevitably produced great losses as well as great—if impermanent—gains. The majority of the country was probably more prosperous, but this redistribution of wealth, on principles which were more mysterious, arbitrary and uncontrollable than ordinary taxation, made adaptation difficult.[1] The state had once been the protector of the saver, and though the *rente* did fluctuate 20 per cent up or down in the course of the nineteenth century, it was possible to rely on the state for a regular income from one's savings.[2] The state did not wish to

[1] A. Sauvy, op. cit. (1965–75), 1. 291; 2. 406–8, 418; 4. 173.
[2] P. Soulaine and L. Deneri, *L'État et l'épargne 1789–1919* (1919) gives the annual price of state bonds.

abandon the saver now, for it generally agreed with him that devaluation was equivalent to national bankruptcy, shameful as well as impolitic, but in practice it sacrificed him, rather than itself. It was in this period, therefore, that the state ceased to regard the preservation of acquired wealth as one of its major functions.[1] This did not mean, as many people believed, the end of the influence of the middle classes, though it did involve a change in their way of life. The radical *Dépêche de Toulouse* declared in 1926 that the cause of the disarray was 'love of lucre', but also 'prodigality'. People were spending more easily, bargaining less, thinking less about economising. The radical leader Herriot sent a circular to teachers urging them to drink less strong coffee and to put less sugar in it, but he was preaching against an inexorable tendency.[2] Inflation meant people had to earn more and spend it while their money was still worth something. This was one of the roots of the expansionist economy that was ultimately adopted. The middle classes made a new kind of deal with the state to achieve this.

Instead of dedicating itself to the preservation of private property, the state began to provide pensions, as an alternative form of security for old age. The law of 1910[3] had made a start, but in so hesitant a way, demanding such small contributions and guaranteeing such totally inadequate pensions, that though 3,430,000 people had entered the scheme by 1913, only 1,728,000 were left in 1922 and these quickly diminished. Old-age insurance schemes run by employers had also generally been regarded with disfavour by the workers, because they were not infrequently used as a way of blackmailing them into obedience, whereas the whole point of saving was that it made one independent of one's boss. The question was debated in parliament from 1924 to 1930, by which time objections to compulsory contributions had virtually disappeared. The law passed in 1930 guaranteed old people 40 per cent of their wages and in 1941 a uniform fixed pension of 3,600 francs was introduced. The retiring age was set at sixty, the lowest in Europe, but this was more a way of combating unemployment

---

[1] André Bouton, *La Fin des rentiers* (1932).
[2] M. Perrot, *La Monnaie et l'opinion publique en France et en Angleterre de 1924 à 1936* (1955), 169, 172.
[3] See vol. 1, 709.

than an institutionalisation of the middle-class ideal of early retirement. Since the number of people over sixty in France had increased between 1881 and 1941 by 25 per cent, the problem of the old had taken on new importance. The pension scheme—a compromise between the English and German systems—was run partly by the state and partly by professional bodies, but because contributions were fixed at a low rate, serious problems of financing would soon arise; and moreover only about half of the working population was affected: peasants and artisans, as usual, resisted these new-fangled ideas.[1] In 1938, likewise, accident insurance, which a law had first sought to encourage in 1898,[2] was made compulsory for all employees, and rates of compensation were substantially raised. It was recognised that accidents at work produced casualties almost as heavy as those sustained in war: between 1920 and 1938 50,000 people were killed and 150,000 permanently incapacitated in this way. The state left it to private insurance companies to provide the cover, before taking on the burden itself by nationalising these in 1945. All these forms of insurance had been pioneered by capitalist employers, as a way, some workers argued, of shielding them from the influence of the revolutionaries; the employers' schemes had been resented, and the state emerged as the impartial guarantor: but this only had the effect of making the masses, in various degrees, civil servants. This was seen most noticeably in the expansion of family allowances. By 1932 virtually all large and middle scale companies were paying these, and they were then made compulsory, but always at the expense of the employers. In 1938 however the state began participating financially in these allowances. The Vichy government so increased the rates that a worker with a large family could get more in family allowances than he earned in wages.[3] The theory developed that a man was entitled to a minimum living wage, a professional wage which recognised his skill and thirdly a wage to maintain his family. What he actually did at work was only part of the

---

[1] P. Waline, *Législation sociale appliquée* (1943), 135–89; Henri Hatzfeld, *Du paupérisme à la sécurité sociale 1850–1940* (1971), on the ideological debates.

[2] See vol. 1, 667. The law of 1898 was extended to cover commerce in 1906, forestry in 1914, agriculture in 1922 and domestic servants in 1923.

[3] The 1941 rate meant that a man with five children received 120 per cent of his salary in family allowances.

reason why he was paid, and when he was out of work, his allowances continued to be paid.

The theorists wondered whether this would mean that people would work less hard. The Vichy regime had just rather optimistically made the cult of work one of its principles. It would take another generation before the implications of this were realised.[1] The problem of why a man should work at all, particularly when he was offered only dull and repetitive work, if he could find charity or the state to support him, could not be raised in this period. The workers, since 1848, had demanded the right to work: they had not been interested in unemployment insurance, except on the basis of mutual aid amongst themselves. Full unemployment insurance was therefore instituted only in 1958; but in the inter-war years the state took unemployment relief out of the hands of private charity. The municipal *bureaux de bienfaisances* were expanded (by decrees of 1926 and 1931), so that the state subsidised them to the extent of between 60 and 90 per cent on what they paid out to the unemployed. In addition the state gave subsidies to a host of union and mutual societies which also helped those out of work. Its intervention was thus cloaked in the garb of favouritism and influence, that characteristic of the Third Republic which perpetuated the arbitrariness of the monarchy.[2] Assistance in illness likewise involved a compromise between free medical treatment and the traditional capitalist system. There was free medicine in the railways and mines, but the doctors disliked this, wishing to keep their status as a liberal profession, and their ability to fix their fees in each case. The law of 1930 instituted a system whereby patients could choose their own doctors, and then get reimbursed by the state. The reimbursement returned roughly half of the fees paid and only 20 per cent of pharmaceutical and hospital expenses. The law covered only ten million people, excluding the self-employed. All this had to be paid for ultimately by taxation, and it was largely through increased charges on employers that the costs were met.[3]

[1] 'Jeunesse en rupture', *Autrement* (Jan. 1975), especially 58–67.

[2] Claude Lasry, *Lutte contre le chômage et finances publiques 1929–1937* (1938).

[3] Henry C. Galant, *Histoire politique de la sécurité sociale française 1945–52* (1955); P. Waline, op. cit. 115–38; C. N. Pipkin, *Social Politics and Modern Democracies* (1931), vol. 2.

It may seem contradictory that this was achieved despite all the obstacles the Third Republic supposedly raised against reform. There are two complementary explanations. On the one hand, this social legislation was pushed through by the determined efforts of a few men, who showed the power that the civil service could exert. It was Millerand who originally got the discussions going, after being impressed by a German insurance scheme he saw functioning in Alsace, and he got the Alsatian deputy Jourdain to produce a bill in co-operation with Georges Cahen (who was in charge of pensions at the ministry of labour) and with Antonelli, a professor of economics who was also a deputy. Together these men proposed a very wide-ranging plan of insurance, embracing all aspects of life, and foreshadowing the grandiose plans of the post-1945 era, which, like it, were the result of the combined efforts of professors, civil servants and technicians. The great problem was to get agreement from vested interests. This was achieved through the efforts of Raoul Péret, who was minister of justice under Tardieu but also president of the Mutualists Organisation, and Gaston Roussel, who was in charge of the Mutuality Department in the ministry of labour. The Mutualists were determined not to lose their dominant position in insurance. Roussel got them to sign an agreement, at the ministry of labour, with the Confédération Générale du Travail for a division of spheres of influence. The employers, through their spokesman Robert Pinot, declared that the proposals of the bill 'tend to nothing less than a modification of the traditional physiognomy of French society in its most characteristic traits' and that 'a totally different mentality would arise' if it was passed. The ministry got them to agree by withdrawing proposals for the equal representation of employers and workers in the management of the insurance scheme and by a reduction of the employers' contributions. The agreement of the peasants and doctors was moreover obtained by various compromises. The law of 1930 was a triumph of negotiation under the guidance of the civil servants.[1]

The second reason why the insurance scheme was introduced was that the 1920s enjoyed exceptional economic prosperity,

[1] René Hubert, 'Histoire philosophique de l'institution des assurances sociales en France', L'Année politique française et étrangère, vol. 5 (1930), 273–315.

comparable to that of the 1850s, and producing a new faith in prosperity through expansion. The basis of this revival was, first, the reconstruction in the territories damaged by the war and secondly the development of a number of new industries. The revival was very uneven, affecting only some sections of the economy.

*Growth of Industrial Production 1913–29* (%)

| | |
|---|---|
| Textiles | −8 |
| Paper | +6 |
| Leather | +19 |
| Mines | +23 |
| Building | +23 |
| Metallurgy | +29 |
| Mechanical Industries | +57 |
| Rubber | +761 |

Coal production rose by 35 per cent (1913–30), though productivity per man-hour fell by 7·7 per cent. In the iron mines, however, productivity per man-hour rose by 41 per cent. Steel production trebled, making France the largest producer in Europe after Germany, and the equal of England: Schneider of Le Creusot modernised its equipment, diversified into shipbuilding and armaments, expanded into Czechoslovakia (Skoda), Hungary (petrol), Romania (aluminium), Poland and elsewhere. The French car industry became the largest in the world after that of the U.S.A. The electrical industry stimulated the growth of a whole variety of new enterprise, significantly organised in large firms and cartels with international links, under the dominance of the American G.E.C.[1] Though the textile industry as a whole failed to adapt itself to new conditions, the rayon industry (which owed its inception to a Frenchman, the comte de Chardonnet, a graduate of the Polytechnic and the École des Ponts et Chaussées who founded the first rayon factory in 1890) grew very fast in the 1920s, when over twenty firms were established to produce 'artificial silk'. In this decade, world production decupled, but France competed successfully, reducing its prices by 70 per cent,

[1] Cf. Robert Lecat, *L'Industrie de la construction électrique en France* (Aix thesis, 1933).

emphasising cheapness rather than quality and seeking large-volume production; it was only after 1932 that it ceased expanding and was overtaken by its rivals.[1] The chemical industry, though not as insignificant before 1914 nor as dependent on Germany as is usually believed (it was in dyes that the French were weak, and to a certain extent in pharmaceuticals, but not in electrochemistry or in the soda industry), not only expanded in scope, but increased its productivity per man-hour by about 60 per cent. Saint-Gobain, once a glass works, became a giant international concern, with subsidiaries in Germany and Italy, producing a wide variety of chemicals. France became Europe's second-largest producer of aluminium. Its banks, which before the war had preferred to finance foreign governments, now gave considerably more backing to domestic industry. The Crédit National founded in 1919 (on the model of Napoleon III's Crédit Foncier) to finance the repair of war damage, added an element of state sponsored and directed industrial investment.[2] The result was that exports of industrial products doubled in volume and the national income increased twice as fast in the 1920s as in the decade before the war.[3]

The most outstanding representative of the new industrial management that was responsible for this was perhaps Ernest Mercier (1878–1955). He had the typical antecedents which made him a favourite of the regime: his grandfather had been a Protestant republican who had emigrated during the Second Empire, to found a pharmacy in Algeria; his father was mayor and a leader of the radical party in Constantine; he himself married the daughter of an anticlerical senator and, secondly, the niece of Captain Dreyfus. He was educated at the Polytechnic, but left the state's service to enter private industry. In course of time he became managing director of France's leading electrical supply company, and later president of the

[1] Léon Robert, *L'Industrie de la rayonne en France* (Paris thesis, 1943), good graph, p. 138. Cf. Pierre Clerget, *Les Industries de la soie en France* (1925).

[2] H. Laufenberger, *Enquête sur les changements de structure de crédit et de la banque*: vol. 1, *Les Banques françaises* (1940), 225; Jacques Alexandre, *Les Grands Établissements financiers et le trésor public de 1919 à 1941* (Montpellier thesis, published Toulouse, 1942).

[3] A. Sauvy, op. cit. 1. 259–74; Claude Fohlen, *La France de l'entre-deux-guerres* (1966), 71–83.

Compagnie française des pétroles. It was indicative of new trends that this child of the republic should have preferred industry to politics or literature. In 1925 he visited the U.S.A., as a guest of the General Electric Company, and was deeply impressed both by American prosperity and by the prestige that businessmen enjoyed there. He made himself the advocate of national reorganisation, in a style which was called neo-Saint-Simonian. He founded a movement Le Redressement français (1927), which won about 20,000 influential subscribers and which produced a host of pamphlets urging the modernisation of industry by the concentration of firms, standardisation in manufacturing, the stimulation of both higher productivity and higher consumption. French individualism, Mercier declared, was very pleasant, but obsolete. He hailed the election of Hoover to the presidency as a sign of the times: 'the most powerful people on earth, the American people, have elected an engineer as their leader'. He argued that government could no longer be left to politicians who spent their time arguing over ideology: more power must be given to the president and he should rely more on experts and technicians for advice. The efficiency of Henry Ford was the best way to triumph over Marx. The workers should be made happy not by giving them equal wealth, but by the possibility of self-realisation: new forms of industrial relations, rule by an élite of managers, rather than more democracy, was the answer. Mercier denounced fascism as giving too much power to the state. Corporatism he at first thought impractical because the workers were too attached to the class struggle, though he later saw virtues in its aim; but his ideal was an economy based on 'collaboration between producers and the state' and relying on planning by consent. He was an ardent European in the 1920s, and became president of the French Pan-Europe Committee, though he maintained that France would always have a special role to play as a nation, exercising its 'moral mission'. Mercier, however, was too obviously a rich man (his annual income in the 1930s was on average 2,500,000 francs) for him not to be regarded as primarily a defender of the interests of big business. Léon Blum denounced his doctrines as 'industrial Bonapartism'. Mercier's sponsorship of a war-veterans' journal *Nos plaisirs* and a workers' sports magazine *Le Muscle*, and his use of money in elections, even though he claimed to be above party, made the charges against him plausible. In fact big business was far from being united behind him, as the perfumer Coty's attacks on him publicly revealed. The variations in emphasis among industrialists, in their attitudes to the state and to democracy, were very considerable. Mercier's own views were probably more liberal than those of many of his supporters. His committee included Marshal Foch, Clémentel and Giscard d'Estaing but also Alibert (minister of justice in 1940), Hubert Lagardelle (minister of labour in 1942) and Lucien Romier (adviser to Pétain). His importance, however, lies not in the precise detail of his doctrine, but in the publicity he gave to the idea of technocracy. His daughter married Wilfred Baumgartner, who became governor of the Bank of France and minister of finance in the Fifth Republic. That was when his hopes, in modified form, became realities, when technocracy found a *modus vivendi* with parliamentary government.[1]

Three different attempts were made, by political methods, to bring about a new relationship between the state and society: Tardieu's 'politics of prosperity', Blum's Popular Front and Pétain's Vichy state. They were quite different in their ideological inspiration and in their character; all three of them failed; but they can be seen in retrospect to have the common element that they all sought to give a new role to the state and to modify, though not altogether or immediately to abolish, capitalism. Their ideas, and their failure, contributed powerfully to the formation of Gaullist France, which was in some ways a compromise between them.

André Tardieu (prime minister 1930–2) was intellectually one of the most brilliant figures of the Third Republic. He won the highest success in every field he entered. He came top in the *concours général*, top in the entrance examination to the École Normale (which he took because it was 'reputedly the hardest'), top in the entrance examination to the foreign service and then in that to the ministry of the interior. He became political secretary to the prime minister at the age of twenty-three and two years later one of the country's highest-paid journalists,

[1] Richard F. Kuisel, *Ernest Mercier, French Technocrat* (Univ. of California Press, 1967).

with regular columns (in the *Figaro* and then *Le Temps*) which had an international reputation and influence. He published a book on contemporary affairs almost every year. He combined with all this professorships at the École des Sciences Politiques and at the École de Guerre, and a guest lectureship at Harvard (for which latter job he learnt English). During the war, he was the main civilian adviser of the commander-in-chief Joffre and after it, he was Clemenceau's right-hand man in the making of the peace treaty; he showed his administrative ability also as High Commissioner in the United States. The legends about his amazing industriousness, fluency and quickness of mind are innumerable: he was 'the most perfect intelligence I have ever known' said General Gamelin. Everything he wrote, he wrote straight off without corrections: it was even reported that when he was in Washington, in an oppressively hot summer, 'though he dozed off from time to time, his hand went on writing'. Clemenceau said to him: 'You are a Napoleon'. Tardieu had thought at first that he could exercise power best behind the scenes, arguing that the real force in democracy was not the government but public opinion, and he would specialise in organising and expressing it. He never claimed or even wished to be original. His gifts were for efficiency, hard work, action, and that is why he had such an admiration for the Americans, in whom he saw these qualities cultivated and valued. However, frustration at the obstacles imposed by parliamentary routine led him, inevitably, to seek ministerial office. After holding a succession of portfolios in the 1920s, he came prime minister, the first one of the interwar years who did not represent continuity with the pre-1914 era. He announced his policy as being the inauguration of a new era and as facing up resolutely to the future.

His policy had two sides to it. First, it sought to get the reforms that had been trailing for years in endless discussion—sent back and forth between the two houses and their committees—passed rapidly. There was no innovation involved here, only more efficiency. He told the radicals, to whom he had vainly offered a large share of the posts in his cabinet, not to shoot him 'when I come before you bearing your children in my arms'. By fifteen laws and fifty decrees, he did indeed dispatch a lot of business rapidly, most notably the social insurance scheme and free education in the bottom form of the *lycées*. Though classified politically as moderate right wing, he carried out, like a punctilious civil servant, the policy of the moderate left which had the majority in the country. Secondly, he proposed a 'plan of national re-equipment' based on unprecedented state investment: the modernisation of agriculture by rural electrification, reafforestation, an institute of agronomic research, credit facilities and a radio network for the countryside (1,750 million francs); the improvement of health to combat depopulation and the stimulation of research and technical education (1,450 millions); the improvement of roads, ports, and transport (1,797 millions); and the development of the colonies (3,600 millions). This was his 'policy of prosperity', which aimed both to make the country richer and to yield such increased revenue for the treasury that no further taxation would be needed to pay for it. On the contrary, he capped his programme with tax reductions of 3,340 million francs. There was virtually no section of the community whose interests he did not promise to advance: he held out the prospect of increased production, profits and wages. This was the expression of the euphoria that the prosperity of the 1920s had created. It was ironical that Tardieu came to power just as the depression set in; but Tardieu's was also a policy to combat the depression, for he declared that 'the old and noble doctrine of *laissez-faire* . . . confronted with the present concentration of capital, size of firms and internationalisation of business, is no longer adequate. Whether we like it or not, the state must henceforth intervene where formerly it did not, it must take charge of things it used to ignore.' He wanted political reform to follow, to concentrate more power in the executive: 'the state must resume consciousness of its duties and of its rights'. The popular will must be given fuller expression by the use of referenda and by the institution of women's suffrage. Civilisation was in crisis and 'to defend our civilisation, France must be in good working order'. For a time Tardieu was able to galvanise parliament into action: he got it to agree to meet three times a day, even including Sundays, but he had to ask for votes of confidence sixty times to force compliance. He failed to win genuine backing for his policy in parliament. He spent too much time abroad, in discussion with the leaders of other nations. He was unable to create the institutions needed to give his policy a chance of success, or to overcome the republic's built-in suspicion of power.[1]

However, though Tardieu was a failure in parliamentary terms, important new developments began to take place off the political stage, and it is behind the scenes that new forces were being created for change. Lucien Romier, the historian whose *Explanation of Our Times* (1925) provided a breviary for the frustrated critics of French conservatism, pointed out that power would increasingly rest not with politicians, but with the civil servants and the administrators. Now some of these began to become more conscious of their role and to exert a new influence in economic affairs. While the parliamentary debates concentrated on the problem of military security and reparations, the inspectors of finance came to realise that their apparently routine functions could provide the basis for new methods in the formulation and execution of ministerial policy. Inspectors of finance, whose original function had been to audit state accounts, had gradually seen the scope of their activities widened to include private firms in receipt of state subsidies; as early as 1855 the railway companies had been subject to their investigations. They were not numerous (there were about seventy or eighty of them at any one time) but promotion was rapid since they were recognised as an élite corps, and inspectors in their thirties could hold very influential positions. About a quarter of them resigned to go into private industry (in the 1890s a half of them), and they came to constitute a kind of freemasonry which extended equally over the civil service and the largest firms in the country. 'It is to them', wrote one of them, 'that is due that sort of loyalty, that discipline and cohesion of a large part of private finance towards the directives and policy of ministers.'[2] Their importance was increased when for the first time in 1926 parliament

[1] Rudolf Binion, *Defeated Leaders* (New York, 1960), 197–337; Michel Missoffe, *La Vie volontaire d'André Tardieu* (1929); Louis Aubert *et al.*, *André Tardieu* (1957); Louis Guitard, 'Portrait sentimental d'André Tardieu', *Les Œuvres libres*, no. 184 (Sept. 1961), 79–96; Marcel Prélot, 'La France en 1930 et 1931', *L'Année politique française et étrangère* (1932), 68–123; André Tardieu, *L'Épreuve du pouvoir* (1931), *La Réforme de l'état* (1934), and *La Révolution à refaire* (2 vols., 1936–7).
[2] François Pietri, *Le Financier* (1931), 85.

began the practice of delegating 'full powers' to the executive, and when in 1932 an under-secretary of state was appointed with the task of co-ordinating economic policy and seeking ways of expanding the economy. The civil service began organising itself for economic planning.[1]

The ideas which inspired it, however, came from outside, and mainly from the graduates of the Polytechnic. In 1930 Jean Coutrot founded the Polytechnic's Centre for Economic Studies with about seven or eight others, and by 1937 it had 1,200 members, 'comprising almost all those in France with economic expertise'. The meetings were originally held at the home of Yves Bouthillier (an inspector of finance who became a minister under both Paul Reynaud and Pétain) but later in the Polytechnic itself and sometimes in the great amphitheatre of the Sorbonne. Members of this centre were to be found as advisers to almost every government from the 1930s to the 1950s. Coutrot himself was brought into the Popular Front government as head of a committee to reorganise labour relations, but he turned up again as an adviser in the Vichy government; he was present in the room when Laval offered Belin (the trade union leader, who also attended these Polytechnic meetings) the ministry of industrial production. Charles Spinasse (originally a professor at the École des Arts et Métiers) became Blum's minister for the national economy, and in daily conferences brought together several others from the same group; Branger, who was still a young student at the Polytechnic, was brought in as adviser on transport policy and Alfred Sauvy, a young graduate of the school, as head of a new information section. It is true that most of the ideas of these men in Blum's government were challenged by the young lawyers whom Blum's radical allies brought into the ministry of commerce: the achievements were very limited. In 1942 Bichelonne, who had been the top graduate of his year at the Polytechnic, succeeded Belin as minister of industrial production, with Gérard Bardet (one of the earlier organisers of the Polytechnic Centre) and Henri Culman (an inspector of finance, who had been a *chef adjoint de cabinet de ministre* in the Popular Front, and whose writings made him one of the theorists of the Vichy regime's economic policy) as particularly influential

[1] Jean Meynaud, *La Technocratie. Mythe ou réalité* (1964).

civil servants behind the scenes. The importance of this Poly-
technic group was due not to its advocacy of a particular
doctrine but to the new approach to government that it caused
to be adopted. It contained many different shades of opinion:
Jacques Rueff, who was an upholder of classical liberal economics and who served as Laval's adviser in 1934, Roland
Boris, the president of the group, later adviser to de Gaulle and
Mendès-France and brother of Blum's minister, and Pierre
Massé, who became a commissioner for planning in the Fifth
Republic. Coutrot introduced the method of research by teams,
each specialising in one aspect of the economy; and this was
gradually adopted as a method for the formulation of government policy. These men differed about details but they were
agreed that economic planning had to play a key role in the
future. Coutrot's friends, the Guillaume brothers, produced
one of the earliest theoretical treatises on economic forecasting
and the use of mathematical techniques.[1]

Jean Coutrot was one of those men who exerted a great
influence on his contemporaries without ever attracting public
attention; even if he had not committed suicide in 1942, he
would probably have remained a source of inspiration rather
than become a public figure. Coutrot believed that France
needed a thorough reassessment of its whole way of life: 'we
need to rethink our epoch, to understand it and to create it'.
The reassessment must extend to the questioning of all accepted
notions, which had not been attempted since the Saint-
Simonians. There was much in his movement which recalled
these utopian thinkers and industrialists, many of whom had
also been graduates of the Polytechnic. Had Coutrot lived to
work out his ideas, he might perhaps have won a place in the
history of thought as important as theirs, for the range of his
interests was unusually wide and he attempted to stimulate a
new synthesis that incorporated the latest findings of the new
sciences. He followed up the creation of his group by establishing a 'centre for the study of human problems'. This
brought together a dazzling collection of thinkers: the political
scientist André Siegfried, the jurist Marcel Prélot, the psychiatrists Henri Wallon and Georges Matisse, the sociologists
Celestin Bouglé, Hyacinthe Dubreuilh and Georges Friedman,

[1] Philippe Bauchard, *Les Technocrates et le pouvoir* (1966).

the trade unionist Robert Lacoste, the industrialist Detoeuf; and Aldous Huxley, whose visions of the future excited them, was also present at their meetings. Coutrot was keen that a new body of technocrats, independent of big business and concerned only with the public welfare, should be formed to plan the new society, and that their efforts should be directed to all 'indispensable' spheres of activity. Though the stress of the Polytechniciens was on economics, in this second group it was more on psychology. The problem of hunger was in the process of being solved; the next obstacle was hate and fear. There should be no more talk about liberty and justice, which were too vague, but rather of concrete difficulties in human relations. These should be seen as having two sides, psychological and social. The time had come to plan for a better kind of human; the emotional development of man was lagging far behind his material progress. The frequency of neuroses showed that the 'equilibrium of the individual' needed much more attention: sexual relations needed to be understood better, to discover whether the sexual act should be dissociated from its sentimental and moral concomitants, so that it would be like a 'sporting match'; the effect of professional specialisation on human nature needed to be investigated, for what was economically progressive was not necessarily emotionally beneficial. He asked whether the family still had a value 'in times like ours, of rapid transition'. Psychology and genetics seemed to hold out the hope of control being achieved over men's sensibilities and internal energies. It would then be possible either to diminish men's need to hate, or to divert it against physical rather than human enemies, or to confine it to an internal struggle against certain aspects of one's own nature. He believed that until personal and national egoisms had been resolved, it was no use founding bodies like the League of Nations, because egoisms could not be reconciled. Contacts between classes would have to be increased, and the new methods of communication, including television (he foresaw its power), needed to be used beneficially so as to mitigate these egoisms. Coutrot wanted much more planning than France has adopted. But he did leave room for private property, arguing that the state should intervene only to prevent the abuse of property rights. As the lawyers pointed out, the courts had already refused to recognise absolute property rights. Coutrot was still in favour of individualism, but 'co-ordinated individualism', not 'anarchic' or 'corporalised' individualism. He gave a lot of attention to economics, but he called his book *Economic Humanism*. He was never precise about what this meant. His life is interesting for the trends of thought it reveals rather than for clear ideas.[1]

The planners of the Polytechnic were still very much a minority. The mass of French economists were opposed to the idea of a planned economy, as they affirmed at their congress in 1933. The tradition of economics teaching in the universities was essentially liberal. It is true that Professor Charles Gide (whose *Principles of Political Economy*, translated into fifteen languages, was said to have been the most successful economics book after Adam Smith and Marx) devoted his life to the co-operative movement.[2] But François Simiand argued that economic progress came from alternate phases of prosperity and depression and that it was wrong to try to abolish the depressions, which, like the floods of the Nile, could be put to good use.[3] The economists claimed that the country lacked the statistics which would be needed as a basis for an economy directed by the government—which was true enough—and that state intervention only caused even more chaos, as recent experience showed. They preferred to maintain their role as critics and analysts of the eclectic school. Gaetan Pirou and Roger Picard, leading economists at the Paris faculty of law, were above all enemies of dogmatism. French economists have been reproached for being ignorant of the work of Keynes, but wrongly so. Keynes, as the author of *The Economic Consequences of the Peace*, had long been unpopular in France, whose claims for reparations he had attacked. In 1938, within two years of the publication of Keynes's *General Theory*, Blum's second government was already incorporating its ideas into its programme. But French economists were faced by a deluge of other theories which kept them fully occupied. Their general attitude was one of suspicion of new-fangled ideas.

[1] Jean Coutrot, *Entretiens sur les sciences de l'homme* (1937), *De Quoi vivre* (1935), *L'Humanisme économique* (1936).
[2] G. Pirou, *Les Doctrines économiques en France depuis 1870* (4th edition, 1941), 208.
[3] F. Simiand, *Le Salaire, l'évolution sociale et la monnaie* (3 vols., 1932).

It was only in the 1950s that they began to train their pupils to assume a directing role in the economy.[1]

In 1904 Veblen argued that the important division in society was not between rich and poor but between the scientists and the defenders of the old rites. He saw in the engineers the representatives of the former, concerned only with efficiency, while businessmen were the conservatives and it was they who, absorbed by the desire for profits, were preventing mechanisation from yielding its full benefits. The engineers of France did indeed begin to see themselves in something like this light in the inter-war years. Apart from the few hundred graduates of the Polytechnic and the other prestigious *grandes écoles*, engineers as a whole still had a humble status. Industrialists treated them as little better than foremen, and even the more advanced ones valued only the engineer who specialised in the commercial side of business. Despite their qualifications, most engineers were subjected to the same factory discipline as workers: they had to clock in four times a day, they had to make excuses as to why they were late to the porter, just like the workers, and in their presence; they were forbidden to wash their hands in the last fifteen minutes of the working day (on the ground that they could not do anything useful with clean hands in so short a time); they had to wear numbers on their coats and have their briefcases searched when they went home. Despite the increasing specialisation of science, they were often unable to use their training, because industry hesitated to employ them, and they were forced to take jobs in any technical capacity that was offered, not necessarily their own. They received wages which were not much higher than those paid to foremen. However, their numbers were increasing. In 1934 the title of *ingénieur diplômé* was created and by 1938 ninety-three different schools were able to confer it. The domination of the Paris schools was not threatened, but there were now also institutions, variously called Engineering Schools (Marseille) or Technical Schools (Strasbourg) or Polytechnics (Institut Polytechnique de l'Ouest), all over the provinces, as well as specialised ones

[1] G. Pirou, *La Crise du capitalisme* (2nd edition, 1936); Bernard Lavergne, *Essor et décadence des idées politiques et sociales en France de 1900 à nos jours. Souvenirs personnels* (1965), memoirs of a professor of economics; Louis Baudin, *Le Corporatisme* (1942), on the 1936 economists' congress.

like the Institut électro-Technique de Grenoble or the École Supérieure d'Aéronautique. By 1938 between 2,500 and 3,000 engineers were graduating every year.[1] They began to demand a higher status. The graduates of the new schools began to question the superiority of the Polytechnic and to criticise it for being too theoretical, for not training its graduates in administration or in industrial relations, for teaching too much mathematics and not enough physics or chemistry. The Paris Chamber of Commerce established a School of Management which used the Harvard Business School's case-study techniques and which gave the ambitious engineers who attended it new pretensions.[2] Henri Fayol, a graduate of the École des Mines of Saint-Étienne who rose to be head of several mining and metallurgical companies, published a treatise on industrial management, which encouraged the engineers in their belief in their own importance.[3] The engineer, it was now said, ought to be the pivot of the new industrial system, the mediator between workers and capitalists, the organiser of wage agreements, the person who could distribute responsibilities and run nationalised industries. He should no longer be seen simply as a technician but as the main component of the new managerial class, the *cadres*. The *cadres*, wrote one of these engineers in 1943, were the new aristocracy, but they were at the same time rebels, rebels against conformity and routine; they were distinguished by the desire to command and to assume responsibility. After 1918 they did indeed begin to organise themselves into trade unions which argued that they were qualified to put France into better order, but were being excluded from making the important decisions.[4] In 1937 they combined into a single Federation of Engineers (F.N.S.I.) with 23,000 members and were able to conclude over thirty collective agreements with their employers within a year, which considerably improved their financial position. This however had the effect of keeping them cut off from the employers. They still had an

---

[1] In 1970 the figure was 7,500.

[2] Pierre Jolly, directeur du centre de perfectionnement dans l'administration des affaires, *L'Éducation du chef d'entreprise* (1931), and *Joie au travail et réformes de structure* (1938).

[3] H. Fayol, *Administration industrielle et générale* (1917).

[4] Syndicat des Ingénieurs chimistes (1918); Syndicat des Ingénieurs électriques (1919); Union des Ingénieurs français (1920), etc.

inferiority complex towards the Polytechniciens and the Inspectors of Finance, and they were mistrustful of the bankers whom they accused both of running and of emasculating industry. These animosities were superficial and gradually disappeared with the widening of the idea of the *cadres* after the Second World War. However the engineers were far from all being dynamic and progressive, just as their accusations against their employers were indiscriminate. The inter-war period, which saw their rise, also filled many of them with a deep desire for security; and the nationalised industries would find ready recruits among them.[1]

These developments were, to a certain extent, superficial, in that they did not alter the attitude of the workers towards the state: but that is what did change during the Popular Front. The trade union movement, as has been seen, was traditionally hostile to all governments and to political parties in general, and sought the liberation of the worker by his own efforts. From 1914 onwards the union leaders co-operated in the drafting of social legislation, participated in some government consultative councils and to a certain extent made the unions instruments of government policy.[2] But this did not mean that the masses as a whole ceased to look on the state as an enemy. In 1936 however the possibility that this might change was glimpsed, though briefly. The advent of the country's first socialist government created a sense of euphoria and libera-tion among the workers, a feeling that they could at last express themselves freely, in a way hardly ever before ex-perienced. The importance of the Popular Front, on the psycho-logical plane, can be compared only to the revolution of 1848 and the 'events' of 1968: in the reaction it stimulated among conservatives, it was like the Commune of 1871. The spon-taneous occupation of factories by workers, which showed how fragile the rights of property owners were, was deeply unnerv-ing and shocking to the rich. All the supporters of the Popular Front remembered this among the most moving experiences

[1] Henri Château, *Le Syndicalisme des techniciens en France* (Paris thesis, 1938); Pierre Alamigeon, *Les Cadres dans l'industrie et notamment dans la métallurgie* (Paris thesis, 1943, published Bar-sur-Aube); Yvon Gattaz, *Les Hommes en gris: ingénieurs, cadres, chefs d'entreprise* (1970); cf. W. H. G. Armitage, *The Rise of the Technocrats* (1965).     [2] See vol. 1. 275–6.

of their lives, and rightly so. For the first time workers and employers met, at a national level, more or less as equals, and for the first time the influence of the government was openly on the side of the workers. The euphoria expressed itself in an atmosphere of carnival, which the grim factories had never produced before. But something of a myth has, as a result, grown around this. Just as important as the occupation of the factories was the fact that in no case was this followed up by a demand for their confiscation or nationalisation. Everywhere the workers took care not to spoil the equipment and machines. In the Galeries Lafayette, the occupiers abstained from using the beds or blankets for sale and slept on the floor. Hierarchy and property were thus only partially transformed; but they were transformed. The workers did not challenge legal ownership, but they acted as though the factories belonged to them also, in the sense that their labour gave them rights in them. What they demanded was greater respect as humans, a better wage as workers and not least security in their jobs, for part of the purpose of the occupations was that they prevented the employers from taking on other 'yellow' workers, which a simple strike would have allowed. Blum's government received all the workers' delegations which came to see it, even to the extent, on one occasion, of interrupting a cabinet meeting to do so. The most important result of the Popular Front was that it established the principle that the workers had a right to express their opinion on all matters concerning them: many consultative councils, of which their representatives were members, had been in existence since the turn of the century, but henceforth consultation of the workers became a necessary part of government. This was a radical change in the way the state functioned. But it took a little longer for the employers to recover from the shock they had received and adjust themselves to a new form of relationship with their employees. The workers for their part were so used to passive obedience to their bosses that they sometimes obeyed the shop stewards they now had to elect in just the same way, without argument. Democracy was not yet introduced into industrial relations.

The main institution which altered the situation was the system of collective bargaining. The state henceforth could impose minimum wages on industry. These wages were agreed by the main trade unions and employers, but the state could apply their agreement to all firms, even when they had taken no part in the negotiations. In cases where agreement could not be reached, the unions and employers could appeal to an arbitrator, but it is significant that the panel of arbitrators they agreed on consisted entirely of civil servants (councillors of state, judges, professors etc.), as did also the Superior Arbitration Court, established in 1938 to reconcile inconsistencies among arbitrations.[1] Workers and employers seldom could agree and the result was that in practice the state imposed its decisions on them. The institution of the *office du blé* (1936–9) enabled the state, also, to fix the price of wheat at rates which would reconcile the interests of producers and consumers, at the expense of hoarders and speculators. Never before in peace-time had it attempted to end the system of free market competition, on such a scale. A law tried, in addition, to prohibit price increases in other goods, 'unjustified by rising costs'. The state's long history of interference in conditions of work was now crowned by the laws instituting two weeks' compulsory paid holiday, and reducing the working week to forty hours. Its control over the Bank of France was greatly strengthened, not by nationalisation, but by abolishing the rights of the 200 largest shareholders, and replacing the plutocratic Regents by a council nominated by the state, who would be mainly civil servants. The influence of civil servants was further increased by the invention of the *loi-cadre*, by which parliament legislated in principle only, outlining a framework (*cadre*), but left the details to be worked out by the administration. Within the administration, Blum tried to impose greater cohesion, by taking no ministerial portfolio himself, and by establishing a secretariat charged with co-ordinating policy, so that the conflicts between ministries, and the delays this produced, should be minimised. Formerly, the ministry of finance almost had a *de facto* veto on reform; this new policy was an attempt to make government more coherent; but it had only very limited success. Everything that has been said about the increase in state power must be qualified by the proviso that bureaucracy, with its rivalries and red tape, had great difficulty

[1] J. Brissaud and T. A. Gueydan, *L'Évolution sociale et la pratique de l'arbitrage* (1939); D. Sarrano, *La Cour supérieure d'arbitrage* (Paris thesis, 1938).

in using that power. The larger the number of regulations forced through its machinery, the more frequent were its attacks of constipation.

The Popular Front is still a living memory and the least criticism of its work still arouses sensitive reactions from its surviving participants. These survivors see themselves as inaugurating a new era, whereas the historian sees precedents, continuities and limits to what was achieved in practice, which make the experience appear less heroic than it was to those who lived through it. In economic terms, the Popular Front was largely unsuccessful. The much-decried deflationary policy of the conservatives (1932–5)—which showed that conservatives also resorted to using state power to influence the economy—had produced a marked revival of production. The Popular Front gave the workers wage increases of unprecedented magnitude—amounting in all to 35 per cent and in some cases up to 50 per cent—but this was accompanied by inflation of 27 per cent within a single year, and by May 1938 workers' real wages were back to what they were in May 1936. Pensioners and civil servants, however, were left about 20 per cent poorer. Despite the shortening of the working week, unemployment fell at a slower rate in France than in neighbouring countries. Whereas elsewhere the depression was lifting, in France it was accentuated: production fell by 6 per cent, whereas it had increased by 8 per cent in the year before Blum came to power. Devaluation, which the workers had long, rather uncomprehendingly, opposed, was eventually forced on Blum, but he carried it out at too low a rate, so that it failed to make French goods competitive again. Blum had postponed it partly because he wished to obtain international agreement to it: he saw his negotiations as heralding new methods in the co-operative regulation of the world's finances. A young socialist, André Philip, declared that this episode had a decisive influence on his life, because it showed him that France was no longer able to solve its economic problems independently of other powers; reforms on a national scale were thus no longer possible. But this was not a lesson that was generally drawn, any more than, in the atmosphere of hostility and recrimination, it was seen that there were narrow limits to what a government could achieve without the full support of public opinion. The Popular Front represented only half the nation. Though it claimed to represent the poor against the rich, and though it is true that most of the rich were against it, there were people of all classes behind the opposition. So long as the state did no more than interfere in the working of the capitalist system, without really controlling it, it was dependent on the good will or 'confidence' of the capitalists. The fundamental change that was to make possible a much greater influence of the state on the workings of capitalism was the policy of planning, which, in effect, bribed the capitalists by financial inducements to invest in a way the state approved. The idea of co-operation based on self-interest—since moral consensus was absent—was a post-war invention.

To criticise the Popular Front government for not doing more is, however, to ignore the limitations within which it had to work. It was not a socialist government, as Blum was at pains to point out. The socialists were asked to form the ministry because they won most seats, but they had to share power with the radicals, and to rely also on the votes of the communists. The radicals remained by far the largest party in the Senate, so that full approval of all legislation had to be secured from them. In due course they overthrew Blum by refusing to allow him to increase taxation: even at modest rates that seemed too socialist for them. The Popular Front had as its policy the implementation of the moderate common programme of the left: it must be judged therefore for the way it achieved this. Its importance should be measured less in terms of legislation than in the emotional impact it had. It represented the revival and reunification of the left. Blum abandoned his reluctance to take office without a majority largely because of the threat of fascism. One of the first laws he passed dissolved the para-military 'fascist' leagues. Like the occupation of the factories, directed partly against 'yellow' workers, the socialist occupation of power was designed to keep the fascists out and to save democratic institutions. But it produced reactions of terror on the part of many conservatives who were in no way fascist. It was not a formula which worked, therefore, first because it immediately created antagonisms based on fear, and second because it involved the resurrection of old labels to solve new problems. The experience of the Popular Front showed that the idea of the left, however powerful emotionally, was in practical terms sterile: from the right wing of the radicals to the left wing of the communist party was too long a road. There was perhaps no other formula available, given the backward-looking character of politics, but, revolutionary though the Popular Front seemed, it was not revolutionary enough to find an alternative.

And yet Blum must be considered one of the most impressive statesmen of the Third Republic. No politician—apart from Gambetta and Jaurès—has been so admired and loved, though it is true none has been more hated and insulted. He was France's first Jewish prime minister but he received none of the tolerance that Disraeli was allowed in England. Anti-Semitic insults of the most vulgar kind were shouted at him while he made his speeches in parliament. On one occasion he was physically assaulted and beaten up: it is this kind of atmosphere that explains why the Popular Front seemed obviously neces-sary. Blum was proud of being a Jew; he believed that Jews had a special role to play in the revolution, because, he claimed, they were practically critical, rationalist and above all devoted to justice. His mother, he said, 'carried the sentiment of justice to such melancholy extremes' that when she gave him and his brother apples for a snack, she cut two apples in half and gave them each one half from each apple. Justice and Judaism, he argued, were one and the same thing: it was no accident that both Marx and Lassalle were Jews. But Blum was not a practising Jew and if he fitted into any stereotype himself, it was rather into that of the typical French intellectual. His father, who was of Alsatian origin, had built up a successful wholesale business in silk ribbons, but Blum never showed any interest in commerce and turned instead to literature and social life. He quickly established a considerable reputation as a literary critic on *La Revue blanche*, championing young writers systematically, arguing that each generation must protest its originality against its elders but also display a wide tolerance to different schools of writing. However, he took a particular interest in seeking out the ideas in literature, equating beauty with truth, and he liked clarity, sincerity and disinterestedness above all else. He won admission to the École Normale Supérieure, but left after a year, having found its work un-congenial and having failed in his examinations. He then gained entry into the Conseil d'État (by competitive examination, at his second attempt) and for twenty-four years he combined his writing with service as a member of the country's highest administrative judiciary, specialising in disputes between the state and the individual; he participated in the process by which, on the one hand, the public interest was gradually allowed to override the sanctity of private contract, and on the other, the administration was forced to account for abuses of its power. At the same time, he took an interest in politics at the theoretical level; and he helped finance the socialist paper *L'Humanité* and Péguy's bookshop, where many socialist academics and writers met to discuss the renovation of the world. Blum led a sociable and varied life. He hated specialisation. He declared that science could no longer be considered the key to the future, because it had become too specialised, and, besides, it increased suffering and injustice even if it also created new wealth. He rejected both the Tolstoian solution of sacrifice and all appeals to violence. He was hostile to simple formulae. His own temperament and talents inclined him to the conciliation of contradictions and animosities. That is what attracted him above all to Jaurès, who had the same inclinations and with whom he formed a deep friendship. It was only a feeling of obligation to carry on Jaurès's work after his death that persuaded Blum to enter active politics himself. Socialism, for both Jaurès and Blum, was a kind of religion, an expression of their character, rather than an economic analysis of society. Blum was even less of a Marxist than Jaurès. He said that Marx was a 'mediocre metaphysician', whose economic doctrines were increasingly outdated every day. Blum's own socialism was much more an extension of the ideas of the eighteenth-century *philosophes*; it was, he said, the result of a 'purely rationalist conception of society' seeking to reduce 'the obscure and evil forces which resist clarity of mind and the action of will based on reflection'; its aim was justice and happiness. He did believe that the collectivisation of property was the fundamental solution, but he was against achieving this by violence, arguing that the revolution should come only when the time for it was ripe. The real revolution was education, which transformed men's minds, not *coups d'état*: the Bolsheviks had confused ends and means and their seizure of power was a fraud. He was against minorities arrogating rights of dictatorship to themselves; he wanted socialism to triumph only when men saw that it was that was best for them, that it was in their own interest. This, however, did not make him a reformist. He argued that reformism and revolution were not alternatives but appealed to different people, depending on how far ahead they were disposed to look: reforms should not be thought of as likely to satisfy the masses and put them off revolution, at least if revolution was understood in his way, as the culmination of change. This is an example of the way Blum reconciled opposing tendencies among socialists; and it was, in large measure, due to his conciliatory efforts that the socialist party was, after the breach with the communists, expanded until it became the largest party in parliament. Blum was accepted as the party leader because he was recognised as having the subtlest brain in it, the greatest skill in developing its policy and enunciating its attitudes to the issues of the day. The result was that French socialism remained above all a humanistic creed, placing its major emphasis on the fulfilment of the individual.

Blum was a man of exceptional sensitivity, whose gentleness and kindness won him deep affection from all those who worked for him, just as his natural authority, firmness and ability to understand complicated problems quickly commanded respect. The preservation of individual liberty remained the foremost aim of the party. To such an extent was Blum attached to parliamentary government, as the indispensable guarantor of that liberty, that, though he saw the need for it to be made much more efficient in France, he was extremely anxious that the strengthening of the executive should be done in a way which would not jeopardise the system. He proposed changes therefore not in the parliamentary system, but simply in the techniques of government. Though he urged nationalisation, he wanted nationalised industries to be run as autonomous institutions, working for the public interest but largely independent of the government. Though he believed that capitalism had failed, in that its crisis was due to its inability to create enough purchasing power among the masses to buy the goods it produced in increasing quantities, he did not propose to overthrow capitalism, but rather to

M m

induce it to increase that purchasing power by raising wages. He kept his party out of office, so long as it did not have a majority, being determined that it should not become contaminated by power; he considered it his duty to pass on its doctrines unsullied to succeeding generations; and when in 1936 he did take office, he limited his ambitions precisely to the execution of the common programme of the left—which did not involve the establishment of socialism. The point on which he was most vulnerable was his foreign policy, for the socialists were by tradition pacifists and the menace of Nazism left them perplexed and indecisive. After 1945, Blum thought that he had made a mistake and that he should have supported a war against it, to destroy it before it caused further trouble. He had, however, seen the dangers inherent in Hitler's rise to power more clearly than most. Blum's enemies were blinded by passion, therefore, when they saw him as a dangerous and fanatical threat to French society as it existed. In many ways, he gave expression to the very generosity, rationality and moderation which that society cherished. But he illustrated also the limits of its rationality. He was no more able to understand his opponents than they to understand him. For all the acuteness of his sensibilities, his imagination was not broad enough to comprehend the reasons, for example, why the antidreyfusards persisted in denying the evidence of Dreyfus's innocence. He was, even as a very young man, remarkable for his awareness of the need for people to find satisfaction for the different sides of their personalities, physical, intellectual and sentimental, but he ultimately considered that the rational side should be dominant, and he could not help thinking that it could be made dominant by the use of rational argument. The weakness of socialism was that it remained fundamentally a doctrine for intellectuals.[1]

Technocracy made further headway under the Vichy regime. But that regime was also a manifestation of the survival of gerontocracy, and it is this that now requires explanation.

[1] Gilbert Ziebura, *Léon Blum et le parti socialiste 1872–1934* (1967); William Logne, *Léon Blum, The Formative Years 1872–1914* (North Illinois U.P., De Kalb, 1973); James Joll, *Three Intellectuals in Politics* (1960); Joel Colton, *Léon Blum, Humanist in Politics* (New York 1966); *Léon Blum, chef du gouvernement 1936–7* (Cahiers de la fondation nationale des sciences politiques no. 155, 1967); Georges Lefranc, *Histoire du Front Populaire* (1965).

# 22. Gerontocracy

NOSTALGIA was more widespread than optimism. The forces resisting change were more powerful than those which accepted or welcomed it. The years after 1914 therefore need to be looked at also from the point of view of those popular reactions which were fundamentally conservative, even when they assumed apparently revolutionary stances. It has been suggested[1] that the division of French politics into left and right was ultimately more confusing than useful, and at no time was this more obviously revealed than in this period. The men who opposed change, or who continued to repeat traditional gestures, were to be found in almost all parties, both left and right.

The reason for this must be sought, first of all, in the effect of the Great War. The war brought revolution to the three great kingdoms of continental Europe, but not to France. Yet this was the war that produced the heaviest loss of life France had ever sustained. One million four hundred thousand French soldiers were killed, i.e. 17·6 per cent of the army (compared with 17·1 per cent killed in the Austrian army, 15·1 per cent in the German and 13 per cent in the British). In economic terms this represented the disappearance of 10·5 per cent of France's active male population (compared with Germany's loss of 9·8 per cent and Britain's 5·1 per cent). The recovery of Alsace and Lorraine was not enough to compensate and the French population fell from 39·6 million to 39·12 million.[2] Though victorious, France was severely mutilated; and just as the defeat of 1871 had produced a conservative reaction, so in 1919 a conservative parliament was elected—the first right-wing majority since the foundation of the republic. The restoration of the pre-1914 world was not only felt as

---

[1] See volume 1, chapter 14. The opposite view is taken by François Goguel, *La Politique des partis sous la 3ᵉ république* (new edition, 1958); this remains an indispensable source, but it should be remembered that it was written in 1942–5.
[2] Germany's population fell from 64·9 to 59 million; Britain's rose from 45·4 to 47·9. Cf. Michel Huber, *La Population de la France pendant la guerre* (1932).

a need, but became an obsession. So many young people were killed in the war that the old politicians were able to survive with less opposition than they might otherwise have encountered, and old ideas were thus given a new lease of life. Resentment was a legacy of the war, more than hope. Three million soldiers were wounded: 1,100,000 suffered permanent disablement. Ex-servicemen's organisations, incapable of forgetting the past, became an important new power in the land.

The experience of the war was of such a nature that it encouraged the desire for revenge rather than for a new start. Sixteen per cent of the population (6·5 million) suffered from occupation by the enemy. Ten departments on the eastern frontier spent most of the war under German rule or served as a battleground: the war on the western front was fought almost entirely on French territory. In 1918 the population of this area had been reduced by 2,880,000 people (44 per cent). The department of the Aisne lost two-thirds of its inhabitants, those of the Marne and Meuse one-half. There were three types of victims: those who fled, those who remained under German rule, and those whose possessions were devastated by battle. About 1,500,000 left their homes at the approach of the German armies and spent the war as refugees. The government attempted to distribute them evenly over the whole country, but many preferred not to move too far away: the population of some departments was swollen by 10 or even 15 per cent. The fate of the occupied regions was more tragic. Some villages, anxious to avoid all provocation, spontaneously handed in their guns to the *mairie*. But during the invasion, whole villages were annihilated when the Germans felt their advance was endangered or resisted by the civilians. German atrocities became a subject of vigorous propaganda and German barbarism in this war was declared to exceed even that of the Thirty Years War. Once the front was stabilised, however, the Germans sought to exploit rather than punish. Military control was firmly established over all economic activity: the occupied regions were organised to produce food and other goods for the benefit of Germany. Forced labour was used to build and maintain the roads, railways and forests and to work the armaments factories. In the villages all were compelled to work in the fields. Men were requisitioned for special jobs by the army through the mayors (for the Germans kept the French administration under their military rule); they were usually allowed to go home in the evenings if their jobs were not too far away; but some were enrolled into the Z.A.B. (Civilian Labour Battalions) which were virtually military and sometimes worked at the front. Dependence on the whim of the commanders, reinforced on occasion by the taking of hostages, maintained a constant state of anxiety. Billeting of German troops, curfews, the confiscation of cars, bicycles, cameras, the imposition of heavy fines for a large number of new offences, compulsory 'loans', taxation and exactions of various sorts, strict control of all travel, the gradual closing of most shops and taverns, the halting of commerce and the disappearance of most fairs, the replacement of money by barter, the prohibition of correspondence with France—all this turned the occupied region into something resembling a vast concentration camp. In Belgium, at least most of the agricultural produce was left to the inhabitants; but France was treated with greater severity by its invaders: after 1915 almost all food was removed. The large towns could obtain neither eggs, nor meat nor milk for three years. Famine was averted by the Americans, working through the Red Cross and through a Committee for the Feeding of the North, to which the Germans readily and naturally gave every facility. An elaborate rationing system was instituted, which provided less than an adequate diet, but enough to sustain life. The death rate rose from 27 per cent in 1915 to 41 per cent in 1918 (compared with 21 per cent in Brussels in 1918). Tuberculosis and malnutrition affected the children in particular.[1]

In the final stages of the war, the Germans systematically destroyed all the steel mills and textile factories and 80 per cent of the mines, after having stripped them of useful machinery. As they retreated, they evacuated and razed the land so as to leave it completely empty. Soissons, twice occupied and twice razed, the scene of fighting for thirty-two months, had by 1918 only 500 of its former 15,000 inhabitants. Reims retained only 15 per cent of its population, who survived in underground caves, where the public authorities, schools and

[1] Paul Collinet and Paul Stahl, *Le Ravitaillement de la France occupée* (1928), 152-3.

churches continued to function. In the sizeable area devastated by battle, the work of many generations was almost completely annihilated, the land rendered unfit for agriculture; half the farm buildings were destroyed, three-quarters of the farm implements lost, most of the animals killed.[1] The actual damage and suffering inflicted was exacerbated by propaganda about German atrocities. This probably produced an even more long-lasting legacy of hate. The most distinguished scholars contributed to the vilification of the enemy. A pamphlet claimed that phrenological study showed that the Germans' brains lacked the organ of comparison, which explained not only the Germans' inability to make reasonable judgements, but also the depression in their skulls, which made room perfectly for the visor of their helmets. One whole floor of the *Maison de la Presse* was given over to the manufacture of false photographs showing horrible mutilations. The Catholic Church had a propaganda association under Mgr Baudrillart, rector of the Catholic Institute of Paris, which spread rumours of atrocities. The French were particularly forceful and imaginative in their invention of these horror stories, which is why the Germans, who engaged less successfully in the same kind of propaganda, emerged as the criminals.[2]

It took about a dozen years for the physical damage of the war to be repaired. There was an opportunity for the building of a new France. Indeed, a compulsory national town-planning law (14 March 1919) required every city of over 10,000 inhabitants to make plans for improvements within three years, and every town or village which had been damaged, irrespective of size, to produce a reconstruction plan within three months. An expropriation law (6 November 1918) allowed the state or a municipality to expropriate for public use a whole zone and not just the land immediately needed. Every new building in the devastated regions had to conform to public sanitation laws; thatched roofs were forbidden, even on barns; measures against damp were required, the ventilation of kitchens, the compulsory installation of water-closets in all new lodgings with two rooms or more, a minimum size for windows; no

---

[1] George B. Ford, *Out of the Ruins* (New York, 1919), I. 57.
[2] J. M. Read, *Atrocity Propaganda 1914–1919* (New Haven, 1941), 24, 142–4, with a good bibliography.

new building was to be higher than the street was wide.[1] But the financial provisions for the reconstruction encouraged profiteering rather than the modernisation and re-equipment of industry. The state undertook to indemnify all losses sustained through enemy action but it offered overwhelming financial inducements to rebuild in the same region. An owner could take his money and not rebuild, but in such a case he would receive only the value of the property in 1914. If he rebuilt, he would get a sum three or four times larger, to compensate for the increased post-war cost of rebuilding—but he had to rebuild in the same commune, or at least within a radius of fifty kilometres of the original site, provided always this was inside the 'devastated battle zone'. This reflected a natural fear that otherwise a whole region of France would remain a desert, but it resulted in the guiding principle being the reconstruction of the France of 1914 in almost identical shape. No attempt was made to consider the national economic interest, to decide, for example, whether a destroyed sugar factory should be replaced by another one, rather than something else. No distinction was made, in allocating compensation, between productive re-equipment and the reconstitution of consumer assets. Twenty-nine milliard gold francs were distributed in war compensation, which was obviously an exaggerated sum, for it was equal to one-tenth of the total private wealth of France in 1914. The idea was that German reparations would pay for it. The committees which assessed damages were therefore generous in their estimates, if only from patriotism; and in addition some found scope for fraud or embezzlement. Germany of course did not pay. Instead of levying a tax on property throughout the country, to share the burden, the state therefore raised the money by loans. The money market was unable to withstand this, and by 1925 the state was virtually bankrupt. Inflation meant that the victims of war damage were replaced by victims of the collapse of the franc.[2]

The French had been exceptionally resourceful in meeting the challenges presented by the war. The population in the unoccupied regions was kept well fed at little below pre-war standards; military supplies were, after initial chaos, produced

[1] Ford, op. cit. 145, 153-4.
[2] Edmond Michel, *Les Dommages de guerre de la France et leur réparation* (1932).

in adequate quantities; and the war was won without any real crisis and without revolution. This very success, however, was to be a principal cause of the failure to reform either the political or economic mechanism when peace came. The success was, of course, to a certain extent illusory, because the French made up the deficiencies of their production by borrowing. The payment of the price of victory was postponed till after peace was made: the crisis came then, rather than during the war. Some people lost all they had, but a great many more survived fairly comfortably and some even prospered in the war. Thus though the peasants suffered enormously in terms of war casualties—673,000 were killed and another half a million were seriously wounded, out of about eight million— the survivors were able to pay off their mortgages, thanks to inflation, and the labourers were able to command much higher wages. Though agricultural production fell drastically during the war, there were large profits to be made, despite the government's efforts at price fixing. In particular wine-growers did well because the army bought up one-third of their production, at prices three times higher than those prevailing in 1914. The peasants were the principal bene-ficiaries of the black market created by food rationing (which really hit only the towns), and though they complained about billeting and the destruction of crops, they made enormous profits from the troops, and foreign ones most of all. The war therefore did not turn the peasants into revolutionaries, but confused their thinking about their situation. While despair or ambition continued to drive large numbers to the towns— so that the number of peasants fell by 14 per cent between 1919 and 1930—the land continued to be a refuge for those who had still not come to terms with the modern economy. Though large farmers increased production—total food production rose by 3 per cent in these years, despite the fall in the agricultural population, and productivity per person rose by 19 per cent— France could no longer claim to be self-sufficient in food, and the peasants were subjected to ruinous international competition.[1]

---

[1] Food consumption (%):

|  | 1910–13 | 1923–31 |
|---|---|---|
| from metropolitan France | 85·1 | 74·8 |
| colonies | 6·8 | 9·5 |
| foreign countries | 8·1 | 15·7 |

Prosperity alternated with crisis: in 1930–5 it was agricultural prices which fell more than those of any other commodity, despite protection; but in the next four years, peasant incomes rose by over a half. Though it is now argued that too many people were trying to live off the land, there were many who were still preaching a return to the land, and that was official policy in 1940–2. Far from higher productivity being the obvious solution to the peasants' problems, governments urged them to reduce production in the 1930s. The confusion resulting from these apparent contradictions prevented any general acceptance of 'modernisation' as the answer. The attempts to establish large-scale co-operative farms under the pressure of war in 1914–18 had failed completely: one near Toulouse, which had received a loan of three million francs interest free from the government failed to make any profits. The co-operative of the Forez lost four million francs. Ministerial exhortations and circulars had no practical results. There was no new or general sense of direction in agriculture, beyond the desire to keep France a predominantly rural nation.[1]

Nostalgia was only one form of conservatism. Another kind of resistance to change came from ignorance about the changes that were taking place, and the inability to understand them. What people thought was happening was, in some ways, as important as what actually did happen. The inability to judge events was partly a question of slow psychological adaptation, an inevitable tendency to find what one was looking for, but partly also a result of the inadequacy of information about the economy. France's statistical service in this period consisted of 120 men, at a time when even Czechoslovakia employed 1,198 in its similar service and Germany 2,358. The cost of living index was compiled on the basis of the retail price of only thirteen articles, ignoring, for example, the cost of clothing and rents. Whereas in the 1920s most countries in Europe established institutes to study the economy, on the model of the Harvard Economic Service, France did not do so.

[1] M. Augé-Laribé, *L'Agriculture française pendant la guerre* (1925), 62; A. Sauvy, *Histoire économique de la France entre les deux guerres* (4 vols., 1967–75), 1. 239–58, 2. 128, 137, 293; G. Perreux, *La Vie quotidienne des civils en France pendant la grande guerre* (1966), 146–7.

In 1938 no one knew, for example, what the national production of chemical products, or agricultural machines, or textiles
was. It was only in that year that a decree-law[1] ordered a
survey of production and distribution. The result was that
Blum was unable to see the damaging effects of the forty-hour
week on the economy. The politicians had to work largely in
the dark. There was no obstacle therefore to bogy men ob-
sessing them and, even more, the public.

Probably the most worrying of these bogy men were the
industrialists and bankers, who moreover did their best to
conceal the facts about themselves. They had only themselves
to blame if their activities were construed in the most un-
favourable way. The phenomenon which attracted particular
attention was the concentration of business into larger units.
The number of firms fell by 35 per cent between 1906 and
1926, which meant that artisans were going out of business.
The number of firms employing between 21 and 100 workers
increased by 60 per cent and those with over 100 workers by
50 per cent.[2] The number of people employed in factories with
over 500 workers doubled between 1900 and 1931 to reach
almost one and a half million. However the proportion of
firms which could be considered large-scale was still small. In
1931 only 13 per cent of the industrial work force were employed by firms large enough to put the bulk of their workers in
factories of 100 or more men. In 1939 there were still 151,044
family firms against 43,080 limited liability companies, even if
the total capital of the latter was larger. Cartels in particular
attracted attention. Much was made of the fact, also, that by
1936 the three largest car manufacturers had won 75 per
cent of the national market, whereas in 1913 they had only
29 per cent (a rather untypical situation). The difficulties of the
economy were thus blamed somewhat uncritically on big
business without a proper appreciation of its real, and rather
limited, role. Battles were fought against imaginary enemies,
or at least enemies whose might and whose unity were grossly
exaggerated.[3] To what extent employers were 'malthusian'

---

[1] A decree issued by the government, without a parliamentary vote, but having
the force of law.         [2] G. Pirou, *Les Cadres de la vie économique* (1940), 1. 143.
[3] M. Lévy-Leboyer, 'Le Patronat français a-t-il été malthusien?', *Le Mouvement
social* (July–Sept. 1974), 3–49, which contains a valuable bibliography of recent
work on industrial developments in the inter-war years.

in these years, and impregnated by the 'Maginot Line' attitude, is debatable, and the tendency, now that more research is being done on employers, is to argue that these accusations cannot be applied indiscriminately to them: neither the government nor the masses had adequate information about their policy. Many employers had great difficulty in understanding the effects of devaluation on industry and on exports, so that they took the most contradictory action.

The workers, for their part, were confused about their own situation by inflation, which made impartial calculation difficult. During the First World War, their real wages had risen considerably, particularly among the poorer paid; 413,000 workers were brought back from the front to the factories, where they earned high civilian wages while the peasants fought and died for a private's pittance. The French workers did much better in the war than the German ones, who, because of industrial mobilisation, had their real wages reduced by 42 per cent in 1914–16, and who had still barely returned to 1914 levels in 1918.[1] The improvement in the French workers' position continued between the wars, and even in the 1930s their real wages rose by no less than 25 per cent: they were the beneficiaries of the collapse of food prices.[2] However, whereas in May–July 1917 96 per cent of strikes were totally or partially successful, the strikes of 1919–20, which many thought might be the presage of revolution, were disastrous failures and, as has been seen,[3] the workers' relations with their employers remained bitter and antagonistic. Though the Popular Front was immensely important in revealing what the workers could achieve by spontaneous action, it was also immensely disappointing: the large gains in wages were quickly cancelled out by price rises; paradoxically 1937 and 1938 were the years when the workers' standard of living did not rise. Unemployment for French workers never rose very high in official figures (which gave a maximum of under half a million unemployed, i.e. 5 per cent of the industrial and commercial work force) but short-time

---

[1] W. Oualid and C. Picquenard, *La Guerre et le travail. Salaires et tarifs* (1928); G. D. Feldman, *Army, Industry and Labour in Germany 1914–18* (Princeton, 1966), 117, 472. Cf. the play *Les Nouveaux Riches* by Abadie and Cesse, first performed at the Sarah Bernhardt Theatre in Paris on 1 March 1917.

[2] Sauvy, op. cit. 2. 25, 406.            [3] See vol. 1. 274–82.

work, which probably affected one-fifth of workers, was a source of profound demoralisation throughout the 1930s, for France was slower to recover from the depression than other countries.[1]

Most of the politicians of the inter-war years offered the country virtually the same programme and solutions that their predecessors had done in the nineteenth century. Indeed most of them had established themselves as ministers long before 1914, and since they continued to win elections, the mass of the people accepted and probably shared their traditional attitudes. Thus it was generally agreed, even by his enemies, that Poincaré, whose life almost spanned the whole Third Republic (1860–1934), owed his success to his being particularly representative of that regime's ideals. Poincaré consciously sought to give expression to these ideals in his policies. He could be attacked for identifying himself, and France, with the middle-class savers, the *rentiers*, and to devoting his life to rescuing them from inflation; but he was proud to acknowledge this as his ambition and he did not consider that this meant he was selfishly serving the interests of a minority class. It is true there were only about 510,000 *rentiers* who owned state bonds.[2] But Poincaré saw them as only one section of the rather larger group of people who had invested their savings in other securities, and of the even wider community which believed in saving. The savers were, to him, the motor force of French society, just as to the socialists the workers were. French society was based on ambition, the ambition to make money, to become educated and to rise in the social scale. It was a society that worked because it kept the road to *embourgeoisement* always open, and leadership was constantly renewed by new recruits, who rose to comfort or eminence on the basis of their savings, usually amassed slowly through several generations. Ambition, Poincaré thought, was a good thing

---

[1] C. Gide and W. Oualid, *Le Bilan de la guerre pour la France* (1931); Arthur Fontaine, *L'Industrie française pendant la guerre* (1925); G. Olphe Gaillard, *Histoire économique et financière de la guerre 1914–1918* (1923); A. Sauvy, op. cit.; C. J. Gignoux, *L'Économie française entre les deux guerres 1919–39* (n.d., about 1940); E. Dussauze, *L'État et les ententes industrielles* (1939); J. Tchernoff, *Les Ententes économiques et financières* (1933–7).

[2] This is the 1911 figure.

because it stimulated progress and the spirit of invention, but also thrift and prudence. Poincaré's dedication to this ideal shows that when Guizot had held up the motto 'Get Rich' to his countrymen, he had found a response and Poincaré indeed repeated Guizot's famous dictum, while modifying it slightly: 'Help yourselves,' he said, 'and the state (which is not Heaven) will help you later, if it can'. He was not as opposed to state interference as Guizot; though he remained basically a liberal, he thought the state should prevent the growth of monopolies and 'capitalist concentration' because these blocked the road of the rising small entrepreneur (failing to see that the large firms were offering the middle classes an alternative method of advancement and a new form of power). He was against the state taking over the role of providence and distributing favours and subsidies to its protégés, but he believed that the state should express the pride and self-satisfaction of its members by an active foreign policy. Nationalism, as his brother-in-law, the philosopher Boutroux said, was not incompatible with liberalism because it represented the reaction of the individual against 'the increasing obliteration of man by impersonal science, matter and chance'. Poincaré saw in the cult of the fatherland a way of reconciling reason and sentiment, self-interest and altruism. He was the heir not only of Guizot but of Thiers also, for whom a strong state, in the monarchical tradition, was necessary both for the dignity of Frenchmen and for the security of their property. Poincaré was, however, profoundly devoted to the republican regime and he never even toyed with possible alternatives. This was partly because he was a lawyer with a deep respect for legality—he was horrified, for example, that the Bank of France should have secretly engaged in financial manipulations which were not entirely legal—and partly because, as a minister, he considered himself a servant of the regime, with a duty to defend it. Honesty was for him one of the very basic virtues. He practised what he preached, moreover, and he owed his long tenure of the highest offices to the respect he inspired as incorruptible. Honesty meant that if ever he asked a civil service messenger to run an errand for him on a private matter, he would pay for it personally. He abandoned politics for a decade in order to make a fortune at the Bar, so that he could be financially independent; and he then used up his savings as president of the republic, refusing to do more than receive his salary. He rejected the offer of a lucrative sinecure which might suggest he was using his political influence for personal benefit. He had no doubts about what was right and wrong. Legality, justice and morality were all one to him. He was not interested in innovation, or in trying to solve insoluble problems. He was content to be the common denominator of his countrymen.

Poincaré was cold, timid, unattractive, unemotional. 'A head of state in the exercise of his duty', he said, 'has not the right to have tears in his eyes.' He was neither loved, nor admired, but he was respected. He was frequently referred to as France's lawyer, employed to get it its rights. Authors like Giraudoux were appalled that a lawyer, concerned above all with the past, quarrelling endlessly with the Germans about money, should claim to personify France, and be widely accepted as doing so; but the preoccupation with money was undoubtedly one national obsession. Poincaré was in fact also a man of considerable culture. He had been more attracted by literature than law in his youth; he had written no less than four novels, never published; he was elected to the French Academy and he always enjoyed the company of writers and artists more than that of politicians. But he had very few friends. He was representative of the tradition that regarded emotion as a private matter, and life as essentially serious, demanding, above all, hard work. He worked twelve hours a day and seldom accepted social invitations; he wrote all his letters by hand even when president of the republic; he answered his correspondence promptly and was always efficient. He concentrated on finance because he believed that sound finances were the essential foundation for an ordered society, and the state's main function (he quoted Thiers on this) was finance and defence. He was not therefore a party man; he offered himself as an arbitrator, a conciliator, who could fulfil national ambitions. He was not entirely conservative in the way he interpreted these. His talent had been recognised when he was still very young and he had first been drawn into a government as early as 1886, as a *chef de cabinet* on a minister's staff; and he became a minister in his thirties.

The ideas that guided him in the 1920s had been acquired forty years before. Poincaré was thus a staunch enemy of socialism, to the extent of voting against Waldeck-Rousseau who had been so rash as to admit a renegade socialist into his ministry. He had started his life as an admirer of Méline. He had opposed even pensions for railway workers. He always saw the reduction of government expenditure as a major objective, and budget deficits as the source of most evils. But in 1899 he had broken with Méline, arguing that anti-socialism could not be the entire programme of a politician. He eventually came to accept the idea of an income tax, provided that the traditional secrecy of business profits and family affairs was respected. He accepted insurance, provided it was run on mutual principles (not by the state). He thus typified the conservative who gradually came to accept that times were changing, and who belatedly adopted ideas that had been fashionable a generation earlier.

Poincaré's greatest achievement was to make the conservative *rentier* come to terms with the fact that his savings had been irrevocably lost in the chaos of the war and its aftermath. Poincaré took a very long time to admit this himself. He had always worked to give the country its rights and he believed in firmness in the exaction of those rights. In 1912–14, as prime minister and then president of the republic, he had not flinched from the idea of a war against Germany, if that was the price that had to be paid for the recognition of France's rights. After the war, he had supported the declaration of German war guilt and the exaction of large reparations. He had demanded the annexation of the Rhineland; and when Germany defaulted, he ordered the occupation of the Ruhr. Whereas Millerand, who had spent his life making compromises, wanted to do a deal with the German industrialists, to establish a Franco-German iron and steel compact, Poincaré insisted on the German state meeting its obligations. British and American historians have generally condemned this attitude as a refusal to face the economic realities, but French ones have maintained that France had a strong case and was shamefully and selfishly let down by its allies. The French middle classes could not see why, in the conflict of interests, they should be the ones to make sacrifices. They were in no mood for sacrifices; they felt their very existence was at stake, and so it was if their aristocratic pretensions—to live off accumulated capital rather than from daily work—were considered an essential part of their values. They gave way only because in 1925 they seemed threatened by total bankruptcy. Poincaré devalued the franc to four-fifths of its pre-war level. He accepted the Locarno treaty which put an end to the policy of sanctions against Germany. He carefully fixed the devaluation at a figure high enough to avoid unemployment and social unrest, but low enough to make French exports very competitive in world markets. In the process, he saved the parliamentary institutions of the republic; and he gave the traditionally influential classes a further lease of life. He did not stop negotiating with the Germans about reparations, and even if no money could be extracted from them, his supporters could still cherish their mistrust or hate of the Germans for another generation. Poincaré for many years collected material for a biography of Thiers, whom he greatly admired. He and Thiers stood in the same tradition, and together they show the continuity of the liberal, chauvinistic, cultured, basically self-satisfied core of middle-class families, who would not admit change unless absolutely forced to.[1]

This was only one kind of conservatism. Another was less readily identifiable, because it called itself radicalism. But in these years radicalism for the first time admitted that the most dangerous enemy was communism, and for the first time it ceased to pay lip-service to all 'advanced' ideas. This was a belated recognition that the radical party had matured into a network of families who, by temperament and tradition, were still hostile to capitalism and Catholicism but who, in practice, had won their place in the world as they found it, were proud of their achievement and thought that it was enough if arrangements could be made for others to follow in their footsteps. They would never proclaim themselves satisfied, but, provided they could criticise, they were. They did not believe in the redistribution of wealth, but only in making it easier for more

[1] Marguerite Perrot, *Le Mode de vie des familles bourgeoises* (1961), for the effects of inflation; Pierre Miquel, *Poincaré* (1961); Fernand Payen, *Raymond Poincaré; l'homme, le parlementaire, l'avocat* (1936); Raymond Poincaré, 'Vues politiques', *La Revue de Paris* (1 Apr. 1898), 638–58; id., *Idées contemporaines* (1906); id., *Au service de la France* (memoirs, covering the years 1912–18, 10 vols. 1926–33).

people to acquire it, in moderate quantities. Their doctrine ultimately reduced itself to the worship of moral virtues, just as the conservatives' did, though they saw salvation through education rather than religion. This enabled them to live on two planes—to be highly critical of society in their speech, but to be highly representative of the virtues of that society and to lead conformist lives according to its rules. France was thus held steady by this central core of people who, though they toyed with ideas, and often accepted that change was desirable, always found good reasons for postponing doing anything about it.

It has been suggested that in these years, the middle class in France divided into two components—the small capitalists (who lived off their private incomes) and the wage earners—and that the socialists gradually drew the latter group away from the radicals. Radicalism was thus left with an essentially conservative clientele, attached to private property and public order, hostile to big business but not to small savers.[1] In several other countries the petty bourgeoisie would have been tempted by fascism. In France the radical tradition prevented this: its stress both on rationalism and on prudence kept them loyal to the republic. But they did not use their influence in the cause of reform. This was partly because they were deeply divided. The radical party included both Clemenceau and Caillaux who advocated diametrically opposed foreign policies, to the extent that the former had the latter arrested and charged with treason. There were at least four major cliques within the party after 1919, grouped around the personalities of Herriot, Daladier, Chautemps and Sarraut, who took different lines largely for reasons of temperament. It was rare for them all to vote in the same way. Once their programme of anticlericalism, parliamentary government and educational opportunity had been achieved, the radicals became, in the inter-war years, essentially the party that acted as the middleman in politics, keeping the system going by arranging compromises, mitigating the effect of inevitable legislation or economic crises. Even their attitude to big business was ambivalent. They received election funds from the insurance companies and most

[1] J. P. Florin, 'Le Radical-socialisme dans le département du Nord 1914–36', *Revue française de science politique* (Apr. 1974), 236–77.

of their newspapers were taken over by press magnates. They held directorships in powerful capitalist companies. They gave protection to financiers who could oil the wheels of government, even to the extent of allowing the famous crook, Stavisky, immunity to pursue his swindles. Though they made electoral alliances with the socialists, they were very reluctant to share power with them and the collaboration of the Popular Front was unpleasant to them, because they were, ultimately, unwilling to launch a serious attack on capitalism: they agreed to participate in Blum's government 'from pride, fear and ignorance'. In 1938 they finally adopted anti-communism as the main plank of their programme. At the same time the new generation of their members formed a group *Jeunesses Radicales*, which made Order, Authority and Nation its motto. They turned to the empire as holding out the hope for a new patriotic salvation. It was not surprising that in 1940 they voted in large majority for Pétain. However, the radicals had room within their ranks for men like Mendès France and Jean Zay whose reforming zeal was unquestionable and genuine.[1] The explanation of this is to be found less in political terms than in character. To explain why so many different kinds of people were radical is like explaining why they got married. One can see this by looking at the radical leader, Herriot.

Édouard Herriot (1872–1957), like Poincaré, lived almost right through the Third Republic and he was one of its heroes. He owed his ascendancy, however, to totally different qualities. Whereas Poincaré was moved by duty, Herriot needed above all affection. He was the leader of the radicals because he exuded fraternity. He was always jovial, hearty, friendly; he was a brilliant and insatiable conversationalist; he loved making emotional speeches and these were so eloquent that even political audiences shouted 'encore' at the end of them. He was deeply sensitive, easily hurt by the least criticism and in constant need of applause, and of a reciprocation of the flattery he showered on all with whom he came into contact. There was no malice in him; but, as he himself said, he was a spoilt child. He was a scholarship boy who had won every academic success and ended up a university professor of literature at Lyon. He was a literary man, who wrote more than

[1] Peter J. Larmour, *The French Radical Party in the 1930s* (Stanford, 1964).

thirty books, and whose first attraction was to beauty rather than to philosophical systems. His conversation was studded with literary quotations; he did not go into politics because he liked arguing, but because he liked the human contact, mutual stimulation, but most of all agreement with others. Even his youth was marked by no political enthusiasms, but rather by a series of rejections: he lost his faith without realising it 'as one loses one's hair'; he was repelled by socialism, in the excessively Germanic form, as it seemed to him, that it was developing; and the doctrines of Maurras also appeared too harsh. Herriot would have liked politics to be based on sympathy, and he even tried to apply this to international relations. That is why his heroes were the utopians of the 1840s and particularly Constantin Pecqueur.

That is why, also, he wrote his two theses about women of the eighteenth century: he adored women who won sympathy by their charm, who were intelligent enough to converse but who acquiesced in male superiority. He would have liked international relations to be based on the same principles of human attraction and was dismayed when dour politicians like Ramsay Macdonald did not respond. Under Herriot's leadership, the radical party became a great club, where a good time was had by all, but whose members were puzzled that not everyone wished to join. Eloquence, said Herriot, was man's beauty. The radicals were content to limit strife to verbal gymnastics. That was to raise an enormous barrier against action or change.

This did not mean that Herriot opposed the reforming ideas of his time. On the contrary, he understood them as well as anyone. He was immensely learned and widely read. In 1919 he published a two-tomed study of the reforms that France needed to undertake: he was very radical indeed in his recommendations, demand nothing less than 'a total transformation of our habits and institutions': 'the time has come', he said, 'to found a Fourth Republic'. His review of detailed problems, with long and comprehensive bibliographies, made his book appear an impressive political treatise. He seemed, moreover, to be in favour of rapid modernisation. He praised the Americans for their dedication to productivity, and combining this with the radical cult of education, he coined the slogan 'to understand and to create' (creation meaning producing, in the widest sense). Technical education should be advanced and scientific management and research encouraged. He embraced Taylorism as a new application of Cartesianism. Despite his own absorption in literature, he proclaimed that science contained the key to the future, and traditional culture should serve rather as a resource for factory and office workers in monotonous jobs. Foreign policy must be based on an acceptance of greater interdependence between nations. There was no real difference between socialism and radicalism, according to Herriot, except in the way it was implemented; radicalism did things more gradually and opportunely. However, though Herriot sometimes said he was an ordinary man (*peuple*)—and he was indeed popular because he was unpretentious—he also said that he was a bourgeois. When it came, therefore, to the question of who would carry out these reforms, Herriot was considerably less conciliatory. He was suspicious of 'technicians' and denounced the Polytechnic as the 'only theology faculty that has not been abolished'.[1] Though he castigated the big capitalists, he was frightened by them. He resigned in 1925 rather than fight them. He declared his ministry had come upon an impregnable *Mur d'Argent*, which stood as an obstacle to progress. That defeat was a traumatic experience, to which he often referred with horror. People accused him of lacking the courage of his convictions, for he could not bring himself to impose an income tax that really worked, that was not the subject of fraud and evasion. But he was restrained by a deeply ingrained liberalism. The prospect of another battle with the capitalists made him unwilling to co-operate with the socialists, and he liked finance ministers to be moderate men who commanded the confidence of the bankers. He was not willing to push his belief in equality beyond equality of opportunity, because he thought (like Poincaré) that individual effort should be recompensed by individual reward and social promotion. He said he deplored the material poverty of the workers less than their spiritual poverty. He was all for female rights, but argued that women were not ready for more than the municipal vote, and though he advanced equality of educational opportunity for girls, he was suspicious of too much 'intellectual

[1] E. Herriot, *Notes et maximes inédites* (1961), 40, 46.

excitement' for them, which could produce 'disequilibrium'.[1] He was not anti-religious, but he could not abandon the traditional anticlericalism of his party, and so he roused much animosity, even though it was his ambition to reconcile Frenchmen. He said he was shocked by a notice he once saw reading: *Restaurant ouvrier, cuisine bourgeoise.*[2] Yet there was the same contradiction within him. Though he was a most amiable, intelligent and friendly man, he was also very difficult to get on with as a colleague. He was ready to rally in times of national crisis, but when it came to taking action, he insisted on formal procedures being adhered to, on parliament debating the matter at length, and he staunchly resisted the right to issue decree-laws being given to governments. He was in favour of European unity, but his sympathy with other nations was superficial: he was sure the French were the most intelligent people in the world.[3] The radical party's support was virtually indispensable to every government, though it was not large enough to form a ministry by itself: the radicals were like the feathers on a duck's back; they kept France warm and caused all reforms to run smoothly off.

This is not to say that the *Mur d'Argent* was entirely a myth and that big business was not also a powerful conservative force, but it was probably less of an obstacle to the radicals than their own hesitations. How the capitalists used their money to influence politics can be seen by taking the case of François de Wendel. He called himself, not without some plausibility, France's leading industrialist. He was the symbol of plutocracy (as Caillaux called him) and of the occult power of international finance, to the extent that an assassination attempt was made on him, with the aim of avenging the shooting of Jaurès. His family's factories were for a time partly French and partly German, as a result of the loss of Alsace and Lorraine, and he was therefore accused (falsely) of putting pressure on the government to avoid damaging his firm's property in Germany during the war. Wendel's position astride the frontier in fact made him not a partisan of co-operation with Germany, but

[1] E. Herriot, *Créer* (1919), 1. 9, 2. 227.    [2] E. Herriot, *Jadis* (1948), 1. 146.
[3] M. Soulié, *La Vie politique d'Édouard Herriot* (1962), 121; P. O. Lapie, *Herriot* (1967).

violently hostile to it. If there was one motive behind his political life, it was his fear of Germany. His *bête noire* was Caillaux, whom he might have approved of for his orthodox views on finance, but whom he detested because Caillaux favoured peace with Germany. Caillaux said to him: 'I am a man from the West. I see the Anglo-Saxon danger more.' Wendel preferred Poincaré who was an easterner, a 'man of the frontier'. Wendel was thus firmly opposed to the Vichy government during the war: he thought the main value of Nazism was that it revealed Germany in its true light. He always considered the national interest and foreign policy more important than the defence of the social order at home. He was attacked in the press, nevertheless, as being anxious not to offend Hitler, since the Wendels owned mines in Germany. It was significant that the newspaper which waged this campaign against him was subsidised by another section of the French plutocracy, notably Ernest Mercier and the electrical industry. The first thing that emerges from a study of the plutocracy is its profound divisions, its inability to act in unison and its failure therefore to make much impact on the course of events. Wendel's private papers show him to have been in almost constant disagreement with the Comité des forges, even though he was its president and even though he contributed 20 per cent of its budget: the interests of its members were too diverse to make a concerted policy possible. In the Bank of France, of which he was a governor, he was likewise at odds with many of his colleagues, because there was a long-standing breach between the bankers and the industrialists. The personal friendship of Wendel and Rothschild cut across this division, but the bankers were themselves divided between those who wished to rescue the small savers and those who were willing to borrow more from America and make a new start, based on a great export drive. The crisis of the franc in 1924–8 has long been regarded as proof of the ability of the Bank of France's governors (the cream of the plutocracy) to dictate to the state. Wendel was determined to get rid of Herriot and considered himself the representative of those who were panic-stricken by the advent of the radicals; he was keen to use his power to save the country from the reds. However, closer examination of the negotiations between the

Bank and the government reveals that it was mainly the government's hesitations that allowed the Bank to appear as an obstacle.

A more accurate accusation is that the plutocrats used their money to finance newspapers and pseudo-fascist movements. The perfumer Coty was particularly active in this way. But the case of Wendel, which has been carefully studied, shows that though a lot of money did change hands, it probably had very little effect on politics. Wendel bought *Le Journal des Débats* and he collected subscriptions from large firms to keep *Le Temps* as a conservative paper; but after a time Rothschild discontinued his contribution saying that it was a waste of money, since these papers made very little difference to public opinion. Wendel did give Pierre Taittinger's Jeunesses Patriotes 50,000 francs; but he was suspicious of anti-parliamentary groups, because he subsidised a parliamentary party himself, the Union des Républicains Démocratiques. This party also received funds from the Union des Intérêts Économiques, an organisation to distribute the political funds of big business, as well as 150,000 from Tardieu when he was prime minister (but Tardieu had himself received donations from the Comité des forges). However, Wendel had a lot of trouble in his own party and at one point found himself in a minority of fifteen out of about a hundred: the party's other leader, Louis Marin, was a *petit bourgeois* who was essentially a nationalist, and not pro-capitalist. Millerand used to be the Comité des forges's attorney, but when he became president he shunned Wendel, determined to show his independence. Wendel indeed found himself discounted and avoided, precisely because he was rich and people were anxious not to appear to be in his pay. He lacked the personal qualities needed to exert a real influence in politics. He said that since he did not have a stable of race-horses or play baccarat, he felt he could afford to pay for the luxury of having an independent opinion. The money he spent in this way reinforced the view that the plutocracy stood in the way of change. Wendel certainly had no developed ideas for reform and he criticised the Vichy government for trying to establish a 'New Order', when it would be better to 'save and defend the old one'. He believed that men were always the same, and nothing would improve them. The traditional organisation of society was therefore best. It is possible that many who were not plutocrats thought the same.[1]

The Vichy regime (1940–4) does not fit into the traditional dichotomy of left or right. It is generally classified as reactionary and backward-looking. It was this; but it was more than this; and it is its complexity that makes it important. If it had simply been a tool of the German conqueror, these four years could perhaps be considered (and some have argued that they should be) as an awful nightmare, to be forgotten as quickly as possible, and 'to be expunged from history'. But the 'National Revolution' it inaugurated represented a genuine attempt at reform, which needs to be taken seriously despite the confusions in it and despite its disastrous failure. It gave expression to a widespread determination to create a new France. The Third Republic had identified progress with parliamentary government and liberalism. Once people took the advantages of these for granted, they became increasingly critical of the concomitant inconveniences. About half the nation always had doubts about the prevailing system. So in 1940, it was not the Germans who overthrew the Third Republic. Parliament voluntarily abdicated and voted all its powers to Marshal Pétain, without reservations. This was an acknowledgement of impotence. It was not, therefore, just the right-wing opposition to the republic which thus gained office. Representatives of virtually all parties, abandoning their old attitudes, sought to co-operate in establishing a new order. For a time, Pétain's government enjoyed a popularity which was perhaps more widespread than that of any previous government.

The basis of the Vichy regime was both hope and despair. There was no need for the French to stop fighting, and a small minority argued that the battle could be continued, if necessary by withdrawing from the mainland to the colonies. But only about 35,000 took this view, or believed it strongly enough to join General de Gaulle's resistance movement in its early, lonely days. The vast majority of the nation was not willing to repeat the traumatic experiences of 1914–18. About ten

[1] J. N. Jeanneney, *François Wendel en République. L'Argent et le pouvoir 1914–40* (1976).

million people fled before the invading Nazi army in the greatest exodus the country had experienced, creating unprecedented conditions of chaos: they did not believe they could stop the Germans and they had no wish to die, heroically or otherwise. The armistice that Pétain signed was therefore greeted with almost universal approval and relief. Pétain believed that France's defeat had been caused not by military mistakes but by moral collapse. It was therefore no use fighting. The defeat should be used as a basis for a complete overhaul of the country. Guilt and shame inspired a search for refuge in traditional values as well as a desire to deny and break away from the immediate past. The depth of this feeling can be judged from the unprecedented powers that parliament voted Pétain, greater than any absolute monarch had enjoyed. All authority was vested in him, without limitation of time, and without responsibility to anyone. Pétain was eighty-four years old. The faith placed in such an old man was a sort of reversion to childhood by the nation, an abandonment of critical faculties and of responsibility brought on by mortal terror.[1]

Pétain was a soldier, not a politician. The Vichy regime was run by soldiers, civil servants and experts, not by politicians, who were largely discarded and some of whom were even put on trial on the charge of being responsible for the disastrous war.[2] Pétain's ministers were mainly civil servants who had already helped to run the country from behind the scenes under the Third Republic and who were now given greater, and visible, power. Inspectors of finance, councillors of state, Polytechniciens were in particular evidence, and they far outnumbered the visionaries and romantics. When Admiral Darlan became prime minister in 1942, he advanced technocracy even further. So though there seems little continuity between the Third and Fourth Republics on the political level, there was in fact an underlying one, because most senior civil servants survived through all these changes. Something like 98 per cent of those who served Vichy remained in state employment under the Fourth Republic. Their experiments

[1] Robert O. Paxton, *Vichy France* (1972); Robert Aron, *The Vichy Regime* (1958); Richard Griffiths, *Marshal Pétain* (1970); Stanley Hoffmann, *Decline and Renewal, France since the 1930s* (1974), 3–60.

[2] On the role of soldiers, see R. O. Paxton, *Parades and Politics at Vichy* (Princeton, 1966).

with the organisation of the state were decisive for the future
character of French society.

They were far from being united in their views, and so their
influence was not obvious. Bouthillier, the inspector of finances
whom Pétain appointed minister of finance (1940–2), was
imbued with what have been called typical middle-class ideas:
a suspicion of the state and of bureaucrats, for even bureaucrats
were self-deprecating, but he was also proud of the independence his status conferred on him, and he bitterly resented
the suggestion that the inspectors of finance were tools of
capitalism. He thus had a two-sided attitude to the state: he
was opposed to the state running everything (*dirigisme*) but he
criticised the business classes for behaving like the parlements
of the *ancien régime* and he declared that capitalism was not
basic to French civilisation. He was orthodox in his financial
ideas, but he also wished to end the class struggle and to force
the capitalists to give the workers more power in the economic
field.[1] By contrast his successor Bichelonne had much less
concern for human considerations. He was regarded as the
Polytechnic's most brilliant graduate, with a 'prodigious
intelligence' but one which saw all problems in their technical
aspect. Bichelonne believed that economic planning by the
state was not just a wartime expedient, but a permanent
necessity. He has been remembered by supporters of Vichy as
a hero, and he was indeed the incarnation of the technocrat
of those days: 'effervescent, always late, always running,
always sweating, jostling people out of the way, his arms always
loaded with files, his desk covered with large piles of them,
behind which he disappeared. He was a little too keen to
show his talents to all who approached him.'[2] Pétain's ministers
of education were university professors and his ministers for
industry people with experience of industry.

Pétain's ideal was that he should give orders in a military
fashion to a few ministers, who would pass them on to their
subordinates, and so on down the chain of command. He thus
had only a small inner cabinet, and met his ministers as a body
infrequently. He had been given virtually absolute power, for it

---

[1] Yves Bouthillier, *Le Drame de Vichy* (1951), 2. 264, 274–5, 293, 303, 379.
[2] *Le Gouvernement de Vichy 1940–2* (colloque de la Fondation Nationale des
Sciences Politiques) (1972), 207.

was limited by no institutions: he was given the right to promulgate a constitution as he pleased, and he never bothered to do so. His speeches were studied as though they were holy writ and collected as the embodiment of the principles that should guide the nation.[1] His speech writers were, however, numerous: some had an Action Française background; others were Personalists or Corporatists. Pétain was moreover surrounded by a sort of royal court in which obscure men, appointed to positions in his household for accidental reasons, wielded considerable influence. The only minister who was admitted to Pétain's intimacy was Alibert, a megalomaniac professor of constitutional law who was put in charge of justice, and who ironically had no scruples about increasing the arbitrariness of the regime. But Pétain was brought into power by the politicians of the Third Republic, and Pierre Laval (his deputy prime minister, July to December 1940 and prime minister April 1942 to August 1944) carried many of the attitudes of that regime into Pétain's. Pétain hated Laval but also felt he needed him: that was another of the complex alliances of Vichy.

Laval's father had been a butcher and innkeeper with a few acres of land. He himself had all the qualities of the tight-fisted, astute Auvergnat peasantry. He got himself a job as an usher in a *lycée*, took a degree in science, determined to be more than a schoolmaster, became a lawyer, offered cheap consultations, made a name as a negotiator who could settle cases out of court and ended up as one of the most successful barristers in the country. He joined the socialist party. He acquired some fame for defending trade unionists who were prosecuted for violent agitation or strike action, proclaiming himself a 'manual lawyer' in the service of 'manual labourers'. In 1914 he was elected to parliament as the youngest socialist deputy. But when the socialists and communists split after the war, he would not choose between them and became an independent socialist. 'My socialism', he said, 'was much more a socialism of the heart than a doctrinal socialism. I was much more interested in men, their jobs, their misfortunes, their conflicts than in the digressions of the great German pontiff.' He did indeed have an uncanny skill at understanding men. He had extraordinary charm. His external appearance, it is true, was unprepossessing

[1] Maréchal Pétain, *La France nouvelle, principes de la communauté* (1941).

and suspicious: even as prime minister he still looked, it was said, like a chestnut vendor in his Sunday best. But he could quickly win sympathy and confidence in tête-à-tête conversation. He has been called one of the most persuasive and plausible people of his day. He was no orator; he could not write well; he lacked elegance; he had no gift for rousing the masses; but he was a master of individual seduction and backstage politics. He never became pompous and always kept his old socialist habits of camaraderie and *tutoiement*. For twenty-one years he was mayor of Aubervilliers where he raised to a fine art the business of doing favours: he handed people who came to his political surgery their letters of recommendation at once, so that they could post them themselves. He bought up two newspapers and a radio station to support him and turned them into profitable enterprises as well. He bought a 300-acre farm in Normandy and made it pay; he acquired the château of his native village, exploited the mineral spring in it and got all the railways to use his bottled water. He became a rich man but kept his simple habits. He had no taste for night life; he went to bed at nine; his wife who spent most of her time at home had the reputation of having only one dress. Laval was one of the few politicians of this period not to be smeared by financial scandal. He had no idealism, but it is perhaps too much to say that he was moved simply by ambition, for there was a strong element of self-defence in his search for power. He never dreamt of becoming a dictator. He knew his limitations and his qualities too well. He was no intellectual. He was guided by his native wit and he confirmed his hunches by consulting an astrologer.

Laval had no illusions about France either. His crime to his countrymen, a generation later, was his pessimism. 'We shall always be thirty-eight to forty millions', he said, 'compared with (Germany's) sixty to seventy millions, and we have a common frontier. Do you know the Arab proverb: If you cannot kill your enemy, give him your daughter in marriage?' His character made it impossible for him to place faith in the League of Nations: he preferred individual bargains with nations. He thought he could apply his skill at personal negotiation to international diplomacy. He had no scruples about dealing with dictators, for he considered that democracy was out of date. 'We are paying today', he declared, 'for the fetishism which chained us to democracy and delivered us to the worst excesses of capitalism, while around us Europe was forging without us a new world inspired by new principles.' Bolshevism was the great danger to him, Russia the main threat to France, and Germany the best safeguard against it. He feared England as a traditional enemy. He was willing to collaborate with Germany, to remodel the French constitution on fascist lines, because otherwise Germany would force a much more unpalatable domination on France. He did not believe that Hitler intended to crush France. Whatever happened, France would inevitably have, because of its sheer size, an important part in a European federation. He believed he could play off Germany and Italy to his own advantage. But he destroyed what popularity he had by saying too bluntly, 'I desire the victory of Germany'.

Laval's defenders have hailed him as a forerunner of Franco-German co-operation and a United Europe. They quote his statement to the American ambassador: 'My policy is founded on reconciliation with Germany. Without this reconciliation I can see no hope of peace, whether for Europe, France or even the world. I am certain that the Germans will be victorious but, even if they were to be defeated, my policy towards them will be the same, because it is the only one which is in the interests of ultimate peace.' His view of Europe had much in common with de Gaulle's, except that he did not wish it to extend to the Urals, for he hated Russia, while on the other hand he was always very favourable to the United States. The trouble with Laval however was that he was too clever, or too simple. He admitted: 'I have always had simple ideas in politics.' He misjudged Hitler and failed to see that co-operation with him on equal terms was impossible. He disregarded the warnings of his wife (who was Jewish) that agreements with Hitler were not worth the paper they were written on. He ended up an intriguer who was duped; a representative of the Third Republic's skill at compromise (a significantly ambiguous word) who carried it to disastrous extremes.[1]

[1] Geoffrey Warner, *Pierre Laval and the Eclipse of France* (1968); Hubert Cole, *Laval, a Biography* (1963); Alfred Mallet, *Pierre Laval* (2 vols., 1955); Georges Saint-Bonnet, *Pierre Laval, Homme d'état* (1931); Maurice Privat, *Pierre Laval* (1931).

Pétain protested that what Laval lacked was 'spiritual values'. This summarises the ambiguity of the Vichy regime. It was an attempt to raise the country's moral level, but never was morality more controversial. It will be a long time before historians are able to disentangle the many different levels of consciousness at which people behaved in these years. The aspects of character brought out by the strains of war and occupation gave life the appearance of being lived under bright stage lights, both distorting normality and revealing its frailty, enabling people to shut out from their vision what they preferred not to know. The Vichy regime has been called the triumph of the *ratés*, the failures, and the revenge of the minorities. It is true that it brought to power many of the right-wing groups that had been excluded from the Third Republic, and that a surprisingly large number of second-rate and dubious people suddenly came into prominence. But this happens with most regimes that follow predecessors who abdicate or collapse. The Bonapartists likewise appeared to be nonentities, vastly inferior in culture and status to the Orleanists they replaced, but the Orleanists had originally been upstart journalists and professors when they seized power. The originality of the Vichy regime was that it was supported not only by failures, but also by some very successful people. The evicted politicians of the Third Republic were replaced partly by men who had hitherto kept out of politics, but who had managed important sectors of the economy or of government. The regime revealed the contradiction that had existed in the Third Republic between the façade of authority and the realities of power behind it. 1940 was one of those revolutions (1848 was another) when the sudden disappearance of a government has the same effect as clothes being torn off a person, revealing in nakedness all the muscles, blemishes, scars and eccentricities that are normally concealed. That is why it cannot be considered an unfortunate lapse, a gap in history, best forgotten.

The political theory of the Vichy regime was thus many-sided and even more at variance with its practice than is usual. To talk about the regime as a coherent entity is misleading. However, beneath the variety, there does seem to have been a common search to 'rediscover the mission' of France, to find its 'true identity'. Christianity, first of all, was considered

an essential part of this. In these four years, the Catholic part
of the nation was reintegrated into it, after over a century of
persecution. This took place, significantly, not only as a result
of the policy of the Vichy government, but also in the Resistance movement, in which practising Christians played a role
side by side with the communists. After the liberation, the
Catholics were at last able to share power on equal terms with
other parties. The Vichy regime ended the prohibition against
religious orders; church property seized in 1905 and still
unsold was restored to the Church; subsidies were given to
church schools and optional religious instruction allowed in
state ones. The government made the Catholic ideal of the
large, hierarchical family its own; it limited divorce; it greatly
increased family allowances, and encouraged mothers to
remain in the home. It was significant that Pétain, who was
himself childless and married to a divorcée, should have led
this campaign, which resembled a confession of guilt and a
renunciation of the individualist values of the Third Republic.
This did not express simply an ephemeral mood. Despite all the
anxiety caused by the war, it was in this period that the French
birth-rate suddenly began rising, and the new attitude to
children was maintained in the Fourth Republic. The Church
gave Pétain its blessing and support, but there was no widespread religious revival, for this altered behaviour was not
specifically religious in origin. The Church was soon disillusioned by the regime when it saw that Pétain had other
allies who were barely compatible with itself. Its harmonious
relations with him were damaged by his persecution of the
Jews, though there were those who defended anti-Semitism
as being in the tradition of Christianity.[1]

The ambiguous relations with the Church illustrated what
varied interpretations were placed on morality. There was
constant talk about the need to strengthen morals. The firmly
established belief in education was not weakened. However,
because the Third Republic's schools had claimed to be
creating a new kind of citizen, they were blamed for all the
disasters that had befallen the country. The Vichy regime,
nevertheless, saw the answer only in more education. It

[1] Mgr Guerry, *L'Église en France sous l'occupation* (1947); Jacques Duquesne,
*Les Catholiques français sous l'occupation* (1966).

attacked 'easy-going' teaching methods, which assumed that
children were naturally good and needed simply to be left to
grow with the minimum of constraint. It argued that such an
attitude left most people without a clear purpose in life, and
certainly without a moral one, and that was why France had
collapsed in 1940. It wanted discipline to be instilled as an
end in itself, and patriotism to be taught without reservations.
The family, rather than the individual, should be the basic
unit in society, so in the schools it wanted the cultivation no
longer of individual critical powers but of the team spirit:
'Learn to work together, to think together, to play your
games together,' said Pétain. 'Bookish learning' was discredited, as was the ideal of education as an impartial search
for truth: 'Life is not neutral: it requires one to take sides
boldly,' declared the Marshal. However, since he was deeply
suspicious of the state's teachers, who had the reputation
of being impious and rebellious, he sought to create the new
moral generation not so much in the schools, which were vexed
with controls rather than developed, but in independent youth
organisations. His policy was in some ways a development of
tendencies in Catholic education, stressing character training
above scholarship. Youth movements were given a large
amount of encouragement, but because the old-established
ones were unwilling to lose their identity, they were allowed to
survive and no unified moral doctrine was preached throughout
all of them. The nearest the regime came to establishing an
original youth organisation of its own was its Chantiers de la
Jeunesse, a civilian replacement for military service. Here young
men of twenty-one spent eight months partly in forestry work
(producing much-needed fuel) and partly attending classes on
morals and history, based on Action Française textbooks. It is
unlikely that this had any effect in so far as indoctrination
was concerned; but the stress on physical effort and on sport did.
Sport, as has been seen, expanded enormously during this war
and its development as a mass activity for children dates more
from Vichy than from the Third Republic. Sport, of course,
did not make the French either more moral, or more Christian.
The new generation, as a whole, was not affected by this
proselytising, any more than it was subdued by the discipline.
To control the rebelliousness of youth, or as one participant

in the effort put it, to end the war between the family and the school, was a very ambitious aim. Even the schools for training leaders (*écoles de cadres*) evolved along different lines, showing how consensus was a vain dream.[1] Pétain did not try to establish a totalitarian state. He was not a fascist. There were fascists who supported his régime, but they were not given important positions of power, except on the propaganda side. The fascists were to be found in Paris much more than in Vichy. Their violently phrased newspapers gave the regime a veneer of fascist verbiage, but the reality was different. Pétain was opposed to the extension of the power of the state. He condemned socialism and liberalism equally. He had a certain admiration for Salazar, but he was too much of a French peasant to be interested in copying foreign models. The political and economic doctrine which enjoyed greatest favour under his government was corporatism. This was an adaptation of the Social Catholic ideas of La Tour du Pin[2] which sought to combine social justice with the preservation of hierarchy, to keep capitalism but to get rid of ruinous competition, to replace both the class struggle and state intervention by self-governing professional and regional corporations.[3] Corporatism was in some ways a new form of solidarism,[4] and like it an attempt to avoid the dilemmas of modern life. There were people who stressed the traditionalist aspects of corporatism, and thought it meant the revival of the medieval corporations. Pétain indeed promised to restore the provinces of the *ancien régime*. But though a commission was appointed, under the historian Lucien Romier, to prepare a law on the subject, nothing was in fact done.[5] The nearest Pétain came to implementing corporatism in anything like its full sense was in agriculture, where it was shown that it was much more subtle than simple reaction. The Peasant Charter organised the rural population into 30,000 local syndicates, united them

---

[1] J. Hervet, *Les Chantiers de la jeunesse* (1962); Janine Bourdin, 'L'École de cadres d'Uriage', *Revue française de science politique* (Dec. 1959), 1029–45; on the educational policy, see the forthcoming work of W. D. Halls and J. Long's Oxford thesis.

[2] Marquis de la Tour du Pin, *Vers un ordre social chrétien* (1907).

[3] M. H. Elbow, *French Corporatist Theory 1789–1948* (New York, 1953).

[4] See vol. 1, chapter 21.

[5] Pierre Barral, 'Idéal et pratique du régionalisme dans le régime de Vichy', *Revue française de science politique* (Oct. 1974), 911–39.

into a hierarchy of regional and national institutions and so for the first time gave the peasants a chance to speak with one voice. It forced the peasants to produce leaders from within their own ranks and these leaders were to survive into the Fourth Republic, when the peasant pressure group was as a result far more powerful. The corporation was supposed to enable the peasants to manage their own affairs, to regulate production and sales. In the eyes of Louis Salleron, the principal theorist behind this reform, the corporation was both an attack against individualism and a liberation from state power. In practice, however, the state appointed the leaders and used the corporation as an instrument for the implementation of its own policies.[1] The results were thus confused: the tendency towards state control was accentuated; the traditional cry of 'back to the land' was given official patronage and the maintenance of a large peasant population remained a strong ideal; but the peasant corporation leaders evolved in the course of these years and by 1944 were talking about combining the preservation of peasant values with modernisation and higher productivity.[2]

The introduction of corporatism into industry likewise both strengthened traditional forces and opened up new possibilities. An attempt was made to save the artisans from extinction by industrialisation. The old Compagnonage was revived. Industry in general was required to organise itself into groups, so that each branch of it could allocate raw materials amongst its members and manage its own affairs. Eventually 321 *comités d'organisation* were set up (about ten times as many as had been intended, for particularism proved to be strong). To a certain extent this meant that the cartels and trade associations that had developed before the war were now generalised, so what was established was not so much self-government, but government by big business, for it was the large firms which dominated the committees. But there were civil servants (like Laroque, a councillor of state specialising in industrial relations) who thought big business employers were

---

[1] Louis Salleron, *Naissance de l'état corporatif. Dix ans de syndicalisme paysan* (1942).
[2] G. Wright, *Rural Revolution in France* (Stanford, 1964), chapter 5; André Bellesort *et al.*, *France 1941: la révolution nationale constructive. Un bilan et un programme* (1941).

unfit to be given such a large share in managing the economy; and the government commissioners who sat on each of these committees used their very considerable powers to the extent that they were accused of autocracy. Here too, therefore, supposedly autonomous institutions were turned into instruments of state control. The hostility of the smaller firms to this was exacerbated by the policy of allocating raw materials in proportion to the size of firms in 1938, so calling a permanent halt to competition or expansion. In 1942, however, Bichelonne changed this rule and created a new criterion, that allocations should be in accordance with a factory's productive efficiency and the quality of its work. This did not always change things, but it did encourage the growth of a new concern with productivity among the smaller employers. Planning took on far more sophisticated forms than in the Third Republic. All firms were required to send in monthly statistics, and to reply to questionnaires asking between 150 and 320 different facts. Punch card machines were installed in a central Paris office to process this information; general production plans were made by industries, standardising and rationalising output (shoes, for example, were to be made in only thirty-seven types, and there was an effort to improve the distribution system for them). A Ten-Year Plan for National Equipment was drawn up by François Lehideux (Renault's nephew and sometime managing director), who was minister of industrial production. The result of this was to stimulate the growth of several new kinds of technocrats. The officials of the old trade associations used to run small offices with tiny staffs. Now they multiplied, acquired far greater importance, and that was the basis of their great power after the war. The state, for its part, increased the number of civil servants at a faster rate than ever before. It sent out commissioners and inspectors to control the activities of business. At first industrialists were hostile to them, rejecting all idea of state control, and speaking contemptuously of the 'insolent and ignorant excise officers' who poked their noses into their affairs. But in time these were replaced by 'distinguished and educated gentlemen' whose inspection of the books could be helpful, and who were often relied on for advice, not only in interpreting regulations but also in improving management. This experience of close state supervision (made necessary by war rationing and price controls) did not win businessmen over to *dirigisme*, which remained a bogy, but it did show them that the state could be used to mitigate the worst horrors of competition. Employers saw that the men in the ministry had a lot in common with them, particularly as it was increasingly the same men who moved in and out of jobs in the public and private sectors indiscriminately. It was on the basis of the mutual confidence that was gradually built up in this way that the planning of the post-war period was developed.

The problem of the relation between employers and workers was, however, not solved, and this was the weakest point in the Vichy economic system. Corporations in theory should have had representatives of workers and managers on the committees that ran them, but the trade unions were virtually abolished, because contaminated by socialism. *Autogestion* (which was one of the ideals of the regime) was a farce and the 'mixed social committees' which replaced the unions were forbidden to discuss wages. The authoritarianism of big business was thus even reinforced. It was no accident that the vast majority of employers sided with the Vichy regime and in the Fourth Republic (for hardly any of them were purged as collaborators) they resumed open battle with the workers. But a new generation of employers, the *Jeunes Patrons*, made their appearance, discontented with the domination of large firms, and willing to buy co-operation from their workers by higher wages, improved conditions and more humane treatment.[1]

Though there were thus important ways in which trends of the inter-war years were developed under Pétain, to be continued in due course by the republics which followed, the regime was a failure because it did not remain faithful to its aim of uniting the nation. In 1940 it had quite exceptionally wide support. But its doctrines involved the eradication of so many elements of French society, which it condemned as pernicious, that its base grew narrower and narrower. The politicians

[1] Paul Leroy, *L'Industrie de la chaussure: économie libérale, économie dirigée* (Nancy thesis, 1943), one of the best descriptions of the detailed working of a *comité d'organisation* by a shoe manufacturer; H. W. Ehrmann, *Organised Business in France* (Princeton, 1957), 58–100; Bernard Mottez, *Systèmes de salaire et politique patronales. Essai sur l'évolution des pratiques et des idéologies patronales* (1966); E. Dussauze, *L'État et les ententes industrielles* (Paris thesis, 1938).

were the first victims. There was widespread disillusionment with them. But when they were put on trial as criminals, they were turned into martyrs. The purge of local councillors hurt the pride of a large number of notables. Pétain's declared aim of replacing hierarchies of birth and wealth by one based on 'merit'—an élite drawn from all classes—was never given the institutional embodiment he promised: the provincial assemblies never materialised; and his own absolutism was maintained. The Jews were quickly singled out as enemies, long before the Germans expressed any desire that the 'final solution' should be applied to France. The Jews were, however, slow to react, because official French anti-Semitism, as introduced by the law of 3 October 1940, simply excluded them from government service, and exempted Jewish war veterans from these discriminatory measures. A sort of apartheid system was envisaged, by which the Jews, distinguished by a yellow star on their clothes, should form an autonomous corporation or ghetto. It was only gradually, as increasingly fanatical racists were placed in charge of Jewish affairs, and only in 1942, when systematic deportation began, that the French Jews were doomed to extermination.[1] In fact most of those deported (about 65,000) were foreigners: only about 6,000 French Jews went to the German concentration camps; about half of these never returned; about 20,000 were interned in French concentration camps. Though various ministers and officials claimed that they tried to minimise the effects of this organised brutality, and though Frenchmen did indeed suffer less from it than other Europeans, the damage it did to the plausibility of the regime was far greater than the cheap popularity it attracted. Equally futile was the regime's war against the freemasons, to whom it attributed absurd machiavellian intentions and vastly exaggerated power.[2] Most dangerous of all was its persecution of communists, which nullified any pretence that it was well disposed to the workers. All this created too many enemies, too many Frenchmen who were not recognised as such.

[1] Xavier Vallat, *Le Nez de Cléopâtre* (1957). For the way the anti-Semitic policy affected one Jewish girl, see Georgette Elgey, *La Fenêtre ouverte* (1973), an outstanding piece of autobiographical writing.

[2] See the vast number of publications on freemasonry in this period.

These atrocities might have been condoned if the country as a whole had benefited from collaboration with Germany. Pétain honestly believed that by making an armistice, he was saving his countrymen from a much worse fate: the preservation of human life was his aim in 1940 as it had been at the battle of Verdun in 1916. But Paul Reynaud, who riposted that the Germany they had to deal with was led not by William II but by 'Genghis Khan', was proved to be right in his argument that France would simply be manipulated by its conquerors. The advantages of the armistice were indeed short-lived. Germany exacted, under the euphemism of 'occupation costs', between a fifth and a third of France's national income. Virtually one-half of public expenditure went to Germany each year in this form. In addition, about 40 per cent of industrial production went to Germany; over half the French labour force was employed on German contracts. Between 1,300,000 and 1,400,000 French workers were transported to Germany to work in factories there, so that one-tenth of the total active labour force in Germany was French. The effect on the French economy was, first, a trebling of the paper money; secondly, a great decline in productivity (partly from lack of labour and raw materials, but partly also from resistance by French workers to German orders); and thirdly a fall of one-third in food consumption. France, as it turned out, was hungrier and colder than any other country involved in this war.[1] Pétain did not dupe his enemy.

But collaboration with Germany had wider implications. There were those who believed that France could no longer survive as an independent nation, that it must make common cause with the victorious Reich and so win for itself a privileged position in a united Europe, that peace was unattainable except by European unity—the League of Nations having failed so miserably—and that Germany was offering Europe a chance not only of unity but also of prosperity. Many collaborationists saw themselves as men of advanced, progressive ideas, as idealistic visionaries, or alternatively as realists accepting the inevitable. The collaborationists came from all parties: their attitude was a matter of temperament,

[1] Alan S. Milward, *The New Order and the French Economy* (Oxford, 1970), 63, 272–88.

an indication of the quality of their optimism. Some were seeking revenge for the lack of recognition they had suffered under the Third Republic; some rejoiced in the collapse of France because they thought that only from death could it be resurrected (as Drieu La Rochelle saw it); some were fanatics to whom the violence of Nazism was intoxicating; some were inspired by a hatred of Jews and of communists. There were groups, parties and militias which made collaboration an organised activity, but these were numerically insignificant. Collaboration was more widespread in a more subtle way, in daily life. Not infrequently it could be combined with resistance.[1] At the liberation, over 100,000 were gaoled for collaborating. There were rumours that as many were killed in private revenge by men of the Resistance who had suffered at the hands of the collaborationists, though only 4,500 murders of this kind seem to be authenticated.[2] The division of France into collaborators and resisters made the liberation, in part, also a civil war. The bitterness that these divisions bequeathed took a whole generation to lose its sharpness. It is still not possible to discuss this period in France with total equanimity.

If the Germans had won the war, the collaboration would now be presented as a sign of the impending collapse of French patriotism. This would be in keeping with the normal tendency to give history the appearance of a great river, always flowing in one direction. The Second World War certainly brought home to more Frenchmen what some of them already began to realise in the First World War, that their national independence was no longer viable in the old way. But it was very difficult to adjust mentally to the implications of this, and people came to accept the different implications at different speeds. That had been the cause of the failure of inter-war diplomacy. There had been men like Briand who saw the solution in European reconciliation. He had shown early on in his career that he was not simply a verbose idealist: in the

[1] Michèle Cotta, *La Collaboration 1940–1944* (1964).
[2] Marcel Ophuls, *Le Chagrin et la pitié* (film, 1972), and the analysis of it by Stanley Hoffmann, op. cit. 45–60; Peter Novick, *The Resistance versus Vichy* (New York, 1968); Louis Noguères, *Histoire de la Résistance* (1967); S. Hawes and R. White, *Resistance in Europe 1939–45* (1957); Robert Aron, *Histoire de l'Épuration* (1967); H. Michel, *Bibliographie critique de la Résistance* (1964); and the important forthcoming work of H. R. Kedward on the Resistance.

dispute over the separation of Church and state, he had carried a policy which had not ended the deep animosities but which had been decisive in enabling the two parties to live henceforth with increasing tolerance of their differences. In 1929 Briand had proposed a European federation, with economic co-operation as a first stage. Both Tardieu and Herriot had talked about establishing an international army. But the desire to extract reparations from Germany, the fear of German rearmament, the apparently conflicting interests and unreliability of allies and the precariousness of the balance of power diplomacy, had confirmed traditional attitudes. The feeling remained that France must use its power—or what was left of it—to get its way. But people were becoming increasingly unsure whether they wished to fight simply for prestige. The divisions during the Vichy regime reflected the country's tension between patriotism and despair.[1]

Inevitably this bred anger, which was indeed the emotion most prominent at the end of this period. The history of anger has yet to be written. The Resistance movement provides a good angle from which it may be approached. Roderick Kedward has shown how anger was one of the major factors that lay at its roots. The angriest people of all now were the communists, who regarded Vichy as the revenge of the rich for the Popular Front, and as an intensification of the class war: they were just as angry with the government as with Germany. Journalists who were censored, teachers who resented aid to the rival church schools, freemasons and Jews who were persecuted, all had immediate cause to be angry, but what is notable is that very frequently, it was often only when they became personally involved that their anger led to action. Anger needed to be shared to express itself, and it became more powerful when it was.[2] Anger was the stimulus behind the desire for a new order, but also the obstacle to seeing clearly the implications of the survival and decay of the principle of gerontocracy.

[1] For a guide to inter-war diplomacy, with an up-to-date bibliography, see J. Neré, *The Foreign Policy of France from 1914 to 1945* (1975, French edition 1974).
[2] H. R. Kedward, 'Anger in the Resistance' (unpublished paper).

# 23. Hypocrisy

FRANCE is supposed to be a country where the intellectual enjoys great prestige and influence. This is true in so far as a large number of people like to think of themselves as intellectuals. A sample survey in the 1950s revealed that 30 per cent of insurance clerks considered themselves as belonging to the intellectual class; and even 20 per cent of typists in another survey described themselves in the same way. This is partly a relic of the age when everybody with a university or school diploma regarded himself as being raised above the masses by that very fact; this is what the Russians meant when they invented the word *intelligentsia* in the 1860s. The definition that every person whose work involves more mental than physical labour is an intellectual was adopted by the International Confederation of Intellectual Workers at their fifth congress in 1927, and following that the French census of 1954 counted 1,100,000 people as intellectuals, including in this category army officers, priests, lawyers, doctors, engineers, teachers and booksellers. The number would have been even larger if students were added. The fact that bodies like the Music Hall Singers' Trade Union and the Association of Stenotypists demanded to be classified in this way shows that the term has won approval beyond literary circles. It is not just that it enables marginal groups to avoid the dilemma of admitting that they are workers, or that they are bourgeois; nor that education gives status. Literature has been highly respected in France as an essential national activity. Literary men have been called to high public office simply because of the prestige their books have given them. Writers moreover have taken to debating publicly about almost every aspect of human affairs, so that they have constituted themselves into a kind of national consultative council, self-appointed, but taken almost as seriously by the press as they take themselves.

The term 'intellectual' has been popular perhaps also because it has been both a term of abuse and a source of pride.

An intellectual was sometimes defined as a person with highly developed critical faculties. He was associated therefore with the left. This was the case at the end of the nineteenth century, when the word was first adopted in France. The literary supporters of Dreyfus, who signed a manifesto in his favour, were heralded as 'the intellectuals' by Clemenceau. Conservatives replied by attacking them as the pretentious, half-baked inhabitants of libraries and laboratories who claimed to be supermen, who sought to raise writers and professors into a new noble caste, proud that they did not think like ordinary men. Cleverness, the intellectuals were told by those on the right, was not everything and certainly not as important as practical experience, character, judgement or will-power. Nevertheless the right wing produced its own intellectuals also. In 1913 Agathon's inquiry at the Sorbonne showed that the students there were attaching themselves to ideals of chivalry and chauvinism which were just as critical of the *status quo* as those of the left.[1] The Camelots du Roi (founded in 1908 to demonstrate, often with violence, in favour of a monarchical restoration) were mainly students, and between the wars the right-wing Action Française was described as 'the party of intelligence', opposing that of the professors. The French Academy and many learned societies were bastions of conservatism and in 1935 Henri Massis was able to collect 850 signatures from intellectuals of the right approving Mussolini's invasion of Abyssinia. The Vichy regime had the support of many intellectuals. It was only because these men were discredited by collaboration with the Germans, and disappeared into obscurity, that, after 1945, intellectuals appeared to be predominantly left wing. But this was a short-lived illusion. The Semaines des écrivains catholiques (an annual congress) now renamed itself the Semaines des intellectuels catholiques. By 1968 it was clear that university professors were not predominantly left-wing—that was a reputation which a vocal and distinguished minority in the faculties of letters and science gave them; but medicine and law were mainly conservative. It is true that attacks on intellectuals came most powerfully from the right— the Poujade movement of small shopkeepers in the 1950s was particularly hostile to them—but in 1956 a member of the

[1] Agathon, *Les Jeunes Gens d'aujourd'hui* (1913).

socialist party could still complain that even among socialists 'there is no more opprobrious epithet than that of intellectual'.

Intellectuals may, paradoxically, perhaps be distinguished less by their intellectual opinions than by their emotional attitudes. They often described themselves as people whose primary concern was with truth and with knowledge, who regarded thought as the most superior form of activity, and who held disinterestedness, originality and critical power in the highest esteem. But precisely because they have been so critical, they have not spared themselves, and every one of these definitions has been attacked by them. They have been in disagreement amongst themselves on almost every subject. However, they have, despite their search for originality, generally shared three characteristics of personality. They have been above all self-conscious, and life for them has had two parts, experience and meditation on experience, with the latter usually taking more time than the former; almost invariably this has meant that they have been personally ill at ease in the world. Secondly, they have been people who have been unable to tolerate the contradictions of life: they have devoted themselves to resolving contradictions and to reducing complexity into simplifications. They have been inventors and adepts of systems and formulae. But they have been more than just followers of a religion or a creed, because, thirdly, they have not normally been concerned simply with their own salvation or welfare, and they have sought solutions of universal scope, and of an abstract nature, applicable to all men. They were not necessarily highly educated, or academics; on the contrary the autodidact, the party militant, the book-loving artisan, the village pharmacist were much more typical examples of rank-and-file intellectuals. Intellectuals were essentially abnormal in their attitudes. Until the twentieth century thinking was regarded as a painful and even dangerous activity and a *Treatise on Nutrition* in 1907 still argued that the energy of the brain had no connection with the other energies developed by the body: it was only later that the processes by which the blood circulated in the brain and oxygen was used by it were established.[1] Intellectuals were

[1] Aron Bacicurinschi, *Contribution à l'étude de l'alimentation des intellectuels* (Paris medical thesis, 1936).

eccentrics, who suffered a special kind of tension as individuals in society. The irony of their situation was that the solutions they proposed often only reinforced the contradictions of which they felt themselves to be the victims. This is what emerged with particular force in the inter-war period.[1]

The idea that intellectuals have been increasingly influential has gained currency mainly through frequent repetition, rather than as a result of any careful analysis of their power. This book has attempted to show that their power manifested itself mainly in the way people looked at the world's problems. The intellectuals raised disagreements on to the abstract plane of principle and so consolidated differing opinions, formulated issues and categorised people in ways which they might not have chosen for themselves and which were not necessarily accurate. In particular, they interpreted history and in doing so greatly simplified it. It is impossible to study the past without being influenced by their interpretations, which have been like rose-coloured spectacles placed on every schoolboy's nose. Their simplications have become a part of national culture; they continue to influence politics; and they are therefore themselves an important part of history. Inevitably, the intellectuals attributed to themselves great influence on the course of events, but in a way that is considerably exaggerated. French history and French life therefore have to be studied on two levels; what happened and what people thought was happening were often very different. The explanation of change in terms of the relatively small set of ideas that interested most intellectuals at any particular time has meant that large segments of life have been ignored as trivial or vulgar, simply because they could not be fitted into the common thought patterns of intellectuals. This book has tried to show that education, which was one of the main ways intellectuals exercised their influence, met with much resistance despite the material benefits it could confer, and that traditional mentalities survived to counterbalance the attitudes that the schools propagated. There was much behaviour intellectuals were unable to alter, or even to touch.

[1] 'Les Intellectuels dans la société française contemporaine', special issue of the *Revue française de science politique* (Dec. 1959). Cf. Richard Hofstadter, *Anti-Intellectualism in American Life* (1962), and R. Pipes, *The Russian Intelligentsia* (Columbia U.P., 1961).

Intellectuals were therefore in an ambiguous situation, and that is perhaps why their view of themselves alternated so dramatically between arrogance and despair. On the one hand, they sometimes claimed to be the new spiritual leaders of the world, replacing the clergy. It has been seen how the 'genius' emerged in the early nineteenth century, challenging traditional hierarchies, seeing himself as destined to be the guide of the masses.[1] Intelligence, it was claimed, gave those who were gifted with it a mission of leadership and the rights of an élite. As one author said in 1855, those who expressed the results of thought—writers most notably—were not 'jugglers with words', but 'flagellators of vice and glorifiers of virtue'. They had to assert themselves as the judges of mankind, and not tolerate being looked on as simply 'literary clowns who are paid to facilitate the digestion'. The trouble was that they were often greedy; they sought reward in easy money rather than in high respect, and debased themselves by writing about sex and crime ('brothel and prison literature').[2] Balzac said that a writer was a prince because he shaped the world; Vigny declared that intellectual deeds are the only great deeds and dreamt of an aristocracy of the intelligence. This was not an exclusively French phenomenon: Carlyle, for example, wrote of the Hero as Man of Letters and (for a time) thought of him as 'our most important modern person'. But the man of letters has become an obsolete category in England, where intellectuals have generally been much more self-effacing. In France, by contrast, the political regime was dubbed in 1927 the *republic of professors*, and the ruling radical party was considered the representative of the 'provincial idealist' who maintained the superiority of spiritual over material values.[3] Education was one of the Third Republic's main obsessions. So French intellectuals have been distinguished by close association with political power. It has frequently been pointed out how large a number of graduates of the École Normale have played a central role in politics. But, at the same time, the intellectuals had much to complain about on the subject of the way they were treated. The U.S.A.,

[1] Volume 1, chapter 16, 'The Genius in Politics'.
[2] Alexandre Weill, *L'Homme de lettres* (1855), 68; cf. Jules Brisson, *De l'influence de l'homme de lettres sur la société* (1862).
[3] Albert Thibaudet, *La République des professeurs* (1927).

supposedly anti-intellectual, was far more generous financially to its authors than France was.[1] Very few French writers were able to live off their books, let alone become rich. The rewards of authorship were always very modest, and remain so, apart from a few exceptions.[2] So, as well as calling themselves demi-gods, intellectuals also lamented that they were a proletariat.

In the mid-nineteenth century, theirs was a proletariat of *bacheliers* (secondary-school leavers); in the twentieth century it was a proletariat of university graduates, who were unable to find jobs to match their exceptional qualifications. Intelligence alone was not enough to obtain employment in a society controlled by family networks. The problem of the overproduction of intellectuals arose very early, but it developed in a cyclical rather than in a gradual way. The first crisis occurred between 1840 and 1870, when the number of secondary-school graduates doubled: it was no accident that the republican party of the Second Empire was swollen by so many frustrated young men. In the Third Republic, the expansion of education was roughly matched by an expansion of career opportunities in the civil service and commerce. But between 1900 and 1939, the number of students in the faculties of letters increased sixfold. This was a symptom of prosperity (in that these were largely the children of well-to-do parents), but also a cause of hardship, for there was no way that all these lovers of literature could put their energies to satisfying use. The number of candidates for posts as teachers of literature rose from 837 in 1922 to 2,067 in 1935, for a roughly constant 180 vacancies a year.[3] In the inter-war years unemployment became a problem, however, not just for students of the arts, but for professional people in general.[4] These years were ones of unprecedented intellectual ferment not only because there were more potential intellectuals than ever before, but also because

[1] Robert Lévy, *Le Mécènat et l'organisation du crédit intellectuel* (1924) complains that only 0·5 per cent of the 1923 French budget was spent on subsidising the arts in all their forms.

[2] Édouard Gaède, 'L'Écrivain et la société'. Unpublished report on an inquiry into the opinions of over 300 living authors (2 vols., University of Nice, 1972).

[3] Ronald Weil, *Le Chômage de la jeunesse intellectuelle diplômée* (Paris law thesis 1937), 119.

[4] Victor Rousset, *La Condition économique et sociale des travailleurs intellectuels* (Paris law thesis, 1934).

the problem of the place of the intellectual in society presented itself as an urgent one in practical terms. In 1914 the intellectuals were described as men who aroused jealousy or hostility, in reaction against their arrogance and their claim to be more knowledgeable than their fellows, but it was pointed out that they were men who were also constantly humiliated by their own inadequacies. They were themselves among the victims of the war against respect that they waged; they were too unsure of themselves to act decisively; and though they were attracted by the company of other intellectuals, it was ideas, rather than real friendship, that held them together: they were unsociable, lonely people.[1] The interest of the interwar years is that intellectuals now tried to escape from this situation.

A sociologist has laid it down as a general rule that the influence of intellectuals depends on the attitudes of people towards intellectual culture.[2] This is either a tautology or not wholly true. It is possible for intellectuals to be influential without the masses being aware of their influence, and without them approving of what the intellectuals stand for. The same sociologist believes that the influence of intellectuals increases with the spread of education. This is likewise too simple, for education is concerned not only with the spread of knowledge, but also with the classification of people (creating both failures and an élite) and with separating them into different kinds of specialists, who can be more conscious of what divides than what unites them. The notion that education encourages dedication to ideas, rather than to material goals, was an illusion only intellectuals suffered from. The first step in any investigation of the influence of intellectuals must be of the varieties of intellectuals, and of the way they influence each other, before they can influence others. Intellectualism (this book has argued[3]) is closely linked with individualism. If intellectuals are self-conscious people, the growth of self-awareness is the basis of their importance. Literature seems to have been a principal factor in the development of self-awareness. Literature in this

---

[1] A. Cartault, *L'Intellectuel: étude psychologique et morale* (1914), 249, 300, 310.
[2] Edward Shils, *The Intellectuals and the Powers and other essays* (Chicago 1972), 155.
[3] Chapter 16 on Individualism.

period was concerned above all with revealing the nature of man and with seeking ways by which he could express his individuality. Intellectuals have therefore been the great enemies of hypocrisy, if by hypocrisy is understood not only the pretence to virtue, but the all-pervading need to play a role. Intellectuals rebelled against the tolerance of contradictions and of compromises that role-playing involved.[1] They made an issue of the difficulties of living. They therefore confirmed themselves as outsiders, and that greatly limited their influence. They influenced each other most of all.

A heretic breed of intellectual developed in the form of technocrats and technicians. These men relegated principle to a secondary place and raised the efficient management of society into a sufficient activity. By concentrating on action, they won a directing position in both the political and economic spheres. The distinction between intellectuals and technocrats was a subtle one; the two were not always mutually exclusive. Just as the intellectual rejected the narrow specialisation of the academic, so the technocrats aspired to the same kind of universal competence or outlook that the intellectuals claimed. Indeed the technocrats carried this eighteenth-century tradition of the *philosophes* further, for whereas the intellectuals often came to despise the practical, the technocrats claimed to be inspired by theory and to be practical at the same time. An inquiry in 1963, asking technocrats what qualities they thought made them successful, revealed that 75 per cent of them placed the major emphasis on 'general culture' and only 25 per cent on technical knowledge.[2] The intellectuals were the guardians of this general culture, even if they were often superficially, also, its most vociferous critics. The technocrats were their pupils, as were all educated men. The intellectuals therefore did indeed, in some ways, occupy a position in society similar to that of the clergy, and their jargon was popularised in the same way that lip-service was paid to Christian morality. But that did not mean that their ideas ruled the country, any more than the fact that most Frenchmen got married in church meant that Christianity ruled their lives. It was always

---

[1] Cf. André Malraux, *Antimémoires* (1967), 13.

[2] F. Bon and M. A. Burnier, *Les Nouveaux Intellectuels* (1966, new edition 1971), 106, 107 n.

even more difficult to measure the influence of intellectuals than
of priests, and that is why intellectuals could entertain illusions
about their own importance. But their position was far weaker
than that of the Catholics, because they were much more
elitist, constantly witch-hunting, refusing to recognise as one
of themselves those with whom they disagreed. Anarchy
reigned amongst them, and that was not the least of their
torments.

In the inter-war years Julien Benda, in a celebrated book,
*The Betrayal of the Intellectuals*, attacked them for abandoning
the high realms of disinterested, abstract speculation and for
descending from their ivory towers into the market-place.[1] Their
justification, he argued, came from their dedication to rational,
universal values. Once they started participating in daily
politics, they became victims of passion, they compromised their
ideals, they lost the prestige that came from maintaining that
their kingdom was not of this world. Benda was correct in his
observation of the new practical concerns of intellectuals, but he
was in a minority when he deplored this. The interest of these
years is that the intellectuals now for a time had a central
role in national life, because they sought practical solutions to
their dilemmas.

The communist party was the creation of intellectuals, and it
showed how much they could achieve, but also how far they
were from being able to win control over those who were
attracted by their ideals. By 1945 over a quarter of the electorate was voting communist. The party became the largest in
the country, overtaking the socialists in 1936.[2] But 1947 marked
the peak of its influence, and it was never able to expand beyond
this minority position, formidable though it remained. The
ultimate failure meant that for a whole generation a very
sizeable portion of the intellectuals, who were intensely
attracted to communism, were kept in permanent opposition,
with very important consequences for their status and their
own image of themselves.

[1] Julien Benda, *La Trahison des clercs* (1927).
[2] Party membership 1921 109,000; 1923 55,000; 1930 39,000; 1933 28,000;
1935 86,000; 1936 280,000; 1937–8 320,000; 1945 387,000; 1947 907,000; 1956–66
just over 400,000.

The failure was not the result of accident, or of tactical mismanagement. The communist party appealed to a wide variety of people, from almost every class. It represented the revival of the traditional French revolutionary ideal but also an abandonment of methods hitherto tried. The failure of the general strike of 1920 showed the need for alternatives and the Russian model, the only successful one in the world, was irresistible. To be a communist meant first of all to accept the leadership of Russia, to see radical change as obtainable only through a global revolutionary movement. The party remained obedient to the directives of Moscow throughout this period, because Soviet achievements were immeasurably more impressive than anything French revolutionaries had been able to do. To be a communist involved a measure of humility. In 1920, 110,000 out of the 180,000 members of the Socialist party broke away to form a separate communist party. Their decision was based on considerable ignorance about Russia. The Syndicalists, who formed a major portion of the new party, imagined that the Russian revolution had been a victory for their doctrines, because it had begun with a strike and had led to the establishment of workers' soviets. Those who negotiated the adherence to the Communist International thought that Bolshevism was not basically different from Jaurèsism, only covered with *sauce tartare*. Léon Blum protested in vain that Bolshevism was autocratic and that he would ultimately prefer France as it was than France run by a disciplined, authoritarian party, that denied both democracy and liberty. The Russians however were at first careful to show great moderation, so that joining the International appeared to involve only a minimum of obligations. These misunderstandings soon came out into the open. The 'Bolshevisation' of the party (1920–4), when dissident and anarchist elements were expelled, led to a loss of one-half of its membership. The abandonment of the tradition of the unity of the left, and the denunciation of the socialists as the prime enemy, led to the loss of half of the remaining faithful in the years following. The party thus came to be a small sect, with little influence on the country at large: nineteen out of its twenty-six deputies in 1924 were elected in the Paris region. However, this contraction enabled it to build itself up in a thoroughly original way, as a disciplined, hierarchical organisation, based on cells which had no means of influencing policy, the orders coming from a virtually self-perpetuating leadership, controlled by emissaries from Moscow. A party school at Bobigny trained the functionaries who ran the system; subsidies from Russia paid their salaries.[1] In the 1930s future leaders were sent to the International Leninist school in Moscow for a course lasting two and a half years, which completed the acceptance of Marxism as an instrument of revolution that transcended national boundaries and traditions.

The domination of Russia was not easy to achieve and in the inter-war years the rate of elimination of members of the central committees for deviations of various kinds was about 50 per cent and only one-tenth of the leading militants survived successive purges to get appointed to the committee four or more times. The long tenure of power by Maurice Thorez contrasted sharply therefore with the instability of his subordinates: his control of the party was accordingly enhanced. Thorez epitomised the originality of the communist party organiser. Whereas in all other parties parliamentary office came as the crowning of an interest in politics that began on an amateur and part-time basis, Thorez was a professional politician all his life, being appointed a local party functionary at the age of twenty-three and head of the national party at thirty-two. The party functionary's task was not to make policy in the way the political leaders of other parties had to, because communist policy was decided in Moscow, and the party's theoretical doctrine had been more or less fixed once and for all. He had no worries therefore about carrying out contradictory orders, even if they involved complete volte-face, because he recognised these as tactical manœuvres, not to be confused with the ultimate principles the party stood for, but which prudence occasionally required it to conceal or gloss over. Communists elected to parliament were bound by written undertakings they had to give in advance, to resign if called upon to do so by the party; they had to give the party a portion of their salaries; they accepted that they were responsible not to their electors but to the central committee. The communists were

[1] Annie Kriegel, *Aux origines du communisme français 1914–1920* (1964) and Robert Wohl, *French Communism in the Making 1914–1924* (Stanford, 1966) are the two excellent standard works on this early period.

not weakened therefore by the friction between the deputies and the constituencies which so hampered other parties, or by compromises other deputies got into the habit of making with their opponents. Thorez was able to remain supreme over the party members not only because he enjoyed the confidence of Moscow, but because he embodied the virtues the party admired. He was, by origin, a genuine worker, the son and grandson of miners, who had gone into the mines himself at the age of twelve; but he had come top in his primary school and, always regretting that he had not had a better education, he was an autodidact intellectual, the kind that the workers respected. He taught himself German in prison so as to be able to read Engels, Goethe and Heine in the original; he learnt not only Russian but also Latin in his efforts to become a cultivated person. He was not tormented by the problem of asserting his individuality or of differentiating himself by originality: he represented the workers' desire to achieve dignity, to overcome their sense of being inferior, to obtain more responsibility. One of the great attractions of communism was that it treated the man who joined the party as the member of an élite, destined to lead his fellows to better things. The result was, however, that the atmosphere in the party was one of comradeliness, rather than of personal friendship. Thorez was admired for his solidity, his dynamism, his oratorical and polemical skill; but it was not held against him that he was secretive, ruthless, hungry for power, unhesitating in abandoning colleagues who were guilty of deviation, however long or close their collaboration had been. The cult of personality was applied only to one leader. This meant that even if everyone else in the party could consider himself something of a political theorist—and all were expected to study Marxist theory—that status did not involve individualistic illusions. There was no room for eccentrics or anarchists. Collective action was the basic creed.

To the party leaders, abrupt changes of tactics were acceptable because, as Maurice Thorez said, their principle was that 'one cannot be tied by a formula or a resolution'; they were 'realists' who 'demand only what is possible in the conditions of each moment'.[1] The balance of idealism and

[1] M. Thorez, *Fils du Peuple* (1960 edition), 46, 128.

practicality was one of communism's major preoccupations. But the changing tactics appealed to different clienteles and the party's membership therefore constantly changed also. To appreciate the appeal, one should add to its membership figures the large numbers who passed through it, leaving disillusioned. In this period, communism was a two-faced phenomenon, presenting a frightening monolithic organisation to its opponents, but internally racked by tensions, exactly like the respectable marriages of the bourgeois society it denounced. This was partly because the relics of various national traditions remained a powerful influence within it. The communist party aimed to be a workers' party. In 1926 it claimed that only 5 per cent of its members were middle class. This was probably inaccurate: in the Limousin region, out of 3,100 members, only 600 were workers, 2,000 were peasants and 500 were small proprietors and artisans. In 1929 four-fifths of the party were said to be workers. It is certain that it obtained massive support from workers in the metal industries (who in the Seine comprised one-third of its total membership) and in state and railway employment. The party never gained many adherents in the private sector of industry as a whole. Its working-class element diminished steadily and in 1959 only 40 per cent were industrial workers.[1]

It was no accident that an increasing proportion consisted of civil servants, given the regimentation that members had to accept. But in the course of these years, a considerable variety of classes were incorporated into the party, so that communism came to mean different things in different parts of the country, beneath its apparently uniform structure. In 1934 the party did a roundabout turn, ceased to consider democratic socialism as the prime enemy and offered itself as the bulwark against fascism. It dropped its internationalism for a fiery patriotism, and claimed to be the most national of French parties, giving asylum to the middle class as well as to the workers, assuming in effect the mantle of the Jacobins. It was thus able to be the principal beneficiary of the enthusiasm engendered by the Popular Front.[2] By refusing to take

[1] M. Perrot and A. Kriegel, *Le Socialisme français et le pouvoir* (1966), 202–8.
[2] Daniel R. Brower, *The New Jacobins. The French Communist Party and the Popular Front* (Cornell U.P., 1968).

office with Blum it remained a party of opposition and was unsullied by the failure of his government. It made the reunification of the left its major objective and when that unity was achieved, it emerged as the leader of the left because it had the best organisation available, to incorporate the mass of hitherto unpolitical workers who flocked into the trade unions. Having won this hold over the workers, it spread its influence into agriculture during the Second World War. Despite the complications caused by its support for the Soviet–Nazi pact, which temporarily put it out of harmony with public opinion, it was able to make enormous gains by then taking a leading part in the Resistance, making itself the champion of patriotism as well as of the poor. Between 1937 and 1945 its membership in industrial regions rose only by about 50 per cent but by three and a half times in rural areas, so that for a short time the peasants comprised over a fifth of the communist electorate. The communists appealed to the industrial workers of the north and to the peasants of the Massif Central and the Mediterranean for rather different reasons, which were very similar to the reasons for the success of the Guesdists before the war in these contrasting situations.[1] The peasant communist was, as the Guesdist ones had been, above all heir to the traditions of the revolution of 1789. He was not interested in the subtleties of Marxism, but voted communist, paradoxically, simply to assert his independence.

There were villages like Épagny (Aisne) which in 1946 gave 60 per cent of its votes to the communists; but this was a purely theoretical protest by the rural proletariat, for in the local elections, not a single communist was put on to the municipal council, which was predominantly conservative, and the largest gentleman landowner continued as mayor without significant opposition. The way communism inherited the traditions of radicalism could be seen in the village of Saint-Pierre-Toirac (Lot) whose smallholders in 1945 abandoned radicalism for communism, but the superficiality of their change was shown a decade later when half of these new communists transferred their vote to Poujade's *small man* movement. Personal considerations could make peasants vote communist, as it could make them vote anything else. Samazan

---

[1] See vol. 1, 745–52.

(Lot-et-Garonne) elected the first peasant communist to parliament as far back as 1920: Renaud Jean, who became the party's expert on agricultural affairs, was mayor of this village, but he did not turn it into a model soviet: the co-operatives all failed, because, as he himself said, the peasants were too individualistic for such things; and the achievement he was particularly proud of, which his political position had won the village, was not only to have had a school established in it, but also to have obtained for it its own village priest.[1] In urban regions, by contrast, an important attraction of communism was that it provided every kind of social facility for its members, curing the very 'alienation' it was supposed to represent. The party's slogan was 'You have to be a communist twenty-four hours a day'. It created organisations to cater for every recreational need, to provide every form of leisure activity; it had its own newspapers and collections of books for members to read, just as the parish libraries kept the Catholics in a separate intellectual world. It not only ensured that the welfare of its members was always looked after; it provided not just clubs for them; it also held out the hope of an alternative career, for the successful militant could become a paid party functionary.

Paradoxically, therefore, communists were frequently people who were not interested in politics, and for whom membership involved abstention from discussion with their opponents. (In the rural south, it was different: communism appealed to political animals, who liked arguing, but who were not necessarily particularly interested by Marxism.) The result was that the revolutionary character of the party was somewhat deceptive. What it demanded from its members was conformity. It did not have the stimulus of youthful radicalism, because it denied that there could be such a thing as a conflict of generations: its attitude to the young was that they should be initiated into the party by a sort of apprenticeship in youth organisations, and there was no question of these challenging the orthodoxy of the leadership. A survey carried out in 1949 among the readers of *L'Humanité* showed that they had almost exactly the same possessions and habits as the readers of *France-Soir*, a popular non-communist paper: the only difference was

[1] Gordon Wright, *Rural Revolution in France* (1964), 187–208.

that the readers of *L'Humanité* were far less frequently subscribers to the telephone.[1] The high ideals of the party were
matched by a concentration on winning practical material
advantages for its members. It was concerned much more
with happiness than with liberty. In the popular mind, as
public opinion polls revealed, it was generally considered the
party which was most concerned with improving the workers'
wages (just as Gaullism was regarded as aiming above all
at the glory and economic prosperity of France).[2] The party's
supporters found in Marxism an explanation of why their
wages were low, and how their exploitation could be ended;
they found in the party the only organisation that seemed
really interested in their well-being and that offered them
comradeship and a sense of being appreciated. But their
votes were very far from being inspired by mainly materialistic
aims. Only a small minority of the communist voters were
party members. Most of these voters were expressing protest
at the established system, which meant that they retained
their sense of independence against all organisations and
institutions. Surprisingly, when questioned in the 1950s, only
14 per cent of industrial workers said that the workers were
happiest in the Soviet Union, whereas 54 per cent said they
were happiest in the U.S.A. Faith in Russia survived this, and
this assertion often went hand in hand with the statement that
the workers were slaves of capitalism in the U.S.A. Truth had
many purposes, and many faces. It required a special mentality—or rather mentalities—to vote communist. Only a
quarter of Frenchmen in the lowest income groups voted
communist at the height of the party's popularity.[3]

The position of intellectuals in a party which, on the one
hand, was so bureaucratic and, on the other, was a coalition
of such disparate elements, could not but be difficult. Yet the
party became increasingly attractive to intellectuals and the
communist temptation was an experience that a large number
of them went through. Opponents of the party have tried to
dismiss this as an essentially emotional or neurotic infatuation,

[1] Annie Kriegel, *The French Communists: Profile of a People* (Chicago, 1972), 23,
58, 172.
[2] *Les Communistes en France* (Cahiers de la Fondation Nationale des Sciences
Politiques no. 175) (1969), 270.
[3] Hadley Cantril, *The Politics of Despair* (New York, 1958), 112.

in which the convert 'systematically deceives himself' about his motives and pretends to himself that he is moved by rational arguments.[1] It is true that Marxism became the subject of serious study only after 1929 when the first French periodical devoted to it, the *Revue marxiste*, was founded; and that it was only in 1934 that the philosopher Henri Lefebvre published his *Selected Texts from Marx*. It was only then that Marxism began to alter the direction of philosophical thought in France, and so of the schoolboys who studied philosophy. By 1945, however, one-quarter of the students of the École Normale Supérieure were party members; and though a decade later this proportion had fallen to only 5 per cent, one-quarter of the students of the Cité Universitaire still voted communist in 1956.[2] The reasons that led so many inquiring and sensitive minds into the party were too numerous and complex to be summarised by any simple explanation. The physical horrors of the Great War filled some with such a violent hate of the generation and the civilisation that had produced it, that they could see hope only in total reconstruction, and the Bolshevik Revolution set a clear example of how this could be attempted. Communism offered the chance of putting dissatisfaction to positive use. The surrealists led the way in transforming the intellectual's individual and largely literary revolt into a search for a more total liberation, which Marxist revolution seemed to offer: this, they hoped, would 'change life' and 'transform the world'. There were those who joined simply because they wished to identify themselves with the Russian Revolution, for even if they knew little of its doctrines, it seemed to be the herald of a new age of justice and of fraternity. Believers in the need for a radical alternative to the *status quo*, or in the need for violence to change it, found in it the exhilarating prospect of unselfish action and dedication.[3] 'We were in search of a mystique' said Froissard, talking of the generation that emerged from the war.

But it was more than that, as the case of Paul Nizan illustrates. He was the son of a bourgeois, but the grandson of a

[1] J. Monnerot, *Sociology and Psychology of Communism* (Boston, 1953).

[2] David Caute, *Communism and the French Intellectuals 1914–60* (1964), 29: a key work for understanding the history of this period.

[3] Nicole Racine and Louis Bodin, *Le Parti communiste français pendant l'entre-deux-guerres* (1972).

railway worker. Nizan was tormented that he could not call himself the brother of the workers: he was tormented by guilt that his family had deserted the class from which it had sprung. He went to the École Normale, but hated being part of a 'factory to produce élites', entrusted by the bourgeoisie with the task of justifying its domination. He revolted against the philosophy professors whom he accused of turning out watch-dogs for the *status quo*, of making philosophy synonymous with understanding, so that it did not require one to do anything about the evils of the world; professors simply brain-washed their pupils—defenceless youths exhausted by examinations—and taught them to play intellectual tricks with words. Nizan fled to Aden in disgust, becoming tutor to the family of Antonin Besse (a French merchant-millionaire who later founded St. Antony's College, Oxford).[1] But he could not escape from his anxieties. He abandoned teaching to work for *L'Humanité*. He saw in Marxism a doctrine that gave 'satisfaction for all the appetites of human nature'. The Communist Manifesto was, in his view, the proclamation that 'man is love and that he is prevented from loving'. Communist literature should therefore 'denounce the scandal of the conditions imposed on man'; it must be responsible, committed, suggesting solutions and not mere reflection; above all it must 'give men self-consciousness', which was how Marx defined philosophy. Nizan illustrated the feeling of intellectuals who were dissatisfied simply with thinking: 'a thought', he said, 'has a desire for something, it wants a purpose'. He hoped to find it in the party. But in 1939 he resigned from the party over the Russo-German pact. He had not ceased to be a patriot. Thorez claimed Nizan had been a police spy all along. This denunciation was typical of the slurs the party heaped on those who broke with it—a practice which was a factor in keeping its relationships charged with high emotion. This explains, in part, why some of those who deserted communism ended up at the opposite extreme of politics, collaborationists with the Germans under Vichy, persecuting their former friends.[2]

In 1945 the pupils of the École Normale explained in a series

---

[1] Another tutor later employed by Besse was Jacques Le Goff.

[2] Paul Nizan, *Intellectuel communiste. Écrits et correspondance 1926–40*, ed. J. J. Brochier (1970).

of public letters what it was that drew them to the party, even if they did not always join it. Marxism, they said, gave them a sense of lucidity, above the contradictions of society: it satisfied their need for coherence and their refusal of passive resignation before the world's problems. It offered optimism, but of a severe kind, based on facts and capable of being translated into daily action. It made sincerity possible, that is to say, the cohesion of thought and action, the abolition of hypocrisy. Some thought disputation and criticism in the way that other parties allowed. In 1924 Rosmer (he adopted this pseudonym from Ibsen's character who could not stand hypocrisy) was among those who complained about the party's excessive discipline: 'It produces a cascade of marching orders to which it expects obedience without understanding and above all without a word of reply except to murmur the sacramental: Captain, you are right! A secret society mentality is being created and the methods of N.C.O.s are being established . . . Soon the party's bureaucracy will surpass that of the French state.' The party replied that intellectuals could not understand how a single ideology could be imposed in a party formed from varied schools of thought, but that the working class was instinctively hostile to the survival of the old intellectual traditions. There followed a period of systematic anti-intellectualism, or rather of opposition to the notion that intellectuals had a special role to play in the party. Ordinary party members thought of themselves as intellectuals of sorts, and they resented the claims of bourgeois intruders (like the surrealists) to a privileged position, or to a special competence. The demands made on intellectuals who joined the party therefore required exceptional sacrifices, which gradually led to accepting that individualism was only a sign of useless pride and that it had had its day: the need now was to seek salvation by collective means. The Second World War had shown the incompetence of the ruling class, but it had failed to dislodge it from its privileges. Only the workers could be creators of a new era: the party offered intellectuals a chance to get away from their isolation, to overcome their guilt about it, to express their longing for greater fraternity, for the communist party seemed the only one which had won genuine enthusiasm among the workers. Some were attracted by the party's 'extraordinary dynamism', its 'idealism, appetite for efficiency, discipline and success', by its determination to do something positive and at once, by the feeling that to be a member was an adventure. Some joined because it became fashionable to do so, just as others abstained because they wished to show that they could resist fashion. Catholic beliefs did restrain many students from taking the final plunge, but not infrequently the temptation of Marxism remained powerful and even obsessive.[1]

There were many intellectuals in the party at its foundation, and they were quickly made aware that it would not tolerate deviations. But after 1936 the party adopted a new line, of welcoming anybody of the left who would join, of infiltrating non-political groups and capturing them for communism. It sought to win prestige by obtaining the adhesion of great names. It had a charming second-rate poet, Paul Vaillant-Couturier, in charge of its relations with intellectuals: he brilliantly combined a concern for the problems that interested intellectuals with an easy-going, eclectic and modest approach to life, being always good-humoured, loving good food, popular songs and revolutionary hymns, aviation, archaeology, hunting and fishing, travel.[2] So Picasso could say that he found in the communist party 'a homeland', and Aragon talked of it as *la famille*. There were intellectuals who claimed that belonging to the party influenced their whole lives, including their physics (as Langevin claimed), but that was not borne out by the way they in fact continued to keep their work and their politics separate. Leger insisted that his art should remain in a distinct compartment when he joined the party. The party, at this stage, turned a blind eye to these heresies. It was only after 1945 that it began to demand a more total obedience of its directives and the production of a special kind of literature and even a special kind of science. It was this tolerance that made possible its popularity among such marginal but important groups as the teachers. In 1955 Raymond Aron launched his attack on communism as the *Opium of the Intellectuals*, deploring that its adherents could not argue without hate and that they

[1] Enquête sur le communisme et les jeunes, *Esprit* (1 Feb. 1946), 191–260.
[2] André Wurmser, 'Paul Vaillant-Couturier', *Europe* (15 Nov. 1937), 396–8; *Vaillant-Couturier. Écrivain*, ed. André Stil (1967); P. Vaillant-Couturier, *Enfance* (1938), illustrated by the author.

saw in argument the 'secret of human destiny'. That probably marked the end of the honeymoon period in the relations of the intellectuals and communism.[1]

In the communist party, the intellectuals tried to lose themselves in a working-class movement. At the same time, other intellectuals, in the so-called right-wing movements, frontally attacked many of the values traditionally sacred to those who believed in the culture of the mind. At the very time when the power of the intellectuals seemed to be higher than it had ever been, they appeared to be bent on suicide. This was a period of exceptionally vigorous intellectual debate, but never perhaps did confusion hold more sway in the minds of intelligent men. Opinions were held with dogmatic violence, until they were discarded like burst balloons. Some intellectuals were attracted, in varying degrees, by fascism, though few were well informed about its development in Europe, and they generally talked of it vaguely as an 'aesthetic' or an 'ethic'. 'We do not know what we ought to do', wrote Drieu La Rochelle, 'but we are going to try to do something, no matter what.' The fascist sympathisers had a longing for action, like the communists, but their view of action was unashamedly romantic: they claimed to wish to overthrow all idols, to shock the society that made them uncomfortable, but they were also deeply attracted by the old French nationalist traditions, even more than by foreign example. They raised physical courage into a fetish and held up youth as the ideal state: they saw themselves as the representatives of a new generation. 'Thanks to us,' wrote Paul Marion, who became Pétain's minister of information, 'the France of camping, of sports, of dances, of travel and of group hikes will sweep away the France of aperitifs, of tobacco dens, of party congresses and of long digestions.'[2] It is important to understand why so many intellectuals came to despair of intelligence.[3]

[1] Henri Lefebvre, *La Somme et le reste* (1959); Paul Langevin, *La Pensée et l'action* (1964); R. Aron, *L'Opium des intellectuels* (1955); J. Touchard and others, 'Le Parti communiste français et les intellectuels 1920–1939', *Revue française de science politique* (June 1967), 468–544; and the forthcoming history of the French communist party by Edward Mortimer.
[2] On Paul Marion, see the unpublished thesis by G. M. Thomas (Oxford 1970).
[3] Raoul Girardet, 'Notes sur l'esprit d'un fascisme français 1934–9', *Revue française de science politique* (1955), 529–46.

Intellectuals had an inheritance of gloom that went back at least to the late eighteenth century. Though they rebelled against Catholicism, they also developed and expanded the pessimistic strand in its teaching which saw the world as the home of sin and corruption. Disenchantment with progress occurred almost as soon as the faith in it arose. The intellectual, as an individual, was assailed by solitude, boredom, dissatisfaction with himself, and guilt, all of which were accentuated because he set himself impossible goals and because the distractions with which he tried to appease his worries—love, glory, travel, religion—never quite satisfied him. Rousseau has been called the father of this *mal de siècle* and Baudelaire is supposed to have reformulated it, as a consciousness of the inescapable solitude of man, tortured by his vices.[1] But, as has been seen, it required more than fashion or the influence of writers to produce it. Already in 1860, at the height of the Second Empire's prosperity, a liberal writer asserted that the pessimists were outnumbering the optimists.[2] The intellectuals were perhaps inevitably prone to pessimism, because while they held out new hopes before mankind, they were particularly sensitive to the conflict of the individual and society and they saw themselves as a minority battling against vulgarity and the errors of the masses.[3] There were those who protested that the French nation, as a whole, 'the nation of wine-drinkers', was essentially gay and vivacious; but even its prosperity was declared to be a sign of decadence: Bergson said that 'humanity groans, half crushed under the weight of the progress it has made'. The intellectuals were nearly always moralists who were worried by pleasure.[4] They had need of heroic measures to extract themselves from their despondency.

The cult of the irrational became, paradoxically, one of their solutions. Bergson (1859–1941), the country's leading philosopher, seemed to have made this respectable. Bergson was, in politics, a moderate liberal, and he was horrified by the conclusions people drew from his philosophy, but misunderstanding was the price he paid for his fame. He was an

[1] Ch. Dédéyan, *Le Nouveau Mal de siècle de Baudelaire à nos jours* (vol. 1, 1968).

[2] Charles de Rémusat, 'Du pessimisme politique', *Revue des Deux Mondes* (1 Aug. 1860), 729–31.

[3] G. Palante, *Individualisme et pessimisme* (1913).

[4] K. W. Swart, *The Sense of Decadence in 19th Century France* (The Hague, 1964).

immensely impressive lecturer and a fluent writer, and his ambition was to produce a philosophy that everybody could understand. He did not in fact invent a great deal. He probably owed his instant success (and his later, almost total, eclipse) to the fact that he combined a number of ideas current in his youth into a general synthesis. He made them more convincing by appearing to base them on the latest scientific discoveries: each of his books dealt with a philosophical problem, in relation to biology, psychology, physics and anthropology. The philosophers Ravaisson, Boutroux, Cournot Fouillée, Guyau had not made much impact outside academic circles. Bergson borrowed from them, but by making himself also a populariser of science, while at the same time vindicating spiritual values against the menace of mechanistic determinism, he was able to provide every man with a new justification for the urges created by emotional hunger. Bergson was not anti-rationalist: what he did was rather to deny that reason necessarily produced clear results, or that emotion was necessarily a source of confusion or obscurity. He gave a new status to the 'inner life', which science appeared to have explained as an amalgam of physical stimuli. Science, he argued, could not penetrate beyond time and space to *la durée*, the permanent core of individuals, built up with memories, known through introspection, and which language was unable to describe. The individual was in a constant state of creativity. His inner life was the source of his liberty. The best reason for action was not to have a reason, but to act 'because it is me'. The *élan vital*, which was a development of the eighteenth-century Montpellier medical doctrine of vitalism (Bergson's science was not always the most modern), became the symbol for a new kind of emotional dynamism. *Bergsonisme* was vigorously denounced as mysticism by many intellectuals, but it was for that very reason attractive to others. It was not surprising that on his death-bed, Bergson (born a Jew) declared his acceptance of Catholicism, refusing to join the Church only because such a course might seem an abandonment of the Jews in their hour of persecution. Bergsonism was not a Christian doctrine, but it seemed to destroy materialism and was therefore a source of inspiration for the religious revival.[1]

---

[1] H. Bergson, *Œuvres* (ed. Robinet, 1959); C. Péguy, *Note sur M. Bergson et la*

Mysticism was particularly acceptable now, partly because, in reaction against the aridity of science and the failure of positivism to provide adequate emotional sustenance, Catholicism found a new appeal among writers and students. This was by no means wholly an emotional revival: Jacques Maritain, basing himself on a new interest in St. Thomas Aquinas, led a movement which was vigorously intellectual. Others found in Catholicism a religion of expiation and sacrifice: Huysmans had died refusing all pain-killing drugs, wishing to suffer for others, to expiate the sins of mankind. The fascination with suffering can be seen in the work, for example, of the painter Rouault; the obsession with guilt in the poetry of Claudel; the rejection of contemporary society in the colonial adventures of Psichari, the grandson of Renan; the rebellion against individualism in Alphonse de Chateaubriant, who became a Nazi because he somehow saw it as the logical conclusion of his Catholicism. Religion was far from pushing people into reactionary or extremist political stances, but it did provide a stimulus for the rejection of materialism, for the acceptance of discipline, for the condemnation of the idea of life as a simple search for happiness. Thus Saint-Exupéry (1900–44) ended up appearing to be a reactionary mainly because of his silences: he was not interested in ideologies, but in self-abnegation. He declared himself in favour of liberty: liberty however meant not doing what one wanted, but 'fulfilling a destiny', 'finding one's way to God'. His cult of the heroic qualities of leadership could easily be debased from the selfless ideals he held dear into sadistic exploitation. Saint-Exupéry's message was ambiguous: he approved of air pilots being punished for mistakes they had not committed, because that would reinforce discipline. It needed the horrors of the Second World War for Catholicism to shake itself free of its traditional sympathies for hierarchical and authoritarian political systems.[1]

*philosophie bergsonienne* (1914); A. Thibaudet, *Le Bergsonisme* (1922); J. Chevalier, *Bergson* (1926); V. Yankélevitch, *Bergson* (1931); B. A. Scharfstein, *The Roots of Bergson's Philosophy* (New York, 1943); M. Barthélemy-Madaule, *Bergson adversaire de Kant* (1964) and *Bergson* (1967); 'Hommage à Bergson', *Bulletin de la société française de philosophie* (Jan.–Mar. 1960); T. Hanna, *The Bergsonian Heritage* (New York, 1962); A. E. Pilkington, *Bergson and his Influence* (Cambridge, 1976).

[1] H. Stuart Hughes, *Consciousness and Society* (1959) and *The Obstructed Path* (1969); Richard Griffiths, *The Reactionary Revolution: the Catholic Revival in French*

Georges Sorel (1847–1922) had very little influence in France, and not much elsewhere, but he illustrates how widely intellectuals were now straying from traditional paths. He adopted in turn the causes of revolutionary syndicalism, royalism, fascism and Bolshevism. Though he cared nothing for the contradictions in his writings, there was a logic behind this, for the one thing he was certain about was that democracy had failed, most of all because it had led to a collapse of morals: 'France', he wrote, 'has ceased to believe in its principles.' He was at bottom an old-fashioned moralist. His early works had been about the Bible. He considered chastity to be an indispensable ingredient of the ethical rejuvenation he wished to bring about. But all the methods so far tried he condemned as hopeless: education simply obscured the issues in 'the verbosity of professors'; peaceful revolutions preserved too much of the past; socialism was a new form of careerism; the bourgeoisie were cowards. Sorel urged the proletariat to revolutionary violence, not because he admired them—he had no illusions about the common man's virtues—but simply because they were the only group powerful enough to change things. He was not clear what he would put in the place of what was overthrown, for he despised utopias. He wanted a revolution not to capture power—that is what he criticised all other revolutionaries for—but to rouse the bourgeoisie from their slumbers, to give an opportunity for heroic action, for fervour and grandeur. Violence, as he preached it, did not mean force (which simply establishes a new power): violence abolished power and brought about a new 'sublime' situation, a new morality. This had to be achieved without the aid of intellectuals, whom he also despised as idle exploiters of other peoples' labour. Sorel was not a practical revolutionary: he spent the first half of his life as a road and bridge engineer in the civil service, and then lived in quiet suburban retirement, with the peasant girl whom his bourgeois family dissuaded him from marrying. The engineer came out both in his quest for 'order' and in his paradoxical disregard for material prosperity. Sorel was significant because he emphasised the

*Literature 1870–1914* (1966) and Micheline Tison-Braun, *La Crise de l'humanisme. Le conflit de l'individu et de la société dans la littérature française moderne* (2 vols., 1967) are invaluable guides, with good bibliographical references.

O O

importance of myth and irrationality in behaviour. He shows
how disillusionment with the established order had gone so far,
that its destruction was preached, simply in the hope that somehow, out of the chaos, a new romantic heroism would emerge.[1]

The various tendencies came together in the Action Française movement, which, more than any other, gave expression
to the anxieties of intellectuals in the inter-war years. The
Catholic historian Daniel-Rops wrote: 'Action Française is
incontestably the only great party of our day that has a place
for intelligence in its programme. In the ranks of that party,
an intellectual, far from feeling suspect as he would be in the
midst of the parties of order, will feel respected. Communism
is less systematic about finding a place for intelligence.'
Action Française was an essentially middle-class organisation,
characterised by a Belgian newspaper as 'a bizarre mixture of
intelligence and vulgarity, science and stupidity'. Its newspaper, which reached a circulation of about 100,000 copies,
was read by Proust, even though he was a Dreyfusard, because
it was so well written, providing 'a cure by elevation of the
mind'. Several of its leaders and supporters were elected
members of the French Academy. It included among its
founders the scientist Quinton (grand-nephew of Danton)
and Fagniez (the co-founder of the 'scientific' Revue historique);
it numbered an exceptionally large proportion of doctors
among its members, as well as teachers, librarians, lawyers,
clergy, army officers and noblemen. It flirted briefly with the
working class, but failed to have much appeal for it, even though
Léon Daudet (one of its most popular writers) believed anti-
Semitism was the way to attract it. University students joined
it enthusiastically, and combined with its brigades of thugs to
beat up hostile professors, break up lectures and unpatriotic
or immoral film shows, fight with opposing groups, and sell
the movement's newspaper in the streets. It established an
Institute, with professorial chairs named after its heroes—
Barrès, Comte, Sainte-Beuve, Louis XI, Pius IX. It was very
much an intellectual movement, financing itself to a not

[1] James H. Meisel, *The Genesis of Georges Sorel* (Ann Arbor, 1951); Richard
Humphreys, *G. Sorel, prophet without honour* (Cambridge, Mass., 1951); P. Andreu,
*Notre maître, M. Sorel* (1953); G. Sorel, *Les Illusions du progrès* (1968), *Réflexions sur
la violence* (1908).

inconsiderable extent from the sale of its publications, though
even more from funds provided by Léon Daudet (to whom the
fortune of the sugar-refining son of Baroche, Minister of
Napoleon III, had passed, by a complicated route) and by
the wife of a director of the Creusot steel works.[1]

Charles Maurras (1868–1952), the movement's main leader,
was a bitter, deeply disillusioned man of letters. Having lost
his father at the age of six, and gone partly deaf at fourteen,
he lost his religious faith, adopting a tragic view of life, obsessed by death and the helplessness of man. He continued to
value Catholicism as a symbol of national unity, as an institution that offered order and beauty: religion was good for
others. But Maurras had no real interest in the masses, opposing education, even primary education, as giving them excessive conceit. He rejected almost every ideal of his time: he
dismissed the class struggle as an invention of intellectuals,
though he never bothered to learn much about the working
class, or about economics. He developed hatreds which nothing
could assuage; he resented ever having to admit he had made
a mistake; he revelled in slandering his enemies. He saw
enemies, indeed, on every side: Jews, Protestants, foreigners,
politicians, intellectuals (there was plenty of self-hate in him
too). All his life he imagined plots and conspiracies everywhere.
He decided that the problems of men could not be solved by
reason. There were only two paths of escape from the 'world
of darkness man carries in him': one was will-power, discipline,
revolt and violence against society as it existed; and the other
was a return into the womb of tradition. Feeling humiliated
by France's poor showing at the Olympic games of 1898
he declared his conversion to royalism. Monarchy, he said, had
made England great; monarchy was also a symbol, and France
had need of symbols, as opposed to the abstract ideas with
which its republican leaders had bemused it. He turned
liberty upside down, demanding not liberty for the individual
but for the government, liberty for fathers to dispose of their
property as they pleased, liberty for the old provinces to be
reconstituted. He was deeply attracted by the 'order' and
stability he imagined to have existed in the medieval world

[1] Eugen Weber, *Action Française. Royalism and Reaction in Twentieth Century France*
(Stanford, 1962) is the best and fullest guide.

and urged a reconstruction of many of its institutions. But he was using monarchy only as a tool: though he attracted many aristocratic supporters, the Pretender was always ill at ease in his relations with Action Française and ultimately condemned it. Likewise, his alliance with the Catholic Church was essentially too cynical and compromising to be successful. Maurras undoubtedly made himself into a political figure, whose writings gained far more attention than the number of votes he might have been able to win would have justified. But his power remained essentially verbal. He could not pass from polemic to action. In the crisis of February 1934, when the demonstrations of his supporters seemed to open up the chance of overthrowing the republic, Maurras dissuaded them from carrying their violence to any conclusion: he busied himself writing his editorial for the next morning's issue of his newspaper. It became uncertain whether Maurras really wanted to change things. After the defeat of 1940, he objected both to collaboration with the Germans and to resistance against them, because that would damage the unity of France. His steady support of Pétain, who acknowledged him as an inspiration, proved sterile.[1]

The consequences of such doctrines did not seem contradictory, because the intellectuals who followed Maurras believed that they were giving life its full meaning: instead of trying to repress violence, it should be accepted, just as the passions in general should not be repressed; they saw themselves as raising these passions to a higher level, accepting the nastiness of life but finding a place for heroism in it all the same.[2] That they did have some echo outside their own ranks was seen in the success of the political language which blossomed in this period as new alternatives to the political parties, offering demonstrations, uniforms, physical fitness and sometimes violence as substitutes for old-fashioned verbal debate. These were able to draw on a whole variety of forces for which

[1] C. Maurras, Enquête sur la monarchie (1900–9); L'Avenir de l'intelligence (1905); H. Bordeaux et al., Charles Maurras, Témoignages (1953); Leon S. Roudiez, Maurras jusqu'à l'Action Française (1957); R. Havard de la Montagne, Histoire de l'Action Française (1950). Mr. Victor Nguyen is writing a doctoral thesis on Maurras and is the editor of an illuminating new series Études maurrasiennes, published by an Institute to study Maurras, founded in 1973.

[2] E. Berth, Les Méfaits des intellectuels (1914).

the parliamentary regime did not cater. Thus the Jeunesses Patriotes (founded in 1924) combined Bonapartist tendencies with the organisation of a youth movement. Its president, Pierre Taittinger, deputy for the old Bonapartist fief of Charente-Inférieure, was assisted by a student of the École Normale, Henri Simon; its demonstrators were partly provided by the Phalanges Universitaires. It claimed a quarter of a million members and obtained one ministry and three under-secretary-ships of state in Tardieu's government of November 1929. But its increasing concentration on parliamentary elections led to its losing its appeal for the young and the impetuous. Georges Valois's Faisceau or Blue Shirts (1925), who claimed to be the first French fascists, was a break-away from Action Française, seeking to win the support of war-veteran organisations to carry out Maurras's programme. Valois believed that Maurras had provided the ideas but could not carry them out. However, Valois had no special political skills either: he ended up dis-illusioned with fascism, as he had been with royalism and syndicalism, and he died, accused of Gaullism, at Belsen con-centration camp.[1] Jacques Doriot's Parti Populaire Français (1936) tried to bring together socialists and nationalists, who were disillusioned with the traditional parties: by being at once anti-capitalist, anti-bolshevik, anti-Semitic and revivalist, by having as its leader a genuine worker with considerable demagogic skill, who managed to give the impression that he would produce a clean sweep of the old order, this party, which was as near as France came to having a fascist party, appealed to many intellectuals on the one hand, but also to workers, clerks and artisans, and it got some rich financial backers too. Doriot was the man whom the author Drieu La Rochelle (1893–1945) hailed as 'the good athlete . . . our champion against death and decadence', a leader, at last, who was not 'a fat-bellied intellectual'. Drieu La Rochelle joined this party because he hated 'the old *gaga* world of left-wing intellectuals' who lived off a 'rationalist conception of life', ignoring the 'bodily self-expression that is the main need of contemporary man'. Drieu thought he wanted action rather

---

[1] G. Valois, *La Monarchie et la classe ouvrière* (1909), *L'Homme qui vient* (1910), *Intelligence et production* (1920), *L'Homme contre l'argent* (1928), *L'Homme devant l'éternel* (1947).

than words; because he was attracted by too many ideas, he rebelled against them, mixed them up and sought an escape from his agitation, and from the real world, in heroism. Doriot tried to rule the tortured or frightened men who followed him in the manner of the fascist dictators, but he did not have their stamina. By becoming an all-out collaborator with the Germans, he undermined his nationalist base. He probably never had more than 60,000 active members and his sympathisers probably did not exceed 300,000.[1]

More important was Colonel de la Rocque's Parti Social Français, which in 1940 claimed three million supporters and may well have had two million, enough to be offered a seat in Paul Reynaud's war cabinet. La Rocque was the son of a general, who sought to express his military ideals, after his own retirement from the army, by forming an association of decorated veterans, the Croix de Feu. This grew from a small sect into a para-military league and then into a political party designed to reconcile Frenchmen in yet another combination of nationalism, social reform and heroism. La Rocque was a reserved man, as were his lieutenants, and his originality has not been fully appreciated because of his superficial fascist links. He was both a woolly idealist, a believer in dedication to the public service, and an astute politician, willing to play with fire but cautious about it. His refusal to seek power himself, or to attempt violent revolution, became an important source of strength. He was an advocate of European union, but thought this would come about only under the threat of the 'Asiatic danger'. He carefully kept religion out of politics; he was respectful towards the Catholic Church and he rejected anti-Semitism. He was not extremist enough for the intellectuals, but he was probably more effective in popularising a mishmash of their doctrines for mass consumption. He lacked the stature of de Gaulle, but he was in some ways a precursor of him; and he might perhaps have become a powerful figure had war not broken out. As it was, he quarrelled with Pétain, and was finally deported by the Nazis.[2]

[1] Paul Serant, Le Romantisme fasciste (1959); J. Plumyène and R. La Sierra, Les Fascismes français 1923–63 (1963); D. Wolf, Doriot (1969); M. Winock, 'Gilles de Drieu La Rochelle', Le Mouvement social (July–Sept. 1972), 29–48.

[2] Lt.-Col. de la Rocque, Service public (1934); id., Au service de l'avenir (1946); Henry Malherbe, La Rocque (1934); François Veuillot, La Rocque et son parti comme

The 1930s, in some respects, resembled the 1840s, and they ended as tragically as the great optimist rising of 1848 did. These were the years when intellectual debate assumed exceptional proportions. The intelligent young men of the 1930s were permanently marked by their youth, as the men of 1848 were by theirs: both remained clearly recognisable. The two periods had this in common, that the established order appeared intolerable, unjust and corrupting to a large number of the rising generation of educated men. Rejecting money-making or pure literature, they sought not just political solutions for their distress, but total solutions, which were ultimately moral, religious or quasi-religious. They did not just give themselves up to talking or writing, though they did a great deal of this, with a seriousness that made their elders and their successors appear quite frivolous, but they were also willing to act. They believed themselves to be on the threshold of great transformations, and they were confident that they could not only influence them but direct them. Never were ideas, as such, more respected, or so freely produced. Within the established political parties, youth movements blossomed to challenge traditional orthodoxy; new parties were founded; little groups of people, publishing their programmes in numerous ephemeral reviews, made the intellectual and political world very conscious of its ferment. Introspection ceased to have any more attraction, still less did gerontocracy, both of which had failed to produce sustainable ideals.[1]

The intellectuals were, nevertheless, no more successful in 1939 than they had been in 1848. Their internecine strife was part of the explanation. This took on new dimensions of violence. People now condemned each other to death because they did not share opinions. Political dispute ended in civil war, in 1944 as it had done in 1849. The search for national

*je les ai vus* (1938); Edith and Gilles de la Rocque, *La Rocque tel qu'il était* (1962). For petit bourgeois opinion, cf. Hubert Ley, *L'Artisanat entité corporative* (1938). For right-wing movements, Malcolm Anderson, *Conservative Politics in France* (1974).

[1] J. L. Loubet del Bayle, *Les Non-conformistes des années 30* (1969); J. P. Maxence, *Histoire de dix ans 1927–37* (1939); Pierre Andreu, 'Les Idées politiques de la jeunesse intellectuelle de 1927 à la guerre', *Revue des travaux de l'académie des sciences morales et politiques* (1957), 2e semestre 17–35; Jean Touchard, 'L'Esprit des années 1930', in Guy Michaud, *Tendances politiques dans la vie française depuis 1789* (1960), 89–120.

reconciliation, or rejuvenation, produced, once more, a division of the country into uncompromisingly opposed factions. So just as the 'sentimentals' were discredited after the fiasco presided over by the poet Lamartine, so the intellectuals of the 1930s found themselves either cast into opposition as communists, into obscurity as fascists, or into disillusionment by the collapse of their ideals. What they had shared was a faith in the importance of commitment. Some continued to preach this, reinforced in their faith by the experience of the war. But this did not enable them to escape from their isolation: they remained a group apart, essentially ill at ease, because of the complexity of their temperaments. They wished to simplify the options before men, but in doing so they ignored the problem of how to deal with those who would not agree with them, who could not fit into their systems. They did not find a remedy for the vicious circle of revolution being followed by reaction. They were not as revolutionary as they thought, for their practical proposals usually remained institutional, even though the faults they wished to remedy were essentially moral, in the sense that what they cared about most was how the individual behaved. But once they placed their faith in institutions, these were taken over by experts in the running of institutions, who perpetuated the old bureaucratic traditions and who were inevitably corrupted by power. In this, the intellectuals made the same mistake as the Catholic Church had done, of believing it would be strengthened by political support. The revolutionaries of 1848 had been as ambitious as their successors of 1930 but their attempt to improve human behaviour by a vague emotional appeal to fraternal instincts could not last more than a few months, if that. Society continued to live with its contradictions and to use hypocrisy as its method of diminishing friction between humans.

The intellectuals had always found this intolerable. They had previously coped by cultivating detachment, but that was something they now found intolerable also. After so many years of critical activity, they wished to escape from the lonely position they had adopted, and which a few of them, like Julien Benda, still urged them to maintain. The crisis in Europe was in any case too grave to allow them to remain aloof. But commitment and detachment were not as incompatible as they believed. Commitment meant that they took themselves with deadly seriousness. They ceased to be able to look dispassionately at themselves. Independence of mind, rather than abstention from worldly concerns, had always been their most valued contribution to society; when expressed as humour, it was one of the ways that they found an echo in the masses; some intellectuals, like Valéry, still appreciated the virtues of this approach. But these years generally appeared too sombre; the mirrors became too darkened for most people to see their own reflections, still less to laugh at them.

If the quality of human behaviour, which was the concern of intellectuals, had not been much advanced between 1848 and 1945, it was perhaps because its history was still being regarded as the record of crime and folly. People had not yet come to see it rather as the record of illusion and weakness, with illusion being understood to involve dreaming as well as miscalculation, and weakness being seen as including sympathy, and stemming from fear. The intellectuals of 1848 were too naïve, too generous in their interpretation of human behaviour. Those of the 1930s were often that also, but they were generally too angry, too tormented themselves to provide the leadership for those who did not share their preoccupations, and who did not feel understood by them.

# Conclusion

WHAT then does French history add up to? I began this book by asking how much truth there was in the traditional generalisations made about France, whether there was a common core of attitudes which Frenchmen shared beneath their endless arguments and what indeed these arguments signified. My answer is that it is not enough to make either of the personifications of France on which conventional wisdom has agreed. It is not enough to select a certain number of achievements by Frenchmen, notably in political theory, the arts and literature, and maintain that France represented 'culture', that it stood for spiritual values, for human dignity and for taste. These were, without doubt, the reasons why Paris could claim to be the capital of the world in this period. France, though financially not richer than other nations, did seem to have greater resources of sympathy and to care more passionately about more universal problems. The France of these years will always remain memorable for the brilliance of its writers and its artists, for the vivacity of its social life, for its inexhaustible curiosity and versatility, for its ability to enjoy life even while it was aware of all that was bitter in life. Its unique combination of intelligence, style and feeling more than compensated for its self-satisfaction and obstinacy and for the qualities which foreigners found ridiculous or disagreeable.

However, such a view categorises a whole nation on the basis of the characteristics of a tiny minority, and it ignores all that could contradict it. The majority of Frenchmen were in fact peasants who cared little for these artistic ideals and who themselves admitted that they were egoistic, rapacious and mistrustful. The bourgeoisie, which claimed to incarnate the nation's values, was also held to symbolise selfishness, philistinism and complacency. The French produced lofty principles and ideas, but they could be brutal and violent and they prided themselves on being a military nation. Their economic and political organisation was chaotic, and even the brilliant writers were continually lamenting the country's decadence.

It is not enough, either, to see France's historical importance in its pioneering role in the establishment of democracy. It was indeed the first country to adopt universal manhood suffrage. It shook the whole world with its declaration of the rights of man, its repeated use of revolution to overthrow arbitrary or unpopular governments, its triple principles of liberty, equality and fraternity and its opening of careers to talent. Its history was therefore of interest not just to its own children, but was inseparable from that of modernisation in every corner of the globe. No nation, no democracy can write its own history without acknowledging some debt, or some indirect influence to France. French history will always remain of universal historical significance. There is no doubt, however, that French society, as it emerged from these revolutions, has increasingly ceased to be a model. Repeated political crises have suggested that democracy, in France itself, has been a failure. The diversity of opinion and interest seems to have ended in stalemate. Social privilege has not been eliminated. There are numerous flagrant contradictions between the high principles the French have proclaimed and the way they have behaved in practice.

There is always a demand for simple answers to large problems, for the chaos of daily life to be given meaning. Intellectuals have derived much of their influence from their specialisation as suppliers of formulae which do just that. Their explanations have not only enabled people to make sense of the world around them but have also determined in large measure what they see around them. They have, as it were, provided the glue that makes events hold together. The first aim of this book has been to separate the glue from the events, the myths from the reality, to distinguish what was said from what was done, to contrast what actually happened with what people thought was happening. Once the facts are allowed to come loose, it is possible to think again about the patterns into which they might fall. There is no reason why historians should accept the frameworks that have been bequeathed to them, or why they should continue to use traditional categories. Old myths, of course, are not to be simply discarded as useless dross: on the contrary, they provide invaluable clues for the understanding of social unity and consensus; but they are misleading because they inevitably see problems from one point of view and their authors usually attribute too much importance to themselves. I have not followed the politicians in thinking that history can be summarised in a series of reforms, for people's lives were not as fundamentally altered by institutional and legislative changes as the politicians believed or hoped they could be.

Because of the way French history has been written, there have been two myths which I have particularly investigated: that of *la France bourgeoise* and that of the political cleavage of Frenchmen into left and right. I approached these notions by pulling them apart, by pointing out the difficulties they caused and how they were created precisely to conceal these difficulties, to give an appearance of coherence. Six case studies of particular sections of the bourgeoisie, and detailed analysis of the divisions and subdivisions of the various political parties, led to the conclusion that it would be useful to put aside these general labels and start again. Rather than begin with preconceived views about the groupings one should use to study men, I have used as my point of departure the individual and the attitudes with which he faces the world. That is why this book is divided into six sections—ambition, love, politics, intellect, taste and anxiety—which are six different ways of looking at the individual. The book thus starts, as a first step, by reducing history into a kind of *pointillisme*, and reducing complex phenomena to their most elementary forms. This serves the purpose of disengaging the facts from what holds them together and making one conscious of the independent existence of interpretations placed on facts, in the way that space between objects can be seen not as a blank but as having a character and colour of its own, apart from what surrounds it. But the more individual people are studied in detail, the more complex do they reveal themselves to be. So I have not sought for a single key to explain their behaviour. Other disciplines may develop 'general theories', but historians fool themselves if they try to do this. Historical theories indeed have always been simplifications, and they need to be revealed as such. Historical analysis inescapably finds the individual the object of many different pressures and often presenting a different face to each of these; he can behave, depending on the circumstances in which he finds himself, in ways which may appear contradictory, and he hardly ever becomes quite predictable. From *pointillisme*, therefore, I have gone on to attempt a portrait of the individual simultaneously from several different sides, as though I were painting not just the obvious face, but the back of the head also, and the features rearranged so that they may all be seen at once. I have been hesitant about claiming to see causal relationships, which historians tend to imagine too freely. To talk of causes means to talk of proof and it is difficult to prove motives, character or interpretations. I prefer juxtaposition, so that the reader can make what links he thinks fit himself. This limitation has the advantage that I can show the whole complexity of each factor, without having to suppress all those that do not fit into the causal pattern. Chronology is the most primitive causal pattern imposed on events: I have sought to avoid its tyranny too, and to show time moving at different speeds in different compartments of life. I have been interested in change but equally in continuities and survivals. I have not sought to prove that change in one sphere necessarily influenced other spheres. I have found all sorts of obstacles that prevented clocks from harmonising: the country was full of stuck barometers and thermometers out of order. People's ability to adapt to change superficially, while preserving their deeper attitudes, has been seen over and over again.

I started the book by probing into the ambitions of Frenchmen as individuals, because that showed how they saw both their present and their future. Superficially, their ambitions seem to have merged into a common obsession with social mobility. The French Revolution established not so much equality, as the principle of equality of opportunity, which meant that competitiveness was raised into a virtue. But competitiveness did not take the same form as it did in America, or at least as legend associated it with America. France was not united by this cult, nor by the optimism it could have engendered. There were always those who had strong doubts about the wisdom of ambition, fearing the conflicts it produced, and maintaining a preference for the traditional idea of following in one's father's footsteps, or using his influence to establish one's own career. There was no one universal ambition. Glory, money, happiness, security, influence were rival attractions. Different occupations led to one or other of these, and when a choice between them was made, it implied also the choice of a distinct way of life. Men were thus separated by their jobs into private worlds, with different aspirations. This fragmentation was seen not only among the bourgeoisie, but also among the peasants and the workers. A psychological study of the ambitions of French people today has confirmed that this fragmentation continues. They are still divided as to what they hope for. Thus 89 per cent of the sons of teachers and of people in commerce admit to being ambitious and 80 per cent of sons of clerks, soldiers and policemen, but the average of all the occupations is only 55 per cent. The nature of ambition in fact varies: on average three-quarters of the population believe that hard work is the way to success, but only one-third of intellectuals and artists think this, and less than half of lawyers: there are those who believe they have a right to get to the top, because they have superior gifts. Manual workers are exactly divided on this subject, hope and despair being equally balanced. Sixty per cent of the sons of soldiers have as their ambition the desire to devote themselves to an ideal, rather than to making money, but only 21 per cent of the population as a whole share this attitude. By contrast 77 per cent of the sons of merchants hope to do well through the influence of their families and parents; whereas the nation as a whole is equally divided on just how much nepotism can achieve.[1] Different social groups thus clearly cultivate different aims; it is not possible to link pressure for change with a whole class. On the contrary, for those groups which are most ambitious are bitterly hostile to each other. Thus teaching, the army and commerce have been the three major avenues for social climbing. Far from being allies, however, the members of each of these professions have held the other two in contempt. France has not entirely thrown off privilege, and the cult of equality is balanced by jealousy. Perhaps it was because rising in the social scale still remained very difficult that rivalry was so pronounced; perhaps it was because there were so many failures, that the success of others was resented as much as it was applauded as proof of the principle of equal opportunity.

The importance of the family, as the basis of French civilisation, was another widely acclaimed myth. People felt so strongly about family life because they experienced its benefits comparatively rarely and they therefore dreamt of it as an ideal. It has

[1] C. Lévy-Leboyer, *L'Ambition professionnelle et la mobilité sociale* (1971).

been shown that, around 1900, 45 per cent of marriages lasted less than fifteen years; to be an orphan, to be illegitimate, to be abandoned or sent away to wet-nurses in one's infancy was a common experience. Nearly 40 per cent of women worked (not all that much less than the 68 per cent of men who did) and so the idea that the wife's place was in the home was something many people could long for, without having known it.[1] How to make family life more satisfactory, for those who did lead such a life, was a source of much worry. Contradictory solutions were proposed. The relations of husband and wife were clearly often unsatisfactory. The two belonged to opposing cultures, and were educated differently. The conflict about religion was partly a conflict between the sexes. The fact that there was no strong feminist movement indicated not that the situation was harmonious but rather that each sex had successfully built up defences around itself, and that it was holding its own in the war between them. In 1960, only a tiny minority found friendship with members of the opposite sex possible. The respectable façade of marriage was maintained only by a well-organised system of prostitution. The relations of parents and children were far from being ones of authority and respect that every generation likes to imagine once existed. The rebellious child was already a problem in 1848, just as the 'permissive society' was. Love was the revolutionary factor in social relations, as 'ideas' were in politics, and love was also counter-revolutionary. Some parents reformed the family by introducing more affection into it, but the affections of father and mother were not necessarily of the same kind. Control of children, and particularly of daughters, was what mothers struggled for, but the over-possessive mother was already being complained about in the Second Empire. Fathers, for their part, had difficulty in expressing their affection, for it did not combine easily with the obedience they also demanded. Love and ambition often conflicted. Parents keen to get on in the world made demands on their children which placed great strains on them: the coldness of the aristocracy towards its children was copied by some members of the petty bourgeoisie, in the hope of instilling the virtues that led to success. In the 1950s, a majority of parents still believed that more severity was needed in bringing up children.

[1] Volume 1, 315 and 351.

Love and discipline thus continued to be alternative and conflicting bases of the family, but family instability did not just
reflect political conflicts in general, for the family was, also, to
some extent, at war with society. Parents appealed to the schools
to establish harmony between the generations. But the educational system they set up developed its own independent ideals.
It told parents that they were incapable of giving children an
adequate upbringing, that the defects children suffered from
were indeed largely due to the laziness, ignorance or faults of
parents themselves. However, a conflict between schools and
children soon also became evident, and the schools were no
more successful than parents in making the young behave as
they were told. The children played off school against parents
and developed defence mechanisms of their own to counteract
both. With the lengthening of the schooling period, and the
ending of child labour, children became almost a separate class
in society. This was only very vaguely perceived. In the inter-
war period, adolescents were declared to have 'special psychological problems', which was the beginning of the recognition
of their autonomy, and of the inability of their elders to understand them, let alone control them. So, even if there was more
love in the family at the end of this period, love had also set up
tensions of its own. It was a disruptive factor, cutting across all
other divisions, as well as the source of conciliations. Shame, or
hypocrisy, prevented an acknowledgement of these difficulties
and it was only in 1968 that the conflict of generations was finally
recognised as a major political problem, but that problem had
long been in existence. The Saint-Simonians had been rebels not
just against the political and economic order, but against its
emotional bases also: they included a large number of orphans
or children of irregular upbringing. Jules Vallès openly stated
that he participated in the rising of the Commune partly to
obtain revenge for the cruelty he had suffered as a child at
his father's hands. The relationship between family and politics
will, however, always remain obscure, because there is no way
of assessing the precise influence of family background, but it
may be that those who engaged actively in politics will be seen
as sharing certain emotional characteristics, as much as dedication to the public good.

The cult of the intellect was another of the pillars of French civilisation. This period was distinguished by the enormous efforts made to spread that cult and to develop a uniform way of thinking among a population which was only just emerging from illiteracy. This was, again, another kind of revolution, which created new forms of prestige and privilege. The state, partly in order to counteract its rival the Church and partly to 'moralise' the masses, embarked on a programme of education which undoubtedly strengthened nationalist sentiment and participation. The influence of Paris was greatly increased; provincialism and patois were cowed into admission of their inferiority; the favours of the state went to those who could pass examinations, showing that they had learnt to admire a select number of literary gods and could more or less imitate their speech and their style. But the uniformity thus created was superficial. The state found that, with the school system, it had brought into being a monster it could not control. The schools developed values of their own, which were not in harmony with thóse of society at large. They preached admiration of the great minds of the past and rejected the commercial, industrial world as corrupting and base. Like the Church, they saw their role as the protection of children against adult temptations; they felt unappreciated and therefore fell on the defensive. Like the bureaucracy, they did not just serve the state but made their own preservation and expansion a primary goal. They were moreover divided amongst themselves and so instead of producing pupils with equal chances in life or ones who accepted the same values, they created a series of élites, separating secondary and primary pupils into two distinct worlds. They made it easier for people to rise in the social scale, but only marginally, for education could not override the influence of the family. Examinations opened the road to success for some, but damned others as failures. The cult of intelligence was corrupted by facile verbalism, by mediocre imitativeness; for many, it meant not acceptance of spiritual values but a way of getting a job and more money. But it also led to the growth of a large class with a vested interest in respect for the intellect, which became a power to be reckoned with, though inevitably it also aroused opposition as well as admiration.

The admiration, and the resistance, could be seen in the country's taste. Books and newspapers, like trains, greatly increased the possibilities of communication, and therefore of uniformity. Science and literature combined to offer people similar experiences, and to give equality probably more practical meaning than politics did. They greatly increased optimism, and intellectuals became the leaders of society in the sense that they formulated its hopes. But they also found that their exhortations were very often shed like water off a duck's back. The literature that gained the widest audience was not always that which seemed to deserve admiration: the masses welcomed books that fitted in with their traditional preoccupations and with their desire for escapism, and they found food for their imagination in trashy novels and popular journalism. To 'elevate' their taste became the intellectuals' hopeless mission. They encountered a further obstacle in the fact that taste got confused with imitation: the furniture the peasants began to fill their houses with, the clothes they ordered from the department stores were parodies of the artistic creations on which they were based. A contradiction between the aims of artists and the tastes of the masses, which refused to be shaped by them, was revealed. Artists became concerned with giving expression to their individuality; only rarely did that result in work with a universal message; artists therefore withdrew into a more or less private world of their own.

The masses did not show themselves receptive to intellectual or sensual originality, first because they had more pressing problems connected with their mere survival, and secondly because beyond that, getting on in the world became a matter not only of acquisition, but also of appearance. In taste, social mobility involved showing off one's wealth, which meant modelling appearances, as far as possible, on those who were better off. This turned into the imitation of mediocrity; but this imitation was not entirely voluntary, and certainly not spontaneous. The role of intermediaries was probably decisive: the masses bought what goods they could. Merchants and manufacturers decided what should be sold and these hidden arbiters of taste were not as responsive to demand as they might claim. Just as in politics, the people got less of what they wanted, in return for their taxes, than the politicians promised them, so the search for cheapness and for profits distorted the benefits that were derived from both artistic and industrial production. Democracy was still in its infancy and it was no more able to express its desires clearly than a child at a fair. It stared with awe at the intellectual jugglers; it envied them their verbal skills, but it was not on the whole attracted by the intellectual way of life, which was too narrow for it. It undoubtedly found the stalls of the materialists, hawking comfort and property, more attractive. But it is wrong to say that it was seduced by them. This was not a materialist society, and not just because it was too complex to have any such simple attachment. It has been shown how the desire for immediate pleasure was firmly repressed in many sectors, how it was the industrial workers, with no hope of rising out of their class, who were willing to spend their money freely, above all on food and entertainment, as soon as they got it; but peasants and clerks preferred to save, in the belief that there were more permanent satisfactions. There was little popular demand for the social benefits that governments organised, like sanitation or cheap housing estates, which segregated the poor. The standard of living was raised not just by pressure from below, for the workers were as interested in independence as in prosperity. The bureaucracy expanded not because it was overworked but because it searched endlessly for more to do. Government expenditure, or inflation, ultimately made saving impossible for the small man, and the consumer society thus became a necessity. Industrialists, for their part, produced goods for the masses less to 'meet demand' than to increase their profits. They were slow to see the need to raise wages if they were to find more buyers for their goods. The expansion of industry led to a reduction in the hours of work, or rather a reorganisation of work, so that work became distinct from leisure. All this proceeded in a very haphazard way: it was certainly not a sign that the masses were able to reorganise their lives according to their taste. They had more money to spend, but they also had more demands on them. Their lives could be far richer, but boredom was also a larger menace in many trades. But if things were not as they would have liked them, they bore with them because they had a large arsenal of defence mechanisms, of which humour was not the least powerful. They were involved in far more defensive battles, of this private nature, than in occasional open rebellion.

The injustices of politics and economics were not their only source of worry: in private anxiety men had to cope also with their own selves. This was a period in which self-awareness increased enormously and the discovery of the individual was as revolutionary as the extension of his physical power through industry. Here again intellectuals led the way, analysing their loneliness, their guilt, and the conflicts of their emotions. They showed how education and the cultivation of sensibility did not necessarily increase happiness. As physical diseases were gradually conquered, nervous maladies proliferated to take their place. Individualism did not lead to a demand for more liberty, for it also made many of those who were affected by it turn for comfort and support to other sources: it revealed that fraternity was a principle even more difficult to implement than equality; and the intellectuals who pondered it were too torn within themselves to offer acceptable solutions. The doctors acted as advisers and consolers, but though they won much influence as a result, they offered palliatives, not solutions. Anxiety therefore split the nation along other lines. The discipline the army offered young men who were compulsorily passed through it was shrugged off, and military ideals remained the private code of an isolated, professional group: it never succeeded in exerting much influence outside times of war. Catholicism, to which the nation nominally adhered, was the object of the century's most vigorous quarrels, concentrating the animosities produced by other disputes too; it has only recently ceased being a source of division, and instead it has become the creed of another minority. Thus society was fragmented by yet another cell. And on its fringes, the criminal world had its own mysterious laws. The fall in population gave the impression that anxiety was sapping the nation's vitality, but that was to measure vitality unfairly: and besides it was not every couple who started having one child only—the nation was divided here also, and there was still a large group who produced large families. There was no one attitude even in the face of death.

Politics reflected these various pressures inadequately. It tried to simplify life by dividing Frenchmen into supporters of left and right. There is no doubt that to a considerable extent it succeeded. These labels have been immensely powerful influences and to that extent they do represent a very definite bifurcation, which makes it almost impossible for people on opposite sides of this barrier to co-operate. To Frenchmen this is something inescapable. No account of politics which does not base itself on it can make sense to them. But to outsiders, who have not been involved in the almost religious emotions this breach has produced, it appears not simply as a distinction between supporters and opponents of change (valid both on the theoretical and traditional levels) but also as a basic source of confusion. Because of it, Frenchmen have been unable to see just how much unites them, or they have tried to fit disagreements into this stereotype which distorts the realities. They have, of course, been partly conscious of this, and the division of left and right has in practice been attenuated by various modifications. The left has had to be split into two, to accommodate the communists, and the right has been forced to recognise as its illegitimate offspring such hybrid forms as Bonapartism or Gaullism; a blind eye has had to be turned to all those politicians who climbed into power on a left-wing programme, only to behave in office indistinguishably from their right-wing opponents. It is legitimate to classify politicians according to the principles they appeal to; but it is equally necessary for historians to judge them by what they do as well as by what they say.

The first step is to differentiate between political philosophers, governments, party militants and the masses. With political philosophers, ideology is all-important; but ideologies are notoriously ambiguous. One cannot divide Frenchmen, for example, into followers and opponents of Rousseau or Proudhon, because they have been interpreted in radically different ways and have been claimed as the founding fathers of both libertarian and totalitarian systems. There are, it is true, clear friends and enemies of Marx, but Marx, as has been shown, was mixed up with so much other ideology, that there are profound and fundamental divergences between those who admired him. Every ideal—democracy, liberty, or socialism—has been twisted into too many shapes to have a clear significance. The clash of theory and practice has confused matters further still. It has been shown how French politicians tacitly divided themselves into those seeking ministerial office and those content to act as middlemen. Those who entered governments very seldom escaped being corrupted by the fascination of power. Their history has to be written in terms of the use they made of the state, which still had many of its *ancien régime* characteristics, and which was almost constantly strengthened, irrespective of the political theory that was supposedly being implemented. This century may be remembered as the great age of liberalism, but the bureaucracy all the same trebled in size. Clemenceau, the staunch radical fighter for liberty, and for long the representative of the individual against authority, was in office as fierce an upholder of governmental power, as ruthless a repressor of trade unions and of strikes, as the dictator Napoleon III, and indeed whereas Clemenceau carried out a certain amount of nationalisation, Napoleon III's was paradoxically one of the rare governments to reduce state regulation of industry and trade. Waldeck-Rousseau, because he was associated with the anticlerical campaign and with the law enfranchising trade unions, has remained a hero of the left, but he despised left-wing politicians, he disliked the revolutionary trade unions, hoping to win the workers away from them; he had little of the left wing's optimism, still less its faith in education: he was a jumble of prejudices, with an authoritarian personality that saw fraternity in distinctly theoretical terms. By contrast, Léon Blum, who terrified the bourgeoisie because he was a socialist, was one of the most sensitive politicians to hold high office, one of the most warmly attached to humane values and indeed the least willing to use violence to enforce his programme, insisting that socialism could work only when everybody was ready for it and accepted it. To suggest that politicians should be distinguished by their temperaments, by their sensibility or their style of behaviour, is not to minimise the importance of ideology, but to place this in a broader perspective, as part of a whole personality and a total situation, and not to see it just in terms of theory.

These confusions were exacerbated by the 'notables', the party militants and those for whom politics was a way of life. At this level, doctrinal issues were constantly invoked and passionately debated. But these men had three different roles: to spread consciousness of general interests and so make the masses as a whole participate more actively in the national community, to act as the intermediaries who arranged the compromises and the deals between government and people, and to fight amongst themselves for power. Whereas the most famous politicians generally had the ambition to overcome national divisions, to go beyond party, and win the approval of all Frenchmen, political divisions were stressed by the local militants, for whom the exclusion of their enemies was always a major preoccupation. Politics had several faces: it showed the general significance and importance of apparently minor disputes, but it also provided a means by which the authority and favours of the state could be used to win personal battles. All sorts of animosities therefore came to group themselves under the banner of lofty principles, which helped to make sordid ambitions respectable. Village rivalries were thus consolidated; family feuds grew into impregnable traditions; people often forgot what they had originally quarrelled about, but they were certain they had to go on fighting. Politics in France was particularly intertwined with history because of this: old divisions were perpetuated even though new solutions had arisen. It was long impossible for left and right, embittered by the anticlerical war and by memories of mutual persecution, to face up to the fact that the redistribution of real economic and political power was making nonsense of many of their prejudices. The masses were not as interested by politics as legend has it, and just how superficial their adherence to the parties was became evident from time to time, when they emerged from their lethargy to show enthusiasm for 'saviours' like Napoleon III, Boulanger or Pétain. The extreme left wing was not so much a party as an opting-out of the party system; syndicalism, and then the 25 per cent communist vote showed how widespread this attitude was. *Apolitism* has been somewhat confused by the fact that some parties have emerged, like Bonapartism, or Gaullism, as the avowed representatives of the 'silent majority'. They have claimed that there was a national consensus, which was concealed by party strife, and to which they could give expression. This was only partly justified, though it was perfectly true that there were many issues on which the people would have agreed, if only party considerations had not stopped them.

It would be more accurate to say that the country was divided between those with a partisan mentality and those with a consensus mentality. The 'national' movements were not truly national, because they appealed only to the latter, and they obtained their cohesion partly by attacking the former: they too always had enemies. It should be possible, however, for the historian to see, with hindsight, what both these mentalities had in common, apart from the difference in temperament. Religion is a good example: this was what divided people as much as anything: but on the practical level, that is to say, on the level of morality, clericals and anticlericals were not really divided: being both puritan, they believed in avoiding temptation, and . in seeking spiritual as opposed to material satisfactions. The masses were unable to express their own opinions on this matter in a clear way, but it is certain that they did not share this puritan philosophy, or at the very least that they were divided about it. The issue of the consumer society, and of pleasure while one could get it, was never put before them, and yet this was perhaps the most fundamental question raised by industrialisation and urbanisation. Democracy therefore only went a certain way: it offered the masses a certain amount of choice, but the choices were not necessarily formulated in a way to allow them to express their aspirations in their entirety. The power of the intellectuals, who formulated the choices, was based on this. But it has been seen that often more portentous choices were forced on the people by the facts of economic life: here it was a different set of men who both offered the options and limited them.

Technocracy was an attempt to produce a compromise between the various pressures in this society, and some coherence between them. It was the old monarchy's benevolent despotism, modernised by meritocracy, democratised by the public opinion poll and a broadened social conscience, but remaining firmly seated in the old traditions of centralisation and bureaucracy. However, even its all-seeing efficiency could not cope with the multitude of human tensions and diversities that could not fit perfectly into its programme of political stability and economic prosperity. It had, besides, no consolations to offer in times of depression, and no emotional attractions to win it forgiveness when it made mistakes. It did not solve the problem of democratic participation. But neither had the traditional form of government it ultimately replaced, or rather absorbed. Gerontocracy had survived so long because it had found subterfuges to absorb the conflict of generations, allowing superficial political changes to mask underlying continuity. The movement of parties to the left gave scope to youthful opportunism, while a compensating institutional conservatism and historical attitudes minimised the consequences and preserved the system as a whole. However, education so strengthened those sections of the community which had hitherto been excluded from political power—women and children—that the hypocrisy about the difficulties of family life could no longer be maintained, and gerontocracy collapsed with it.

The conclusion need not necessarily be, as some political analysts have argued,[1] that this was a 'stalemate society'. It appears so only if one holds up certain liberal ideals to it and wonders why it has failed to meet them. By this criterion, some people were indeed frustrated, but one should not assume that participation or efficiency were universal aspirations, nor that Frenchmen as a whole knew what it was that they wanted, even if the political system had allowed them to achieve it. If one wishes to characterise this society with a label of this sort one could call it rather a cellular society. The occupational, ideological, regional and social groups of which it was composed absorbed themselves deeply in sectional interests, and developed ways of life which made these groups as near as possible private worlds, each with its own satisfactions. Artists, businessmen, teachers, soldiers, each pursued different goals; people grouped themselves in family and client networks; mentally, they functioned at different times rationally, emotionally, superstitiously, humorously. The frustrations of national politics were thus made more remote. Tocqueville's idea of the Frenchman as an isolated individual, helpless before the centralised state, and the modern sociologists' vision of him as tormented by alienation, were true only if one ignored whole aspects of his life, in which he found ample scope to express himself and to make something even out of his misfortunes. He may not have been able to attain his ideals, but he found many substitutes for them. It is legitimate to show in what respects the political system did not work, but one should not forget also that in practice, somehow or other, people managed. How they did says as much about their culture as their ideals and their institutions.

These six different approaches to life have shown divisions cutting across Frenchmen in so many ways that there were an almost infinite number of permutations. If enough aspects of

[1] See the suggestive writings of S. Hoffmann, *In Search of France* (1963) and *Decline or Renewal?* (1974).

their lives are taken into account, Frenchmen cannot be classified or categorised. The political and economic myths which sought to make common action possible or to give them the hope that there was a universal solution for their troubles were too partial, too restricted to a limited range of problems, to dominate general behaviour and attitudes. What this book has tried to show is that the individual had not learnt to cope with himself, let alone with the political and economic institutions surrounding him; the emotional stability was lacking to make these work as the theorists planned. The problems of human relations, of dealing with family, friends and strangers, were baffling because self-knowledge was still in a very primitive stage. Frenchmen were not short of ideas, nor of banners behind which they could march, but they were short of mirrors in which they could see themselves. The mirrors that existed were generally misted up by the fog of principles which made it difficult to see the realities, and in any case people looked at their mirrors through coloured spectacles, having chosen a colour to suit them in early youth and seldom changing. The compartmentalisation of society meant that, in addition, people were fitted with blinkers. The nineteenth century opened up new opportunities for everyone, but people seized them with caution. They bolstered themselves up by playing roles, which simplified things in some ways. But this meant also that new barriers were raised up between men, for specialisation affected not only their jobs, through the division of labour and the rise of the professions, but life in general. The young and the old began to split off as separate classes. Male and female maintained separate ideals. The twentieth century's answer to this was to seek an escape from these barriers through distractions, entertainment, leisure. But the growth of leisure only created a new compartmentalisation in that work and leisure were now separated too. Durkheim thought the answer to the dissatisfaction which this was causing was to strengthen the institutions of these small worlds, but that would only have accentuated their isolation and would have done nothing to improve communication between them.

The problem that remained unsolved at the end of this period was how individuals could escape from their private worries, transcend the specialisation that industrialisation and technocracy demanded, and acquire some detachment from pressures upon them. They could not obtain that mastery of the environment that the scientists promised them, nor even that control over their own destinies that the politicians claimed universal suffrage gave them, until they had ceased to be slaves of their history, their self-deceptions, their passions and their worries. It is in this sense that the political, economic, social and moral strands of the history recounted in this book converge: each of them forced the individual to define himself in his allegiance, his specialisation and his tastes. I have shown how people got round the inconveniences this caused, but they found only palliatives for the pressure that they should be consistent and predictable. The search for prosperity was necessary and inevitable, but the preoccupation with it allowed people to forget what their goals were, or to avoid asking the question. At the end of this period, Frenchmen still had not worked out clearly where their priorities lay.

So one cannot sum up modern French history simply by talking about democracy and art. One can, alternatively, see it as being dominated by competitiveness and anxiety. To do this is to distinguish between two kinds of history, between the spoken and the unspoken, between the way people liked to see themselves, and the side of them they preferred to keep quiet about. That is what I have tried to do in this book. I have tried to show that if one ceases to look on Frenchmen's actions simply through the categories which they liked to employ, then the inspiration of their daily lives turns out to be also the bane that tormented them. Competitiveness distracted them from the principles they preached; it often became a partial substitute for those principles; but it opened the door only to new worries. This has therefore been a history of an infant democracy, characterised by confusion about its direction, and with a tendency to get lost in conflicts whose meaning often became obscure. It has also been a commentary on the difficulty, for a nation, of making choices, of forging its identity and of finding the detachment to judge what it is doing.

This book has been not quite a post-mortem examination of French nationalism, but rather a summing-up of its achievement as it reaches the age for retirement, or as it prepares to merge itself in a new European nationalism, whose character is even more uncertain. Europe will undoubtedly inherit an ambivalent legacy from it. The nationalism of France was based on a euphoria which gave people the illusion that they had found a purpose, but the closer examination of that purpose, attempted here, suggests that the choices were only dimly beginning to be seen. The euphoria was, to a certain extent, artificially stimulated. It undoubtedly made possible the achievement of noble and plausible goals, but it also diverted a great deal of energy into sterile pursuits. French nationalism in this period, though it was progressive and liberal, was still the child of the monarchs of the *ancien régime*; it was obsessed by power and vanity. Its ambitions were constantly disrupted by emotion, because it had only a limited understanding of the individual imagination: it placed its faith in laws and institutions. Individuals learnt to shrug these off, and this, as much as the efforts of the politicians, explains why France was, to a certain extent, or sometimes, a free country.

In writing this book, I have seen my main purpose as one of clarification. I have tried to do this not by simplification—for the problems dealt with have shown themselves to be more complex as they are more deeply pursued—but above all by distinguishing between different levels of historical reality—ideological, social, institutional, emotional. The way to get a picture of the whole wood, while surrounded by a mass of trees, is to learn how to see it in different ways, to allow the light to illuminate different aspects, and so to become aware of its changing, complementary and even contradictory variety.

Every generation is confused by its past and uncertain about the significance of its own times. The historian questions the generalisations that have become current about the past and its relations with the present. He tries to discover what people have been trying to do, which is not necessarily what they said or thought they were doing, and to show why plans went astray, why situations no one wanted came about. Historical study is a necessary preliminary to an understanding of the choices that each generation has to make, and to a reordering of the priorities it must have before it. The historian is not a soothsayer, he cannot tell what is going to happen next; but he may perhaps have some use all the same, in the sense that he can be a kind of court jester. He cultivates detachment. Humour, as has been shown, is one form of detachment. The historian tries to interest and entertain, but also to say what his readers may not wish to hear.

For myself, not the least reward for having devoted twenty-one years to research on this subject, is that I do not feel that I have ceased to be concerned with the universal by studying the ideas, manners and achievements of France in such detail. France has always had something interesting to say about virtually every aspect of life; I have found it an unfailing source of stimulation. So, though I have not hesitated to paint a true likeness, as I see it, warts and all, this is a work composed with affection. It is offered to its sitter, in all modesty, with gratitude.

# BIBLIOGRAPHY

PRESSURE of space makes it impossible to place here bibliographical references additional to those in the footnotes: since these will be of interest only to specialists, they can be reserved for a separate volume. This note will simply indicate how the reader can find out more on particular topics.

Books published in France have been listed since 1811 in the *Bibliographie de la France. Journal officiel de la librairie.* From 1934 *Biblio* has performed a similar function. These, however, are not as convenient to use as Otto Lorenz (a German who became a naturalised Frenchman), *Catalogue général de la librairie française*, which first appeared in 1867 with four volumes covering the years 1840–65; it continued to come out every decade or so after that; but unfortunately stopped in 1925. The great merit of this work is that it has a subject index, which must be the starting-point of every piece of research. To supplement it, one should use the catalogues of the Bibliothèque Nationale, though that again is complicated. The author catalogue was started in 1896 and has now reached the letter V. This means that twentieth-century books published by an author whose name begins with a letter from the beginning of the alphabet are not to be found in it. Books published after 1960 have, however, separate published catalogues. For the gap left in this way, a visit to the B.N. is indispensable, to consult its card catalogue. The unpublished subject catalogue in the B.N. is invaluable (for books published after 1882). The general rule is in fact that a bibliography for research on France can only be properly compiled by a visit to Paris, not only for this unpublished subject catalogue, but also for those to be found in other, specialised, libraries. A descriptive list of these can be found in *Répertoire des bibliothèques de France* (new edition, 1970). For example, the Bibliothèque Marie Durand is where everyone wanting to work on women's history must go; subject catalogues on cards in the Institut Pédagogique and the Musée Social are indispensable for research on education and social questions; the library of Nanterre University has a collection on the First World War and politics and economics since then, which is unrivalled.

When it comes to discovering what articles have been written, things are much harder. Simply to know what periodicals existed, one needs to visit the B.N. to consult its *Catalogue collectif des périodiques conservés dans les bibliothèques de Paris et dans les bibliothèques universitaires de province*, which lists those that came out before 1939. Three volumes of this catalogue have been published; the final volume (A–C) is awaited. For more recent periodicals, H. F. Raux, *Répertoire de la presse et des publications périodiques françaises* (1958, new edition 1961) lists 15,000. The *Annuaire de la presse* (1878, annual) is also useful. But there is no full index to articles in periodicals, and indeed few periodicals printed indexes. The *Revue des Deux Mondes* is an important exception. *Le Monde* is being indexed at the moment and the years 1861–80 have so far been done. This is the nearest there is to an equivalent of the index of the London *Times*, which can be useful for France; but the most important indexes to French periodicals are to be found on a single shelf in the Salle de bibliographie of the B.N. There is no alternative but to leaf through periodicals and newspapers, which is always rewarding, even if time-consuming. An additional snag is that many newspapers, particularly provincial ones, are kept at Versailles, and have to be ordered in advance for consultation in Paris.

For the more straightforward kinds of history, there are the historical bibliographies. These began with the *Catalogue de l'histoire de France* (1885–95) in twenty-two volumes, listing the B.N.'s holdings, by subject. (This is continued on card indexes in the basement of the B.N.) Then came G. Brière and P. Caron, *Répertoire méthodique de l'histoire moderne et contemporaine de la France 1899–1906* (1907); P. Caron, *Bibliographie des travaux publiés de 1866 à 1897 sur l'histoire de France depuis 1789* (1912) and P. Caron and H. Stein, *Répertoire bibliographique de l'histoire de France* (1920–9). The Comité Français des Sciences Historiques published a good guide to *La Recherche historique en France de 1940 à 1965* (1965). Since 1953 there has been an excellent *Bibliographie annuelle de l'histoire de France*, which has sections on political, institutional, economic and social, religious, colonial, 'civilisation' and local history. This gives obscure articles as well as virtually all significant books. But one needs to supplement it by investigating what unpublished memoirs and theses have been produced. This can be done in part by consulting the lists published in the *Revue historique* and more systematically by going through the universities' official catalogues of theses, *Catalogue des thèses de doctorat soutenues devant les universités françaises*, another time-consuming activity, since they are arranged not by subject but by faculty. For work in progress, there is the *Répertoire raisonné des doctorats d'état, lettres et sciences humaines, inscrits d'octobre 1970 à mai 1975* (1975), which is published by the Fichier Central des thèses at the University of Paris X—Nanterre, a visit to which is also desirable, since they keep a useful subject catalogue. For masters' theses, there is no real substitute for personal contact with the supervisors, because many of them used to be kept by the supervisors and never found their way into any library.

The specifically historical bibliographies should be supplemented by others, whose great value is not sufficiently recognised. A. Grandin, *Bibliographie des sciences juridiques, politiques, économiques et sociales* (1926), published in three volumes, and supplemented with annual volumes which take it up to the end of the war, is particularly useful for references to law theses and to official publications. There are interesting subject classifications in Otto Klapp, *Bibliographie der französischen Literaturwissenschaft* (Frankfurt am Main, published annually since 1956) and René Rancoeur, *Bibliographie de la littérature française moderne, 16ᵉ-20ᵉ siècles* (1962 onwards). The third volume of Hugo P. Thieme, *Bibliographie de la littérature française de 1800 à 1930* (1933) is a subject catalogue on 'Civilisation', but this work is also very valuable for the lists of books and articles written by and about all the major and many minor 'literary' authors. It was continued by S. Dreher and M. Rolli, *Bibliographie de la littérature française, 1930-9* (Geneva, 1948), and then by M. Drevet for 1940-9 (1954). The fullest literary bibliography is H. Talvant and J. Place, *Bibliographie des auteurs modernes de langue française 1801-1927* (started in 1928 and reaching volume 21, letter M, by 1975). Other useful specialised bibliographies have been given in the footnotes of this book. Among the fullest ones for recent work are the *Répertoire général des sciences religieuses* (1950 ff.) and the *Bulletin signalétique du C.N.R.S.* which since 1956 has had a series on the human sciences. Léon Vallée, *Bibliographie des bibliographies* (1883) and L. N. Malclès, *Manuel de bibliographie* (1963) and *Les Services du travail bibliographique* (1950-8, four volumes) can give further guidance. One can often find unexpected information in such specialised works as J. Leguy, *Catalogue bibliographique des livres de langue française sur la musique* (1954); the *Bibliographie géographique internationale* (1931 ff.) which used to be a supplement to the *Annales de géographie française* (1893-1930) and which is particularly useful for local and economic history. For science, see F. Russo, *Histoire des sciences et des techniques. Bibliographie* (1954), and the bibliographies in R. Taton, *Histoire générale des sciences* (1957 ff.) and M. Daumas, *Histoire générale des techniques* (1962 ff.). For medicine, the best thing to do is to go to the library of the Paris faculty of medicine, which is full of curious things. Medical theses are a vast untapped source, and rather difficult to get hold of: they have to be ordered in advance at the B.N.: A. Hahn, *La Bibliothèque de la faculté de médecine de Paris*

(1929) and *Table des thèses soutenues devant la faculté de médecine de Paris* (1939) may help. The best encyclopedia to start one off on research is P. Larousse, *Grand Dictionnaire universel du 19e siècle* (1866–76, fifteen volumes and two supplements), as fascinating as the early editions of the *Encyclopaedia Britannica*. Several more recent editions are of varying quality and depth. A. de Monzie and Lucien Febvre, *Encyclopédie française* (1937) is the most instructive for the early twentieth century, and it also has long bibliographies. There are some good religious encyclopedias, notably A. Vacant, *Dictionnaire de théologie catholique* (1903–50, thirty volumes); A. Baudrillart and R. Aubert, *Dictionnaire d'histoire et de géographie ecclésiastiques* (1912 ff.); J. Bricourt, *Dictionnaire pratique des connaissances religieuses* (1925–33, seven volumes), and G. Jacquemet, *Catholicisme* (1947 ff.). To discover quickly what a place is like, consult P. Joanne, *Dictionnaire géographique et administratif de la France* (1890–1905 in seven volumes), or his one-volume *Dictionnaire géographique, administratif, postal, statistique, archéologique de la France, de l'Algérie et des colonies* (second edition, 1872), which is an indispensable reference work; to bring it up to date, there are the *Dictionnaires des communes*, which however are far less informative. For urban history, see P. Wolff and P. Dollinger, *Bibliographie d'histoire des villes de France* (1967). There are a large number of local bibliographies, which need to be supplemented by leafing through local periodicals: here again nothing can replace a visit to the local departmental or municipal libraries, from which one always emerges with new ideas.

For political history, M. Block, *Dictionnaire de l'administration française* (third edition, 1891) and *Petit Dictionnaire politique et social* (1896) are useful for the definition of terms and the details of laws. Legislation needs to be looked up in J. B. and J. Duverger's *Collection complète des lois, décrets etc.* (annual), but a visit to the library of the faculty of law in Paris will always prove useful: there is virtually no law which has not had some commentary written upon it by a law student, and the encyclopedias there show one further complications and links. The parliamentary debates are easily followed both in the *Moniteur universel*, later the *Journal officiel* (which also published laws and decrees), and in separate series, one for the lower and one for the upper house, variously entitled *Compte-rendu des séances du corps législatif* and *Procès-verbaux des séances du corps législatif* for 1852–60, *Annales du Sénat et du Corps législatif* 1861–70 and *Débats parlementaires* for the Third Republic. For diplomatic history, see D. H. Thomas and L. M. Case, *Guide to the Diplomatic Archives of Western Europe* (Philadelphia, 1959).

France is poorer in biographical dictionaries than other countries. The *Dictionnaire de biographie française* (started in 1933 by J. Balteau and continued by Roman d'Amat) had by 1975 reached the letter F. It is indispensable and also has bibliographies, but needs to be supplemented by A. Robert and G. Cougny, *Dictionnaire des parlementaires français 1789–1889* (five volumes, 1889–91), continued by J. Jolly, for the years 1889–1940, in a series which started in 1960 and is not quite complete. In addition, L. C. Vapereau, *Dictionnaire des contemporains* (third edition 1865, sixth edition 1893, the different editions all remain valuable); Nath Imbert, *Dictionnaire national des contemporains* (1936); E. Bénézit, *Dictionnaire des peintres, sculpteurs, dessinateurs et graveurs* (eight volumes, 1955–61). There is a full list of all these biographical dictionaries in J. Auffray, 'Bibliographie des recueils biographiques des contemporains aux 19ᵉ et 20ᵉ siècles' (unpublished mémoire, Institut National des Techniques de Documentation, 1963). The I.N.T.D., which trains people to produce bibliographies, has a large number of unpublished ones in its library, on the most diverse subjects, compiled by students as part of their course, and many are extremely interesting. For almanacs, beginning with the major political one which lists all office holders, *L'Almanach national* (annual, called *l'Almanach royal* or *Impérial* at different times), see G. Saffroy, *Bibliographie des almanachs et annuaires* (1959).

The information to be found in manuscript and in archival depositories is only very partially catalogued. The *Catalogue général des manuscrits des bibliothèques publiques en France*, which was started at the end of the nineteenth century, is of little use for this period except in its very latest volumes, which means that there is no ready way of discovering, except by direct inquiry, what manuscript collections are to be found in most provincial towns. The Bibliothèque Nationale's *Nouvelles Acquisitions du département des manuscrits* (issued every few decades, starting 1891) is important, but it needs to be supplemented by the latest catalogue in the manuscript reading room itself. The largest depository of manuscripts is of course the Archives Nationales. The collections in Paris include the papers of parliament and the ministries, divided by series. The most important ones for this period are: F1 Administration in general and personnel; F1c Elections, including prefects' reports on public opinion; F1d decorations; F2 and 3 local administration; F4–6 administrative accounts; F7 police; F8 sanitary control; F9 military; F10 agriculture; F11 food supplies; F12 commerce and industry; F13 public buildings; F14 public works; F15 poor assistance; F16 prisons; F17 education; F18 printing and bookselling;

F19 religion; F20 statistics; F21 fine arts; F22 labour and insurance; F23 extraordinary services in war-time; F30–4 finance; F35 state industries; F36 economic affairs; F70 Minister of State; F80 Algeria (but most archives concerning it are in Aix-en-Provence); F90 posts and telegraphs; C election results and frauds; O5 Napoleon III's household; AJ5–10 inter-war reparations; AJ12 Panama Company; AJ13 Opéra (but see also those in the Opéra's own library, and those in the Bibliothèque de l'Arsenal); AJ16 Academy of Paris; AJ17 Imprimerie Nationale; AJ21, 24 and 25 economic reconstruction after World War I; AK Cour des Comptes; AM Cour de Cassation. The BB series of the Ministry of Justice is important: 1 and 5 personnel, 6 files on magistrates, 7 files on tribunaux de commerce, 8 juges de paix, 9 solicitors, auctioneers and huissiers, 10 notaries; 11 naturalisations, 11 and 12 changes of name; 15 dispensations for marriages; 2 and 16 civil division; 17 Minister of Justice; 3, 18 and 19 criminal division, 20 assize courts, 21–4 pardons, 31 Alsace-Lorraine in 1871. Printed public documents are to be found in the AD series, arranged by ministry. The archives of the former ministry of the colonies are very rich; the records of the navy, which are incomplete but contain much still untouched, are partly in the National Archives and partly in its own archives; those of the army are in the Château de Vincennes where the Service historique de l'Armée is situated. Just as the navy has interesting information on the colonies, so the army's archives are indispensable for French political history.

The archives of local government are divided into the following series, situated in the provincial *départements'* capitals: M politics, P finances, R army, S public works, T education, U justice, V religion, X poor, Y prisons, Z miscellaneous and with all sorts of interesting things in it. The archives of the communes are sometimes in the departmental archives and sometimes in the *mairie*. In local research one needs to discover how much has been destroyed by enemy action during wars, or simply lost. Only a small part of the collections are catalogued. See the A.N.'s publications: *L'État des inventaires des archives nationales, départementales, communales et hospitalières au 1er janvier 1937*, with supplements since then.

M. Rambaud, *Les Sources de l'histoire de l'art aux archives nationales* (1955), supplemented by periodical reports on further acquisitions, is indispensable. For the theatre, the Bibliothèque de l'Arsenal is a starting-point; for music halls the Collection Gustave Fréjaville. For music see C. Pierre, *Le Conservatoire national de musique* (1900), and the archives of the institution, and J. Chailley on 'Recherches musicologiques' in *Précis de musicologie* (1958). For literature,

D. Gallet-Guerne, *Les Sources de l'histoire littéraire aux archives nationales* (1961). For social history in general, Colloque de l'École Normale Supérieure de Saint-Cloud, *L'Histoire sociale, sources et méthodes* introduced by E. Labrousse (1967); J. Le Goff and P. Nora, *Faire l'histoire* (three volumes, 1974). For statistics, B. Gille, *Les Sources statistiques de l'histoire de France* (1964) which unfortunately stops at 1870, and for the way to use them, see the works of A. Daumard; also C. Legeard, *Guide de recherches documentaires en démographie* (1966). For trade union history, R. Brécy, *Le Mouvement syndical en France 1871–1921, essai bibliographique* (1963). The *Annuaire statistique* (annual since 1878) is a mine of curious information, and a starting-point for using the larger, full series of official statistical publications.

Private papers are harder to find than they are in many other countries. There is no central register. But the Archives Nationales now has four important series: AB xix for private documents it has acquired by extraordinary means, AP for private papers bought or donated; AQ for business archives and AS for archives of associations. It has published a catalogue of these, but again a visit is necessary to secure more up-to-date information.

Finally, P. Guiral, R. Pillorget and M. Agulhon, *Guide de l'étudiant en histoire moderne et contemporaine* (1971) lists the most important standard works, major articles, textbooks and reference books, as well as containing much useful general advice. It is worth looking too at similar works on other branches of study, such as those on sociology, philosophy, literature, etc.

All this may seem somewhat chaotic, and so it is, but then finding one's way through the chaos produces a good part of the pleasure of writing history.

# ACKNOWLEDGEMENTS

I should like to record my gratitude to the institutions whose indulgence and encouragement have enabled me to write this book: first of all, at Oxford, my two Colleges, St. Antony's and Christ Church, the Faculty of Modern History, and the University Press; also the Centre National de la Recherche Scientifique in Paris, the French Embassy in London, the British Academy, the Leverhulme Trust, the Wolfson Literary Trust and the History Department of Harvard University.

In addition I wish to thank the editors of this series, Lord Bullock and Sir William Deakin, for their kindness to me. I am grateful to Miss Margot Charlton for typing my manuscript. Finally, I owe more than I can say to my wife, whose help and advice have been invaluable, to my brother, from whose extensive reading in his own subject I have derived much benefit, and, not least, to my parents.

# INDEX